Contemporary Moral Arguments

Second Edition

Contemporary Moral Arguments

Readings in Ethical Issues

Second Edition

Lewis Vaughn

New York Oxford
OXFORD UNIVERSITY PRESS

Oxford University Press is a department of the University of Oxford. It furthers the University's
objective of excellence in research, scholarship, and education by publishing worldwide.

Oxford   New York
Auckland   Cape Town   Dar es Salaam   Hong Kong   Karachi
Kuala Lumpur   Madrid   Melbourne   Mexico City   Nairobi
New Delhi   Shanghai   Taipei   Toronto

With offices in
Argentina   Austria   Brazil   Chile   Czech Republic   France   Greece
Guatemala   Hungary   Italy   Japan   Poland   Portugal   Singapore
South Korea   Switzerland   Thailand   Turkey   Ukraine   Vietnam

For titles covered by Section 112 of the US Higher Education Opportunity
Act, please visit www.oup.com/us/he for the latest information about
pricing and alternate formats.

Published by Oxford University Press
198 Madison Avenue, New York, NY 10016
www.oup.com

Oxford is a registered trademark of Oxford University Press.

Library of Congress Cataloging-in-Publication Data
Vaughn, Lewis.
    Contemporary moral arguments : readings in ethical issues / Lewis Vaughn.—2nd ed.
        p. cm.
    Includes index.
    ISBN 978-0-19-992226-0
1. Ethics—Textbooks.   2. Applied ethics—Textbooks.   I. Title.
    BJ1012.V384 2013
    170—dc23

                                            2012030393

CONTENTS

This second edition of *Contemporary Moral Arguments* is true to the mission of the first but has taken to heart a few lessons from the teachers who use it. From the beginning, the assumption underlying this text has been that much of the satisfaction and understanding to be gained from studying (and teaching) applied ethics comes from *arguments*—specifically the many well-known arguments that have provoked the most debate and reflection on contemporary issues. We know that in each of the major moral disputes—from abortion to terrorism to world poverty—there are certain influential arguments that have become must-see landmarks on the ethical terrain. *Contemporary Moral Arguments* zeroes in on many of these key arguments and uses them as guideposts and entry points for the traditional and contemporary readings that discuss them.

This controlling idea results in a clear organization that puts arguments at the center of attention: The book's readings are sorted into 10 topical chapters, with the readings within those chapters organized by argument. Each argument is introduced by a briefing that (1) sketches the argument, (2) provides ethical and conceptual background for it, and (3) reviews some of the main philosophical responses to it. After the briefing come two to four essays presenting the classic statement of the argument, critiques and defenses of it, and discussions of related debates. Each chapter has an extensive introduction to the issue, text boxes supplying basic facts on the issue, and essay questions following each argument section.

The main benefits of this approach are that (1) it helps students focus on argumentation, where much of the philosophical work gets done, (2) it gives them clear points of reference for navigating material in which they often get lost, and (3) it helps them understand and appreciate the ethical dialectic—the interplay of argument and counterargument among articles and authors. In short, it shows them by example how we do ethics.

MAIN FEATURES

- In-depth treatment of 27 important arguments in 16 major issues of applied ethics, investigated by 68 readings (plus 7 selections in the introductory chapters). The issues include abortion, drugs and autonomy, euthanasia and assisted suicide, genetic engineering and cloning, capital punishment, war, terrorism, torture, pornography, free speech, health care, animal rights, environmental issues, and global justice.
- Two substantial introductory chapters relating moral problems to ethical concepts, moral theory, and critical reasoning. Chapter 1 introduces ethics, spells out the fundamentals, critiques moral relativism, clarifies the relationship between ethics

and religion, and covers the basics of reading, constructing, and assessing moral arguments in context. Chapter 2 explains the nature of moral theory, provides an overview of the major theories, and shows how to apply plausible criteria to evaluate them. The chapter covers utilitarianism, ethical egoism, Kantian ethics, natural law theory, Rawls's contractarianism, virtue ethics, the ethics of care, and feminist ethics.

- Essay questions at the end of each argument section. The discussions of arguments and the related readings are prime material for writing assignments, so each argument section (numbered 1 to 27) concludes by asking students to write critiques of the arguments and counterarguments found in the selections.

- Pedagogical devices. Every chapter contains a list of key terms (linked to an end-of-book glossary), suggestions for further reading, and a variety of informative text boxes. The boxes are of four types:

  - "Facts and Figures"—statistics on the social, historical, and scientific aspects of the chapter's topic
  - "Public Opinion"—recent opinion polls tracking people's views on moral issues
  - "Legalities"—summaries of important court rulings or other legal matters
  - "Time Line"—a rundown of important events relating to the topic

NEW TO THIS EDITION

- Probably the most important change is an *expanded introductory chapter* that gives students more help in evaluating arguments in the rough—that is, in the sometimes bumpy terrain of essays and excerpts. There's a new section that shows by example how to do just that, with a sample essay dissected step by step, followed by argument exercises for student practice.

- A new chapter on drugs and autonomy makes its debut here, focusing on the harm argument against drug use and the argument against paternalism. The readings offered are classics in the field: "Against Legalization of Drugs" by James Q. Wilson; "A Moral Right to Use Drugs" by Douglas N. Husak; "Paternalism" by Gerald Dworkin; and "What Libertarianism Is" by John Hospers.

- Three additional readings supplement other chapters: Hursthouse's "Virtue Theory and Abortion" in the abortion chapter; John Arthur's "Sticks and Stones" in the chapter on pornography and free speech; and Baxter's "People or Penguins" in the animal rights and environmental chapter.

- A new section on ethical egoism now appears in Chapter 2 (Moral Theories).

- Many text boxes, including "Facts and Figures" and "Public Opinion," have been updated to reflect the latest information on abortion, euthanasia and assisted suicide, genetic engineering, capital punishment, war and terrorism, and economic and global justice.

- Essay questions have been revised to prompt more critical thinking and reflection on moral issues.

- In keeping with another suggestion by reviewers, several readings are now shorter to make them more manageable for students.

ANCILLARIES

- An Instructor's Manual with test bank on CD
- An online Student Study Guide that includes study questions, flashcards with key words, essay questions for each reading, and helpful web links at www.oup.com/us/vaughn

ACKNOWLEDGMENTS

This edition has been helped along by many able professionals. First among them are the hard-working people at Oxford University Press—most notably my very worthy editor Robert Miller and the long-suffering editorial assistants Kristin Maffei and Emily Krupin. Through their astute critiques, a platoon of reviewers also helped hew and smooth this book for the better. Many thanks to Robert L. Borton, Orange Coast College and Mt. San Antonio College; Travis Butler, Iowa State University; Charles R. Carlson, Texas A&M University; Kenneth Daley, Southern Methodist University; Frank K. Fair, Sam Houston State University; Stephen Finlay, University of Southern California; Gary L. Francione, Rutgers University School of Law at Newark; Charles Hermes, University of Texas at Arlington; David R. Hiley, University of New Hampshire; Stephen C. Hiltz, Southern Methodist University and University of Texas at Dallas; Robert Hull, West Virginia Wesleyan College; Eva Deane Kort, University of North Carolina at Wilmington; Scott A. Merlino, California State University at Sacramento; Matthew Pamental, Northern Illinois University; Joseph Pappin III, University of South Carolina at Columbia; Max Pensky, Binghamton University; Mark Rigstad, Oakland University; Leland Saunders, University of Maryland; and Michael Spicher, University of South Carolina.

CHAPTER I

Moral Reasoning

As you begin a serious study of ethics, you can take heart from two facts. First, the subject—however forbidding or peculiar it may seem to you—is not exactly alien territory. Ethics is about morality, and morality is about life—your life. More precisely, **ethics** (also called moral philosophy) is the study of morality using the methods of philosophy, and **morality** concerns beliefs about right and wrong actions and good and bad persons or character. Like it or not, to make your way through life, you must cross the dense, thorny realm of morality. It is very difficult or impossible for you to avoid thinking about right and wrong, judging people to be good or bad, debating with others about moral issues, accepting or rejecting the moral beliefs of your family or culture, or coming to some general understanding (a moral theory) about the nature of morality itself. Ethics can help you navigate this tough terrain, but the landscape itself is familiar: you have roamed over it many times before.

Second, ethics does work—it labors in morality. It is a systematic, rational search for answers to moral questions, often the hardest and most momentous questions we can ask. The moral issues discussed in this text are difficult, contentious, and persistent. Yet ethics holds out the hope of making headway even in these turbulent waters. Through careful reflection, critical analysis, and the close examination of moral arguments, we can often make good progress. Ethics may not be easy, but neither is it futile.

ETHICS AND THE MORAL DOMAIN

Morality consists mostly of our moral judgments, principles, values, and theories; and ethics is the careful, philosophical examination of these. There are many ways to study morality, but the deepest and most enlightening is the philosophical way. Philosophy is the systematic exploration of life's big questions using critical thinking and logical argument. Using its methods, we can examine the heart of moral issues, judge the worth of moral judgments or principles, and—above all—work to ensure that our moral beliefs rest on the solid ground of good reasons.

Our distinction between morality and ethics seems clear enough, but everyday language sometimes blurs it. People often use *morality* and *ethics* as synonyms for moral beliefs or practices generally (as in "Morality is the foundation of civilization" or "Ethics cannot be ignored"). Or they may use the words to refer to the moral beliefs or practices of specific groups or persons (for example, "Muslim morality," "Chinese ethics," or the "ethics of John Stuart Mill"). They may maintain our distinction (as we will generally in this text) and use the adjective forms *moral* and *ethical* accordingly. Or they may consider these terms equivalent to right or good ("That was the ethical thing to do") and use *immoral* or *unethical* as synonyms for wrong or bad ("abortion is immoral," "cheating on an exam is unethical").

We all sense that morality is somehow crucially different from other aspects of life. But how? For starters, it is *normative*, or evaluative. It provides us with norms, or standards, for judging actions and persons—standards in the form of moral judgments, principles, rules, or theories. With moral standards in hand, we decide whether an action is morally right or wrong and whether a person is morally good or bad. The main business of morality is therefore not to describe how things are, but to prescribe how things should be.

Morality, of course, is not the only normative realm. Just as morality is preoccupied with moral norms, other normative endeavors are concerned with nonmoral norms. The art world may use aesthetic norms to judge painting and sculpture. The law applies legal norms (laws and regulations) to judge the lawfulness of people's actions. Society insists on norms of etiquette to judge the politeness of social behavior.

But even in the crowded domain of the normative, morality is unique, deriving its distinctiveness from the combination of several characteristics. First, moral norms seem to have a much stronger hold on us than nonmoral ones do. The former are thought generally to dominate the latter, to have the property of *overridingness*. If a law enjoined us to commit a seriously immoral act, we would probably think the law illegitimate and might even flout it in an act of civil disobedience. If a rule of etiquette prevented us from performing an action that we regarded as morally obligatory, we would likely ignore the rule. Whatever we actually do when confronted with a conflict between a moral and a nonmoral norm, we tend to believe that the moral norm must override the nonmoral.

Second, moral norms have the feature of *impartiality*, the idea that they apply to everyone equally, that everyone should be considered of equal moral worth and that each person's interests must be given equal weight. One familiar way to express this requirement is that equals should be treated equally unless there is a morally relevant reason to treat them differently. If we have a moral rule that says we must not assault innocent persons, then it applies to everyone regardless of his or her social standing, income, race, skin color, gender, age, or occupation. We would consider it unjust—a clear-cut case of discrimination—to apply the rule to some people but not to others when there is no morally relevant difference between them. Social standing, race, gender, and the like mark differences among people, but they are not morally relevant differences, not the sort of differences that affect their moral standing as persons.

Some differences, of course, are morally relevant and may justify our treating people differently. Ordinarily we would think it unjust to single out a law-abiding person and forcibly take away her freedom of movement by confining her to a medical facility. But if she is a carrier of a deadly contagious disease, we might think her condition marked a morally relevant difference that justified her being quarantined by public health authorities.

Third, like nonmoral norms, moral norms have *universality*. They apply not just in one unique circumstance, but in all circumstances that are relevantly similar. Logically, it makes no sense to say that Anne's deliberately injuring someone in a particular situation is wrong but that Eduardo's deliberately injuring someone in a nearly identical situation is right. Morality demands consistency among similar cases.

Fourth, morality is *reason driven*. To be fully involved in the moral life, to make informed moral judgments, to use the resources of ethics to fathom the nature of morality itself is to engage in *moral reasoning*—critical thinking applied to the moral sphere. To do moral reasoning is to ensure that our moral judgments are not wrought out of thin air or concocted from prejudice or blind emotion—but are supported by good reasons. The entire enterprise of ethics is devoted to the search for moral understanding, which can only be attained through careful reflection and the sifting of reasons for belief.

From the dictates of logic and our commonsense moral experience we know that moral assertions uncoupled from reasons are usually suspect. What would we think of someone who declares that torturing innocent people is morally permissible (or impermissible) and that he has no reasons whatsoever for believing this? Or worse, he believes what he does because he wishes it to be true? We would likely not take him seriously and would not think much of his opinion, for he has given us no good reason to. He has told us something about himself—but nothing about the trustworthiness of his view.

None of this should lead us to conclude that moral reasoning is a mechanical process cut off from human emotion. Feelings are an essential element in the moral life. The kinds of moral issues discussed in this text—abortion, capital punishment, terrorism, war, assisted suicide, and others—are bound to evoke emotions in us. And that can be a good thing. Emotions can help us empathize with others and enlarge our understanding of the stakes involved in moral decisions. But our feelings are too often the product of our psychological needs, cultural conditioning, and selfish motivations. Critical thinking is the corrective, giving us the power to examine and guide our feelings to achieve a more balanced view.

What about our conscience—can we trust it? Our conscience is conditioned by our upbringing, cultural background, and other influences. At times, it seems to speak to us in an imaginary though authoritative voice, telling us to do or not to do something. But conscience is like our feelings in that it may be the result of irrelevant influences and is therefore no infallible indicator of moral truth. In the name of conscience, people have done noble deeds—and committed horrible acts. Like our feelings, the voice of conscience should not be ignored; it can often alert us to something of moral importance—something we need to submit to critical examination. Only through critical thinking can we rise above our feelings, our conscience, and our personal interests to see with moral clarity.

The moral norms that permeate our lives and to which we apply moral reasoning are of two kinds: norms of *obligation* and norms of *value*. The former refer to what we are obligated to do, our obligatory conduct or duty; the latter have to do with our estimations of moral worth, what we think is good or bad. We generally apply norms of obligation to *actions*, judging particular acts to be right or wrong according to a relevant moral concept, principle, or theory. Thus we say, "He should not have stolen the book" or "Breaking her promise was wrong." We use norms of value to judge the moral worth of *persons*, their *character*, or their *motives*, finding them to be good, bad, praiseworthy, or blameworthy. We say, "He was a good man," "She is compassionate," or "He acted out of greed." Acknowledging the complexity of the moral life, we sometimes insist that a right action was performed by a bad person or that a wrong action was performed by a good person.

We can also make some important distinctions about the seemingly straightforward terms *right* and *wrong*. *Right* can mean "permissible"; a permissible action is allowed, one that is not wrong to perform. Or *right* can mean "obligatory"; an obligatory action is required, one that would be wrong *not* to perform. *Wrong* means "prohibited"; a prohibited action would be wrong to perform. An action that is "above and beyond" our duty—one that is not required but is praiseworthy—is *supererogatory*. Some believe that telling a "white lie" to spare a friend's feelings is right (permissible); some think the action is right (obligatory); some insist that telling any kind of lie is wrong (prohibited). For many people, giving to charity is obligatory; for others, it is supererogatory.

As you can see, the field of ethics encompasses a wide philosophical expanse—so wide that it has been subdivided into three main branches and many specialty areas. The branch known as **normative ethics** involves the exploration and evaluation of moral norms (principles, virtues, values, and theories). Its goal is to use critical thinking to search for norms that we are justified in using as guides to the moral life. In normative ethics we ask: What moral principles or virtues, if any, should govern our actions? How should we resolve conflicts between moral principles? What makes an action right? What values in life are most important? What moral theory best explains our moral experience?

Another branch, **metaethics**, examines the philosophical underpinnings of these vital questions. It is the study of the fundamental assumptions, concepts, and reasoning involved in the field of ethics. Instead of asking how we should live or what actions are right, metaethics asks: What is goodness? What is rightness? What is a virtue? Are there such things as moral facts? If so, how can we know them? How can a moral judgment be supported?

Applied ethics, the third branch, is the application of moral principles, virtues, or theories to real-life cases or issues. Its aim is to arrive at informed, well-reasoned answers to specific moral questions or problems—which is also the object of this text, an anthology in applied ethics. Subfields in applied ethics focus on moral questions related to a specific profession or subject—for example, medical ethics, business ethics, legal ethics, or environmental ethics.

Descriptive ethics is also a formal enquiry into morality, but it uses the methodology of science, not philosophy. Its aim is to examine the empirical facts of the moral life—the descriptive details of people's moral beliefs and behavior. Descriptive ethics is mainly the job of anthropologists, sociologists, historians, and psychologists. They want to know *what* people believe. Moral philosophers want to know whether people *should* believe.

ETHICS, LAW, AND RELIGION

What is the connection between ethics and the normative realms of law and religion? Laws are norms of behavior established and enforced by the state. They are often in agreement with moral norms (murder is both legally and morally wrong, for example), and some people believe that legal norms coincide (or should coincide) with moral norms. But these two kinds of standards are distinct. An action may be legally permissible but morally impermissible, and vice versa. Lying to your best friend or wasting your life in pointless endeavors may be immoral—but not illegal. According to some, gay marriage is moral—but in many states, it is illegal. The struggle for the civil rights of African Americans in the 1960s is widely believed to have been a righteous cause—yet in many states those rights were prohibited by law.

Most people see the wisdom of outlawing actions that cause substantial harm to others, but they disagree about whether harmless actions that are thought to be immoral should also be made illegal. Some insist that any action they consider seriously immoral should be outlawed regardless of its harmlessness, a controversial view known as *legal moralism.* This doctrine often enters into debates about legalizing abortion, assisted suicide, gay marriage, stem cell research, and pornography.

The relationship between ethics and religion is more complicated. Historically every religion has offered its adherents moral content in the form of commandments or precepts. Christianity, Judaism, Islam, Hinduism, and others all contain normative standards for right conduct. (Of course, we can say the same of secular or nontheistic systems of morality, including Aristotelian ethics, Stoicism, Confucianism, Buddhism, Kantianism, utilitarianism, and contractarianism.) None of this is controversial. But from the fact that religion contains a system of morality, many have concluded that religion must be the *source* of morality. More precisely, the idea is that God *makes* the moral law; right and wrong are constituted by the will of God. Right actions are those commanded by God; wrong actions are those prohibited by God. The doctrine that God is the creator of morality is known as the **divine command theory**, and both religious and nonreligious thinkers have found its implications disturbing.

The central difficulty is that the doctrine forces a troubling dilemma on us, one outlined for us by Socrates. In Plato's dialogue *Euthyphro,* Socrates asks, in effect, Are actions right because God commands them, or does God command them because they are right? To choose the first option is to say that God makes morality and to accept the divine command theory. To choose the second is to say that morality exists independently of God's will, and even he must obey it. For many theists, the second option (the denial of the divine command theory) is far more palatable than the first, for the first one implies that morality is completely arbitrary.

If an action is morally right only because God says so, then any action at all could be morally right. If God so willed, the torture and slaughter of innocents would be morally right. As the divine command theory would have it, there could be no reasons for God's willing one way or the other. He just commands, and that makes an action right (or wrong). But if God has no reasons for his commands, no standards other than his say-so, his commands are arbitrary.

A divine command theorist might reply that God would never command something as evil as the torture and slaughter of innocents because God is all-good. But this response seems to make the idea of the goodness of God meaningless. One critic makes the point like this:

> No, you say, such a thing is impossible. A *good* God would never allow such a thing [wicked deeds]. Right enough. But what does it mean to be good? If the Divine Command Theory is correct, then something is good just in case it is favored by God. But then look what happens: to say that God is good is just to say that God is favored by God. Is that really what we mean when we say that God is good?[1]

The arbitrariness problem has led both theists and nontheists to reject the divine command theory and to accept the second option of the dilemma, the view that morality is not dependent on God's will. Right and wrong must then exist independently of God and are binding on everyone, including God himself. In this way, the notion of God's goodness has real meaning, and the religious can coherently claim that God is

---

[1] Russ Shafer-Landau, *Whatever Happened to Good and Evil?* (New York: Oxford University Press, 2004), 81–82.

good, that he unerringly observes the moral law, and that he urges mortals to strive to do the same.

MORAL RELATIVISM

Most people are moral objectivists, though they may not call themselves that. **Moral objectivism** is the view that there are moral standards that are true or correct for everyone. That is, they are objective—they are true independently of what individuals or societies happen to believe regarding them. If an act is morally wrong, it is wrong regardless of whether you or anyone else agrees that it is wrong. The doctrine does not entail *moral absolutism*, the notion that moral principles must apply without exceptions in all cases or without adaptation to particular circumstances. A moral objectivist could interpret moral principles in an absolutist way, or she could (as most objectivists probably do) believe that moral principles are **prima facie**—applicable unless exceptions are warranted (as when two principles conflict and one must be given more weight than the other). And she could also hold that the same moral principles may need to be applied differently in different cultures because of varying sociological or historical conditions.

Moral relativism is the rejection of the objectivist view. It says that moral standards do not have independent status but are relative to what individuals or cultures believe. An action is morally right if an individual or a culture condones it; it is morally wrong if an individual or culture condemns it. Objective moral truth is nonexistent. When the individual is the arbiter of rightness, the view is called **subjective relativism**; when culture is the arbiter it is **cultural relativism**.

According to subjective relativism, to find out what is right or wrong, a person needs only to consult his or her own beliefs. Morality is essentially a matter of personal taste. If you condone capital punishment, then it is morally right. Your endorsement makes it right. If you condemn it, then it is morally wrong. Your condemnation makes it wrong. Ethical inquiry then consists of simply determining what your sincere moral beliefs are.

But subjective relativism has unpalatable implications. Consider these:

- The doctrine implies that on moral matters, individuals are *infallible*. If you sincerely approve of an action, then it is morally right—and you cannot be mistaken. If your approval is genuine, the issue is settled, and your verdict is unerring. But this view of things flies in the face of our commonsense moral experience. We know that when we make moral judgments, we often are seriously mistaken. We judge someone's actions to be morally right (or wrong) or decide to guide our lives by a moral principle—then discover that we made a regrettable, horrible error. Our fallibility is an obvious fact of the moral life.

- The doctrine entails an implausible *moral equivalence*. It says that the sincere moral views of any individual are as good or as true as those of any other. If the serial killer and cannibal Jeffrey Dahmer approved of his slaughtering seventeen people, then it is morally right. If you disapprove of the slaughter, then it is morally wrong. By the lights of moral subjectivism, Dahmer's view is no better or worse than yours. Does anyone really believe that all moral judgments are created equal?

- The doctrine implies that *moral disagreement* is virtually impossible. Suppose a friend tells you that the terrorists who perpetrated the September 11 attacks on the United States were morally justified in doing so. And you respond that the terrorists were not morally justified. This would seem like an obvious example of two people having a disagreement about an important moral matter. But no disagreement at all is taking place, according to subjective relativism. You and your friend are merely expressing your approval and disapproval, your respective likes and dislikes. And because the two of you are just expressing your personal tastes, you are not really disagreeing on an issue—just as you would not be disagreeing if you said you like chocolate ice cream and your friend said he likes vanilla. But our moral experience suggests that genuine disagreement over moral issues is not only possible but common.

These absurdities raise serious doubts about subjective relativism. Many think cultural relativism is more plausible, and some assume it without question, in part because it seems to provide a basis for social tolerance and respectful pluralism. The main argument in its favor goes like this: if people's moral judgments differ between cultures, then moral standards are relative to culture (there are no objective truths); people's moral judgments do in fact differ between cultures; therefore, moral standards are relative to culture (cultural relativism).

Does this argument prove its case? We examine the basics of logical argument later in this chapter. For now, we can just note that for an argument to be good (to establish the truth of its conclusion), its conclusion must follow logically from its supporting statements (premises), and the supporting statements must be true. As it turns out, the conclusion of the cultural relativism argument does follow logically from the premises. But are the premises true? The second premise seems undeniable: anthropological and sociological evidence shows that judgments about right and wrong by people from different cultures often differ greatly. Some societies condone abortion, infanticide, polygamy, the killing of elders, the stoning of women, female circumcision, and religious intolerance—and some abhor these practices.

So the second premise is true, but the first premise (if people's moral judgments differ between cultures, then moral standards are relative to culture) is false. We cannot conclude from the diversity of moral judgments among cultures that there are no objective moral standards—just as we cannot conclude from disagreement about an historical event that no statement about the event could be objectively true. Disagreement on a moral issue could arise simply because one or more cultures are wrong about the objective moral facts.

The first premise assumes that conflicting moral judgments must indicate a disagreement about moral standards. But it's possible for cultures to accept the same fundamental moral principles but differ in their understanding of nonmoral reality. For example, two different cultures could agree completely on the moral principle of respect for persons. But because of different beliefs about death, the soul, and immortality, they could disagree on how this respect is best expressed. One culture might insist that respect is properly shown by cremating the dead; another by mummifying the dead; another by eating the dead. Just as anthropology has demonstrated the diversity of moral judgments among cultures, it has also documented common moral standards among otherwise diverse societies.

So the argument for cultural relativism founders because its key premise is false. Moreover, the doctrine undermines itself by implying statements that are doubtful:

- Just as subjective relativism does, cultural relativism would have us believe that cultures are morally infallible. If a society says that certain actions are morally permissible, then they *are* morally permissible. If a society genuinely approves of the actions, they are right—and the society cannot be in error. But we know that cultures are as fallible as individuals are, often endorsing morally repugnant acts of all kinds—persecution of minorities, racism, sexism, slavery, holocausts, ethnic cleansing, imprisonment of dissidents, and on and on.

- Cultural relativism implies that other cultures are beyond criticism; we cannot legitimately criticize them because each culture is the maker of its own moral truth. We cannot accuse another culture of immoral behavior because whatever behavior that culture genuinely endorses *is* moral. To accept this implication of cultural relativism is to say that if the people of Germany approved of the extermination of millions of Jews in World War II, then the extermination was morally right. Or if the culture of the September 11 hijackers approved of the attacks that killed 3,000 people, then the attacks were morally right. But this is implausible. Our moral experience suggests that we can and do condemn other societies for morally heinous acts.
- Cultural relativism implies that there is no such thing as moral progress. Most of us do believe in moral progress, instances in which immoral acts are no longer committed, or today's practices and policies are morally better than those of the past. We see evidence of moral progress in the fact that society no longer condones slavery, lynchings, racial discrimination, and wanton destruction of the environment. But moral progress requires a stable, objective moral standard for comparing cultures of the past and present. Cultural relativism denies that there are any such standards; there are only moral norms relative to individual cultures.
- According to cultural relativism, all social reformers—Martin Luther King, Jr., Mahatma Gandhi, John Stuart Mill, Margaret Sanger, and all the rest—are never right. Since society determines by consensus what is morally right, anyone who disagrees with society must automatically be wrong. But this view conflicts dramatically with our moral experience. We tend to think that sometimes society is wrong and the reformers are right.

There is a good chance that if you are a cultural relativist, these considerations will not move you very much. That's because you probably think that cultural relativism strongly supports your belief in the important virtue of tolerance toward other cultures and that moral objectivism does not. If the values of one culture are no better or worse than those of another, then there is no basis for hatred or hostility toward any culture anywhere. Tolerance is of course both morally praiseworthy and beneficial to our fractured planet of conflicting values. But cultural relativism has no advantage over moral objectivism in promoting tolerance—and may have a critical disadvantage.

First note that moral objectivism does not entail intolerance. It says only that some moral beliefs are better than others; it does not imply anything about how objectivists should behave toward those they think are in moral error. Some objectivists are intolerant; many are not. But cultural relativism can easily justify intolerance and cannot consistently advocate tolerance. If there are intolerant cultures (and there surely are), then since cultures make rightness, intolerance in those cultures is morally right. For sincerely intolerant societies, the persecution of minorities and the killing of dissidents may be the height of moral rectitude. In addition, cultural relativists who insist that everyone should embrace tolerance are contradicting themselves. To say that tolerant behavior is right for everyone is to assert an objective moral norm—but cultural relativism says there are no objective moral norms. The moral objectivist, however, can plausibly claim that the moral requirement of tolerance is universal.

MORAL ARGUMENTS

Critical thinking is the systematic evaluation or formulation of beliefs, or statements, by rational standards. We employ it every time we carefully and systematically assess the truth of a statement or the merits of a logical argument. We ask, Are there good reasons for believing this statement? Is this a good argument—does it prove its case? These sorts of questions are asked in every academic field and in every serious human endeavor. Wherever there is a need to acquire knowledge, to separate truth from falsity, and to come to a reliable understanding of how the world works, such questions are asked and answers are sought. Ethics is no exception. Critical thinking in ethics—*moral reasoning*—employs the same general principles of logic and evidence that guide the search for truth in every other field. So we need not wonder whether we use critical thinking in ethics but whether we use it well.

Argument Basics

Moral reasoning, just like any other kind of critical thinking, is largely concerned with the construction and evaluation of arguments. As you may have guessed, here **argument** denotes not a verbal fight but a set pattern of assertions: at least one statement providing support for another statement. We have an argument when one or more statements try to give us reasons for believing another one. The supporting statements are **premises**, and the supported statement is the **conclusion**. In critical thinking, the term **statement** also has a technical meaning. A statement (or claim) is an assertion that something is or is not the case and is therefore the kind of utterance that is either true or false.

You need to understand at the outset that *argument* in this sense is not synonymous with *persuasion*. An argument provides us with reasons for accepting a claim; it is an attempted "proof" for an assertion. But persuasion does not necessarily involve giving any reasons at all for accepting a claim. To persuade is to influence people's opinions, which can be accomplished by offering a good argument but also by misleading with logical fallacies, exploiting emotions and prejudices, dazzling with rhetorical gimmicks, hiding or distorting the facts, threatening or coercing people—the list is long. Good arguments prove something whether or not they persuade. Persuasive ploys can change minds but do not necessarily prove anything.

So we formulate an argument to try to show that a particular claim (the conclusion) should be believed, and we analyze an argument to see if it really does show what it purports to show. If the argument is good, we are entitled to believe its conclusion. If it is bad, we are not entitled to believe it.

Consider these two simple arguments:

Argument 1

Law enforcement in the city is a complete failure. Incidents of serious crime have doubled.

Argument 2

It's wrong to take the life of an innocent person. Abortion takes the life of an innocent person. So abortion is wrong.

In Argument 1, the conclusion is "Law enforcement in the city is a complete failure," which is supported by the premise "Incidents of serious crime have doubled." The conclusion of Argument 2 is "abortion is wrong," and it is backed by two premises: "It's wrong to take the life of an innocent person" and "Abortion takes the life of an innocent person." Despite the differences between these two passages (differences in content, the number of premises, and the order of their parts), they are both arguments because they exemplify basic argument structure: a conclusion supported by at least one premise.

Though the components of an argument seem clear enough, people often fail to distinguish between arguments and strong statements that contain no arguments at all. Suppose we change Argument 1 into this:

> Law enforcement in the city is a complete failure. Nothing seems to work anymore. We've seen this kind of bad situation before.

Now there is no argument, just an expression of annoyance or anger. There are no statements giving us reasons to believe a conclusion. What we have are some unsupported assertions that may merely *appear* to make a case. If we ignore the distinction between genuine arguments and nonargumentative material, critical reasoning is undone.

Assuming we can recognize an argument when we see it, how can we tell if it is a good one? Fortunately, the general criteria for judging the merits of an argument are simple and clear. A good argument—one that gives us good reasons for believing a claim—must have (1) solid logic and (2) true premises. Requirement (1) means that the conclusion should follow logically from the premises, that there must be a proper logical connection between supporting statements and the statement supported. Requirement (2) says that what the premises assert must in fact be the case. An argument that fails in either respect is a bad argument.

There are two basic kinds of arguments—deductive and inductive—and our two requirements hold for both of them, even though the logical connections in each type are distinct. **Deductive arguments** are intended to give *logically conclusive* support to their conclusions so that if the premises are true, the conclusion absolutely must be true. Argument 2 is a deductive argument and is therefore supposed to be constructed so that if the two premises are true, its conclusion cannot possibly be false. Here it is with its structure laid bare:

Argument 2
1. It's wrong to take the life of an innocent person.
2. Abortion takes the life of an innocent person.
3. Therefore, abortion is wrong.

Do you see that, given the form or structure of this argument, if the premises are true, then the conclusion *has to be true*? It would be very strange—illogical, in fact—to agree that the two premises are true but that the conclusion is false.

Now look at this one:

Argument 3
1. All dogs are mammals.
2. Rex is a dog.
3. Therefore, Rex is a mammal.

Again, there is no way for the premises to be true while the conclusion is false. The deductive form of the argument guarantees this.

So a deductive argument is intended to have this sort of airtight structure. If it actually does have this structure, it is said to be *valid*. Argument 2 is deductive because it is intended to provide logically conclusive support to its conclusion. It is valid because, as a matter of fact, it does offer this kind of support. A deductive argument that fails to provide conclusive support to its conclusion is said to be *invalid*. In such an argument, it is possible for the premises to be true and the conclusion false. Argument 3 is intended to have a deductive form, and because it actually does have this form, the argument is also valid.

An elementary fact about deductive arguments is that their validity (or lack thereof) is a separate issue from the truth of the premises. Validity is a structural matter, depending on how an argument is put together. Truth concerns the nature of the claims made in the premises and conclusion. A deductive argument is supposed to be built so that *if* the premises are true, the conclusion must be true—but in a particular case, the premises might *not* be true. A valid argument can have true or false premises and a true or false conclusion. (By definition, of course, it cannot have true premises and a false conclusion.) In any case, being invalid or having false premises dooms a deductive argument.

Inductive arguments are supposed to give *probable* support to their conclusions. Unlike deductive arguments, they are not designed to support their conclusions decisively. They can establish only that, if their premises are true, their conclusions are probably true (more likely to be true than not). Argument 1 is an inductive argument meant to demonstrate the probable truth that "Law enforcement in the city is a complete failure." Like all inductive arguments (and unlike deductive ones), it can have true premises and a false conclusion. So the sole premise—"incidents of serious crime have doubled"—can be true while the conclusion is false.

If inductive arguments succeed in lending probable support to their conclusions, they are said to be *strong*. Strong arguments are such that if their premises are true, their conclusions are probably true. If they fail to provide this probable support, they are termed *weak*. Argument 1 is a weak argument because its premise, even if true, does not show that more likely than not law enforcement in the city is a complete failure. After all, even if incidents of serious crime have doubled, law enforcement may be successful in other ways, or incidents of serious crime may be up for reasons unrelated to the effectiveness of law enforcement.

But consider this inductive argument:

Argument 4
1. Eighty-five percent of the students at this university are Republicans.
2. Sonia is a student at this university.
3. Therefore, Sonia is probably a Republican.

This argument is strong. If its premises are true, its conclusion is likely to be true. If eighty-five percent of the university's students are Republicans, and Sonia is a university student, she is more likely than not to be a Republican too.

When a valid (deductive) argument has true premises, it is a good argument. A good deductive argument is said to be *sound*. Argument 2 is valid, but we cannot say whether it is sound until we determine the truth of the premises. Argument 3 is valid, and if its premises are true, it is sound. When a strong (inductive) argument has true premises, it is also a good argument. A good inductive argument is said to be *cogent*. Argument 1 is weak, so there is no way it can be cogent. Argument 4 is strong, and if its premises are true, it is cogent.

Checking the validity or strength of an argument is often a plain, commonsense undertaking. Using our natural reasoning ability, we can examine how the premises are linked to the conclusion and can see quickly whether the conclusion follows from the premises. We are most likely to make an easy job of it when the arguments are simple. Many times, however, we need some help, and help is available in the form of methods and guidelines for evaluating arguments.

Having a familiarity with common argument patterns, or forms, is especially useful when assessing the validity of deductive arguments. We are likely to encounter these forms again and again. Here is a prime example:

Argument 5
1. If the surgeon operates, then the patient will be cured.
2. The surgeon is operating.
3. Therefore, the patient will be cured.

This argument form contains a *conditional* premise—that is, a premise consisting of a conditional, or if-then, statement (actually a compound statement composed of two constituent statements). Premise 1 is a conditional statement. A conditional statement has two parts: the part beginning with *if* (called the *antecedent*) and the part beginning with *then* (known as the *consequent*). So the antecedent of Premise 1 is "If the surgeon operates," and the consequent is "then the patient will be cured."

The best way to appreciate the structure of such an argument (or any deductive argument, for that matter) is to translate it into traditional argument symbols in which each statement is symbolized by a letter. Here is the symbolization for Argument 5:

1. If p, then q.
2. p.
3. Therefore, q.

We can see that p represents "the surgeon operates," and q represents "the patient will be cured." But notice that we can use this same symbolized argument form to represent countless other arguments—arguments with different statements but having the same basic structure.

It just so happens that the underlying argument form for Argument 5 is extremely common—common enough to have a name, *modus ponens* (or affirming the antecedent). The truly useful fact about *modus ponens* is that any argument having this form is valid. We can plug any statements we want into the formula and the result will be a valid argument, a circumstance in which if the premises are true, the conclusion must be true.

An equally prevalent argument form is *modus tollens* (or denying the consequent). For example:

Argument 6
1. If the dose is low, then the healing is slow.
2. The healing is not slow.
3. Therefore, the dose is not low.

1. If *p*, then *q*.
2. Not *q*.
3. Therefore, not *p*.

Modus tollens is also a valid form, and any argument using this form must also be valid.

There are also common argument forms that are *invalid*. Here are two of them:

Affirming the Consequent

Argument 7
1. If the patient is getting better, then drugs are unnecessary.
2. Drugs are unnecessary.
3. Therefore, the patient is getting better.

1. If *p*, then *q*.
2. *q*.
3. Therefore, *p*.

Denying the Antecedent

Argument 8
1. If the rate of infection is increasing, then the patients will die.
2. The rate of infection is not increasing.
3. Therefore, the patients will not die.

1. If *p*, then *q*.
2. Not *p*.
3. Therefore, not *q*.

The advantage of being able to recognize these and other common argument forms is that you can use that skill to readily determine the validity of many deductive arguments. You know, for example, that any argument having the same form as *modus ponens* or *modus tollens* must be valid, and any argument in one of the common invalid forms must be invalid.

The Structure of Moral Arguments

A **moral argument** is an argument whose conclusion is a moral statement (a moral judgment), an assertion that an action is right or wrong or that a person or motive is good or bad. We utter a moral statement when we say such things as "Physician-assisted suicide is wrong" or "Maria should not have had an abortion" or "Henry is a good person." We are constantly making moral statements and including them in our moral arguments, which we frequently devise and hold up for inspection and evaluation.

Recall Argument 2, a simple (and common) moral argument:

1. It's wrong to take the life of an innocent person.
2. Abortion takes the life of an innocent person.
3. Therefore, abortion is wrong.

Here we can see all the standard features of a typical moral argument:

(1) At least one premise (premise 1) is a moral statement asserting a general moral norm such as a moral principle;

(2) at least one premise (premise 2) is a nonmoral statement describing an action or circumstance; and

(3) the conclusion is a moral statement expressing a moral judgment about a specific action or circumstance.

Notice how natural this pattern seems. If we want to argue that a particular action (or kind of action) is wrong, for example, we must provide a reason for this moral judgment. The natural (and logical) move is to reach for a general moral principle that supports the judgment. Why is Joan's getting an abortion morally wrong? Because, someone might argue, it is wrong to take the life of an innocent person (a moral principle), and Joan's abortion would be taking of the life of an innocent person (a non-moral fact).

This natural way of proceeding reflects the logical realities of moral reasoning. In a moral argument, we *must* have at least one moral premise to draw a conclusion about the morality of a particular state of affairs. Without a moral premise, we cannot legitimately arrive at a moral conclusion, or judgment. That is, from a nonmoral premise alone, a moral conclusion does not logically follow. For example, from the nonmoral fact that abortions are frequently performed, we cannot conclude that abortion is immoral. Nonmoral premises cannot support a conclusion expressing a moral judgment. Likewise, we cannot reason from a moral premise alone (one affirming a general moral principle) to a conclusion about the morality of a particular action. We need a nonmoral premise affirming that the particular action in question is an instance of the general class of actions referred to in the general moral premise. In Argument 2, the moral premise tells us it's wrong to take the life of an innocent person, but we need the nonmoral premise to assert that abortion is an instance of taking the life of an innocent person. After all, that a fetus is a person—the kind of entity that is deserving of full moral rights—is not obviously true and not assented to by everyone. We must spell out in a premise what we take to be the nonmoral fact of the matter.

This discussion underscores a previously mentioned fact about moral disagreements. When people disagree on a moral issue, they may or may not be disagreeing about moral principles. They may actually share the relevant moral principles but disagree about the nonmoral facts—or vice versa. So when people take contradictory stands on the conclusion of a moral argument, the source of the conflict could lie with the moral premises or the nonmoral premises or both.

Unfortunately, in everyday life moral arguments do not come with their premises clearly labeled, so we need to be able to identify the premises ourselves. This job is made more difficult by a simple fact of the moral life: often premises (moral and nonmoral) are left unsaid and are merely implied. Sometimes premises are unstated because they are obvious assumptions that need not be mentioned. But if we are to perform a thorough evaluation of an argument, we must drag the implicit premises into the open so they can be fully assessed. Such careful scrutiny is especially important in moral arguments because the implicit premises are often questionable assumptions—the secret, weak links in the chain of reasoning. For example:

Argument 9

1. In vitro fertilization is an entirely unnatural process, as far from natural reproduction as one could imagine.

2. Therefore, in vitro fertilization should not be used.

As it stands, this is a bad argument; the conclusion does not follow from the premise. But there is an implied (moral) premise lurking here, and if we make it explicit, the argument will be valid:

1. In vitro fertilization is an entirely unnatural process, as far from natural reproduction as one could imagine.
2. Any process that is unnatural should not be used.
3. Therefore, in vitro fertilization should not be used.

Now the argument is complete, and we can see both the nonmoral premise (premise 1) and the moral premise (premise 2), which is a moral principle. But now that we have brought the moral premise into the light of day, we can see that it is false or at least debatable. We use many processes and products that are unnatural, but we generally do not regard them as morally impermissible. Some examples are modern pharmaceuticals, intravenous feeding, surgery, CAT scans, artificial limbs, and contact lenses.

Very often we can tell that an argument has an unstated premise because there is a logical leap between the stated premises and the conclusion. The inference from stated premises to conclusion does not work unless the missing premise is supplied. A good candidate for the implicit premise will make the argument valid or strong and will be plausible in the context of the argument. The most straightforward approach, however, is to treat the argument as deductive and look for a premise that will make the argument valid, as we did in Argument 9.

Evaluating Moral Premises
To reiterate: determining whether an argument is good—whether it gives you good reasons to accept its conclusion—involves (1) checking the logic and (2) assessing the truth of the premises. How you go about evaluating the truth of the premises depends on whether those premises are nonmoral or moral.

Checking the truth of nonmoral premises can involve the exploration of either *empirical* or *conceptual* matters. An empirical belief, or claim, is one that can be confirmed by sense experience—that is, by observation or scientific investigation. Most nonmoral premises are empirical claims that we can check by examining our own experience or that of others or by consulting the relevant experts or scientific findings. By these methods we can test (and support) a wide variety of empirical assertions, such as many of the nonmoral premises examined earlier: "Incidents of serious crime have doubled"; "Eighty-five percent of the students at this university are Republicans"; "If the patient is getting better, then drugs are unnecessary." Moral reasoning demands that we always seek the most reliable evidence available for empirical claims and try to assess its worth objectively.

A conceptual matter has to do with the meaning of terms, something we need to pay attention to because disputes in ethics sometimes hinge on the meaning of a concept. For example, in disagreements about the moral permissibility of abortion, the crux of the matter is often how the disputants define *person* (as in Argument 2), or *human life*, or *human being*. Similarly, whether someone supports or opposes euthanasia often hangs on how it is defined. Some, for example, define it in the narrow sense of taking direct action to kill someone for his or her sake (mercy killing) while others insist on a wider sense that encompasses both mercifully killing and allowing to die. Whether we are devising our own arguments or evaluating those of others, being clear on the meaning of terms is essential, and any proposed definition must be backed by good reasons.

Moral premises are like nonmoral ones in that they too should be supported by good reasons and be subjected to serious scrutiny. But just how are moral premises supported and scrutinized?

Support for a moral premise (a moral principle or standard) can come from at least three sources: other moral principles, moral theories, or our most reliable moral judgments. Probably the most common way to support a moral principle is to appeal to a higher-level principle. Suppose the moral premise in question is "A woman should not be forced to have an abortion against her will." Some would argue that this principle is derived from, or is based on, the higher principle that autonomous persons should be allowed to exercise their capacity for self-determination. Or let's say the premise is "Individuals in a persistent vegetative state should never have their feeding tubes removed for the purpose of letting them 'die with dignity.'" Many would base this assertion on the principle that human life is sacred and should be preserved at all costs. Frequently, the higher principle appealed to is plausible, seemingly universal, or accepted by all parties so that further support for the principle is not necessary. At other times, the higher principle itself may be controversial and in need of support.

Moral premises can also be supported by a moral theory, a general explanation of what makes an action right or a person or motive good. (In the next chapter we discuss moral theories in depth.) For example, traditional utilitarianism is a moral theory affirming that right actions are those that produce the greatest happiness for all concerned. Appealing to utilitarianism, then, someone might insist that a baby born with severe brain damage who will die within a few days should not be allowed to wither slowly away in pain but should be given a lethal injection. The justification for this policy is that it would produce the least amount of unhappiness (including pain and suffering) for all concerned, including baby, parents, and caregivers. Those who reject this policy would have to argue that there was something wrong with utilitarianism or that other considerations (including alternative theories) outweigh utilitarian concerns.

Another possible source of support for moral premises is what philosophers call our *considered moral judgments*. These are moral judgments we deem plausible or credible after careful reflection that is as unbiased as possible. They may apply to both particular cases and more general moral statements. For example, after deliberation we might conclude that "Inflicting undeserved and unnecessary pain on someone is wrong," "Deliberately killing a person is permissible only in self-defense or in war," or "Equals should be treated equally." Like moral principles and theories, such judgments can vary in how much weight they carry in moral arguments and can be given more or less credibility (or undermined completely) by relevant reasons. (We examine more closely the relationships among theories, principles, and considered judgments in Chapter 2.)

Moral premises can be called into question by showing that they somehow conflict with credible principles, theories, or judgments. One way to do this is to cite *counterexamples*, instances in which the moral principle in question seems not to hold. Recall that a counterexample helps us see that the moral premise in Argument 9 is dubious. The premise says "Any process that is unnatural should not be used," but we often use unnatural products or processes (CAT scans and contact lenses, for instance) and do not think these actions morally wrong. In the same way, we can use counterexamples to evaluate the moral premise in Argument 2:

1. It's wrong to take the life of an innocent person.
2. Abortion takes the life of an innocent person.
3. Therefore, abortion is wrong.

Are there no exceptions to premise 1? Is it always wrong to kill an innocent person? We can imagine cases in which this premise seems either doubtful or at least not obviously true. What about situations in which many lives can be saved by taking the life of one person? What if all fifty people in a lifeboat at sea will drown unless one of them is cast overboard? What if the one unlucky person *agrees* to be cast overboard to save all the others? Or suppose a person is dying of cancer and is suffering unspeakable pain that cannot be relieved by any medical means—and she begs for a lethal injection of morphine? Some would argue that these scenarios raise serious questions about premise 1, suggesting that at least in its current form, it may not be true. In response to these counterexamples, some who wish to defend the premise might modify it to take the scenarios into account or even try to show that despite its implications premise 1 is justified.

READING AND EVALUATING ARGUMENTS
It's one thing to understand the workings of arguments; it's quite another to be able to identify arguments in an essay and make a reasonable judgment about their worth. Mastering this skill can be challenging because in argumentative essays (like the ones in this text), arguments can be simple or complex, clearly stated or perplexing, and apparent or hidden. This is true for essays in ethics as well as for any other kind of writing that contains arguments. In some essays, the relationship between the conclusion (or conclusions) and the premises can be complicated, and even good arguments can be surrounded by material irrelevant to the arguments at hand. The remedy for these difficulties is instructive examples and plenty of practice, some of which you can get in this chapter and in the readings to come.

We will get to the examples in a moment, but for now let's focus on a few general guidelines for the productive reading and assessing of moral arguments in argumentative contexts.

1. Approach the Text With an Open Mind
If you are studying ethics for the first time, you are likely—at least at first—to find a good bit of the material difficult, strange, or exasperating, sometimes all three at once. That's normal. Ethics is an exploration of the rugged frontiers of moral knowledge, where controversies thrive and moral ideas are tested by fire. So much of this new territory is likely to seem daunting or unfamiliar. There's also an excellent chance that your first visits to this terrain will be vexing, perhaps even infuriating, because you may sometimes disagree with what you read.

There is no shame in experiencing any of these reactions. They come with the territory. But if you are to make any headway in ethics, you need to try your best to counteract these attitudes and feelings. Remember, ethics at its best is a fair-minded, fearless search for moral understanding. Anything that interferes with this noble quest must be overcome and cast aside. So as you read, keep the following in mind:

- *Avoid making a judgment about an essay's ideas or arguments until you fully understand them and have fairly considered them.* Make sure you are not reading with the intent to prove the conclusions false (or true). Be open to the possibility that the essay could give you good reasons to change your mind about something.
- *Try to maintain a neutral attitude toward the writer, presuming neither that she is right nor wrong, neither sinner nor saint.* Don't assume that everything a renowned philosopher says must be true, and don't presuppose that everything a philosopher you dislike says must be false. Give the writer the same attention and respect that you would give a friend who is discussing a serious issue with you.
- *If you are reading the work of a famous philosopher and you find yourself thinking that his or her ideas are obviously silly or ridiculous, think again.* The odds are good that you are misunderstanding what you read. It is wiser to assume that the text offers something of value (even if you disagree with it) and that you need to read more carefully.

2. Read Actively and Critically

The reading of moral philosophy is intense. It cannot be rushed. It cannot be crammed. It cannot be done while your mind is on automatic pilot.

Philosophical reading is *active* reading. Instead of reading just to get through a piece of writing, you must take your time and ask yourself what key terms and passages mean, how the argument is structured, what the central thesis is, where the premises are, how certain key ideas are related, whether the main conclusion conflicts with propositions you know are true, even how the material compares with other writing on the same subject.

Reading ethics is also *critical* reading. In critical reading, you ask not just what something means but whether a statement is true and if the reasoning is solid. You ask if the conclusion really follows from the premises, whether the premises are true, if the analysis of a term really makes sense, and whether there are counterexamples to moral premises.

An ethics essay, of course, contains more than just a bare-bones argument. Often a considerable amount of space is devoted to explaining the background or history of the topic being addressed, elaborating on each of the premises, discussing the implications of the argument's conclusion, and answering possible criticisms of the essay's main points. Certainly you must take these into account when you are reading and evaluating an ethics article. But your primary task is to arrive at an honest and well-reasoned assessment of the text's central claim.

3. Identify the Conclusion First, Then the Premises

When you first begin reading essays in moral philosophy, they may seem to you like dark thickets of propositions into which you may not enter without losing your way. But your situation is really not that bad. In argumentative writing (the kind you are most likely to encounter in ethics), you can depend on there being, well, an argument, a conclusion backed by premises. There could, of course, be several arguments that support the main argument, and the arguments could be complex, but these sets of conclusion-plus-premises will all serve as recognizable guideposts. If you want to penetrate the thicket, then, you must first identify the argument (or arguments). And the key to doing that is to *find the conclusion first, then look for the premises.*

Zeroing in on conclusions and premises can be a lot easier if you keep an eye out for *indicator words.* Indicator words often tag along with arguments and indicate that a conclusion or premise may be nearby.

Here are a few conclusion indicator words:

consequently	*as a result*
thus	*hence*
therefore	*so*
it follows that	*which means that*

Here are some premise indicator words:

in view of the fact	*assuming that*
because	*since*
due to the fact that	*for*
because	*given that*

Just remember that indicator words do not *guarantee* the presence of conclusions and premises. They are simply telltale signs.

When you find the main conclusion, you thereby identify the main point of the essay, and you then have the number-one clue to the function of all the rest of the text. Once you uncover the point that the writer is trying to prove, finding the supporting premises becomes much easier. And when you isolate the premises, locating the text that explains and amplifies the premises gets easier too. Therefore, the first—and most important—question you can ask about an argumentative essay is, *"What claim is the writer trying to prove?"*

4. Outline, Paraphrase, or Summarize the Argument

Understanding an essay's argument is so important that testing whether you really "get it" is crucial. You can test your grasp of the argument by outlining, paraphrasing, or summarizing it. If you can lay out an argument's premises and conclusion in an outline, or if you can accurately paraphrase or summarize the argument, you probably have a pretty good understanding of it. Very often students who think they comprehend an argument are surprised to see that they cannot devise an adequate outline or summary of it. Such failures suggest that although outlining, paraphrasing, or summarizing may seem to some to be unnecessary, it is not—at least not to those new to ethics.

With these guidelines in mind, let's examine a short essay on a familiar topic in ethics. Read it and review the comments that follow. (The sentences have been numbered for easy reference, and the footnotes have been removed.)

The Divine Command Theory

(1) Many people believe that God is a lawgiver who alone defines what actions are right and wrong. (2) God, in other words, is the author of morality; an action is right if and only if God commands it to be done. (3) According to this view, there is no right or wrong until God says so, and nothing is moral or immoral independently of

God's willing it to be thus. (4) God, and only God, *makes* rightness and wrongness. (5) This view is known as the divine command theory of morality.

(6) A simple version of the theory is widely accepted today, among both the religious and nonreligious. (7) In this version, God is thought to be the source of all moral principles and values. (8) He can be the source of all morality because he is omnipotent, being able to do anything whatsoever, including create the very foundations of right and wrong.

(9) In the *Euthyphro*, Socrates brings out what is probably the oldest and strongest criticism of the theory. (10) He asks, in effect, is an action right because God commands it to be done, or does God command it to be done because it is right? (11) This question lays bare the dilemma that is inherent in the theory: (12) If an action is right because God commands it, then there is nothing in the action itself that makes it right, and God's command is arbitrary. (13) If God commands the action because it is right (that is, he does not *make* it right), then rightness would seem to be independent of (or prior to) God, and the divine command theory is false. (14) I contend that, at least in the simplest version of the theory, this ancient dilemma still stands and that the most plausible way to resolve it is to reject the theory by accepting that moral standards must exist independently of God's commands.

(15) The central argument against the notion that rightness is whatever God commands is this: (16) If an action is right only because God commands it (that is, nothing is right or wrong in itself, or independent of God), then cruelty, murder, torture, and many other terrible actions would be right if God commanded them. (17) If God commanded such acts, then they would be right, and no one would be committing a wrong by doing them. (18) On the simple version of the theory, there are no limits whatsoever to God's power, so he could indeed command such things. (19) If nothing would be right or wrong until God wills it, he could have no reason to either command murder or forbid it, to sanction the torture of innocents or prohibit it. (20) If God commands rightness, God's commands would be arbitrary—an impossible result for the religious and nonreligious alike. (21) So it follows that the divine command theory must be mistaken.

(22) A parallel argument is also possible. As stated above, if an action is right only because God commands it, then cruelty, murder, torture, and many other terrible actions would be right if God commanded them. (23) This means that such immoral actions—immoral in light of common moral standards—could be transformed by God into moral actions. (24) This outcome, however, is also impossible. (25) So again the divine command theory seems implausible.

(26) The main objection to the above arguments is that God would never command us to commit heinous acts. (27) He would not because he is morally perfect— all-good in all ways. (28) This counterargument, however, begs the question; it is a circular argument. (29) The divine command theory is offered to explain what makes an action right—what makes something morally good. (30) But to try to define what good is by saying that God is good is to talk in a circle: (31) God's commands are good, and they are good because they are God's commands. (32) This definition reduces the divine command theory to empty doubletalk. (33) If we wish to have a better understanding of what makes an action right, we cannot be satisfied with such a definition.

(34) Moral philosopher James Rachels makes this same argument in a slightly different way:

(35) [If] we accept the idea that good and bad are defined by reference to God's will, this notion is deprived of any meaning. (36) What could it mean to say that God's commands are good? (37) If "X is good" means "X is commanded by God," then "God's commands are good" would mean only "God's commands are commanded by God," an empty truism.

(38) To return to Socrates' dilemma, either an action is right only because God commands it, or an action is right (or wrong) independently of God's commands. (39) As we have seen, if an action is right only because God commands it, then God's commands must be arbitrary, and it is possible for him to sanction obviously immoral acts. (40) Since both these consequences are unacceptable, we must accept the second alternative. (41) Rightness, therefore, must be independent of (or prior to) God's commands.

The first question to ask is, What is the author trying to prove? What is the conclusion being argued for? A few conclusion indicator words point the way: "so it follows" in sentence 21; "so" in sentence 25; and "therefore" in sentence 41. These clues indicate that a single conclusion is being put forth, supported by two separate arguments (in the fourth and fifth paragraphs). The conclusion to be proved is that the divine command theory is false. It is previewed in sentence 14 and stated in sentence 21 in the first argument; in sentence 25 in the second; and in sentence 41, which reiterates the conclusion for the whole essay.

Knowing the conclusion enables us to pick out the premises. Premises of the first argument are both stated in sentence 20: "If God commands rightness, God's commands would be arbitrary—an impossible result for the religious and nonreligious alike." The extracted (and paraphrased) argument looks like this:

1. If God commands rightness (the divine command theory), God's commands would be arbitrary.
2. Such arbitrariness would be impossible.
3. Therefore, the divine command theory must be false.

Premises of the second argument are in sentences 23 and 24, so the paraphrased argument would be:

1. If the divine command theory were true, God could transform immoral actions into moral ones.
2. This outcome would be impossible.
3. Therefore, the divine command theory must be false.

To better reveal the argumentative structure of the essay, we can underline the premises and double-underline the conclusion:

(1) Many people believe that God is a lawgiver who alone defines what actions are right and wrong. (2) God, in other words, is the author of morality; an action is right if and only if God commands it to be done. (3) According to this view, there is no right or wrong until God says so, and nothing is moral or immoral independently of God's willing it to be thus. (4) God, and only God, *makes* rightness and wrongness. (5) This view is known as the divine command theory of morality.

(6) A simple version of the theory is widely accepted today, among both the religious and nonreligious. (7) In this version, God is thought to be the source of

all moral principles and values. (8) He can be the source of all morality because he is omnipotent, being able to do anything whatsoever, including create the very foundations of right and wrong.

(9) In the *Euthyphro*, Socrates brings out what is probably the oldest and strongest criticism of the theory. (10) He asks, in effect, is an action right because God commands it to be done, or does God command it to be done because it is right? (11) This question lays bare the dilemma that is inherent in the theory: (12) If an action is right because God commands it, then there is nothing in the action itself that makes it right, and God's command is arbitrary. (13) If God commands the action because it is right (that is, he does not *make* it right), then rightness would seem to be independent of (or prior to) God, and the divine command theory is false. (14) I contend that, at least in the simplest version of the theory, this ancient dilemma still stands and that the most plausible way to resolve it is to reject the theory by accepting that moral standards must exist independently of God's commands.

(15) The central argument against the notion that rightness is whatever God commands is this: (16) If an action is right only because God commands it (that is, nothing is right or wrong in itself, or independent of God), then cruelty, murder, torture, and many other terrible actions would be right if God commanded them. (17) If God commanded such acts, then they would be right, and no one would be committing a wrong by doing them. (18) On the simple version of the theory, there are no limits whatsoever to God's power, so he could indeed command such things. (19) If nothing would be right or wrong until God wills it, he could have no reason to either command murder or forbid it, to sanction the torture of innocents or prohibit it. (20) If God commands rightness, God's commands would be arbitrary—an impossible result for the religious and nonreligious alike. (21) So it follows that the divine command theory must be mistaken.

(22) A parallel argument is also possible. As stated above, if an action is right only because God commands it, then cruelty, murder, torture, and many other terrible actions would be right if God commanded them. (23) This means that such immoral actions—immoral in light of common moral standards—could be transformed by God into moral actions. (24) This outcome, however, is also impossible. (25) So again the divine command theory seems implausible.

(26) The main objection to the above arguments is that God would never command us to commit heinous acts. (27) He would not because he is morally perfect—all-good in all ways. (28) This counterargument, however, begs the question; it is a circular argument. (29) The divine command theory is offered to explain what makes an action right—what makes something morally good. (30) But to try to define what good is by saying that God is good is to talk in a circle: (31) God's commands are good, and they are good because they are God's commands. (32) This definition reduces the divine command theory to empty doubletalk. (33) If we wish to have a better understanding of what makes an action right, we cannot be satisfied with such a definition.

(34) Moral philosopher James Rachels makes this same argument in a slightly different way:

(35) [If] we accept the idea that good and bad are defined by reference to God's will, this notion is deprived of any meaning. (36) What could it mean to say

that God's commands are good? (37) If "X is good" means "X is commanded by God," then "God's commands are good" would mean only "God's commands are commanded by God," an empty truism.

(38) To return to Socrates' dilemma, either an action is right only because God commands it, or an action is right (or wrong) independently of God's commands. (39) As we have seen, if an action is right only because God commands it, then God's commands must be arbitrary, and it is possible for him to sanction obviously immoral acts. (40) Since both these consequences are unacceptable, we must accept the second alternative. <u>(41) Rightness, therefore, must be independent of (or prior to) God's commands.</u>

With the premises and conclusion identified, we can discern the function of the other parts of the essay. Sentences 1 through 13 introduce and explain the central issue (Is the divine command theory true?), providing background for the discussion to come. Sentences 15 through 19 explain and elaborate on the premises of the first argument. Sentence 22 introduces the first premise of the second argument. Sentences 26 through 34 discuss the main objection to the two arguments (God is good and would not command evil), asserting that if it were true, the notion of God's goodness would be meaningless. Sentences 35 through 37 introduce a quotation to back up the charge of meaninglessness. Sentences 38 through 40 reiterate and summarize the two arguments presented, and sentence 41 is a final reiteration of the essay's conclusion.

Should you accept it? That depends on the worth of the arguments—that is, whether the logic is good and the premises are true. Both arguments are deductively valid, so the truth of the premises is the key concern. Here is the first argument:

1. If God commands rightness (the divine command theory), God's commands would be arbitrary.
2. Such arbitrariness would be impossible.
3. Therefore, the divine command theory must be false.

Premise 2 would likely be accepted by all parties to this debate; premise 1 is the sticking point. Is it true that the divine command theory implies arbitrariness in God's commands? We won't try to answer that question now, but it's clear that if the premise were true, the essay's main conclusion would be established. But if there were good reasons to doubt the premise (because, say, counterexamples undermine it), we would have to reject it.

Much the same can be said about the second argument—premise 2 seems undeniable, but premise 1 is less certain:

1. If the divine command theory were true, God could transform immoral actions into moral ones.
2. This outcome would be impossible.
3. Therefore, the divine command theory must be false.

ARGUMENT EXERCISES

1. From the list below, select the conclusion that is supported by the premises in the following argument:

When conservative Newt Gingrich last spoke on this campus, he was shouted down by several people in the audience who do not approve of his politics. He tried to continue but finally had to give up and walk away. That was unfortunate, but he's not the only one. This kind of treatment has also happened to other unpopular guest speakers. How easily the students at this university forget that free speech is guaranteed by the Bill of Rights. University regulations also support free speech for all students, faculty, and visitors and strictly forbid the harassment of speakers. And this country was founded on the idea that citizens have the right to freely express their views—even when those views are unpopular.

    a. Newt Gingrich is a fascist.
    b. We should never have guest speakers on campus.
    c. Campus speakers should be allowed to speak freely without being shouted down.
    d. Some guest speakers deserve to have the right of free speech and some don't.

For each passage below, determine if there is an argument present. If so, identify the premises and the conclusion.

2. [T]he Religious Right is not "pro-family"...Concerned parents realize that children are curious about how their bodies work and need accurate, age-appropriate information about the human reproductive system. Yet, thanks to Religious Right pressure, many public schools have replaced sex education with fear-based "abstinence only" programs that insult young people's intelligence and give them virtually no useful information.—Rob Boston, *Free Inquiry Magazine*

3. [Francis Bacon] is the father of experimental philosophy...In a word, there was not a man who had any idea of experimental philosophy before Chancellor Bacon; and of an infinity of experiments which have been made since his time, there is hardly a single one which has not been pointed out in his book. He had even made a good number of them himself.—Voltaire, *On Bacon and Newton*

4. Is there archaeological evidence for the [Biblical] Flood? If a universal Flood occurred between five and six thousand years ago, killing all humans except the eight on board the Ark, it would be abundantly clear in the archaeological record. Human history would be marked by an absolute break. We would see the devastation wrought by the catastrophe in terms of the destroyed physical remains of pre-Flood human settlements...Unfortunately for the Flood enthusiasts, the destruction of all but eight of the world's people left no mark on the archaeology of human cultural evolution.—Kenneth L. Feder, *Frauds, Myths, and Mysteries*

5. Subjectivism claims that what makes an action [morally] right is that a person approves of it or believes that it's right. Although subjectivism may seem admirably egalitarian in that it takes everyone's moral judgments to be as good as everyone else's, it has some rather bizarre consequences. For one thing, it implies that each of us is morally infallible. As long as we approve of or believe in what we are doing, we can do no wrong. But this cannot be right. Suppose that Hitler believed that it was right to exterminate the Jews. Then it was right for Hitler to exterminate the Jews...But what...Hitler did was wrong, even if [he] believed otherwise.—Theodore Schick, Jr., *Free Inquiry Magazine*

6. "War doesn't solve problems; it creates them," said an Oct. 8 letter about Iraq. World War II solved problems called Nazi Germany and militaristic Japan and created alliances with the nations we crushed...The Persian Gulf war solved the problem of the Iraqi invasion of Kuwait. The Civil War solved the problem of slavery. These wars created a better world. War, or the threat of it, is the only way to defeat evil enemies who are a threat to us. There is no reasoning with them. There can be no peace with them...so it's either us or them. What creates true peace is victory.—Letter to the editor, *The New York Times*

For the following argument, indicate which conclusion from the accompanying list would be strongly supported by the premise given. Assume that all statements are true.

7. Seventy-two percent of the 300 university students who responded to a questionnaire published in the campus newspaper are opposed to the U.S. president's economic policies.

> a. Some readers of the campus newspaper are opposed to the U.S. president's economic policies.
> b. Seventy-two percent of the students attending this school are opposed to the U.S. president's economic policies.
> c. Some students attending this school are opposed to the U.S. president's economic policies.
> d. Most readers of the campus newspaper are opposed to the U.S. president's economic policies.
> e. Seventy-two percent of the readers of the campus newspaper are opposed to the U.S. president's economic policies.

Read the argument below. Then in questions 8 through 12, supply the information requested. Each question asks you to identify by number all the sentences in the argument that fulfill a particular role—conclusion, premise, background information, example or illustration, or reiteration of a premise or the conclusion. Just write down the appropriate sentence numbers.

[1] Is global warming a real threat? [2] Or is it hype propagated by tree-hugging, daft environmentalists? [3] The president apparently thinks that the idea of global climate change is bunk. [4] But recently his own administration gave the lie to his bunk theory. [5] His own Administration issued a report on global warming called the *U.S. Climate Action Report 2002*. [6] It gave no support to the idea that global warming doesn't happen and we should all go back to sleep. [7] Instead, it asserted that global warming was definitely real and that it could have catastrophic consequences if ignored. [8] For example, global climate change could cause heat waves, extreme weather, and water shortages right here in the United States. [9] The report is also backed by many other reports, including a very influential one from the United Nations. [10] Yes, George, global warming is real. [11] It is as real as typhoons and ice storms.

> 8. Conclusion
> 9. Premise or premises
> 10. Background information
> 11. Example or illustration
> 12. Repetition of conclusion or premise

KEY WORDS

ethics	morality	normative ethics
metaethics	applied ethics	descriptive ethics
divine command theory	moral objectivism	prima facie
moral relativism	subjective relativism	argument
cultural relativism	premise	conclusion
statement	deductive argument	
inductive argument	moral argument	

SUMMARY

Ethics is the study of morality using the methods of philosophy, and morality concerns beliefs about right and wrong actions and good and bad persons or character. Morality is a normative domain, having the properties of overridingness, impartiality, universality, and reasonableness.

Legal norms are distinct from moral norms, although these two often coincide. Those who insist that actions that are considered seriously immoral should also be made illegal are known as legal moralists. Religion and morality are linked by virtue of the former having moral content. But both religious and nonreligious thinkers have serious reservations about the divine command theory, the doctrine that God makes the moral law. Moral objectivism is the view that there are moral standards that are true or correct for everyone. Moral relativism rejects moral objectivism, but it has been criticized for its implausible implications.

Moral reasoning involves the evaluation and creation of moral arguments. A moral argument is one whose conclusion is a moral statement. Moral premises can be evaluated just as nonmoral premises can. One way to assess the truth of a moral premise is to cite counterexamples.

READINGS

The Ring of Gyges

PLATO

BOOK 2

With these words I was thinking that I had made an end of the discussion; but the end, in truth, proved to be only a beginning. For Glaucon, who is always the most pugnacious of men, was dissatisfied at Thrasymachus' retirement; he wanted to have the battle out. So he said to me: Socrates, do you wish really to persuade us; or only to seem to have persuaded us, that to be just is always better than to be unjust?

Reprinted from *The Dialogues of Plato*, trans. Benjamin Jowett (Charles Scribner's, 1889).

I should wish really to persuade you, I replied, if I could.

Then you certainly have not succeeded. Let me ask you now:—How would you arrange goods—are there not some which we welcome for their own sakes, and independently of their consequences, as, for example, harmless pleasures and enjoyments, which delight us at the time, although nothing follows from them?

I agree in thinking that there is such a class, I replied.

Is there not also a second class of goods, such as knowledge, sight, health, which are desirable not only in themselves, but also for their results?

Certainly, I said.

And would you not recognize a third class, such as gymnastic, and the care of the sick, and the physician's art; also the various ways of money-making—these do us good but we regard them as disagreeable; and no one would choose them for their own sakes, but only for the sake of some reward or result which flows from them?

There is, I said, this third class also. But why do you ask?

Because I want to know in which of the three classes you would place justice?

In the highest class, I replied, among those goods which he who would be happy desires both for their own sake and for the sake of their results.

Then the many are of another mind; they think that justice is to be reckoned in the troublesome class, among goods which are to be pursued for the sake of rewards and of reputation, but in themselves are disagreeable and rather to be avoided.

I know, I said, that this is their manner of thinking, and that this was the thesis which Thrasymachus was maintaining just now, when he censured justice and praised injustice. But I am too stupid to be convinced by him.

I wish, he said, that you would hear me as well as him, and then I shall see whether you and I agree. For Thrasymachus seems to me, like a snake, to have been charmed by your voice sooner than he ought to have been; but to my mind the nature of justice and injustice have not yet been made clear. Setting aside their rewards and results, I want to know what they are in themselves, and how they inwardly work in the soul. If you please, then, I will revive the argument of Thrasymachus. And first I will speak of the nature and origin of justice according to the common view of them. Secondly, I will show that all men who practice justice do so against their will, of necessity, but not as a good. And thirdly, I will argue that there is reason in this view, for the life of the unjust is after all better far than the life of the just—if what they say is true, Socrates, since I myself am not of their opinion. But still I acknowledge that I am perplexed when I hear the voices of Thrasymachus and myriads of others dinning in my ears; and, on the other hand, I have never yet heard the superiority of justice to injustice maintained by any one in a satisfactory way. I want to hear justice praised in respect of itself; then I shall be satisfied, and you are the person from whom I think that I am most likely to hear this; and therefore I will praise the unjust life to the utmost of my power, and my manner of speaking will indicate the manner in which I desire to hear you too praising justice and censuring injustice. Will you say whether you approve of my proposal?

Indeed I do; nor can I imagine any theme about which a man of sense would oftener wish to converse.

I am delighted, he replied, to hear you say so, and shall begin by speaking, as I proposed, of the nature and origin of justice.

They say that to do injustice is, by nature, good; to suffer injustice, evil; but that the evil is greater than the good. And so when men have both done and suffered injustice and have had experience of both, not being able to avoid the one and obtain the other, they think that they had better agree among themselves to have neither; hence there arise laws and mutual covenants; and that which is ordained by law is termed by them lawful and just. This they affirm to be the origin and nature of justice:—it is a mean or compromise, between the best of all, which is to do injustice and not be punished, and the worst of all, which is to suffer injustice without the power of retaliation; and justice, being at a middle point between the two, is tolerated not as a good, but as the lesser evil, and honoured by reason of the inability of men to do injustice. For no man who is worthy to be called a man would ever submit to such an agreement if he were able to resist; he would be mad if he did. Such is the received account, Socrates, of the nature and origin of justice.

Now that those who practice justice do so involuntarily and because they have not the power to be unjust will best appear if we imagine something of this kind: having given both to the just and the unjust power to do what they will, let us watch and see whither desire will lead them; then we shall discover in the very act the just and unjust man to be proceeding along the same road, following their interest, which all natures deem to be their good, and are only diverted into the path of justice by the force of law. The liberty which we are supposing may be most completely given to them in the form of such a power as is said to have been possessed by Gyges the ancestor of Croesus the Lydian. According to the tradition, Gyges was a shepherd in the service of the king of Lydia; there was a great storm, and an earthquake made an opening in the earth at the place where he was feeding his flock. Amazed at the sight, he descended into the opening, where, among other marvels, he beheld a hollow brazen horse, having doors, at which he stooping and looking in saw a dead body of stature, as appeared to him, more than human, and having nothing on but a gold ring; this he took from the finger of the dead and reascended. Now the shepherds met together, according to custom, that they might send their monthly report about the flocks to the king; into their assembly he came having the ring on his finger, and as he was sitting among them he chanced to turn the collet of the ring inside his hand, when instantly he became invisible to the rest of the company and they began to speak of him as if he were no longer present. He was astonished at this, and again touching the ring he turned the collet outwards and reappeared; he made several trials of the ring, and always with the same result—when he turned the collet inwards he became invisible, when outwards he reappeared. Whereupon he contrived to be chosen one of the messengers who were sent to the court; where as soon as he arrived he seduced the queen, and with her help conspired against the king and slew him, and took the kingdom. Suppose now that there were two such magic rings, and the just put on one of them and the unjust the other; no man can be imagined to be of such an iron nature that he would stand fast in justice. No man would keep his hands off what was not his

own when he could safely take what he liked out of the market, or go into houses and lie with any one at his pleasure, or kill or release from prison whom he would, and in all respects be like a God among men. Then the actions of the just would be as the actions of the unjust; they would both come at last to the same point. And this we may truly affirm to be a great proof that a man is just, not willingly or because he thinks that justice is any good to him individually, but of necessity, for wherever any one thinks that he can safely be unjust, there he is unjust. For all men believe in their hearts that injustice is far more profitable to the individual than justice, and he who argues as I have been supposing, will say that they are right. If you could imagine any one obtaining this power of becoming invisible, and never doing any wrong or touching what was another's, he would be thought by the lookers-on to be a most wretched idiot, although they would praise him to one another's faces, and keep up appearances with one another from a fear that they too might suffer injustice. Enough of this.

Now, if we are to form a real judgment of the life of the just and unjust, we must isolate them; there is no other way; and how is the isolation to be effected? I answer: Let the unjust man be entirely unjust, and the just man entirely just; nothing is to be taken away from either of them, and both are to be perfectly furnished for the work of their respective lives. First, let the unjust be like other distinguished masters of craft; like the skillful pilot or physician, who knows intuitively his own powers and keeps within their limits, and who, if he fails at any point, is able to recover himself. So let the unjust make his unjust attempts in the right way, and lie hidden if he means to be great in his injustice (he who is found out is nobody): for the highest reach of injustice is: to be deemed just when you are not. Therefore I say that in the perfectly unjust man we must assume the most perfect injustice; there is to be no deduction, but we must allow him, while doing the most unjust acts, to have acquired the greatest reputation for justice. If he have taken a false step he must be able to recover himself; he must be one who can speak with effect, if any of his deeds come to light, and who can force his way where force is required by his courage and strength, and command of money and friends. And at his side let us place the just man in his nobleness and simplicity, wishing, as Aeschylus says, to be and not to seem good. There must be no seeming, for if he seem to be just he will be honoured and rewarded, and then we shall not know whether he is just for the sake of justice or for the sake of honours and rewards; therefore, let him be clothed in justice only, and have no other covering; and he must be imagined in a state of life the opposite of the former. Let him be the best of men, and let him be thought the worst; then he will have been put to the proof; and we shall see whether he will be affected by the fear of infamy and its consequences. And let him continue thus to the hour of death; being just and seeming to be unjust. When both have reached the uttermost extreme, the one of justice and the other of injustice, let judgment be given which of them is the happier of the two.

Heavens! my dear Glaucon, I said, how energetically you polish them up for the decision, first one and then the other, as if they were two statues.

I do my best, he said. And now that we know what they are like there is no difficulty in tracing out the sort of life which awaits either of them. This I will proceed to describe; but as you may think the description a little too coarse, I ask you to suppose, Socrates, that the words which follow are not mine.— Let me put them into the mouths of the eulogists of injustice: they will tell you that the just man who is thought unjust will be scourged, racked, bound— will have his eyes burnt out; and, at last, after suffering every kind of evil, he will be impaled: Then he will understand that he ought to seem only, and not to be, just; the words of Aeschylus may be more truly spoken of the unjust than of the just. For the unjust is pursuing a reality; he does not live with a view to appearances—he wants to be really unjust and not to seem only—

His mind has a soil deep and fertile,
Out of which spring his prudent counsels.

In the first place, he is thought just, and therefore bears rule in the city; he can marry whom he will, and give in marriage to whom he will; also he can trade and deal where he likes, and always to his own advantage, because he has no misgivings about injustice, and at every contest, whether in public or private, he gets the better of his antagonists, and gains at their expense, and is rich, and out of his gains he can benefit his friends, and harm his enemies; moreover, he can offer sacrifices, and dedicate gifts to the gods abundantly and magnificently, and can honour the gods or any man whom he wants to honour in a far better style than the just, and therefore he is likely to be dearer than they are to the gods. And thus, Socrates, gods and men are said to unite in making the life of the unjust better than the life of the just....

[We pick up the discussion in Book 9]

BOOK 9

"Now that we've gotten this far," I said, "let's go back to that statement made at the beginning, which brought us here: that it pays for a man to be perfectly unjust if he appears to be just. Isn't that what someone said?"

"Yes."

"Then since we've agreed what power justice and injustice each have, let's have a discussion with him."

"How?"

"By molding in words an image of the soul, so that the one who said that will realize what he was saying."

"What kind of image?"

"Oh, something like those natures the myths tell us were born in ancient times—the Chimaera, Scylla, Cerberus, and others in which many different shapes were supposed to have grown into one."

"So they tell us," he said.

"Then mold one figure of a colorful, many-headed beast with heads of wild and tame animals growing in a circle all around it; one that can change and grow all of them out of itself."

"That's a job for a skilled artist. Still, words mold easier than wax or clay, so consider it done."

"And another of a lion, and one of a man. Make the first by far the biggest, the second second largest."

"That's easier, and already done."

"Now join the three together so that they somehow grow."

"All right."

"Next mold the image of one, the man, around them all, so that to someone who can't see what's inside but looks only at the container it appears to be a single animal, man."

"I have."

"Then shall we inform the gentleman that when he says it pays for this man to be unjust, he's saying that it profits him to feast his multifarious beast and his lion and make them grow strong, but to starve and enfeeble the man in him so that he gets dragged wherever the animals lead him, and instead of making them friends and used to each other, to let them bite and fight and eat each other?"

"That's just what he's saying by praising injustice."

"The one who says justice pays, however, would be saying that he should practice and say whatever will give the most mastery to his inner man, who should care for the many-headed beast like a farmer, raising and domesticating its tame heads and preventing the wild ones from growing, making the lion's nature his partner and ally, and so raise them both to be friends to each other and to him."

"That's exactly what he means by praising justice."

"So in every way the commender of justice is telling the truth, the other a lie. Whether we examine pleasure, reputation, or profit, we find that the man who praises justice speaks truly, the one who disparages it disparages sickly and knows nothing of what he disparages."

"I don't think he does at all."

"Then let's gently persuade him—his error wasn't intended—by asking him a question: 'Shouldn't we say that the traditions of the beautiful and the ugly have come about like this: Beautiful things are those that make our bestial parts subservient to the human—or rather, perhaps, to the divine—part of our nature, while ugly ones are those that enslave the tame to the wild?' Won't he agree?"

"If he takes my advice."

"On this argument then, can it pay for a man to take money unjustly if that means making his best part a slave to the worst? If it wouldn't profit a man to sell his son or his daughter into slavery—to wild and evil men at that—even if he got a fortune for it,

then if he has no pity on himself and enslaves the most godlike thing in him to the most godless and polluted, isn't he a wretch who gets bribed for gold into a destruction more horrible than Euriphyle's, who sold her husband's life for a necklace?"

"Much more horrible," said Glaucon.

"... [E]veryone is better off being ruled by the godlike and intelligent; preferably if he has it inside, but if not, it should be imposed on him from without so that we may all be friends and as nearly alike as possible, all steered by the same thing."

"Yes, and we're right," he said.

"Law, the ally of everyone in the city, clearly intends the same thing, as does the rule of children, which forbids us to let them be free until we've instituted a regime in them as in a city. We serve their best part with a similar part in us, install a like guardian and ruler in them, and only then set them free."

"Clearly."

"Then how, by what argument, Glaucon, can we say that it pays for a man to be unjust or self-indulgent or to do something shameful to get more money or power if by doing so he make himself worse?"

"We can't," he said.

"And how can it pay to commit injustice without getting caught and being punished? Doesn't getting away with it make a man even worse? Whereas if a man gets caught and punished, his beastlike part is taken in and tamed, his tame part is set free, and his whole soul acquires justice and temperance and knowledge. Therefore his soul recovers its best nature and attains a state more honorable than the state the body attains when it acquires health and strength and beauty, by as much as the soul is more honorable than the body."

"Absolutely."

"Then won't a sensible man spend his life directing all his efforts to this end?"

The Case Against Moral Relativism

LOUIS P. POJMAN

"WHO'S TO JUDGE WHAT'S RIGHT OR WRONG?"

Like many people, I have always been instinctively a moral relativist. As far back as I can remember…it has always seemed to be obvious that the dictates of morality arise from some sort of convention or understanding among people, that different people arrive at different understandings, and that there are no basic moral demands that apply to everyone. This seemed so obvious to me I assumed it was everyone's instinctive view, or at least everyone who gave the matter any thought in this day and age.

—Gilbert Harman[1]

Ethical relativism is the doctrine that the moral rightness and wrongness of actions vary from society to society and that there are not absolute universal moral standards on all men at all times. Accordingly, it holds that whether or not it is right for an individual to act in a certain way depends on or is relative to the society to which he belongs.

—John Ladd[2]

Gilbert Harman's intuitions about the self-evidence of ethical relativism contrast strikingly with Plato's or Kant's equal certainty about the truth of objectivism, the doctrine that universally valid or true ethical principles exist.[3] "Two things fill the soul with ever new and increasing wonder and reverence the oftener and more fervently reflection ponders on it: the starry heavens above and the moral law within," wrote Kant. On the basis of polls taken in my ethics and introduction to philosophy classes in recent years, Harman's views may signal a shift in contemporary society's moral understanding. The polls show a two-to-one ratio in favor of moral relativism over moral absolutism, with fewer than five percent of the respondents recognizing that a third position between these two polar opposites might exist. Of course, I'm not suggesting that all of these students had a clear understanding of what

relativism entails, for many who said they were relativists also contended in the same polls that abortion except to save the mother's life is always wrong, that capital punishment is always wrong, or that suicide is never morally permissible.

Among my university colleagues, a growing number also seem to embrace moral relativism. Recently one of my nonphilosopher colleagues voted to turn down a doctoral dissertation proposal because the student assumed an objectivist position in ethics. (Ironically, I found in this same colleague's work rhetorical treatment of individual liberty that raised it to the level of a non-negotiable absolute). But irony and inconsistency aside, many relativists are aware of the tension between their own subjective positions and their metatheory that entails relativism. I confess that I too am tempted by the allurements of this view and find some forms of it plausible and worthy of serious examination. However, I also find it deeply troubling.

In this essay I will examine the central notions of ethical relativism and look at the implications that seem to follow from it. Then I will present the outline of a very modest objectivism, one that takes into account many of the insights of relativism and yet stands as a viable option to it.

1. An Analysis of Relativism

Let us examine the theses contained in John Ladd's succinct statement on ethical (conventional) relativism that appears at the beginning of this essay. If we analyze it, we derive the following argument:

1. Moral rightness and wrongness of actions vary from society to society, so there are no universal moral standards held by all societies.
2. Whether or not it is right for individuals to act in a certain way depends on (or is relative to) the society to which they belong.

3. Therefore, there are no absolute or objective moral standards that apply to all people everywhere.

1. The first thesis, which may be called the *diversity thesis*, is simply a description that acknowledges the fact that moral rules differ from society to society. The Spartans of ancient Greece and the Dobu of New Guinea believe that stealing is morally right, but we believe it is wrong. The Roman father had the power of life and death (*just vitae necisque*) over his children, whereas we condemn parents for abusing their children. A tribe in East Africa once threw deformed infants to the hippopotamuses, and in ancient Greece and Rome infants were regularly exposed, while we abhor infanticide. Ruth Benedict describes a tribe in Melanesia that views cooperation and kindness as vices, whereas we see them as virtues. While in ancient Greece, Rome, China and Korea parricide was condemned as "the most execrable of crimes," among Northern Indians aged persons, persons who were no longer capable of walking, were left alone to starve. Among the California Gallinomero, when fathers became feeble, a burden to their sons, "the poor old wretch is not infrequently thrown down on his back and securely held while a stick is placed across his throat, and two of them seat themselves on the ends of it until he ceases to breathe."[4] Sexual practices vary over time and place. Some cultures permit homosexual behavior, while others condemn it. Some cultures practice polygamy, while others view it as immoral. Some cultures condone while others condemn premarital sex. Some cultures accept cannibalism, while the very idea revolts us. Some West African tribes perform clitoridectomies on girls, whereas we deplore such practices. Cultural relativism is well documented, and "custom is the king o'er all." There may or may not be moral principles that are held in common by every society, but if there are any, they seem to be few at best. Certainly it would be very difficult to derive any single "true" morality by observing various societies' moral standards.

2. The second thesis, *the dependency thesis*, asserts that individual acts are right or wrong depending on the nature of the society from which they emanate. Morality does not occur in a vacuum, and what is considered morally right or wrong must be seen in a context that depends on the goals, wants, beliefs, history, and environment of the society in question. As William G. Sumner says,

> We learn the morals as unconsciously as we learn to walk and hear and breathe, and [we] never know any reason why the [morals] are what they are. The justification of them is that when we wake to consciousness of life we find them facts which already hold us in the bonds of tradition, custom, and habit.[5]

Trying to see things from an independent, noncultural point of view would be like taking out our eyes in order to examine their contours and qualities. There is no "innocent eye." We are simply culturally determined beings.

We could, of course, distinguish between a weak and a strong thesis of dependency, for the nonrelativist can accept a certain degree of relativity in the way moral principles are *applied* in various cultures, depending on beliefs, history, and environment. For example, Jewish men express reverence for God by covering their heads when entering places of worship, whereas Christian men uncover their heads when entering places of worship. Westerners shake hands upon greeting each other, whereas Hindus place their hands together and point them toward the person to be greeted. Both sides adhere to principles of reverence and respect but apply them differently. But the ethical relativist must maintain a stronger thesis, one that insists that the moral principles themselves are products of the cultures and may vary from society to society. The ethical relativist contends that even beyond environmental factors and differences in beliefs, a fundamental disagreement exists among societies. One way for the relativist to support this thesis is by appealing to an indeterminacy of translation thesis, which maintains that there is a conceptual relativity among language groups so that we cannot even translate into our language the worldviews of a culture with a radically different language.

In a sense we all live in radically different worlds. But the relativist wants to go further and maintain that there is something conventional about *any* morality, so that every morality really depends on a level of social acceptance. Not only do various societies adhere to different moral systems, but the very same society could (and often does) change its moral views over place and time. For example, the majority of people in the southern United States now view slavery as immoral, whereas one hundred and forty years ago they did not. Our society's views on divorce, sexuality, abortion, and assisted suicide have changed somewhat as well—and they are still changing.

3. The conclusion that there are no absolute or objective moral standards binding on all people follows from the first two propositions. Combining cultural relativism (*the diversity thesis*) with *the dependency thesis* yields ethical relativism in its classic form. If there are different moral principles from culture to culture and if all morality is rooted in culture, then it follows that there are no universal moral principles that are valid (or true) for all cultures and peoples at all times.

2. Subjectivism

Some people think that this conclusion is still too tame, and they maintain that morality is dependent not on the society but rather on the individual. As my students sometimes maintain, "Morality is in the eye of the beholder." They treat morality like taste or aesthetic judgments—person relative. This form of moral subjectivism has the sorry consequence that it makes morality a very useless concept, for, on its premises, little or no interpersonal criticism or judgment is logically possible. Suppose that you are repulsed by observing John torturing a child. You cannot condemn him if one of his principles is "torture little children for the fun of it." The only basis for judging him wrong might be that he was a hypocrite who condemned others for torturing. But suppose that another of his principles is that hypocrisy is morally permissible (for him); thus we cannot condemn him for condemning others for doing what he does.

On the basis of subjectivism Adolf Hitler and the serial murderer Ted Bundy could be considered as moral as Gandhi, so long as each lived by his own standards, whatever those might be. Witness the following paraphrase of a tape-recorded conversation between Ted Bundy and one of his victims in which Bundy justifies his murder:

Then I learned that all moral judgments are "value judgments," that all value judgments are

subjective, and that none can be proved to be either "right" or "wrong." I even read somewhere that the Chief Justice of the United States had written that the American Constitution expressed nothing more than collective value judgments. Believe it or not, I figured out for myself—what apparently the Chief Justice couldn't figure out for himself— that if the rationality of one value judgment was zero, multiplying it by millions would not make it one whit more rational. Nor is there any "reason" to obey the law for anyone, like myself, who has the boldness and daring—the strength of character—to throw off its shackles.... I discovered that to become truly free, truly unfettered, I had to become truly uninhibited. And I quickly discovered that the greatest obstacle to my freedom, the greatest block and limitation to it, consists in the insupportable "value judgment" that I was bound to respect the rights of others. I asked myself, who were these "others"? Other human beings, with human rights? Why is it more wrong to kill a human animal than any other animal, a pig or a sheep or a steer? Is your life more to you than a hog's life to a hog? Why should I be willing to sacrifice my pleasure more for the one than for the other? Surely you would not, in this age of scientific enlightenment, declare that God or nature has marked some pleasures as "moral" or "good" and others as "immoral" or "bad"? In any case, let me assure you, my dear young lady, that there is absolutely no comparison between the pleasure I might take in eating ham and the pleasure I anticipate in raping and murdering you. That is the honest conclusion to which my education has led me—after the most conscientious examination of my spontaneous and uninhibited self.[6]

Notions of good and bad, or right and wrong, cease to have interpersonal evaluative meaning. We might be revulsed by the views of Ted Bundy, but that is just a matter of taste. A student might not like it when her teacher gives her an F on a test paper, while he gives another student an A for a similar paper, but there is no way to criticize him for injustice, because justice is not one of his chosen principles.

Absurd consequences follow from subjectivism. If it is correct, then morality reduces to aesthetic tastes about which there can be neither argument nor interpersonal judgment. Although many students say they espouse subjectivism, there is evidence that it conflicts with other of their moral views. They typically condemn Hitler as an evil man for his genocidal policies. A contradiction seems to exist between subjectivism and the very concept of morality, which it is supposed to characterize, for morality has to do with *proper* resolution of interpersonal conflict and the amelioration of the human predicament (both deontological and teleological systems do this, but in different ways—see chapters 4 and 5 of Part II). Whatever else it does, morality has a minimal aim of preventing a Hobbesian state of nature (see chapter 1), wherein life is "solitary, poor, nasty, brutish, and short." But if so, subjectivism is no help at all, for it rests neither on social agreement of principle (as the conventionalist maintains) nor on an objectively independent set of norms that bind all people for the common good. If there were only one person on earth, there would be no occasion for morality, because there wouldn't be any interpersonal conflicts to resolve or others whose suffering he or she would have a duty to ameliorate. Subjectivism implicitly assumes something of this solipsism, an atomism in which isolated individuals make up separate universes.

Subjectivism treats individuals like billiard balls on a societal pool table where they meet only in radical collisions, each aimed at his or her own goal and striving to do in the others before they themselves are done in. This atomistic view of personality is belied by the facts that we develop in families and mutually dependent communities in which we share a common language, common institutions, and similar rituals and habits, and that we often feel one another's joys and sorrows. As the poet John Donne wrote, "No man is an island, entire of itself; every man is a piece of the continent."

Radical individualistic ethical relativism is incoherent. If so, it follows that the only plausible view of ethical relativism must be one that grounds morality in the group or culture. This form is called *conventionalism.*

3. Conventionalism

Conventional ethical relativism, the view that there are no objective moral principles but that all valid

moral principles are justified (or are made true) by virtue of their cultural acceptance, recognizes the social nature of morality. That is precisely its power and virtue. It does not seem subject to the same absurd consequences which plague subjectivism. Recognizing the importance of our social environment in generating customs and beliefs, many people suppose that ethical relativism is the correct metaethical theory. Furthermore, they are drawn to it for its liberal philosophical stance. It seems to be an enlightened response to the sin of ethnocentricity, and it seems to entail or strongly imply an attitude of tolerance toward other cultures. Anthropologist Ruth Benedict says, that in recognizing ethical relativity, "We shall arrive at a more realistic social faith, accepting as grounds of hope and as new bases for tolerance the coexisting and equally valid patterns of life which mankind has created for itself from the raw materials of existence."[7] The most famous of those holding this position is the anthropologist Melville Herskovits, who argues even more explicitly than Benedict that ethical relativism entails intercultural tolerance.

1. If morality is relative to its culture, then there is no independent basis for criticizing the morality of any other culture but one's own.
2. If there is no independent way of criticizing any other culture, we ought to be *tolerant* of the moralities of other cultures.
3. Morality is relative to its culture. Therefore,
4. We ought to be *tolerant* of the moralities of other cultures.[8]

Tolerance is certainly a virtue, but is this a good argument for it? I think not. If morality simply is relative to each culture, then if the culture in question does not have a principle of tolerance, its members have no obligation to be tolerant. Herskovits seems to be treating the *principle of tolerance* as the one exception to his relativism. He seems to be treating it as an absolute moral principle. But from a relativistic point of view there is no more reason to be tolerant than to be intolerant and neither stance is objectively morally better than the other.

Not only do relativists fail to offer a basis for criticizing those who are intolerant, but they cannot rationally criticize anyone who espouses what they might regard as a heinous principle. If, as seems to be the case, valid criticism supposes an objective or impartial standard, relativists cannot morally criticize anyone outside their own culture. Adolf Hitler's genocidal actions, so long as they are culturally accepted, are as morally legitimate as Mother Teresa's works of mercy. If Conventional Relativism is accepted, racism, genocide of unpopular minorities, oppression of the poor, slavery, and even the advocacy of war for its own sake are as equally moral as their opposites. And if a subculture decided that starting a nuclear war was somehow morally acceptable, we could not morally criticize these people. Any actual morality, whatever its content, is as valid as every other, and more valid than ideal moralities—since the latter aren't adhered to by any culture.

There are other disturbing consequences of ethical relativism. It seems to entail that reformers are always (morally) wrong since they go against the tide of cultural standards. William Wilberforce was wrong in the eighteenth century to oppose slavery; the British were immoral in opposing *suttee* in India (the burning of widows, which is now illegal in India). The early Christians were wrong in refusing to serve in the Roman army or to bow down to Caesar since the majority in the Roman Empire believed that these two acts were moral duties. In fact, Jesus himself was immoral in breaking the law of His day by healing on the Sabbath day and by advocating the principles of the Sermon on the Mount, since it is clear that few in His time (or in ours) accepted them.

Yet we normally feel just the opposite, that the reformer is a courageous innovator who is right, who has the truth, against the mindless majority. Sometimes the individual must stand alone with the truth, risking social censure and persecution. As Dr. Stockman says in Ibsen's *Enemy of the People*, after he loses the battle to declare his town's profitable but polluted tourist spa unsanitary, "The most dangerous enemy of the truth and freedom among us—is the compact majority. Yes, the damned, compact and liberal majority. The majority has *might*—unfortunately—but *right* it is not. Right—are I and a few others." Yet if relativism is correct, the opposite is necessarily the case. Truth is with the crowd and error with the individual.

Similarly, conventional ethical relativism entails disturbing judgments about the law. Our normal view is that we have a prima facie duty to obey the law, because law, in general, promotes the human good. According to most objective systems, this obligation is not absolute but relative to the particular law's relation to a wider moral order. Civil disobedience is warranted in some cases where the law seems to be in serious conflict with morality. However, if moral relativism is true, then neither law nor civil disobedience has a firm foundation. On the one hand, from the side of the society at large, civil disobedience will be morally wrong, so long as the majority culture agrees with the law in question. On the other hand, if you belong to the relevant subculture which doesn't recognize the particular law in question (because it is unjust from your point of view), disobedience will be morally mandated. The Ku Klux Klan, which believes that Jews, Catholics and Blacks are evil or undeserving of high regard, are, given conventionalism, morally permitted or required to break the laws which protect these endangered groups. Why should I obey a law that my group doesn't recognize as valid?

To sum up, unless we have an independent moral basis for law, it is hard to see why we have any general duty to obey it; and unless we recognize the priority of a universal moral law, we have no firm basis to justify our acts of civil disobedience against "unjust laws." Both the validity of law and morally motivated disobedience of unjust laws are annulled in favor of a power struggle.

There is an even more basic problem with the notion that morality is dependent on cultural acceptance for its validity. The problem is that the notion of a *culture* or *society* is notoriously difficult to define. This is especially so in a pluralistic society like our own where the notion seems to be vague with unclear boundary lines. One person may belong to several societies (subcultures) with different value emphases and arrangements of principles. A person may belong to the nation as a single society with certain values of patriotism, honor, courage, laws (including some which are controversial but have majority acceptance, such as the current law on abortion). But he or she may also belong to a church which opposes some of the laws of the State. He may also be an integral member of a socially mixed community where different principles hold sway, and he may belong to clubs and a family where still other rules are adhered to. Relativism would seem to tell us that where he is a member of societies with conflicting moralities he must be judged both wrong and not-wrong whatever he does. For example, if Mary is a U.S. citizen and a member of the Roman Catholic Church, she is wrong (qua Catholic) if she chooses to have an abortion and not-wrong (qua citizen of the U.S.A.) if she acts against the teaching of the Church on abortion. As a member of a racist university fraternity, KKK, John has no obligation to treat his fellow Black student as an equal, but as a member of the university community itself (where the principle of equal rights is accepted) he does have the obligation; but as a member of the surrounding community (which may reject the principle of equal rights) he again has no such obligation; but then again as a member of the nation at large (which accepts the principle) he is obligated to treat his fellow with respect. What is the morally right thing for John to do? The question no longer makes much sense in this moral Babel. It has lost its action-guiding function.

Perhaps the relativist would adhere to a principle which says that in such cases the individual may choose which group to belong to as primary. If Mary chooses to have an abortion, she is choosing to belong to the general society relative to that principle. And John must likewise choose among groups. The trouble with this option is that it seems to lead back to counter-intuitive results. If Murder Mike of Murder, Incorporated, feels like killing Bank President Ortcutt and wants to feel good about it, he identifies with the Murder, Incorporated society rather than the general public morality. Does this justify the killing? In fact, couldn't one justify anything simply by forming a small subculture that approved of it? Ted Bundy would be morally pure in raping and killing innocents simply by virtue of forming a little coterie. How large must the group be in order to be a legitimate subculture or society? Does it need ten or fifteen people? How about just three? Come to think about it, why can't my burglary partner and I found our own society with a morality of its own? Of course, if my partner dies, I could still claim that I was acting from an originally social set of norms. But why can't I dispense with the interpersonal agreements altogether and invent my own morality—since morality, on this view, is only an invention anyway? Conventionalist relativism seems to reduce to subjectivism. And subjectivism leads, as we have seen, to moral solipsism, to the demise of morality altogether.

Should one object that this is an instance of the *Slippery Slope Fallacy*,[9] let that person give an alternative analysis of what constitutes a viable social basis for generating valid (or true) moral principles. Perhaps we might agree (for the sake of argument, at least) that the very nature of morality entails two people making an agreement. This move saves the conventionalist from moral solipsism, but it still permits almost any principle at all to count as moral. And what's more, those principles can be thrown out and their contraries substituted for them as the need arises. If two or three people decide that they will make cheating on exams morally acceptable for themselves, via forming a fraternity "Cheaters Anonymous" at their university, then cheating becomes moral. Why not? Why not rape, as well?

However, I don't think you can stop the move from conventionalism to subjectivism. The essential force of the validity of the chosen moral principle is that it is dependent on *choice*. The conventionalist holds that it is the choice of the group, but why should I accept the group's silly choice, when my own is better (for me)? Why should anyone give such august authority to a culture of society? If this is all morality comes to, why not reject it altogether—even though one might want to adhere to its directives when others are looking in order to escape sanctions?

4. A Critique of Ethical Relativism

However, while we may fear the demise of morality, as we have known it, this in itself may not be a good reason for rejecting relativism. That is, for judging it false. Alas, truth may not always be edifying. But the consequences of this position are sufficiently alarming to prompt us to look carefully for some weakness in the relativist's argument. So let us examine the premises and conclusion listed at the beginning of this essay as the three theses of relativism.

1. *The Diversity Thesis.* What is considered morally right and wrong varies from society to society, so that there are no moral principles accepted by all societies.
2. *The Dependency Thesis.* All moral principles derive their validity from cultural acceptance.
3. *Ethical Relativism.* Therefore, there are no universally valid moral principles, objective standards which apply to all people everywhere and at all times.

Does any one of these seem problematic? Let us consider the first thesis, the diversity thesis, which we have also called cultural relativism. Perhaps there is not as much diversity as anthropologists like Sumner and Benedict suppose. One can also see great similarities between the moral codes of various cultures. E. O. Wilson has identified over a score of common features,[10] and before him Clyde Kluckhohn has noted much significant common ground between cultures.

> Every culture has a concept of murder, distinguishing this from execution, killing in war, and other "justifiable homicides." The notions of incest and other regulations upon sexual behavior, the prohibitions upon untruth under defined circumstances, of restitution and reciprocity, of mutual obligations between parents and children—these and many other moral concepts are altogether universal.[11]

Colin Turnbull's description of the sadistic, semidisplaced, disintegrating Ik in Northern Uganda supports the view that a people without principles of kindness, loyalty, and cooperation will degenerate into a Hobbesian state of nature.[12] But he has also produced evidence that underneath the surface of this dying society, there is a deeper moral code from a time when the tribe flourished, which occasionally surfaces and shows its nobler face.

On the other hand, there is enormous cultural diversity and many societies have radically different moral codes. Cultural relativism seems to be a fact, but, even if it is, it does not by itself establish the truth of ethical relativism. Cultural diversity in itself is neutral between theories. For the objectivist could concede complete cultural relativism, but still defend a form of universalism; for he or she could

argue that some cultures simply lack correct moral principles.

On the other hand, a denial of complete cultural relativism (i.e., an admission of some universal principles) does not disprove ethical relativism. For even if we did find one or more universal principles, this would not prove that they had any objective status. We could still *imagine* a culture that was an exception to the rule and be unable to criticize it. So the first premise doesn't by itself imply ethical relativism and its denial doesn't disprove ethical relativism.

We turn to the crucial second thesis, the dependency thesis. Morality does not occur in a vacuum, but rather what is considered morally right or wrong must be seen in a context, depending on the goals, wants, beliefs, history, and environment of the society in question. We distinguished a *weak* and a *strong* thesis of dependency. The weak thesis says that the application of principles depends on the particular cultural predicament, whereas the strong thesis affirms that the principles themselves depend on that predicament. The nonrelativist can accept a certain relativity in the way moral principles are *applied* in various cultures, depending on beliefs, history, and environment. For example, a raw environment with scarce natural resources may justify the Eskimos' brand of euthanasia to the objectivist, who in another environment would consistently reject that practice. The members of a tribe in the Sudan throw their deformed children into the river because of their belief that such infants *belong* to the hippopotamus, the god of the river. We believe that they have a false belief about this, but the point is that the same principles of respect for property and respect for human life are operative in these contrary practices. They differ with us only in belief, not in substantive moral principle. This is an illustration of how nonmoral beliefs (e.g., deformed children belong to the hippopotamus) when applied to common moral principles (e.g., give to each his due) generate different actions in different cultures. In our own culture the difference in the nonmoral belief about the status of a fetus generates opposite moral prescriptions. The major difference between pro-choicers and pro-lifers is not whether we should kill persons but whether fetuses are really persons. It is a debate about the facts of the matter, not the principle of killing innocent persons.

So the fact that moral principles are weakly dependent doesn't show that ethical relativism is valid. In spite of this weak dependency on nonmoral factors, there could still be a set of general moral norms applicable to all cultures and even recognized in most, which are disregarded at a culture's own expense.

What the relativist needs is a strong thesis of dependency, that somehow all principles are essentially cultural inventions. But why should we choose to view morality this way? Is there anything to recommend the strong thesis over the weak thesis of dependency? The relativist may argue that in fact we don't have an obvious impartial standard from which to judge. "Who's to say which culture is right and which is wrong?" But this seems to be dubious. We can reason and perform thought experiments in order to make a case for one system over another. We may not be able to *know* with certainty that our moral beliefs are closer to the truth than those of another culture or those of others within our own culture, but we may *be justified* in believing that they are. If we can be closer to the truth regarding factual or scientific matters, why can't we be closer to the truth on moral matters? Why can't a culture be simply confused or wrong about its moral perceptions? Why can't we say that the society like the Ik which sees nothing wrong with enjoying watching its own children fall into fires is less moral in that regard than the culture that cherishes children and grants them protection and equal rights? To take such a stand is not to commit the fallacy of ethnocentricism, for we are seeking to derive principles through critical reason, not simply uncritical acceptance of one's own mores.

Many relativists embrace relativism as a default position. Objectivism makes no sense to them. I think this is Ladd and Harman's position, as the latter's quotation at the beginning of this article seems to indicate. Objectivism has insuperable problems, so the answer must be relativism. The only positive argument I know for the strong dependency thesis upon which ethical relativism rests is that of the indeterminacy of translation thesis. This theory, set forth by B. L. Whorf and W. V. Quine,[13] holds that languages are often so fundamentally

different from one another that we cannot accurately translate concepts from one to another. But this thesis, while relatively true even within a language (each of us has an idiolect), seems falsified by experience. We do learn foreign languages and learn to translate across linguistic frameworks. For example, people from a myriad of language groups come to the United States and learn English and communicate perfectly well. Rather than a complete hiatus, the interplay between these other cultures eventually enriches the English language with new concepts (for example, *forte/foible, taboo* and *coup de grâce*), even as English has enriched (or "corrupted" as the French might argue) other languages. Even if it turns out that there is some indeterminacy of translation between language users, we should not infer from this that no translation or communication is possible. It seems reasonable to believe that general moral principles are precisely those things that can be communicated transculturally. The kind of common features that Kluckhohn and Wilson advance—duties of restitution and reciprocity, regulations on sexual behavior, obligations of parents to children, a no-unnecessary-harm principle, and a sense that the good should flourish and the guilty be punished—these and others constitute a common human experience, a common set of values within a common human predicament of struggling to survive and flourish in a world of scarce resources.[14] So it is possible to communicate cross-culturally and find that we agree on many of the important things in life. If this is so, then the indeterminacy of translation thesis, upon which relativism rests, must itself be relativized to the point where it is no objection to objective morality.

5. The Case for Moral Objectivism

If nonrelativists are to make their case, they will have to offer a better explanation of cultural diversity and why we should nevertheless adhere to moral objectivism. One way of doing this is to appeal to a divine law, and human sin, which causes deviation from that law. Although I think that human greed, selfishness, pride, self-deception and other maladies have a great deal to do with moral differences and that religion may lend great support to morality, I don't think that a religious justification is necessary for the validity of moral principles. In any case, in this section I shall outline a modest nonreligious objectivism, first by appealing to our intuitions and secondly by giving a naturalist account of morality that transcends individual cultures.

First, I must make it clear that I am distinguishing moral *absolutism* from moral *objectivism*. The absolutist believes that there are nonoverrideable moral principles which ought never to be violated. Kant's system, or one version of it, is a good example. One ought never to break a promise, no matter what. Act utilitarianism also seems absolutist, for the principle, Do that act that has the most promise of yielding the most utility, is nonoverrideable. An objectivist need not posit any nonoverrideable principles, at least not in unqualified general form, and so need not be an absolutist. As Renford Bambrough put it,

> To suggest that there is a *right* answer to a moral problem is at once to be accused of or credited with a belief in moral absolutes. But it is no more necessary to believe in moral absolutes in order to believe in moral objectivity than it is to believe in the existence of absolute space or absolute time in order to believe in the objectivity of temporal and spatial relations and of judgments about them.[15]

On the objectivist's account moral principles are what William Ross refers to as *prima facie* principles, valid rules of action which should generally be adhered to, but which may be overridden by another moral principle in cases of moral conflict. For example, while a principle of justice may generally outweigh a principle of benevolence, there are times when enormous good could be done by sacrificing a small amount of justice, so that an objectivist would be inclined to act according to the principle of benevolence. There may be some absolute or nonoverrideable principles, but there need not be many or any for objectivism to be true.[16]

If we can establish or show that it is reasonable to believe that there is at least one objective moral principle which is binding on all people everywhere in some ideal sense, we shall have shown that relativism is probably false and that a limited objectivism is true. Actually, I believe that there are many qualified general ethical principles which are binding on all rational beings, but one will suffice to

refute relativism. The principle I've chosen is the following:

A. It is morally wrong to torture people for the fun of it.

I claim that this principle is binding on all rational agents, so that if some agent, S, rejects A, we should not let that affect our intuition that A is a true principle but rather try to explain S's behavior as perverse, ignorant, or irrational instead. For example, suppose Adolf Hitler doesn't accept A. Should that affect our confidence in the truth of A? Is it not more reasonable to infer that Adolf is morally deficient, morally blind, ignorant, or irrational than to suppose that his noncompliance is evidence against the truth of A?

Suppose further that there is a tribe of Hitlerites somewhere who enjoy torturing people. The whole culture accepts torturing others for the fun of it. Suppose that Mother Teresa or Gandhi tries unsuccessfully to convince them that they should stop torturing people altogether, and they respond by torturing the reformers. Should this affect our confidence in A? Would it not be more reasonable to look for some explanation of Hitlerite behavior? For example, we might hypothesize that this tribe lacked a developed sense of sympathetic imagination which is necessary for the moral life. Or we might theorize that this tribe was on a lower evolutionary level than most *Homo sapiens*. Or we might simply conclude that the tribe was closer to a Hobbesian state of nature than most societies, and as such probably would not survive. But we need not know the correct answer as to why the tribe was in such bad shape in order to maintain our confidence in A as a moral principle. If A is a basic or core belief for us, we will be more likely to doubt the Hitlerites' sanity or ability to think morally than to doubt the validity of A.

We can perhaps produce other candidates for membership in our minimally basic objective moral set. For example:

1. Do not kill innocent people.
2. Do not cause unnecessary pain or suffering.
3. Do not cheat or steal.
4. Keep your promises and honor your contracts.

5. Do not deprive another person of his or her freedom.
6. Do justice, treating equals equally and unequals unequally.
7. Tell the truth.
8. Help other people, at least when the cost to oneself is minimal.
9. Reciprocate (show gratitude for services rendered).
10. Obey just laws.

These ten principles are examples of the *core morality*, principles necessary for the good life. They are not arbitrary, for we can give reasons why they are necessary to social cohesion and human flourishing. Principles like the Golden Rule, not killing innocent people, treating equals equally, truth telling, promise keeping, and the like are central to the fluid progression of social interaction and the resolution of conflicts of which ethics are about (at least minimal morality is, even though there may be more to morality than simply these kinds of concerns). For example, language itself depends on a general and implicit commitment to the principle of truth telling. Accuracy of expression is a primitive form of truthfulness. Hence, every time we use words correctly we are telling the truth. Without this behavior, language wouldn't be possible. Likewise, without the recognition of a rule of promise keeping, contracts are of no avail and cooperation is less likely to occur. And without the protection of life and liberty, we could not secure our other goals.

A moral code or theory would be adequate if it contained a requisite set of these objective principles or the core morality, but there could be more than one adequate moral code or theory which contained different rankings of these principles and other principles consistent with *core morality*. That is, there may be a certain relativity to secondary principles (whether to opt for monogamy rather than polygamy, whether to include a principle of high altruism in the set of moral duties, whether to allocate more resources to medical care than to environmental concerns, whether to institute a law to drive on the left side of the road or the right side of the road, and so forth), but in every morality a certain core will remain, though applied somewhat

differently because of differences in environment, belief, tradition, and the like.

The core moral rules are analogous to the set of vitamins necessary for a healthy diet. We need an adequate amount of each vitamin—some humans more of one than another—but in prescribing a nutritional diet we don't have to set forth recipes, specific foods, place settings, or culinary habits. Gourmets will meet the requirements differently than ascetics and vegetarians, but the basic nutrients may be had by all without rigid regimentation or an absolute set of recipes.

Stated more positively, an objectivist who bases his or her moral system on a common human nature with common needs and desires might argue for objectivism somewhat in this manner:

1. Human nature is relatively similar in essential respects, having a common set of needs and interests.
2. Moral principles are functions of human needs and interests, instituted by reason in order to promote the most significant interests and needs of rational beings (and perhaps others).
3. Some moral principles will promote human interests and meet human needs better than others.
4. Those principles which will meet essential needs and promote the most significant interests of humans in optimal ways can be said to be objectively valid moral principles.
5. Therefore, since there is a common human nature, there is an objectively valid set of moral principles, applicable to all humanity.

This argument assumes that there is a common human nature. In a sense, I accept a *strong dependency thesis*—morality *depends* on human nature and the needs and interests of humans in general, but not on any specific cultural choice. There is only one large human framework to which moral principles are relative.[17] I have considered the evidence for this claim toward the end of Section 4, but the relativist may object. I cannot defend it any further in this paper, but suppose we content ourselves with a less controversial first premise, stating that some principles will tend to promote the most significant interests of persons. The revised argument would go like this:

1. Objectively valid moral principles are those adherence to which meets the needs and promotes the most significant interests of persons.
2. Some principles are such that adherence to them meets the needs and promotes the most significant interests of persons.
3. Therefore, there are some objectively valid moral principles.

Either argument would satisfy objectivism, but the former makes it clearer that it is our common human nature that generates the common principles.[18] However, as I mentioned, some philosophers might not like to be tied down to the concept of a common human nature, in which case the second version of the argument may be used. It has the advantage that even if it turned out that we did have somewhat different natures or that other creatures in the universe had somewhat different natures, some of the basic moral principles would still survive.

If this argument succeeds, there are ideal moralities (and not simply adequate ones). Of course, there could still be more than one ideal morality, from which presumably an ideal observer would choose under optimal conditions. The ideal observer may conclude that out of an infinite set of moralities two, three, or more combinations would tie for first place. One would expect that these would be similar, but there is every reason to believe that all of these would contain the set of core principles.

Of course, we don't know what an ideal observer would choose, but we can imagine that the conditions under which such an observer would choose would be conditions of maximal knowledge about the consequences of action-types and impartiality, second-order qualities which ensure that agents have the best chance of making the best decisions. If this is so, then the more we learn to judge impartially and the more we know about possible forms of life, the better chance we have to approximate an ideal moral system. And if there is the possibility of approximating ideal moral systems with an objective core and other objective components, then ethical relativism is certainly false. We can confidently dismiss it as an aberration and get on with the job of working out better moral systems.

Let me make the same point by appealing to your intuitions in another way. Imagine that you have been miraculously transported to the dark kingdom of hell, and there you get a glimpse of the sufferings of the damned. What is their punishment? Well, they have eternal back itches which ebb and flow constantly. But they cannot scratch their backs, for their arms are paralyzed in a frontal position, so they writhe with itchiness throughout eternity. But just as you are beginning to feel the itch in your own back, you are suddenly transported to heaven. What do you see in the kingdom of the blessed? Well, you see people with eternal back itches, who cannot scratch their own backs. But they are all smiling instead of writhing. Why? Because everyone has his or her arms stretched out to scratch someone else's back, and, so arranged in one big circle, a hell is turned into a heaven of ecstasy.

If we can imagine some states of affairs or cultures that are better than others in a way that depends on human action, we can ask what are those character traits that make them so. In our story people in heaven, but not in hell, cooperate for the amelioration of suffering and the production of pleasure. These are very primitive goods, not sufficient for a full-blown morality, but they give us a hint as to the objectivity of morality. Moral goodness has something to do with the ameliorating of suffering, the resolution of conflict, and the promotion of human flourishing. If our heaven is really better than the eternal itchiness of hell, then whatever makes it so is constitutively related to moral rightness.

6. An Explanation of the Attraction of Ethical Relativism

Why, then, is there such a strong inclination toward ethical relativism? I think that there are four reasons, which haven't been adequately emphasized. One is the fact that the options are usually presented as though absolutism and relativism were the only alternatives, so conventionalism wins out against an implausible competitor. At the beginning of this paper I referred to a student questionnaire that I have been giving for twenty years. It reads as follows: "Are there any ethical absolutes, moral duties binding on all persons at all times, or are moral duties relative to culture? Is there any alternative to these two positions?" Fewer than five percent suggest a third position and very few of them identify objectivism. Granted, it takes a little philosophical sophistication to make the crucial distinctions, and it is precisely for lack of this sophistication or reflection that relativism has procured its enormous prestige. But, as Ross and others have shown and as I have argued in this paper, one can have an objective morality without being absolutist.

The second reason for an inclination toward ethical relativism is the confusion of moral objectivism with moral realism. A realist is a person who holds that moral values have independent existence, if only as emergent properties. The anti-realist claims that they do not have independent existence. But objectivism is compatible with either of these views. All it calls for is deep intersubjective agreement among humans because of a common nature and common goals and needs.

An example of a philosopher who confuses objectivity with realism is the late J. L. Mackie, who rejects objectivism because there are no good arguments for the independent existence of moral values. He admits, however, that there is a great deal of intersubjectivity in ethics. "There could be agreement in valuing even if valuing is just something people do, even if this activity is not further validated. Subjective agreement would give intersubjective values, but intersubjectivity is not objectivity."[19] But Mackie fails to note that there are two kinds of intersubjectivity, and that one of them gives all that the objectivist wants for a moral theory. Consider the following situations of intersubjective agreement:

Set A
A1. All the children in first grade at School S would agree that playing in the mud is preferable to learning arithmetic.

A2. All the youth in the district would rather take drugs than go to school.

A3. All the people in Jonestown, British Guiana, agree that the Rev. Jones is a prophet from God, and they love him dearly.

A4. Almost all the people in community C voted for George Bush.

Set B
B1. All the thirsty desire water to quench their thirst.

B2. All humans (and animals) prefer pleasure to pain.

B3. Almost all people agree that living in society is more satisfying than living as hermits alone.

The naturalist contrasts these two sets of intersubjective agreements and says that the first set is accidental, not part of what it means to be a person, whereas the agreements in the second set are basic to being a person, basic to our nature. Agreement on the essence of morality, the core set, is the kind of intersubjective agreement more like the second kind, not the first. It is part of the essence of a human in community, part of what it means to flourish as a person, to agree and adhere to the moral code.

The third reason is that our recent sensitivity to cultural relativism and the evils of ethnocentrism, which have plagued the relations of Europeans and Americans with those of other cultures, has made us conscious of the frailty of many aspects of our moral repertoire, so that there is a tendency to wonder "Who's to judge what's really right or wrong?" However, the move from a reasonable cultural relativism, which rightly causes us to rethink our moral systems, to an ethical relativism, which causes us to give up the heart of morality altogether, is an instance of the fallacy of confusing factual or descriptive statements with normative ones. Cultural relativism doesn't entail ethical relativism. The very reason that we are against ethnocentricism constitutes the same basis for our being for an objective moral system: that impartial reason draws us to it.

We may well agree that cultures differ and that we ought to be cautious in condemning what we don't understand, but this in no way need imply that there are not better and worse ways of living. We can understand and excuse, to some degree at least, those who differ from our best notions of morality, without abdicating the notion that cultures without principles of justice or promise keeping or protection of the innocent are morally poorer for these omissions.

A fourth reason, which has driven some to moral nihilism and others to relativism, is the decline of religion in Western society. As one of Dostoevski's characters has said, "If God is dead, all things are permitted." The person who has lost religious faith feels a deep vacuum and understandably confuses it with a moral vacuum, or he or she finally resigns to a form of secular conventionalism. Such people reason that if there is no God to guarantee the validity of the moral order, there must not be a universal moral order. There is just radical cultural diversity and death at the end. But even if there turns out to be no God and no immortality, we still will want to live happy, meaningful lives during our fourscore years on earth. If this is true, then it matters by which principles we live, and those which win out in the test of time will be objectively valid principles.

In conclusion I have argued (1) that cultural relativism (the fact that there are cultural differences regarding moral principles) does not entail ethical relativism (the thesis that there are no objectively valid universal moral principles); (2) that the dependency thesis (that morality derives its legitimacy from individual cultural acceptance) is mistaken; and (3) that there are universal moral principles based on a common human nature and a need to solve conflicts of interest and flourish.

So "Who's to judge what's right or wrong?" We are. We are to do so on the basis of the best reasoning we can bring forth, and with sympathy and understanding.

NOTES

1. Gilbert Harman, "Is There a Single True Morality?" in *Morality, Reason and Truth*, eds. David Copp and David Zimmerman (Rowman & Allenheld, 1984).
2. John Ladd, *Ethical Relativism* (Wadsworth, 1973).
3. Lest I be misunderstood, in this essay I will generally be speaking about the validity rather than the truth of moral principles. Validity holds that they are proper guides to action, whereas truth presupposes something more. It presupposes Moral Realism, the theory that moral principles have special ontological status. Although this may be true, not all objectivists agree. R. M. Hare, for instance, argues that moral principles, while valid, do not have truth value. They are like imperatives which have practical application but cannot be said to be true. Also, I am mainly concerned with the status of *principles*, not theories themselves. There may be a plurality of valid moral theories, all containing the same objective principles. I am grateful to Edward Sherline for drawing this distinction to my attention.
4. Reported by the anthropologist Powers, *Tribes of California*, p. 178. Quoted in E. Westermarck, *Origin and Development of Moral Ideals* (London, 1906), p. 336. This work is a mine of examples of cultural diversity.
5. W. G. Sumner, *Folkways* (Ginn & Co., 1906), p. 76.
6. This is a paraphrased and rewritten statement of Ted Bundy by Harry V. Jaffa, *Homosexuality and the Natural Law* (Claremont, CA: The Claremont Institute of the Study of Statesmanship and Political Philosophy, 1990), 3–4.
7. Ruth Benedict, *Patterns of Culture* (New American Library, 1934), p. 257.
8. Melville Herskovits, *Cultural Relativism* (Random House, 1972).
9. The fallacy of objecting to a proposition on the erroneous grounds that, if accepted, it will lead to a chain of states of affairs which are absurd or unacceptable.
10. E. O. Wilson, *On Human Nature* (Bantam Books, 1979), pp. 22–23.
11. Clyde Kluckhohn, "Ethical Relativity: Sic et Non," *Journal of Philosophy*, III (1955).
12. Colin Turnbull, *The Mountain People* (New York: Simon & Schuster, 1972).
13. See Benjamin Whorf, *Language, Thought and Reality* (MIT Press, 1956); and W. V. Quine, *Word and Object* (MIT Press, 1960), and *Ontological Relativity* (Columbia University Press, 1969).
14. David Hume gave the classic expression to this idea of a common human nature when he wrote:

It is universally acknowledged that there is a great uniformity among the actions of men, in all nations and ages, and that human nature remains still the same, in its principles and operations. The same events follow from the same causes. Ambition, avarice, self-love, vanity, friendship, generosity, public spirit; these passions, mixed in various degrees, and distributed through society, have been, from the beginning of the world, and still are, the source of all the actions and enterprises which have ever been observed among mankind. Would you know the sentiments, inclinations, and course of life of the Greeks and Romans? Study well the temper and actions of the French and English: you cannot be much mistaken in transferring to the former most of the observations which you have made with regard to the latter. Mankind are so much the same, in all times and places, that history informs us of nothing new or strange in that particular. Its chief use is only to discover the constant and universal principles of human nature, by showing men in all varieties of circumstances and situations, and furnishing us with materials, from which we may form our observations, and become acquainted with the regular springs of human action and behavior. These records of wars, intrigues, factions, and revolutions, are so many collections of experiments by which the politician or moral philosopher fixes the principles of his science; in the same manner as the physician or natural philosopher becomes acquainted with the nature of plants, minerals, and other external objects, by the experiments which he forms concerning them. Nor are the earth, water, and other elements examined by Aristotle and Hippocrates more like to those which at present lie under our observation than the men described by Polybius and Tacitus are to those who now govern the world. *Essays, Moral, Political and Literary* (Longman, Green, 1875).

15. Renford Bambrough, *Moral Skepticism and Moral Knowledge* (London: Routledge & Kegan Paul, 1979), p. 33.

16. William Ross, *The Right and the Good* (Oxford University Press, 1930), p. 18f.

17. In his essay "Moral Relativism" in *Moral Relativism and Moral Objectivity* (Blackwell, 1996) by Gilbert Harman and Judith Jarvis Thomson, Harman defines moral relativism as the claim that "There is no single true morality. There are many different moral frameworks, none of which is more correct than the others." (p. 5) I hold that morality has a function of serving the needs and interests of human beings, so that some frameworks do this better than others. Essentially, all adequate theories will contain the principles I have identified in this essay.

18. I owe the reformulation of the argument to Bruce Russell. Edward Sherline has objected (in correspondence) that assuming a common human nature in the first argument begs the question against the relativist. You may be the judge.

19. J. L. Mackie, *Ethics: Inventing Right and Wrong* (Penguin, 1977), p. 22.

Can Ethics Provide Answers?

JAMES RACHELS

I once saw a proposal written by a distinguished professor of business to add a course in "business ethics" to his school's curriculum. It was an enthusiastic document, detailing the virtues and benefits of such an offering. But it concluded with the remark that "since there are no definite answers in ethics, the course should be offered on a pass-fail basis." I don't know why he thought that, lacking definite answers, it would be easier to distinguish passing from failing work than B work from C work, but what was most striking was the casual, offhand manner of the remark—as though it were obvious that no matter how important ethical questions might be, no "definite answers" are possible.

Can ethics provide answers? Philosophers have given a great deal of attention to this question, but the result has been a great deal of disagreement. There are generally two schools of thought. On one side are those who believe that ethics is a subject, like history or physics or mathematics, with its own distinctive problems and its own methods of solving them. The fundamental questions of ethics are questions of conduct—what, in particular cases, should we

"Can Ethics Provide Answers" in *Can Ethics Provide Answers? And Other Essays in Moral Philosophy* by James Rachels, 21–48. © 1997 Lanham, MD: Rowman and Littlefield.

do?—and the study of ethics provides the answers. On the other side are those who, like the professor of business, deny that ethics is a proper subject. There are ethical questions, to be sure, and they are important; but since those questions have no definite answers, there cannot be a subject whose business it is to provide them. The debate between these two points of view has grown enormously complicated, and we will examine some of those complications at various points in this book. But at the outset it may be useful to consider the main sorts of reasons that lead people to be skeptical about ethics.

THE CASE AGAINST ETHICS

It is remarkable that every day people make ethical judgments every day about which they feel strongly—sometimes even becoming angry and indignant with those who disagree—and yet, when they reflect on what they are doing, they profess that their opinions are no more "correct" than the contrary opinions they reject so vehemently. How can this be? What could persuade people to adopt such a peculiar stance?

Ethics and Culture

An appreciation of human diversity seems to many people incompatible with a belief in the reality of right and wrong. Sociologists and anthropologists have impressed upon us that moral standards differ from culture to culture and that what the "natural light of reason" reveals to one people may be radically different from what seems obvious to another. This, of course, has been known for a long time. Herodotus made the point clearly in the fifth century BC:

Darius, after he had got the kingdom, called into his presence certain Greeks who were at hand, and asked—"What he should pay them to eat the bodies of their fathers when they died?" To which they answered, that there was no sum that would tempt them to do such a thing. He then sent for certain Indians, of the race called Callatians, men who eat their fathers, and asked them, while the Greeks stood by, and knew by the help of an interpreter all that was said—"What he should give them to burn the bodies of their fathers at their decease?" The Indians exclaimed aloud, and bade him forbear such language. Such is men's wont herein; and

Pindar was right, in my judgment, when he said, "Custom is the king o'er all."[1]

Today any educated person could list countless other examples of cultural variations in ethics: the Eskimos allow firstborn daughters to die of exposure; the Muslims practice polygamy; the Jains will not eat meat. In light of such variations, it seems merely naïve to think that our moral views are anything more than one particular cultural product.

In its crudest form, cultural relativism says simply: "Different cultures have different moral codes; therefore there is no objective truth in ethics." This, however, is most certainly mistaken. In the first place, the fact that different societies have different moral codes proves nothing. There is also disagreement from society to society about scientific matters: in some cultures it is believed that the earth is flat and in others that disease is caused by evil spirits. We do not on that account conclude that there is no truth in geography or in medicine. Instead, we conclude that in some cultures people are not well informed. Similarly, disagreement in ethics might signal nothing more than that some people are less enlightened than others. Why should we assume that, if ethical truth exists, everyone must know it?

Moreover, it may be that some values are relative to culture while others are not. Herodotus was probably right to think that the treatment of the dead—whether to eat or to burn them—is not a matter governed by objectively true standards. It may be simply a matter of convention that respect for the dead is shown in one way rather than another; and if so, the Callatians and the Greeks were equally naïve to be horrified by each other's customs. Alternative sexual customs—another favorite example of relativists—might also be equally acceptable. But this does not mean that there are *no* practices that are objectively wrong. Torture and slavery could still be wrong, independent of cultural standards, even if those other types of behavior are not. It is a mistake to think that because some standards are relative to culture, all must be.

We can, in fact, explain *why* some standards are relative to culture and some are not. It is a matter of the availability of reasons. In some cases, no good reason can be given to show that one custom is better than another. Can any good reason be given to show that burning the dead is better than burying them? Or that clothing that conceals women's knees is preferable to clothing that exposes the knee? If not, the acceptability of these practices is merely culture-relative. On the other hand, in other cases reasons *can* be given to show that some customs are better than others. We can, for example, give reasons to show that slavery is unacceptable, regardless of the conventions of the society in which it is practiced. Thus, the acceptability of this practice is not merely culture-relative.

MacIntyre's Argument

Yet one might easily doubt that reason is such a powerful tool. In his book *Whose Justice? Which Rationality?* Alasdair MacIntyre warns that we should not expect so much from reason. The idea of impartial reason justifying norms of conduct binding on all people is, he says, an illusion fostered by the Enlightenment. In reality there is no such thing. Rationality is possible only within a historical tradition, which sets standards of inquiry for those working within it. But the standards of rational thinking differ from tradition to tradition; and so we cannot speak of "what reason requires" in any universal sense. MacIntyre writes:

> What the enlightenment made us for the most part blind to and what we now need to recover is, so I shall argue, a conception of rational enquiry as embodied in a tradition; a conception according to which the standards of rational justification themselves emerge from and are part of a history in which they are vindicated by the way in which they transcend the limitations of and provide remedies for the defects of their predecessors within the history of the same tradition.[2]

Thus, in MacIntyre's view, the reasons that would be adduced by a modern liberal in arguing, say, that slavery is unjust would not necessarily be acceptable to an Aristotelian, whose standards of rationality are different; and the search for standards that transcend the two traditions is a fool's quest. No such tradition-neutral standards exist, except, perhaps, for purely formal principles such as noncontradiction that are far too weak to yield substantive ethical results.

At first hearing, this sounds like a sophisticated version of cultural relativism. But MacIntyre insists he is no relativist—relativism is one of the modern ideas that he rejects. One of the major challenges confronting the reader of *Whose Justice? Which Rationality?* is to figure out how, after embracing this view of rationality, MacIntyre can escape being a relativist. His idea seems to be this: traditions confront one another historically, and one tradition succeeds in establishing its superiority over its rival by demonstrating that it can solve the problems internal to the other tradition while at the same time incorporating within itself everything in the other tradition that survives the dialectical examination.

This, however, only invites an awkward question. MacIntyre represents the confrontation as involving rational debate and not mere institutional power—Augustinian Christianity displaces Aristotelianism, on his view, not merely because of the combined political power of church and state, but because it could be demonstrated to be superior, even to the partisans of the other tradition. But if there are no standards of practical rationality that are neutral between the two traditions, how is this possible?

MacIntyre believes that an abstract answer to this question is not to be found; for an answer one must look to history for examples of how the process has actually taken place. So the bulk of his book is occupied by an examination of four traditions (the Aristotelian, the Augustinian-Christian, the Scottish, and the modern liberal) and the various clashes between them. To meet MacIntyre's argument head on, then, we would have to examine the details of the historical debates and see whether their outcomes did or did not depend on the application of standards of rationality that were not merely tradition bound. That would be a big project, which will probably never be undertaken by anyone—there is only one Alasdair MacIntyre. Nevertheless, there are several relevant points that might be made.

First, the type of confrontation that MacIntyre pictures as taking place between traditions is possible only because the partisans of the different traditions have a lot in common. If they were not trying to solve the same problems, then it would make no sense to say that one tradition does a better job of solving a problem than does another; and if the traditions had no common content, it would make no sense to talk about one tradition's incorporating within itself the worthy aspects of its rivals. This suggests that what the people in the different traditions have in common might form the basis of a shared rationality that would make possible the development of norms applicable to them all.

Aristotle, who epitomized a tradition that MacIntyre rejects, believed that this is so. Surveying various ancient societies, Aristotle declared, "One can see in one's travels to distant countries the experiences of recognition and affiliation that link every human being to every other human being."[3] He observed that all humans face danger and fear death, and so all have need of courage; that all have bodily appetites that are sometimes difficult to control, and so all have need of ways to manage themselves; that none are self-sufficient, and so all have need of friends. Aristotle thought that such universal elements of human experience provided the basis for an ethic that was not simply local to one culture. He did not, however, expect universal agreement about that ethic. (He did not make the mistake of confusing the question of whether a moral argument of universal validity can be constructed with the different question of whether people can be persuaded to accept that argument.) The fact that people do disagree about norms—the endless disputation that MacIntyre says is typical of modern, rootless humans—was as familiar to Aristotle as it is to us. But as Aristotle realized, there is more than one possible explanation of that disagreement. The disagreement is not necessarily the result of differences in standards of rationality. The best explanation may be that such disagreement stems from a combination of causes, significantly including the ignorance, poverty, disease, and political and religious oppression that have plagued a large proportion of human beings throughout their history.

But the argument cannot be settled at such an abstract level. If we think that there are norms binding on all rational agents—if we think that reasons can be given to show that a particular practice is right or wrong such that those reasons must be accepted by every rational person, regardless of the tradition in which he or she participates—then we should be able to provide an example of such a

norm. A good test case might be slavery. It is easy, of course, to construct an argument against slavery from a modern liberal point of view. But is that argument tied only to modern liberal values? Or does it appeal rather to considerations that any reasonable person should accept?

The primary argument against slavery is, in bare outline, the following. All forms of slavery involve setting apart a class of humans for treatment that is systematically different from that accorded other members of the community. Deprivation of liberty is the feature that these various practices have most in common, although slaves have also been subject to a variety of other unwelcome treatments. Now, the argument is that it is unjust to set some people apart for different treatment unless there is a relevant difference between them that justifies the difference in treatment. But there is no general difference between humans that would justify setting some of them apart as slaves. Therefore slavery is unjust.

Is this argument only a product of modern liberal thought? Or should it be compelling even to those who live in different sorts of societies, with different sorts of traditions? To test this, we might consider a slave society such as Aristotle's. According to one estimate, there were as many slaves in Aristotle's Athens, in proportion to the population, as there were in the slave states of America before the Civil War. Aristotle himself defended slavery. Yet the rational resources available within his tradition seem to have been sufficient for an appreciation of its injustice. Aristotle reports that "some regard the control of a slave by a master as contrary to nature. In their view the distinction of master and slave is due to law or convention; there is no natural difference between them: the relation of master and slave is based on force, and being so based has no warrant in justice."[4]

But, as is well known, Aristotle did not share this enlightened view. A slave owner himself, he held that slavery is justified by the inferior rationality of the slave. Because they are not so rational as other humans, slaves are fitted by nature to be ruled rather than to rule. Aristotle knew that many slaves are inclined to revolt, but he attributed this not to any sense they might have of the injustice of their position but to an excess of "spiritedness." In his sketch of the ideal state, near the end of his *Politics*, he suggests that farm labor should be provided by slaves, "but slaves not drawn from a single stock, or from stocks of a spirited temper. This will at once secure the advantage of a good supply of labour and eliminate any danger of revolutionary designs."⁵ But Aristotle was not of a single mind about this, for he also supported provisions for manumission. After recommending that farm labor be performed by slaves, he adds, "It is wise to offer all slaves the eventual reward of emancipation." In his will, Aristotle provided for the emancipation of his own slaves. This is an unexpected concession from someone who held that slaves are fitted for their station by nature itself.

Plainly, Aristotle accepted the principle that differences in treatment are unjustified unless they are correlated with differences between individuals that justify those differences in treatment. In fact, this is just a modern version of an idea that he advances in the *Nicomachean Ethics*, namely, that like cases should be treated alike and different cases differently. That is why he felt it necessary to defend slavery by contending that slaves possess an inferior degree of rationality. But this is a claim that can be shown to be false by evidence that should be counted as evidence as much by him as by us. Therefore, even on Aristotle's own terms, slavery should be recognizable as unjust. In arguing this, we are not simply transporting our standards of rationality back into a culture that was "different," although we might well cite information about the nature of human beings that we have now but that was unavailable to him.

Of course, showing that this argument should be accepted by Aristotle is not the same as showing that it should be accepted by all reasonable people. The possibility still remains that MacIntyre is right and that there are partisans of some traditions for whom this type of argument could have no effect. But I see no good reason to believe this; the argument I have outlined appeals to such a basic principle of reasoning that it should always have some force for reasonable people. At any rate, as we have seen, Aristotle held the sensible view that people in different traditions have enough in common, in virtue of their shared humanity, to make the achievement of common norms a realistic goal. On its face,

this seems at least as plausible as the idea that the incompatible standards of different traditions cannot be overcome.

The Psychological Argument

Psychological studies tend to undermine confidence in ethics in a different way, by making us aware of the nonrational ways in which moral beliefs are formed in the individual. The story of how this happens remains remarkably constant, even when we consider radically different psychological theories. Freud was one of the first to set out the central idea. He emphasized that children are utterly dependent on their parents—without the parent's constant attention and help, the child cannot satisfy its most basic needs (it cannot obtain food, for example). Thus, retaining the parent's love becomes the most important thing in the child's life. For their part, parents have definite ideas about how children should behave. They are ready to reward children when they behave in desired ways and to punish them when they behave in unwanted ways. The rewards and punishments may be subtle; they may consist of nothing more than smiles, frowns, and harsh words. But that is enough because, as Freud notes, the parent's disapproval is the thing the child fears most.

This little drama is played out over and over again as the child grows up. As a result, the child learns to behave in "accepted" ways. The child also learns how to talk about her behavior: she learns to call the approved ways "right" and the disapproved ways "wrong." That is the origin of our moral concepts. "Moral" and "immoral" are simply names for the approved and disapproved forms of conduct.

To this is added a distinctively "Freudian" idea. Freud says that there exists within us a psychic mechanism for internalizing the role of the parent. After a while, we no longer need the parent to punish us for acting badly—we come to punish ourselves, through feelings of guilt. This mechanism he calls the "superego." It is, Freud says, the same thing that is commonly called the conscience. But in reality it is nothing more than the internalized voice of the parent.

The story has been repeated often, with minor variations. The behaviorists had no patience with

Freudian speculations; nevertheless, their fundamental ideas concerning moral development were
quite similar. Where Freud spoke of "the pleasure
principle" and of parental approval, the behaviorists spoke of "positive reinforcements." The child is
positively reinforced (rewarded) when he behaves in
certain ways, and so he tends to repeat that behavior. He is negatively reinforced (punished) for
other actions, which he subsequently tends not to
repeat. Thus patterns of behavior are established:
some types of conduct come to be accepted, others
come to be rejected. When the child's vocabulary
becomes sufficiently rich, he learns to speak of the
former behavior as right and the latter as wrong.
Indeed, B. F. Skinner went so far as to suggest that
the word "good" could be *defined as* "positively
reinforcing."

All this suggests that our values are simply the
result of our having been conditioned to behave in
certain ways. We may feel that certain actions are
good and others are evil, but that is only because
we have been trained to have those feelings. If we
had been trained differently, we would have different values, and we would feel just as strongly about
them. Therefore, to believe that one's values are
anything more than the result of this conditioning
is simply naïve.

Thus, in many people's minds, psychology swal-
lows up ethics. It does not simply explain ethics;
it explains it away. Ethics can no longer exist as a
subject having as its aim the discovery of what is
right and what is wrong, for this supposes that there
is a right and wrong independent of what people
already happen to believe. Ethics as a subject matter must disappear, to be replaced, perhaps, by the
scientific study of why we have the values we do.
We can try to become clearer about what our values are and about the possible alternatives. But we
can no longer ask questions about the truth of our
convictions.

Yet these psychological facts, like the facts
about cultural variations, turn out to be irrelevant
to the status of ethics as an autonomous subject.
Psychology may tell us that beliefs are acquired in a
certain way, but nothing follows from this about the
nature or validity of those beliefs. After all, every
belief is acquired through the operation of some
psychological mechanism or other. A child may

learn to respond "George Washington" when asked
to name the first American president because she
fears the disapproval of the teacher should she say
anything else, And, we might add, if she were reinforced differently she might grow up believing that
someone else first held that office. Yet it remains a
matter of fact that Washington was the first president. The same goes for one's moral beliefs; the
manner of their acquisition is logically independent
of their status as objectively true or false.

The example of learning history is instructive in
another way. In learning history, a student might go
through two stages. In the first, he learns by rote.
He learns to say things like "George Washington
was the first president" even though he has no idea
why we think this is true. He has no conception of
historical evidence and no understanding of the
methods historians use to verify such things. Later,
however, he may learn about evidence and historical method. Then he not only believes Washington
was the first president; he has good reasons for that
belief. Thus he can be confident that this belief is
not "merely a matter of opinion."

Something very much like this is true of a child's
instruction in how to behave. When a child is very
young, she will respond to the parent's instructions
even though she has no idea of the reasons behind
those instructions. The mother may say, "Don't play
in the street," and the child may obey, even though
she does not understand why playing in the street is
undesirable. She may obey simply because she fears
punishment. Later, however, she will become capable of understanding the reasons: she will see that,
if she plays in the street, she may be seriously hurt
or even killed.

Again, when the child is very young, the mother
may say, "Don't kick your brother," and the child
may obey because otherwise she will be punished.
But later, when she is older, her mother may say
something very different. She may say, "When you
kick your brother, it *hurts* him," or "How would you
like it if someone went around kicking *you*?" In saying these things, and others like them, the mother
is bringing the child to understand the most elementary reasons why little brother should not be
abused.

At one stage of development, the child learns to
behave in certain ways because he will be rewarded

if he does and punished if he doesn't. At a later, more mature stage, he learns that there are good reasons for behaving in those ways. At which stage is he learning morality? In one sense, of course, he is learning to behave morally even at the earlier stage: he is learning to do things that it is morally good to do. But in a deeper sense, moral instruction begins only at the later stage. Only at the later stage does the child begin to learn how to reason and act as a moral agent. Rewards and punishments just keep him in line until he is old enough to understand reasons.

Thus the outcome of the psychological account of ethics is reminiscent of the fate of nineteenth-century attempts to reduce mathematics to psychology. In the late 1800s there was considerable interest in explaining mathematics by reference to psychological theories of human thought—but that interest waned when it was realized that little light was being shed on mathematics itself. Regardless of how it might be related to our thought processes, mathematics remained a subject with its own integrity—its own internal rules, procedures, problems, and solutions. The reason ethics resists explanation by sociology or psychology is that, like mathematics, it is also a subject with its own integrity.

The Question of Proof

There is one further skeptical argument that rivals the cultural relativist argument and the psychological argument in influence. To many people, it seems to be a great deficiency of ethics that there is no proof where ethical opinions are concerned. This appears to be a crucial difference between ethics and science. We can prove that the world is round, that there is no largest prime number, and that dinosaurs and human beings did not live at the same time. But can we prove that abortion is right or wrong? The No-Proof Argument, as we might call it, goes like this: "If there were any such thing as objective truth in ethics, we should be able to prove that some moral opinions are true and others are false. But in fact we cannot prove which moral opinions are true and which are false. Therefore, there is no such thing as objective truth in ethics."

The general claim that moral judgments can't be proved sounds right: anyone who has ever argued about a matter like abortion knows how frustrating it can be to try to "prove" that one's point of view is correct. However, if we inspect this claim more closely, it turns out to be dubious.

Suppose we consider a matter that is much simpler than abortion. A student says that a test given by a teacher was unfair. This is clearly a moral judgment—fairness is a basic moral value. Can this judgment be proved? The student might point out that the test was so long that not even the best students could complete it in the time allowed (and the test was to be graded on the assumption that it should be completed). Moreover, the test covered in detail matters that were quite trivial, while ignoring matters the teacher had stressed as important. And the test included questions about some matters that were not covered in either the assigned readings or the class discussions.

Suppose all this is true. And further suppose that the teacher, when asked to explain, has no defense to offer. (In fact, the teacher, who is rather inexperienced, seems muddled about the whole thing and doesn't seem to have had any very clear idea of what he was doing.) Now hasn't the student proved the test was unfair? What more in the way of proof could we possible want?

It is easy to think of other examples that make the same point:

Jones is a bad man. Jones is a habitual liar; he manipulates people; he cheats when he thinks he can get away with it; he is cruel to other people; and so on.

Dr. Smith is irresponsible. He bases his diagnoses on superficial considerations; he drinks before performing delicate surgery; he refuses to listen to other doctors' advice; and so on.

A certain used-car salesman is unethical. She conceals defects in her cars; she takes advantage of poor people by pressuring them into paying exorbitant prices for cars she knows to be defective; she runs misleading advertisements in any newspaper that will carry them; and so on.

We can, and often do, back up our ethical judgments with good reasons. Thus it does not seem right to say that they are all unprovable, as though they were nothing more than "mere opinions." If a person has good reasons for her judgments, then she is not merely giving "her opinion." On the contrary, she may be making a judgment with which any reasonable person would have to agree.

The process of giving reasons might be taken a step futher. If one of our reasons for saying that Jones is a bad man is that he is a habitual liar, we can go on to explain why lying is bad. Lying is bad because it harms people, because it is a violation of trust, and because the rule requiring truthfulness is necessary for society to exist. (I will not elaborate on these matters here, because they are detailed in chapter 9. The point here is just that such explanations not only are possible in ethics, they are common. There are many examples scattered throughout this book.) So, if we can support our judgments with good reasons, and provide explanations of why these reasons matter, and show that the case on the other side is weak, what more in the way of "proof" could anyone possibly want?

Nevertheless, the impression that moral judgments are "unprovable" is remarkably persistent. What accounts for this persistence? Why is the No-Proof Argument so persuasive? Three reasons might be mentioned.

First, when proof is demanded, people might have in mind an inappropriate standard. They might be thinking, in a vague way, about observations and experiments in science; and when there are no comparable observations and experiments in ethics, they might conclude that there is no proof. But in ethics, rational thinking consists of giving reasons, analyzing arguments, setting out and justifying principles, and the like. The fact that ethical reasoning differs in some way from reasoning in science does not make it deficient.

Second, when we think of "proving our ethical opinions to be correct," we tend to think automatically of the most difficult moral issues. The question of abortion, for example, is an enormously complicated and difficult matter. No one, to my knowledge, has yet produced a perfectly convincing analysis that would show once and for all where the truth lies. If we think of questions like this, it is easy to believe that "proof" in ethics is impossible. But the same could be said of the sciences. There are complicated matters on which physicists cannot agree, and if we focused our attention entirely on them we might conclude that there is no proof in physics either. But

of course there are many simpler matters in physics that can be proved and about which all competent physicists agree. Similarly, in ethics there are many matters far simpler than abortion about which all reasonable people must agree. The examples given above are examples of this type.

Finally, it is easy to conflate two matters that are really very different: (1) proving an opinion to be correct; and (2) persuading someone to accept your proof. It is a common, if frustrating, experience to have an impeccable argument that someone refuses to accept. But that does not mean there is something wrong with the argument or that "proof" is somehow unattainable. It may mean only that someone is being unreasonable. And in ethics we should often expect people not to listen to reason: after all, ethics requires that people do things they don't want to do; so it is only to be expected that sometimes they will try to avoid hearing its demands.

THE DIFFERENCE SCIENCE MAKES

Somehow it seems *natural*, at the end of the twentieth century, to be skeptical about ethics. It is hard to shake this feeling, regardless of what one makes of arguments such as those we have considered so far. Moral skepticism seems to be our lot. The explanation of why this should be so goes deep into our history and into our understanding of the world and our place in it. The most salient part of this history concerns the rise of modern science. Before modern science, people could reasonably believe that their moral judgments were warranted by the facts of nature. The prevailing view of what the world was like supported such a belief. Today this is no longer true.

Understanding What the World Is Like

The Greeks conceived the world to be an orderly system in which everything has its proper place. A central feature of this conception was the idea that *everything in nature exists for a purpose*. Aristotle incorporated this idea into his system of thought when he said that in order to understand anything, we must ask four questions: What is it? What is it made of? How did it come to exist? And what is it for? (The answers might be: this is a knife, it is made of steel, it was made by a craftsman, and it is used for cutting.) Aristotle assumed that the last question—What is it for?—could sensibly be asked of anything whatever. "Nature," he said, "belongs to the class of causes which act for the sake of something."[6]

It seems obvious that artifacts such as knives have purposes, because we have a purpose in mind when we make them. But what about natural objects that we do not make? Do they have purposes too? Aristotle thought so. One of his examples was that we have teeth so that we can chew. Such biological examples can be quite persuasive; the parts of bodies do seem, intuitively, to have particular purposes—eyes are for seeing, the heart is for pumping blood, and so on. But Aristotle's thesis was not limited to organic beings. He also thought, to take a different sort of example, that rain falls so that plants can grow. As odd as it may seem to a modern reader, Aristotle was perfectly serious about this. He considered other alternatives, such as that the rain falls "of necessity" and that this helps the plants only by "coincidence," and rejected them. He even considered a hypothesis strikingly like Darwinian natural selection: "Wherever then all the parts [of plants and animals] came about just what they would have been if they had come to be for an end, such things survived, being organized spontaneously in a fitting way; whereas those which grew otherwise perished and continue to perish, as Empedocles says his 'man-faced ox-progeny' did."[7] But Aristotle rejects this, too. His considered view was that plants and animals are what they are and that the rain falls as it does "because it is better so."

The world, therefore, is an orderly, rational system, with each thing having its own proper place and serving its own special purpose. There is a neat hierarchy: the rain exists for the sake of the plants, the plants exist for the sake of the animals, and the animals exist—of course—for the sake of people, whose well-being is the point of the whole arrangement:

> [W]e must believe, first that plants exist for the sake of animals, second that all other animals exist for the sake of man, tame animals for the use he can make of them as well as for the food they provide; and as for wild animals, most though not all of these can be used for food or are useful in other ways; clothing and instruments can be made out of

them. If then we are right in believing that nature makes nothing without some end in view, nothing to no purpose, it must be that nature has made all things specifically for the sake of man.[8]

It was a stunningly anthropocentric view. Aristotle may be forgiven, however, when we consider that virtually every important thinker in our history has entertained some such thought. Humans are a remarkably vain species.

The Christian thinkers who came later found this view of the world to be perfectly congenial. Only one thing was missing: God was needed to make the picture complete. (Aristotle had denied that God was a necessary part of the picture. For him, the worldview we have outlined was not religious; it was simply a description of how things are.) Thus, the Christian thinkers said that rain falls to help the plants *because that is what the Creator intended* and the animals are for human use *because that is what God made them for.* Values and purposes were, therefore, conceived to be a fundamental part of the nature of things, because the world was believed to have been created according to a divine plan.

The Aristotelian-Christian view of the world had a number of consequences for ethics. On the most general level, it affirmed the supreme value of human life, and it explained why humans are entitled to do whatever they please with the rest of nature. The basic moral arrangement—human beings, whose lives are sacred, dominating a world made for their benefit—was enshrined as the Natural Order of Things.

At a more detailed level, a corollary of this outlook was that the "laws of nature" specify how things ought to be as well as describing how things are. In turn, knowing how things ought to be enables us to evaluate states of affairs as objectively good or bad. Things are as they ought to be when they are serving their natural purposes; when they do not or cannot serve those purposes, things have gone wrong. Thus, teeth that have decayed and cannot be used for chewing are defective and drought, which deprives plants of the rain they need, is a natural objective evil.

There were also implications for human action. Moral rules could be viewed as one type of law of nature. A leading idea was that some forms of human behavior are "natural," while others are not; and "unnatural" acts are said to be wrong. Beneficence, for example, is natural for us because God has made social creatures. We want and need the friendship of other people and we have natural affections for them; hence, behaving brutishly toward them is unnatural. Or, to take a different sort of example, the purpose of the sex organs is procreation. Thus, the use of them for other purposes is "contrary to nature"—that is why the Christian church has traditionally regarded as impermissible any form of sexual activity that does not result in procreation, such as masturbation, gay sex, or the use of contraceptives.

The Aristotelian worldview began to break up in the sixteenth century when it was discovered that the earth orbits the sun, rather than the other way around. This was an alarming development, because the earth's being at the center of things was an important symbol of mankind's central place in the divine plan. But the heliocentric solar system was by no means the most subversive aspect of the emerging new science. Galileo, Newton, and others developed ways of understanding natural phenomena that made no use of evaluative notions. To their way of thinking, the rain has no purpose. It does not fall in order to help the plants grow. Instead, it falls as a result of physical causes. Is it, then, a mere coincidence that there happen to be plants growing beneath the rain to benefit from it? The Aristotelians and the Christians had found this too far-fetched to believe: how can the wonderful arrangement of nature, with each part supplementing and benefiting the other, be mere coincidence? But the modern thinkers eventually found a way to explain the whole setup: the plants are there because they have evolved, by natural selection, in the rainy climate. Natural selection produces an orderly arrangement that appears to have been designed, but, as Darwin emphasized, that is only an illusion. To explain nature, there is no need to assume teleological principles, neither Aristotle's "final causes" nor the Christians' God. This was by far the most insidious feature of the new science.

This style of explanation—appealing only to physical laws devoid of any evaluative content—was developed in such great and persuasive detail, in connection with so many natural phenomena, that educated people universally gravitated to it.

With its superior predictive and explanatory power, this way of thinking transformed people's view of what the world is like. But part of the transformation, inseparable from the rest, was an altered view of the nature of ethics. Right and wrong could no longer be deduced from the nature of things in themselves, for on the new view, the natural world does not, in and of itself, manifest value and purpose. The inhabitants of the world may have needs and desires that generate values special to them, but that is all. The world apart from those inhabitants knows and cares nothing for their values, and it has no values of its own. A hundred and fifty years before Nietzsche declared, "There are no moral facts," David Hume had reached the same conclusion. Hume summed up the moral implications of the new worldview when he wrote: "Take any action allow'd to be vicious: Willful murder, for instance. Examine it in all lights, and see if you can find that matter of fact, or real existence, which you call *vice*. In whichever way you take it, you find only certain passions, motives, volitions and thoughts. There is no other matter of fact in the case."[9] And what of the old idea that "nature has made all things for the sake of man?" In his great essay on suicide, published posthumously in 1783, Hume replied: "The life of a man is of no greater importance to the universe than that of an oyster."[10]

Emotivism and the Eclipse of Ethics

Hume considered belief in an objectively correct ethical system to be part of the old "superstition and false religion." Stripped of false theology, Hume said, we should come to see our morality as nothing more than the expression of our feelings. "When you pronounce any action or character to be vicious," he wrote, "you mean nothing, but that from the constitution of your nature you have a feeling or sentiment of blame from the contemplation of it."[11]

In the twentieth century Hume's thoughts were adapted to support a theory known as *emotivism*. The development of emotivism was one of the great achievements of twentieth-century philosophy. It represented the final, fully worked out form of one of the major options in human thought, ethical subjectivism. Emotivism differed from previous versions of ethical subjectivism in its more sophisticated view of language. A key idea was that not every sentence is meant to be true or false. Utterances such as "Don't do that!" "Hooray for our team!" and "Would that there were more men like Gandhi" are not used to state facts. But that does not mean there is anything defective about them. They serve other purposes. They give instructions about what to do, and they express (not report) our attitudes and commitments, while encouraging others to adopt similar attitudes and commitments. According to the emotivists, ethical "statements" are like this. They are not used to state facts; they are, really, in the same general family as imperatives and avowals. Even though they may be sincere or insincere, imperatives and avowals are neither true nor false—and similarly, moral judgments are neither true or false.

To its supporters, emotivism seemed in keeping with a properly scientific outlook. Science describes the facts in an exhaustive way: any state of affairs, any "fact" that is part of the objective world, must be discoverable by scientific methods and describable in the language of science, broadly speaking. The emotivists denied that there are moral facts. One way of putting their argument is this: Facts are the counterparts of true statements; the fact that Buster Keaton made movies is what makes the statement "Buster Keaton made movies" true. We might think there are moral facts because we mistakenly assume that moral "statements" are the kinds of utterances that could be true. Thus, if in saying that Hitler is wicked we are saying something true, there must be a corresponding fact, Hitler's being wicked, that makes it true. However, once we understand that moral "statements" are not really statements at all and, indeed, are not even the sorts of utterances that could be true, the temptation to think there are moral facts disappears. Thus, the belief in moral facts could now be seen not only as the legacy of discarded scientific and religious view but as the symptom of a mistaken assumption about moral language as well.

With the arrival of emotivism as the dominant theory of ethics, many philosophers believed that the final truth about morality had at last been discovered. We can now understand, they said, why ethical disputes go on endlessly, with neither side being able to convert the other. In an ethical dispute, neither side is "correct," because ethical utterances are not the kinds of utterances that are correct or incorrect. Moreover, there are no "proofs" in ethics, because matters of fact and matters of attitude are logically distinct. Two people can agree on all the facts about a situation and yet have utterly different attitudes toward it. Ethical disagreement is like disagreeing about the choice of a restaurant: people might agree on all the facts about restaurants and yet disagree about where to eat, because some prefer Chinese food while others prefer Italian. That's the way ethics is, and that's all there is to it.

During the middle decades of the twentieth century, while emotivism dominated moral philosophy, philosophers rarely wrote about practical issues. Ethics was a nonsubject, beyond the reach of rational methods. For self-respecting philosophers it became a point of pride that, while they might expound upon ethical theory, ethics itself was not to be broached. "A philosopher is not a parish priest or Universal Aunt or Citizens' Advice Bureau,"[12] said P. H. Nowell-Smith in his widely-read book *Ethics*. A moral philosopher might tell you that "Chastity is good" means something like "Hurrah for chastity!" but it was not his business to join in the cheers.

Eventually, however, emotivism fell out of favor, and today it has few adherents. The theory's demise was partly a matter of intellectual fashion. Before his death in 1979, Charles Stevenson, whose book *Ethics and Language* was the definitive statement of emotivism,[13] remarked that while philosophers had abandoned the theory, no one had actually refuted it. But emotivism had failed because it did not do one of the main things that a theory of ethics must do: it did not provide a satisfactory account of the place of reason in ethics. It is a point of logic that moral judgments, if they are to be acceptable, must be founded on good reasons. If I tell you that such-and-such action is wrong, you are entitled to ask why it is wrong; and if I have no adequate reply, you may reject my advice as unfounded. This is what separates moral judgments from mere statements of preference. If I only say "I like so-and-so," I do not need to have a reason; it may just be a brute fact about me that I happen to like it. In making a moral judgment, however, one is at least implicitly claimmg that there is some reason for or against what is being recommended or rejected.

The emotivists were able to give only the most anemic account of the relation between moral judgments and the reasons that support them. Moral reasoning, on their view, turned out to be indistinguishable from propaganda—giving reasons is just an effort to persuade someone to do something or to adopt an attitude. If that is all moral reasoning is, then *good* reasons are merely considerations that will have the desired effect. If the thought that Goldberg is Jewish causes someone to distrust him, then "Goldberg is a Jew" becomes a reason in support of the judgment that he is a shady character. Stevenson embraced this consequence of his view without flinching: "Any statement," he said, "about any fact which any speaker considers likely to alter attitudes may be adduced as a reason for or against an ethical judgment."[14]

Something had gone wrong. In the end, not many philosophers could seriously believe that any fact can count as a reason in support of any judgment. For one thing, the facts must be relevant to the judgment, and psychological influence does not necessarily bring relevance with it: Jewishness is irrelevant to shadiness, regardless of the psychological connections in anyone's mind. Moreover, it seems obvious that some facts are reasons in support of some actions, regardless of what anyone thinks. In a moment of rhetorical abandon, Hume had said, "'Tis not contrary to reason to prefer the destruction of the whole world to the scratching of my finger."[15] But surely the fact that doing X will cause the destruction of the world, while doing Y will scratch my finger, must be a reason in favor of doing Y, not X. An adequate theory of morality must explain why this is so. But this is only the tip of an iceberg. Moral judgements can be supported by arguments, and those arguments can be criticized and found adequate or inadequate on any number of grounds. Once this is realized, we have taken a big step away from emotivism and all the other trends or thought I have been describing, toward the recognition of ethics as an autonomous subject.

ETHICS AND RATIONALITY

Ultimately the case against ethics can be answered only by demonstrating how moral problems are solvable by rational methods. Some of the essays in this book attempt to do that directly, by providing arguments about particular moral issues. But what can be said of a more general nature? How does one go about establishing what is the right thing to do? If there are answers in ethics, how are they to be found? Considered abstractly, these may seem to be impossibly difficult questions. But they are not so hard as one might think.

We have already alluded to the key idea: In any particular case, the right course of action is the one that is backed by the best reason. Solving moral problems, then, is largely a matter of weighing the reasons, or arguments, that can be given for or against the various alternatives. Consider, for example, euthanasia. Many people feel that mercy killing is wicked, and the American Medical Association condemns it as "contrary to that for which the medical profession stands." Others feel that, in the appropriate circumstances, there is nothing wrong with it. Who is right? We may determine whether euthanasia is right or wrong by formulating and assessing the arguments that can be given for and against it. This is at bottom what is wrong with psychological and cultural relativism: if we can produce good reasons for thinking that this practice (or any other) is wrong and show that the arguments in its support are unsound, then we have proved it wrong, regardless of what belief one has been conditioned to have or what one's cultural code might say. And emotivism runs afoul of the same fact: if a stronger case can be made for euthanasia than against it, then mercy killing is permissible, no matter what one's attitude might be.

But how are arguments to be tested? What distinguishes strong arguments from weak ones? The first and most obvious way that a moral argument can go wrong is by misrepresenting the facts. A rational case for or against a course of conduct must rest on some understanding of the facts of the case—minimally, facts about the nature of the action, the circumstances in which it would be done, and its likely consequences. If the facts are misrepresented, the argument is no good. Even the most skeptical thinkers agree that reason has this role to play in moral judgment.

Unfortunately, however, attaining a clear view of the facts is not always a simple matter. In the first place, we often need to know what the consequences of a course of action will be, and this may be impossible to determine with any precision or certainty. Opponents of euthanasia sometimes claim that if mercy killing were legalized, it would lead to a diminished respect for life throughout society and we would end up caring less about the elderly, the physically handicapped, and the mentally retarded. Defenders of euthanasia, on the other hand, heatedly deny this. What separates the two camps here is a disagreement about "the facts," but we cannot settle the issue in the same easy way we could settle an argument about the melting point of lead. We seem to be stuck with different estimates—all more or less reasonable, with no easy way to decide which to accept—of what would happen if euthanasia were legalized.

Moreover, it is often difficult to determine the facts because the facts are distressingly complex. Take, for example, the question of whether someone who requests euthanasia is "competent"—that is, whether they are rational and in full control of their faculties. I take this to be a question of fact, but it is not a simple matter of fact. In order to decide the matter, we must fit together into a pattern all sorts of other facts about the individual—her state of mind, her attitudes, the quality of her reasoning, the pressures influencing her, and so on. That she is, or is not, competent is a kind of conclusion resting on these other facts; it is a matter of what the simpler facts add up to.

Suppose though, that we have a clear view of the relevant facts, and so our arguments cannot be faulted on that ground. Is there any other test of rationality the arguments must pass? Hume's official view was that, at this point, reason has done all it can do, and the rest is up to our "sentiments." Reason sets out the facts; then sentiment takes over and the choice is made. This is a tempting idea, but it only illustrates a common trap into which people may fall. Philosophical theses may seduce with their beautiful simplicity. An idea may be accepted because of its appeal at a high level of generality, even though it does not conform to what we know to be the case at a lower level.

In fact, when Hume was considering actual ethical issues and not busy overemphasizing the role of sentiment, he knew very well that appeals to reason

are often decisive in other ways. In the essay on suicide, he produced a number of powerful arguments in support of his view that a person has the right to take his own life when he is suffering without hope from a painful illness. Hume specifically opposed the traditional religious view that since life is a gift from God, only God may decide when it shall end. About this he made the simple but devastating observation that we "play God" as much when we save life as when we take it. Each time a doctor treats an illness and thereby prolongs a life, he decrees that this life should not end *now*. Thus if we take seriously that only God may determine the length of a life, we have to renounce not only killing but saving life as well.

Hume's point has force because of the general requirement that our arguments be consistent, and consistency, of course, is the prime requirement of rationality. Hume did not argue that the religious opponent of euthanasia has got his facts wrong—he did not insist that there is no God or that God's will has been misunderstood. If Hume's objection were no more than that, there would be little reason for the religious person to be bothered by it. Hume's objection was much stronger, for he was pointing out that we may appeal to a general principle ("Only God has the right to decide when a life shall end") only if we are willing to accept its consequences. If we accept some of them (the prohibition of suicide and euthanasia) but not others (the abandonment of medicine), then we are inconsistent. This fundamentally important point will be missed if we are bewitched by overly simple doctrines like "Reason establishes the facts; sentiment makes the choice."

There are other ways an ethical view may fail to pass the test of consistency. An ethical view may be based on one's "intuitions"—prereflective hunches about what is right or wrong in particular cases—and, on examination, these may turn out to be incompatible with one another. Consider the difference between killing someone and "merely" allowing someone to die. Many people feel intuitively that there is a big moral difference between these two. The thought of actively killing someone has a kind of visceral repulsiveness about it that is missing from the more passive (but still unpleasant) act of standing by and doing nothing while someone dies. Thus it may be held that although euthanasia is wrong, since it involves direct killing, nevertheless it is sometimes permissible to allow death by refraining from life-prolonging treatment.

To be sure, if we do nothing more than consult our intuitions, there seems to be an important difference here. However, it is easy to describe cases of killing and letting die in which there does *not* seem to be such a difference. Suppose a patient is brought into an emergency room and turned over to a doctor who recognizes him as a man against whom he has a grudge. A quick diagnosis reveals that the patient is about to die but can be saved by a simple procedure—say, an appendectomy. The doctor, seeing his chance, deliberately stalls until it is too late to perform the life-saving procedure, and the patient dies. Now, most of us would think, intuitively, that the doctor is no better than a murderer and that the fact that he did not directly kill the patient, but merely let him die, makes no difference whatever.

In the euthanasia case, the difference between killing and letting die seems important. In the grudge case, the difference seems unimportant. But what is the truth? Is the difference important, or isn't it? Such cases show that unexamined intuitions cannot be trusted. That is not surprising. Our intuitions may be nothing more than the product of prejudice, selfishness, or cultural conditioning; we have no guarantee that they are perceptions of the truth. And when they are not compatible with one another, we can be sure that one or the other of them is mistaken.

Let me mention one other way in which the requirement of consistency can force a change in one's moral views. I have been emphasizing that a moral judgment, if it is to be acceptable, must be backed by reasons. Consistency requires, then, that if there are exactly the same reasons in support of one course of conduct as there are in support of another, those actions are equally right, or equally wrong. We cannot say that X is right but that Y is wrong unless there is a relevant difference between them. This is a familiar principle in many contexts: it cannot be right for a teacher to give students different grades unless there is a relevant difference in the work they have done; it cannot be right to pay workers differently unless there is some relevant difference between the jobs they do; and so on. In general, it is this principle that underlies the social ideal of equality.

But this principle has some surprising consequences. Its implications are much more radical than egalitarians have often realized; for, if applied consistently, it would not only require us to treat our fellow humans better, it would require us to rethink our treatment of nonhuman animals as well. To cite only one instance: We routinely perform experiments on chimpanzees that we would never perform on humans—but what is the difference between the chimps and the humans that justifies this difference in treatment? It might be said that humans are far more intelligent and sensitive than chimpanzees; but this only invites a further query: suppose the humans are mentally retarded and so are *less* intelligent and sensitive than the chimps? Would we be willing to experiment on retarded humans in the same way? And if not, why not? What is the difference between the individuals in question that makes it all right to experiment on one but not the other? At this point, the defender of the status quo may be reduced to asserting that, after all, the humans are *human* and that is what makes the difference. This, however, is uncomfortably like asserting that, after all, women are women, or blacks are black, and that is why they may be treated differently. It is the announcement of a prejudice, and nothing more.

This brings us back to the point at which we started. We have adjusted in many ways to the idea that the earth is not the center of the universe and that we humans are but one race among others that have developed here. But where ethics is concerned, we cling to the idea that humanity is still at the center of the cosmos. The idea that every human life is sacred has been replaced by its secular equivalent, that every human life has special value and dignity just in virtue of being human. As a plea for equality among people, the idea has done noble service; but as a justification for our treatment of the nonhuman world, it won't do.

THE LIMITS OF RATIONALITY

This discussion will not have dispelled all the nagging doubts about ethics. Rational methods can be used to construct arguments and to expose factual error and inconsistency in the ways we have described, but is that enough to save ethics from the charge that, at bottom, there is no "truth" in its domain? Couldn't two people who are equally rational—who have all the relevant facts, whose principles are consistent, and so on—still disagree? And if "reason" were inadequate to resolve the disagreement, wouldn't this show that, in the end, ethics really is only a matter of opinion? These questions will not go away.

There is a limit to what rational methods can achieve, which Hume described in the first appendix to his *Inquiry Concerning the Principles of Morals:*

> Ask a man *why he uses exercise;* he will answer, because *he desires to keep his health.* If you then inquire *why he desires health,* he will readily reply, *Because sickness is painful.* If you push your inquiries further and desire a reason *why he hates pain,* it is impossible he can ever give any. This is an ultimate end, and is never referred to any other object.
>
> Perhaps to your second question, *why he desires* health, he may also reply that *it is necessary for the exercise of his calling.* If you ask *why he is anxious on that head,* he will answer, *because he desires to get money.* If you demand, *Why? It is the instrument of pleasure,* says he. And beyond this, it is an absurdity to ask for a reason. It is impossible there can be a progress *in infinitum* and that one thing can always be a reason why another is desired. Something must be desirable on its own account, and because of its immediate accord or agreement with human sentiment and affection.[16]

The impossibility of an infinite regress of reasons is not peculiar to ethics; the point applies in all areas. Mathematical reasoning eventually ends with axioms that are not themselves justified, and reasoning in science ultimately depends on assumptions that are not proved. It could not be otherwise. At some point, reasoning must always come to an end, no matter what one is reasoning about.

But there is a difference between ethics and other subjects, and that difference is in the involvement of the emotions. As Hume observed, when we come to the last reason, we must mention something we care about. Thus, even though "the right thing to do" always depends on what there are the best reasons for doing, *what counts as a reason* itself depends on our emotions. Nothing can count as an ultimate

reason for or against a course of conduct unless we care about that thing in some way. In the absence of any emotional involvement, there are no reasons for action. On this point the emotivists were right, whatever defects their overall theory might have had. And it is the possibility that people might care about different things, and so accept different ultimate principles between which reason cannot adjudicate, that continues to undermine confidence in ethics.

I believe this possibility cannot ever be ruled out entirely and that it will always be the source of a kind of nervousness about ethics. The nervousness cannot be eliminated; we have to live with it. There is, however, one further point to be considered—a point that goes some way toward minimizing the worry.[17]

What people care about is itself sensitive to pressure from deliberative process and can change as a result of thought. This applies as much to people's "ultimate" cares and desires as to their more passing fancies. Someone might not care very much about something before he thinks it through but come to feel differently once he has thought it over. This has been considered extremely important by some of the major philosophers. Aristotle, Butler, and others emphasized that responsible moral judgment must be based on a full understanding of the facts; but, they added, after the facts are established, a separate cognitive process is required for the agent to understand fully the import of what he or she knows. It is necessary not merely to know the facts but also to rehearse them carefully in one's mind, in an impartial, nonevasive way. Only then will one have the kind of knowledge on which moral judgment may be based.

Aristotle even suggested that there are two distinct species of knowledge: first, the sort of knowledge had by one who is able to recite facts, "like the drunkard reciting the verses of Empedocles," but without understanding their meaning; and, second, the sort of knowledge had when one has thought carefully about what one knows. An example might make this clearer. We all know, in an abstract sort of way, that many children in the world are starving; yet for most of us this makes little difference to our conduct. We will spend money on trivial things for ourselves, rather than allowing it to be spent on food for them. How are we to explain this? The Aristotelian explanation is that we "know" the children are starving only in the sense in which the drunkard knows Empedocles' verses—we simply recite the fact.[18] Suppose, though, that we thought carefully about what it must be like to be a starving orphan. Our attitudes, our conduct, and the moral judgments we are willing to make might be substantially altered.

Some years ago, during the Vietnam War, a wire-service photograph of two Vietnamese orphans appeared in American newspapers. They were sleeping on a Saigon street; the younger boy, who seemed to be about four, was inside a tattered cardboard box, while his slightly older brother was curled up around the box. The explanation beneath the photograph said that while they begged for food during the day, the older boy would drag the box with them, because he didn't want his brother to have to sleep on the sidewalk at night.

After this photograph appeared, a large number of people wrote to relief agencies offering help. What difference did the picture make? It was not a matter of people's being presented with new information—it wasn't as though they did not know that starving orphans have miserable lives. Rather, the picture brought home to them in a vivid way things they already knew. It is easy to think of starving children in an abstract, statistical way; the picture forced people to think of them concretely, and it made a difference to people's attitudes.

In moral discussion we often recognize that thinking through what one knows is a separate matter from merely knowing; and we exploit this in a certain strategy of argument. It is the strategy that begins "Think what it is like…"

- Those who favor voluntary euthanasia ask us to consider what it is like, from the point of view of the dying patient, to suffer horribly. If we did, they imply, we would feel more favorably disposed toward mercy killing.
- Albert Camus, in his essay on capital punishment, "Reflections on the Guillotine," argued that people tolerate the death penalty only because they think of it in euphemistic terms ("Pierre paid his debt to society") rather than attending to the sound of the head falling into the basket.[19] If we thought

about it nonevasively, he says, we could not avoid detesting it.
- Opponents of abortion show pictures of fetuses to force us to pay attention to what it is that is killed. The assumption is that if we did, we could not approve of killing it.

Often this method of argument is dismissed as nothing more than a demagogic appeal to emotion. Sometimes the charge is true. But this type of argument may also serve as an antidote for the self-deception that Bishop Butler saw as corrupting moral thought. When we do not want to reach a certain conclusion about what is to be done—perhaps we would rather spend money on ourselves than give it for famine relief—we may refuse to face up in a clear-minded way to what we know. Facts that would have the power to move us are put out of mind or are thought of only bloodlessly and abstractly. Rehearsing the facts in a vivid and imaginative way is the needed corrective.

Now let us return to the question of ethical disagreement. When disagreement occurs, two explanations are possible. First, we might disagree because there has been some failure of rationality on the part of one of us. Or, second, the people who disagree might simply be different kinds of people, who care about different things. In principle, either explanation may be correct. But, in practice, when important matters are at issue, we always proceed on the first hypothesis. We present arguments to those who disagree with us on the assumption (in the hope?) that they have missed something: they are ignorant of relevant facts, they have not thought through what they know, they are inconsistent, and so on. We do not, as a practical matter, credit the idea that we are simply and irreconcilably "different."

Is this assumption reasonable? Isn't it possible that sometimes people just care about different things? It is possible; but if such cases do exist, they are notoriously hard to find. The familiar examples of the cultural anthropologists turn out upon analysis to have other explanations. The Eskimos who allow their firstborn daughters to die of exposure and who abandon feeble old people to a similar fate do not have less concern for life than peoples who reject such practices. They live in different circumstances, under threat of starvation in a hostile environment, and the survival of the community requires policies that otherwise they would happily renounce. Or consider the Ik, a tribe of Africans who during the 1970s were observed to be indifferent even to the welfare of their own children. They would not share food with their children and they laughed when others were sick. Surely, one might think, the Ik are radically different from us. But not so: they took on those characteristics only after a prolonged period of near-starvation that virtually destroyed their tribal culture. Of course human behavior will be modified by calamity; but before their calamity, the Ik were much too "normal" to attract attention. To be sure, there may be some disagreements that reflect cultural variables—Herodotus's Greeks and Callatians, for example—but, beyond that, and barring the kind of disaster that reduced the Ik, it is plausible to think that people are enough alike to make ethical agreement possible, if only full rationality were possible.

The fact that rationality has limits does not subvert the objectivity of ethics, but it does suggest the need for a certain modesty in what can be claimed for it. Ethics provides answers about what we ought to do, given that we are the kinds of creatures we are, caring about the things we will care about when we are as reasonable as we can be, living in the sort of circumstances in which we live. This is not as much as we might want, but it is a lot. And it is as much as we can hope for in a subject that must incorporate not only our beliefs but our ideals.

NOTES

1. *The History of Herodotus*, trans. George Rawlinson, adapted by John Ladd in *Ethical Relativism* (Belmont, Calif.: Wadsworth, 1973), 12.

2. Alasdair MacIntyre, *Whose Justice? Which Rationality?* (Notre Dame, Ind.: University of Notre Dame Press, 1988), 7.

3. Quoted in Martha Nussbaum, "Recoiling from Reason" (a review of MacIntyre), *New York Review of Books*, 7 December 1989, 41. In this paragraph I am heavily indebted to Nussbaum's excellent discussion.

4. *The Politics of Aristotle*, trans. Ernest Barker (London: Oxford University Press, 1946), 9.

5. *Politics of Aristotle*, 306.

6. Aristotle, *Physics*, in *The Basic Works of Aristotle*, ed. Richard McKeon (New York: Random House, 1941), 249.

7. Aristotle, *Physics*, 249.

8. Aristotle, *Politics*, trans. T. A. Sinclair (Harmondsworth, England: Penguin Books, 1962), 40.

9. David Hume, *A Treatise of Human Nature* (Oxford: Oxford University Press, 1888), 468. Originally published in 1739.

10. David Hume, *Essays Moral, Political, and Literary* (Oxford: Oxford University Press, 1963), 590. Originally published in 1741–42.

11. Hume, *Treatise*, 469.

12. P. H. Nowell-Smith, *Ethics* (Baltimore: Penguin Books, 1954), 12.

13. C. L. Stevenson, *Ethics and Language* (New Haven: Yale University Press, 1944).

14. Stevenson, *Ethics*, 114.

15. Hume, *Treatise*, 416.

16. David Hume, *An Inquiry Concerning the Principles of Morals* (Indianapolis: Bobbs-Merrill, 1957), 111. Originally published in 1752.

17. Among contemporary moral philosophers, W. D. Falk has made this point most forcefully; see, for example, his essay "Action-Guiding Reasons," *Journal of Philosophy* 60 (1963): 702–18.

18. Aristotle, *Nicomachean Ethics*, 1147b.

19. Albert Camus, "Reflections on the Guillotine," in *Resistance, Rebellion, and Death* (New York: Knopf, 1961), 175–234.

SUGGESTIONS FOR FURTHER READING

Robert Audi, *Moral Knowledge and Ethical Character* (New York: Oxford University Press, 1997).

Fred Feldman, *Introductory Ethics* (Englewood Cliffs, NJ: Prentice-Hall, 1978).

Richard M. Fox, Joseph P. DeMarco, *Moral Reasoning*, 2nd ed. (New York: Harcourt, 2001).

William K. Frankena, *Ethics*, 2nd ed. (Englewood Cliffs, NJ: Prentice-Hall, 1973).

Bernard Gert, *Morality: Its Nature and Justification* (New York: Oxford University Press, 1998).

Chris Gowans, "Moral Relativism," *The Stanford Encyclopedia of Philosophy* (Spring 2004 ed.), Edward N. Zalta (ed.), URL= <http://plato.stanford.edu/archives/spr2004/entries/moral-relativism/>.

Melville Herskovits, *Cultural Relativism: Perspectives in Cultural Pluralism* (New York: Vintage, 1972).

Kai Nielsen, *Ethics Without God* (Buffalo, NY: Prometheus, 1973).

Louis P. Pojman, *Ethics: Discovering Right and Wrong*, 4th ed. (Belmont, CA: Wadsworth, 2002).

Louis P. Pojman and Lewis Vaughn, ed., *The Moral Life*, 3rd ed. (New York: Oxford University Press, 2007).

James Rachels, *The Elements of Moral Philosophy*, 4th ed. (New York: McGraw-Hill, 2003).

Russ Shafer-Landau, *Whatever Happened to Good and Evil?* (New York: Oxford University Press, 2004).

Theodore Schick, Jr., and Lewis Vaughn, *Doing Philosophy*, 2nd ed., chap. 5 (New York: McGraw-Hill, 2002).

Peter Singer, ed., *A Companion to Ethics* (Cambridge, England: Blackwell, 1993).

Walter T. Stace, "Ethical Relativism" in *The Concept of Morals* (New York: Macmillan, 1965).

Paul Taylor, *Principles of Ethics* (Encino, CA: Dickenson, 1975).

Lewis Vaughn, *Doing Ethics: Moral Reasoning and Contemporary Issues* (New York: W. W. Norton, 2008).

Lewis Vaughn, *The Power of Critical Thinking*, 2nd ed. (New York: Oxford University Press, 2008).

Thomas F. Wall, *Thinking Critically About Moral Problems* (Belmont, CA: Wadsworth, 2003).

CHAPTER 2

Moral Theories

As a thinking, feeling, choosing person, you are unavoidably in the thick of the moral life. You are constantly confronted with momentous questions of moral value and moral rightness. You assert, challenge, accept, or reject moral statements. You make moral judgments about the rightness of actions, the goodness of persons or their character, and the moral quality and worth of your life. Through general moral norms or principles, you try to direct your actions and inform your choices. You make or evaluate moral arguments, testing what you know or think you know about moral realities. And you do something else: you theorize.

As participants in the inescapable drama of the moral life, we all theorize. We all naturally and inevitably venture into the realm of moral theory, trying to see the larger moral meaning behind particular situations and precepts. The question, then, is not whether we theorize—but how well.

WHY MORAL THEORIES?

In science, theories help us understand the empirical world by explaining the causes of events, why things are the way they are. The germ theory of disease explains how particular diseases arise and spread in a human population. The heliocentric (sun-centered) theory of planetary motion explains why the planets in our solar system behave the way they do. In ethics, moral theories have a similar explanatory role. A **moral theory** explains not why one event causes another but why an action is right or wrong or why a person or a person's character is good or bad. A moral theory tells us what it is about an action that *makes it right*, or what it is about a person that *makes him or her good*. The divine command theory of morality, for example, says that right actions are those commanded or willed by God. Traditional utilitarianism says that right actions are those that produce the greatest happiness for all concerned. These and other moral theories are attempts to define rightness or goodness. In this way, they are both more general and more basic than moral principles or other general norms.

Moral theorizing—that is, devising, using, or assessing moral theories or parts of theories—is normal and pervasive in the moral life, though it is often done without much recognition that theory is playing a part in the deliberations. Whenever we try to understand what a moral property such as rightness or goodness means, or justify a moral principle or other norm, or resolve a conflict between two credible principles, or explain why a particular action or practice is right or wrong, or evaluate the plausibility of specific moral intuitions or assumptions, we do moral theorizing. In fact, we *must* theorize if we are to make headway in such investigations. We must stand back from the situation at hand and try to grasp the larger pattern that only theory can reveal.

Moral theories that concentrate on right and wrong actions are known as theories of obligation (or duty) or simply *theories of right action*. The divine command theory and utilitarianism are theories of right action. Philosophers often distinguish these from moral theories that focus on good and bad persons or character—so-called *virtue-based theories*. Virtue ethics (covered later in this chapter) is a prime example.

How do moral theories fit into our everyday moral reasoning? In answering that, let's focus on theories of right action, probably the most influential type in ethics. First, moral theories can figure directly in our moral arguments. As we saw earlier, moral arguments contain both moral and nonmoral premises. A moral premise can consist of a moral principle, a moral rule (a less general norm derived from or based on a principle), or a claim expressing a central tenet of a moral theory. Using such a tenet, someone might argue, for example, that stem-cell research should be fully funded rather than halted altogether because such a step would eventually lead to a greater benefit for more people, and right actions (according to utilitarianism) are those that result in the greatest overall benefit for the greatest number. Thus the fundamental moral standard of utilitarianism becomes a premise in an argument for a specific action in a particular case.

Second, theories can have an indirect impact on moral arguments because principles appealed to are often supported in turn by a moral theory. The principles can be either derived from or supported by the theory's account of right and wrong action. Consider the prohibition against murder, the basic precept that it is wrong to take the life of an innocent person. This principle can be drawn from theories built around the fundamental notion of respect for persons. As one such theory would have it, murder is wrong because it treats people not as persons with inherent worth but as mere things to be used or dispensed with as one wishes.

Some people are tempted to deduce from all this that moral theories are the dominant force in moral reasoning as well as in the moral life. This view would be an oversimplification. By design, moral theories are certainly more general in scope than moral principles, rules, or judgments. But from this fact, it does not follow that theories alone are the ultimate authority in moral deliberations. For one thing, to be truly useful, moral theories must be filled out with details about how to apply them in real life and what kinds of cases to which they are relevant. For another, there is more to morality than what can be captured in the general norms of a theory. There is also the testimony of the particular, the evidence of individual moral judgments.

Our moral deliberations, then, involve both the general and the particular. Suppose we embrace a moral theory that seems to offer us a plausible explanation of what makes an action right or wrong. When we must decide which action is morally right in a particular situation, we look to our theory for general guidance. From our theory we may glean a set of moral principles that seem to apply to the case at hand. If the principles lead us to conflicting choices, we look again to the theory for insight in resolving the conflict. But we also must take into account our considered judgments about the case. (We may also formulate considered judgments about the relevant principles or rules.) If our considered judgments and the deliverances of our theory are consistent with one another, we have additional assurance that our decision in the case is correct. If our judgments clash with our theory or principles, we must decide which to revise or discard—for critical reasoning demands that our beliefs be coherent, that they do not harbor contradictions. If we believe our judgments to be more credible than the implications of our theory (or principles), we may modify the theory accordingly (or, rarely, regard the theory as irreparable and give it up). But if the theory seems more credible in this case, we may conclude that our judgment is untrustworthy and set it aside.

So a moral theory can show us what is important and reasonable in morality, guiding our judgments through overarching insights that may help us with specific cases and issues, sometimes correcting erring judgments along the way. Our considered judgments are fallible indicators of moral common sense and are checks against wayward theory or flawed principle. In ethics, both these moral resources are highly respected and widely used.

IMPORTANT MORAL THEORIES
Several moral theories have played major roles in ethics. Theories of right action (in contrast to virtue-based theories) have dominated the field, each usually based on one of two broad views about the essential character of right actions. **Consequentialist theories** insist that the rightness of actions depends solely on their consequences or results. The key question is what or how much good the actions produce, however *good* is defined. **Deontological** (or nonconsequentialist) **theories** say that the rightness of actions is determined not solely by their consequences but partly or entirely by their intrinsic nature. For some or all actions, rightness depends on the kind of actions they are, not on how much good they produce. A consequentialist theory, then, may say that stealing is wrong because it causes more harm than good. But a deontological theory may contend that stealing is inherently wrong regardless of its consequences, good or bad.

Utilitarianism
The leading consequentialist theory is **utilitarianism**, the view that right actions are those that result in the most beneficial balance of good over bad consequences for everyone involved. It says we should maximize the nonmoral good (the *utility*) of everyone affected, regardless of the contrary urgings of moral rules or unbending moral principles. Various forms of utilitarianism differ in how they define utility, with some equating it with happiness or pleasure (the hedonistic view), others with satisfaction of preferences or desires or some other intrinsically valuable things or states such as knowledge or perfection.

In applying the utilitarian moral standard (the greatest good, everyone considered), some moral philosophers concentrate on specific acts and some on rules covering kinds of acts. The former approach is called **act-utilitarianism**, the idea that the rightness of actions depends solely on the relative good produced by *individual actions*. An act is right if in a particular situation it produces a greater balance of good over bad than any alternative acts; determining rightness is a matter of weighing the effects of each possible act. The latter approach, known as **rule-utilitarianism**, avoids judging rightness by specific acts and focuses instead on *rules governing categories of acts*. It says a right action is one that conforms to a rule that, if followed consistently, would create for everyone involved the most beneficial balance of good over bad. We are to adhere to the rules because they maximize the good for everyone considered—even though a given act may produce bad effects in a particular situation.

The classic, or traditional, version of utilitarianism was devised by English philosopher Jeremy Bentham (1748–1832) and given more detail and plausibility by another English philosopher, John Stuart Mill (1806–1873). Classic utilitarianism is hedonistic in that the utility to be maximized is pleasure, broadly termed happiness, the only intrinsic good. A right action produces more net happiness (amounts of happiness minus unhappiness) than any alternative action, everyone considered. As Mill put it,

> [Actions] are right in proportion as they tend to promote happiness, wrong as they tend to produce the reverse of happiness. By "happiness" is intended pleasure, and the absence of pain; by "unhappiness," pain and the privation of pleasure.[1]

Bentham and Mill, however, had different ideas about what happiness entailed, as do many philosophers today. Bentham thinks that happiness is one-dimensional: it is pleasure, pure and simple, something that varies only in the amount that an agent can experience. On this scheme, it seems that the moral ideal would be to experience maximum amounts of pleasure, as does the glutton or the debauchee. But Mill thinks that pleasures can vary in quality as well as quantity. For him, there are lower and higher pleasures—the lower and inferior ones indulged in by the glutton and his ilk and the higher and more satisfying ones found in such experiences as the search for knowledge and the appreciation of art and music. Mill famously sums up this contrast by saying, "It is better to be a human being dissatisfied than a pig satisfied; better to be Socrates dissatisfied than a fool satisfied."[2]

Like all forms of utilitarianism, the classic formulation demands a strong sense of impartiality. When promoting happiness, we must not only take into account the happiness of everyone affected, but also give everyone's needs or interests equal weight. Mill explains:

> [The] happiness which forms the utilitarian standard of what is right conduct, is not the agent's own happiness, but that of all concerned. As between his own happiness and that of others, utilitarianism requires him to be as strictly impartial as a disinterested and benevolent spectator.[3]

In classic utilitarianism, the emphasis is on maximizing the total quantity of net happiness, not on ensuring that it is rationed in any particular amounts among the people involved. This means that an action resulting in one thousand units of happiness for ten people is better than an action yielding only nine hundred units of happiness for those same ten people—regardless of how the units of happiness are distributed among them. Classic utilitarians do want to allocate the total amount of happiness among as many people as possible (thus their motto, "the greatest happiness for the greatest number"). But maximizing total happiness is the fundamental concern whether everyone gets an equal portion or one person gets the lion's share.

[1] John Stuart Mill, "What Utilitarianism Is," *Utilitarianism* (1863).
[2] Mill, "What Utilitarianism Is."
[3] Mill, "What Utilitarianism Is."

Consider how utilitarianism could apply to euthanasia. An act-utilitarian might conclude that euthanasia for someone suffering horrible, inescapable pain would be permissible because ending life would bring about the most net happiness. In her calculations, she would also include factors such as the psychological, social, and financial impact on the patient's family, friends, and caregivers. A rule-utilitarian might insist that more net happiness would be produced by consistently following a rule that disallowed euthanasia. He could argue that permitting mercy killings would have terrible consequences overall—increases in nonvoluntary or involuntary euthanasia, erosion of respect for the medical profession, and a weakening of society's abhorrence of homicide.

Ethical Egoism

Another consequentialist theory is **ethical egoism**, the view that right actions are those that further one's own best interests. Your duty is to look out for yourself by doing what yields the most favorable consequences for you, even if the interests of others are ignored or thwarted. Ethical egoists may equate their interests with pleasure, happiness, self-realization, or other valued states, but they all agree that promoting these things for oneself is the essence of morality. Selfishness and wild abandon, however, are not entailed by ethical egoism, for ignoring the needs of others or acting without restraint may not be in one's best interests.

Ethical egoism, though consequentialist, is a conceptual mile away from utilitarianism. The utilitarian says we have a duty to maximize the well-being of everyone within our reach, and that we must treat everyone (including ourselves) impartially and with equal regard. Ethical egoism says that you have a moral obligation to maximize the well-being of just one person—yourself—and that you act morally only when you play favorites and give special treatment to number one. Whether you help or harm others, cooperate with them or oppose them, you must always do what produces the most favorable consequences for *you*. Doing what is in your own best interest is the essence of the moral life.

Ethical egoists have argued that the theory is on solid ground because it reflects what they believe is an obvious psychological fact about human nature: *people always act out of self-interest*. Altruism—the disinterested concern for the well-being of others—is never a motive for action. This claim about human motives is an empirical theory called **psychological egoism**. It is the starting point for the ethical egoist's main argument, which says that (1) we are obligated to act only if we *can* act; (2) we can act only when motivated by self-interest; (3) therefore, we are obligated to act only when motivated by self-interest. The argument is based on a simple fact about the moral life: we are not morally obligated to do the impossible. We have no duty to make our loved ones live two hundred years, because that is beyond our power. We have no obligation to ensure that everyone is healthy, because that feat is not possible. Likewise we are not capable of acting altruistically, so we have no obligation to do so. We are duty bound to do only what we can do—which is to act purely out of self-interest.

Critics have rebutted this argument by rejecting psychological egoism (premise 2). They point out that our experience suggests that we don't always act out of self-interest. We often look out for number one, but we also sometimes choose to inconvenience ourselves, incur serious disadvantages, or put ourselves at risk—to help someone else. People rush into burning buildings to save a complete stranger. Mothers starve themselves so their children will have food. Husbands and wives sell everything they own to pay for their spouses' urgent medical care.

Ethical egoists are likely to respond to this line by declaring that such experiences are deceptive, for actions that seem purely altruistic are in fact done to achieve social advantage, to feel personal satisfaction, or to prevent some future calamity. In fact, for every instance of apparent altruistic behavior, ethical egoists must say that we are seriously mistaken about the motivation behind it.

This reply may save psychological egoism from refutation, but it does so at a cost. It means that the theory is untestable. No evidence could ever count against it; all possible evidence is consistent with it. Psychological egoism is thus completely uninformative and conceptually worthless, so it cannot be used as a premise in the argument for ethical egoism.

On the other hand, if we have no preconceptions about which way the evidence points, and we take it at face value, it seems to count against psychological egoism. The only evidence we have regarding our motivations for acting is people's behavior and their introspective reports about why they behave as they do. And this evidence, though not always reliable, suggests that we sometimes do act selflessly and altruistically.

A common form of psychological egoism says that people perform actions solely to obtain satisfaction, happiness, or pleasure—even actions that appear to be altruistic or selfless. But this view of the matter, philosophers insist, is muddled. It is much more likely that we act to obtain particular things, not satisfaction itself, and that we experience satisfaction as a by-product of obtaining those things. We don't seek satisfaction; we seek certain things that give us satisfaction when we acquire them. If the things themselves were not the object of our desires, it would be difficult to see how we could get any satisfaction from our attaining them.

Of all the arguments put forth against ethical egoism, the one that is probably most damaging boils down to this: the theory runs afoul of moral common sense. In judging a moral theory, we have good reason to doubt its worth if it conflicts with what we take to be our plausible moral intuitions. As we have seen, our intuitions may be mistaken, but we are entitled to accept them at face value unless we have good reason to mistrust them. Critics maintain that ethical egoism clashes with moral common sense in two important ways.

First, the theory seems to be inconsistent with our considered moral judgments. Ethical egoism implies that if secretly murdering and robbing a rich stranger would be in your best interests, then you should do so. The same could be said about your betraying your best friend, or falsely accusing someone of a serious crime, or burning down a factory owned by your business competitor. All these actions would be condemned by our considered moral judgments, but ethical egoism could countenance them. Commonsense morality says they are wrong; ethical egoism says they may be right. This objection to the theory is not undercut by the claim that morally wrong actions are never in one's best interests, for we can easily imagine counterexamples in which immoral acts are to a person's advantage.

Second, ethical egoism appears to conflict with an essential element of the moral life: impartiality. As we saw earlier, morality entails that equals be treated equally unless there is a morally relevant reason to treat them differently. Each person's interests must be given equal weight. But, by definition, ethical egoism insists that some people's interests should be regarded as more worthy of consideration than those of others—specifically, one's *own* interests are to be given higher priority than those of anyone else in the world. Discrimination against others for no good reason is required by the theory.

Kantian Ethics

From the great German philosopher Immanuel Kant (1724–1804) comes what is widely regarded as probably the most sophisticated and influential deontological theory ever devised. **Kant's theory** is the very antithesis of utilitarianism, holding that right actions do not depend in the least on consequences, the maximization of utility, the production of happiness, or the desires and needs of human beings. For Kant, the core of morality consists in following a rational and universally applicable moral rule and doing so solely out of a sense of duty. An action is right only if it conforms to such a rule, and we are morally praiseworthy only if we perform it for duty's sake alone.

In Kant's system, all our moral duties are expressed in the form of *categorical imperatives*. An imperative is a command to do something; it is categorical if it applies without exception and without regard for particular needs or purposes. A categorical imperative says, "Do this—regardless." In contrast, a *hypothetical imperative* is a command to do something if we want to achieve particular aims, as in "If you want good pay, work hard." The moral law, then, rests on absolute directives that do not depend on the contingencies of desire or utility.

Kant says that through reason and reflection we can derive our duties from a single moral principle, what he calls *the* categorical imperative. He formulates it in different ways, the first one being "Act only on that maxim through which you can at the same time will that it should become a universal law."[4] For Kant, our actions have logical implications—they imply general rules, or maxims, of conduct. If you tell a lie for financial gain, you are in effect acting according to a maxim like "I shall lie when doing so benefits me financially." The question is whether the maxim corresponding to an action is a legitimate moral law. To find out, we must ask if we could consistently will that the maxim become a universal law applicable to everyone—that is, if everyone could consistently act on the maxim and we would be willing to have them do so. If we could do this, then the action described by the maxim is morally permissible; if not, it is prohibited. Thus moral laws embody two characteristics thought to be essential to morality itself: universality and impartiality.

To show us how to apply this formulation of the categorical imperative to a specific situation, Kant uses the example of a lying promise. Suppose you need to borrow money from a friend, but you know you could never pay her back. So to get the loan, you decide to lie, falsely promising to repay the money. To find out if such a lying promise is morally permissible, Kant would have you ask if you could consistently will the maxim of your action to become a universal law, to ask in effect "What if everyone did this?" The maxim is "Whenever you need to borrow money you cannot pay back, make a lying promise to repay." So what *would* happen if everyone in need of a loan acted in accordance with this maxim? People would make lying promises to obtain loans, but everyone would also know that such promises were worthless, and the custom of loaning money on promises would disappear. So willing the maxim to be a universal law involves a contradiction: if everyone

---

4 Immanuel Kant, *Groundwork of the Metaphysic of Morals*, trans. H. J. Paton (New York: Harper & Row, 1964), 88.

made lying promises, promise-making itself would be no more; you cannot consistently will the maxim to become a universal law. Therefore, your duty is clear: making a lying promise to borrow money is morally wrong.

Kant's first formulation of the categorical imperative yields several other duties, some of which are particularly relevant to bioethics. Notably he argues that there is an absolute moral prohibition against killing the innocent, lying, committing suicide, and failing to help others when feasible.

Perhaps the most renowned formulation of the categorical imperative is the principle of respect for persons (a formulation distinct from the first one although Kant thought them equivalent). As he puts it, "Act in such a way that you always treat humanity, whether in your own person or in the person of any other, never simply as a means, but always at the same time as an end."[5] People must never be treated as if they were mere instruments for achieving some further end, for people are ends in themselves, possessors of ultimate inherent worth. People have ultimate value because they are the ultimate source of value for other things. They bestow value; they do not have it bestowed upon them. So we should treat both ourselves and other persons with the respect that all inherently valuable beings deserve.

According to Kant, the inherent worth of persons derives from their nature as free, rational beings capable of directing their own lives, determining their own ends, and decreeing their own rules by which to live. Thus, the inherent value of persons does not depend in any way on their social status, wealth, talent, race, or culture. Moreover, inherent value is something that all persons possess equally. Each person deserves the same measure of respect as any other.

Kant explains that we treat people merely as a means instead of an end-in-themselves if we disregard these characteristics of personhood—if we thwart people's freely chosen actions by coercing them, undermine their rational decision-making by lying to them, or discount their equality by discriminating against them.

Notice that this formulation of the categorical imperative does not actually prohibit treating a person as a means but forbids treating a person *simply*, or *merely*, as a means—as nothing but a means. Kant recognizes that in daily life we often must use people to achieve our various ends. To buy milk, we use the cashier; to find books, we use the librarian; to get well, we use the doctor. But because their actions are freely chosen and we do not undermine their status as persons, we do not use them *solely* as instruments of our will. Medical researchers use their human subjects as a means to an end—but not merely as a means to an end if the subjects give their informed consent to participate in the research.

Natural Law Theory

From ancient times to the present day, many people have thought that the outlines of the moral law are plain to see because they are written large and true in nature itself. This basic notion has been developed over the centuries into what is known as **natural law theory**, the view that right actions are those that conform to moral standards discerned in nature through human reason. Undergirding this doctrine is the belief that all of nature (including humankind) is teleological, that it is somehow directed toward particular goals

---

[5] Kant, *Groundwork*, 96.

or ends, and that humans achieve their highest good when they follow their true, natural inclinations leading to these goals or ends. There is, in other words, a way things *are*—natural processes and functions that accord with the natural law—and how things are shows how things *should be*. The prime duty of humans, then, is to guide their lives toward these natural ends, acting in accordance with the requirements of natural law.

Implicit in all this is the element of rationality. According to natural law theory, humans are rational beings empowered by reason to perceive the workings of nature, determine the natural inclinations of humans, and recognize the implications therein for morally permissible actions. That is, reason enables human beings to ascertain the moral law implicit in nature and to apply that objective, universal standard to their lives.

Though natural law theory has both religious and nonreligious forms, the theistic formulation of theologian-philosopher Thomas Aquinas (1225–1274) has been the theory's dominant version. It is not only the official moral outlook of the Roman Catholic Church, but it has also been the intellectual starting point for many contemporary variations of the theory, secular and otherwise. For Aquinas, God is the author of the natural law who gave humans the gift of reason to discern the law for themselves and live accordingly. Aquinas argues that human beings naturally tend toward—and therefore have a duty of—preserving human life and health (and so must not kill the innocent), producing and raising children, seeking knowledge (including knowledge of God), and cultivating cooperative social relationships. In all this, Aquinas says, the overarching aim is to do and promote good and avoid evil.

Natural law theory does not provide a relevant moral rule covering every situation, but it does offer guidance through general moral principles, some of which are thought to apply universally and absolutely (admitting no exceptions). Among these principles are absolutist prohibitions against directly killing the innocent, lying, and using contraceptives. In his list of acts considered wrong no matter what, Aquinas includes adultery, blasphemy, and sodomy.

Of course, moral principles or rules often conflict, demanding that we fulfill two or more incompatible duties. We may be forced, for example, to either tell a lie and save people's lives or tell the truth and cause their death—but we cannot do both. Some moral theories address these problems by saying that all duties are prima facie: when duties conflict, we must decide which ones override the others. Theories that posit absolute duties—natural law theory being a prime example—often do not have this option. How does the natural law tradition resolve such dilemmas? Among other resources, it uses the **doctrine of double effect**.

This principle, a cornerstone of Roman Catholic ethics, affirms that performing a bad action to bring about a good effect is never morally acceptable but that performing a good action may sometimes be acceptable even if it produces a bad effect. More precisely, the principle says it is always wrong to intentionally perform a bad action to produce a good effect, but doing a good action that results in a bad effect may be permissible if the bad effect is not intended although foreseen. In the former case, a bad thing is said to be directly intended; in the latter, a bad thing is not directly intended.

These requirements have been detailed in four "tests" that an action must pass to be judged morally permissible. We can express a traditional version of these tests like this:

1. The action itself must be morally permissible.
2. Causing a bad effect must not be used to obtain a good effect (the end does not justify the means).

3. Whatever the outcome of an action, the intention must be to cause only a good effect. (The bad effect can be foreseen but never intended.)

4. The bad effect of an action must not be greater in importance than the good effect.

Consider the application of these tests to euthanasia. Suppose an 80-year-old hopelessly ill patient is in continuous, unbearable pain and begs to be put out of her misery. Is it morally permissible to grant her request (either by giving a lethal injection or ending all ordinary life-sustaining measures)? If we apply the doctrine of double effect as just outlined, we must conclude that the answer is *no*: euthanasia—either active or passive—is not a morally permissible option here. (In the Roman Catholic view, all forms of euthanasia are wrong, although it is permissible not to treat a hopelessly ill person for whom ordinary life-sustaining treatments are useless.) Failing even one of the tests would render an action impermissible, but in this case let us run through all four as a natural law theorist might:

1. Taking steps to terminate someone's life is a clear violation of test 1. Whatever its effects, the action of taking a life is in itself immoral, a violation of the cardinal duty to preserve innocent life.

2. Ending the woman's life to save her from terrible suffering is an instance of causing a bad effect (the woman's death) as a means of achieving a good effect (cessation of pain)—a failure of test 2.

3. The death of the woman is intended; it is not merely a tragic side effect of the attempt solely to ease her pain. So the action fails test 3.

4. Causing the death of an innocent person is a great evil that cannot be counterbalanced by the good of pain relief. So the action does not pass test 4.

The verdict in such a case would be different, however, if the patient's death were not intentionally caused but unintentionally brought about. Suppose, for example, that the physician sees that the woman is in agony and so gives her a large injection of morphine to minimize her suffering—knowing full well that the dose will also probably speed her death. In this scenario, the act of easing the woman's pain is itself morally permissible (test 1). Her death is not a means to achieve some greater good; the goal is to ease her suffering (test 2). Her death is not intended; the intention is to alleviate her pain, though the unintended (but foreseen) side effect is her hastened death (test 3). Finally, the good effect of an easier death seems more or less equivalent in importance to the bad effect of a hastened death. Therefore, unintentionally but knowingly bringing about the woman's death in this way is morally permissible.

We get similar results if we apply the double-effect principle in the traditional way to abortion. We find that as the intentional destruction of an innocent human life, (so-called direct) abortion is always immoral (test 1). Moreover, it is wrong even (or especially) if it is performed to bring about some good result, such as saving the mother's life or preventing serious harm to her (tests 2 and 3). On the other hand, actions leading unintentionally to the death of a fetus (so-called indirect abortion) may be permissible in rare cases. Say a pregnant woman has an infectious disease that will kill her unless she gets injections of a powerful drug. But the drug will abort the fetus. According to the doctrine of double effect, receiving the injections may be morally permissible if the action itself is morally permissible, which it is (test 1); if the death of the fetus is not used to rescue the woman (test 2); if the injections are given with the intention of curing the woman's disease, not of inducing an abortion (test 3); and if the death of the fetus is balanced by the life of the woman (test 4).

Rawls's Contractarianism

In its broadest sense, **contractarianism** refers to moral theories based on the idea of a social contract, or agreement, among individuals for mutual advantage. The most influential contemporary form of contractarianism is that of philosopher John Rawls (1921–2002), who uses the notion of a social contract to generate and defend moral principles governing how members of a society should treat one another. He asks, in effect, by what principles should a just society structure itself to ensure a fair distribution of rights, duties, and advantages of social cooperation?

His answer is that the required principles—essentially principles of justice—are those that people would agree to under hypothetical conditions that ensure fair and unbiased choices. Rawls believes that if the starting point for the social contract is fair—if the initial conditions and bargaining process for producing the principles are fair—then the principles themselves will be just and will define the essential makeup of a just society. As he says,

> [The] guiding idea is that the principles of justice for the basic structure of society are the object of the original agreement. They are the principles that free and rational persons concerned to further their own interests would accept in an initial position of equality as defining the fundamental terms of their association. These principles are to regulate all further agreements; they specify the kinds of social cooperation that can be entered into and the forms of government that can be established.[6]

At the hypothetical starting point—what Rawls calls the "original position"—a group of normal, self-interested, rational individuals come together to choose the principles that will determine their basic rights and duties and their share of society's benefits and burdens. But to ensure that their decisions are as fair and impartial as possible, they must meet behind a metaphorical "veil of ignorance." Behind the veil, no one knows his or her own social or economic status, class, race, sex, abilities, talents, level of intelligence, or psychological makeup. Since the participants are rational and self-interested but ignorant of their situation in society, they will not agree to principles that will put any particular group at a disadvantage because they might very well be members of that group. They will choose principles that are unbiased and nondiscriminatory. The assumption is that since the negotiating conditions in the original position are fair, the agreements reached will also be fair—the principles will be just.

Rawls contends that given the original position, the participants would agree to arrange their social relationships according to these fundamental principles:

1. Each person is to have an equal right to the most extensive total system of equal basic liberties compatible with a similar system of liberty for all.
2. Social and economic inequalities are to be arranged so that they are both:
   (a) to the greatest benefit of the least advantaged . . . and
   (b) attached to offices and positions open to all under conditions of fair equality of opportunity.[7]

The first principle—the equal liberty principle—says that everyone is entitled to the most freedom possible in exercising basic rights and duties (for example, the right to vote and hold office and freedom of speech, assembly, and thought). Each person should get

---

[6] John Rawls, *A Theory of Justice*, rev. ed. (Cambridge, MA: Harvard University Press, 1999), 10.
[7] Rawls, 266.

a maximum degree of basic liberties but no more than anyone else. This principle takes precedence over all other considerations (including the second principle) so that basic liberties cannot be reduced or cancelled just to improve economic well-being.

The second principle concerns social and economic goods such as income, wealth, opportunities, and positions of authority. Part (b) says that everyone is entitled to an equal chance to try to acquire these basic goods. No one is guaranteed an equal share of them, but opportunities to obtain these benefits must be open to all, regardless of social standing.

Rawls knows that social and economic inequalities will naturally arise in society. But as he asserts in part (a), they are not unjust if they work to everyone's benefit, especially to the benefit of the least well off in society. "[There] is no injustice," he says, "in the greater benefits earned by a few provided that the situation of persons not so fortunate is thereby improved."[8] For Rawls, such a policy is far more just than one in which some people are made to suffer for the greater good of others: "[I]t is not just that some should have less in order that others may prosper."

In Rawls's scheme, the demands of the first principle must be satisfied before satisfying the second, and the requirements of part (b) must be met before those of part (a). In any just distribution of benefits and burdens, then, the first priority is to ensure equal basic liberties for all concerned, then equality of opportunity, then the arrangement of any inequalities to the benefit of the least advantaged.

As a theory of distributive justice, Rawls's contractarianism seems to have significant implications for the allocation of society's health care resources (see Chapter 10). For example, one prominent line of argument goes like this: as Rawls claims, everyone is entitled to fair equality of opportunity, and adequate (basic) health care enables fair equality of opportunity (by ensuring "normal species functioning"). Therefore, everyone is entitled to adequate health care, which includes all appropriate measures for eliminating or compensating for the disadvantages of disease and impairment.[9] In such a system, there would be universal access to a basic level of health care, while more elaborate or elective services would be available to anyone who could afford them.

Virtue Ethics

Most moral theories—including all those just discussed—are theories of obligation. They emphasize the rightness of actions and the duties of moral agents. Their main concern is knowing and doing what's right, and their chief guide to these aims is moral principles or directives. **Virtue ethics**, however, is a radically different kind of moral theory: it focuses on the development of virtuous character. According to virtue ethics, character is the key to the moral life, for it is from a virtuous character that moral conduct and values naturally arise. Virtues are engrained dispositions to act by standards of excellence, so having the proper virtues leads as a matter of course to right actions properly motivated. The central task in morality, then, is not knowing and applying principles, but being and becoming a good person, someone possessing the virtues that define moral excellence. In virtue ethics, someone determines right action not by consulting rules but by asking what a truly virtuous person would do or whether an action would accord with the relevant virtues.

[8] Rawls, 13.
[9] Norman Daniels, "Health Care Needs and Distributive Justice," in *Justice and Justification* (Cambridge, England: Cambridge University Press, 1996).

Aristotle (384–322 BCE) is the primary inspiration for contemporary versions of virtue ethics. For him, as for many modern virtue ethicists, the highest goal of humanity is the good life or "human flourishing" (what Aristotle calls *eudaimonia*, or happiness), and developing virtues is the way to achieve such a rich and satisfying life. Thus virtues are both the traits that make us good persons and the dispositions that enable us to live good lives. The good life is the virtuous life.

Unlike many theories of obligation, virtue ethics asks us to do more than just observe minimal moral rules—it insists that we *aspire to moral excellence*, that we cultivate the virtues that will make us better persons. In this sense, virtue ethics is goal directed, not rule guided. The moral virtues—benevolence, honesty, loyalty, compassion, fairness, and the like—are ideals that we must ever strive to attain. (There are also nonmoral virtues such as patience, prudence, and reasonableness, which need not concern us here.) By the lights of both Aristotle and modern virtue ethicists, character is not static. We can become more virtuous by reflecting on our lives and those of others, practicing virtuous behavior, or imitating moral exemplars such as Gandhi, Buddha, Jesus, Muhammad, and Socrates. We can—and should—be better than we are.

To the virtue ethicist, possessing the right virtues means having the proper motivations that naturally accompany those virtues. To act morally, we must act from virtue, and acting from virtue means acting with the appropriate motives. It is not enough to do right; we must do right for the right motivating reasons. If we save a drowning friend, we should do so out of genuine feelings of compassion, kindness, or loyalty—not because of the prodding of moral rules or social expectations. In contrast, some moral theories (notably Kant's) maintain that acting morally is solely a matter of acting for duty's sake—performing an action simply because duty requires it. Virtuous motives are irrelevant; we act morally if we do our duty regardless of our motivations. But this notion seems to many to offer a barren picture of the moral life. Surely, they say, motivations for acting are often relevant to our evaluations of people's character and actions. The friend we saved from drowning would probably be appalled if we declared that we saved her out of duty even though we did not really care whether she lived or died. Many moral philosophers agree that motivations are indeed important considerations in moral judgments, and they have incorporated virtues into their theories of obligation.

The virtue ethics approach to ethical issues is distinctive. On abortion, for example, the virtue ethicist might argue that a woman's decision to have an abortion should be judged by the virtues (or lack thereof) that she draws on in deciding what to do. If she decides to have an abortion just because she is afraid of the responsibilities of parenthood, she shows cowardice. If she wants to go through with an abortion merely because pregnancy would disrupt her vacation plans, she shows self-centeredness and callousness. In neither case is the virtue ethicist likely to call the woman's decision virtuous.[10]

The Ethics of Care
The ethics of care is a distinctive moral perspective that arose out of feminist concerns and grew to challenge core elements of most other moral theories. Generally those theories emphasize abstract principles, general duties, individual rights, impartial judgments,

---

[10] Examples from Rosalind Hursthouse, *Beginning Lives* (Oxford: Blackwell, 1987), cited in Justin Oakley, "A Virtue Ethics Approach," in *A Companion to Bioethics* (Oxford: Blackwell, 2001), 86–97.

and deliberative reasoning. But the ethics of care shifts the focus to the unique demands of specific situations and to the virtues and feelings that are central to close personal relationships—empathy, compassion, love, sympathy, and fidelity. The heart of the moral life is feeling for and caring for those with whom you have a special, intimate connection.

Early on, the ethics of care drew inspiration from the notion that men and women have dramatically different styles of moral decision making, with men seizing on principles, duties, and rights, and women homing in on personal relationships, caring, and empathy. This difference was highlighted in research done by psychologist Carol Gilligan and published in her 1982 book *In a Different Voice*.[11] Typically men recognize an ethic of justice and rights, she says, and women are guided by an ethic of compassion and care. In her view the latter is as legitimate as the former, and both have their place in ethics.

Other research has suggested that the differences between men and women in styles of moral thinking may not be as great as Gilligan suggests. But the credibility of the empirical claim does not affect the larger insight that the research seemed to some writers to suggest: caring is an essential part of morality, and the most influential theories have not fully taken it into account.

These points get support along several lines. First, virtue ethics reminds us that virtues are part of the moral life. If caring is viewed as a virtue—in the form of compassion, empathy, or kindness—then caring too must be an element of morality. A moral theory then would be deficient if it made no room for care.

Moreover many argue that unlike the ethics of care, most moral theories push the principle of impartiality too far. Recall that impartiality in morality requires us to consider everyone as equal, counting everyone's interests the same. The principle applies widely, especially in matters of public justice, but less so in personal relationships of love, family, friendship, and the like. We seem to have special obligations (partiality) to close friends, family members, and others we care for, duties that we do not have to strangers or to universal humanity. As one philosopher explains it,

> May I devote my time and resources to caring for my own friends and family, even if this means ignoring the needs of other people whom I could also help? From an impartial point of view, our duty is to promote the interests of everyone alike. But few of us accept that view. The ethics of care confirms the priority that we naturally give to our family and friends, and so it seems a more plausible moral conception.[12]

Most moral theories emphasize duties and downplay the role of emotions, attitudes, and motivations. Kant, for example, would have us do our duty for duty's sake, whatever our feelings. For him, to be a morally good parent, we need only act from duty. But taking care of our children as a matter of moral obligation alone seems an empty exercise. Surely being a morally good parent also involves having feelings of love and attitudes of caring. The ethics of care eagerly takes these emotional elements into account.

Many philosophers, including several writing from a feminist perspective, have lodged such criticisms against the most influential moral theories while suggesting that

[11] Carol Gilligan, *In a Different Voice: Psychological Theory and Women's Development* (Cambridge, MA: Harvard University Press, 1982).
[12] James Rachels, *The Elements of Moral Philosophy* (New York: McGraw-Hill, 2003), 168.

a mature morality should accommodate both an ethic of obligation and an ethic of care. Annette Baier, for example, has taken this approach:

> It is clear, I think, that the best moral theory has to be a cooperative product of women and men, has to harmonize justice and care. The morality it theorizes about is after all for all persons, for men and for women, and will need their combined insights. As Gilligan said, what we need now is a "marriage" of the old male and the newly articulated female insights.[13]

Feminist Ethics

Feminist ethics is an approach to morality aimed at advancing women's interests and correcting injustices inflicted on women through social oppression and inequality. It is defined by a distinctive focus on these issues, rather than by a set of doctrines or common ideology among feminists, many of whom may disagree on the nature of feminist ethics or on particular moral issues. A variety of divergent perspectives have been identified as examples of feminist ethics, including the ethics of care.

Feminist ethics generally downplays the role of moral principles and traditional ethical concepts, insisting instead that moral reflection must take into account the social realities—the relevant social practices, relationships, institutions, and power arrangements. Many feminists think that the familiar principles of Western ethics—autonomy, utility, freedom, equality, and the like—are too broad and abstract to help us make moral judgments about specific persons who are enmeshed in concrete social situations. It is not enough, for example, to respect a woman's decision to have an abortion if she is too poor to have one, or if her culture is so oppressive (or oppressed) as to make abortion impossible to obtain, or if social conditioning leads her to believe that she has no choice or that her views don't count. Theoretical autonomy does not mean much if it is so thoroughly undermined in reality.

Many theorists in feminist ethics also reject the traditional concept of the moral agent. Jan Crosthwaite says that the old notion is that of "abstract individuals as fundamentally autonomous agents, aware of their own preferences and values, and motivated by rational self-interest (though not necessarily selfish)."[14] But, she says, many feminists

> present a richer conception of persons as historically and culturally located, socially related and essentially embodied. Individuals are located in and formed by specific relationships (chosen and unchosen) and ties of affection and responsibility.... Such a conception of socially embedded selves refocuses thinking about autonomy, shifting the emphasis from independent self-determination towards ideals of integrity within relatedness.... Respecting autonomy becomes less a matter of protecting individuals from "coercive" influences than one of positive empowerment, recognizing people's interdependence and supporting individuals' development of their own understanding of their situation and options.[15]

---

[13] Annette C. Baier, "The Need for More Than Justice," *Canadian Journal of Philosophy*, suppl. vol. 13 (1988): 56.

[14] Jan Crosthwaite, "Gender and Bioethics," in *A Companion to Bioethics*, ed. Helga Kuhse and Peter Singer (Malden, MA: Blackwell Publishing, 2001), 32–40.

[15] Crosthwaite, 37.

Though all adherents of feminist ethics support liberation and equality for women, they disagree on how these values apply to specific moral issues. Most support unimpeded access to abortion, for example, but some do not.

JUDGING MORAL THEORIES

As you can see, as explanations of what makes actions right or character good, moral theories can differ dramatically in both content and quality. In their own fashion, they try to identify the true determinants of rightness or goodness, and they vary in how close they seem to get to the mark. Most moral philosophers would readily agree: some moral theories are better than others, and a vital task in ethics is to try to tell which is which. Moral theories can be useful and valuable to us only if there are criteria for judging their worth—and fortunately there are such standards and straightforward ways of applying them.

The Moral Criteria of Adequacy

In several ways, moral theories are analogous to scientific theories. Scientists devise theories to explain the causes of events. The germ theory is offered to explain the cause and spread of infectious diseases. The Big Bang theory is used to explain the structure and expansion of the universe. The "greenhouse effect" is put forth to explain climate change. For each phenomenon to be explained, scientists usually have several possible theories to consider, and the challenge is to determine which one is best (and is therefore most likely to be correct). The superior theory is the one that fares best when judged by generally accepted yardsticks known as the *scientific criteria of adequacy*. One criterion that is often invoked is *fruitfulness*—whether the theory makes successful predictions of previously unknown phenomena. All things being equal, a theory that makes successful predictions of novel phenomena is more likely to be true than one that does not. Another important criterion is *conservatism*—how well a theory fits with established facts, with what scientists already know. All things being equal, a theory that conflicts with what scientists already have good reasons to believe is less likely to be true than a theory that has no such conflicts. Of course, an unconservative theory can turn out to be correct, and a conservative theory wrong, but the odds are against this outcome. Analogously, moral theories are meant to explain what makes an action right or a person good, and to try to determine which moral theory is most likely correct, we apply conceptual yardsticks—the *moral criteria of adequacy*. Any plausible moral theory must measure up to these critical standards.

An important criterion of adequacy for moral theories is *Criterion 1: consistency with our considered moral judgments*. Any plausible scientific theory must be consistent with the data that the theory is supposed to explain; there should be no conflicts between the theory and the relevant facts. A theory put forth to explain planetary motion, for example, must account for the relevant data—scientific observations of the movements of the planets and related objects. Likewise, a moral theory must also be consistent with the data it is supposed to explain: our considered moral judgments, what some call our moral common sense. We arrive at them after careful deliberation that is as free of bias, self-interest, and other distorting influences as possible. Moral philosophers grant them considerable respect and try to take them into account in their moral theorizing. As we have seen, these judgments are fallible, and they are often revised under pressure from trustworthy principles or theories. But we are entitled to trust them unless we have good reason to doubt them. Therefore, any moral theory that is seriously inconsistent with our considered judgments must generally be regarded as badly flawed, perhaps fatally so, and in need of revision. Our considered judgments, for example, tell us that slavery, murder, rape, and genocide are wrong. A moral theory that implies otherwise fails this criterion and is a candidate for rejection.

In applying this standard, we must keep in mind that in both science and ethics, there is tension between theory and data. A good theory explains the data, which in turn influence the shape of the theory. Particularly strong data can compel scientists to alter a theory to account for the information, but a good theory can also give scientists reasons to question or reject particular data. In the same way, there is a kind of give and take between a moral theory and the relevant data. Our considered moral judgments may give us good reasons for altering or even rejecting our moral theory. But if our moral theory is coherent and well supported, it may oblige us to rethink or reject our considered judgments. In both science and ethics, the goal is to ensure that the fit between theory and data is as tight as possible. The fit is acceptably close when no further changes in the theory or the data are necessary—when there is a kind of balance between the two that moral philosophers call "reflective equilibrium."

Another test of adequacy is *Criterion II: consistency with the facts of the moral life*. In science, good theories are consistent with scientific background knowledge, with what scientists already have good reasons to believe. Such theories are, as mentioned earlier, conservative. This background knowledge includes other well-founded theories, highly reliable findings, and scientific (natural) laws. Moral theories should also be consistent with background knowledge—the *moral* background knowledge, the basic, inescapable experiences of the moral life. These experiences include making moral judgments, disagreeing with others on moral issues, being mistaken in our moral beliefs, and giving reasons for accepting moral beliefs. That we do in fact experience these things from time to time is a matter of moral common sense—seemingly obvious facts of the moral life. Thus, any moral theory that is inconsistent with these aspects of the moral life is deeply problematic. It is possible that we are deluded about the moral life—that we, for example, merely think we are disagreeing with others on moral issues but are actually just venting our feelings. But our experience gives us good grounds for taking the commonsense view until we are given good reasons to believe otherwise.

Finally, we have *Criterion III: resourcefulness in moral problem solving*. If a scientific theory helps scientists answer questions, solve problems, and control facets of the natural world, it demonstrates both its plausibility and usefulness. All things being equal, such a resourceful theory is better than one that has none of these advantages. Much the same is true for moral theories. A resourceful moral theory helps us solve moral problems. It can help us identify morally relevant aspects of conduct, judge the rightness of actions, resolve conflicts among moral principles and judgments, test and correct our moral intuitions, and understand the underlying point of morality itself. Any moral theory that lacks problem-solving resourcefulness is neither useful nor credible.

Applying the Criteria

Let's apply the three moral criteria of adequacy to two theories we discussed earlier (one consequentialist; the other deontological). As we do, keep in mind that evaluating moral theories using these yardsticks is not a rote process. There is no standard procedure for applying the criteria to a theory and no set of instructions for assigning conceptual weight to each criterion as we judge a theory's worth. But the criteria do help us make broad judgments on rational grounds about a theory's strengths and weaknesses. We must use them as guides, relying on our best judgment in applying them, just as scientists must use their own educated judgment in wielding their kind of criteria of adequacy. In neither case is there a neat algorithm for theory assessment, but nonetheless in both arenas the process is objective, reasonable, and essential.

We should also remember that no moral theory is perfect, and none is likely to get the highest marks on every test. But there is much to learn even from flawed theories. If we look closely, we can see that each of the most influential theories of past centuries, even with its faults apparent, seems to have grasped at least a modest, gleaming piece of the truth about the moral life.

Utilitarianism

For simplicity's sake, let us try to apply the criteria to classic act-utilitarianism, the view that right actions are those that result in the greatest overall happiness for everyone involved. First, note that the theory seems to pass the test suggested by Criterion II (consistency with the facts of the moral life). Utilitarianism assumes that we can indeed make moral judgments, have moral disagreements, be mistaken in our moral beliefs, and provide supporting reasons for our moral judgments.

The theory, however, has been accused of a lack of usefulness—failing Criterion III (resourcefulness in moral problem solving). The usual charge is that utilitarianism is a poor guide to the moral life because the theory demands too much of us and blurs the distinction between obligatory and supererogatory actions. Utilitarianism says that we should always try to maximize happiness for everyone considered, to do our utmost to increase overall utility. But some say this requirement would lead us to extreme beneficence—to, for example, give away most of our possessions, spend most of our time in charity work, and deem mandatory many acts that we would normally consider above and beyond the call of duty. Some defenders of the theory have suggested that it can be easily modified to ease the demands that it places on us. A few utilitarians have insisted that, contrary to the popular view, the commonsense distinction between obligatory and supererogatory acts is mistaken and that morality does demand the kind of sacrifice that utilitarianism implies.

The most serious accusation against classic utilitarianism is that it flies in the face of our considered moral judgments (Criterion I), especially concerning issues of justice and rights. Consider the case of a man arrested for murder who is in fact innocent of the crime. Angry citizens demand that he be lynched immediately, and they threaten riots and reprisal killings against the man's family. The local police chief knows that by lynching the man, the overall happiness of the people would be increased far more than if the man got a fair trial—the mob would be satisfied, lives would be saved, and property would be spared destruction. So the chief lets the town string the man up. Does the chief do right? The utilitarian seems obliged to say yes. But our commonsense judgment would likely be that the chief did wrong by violating the man's rights and perpetrating an injustice.

Some utilitarians have replied to such Criterion I criticisms by saying that scenarios like the one just presented are unrealistic and misleading. In the real world, they say, actions that seem to conflict with our moral intuitions almost always produce such bad consequences that the actions cannot be justified even on utilitarian grounds. Once *all* the possible consequences are taken into account, it becomes clear that the proposed actions do not maximize happiness and that commonsense morality and utilitarianism coincide.

Critics respond to the utilitarians by admitting that many times the judgments of commonsense morality and utilitarianism do in fact coincide when all the facts are known—but not always. Even the utilitarian must admit that there could be cases in which actions that maximize utility do clash with our considered moral judgments, and this possibility raises doubts about the utilitarian standard.

Kant's Theory

Like utilitarianism, Kant's theory seems generally consistent with the basic facts of the moral life (Criterion II), but many philosophers argue that it is not consistent with moral common sense (Criterion I). A major cause of the problem, they say, is Kant's insistence that we have absolute (or "perfect") duties—obligations that must be honored without exception. Thus in Kantian ethics, we have an absolute duty not to lie or to break a promise or to kill the innocent, come what may. Imagine that a band of killers wants to murder an innocent man who has taken refuge in your house, and the killers come to your door and ask you point blank if he is in your house. To say no is to lie; to answer truthfully is to guarantee the man's death. What should you do? In a case like this, says Kant, you must *do your duty*—you must tell the truth though murder is the result and a lie would save a life. But in this case such devotion to moral absolutes seems completely askew, for saving an innocent life seems far more important morally than blindly obeying a rule. Our considered judgments suggest that sometimes the consequences of our actions do matter more than adherence to the letter of the moral law, even if the moral law is generally worthy of our respect and obedience.

Some have thought that Kant's theory can yield implausible results for another reason. Recall that the first formulation of the categorical imperative says that an action is permissible if persons could consistently act on the relevant maxim, and we would be willing to have them do so. This requirement seems to make sense if the maxim in question is something like, "do not kill the innocent" or "treat equals equally." But what if the maxim is "Enslave all Christians" or "Kill all Ethiopians"? We could—without contradiction—will either one of these precepts to become a universal law. And if we were so inclined, we could be willing for everyone to act accordingly, even if we ourselves were Christians or Ethiopians. So by Kantian lights, these actions could very well be morally permissible, and their permissibility would depend on whether someone was willing to have them apply universally. Critics conclude that because the first formulation of the categorical imperative seems to sanction such obviously immoral acts, the theory is deeply flawed. Defenders of Kant's theory, on the other hand, view the problems as repairable and have proposed revisions.

This apparent arbitrariness in the first formulation can significantly lessen the theory's usefulness (Criterion III). The categorical imperative is supposed to help us discern moral directives that are rational, universal, and objective. But if it is subjective in the way just described, its helpfulness as a guide for living morally is dubious. There may be remedies for this difficulty, but Kant's theory in its original form seems problematic.

KEY WORDS

moral theory	consequentialist theories	deontological theories
utilitarianism	act-utilitarianism	rule-utilitarianism
natural law theory	doctrine of double effect	contractarianism
virtue ethics	Kant's theory	psychological egoism
ethical egoism		

SUMMARY

A moral theory explains why an action is right or wrong or why a person or a person's character is good or bad. Making, using, or assessing moral theories is a normal, pervasive feature of the moral life.

Consequentialist moral theories assume that the rightness of actions depends on their consequences or results. Deontological theories say that the rightness of actions is determined partly or wholly by their intrinsic nature. The leading consequentialist theory is utilitarianism, the view that right actions are those that result in the most beneficial balance of good over bad consequences for everyone involved. Kantian ethics is opposed to consequentialist theories, holding that morality consists in following a rational and universally applicable moral rule and doing so solely out of a sense of duty. An action is right only if it conforms to such a rule, and we are morally praiseworthy only if we perform it for duty's sake alone. Natural law theory is a centuries-old view of ethics that maintains that right actions are those conforming to moral standards discerned in nature through human reason. Rawls's theory is a form of contractarianism, which means it is based on the idea of a social contract, or agreement, among individuals for mutual advantage. Rawls argues for a set of moral principles that he believes would be arrived at through a fair, but hypothetical bargaining process. Virtue ethics focuses on the development of virtuous character. The central task in morality is not knowing and applying principles, but being and becoming a good person, someone possessing the virtues that define moral excellence. The ethics of care emphasizes the virtues and feelings that are central to close personal relationships.

The worth of moral theories can be assessed through the application of the moral criteria of adequacy. Criterion I is consistency with our considered moral judgments; Criterion II, consistency with the facts of the moral life; and Criterion III, resourcefulness in moral problem solving.

READINGS

Utilitarianism

JOHN STUART MILL

A passing remark is all that needs be given to the ignorant blunder of supposing that those who stand up for utility as the test of right and wrong, use the term in that restricted and merely colloquial sense in which utility is opposed to pleasure. An apology is due to the philosophical opponents of utilitarianism, for even the momentary appearance itarianism, for even the momentary appearance of confounding them with any one capable of so absurd a misconception; which is the more extraordinary, inasmuch as the contrary accusation, of referring everything to pleasure, and that too in its

From John Stuart Mill, *Utilitarianism* (London: Longmans, Green, and Company, 1879).

grossest form, is another of the common charges against utilitarianism: and, as has been pointedly remarked by an able writer, the same sort of persons, and often the very same persons, denounce the theory "as impracticably dry when the word utility precedes the word pleasure, and as too practically voluptuous when the word pleasure precedes the word utility." Those who know anything about the matter are aware that every writer, from Epicurus to Bentham, who maintained the theory of utility, meant by it, not something to be contradistinguished from pleasure, but pleasure itself, together with exemption from pain; and instead of opposing the useful to the agreeable or the ornamental, have always declared that the useful means these, among other things. Yet the common herd, including the herd of writers, not only in newspapers and periodicals, but in books of weight and pretension, are perpetually falling into this shallow mistake. Having caught up the word utilitarian, while knowing nothing whatever about it but its sound, they habitually express by it the rejection, or the neglect, of pleasure in some of its forms; of beauty, of ornament, or of amusement. Nor is the term thus ignorantly misapplied solely in disparagement, but occasionally in compliment; as though it implied superiority to frivolity and the mere pleasures of the moment. And this perverted use is the only one in which the word is popularly known, and the one from which the new generation are acquiring their sole notion of its meaning. Those who introduced the word, but who had for many years discontinued it as a distinctive appellation, may well feel themselves called upon to resume it, if by doing so they can hope to contribute anything towards rescuing it from this utter degradation.

The creed which accepts as the foundation of morals, Utility, or the Greatest Happiness Principle, holds that actions are right in proportion as they tend to promote happiness, wrong as they tend to produce the reverse of happiness. By happiness is intended pleasure, and the absence of pain; by unhappiness, pain, and the privation of pleasure. To give a clear view of the moral standard set up by the theory, much more requires to be said; in particular, what things it includes in the ideas of pain and pleasure; and to what extent this is left an open question. But these supplementary explanations do not affect the theory of life on which this theory of morality is grounded—namely, that pleasure, and freedom from pain, are the only things desirable as ends; and that all desirable things (which are as numerous in the utilitarian as in any other scheme) are desirable either for the pleasure inherent in themselves, or as means to the promotion of pleasure and the prevention of pain.

Now, such a theory of life excites in many minds, and among them in some of the most estimable in feeling and purpose, inveterate dislike. To suppose that life has (as they express it) no higher end than pleasure—no better and nobler object of desire and pursuit—they designate as utterly mean and groveling; as a doctrine worthy only of swine, to whom the followers of Epicurus were, at a very early period, contemptuously likened; and modern holders of the doctrine are occasionally made the subject of equally polite comparisons by its German, French, and English assailants.

When thus attacked, the Epicureans have always answered, that it is not they, but their accusers, who represent human nature in a degrading light; since the accusation supposes human beings to be capable of no pleasures except those of which swine are capable. If this supposition were true, the charge could not be gainsaid, but would then be no longer an imputation; for if the sources of pleasure were precisely the same to human beings and to swine, the rule of life which is good enough for the one would be good enough for the other. The comparison of the Epicurean life to that of beasts is felt as degrading, precisely because a beast's pleasures do not satisfy a human being's conceptions of happiness. Human beings have faculties more elevated than the animal appetites, and when once made conscious of them, do not regard anything as happiness which does not include their gratification. I do not, indeed, consider the Epicureans to have been by any means faultless in drawing out their scheme of consequences from the utilitarian principle. To do this in any sufficient manner, many Stoic, as well as Christian elements require to be included. But there is no known Epicurean theory of life which does not assign to the pleasures of the intellect; of the feelings and imagination, and of the moral sentiments, a much higher value as pleasures than to those of mere sensation. It must be admitted, however, that utilitarian writers in general have placed the superiority of mental over bodily pleasures chiefly in the greater permanency, safety, uncostliness, &c., of the former—that is, in their circumstantial advantages rather than in their intrinsic nature. And on all these points utilitarians have fully proved their case; but they might have taken the other, and, as it may be called, higher ground, with entire consistency. It is quite compatible with the principle of utility to recognise the fact, that some *kinds* of pleasure are more desirable and more valuable than others. It would be absurd that while, in estimating all other things, quality is considered as well as quantity, the estimation of pleasures should be supposed to depend on quantity alone.

If I am asked, what I mean by difference of quality in pleasures, or what makes one pleasure more valuable than another, merely as a pleasure, except its being greater in amount, there is but one possible answer. Of two pleasures, if there be one to which all or almost all who have experience of both give a decided preference, irrespective of any feeling of moral obligation to prefer it, that is the more desirable pleasure. If one of the two is, by those who are competently acquainted with both, placed so far above the other that they prefer it, even though knowing it to be attended with a greater amount of discontent, and would not resign it for any quantity of the other pleasure which their nature is capable of, we are justified in ascribing to the preferred enjoyment a superiority in quality, so far outweighing quantity as to render it, in comparison, of small account.

Now it is an unquestionable fact that those who are equally acquainted with, and equally capable of appreciating and enjoying, both, do give a most marked preference to the manner of existence which employs their higher faculties. Few human creatures would consent to be changed into any of the lower animals, for a promise of the fullest allowance of a beast's pleasures; no intelligent human being would consent to be a fool, no instructed person would be an ignoramus, no person of feeling and conscience would be selfish and base, even though they should be persuaded that the fool, the dunce, or the rascal is better satisfied with his lot than they are with theirs. They would not resign what they possess more than he, for the most complete satisfaction of all the desires which they have in common with him. If they ever fancy they would, it is only in cases of unhappiness so extreme, that to escape from it they would exchange their lot for almost any other, however undesirable in their own eyes. A being of higher faculties requires more to make him happy, is capable probably of more acute suffering, and is certainly accessible to it at more points, than one of an inferior type; but in spite of these liabilities, he can never really wish to sink into what he feels to be a lower grade of existence. We may give what explanation we please of this unwillingness; we may attribute it to pride, a name which is given indiscriminately to some of the most and to some of the least estimable feelings of which mankind are capable; we may refer it to the love of liberty and personal independence, an appeal to which was with the Stoics one of the most effective means for the inculcation of it; to the love of power, or to the love of excitement, both of which do really enter into and contribute to it: but its most appropriate appellation is a sense of dignity, which all human beings possess in one form or other, and in some, though by no means in exact, proportion to their higher faculties, and which is so essential a part of the happiness of those in whom it is strong, that nothing which conflicts with it could be, otherwise than momentarily, an object of desire to them. Whoever supposes that this preference takes place at a sacrifice of happiness—that the superior being, in anything like equal circumstances, is not happier than the inferior—confounds the two very different ideas, of happiness, and content. It is indisputable that the being whose capacities of enjoyment are low, has the greatest chance of having them fully satisfied; and a highly-endowed being will always feel that any happiness which he can look for, as the world is constituted, is imperfect. But he can learn to bear its imperfections, if they are at all bearable; and they will not make him envy the being who is indeed unconscious of the imperfections, but only because he feels not at all the good which those imperfections qualify. It is better to be a human being dissatisfied than a pig satisfied; better to be Socrates dissatisfied than a fool satisfied. And if the fool, or the pig, is of a different opinion, it is because they only know their own side of the question. The other party to the comparison knows both sides.

It may be objected, that many who are capable of the higher pleasures, occasionally, under the influence of temptation, postpone them to the lower. But this is quite compatible with a full appreciation of the intrinsic superiority of the higher. Men often, from infirmity of character, make their election for the nearer good, though they know it to be the less valuable; and this no less when the choice is between two bodily pleasures, than when it is between bodily and mental. They pursue sensual indulgences to the injury of health, though perfectly aware that health is the greater good. It may be further objected, that many who begin with youthful enthusiasm for everything noble, as they advance in years sink into indolence and selfishness. But I do not believe that those who undergo this very common change, voluntarily choose the lower description of pleasures in preference to the higher. I believe that before they devote themselves exclusively to the one, they have already become incapable of the other. Capacity for the nobler feelings is in most natures a very tender plant, easily killed, not only by hostile influences, but by mere want of sustenance; and in the majority of young persons it speedily dies away if the occupations to which their position in life has devoted them, and the society into which it has thrown them, are not favourable to keeping that higher capacity in exercise. Men lose their high aspirations as they lose their intellectual tastes, because they have not time or opportunity for indulging them; and they addict themselves to inferior pleasures, not because they deliberately prefer them, but because they are either the only ones to which they have access, or the only ones which they are any longer capable of enjoying. It may be questioned whether any one who has remained equally susceptible to both classes of pleasures, ever knowingly and calmly preferred the lower; though many, in all ages, have broken down in an ineffectual attempt to combine both.

From this verdict of the only competent judges, I apprehend there can be no appeal. On a question which is the best worth having of two pleasures, or which of two modes of existence is the most grateful to the feelings, apart from its moral attributes and from its consequences, the judgment of those who are qualified by knowledge of both, or, if they differ, that of the majority among them, must be admitted as final. And there needs be the less hesitation to accept this judgment respecting the quality of pleasures, since there is no other tribunal to be referred to even on the question of quantity. What means are there of determining which is the acutest of two pains, or the intensest of two pleasurable sensations, except the general suffrage of those who are familiar with both? Neither pains nor pleasures are homogeneous, and

pain is always heterogeneous with pleasure. What is there to decide whether a particular pleasure is worth purchasing at the cost of a particular pain, except the feelings and judgment of the experienced? When, therefore, those feelings and judgment declare the pleasures derived from the higher faculties to be preferable *in kind*, apart from the question of intensity, to those of which the animal nature, disjoined from the higher faculties, is susceptible, they are entitled on this subject to the same regard.

I have dwelt on this point, as being a necessary part of a perfectly just conception of Utility or Happiness, considered as the directive rule of human conduct. But it is by no means an indispensable condition to the acceptance of the utilitarian standard; for that standard is not the agent's own greatest happiness, but the greatest amount of happiness altogether, and if it may possibly be doubted whether a noble character is always the happier for its nobleness, there can be no doubt that it makes other people happier, and that the world in general is immensely a gainer by it. Utilitarianism, therefore, could only attain its end by the general cultivation of nobleness of character, even if each individual were only benefited by the nobleness of others, and his own, so far as happiness is concerned, were a sheer deduction from the benefit. But the bare enunciation of such an absurdity as this last, renders refutation superfluous.

According to the Greatest Happiness Principle, as above explained, the ultimate end, with reference to and for the sake of which all other things are desirable (whether we are considering our own good or that of other people), is an existence exempt as far as possible from pain, and as rich as possible in enjoyments, both in point of quantity and quality; the test of quality, and the rule for measuring it against quantity, being the preference felt by those who, in their opportunities of experience, to which must be added their habits of self-consciousness and self-observation, are best furnished with the means of comparison. This, being, according to the utilitarian opinion, the end of human action, is necessarily also the standard of morality; which may accordingly be defined, the rules and precepts for human conduct, by the observance of which an existence such as has been described might be, to the greatest extent possible, secured to all mankind; and not to them only, but, so far as the nature of things admits, to the whole sentient creation....

Fundamental Principles of the Metaphysic of Morals

IMMANUEL KANT

Nothing can possibly be conceived in the world, or even out of it, which can be called good, without qualification, except a Good Will. Intelligence, wit, judgment, and the other *talents* of the mind, however they may be named, or courage, resolution, perseverance, as qualities of temperament, are undoubtedly good and desirable in many respects; but these gifts of nature may also become extremely bad and mischievous if the will which is to make use of them, and which, therefore, constitutes what is called *character*, is not good. It is the same with the *gifts of fortune*. Power, riches, honour, even health, and the general well-being and contentment with one's condition which is called *happiness*, inspire pride, and often presumption, if there is not a good will to correct the influence of these on the mind, and with this also to rectify the whole principle of acting, and adapt it to its end. The sight of a being who is not adorned with a single feature of a pure and good will, enjoying unbroken prosperity, can never give pleasure to an impartial rational spectator. Thus a good will appears to constitute the indispensable condition even of being worthy of happiness.

There are even some qualities which are of service to this good will itself, and may facilitate its action, yet which have no intrinsic unconditional value, but always presuppose a good will, and this qualifies the esteem that we justly have for them, and does not permit us to regard them as absolutely good. Moderation in the affections and passions, self-control, and calm deliberation are not only good in many respects, but even seem to constitute part of the intrinsic worth of the person; but they are far from deserving to be called good without qualification, although they have been so unconditionally praised by the ancients. For without the principles of a good will, they may become extremely bad; and the coolness of a villain not only makes him far more dangerous, but also directly makes him more abominable in our eyes than he would have been without it.

A good will is good not because of what it performs or effects, not by its aptness for the attainment of some proposed end, but simply by virtue of the volition, that is, it is good in itself, and considered by itself is to be esteemed much higher than all that can be brought about by it in favour of any inclination, nay, even of the sum-total of all inclinations. Even if it should happen that, owing to special disfavour of fortune, or the niggardly provision of a step-motherly nature, this will should wholly lack power to accomplish its purpose, if with its greatest efforts it should yet achieve nothing, and there should remain only the good will (not, to be sure, a mere wish, but the summoning of all means in our power), then, like a jewel, it would still shine by its own light, as a thing which has its whole value in itself. Its usefulness or fruitlessness can neither add to nor take away anything from this value. It would be, as it were, only the setting to enable us to handle it the more conveniently in common commerce, or to attract to it the attention of those who are not yet connoisseurs, but not to recommend it to true connoisseurs, or to determine its value.

There is, however, something so strange in this idea of the absolute value of the mere will, in which no account is taken of its utility, that notwithstanding the thorough assent of even common reason to the idea, yet a suspicion must arise that it may perhaps really be the product of mere high-flown fancy, and that we may have misunderstood the purpose of nature in assigning reason as the governor of our will. Therefore we will examine this idea from this point of view.

In the physical constitution of an organized being, that is, a being adapted suitably to the purposes of life, we assume it as a fundamental principle that no organ for any purpose will be found but what is also the fittest and best adapted for that

From Kant, *Critique of Practical Reason*, trans. Thomas Kingswill Abbott (London: Longmans, Green, & Co., 1909).

purpose. Now in a being which has reason and a will, if the proper object of nature were its *conservation*, its *welfare*, in a word, its *happiness*, then nature would have hit upon a very bad arrangement in selecting the reason of the creature to carry out this purpose. For all the actions which the creature has to perform with a view to this purpose, and the whole rule of its conduct, would be far more surely prescribed to it by instinct, and that end would have been attained thereby much more certainly than it ever can be by reason. Should reason have been communicated to this favoured creature over and above, it must only have served it to contemplate the happy constitution of its nature, to admire it, to congratulate itself thereon, and to feel thankful for it to the beneficent cause, but not that it should subject its desires to that weak and delusive guidance, and meddle bunglingly with the purpose of nature. In a word, nature would have taken care that reason should not break forth into *practical exercise*, nor have the presumption, with its weak insight, to think out for itself the plan of happiness, and of the means of attaining it. Nature would not only have taken on herself the choice of the ends, but also of the means, and with wise foresight would have entrusted both to instinct.

And, in fact, we find that the more a cultivated reason applies itself with deliberate purpose to the enjoyment of life and happiness, so much the more does the man fail of true satisfaction. And from this circumstance there arises in many, if they are candid enough to confess it, a certain degree of *misology*, that is, hatred of reason, especially in the case of those who are most experienced in the use of it, because after calculating all the advantages they derive, I do not say from the invention of all the arts of common luxury, but even from the sciences (which seem to them to be after all only a luxury of the understanding), they find that they have, in fact, only brought more trouble on their shoulders, rather than gained in happiness; and they end by envying, rather than despising, the more common stamp of men who keep closer to the guidance of mere instinct, and do not allow their reason much influence on their conduct. And this we must admit, that the judgment of those who would very much lower the lofty eulogies of the advantages which reason gives us in regard to the happiness and satisfaction of life, or who would even reduce them below zero, is by no means morose or ungrateful to the goodness with which the world is governed, but that there lies at the root of these judgments the idea that our existence has a different and far nobler end, for which, and not for happiness, reason is properly intended, and which must, therefore, be regarded as the supreme condition to which the private ends of man must, for the most part, be postponed.

For as reason is not competent to guide the will with certainty in regard to its objects and the satisfaction of all our wants (which it to some extent even multiplies), this being an end to which an implanted instinct would have led with much greater certainty; and since, nevertheless, reason is imparted to us as a practical faculty, i.e. as one which is to have influence on the *will*, therefore, admitting that nature generally in the distribution of her capacities has adapted the means to the end, its true destination must be to produce a *will*, not merely good as a *means* to something else, but *good in itself*, for which reason was absolutely necessary. This will then, though not indeed the sole and complete good, must be the supreme good and the condition of every other, even of the desire of happiness. Under these circumstances, there is nothing inconsistent with the wisdom of nature in the fact that the cultivation of the reason, which is requisite for the first and unconditional purpose, does in many ways interfere, at least in this life, with the attainment of the second, which is always conditional, namely, happiness. Nay, it may even reduce it to nothing, without nature thereby failing of her purpose. For reason recognizes the establishment of a good will as its highest practical destination, and in attaining this purpose is capable only of a satisfaction of its own proper kind, namely, that from the attainment of an end, which end again is determined by reason only, notwithstanding that this may involve many a disappointment to the ends of inclination.

We have then to develop the notion of a will which deserves to be highly esteemed for itself, and is good without a view to anything further, a notion which exists already in the sound natural understanding, requiring rather to be cleared up than to be taught, and which in estimating the value of our actions always takes the first place, and constitutes the condition of all the rest. In order to do this, we will take the notion of duty, which includes that of a good will, although implying certain subjective restrictions and hindrances. These, however, far from concealing it, or rendering it unrecognizable, rather bring it out by contrast, and make it shine forth so much the brighter.

I omit here all actions which are already recognized as inconsistent with duty, although they may be useful for this or that purpose, for with these the question whether they are done *from duty* cannot arise at all, since they even conflict with it. I also set aside those actions which really conform to duty, but to which men have *no* direct *inclination*, performing them because they are impelled thereto by some other inclination. For in this case we can readily distinguish whether the action which agrees with duty is done *from duty*, or from a selfish view. It is much harder to make this distinction when the action accords with duty, and the subject has besides a *direct* inclination to it. For example, it is always a matter of duty that a dealer should not overcharge an inexperienced purchaser; and wherever there is much commerce the prudent tradesman does not overcharge; but keeps a fixed price for everyone, so that a child buys of him as well as any other. Men are thus *honestly* served; but this is not enough to make us believe that the tradesman has so acted from duty and from principles of honesty: his own advantage required it; it is out of the question in this case to suppose that he might besides have a direct inclination in favour of the buyers, so that, as it were, from love he should give no advantage to one over another. Accordingly the action was done neither from duty nor from direct inclination, but merely with a selfish view.

On the other hand, it is a duty to maintain one's life; and, in addition, everyone has also a direct inclination to do so. But on this account the often anxious care which most men take for it has no intrinsic worth, and their maxim has no moral import. They preserve their life *as duty requires*, no doubt, but not *because duty requires*. On the other hand, if adversity and hopeless sorrow have completely taken away the relish for life; if the unfortunate one, strong in mind, indignant at his fate rather than desponding or dejected, wishes for death, and yet preserves his life without loving it—not from inclination or fear, but from duty—then his maxim has a moral worth.

To be beneficent when we can is a duty; and besides this, there are many minds so sympath-

etically constituted that, without any other motive of vanity or self-interest, they find a pleasure in spreading joy around them, and can take delight in the satisfaction of others so far as it is their own work. But I maintain that in such a case an action of this kind, however proper, however amiable it may be, has nevertheless no true moral worth, but is on a level with other inclinations, e.g. the inclination to honour which, if it is happily directed to that which is in fact of public utility and accordant with duty, and consequently honourable, deserves praise and encouragement, but not esteem. For the maxim lacks the moral import, namely, that such actions be done *from duty*, not from inclination. Put the case that the mind of that philanthropist was clouded by sorrow of his own, extinguishing all sympathy with the lot of other's, and that while he still has the power to benefit others in distress, he is not touched by their trouble because he is absorbed with his own; and now suppose that he tears himself out of this dead insensibility, and performs the action without any inclination to it, but simply from duty, then first has his action its genuine moral worth, Further still; if nature has put little sympathy in the heart of this or that man; if he, supposed to be an upright man, is by temperament cold and indifferent to the sufferings of others, perhaps because in respect of his own he is provided with the special gift of patience and fortitude, and supposes, or even requires, that others should have the same—and such a man would certainly not be the meanest product of nature—but if nature had not specially framed him for a philanthropist, would he not still find in himself a source from whence to give himself a far higher worth than that of a good-natured temperament could be? Unquestionably. It is just in this that the moral worth of the character is brought out which is incomparably the highest of all, namely, that he is beneficent, not from inclination, but from duty.

To secure one's own happiness is a duty, at least indirectly; for discontent with one's condition, under a pressure of many anxieties and amidst unsatisfied wants, might easily become a great *temptation to trangression of duty*. But here again, without looking to duty, all men have already the strongest and most intimate inclination to happiness, because it is just in this idea that all inclinations are combined in one total. But the precept of happiness is often of such a sort that it greatly interferes with some inclinations, and yet a man cannot form any definite and certain conception of the sum of satisfaction of all of them which is called happiness. It is not then to be wondered at that a single inclination, definite both as to what it promises and as to the time within which it can be gratified, is often able to overcome such a fluctuating idea, and that a gouty patient, for instance, can choose to enjoy what he likes, and to suffer what he may, since, according to his calculation, on this occasion at least, he has [only] not sacrificed the enjoyment of the present moment to a possibly mistaken expectation of a happiness which is supposed to be found in health. But even in this case, if the general desire for happiness did not influence his will, and supposing that in his particular case health was not a necessary element in this calculation, there yet remains in this, as in all other cases, this law, namely, that he should promote his happiness not from inclination but from duty, and by this would his conduct first acquire true moral worth.

It is in this manner, undoubtedly, that we are to understand those passages of Scripture also in which we are commanded to love our neighbour, even our enemy. For love, as an affection, cannot be commanded, but beneficence for duty's sake may; even though we are not impelled to it by any inclination—nay, are even repelled by a natural and unconquerable aversion. This is *practical* love, and not *pathological*—a love which is seated in the will, and not in the propensions of sense—in principles of action and not of tender sympathy; and it is this love alone which can be commanded.

The second proposition is: That an action done from duty derives its moral worth, *not from the purpose* which is to be attained by it, but from the maxim by which it is determined, and therefore does not depend on the realization of the object of the action, but merely on the *principle of volition* by which the action has taken place, without regard to any object of desire. It is clear from what precedes that the purposes which we may have in view in our actions, or their effects regarded as ends and springs of the will, cannot give to actions any unconditional or moral worth. In what, then, can their worth lie, if it is not to consist in the will and in reference to its expected effect? It cannot lie anywhere but in the *principle of the will* without regard to the ends which can be attained by the action. For the will stands between its a priori principle, which is formal, and its a posteriori spring, which is material, as between two roads, and as it must be determined by something, it follows that it must be determined by the formal principle of volition when an action is done from duty, in which case every material principle has been withdrawn from it.

The third proposition, which is a consequence of the two preceding, I would express thus: *Duty is the necessity of acting from respect for the law.* I may have *inclination* for an object as the effect of my proposed action, but I cannot have *respect* for it, just for this reason, that it is an effect and not an energy of will. Similarly, I cannot have respect for inclination, whether my own or another's; I can at most, if my own, approve it; if another's, sometimes even love it; i.e. look on it as favourable to my own interest. It is only what is connected with my will as a principle, by no means as an effect—what does not subserve my inclination, but overpowers it, or at least in case of choice excludes it from its calculation—in other words, simply the law of itself, which can be an object of respect, and hence a command. Now an action done from duty must wholly exclude the influence of inclination, and with it every object of the will, so that nothing remains which can determine the will except objectively the *law*, and subjectively *pure respect* for this practical law, and consequently the maxim that I should follow this law even to the thwarting of all my inclinations.

Thus the moral worth of an action does not lie in the effect expected from it, nor in any principle of action which requires to borrow its motive from this expected effect. For all these effects—agreeableness of one's condition, and even the promotion of the happiness of others—could have been also brought about by other causes, so that for this there would have been no need of the will of a rational being; whereas it is in this alone that the supreme and unconditional good can be found. The pre-eminent good which we call moral can therefore consist in nothing else than *the conception of law* in itself, *which certainly is only possible in a rational being*, in so far as this conception, and not the expected effect, determines the will. This is a good which is already present in the person who acts accordingly, and we have not to wait for it to appear first in the result.

But what sort of law can that be, the conception of which must determine the will, even without paying any regard to the effect expected from it, in order that this will may be called good absolutely and without qualification? As I have deprived the will of every impulse which could arise to it from obedience to any law, there remains nothing but the universal conformity of its actions to law in general, which alone is to serve the will as a principle, i.e. I am never to act otherwise than so *that I could also will that my maxim should become a universal law.* Here, now, it is the simple conformity to law in general, without assuming any particular law applicable to certain actions, that serves the will as its principle, and must so serve it, if duty is not to be a vain delusion and a chimerical notion. The common reason of men in its practical judgments perfectly coincides with this, and always has in view the principle here suggested. Let the question be, for example: May I when in distress make a promise with the intention not to keep it? I readily distinguish here between the two significations which the question may have: Whether it is prudent, or whether it is right, to make a false promise? The former may undoubtedly often be the case. I see clearly indeed that it is not enough to extricate myself from a present difficulty by means of this subterfuge, but it must be well considered whether there may not hereafter spring from this lie much greater inconvenience than that from which I now free myself, and as, with all my supposed *cunning,* the consequences cannot be so easily foreseen but that credit once lost may be much more injurious to me than any mischief which I seek to avoid at present, it should be considered whether it would not be more *prudent* to act herein according to a universal maxim, and to make it a habit to promise nothing except with the intention of keeping it. But it is soon clear to me that such a maxim will still only be based on the fear of consequences. Now it is a wholly different thing to be truthful from duty, and to be so from apprehension of injurious consequences. In the first case, the very notion of the action already implies a law for me; in the second case, I must first look about elsewhere to see what results may be combined with it which would affect myself. For to deviate from the principle of duty is beyond all doubt wicked; but to be unfaithful to my maxim of prudence may often be very advantageous to me, although to abide by it is certainly safer. The shortest way, however, and an unerring one, to discover the answer to this question whether a lying promise is consistent with duty, is to ask myself, Should I be content that my maxim (to extricate myself from difficulty by a false promise) should hold good as a universal law, for myself as well as for others? and should I be able to say to myself, "Every one may make a deceitful promise when he finds himself in a difficulty from which he cannot otherwise extricate himself"? Then I presently become aware that while I can will the lie, I can by no means will that lying should be a universal law. For with such a law there would be no promises at all, since it would be in vain to allege my intention in regard to my future actions to those who would not believe this allegation, or if they over-hastily did so, would pay me back in my own coin. Hence my maxim, as soon as it should be made a universal law, would necessarily destroy itself.

I do not, therefore, need any far-reaching penetration to discern what I have to do in order that my will may be morally good. Inexperienced in the course of the world, incapable of being prepared for all its contingencies, I only ask myself: Canst thou also will that thy maxim should be a universal law? If not, then it must be rejected, and that not because of a disadvantage accruing from it to myself or even to others, but because it cannot enter as a principle into a possible universal legislation, and reason extorts from me immediate respect for such legislation. I do not indeed as yet *discern* on what this respect is based (this the philosopher may inquire), but at least I understand this, that it is an estimation of the worth which far outweighs all worth of what is recommended by inclination, and that the necessity of acting from *pure* respect for the practical law is what constitutes duty, to which every other motive must give place, because it is the condition of a will being good *in itself,* and the worth of such a will is above everything.

Thus, then, without quitting the moral knowledge of common human reason, we have arrived at its principle. And although, no doubt, common men do not conceive it in such an abstract and universal form, yet they always have it really before their eyes, and use it as the standard of their decision....

Nor could anything be more fatal to morality than that we should wish to derive it from examples. For every example of it that is set before me must be first itself tested by principles of morality, whether it is worthy to serve as an original example, i.e. as a pattern, but by no means can it authoritatively furnish the conception of morality. Even the Holy One of the Gospels must first be compared with our ideal of moral perfection before we can recognize Him as such; and so He says of Himself, "Why call ye Me [whom you see] good; none is good [the model of good] but God only [whom ye do not see]?" But whence have we the conception of God as the supreme good? Simply from the *idea* of moral perfection, which reason frames a priori, and connects inseparably with the notion of a free will. Imitation finds no place at all in morality, and examples serve only for encouragement, i.e. they put beyond doubt the feasibility of what the law commands, they make visible that which the practical rule expresses more generally, but they can never authorize us to set aside the true original which lies in reason, and to guide ourselves by examples....

From what has been said, it is clear that all moral conceptions have their seat and origin completely a priori in the reason, and that, moreover, in the commonest reason just as truly as in that which is in the highest degree speculative; that they cannot be obtained by abstraction from any empirical, and therefore merely contingent knowledge; that it is just this purity of their origin that makes them worthy to serve as our supreme practical principle, and that just in proportion as we add anything empirical, we detract from their genuine influence, and from the absolute value of actions; that it is not only of the greatest necessity, in a purely speculative point of view, but is also of the greatest practical importance, to derive these notions and laws from pure reason, to present them pure and unmixed, and even to determine the compass of this practical or pure rational knowledge, i.e. to determine the whole faculty of pure practical reason; and, in doing so, we must not make its principles dependent on the particular nature of human reason, though in speculative philosophy this may be permitted, or may even at times be necessary; but since moral laws ought to hold good for every rational creature, we must derive them from the general concept of a rational being. In this way, although for its *application* to man morality has need of anthropology, yet, in the first instance, we must treat it independently as pure philosophy, i.e. as metaphysic, complete in itself (a thing which in such distinct branches of science is easily done); knowing well that unless we are in possession of this, it would not only be vain to determine the moral element of duty in right actions for purposes of speculative criticism, but it would be impossible to base morals on their genuine principles, even for common practical purposes, especially of moral instruction, so as to produce pure moral dispositions, and to engraft them on men's minds to the promotion of the greatest possible good in the world.....

On the other hand, the question, how the imperative of *morality* is possible, is undoubtedly one, the only one, demanding a solution, as this is not at all hypothetical, and the objective necessity which it presents cannot rest on any hypothesis, as is the case with the hypothetical imperative. Only here we must never leave out of consideration that we *cannot* make out *by any example*, in other words empirically, whether there is such an imperative at all; but it is rather to be feared that all those which seem to be categorical may yet be at bottom hypothetical. For instance, when the precept is: Thou shalt not promise deceitfully; and it is assumed that the necessity of this is not a mere counsel to avoid some other evil, so that it should mean: Thou shalt not make a lying promise, lest if it become known thou shouldst destroy thy credit, but that an action of this kind must be regarded as evil in itself, so that the imperative of the prohibition is categorical; then we cannot show with certainty in any example that the will was determined merely by the law, without any other spring of action, although it may appear to be so. For it is always possible that fear of disgrace, perhaps also obscure dread of other dangers, may have a secret influence on the will. Who can prove by experience the non-existence of a cause when all that experience tells us is that we do not perceive it? But in such a case the so-called moral imperative, which as such appears to be categorical and unconditional, would in reality be only a pragmatic precept, drawing our attention to our own interests, and merely teaching us to take these into consideration.

We shall therefore have to investigate a priori the possibility of a categorical imperative, as we have not in this case the advantage of its reality being given in experience, so that [the elucidation of] its possibility should be requisite only for its explanation, not for its establishment. In the meantime it may be discerned beforehand that the categorical imperative alone has the purport of a practical law: all the rest may indeed be called *principles* of the will but not laws, since whatever is only necessary for the attainment of some arbitrary purpose may be considered as in itself contingent, and we can at any time be free from the precept if we give up the purpose: on the contrary, the unconditional command leaves the will no liberty to choose the opposite; consequently it alone carries with it that necessity which we require in a law.

Secondly, in the case of this categorical imperative or law of morality, the difficulty (of discerning its possibility) is a very profound one. It is an a priori synthetical practical proposition; and as there is so much difficulty in discerning the possibility of speculative propositions of this kind, it may readily be supposed that the difficulty will be no less with the practical.

In this problem we will first inquire whether the mere conception of a categorical imperative may not perhaps supply us also with the formula of it, containing the proposition which alone can be a categorical imperative; for even if we know the tenor of such an absolute command, yet how it is possible will require further special and laborious study, which we postpone to the last section.

When I conceive a hypothetical imperative, in general I do not know beforehand what it will contain until I am given the condition. But when I conceive a categorical imperative, I know at once what it contains. For as the imperative contains besides the law only the necessity that the maxims shall conform to this law, while the law contains no conditions restricting it, there remains nothing but the general statement that the maxim of the action should conform to a universal law, and it is this conformity alone that the imperative properly represents as necessary.

There is therefore but one categorical imperative, namely, this: *Act only on that maxim whereby thou canst at the same time will that it should become a universal law.*

Now if all imperatives of duty can be deduced from this one imperative as from their principle, then, although it should remain undecided whether what is called duty is not merely a vain notion, yet at least we shall be able to show what we understand by it and what this notion means.

Since the universality of the law according to which effects are produced constitutes what is properly called *nature* in the most general sense (as to form), that is the existence of things so far as it is determined by general laws, the imperative of duty may be expressed thus: *Act as if the maxim of thy action were to become by thy will a universal law of nature.*

We will now enumerate a few duties, adopting the usual division of them into duties to ourselves and to others, and into perfect and imperfect duties.

1. A man reduced to despair by a series of misfortunes feels wearied of life, but is still so far in possession of his reason that he can ask himself whether it would not be contrary to his duty to himself to take his own life. Now he inquires whether the maxim of his action could become a universal law of nature. His maxim is: From self-love I adopt it as a principle to shorten my life when its longer duration is likely to bring more evil than satisfaction. It is asked then simply whether this principle founded on self-love can become a universal law of nature. Now we see at once that a system of nature of which it should be a law to destroy life by means of the very feeling whose special nature it is to impel to the improvement of life would contradict itself, and therefore could not exist as a system of nature; hence that maxim cannot possibly exist as a universal law of nature, and consequently would be wholly inconsistent with the supreme principle of all duty.

2. Another finds himself forced by necessity to borrow money. He knows that he will not be able to repay it, but sees also that nothing will be lent to him, unless he promises stoutly to repay it in a definite time. He desires to make this promise, but he has still so much conscience as to ask himself: Is it not unlawful and inconsistent with duty to get out of a difficulty in this way? Suppose, however, that he

resolves to do so, then the maxim of his action would be expressed thus: When I think myself in want of money, I will borrow money and promise to repay it, although I know that I never can do so. Now this principle of self-love or of one's own advantage may perhaps be consistent with my whole future welfare; but the question now is, Is it right? I change then the suggestion of self-love into a universal law, and state the question thus: How would it be if my maxim were a universal law? Then I see at once that it could never hold as a universal law of nature, but would necessarily contradict itself. For supposing it to be a universal law that everyone when he thinks himself in a difficulty should be able to promise whatever he pleases, with the purpose of not keeping his promise, the promise itself would become impossible, as well as the end that one might have in view in it, since no one would consider that anything was promised to him, but would ridicule all such statements as vain pretences.

3. A third finds in himself a talent which with the help of some culture might make him a useful man in many respects. But he finds himself in comfortable circumstances, and prefers to indulge in pleasure rather than to take pains in enlarging and improving his happy natural capacities. He asks, however, whether his maxim of neglect of his natural gifts, besides agreeing with his inclination to indulgence, agrees also with what is called duty. He sees then that a system of nature could indeed subsist with such a universal law although men (like the South Sea islanders) should let their talents rest, and resolve to devote their lives merely to idleness, amusement, and propagation of their species—in a word, to enjoyment; but he cannot possibly *will* that this should be a universal law of nature, or be implanted in us as such by a natural instinct. For, as a rational being, he necessarily wills that his faculties be developed, since they serve him, and have been given him, for all sorts of possible purposes.

4. A fourth, who is in prosperity, while he sees that others have to contend with great wretchedness and that he could help them, thinks: What concern is it of mine? Let everyone be as happy as Heaven pleases, or as he can make himself; I will take nothing from him nor even envy him, only I do not wish to contribute anything to his welfare or to his assistance in distress! Now no doubt if such a mode

of thinking were a universal law, the human race might very well subsist, and doubtless even better than in a state in which everyone talks of sympathy and good-will, or even takes care occasionally to put it into practice, but, on the other side, also cheats when he can, betrays the rights of men, or otherwise violates them. But although it is possible that a universal law of nature might exist in accordance with that maxim, it is impossible to *will* that such a principle should have the universal validity of a law of nature. For a will which resolved this would contradict itself, inasmuch as many cases might occur in which one would have need of the love and sympathy of others, and in which, by such a law of nature, sprung from his own will, he would deprive himself of all hope of the aid he desires.

These are a few of the many actual duties, or at least what we regard as such, which obviously fall into two classes on the one principle that we have laid down. We must be *able to will* that a maxim of our action should be a universal law. This is the canon of the moral appreciation of the action generally. Some actions are of such a character that their maxim cannot without contradiction be even *conceived* as a universal law of nature, far from it being possible that we should *will* that it *should* be so. In others this intrinsic impossibility is not found, but still it is impossible to *will* that their maxim should be raised to the universality of a law of nature, since such a will would contradict itself. It is easily seen that the former violate strict or rigorous (inflexible) duty; the latter only laxer (meritorious) duty. Thus it has been completely shown by these examples how all duties depend as regards the nature of the obligation (not the object of the action) on the same principle....

Now I say: man and generally any rational being *exists* as an end in himself, *not merely as a means* to be arbitrarily used by this or that will, but in all his actions, whether they concern himself or other rational beings, must be always regarded at the same time as an end. All objects of the inclinations have only a conditional worth; for if the inclinations and the wants founded on them did not exist, then their object would be without value. But the inclinations themselves being sources of want are so far from having an absolute worth for which they should be desired, that, on the contrary, it must be the universal wish of every rational being to be wholly free from them. Thus the worth of any object which is *to be acquired* by our action is always conditional. Beings whose existence depends not on our will but on nature's, have nevertheless, if they are rational beings, only a relative value as means, and are therefore called *things*; rational beings, on the contrary, are called *persons,* because their very nature points them out as ends in themselves, that is as something which must not be used merely as means, and so far therefore restricts freedom of action (and is an object of respect). These, therefore, are not merely subjective ends whose existence has a worth *for us* as an effect of our action, but *objective ends,* that is things whose existence is an end in itself: an end moreover for which no other can be substituted, which they should subserve *merely* as means, for otherwise nothing whatever would possess *absolute worth*; but if all worth were conditioned and therefore contingent, then there would be no supreme practical principle of reason whatever.

If then there is a supreme practical principle or, in respect of the human will, a categorical imperative, it must be one which, being drawn from the conception of that which is necessarily an end for everyone because it is *an end in itself,* constitutes an *objective* principle of will, and can therefore serve as a universal practical law. The foundation of this principle is: *rational nature exists as an end in itself.* Man necessarily conceives his own existence as being so: so far then this is a *subjective* principle of human actions. But every other rational being regards its existence similarly, just on the same rational principle that holds for me: so that it is at the same time an objective principle, from which as a supreme practical law all laws of the will must be capable of being deduced. Accordingly the practical imperative will be as follows: *So act as to treat humanity, whether in thine own person or in that of any other, in every case as an end withal, never as means only....*

Looking back now on all previous attempts to discover the principle of morality, we need not wonder why they all failed. It was seen that man was bound to laws by duty, but it was not observed that the laws to which he is subject are *only those of his own giving*, though at the same time they are

universal, and that he is only bound to act in conformity with his own will; a will, however, which is designed by nature to give universal laws. For when one has conceived man only as subject to a law (no matter what), then this law required some interest, either by way of attraction or constraint, since it did not originate as a law from *his own* will, but this will was according to a law obliged by *something else* to act in a certain manner. Now by this necessary consequence all the labour spent in finding a supreme principle of *duty* was irrevocably lost. For men never elicited duty, but only a necessity of acting from a certain interest. Whether this interest was private or otherwise, in any case the imperative must be conditional, and could not by any means be capable of being a moral command. I will therefore call this the principle of *Autonomy* of the will, in contrast with every other which I accordingly reckon as *Heteronomy*.

The conception of every rational being as one which must consider itself as giving in all the maxims of its will universal laws, so as to judge itself and its actions from this point of view—this conception leads to another which depends on it and is very fruitful, namely, that of a *kingdom of ends.*

By a *kingdom* I understand the union of different rational beings in a system by common laws. Now since it is by laws that ends are determined as regards their universal validity, hence, if we abstract from the personal differences of rational beings, and likewise from all the content of their private ends, we shall be able to conceive all ends combined in a systematic whole (including both rational beings as ends in themselves, and also the special ends which each may propose to himself), that is to say, we can conceive a kingdom of ends, which on the preceding principles is possible.

For all rational beings come under the *law* that each of them must treat itself and all others *never merely as means*, but in every case *at the same time as ends in themselves.* Hence results a systematic union of rational beings by common objective laws, i.e., a kingdom which may be called a kingdom of ends, since what these laws have in view is just the relation of these beings to one another as ends and means.

Nicomachean Ethics

ARISTOTLE

BOOK I

All Human Activities Aim at Some Good

Chapter 1

Every art and every scientific inquiry, and similarly every action and purpose, may be said to aim at some good. Hence the good has been well defined as that at which all things aim. But it is clear that there is a difference in ends; for the ends are sometimes activities, and sometimes results beyond the mere activities. Where there are ends beyond the action, the results are naturally superior to the action.

As there are various actions, arts, and sciences, it follows that the ends are also various. Thus health is the end of the medical art, a ship of shipbuilding, victory of strategy, and wealth of economics. It often happens that a number of such arts or sciences combine for a single enterprise, as the art of making bridles and all such other arts as furnish the implements of horsemanship combine for horsemanship, and horsemanship and every military action for strategy; and in the same way, other arts or sciences combine for others. In all these cases, the ends of the master arts or sciences, whatever they may be, are more desirable than those of the subordinate arts or sciences, as it is for the sake of the former that the latter are pursued. It makes no difference to the argument whether the activities themselves are the ends of the action, or something beyond the activities, as in the above-mentioned sciences.

If it is true that in the sphere of action there is some end which we wish for its own sake, and for the sake of which we wish everything else, and if we do not desire everything for the sake of something else (for, if that is so, the process will go on *ad infinitum,* and our desire will be idle and futile), clearly this end will be good and the supreme good. Does it not follow then that the knowledge of this good is of great importance for the conduct of life? Like archers who have a mark at which to aim, shall we not have a better chance of attaining what we want?

If this is so, we must endeavor to comprehend, at least in outline, what this good is, and what science or faculty makes it its object.

It would seem that this is the most authoritative science. Such a kind is evidently the political, for it is that which determines what sciences are necessary in states, and what kinds should be studied, and how far they should be studied by each class of inhabitant. We see too that even the faculties held in highest esteem, such as strategy, economics, and rhetoric, are subordinate to it. Then since politics makes use of the other sciences and also rules what people may do and what they may not do, it follows that its end will comprehend the ends of the other sciences, and will therefore be the good of mankind. For even if the good of an individual is identical with the good of a state, yet the good of the state is evidently greater and more perfect to attain or to preserve. For though the good of an individual by himself is something worth working for, to ensure the good of a nation or a state is nobler and more divine.

These then are the objects at which the present inquiry aims, and it is in a sense a political inquiry....

The Science of the Good for Man Is Politics

Chapter 2

As every science and undertaking aims at some good, what is in our view the good at which political science aims, and what is the highest of all practical goods? As to its name there is, I may say, a general agreement. The masses and the cultured classes agree in calling it happiness, and conceive that "to live well" or "to do well" is the same thing as "to be happy." But as to what happiness is they do not agree, nor do the masses give the same account of it as the philosophers. The former take it to be something visible and palpable, such as pleasure, wealth,

From James E. C. Weldon, trans. *Aristotle's Nicomachean Ethics* (New York: Macmillan, 1897).

or honor; different people, however, give different definitions of it, and often even the same man gives different definitions at different times. When he is ill, it is health, when he is poor, it is wealth; if he is conscious of his own ignorance, he envies people who use grand language above his own comprehension. Some philosophers, on the other hand, have held that, besides these various goods, there is an absolute good which is the cause of goodness in them all.[1] It would perhaps be a waste of time to examine all these opinions; it will be enough to examine such as are most popular or as seem to be more or less reasonable.

Chapter 3

Men's conception of the good or of happiness may be read in the lives they lead. Ordinary or vulgar people conceive it to be a pleasure, and accordingly choose a life of enjoyment. For there are, we may say, three conspicuous types of life, the sensual, the political, and, thirdly, the life of thought. Now the mass of men present an absolutely slavish appearance, choosing the life of brute beasts, but they have ground for so doing because so many persons in authority share the tastes of Sardanapalus.[2] Cultivated and energetic people, on the other hand, identify happiness with honor, as honor is the general end of political life. But this seems too superficial an idea for our present purpose; for honor depends more upon the people who pay it than upon the person to whom it is paid, and the good we feel is something which is proper to a man himself and cannot be easily taken away from him. Men too appear to seek honor in order to be assured of their own goodness. Accordingly, they seek it at the hands of the sage and of those who know them well, and they seek it on the ground of their virtue; clearly then, in their judgment at any rate, virtue is better than honor. Perhaps then we might look on virtue rather than honor as the end of political life. Yet even this idea appears not quite complete; for a man may possess virtue and yet be asleep or inactive throughout life, and not only so, but he may experience the greatest calamities and misfortunes. Yet no one would call such a life a life of happiness, unless he were maintaining a paradox. But we need not dwell further on this subject, since it is sufficiently discussed in popular philosophical treatises. The third life is the life of thought, which we will discuss later.

The life of money making is a life of constraint; and wealth is obviously not the good of which we are in quest; for it is useful merely as a means to something else. It would be more reasonable to take the things mentioned before—sensual pleasure, honor, and virtue—as ends than wealth, since they are things desired on their own account. Yet these too are evidently not ends, although much argument has been employed to show that they are....

Characteristics of the Good

Chapter 5

But leaving this subject for the present, let us revert to the good of which we are in quest and consider what it may be. For it seems different in different activities or arts; it is one thing in medicine, another in strategy, and so on. What is the good in each of these instances? It is presumably that for the sake of which all else is done. In medicine this is health, in strategy victory, in architecture a house, and so on. In every activity and undertaking it is the end, since it is for the sake of the end that all people do whatever else they do. If then there is an end for all our activity, this will be the good to be accomplished; and if there are several such ends, it will be these.

Our argument has arrived by a different path at the same point as before; but we must endeavor to make it still plainer. Since there are more ends than one, and some of these ends—for example, wealth, flutes, and instruments generally—we desire as means to something else, it is evident that not all are final ends. But the highest good is clearly something final. Hence if there is only one final end, this will be the object of which we are in search; and if there are more than one, it will be the most final. We call that which is sought after for its own sake more final than that which is sought after as a means to something else; we call that which is never desired as a means to something else more final than things that are desired both for themselves and as means to something else. Therefore, we call absolutely final that which is always desired for itself and never as a means to something else. Now happiness more than anything else answers to this description. For happiness we always desire for its own sake and never as a means to something else, whereas honor, pleasure, intelligence, and every virtue we desire partly for their own sakes (for we should desire them independently of what might result from them), but partly also as means to happiness, because we suppose they will prove instruments of happiness. Happiness, on the other hand, nobody desires for the sake of these things, nor indeed as a means to anything else at all.

If we start from the point of view of self-sufficiency, we reach the same conclusion; for we assume that the final good is self-sufficient. By self-sufficiency we do not mean that a person leads a solitary life all by himself, but that he has parents, children, wife and friends and fellow citizens in general, as man is naturally a social being. Yet here it is necessary to set some limit; for if the circle must be extended to include ancestors, descendants, and friends' friends, it will go on indefinitely. Leaving this point, however, for future investigation, we call the self-sufficient that which, taken even by itself, makes life desirable and wanting nothing at all; and this is what we mean by happiness.

Again, we think happiness the most desirable of all things, and that not merely as one good thing among others. If it were only that, the addition of the smallest more good would increase its desirableness; for the addition would make an increase of goods, and the greater of two goods is always the more desirable. Happiness is something final and self-sufficient and the end of all action.

Chapter 6

Perhaps, however, it seems a commonplace to say that happiness is the supreme good; what is wanted is to define its nature a little more clearly. The best way of arriving at such a definition will probably be to ascertain the function of man. For, as with a flute player, a sculptor, or any artist, or in fact anybody who has a special function or activity, his goodness and excellence seem to lie in his function, so it would seem to be with man, if indeed he has a special function. Can it be said that, while a carpenter and a cobbler have special functions and activities, man, unlike them, is naturally functionless? Or, as the eye, the hand, the foot, and similarly each part of the body has a special function, so may man be regarded as having a special function

apart from all these? What, then, can this function be? It is not life; for life is apparently something that man shares with plants; and we are looking for something peculiar to him. We must exclude therefore the life of nutrition and growth. There is next what may be called the life of sensation. But this too, apparently, is shared by man with horses, cattle, and all other animals. There remains what I may call the active life of the rational part of man's being. Now this rational part is twofold; one part is rational in the sense of being obedient to reason, and the other in the sense of possessing and exercising reason and intelligence. The active life too may be conceived of in two ways, either as a state of character, or as an activity; but we mean by it the life of activity, as this seems to be the truer form of the conception.

The function of man then is activity of soul in accordance with reason, or not apart from reason. Now, the function of a man of a certain kind, and of a man who is good of that kind—for example, of a harpist and a good harpist—are in our view the same in kind. This is true of all people of all kinds without exception, the superior excellence being only an addition to the function; for it is the function of a harpist to play the harp, and of a good harpist to play the harp well. This being so, if we define the function of man as a kind of life, and this life as an activity of the soul or a course of action in accordance with reason, and if the function of a good man is such activity of a good and noble kind, and if everything is well done when it is done in accordance with its proper excellence, it follows that the good of man is activity of soul in accordance with virtue, or, if there are more virtues than one, in accordance with the best and most complete virtue. But we must add the words "in a complete life." For as one swallow or one day does not make a spring, so one day or a short time does not make a man blessed or happy....

Inasmuch as happiness is an activity of soul in accordance with perfect virtue, we must now consider virtue, as this will perhaps be the best way of studying happiness....Clearly it is human virtue we have to consider; for the good of which we are in search is, as we said, human good, and the happiness, human happiness. By human virtue or excellence we mean not that of the body, but that of the soul, and by happiness we mean an activity of the soul....

BOOK II

Chapter 1

Virtue then is twofold, partly intellectual and partly moral, and intellectual virtue is originated and fostered mainly by teaching; it demands therefore experience and time. Moral virtue on the other hand is the outcome of habit, and accordingly its name, *ethike,* is derived by a slight variation from *ethos,* habit. From this fact it is clear that moral virtue is not implanted in us by nature; for nothing that exists by nature can be transformed by habit. Thus a stone, that naturally tends to fall downwards, cannot be habituated or trained to rise upwards, even if we tried to train it by throwing it up ten thousand times. Nor again can fire be trained to sink downwards, nor anything else that follows one natural law be habituated or trained to follow another. It is neither by nature then nor in defiance of nature that virtues grow in us. Nature gives us the capacity to receive them, and that capacity is perfected by habit.

Again, if we take the various natural powers which belong to us, we first possess the proper faculties and afterwards display the activities. It is obviously so with the senses. Not by seeing frequently or hearing frequently do we acquire the sense of seeing or hearing; on the contrary, because we have the senses we make use of them; we do not get them by making use of them. But the virtues we get by first practicing them, as we do in the arts. For it is by doing what we ought to do when we study the arts that we learn the arts themselves; we become builders by building and harpists by playing the harp. Similarly, it is by doing just acts that we become just, by doing temperate acts that we become temperate, by doing brave acts that we become brave. The experience of states confirms this statement, for it is by training in good habits that lawmakers make the citizens good. This is the object all lawmakers have at heart; if they do not succeed in it, they fail of their purpose; and it makes the distinction between a good constitution and a bad one.

Again, the causes and means by which any virtue is produced and destroyed are the same; and equally so in any part. For it is by playing the harp that both good and bad harpists are produced; and the case of builders and others is similar, for it is by building well that they become good builders and by building badly that they become bad builders. If it were not so, there would be no need of anybody to teach them; they would all be born good or bad in their several crafts. The case of the virtues is the same. It is by our actions in dealings between man and man that we become either just or unjust. It is by our actions in the face of danger and by our training ourselves to fear or to courage that we become either cowardly or courageous. It is much the same with our appetites and angry passions. People become temperate and gentle, others licentious and passionate, by behaving in one or the other way in particular circumstances. In a word, moral states are the results of activities like the states themselves. It is our duty therefore to keep a certain character in our activities, since our moral states depend on the differences in our activities. So the difference between one and another training in habits in our childhood is not a light matter, but important, or rather, all-important.

Chapter 2

Our present study is not, like other studies, purely theoretical in intention; for the object of our inquiry is not to know what virtue is but how to become good, and that is the sole benefit of it. We must, therefore, consider the right way of performing actions, for it is acts, as we have said, that determine the character of the resulting moral states.

That we should act in accordance with right reason is a common general principle, which may here be taken for granted. The nature of right reason, and its relation to the virtues generally, will be discussed later. But first of all it must be admitted that all reasoning on matters of conduct must be like a sketch in outline; it cannot be scientifically exact. We began by laying down the principle that the kind of reasoning demanded in any subject must be such as the subject matter itself allows; and questions of conduct and expediency no more admit of hard and fast rules than questions of health.

If this is true of general reasoning on ethics, still more true is it that scientific exactitude is impossible in treating of particular ethical cases. They do not fall under any art or law, but the actors themselves have always to take account of circumstances, as much as in medicine or navigation. Still, although such is the nature of our present argument, we must try to make the best of it.

The first point to be observed is that in the matters we are now considering deficiency and excess are both fatal. It is so, we see, in questions of health and strength. (We must judge of what we cannot see by the evidence of what we do see.) Too much or too little gymnastic exercise is fatal to strength. Similarly, too much or too little meat and drink is fatal to health, whereas a suitable amount produces, increases, and sustains it. It is the same with temperance, courage, and other moral virtues. A person who avoids and is afraid of everything and faces nothing becomes a coward; a person who is not afraid of anything but is ready to face everything becomes foolhardy. Similarly, he who enjoys every pleasure and abstains from none is licentious; he who refuses all pleasures, like a boor, is an insensible sort of person. For temperance and courage are destroyed by excess and deficiency but preserved by the mean.

Again, not only are the causes and agencies of production, increase, and destruction in moral states the same, but the field of their activity is the same also. It is so in other more obvious instances, as, for example, strength; for strength is produced by taking a great deal of food and undergoing a great deal of exertion, and it is the strong man who is able to take most food and undergo most exertion. So too with the virtues. By abstaining from pleasures we become temperate, and, when we have become temperate, we are best able to abstain from them. So again with courage; it is by training ourselves to despise and face terrifying things that we become brave, and when we have become brave, we shall be best able to face them.

The pleasure or pain which accompanies actions may be regarded as a test of a person's moral state. He who abstains from physical pleasures and feels pleasure in so doing is temperate; but he who feels pain at so doing is licentious. He who faces dangers with pleasure, or at least without pain, is brave; but he who feels pain at facing them is a coward. For moral virtue is concerned with pleasures and pains. It is pleasure which makes us do what is base, and pain which makes us abstain from doing what is noble. Hence the importance of having a certain training from very early days, as Plato says, so that

we may feel pleasure and pain at the right objects; for this is true education....

Chapter 3

But we may be asked what we mean by saying that people must become just by doing what is just and temperate by doing what is temperate. For, it will be said, if they do what is just and temperate they are already just and temperate themselves, in the same way as, if they practice grammar and music, they are grammarians and musicians.

But is this true even in the case of the arts? For a person may speak grammatically either by chance or at the suggestion of somebody else; hence he will not be a grammarian unless he not only speaks grammatically but does so in a grammatical manner, that is, because of the grammatical knowledge which he possesses.

There is a point of difference too between the arts and the virtues. The productions of art have their excellence in themselves. It is enough then that, when they are produced, they themselves should possess a certain character. But acts in accordance with virtue are not justly or temperately performed simply because they are in themselves just or temperate. The doer at the time of performing them must satisfy certain conditions; in the first place, he must know what he is doing; secondly, he must deliberately choose to do it and do it for its own sake; and thirdly, he must do it as part of his own firm and immutable character. If it be a question of art, these conditions, except only the condition of knowledge, are not raised; but if it be a question of virtue, mere knowledge is of little or no avail; it is the other conditions, which are the results of frequently performing just and temperate acts, that are not slightly but all-important. Accordingly, deeds are called just and temperate when they are such as a just and temperate person would do; and a just and temperate person is not merely one who does these deeds but one who does them in the spirit of the just and the temperate.

It may fairly be said that a just man becomes just by doing what is just, and a temperate man becomes temperate by doing what is temperate, and if a man did not so act, he would not have much chance of becoming good. But most people, instead of acting, take refuge in theorizing; they imagine that they are philosophers and that philosophy will make them virtuous; in fact, they behave like people who listen attentively to their doctors but never do anything that their doctors tell them. But a healthy state of the soul will no more be produced by this kind of philosophizing than a healthy state of the body by this kind of medical treatment.

Chapter 4

We have next to consider the nature of virtue. Now, as the properties of the soul are three, namely, emotions, faculties, and moral states, it follows that virtue must be one of the three. By emotions I mean desire, anger, fear, pride, envy, joy, love, hatred, regret, ambition, pity—in a word, whatever feeling is attended by pleasure or pain. I call those faculties through which we are said to be capable of experiencing these emotions, for instance, capable of getting angry or being pained or feeling pity. And I call those moral states through which we are well or ill disposed in our emotions, ill disposed, for instance, in anger, if our anger be too violent or too feeble, and well disposed, if it be rightly moderate; and similarly in our other emotions.

Now neither the virtues nor the vices are emotions; for we are not called good or bad for our emotions but for our virtues or vices. We are not praised or blamed simply for being angry, but only for being angry in a certain way; but we are praised or blamed for our virtues or vices. Again, whereas we are angry or afraid without deliberate purpose, the virtues are matters of deliberate purpose, or require deliberate purpose. Moreover, we are said to be moved by our emotions, but by our virtues or vices we are not said to be moved but to have a certain disposition.

For these reasons the virtues are not faculties. For we are not called either good or bad, nor are we praised or blamed for having simple capacity for emotion. Also while Nature gives us our faculties, it is not Nature that makes us good or bad; but this point we have already discussed. If then the virtues are neither emotions nor faculties, all that remains is that they must be moral states.

Chapter 5

The nature of virtue has been now described in kind. But it is not enough to say merely that virtue is a moral state; we must also describe the character of that moral state.

We may assert then that every virtue or excellence puts into good condition that of which it is a virtue or excellence, and enables it to perform its work well. Thus excellence in the eye makes the eye good and its function good, for by excellence in the eye we see well. Similarly, excellence of the horse makes a horse excellent himself and good at racing, at carrying its rider and at facing the enemy. If then this rule is universally true, the virtue or excellence of a man will be such a moral state as makes a man good and able to perform his proper function well. How this will be the case we have already explained, but another way of making it clear will be to study the nature or character of virtue.

Now of everything, whether it be continuous or divisible, it is possible to take a greater, a smaller, or an equal amount, and this either in terms of the thing itself or in relation to ourselves, the equal being a mean between too much and too little. By the mean in terms of the thing itself, I understand that which is equally distinct from both its extremes, which is one and the same for every man. By the mean relatively to ourselves, I understand that which is neither too much nor too little for us; but this is not one nor the same for everybody. Thus if 10 be too much and 2 too little, we take 6 as a mean in terms of the thing itself; for 6 is as much greater than 2 as it is less than 10, and this is a mean in arithmetical proportion. But the mean considered relatively to ourselves may not be ascertained in that way. It does not follow that if 10 pounds of meat is too much and 2 too little for a man to eat, the trainer will order him 6 pounds, since this also may be too much or too little for him who is to take it; it will be too little, for example, for Milo but too much for a beginner in gymnastics. The same with running and wrestling; the right amount will vary with the individual. This being so, the skillful in any art avoids alike excess and deficiency; he seeks and chooses the mean, not the absolute mean, but the mean considered relatively to himself.

Every art then does its work well, if it regards the mean and judges the works it produces by the mean. For this reason we often say of successful works of art that it is impossible to take anything from them or to add anything to them, which implies that excess or deficiency is fatal to excellence but that the mean state ensures it. Good artists too, as we say, have an eye to the mean in their works. Now virtue, like Nature herself, is more accurate and better than any art; virtue, therefore, will aim at the mean. I speak of moral virtue, since it is moral virtue which is concerned with emotions and actions, and it is in these we have excess and deficiency and the mean. Thus it is possible to go too far, or not far enough in fear, pride, desire, anger, pity, and pleasure and pain generally, and the excess and the deficiency are alike wrong; but to feel these emotions at the right times, for the right objects, towards the right persons, for the right motives, and in the right manner, is the mean or the best good, which signifies virtue. Similarly, there may be excess, deficiency, or the mean, in acts. Virtue is concerned with both emotions and actions, wherein excess is an error and deficiency a fault, while the mean is successful and praised, and success and praise are both characteristics of virtue.

It appears then that virtue is a kind of mean because it aims at the mean.

On the other hand, there are many different ways of going wrong; for evil is in its nature infinite, to use the Pythagorean phrase, but good is finite and there is only one possible way of going right. So the former is easy and the latter is difficult; it is easy to miss the mark but difficult to hit it. And so by our reasoning excess and deficiency are characteristics of vice and the mean is a characteristic of virtue,

"For good is simple, evil manifold."

Chapter 6
Virtue then is a state of deliberate moral purpose, consisting in a mean relative to ourselves, the mean being determined by reason, or as a prudent man would determine it. It is a mean, firstly, as lying between two vices, the vice of excess, on the one hand, the vice of deficiency on the other, and, secondly, because, whereas the vices either fall short of or go beyond what is right in emotion and action, virtue discovers and chooses the mean. Accordingly, virtue, if regarded in its essence or theoretical definition, is a mean, though, if regarded from the point of view of what is best and most excellent, it is an extreme.

But not every action or every emotion admits of a mean. There are some whose very name implies wickedness, as, for example, malice, shamelessness, and envy among the emotions, and adultery, theft, and murder among the actions. All these and others like them are marked as intrinsically wicked, not merely the excesses or deficiencies of them. It is never possible then to be right in them; they are always sinful. Right or wrong in such acts as adultery does not depend on our committing it with the right woman, at the right time, or in the right manner; on the contrary, it is wrong to do it at all. It would be equally false to suppose that there can be a mean or an excess or deficiency in unjust, cowardly or licentious conduct; for, if that were so, it would be a mean of excess and deficiency, an excess of excess and a deficiency of deficiency. But as in temperance and courage there can be no excess or deficiency, because the mean there is in a sense an extreme, so too in these other cases there cannot be a mean or an excess or a deficiency, but however the acts are done, they are wrong. For in general an excess or deficiency does not have a mean, nor a mean an excess or deficiency....

Chapter 8
There are then three dispositions, two being vices, namely, excess and deficiency, and one virtue, which is the mean between them; and they are all in a sense mutually opposed. The extremes are opposed both to the mean and to each other, and the mean is opposed to the extremes. For as the equal if compared with the less is greater, but if compared with the greater is less, so the mean state, whether in emotion or action, if compared with deficiency is excessive, but if compared with excess is deficient. Thus the brave man appears foolhardy compared with the coward, but cowardly compared with the foolhardy. Similarly, the temperate man appears licentious compared with the insensible man but insensible compared with the licentious; and the liberal man appears extravagant compared with the stingy man but stingy compared with the spendthrift. The result is that the extremes each denounce the mean as belonging to the other extreme; the coward calls the brave man foolhardy, and the foolhardy man calls him cowardly; and so on in other cases.

But while there is mutual opposition between the extremes and the mean, there is greater opposition between the two extremes than between extreme and the mean; for they are further removed from each other than from the mean, as the great is further from the small and the small from the great than either from the equal. Again, while some extremes show some likeness to the mean, as foolhardiness to courage and extravagance to liberality, there is the greatest possible dissimilarity between extremes. But things furthest removed from each other are called opposites; hence the further things are removed, the greater is the opposition between them.

In some cases it is deficiency and in others excess which is more opposed to the mean. Thus it is not foolhardiness, an excess, but cowardice, a deficiency, which is more opposed to courage, nor is it insensibility, a deficiency, but licentiousness, an excess, which is more opposed to temperance. There are two reasons why this should be so. One lies in the nature of the matter itself; for when one of two extremes is nearer and more like the mean, it is not this extreme but its opposite that we chiefly contrast with the mean. For instance, as foolhardiness seems more like and nearer to courage than cowardice, it is cowardice that we chiefly contrast with courage; for things further removed from the mean seem to be more opposite to it. This reason lies in the nature of the matter itself; there is a second which lies in our own nature. The things to which we ourselves are naturally more inclined we think more opposed to the mean. Thus we are ourselves naturally more inclined to pleasures than to their opposites, and are more prone therefore to self-indulgence than to moderation. Accordingly we speak of those things in which we are more likely to run to great lengths as more opposed to the mean. Hence licentiousness, which is an excess, seems more opposed to temperance than insensibility.

Chapter 9

We have now sufficiently shown that moral virtue is a mean, and in what sense it is so; that it is a mean as lying between two vices, a vice of excess on the one side and a vice of deficiency on the other, and as aiming at the mean in emotion and action.

That is why it is so hard to be good; for it is always hard to find the mean in anything; it is not everyone but only a man of science who can find the mean or center of a circle. So too anybody can get angry—that is easy—and anybody can give or spend money, but to give it to the right person, to give the right amount of it, at the right time, for the right cause and in the right way, this is not what anybody can do, nor is it easy. That is why goodness is rare and praise worthy and noble. One then who aims at a mean must begin by departing from the extreme that is more contrary to the mean; he must act in the spirit of Calypso's advice,

"Far from this spray and swell hold thou thy ship,"

for of the two extremes one is more wrong than the other. As it is difficult to hit the mean exactly, we should take the second best course, as the saying is, and choose the lesser of two evils. This we shall best do in the way described, that is, steering clear of the evil which is further from the mean. We must also note the weaknesses to which we are ourselves particularly prone, since different natures tend in different ways; and we may ascertain what our tendency is by observing our feelings of pleasure and pain. Then we must drag ourselves away towards the opposite extreme; for by pulling ourselves as far as possible from what is wrong we shall arrive at the mean, as we do when we pull a crooked stick straight.

In all cases we must especially be on our guard against the pleasant, or pleasure, for we are not impartial judges of pleasure. Hence our attitude towards pleasure must be like that of the elders of the people in the *Iliad* towards Helen, and we must constantly apply the words they use; for if we dismiss pleasure as they dismissed Helen, we shall be less likely to go wrong. By action of this kind, to put it summarily, we shall best succeed in hitting the mean.

Undoubtedly this is a difficult task, especially in individual cases. It is not easy to determine the right manner, objects, occasion and duration of anger. Sometimes we praise people who are deficient in anger, and call them gentle, and at other times we praise people who exhibit a fierce temper as high spirited. It is not however a man who deviates a little from goodness, but one who deviates a great deal, whether on the side of excess or of deficiency, that is blamed; for he is sure to call attention to himself. It is not easy to decide in theory how far and to what extent a man may go before he becomes blameworthy, but neither is it easy to define in theory anything else in the region of the senses; such things depend on circumstances, and our judgment of them depends on our perception.

So much then is plain, that the mean is everywhere praiseworthy, but that we ought to aim at one time towards an excess and at another towards

a deficiency; for thus we shall most easily hit the mean, or in other words reach excellence.

NOTES

1. Plato.
2. A half-legendary ruler whose name to the Greeks stood for extreme mental luxury and extravagance.

A Theory of Justice

JOHN RAWLS

1. THE ROLE OF JUSTICE

Justice is the first virtue of social institutions, as truth is of systems of thought. A theory however elegant and economical must be rejected or revised if it is untrue; likewise laws and institutions no matter how efficient and well-arranged must be reformed or abolished if they are unjust. Each person possesses an inviolability founded on justice that even the welfare of society as a whole cannot override. For this reason justice denies that the loss of freedom for some is made right by a greater good shared by others. It does not allow that the sacrifices imposed on a few are outweighed by the larger sum of advantages enjoyed by many. Therefore in a just society the liberties of equal citizenship are taken as settled; the rights secured by justice are not subject to political bargaining or to the calculus of social interests. The only thing that permits us to acquiesce in an erroneous theory is the lack of a better one; analogously, an injustice is tolerable only when it is necessary to avoid an even greater injustice. Being first virtues of human activities, truth and justice are uncompromising.

These propositions seem to express our intuitive conviction of the primacy of justice. No doubt they are expressed too strongly. In any event I wish to inquire whether these contentions or others similar to them are sound, and if so how they can be accounted for. To this end it is necessary to work out a theory of justice in the light of which these

assertions can be interpreted and assessed. I shall begin by considering the role of the principles of justice. Let us assume, to fix ideas, that a society is a more or less self-sufficient association of persons who in their relations to one another recognize certain rules of conduct as binding and who for the most part act in accordance with them. Suppose further that these rules specify a system of cooperation designed to advance the good of those taking part in it. Then, although a society is a cooperative venture for mutual advantage, it is typically marked by a conflict as well as by an identity of interests. There is an identity of interests since social cooperation makes possible a better life for all than any would have if each were to live solely by his own efforts. There is a conflict of interests since persons are not indifferent as to how the greater benefits produced by their collaboration are distributed, for in order to pursue their ends they each prefer a larger to a lesser share. A set of principles is required for choosing among the various social arrangements which determine this division of advantages and for underwriting an agreement on the proper distributive shares. These principles are the principles of social justice: they provide a way of assigning rights and duties in the basic institutions of society and they define the appropriate distribution of the benefits and burdens of social cooperation.

Now let us say that a society is well-ordered when it is not only designed to advance the good of its members but when it is also effectively regulated by a public conception of justice. That is, it is a society in which (1) everyone accepts and knows that the others accept the same principles of justice, and (2) the basic social institutions generally satisfy and are generally known to satisfy these principles. In this case while men may put forth excessive demands on one another, they nevertheless acknowledge a common point of view from which their claims may be adjudicated. If men's inclination to self-interest makes their vigilance against one another necessary, their public sense of justice makes their secure association together possible. Among individuals with disparate aims and purposes a shared conception of justice establishes the bonds of civic friendship; the general desire for justice limits the pursuit of other ends. One may think of a public conception of justice as constituting the fundamental charter of a well-ordered human association.

Existing societies are of course seldom well-ordered in this sense, for what is just and unjust is usually in dispute. Men disagree about which principles should define the basic terms of their association. Yet we may still say, despite this disagreement, that they each have a conception of justice. That is, they understand the need for, and they are prepared to affirm, a characteristic set of principles for assigning basic rights and duties and for determining what they take to be the proper distribution of the benefits and burdens of social cooperation. Thus it seems natural to think of the concept of justice as distinct from the various conceptions of justice and as being specified by the role which these different sets of principles, these different conceptions, have in common.[1] Those who hold different conceptions of justice can, then, still agree that institutions are just when no arbitrary distinctions are made between persons in the assigning of basic rights and duties and when the rules determine a proper balance between competing claims to the advantages of social life. Men can agree to this description of just institutions since the notions of an arbitrary distinction and of a proper balance, which

are included in the concept of justice, are left open for each to interpret according to the principles of justice that he accepts. These principles single out which similarities and differences among persons are relevant in determining rights and duties and they specify which division of advantages is appropriate. Clearly this distinction between the concept and the various conceptions of justice settles no important questions. It simply helps to identify the role of the principles of social justice.

Some measure of agreement in conceptions of justice is, however, not the only prerequisite for a viable human community. There are other fundamental social problems, in particular those of coordination, efficiency, and stability. Thus the plans of individuals need to be fitted together so that their activities are compatible with one another and they can all be carried through without anyone's legitimate expectations being severely disappointed. Moreover, the execution of these plans should lead to the achievement of social ends in ways that are efficient and consistent with justice. And finally, the scheme of social cooperation must be stable: it must be more or less regularly complied with and its basic rules willingly acted upon; and when infractions occur, stabilizing forces should exist that prevent further violations and tend to restore the arrangement. Now it is evident that these three problems are connected with that of justice. In the absence of a certain measure of agreement on what is just and unjust, it is clearly more difficult for individuals to coordinate their plans efficiently in order to insure that mutually beneficial arrangements are maintained. Distrust and resentment corrode the ties of civility, and suspicion and hostility tempt men to act in ways they would otherwise avoid. So while the distinctive role of conceptions of justice is to specify basic rights and duties and to determine the appropriate distributive shares, the way in which a conception does this is bound to affect the problems of efficiency, coordination, and stability. We cannot, in general, assess a conception of justice by its distributive role alone, however useful this role may be in identifying the concept of justice. We must take into account its wider connections; for even though justice has a certain priority, being the most important virtue of institutions, it is still true that, other things equal, one conception of justice is preferable to another when its broader consequences are more desirable.

.....

3. THE MAIN IDEA OF THE THEORY OF JUSTICE

My aim is to present a conception of justice which generalizes and carries to a higher level of abstraction the familiar theory of the social contract as found, say, in Locke, Rousseau and Kant.[2] In order to do this we are not to think of the original contract as one to enter a particular society or to set up a particular form of government. Rather, the guiding idea is that the principles of justice for the basic structure of society are the object of the original agreement. They are the principles that free and rational persons concerned to further their own interests would accept in an initial position of equality as defining the fundamental terms of their association. These principles are to regulate all further agreements; they specify the kinds of social cooperation that can be entered into and the forms of government that can be established. This way of regarding the principles of justice I shall call justice as fairness.

Thus we are to imagine that those who engage in social cooperation choose together, in one joint act, the principles which are to assign basic rights and duties and to determine the division of social benefits. Men are to decide in advance how they are to regulate their claims against one another and what is to be the foundation charter of their society. Just as each person must decide by rational reflection what constitutes his good, that is, the system of ends which it is rational for him to pursue, so a group of persons must decide once and for all what is to count among them as just and unjust. The choice which rational men would make in this hypothetical situation of equal liberty, assuming for the present that this choice problem has a solution, determines the principles of justice.

In justice as fairness the original position of equality corresponds to the state of nature in the traditional theory of the social contract. This original position is not, of course, thought of as an actual historical state of affairs, much less as a primitive condition of culture. It is understood as a purely hypothetical situation characterized so as to lead to a certain conception of justice.[3] Among the essential features of this situation is that no one knows his place in society, his class position or social status, nor does any one know his fortune in the distribution of natural assets and abilities, his intelligence, strength, and the like. I shall even assume that the parties do not know their conceptions of the good or their special psychological propensities. The principles of justice are chosen behind a veil of ignorance. This ensures that no one is advantaged or disadvantaged in the choice of principles by the outcome of natural chance or the contingency of social circumstances. Since all are similarly situated and no one is able to design principles to favor his particular condition, the principles of justice are the result of a fair agreement or bargain. For given the circumstances of the original position, the symmetry of everyone's relations to each other, this initial situation is fair between individuals as moral persons, that is, as rational beings with their own ends and capable, I shall assume, of a sense of justice. The original position is, one might say, the appropriate initial status quo, and thus the fundamental agreements reached in it are fair. This explains the propriety of the name "justice as fairness": it conveys the idea that the principles of justice are agreed to in an initial situation that is fair. The name does not mean that the concepts of justice and fairness are the same, any more than the phrase "poetry as metaphor" means that the concepts of poetry and metaphor are the same.

Justice as fairness begins, as I have said, with one of the most general of all choices which persons might make together, namely, with the choice of the first principles of a conception of justice which is to regulate all subsequent criticism and reform of institutions. Then, having chosen a conception of justice, we can suppose that they are to choose a constitution and a legislature to enact laws, and so on, all in accordance with the principles of justice initially agreed upon. Our social situation is just if it is such that by this sequence of hypothetical agreements we would have contracted into the general system of rules which defines it. Moreover, assuming that the original position does determine a set of principles (that is, that a particular conception of justice would be chosen), it will then be true that whenever social institutions satisfy these principles those engaged in them can say to one another that they are cooperating on terms to which they would agree if they were free and equal persons whose relations with respect to one another were fair. They could all view their arrangements as meeting the stipulations which they would acknowledge in an initial situation that embodies widely accepted and reasonable constraints on the choice of principles. The general recognition of this fact would provide the basis for a public acceptance of the corresponding principles of justice. No society can, of course, be a scheme of cooperation which men enter voluntarily in a literal sense; each person finds himself placed at birth in some particular position in some particular society, and the nature of this position materially affects his life prospects. Yet a society satisfying the principles of justice as fairness comes as close as a society can to being a voluntary scheme, for it meets the principles which free and equal persons would assent to under circumstances that are fair. In this sense its members are autonomous and the obligations they recognize self-imposed.

One feature of justice as fairness is to think of the parties in the initial situation as rational and mutually disinterested. This does not mean that the parties are egoists, that is, individuals with only certain kinds of interests, say in wealth, prestige, and domination. But they are conceived as not taking an interest in one another's interests. They are to presume that even their spiritual aims may be opposed, in the way that the aims of those of different religions may be opposed. Moreover, the concept of rationality must be interpreted as far as possible in the narrow sense, standard in economic theory, of taking the most effective means to given ends. I shall modify this concept to some extent, as explained later (§25), but one must try to avoid introducing into it any controversial ethical elements. The initial situation must be characterized by stipulations that are widely accepted.

In working out the conception of justice as fairness one main task clearly is to determine which principles of justice would be chosen in the original position. To do this we must describe this situation in some detail and formulate with care the problem of choice which it presents. These matters I shall take up in the immediately succeeding chapters. It may be observed, however, that once the principles

of justice are thought of as arising from an original agreement in a situation of equality, it is an open question whether the principle of utility would be acknowledged. Offhand it hardly seems likely that persons who view themselves as equals, entitled to press their claims upon one another, would agree to a principle which may require lesser life prospects for some simply for the sake of a greater sum of advantages enjoyed by others. Since each desires to protect his interests, his capacity to advance his conception of the good, no one has a reason to acquiesce in an enduring loss for himself in order to bring about a greater net balance of satisfaction. In the absence of strong and lasting benevolent impulses, a rational man would not accept a basic structure merely because it maximized the algebraic sum of advantages irrespective of its permanent effects on his own basic rights and interests. Thus it seems that the principle of utility is incompatible with the conception of social cooperation among equals for mutual advantage. It appears to be inconsistent with the idea of reciprocity implicit in the notion of a well-ordered society. Or, at any rate, so I shall argue.

I shall maintain instead that the persons in the initial situation would choose two rather different principles: the first requires equality in the assignment of basic rights and duties, while the second holds that social and economic inequalities, for example inequalities of wealth and authority, are just only if they result in compensating benefits for everyone, and in particular for the least advantaged members of society. These principles rule out justifying institutions on the grounds that the hardships of some are offset by a greater good in the aggregate. It may be expedient but it is not just that some should have less in order that others may prosper. But there is no injustice in the greater benefits earned by a few provided that the situation of persons not so fortunate is thereby improved. The intuitive idea is that since everyone's well-being depends upon a scheme of cooperation without which no one could have a satisfactory life, the division of advantages should be such as to draw forth the willing cooperation of everyone taking part in it, including those less well situated. The two principles mentioned seem to be a fair basis on which those better endowed, or more fortunate in their social position, neither of which we can be said to deserve, could expect the willing cooperation of others when some workable scheme is a necessary condition of the welfare of all.[4] Once we decide to look for a conception of justice that prevents the use of the accidents of natural endowment and the contingencies of social circumstance as counters in a quest for political and economic advantage, we are led to these principles. They express the result of leaving aside those aspects of the social world that seem arbitrary from a moral point of view.

The problem of the choice of principles, however, is extremely difficult. I do not expect the answer I shall suggest to be convincing to everyone. It is, therefore, worth noting from the outset that justice as fairness, like other contract views, consists of two parts: (1) an interpretation of the initial situation and of the problem of choice posed there, and (2) a set of principles which, it is argued, would be agreed to. One may accept the first part of the theory (or some variant thereof), but not the other, and conversely. The concept of the initial contractual situation may seem reasonable although the particular principles proposed are rejected. To be sure, I want to maintain that the most appropriate conception of this situation does lead to principles of justice contrary to utilitarianism and perfectionism, and therefore that the contract doctrine provides an alternative to these views. Still, one may dispute this contention even though one grants that the contractarian method is a useful way of studying ethical theories and of setting forth their underlying assumptions.

Justice as fairness is an example of what I have called a contract theory. Now there may be an objection to the term "contract" and related expressions, but I think it will serve reasonably well. Many words have misleading connotations which at first are likely to confuse. The terms "utility" and "utilitarianism" are surely no exception. They too have unfortunate suggestions which hostile critics have been willing to exploit; yet they are clear enough for those prepared to study utilitarian doctrine. The same should be true of the term "contract" applied to moral theories. As I have mentioned, to understand it one has to keep in mind that it implies a certain level of abstraction. In particular, the content of the relevant agreement is not to enter a given

society or to adopt a given form of government, but to accept certain moral principles. Moreover, the undertakings referred to are purely hypothetical: a contract view holds that certain principles would be accepted in a well-defined initial situation.

The merit of the contract terminology is that it conveys the idea that principles of justice may be conceived as principles that would be chosen by rational persons, and that in this way conceptions of justice may be explained and justified. The theory of justice is a part, perhaps the most significant part, of the theory of rational choice. Furthermore, principles of justice deal with conflicting claims upon the advantages won by social cooperation; they apply to the relations among several persons or groups. The word "contract" suggests this plurality as well as the condition that the appropriate division of advantages must be in accordance with principles acceptable to all parties. The condition of publicity for principles of justice is also connoted by the contract phraseology. Thus, if these principles are the outcome of an agreement, citizens have a knowledge of the principles that others follow. It is characteristic of contract theories to stress the public nature of political principles. Finally there is the long tradition of the contract doctrine. Expressing the tie with this line of thought helps to define ideas and accords with natural piety. There are then several advantages in the use of the term "contract." With due precautions taken, it should not be misleading.

A final remark. Justice as fairness is not a complete contract theory. For it is clear that the contractarian idea can be extended to the choice of more or less an entire ethical system, that is, to a system including principles for all the virtues and not only for justice. Now for the most part I shall consider only principles of justice and others closely related to them; I make no attempt to discuss the virtues in a systematic way. Obviously if justice as fairness succeeds reasonably well, a next step would be to study the more general view suggested by the name "rightness as fairness." But even this wider theory fails to embrace all moral relationships, since it would seem to include only our relations with other persons and to leave out of account how we are to conduct ourselves toward animals and the rest of nature. I do not contend that the contract notion offers a way to approach these questions which are certainly of the first importance; and I shall have to put them aside. We must recognize the limited scope of justice as fairness and of the general type of view that it exemplifies. How far its conclusions must be revised once these other matters are understood cannot be decided in advance.

......

11. TWO PRINCIPLES OF JUSTICE

I shall now state in a provisional form the two principles of justice that I believe would be agreed to in the original position. The first formulation of these principles is tentative. As we go on I shall consider several formulations and approximate step by step the final statement to be given much later. I believe that doing this allows the exposition to proceed in a natural way.

The first statement of the two principles reads as follows.

First: each person is to have an equal right to the most extensive scheme of equal basic liberties compatible with a similar scheme of liberties for others.

Second: social and economic inequalities are to be arranged so that they are both (a) reasonably expected to be to everyone's advantage, and (b) attached to positions and offices open to all.

There are two ambiguous phrases in the second principle, namely "everyone's advantage" and "open to all." Determining their sense more exactly will lead to a second formulation of the principle in §13. The final version of the two principles is given in §46: §39 considers the rendering of the first principle.

These principles primarily apply, as I have said, to the basic structure of society and govern the assignment of rights and duties and regulate the distribution of social and economic advantages. Their formulation presupposes that, for the purposes of a theory of justice, the social structure may be viewed as having two more or less distinct parts, the first principle applying to the one, the second principle to the other. Thus we distinguish between the aspects of the social system that define and secure the equal basic liberties and the aspects that specify and establish social and economic inequalities. Now it is essential to observe that the basic liberties are given by a list of such liberties. Important among these are political liberty (the right to vote and to hold

public office) and freedom of speech and assembly; liberty of conscience and freedom of thought; freedom of the person, which includes freedom from psychological oppression and physical assault and dismemberment (integrity of the person); the right to hold personal property and freedom from arbitrary arrest and seizure as defined by the concept of the rule of law. These liberties are to be equal by the first principle.

The second principle applies, in the first approximation, to the distribution of income and wealth and to the design of organizations that make use of differences in authority and responsibility. While the distribution of wealth and income need not be equal, it must be to everyone's advantage, and at the same time, positions of authority and responsibility must be accessible to all. One applies the second principle by holding positions open, and then, subject to this constraint, arranges social and economic inequalities so that everyone benefits.

These principles are to be arranged in a serial order with the first principle prior to the second. This ordering means that infringements of the basic equal liberties protected by the first principle cannot be justified, or compensated for, by greater social and economic advantages. These liberties have a central range of application within which they can be limited and compromised only when they conflict with other basic liberties. Since they may be limited when they clash with one another, none of these liberties is absolute; but however they are adjusted to form one system, this system is to be the same for all. It is difficult, and perhaps impossible, to give a complete specification of these liberties independently from the particular circumstances—social, economic, and technological—of a given society. The hypothesis is that the general form of such a list could be devised with sufficient exactness to sustain this conception of justice. Of course, liberties not on the list, for example, the right to own certain kinds of property (e.g., means of production) and freedom of contract as understood by the doctrine of laissez-faire are not basic; and so they are not protected by the priority of the first principle. Finally, in regard to the second principle, the distribution of wealth and income, and positions of authority and responsibility, are to be consistent with both the basic liberties and equality of opportunity.

The two principles are rather specific in their content, and their acceptance rests on certain assumptions that I must eventually try to explain and justify. For the present; it should be observed that these principles are a special case of a more general conception of justice that can be expressed as follows.

> All social values—liberty and opportunity, income and wealth, and the social bases of self-respect—are to be distributed equally unless an unequal distribution of any, or all, of these values is to everyone's advantage.

Injustice, then, is simply inequalities that are not to the benefit of all. Of course, this conception is extremely vague and requires interpretation.

NOTES

1. Here I follow H. L. A. Hart, *The Concept of Law* (Oxford, The Clarendon Press, 1961), pp. 155–159.
2. As the text suggests, I shall regard Locke's *Second Treatise of Government*, Rousseau's *The Social Contract*, and Kant's ethical works beginning with *The Foundations of the Metaphysics of Morals* as definitive of the contract tradition. For all of its greatness, Hobbes's *Leviathan* raises special problems. A general historical survey is provided by J. W. Gough, *The Social Contract*, 2nd ed. (Oxford, The Clarendon Press, 1957), and Otto Gierke, *Natural Law and the Theory of Society*, trans. with an introduction by Ernest Barker (Cambridge, The University Press, 1934). A presentation of the contract view as primarily an ethical theory is to be found in G. R. Grice, *The Grounds of Moral Judgment* (Cambridge, The University Press, 1967). See also §19, note 30.
3. Kant is clear that the original agreement is hypothetical. See *The Metaphysics of Morals*, pt. I (*Rechisiehre*), especially §§47, 52; and pt. II of the essay "Concerning the Common Saying: This May Be True in Theory but It Does Not Apply in Practice," in *Kant's Writings*, ed. Hans Reiss and trans. by H. B. Nisbet (Cambridge, The University Press. 1970). pp. 73–87. See Georges Vlachos, *La Pensée politique de Kant* (Paris, Presses Universitaires de France, 1962), pp. 326–335; and J. G. Murphy. *Kant: The Philosophy of Right* (London, Macmillan, 1970), pp. 109–112, 133–136, for a further discussion.
4. For the formulation of this intuitive idea I am indebted to Allan Gibbard.

The Need for More Than Justice

ANNETTE C. BAIER

In recent decades in North American social and moral philosophy, alongside the development and discussion of widely influential theories of justice, taken as Rawls takes it as the "first virtue of social institutions,"[1] there has been a counter-movement gathering strength, one coming from some interesting sources. For some of the most outspoken of the diverse group who have in a variety of ways been challenging the assumed supremacy of justice among the moral and social virtues are members of those sections of society whom one might have expected to be especially aware of the supreme importance of justice, namely blacks and women. Those who have only recently won recognition of their equal rights, who have only recently seen the correction or partial correction of longstanding racist and sexist injustices to their race and sex, are among the philosophers now suggesting that justice is only one virtue

Annette C. Baier, "The Need for More Than Justice" from *Canadian Journal of Philosophy*, Supp. Vol. 13, "On Science, Ethics, and Feminism," edited by Marsha Hanen and Kai Nielsen. Copyright © 1987. Published with permission by the University of Calgary Press.

among many, and one that may need the presence of the others in order to deliver its own undenied value. Among these philosophers of the philosophical counterculture, as it were—but an increasingly large counterculture—I include Alasdair MacIntyre,[2] Michael Stocker,[3] Lawrence Blum,[4] Michael Slote,[5] Laurence Thomas,[6] Claudia Card,[7] Alison Jaggar,[8] Susan Wolf[9] and a whole group of men and women, myself included, who have been influenced by the writings of Harvard educational psychologist Carol Gilligan, whose book *In a Different Voice* (Harvard 1982; hereafter D.V.) caused a considerable stir both in the popular press and, more slowly, in the philosophical journals.[10]

Let me say quite clearly at this early point that there is little disagreement that justice is *a* social value of very great importance, and injustice an evil. Nor would those who have worked on theories of justice want to deny that other things matter besides justice. Rawls, for example, incorporates the value of freedom into his account of justice, so that denial of basic freedoms counts as injustice. Rawls also leaves room for a wider theory of the right, of which the theory of justice is just a part. Still, he does claim that justice is the 'first' virtue of social institutions, and it is only that claim about priority that I think has been challenged. It is easy to exaggerate the differences of view that exist, and I want to avoid that. The differences are as much in emphasis as in substance, or we can say that they are differences in tone of voice. But these differences do tend to make a difference in approaches to a wide range of topics not just in moral theory but in areas like medical ethics, where the discussion used to be conducted in terms of patients' rights, of informed consent, and so on, but now tends to get conducted in an enlarged moral vocabulary, which draws on what Gilligan calls the ethics of *care* as well as that of *justice*.

For "care" is the new buzz-word. It is not, as Shakespeare's Portia demanded, mercy that is to season justice, but a less authoritarian humanitarian supplement, a felt concern for the good of others and for community with them. The "cold jealous virtue of justice" (Hume) is found to be too cold, and it is "warmer" more communitarian virtues and social ideals that are being called in to supplement it. One might say that liberty and equality are being found

inadequate without fraternity, except that "fraternity" will be quite the wrong word, if as Gilligan initially suggested, it is *women* who perceive this value most easily. ("Sorority" will do no better, since it is too exclusive, and English has no gender-neuter word for the mutual concern of siblings.) She has since modified this claim, allowing that there are two perspectives on moral and social issues that we all tend to alternate between, and which are not always easy to combine, one of them what she called the justice perspective, the other the care perspective. It is increasingly obvious that there are many male philosophical spokespersons for the care perspective (Laurence Thomas, Lawrence Blum, Michael Stocker) so that it cannot be the prerogative of women. Nevertheless Gilligan still wants to claim that women are most unlikely to take *only* the justice perspective, as some men are claimed to, at least until some mid-life crisis jolts them into "bifocal" moral vision (see D.V., ch. 6).

Gilligan in her book did not offer any explanatory theory of why there should be any difference between female and male moral outlook, but she did tend to link the naturalness to women of the care perspective with their role as primary care-takers of young children, that is with their parental and specifically maternal role. She avoided the question of whether it is their biological or their social role that is relevant, and some of those who dislike her book are worried precisely by this uncertainty. Some find it retrograde to hail as a special sort of moral wisdom an outlook that may be the product of the socially enforced restriction of women to domestic roles (and the reservation of such roles for them alone). For that might seem to play into the hands of those who still favor such restriction. (Marxists, presumably, will not find it so surprising that moral truths might depend for their initial clear voicing on the social oppression, and memory of it, of those who voice the truths.) Gilligan did in the first chapter of D.V. cite the theory of Nancy Chodorow (as presented in *The Reproduction of Mothering* [Berkeley 1978]) which traces what appears as gender differences in personality to early social development, in particular to the effects of the child's primary caretaker being or not being of the same gender as the child. Later, both in "The Conquistador and the Dark Continent: Reflections on the Nature of Love"

(*Daedalus* [Summer 1984]), and "The Origins of Morality in Early Childhood" (in press), she develops this explanation. She postulates two evils that any infant may become aware of, the evil of detachment or isolation from others whose love one needs, and the evil of relative powerlessness and weakness. Two dimensions of moral development are thereby set— one aimed at achieving satisfying community with others, the other aiming at autonomy or equality of power. The relative predominance of one over the other development will depend both upon the relative salience of the two evils in early childhood, and on early and later reinforcement or discouragement in attempts made to guard against these two evils. This provides the germs of a theory about *why,* given current customs of childrearing, it should be mainly women who are not content with only the moral outlook that she calls the justice perspective, necessary though that was and is seen by them to have been to their hard won liberation from sexist oppression. They, like the blacks, used the language of rights and justice to change their own social position, but nevertheless see limitations in that language, according to Gilligan's findings as a moral psychologist. She reports their discontent with the individualist more or less Kantian moral framework that dominates Western moral theory and which influenced moral psychologists such as Lawrence Kohlberg, to whose conception of moral maturity she seeks an alternative. Since the target of Gilligan's criticism is the dominant Kantian tradition, and since that has been the target also of moral philosophers as diverse in their own views as Bernard Williams, Alasdair MacIntyre, Philippa Foot, Susan Wolf, Claudia Card, her book is of interest as much for its attempt to articulate an alternative to the Kantian justice perspective as for its implicit raising of the question of male bias in Western moral theory, especially liberal-democratic theory. For whether the supposed blind spots of that outlook are due to male bias, or to non-parental bias, or to early traumas of powerlessness or to early resignation to "detachment" from others, we need first to be persuaded that they *are* blind spots before we will have any interest in their cause and cure. Is justice blind to important social values, or at least only one-eyed? What is it that comes into view from the "care perspective" that is not seen from the "justice perspective"?

Gilligan's position here is mostly easily described by contrasting it with that of Kohlberg, against which she developed it. Kohlberg, influenced by Piaget and the Kantian philosophical tradition as developed by John Rawls, developed a theory about typical moral development which saw it to progress from a pre-conventional level, where what is seen to matter is pleasing or not offending parental authority-figures, through a conventional level in which the child tries to fit in with a group, such as a school community, and conform to its standards and rules, to a post-conventional critical level, in which such conventional rules are subjected to tests, and where those tests are of a Utilitarian, or, eventually, a Kantian sort—namely ones that require respect for each person's individual rational will, or autonomy, and conformity to any implicit social contract such wills are deemed to have made, or to any hypothetical ones they would make if thinking clearly. What was found when Kohlberg's questionnaires (mostly by verbal response to verbally sketched moral dilemmas) were applied to female as well as male subjects, Gilligan reports, is that the girls and women not only scored generally lower than the boys and men, but tended to *revert* to the lower stage of the conventional level even after briefly (usually in adolescence) attaining the post conventional level; Piaget's finding that girls were deficient in "the legal sense" was confirmed.

These results led Gilligan to wonder if there might not be a quite different pattern of development to be discerned, at least in female subjects. She therefore conducted interviews designed to elicit not just how far advanced the subjects were towards an appreciation of the nature and importance of Kantian autonomy, but also to find out what the subjects themselves saw as progress or lack of it, what conceptions of moral maturity they came to possess by the time they were adults. She found that although the Kohlberg version of moral maturity as respect for fellow persons, and for their rights as equals (rights including that of free association), did seem shared by many young men, the women tended to speak in a different voice about morality itself and about moral maturity. To quote Gilligan, "Since the reality of interconnexion is experienced by women as given rather than freely contracted, they arrive at an understanding of life that reflects the limits of autonomy and control. As a result, women's development delineates the path not only to a less violent life but also to a maturity realized by interdependence and taking care" (D.V., 172). She writes that there is evidence that "women perceive and construe social reality differently from men, and that these differences center around experiences of attachment and separation...because women's sense of integrity appears to be intertwined with an ethics of care, so that to see themselves as women is to see themselves in a relationship of connexion, the major changes in women's lives would seem to involve changes in the understanding and activities of care" (D.V., 171). She contrasts this progressive understanding of care, from merely pleasing others to helping and nurturing, with the sort of progression that is involved in Kohlberg's stages, a progression in the understanding, not of mutual care, but of mutual *respect,* where this has its Kantian overtones of distance, even of some fear for the respected, and where personal autonomy and independence, rather than more satisfactory interdependence, are the paramount values.

This contrast, one cannot but feel, is one which Gilligan might have used the Marxist language of alienation to make. For the main complaint about the Kantian version of a society with its first virtue justice, construed as respect for equal rights to formal goods such as having contracts kept, due process, equal opportunity including opportunity to participate in political activities leading to policy and law-making, to basic liberties of speech, free association and assembly, religious worship, is that none of these goods do much to ensure that the people who have and mutually respect such rights will have any other relationships to one another than the minimal relationship needed to keep such a "civil society" going. They may well be lonely, driven to suicide, apathetic about their work and about participation in political processes, find their lives meaningless and have no wish to leave offspring to face the same meaningless existence. Their rights, and respect for rights, are quite compatible with very great misery, and misery whose causes are not just individual misfortunes and psychic sickness, but social and moral impoverishment.

What Gilligan's older male subjects complain of is precisely this sort of alienation from some dimly glimpsed better possibility for human beings, some richer sort of network of relationships. As one of Gilligan's male subjects put it, "People have real emotional needs to be attached to something, and equality does not give you attachment. Equality fractures society and places on every person the burden of standing on his own two feet" (D.V., 167). It is not just the difficulty of self reliance which is complained of, but its socially "fracturing" effect. Whereas the younger men, in their college years, had seen morality as a matter of reciprocal non-interference, this older man begins to see it as reciprocal attachment. "Morality is...essential...for creating the kind of environment, interaction between people, that is a prerequisite to the fulfillment of individual goals. If you want other people not to interfere with your pursuit of whatever you are into, you have to play the game," says the spokesman for traditional liberalism (D.V. 98). But if what one is "into" is interconnexion, interdependence rather than an individual autonomy that may involve "detachment," such a version of morality will come to seem inadequate. And Gilligan stresses that the interconnexion that her mature women subjects, and some men, wanted to sustain was not merely freely chosen interconnexion; nor interconnexion between equals, but also the sort of interconnexion that can obtain between a child and her unchosen mother and father, or between a child and her unchosen older and younger siblings, or indeed between most workers and their unchosen fellow workers, or most citizens and their unchosen fellow citizens.

A model of a decent community different from the liberal one is involved in the version of moral maturity that Gilligan voices. It has in many ways more in common with the older religion-linked versions of morality and a good society than with the modern Western liberal ideal. That perhaps is why some find it so dangerous and retrograde. Yet it seems clear that it also has much in common with what we can call Hegelian versions of moral maturity and of social health and malaise, both with Marxist versions and with so-called right-Hegelian views.

Let me try to summarize the main differences, as I see them, between on the one hand Gilligan's version of moral maturity and the sort of social structures that would encourage, express and protect it, and on the other the orthodoxy she sees herself to be challenging. I shall from now on be giving my own interpretation of the significance of her challenges, not merely reporting them.[11] The most obvious point is the challenge to the individualism of the Western tradition, to the fairly entrenched belief in the possibility and desirability of each person pursuing his own good in his own way, constrained only by a minimal formal common good, namely a working legal apparatus that enforces contracts and protects individuals from undue interference by others. Gilligan reminds us that noninterference can, especially for the relatively powerless, such as the very young, amount to neglect, and even between equals can be isolating and alienating. On her less individualist version of individuality, it becomes defined by responses to dependency and to patterns of interconnexion, both chosen and unchosen. It is not something a person *has*, and which she then chooses relationships to suit, but something that develops out of a series of dependencies and inter-dependencies, and responses to them. This conception of individuality is not flatly at odds with, say, Rawls' Kantian one, but there is at least a difference of tone of voice between speaking as Rawls does of each of us having our own rational life plan, which a just society's moral traffic rules will allow us to follow, and which may or may not include close association with other persons, and speaking as Gilligan does of a satisfactory life as involving "progress of affiliative relationship" (D.V., 170) where "the concept of identity expands to include the experience of interconnexion" (D.V., 173). Rawls can allow that progress to Gilligan-style moral maturity may be *a* rational life plan, but not a moral constraint on every life-pattern. The trouble is that it will not do just to say "let this version of morality be an optional extra. Let us agree on my essential minimum, that is on justice and rights, and let whoever wants to go further, and cultivate this more demanding ideal of responsibility and care." For, first, it cannot be satisfactorily cultivated without closer cooperation from others than respect for rights and justice will ensure, and, second, the encouragement of some to cultivate it while others do not could easily lead to exploitation of those who do. It obviously *has* suited some in most societies

well enough that others take on the responsibilities of care (for the sick, the helpless, the young) leaving them free to pursue their own less altruistic goods. Volunteer forces of those who accept an ethic of care, operating within a society where the power is exercised and the institutions designed, redesigned, or maintained by those who accept a less communal ethic of minimally constrained self-advancement, will not be the solution. The liberal individualists may be able to "tolerate" the more communally minded, if they keep the liberals' rules, but it is not so clear that the more communally minded can be content with just those rules, nor be content to be tolerated and possibly exploited.

For the moral tradition which developed the concept of rights, autonomy and justice is the same tradition that provided "justifications" of the oppression of those whom the primary right-holders depended on to do the sort of work they themselves preferred not to do. The domestic work was left to women and slaves, and the liberal morality for right-holders was surreptitiously supplemented by a different set of demands made on domestic workers. As long as women could be got to assume responsibility for the care of home and children, and to train their children to continue the sexist system, the liberal morality could continue to be the official morality, by turning its eyes away from the contribution made by those it excluded. The long unnoticed moral proletariat were the domestic workers, mostly female. Rights have usually been for the privileged. Talking about laws, and the rights those laws recognize and protect, does not in itself ensure that the group of legislators and rights-holders will not be restricted to some elite. Bills of rights have usually been proclamations of the rights of some in-group, barons, landowners, males, whites, non-foreigners. The "justice perspective," and the legal sense that goes with it, are shadowed by their patriarchal past. What did Kant, the great prophet of autonomy, say in his moral theory about women? He said they were incapable of legislation, not fit to vote, that they needed the guidance of more "rational" males.[12] Autonomy was not for them, only for first class, really rational, persons. It is ironic that Gilligan's original findings in a way confirm Kant's views—it seems that autonomy really may not be for women. Many of them reject that ideal (D.V., 48), and have been found not as good at making rules as are men. But where Kant concludes—"so much the worse for women," we can conclude—"so much the worse for the male fixation on the special skill of drafting legislation, for the bureaucratic mentality of rule worship, and for the male exaggeration of the importance of independence over mutual interdependence."

It is however also true that the moral theories that made the concept of a person's rights central were not just the instruments for excluding some persons, but also the instruments used by those who demanded that more and more persons be included in the favored group. Abolitionists, reformers, women, used the language of rights to assert their claims to inclusion in the group of full members of a community. The tradition of liberal moral theory has in fact developed so as to include the women it had for so long excluded, to include the poor as well as rich, blacks and whites, and so on. Women like Mary Wollstonecraft used the male moral theories to good purpose. So we should not be wholly ungrateful for those male moral theories, for all their objectionable earlier content. They were undoubtedly patriarchal, but they also contained the seeds of the challenge, or antidote, to this patriarchal poison.

But when we transcend the values of the Kantians, we should not forget the facts of history—that those values were the values of the oppressors of women. The Christian church, whose version of the moral law Aquinas codified, in his very legalistic moral theory, still insists on the maleness of the God it worships, and jealously reserves for males all the most powerful positions in its hierarchy. Its patriarchical prejudice is open and avowed. In the secular moral theories of men, the sexist patriarchal prejudice is today often less open, not as blatant as it is in Aquinas, in the later natural law tradition, and in Kant and Hegel, but is often still there. No moral theorist today would say that women are unfit to vote, to make laws, or to rule a nation without powerful male advisors (as most queens had), but the old doctrines die hard. In one of the best male theories we have, John Rawls's theory, a key role is played by the idea of the "head of a household." It is heads of households who are to deliberate behind a "veil of ignorance" of historical details, and of details of their own special situation, to arrive at the "just" constitution for a society. Now of course Rawls does

not think or say that "heads" are fathers rather than mothers. But if we have really given up the age-old myth of women needing, as Grotius put it, to be under the "eye" of a more "rational" male protector and master, then how do families come to have any one "head," except by the death or desertion of one parent? They will either be two-headed, or headless. Traces of the old patriarchal poison still remain in even the best contemporary moral theorizing. Few may actually say that women's place is in the home, but there is much muttering, when unemployment figures rise, about how the relatively recent flood of women into the workforce complicates the problem, as if it would be a good thing if women just went back home whenever unemployment rises, to leave the available jobs for the men. We still do not really have a wide acceptance of the equal right of women to employment outside the home. Nor do we have wide acceptance of the equal duty of men to perform those domestic tasks which in no way depend on special female anatomy, namely cooking, cleaning, and the care of weaned children. All sorts of stories (maybe true stories), about children's need for one "primary" parent, who must be the mother if the mother breast feeds the child, shore up the unequal division of domestic responsibility between mothers and fathers, wives and husbands. If we are really to transvalue the values of our patriarchal past, we need to rethink all of those assumptions, really test those psychological theories. And how will men ever develop an understanding of the "ethics of care" if they continue to be shielded or kept from that experience of caring for a dependent child, which complements the experience we all have had of being cared for as dependent children? These experiences form the natural background for the development of moral maturity as Gilligan's women saw it.

Exploitation aside, why would women, once liberated, not be content to have their version of morality merely tolerated? Why should they not see themselves as voluntarily, for their own reasons, taking on *more* than the liberal rules demand, while having no quarrel with the content of those rules themselves, nor with their remaining the only ones that are expected to be generally obeyed? To see why, we need to move on to three more differences between the Kantian liberals (usually contractarians) and their critics. These concern the relative weight put on relationships between equals, and the relative weight put on freedom of choice, and on the authority of intellect over emotions. It is a typical feature of the dominant moral theories and traditions, since Kant, or perhaps since Hobbes, that relationships between equals or those who are deemed equal in some important sense, have been the relations that morality is concerned primarily to regulate. Relationships between those who are clearly unequal in power, such as parents and children, earlier and later generations in relation to one another, states and citizens, doctors and patients, the well and the ill, large states and small states, have had to be shunted to the bottom of the agenda, and then dealt with by some sort of "promotion" of the weaker so that an appearance of virtual equality is achieved. Citizens collectively become equal to states, children are treated as adults-to-be, the ill and dying are treated as continuers of their earlier more potent selves, so that their "rights" could be seen as the rights of equals. This pretence of an equality that is in fact absent may often lead to desirable protection of the weaker, or more dependent. But it somewhat masks the question of what our moral relationships *are* to those who are our superiors or our inferiors in power. A more realistic acceptance of the fact that we begin as helpless children, that at almost every point of our lives we deal with both the more and the less helpless, that equality of power and interdependency, between two persons or groups, is rare and hard to recognize when it does occur, might lead us to a more direct approach to questions concerning the design of institutions structuring these relationships between unequals (families, schools, hospitals, armies) and of the morality of our dealings with the more and the less powerful. One reason why those who agree with the Gilligan version of what morality is about will not want to agree that the liberals' rules are a good minimal set, the only ones we need pressure *everyone* to obey, is that these rules do little to protect the young or the dying or the starving or any of the relatively powerless against neglect, or to ensure an education that will form persons to be *capable* of conforming to an ethics of care and responsibility. Put baldly, and in a way Gilligan certainly has not put it, the liberal morality, if unsupplemented, may *unfit* people to be anything other than what its justifying theories suppose

them to be, ones who have no interest in each others' interests. Yet some must take an interest in the next generation's interests. Women's traditional work, of caring for the less powerful, especially for the young, is obviously socially vital. One cannot regard any version of morality that does not ensure that it gets well done as an adequate "minimal morality," any more than we could so regard one that left any concern for more distant future generations an optional extra. A moral theory, it can plausibly be claimed, cannot regard concern for new and future persons as an optional charity left for those with a taste for it. If the morality the theory endorses is to sustain itself, it must provide for its own continuers, not just take out a loan on a carefully encouraged maternal instinct or on the enthusiasm of a self-selected group of environmentalists, who make it their business or hobby to be concerned with what we are doing to mother earth.

The recognition of the importance for all parties of relations between those who are and cannot but be unequal, both of these relations in themselves and for their effect on personality formation and so on other relationships, goes along with a recognition of the plain fact that not all morally important relationships can or should be freely chosen. So far I have discussed three reasons women have not to be content to pursue their own values within the framework of the liberal morality. The first was its dubious record. The second was its inattention to relations of inequality or its pretence of equality. The third reason is its exaggeration of the scope of choice, or its inattention to unchosen relations. Showing up the partial myth of equality among actual members of a community, and of the undesirability of trying to pretend that we are treating all of them as equals, tends to go along with an exposure of the companion myth that moral obligations arise from freely *chosen* associations between such equals. Vulnerable future generations do not choose their dependence on earlier generations. The unequal infant does not choose its place in a family or nation, nor is it treated as free to do as it likes until some association is freely entered into. Nor do its parents always choose their parental role, or freely assume their parental responsibilities any more than we choose our power to affect the conditions in which later generations will live. Gilligan's attention to the version of morality and moral maturity found in women, many of whom had faced a choice of whether or not to have an abortion, and who had at some point become mothers, is attention to the perceived inadequacy of the language of rights to help in such choices or to guide them in their parental role. It would not be much of an exaggeration to call the Gilligan "different voice" the voice of the potential parents. The emphasis on care goes with a recognition of the often unchosen nature of the responsibilities of those who give care, both of children who care for their aged or infirm parents, and of parents who care for the children they in fact have. Contract soon ceases to seem the paradigm source of moral obligation once we attend to parental responsibility, and justice as a virtue of social institutions will come to seem at best only first equal with the virtue, whatever its name, that ensures that each new generation is made appropriately welcome and prepared for their adult lives.

This all constitutes a belated reminder to Western moral theorists of a fact they have always known, that as Adam Ferguson, and David Hume before him emphasized, we are born into families, and the first society we belong to, one that fits or misfits us for later ones, is the small society of parents (or some sort of child-attendants) and children, exhibiting as it may both relationships of near equality and of inequality in power. This simple reminder, with the fairly considerable implications it can have for the plausibility of contractarian moral theory, is at the same time a reminder of the role of human emotions as much as human reason and will in moral development as it actually comes about. The fourth feature of the Gilligan challenge to liberal orthodoxy is a challenge to its typical *rationalism,* or intellectualism, to its assumption that we need not worry what passions persons have, as long as their rational wills can control them. This Kantian picture of a controlling reason dictating to possibly unruly passions also tends to seem less useful when we are led to consider what sort of person we need to fill the role of parent, or indeed want in any close relationship. It might be important for father figures to have rational control over their violent urges to beat to death the children whose screams enrage them, but more than control of such nasty passions seems needed in the mother or primary parent, or

parent-substitute, by most psychological theories. They need to love their children, not just to control their irritation. So the emphasis in Kantian theories on rational control of emotions, rather than on cultivating desirable forms of emotion, is challenged by Gilligan, along with the challenge to the assumption of the centrality of autonomy, or relations between equals, and of freely chosen relations.

The same set of challenges to "orthodox" liberal moral theory has come not just from Gilligan and other women, who are reminding other moral theorists of the role of the family as a social institution and as an influence on the other relationships people want to or are capable of sustaining, but also, as I noted at the start, from an otherwise fairly diverse group of men, ranging from those influenced by both Hegelian and Christian traditions (MacIntyre) to all varieties of other backgrounds. From this group I want to draw attention to the work of one philosopher in particular, namely Laurence Thomas, the author of a fairly remarkable article[13] in which he finds sexism to be a more intractable social evil than racism. In a series of articles, and a forthcoming book,[14] Thomas makes a strong case for the importance of supplementing a concern for justice and respect for rights with an emphasis on equally needed virtues, and on virtues seen as appropriate *emotional* as well as rational capacities. Like Gilligan (and unlike MacIntyre) Thomas gives a lot of attention to the childhood beginnings of moral and social capacities, to the role of parental love in making that possible, and to the emotional as well as the cognitive development we have reason to think both possible and desirable in human persons.

It is clear, I think, that the best moral theory has to be a cooperative product of women and men, has to harmonize justice and care. The morality it theorizes about is after all for all persons, for men and for women, and will need their combined insights. As Gilligan said (D.V., 174), what we need now is a "marriage" of the old male and the newly articulated female insights. If she is right about the special moral aptitudes of women, it will most likely be the women who propose the marriage, since they are the ones with more natural empathy, with the better diplomatic skills, the ones more likely to shoulder responsibility and take moral initiative, and the ones who find it easiest to empathize and care about how the other party feels. Then, once there is this union of male and female moral wisdom, we maybe can teach each other the moral skills each gender currently lacks, so that the gender difference in moral outlook that Gilligan found will slowly become less marked.

NOTES

1. John Rawls, *A Theory of Justice* (Harvard University Press).
2. Alasdair MacIntyre, *After Virtue* (Notre Dame: Notre Dame University Press).
3. Michael Stocker "The Schizophrenia of Modern Ethical Thieories," *Journal of Philosophy* 73, 14, 453–66, and "Agent and Other: Against Ethical Universalism," *Australasian Journal of Philosophy* 54, 206–20.
4. Lawrence Blum, *Friendship, Altruism and Morality* (London: Routledge & Kegan Paul 1980).
5. Michael Slote, *Goods and Virtues* (Oxford: Oxford University Press 1983).
6. Laurence Thomas, "Love and Morality," in *Epistemology and Sociobiology,* James Fetzer, ed. (1985); and "Justice, Happiness and Self Knowledge," *Canadian Journal of Philosophy* (March, 1986).

Also "Beliefs and the Motivation to be Just," *American Philosophical Quarterly* 22 (4), 347–52.
7. Claudia Card, "Mercy," *Philosophical Review* 81, 1, and "Gender and Moral Luck," forthcoming.
8. Alison Jaggar, *Feminist Politics and Human Nature* (London: Rowman and Allenheld 1983).
9. Susan Wolf, "Moral Saints," *Journal of Philosophy* 79 (August, 1982), 419–39.
10. For a helpful survey article see Owen Flanagan and Kathryn Jackson, "Justice, Care & Gender: The Kohlberg-Gilligan Debate Revisited," *Ethics*.
11. I have previously written about the significance of her findings for moral philosophy in "What Do Women Want in a Moral Theory?" *Nous* 19 (March 1985), "Trust and Antitrust", *Ethics* 96 (1986), and in "Hume the Women's Moral Theorist" in *Women and Moral Theory*, Kittay and Meyers, ed., forthcoming.
12. Immanuel Kant, *Metaphysics of Morals,* sec. 46.
13. Laurence Thomas, "Sexism and Racism: Some Conceptual Differences," *Ethics* 90 (1980), 239–50; republished in *Philosophy, Sex and Language,* Vetterling-Braggin, ed. (Totowa, NJ: Littlefield Adams 1980).
14. See articles listed in note 6, above. The forthcoming book has the title *A Psychology of Moral Character.*

SUGGESTIONS FOR FURTHER READING

Anita L. Allen, *New Ethics: A Guided Tour of the Twenty-First Century Moral Landscape* (New York: Miramax, 2004).

Thomas Aquinas, *Summa Theologica* in *Basic Writings of St. Thomas Aquinas*, trans. A. C. Pegis (New York: Random House, 1945).

Jeremy Bentham, "Of the Principle of Utility," *An Introduction to the Principles of Morals and Legislation* (Oxford: Clarendon Press, 1879) 1–7.

Stephen Buckle, "Natural Law," in *A Companion to Ethics,* ed. Peter Singer (Cambridge: Blackwell, 1993) 161–74.

Steven M. Cahn and Joram G. Haber, *Twentieth Century Ethical Theory* (Upper Saddle River, NJ: Prentice-Hall, 1995).

Fred Feldman, "Act Utilitarianism: Pro and Con" in *Introductory Ethics* (Englewood Cliffs, NJ: Prentice-Hall, 1978).

John Finnis, *Natural Law and Natural Rights* (New York: Oxford University Press, 1980).

William K. Frankena, *Ethics*, 2nd ed. (Englewood Cliffs, NJ: Prentice-Hall, 1973).

C.E. Harris, *Applying Moral Theories* (Belmont, CA: Wadsworth, 1997).

Dale Jamieson, "Method and Moral Theory," in *A Companion to Ethics,* ed. Peter Singer (Cambridge: Blackwell, 1993) 476–87.

Mark Murphy, "The Natural Law Tradition in Ethics," *The Stanford Encyclopedia of Philosophy* (Winter 2002 ed.), Edward N. Zalta, ed. <http://plato.stanford.edu/archives/win2002/entries/natural-law-ethics>.

Kai Nielsen, "A Defense of Utilitarianism," *Ethics* 82 (1972) 113–24.

Kai Nielsen, *Ethics Without God* (Buffalo, NY: Prometheus, 1973).

Robert Nozick, "The Experience Machine," in *Anarchy, State and Utopia* (New York: Basic Books, 1974).

Onora O'Neill, "Kantian Ethics," in *A Companion to Ethics*, ed. Peter Singer (Cambridge: Blackwell, 1993) 175–85.

Louis P. Pojman and Lewis Vaughn, ed., *The Moral Life*, 3rd ed. (New York: Oxford University Press, 2007).

James Rachels, *The Elements of Moral Philosophy*, 4th ed. (New York: McGraw-Hill, 2003).

James Rachels, ed., *Ethical Theory 2: Theories About How We Should Live* (Oxford: Oxford University Press, 1998).

John Rawls, "Some Remarks about Moral Theory" in *A Theory of Justice* (Cambridge: Harvard University Press, 1999), 40–46.

J. J. C. Smart, "Extreme and Restricted Utilitarianism," in *Essays Metaphysical and Moral* (Oxford: Blackwell, 1987).

Paul Taylor, *Principles of Ethics* (Encino, CA: Dickenson, 1975).

Lewis Vaughn, *Doing Ethics: Moral Reasoning and Contemporary Issues* (New York: W. W. Norton, 2008).

Bernard Williams, "A Critique of Utilitarianism," in *Utilitarianism: For and Against*, ed. J. J. C. Smart and Bernard Williams (New York: Cambridge University Press, 1973).

Abortion

Views on abortion—whether held by church, state, or citizenry—have varied dramatically through time and across cultures. Abortions in the ancient world were common, and there was no shortage of methods for effecting them. Some writers of the time condemned the practice, and some recommended it. "Let there be a law that no deformed child shall live," says Aristotle, "and if couples have children in excess, let abortion be procured before life and sense have begun."[1] The Hippocratic Oath proscribed the use of abortifacients (substances or devices for inducing abortions), a prohibition respected by many physicians but ignored by others.

The Hebrew and Christian scriptures do not denounce abortion and do not suggest that the fetus is a person. A passage in Exodus chapter 21 touches on the topic and implies that the unborn entity is not a full human being. The passage comes after the emphatic "You shall not murder" of the Ten Commandments and after a warning that the penalty for murder is death. But Exodus 21:22 says that if a man causes a woman to have a miscarriage "but [she] is not harmed in any other way," the penalty is just a fine. Causing the death of a fetus was not considered murder.

Christians have generally condemned abortion, though their ideas about the personhood of the fetus have changed through the centuries. Many contemporary Christians, especially Roman Catholics, assume that the unborn is a full human being from the moment of conception. But in the twelfth century, the church came to the view that an embryo cannot have a soul until several weeks after conception. The rationale, inspired by Aristotle, was that the unborn cannot have a soul until it is "formed"—that is, until it has a human shape, a stage that is reached long after conception. Thomas Aquinas accepted this view and maintained that male embryos are formed (and thus given a soul, or "ensouled") 40 days after conception; female embryos, 90 days. Thus, killing a fetus, though always sinful, is not murder until after it is formed. In 1312, this doctrine became the church's official position. Only in the late nineteenth century did the church decide that ensoulment happens at conception and that any abortion after that point is the killing of a human person.

---

[1] Aristotle, *Politics* VII, 16, 1335b.

FACTS AND FIGURES: Abortion

- In 2008, 1.21 million abortions were performed; in 2000, 1.31 million.
- Most Western industrialized countries have lower abortion rates than the United States does.
- Almost half of all pregnancies are unintended.
- Four in ten unintended pregnancies end in abortions.
- Each year, approximately 2 percent of women aged 15 to 44 have an abortion.
- 37 percent of women having abortions say they are Protestant; 28 percent, Catholic.
- 54 percent of women who have abortions had used contraception during the month they became pregnant.

- The risk of death associated with abortion is one death per million abortions performed at 8 weeks or earlier; one death in 29,000 abortions performed at 16 to 20 weeks; and one death per 11,000 performed at 21 weeks or later.[2]
- Less than 0.3 percent of women having abortions suffer medical complications requiring hospitalization.[3]
- Over 50 percent of women who have abortions are in their twenties; 18 percent are teenagers.

Data for the United States, compiled and developed by The Alan Guttmacher Institute, "Facts on Induced Abortion in the United States," August 2011, http://www.guttmacher.org/pubs/fb_induced_abortion.html#14 (22 February 2012). Some sources further specified in endnotes.

In English common law, abortion was considered a crime only if performed after **quickening** (when the mother first detects fetal movement). From its beginnings through the nineteenth century, American law mostly reflected this tradition. Accordingly, in the early 1800s, several states passed statutes outlawing abortion after quickening except to save the life of the mother. But in the next 100 years, abortion laws gradually became stricter, dropping the quickening cutoff point and banning all abortions but those thought to preserve the life (or rarely, the health) of the mother. The medical profession generally supported the tougher laws, and the views of physicians on abortion carried great weight.

In the 1950s, a trend toward liberalized laws began, and by 1970 the American Medical Association (AMA) and the American College of Obstetricians and Gynecologists were officially advocating less severe abortion policies. The latter declared that "It is recognized that abortion may be performed at a patient's request, or upon a physician's recommendation."[4] By that time, twelve states had amended their abortion statutes to make them less restrictive, and the public had warmed considerably to the idea of legalized abortion. The culmination of all these changes was the 1973 Supreme Court case of *Roe v. Wade*, which made abortions before viability legal.

[2] Bartlett, L. A., et al., "Risk Factors for Legal Induced Abortion-Related Mortality in the United States," *Obstetrics & Gynecology*, 2004, 103(4): 729–37.

[3] Henshaw, S. K., "Unintended Pregnancy and Abortion: A Public Health Perspective," in ed. M. Paul et al., *A Clinician's Guide to Medical and Surgical Abortion* (New York: Churchill Livingstone, 1999, 11–22); American College of Obstetricians and Gynecologists, *Induced Abortion*, June 2007.

[4] American College of Obstetricians and Gynecologists, *Standards for Obstetric-Gynecological Hospital Services* (Washington, D.C.: ACOG, August, 1970), 53; *Statement of Policy: Abortion* (Washington, DC: ACOG, August, 1970). Quoted in Albert R. Jonsen, *The Birth of Bioethics* (New York: Oxford University Press).

The abortion policies of previous eras were handicapped by poor understanding of human development. In modern times, however, the facts are clear: *fertilization*, or conception, happens when a sperm cell penetrates an egg, or ovum, forming a single cell known as a *zygote*, or conceptus. This meeting of sperm and egg usually takes place in one of the two fallopian tubes, the narrow tunnels linking the egg-producing ovaries with the uterus. For three to five days, the zygote moves down the fallopian tube to the uterus, dividing continually and thus getting larger along the way. In the fluid-filled uterus, it divides further, becoming a hollow sphere of cells known as a *blastocyst*. Within about five days, the blastocyst lodges firmly in the lining of the uterus (a feat called implantation) and is then known as an *embryo*.

The embryonic stage lasts until eight weeks after fertilization. During this time most of the embryo's internal organs form, the brain and spinal cord start to generate, and external features such as limbs and ears begin to appear. At eight weeks, though it is only about the size of a raspberry, the embryo has a rudimentary human shape.

From the end of the eighth week until birth, the unborn is technically known as a *fetus*. (In this text, however, we use the term to refer to the unborn at any stage from conception to birth.) At about fourteen weeks of pregnancy, doctors can determine the fetus's sex. Around 16 to 20 weeks, the mother can feel the fetus moving inside her. Quickening was once thought to be a threshold event in pregnancy, signaling ensoulment or the presence of a human being. But it is of doubtful importance (except to the mother) since the fetus moves undetected before quickening, and the mother's sensing fetal movement is not associated with any significant change in development. A more meaningful benchmark is **viability**, the development stage at approximately 23 to 24 weeks of pregnancy when the fetus may survive outside the uterus. Babies born at this point, however, are at a high risk of severe disabilities (mental retardation and blindness, among others) and death.

Development from fertilization to birth (called gestation) is nine months long, or about 40 weeks. This span of pregnancy is calculated from the first day of the woman's last menstrual period and is traditionally divided into three three-month intervals—first trimester (0–12 weeks), second trimester (13–24 weeks), and third trimester (25 weeks to delivery). Babies delivered in the third trimester but before thirty-seven weeks are considered premature.

Abortion is the ending of a pregnancy. Abortion due to natural causes—birth defect or injury, for example—is known as **spontaneous abortion** or miscarriage. The intentional termination of pregnancy through drugs or surgery is called **induced abortion** or, more commonly, simply abortion. Abortion in this sense is the issue over which most of the philosophical and judicial struggles are waged. Such is generally not the case for **therapeutic abortion**—abortion performed to preserve the life or health of the mother. Most people believe therapeutic abortion to be morally permissible.

Several methods are used to perform abortions, some of them surgical and some pharmaceutical. The method used depends on, among other things, the woman's health and the length of her pregnancy. The most common technique is known as *suction curettage* (also, *vacuum aspiration*), which is used in the first twelve weeks of pregnancy (when nearly 90 percent of abortions are performed). A doctor inserts a thin, bendable tube through the opening of the cervix into the uterus and, using a vacuum syringe or a machine or hand pump, suctions the contents of the uterus out through the tube. The method used most often after the first twelve weeks is *dilation and evacuation*. It involves widening the cervix and employing both suction and forceps to extract the fetus and placenta.

Abortions can be induced with drugs (often referred to as "medical abortions") but only in the first seven to nine weeks of pregnancy. The most common regimen uses two medications: mifepristone (RU-486, the so-called abortion pill) and misoprostol, a prosta-glandin (hormonelike substance). Mifepristone interferes with the hormone progesterone, thinning the lining of the uterus and preventing implantation of the embryo. Misoprostol prompts the uterus to contract, forcing the embryo out. A woman sees her physician to take mifepristone, then up to three days later takes misoprostol (either at home or in the physician's office). This two-step procedure causes abortion about 95 percent of the time.

The risk of complications (such as serious bleeding or internal injury) from abortion is low and varies directly with the length of pregnancy—the earlier an abortion is performed, the lower the risk. Less than 1 percent of women having early abortions experience complications; up to 2 percent of those having later abortions do.[5] Death is a risk in any surgical procedure; the risk of death associated with abortion is one death per million abortions performed at eight weeks or earlier, one death in 29,000 abortions performed at 16–20 weeks, and one death per 11,000 performed at 21 weeks or later.[6] The chances of a woman dying in childbirth is at least ten times higher than the risk of dying from an early abortion.[7]

Half of women having abortions are under twenty-five years old, 33 percent are age twenty to twenty-four, and 17 percent are teenagers. Two-thirds of abortions are performed on women who have never married.[8]

Their reasons for terminating a pregnancy are varied. According to a recent survey of women who had abortions, the reasons include:

- Having a baby would change my life (interfere with education, employment, etc.).—74 percent
- I can't afford a baby now (I'm unmarried, unemployed, destitute, etc.).—73 percent
- I don't want to be a single mother, or I'm having relationship problems.—48 percent
- My relationship or marriage may break up soon.—11 percent
- I've already completed my childbearing.—38 percent
- My husband or partner wants me to have an abortion.—14 percent
- There are possible problems affecting the health of the fetus.—13 percent

---

[5] American College of Obstetricians and Gynecologists, *Induced Abortion*, June 2007; Henshaw, S. K., "Unintended Pregnancy and Abortion: A Public Health Perspective," in ed. M. Paul et al., *A Clinician's Guide to Medical and Surgical Abortion* (New York: Churchill Livingstone, 1999, 11–22); American College of Obstetricians and Gynecologists, *Induced Abortion*, June 2007.
[6] Bartlett, L. A., et al., "Risk Factors for Legal Induced Abortion-Related Mortality in the United States," *Obstetrics & Gynecology*, 2004, 103(4): 729–737.
[7] D. A. Grimes, "Estimation of Pregnancy-Related Mortality Risk by Pregnancy Outcome, United States, 1991–1999," *American Journal of Obstetrics & Gynecology*, 2006, 194(1): 92–94; American College of Obstetricians and Gynecologists, *Induced Abortion*, June 2007.
[8] Data from the Centers for Disease Control and Prevention, compiled and developed in R. K. Jones et al., "Abortion in the United States: Incidence and Access to Services, 2005," *Perspectives on Sexual and Reproductive Health*, 2008.

- There are physical problems with my health.—12 percent
- I was a victim of rape.—1 percent
- I became pregnant as a result of incest.—less than 0.5 percent[9]

Polls gauging the attitudes of the American public toward abortion have revealed many divisions but also remarkable agreement on some points. Only a small minority of people (5–20 percent) think that abortion should be illegal or unavailable in all circumstances. Most reject a total ban but differ on the existence or extent of restrictions placed on abortion. Roughly half consider themselves to be "pro-life," and half "pro-choice." A sizable majority would not like to see *Roe v. Wade* completely overturned.[10]

The legal conflicts over abortion have influenced the ethical arguments, and vice versa. The former seized the attention of the nation when *Roe v. Wade* was handed down. Roe was "Jane Roe," a.k.a. Norma McCorvey, who had sought a nontherapeutic abortion in Texas where she lived. But Texas law forbade all abortions except those necessary to save the mother's life. So Roe sued the state of Texas in federal court, which ruled that the law was unconstitutional. Texas appealed the decision to the U.S. Supreme Court, and the Court sided with the federal court, declaring in *Roe v. Wade* that no state can ban abortions that are performed before viability.

The Court saw in the Constitution (most notably the Fourteenth Amendment, which grants due process and equal protection under the law) a guaranteed right of personal privacy that limits interference by the state in people's private lives, and the majority believed that the right encompassed a woman's decision to terminate her pregnancy. But, the Court noted, "this right is not unqualified and must be considered against important state interests in regulation." So it balanced the woman's right and state interests according to trimester of pregnancy. In the first trimester, the woman's right to end her pregnancy cannot be curtailed by the state. Her decision must be respected, and "its effectuation must be left to the medical judgment of the pregnant woman's attending physician." In the second trimester, the state may limit—but not entirely prohibit—the woman's right by regulating abortion for the sake of her health. After viability, the state may regulate and even ban abortion except when it's necessary to preserve her life or health. The Court affirmed that its ruling "leaves the State free to place increasing restrictions on abortion as the period of pregnancy lengthens, so long as those restrictions are tailored to the recognized state interests."

The Court noted that the Constitution does not define "person" and that "the word 'person,' as used in the Fourteenth Amendment, does not include the unborn." In fact, the law has never maintained that the unborn are persons "in the whole sense."

After this historic case, the Supreme Court handed down numerous other decisions that circumscribed, but did not invalidate, the right to abortion defined in *Roe*. In these rulings, the Court held that (1) a woman can be required to give her written informed consent to abortion, (2) the government is not obliged to use taxpayer money to fund abortion services, (3) parental consent or a judge's authorization can be demanded of minors under age eighteen who seek abortions, (4) a state can forbid the use of public facilities to perform abortions (except to save the woman's life), (5) a woman who consents to an

---

[9] Lawrence B. Finer, et al., "Reasons U.S. Women Have Abortions: Quantitative and Qualitative Perspectives," *Perspectives on Sexual and Reproductive Health*, 2005, 37(3):110–18.
[10] Several polls including Gallup Poll, May 10–13, 2007.

PUBLIC OPINION: **Abortion**

"Do you think abortion should be legal in all cases, legal in most cases, illegal in most cases, or illegal in all cases?"

Legal in all cases	Legal in most cases	Illegal in most cases	Illegal in all cases	Unsure
19%	35%	30%	15%	2%

ABC News/*Washington Post* Poll. July 14–17, 2011. N=1,001 adults nationwide. Margin of error ± 3.5.

"Which of these comes closest to your view? Abortion should be generally available to those who want it. OR, Abortion should be available, but under stricter limits than it is now. OR, Abortion should not be permitted."

Generally available	Available under stricter limits	Not permitted	Unsure
37%	37%	23%	4%

CBS News/*New York Times* Poll. Jan. 12–17, 2012. N=1,154 adults nationwide. Margin of error ± 3.

"On the issue of abortion, would you say you are more pro-life or more pro-choice?"

Pro-Life	Pro-Choice	Both/Mix	Unsure
50%	42%	5%	3%

FOX News/Opinion Dynamics Poll. Jan. 18–19, 2011. N=900 registered voters nationwide. Margin of error ± 3.

abortion can be required to wait twenty-four hours before the procedure is performed, and (6) a state can mandate that a woman be given abortion information. Eventually the Court came to a key doctrine concerning such limitations: before viability, abortion can be restricted in many ways as long as the constraints do not amount to an "undue burden" on a woman trying to get an abortion. A state regulation constitutes an undue burden if it "has the purpose or effect of placing a substantial obstacle in the path of a woman seeking an abortion of a nonviable fetus."

Abortions performed late in pregnancy using a controversial surgical procedure have been the flashpoint for intense debate, legislative action, and court rulings. The procedure is known technically as *intact dilation and extraction* (D&X) and disparagingly as *partial-birth abortion*. Physicians use the first term; abortion opponents tend to use the latter. Late-term abortions are performed after the twentieth week of gestation and are uncommon, comprising around 1 percent of all abortions. Some women have them to protect their life or health and some to avoid having a severely impaired infant. Others have late abortions because they would not or could not have them earlier (these include teenagers, the poor, drug addicts, and women who were unaware of their pregnancy).

In 2003 President Bush signed the Partial-Birth Abortion Ban Act, which outlawed a type of late-term abortion. Several federal courts, however, declared the law unconstitutional because it lacks a "health exception" for women whose health is threatened. In 2007 the U.S. Supreme Court upheld the law, effectively banning D&X abortions (and arguably some other late-term procedures).

People generally take one of three positions on the moral permissibility of abortion. The conservative view is that abortion is never morally acceptable (except possibly to preserve the mother's life), for the unborn is a human being in the full sense. The liberal view is that abortion is acceptable whenever the woman wants it, for the unborn is not a human being in the full sense. The moderate stance falls between these two stands, rejecting both the conservative's zero-tolerance for abortion and the liberal's idea of abortion on request. For the moderate, some—but not all—abortions may be morally justified. (These labels are common but sometimes misleading; being a conservative or liberal on the abortion issue does not necessarily mean you are a conservative or liberal in the broader political sense.)

KEY TERMS

abortion

spontaneous abortion

induced abortion

therapeutic abortion

quickening

viability

ARGUMENTS AND READINGS

I. WARREN'S PERSONHOOD ARGUMENT FOR ABORTION

The liberal says that the unborn is not a person, not a full human being, and therefore does not have a right to life. If the unborn is a person, then killing it would be murder, and its right to life would be at least as weighty as the mother's. How can the liberal show that fetuses are not persons?

To start, the liberal will insist that merely being a *Homo sapiens*—a creature with human DNA—is not sufficient for personhood. To think so is to be guilty of a kind of prejudice called *speciesism*. The liberal argues that since whatever properties make us persons (and thus grant us a right to life) could conceivably be manifested by a nonhuman species, merely being a member of the human species cannot be sufficient for personhood status. If we assume that an entity is a person just because it happens to belong to our favored biological classification, we stand convicted of speciesism, close cousin to racism. There are properties that do qualify an entity as a person, but simply being human is not one of them.

The liberal tack is to identify these traits and point out that a fetus does not possess them. In "On the Moral and Legal Status of Abortion," Mary Anne Warren famously identifies five traits that are "most central" to personhood: (1) consciousness and the capacity to feel pain, (2) reasoning, (3) self-motivated activity, (4) the capacity to communicate, and (5) "the presence of self-concepts, and self-awareness, either individual or racial or both." To be considered a person, she says, a being need not possess all these traits, but surely "any being which satisfies *none* of (1)–(5) is certainly not a person." She argues that a fetus in fact satisfies none and is therefore not yet a person and "cannot coherently be said to have full moral rights."[11]

The conservative will counter that the liberal's standards for personhood are set too high, for they imply that cognitively impaired individuals—victims of serious dementia, retardation, or schizophrenia, for instance—are not persons and therefore do not have a right to life. The liberal view seems to condone the killing of these unfortunates, a repugnant implication. The liberal response is that even if cognitively impaired individuals do not qualify as persons, we may still have good reasons for not killing them—for example, because people value them or because a policy allowing them to be killed would be harmful to society (perhaps encouraging unnecessary killings or causing a general devaluing of life). In addition, the liberal points out that the personhood status of many (or most) cognitively impaired individuals is unclear, so a policy of regarding them as less than persons would be risky.

Perhaps the biggest challenge to the liberal notion of personhood is the charge that it sanctions infanticide. The argument is that if killing a fetus is morally permissible because it is not a person, then killing an infant must be acceptable as well, for it is not a person either. According to the liberal's personhood criteria mentioned earlier, neither a fetus nor an infant is a person. Moreover, there is a glaring problem with the common liberal assumption that birth is the point at which a fetus becomes a person: the fetus just before birth and the infant just after are biologically almost indistinguishable. Saying that the former has no right to life but the latter does seems hard to justify.

Liberals contend that even if infants are not persons, infanticide is rarely permissible (possible exceptions include cases of horrendous birth defects and terminal illness). Warren contends that that this is so because infants, though not persons, do have some moral standing:

> In this country, and in this period of history, the deliberate killing of viable newborns is virtually never justified. This is in part because neonates are so very *close* to being persons that to kill them requires a very strong moral justification—as does the killing of dolphins, whales, chimpanzees, and other highly personlike creatures. It is certainly wrong to kill such beings just for the sake of convenience, or financial profit, or "sport."[12]

---

[11] Mary Anne Warren, "On the Moral and Legal Status of Abortion," *The Monist*, vol. 57., no. 1, 1973, 43–61.

[12] Mary Anne Warren, "Postscript on Infanticide," in *The Problem of Abortion*, 2nd ed., ed. Joel Feinberg (Belmont, CA: Wadsworth, 1984).

On the Moral and Legal Status of Abortion

MARY ANNE WARREN

The question which we must answer in order to produce a satisfactory solution to the problem of the moral status of abortion is this: How are we to define the moral community, the set of beings with full and equal moral rights, such that we can decide whether a human fetus is a member of this community or not? What sort of entity, exactly, has the inalienable rights to life, liberty, and the pursuit of happiness? Jefferson attributed these rights to all *men*, and it may or may not be fair to suggest that he intended to attribute them *only* to men. Perhaps he ought to have attributed them to all human beings. If so, then we arrive, first, at Noonan's problem of defining what makes a being human, and, second, at the equally vital question which Noonan does not consider, namely, What reason is there for identifying the moral community with the set of all human beings, in whatever way we have chosen to define that term?

1. ON THE DEFINITION OF "HUMAN"

One reason why this vital second question is so frequently overlooked in the debate over the moral status of abortion is that the term "human" has two distinct, but not often distinguished, senses. This fact results in a slide of meaning, which serves to conceal the fallaciousness of the traditional argument that since (1) it is wrong to kill innocent human beings, and (2) fetuses are innocent human beings, then (3) it is wrong to kill fetuses. For if "human" is used in the same sense in both (1) and (2) then, whichever of the two senses is meant, one of these premises is question-begging. And if it is used in two different senses then of course the conclusion doesn't follow.

Thus, (1) is a self-evident moral truth, and avoids begging the question about abortion, only if "human being" is used to mean something like "a full-fledged member of the moral community." (It may or may not also be meant to refer exclusively to members of the species *Homo sapiens*.) We may call this the *moral* sense of "human." It is not to be confused with what we will call the *genetic* sense, i.e., the sense in which *any* member of the species is a human being, and no member of any other species could be. If (1) is acceptable only if the moral sense is intended, (2) is nonquestion-begging only if what is intended is the genetic sense.

In "Deciding Who Is Human," Noonan argues for the classification of fetuses with human beings by pointing to the presence of the full genetic code, and the potential capacity for rational thought. It is clear that what he needs to show, for his version of the traditional argument to be valid, is that fetuses are human in the moral sense, the sense in which it is analytically true that all human beings have full moral rights. But, in the absence of any argument showing that whatever is genetically human is also morally human, and he gives none, nothing more than genetic humanity can be demonstrated by the presence of the human genetic code. And, as we will see, the *potential* capacity for rational thought can at most show that an entity has the potential for *becoming* human in the moral sense.

2. DEFINING THE MORAL COMMUNITY

Can it be established that genetic humanity is sufficient for moral humanity? I think that there are very good reasons for not defining the moral community in this way. I would like to suggest an alternative way of defining the moral community, which I will argue for only to the extent of explaining why it is, or should be, self-evident. The suggestion is simply that the moral community consists of all and only *people*, rather than all and only human beings; and probably the best way of demonstrating its self-evidence is by considering the concept of personhood, to see what sorts of entity are and are not persons, and what the decision that a being is or is not a person implies about its moral rights.

What characteristics entitle an entity to be considered a person? This is obviously not the place to attempt a complete analysis of the concept of personhood, but we do not need such a fully adequate analysis just to determine whether and why a fetus is or isn't a person. All we need is a rough and approximate list of the most basic criteria of personhood, and some idea of which, or how many, of these an entity must satisfy in order to properly be considered a person.

In searching for such criteria, it is useful to look beyond the set of people with whom we are acquainted, and ask how we would decide whether a totally alien being was a person or not. (For we have no right to assume that genetic humanity is necessary for personhood.) Imagine a space traveler who lands on an unknown planet and encounters a race of beings utterly unlike any he has ever seen or heard of. If he wants to be sure of behaving morally toward these beings, he has to somehow decide whether they are people, and hence have full moral rights, or whether they are the sort of thing which he need not feel guilty about treating as, for example, a source of food.

How should he go about making this decision? If he has some anthropological background, he might look for such things as religion, art, and the manufacturing of tools, weapons, or shelters, since these factors have been used to distinguish our human from our prehuman ancestors, in what seems to be closer to the moral than the genetic sense of "human." And no doubt he would be right to consider the presence of such factors as good evidence that the alien beings were people, and morally human. It would, however, be overly anthropocentric of him to take the absence of these things as adequate evidence that they were not, since we can imagine people who have progressed beyond, or evolved without ever developing, these cultural characteristics.

I suggest that the traits which are most central to the concept of personhood, or humanity in the moral sense, are, very roughly, the following:

1. Consciousness (of objects and events external and/or internal to the being), and in particular the capacity to feel pain;

2. Reasoning (the *developed* capacity to solve new and relatively complex problems);
3. Self-motivated activity (activity which is relatively independent of either genetic or direct external control);
4. The capacity to communicate, by whatever means, messages of an indefinite variety of types, that is, not just with an indefinite number of possible contents, but on indefinitely many possible topics;
5. The presence of self-concepts, and self-awareness, either individual or racial, or both.

Admittedly, there are apt to be a great many problems involved in formulating precise definitions of these criteria, let alone in developing universally valid behavioral criteria for deciding when they apply. But I will assume that both we and our explorer know approximately what (1)–(5) mean, and that he is also able to determine whether or not they apply. How, then, should he use his findings to decide whether or not the alien beings are people? We needn't suppose that an entity must have *all* of these attributes to be properly considered a person; (1) and (2) alone may well be sufficient for personhood, and quite probably (1)–(3) are sufficient. Neither do we need to insist that any one of these criteria is *necessary* for personhood, although once again (1) and (2) look like fairly good candidates for necessary conditions, as does (3), if "activity" is construed so as to include the activity of reasoning.

All we need to claim, to demonstrate that a fetus is not a person, is that any being which satisfies *none* of (1)–(5) is certainly not a person. I consider this claim to be so obvious that I think anyone who denied it, and claimed that a being which satisfied *none* of (1)–(5) was a person all the same, would thereby demonstrate that he had no notion at all of what a person is—perhaps because he had confused the concept of a person with that of genetic humanity. If the opponents of abortion were to deny the appropriateness of these five criteria, I do not know what further arguments would convince them. We would probably have to admit that our conceptual schemes were indeed irreconcilably different, and that our dispute could not be settled objectively.

I do not expect this to happen, however, since I think that the concept of a person is one which is very nearly universal (to people), and that it is common to both proabortionists and antiabortionists, even though neither group has fully realized the relevance of this concept to the resolution of their dispute. Furthermore, I think that on reflection even the antiabortioninsts ought to agree not only that (1)–(5) are central to the concept of personhood, but also that it is a part of this concept that all and only people have full moral rights. The concept of a person is in part a moral concept; once we have admitted that x is a person we have recognized, even if we have not agreed to respect, x's right to be treated as a member of the moral community. It is true that the claim that *x is a human being* is more commonly voiced as part of an appeal to treat x decently than is the claim that x is a person, but this is either because "human being" is here used in the sense which implies personhood, or because the genetic and moral senses of "human" have been confused.

Now if (1)–(5) are indeed the primary criteria of personhood, then it is clear that genetic humanity is neither necessary nor sufficient for establishing that an entity is a person. Some human beings are not people, and there may well be people who are not human beings. A man or woman whose consciousness has been permanently obliterated but who remains alive is a human being which is no longer a person; defective human beings, with no appreciable mental capacity, are not and presumably never will be people, and a fetus is a human being which is not yet a person, and which therefore cannot coherently be said to have full moral rights. Citizens of the next century should be prepared to recognize highly advanced, self-aware robots or computers, should such be developed, and intelligent inhabitants of other worlds, should such be found, as people in the fullest sense, and to respect their moral rights. But to ascribe full moral rights to an entity which is not a person is as absurd as to ascribe moral obligations and responsibilities to such an entity.

3. FETAL DEVELOPMENT AND THE RIGHT TO LIFE

Two problems arise in the application of these suggestions for the definition of the moral community to the determination of the precise moral status of a human fetus. Given that the paradigm example of a person is a normal adult human being, then (1) How like this paradigm, in particular how far advanced since conception, does a human being need to be before it begins to have a right to life by virtue, not of being fully a person as of yet, but of being *like* a person? and (2) To what extent, if any, does the fact that a fetus has the *potential* for becoming a person endow it with some of the same rights? Each of these questions requires some comment.

In answering the first question, we need not attempt a detailed consideration of the moral rights of organisms which are not developed enough, aware enough, intelligent enough, etc., to be considered people, but which resemble people in some respects. It does seem reasonable to suggest that the more like a person, in the relevant respects, a being is, the stronger is the case for regarding it as having a right to life, and indeed the stronger its right to life is. Thus we ought to take seriously the suggestion that, insofar as "the human individual develops biologically in a continuous fashion…the rights of a human person might develop in the same way." But we must keep in mind that the attributes which are relevant in determining whether or not an entity is enough like a person to be regarded as having some of the same moral rights are no different from those which are relevant to determining whether or not it is fully a person—i.e., are no different from (1)–(5)—and that being genetically human, or having recognizably human facial and other physical features, or detectable brain activity, or the capacity to survive outside the uterus, are simply not among these relevant attributes.

Thus it is clear that even though a seven- or eight-month fetus has features which make it apt to arouse in us almost the same powerful protective instinct as is commonly aroused by a small infant, nevertheless it is not significantly more personlike than is a very small embryo. It is *somewhat* more personlike; it can apparently feel and respond to pain, and it may even have a rudimentary form of consciousness, insofar as its brain is quite active. Nevertheless, it seems safe to say that it is not fully conscious, in the way that an infant of a few months is, and that it cannot reason, or communicate messages of indefinitely many sorts, does not engage in self-motivated activity, and has no self-awareness. Thus, in the *relevant* respects, a fetus, even a fully developed one, is considerably less personlike than is the average mature mammal, indeed the average fish. And I think that a rational person must conclude that if the right to life of a fetus is to be based upon its resemblance to a person, then it cannot be said to have any more right to life than, let us say, a newborn guppy (which also seems to be capable of feeling pain), and that a right of that magnitude could never override a woman's right to obtain an abortion, at any stage of her pregnancy.

There may, of course, be other arguments in favor of placing legal limits upon the stage of pregnancy in which an abortion may be performed. Given the relative safety of the new techniques of artificially inducing labor during the third trimester, the danger to the woman's life or health is no longer such an argument. Neither is the fact that people tend to respond to the thought of abortion in the later stages of pregnancy with emotional repulsion, since mere emotional responses cannot take the place of moral reasoning in determining what ought to be permitted. Nor, finally, is the frequently heard argument that legalizing abortion, especially late in the pregnancy, may erode the level of respect for human life, leading, perhaps, to an increase in unjustified euthanasia and other crimes. For this threat, if it is a threat, can be better met by educating people to the kinds of moral distinctions which we are making here than by limiting access to abortion (which limitation may, in its disregard for the rights of women, be just as damaging to the level of respect for human rights).

Thus, since the fact that even a fully developed fetus is not personlike enough to have any significant right to life on the basis of its personlikeness shows that no legal restrictions upon the stage of pregnancy in which an abortion may be performed can be justified on the grounds that we should protect the rights of the older fetus, and since there is no other apparent justification for such restrictions, we may conclude that they are entirely unjustified. Whether or not it would be *indecent* (whatever that means) for a woman in her seventh month to obtain an abortion just to avoid having to postpone a trip to Europe, it would not, in itself, be *immoral*, and therefore it ought to be permitted.

4. POTENTIAL PERSONHOOD AND THE RIGHT TO LIFE

We have seen that a fetus does not resemble a person in any way which can support the claim that it has even some of the same rights. But what about its *potential*, the fact that if nurtured and allowed to develop naturally it will very probably become a person? Doesn't that alone give it at least some right to life? It is hard to deny that the fact that an entity is a potential person is a strong prima facie reason for not destroying it; but we need not conclude from this that a potential person has a right to life, by virtue of the potential. It may be that our feeling that it is better, other things being equal, not to destroy a potential person is better explained by the fact that potential people are still (felt to be) an invaluable resource, not to be lightly squandered. Surely, if every speck of dust were a potential person, we would be much less apt to conclude that every potential person has a right to become actual.

Still, we do not need to insist that a potential person has no right to life whatever. There may well be something immoral, and not just imprudent, about wantonly destroying potential people, when doing so isn't necessary to protect anyone's rights. But even if a potential person does have some *prima facie* right to life, such a right could not possibly outweigh the right of a woman to obtain an abortion, since the rights of any actual person invariably outweigh those of any potential person, whenever the two conflict. Since this may not be immediately obvious in the case of a human fetus, let us look at another case.

Suppose that our space explorer falls into the hands of an alien culture, whose scientists decide to create a few hundred thousand or more human beings, by breaking his body into its component cells, and using these to create fully developed human beings, with, of course, his genetic code. We may imagine that each of these newly created men will have all of the original man's abilities, skills, knowledge, and so on, and also have an individual self-concept, in short that each of them will be a bona fide (though hardly unique) person. Imagine that the whole project will take only seconds, and that its chances of success are extremely high, and that our explorer knows all of this, and also knows that these people will be treated fairly. I maintain that in such a situation he would have every right to escape if he could, and thus to deprive all of these potential people of their potential lives; for his right to life outweighs all of theirs together, in spite of the fact that they are all genetically human, all innocent, and all have a very high probability of becoming people very soon, if only he refrains from acting.

Indeed, I think he would have a right to escape even if it were not his life which the alien scientists planned to take, but only a year of his freedom, or, indeed, only a day. Nor would he be obligated to stay if he had gotten captured (thus bringing all these people-potentials into existence) because of his own carelessness, or even if he had done so deliberately, knowing the consequences. Regardless of how he got captured, he is not morally obligated to remain in captivity for *any* period of time for the sake of permitting any number of potential people to come into actuality, so great is the margin by which one actual person's right to liberty outweighs whatever

right to life even a hundred thousand potential people have. And it seems reasonable to conclude that the rights of a woman will outweigh by a similar margin whatever right to life a fetus may have by virtue of its potential personhood.

Thus, neither a fetus's resemblance to a person, nor its potential for becoming a person provides any basis whatever for the claim that it has any significant right to life. Consequently, a woman's right to protect her health, happiness, freedom, and even her life, by terminating an unwanted pregnancy, will always override whatever right to life it may be appropriate to ascribe to a fetus, even a fully developed one. And thus, in the absence of any overwhelming social need for every possible child, the laws which restrict the right to obtain an abortion, or limit the period of pregnancy during which an abortion may be performed, are a wholly unjustified violation of a woman's most basic moral and constitutional rights.

The Being in the Womb Is a Person

STEPHEN SCHWARZ

A THEORY ABOUT HUMAN BEINGS AND PERSONS

Let us now examine a theory that defends abortion on the grounds that the child in the womb, though undoubtedly a human being, is not a person, and that it is only the killing of persons that is intrinsically and seriously wrong. The theory consists of two major theses: First, that killing human beings is not wrong; second, that the child (in the womb and for a time after birth) is human but not a person. I shall argue that both of these theses are mistaken.

This theory recognizes that abortion is the deliberate killing of an innocent human being, but it denies this is wrong because it denies that it is wrong to deliberately kill human beings. What *is* wrong is killing human beings who are persons. Now, of course, many human beings are persons,

for example, normal adult human beings, and it is wrong to kill them because they are persons. But small infants, such as newborn babies or babies in the womb, though they are undoubtedly human, are not, according to this theory, persons. And so it is not intrinsically wrong to kill them. That is, it is not wrong in itself, though it may be wrong because of adverse consequences. A small child, therefore, has no right to life as a normal adult does, and if the child is unwanted, he may be killed.

Thus, the theory allows for abortion and infanticide alike. It rejects the typical pro-abortion lines, such as viability and birth. It agrees that there is no morally significant difference between "before" and

Reprinted by permission of Stephen D. Schwarz.

"after." But instead of saying that killing a human being is *wrong* on both sides of such a line, it claims that it is *right* (or can be right) on both sides of the line.

Joseph Fletcher expresses this view when he remarks, "I would support the…position…that both abortion and infanticide can be justified if and when the good to be gained outweighs the evil—that neither abortion nor infanticide is as such immoral."

Michael Tooley has an essay entitled, "A Defense of Abortion and Infanticide." If the idea that killing babies is morally right is shocking to most people, Tooley replies in his essay that this is merely an emotional response, not a reasoned one. "The response, rather than appealing to carefully formulated moral principles, is primarily visceral," he says. And, "It is reasonable to suspect that one is dealing with a taboo rather than with a rational prohibition." His position is: "Since I do not believe human infants are persons, but only potential persons, and since I think that the destruction of potential persons is a morally neutral action, the correct conclusion seems to me to be that infanticide is in itself morally acceptable."

I want to show that the theories held by Fletcher, Tooley, and others are absolutely wrong. Infanticide and abortion are both morally wrong, as wrong as the deliberate killing of an older child or an adult, and thus our emotional response of shock and horror at killing babies is completely grounded in reason and moral principles. I want to show that a small child, after birth or still in the womb, *is* a person, as much a person as the rest of us; that the notion of person as used by these writers is a special one, a narrower concept, and not the one that is crucial for morality. I want to make clear why the attempts to show that a small child is not a person are mistaken, and that all human beings as such are persons.

ARGUMENT OF MARY ANN WARREN

In an argument for this theory, Mary Ann Warren examines "the traditional argument that since (1) it is wrong to kill innocent human beings, and (2) fetuses are innocent human beings, then (3) it is wrong to kill fetuses." This argument, she claims, is "fallacious," because "the term 'human' has two distinct, but not often distinguished, senses. In premise

one, human means person, or full-fledged member of the moral community, a being whom it is wrong to kill. In premise two, on the other hand, the term human refers merely to a member of the biological species human, as opposed, say, to a rabbit or an eagle. Warren's claim is that mere membership in a biological species is morally irrelevant and thus does not confer on the being in question a right to life.

"Yes, a fetus is biologically human (human in the genetic sense), but that does not make it the kind of being who has a right to life. It is only persons (those who are human in the moral sense) who have such a right. It is wrong to kill persons, and if a human being is not also a person he does not have a right to life, and it is, or often can be, morally right to destroy him." This, in essence, is Warren's argument.

Warren offers an analysis of what is a person, a full-fledged member of the moral community:

I suggest that the traits which are most central to the concept of personhood, or humanity in the moral sense, are, very roughly, the following:

1. consciousness (of objects and events external and/or internal to the being), and in particular the capacity to feel pain;

2. reasoning (the *developed* capacity to solve new and relatively complex problems);

3. self-motivated activity (activity which is relatively independent of either genetic or direct external control);

4. the capacity to communicate, by whatever means, messages of an indefinite variety of types, that is, not just with an indefinite number of possible contents, but on indefinitely many possible topics;

5. the presence of self-concepts, and self-awareness, either individual or racial, or both.

This, she acknowledges, is not a full analysis of the concept of a person. It is not a list of necessary and sufficient conditions for being a person. But, she says, this does not matter.

All we need to claim, to demonstrate that a fetus is not a person, is that any being which satisfies *none* of (1)–(5) is certainly not a person. I consider this claim to be so obvious that I think anyone who denied it, and claimed that a being which satisfied none of (1)–(5) was a person all the same, would thereby demonstrate that he had no notion at all of what a person is—perhaps because he had confused the concept of a person with that of genetic humanity.

We can now see Warren's argument for abortion in its entirety. A fetus is human in the genetic sense; that is morally irrelevant. A fetus is not human in the moral sense: he is not a person since he satisfies none of the criteria she has outlined. Not being a person, he has no right to life, and abortion is morally permissible. The same applies to the child after birth. "Killing a newborn infant isn't murder." Infanticide is wrong, according to Warren, only to the extent that the child is wanted, that there are couples who would like to adopt or keep him. "Thus, infanticide is wrong for reasons analogous to those which make it wrong to wantonly destroy natural resources, or great works of art."

But destroying natural resources or works of art is not always wrong, and certainly not wrong in the sense in which murder is wrong. Warren acknowledges this when she says, "It follows from my argument that when an unwanted or defective infant is born into a society which cannot afford and/or is not willing to care for it, then its destruction is permissible."

BEING A PERSON AND FUNCTIONING AS A PERSON

The failure of Warren's argument can be seen in light of the distinction between being a person and functioning as a person. Consider Warren's five characteristics of a person: consciousness, reasoning, self-motivated activity, the capacity to communicate, and the presence of self-concepts. Imagine a person in a deep, dreamless sleep. She is not conscious, she cannot reason, etc.; she lacks all five of these traits. She is not functioning as a person; that is part of what being asleep means. But of course she is a person, she retains fully her status of being a person, and killing her while asleep is just as wrong as killing her while she is awake and functioning as a person.

Functioning as a person refers to all the activities proper to persons as persons, to thinking in the broadest sense. It includes reasoning, deciding, imagining, talking, experiencing love and beauty, remembering, intending, and much more. The term *function* does not refer here to bodily functions, but rather to those of the mind, though certain bodily functions, especially those of the brain, are necessary conditions for functioning as a person.

When Warren points out that a fetus satisfies none of the five traits she mentions, she shows only that a fetus does not function as a person, not that it lacks the being of a person, which is the crucial thing.

At this point several objections are likely to be raised: First, the sleeping person will soon wake up and function as a person, while the being in the womb will not.

In reply, neither the sleeping person nor the being in the womb now display the qualities of a functioning person. Both will display them. It is only a matter of time. Why should the one count as a real person because the time is short, while the other does not, simply because in her case the time is longer?

Second, the sleeping adult was already self-conscious, had already solved some problems. Therefore, she has a history of functioning as a person. The child in the womb has no such history. Thus Tooley argues that "an organism cannot have a serious right to life [be a person] unless it either now possesses, or did possess at some time in the past, the concept of a self…[what is required for functioning as a person]." The human being sound asleep counts as a person because she once functioned as a person; the child never did, so she does not count as a person.

True, there is a difference with respect to past functioning, but the difference is not morally relevant. The reason the child never functioned as a person is because her capacity to do so is not yet sufficiently developed. It cannot be, for she is near the beginning of her existence, in the first phase of her life.

Imagine a case of two children. One is born comatose, and he will remain so until the age of nine. The other is healthy at birth, but as soon as she achieves the concept of a continuing self for a brief time, she, too, lapses into a coma, from which she will not emerge until she is nine. Can anyone seriously hold that the second child is a person with a right to life, while the first child is not? In one case, self-awareness will come only after nine years have elapsed, in the other, it will return. In both cases, self-awareness will grow and develop. Picture the two unconscious children lying side by side. Almost nine years have passed. Would it not be absurd to say that only one of them is a person, that there is some essential, morally relevant, difference between them? Imagine someone about to kill both of them. Consistent with his theory, Tooley would have to say: "You may kill the first, for he is not a person. He is human only in the genetic sense, since he has no history of functioning as a person. You may not kill the second, since she does have such a history." If this distinction is absurd when applied to the two born human beings, is it any less absurd when applied to two human beings, one born (asleep in a bed), the other preborn (sleeping in the womb)?

In short, when it comes to functioning as a person, there is no moral difference between "did, but does not" (the sleeping adult) and "does not, but will." (the small child).

Third, a sleeping person has the capacity to function as a person and therefore counts as being a person, even though this capacity is not now actualized. In contrast, a child in the womb lacks this capacity, so he does not count as being a person.

This is the most fundamental objection, and probably underlies the preceding two objections. In considering it, compare the following beings:

A. A normal adult, sound asleep, not conscious.
B. An adult in a coma from which he will emerge in, say, six months and function normally as a person.
C. A normal newborn baby.
D. A normal baby soon to be born.
E. A normal "well proportioned small scale baby" in the womb at seven weeks.
F. A normal embryo or zygote.

Case A, the normal adult sound asleep, is someone who has the being of a person, who is not now functioning as a person, and who clearly has the capacity to function as a person. I want to show now that all the other cases are essentially similar to this one. That is, if case A is a person—a full-fledged member of the moral community, a being with a right to life, whose value lies in his own being

and dignity, and not merely in his significance for others (like natural resources and works of art), a being whose willful destruction is murder—each of the other cases is a person as well.

The objection claims that the being in the womb lacks the capacity to function as a person. True, it lacks what I shall call the *present immediate capacity* to function, where responses may be immediately elicited. Such a capacity means the capability of functioning, where such a capability varies enormously among people, and normally develops and grows (as a result of learning and other experiences).

The capability of functioning as a person is grounded in the *basic inherent capacity* to function. This is proper to the being of a person and it has a physical basis, typically the brain and nervous system. It is a capacity that grows and develops as the child grows and develops.

This basic inherent capacity may be fully accessible, as in a normal sleeping adult. It then exists in its present immediate form. It may also exist in other forms where it is latent, as in reversible coma. I shall call this the latent-1 capacity, where the basic inherent capacity is present but temporally damaged or blocked. In a small child, the basic inherent capacity is there but insufficiently developed for the child to function in the manner of a normal adult. I shall call this the latent-2 capacity.

Let me turn to the actual refutation of this objection. I will begin with cases A through E (replies 1 and 2), then case F (3), then abnormal or handicapped human beings (4).

(1) The beings on our list, A through E, differ only with respect to their present immediate capacity to function. They are all essentially similar with respect to their basic inherent capacity, and through this, their being as persons.

Thus the adult in a coma, case B, is not essentially different from the sleeping person in case A. Person B is in a deep, deep sleep; person A in a comparatively superficial sleep. Person B cannot be awakened easily; person A can be. Person B is in a very long sleep; person A is in a short sleep, say 8 hours. Both have the basic inherent capacity: in A it is present immediate; in B it is latent-1. That is certainly not a morally relevant difference. If the status of persons is to be viewed in terms of capacity to function as a person, then surely a latent-1 capacity (temporarily blocked—person B) qualifies as much as a non-latent capacity (present immediate—person A).

Consider now the newborn baby, case C. He too has the physical basis for functioning as a person (brain, nervous system, etc.). Only his overall development is insufficient for him to actually function on the level of the normal adult. He has a latent-2 capacity. Thus there is an essential similarity between cases B and C, the adult in a coma and the newborn baby. Neither has the present immediate capacity to function as a person. Both take longer than the sleeping adult (case A) to wake up from their slumber. But both have a latent capacity to function, because they both have the basic inherent capacity to function. In the case of B, the impossibility of eliciting an immediate response is due to an abnormality, which brought on the coma. In the other, case C, this is due to the fact that the being is not yet far enough along in his process of development. In both cases the basic inherent capacity is there, it is merely latent.

Cases C and D, babies just after birth and just before birth, are clearly the same in terms of their capacity to function as persons. Birth is, among other things, the beginning of vast new opportunities to develop the basic inherent capacity to function by seeing, hearing, touching, etc., a capacity that is equally present just before birth.

Case E, a baby at seven weeks, has "all the internal organs of the adults"; and "after the eighth week no further primordia will form; *everything* is already present that will be found in the full term baby." It is these "internal organs" and "primordia" that constitute the physical base for the basic inherent capacity to function as a person. They are substantially present in both the very young preborn child, at seven and eight weeks (case E), and the older preborn child (case D). Thus the cases D and E are essentially similar with respect to their basic inherent capacity, and because of this, their being as persons.

In brief, cases A through E are essentially similar. Cases B through E are similar in themselves (each represents a latent capacity); and, taken together, in comparison with A (present immediate capacity). There is no essential difference among

cases B through E. If a person whose lack of present immediate capacity to function is due to a disorder (as in case B) should be respected as a person, then surely a being whose lack of this capacity to function is due to insufficient development (cases C through E) should also be respected as a person. Both are beings with the potential to function as a person; and this they can only have if they have the basis for it, that is, the being of a person. Case B represents a latent-1 capacity, cases C through E, a latent-2 capacity; both are forms of the basic inherent capacity to function, proper to the nature of a person. If a latent-1 capacity (B) is a mark of a person, then surely a latent-2 capacity (C through E) is also a mark of a person. Both B and C through E represent beings who will have the capability to function as persons, who lack this capability now because of the condition of the working basis of this capability (brain, nervous system, etc.). In one, that condition is one of disorder or blockage, in the other, the lack of development proper to the age of the being in question.

(2) The essential similarity among the beings A through E is also established if they are imagined as the same being: a being in the womb developing from seven weeks to birth (E to C), then lapsing into a coma (B), then recovering (A). Thus if there is a person at the end (A), there is also that same person at the beginning (E). It is the same person going through various stages, representing first a latent-2 capacity, then a latent-1 capacity, and finally a present immediate capacity.

I am now a being capable of functioning as a person (present immediate capacity). Many years ago I was a small newborn baby, and before that a smaller child in my mother's womb. My capabilities have changed, they have increased as my basic inherent capacity to function as a person has developed; but I remain always *the same person*, the same essential being, the being who has these growing capabilities. If I am essentially a person now, I was essentially a person then, when I was a baby. The fact that my capabilities to function as a person have changed and grown does not alter the absolute continuity of my essential being, that of a person. In fact, this variation in capabilities presupposes the continuity of my being as a person. It is *as a person* that I develop my capabilities to function as a person. It is because I am a person that I have these capabilities, to whatever degree.

And so the basic reality is being as a person. This is what entails your right to life, the wrongness of killing you, the necessity of respecting you as a person, and not just as a desired commodity like a natural resource. It is *being* a person that is crucial morally, not *functioning* as a person. The very existence and meaning of functioning as a person can have its basis only in the being of a person. It is because you have the being of a person that you can function as a person, although you might fail to function as a person and still retain your full being as a person.

(3) Let us turn now to case F, the zygote or embryo. There are three considerations that show the essential similarity between this case and cases A through E.

First: The continuum argument applies here as well. The adult now sleeping is the same being who was once an embryo and a zygote. There is a direct continuity between the zygote at F and the child at E, through to the adult at A. If the being at the later stages should be given the respect due to persons, then that same being should also be given this respect when he is at an earlier stage.

Second: It may be objected that the zygote lacks "a well-developed physical substratum of consciousness"—that it lacks the actual physical basis (brain, nervous system, etc.) for the basic inherent capacity to function as a person. This is incorrect. The zygote does not lack this physical basis; it is merely that it is now in a primitive, undeveloped form. The zygote has the essential structure of this basis; a structure that will unfold, grow, develop, mature, which takes time. As Blechschmidt states, "...the fertilized ovum (zygote) is already a form of man. Indeed, it is already active....All the organs of the developing organism are differentiation products of each unique [fertilized] human ovum." That is, the organs that form the physical basis for the more developed basic inherent capacity to function as a person (at various stages, E to A) are "differentiation products" of what is already present in the zygote. Thus the zygote has, in primitive form, the physical basis of his basic inherent capacity to function as a person. In the adult this same basis exists in developed form.

The zygote actually has the basic inherent capacity to function as a person because he has the essential physical structure for this. This structure is merely undeveloped:

The zygotic self cannot actually breathe, but he *actually has* the undeveloped capacity for breathing. Nor can this zygotic self actually think and love as an adult does, but he *actually has* the undeveloped capacity for thinking and loving. And the human zygote could not actually have such undeveloped capacities unless he actually IS the kind of being that *has* such capacities. Just as it is obviously true that only a human being can have the *developed* capacities for thinking and loving, it should be obviously true that only a human being can have the *undeveloped* capacities for thinking and loving.

Elsewhere, Robert Joyce remarks:

A person is not an individual with a *developed* capacity for reasoning, willing, desiring, and relating to others. A person is an individual with a natural capacity for these activities and relationships, whether this natural capacity is ever developed or not—i.e., whether he or she ever attains the functional capacity or not. Individuals of a rational, volitional, self-conscious *nature* may never attain or may lose the functional capacity for fulfilling this nature to any appreciable extent. But this inability to fulfill their nature does not negate or destroy the nature itself.

A being at the beginning of his development cannot be expected to possess what only that development can provide for him. He is already the being who will later function as a person, given time. The sleeping person is also a being who will later function as a person, only he will do it much sooner. What they each have now—a fully developed brain in one case, and a potential brain, that which will grow into a developed brain, in the other—is a basis for their capacity to function as persons. It is the same essential basis, one undeveloped, the other developed. It is merely a matter of degree; there is no difference in kind.

One must already *be* a human person in order to develop the human brain necessary for the present and immediate capacity to function as a person. As we noted earlier, *"only a human being can develop a human brain, a human brain cannot develop before a human exists."* "Human being" means of course "human person," the same being in different phases of his existence.

Third: Imagine a person J solving new and relatively complex problems (item 2 on Mary Ann Warren's list).

1. Person J *is doing* this.
2. Person K *has the capacity* to do this (like the sleeping person A on the list).
3. Person L *has the capacity to learn* to do this (to learn what is necessary for having this capacity; for example, a child in school).
4. Person M *has the capacity to acquire*, by natural development, what is necessary for the capacity to learn to do this.

What is true of person M applies to a newborn baby (C), or a baby about to be born (D), or a much younger baby, at seven weeks (E). It applies equally to that same being at a still earlier stage of her development, as a zygote (F).

There is a continuity here. If being a person is approached from the point of view of capacity to function as a person, then clearly persons K, L, and M are essentially alike. Each is removed by one or more steps from the person J, who is actually functioning as a person. None of these steps is of moral or metaphysical significance. In reverse order from M to J, there is, respectively, a capacity to acquire, a capacity to learn, and a capacity to do what the next being represents. If doing is to count for being a person, then surely the capacity to do, the capacity to learn to do, and the capacity to acquire what is needed to learn to do must also count.

This chain argument shows not only the essential similarity between the zygote (F) and the child at later stages (C through E) but also the essential similarity among the beings A through F.

We are now in a better position to understand the real significance of past functioning as a person, which is present in the adult (asleep or in a coma), and absent from the child. It is a sign that the being in question is a person. Because a certain being has functioned in the past, he must be a person. But if

he has not, or we do not know it, it does not follow that he is not a person. Other indications must also be examined. In the case of a small baby, born or preborn, including the zygote stage of a baby's existence, there are three such indications.

One, the *continuum of being*, the identity of the person. The baby is now the same being, the same "self" that the child will be later on. "I was once a newborn baby and before that, a baby inside my mother." Since it is a human being's essential nature to be a person, this being—as a zygote, as a seven-week-old baby, as a newborn—is always a person.

Two, the *continuum of essential structure* for the basic inherent capacity to function as a person. The baby as a zygote has the essential physical structure that represents this capacity. Both in the primitive form of development and in all later stages of development, there exists the same essential structure.

Three, the *continuum of capacities*, to acquire, learn, and do. The zygote has the capacity to acquire what is needed to learn to function as a person.

If a being is not now functioning as a person, is he a person? Two perspectives can be used in answering this question: present to past and present to future. An affirmative answer in either case suffices to indicate that the being in question is a person. Present to past: yes, he is a person because he functioned as a person in the past. Present to future: yes, he is a person because he will function as a person in the future, based on the three-fold continuum. The mistake of writers such as Tooley is to ignore the second of these.

(4) Let us turn, finally, to the case of abnormal, or handicapped, human beings. Does the analysis offered here—that the beings A through F are essentially similar with respect to their being as persons, and their basic inherent capacity to function as persons—apply equally to abnormal, or handicapped, human beings?

It certainly does. A handicapped person (physically, mentally, or both) has the same being of a person as the rest of us who are fortunate enough not to be so afflicted. He has, with this, the same dignity, the same rights as the rest of us. We must "do unto him" as we would want others to "do unto us" if we were afflicted with a handicap. Just as there is no morally relevant difference between a normal functioning person and a small child who cannot yet function as a person because of his lack of development, there is also no morally relevant difference between the normal functioning person and one incapable, or less capable, of doing so. Anyone of us who now has the present immediate capacity to function as a person may lose it through a severe illness or accident. If that happened to you, you would still have the same status of being a person, the same dignity and rights of a person.

Even a very severely abnormal or handicapped human being has the basic inherent capacity to function as a person, which is a sign that he is a person. The abnormality represents a hindrance to the actual working of this capacity, to its manifestation in actual functioning. It does not imply the absence of this capacity, as in a nonperson.

The normal adult and child were selected for this analysis because it is in them that the essence of functioning as a person, or its usual absence because of (normal) lack of development, can most easily be seen and understood. Once recognized there, it applies equally to all persons, regardless of the degree to which they are able to accomplish it.

To conclude this part of the main argument: would Mary Ann Warren admit the adult sound asleep to the status of person? If not, she is saying it is acceptable to kill people in their sleep. Suppose she admits sleeping person A. She must then admit sleeping person B, the one in a longer, deeper sleep. The only differences are the length and nature of the sleep. In each case there is a being with a capacity to function as a person, who will, if not killed, wake up to exercise it. Clearly there is no morally relevant difference between them. This proves decisively that present immediate capacity to function as a person is not necessary to being a person. This is plainly true of the newborn baby C. Having then admitted B as a person, Warren is forced to admit C as well, for the two cases are essentially the same: no present immediate capacity to function as a person, the presence of a latent capacity, rooted in the basic inherent capacity.

With this, Warren's whole argument is destroyed. For she herself claims that, in terms of their intrinsic nature, their being (as persons or nonpersons), the newborn baby (C) and the preborn baby (D through F) are morally on a par. Neither (her argument shows) can now function as a person. Both, I have

shown, have the basic inherent capacity to function as persons. In all of these cases, there is the same being, with the same essential structure of a person, differing only with respect to the degree of development of the capacity to function as a person.

Views like those of Warren and Tooley do not reach the crucial point: the fact that a human being functions as a person or has the present and immediate capacity to do so, is not the ground for his dignity, preciousness, and right to life; rather, that decisive ground is the fact of his *being* a person.

THE REALITY OF THE PERSON SEEN THROUGH LOVE

Imagine a person you deeply love in a coma from which he will emerge in about thirty weeks, perfectly normal. Apply Warren's five criteria. He fails them all. He is not conscious, he cannot reason, he is incapable of self-motivated activity, he cannot communicate, he has no self-concepts or awareness of himself. This doesn't mean he is not a person; that he has no right to life of his own; that he could be killed if no one cared. He is just as real, just as precious, just as much a full person as if he were now capable of functioning as a person. It is just as important and necessary to respect him and care for him as if he were awake.

The child in the womb is in a comparable state, only his "sleep" is normal and is not preceded by a phase where he is able to function as a person. He is also unseen. But none of these makes a morally relevant difference. If one person in "deep sleep" (inability to function as a person) is to be respected and cared for, then the other person should be cared for and respected as well.

THE DISTINCTION APPLIED TO SOME PRO-ABORTION VIEWS

Given our understanding of the distinction between being a person and functioning as a person, we can now come to a better understanding of some of the things put forward by defenders of abortion.

1. Drawing Lines

We examined ten suggested places to draw the line between what is supposed to be merely a *preparation* for a person and the actual person. Every line proved false. In each case the same fully real person is clearly present on both sides of it. No line marks any real difference with regard to *being* a person: the person is there before as well as after. But many of these lines do have a bearing on *functioning* as a person. Thus a baby after birth interacts with others in a way not possible before birth. A baby who has reached sentience has developed an important dimension of his capacity to function as a person. And the presence of a functioning brain marks a significant milestone in the child's development as a functioning person. If these lines seem to have any plausibility, it is because one has in mind functioning as a person. But the plausibility evaporates when one realizes that the crucial thing is not functioning as a person, but being a person.

2. *The Agnostic Position*
Realizing that these lines do not work, some people say that it is simply not known when a human person begins to exist. What should be said is, rather, that it is not known when *functioning* as a person begins, for there is indeed no single place on the continuum of human life at which this begins. It is a gradual development. But the *being* of the person is there all along. And the development is what it is because the being of the person is there all the way through: it is the person's development. Agnosticism regarding functioning as a person should not lead to agnosticism regarding being a person.

3. *The Gradualist Position*
False when applied to the *being* of a person, the gradualist position is absolutely valid when applied to *functioning* as a person. That is indeed a matter of degree. We gradually develop our basic inherent capacity to think and to communicate.

4. *The Notion of Potential Person*
False when applied to *being* a person, the notion of potential person has a validity when applied to *functioning* as a person. If by "person" we mean "functioning person," for example, a normal adult making a complex decision or reading a book, then clearly a child in the womb, or just born, or even at age one, is only potentially such a person. A baby is a potential functioning person; but he is that only because he has the actual being of a person.

HUMAN IS NOT MERELY A BIOLOGICAL CATEGORY
The theory advanced by writers such as Fletcher, Tooley, and Warren holds that killing babies is permissible because they are not persons; whereas, in fact, they are nonfunctioning persons. A functioning person is one who either is now actually functioning as a person, or has the present immediate capacity to do so. What the theory holds is that only functioning persons (and those who were once such persons) are truly persons. It may, therefore, be called the *functioning-person theory.*

Advocates of the functioning-person theory hold that it is not in itself wrong to kill human beings; that this can only be wrong when the being in question is a "person," as defined by the theory (one who has the present immediate capacity to function as a person, or has had it in the past). Such advocates hold that the single fact that a being is human does not constitute any reason for not deliberately killing it. Hence, they say, killing babies, born or preborn, is not in itself wrong. *If* it is ever wrong, it is so because these babies are wanted and would be missed by adults. The thesis, as Tooley puts it, is that "membership in a biological species is not morally significant *in itself.*" In the words of Singer, "Whether a being is or is not a member of our species is in itself no more relevant to the wrongness of killing it than whether it is or is not a member of our race." Warren says that being human in the genetic sense does not give the being in question a right to life.

The thrust of this is to drive a wedge between two categories of beings—persons and human beings—and to hold that it is the former, not the latter, that is of moral significance. There are two fundamental and disastrous errors in this approach. The first concerns the category of persons, and consists in equating this term with functioning persons (present or past), thereby excluding babies who have not yet developed the present immediate capacity to function as persons. The second error, closely related to the first, is to dismiss the category of human being as not (in itself) morally significant.

Proponents of the functioning-person theory are quite right in maintaining that there is a distinction between persons and human beings. They point out that there could be persons who are not human beings, for example, creatures on distant planets who can think, make decisions, feel gratitude, and so forth. They would certainly be persons, without being human beings. In the Christian faith, angels are persons, but not human beings. So, not all persons are necessarily human beings. But, I shall maintain, all human beings are persons (though not necessarily functioning persons). Being human is not necessary to being a person (there could be others), but it is sufficient, for all human beings are persons.

The fundamental error here is the notion that human is a mere biological category, that it designates simply one of many zoological species. If this were so, if the difference between human and other species were like the difference between, say, cats and dogs, or tigers and bears, then of course it would be morally irrelevant. But human—though it may be viewed as a zoological species, and compared to other species in the study of anatomy and physiology—is not simply a biological category. It is rather a mode of being a person.

Human designates, in its most significant meaning, a type of being whose nature it is to be a person. A person is a being who has the basic inherent capacity to function as a person, regardless of how developed this capacity is, or whether or not it is blocked, as in severe senility. We respect and value human beings, not because they are a certain biological species, but because they are persons; because it is the nature of a human being to be a person. All human beings are persons, even if they can no longer function as persons (severe senility), or cannot yet function as persons (small babies), or cannot now function as persons (sound asleep or under anesthesia or in a coma).

The theory is correct when it says that it is persons who are of moral significance; and that persons need not be human persons (they may be martians or angels). The error is to fail to recognize that humans are persons. Being human is a mode of existence of persons. So we should respect human beings—all human beings, regardless of race, degree of intelligence, degree of bodily health, degree of development as functioning persons—because they are persons.

"Do unto others as you would have them do unto you." Surely the class of others is not limited to functioning persons. It includes all human beings; perhaps others as well, but at least all human beings. "Do unto others" must include, very specifically, the lame, the retarded, the weak. It must include those no longer able to function as persons, as well as those not yet able to do so.

When we love another person, it is the *total human being* that we love, not just his or her rationality, or that which makes him or her capable of functioning as a person. We love their individual mode of being, expressed in many ways, such as gestures, facial features, tone of voice, expressions in the eyes, etc. These are, of course, in one respect, bodily features. This does not render them merely biological in the sense dismissed by Singer, Tooley, and others. They are dimensions of the total human person.

The present immediate capacity to function as a person is not essential to this fundamental reality, the total human being. When a loved one is under anesthesia, he is still fully that person, that total human being. More than that, part of the beauty, the charm, the lovableness of a small child is that he is *only a child*, not yet matured, not yet (fully) capable of functioning as a person. The total human being in such a case does not even require the present capacity to function as a person.

Warren, Tooley, and Singer fall into the trap of seeing "human" as a mere biological category because of an earlier, and more fundamental, error: confusing person and functioning person (present or past), indeed, grouping the two together. For if it is assumed that "person" equals "functioning person," and if a small child is not a (fully) functioning person, it follows that the child is not a person. If the child is not a human *person*, "human" can then refer only to a biological species. Once one strips the child of his status as a person (on the grounds that he cannot now function as a person), what is there left except his being a member of a biological species? Separated from the notion of person, the notion of "human" is indeed only a biological species, and as such morally irrelevant.

The fallacy is, then, the separation of human and person, the failure to see that humans are precisely *human persons*. Humans are human persons, where "persons" includes nonfunctioning persons as well as functioning persons....

Abortion: A Defense of the Personhood Argument

LOUIS P. POJMAN

> Every unborn child must be regarded as a human person with all the rights of a human person, from the moment of conception.
>
> (Ethical and Religious Directive from Catholic Hospitals)

> [Abortion] during the first two or three months of gestation [is morally equivalent] to removal of a piece of tissue from the woman's body.
>
> (Thomas Szasz, "The Ethics of Abortion," *Humanist*, 1966)

No social issue divides our society as does the moral and legal status of the human fetus and the corresponding question of the moral permissibility of abortion. On the one hand, such organizations as the Roman Catholic Church and the Right-to-Life Movement, appalled by the 1.5 million abortions that take place in the United States each year, have exerted significant political pressure toward introducing a constitutional amendment that would grant full, legal rights to fetuses. On the other hand, prochoice groups, such as the National Organization of Women (NOW), the National Abortion Rights Action League (NARAL), and feminist organizations have exerted enormous pressure on politicians to support pro-abortion legislation. The Republican and Democratic political platforms of the past three elections took diametrically opposite sides on this issue.

Opponents of abortion, like John Noonan and Stephen Schwarz, argue that because there is no non-arbitrary cutoff point between conception of the single-cell zygote and the full adult where we can say, "Here we do not have a human being and here we do," to draw the line anywhere but at conception is to justify infanticide, the killing of small children, the killing of teenagers, and the killing of the elderly.

In this essay I will examine the problem of abortion. But first I want to prove that no poor people exist in the world! I know you will agree that having a single penny does not make the difference between being wealthy or poor. Perhaps having a penny will make the difference in purchasing something, but that in itself does not constitute the difference between poverty and wealth. Then I hope you will agree that possessing a billion dollars constitutes being wealthy. Now take a penny away from our billionaire. Does the loss of one cent make him poor? Of course not. We have already agreed that the gain or loss of one penny does not make a difference with regard to whether someone is poor or wealthy. Now take another penny from him and another and another until he only is worth $1.25, the price of *The Sunday New York Times*. He is homeless and cannot even afford a half-gallon of milk, but by our argument, he is not poor, for all we did was subtract pennies from him one by one and such small increments cannot make a difference.

Of course, we could work the argument the other way around and prove that no one is rich— that everyone is poor. We will agree to the same crucial premise that a penny does not make a difference between wealth and poverty. We will agree that possessing only a penny makes no one rich. Then we will give a penny to our poor man, one by one, until he possesses a hundred billion pennies or a billion dollars.

Or consider this argument. No one is really bald, for taking a single hair from anyone with a complete head of hair cannot produce baldness, so we begin to take hairs from your head one by one until you have no hair at all on your head. At what point were you really bald? Surely, having merely one strand of hair is being bald, and adding a second makes no difference to the designation of being bald. So we can go from baldness to a full head of hair without ever finding a cutoff point where baldness ends and hairiness begins. Yet we are sure that there is a

From Pojman/Beckwith, *The Abortion Controversy: A Reader*, 2E. © 1998 Wadsworth, a part of Cengage Learning, Inc. Reproduced by permission.

difference between baldness and having a full head of hair.

When does an accumulation of sand, soil, and rock become a mountain? A piece of sand, a speck of soil, and a tiny stone do not constitute a mountain, but if we keep adding sand, soil, and rocks long enough we will eventually end up with a structure as large as Mt. Everest!

You get the point. Concepts are not clear and do not fit easily onto reality, so that it may not make sense to speak of drawing a line between stages of development. These are examples of Slippery Slope Arguments, sometimes called "Edge of the Wedge Arguments." Such arguments have been used as the trump card of traditionalists opposed to social change. Give innovation an inch and it will take a mile. The first step to Auschwitz begins with a seemingly innocent concession to those who would promote social considerations over the sanctity of life.

The slippery slope arguments trade on the difficulty of applying concepts, which are vague, to reality, which is precise. That is, I have an absolutely precise number of hairs on my head, but the concept of baldness is imprecise. The fallacy of the slippery slope argument is to suppose that because there is no distinct cutoff point in reality where concepts change (rich to poor, and so forth), there is no real difference between state A and B. But there is. We know the difference between wealth and poverty even though we cannot define it in absolute monetary terms. We know the difference between a full head of hair and baldness even though we cannot say exactly where baldness begins. We know the difference between a hill and a mountain even though there is a grey area in between where we are not sure what to call it.

Now apply this point to the moral problem of abortion. Simply because we cannot discover a bright line separating a person from a nonperson does not rule out the existence of such a distinction. If we judge on the merits of the case that a relevant moral difference exists between fetal life and self-conscious human life, that difference can be as real as the difference between poverty and wealth or a mole hill and Mt. Whitney. Even though no perceptible difference might exist between any two successive stages, a real difference can appear between nonsuccessive stages.

THE LIBERAL POSITION

The liberal position asserts that it is always or almost always morally permissible for a woman to have an abortion. It allows abortion on demand. Four arguments for this position have been offered. They are as follows:

1. Subjectivism: Radical Relativism
2. Absolute Right to Privacy Argument (reproductive freedom)
3. The Quality of Life Argument (in cases of the probability of defective neonates)
4. The Personhood Argument

1. Subjectivism: Radical Relativism

Abortion is a private matter into which the law should not enter. No one should be forced to have children. H. Schur in his book, *Crimes without Victims*, calls abortion a victimless crime. Unfortunately, he supplies no argument for his view that fetuses are nonpersons. Schur assumes that morality is merely a matter of individual choice. Who are we to judge?

But subjectivism is a dubious doctrine. If fetuses are persons, then is not what we are doing tantamount to killing innocent people? Are not we all engaged in mass killings? And is not the killing of innocents to be condemned?

2. The Absolute Right to Privacy Argument

The National Organization of Women (NOW) and many radical feminists hold that because a woman has an absolute right to her own body on which a fetus is dependent, she may do whatever is necessary to detach the fetus from her, including putting it to death.

The first problem with this argument is that it is unclear whether we have any *absolute* rights at all. An absolute right always overrides all other considerations. It is doubtful whether we have many of these. The only ones I can think of are rights like the right not to be unnecessarily harmed or tortured. We have no reason to believe that our right to use our own body as we wish is an absolute right. Consider 500-pound Fat Fred who decides to sit down, but your money-packed wallet happens to be directly on the spot where he sits. You request him to move his body so that you can get your wallet, but he refuses, claiming that he has an absolute right to do with his body what he wills.

The doctrine of absolute rights to privacy or body use suffers from lack of intelligent support. Because our bodies are public and interact with other people's bodies and property, we need ways of adjudicating conflicts between them, but there is no such thing as an absolute right to do whatever we want with our bodies. The parent of dependent children does not have a right to remove his or her body to a different locale, abandoning the children. A citizen may be morally obligated to take his or her body to the army recruitment center when his or her nation is in danger and the draft board picks his or her number.

Although my right to do what I please with my body can include my right to deny its use to a creature who needs it (for example, the mayor of my town needs to attach himself to someone with a functioning liver), it does *not* give me a right to kill the mayor. I only have a right to disengage from him, not kill him. Because all current methods of abortion involve killing the fetus before disengagement, none of them can be justified by the libertarian argument.

The case is even more serious for the libertarian argument because the woman wanting an abortion has typically voluntarily put herself at risk for pregnancy. Suppose that President Clinton suddenly has a rare form of liver and double kidney failure, so that he needs to be plugged into a human being's kidneys and liver. The person will have to walk around with the President, sleep in his bed, and eat at his table for nine months. One hundred people with the right kinds of kidneys and livers are rounded up and invited to participate in a lottery. One person, the loser, will get plugged in to the president. Each of the one hundred people will win $1,000 for playing the game. You are one of the people invited to play. Would you play?

Most people asked, including myself, say that they would take the risk of playing the lottery. Once we agree to play we are obligated to accept the inconvenience if we lose. It would be absurd to back out, claiming an absolute right to privacy or bodily use.

The implications of the lottery game for abortion are obvious. Once people voluntarily engage in sex, they are engaged in the lottery game. Even if they use birth control devices, pregnancy might result. If the fetus is a person, with a right to life, the woman cannot simply dismiss that right by invoking a superior right to privacy. She has suspended that right by engaging in an act that brought the new being into existence.

3. The Quality of Life Argument

One strategy available to the liberal is to deny that life is of absolute value. Life may be a necessary condition for happiness and whatever makes life worth living, but not all life is worth living. The severely deformed, retarded, anencephalic or hydrocephalic child might live a negative existence, in which case abortion might be warranted. Or suppose that a pregnant woman is informed that the fetus she is carrying has Tay-Sachs disease or *spina bifida* and is told that if she aborts, in five months she will be able to conceive a normal child. If it is quality that counts, the woman not only may abort, but she has a positive duty to do so.

This argument can be extended to cover cases where the woman is incapable of providing an adequate upbringing for the child to be born, the case of the teenage pregnancy, the family with children which cannot afford another child. That the world is already overpopulated is another consideration arguing for abortion of unwanted children. No unwanted child should enter the world.

The Quality of Life Argument has merit—quality does count—but it has weaknesses that need to be examined. First, the argument against bringing unwanted children into the world can be offset by the availability of adoption. Many childless couples *want* these children. Nevertheless, not all children are likely to be adopted into loving homes, so that some abortions would still be permitted.

A more significant objection is that the Quality of Life Argument leaves the status of the fetus untouched. If the fetus is a person, then it makes no more sense to speak of aborting it because you do not think it will have an adequate quality of life than it does to kill a baby or ten-year old or ninety-year-old because you do not think he or she will have an adequate quality of life. Although quality counts, the critic contends, we do not have the right to "play God" in this way with people's lives. It is too dangerous.

The prochoice adherent has a response here—sometimes we must play God, for sometimes the prospects of suffering for all concerned are so dire and so likely that abortion, even if the fetus is a person, is permissible. In this sense, abortion is the lesser of evils, though still an evil.

This is essentially the moderate position as set forth by Daniel Callahan, L. W. Sumner, Baruch Brody, and Caroline Whitbeck.

4. The Personhood Argument

Our intuitions generally tell us that the fetus does not have the same moral status as the mother. Anti-abortionists often base their conclusions on our religious heritage, but even there the case is ambiguous. Although the notion of ensoulment argues for the personhood of the fetus, earlier Biblical ideas lend support for a distinction of status. For example, Exodus (21:22) says that if a man causes a woman to abort, he shall be punished, but if the woman's death follows, those responsible shall give "life for life, eye for eye, tooth for tooth."

Moreover, a tradition within the Roman Catholic Church, going at least as far back as Thomas Aquinas (1225–1274) and adopted at the Council of Vienna in 1312, called *hylomorphism*, holds that the human soul is to the body somewhat as the shape of a statue is to the actual statue. Thus, without a fully formed human shape, no human soul exists.

Furthermore, serious difficulties arise in viewing the single-cell zygote or the conceptus as a person, given the phenomenon of twinning that can take place up to the third week of pregnancy. If the embryo splits into two (or three, four, or more) embryos, does one person (soul) become two (or more)? How can personhood, with its characteristic of complete unity, be divided?

But it is not enough for liberals to point out problems in the conservative position. The liberal must go to the heart of the matter and dismantle the conservative arguments for the fetus's right to life. The central one is offered by Noonan:

1. We ought never to kill innocent human beings.
2. Fetuses are innocent human beings.

3. Therefore we ought never to kill fetuses (that is, have abortions).

The liberal points out that the term *human being* is used ambiguously in the argument. Note that sometimes by *human being* we have a biological concept in mind, the species *Homo sapiens*, that at other times we have a psychological-moral concept in mind, someone with the characteristics of humans as we typically find them, characteristics such as rationality, freedom, and self-consciousness, which mark them off from other animals. In philosophy we sometimes refer the word *person* to this type of being. A person is someone who has an intrinsic right to life. If we apply this distinction to Noonan's argument, we see that it trades on this ambiguity.

In the first premise "human beings" refers to persons, while in the second it refers to *Homo sapiens*. The argument should read as follows:

1. We ought never to kill innocent *persons*.
2. Fetuses are innocent *Homo sapiens*.
3. Therefore we ought never to kill fetuses.

But this is an invalid argument, since it is not obvious that all *Homo sapiens* are persons.

The question is this: by virtue of what characteristics does someone have a right to life? The liberal will point out that it is a form of prejudice, similar to racism, sexism, nationalism, religionism, and ethnocentrism, to prefer one species to another simply because it is your species or to grant someone a right simply because he or she is a member of a biological group. Richard Ryder and Peter Singer in their works on animal rights call this prejudice *Speciesism*.

Speciesism violates the first principle of justice: Treat equals equally and unequals unequally. Suppose it turned out that one ethnic group or gender on average made better musicians than other groups. It would still be unjust automatically to allow all and only members of that group to enter music schools. Individuals have a right to be judged according to their ability, and so we would want to test individuals independently of ethnic group or gender to ascertain a candidate's capacity for musical performance.

What are the characteristics that give beings a right to life analogous to the characteristics that give candidates a right to enter music school? The liberal argues that certain properties that most adult humans have are the proper criteria for this distinction. These properties are intrinsically valuable traits that allow us to view ourselves as selves with plans and projects over time, properties like self-consciousness and rationality. Both conservatives and liberals agree that these qualities are intrinsically good. The liberal, however, tries to draw out their implications: that our ability to make plans, to think rationally, and to have a self over time give us a special right to life. Although it is difficult to specify exactly what are the necessary and sufficient conditions for personhood, and liberals have described these conditions differently—some emphasizing desires and interests, others emphasizing agency or the ability to project into the future, others emphasizing the capacity for a notion of the self—they all point to a cluster of characteristics which distinguish children and adults from fetuses, infants, and most animals. And those characteristics enable us to interact and reciprocate on the social playing field of civilized existence.

Joel Feinberg describes personhood this way:

> What makes me certain that my parents, siblings, and friends are people is that they give evidence of being conscious of the world and of themselves; they have inner emotional lives, just like me; they can understand things, and reason about them, make plans, and act; they can communicate with me, argue, negotiate, express themselves, make agreements, honor commitments, and stand in relationships of mutual trust; they have tastes and values of their own; they can be frustrated or fulfilled, pleased or hurt....

A certain vagueness inheres in the specification of these qualities, and individuals possess them to different degrees—life is not neat and tidy—but we have an adequate idea of what they are. Practically, a typical test of whether someone is a person is the ability to reason about or emphatically communicate about interpersonal relations. Studies show that not only humans but gorillas, chimpanzees, and dogs have this ability.

I think that the phrase "rational self-consciousness" captures what we typically mean by this property. It distinguishes the average adult human from most of the animal kingdom. But not all humans have these qualities, whereas some animals may possess them. Severely retarded children, anencephalic babies, severely senile adults, and people in persistent vegetative states do not possess these properties, but dolphins, whales, chimpanzees, apes, and even some dogs and pigs may possess them. The following diagram represents the relationship between humans and animals with regard to personhood.

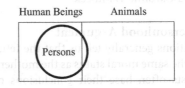

If rational self-consciousness marks the criterion for having a right to life, then fetuses do not have a right to life, since they are neither rational nor self-conscious.

THE CONSERVATIVE RESPONSE AND LIBERAL COUNTERRESPONSE

How do conservatives respond to this argument? First, they point out two counterintuitive implications of the liberal position, and then they point out something missing that changes the liberal's logic.

If the personhood argument were followed, we would be permitted to kill unconscious and severely retarded and senile humans—even normal people when they sleep, for none of these have the required characteristics for personhood. Second, the argument ignores the fact that the fetus is a *potential* person, and potentiality for self-consciousness should be seen as granting a being similar rights as an actual person. Finally, the argument would also sanction infanticide, something that most liberals are loath to allow.

Poignant as these objections are, the liberal has an adequate response to each of them. Regarding the killing of the retarded and senile, the liberal would point out that most of these people still have an adequate amount of self-consciousness and rationality and that it would be dangerous to put into practice a policy of doing away with all but the most obvious cases of irretrievable loss of selfhood. With regard to those who sleep or are unconscious, they still have the capacity for rational self-consciousness, so we may not kill them.

Potentiality is not enough, only actuality or capacity for self-consciousness is sufficient for granting someone a right to life. Let me illustrate this with an example from the 1992 presidential campaign. Suppose that during that campaign of the Democratic Party for the presidential nomination, Jerry Brown had suddenly appeared at the White House with his family and furniture. "I'm moving in here," he announces to an incredulous White House staff.

"You can't do. It's unlawful! President Bush rightly lives here," objects the staff member.

"You don't know what you're talking about. Don't you Republicans believe that a potential person has all the rights of an actual person? Well, on that same logic, a potential president has the same rights as an actual president. Since I am potentially the president, I'm taking advantage of my rights, so let me in."

Although the fetus may be a potential person, it is not yet an actual one; hence, it does not have the same rights as an actual person.

In this regard, Mary Anne Warren offers the following thought experiment:

Suppose that our space explorer falls into the hands of an alien culture, whose scientists decide to create a few hundred thousand or more human beings, by breaking his body into its component cells, and using these to create fully developed human beings, with, of course, his genetic code. We may imagine that each of these newly created men will have all of the original man's abilities, skills, knowledge, and so on, and also have an individual self-concept, in short that each of them will be a bona fide (though hardly unique) person. Imagine that the whole project will take only seconds, and that its chances of success are extremely high, and that our explorer knows all of this, and also knows that these people will be treated fairly. I maintain that in such a situation he would have every right to escape if he could, and thus to deprive all of these potential people of their potential lives; for his right to life outweighs all of theirs together, in spite of the fact that they are all genetically human,

all innocent, and all have a very high probability of becoming people very soon, if only he refrains from acting.

Warren, in a later article, seems to have lost confidence in this argument, conceding that such bizarre situations are inadequate grounds for the refutation of the potentiality principle. But the situation is not as bizarre as we might suppose.

Consider the implications of the thesis held by virtually all conservatives that the single-cell zygote has the same right to life as a fully conscious moral agent. If you believe that a single-cell zygote has a right to life, then you should refrain from washing, scratching, and brushing your teeth. Why? Because in doing so, you are killing thousands of single cells of *exactly the same nature* as the zygote. The only difference between other diploid cells in our body and the zygote is the location. The zygote fortuitously has gotten into the incubator, whereas the others have not. But that is an irrelevant distinction, having nothing to do with inherent rights or the quality of the cell itself. Given the prospects of cloning, any cell of your body could be developed into a fetus, a baby, and, finally, into an adult. If the zygote is sacred and possesses a right to life, the same goes for every other human cell in the world.

Some conservatives, like Stephen Schwarz, argue that the fetus is not a potential person but an actual person, an essential person, who simply is not functioning as an adult.

Schwarz raises an important issue. If a sleeping person or temporarily comatose person is not to be killed because he or she has the potential for rational self-consciousness, should not the fetus be likewise protected since it too will eventually become rationally self-conscious? "Neither the sleeping person nor the being in the womb now display the qualities of a functioning person. Both will display them. It is only a matter of time. Why should the one count as a real person because the time is short, while the other does not, simply because in her case the time is longer?"

Rejecting the idea of potentiality altogether, Schwarz divides the relevant categories into varieties of capacities. Personhood is grounded in the *basic inherent capacity* to function as rational beings. But this basic capacity may not be presently operative, but only latent, as in a reversible coma, which Schwarz calls *latent-1 capacity*, or where it is insufficiently developed, as in a small child, which Schwarz calls *latent-2 capacity*. All of these capacities are sufficient for personhood. Schwarz argues that the single-cell zygote has the physical basis of the required capacities (that is, it has latent-2 capacity). "It is merely that it is now in a primitive, undeveloped form. The zygote has the essential structure of this basis; a structure that will unfold, grow, develop, mature, which takes time…The zygote actually has the basic inherent capacity to function as a person because he has the essential physical structure for this." So the single-cell zygote is a full person.

But if every human zygote is a full person whose latent-2 capacity grants an inalienable right to life, every cell in our bodies must merit that same protection, since essentially it has the same structure as the cell in the pregnant woman's uterus. In fact, the ovum and the spermatozoon also have the essential genetic make-up, so that they would qualify as persons, and as such deserve full protection.

With regard to the matter of treating the fetus as a person with "latent-2 capacities" rather than as a potential person, Schwarz seems to be playing with words. "Latent-2 capacity" obscures the distinction between potentiality and actuality. The crucial distinction between a capacity and a potentiality goes like this. Consider a lump of clay. It does not have the capacity to hold water, but it has the potentiality for that capacity (Schwarz's latent-2 capacity). Suppose that I mold it into a cup. Now it has the capacity for holding water even though at present it is not holding any (what Schwarz calls a latent-1 capacity). The fetus only has the potentiality for self-consciousness, whereas the unconscious person has the capacity for it. The seemingly innocuous latent-1 and latent-2 capacities slur over the essential difference between having the potential for becoming a rational self-conscious person and actually being one who is not functioning as such. It makes all the difference in the world—as much difference as between a mere pack of clay and a clay cup with a lid on it so that it cannot presently take in liquid.

Although Schwarz is aware that liberals want to make something like this distinction, he thinks that on reflection our intuitions will lead us to a contrary judgment. Here is his thought experiment.

Consider the case of two children. "One is born comatose, and he will remain so until the age of nine. The other is healthy at birth, but as soon as she achieves the concept of a continuing self for a brief time, she, too, lapses into a coma, from which she will not emerge until she is nine." Then Schwarz asks, "Can anyone seriously hold that the second child is a person with a right to life, while the first child is not?" My response is, "Yes, indeed, I can!"

My intuitions are exactly the opposite of Schwarz's, which makes me suspect that our intuitions are partly a function of the wider theories about human nature, personal identity, religion, and morality. Here is my assessment of Schwarz's counter example. First of all, children are not born with a sense of selfhood. They gradually achieve this property as they interact with their parents and older siblings. Piaget and other psychologists think that the child only attains such a sense in the second year of life. Schwarz's counter example presupposes that the sense of selfhood is a *fiat*, which reveals a deep misunderstanding of the psychological process of becoming self-aware.

Second, one must question the relevance of Schwarz's counter example. If the pro-abortionist believes that a sense of selfhood is the decisive property separating personhood from nonpersonhood, why should the fact that someone only enjoyed it for a short time be a reason for discounting it at all? Suppose Albert Einstein went into a nine-year comatose state immediately after arriving at his theory of relativity. He still possessed something valuable, which his fellow comatosee lacked. The question is not whether the girl in Schwarz's example possessed a sense of selfhood for a long time, but whether the sense of selfhood is a necessary and sufficient criterion for deontological personhood. The liberal argues that it is, and so he or she should not be moved by such counter examples.

Schwarz holds that an adult person is identical with his or her single-cell zygote. "My capabilities have changed; they have increased as my basic inherent capacity to function as a person has developed; but I remain always *the same person*, the same essential being." But this identity of the adult with the zygote or blastocyst creates staggering difficulties. If I am exactly identical to my zygote, then I am exactly identical to whatever my zygote develops into. But early in the fetus's life, twinning sometimes occurs (not to speak of quintupling!). So, if I am an identical twin, I must be identical to my identical twin. So if my twin commits a murder, I may be executed for it, and if I marry Joan, my twin may properly sleep with her.

Unless one is willing to swallow such implications, this kind of conservative position on personal identity from the zygote to the adult is doomed to incoherence.

Infanticide

The most serious objection to the liberal position on abortion is that it leads to the permissibility of infanticide. Since there is no relevant difference between a fetus one day before birth and a baby one day after birth, if abortion of a fetus is permissible, so is the killing of a baby. What is the liberal's response to this charge?

The liberal's reply is a qualified, "Yes, but not necessarily." In a sense liberalism does lead to the permissibility of infanticide, but it need not. Let me explain.

The liberal can distinguish between *natural right* (or deontological right) and a *social right* (or utilitarian right). A natural right is one that a person has simply by virtue of intrinsic qualities. A social right, on the other hand, is not intrinsic to the being, but bestowed by society. Society has the privilege and right of protecting things that it deems valuable or useful to its purposes. Just as it can grant a forest or endangered animal species a protective right, so it can give fetuses or infants such rights if it so chooses. The only necessary condition for granting something a social right is that we give a utilitarian reason for doing so. Since the entity at issue does not have sufficient intrinsic value to claim the right, there must be an instrumental reason for doing so.

We are more willing to extend a social right to infants than to fetuses because they are closer to personhood and because they are independent of the mother's body and can be adopted. If a state decided that good reasons existed to extend the social right to life to fetuses, it would be justified in doing so. But it does not have to, and if there were good utilitarian reasons for doing so, the state could remove the social right to life from infants. Because removing that right would most likely cause a social upheaval far beyond the present uproar over the legalization of abortion, this is unlikely to happen. Nonetheless, on the liberal argument, such a move could not be ruled out as morally unacceptable.

Let me succinctly set forth this argument in six steps so that you will be able to examine it carefully.

1. All and only actual persons have a deontological moral *right* to life (that is, potentiality or "latent-2 capacities" do not count).
2. Persons may be defined as beings who have the capacity for reason and self-conscious desire ("Reason Capacity").
3. Fetuses and infants do not have Reason Capacities and so do not have a deontological moral right to life.
4. However, there are social rights (utilitarian rights) that society may bestow on classes of beings for utilitarian reasons. This includes treating some potential persons as though they had full deontological rights.
5. There are good utilitarian reasons for treating infants (and perhaps fetuses in the latter stages of pregnancy) as "persons," giving them social rights.
6. Therefore, we ought to bestow a social right on infants and perhaps on viable fetuses. That is, once past a fixed time a woman loses her right to abort potential persons, except where they will be seriously defective or where the mother's life or health is endangered.

The distinction between a deontological right and a social or utilitarian right means that certain rights are largely beyond the authority of society to tamper with. The basic rights of persons are within this domain. However, optional rights, social rights, may be extended or withheld from beings not yet fully human but on the way to becoming so. . . .

Why Abortion Is Immoral

DON MARQUIS

The view that abortion is, with rare exceptions, seriously immoral has received little support in the recent philosophical literature. No doubt most philosophers affiliated with secular institutions of higher education believe that the anti-abortion position is either a symptom of irrational religious dogma or a conclusion generated by seriously confused philosophical argument. The purpose of this essay is to undermine this general belief. This essay sets out an argument that purports to show, as well as any argument in ethics can show, that abortion is, except possibly in rare cases, seriously immoral, that it is in the same moral category as killing an innocent adult human being.

The argument is based on a major assumption. Many of the most insightful and careful writers on the ethics of abortion—such as Joel Feinberg, Michael Tooley, Mary Anne Warren, H. Tristram Engelhardt, Jr., L. W. Sumner, John T. Noonan, Jr., and Philip Devine[1]—believe that whether or not abortion is morally permissible stands or falls on whether or not a fetus is the sort of being whose life it is seriously wrong to end. The argument of this essay will assume, but not argue, that they are correct.

Also, this essay will neglect issues of great importance to a complete ethics of abortion. Some anti-abortionists will allow that certain abortions, such as abortion before implantation or abortion when the life of a woman is threatened by a pregnancy or abortion after rape, may be morally permissible. This essay will not explore the casuistry of these hard cases. The purpose of this essay is to develop a general argument for the claim that the overwhelming majority of deliberate abortions are seriously immoral.

I

A sketch of standard anti-abortion and pro-choice arguments exhibits how those arguments possess certain symmetries that explain why partisans of those positions are so convinced of the correctness of their own positions, why they are not successful in convincing their opponents, and why, to others, this issue seems to be unresolvable. An analysis of the nature of this standoff suggests a strategy for surmounting it.

Consider the way a typical anti-abortionist argues. She will argue or assert that life is present from the moment of conception or that fetuses look like babies or that fetuses possess a characteristic such as a genetic code that is both necessary and sufficient for being human. Anti-abortionists seem to believe that (1) the truth of all of these claims is quite obvious, and (2) establishing any of these claims is sufficient to show that abortion is morally akin to murder.

A standard pro-choice strategy exhibits similarities. The pro-choicer will argue or assert that fetuses are not persons or that fetuses are not rational agents or that fetuses are not social beings. Pro-choicers seem to believe that (1) the truth of any of these claims is quite obvious, and (2) establishing any of these claims is sufficient to show that an abortion is not a wrongful killing.

In fact, both the pro-choice and the anti-abortion claims do seem to be true, although the "it looks like a baby" claim is more difficult to establish the earlier the pregnancy. We seem to have a standoff. How can it be resolved?

As everyone who has taken a bit of logic knows, if any of these arguments concerning abortion is a good argument, it requires not only some claim characterizing fetuses, but also some general moral principle that ties a characteristic of fetuses to having or not having the right to life or to some other moral characteristic that will generate the obligation or the lack of obligation not to end the life of a fetus. Accordingly, the arguments of the anti-

Don Marquis, "Why Abortion Is Immoral," *Journal of Philosophy*, LXXXVI, 4 (April 1989): 183–202. © Journal of Philosophy.

abortionist and the pro-choicer need a bit of filling in to be regarded as adequate.

Note what each partisan will say. The anti-abortionist will claim that her position is supported by such generally accepted moral principles as "It is always prima facie seriously wrong to take a human life" or "It is always prima facie seriously wrong to end the life of a baby." Since these are generally accepted moral principles, her position is certainly not obviously wrong. The pro-choicer will claim that her position is supported by such plausible moral principles as "Being a person is what gives an individual intrinsic moral worth" or "It is only seriously prima facie wrong to take the life of a member of the human community." Since these are generally accepted moral principles, the pro-choice position is certainly not obviously wrong. Unfortunately, we have again arrived at a standoff.

Now, how might one deal with this standoff? The standard approach is to try to show how the moral principles of one's opponent lose their plausibility under analysis. It is easy to see how this is possible. On the one hand, the anti-abortionist will defend a moral principle concerning the wrongness of killing which tends to be broad in scope in order that even fetuses at an early stage of pregnancy will fall under it. The problem with broad principles is that they often embrace too much. In this particular instance, the principle "It is always prima facie wrong to take a human life" seems to entail that it is wrong to end the existence of a living human cancer-cell culture, on the grounds that the culture is both living and human. Therefore, it seems that the anti-abortionist's favored principle is too broad.

On the other hand, the pro-choicer wants to find a moral principle concerning the wrongness of killing which tends to be narrow in scope in order that fetuses will *not* fall under it. The problem with narrow principles is that they often do not embrace enough. Hence, the needed principles such as "It is prima facie seriously wrong to kill only persons" or "It is prima facie wrong to kill only rational agents" do not explain why it is wrong to kill infants or young children or the severely retarded or even perhaps the severely mentally ill. Therefore, we seem again to have a standoff. The anti-abortionist charges, not unreasonably, that pro-choice principles concerning killing are too narrow to be

acceptable; the pro-choicer charges, not unreasonably, that anti-abortionist principles concerning killing are too broad to be acceptable.

Attempts by both sides to patch up the difficulties in their positions run into further difficulties. The anti-abortionist will try to remove the problem in her position by reformulating her principle concerning killing in terms of human beings. Now we end up with: "It is always prima facie seriously wrong to end the life of a human being." This principle has the advantage of avoiding the problem of the human cancer-cell culture counterexample. But this advantage is purchased at a high price. For although it is clear that a fetus is both human and alive, it is not at all clear that a fetus is a human *being*. There is at least something to be said for the view that something becomes a human being only after a process of development, and that therefore first trimester fetuses and perhaps all fetuses are not yet human beings. Hence, the anti-abortionist, by this move, has merely exchanged one problem for another.[2]

The pro-choicer fares no better. She may attempt to find reasons why killing infants, young children, and the severely retarded is wrong which are independent of her major principle that is supposed to explain the wrongness of taking human life, but which will not also make abortion immoral. This is no easy task. Appeals to social utility will seem satisfactory only to those who resolve not to think of the enormous difficulties with a utilitarian account of the wrongness of killing and the significant social costs of preserving the lives of the unproductive.[3] A pro-choice strategy that extends the definition of "person" to infants or even to young children seems just as arbitrary as an anti-abortion strategy that extends the definition of "human being" to fetuses. Again, we find symmetries in the two positions and we arrive at a standoff.

There are even further problems that reflect symmetries in the two positions. In addition to counterexample problems, or the arbitrary application problems that can be exchanged for them, the standard anti-abortionist principle "It is prima facie seriously wrong to kill a human being," or one of its variants, can be objected to on the grounds of ambiguity. If "human being" is taken to be a *biological* category, then the anti-abortionist is left with the problem of explaining why a merely biological category should make a moral difference. Why, it is asked, is it any more reasonable to base a moral conclusion on the number of chromosomes in one's cells than on the color of one's skin?[4] If "human being," on the other hand, is taken to be a *moral* category, then the claim that a fetus is a human being cannot be taken to be a premise in the anti-abortion argument, for it is precisely what needs to be established. Hence, either the anti-abortionist's main category is a morally irrelevant, merely biological category, or it is of no use to the anti-abortionist in establishing (noncircularly, of course) that abortion is wrong.

Although this problem with the anti-abortionist position is often noticed, it is less often noticed that the pro-choice position suffers from an analogous problem. The principle "Only persons have the right to life" also suffers from an ambiguity. The term "person" is typically defined in terms of psychological characteristics, although there will certainly be disagreement concerning which characteristics are most important. Supposing that this matter can be settled, the pro-choicer is left with the problem of explaining why *psychological* characteristics should make a *moral* difference. If the pro-choicer should attempt to deal with this problem by claiming that an explanation is not necessary, that in fact we do treat such a cluster of psychological properties as having moral significance, the sharp-witted anti-abortionist should have a ready response. We do treat being both living and human as having moral significance. If it is legitimate for the pro-choicer to demand that the anti-abortionist provide an explanation of the connection between the biological character of being a human being and the wrongness of being killed (even though people accept this connection), then it is legitimate for the anti-abortionist to demand that the pro-choicer provide an explanation of the connection between psychological criteria for being a person and the wrongness of being killed (even though that connection is accepted).[5]

Feinberg has attempted to meet this objection (he calls psychological personhood "commonsense personhood"):

The characteristics that confer commonsense personhood are not arbitrary bases for rights and duties, such as race, sex or species membership; rather they are traits that make sense out of rights and duties and without which those moral attributes would have no point or function. It is because people are conscious; have a sense of their personal identities; have plans, goals, and projects; experience emotions; are liable to pains, anxieties, and frustrations; can reason and bargain, and so on—it is because of these attributes that people have values and interests, desires and expectations of their own, including a stake in their own futures, and a personal well-being of a sort we cannot ascribe to unconscious or nonrational beings. Because of their developed capacities they can assume duties and responsibilities and can have and make claims on one another. Only because of their sense of self, their life plans, their value hierarchies, and their stakes in their own futures can they be ascribed fundamental rights. There is nothing arbitrary about these linkages (op. cit., p. 270).

The plausible aspects of this attempt should not be taken to obscure its implausible features. There is a great deal to be said for the view that being a psychological person under some description is a necessary condition for having duties. One cannot have a duty unless one is capable of behaving morally, and a being's capability of behaving morally will require having a certain psychology. It is far from obvious, however, that having rights entails consciousness or rationality, as Feinberg suggests. We speak of the rights of the severely retarded or the severely mentally ill, yet some of these persons are not rational. We speak of the rights of the temporarily unconscious. The New Jersey Supreme Court based their decision in the Quinlan case on Karen Ann Quinlan's right to privacy, and she was known to be permanently unconscious at that time. Hence, Feinberg's claim that having rights entails being conscious is, on its face, obviously false.

Of course, it might not make sense to attribute rights to a being that would never in its natural history have certain psychological traits. This modest connection between psychological personhood and moral personhood will create a place for Karen Ann Quinlan and the temporarily unconscious. But then it makes a place for fetuses also. Hence, it does not serve Feinberg's pro-choice purposes. Accordingly, it seems that the pro-choicer will have as much difficulty bridging the gap between psychological personhood and personhood in the moral sense as the anti-abortionist has bridging the gap between being a biological human being and being a human being in the moral sense.

Furthermore, the pro-choicer cannot any more escape her problem by making person a purely moral category than the anti-abortionist could escape by the analogous move. For if person is a moral category, then the pro-choicer is left without the resources for establishing (noncircularly, of course) the claim that a fetus is not a person, which is an essential premise in her argument. Again, we have both a symmetry and a standoff between pro-choice and anti-abortion views.

Passions in the abortion debate run high. There are both plausibilities and difficulties with the standard positions. Accordingly, it is hardly surprising that partisans of either side embrace with fervor the moral generalizations that support the conclusions they preanalytically favor, and reject with disdain the moral generalizations of their opponents as being subject to inescapable difficulties. It is easy to believe that the counterexamples to one's own moral principles are merely temporary difficulties that will dissolve in the wake of further philosophical research, and that the counterexamples to the principles of one's opponents are as straightforward as the contradiction between A and O propositions in traditional logic. This might suggest to an impartial observer (if there are any) that the abortion issue is unresolvable.

There is a way out of this apparent dialectical quandary. The moral generalizations of both sides are not quite correct. The generalizations hold for the most part, for the usual cases. This suggests that they are all *accidental* generalizations, that the moral claims made by those on both sides of the dispute do not touch on the *essence* of the matter.

This use of the distinction between essence and accident is not meant to invoke obscure metaphysical categories. Rather, it is intended to reflect the rather atheoretical nature of the abortion discussion. If the generalization a partisan in the abortion dispute adopts were derived from the reason why ending the life of a human being is wrong, then there could not be exceptions to that generalization unless some special case obtains in which there are even more powerful countervailing reasons. Such generalizations would not be merely accidental generalizations; they would point to, or be based upon, the essence of the wrongness of killing, what it is that makes killing wrong. All this suggests that a necessary condition of resolving the abortion controversy is a more theoretical account of the wrongness of killing. After all, if we merely believe, but do not understand, why killing adult human beings such as ourselves is wrong, how could we conceivably show that abortion is either immoral or permissible?

II

In order to develop such an account, we can start from the following unproblematic assumption concerning our own case: it is wrong to kill *us*. Why is it wrong? Some answers can be easily eliminated. It might be said that what makes killing us wrong is that a killing brutalizes the one who kills. But the brutalization consists of being inured to the performance of an act that is hideously immoral; hence, the brutalization does not explain the immorality. It might be said that what makes killing us wrong is the great loss others would experience due to our absence. Although such hubris is understandable, such an explanation does not account for the wrongness of killing hermits, or those whose lives are relatively independent and whose friends find it easy to make new friends.

A more obvious answer is better. What primarily makes killing wrong is neither its effect on the murderer nor its effect on the victim's friends and relatives, but its effect on the victim. The loss of one's life is one of the greatest losses one can suffer. The loss of one's life deprives one of all the experiences, activities, projects, and enjoyments that would otherwise have constituted one's future. Therefore, killing someone is wrong, primarily because the killing inflicts (one of) the greatest possible losses on the victim. To describe this as the loss of life can be misleading, however. The change in my biological state does not by itself make killing me wrong. The effect of the loss of my biological life is the loss to me of all those activities, projects, experiences, and enjoyments which would otherwise have constituted my future personal life. These activities, projects, experiences, and enjoyments are either valuable for their own sakes or are means to something else that is valuable for its own sake. Some parts of my future are not valued by me now, but will come to be valued by me as I grow older and as my values and capacities change. When I am killed, I am deprived both of what I now value which would have been part of my future personal life, but also what I would come to value. Therefore, when I die, I am deprived of all of the value of my future. Inflicting this loss on me is ultimately what makes killing me wrong. This being the case, it would seem that what makes killing *any* adult human being prima facie seriously wrong is the loss of his or her future.[6]

How should this rudimentary theory of the wrongness of killing be evaluated? It cannot be faulted for deriving an "ought" from an "is," for it does not. The analysis assumes that killing me (or you, reader) is prima facie seriously wrong. The point of the analysis is to establish which natural property ultimately explains the wrongness of the killing, given that it is wrong. A natural property will ultimately explain the wrongness of killing, only if (1) the explanation fits with our intuitions about the matter and (2) there is no other natural property that provides the basis for a better explanation of the wrongness of killing. This analysis rests on the intuition that what makes killing a particular human or animal wrong is what it does to that particular human or animal. What makes killing wrong is some natural effect or other of the killing. Some would deny this. For instance, a divine-command theorist in ethics would deny it. Surely this denial is, however, one of those features of divine-command theory which renders it so implausible.

The claim that what makes killing wrong is the loss of the victim's future is directly supported by two considerations. In the first place, this theory explains why we regard killing as one of the worst of crimes. Killing is especially wrong, because it deprives the victim of more than perhaps any other crime. In the second place, people with AIDS or cancer who know they are dying believe, of course, that dying is a very bad thing for them. They believe that the loss of a future to them that they would otherwise have experienced is what makes their premature death a very bad thing for them. A better theory of the wrongness of killing would require a different natural property associated with killing which better fits with the attitudes of the dying. What could it be?

The view that what makes killing wrong is the loss to the victim of the value of the victim's future gains additional support when some of its implications are examined. In the first place, it is incompatible with the view that it is wrong to kill only beings who are biologically human. It is possible that there exists a different species from another planet whose members have a future like ours. Since having a future like that is what makes killing someone wrong, this theory entails that it would be wrong to kill members of such a species. Hence, this theory is opposed to the claim that only life that is biologically human has great moral worth, a claim which many anti-abortionists have seemed to adopt. This opposition, which this theory has in common with personhood theories, seems to be a merit of the theory.

In the second place, the claim that the loss of one's future is the wrong-making feature of one's being killed entails the possibility that the futures of some actual nonhuman mammals on our own planet are sufficiently like ours that it is seriously wrong to kill them also. Whether some animals do have the same right to life as human beings depends on adding to the account of the wrongness of killing some additional account of just what it is about my future or the futures of other adult human beings which makes it wrong to kill us. No such additional account will be offered in this essay. Undoubtedly, the provision of such an account would be a very difficult matter. Undoubtedly, any such account would be quite controversial. Hence, it surely should not reflect badly on this sketch of an elementary theory of the wrongness of killing that it is indeterminate with respect to some very difficult issues regarding animal rights.

In the third place, the claim that the loss of one's future is the wrong-making feature of one's being killed does not entail, as sanctity of human life theories do, that active euthanasia is wrong. Persons who are severely and incurably ill, who face a future of pain and despair, and who wish to die will not have suffered a loss if they are killed. It is, strictly speaking, the value of a human's future which makes killing wrong in this theory. This being so, killing does not necessarily wrong some persons who are sick and dying. Of course, there may be other reasons for a prohibition of active euthanasia, but that is another matter. Sanctity-of-human-life theories seem to hold that active euthanasia is seriously wrong even in an individual case where there seems to be good reason for it independently of public policy considerations. This consequence is most implausible, and it is a plus for the claim that the loss of a future of value is what makes killing wrong that it does not share this consequence.

In the fourth place, the account of the wrongness of killing defended in this essay does straightforwardly entail that it is prima facie seriously wrong to kill children and infants, for we do presume that they have futures of value. Since we do believe that it is wrong to kill defenseless little babies, it is important that a theory of the wrongness of killing easily account for this. Personhood theories of the wrongness of killing, on the other hand, cannot straightforwardly account for the wrongness of killing infants and young children.[7] Hence, such theories must add special ad hoc accounts of the wrongness of killing the young. The plausibility of such ad hoc theories seems to be a function of how desperately one wants such theories to work. The claim that the primary wrong-making feature of a killing is the loss to the victim of the value of its future accounts for the wrongness of killing young children and infants directly; it makes the wrongness of such acts as obvious as we actually think it is. This is a further merit of this theory. Accordingly, it seems that this value of a future-like-ours theory of the wrongness of killing shares strengths of both sanctity-of-life and personhood accounts while avoiding weaknesses of both. In addition, it meshes with a central intuition concerning what makes killing wrong.

The claim that the primary wrong-making feature of a killing is the loss to the victim of the value of its future has obvious consequences for the ethics of abortion. The future of a standard fetus includes a set of experiences, projects, activities, and such which are identical with the futures of adult human beings and are identical with the futures of young children. Since the reason that is sufficient to explain why it is wrong to kill human beings after the time of birth is a reason that also applies to fetuses, it follows that abortion is prima facie seriously morally wrong.

This argument does not rely on the invalid inference that, since it is wrong to kill persons, it is wrong to kill potential persons also. The category that is morally central to this analysis is the category of having a valuable future like ours; it is not the category of personhood. The argument to the conclusion that abortion is prima facie seriously morally wrong proceeded independently of the notion of person or potential person or any equivalent. Someone may wish to start with this analysis in terms of the value of a human future, conclude that abortion is, except perhaps in rare circumstances, seriously morally wrong, infer that fetuses have the right to life, and then call fetuses "persons" as a result of their having the right to life. Clearly, in this case, the category of person is being used to state the *conclusion* of the analysis rather than to generate the *argument* of the analysis.

The structure of this anti-abortion argument can be both illuminated and defended by comparing it to what appears to be the best argument for the wrongness of the wanton infliction of pain on animals. This latter argument is based on the assumption that it is prima facie wrong to inflict pain on me (or you, reader). What is the natural property associated with the infliction of pain which makes such infliction wrong? The obvious answer seems to be that the infliction of pain causes suffering and that suffering is a misfortune. The suffering caused by the infliction of pain is what makes the wanton infliction of pain on me wrong. The wanton infliction of pain on other adult humans causes suffering. The wanton infliction of pain on animals causes suffering. Since causing suffering is what makes the wanton infliction of pain wrong and since the wanton infliction of pain on animals causes suffering, it follows that the wanton infliction of pain on animals is wrong.

This argument for the wrongness of the wanton infliction of pain on animals shares a number of structural features with the argument for the serious prima facie wrongness of abortion. Both arguments start with an obvious assumption concerning what it is wrong to do to me (or you, reader). Both then look for the characteristic or the consequence of the wrong action which makes the action wrong. Both recognize that the wrong-making feature of these immoral actions is a property of actions sometimes directed at individuals other than postnatal human beings. If the structure of the argument for the wrongness of the wanton infliction of pain on animals is sound, then the structure of the argument for the prima facie serious wrongness of abortion is also sound, for the structure of the two arguments is the same. The structure common to both is the key to the explanation of how the wrongness of abortion can be demonstrated without recourse to the category of person. In neither argument is that category crucial.

This defense of an argument for the wrongness of abortion in terms of a structurally similar argument for the wrongness of the wanton infliction of pain on animals succeeds only if the account regarding animals is the correct account. Is it? In the first place, it seems plausible. In the second place, its major competition is Kant's account. Kant believed that we do not have direct duties to animals at all, because they are not persons. Hence, Kant had to explain and justify the wrongness of inflicting pain on animals on the grounds that "he who is hard in his dealings with animals becomes hard also in his dealing with men."[8] The problem with Kant's account is that there seems to be no reason for accepting this latter claim unless Kant's account is rejected. If the alternative to Kant's account is accepted, then it is easy to understand why someone who is indifferent to inflicting pain on animals is also indifferent to inflicting pain on humans, for one is indifferent to what makes inflicting pain wrong in both cases. But, if Kant's account is accepted, there is no intelligible reason why one who is hard in his dealings with animals (or crabgrass or stones) should also be hard in his dealings with men. After all, men are persons: animals are no more persons than crabgrass or stones. Persons are Kant's crucial moral category. Why, in short, should a Kantian accept the basic claim in Kant's argument?

Hence, Kant's argument for the wrongness of inflicting pain on animals rests on a claim that, in a world of Kantian moral agents, is demonstrably false. Therefore, the alternative analysis, being more plausible anyway, should be accepted. Since this alternative analysis has the same structure as the anti-abortion argument being defended here, we have further support for the argument for the immorality of abortion being defended in this essay.

Of course, this value of a future-like-ours argument, if sound, shows only that abortion is prima facie wrong, not that it is wrong in any and all circumstances. Since the loss of the future to a standard fetus, if killed, is, however, at least as great a loss as the loss of the future to a standard adult human being who is killed, abortion, like ordinary killing, could be justified only by the most compelling reasons. The loss of one's life is almost the greatest misfortune that can happen to one. Presumably abortion could be justified in some circumstances, only if the loss consequent on failing to abort would be at least as great. Accordingly, morally permissible abortions will be rare indeed unless, perhaps, they occur so early in pregnancy that a fetus is not yet definitely an individual. Hence, this argument should be taken as showing that abortion is presumptively very seriously wrong, where the presumption is very strong—strong as the presumption that killing another adult human being is wrong. ...

VI

The purpose of this essay has been to set out an argument for the serious presumptive wrongness of abortion subject to the assumption that the moral permissibility of abortion stands or falls on the moral status of the fetus. Since a fetus possesses a property, the possession of which in adult human beings is sufficient to make killing an adult human being wrong, abortion is wrong. This way of dealing with the problem of abortion seems superior to other approaches to the ethics of abortion, because it rests on an ethics of killing which is close to self-evident, because the crucial morally relevant property clearly applies to fetuses, and because the argument avoids the usual equivocations on "human life," "human being," or "person." The argument rests neither on religious claims nor on Papal dogma. It is not subject to the objection of "speciesism." Its soundness is compatible with the moral permissibility of euthanasia and contraception. It deals with our intuitions concerning young children.

Finally, this analysis can be viewed as resolving a standard problem—indeed, *the* standard problem—concerning the ethics of abortion. Clearly, it is wrong to kill adult human beings. Clearly, it is not wrong to end the life of some arbitrarily chosen single human cell. Fetuses seem to be like arbitrarily chosen human cells in some respects and like adult humans in other respects. The problem of the ethics of abortion is the problem of determining the fetal property that settles this moral controversy. The thesis of this essay is that the problem of the ethics of abortion, so understood, is solvable.

NOTES

1. Feinberg, "Abortion," in *Matters of Life and Death: New Introductory Essays in Moral Philosophy*, Tom Regan, ed. (New York: Random House, 1986), pp. 256–293; Tooley, "Abortion and Infanticide," *Philosophy and Public Affairs*, II, 1 (1972): 37–65; Tooley, *Abortion and Infanticide* (New York: Oxford, 1984): Warren, "On the Moral and Legal Status of Abortion," *The Monist*, LVII, 1 (1973): 43–61; Engelhardt, "The Ontology of Abortion," *Ethics*, LXXXIV, 3 (1974): 217–234; Sumner, *Abortion and Moral Theory* (Princeton: University Press, 1981); Noonan, "An Almost Absolute Value in History," in *The Morality of Abortion: Legal and Historical Perspectives*, Noonan, ed. (Cambridge: Harvard, 1970); and Devine, *The Ethics of Homicide* (Ithaca: Cornell, 1978).

2. For interesting discussions of this issue, see Warren Quinn, "Abortion: Identity and Loss," *Philosophy and Public Affairs*, XIII, 1 (1984):24–54; and Lawrence C. Becker, "Human Being: The Boundaries of the Concept," *Philosophy and Public Affairs*, IV, 4 (1975):334–359.

3. For example, see my "Ethics and The Elderly: Some Problems," in Stuart Spicker, Kathleen Woodward, and David Van Tassel, eds., *Aging and the Elderly: Humanistic Perspectives* in *Gerontology* (Atlantic Highlands, NJ: Humanities, 1978), pp. 341–355.

4. See Warren, op cit., and Tooley, "Abortion and Infanticide."

5. This seems to be the fatal flaw in Warren's treatment of this issue.

6. I have been most influenced on this matter by Jonathan Glover, *Causing Death and Saving Lives* (New York: Penguin, 1977), ch. 3; and Robert Young, "What Is So Wrong with Killing People?" *Philosophy*, LIV, 210 (1979):515–528.

7. Feinberg, Tooley, Warren, and Engelhardt have all dealt with this problem.

8. "Duties to Animals and Spirits," in *Lectures on Ethics*, Louis Infeld, trans. (New York: Harper, 1963), p. 239.

ARGUMENT 1 ESSAY QUESTIONS

1. Who makes the stronger case for their view on abortion—Mary Anne Warren or Don Marquis? Why? Does either argument contain a problematic premise? If so, what is it?
2. What is Pojman's argument for abortion? Is his argument sound? Explain.
3. How does Schwarz's view of personhood differ from Warren's? Which view is more plausible? Why?

2. NOONAN'S PERSONHOOD-AT-CONCEPTION ARGUMENT AGAINST ABORTION

The main conservative argument against abortion goes like this: (1) The killing of an innocent person is wrong; (2) the unborn is an innocent person from the moment of conception; (3) therefore, it is wrong to kill the unborn (abortion is immoral). This argument is valid, and premise 1 is obviously true. The crux of the matter is premise 2, which the conservative asserts and the liberal denies. What arguments can the conservative offer to support it?

In "An Almost Absolute Value in History," the approach of John T. Noonan is to start by showing that in the continuous process of development from zygote to adult human, there seems to be no precise point at which the entity becomes unmistakably a bona fide human being (with a right to life). No clear line between nonperson and person can be found. The commonly proposed demarcations between person and nonperson—viability, experience, the sentiments of adults, quickening, and social visibility—are arbitrary and unsupportable. Noonan argues that the most plausible view then is that personhood begins at conception, for it is at conception that there is a dramatic increase in the probability that the unborn entity will develop into a mature human being with undeniable moral rights. What propels this jump in probabilities is the sudden appearance of a full complement of genetic information. As he puts it,

> The positive argument for conception as the decision moment of humanization is that at conception the new being receives the genetic code. It is this genetic information which determines his characteristics, which is the biological carrier of the possibility of human wisdom, which makes him a self-evolving being. A being with a human genetic code is man.[13]

Critics respond in various ways to this view. They point out, for example, that just because no nonperson/person line can be drawn, that doesn't mean there is no difference to be observed between the two phenomena. We may not be able to specify the precise moment when a tadpole turns into a frog, but we know there is a real difference between the two states. The failure to pinpoint a distinct moment after conception when the unborn becomes a person does not show that it must be a person from the moment of conception.

Some philosophers argue on empirical grounds that the zygote cannot be an individual human being:

> [T]he very early conceptus cannot be identified with the embryo that may develop from it. This is because, for about the first two weeks of existence, it consists of a set of undifferentiated cells, any one of which could give rise to an embryo under certain circumstances. This 'pre-embryo' may spontaneously divide, resulting in twins or triplets; alternatively, it may combine with another pre-embryo, giving rise to a single fetus.[14]

Conservatives avoid such complications by arguing not that the fetus is a person, but that it is a *potential* person and thus has the same right to life as any existing person. The unborn may not be a person now, but its status as a possible future person puts it in the same moral category as any normal adult human being. Philip Devine expresses the point like this:

---

[13] John T. Noonan, Jr., "An Almost Absolute Value in History," in *The Morality of Abortion: Legal and Historical Perspectives*, John T. Noonan, Jr., ed. (Cambridge, MA: Harvard University Press, 1970), 51–59.

[14] Mary Anne Warren, "Abortion," in *A Companion to Bioethics*, ed. Helga Kuhse and Peter Singer (Oxford: Blackwell, 2001), 130.

What makes the difference between human beings and other life is the capacity human beings enjoy for a specially rich kind of life. The life already enjoyed by a human being cannot be taken away from him, only the prospect of such life in the future. But this prospect is possessed as much by an infant or fetus as by a full-grown adult.[15]

A common response to this potentiality argument is that there is a world of difference between (1) possessing a particular trait that gives you a right and (2) *having the potential* to develop a trait that gives you a right. "[T]he right to vote in political elections may be granted to citizens who have reached the age of 18," says Mary Anne Warren, "but not to pre-adolescents—even though most of them clearly have the potential to reach the age of 18." From the fact that someone has the potential to become a Supreme Court justice, it does not follow that we should treat her as if she were a justice now.

An Almost Absolute Value in History

JOHN T. NOONAN, JR.

The most fundamental question involved in the long history of thought on abortion is: How do you determine the humanity of a being? To phrase the question that way is to put in comprehensive humanistic terms what the theologians either dealt with as an explicitly theological question under the heading of "ensoulment" or dealt with implicitly in their treatment of abortion. The Christian position as it originated did not depend on a narrow theological or philosophical concept. It had no relation to theories of infant baptism.[1] It appealed to no special theory of instantaneous ensoulment. It took the world's view on ensoulment as that view changed from Aristotle to Zacchia. There was, indeed, theological influence affecting the theory of ensoulment finally adopted, and, of course, ensoulment itself was a theological concept, so that the position was always explained in theological terms. But the theological notion of ensoulment could easily be translated into humanistic language by substituting "human" for "rational soul"; the problem of knowing when a man is a man is common to theology and humanism.

If one steps outside the specific categories used by theologians, the answer they gave can be analyzed as a refusal to discriminate among human beings on the basis of their varying potentialities. Once conceived, the being was recognized as man because he had man's potential. The criterion for humanity, thus, was simple and all-embracing: if you are conceived by human parents, you are human.

---

[15] Philip Devine, "The Scope of the Prohibition against Killing," in *The Ethics of Homicide* (Ithaca, NY: Cornell University Press, 1978).

The strength of this position may be tested by a review of some of the other distinctions offered in the contemporary controversy over legalizing abortion. Perhaps the most popular distinction is in terms of viability. Before an age of so many months, the fetus is not viable, that is, it cannot be removed from the mother's womb and live apart from her. To that extent, the life of the fetus is absolutely dependent on the life of the mother. This dependence is made the basis of denying recognition to its humanity.

There are difficulties with this distinction. One is that the perfection of artificial incubation may make the fetus viable at any time: it may be removed and artificially sustained. Experiments with animals already show that such a procedure is possible.[2] This hypothetical extreme case relates to an actual difficulty: there is considerable elasticity to the idea of viability. Mere length of life is not an exact measure. The viability of the fetus depends on the extent of its anatomical and functional development.[3] The weight and length of the fetus are better guides to the state of its development than age, but weight and length vary.[4] Moreover, different racial groups have different ages at which their fetuses are viable. Some evidence, for example, suggests that Negro fetuses mature more quickly than white fetuses.[5] If viability is the norm, the standard would vary with race and with many individual circumstances.

The most important objection to this approach is that dependence is not ended by viability. The fetus is still absolutely dependent on someone's care in order to continue existence; indeed a child of one or three or even five years of age is absolutely dependent on another's care for existence; uncared for, the older fetus or the younger child will die as surely as the early fetus detached from the mother. The unsubstantial lessening in dependence at viability does not seem to signify any special acquisition of humanity.

A second distinction has been attempted in terms of experience. A being who has had experience, has lived and suffered, who possesses memories, is more human than one who has not. Humanity depends on formation by experience. The fetus is thus "unformed" in the most basic human sense.[6]

This distinction is not serviceable for the embryo which is already experiencing and reacting. The embryo is responsive to touch after eight weeks[7] and at least at that point is experiencing. At an earlier stage the zygote is certainly alive and responding to its environment.[8] The distinction may also be challenged by the rare case where aphasia has erased adult memory: has it erased humanity? More fundamentally, this distinction leaves even the older fetus or the younger child to be treated as an unformed inhuman thing. Finally, it is not clear why experience as such confers humanity. It could be argued that certain central experiences such as loving or learning are necessary to make a man human. But then human beings who have failed to love or to learn might be excluded from the class called man.

A third distinction is made by appeal to the sentiments of adults. If a fetus dies, the grief of the parents is not the grief they would have for a living child. The fetus is an unnamed "it" till birth, and is not perceived as personality until at least the fourth month of existence when movements in the womb manifest a vigorous presence demanding joyful recognition by the parents.

Yet feeling is notoriously an unsure guide to the humanity of others. Many groups of humans have had difficulty in feeling that persons of another tongue, color, religion, sex, are as human as they. Apart from reactions to alien groups, we mourn the loss of a ten-year-old boy more than the loss of his one-day-old brother or his 90-year-old grandfather. The difference felt and the grief expressed vary with the potentialities extinguished, or the experience wiped out; they do not seem to point to any substantial difference in the humanity of baby, boy, or grandfather.

Distinctions are also made in terms of sensation by the parents. The embryo is felt within the womb only after about the fourth month.[9] The embryo is seen only at birth. What can be neither seen nor felt is different from what is tangible. If the fetus cannot be seen or touched at all, it cannot be perceived as man.

Yet experience shows that sight is even more untrustworthy than feeling in determining humanity. By sight, color became an appropriate index for saying who was a man, and the evil of facial discrimination was given foundation. Nor can touch provide the test; a being confined by sickness, "out of touch" with others, does not thereby seem to lose his humanity. To the extent that touch still has appeal as a criterion, it appears to be a survival of the old English idea of "quickening"—a possible mistranslation of the Latin *animatus* used in the canon law.[10] To that extent touch as a criterion seems to be dependent on the Aristotelian notion of ensoulment, and to fall when this notion is discarded.

Finally, a distinction is sought in social visibility. The fetus is not socially perceived as human. It cannot communicate with others. Thus, both subjectively and objectively, it is not a member of society. As moral rules are rules for the behavior of members of society to each other, they cannot be made for behavior toward what is not yet a member. Excluded from the society of men, the fetus is excluded from the humanity of men.[11]

By force of the argument from the consequences, this distinction is to be rejected. It is more subtle than that founded on an appeal to physical sensation, but it is equally dangerous in its implications. If humanity depends on social recognition, individuals or whole groups may be dehumanized by being denied any status in their society. Such a fate is fictionally portrayed in *1984* and has actually been the lot of many men in many societies. In the Roman empire, for example, condemnation to slavery meant the practical denial of most human rights; in the Chinese Communist world, landlords have been classified as enemies of the people and so treated as non-persons by the state. Humanity does not depend on social recognition, though often the failure of society to recognize the prisoner, the alien, the heterodox as human has led to the destruction of human beings. Anyone conceived by a man and a woman is human. Recognition of this condition by society follows a real event in the objective order, however imperfect and halting the recognition. Any attempt to limit humanity to exclude some group runs the risk of furnishing authority and precedent for excluding other groups in the name of the consciousness or perception of the controlling group in the society.

A philosopher may reject the appeal to the humanity of the fetus because he views "humanity" as a secular view of the soul and because he doubts the existence of anything real and objective which can be identified as humanity.[12] One answer to such a philosopher is to ask how he reasons about moral questions without supposing that there is a sense in which he and the others of whom he speaks are human. Whatever group is taken as the society which determines who may be killed is thereby taken as human. A second answer is to ask if he does not believe that there is a right and wrong way of deciding moral questions. If there is such a difference, experience may be appealed to: to decide who is human on the basis of the sentiment of a given society has led to consequences which rational men would characterize as monstrous.[13]

The rejection of the attempted distinctions based on viability and visibility, experience and feeling, may be buttressed by the following considerations: Moral judgments often rest on distinctions, but if the distinctions are not to appear arbitrary fiat, they should relate to some real difference in probabilities. There is a kind of continuity in all life, but the earlier stages of the elements of human life possess tiny probabilities of development. Consider for example, the spermatozoa in any normal ejaculate: There are about 200,000,000 in any single ejaculate, of which one has a chance of developing into a zygote.[14] Consider the oocytes which may become ova: there are 100,000 to 1,000,000 oocytes in a female infant, of which a maximum of 390 are ovulated.[15] But once spermatozoon and ovum meet and the conceptus is formed, such studies as have been made show that roughly in only 20 percent of the cases will spontaneous abortion occur.[16] In other words, the chances are about 4 out of 5 that this new being will develop. At this stage in the life of the being there is a sharp shift in probabilities, an immense jump in potentialities. To make a distinction between the rights of spermatozoa and the rights of the fertilized ovum is to respond to an enormous shift in possibilities. For about twenty days after conception the egg may split to form twins or combine with another egg to form a chimera, but the probability of either event happening is very small.

It may be asked, What does a change in biological probabilities have to do with establishing humanity? The argument from probabilities is not aimed at establishing humanity but at establishing an objective discontinuity which may be taken into account in moral discourse. As life itself is a matter of probabilities, as most moral reasoning is an estimate of probabilities, so it seems in accord with the structure of reality and the nature of moral thought to found a moral judgment on the change in probabilities at conception. The appeal to probabilities is the most commensensical of arguments, to a greater or smaller degree all of us base our actions on probabilities, and in morals, as in law, prudence and negligence are often measured by the account one has taken of the probabilities. If the chance is 200,000,000 to 1 that the movement in the bushes into which you shoot is a man's, I doubt if many persons would hold you careless in shooting; but if the chances are 4 out of 5 that the movement is a human being's, few would acquit you of blame. Would the argument be different if only one out of ten children conceived came to term? Of course this argument would be different. This argument is an appeal to probabilities that actually exist, not to any and all states of affairs which may be imagined.

The probabilities as they do exist do not show the humanity of the embryo in the sense of a demonstration in logic any more than the probabilities of the movement in the bush being a man demonstrate beyond all doubt that the being is a man. The appeal is a "buttressing" consideration, showing the plausibility of the standard adopted. The argument focuses on the decisional factor in any moral judgment and assumes that part of the business of a moralist is drawing lines. One evidence of the nonarbitrary character of the line drawn is the difference of probabilities on either side of it. If a spermatozoon is destroyed, one destroys a being which had a chance of far less than 1 in 200 million of developing into a reasoning being, possessed of the genetic code, a heart and other organs, and capable of pain. If a fetus is destroyed, one destroys a being already possessed of the genetic code, organs, and sensitivity to pain, and one which had an 80 percent chance of developing further into a baby outside the womb who, in time, would reason.

The positive argument for conception as the decisive moment of humanization is that at conception the new being receives the genetic code.[17] It is this genetic information which determines his characteristics, which is the biological carrier of the possibility of human wisdom, which makes him a self-evolving being. A being with a human genetic code is man.

This review of current controversy over the humanity of the fetus emphasizes what a fundamental question the theologians resolved in asserting the inviolability of the fetus. To regard the fetus as possessed of equal rights with other humans was not, however, to decide every case where abortion might be employed. It did decide the case where the argument was that the fetus should be aborted for its own good. To say a being was human was to say it had a destiny to decide for itself which could not be taken from it by another man's decision. But human beings with equal rights often come in conflict with each other, and some decision must be made as whose claims are to prevail. Cases of conflict involving the fetus are different only in two respects: the total inability of the fetus to speak for itself and the fact that the right of the fetus regularly at stake is the right to life itself.

The approach taken by the theologians to these conflicts was articulated in terms of "direct" and "indirect." Again, to look at what they were doing from outside their categories, they may be said to have been drawing lines or "balancing values." "Direct" and "indirect" are spatial metaphors; "line-drawing" is another. "To weigh" or "to balance" values is a metaphor of a more complicated mathematical sort hinting at the process which goes on in moral judgments. All the metaphors suggest that, in the moral judgments made, comparisons were necessary, that no value completely controlled. The principle of double effect was no doctrine fallen from heaven, but a method of analysis appropriate where two relative values were being compared. In Catholic moral theology, as it developed, life even of the innocent was not taken as an absolute. Judgments on acts affecting life issued from a process of weighing. In the weighing, the fetus was always given a value greater than zero, always a value separate and independent from its parents. This valuation was crucial and fundamental in all Christian thought on the subject and marked it off from any approach which considered that only the parents' interests needed to be considered.

Even with the fetus weighed as human, one interest could be weighed as equal or superior: that of the mother in her own life. The casuists between 1450 and 1895 were willing to weigh this interest as superior. Since 1895, that interest was given decisive weight only in the two special cases of the cancerous uterus and the ectopic pregnancy. In both of these cases the fetus itself had little chance of survival even if the abortion were not performed. As the balance was once struck in favor of the mother whenever her life was endangered, it could be so struck again. The balance reached between 1895 and 1930 attempted prudentially and pastorally to forestall a multitude of exceptions for interests less than life.

The perception of the humanity of the fetus and the weighing of fetal rights against other human rights constituted the work of the moral analysts. But what spirit animated their abstract judgments? For the Christian community it was the injunction of Scripture to love your neighbor as yourself. The fetus as human was a neighbor; his life had parity with one's own. The commandment gave life to what otherwise would have been only rational calculation.

The commandment could be put in humanistic as well as theological terms: Do not injure your fellow man without reason. In these terms, once the humanity of the fetus is perceived, abortion is never right except in self-defense. When life must be taken to save life, reason alone cannot say that a mother must prefer a child's life to her own. With this exception, now of great rarity, abortion violates the rational humanist tenet of the equality of human lives.

For Christians the commandment to love had received a special imprint in that the exemplar proposed of love was the love of the Lord for his disciples. In the light given by this example, self-sacrifice carried to the point of death seemed in the extreme situations not without meaning. In the less extreme cases, preference for one's own interests to the life of another seemed to express cruelty or selfishness irreconcilable with the demands of love.

NOTES

1. According to Glanville Williams (*The Sanctity of Human Life* supra n. 169, at 193), "The historical reason for the Catholic objection to abortion is the same as for the Christian Church's historical opposition to infanticide: the horror of bringing about the death of an unbaptized child." This statement is made without any citation of evidence. As has been seen, desire to administer baptism could, in the Middle Ages, even be urged as a reason for

procuring an abortion. It is highly regrettable that the American Law Institute was apparently misled by Williams' account and repeated after him the same baseless statement. See American Law Institute, *Model Penal Code: Tentative Draft No. 9* (1959), p. 148, n. 12.

2. E.g., R. L. Brinster and J. L. Thomson, "Development of Eight-Cell Mouse Embryos in Vitro," 42 *Experimental Cell Research* 308 (1966).

3. J. Edgar Morison, *Fetal and Neonatal Pathology* 99–100 (1963).

4. Peter Gruenwald, "Growth of the Human Fetus," 94 *American Journal of Obstetrics and Gynecology* 1112 (1966).

5. Morison, *Fetal and Neonatal Pathology* supra n. 3, at 101.

6. This line of thought was advanced by some participants at the International Conference on Abortion sponsored by the Harvard Divinity School in cooperation with the Joseph P. Kennedy, Jr., Foundation in Washington, D.C., Sept. 8–10, 1967.

7. Frank D. Allan, *Essentials of Human Embryology* 165 (1960).

8. Frederick J. Gottleib, *Developmental Genetics* 28 (1966).

9. Allan, *Essentials of Human Embryology* supra n. 7, at 165.

10. See David W. Louisell and John T. Noonan, Jr., "Constitutional Balance," *infra.*

11. Another line of thought advanced at the Conference mentioned in n. 6. Thomas Aquinas gave an analogous reason against baptizing a fetus in the womb: "As long as it exists in the womb of the mother, it cannot be subject to the operation of the ministers of the Church as it is not known to men" (*In sententias Petri Lombardi* 4.6 1.1.2).

12. Compare John O'Connor, "Humanity and Abortion," 12 *Natural Law Forum* 128–130 (1968), with John T. Noonan, Jr. "Deciding Who Is Human," 12 *Natural Law Forum* 134–138.

13. A famous passage of Montesquien reads:
"Ceux dont il s'agit sont noirs depuis les pieds jusqu'à la tête; et ils ont le nez si écrasé qu'il est presque impossible de les plaindre.
"On ne peut se mettre dans l'esprit que Dieu qui est un être très-sage, ait mis une âme, surtout une âme bonne, dans un corps tout noir.
"Il est si naturel de penser que c'est la couleur qui constitue l'essence de l'humanité, que les

peuples d'Asle, qui font des eunuques, privent toujours les noirs du rapport qu'ils ont avec nous d'une façon plus marquée." *Montesquieu, De l'esprit des lois,* in *Oeuvres Complètes* book 15, chap. 5 (Paris, 1843).

14. J. S. Baxter, *Frazer's Manual of Embryology* 5 (1963).
15. Gregory Pancus, *The Control of Fertility* 197 (1965).
16. Idem. Apparently there is some small variation by region.
17. Gottleib, *Developmental Genetics* supra n. 8, at 17.

In Defense of Abortion and Infanticide

MICHAEL TOOLEY

ABORTION AND INFANTICIDE

What reason is there for raising the question of the morality of infanticide? One reason is that it seems very difficult to formulate a completely satisfactory pro-abortion position without coming to grips with the infanticide issue. For the problem that the liberal on abortion encounters here is that of specifying a cutoff point that is not arbitrary: At what stage in the development of a human being does it cease to be morally permissible to destroy it, and why?

It is important to be clear about the difficulty here. The problem is not, as some have thought, that since there is a continuous line of development from a zygote to a newborn baby, one cannot hold that it is seriously wrong to destroy a newborn baby without also holding that it is seriously wrong to destroy a zygote, or any intermediate stage in the development of a human being. The problem is rather that if one says that it is wrong to destroy a newborn baby but not a zygote or some intermediate stage, one should be prepared to point to a *morally relevant* difference between a newborn baby and the earlier stage in the development of a human being.

Precisely the same difficulty can, of course, be raised for a person who holds that infanticide is morally permissible, since one can ask what morally relevant difference there is between an adult human being and a newborn baby. What makes it morally permissible to destroy a baby, but wrong to kill an adult? So the challenge remains. But I shall argue that in the latter case there is an extremely plausible answer.

Reflecting on the morality of infanticide forces one to face up to this challenge. In the case of abortion a number of events—quickening or viability, for instance—might be taken as cutoff points, and it is easy to overlook the fact that none of these events involves any morally significant change in the developing human. In contrast, if one is going to defend infanticide, one has to get very clear about what it is that gives something a right to life.

One of the interesting ways in which the abortion issue differs from most other moral issues is that the plausible positions on abortion appear to be extreme ones. For if a human fetus has a right to life, one is inclined to say that, in general, one would be justified in killing it only to save the life of the mother, and perhaps not even in that case. Such is the extreme anti-abortion position. On the other hand, if the fetus does not have a right to life, why should it be seriously wrong to destroy it? Why would one need to point to special circumstance—such as the presence of genetic disease, or a threat to the woman's health—in order to justify such action? The upshot is that there does not appear to be any room for a moderate position on abortion as one finds, for example, in the Model Penal Code recommendations.

Aside from the light it may shed on the abortion question, the issue of infanticide is both interesting and important in its own right. The theoretical

Reprinted by permission of Michael Tooley.

interest has been mentioned earlier: It forces one to face up to the question of what it is that gives something a right to life. The practical importance need not be labored. Most people would prefer to raise children who do not suffer from gross deformities or from severe physical, emotional, or intellectual handicaps. If it could be shown that there is no moral objection to infanticide, the happiness of society could be significantly and justifiably increased.

The suggestion that infanticide may be morally permissible is not an idea that many people are able to consider dispassionately. Even philosophers tend to react in a way that seems primarily visceral—offering no arguments and dismissing infanticide out of hand.

Some philosophers have argued, however, that such a reaction is not inappropriate, on the ground that, first, moral principles must, in the final analysis, be justified by reference to our moral feelings, or intuitions, and secondly, infanticide is one practice that is judged wrong by virtually everyone's moral intuition. I believe, however, that this line of thought is unsound, and I have argued elsewhere that even if one grants, at least for the sake of argument, that moral intuitions are the final court of appeal regarding the acceptability of moral principles, the question of the morality of infanticide is not one that can be settled by an appeal to our intuitions concerning it. If infanticide is to be rejected, an argument is needed, and I believe that the considerations advanced in this essay show that it is unlikely that such an argument is forthcoming.

WHAT SORT OF BEING CAN POSSESS A RIGHT TO LIFE?

The issues of the morality of abortion and of infanticide seem to turn primarily upon the answers to the following four questions:

1. What properties, other than potentialities, give something a right to life?
2. Do the corresponding potentialities also endow something with a right to life?
3. If not, do they at least make it seriously wrong to destroy it?
4. At what point in its development does a member of the biologically defined species *Homo*

sapiens first possess those nonpotential properties that give something a right to life?

The argument to be developed in the present section bears upon the answers to the first two questions.

How can one determine what properties endow a being with a right to life? An approach that I believe is very promising starts from the observation that there appear to be two radically different sorts of reasons why an entity may lack a certain right. Compare, for example, the following two claims:

1. A child does not have a right to smoke.
2. A newspaper does not have a right not to be torn up.

The first claim raises a substantive moral issue. People might well disagree about it, and support their conflicting views by appealing to different moral theories. The second dispute, in contrast, seems an unlikely candidate for moral dispute. It is natural to say that newspapers just are not the sort of thing that can have any rights at all, including a right not to be torn up. So there is no need to appeal to a substantive moral theory to resolve the question whether a newspaper has a right not to be torn up.

One way of characterizing this difference, albeit one that will not especially commend itself to philosophers of a Quinean bent, is to say that the second claim, unlike the first, is true in virtue of a certain *conceptual* connection, and that is why no moral theory is needed in order to see that it is true. The explanation, then, of why it is that a newspaper does not have a right not to be torn up, is that there exists some property P such that, first, newspapers lack property P, and, second, it is a conceptual truth that only things with property P can be possessors of rights.

What might property P be? A plausible answer, I believe, is set out and defended by Joel Feinberg in his paper, "The Rights of Animals and Unborn Generations." It takes the form of what Feinberg refers to as the *interest principle*: "...the sorts of beings who *can* have rights are precisely those who have (or can have) interests." And then, since "interests must be compounded somehow out of conations," it follows that things devoid of desires, such as newspapers, can have neither interests nor rights. Here, then, is one account of the difference in status between judgments such as (1) and (2) above.

Let us now consider the right to life. The interest principle tells us that an entity cannot have any rights at all, and, *a fortiori*, cannot have a right to life, unless it is capable of having interests. This in itself may be a conclusion of considerable importance. Consider, for example, a fertilized human egg cell. Someday it will come to have desires and interests. As a zygote, however, it does not have desires, nor even the *capacity* for having desires. What about interests? This depends upon the account one offers of the relationship between desires and interests. It seems to me that a zygote cannot be properly spoken of as a subject of interests. My reason is roughly this. What is in a thing's interest is a function of its present and future desires, both those it will actually have and those it could have. In the case of an entity that is not presently capable of any desires, its interests must be based entirely upon the satisfaction of future desires. Then, since satisfaction of future desires presupposes the continued existence of the entity in question, anything which has an interest that is based upon the satisfaction of future desires must also have an interest in its own continued existence. Therefore, something that is not presently capable of having any desires at all—like a zygote—cannot have any interests at all unless it has interest in its own continued existence. I shall argue shortly, however, that a zygote cannot have such an interest. From this it will follow that it cannot have any interests at all, and this conclusion, together with the interest principle, entails that not all members of the species *Homo sapiens* have a right to life.

The interest principle involves, then, a thesis concerning a necessary condition that something must satisfy if it is to have a right to life, and it is a thesis that has important moral implications. It implies, for example, that abortions, if performed sufficiently early, do not involve any violation of a right to life. But on the other hand, the interest principle provides no help with the question of the moral status of human organisms once they have developed to the point where they do have desires, and thus are capable of having interests. The interest principle states that they *can* have

rights. It does not state whether they *do* have rights—including, in particular, a right not to be destroyed.

It is possible, however, that the interest principle does not exhaust the connections between rights and interests. It formulates only a very general connection: A thing cannot have any rights at all unless it is capable of having at least some interest. May there not be more specific connections, between particular rights and particular sorts of interests? The following line of thought lends plausibility to this suggestion. Consider animals such as cats. Some philosophers are inclined to hold that animals such as cats do not have any rights at all. But let us assume, for the purpose of the present discussion, that cats do have some rights, such as a right not to be tortured, and consider the following claim:

3. A cat does not have a right to a university education.

How is this statement to be regarded? In particular, is it comparable in status to the claim that children do not have a right to smoke, or, instead, to the claim that newspapers do not have a right to be torn up? To the latter, surely. Just as a newspaper is not the sort of thing that can have any rights at all, including a right not to be destroyed, so one is inclined to say that a cat, though it may have some rights, such as a right not to be tortured, is not the sort of thing that can possibly have a right to a university education.

This intuitive judgment about the status of claims such as (3) is reinforced, moreover, if one turns to the question of the grounds of the interest principle. Consider, for example, the account offered by Feinberg, which he summarizes as follows:

> Now we can extract from our discussion of animal rights a crucial principle for tentative use in the resolution of the other riddles about the applicability of the concept of a right, namely, that the sorts of beings who *can* have rights are precisely those who have (or can have) interests. I have come to this tentative conclusion for two reasons: (1) because a right holder must be capable of being represented and it is impossible to represent a being that has no interests, and (2) because a right holder must be capable of being a beneficiary in his own person, and a being without interests is a being that is incapable of being harmed or benefited, having

no good or "sake" of its own. Thus a being without interests has no "behalf" to act in, and no "sake" to act for.

If this justification of the interest principle is sound, it can also be employed to support principles connecting particular rights with specific sorts of interests. Just as one cannot represent a being that has no interest at all, so one cannot, in demanding a university education for a cat, be representing the cat unless one is thereby representing some interest that the cat has, and that would be served by its receiving a university education. Similarly, one cannot be acting for the sake of a cat in arguing that it should receive a university education unless the cat has some interest that will thereby be furthered. The conclusion, therefore, is that if Feinberg's defense of the interest principle is sound, other, more specific principles must also be correct. These more specific principles can be summed up, albeit somewhat vaguely, by the following, *particular-interests principle*.

It is a conceptual truth that an entity cannot have a particular right, R, unless it is at least capable of having some interest, I, which is furthered by its having right R.

Given this particular-interests principle, certain familiar facts, whose importance has not often been appreciated, become comprehensible. Compare an act of killing a normal adult human being with an act of torturing one for five minutes. Though both acts are seriously wrong, they are not equally so. Here, as in most cases, to violate an individual's right to life is more seriously wrong than to violate his right not to have pain inflicted upon him. Consider, however, the corresponding actions in the case of a newborn kitten. Most people feel that it is seriously wrong to torture a kitten for five minutes, but not to kill it painlessly. How is this difference in the moral ordering of the two types of acts, between the human case and the kitten case, to be explained? One answer is that while normal adult human beings have both a right to life and a right not to be tortured, a kitten has only the latter. But why should this be so? The particular-interest principle, however, suggests a possible explanation. Though kittens have some interests, including, in

particular, an interest in not being tortured, which derives from their capacity to feel pain, they do not have an interest in their own continued existence and, hence, do not have a right not to be destroyed. This answer contains, of course, a large promissory element. One needs a defense of the view that kittens have no interest in continued existence. But the point here is simply that there is an important question about the rationale underlying the moral ordering of certain sorts of acts, and that the particular-interests principle points to a possible answer.

This fact lends further plausibility, I believe, to the particular-interests principle. What one would ultimately like to do, of course, is to set out an analysis of the concept of a right, show that the analysis is indeed satisfactory, and then show that the particular-interests principle is entailed by the analysis. Unfortunately, it will not be possible to pursue such an approach here, since formulating an acceptable analysis of the concept of a right is a far from trivial matter. What I should like to do, however, is to touch briefly upon the problem of providing such an analysis, and then to indicate the account that seems to me most satisfactory—an account which does entail the particular-interests principle.

It would be widely agreed, I believe, both that rights impose obligations and that the obligations they impose upon others are *conditional* upon certain factors. The difficulty arises when one attempts to specify what the obligations are conditional upon. There seems to be two main views in this area. According to the one, rights impose obligations that are conditional upon the interests of the possessor of the right. To say that Sandra has a right to something is thus to say, roughly, that if it is in Sandra's interest to have that thing, then others are under an obligation not to deprive her of it. According to the second view, rights impose obligations that are conditional upon the right's not having been waived. To say that Sandra has a right to something is to say, roughly, that if Sandra has not given others permission to take the thing, then they are under an obligation not to deprive her of it.

Both views encounter serious difficulties. On the one hand, in the case of minors, and nonhuman animals, it would seem that the obligations that rights impose must be taken as conditional upon the interests of those individuals, rather than upon whether they have given one permission to do certain things. On the other, in the case of individuals who are capable of making informed and rational decisions, if that person has not given one permission to take something that belongs to him, it would seem that one is, in general, still under an obligation not to deprive him of it, even if having that thing is no longer in his interest.

As a result, it seems that a more complex account is needed of the factors upon which the obligations imposed by rights are conditional. The account which I now prefer, and which I have defended elsewhere, is this: "A has a right to X" means the same as:

A is such that it can be in A's interest to have X, and either (1) A is not capable of making an informed and rational choice whether to grant others permission to deprive him of X, in which case, if it is in A's interest not to be deprived of X, then, by this fact alone, others are under a prima facie obligation not to deprive A of X, *or* (2) A is capable of making an informed and rational choice whether to grant others permission to deprive him of X, in which case the others are under a prima facie obligation not to deprive A of X if and only if A has not granted them permission to do so.

And if this account, or something rather similar is correct, then so is the particular-interests principle.

What I now want to do is simply apply the particular-interests principle to the case of the right to life. First, however, one needs to notice that the expression, "right to life," is not entirely happy, since it suggests that the right in question concerns the continued existence of a biological organism. That this is incorrect can be brought out by considering possible ways of violating an individual's right to life. Suppose, for example, that future technological developments make it possible to change completely the neural networks in a brain, and that the brain of some normal adult human being is thus completely reprogrammed so that the organism in question winds up with memories (or rather, apparent memories), beliefs, attitudes, and personality traits totally different from those associated with it before it was subjected to reprogramming. (The Pope is reprogrammed, say, on the model of

Bertrand Russell.) In such a case, however beneficial the change might be, one would surely want to say that *someone* had been destroyed, that an adult human being's right to life had been violated, even though no biological organism had been killed. This shows that the expression, "right to life," is misleading, since what one is concerned about is not just the continued existence of a biological organism.

How, then, might the right in question be more accurately described? A natural suggestion is that the expression, "right to life," refers to the right of a subject of experiences and other mental states to continue to exist. It might be contended, however, that this interpretation begs the question against certain possible views. For someone might hold— and surely some people in fact do—that while continuing subjects of experiences and other mental states certainly have a right to life, so do some other organisms that are only potentially such continuing subjects, such as human fetuses. A right to life, on this view, is *either* the right of a subject of experiences to continue to exist *or* the right of something that is only potentially a continuing subject of experiences to become such an entity.

This view is, I believe, to be rejected, for at least two reasons. First, this view appears to be clearly incompatible with the interest principle. Second, this position entails that the destruction of potential persons is, in general, prima facie seriously wrong, and I shall argue, in the next section, that the latter view is incorrect.

Let us consider, then, the right of a subject of experiences and other mental states to continue to exist. The particular-interests principle implies that something cannot possibly have such a right unless its continued existence can be in its interest. We need to ask, then, what must be the case if the continued existence of something is to be in its interest.

It will help to focus our thinking, I believe, if we consider a crucial case, stressed by Derek Parfit. Imagine a human baby that has developed to the point of being sentient, and of having simple desires, but that is not yet capable of having any desire for continued existence. Suppose, further, that the baby will enjoy a happy life and will be glad that it was not destroyed. Can we or can we not say that it is in the baby's interest not to be destroyed?

To approach this case, let us consider a closely related one, namely, that of a human embryo that has not developed sufficiently far to have any desires, or even any states of consciousness at all, but that will develop into an individual who will enjoy a happy life, and who will be glad that his mother did not have an abortion. Can we or can we not say that it is the embryo's interest not to be destroyed?

Why might someone be tempted to say that it is in the embryo's interest that it not be destroyed? One line of thought which, I believe, tempts some people, is this. Let Mary be an individual who enjoys a happy life. Then, though some philosophers have expressed serious doubts about this, it might very well be said that it was certainly in Mary's interest that a certain embryo was not destroyed several years earlier. And this claim, together with the tendency to use expressions such as "Mary before she was born" to refer to the embryo in question, may lead one to think that it was in the embryo's interest not to be destroyed. But this way of thinking involves conceptual confusion. A subject of interests, in the relevant sense of "interest," must necessarily be a subject of conscious states, including experiences and desires. This means that in identifying Mary with the embryo, and attributing to it her interest in its earlier nondestruction, one is treating the embryo as if it were itself a subject of consciousness. But by hypothesis, the embryo being considered has not developed to the point where there is any subject of consciousness associated with it. It cannot, therefore, have any interests at all, and *a fortiori*, it cannot have any interest in its own continued existence.

Let us now return to the first case—that of a human baby that is sentient, and that has simple desires, but which is not yet capable of having more complex desires, such as a desire for its own continued existence. Given that it will develop into an individual who will lead a happy life and who will be glad that the baby was not destroyed, does one want to say that the baby's not being destroyed is in the baby's own interest?

Again, the following line of thought may seem initially tempting. If Mary is the resulting individual, then it was in Mary's interest that the baby not have been destroyed. But the baby just *is* Mary when she was young. So it must have been in the baby's interest that it not have been destroyed.

Indeed, this argument is considerably more tempting in the present case than in the former, since here there is something that is a subject of consciousness, and which it is natural to identify with Mary. I suggest, however, that when one reflects upon the case, it becomes clear that such an identification is justified only if certain further things are the case. Thus, on the one hand, suppose that Mary is able to remember quite clearly some of the experiences that the baby enjoyed. Given that sort of causal and psychological connection, it would seem perfectly reasonable to hold that Mary and the baby are one and the same subject of consciousness, and thus, that if it is in Mary's interest that the baby not have been destroyed, then this must also have been in the baby's interest. On the other hand, suppose that not only does Mary, at a much later time, not remember any of the baby's experiences, but the experiences in question are not psychologically linked, either via memory or in any other way, to mental states enjoyed by the human organism in question at *any* later time. Here it seems to me clearly incorrect to say that Mary and the baby are one and the same subject of consciousness, and therefore it cannot be correct to transfer, from Mary to the baby, Mary's interest in the baby's not having been destroyed.

Let us now return to the question of what must be the case if the continued existence of something is to be in its own interest. The picture that emerges from the two cases just discussed is this. In the first place, nothing at all can be in an entity's interest unless it has desires at some time or other. But more than this is required if the continued existence of the entity is to be in its own interest. One possibility, which will generally be sufficient, is that the individual have, at the time in question, a desire for its own continued existence. Yet it also seems clear that an individual's continued existence can be in its own interest even when such a desire is not present. What is needed, apparently, is that the continued existence of the individual will make possible the satisfaction of some desires existing at other times. But not just any desires existing at other times will do. Indeed, as is illustrated both by the case of the baby just discussed and by the deprogramming/reprogramming example, it is not even sufficient that they be desires associated with the same physical organism. It is crucial that they be desires that belong to one and the same subject of consciousness.

The critical question, then, concerns the conditions under which desires existing at different times can be correctly attributed to a single, continuing subject of consciousness. This question raises a number of difficult issues that cannot be considered here. Part of the rationale underlying the view I wish to advance will be clear, however, if one considers the role played by memory in the psychological unity of an individual over time. When I remember a past experience, what I know is not merely that there was a certain experience which someone or other had, but that there was an experience that belonged to the *same* individual as the present memory beliefs, and it seems clear that this feature of one's memories is, in general, a crucial part of what it is that makes one a continuing subject of experiences, rather than merely a series of psychologically isolated, momentary subjects of consciousness. This suggests something like the following principle:

Desires existing at different times can belong to a single, continuing subject of consciousness only if that subject of consciousness possesses, at some time, the concept of a continuing self or mental substance.

Given this principle, together with the particular-rights principle, one can set out the following argument in support of a claim concerning a necessary condition that an entity must satisfy if it is to have a right to life:

1. The concept of a right is such that an individual cannot have a right at time *t* to continued existence unless the individual is such that it can be in its interest at time *t* that it continue to exist.

2. The continued existence of a given subject of consciousness cannot be in that individual's interest at time *t* unless *either* that individual has a desire, at time *t*, to continue as a subject of consciousness, *or* that individual can have desires at other times.

3. An individual cannot have a desire to continue to exist as a subject of consciousness unless it possesses the concept of continuing self or mental substance.

4. An individual existing at one time cannot have desires at other times unless there is at least one time at which it possesses the concept of a continuing self or mental substance.

Therefore,

5. An individual cannot have a right to continued existence unless there is at least one time at which it possesses the concept of a continuing self or mental substance.

This conclusion is obviously significant. But precisely what implications does it have with respect to the morality of abortion and infanticide? The answer will depend upon what relationship there is between, on the one hand, the behavioral and neurophysiological development of a human being, and, on the other, the development of that individual's mind. Some people believe that there is no relationship at all. They believe that a human mind, with all its mature capacities, is present in a human from conception onward, and so is there before the brain has even begun to develop, and before the individual has begun to exhibit behavior expressive of higher mental functioning. Most philosophers, however, reject this view. They believe, on the one hand that there is, in general, a rather close relation between an individual's behavioral capacities and its mental functioning, and, on the other, that there is a very intimate relationship between the mind and the brain. As regards the latter, some philosophers hold that the mind is in fact identical with the brain. Others maintain that the mind is distinct from the brain, but causally dependent upon it. In either case, the result is a view according to which the development of the mind and the brain are necessarily closely tied to one another.

If one does adopt the view that there is a close relation between the behavioral and neurophysiological development of a human being, and the development of its mind, then the previous conclusion has a very important, and possibly decisive implication with respect to the morality of abortion and infanticide. For when human development, both behavioral and neurophysiological, is closely examined, it is seen to be most unlikely that human fetuses, or even newborn babies, possess any concept of a continuing self. And in the light of the above conclusion, this means that such individuals do not possess a right to life.

But is it reasonable to hold that there is a close relation between human behavioral and neurophysiological development, and the development of the human mind? Approached from a scientific perspective, I believe that there is excellent reason for doing so. Consider, for example, what is known about how, at later stages, human mental capacities proceed in step with brain development, or what is known about how damage to different parts of the brain can affect, in different ways, an individual's intellectual capacities.

Why, then, do some people reject the view that there is a close relationship between the development of the human mind, and the behavioral and neurophysiological development of human beings? There are, I think, two main reasons. First, some philosophers believe that the scientific evidence is irrelevant because they believe that it is possible to establish, by means of a purely metaphysical argument, that a human mind, with its mature capacities, is present in a human from conception onward. I have argued elsewhere that the argument in question is unsound.

Second, and more commonly, some people appeal to the idea that it is a divinely revealed truth that human beings have minds from conception onward. There are a number of points to be made about such an appeal. First, the belief that a mind, or soul, is infused into a human body at conception by God is not an essential belief within many of the world's religions. Second, even with religious traditions, such as Roman Catholicism, where the belief is a very common one, it is by no means universally accepted. Thus, for example, the well-known Catholic philosopher, Joseph Donceel, has argued very strongly for the claim that the correct position on the question of ensoulment is that the soul enters the body only when the human brain has undergone a sufficient process of development. Third, there is the question of whether it is reasonable to accept the religious outlook that is being appealed to in support of the contention that humans have minds that are capable of higher intellectual activities from conception onward. This question raises very large

issues in philosophy of religion, which cannot be pursued here. But it should at least be said that most contemporary philosophers who have reflected upon religious beliefs have come to the view that there is not sufficient reason even for believing in the existence of God, let alone for accepting the much more detailed religious claims which are part of a religion such as Christianity. Finally, suppose that one nonetheless decides to accept the contention that it is a divinely revealed truth that humans have, from conception onward, minds that are capable of higher mental activities, and that one appeals to this purported revelation in order to support the claim that all humans have a right to life. One needs to notice that if one then goes on to argue, not merely that abortion is wrong, but that there should be a law against it, one will encounter a very serious objection. For it is surely true that it is inappropriate, at least in a pluralistic society, to appeal to specific religious beliefs of a nonmoral sort—such as the belief that God infuses souls into human bodies at conception—in support of legislation that will be binding upon everyone, including those who either accept different religious beliefs, or none at all.

IS IT MORALLY WRONG TO DESTROY POTENTIAL PERSONS?

In this section I shall consider the question of whether it can be seriously wrong to destroy an entity, not because of the nonpotential properties it presently possesses but because of the properties it will later come to have, if it is not interfered with. First, however, we need to be clear why this is such a crucial question. We can do this by considering a line of thought that has led some people to feel that the anti-abortionist position is more defensible than that of the pro-abortionist. The argument in question rests upon the gradual and continuous development of an organism as it changes from a zygote into an adult human being. The anti-abortionist can point to this development, and argue that it is morally arbitrary for a pro-abortionist to draw a line at some point in this continuous process—such as at birth, or viability—and to say that killing is permissible before, but not after, that particular point.

The pro-abortionist reply would be, I think, that the emphasis on the continuity of the process is misleading. What the anti-abortionist is really doing is simply challenging the pro-abortionist to specify what properties a thing must have in order to have a right to life, and to show that the developing organism does acquire those properties at the point in question. The pro-abortionist may then be tempted to argue that the difficulty in meeting this challenge should not be taken as grounds for rejecting his position. For the anti-abortionist cannot meet this challenge either; he is equally unable to say what properties something must have if it is to have a right to life.

Although this rejoinder does not dispose of the anti-abortionist argument, it is not without bite. For defenders of the view that abortion is almost always wrong have failed to face up to the question of the *basic* moral principles on which their position rests, where a basic moral principle is one whose acceptability does not rest upon the truth of any factual claim of a nonmoral sort. They have been content to assert the wrongness of killing any organism, from a zygote on, if that organism is a member of the biologically defined species *Homo sapiens.* But they have overlooked the point that this cannot be an acceptable *basic* moral principle, since difference in species is not in itself a morally relevant difference.

The anti-abortionist can reply that it is possible to defend his position, but not a pro-abortionist position, *without* getting clear about the properties a thing must possess if it is to have a right to life. For one can appeal to the following two claims: First, that there is a property, even if one is unable to specify what it is, that (1) is possessed by normal adult humans, and (2) endows any being possessing it with a right to life. Second, that there are properties that satisfy (1) and (2), at least one of those properties will be such that any organism potentially possessing that property has a right to life even now, simply in virtue of that potentiality—where an organism possesses a property potentially if it will come to have it in the normal course of its development.

The second claim—which I shall refer to as the potentiality principle—is crucial to the anti-abortionist's defense of his position. Given that principle, the anti-abortionist can defend his position without grappling with the very difficult question of what nonpotential properties an entity must possess in order to have a right to life. It is enough to

know that adult members of *Homo sapiens* do have such a right. For then one can employ the potentiality principle to conclude that any organism that belongs to the species *Homo sapiens,* from a zygote on—with the possible exception of those that suffer from certain gross neurophysiological abnormalities—must also have a right to life.

The pro-abortionist, in contrast, cannot mount a comparable argument. He cannot defend his position without offering at least a partial answer to the question of what properties a thing must possess in order to have a right to life.

The importance of the potentiality principle, however, goes beyond the fact that it provides support for an anti-abortion position. For it seems that if the potentiality principle is unsound, then there is no acceptable defense of an extreme conservative view on abortion.

The reason is this: Suppose that the claim that an organism's having certain potentialities is sufficient grounds for its having a right to life cannot be sustained. The claim that a fetus that is a member of *Homo sapiens* has a right to life can then be attacked as follows. The reason an adult member of *Homo sapiens* has a right to life, but an infant ape, say, does not, is that there are certain physiological properties that the former possesses and the latter does not. Now even if one is unsure exactly what the relevant psychological characteristics are, it seems clear that an organism in the early stages of development from a zygote into an adult member of *Homo sapiens* does not possess those properties. One need merely compare a human fetus with an ape fetus. In early stages of development, neither will have any mental life at all. (Does a zygote have a mental life? Does it have experiences? Or beliefs? Or desires?) In later stages of fetal development some mental events presumably occur, but these will be of a very rudimentary sort. The crucial point, however, is that given what we know through comparative studies of, on the one hand, brain development and, on the other, behavior after birth, it is surely reasonable to hold that there are no significant differences in the respective mental lives of a human fetus and an ape fetus. There are, of course, physiological differences, but these are not in themselves morally significant. *If* one held that potentialities were relevant to the ascription of a right to life, one could argue that the physiological differences, though not morally relevant in themselves, are morally relevant in virtue of their causal consequences: They will lead to later psychological differences that are morally relevant, and for this reason the physiological differences are themselves morally significant. But if the potentiality principle is not available, this line of argument cannot be used, and there will then be no differences between a human and an ape fetus that the anti-abortionist can use as grounds for ascribing a right to life to the former but not to the latter.

This argument assumes, of course, that the anti-abortionist cannot successfully argue that there are religious reasons for holding that, even when potentialities are set aside, there is a morally relevant difference between human fetuses and ape fetuses. In the previous section I indicated, however, why it is very unlikely that any religious line of argument can be satisfactory in the present context.

The conclusion seems to be then, that the anti-abortionist position is defensible only if the potentiality principle is sound. Let us now consider what can be said against that principle. One way of attacking it is by appealing to the conclusion advanced in the previous section, to the effect that an individual cannot have a right to continued existence unless there is at least one time at which it possesses the concept of continuing self or mental substance. This principle entails the denial of the potentiality principle. Or more precisely, it does so in conjunction with the presumably uncontroversial empirical claim that a fertilized human egg cell, which does possess the relevant potentialities, does not possess the concept of a continuing self or mental substance.

Alternatively, one could appeal to the more modest claim involved in the interest principle and use it to argue that since a fertilized human egg cell cannot have any interests at all, it cannot have any rights, and a fortiori cannot have a right to life. So potentialities alone cannot endow something with a right to life. . . .

My argument against the modified potentiality principle can now be stated. Suppose at some future time a chemical were to be discovered which, when injected into the brain of a kitten, would cause the kitten to develop into a cat possessing a brain of the sort possessed by humans,

and consequently into a cat having all the psychological capabilities characteristic of normal adult humans. Such cats would be able to think, to use language, and so on. Now it would surely be morally indefensible in such a situation to hold that it is seriously wrong to kill an adult member of the species *Homo sapiens* without also holding that it is wrong to kill any cat that has undergone such a process of development: There would be no morally significant differences.

Second, imagine that one has two kittens, one of which has been injected with a special chemical, but which has not yet developed those properties that in themselves endow something with a right to life, and the other of which has not been injected with the special chemical. It follows from the moral symmetry principle that the action of injecting the former with a "neutralizing" chemical that will interfere with the transformation process and prevent the kitten from developing those properties that in themselves would give it a right to life is prima facie no more seriously wrong than the action of intentionally refraining from injecting the second kitten with the special chemical.

It perhaps needs to be emphasized here that the moral symmetry principle does not imply that neither action is morally wrong. Perhaps both actions are wrong, even seriously so. The moral symmetry principle implies only that if they are wrong, they are so to precisely the same degree.

Third, compare a kitten that has been injected with the special chemical and then had it neutralized, with a kitten that has never been injected with the chemical. It is clear that it is no more seriously wrong to kill the former than to kill the latter. For although their bodies have undergone different processes in the past, there is no reason why the kittens need differ in any way with respect to either their present properties or their potentialities.

Fourth, again consider two kittens, one of which has been injected with the special chemical, but which has not yet developed those properties that in themselves would give it a right to life, and the other of which has not been injected with the chemical. It follows from the previous two steps in the argument that the combined action of injecting the first kitten with a neutralizing chemical and then killing it is no more seriously wrong than the combined action of intentionally refraining from injecting the second kitten with the special chemical and then killing it.

Fifth, one way of neutralizing the action of the special chemical is simply to kill the kitten. And since there is surely no reason to hold that it is more seriously wrong to neutralize the chemical and to kill the kitten in a single step than in two successive steps, it must be the case that it is no more seriously wrong to kill a kitten that has been injected with the special chemical, but which has not developed those properties that in themselves would give it a right to life, than it is to inject such a kitten with a neutralizing chemical and then to kill it.

Next, compare a member of *Homo sapiens* that has not developed far enough to have those properties that in themselves give something a right to life, but which later will come to have them, with a kitten that has been injected with the special chemical but which has not yet had the chance to develop the relevant properties. It is clear that it cannot be any more seriously wrong to kill the human than to kill the kitten. The potentialities are the same in both cases. The only difference is that in the case of a human fetus the potentialities have been present from the beginning of the organism's development, while in the case of the kitten they have been present only from the time it was injected with the special chemical. This difference in the time at which the potentialities were acquired is not a morally relevant one.

It follows from the previous three steps in the argument that it is no more seriously wrong to kill a human being that lacks properties that in themselves, and irrespective of their causal consequences, endow something with a right to life, but which will naturally develop those properties, than it would be to intentionally refrain from injecting a kitten with the special chemical, and to kill it. But if it is the case that normal adult humans do possess properties that in themselves give them a right to life, it follows in virtue of the modified potentiality principle that it is seriously wrong to kill any human organism that will naturally develop the properties in question. Thus, if the modified potentiality principle is sound, we are forced by this argument to conclude that if there were a chemical that would transform kittens into animals having the psychological capabilities possessed by adult humans, it would be seriously

wrong to intentionally refrain from injecting kittens with the chemical and to kill them instead.

But is it clear that this final conclusion is unacceptable? I believe that it is. It turns out, however, that this issue is *much* more complex than most people take it to be. Here, however, it will have to suffice to note that the vast majority of people would certainly view this conclusion as unacceptable. For although there are at present no special chemicals that will transform kittens in the required way, there are other biological organisms, namely unfertilized human egg cells, and special chemicals, namely human spermatozoa, that will transform those organisms in the required way. So if one were to hold that it was seriously wrong to intentionally refrain from injecting kittens with the special chemical and instead to kill them, one would also have to maintain that it was prima facie seriously wrong to refrain from injecting human egg cells with spermatozoa, and instead to kill them. So unless the anti-abortionist is prepared to hold that any woman, married or unmarried, does something seriously wrong every month that she intentionally refrains from getting pregnant, he cannot maintain that it would be seriously wrong to refrain from injecting the kitten with the special chemical, and instead to kill it. ....

SUMMARY AND CONCLUSIONS
In this paper I have advanced three main philosophical contentions:

1. An entity cannot have a right to life unless it is capable of having an interest in its own continued existence.
2. An entity is not capable of having an interest in its own continued existence unless it possesses, at some time, the concept of a continuing self, or subject of experiences and other mental states.
3. The fact that an entity will, if not destroyed, come to have properties that would give it a right to life does not in itself make it seriously wrong to destroy it.

If these philosophical contentions are correct, the crucial question is a factual one: At what point does a developing human being acquire the concept of a continuing self, and at what point is it capable of having an interest in its own continued existence? I have not examined this issue in detail here, but I have suggested that careful scientific studies of human development both behavioral and neurophysiological, strongly support the view that

The Scope of the Prohibition Against Killing

PHILIP DEVINE

In what follows, I distinguish three principles of interpretation determining the limits of the moral rule against homicide and other moral rules protecting distinctively human rights. One of these, the *species principle*, will be founded on the kinship or solidarity that obtains among members of the same species. It seems best understood as a more precise version of the "Standard Belief" which Roger Wertheimer attributes to nearly everyone: that what warrants the ascription of human moral status to a creature is simply that creature's being human. (I say a more precise version, since Wertheimer believes that one can deny that a biologically human creature is a member of "the family of man," although why he thinks this is not completely clear.) The second, the *present enjoyment* (or present possession) *principle*, rests on the ability of human beings to assert their personhood by appeals or resistance. And the third, the *potentiality principle*, rests on the uniquely rich kinds of action and experience of which human beings are capable, and the uniquely severe loss suffered when the prospect of such a life is frustrated, whether or not the organism whose existence has been ended or whose capacity for such life has been impaired has had some experience of it. The potentiality and present enjoyment principles seem best viewed as attempts to replace the Standard Belief with something thought more satisfactory. Our choice among these principles will determine our judgment of the moral status of fetuses, infants, and the moribund, and thus make a crucial difference to our judgments concerning abortion, infanticide, and euthanasia.

even newborn humans do not have the capacities in question. If this is right, then it would seem that infanticide during a time interval shortly after birth must be viewed as morally acceptable.

7. THE SPECIES PRINCIPLE

A first statement of the species principle as it applies to killing is as follows: those creatures protected by the moral rule against homicide are the members of the human species, and only the members of the human species. This version of the principle protects all human organisms, whatever their degree of maturity or decay, including fetuses and embryos, but not robots or nonhuman animals, whatever the attainments of such beings might be.

The species principle does not mean, as Joseph Fletcher thinks, that "we would be human if we have opposable thumbs, are capable of face-to-face coitus and have a brain weighing 1400 grams, whether a particular brain functions cerebrally or not." Obviously a creature might be morally and biologically human while lacking one of these traits—say a child born without hands (and thus without thumbs)—and it is easy to imagine a species that met the suggested criteria without being in any sense human. Membership in a biological species is a complex matter, but scientists are now well able to recognize biological humanity in the fine structure of an organism, without reference to such things as opposable thumbs. Jérôme Lejeune puts the point nicely:

> Let us take the example of trisomy 21 [a chromosome disorder], observed by amniocentesis.

From *The Ethics of Homicide* by Philip Devine. Notes deleted. © 1978, Ithaca, NY: Cornell University Press.

Looking at the chromosomes and detecting the extra 21, we say very safely "The child who will develop here will be a trisomic 21." But this phrase does not convey all the information. We have not seen only the extra 21; we have also seen all the 46 other chromosomes and concluded that they were human, because if they had been mouse or monkey chromosomes, we would have noticed.

In other words, even a human defective is a defective *human,* and this biological humanity is recognizable in the genetic structure of the organism even when the genetic structure itself is defective.

Some vagueness does afflict the species principle when it comes to deciding precisely when—at conception or shortly thereafter, when the unity and uniqueness of the nascent creature is secured—a human organism comes into existence, as well as how much breakdown is necessary before we say that a human organism has ceased to be. Ape-human hybrids and the like also pose a knotty problem. But none of these zones of vagueness render the principle unusable, nor do they provide any grounds for refusing to use the principle to condemn killing where the victim is unambiguously a human organism.

Finally, the species principle provides an adequate answer to the "acorn" argument, which has a surprising persistence in disputes about abortion. Whatever may be the case with dormant acorns, a germinating acorn is, while not an oak *tree,* still a member of the appropriate species of oak. If oaks had a serious right to life in their own right, so would oak saplings and germinating acorns. And the same reply can be made to those who would argue about abortion from the premise that a caterpillar is not a butterfly.

An unsound objection to the species principle is that it employs a biological category, that of the species, in the derivation of moral conclusions. This objection takes two forms: that such derivation is an illegitimate inference from an "is" to an "ought," and that to rely on such categories is to offend human dignity by subjecting human beings, like beasts, to the tyranny of animal nature. Neither version of the objection is plausible.

At most, what cannot be done in deriving an "ought" from an "is" is to assert an *entailment.* Modes of inference weaker than entailment cannot be barred as instances of the naturalistic fallacy lost all moral reasoning be made impossible. "X is a human organism; therefore X ought not to be killed" may be as good as any other significant moral inference. Of course one could treat this inference as elliptical, its missing premise being the moral rule against homicide as interpreted in accordance with the species principle ("One ought not to kill a human organism"). But to spell out this argument in this way may be no more illuminating than treating inductive inference as deductive inference with the principle of induction as a suppressed premise. In any case, this reading does nothing to strengthen the objection to the species principle.

As for the version of this contention which turns on human dignity, the answer to it is best put in the form of a question. Why is it wounding to human dignity to recognize that human beings are, among other things, animals, and to call for some respect for the animal aspect of man's being? Is the sanctioning of unlimited assaults on the characteristic modes of coming to be and passing away of the human species more in keeping with respect for human dignity than the placing of restraints on such activity? To regard the according of moral significance to the animal aspect of man's existence as wounding to his dignity seems to make man's dignity contingent upon his being regarded as something he is not.

A more troubling charge is that of species chauvinism: the charge, that is, that the giving of a higher moral status to members of one's own species than to those of others is akin to regarding members of other races as subhuman. It would not be chauvinism in the strict sense to argue that between two intelligent species, members of one have no rights which members of the other are bound to respect, while each agent is morally required to respect the rights of members of his own species, in particular not to kill them unless he has a very compelling justification. It is, after all, considered worse (all other things being equal) to kill one's brother than a stranger, not because one's brother in himself is morally more worthy than the stranger, but because the relationship between brothers is itself morally significant. Nonetheless we would certainly want intelligent Martians to respect our rights, and might be prepared to respect theirs in return. And, if Martians were enough like human beings that the notion of human individuality could be extended to them, this respect for their rights would naturally take the form, *inter alia,* of regarding Martians as protected by our moral (and quite possibly our legal) rules against homicide.

But this line of thought can be accommodated by a modification of the species principle which does not alter its essential structure. According to this modification, what the moral rule against homicide protects is all members of intelligent species, including, but not limited to, the human. On this account determining whether a given creature is protected by the moral rule against homicide is a two-step process: first, identifying the species to which the creature belongs, and second, deciding whether this species is in fact intelligent. For members of the human species, the human species continues to play a somewhat paradigmatic role, in setting the standard of intelligence which must be approached or exceeded for a species to be considered intelligent, and the same is true for members of other intelligent species. A human being will ask whether Martians as a species are intelligent enough by human standards to be regarded as persons, and an intelligent Martian will make the corresponding inquiry concerning human beings. In any case, all creatures protected by the original species principle are protected by the modified species principle as well.

Three problems of application arise for the modified species principle, of particular importance in assessing the claims which might be made on behalf of chimpanzees, whales, and dolphins. First, supposing one member of a species reaches the human level, what effect does this achievement have on the status of the other members of the species? Second, what kind of standards are to be employed in determining whether a given species is to be regarded as intelligent? Since we cannot, in answering these questions, rely on the considerations of lineage which settle nearly all questions of species membership, they will require very careful examination.

It seems that we want to regard an individual cat which has, through some chance or other, attained human intelligence as protected by the moral rule against homicide. To do so consistently with the species principle requires the adoption of one of two strategies: (1) the existence of such a cat renders the entire species *Felis domestica* an intelligent species, and all of its members protected by the moral rule against homicide (consider the plea such a cat might make on behalf of its less intelligent brethren) or (2) the intelligence of our super-cat might be considered as producing a different species, consisting of him alone, although he is still capable of breeding fertilely with other, less favored, cats. (He may wish to disassociate himself from other cats, and feel humiliated by his bodily likeness to subhuman creatures.) The first of these strategies would be plausible for the claims of dolphins and the like, all of which at least come somewhat close to human intelligence. The second would be more plausible for the claims of cats and dogs.

The second question is what traits are decisive for regarding a given individual as rendering his species intelligent. Self-consciousness (or consciousness of oneself as a subject of conscious states) might be suggested, as a necessary condition of the desire to live. Moral agency is another contender, since moral agents are presupposed by moral discourse as such. Finally, the use of language is the key to the rich kind of life enjoyed by human beings, so that it may be taken as what distinguishes the human from the subhuman. An attractive blend of these last two possibilities is participation in moral discourse: if we discover that Martians argue about the issues discussed in this book, we should be obliged to regard them for moral purposes as human.

The question of which traits are crucial is less important for the species than for other interpretations of the moral rule against homicide, since no attempt is made to draw lines within the human species. But even here it may be crucial—especially on some interpretations of what it is to speak a language—to the status of some nonhumans such as chimpanzees. What seems to be the case is that the distinction between human and nonhuman rests not on any one trait, but on an interlocking set of traits, which will wax and wane as a whole.

Finally, we need to ask (supposing that the relevant traits admit of degree) how much of them is required to make a species one of the human level. (If they do not, we will still have to adjudicate borderline cases.) It is worth noticing that our standards can be more demanding here than for either of the species principle's two rivals. In order to reach minimally tolerable results, the present enjoyment principle will have to demand very little of a creature before treating it as a person; the potentiality principle can ask for more, since what the creature will attain in due course, not what it attains now, is the standard. But the species principle can demand the production of saints, philosophers, musicians, scientists, or whatever else is thought to be the highest embodiment of human nature, since the bulk of the species can gain their morally privileged status through the achievements of their best members, so long as there is not a sharp break between the capacities of the best of a species and members of that species generally....

8. THE PRESENT ENJOYMENT PRINCIPLE

The appeal of the species principle, especially as modified and expanded to encompass intelligent nonhumans, to those who are prepared to be generous in their ascriptions of personhood is very great. To the extent, for instance, that we are prepared to regard even the most hopelessly retarded human being as a person, and the killing of such a one as murder, the species principle appears to provide the only plausible grounds for so doing. And even when its full effect is denied, the species principle still has important residues: many who are prepared to defend both abortion and capital punishment balk at the execution of pregnant women, and some defenders of abortion also disapprove of experiments on live aborted "fetuses," as well as experiments on fetuses *in utero* when abortion is intended. And even if we were prepared to admit that the hopelessly retarded might be painlessly killed rather than cared for, still we would be most reluctant to countenance the use of such creatures for the kinds of experiments that are performed on animals, or their being killed for food. Finally, to the extent that we tend to think that there are organisms of the human species that may rightfully be treated as other than human—that may, for instance, be killed to relieve us of the burden of caring for and feeding them—we think in terms of human vegetables, not human brutes. The latter is quite as logical from the standpoint of a denial of the species principle.

Many, however, are not prepared to be so generous in extending the protection of the moral rule against homicide. Nor is this surprising, for the admission that a given creature is a person is morally very expensive, and becomes more so as the lists of human rights grow longer. And caring for those who are persons on the species principle frequently places burdens on those who are persons on narrower principles, of which an unwanted pregnancy may be taken as emblematic. It is therefore well worth asking whether a narrower version of the rule against homicide is possible, one, that is, which is not merely an ad hoc modification of the rule designed to allow us to kill those whose existence we find particularly burdensome.

An obvious possibility is to drop the reference to the species and to require that a creature be in present possession of distinctively human traits before the killing of such a creature will be deemed homicide. Assuming that what we value human beings for is their capacities for rational and social life, perhaps we should place the kind of value which grounds the moral rule against homicide only on those that (now) have these capacities. Or again, we may be impressed by the various ways human beings (and not animals) insist upon respect for their rights (including the right not to be killed), and feel that those who are incapable of making such appeals (or engaging in such resistance) do not deserve to be treated as persons. Let us call this principle the present enjoyment principle.

One consequence of the present enjoyment principle is that the killing of infants is never (morally speaking) murder, never a violation of someone's (serious) right to live, although in many contexts it will be a violation of the quasi-proprietary rights of the parents. One might expect this attitude to carry over into other contexts, so that defenders of infanticide will be more concerned with questions of "ownership" of war orphans, say, and less concerned with the welfare of the infant orphans themselves than the rest of us. This issue is very complex, however, as will become clear later on.

Once the species principle, and consequently the human rights of infants, is questioned, the problem of terminology needs to be discussed. "Human beings," in this context, ceases to be a very useful expression for those protected by the moral rule against homicide. Whatever might be said of fetuses, "infants are not human beings" sounds just too odd. Indeed, I suspect that "human beings" and "human organisms" differ in meaning only as do "baby" and "infant": in other words, that while the evaluations implicit in the two terms are different, all human beings are human organisms and all human organisms are human beings. If I am right about this, it will not be possible—without biological or conceptual confusion—to defend abortion on the grounds that an embryo or fetus is not a human being, but it still might be possible to defend the practice on the grounds that such human organisms are not persons.

On the other hand, Michael Tooley's suggestion that the word "person" be used in a purely moral way, to denote those possessing a serious right to live, will not work either, expect of course as a purely technical usage. (Compare the legal use of the word "person," for which personality belongs to those entities which are recognized as having rights and duties in law.) The word "person" is less tied to the human organism than is "human being," so that whether infants or fetuses are persons can be treated more or less as a straightforward moral question. But it still has a core of descriptive meaning resistant to eccentric moral views. Even if one holds that no one has a right to live, one must still call oneself a person if one uses the concept at all. On the other hand, no matter how passionate a defender one might be of the rights of trees, to say that trees are people would justify a smile. I shall thus continue to use the expressions "human being," "person," and "human person" to denote those protected by the moral rule against homicide, postponing further clarification to a later point. It is first necessary to develop the central objection to the present enjoyment principle.

9. INFANTICIDE AND OUR INTUITIONS

The most striking conflict between the present enjoyment principle and our intuitions—the implication of the principle that infants have no right to live—arises in the specific context of debates about abortion. Many such debates have been conducted within limits imposed by agreed-upon judgments concerning contraception and infanticide.

Contraception, it has been agreed, is a morally legitimate way of avoiding undesired parenthood, and infanticide is not. The participants in the controversy have limited themselves to arguing that abortion (or a practice on the borderline between contraception and abortion) is more closely analogous to contraception than to infanticide, or more closely analogous to infanticide than to contraception. But some defenders of abortion have conceded—or even, like Tooley, insisted on and argued for—what has hitherto been the principal contention of opponents of abortion, that abortion and infanticide are essentially the same, and maintained that there are no good grounds for regarding infanticide as a violation of anyone's right to live.

I shall be considering Tooley's views in some detail, since by his willingness to carry the case against fetal rights to its logical extreme, he manages to present the issues underlying the abortion debate with more than ordinary clarity. An examination of the arguments employed by those who have rested their defense of abortion on the fact that the fetus (and not the woman) is unable to envisage a future for itself, talk, enter into social relations, and so on, will show that their premises are brought to their logical conclusion in Tooley's articles.

I shall not here attempt a direct proof that Tooley is wrong, and that infants have a right to live, but shall limit myself to showing that Tooley's attempt to show that the infant cannot be correctly ascribed a right to live (i.e., accorded the protection of the moral rule against homicide) does not succeed. How serious a limitation this is on a moral case against infanticide depends on one's view of the relationship between moral principles formulated by philosophers and socially established moral intuitions of a relatively concrete sort. In my view, the concrete intuitions embodied in our laws and customs, at least insofar as they are shared by the philosopher in his prereflective moments, are entitled to at least as much weight as the moral principles he finds plausible when they are stated in an abstract manner.

Hence, the feeling that exists against infanticide among persons of widely varying religious, political, and cultural attitudes will be taken as a datum for our inquiry. If it persistently resists attempts to accommodate it within our moral theories, we may be entitled to reject it. But if the arguments of this chapter are sound, we have no good reason to abandon our intuitions in this case.

The acceptability of an appeal to socially current intuitions may well be the chief issue between defenders of infanticide and me. But I think it can be shown that it is reasonable to appeal to such intuitions, and unreasonable to bar such appeals. That our moral intuitions are shaped by others—our parents, teachers, peers, and so on—before we are capable of thinking about morality for ourselves, I do not deny. But to regard this fact as in some way constituting an argument for the conclusion that the beliefs and attitudes so formed are as likely to be false as true is to deprive ourselves of any basis whatever for a moral theory. For there are indefinitely many moral theories, the doctrine that right conduct consists in maximizing pain and minimizing pleasure for instance which are never seriously entertained by philosophers, because they deviate so wildly from the moral intuitions shared by the philosopher and his community. And there are results, such as that it is our duty to kill as many people painlessly as we can, which suffice to invalidate even the most superficially attractive moral theory if they follow from this theory as a result. Moreover, to argue that a moral intuition is suspect because of its source in family or social life is to render one's moral conclusions irrelevant to that life, and thus to moral problems as human beings in fact experience them....

10. INFANTICIDE AND RIGHTS

Tooley's strategy for showing that an infant should not be ascribed a serious right to live is indicated in the following passage: "My approach will be to set out and defend some basic moral principles specifying conditions an organism must satisfy if it is to have a serious right to life. It will be seen that these conditions are not satisfied by human fetuses and infants, and thus that they do not have a right to live." Tooley's account of these basic moral principles gets quite complex, but for the purposes of the present critique the following simplified version will prove sufficient: "An organism possesses a serious right to live only if it possesses the concept of a self as a continuing subject of experiences and other

mental states, and believes that it is itself such a continuing entity." The underlying premise of Tooley's argument is his account of the concept of a right. Again, his analysis is complicated, but the following statement will suffice for our purposes: "My basic argument...rests upon the claim that there is a conceptual connection between the rights an individual can have and the circumstances under which they can be violated,...and that, in general, violation of an individual's right to something involves frustrating the corresponding desire." The central thesis of Tooley's discussion follows immediately from this basic premise: since infants lack consciousness of themselves as continuing beings, they are incapable of desiring that they continue in existence. Accordingly they do not have a right to continue to live.

Against this reasoning I argue, first, that a man may have a right to something he does not desire, and second, that an organism can have a right to something it cannot desire.

Consider the (moral) right not to be punished as a criminal except in accordance with the law. This is a right that can be violated even when the person so punished is a neurotic seeking punishment or a religious fanatic seeking to emulate Christ. It would certainly be prima facie wrong to punish someone as a criminal for a crime he did not commit, or for an act not made criminal by law, just because he consents to and indeed ardently desires such a result, even if this desire is in no sense a temporary aberration but represents his considered decision as to the sort of life he wants to live. And it would seem (to me at least) that the reason it is wrong is that it is a violation of the neurotic's or the fanatic's rights.

(A possible other explanation is that the legal system does not exist to provide this kind of service. It is easy enough to imagine a situation where the exchange would be mutually beneficial, however. Suppose the police have given up hope of uncovering a brutal killer, and there is a danger of lynchings.)

To be sure, to hold that this is the case requires at least an exception to the principle *volenti non fit injuria* as employed by moralists, but this maxim will require heavy qualification in any case. One would hardly wish to apply it to children. Philosophers should resist the temptation to regard a proposition as self-evident because it is expressed in lapidary Latin.

But, of course, the neurotic or the fanatic possesses the concept of not being punished except in accordance with law. So that Tooley's central contention—that for someone to have a right, he must possess a concept of that to which he has a right—remains. A number of counterexamples to this contention are available.

1. Consider once again the right not to be punished except by due process of law. If the infant children of a man convicted of treason were considered traitors themselves, and punished in some way as a result, their moral as well as their legal rights would clearly have been violated, even though they lacked any concept of due process or that of which they were deprived by their punishment.

2. Tooley himself cites the right of a child to an estate, which he is not now capable of wanting. He responds: "My inclination is to say that the correct description is not that the child now has a right to the estate, but that he will come to have such a right when he is mature, and in the meantime no one else has a right to the estate." But this account will not do, given Tooley's account of what a right is, or indeed any reasonable account. For by no means is it always wrong, even prima facie, to take something to which one does not have any right. If I am gathering (unowned) blackberries, I do not have any right to blackberries I have not gathered, but both I and others who do not have any right to them may with perfect rectitude take them and thus deprive each other of the ones we take. (The idiomatic "have no right" implies [roughly] that I would be breaching someone's rights if I took that to which I had no right.)

True, Tooley might adapt a remark of Joel Feinberg's and argue that the property rights of an infant are "placeholders or reservations for the rights he shall inherit when he becomes a full-fledged interested being." But while there is no strict logical difficulty about this proposal (a position of advantage or power can be kept open for someone not now in being, to hold when he comes into being) the application of it to our case is most implausible. For surely the infant has interests even now, in getting enough food if nothing else, for the sake of which his estate could be expended. That is

to say, even an infant can enjoy wealth, although he is not yet capable of understanding that this is what he is doing.

If either of the foregoing examples is accepted, the close connection Tooley attempts to establish between right and desire and hence self-consciousness will be defeated. A being can have rights without a consciousness of that to which it has rights, and even without any consciousness at all. Hence no argument of Tooley's will succeed in showing that an infant does not have the right to continue its existence. Of course one does not *have* to accept them; one might hold that infants have no rights at all. But this position is grossly implausible, and in any case it is not Tooley's position.

Tooley wants to hold that infants have rights—for instance, a right not to be mutilated—and lack only a right not to be killed. He thus admits the soundness of objections of the above sort, and attempts to meet them (1) by asserting that someone's rights can be violated because the person will in the future come to desire that the act which constituted their violation had not taken place, and (2) by adding to his account of rights a complicated stipulation concerning potential desires, which Tooley sums up as follows:

> The basic idea…is simply that actions to which an individual doesn't object—either because he is incapable of desiring at the time that they not occur, or because he lacks relevant information, or because his desires have been "warped" by psychological or physiological means—may nevertheless violate his rights if there is some time at which he is or will be capable of wishing that the action had not occurred, and at which he *would* so wish if he had all the relevant information and had not been subjected to influences that distort his preferences.

But Tooley's theory of rights, even as modified, cannot deal with a child's right to an education. Such a right cannot be treated as a right contingent upon maturity, since being educated is a way of achieving maturity. And it is not because the child's desires are "warped," but only because they are unformed, that he does not desire the things, the subtler kinds of aesthetic experience for instance, which it is one of the functions of an education to get him to desire. The most hopeful part of Tooley's account is the "lack of information" clause. But since education consists in important part in *giving* the child the information that (it is hoped) will make him desire certain things, to explain his lack of a desire for an education in terms of his lack of information is rather unsatisfactory from Tooley's standpoint. Arguing that a child has the right to the information that will make him glad to have received this information, and desirous of receiving more, is rather close to arguing that a baby has a right to live, since letting him live will make him glad to have been let live, and desirous of living longer.

I shall not pursue this line of reasoning any further, however, since it should be clear that, given sufficient equants and epicycles, all our common moral beliefs except that infants have a right to live can be accommodated. Making the points above is still worthwhile, however, since the extreme complexity of the connection between the concept of a right and that of a desire prepares us for the further complexity, and ultimate greater simplicity, of ascribing rights based directly on interests to those who now have no desires, but would eventually have them if we did not now kill them.

For, if, when considering the morality of mutilation or deprivation of property, "one should take into account not merely *future* desires...but also *potential* desires," it seems arbitrary to exclude from consideration those potential desires which are kept from becoming actual not by warping the preferences of the person whose desires they are, but by seeing to it that he never develops these preferences by killing him. (Compare my killing of a female infant with my conditioning her so that she will throw herself on her husband's funeral pyre.) And it is on the face of it extremely paradoxical that it should be permissible to kill but not to mutilate, to remove the head because it will not be missed but not remove the testicles which will. For instance it follows from Tooley's account that if one injures an infant one is well advised to finish it off, since the injury is for Tooley a violation of a right, the injury-plus-killing not. And mutilation is no violation of a right, for Tooley if the infant is known to have a disease which will kill it

before it comes to miss its lost organs or powers, since there will then be no actual individual whose interests will have been violated. But if we castrate a boy child, who is then run over by a bus on the way to choir school, a wrong will be turned into a non-wrong by accident, although one might still hold that those who castrated the infant did wrong by creating a *danger* that there would be a discontented adult eunuch.

The chief point, however, is that since an infant normally will come to be glad that he wasn't killed at birth, it is at least bizarre to maintain that it is all right to kill him at birth since he will not miss the life that he thereby loses. Tooley's argument seems, in the end, to amount to little more than the saying that dead men—or dead babies—tell no tales. In any case, if one asks *why* one should accept Tooley's theory of rights, in all its complexity, the answer turns out to be that it supports the moral conclusions Tooley wishes to reach, including, of course, the conclusion that it is all right to kill babies. That it supports this conclusion is for many of us sufficient reason to reject his theory.

At this point a restatement of the principal issue in contention is desirable. It seems to be common ground that only those creatures which have interests can have rights, and that one can have a right only to that which is in one's interest. The difference between Tooley and myself seems to be that Tooley thinks that an interest must be grounded in a desire, albeit in some cases the desire may only be a possible or future desire of an existing individual. That is to say, if an act is to be a violation of someone's rights, it must be contrary to desires he could experience *now*, or desires he *will* experience in the future. I am maintaining, to the contrary, that at least sometimes desires are expressions of pre-existing interests, and that it is unnecessarily strained, when someone entertains clearly self-destructive desires, to refer to his potential desires to explain how his desires and interests are in conflict. (I do not suppose that someone could have an interest in having something he could never view except with aversion.) Accordingly, an infant can have an interest in continuing to live, although he can possess no articulate desires of any sort, and if we kill him he will never develop any. His existence as a self-maintaining system of a complex sort is sufficient to ground the claim that he has an interest in continuing to live, and hence also (if our common moral notions are not in error) a right to do so.

I have framed my critique of Tooley in terms of his analysis of the concept of a right. But the criticism might also be made in terms of his concept of a self. Tooley comes close to identifying a person with his consciousness, so that either we cease to exist during periods of unconsciousness (as Hume came close to holding) or else (as Descartes held) despite appearances we are never unconscious. A Cartesian standpoint might explain Tooley's rejection of the species and potentiality principles, since it is by virtue of his body that an infant is potentially self-conscious and belongs to the human species. Those whose concept of the self is different can accept these principles (or one of them) and hold that infants have a right to live.

ARGUMENT 2 ESSAY QUESTIONS

1. Contrast Noonan's and Tooley's view of fetal personhood. Which view seems more plausible? Why?
2. What is Devine's argument against abortion? On what grounds does he reject Tooley's view?
3. Who makes the stronger case for their position, Tooley or Devine? Explain.

3. THOMSON'S SELF-DEFENSE ARGUMENT FOR ABORTION

Personhood arguments seem laden with complications for both conservatives and liberals, but they also challenge moderates. Some philosophers have therefore tried to lay out moderate positions without appealing to fetal personhood. The most famous example of the latter comes from Judith Jarvis Thomson in "A Defense of Abortion." She argues that even if the conservative view is correct that the unborn is a person from the moment of conception, abortion may still be morally justified. A fetus may have a right to life, but this right "does not guarantee having either a right to be given the use of or a right to be allowed continued use of another person's body—even if one needs it for life itself."[16] The unborn's right to life is not absolute. It implies not that killing a fetus is always wrong, but that killing it unjustly is always wrong. Thomson argues her point with this striking analogy:

> You wake up in the morning and find yourself back to back in bed with an unconscious violinist. A famous unconscious violinist. He has been found to have a fatal kidney ailment, and the Society of Music Lovers has canvassed all the available medical records and found that you alone have the right blood type to help. They have therefore kidnapped you, and last night the violinist's circulatory system was plugged into yours, so that your kidneys can be used to extract poisons from his blood as well as your own. The director of the hospital now tells you, "Look, we're sorry the Society of Music Lovers did this to you—we would never have permitted it if we had known. But still, they did it, and the violinist now is plugged into you. To unplug you would be to kill him. But never mind, it's only for nine months. By then he will have recovered from his ailment, and can safely be unplugged from you."[17]

Thomson believes that our intuitions would tell us that this arrangement is outrageous, that the violinist's right to life would not give him the right to exploit someone's body against her will. Analogously, a fetus's right to life would not guarantee it unauthorized use of the mother's body; the mother has a right of self-defense. Abortion, therefore, is justified when the fetus takes up residence without the woman's consent, as when pregnancy is due to rape or failed contraception.

Some reject Thomson's argument by contending that it holds only if the woman bears no responsibility for her predicament, if the attached violinist or fetus takes up residence through no fault of her own. She may not be responsible for the fetus if she

---

[16] Judith Jarvis Thomson, "A Defense of Abortion," *Philosophy and Public Affairs*, vol. 1, no. 1 (1971): 47–50, 54–66.
[17] Thomson, "A Defense of Abortion."

becomes pregnant through rape; she does not, after all, consent to be raped. But she can be held responsible if she voluntarily engages in sexual intercourse; she therefore is obligated to carry the fetus to term. Others maintain that the woman is obliged to sustain the life of the unborn because she has a filial obligation to it. The unborn has a natural claim to the woman's body.

A Defense of Abortion[1]

JUDITH JARVIS THOMSON

Most opposition to abortion relies on the premise that the fetus is a human being, a person, from the moment of conception. The premise is argued for, but, as I think, not well. Take, for example, the most common argument. We are asked to notice that the development of a human being from conception through birth into childhood is continuous; then it is said that to draw a line, to choose a point in this development and say "before this point the thing is not a person, after this point it is a person" is to make an arbitrary choice, a choice for which in the nature of things no good reason can be given. It is concluded that the fetus is, or anyway that we had better say it is, a person from the moment of conception. But this conclusion does not follow. Similar things might be said about the development of an acorn into an oak tree, and it does not follow that acorns are oak trees, or that we had better say they are. Arguments of this form are sometimes called "slippery slope arguments"—the phrase is perhaps self-explanatory—and it is dismaying that opponents of abortion rely on them so heavily and uncritically.

I am inclined to agree, however, that the prospects for "drawing a line" in the development of the fetus look dim. I am inclined to think also that we shall probably have to agree that the fetus has already became a human person well before birth. Indeed, it comes as a surprise when one first learns how early in its life it begins to acquire human characteristics. By the tenth week, for example, it already has a face, arms and legs, fingers and toes; it has internal organs, and brain activity is detectable.[2] On the other hand, I think that the premise is false, that the fetus is not a person from the moment of conception. A newly fertilized ovum, a newly implanted clump of cells, is no more a person than an acorn is an oak tree. But I shall not discuss any of this. For it seems to me to be of great interest to ask what happens if, for the sake of argument, we allow the premise. How, precisely, are we supposed to get from there to the conclusion that abortion is morally impermissible? Opponents of abortion commonly spend most of their time establishing that the fetus is a person, and hardly any time explaining the step from there to the impermissibility of abortion. Perhaps they think the step too simple and obvious to require much comment. Or perhaps instead they are simply being economical in argument. Many of those who defend abortion rely on the premise that the fetus is not a person, but only a bit of tissue that will become a person at birth; and why pay out more arguments than you have to? Whatever the explanation, I suggest that the step they take is neither easy nor obvious, that it calls for closer examination than it is commonly given, and that when we do give it this closer examination we shall feel inclined to reject it.

I propose, then, that we grant that the fetus is a person, from the moment of conception. How does the argument go from here? Something like this, I take it. Every person has a right to life. So the fetus has a right to life. No doubt the mother has a right to decide what shall happen in and to her body; everyone would grant that. But surely a person's right to life is stronger and more stringent than the mother's right to decide what happens in and to her body, and so outweighs it. So the fetus may not be killed; an abortion may not be performed.

It sounds plausible. But now let me ask you to imagine this. You wake up in the morning and find yourself back to back in bed with an unconscious violinist. A famous unconscious violinist. He has been found to have a fatal kidney ailment, and the Society of Music Lovers has canvassed all the available medical records and found that you alone have the right blood type to help. They have therefore kidnapped you, and last night the violinist's circulatory system was plugged into yours, so that your kidneys can be used to extract poisons from his blood as well as your own. The director of the hospital now tells you, "Look, we're sorry the Society of Music Lovers did this to you—we would never have permitted it if we had known. But still, they did it, and the violinist now is plugged into you. To unplug you would be to kill him. But never mind, it's only for nine months. By then he will have recovered from his ailment, and can safely be unplugged from you." Is it morally incumbent on you to accede to this situation? No doubt it would be very nice of you if you did, a great kindness. But do you *have* to accede to it? What if it were not nine months, but nine years? Or longer still? What if the director of the hospital says, "Tough luck, I agree, but you've now got to stay in bed, with the violinist plugged into you, for the rest of your life. Because remember this. All persons have a right to life, and violinists are persons. Granted you have a right to decide what happens in and to your body, but a person's right to life outweighs your right to decide what happens in and to your body. So you cannot ever be unplugged from him." I imagine you would regard this as outrageous, which suggests that something really is wrong with that plausible-sounding argument I mentioned a moment ago.

In this case, of course, you were kidnapped; you didn't volunteer for the operation that plugged the violinist into your kidneys. Can those who oppose abortion on the ground I mentioned make an exception for a pregnancy due to rape? Certainly. They can say that persons have a right to life only if they didn't come into existence because of rape; or they can say that all persons have a right to life, but that some have less of a right to life than others, in particular, that those who came into existence because of rape have less. But these statements have a rather unpleasant sound. Surely the question of whether you have a right to life at all, or how much of it you have, shouldn't turn on the question of whether or not you are the product of a rape. And in fact the people who oppose abortion on the ground I mentioned do not make this distinction, and hence do not make an exception in case of rape.

Nor do they make an exception for a case in which the mother has to spend the nine months of her pregnancy in bed. They would agree that would be a great pity, and hard on the mother; but all the same, all persons have a right to life, the fetus is a person, and so on. I suspect, in fact, that they would not make an exception for a case in which, miraculously enough, the pregnancy went on for nine years, or even the rest of the mother's life.

Some won't even make an exception for a case in which continuation of the pregnancy is likely to shorten the mother's life; they regard abortion as impermissible even to save the mother's life. Such cases are nowadays very rare, and many opponents of abortion do not accept this extreme view. All the same, it is a good place to begin: a number of points of interest come out in respect to it.

1. Let us call the view that abortion is impermissible even to save the mother's life "the extreme view." I want to suggest first that it does not issue from the argument I mentioned earlier without the addition of some fairly powerful premises. Suppose a woman has become pregnant, and now learns that she has a cardiac condition such that she will die if she carries the baby to term. What may be done for her? The fetus, being a person, has a right to life, but as the mother is a person too, so has she a right to life. Presumably they have an equal right to life. How is it supposed to come out that an abortion may not be performed? If mother and child have an

equal right to life, shouldn't we perhaps flip a coin? Or should we add to the mother's right to life her right to decide what happens in and to her body, which everybody seems to be ready to grant—the sum of her rights now outweighing the fetus' right to life?

The most familiar argument here is the following. We are told that performing the abortion would be directly killing[3] the child, whereas doing nothing would not be killing the mother, but only letting her die. Moreover, in killing the child, one would be killing an innocent person, for the child has committed no crime, and is not aiming at his mother's death. And then there are a variety of ways in which this might be continued. (1) But as directly killing an innocent person is always and absolutely impermissible, an abortion may not be performed. Or, (2) as directly killing an innocent person is murder, and murder is always and absolutely impermissible, an abortion may not be performed.[4] Or, (3) as one's duty to refrain from directly killing an innocent person is more stringent than one's duty to keep a person from dying, an abortion may not be performed. Or, (4) if one's only options are directly killing an innocent person or letting a person die, one must prefer letting the person die, and thus an abortion may not be performed.[5]

Some people seem to have thought that these are not further premises which must be added if the conclusion is to be reached, but that they follow from the very fact that an innocent person has a right to life.[6] But this seems to me to be a mistake, and perhaps the simplest way to show this is to bring out that while we must certainly grant that innocent persons have a right to life, the theses in (1) through (4) are all false. Take (2), for example. If directly killing an innocent person is murder, and thus is impermissible, then the mother's directly killing the innocent person inside her is murder, and thus is impermissible. But it cannot seriously be thought to be murder if the mother performs an abortion on herself to save her life. It cannot seriously be said that she *must* refrain, that she *must* sit passively by and wait for her death. Let us look again at the case of you and the violinist. There you are, in bed with the violinist, and the director of the hospital says to you, "It's all most distressing, and I deeply sympathize, but you see this is putting an additional strain on your kidneys, and you'll be dead within the month. But you *have* to stay where you are all the same. Because unplugging you would be directly killing an innocent violinist, and that's murder, and that's impermissible." If anything in the world is true, it is that you do not commit murder, you do not do what is impermissible, if you reach around to your back and unplug yourself from that violinist to save your life.

The main focus of attention in writings on abortion has been on what a third party may or may not do in answer to a request from a woman for an abortion. This is in a way understandable. Things being as they are, there isn't much a woman can safely do to abort herself. So the question asked is what a third party may do, and what the mother may do, if it is mentioned at all, is deduced, almost as an afterthought, from what it is concluded that third parties may do. But it seems to me that to treat the matter in this way is to refuse to grant to the mother that very status of person which is so firmly insisted on for the fetus. For we cannot simply read off what a person may do from what a third party may do. Suppose you find yourself trapped in a tiny house with a growing child. I mean a very tiny house, and a rapidly growing child—you are already up against the wall of the house and in a few minutes you'll be crushed to death. The child on the other hand won't be crushed to death; if nothing is done to stop him from growing he'll be hurt, but in the end he'll simply burst open the house and walk out a free man. Now I could well understand it if a bystander were to say, "There's nothing we can do for you. We cannot choose between your life and his, we cannot be the ones to decide who is to live, we cannot intervene." But it cannot be concluded that you too can do nothing, that you cannot attack it to save your life. However innocent the child may be, you do not have to wait passively while it crushes you to death. Perhaps a pregnant woman is vaguely felt to have the status of house, to which we don't allow the right of self-defense. But if the woman houses the child, it should be remembered that she is a person who houses it.

I should perhaps stop to say explicitly that I am not claiming that people have a right to do anything whatever to save their lives. I think, rather, that there are drastic limits to the right of self-defense.

If someone threatens you with death unless you torture someone else to death, I think you have not the right, even to save your life, to do so. But the case under consideration here is very different. In our case there are only two people involved, one whose life is threatened, and one who threatens it. Both are innocent: the one who is threatened is not threatened because of any fault, the one who threatens does not threaten because of any fault. For this reason we may feel that we bystanders cannot intervene. But the person threatened can.

In sum, a woman surely can defend her life against the threat to it posed by the unborn child, even if doing so involves its death. And this shows not merely that the theses in (1) through (4) are false; it shows also that the extreme view of abortion is false, and so we need not canvass any other possible ways of arriving at it from the argument I mentioned at the outset.

2. The extreme view could of course be weakened to say that while abortion is permissible to save the mother's life, it may not be performed by a third party, but only by the mother herself. But this cannot be right either. For what we have to keep in mind is that the mother and the unborn child are not like two tenants in a small house which has, by an unfortunate mistake, been rented to both: the mother *owns* the house. The fact that she does adds to the offensiveness of deducing that the mother can do nothing from the supposition that third parties can do nothing. But it does more than this: it casts a bright light on the supposition that third parties can do nothing. Certainly it lets us see that a third party who says "I cannot choose between you" is fooling himself if he thinks this is impartiality. If Jones has found and fastened on a certain coat, which he needs to keep him from freezing, but which Smith also needs to keep him from freezing, then it is not impartiality that says "I cannot choose between you" when Smith owns the coat. Women have said again and again "This body is *my* body!" and they have reason to feel angry, reason to feel that it has been like shouting into the wind. Smith, after all, is hardly likely to bless us if we say to him, "Of course it's your coat, anybody would grant that it is. But no one may choose between you and Jones who is to have it."

We should really ask what it is that says "no one may choose" in the face of the fact that the body that houses the child is the mother's body. It may be simply a failure to appreciate this fact. But it may be something more interesting, namely the sense that one has a right to refuse to lay hands on people, even where it would be just and fair to do so, even where justice seems to require that somebody do so. Thus justice might call for somebody to get Smith's coat back from Jones, and yet you have a right to refuse to be the one to lay hands on Jones, a right to refuse to do physical violence to him. This, I think, must be granted. But then what should be said is not "no one may choose," but only "I cannot choose," and indeed not even this, but "I will not *act*," leaving it open that somebody else can or should, and in particular that anyone in a position of authority, with the job of securing people's rights, both can and should. So this is no difficulty. I have not been arguing that any given third party must accede to the mother's request that he perform an abortion to save her life, but only that he may.

I suppose that in some views of human life the mother's body is only on loan to her, the loan not being one which gives her any prior claim to it. One who held this view might well think it impartiality to say "I cannot choose." But I shall simply ignore this possibility. My own view is that if a human being has any just, prior claim to anything at all, he has a just, prior claim to his own body. And perhaps this needn't be argued for here anyway, since, as I mentioned, the arguments against abortion we are looking at do grant that the woman has a right to decide what happens in and to her body.

But although they do grant it, I have tried to show that they do not take seriously what is done in granting it. I suggest the same thing will reappear even more clearly when we turn away from cases in which the mother's life is at stake, and attend, as I propose we now do, to the vastly more common cases in which a woman wants an abortion for some less weighty reason than preserving her own life.

3. Where the mother's life is not at stake, the argument I mentioned at the outset seems to have a much stronger pull. "Everyone has a right to life, so the unborn person has a right to life." And isn't the child's right to life weightier than anything other than the mother's own right to life, which she might put forward as ground for an abortion?

This argument treats the right to life as if it were unproblematic. It is not, and this seems to me to be precisely the source of the mistake.

For we should now, at long last, ask what it comes to, to have a right to life. In some views having a right to life includes having a right to be given at least the bare minimum one needs for continued life. But suppose that what in fact *is* the bare minimum a man needs for continued life is something he has no right at all to be given? If I am sick unto death, and the only thing that will save my life is the touch of Henry Fonda's cool hand on my fevered brow, then all the same, I have no right to be given the touch of Henry Fonda's cool hand on my fevered brow. It would be frightfully nice of him to fly in from the West Coast to provide it. It would be less nice, though no doubt well meant, if my friends flew out to the West Coast and carried Henry Fonda back with them. But I have no right at all against anybody that he should do this for me. Or again, to return to the story I told earlier, the fact that for continued life that violinist needs the continued use of your kidneys does not establish that he has a right to be given the continued use of your kidneys. He certainly has no right against you that *you* should give him continued use of your kidneys. For nobody has any right to use your kidneys unless you give him such a right; and nobody has the right against you that you shall give him this right—if you do allow him to go on using your kidneys, this is a kindness on your part, and not something he can claim from you as his due. Nor has he any right against anybody else that *they* should give him continued use of your kidneys. Certainly he had no right against the Society of Music Lovers that they should plug him into you in the first place. And if you now start to unplug yourself, having learned that you will otherwise have to spend nine years in bed with him, there is nobody in the world who must try to prevent you, in order to see to it that he is given something he has a right to be given.

Some people are rather stricter about the right to life. In their view, it does not include the right to be given anything, but amounts to, and only to, the right not to be killed by anybody. But here a related difficulty arises. If everybody is to refrain from killing that violinist, then everybody must refrain from doing a great many different sorts of things. Everybody must refrain from slitting his throat, everybody must refrain from shooting him—and everybody must refrain from unplugging you from him. But does he have a right against everybody that they shall refrain from unplugging you from him? To refrain from doing this is to allow him to continue to use your kidneys. It could be argued that he has a right against us that *we* should allow him to continue to use your kidneys. That is, while he had no right against us that we should give him the use of your kidneys, it might be argued that he anyway has a right against us that we shall not now intervene and deprive him of the use of your kidneys. I shall come back to third-party interventions later. But certainly the violinist has no right against you that *you* shall allow him to continue to use your kidneys. As I said, if you do allow him to use them, it is a kindness on your part, and not something you owe him.

The difficulty I point to here is not peculiar to the right to life. It reappears in connection with all the other natural rights; and it is something which an adequate account of rights must deal with. For present purposes it is enough just to draw attention to it. But I would stress that I am not arguing that people do not have a right to life—quite to the contrary, it seems to me that the primary control we must place on the acceptability of an account of rights is that it should turn out in that account to be a truth that all persons have a right to life. I am arguing only that having a right to life does not guarantee having either a right to be given the use of or a right to be allowed continued use of another person's body—even if one needs it for life itself. So the right to life will not serve the opponents of abortion in the very simple and clear way in which they seem to have thought it would.

4. There is another way to bring out the difficulty. In the most ordinary sort of case, to deprive someone of what he has a right to is to treat him unjustly. Suppose a boy and his small brother are jointly given a box of chocolates for Christmas. If the older boy takes the box and refuses to give his brother any of the chocolates, he is unjust to him, for the brother has been given a right to half of them. But suppose that, having learned that otherwise it means nine years in bed with that violinist, you unplug yourself from him. You surely are not

being unjust to him, for you gave him no right to use your kidneys, and no one else can have given him any such right. But we have to notice that in unplugging yourself, you are killing him; and violinists, like everybody else, have a right to life, and thus in the view we were considering just now, the right not to be killed. So here you do what he supposedly has a right you shall not do, but you do not act unjustly to him in doing it.

The emendation which may be made at this point is this: the right to life consists not in the right not to be killed, but rather in the right not to be killed unjustly. This runs a risk of circularity, but never mind: it would enable us to square the fact that the violinist has a right to life with the fact that you do not act unjustly toward him in unplugging yourself, thereby killing him. For if you do not kill him unjustly, you do not violate his right to life, and so it is no wonder you do him no injustice.

But if this emendation is accepted, the gap in the argument against abortion stares us plainly in the face: it is by no means enough to show that the fetus is a person, and to remind us that all persons have a right to life—we need to be shown also that killing the fetus violates its right to life, i.e., that abortion is unjust killing. And is it?

I suppose we may take it as a datum that in a case of pregnancy due to rape the mother has not given the unborn person a right to the use of her body for food and shelter. Indeed, in what pregnancy could it be supposed that the mother has given the unborn person such a right? It is not as if there were unborn persons drifting about the world, to whom a woman who wants a child says "I invite you in."

But it might be argued that there are other ways one can have acquired a right to the use of another person's body than by having been invited to use it by that person. Suppose a woman voluntarily indulges in intercourse, knowing of the chance it will issue in pregnancy, and then she does become pregnant; is she not in part responsible for the presence, in fact the very existence, of the unborn person inside her? No doubt she did not invite it in. But doesn't her partial responsibility for its being there itself give it a right to the use of her body?[7] If so, then her aborting it would be more like the boy's taking away the chocolates, and less like your unplugging yourself from the violinist—doing so

would be depriving it of what it does have a right to, and thus would be doing it an injustice.

And then, too, it might be asked whether or not she can kill it even to save her own life: If she voluntarily called it into existence, how can she now kill it, even in self-defense?

The first thing to be said about this is that it is something new. Opponents of abortion have been so concerned to make out the independence of the fetus, in order to establish that it has a right to life, just as its mother does, that they have tended to overlook the possible support they might gain from making out that the fetus is *dependent* on the mother, in order to establish that she has a special kind of responsibility for it, a responsibility that gives it rights against her which are not possessed by any independent person—such as an ailing violinist who is a stranger to her.

On the other hand, this argument would give the unborn person a right to its mother's body only if her pregnancy resulted from a voluntary act, undertaken in full knowledge of the chance a pregnancy might result from it. It would leave out entirely the unborn person whose existence is due to rape. Pending the availability of some further argument, then, we would be left with the conclusion that unborn persons whose existence is due to rape have no right to the use of their mothers' bodies, and thus that aborting them is not depriving them of anything they have a right to and hence is not unjust killing.

And we should also notice that it is not at all plain that this argument really does go even as far as it purports to. For there are cases and cases, and the details make a difference. If the room is stuffy, and I therefore open a window to air it, and a burglar climbs in, it would be absurd to say, "Ah, now he can stay, she's given him a right to the use of her house—for she is partially responsible for his presence there, having voluntarily done what enabled him to get in, in full knowledge that there are such things as burglars, and that burglars burgle." It would be still more absurd to say this if I had had bars installed outside my windows, precisely to prevent burglars from getting in, and a burglar got in only because of a defect in the bars. It remains equally absurd if we imagine it is not a burglar who climbs in, but an innocent person who blunders or falls in. Again, suppose it were like this: people-seeds drift about in the air like pollen, and if you open your windows, one may drift in and take root in your carpets or upholstery. You don't want children, so you fix up your windows with fine mesh screens, the very best you can buy. As can happen, however, and on very, very rare occasions does happen, one of the screens is defective; and a seed drifts in and takes root. Does the person-plant who now develops have a right to the use of your house? Surely not—despite the fact that you voluntarily opened your windows, you knowingly kept carpets and upholstered furniture, and you knew that screens were sometimes defective. Someone may argue that you are responsible for its rooting, that it does have a right to your house, because after all you *could* have lived out your life with bare floors and furniture, or with sealed windows and doors. But this won't do—for by the same token anyone can avoid a pregnancy due to rape by having a hysterectomy, or anyway by never leaving home without a (reliable!) army.

It seems to me that the argument we are looking at can establish at most that there are *some* cases in which the unborn person has a right to the use of its mother's body, and therefore *some* cases in which abortion is unjust killing. There is room for much discussion and argument as to precisely which, if any. But I think we should sidestep this issue and leave it open, for at any rate the argument certainly does not establish that all abortion is unjust killing.

5. There is room for yet another argument here, however. We surely must all grant that there may be cases in which it would be morally indecent to detach a person from your body at the cost of his life. Suppose you learn that what the violinist needs is not nine years of your life, but only one hour: all you need do to save his life is to spend one hour in that bed with him. Suppose also that letting him use your kidneys for that one hour would not affect your health in the slightest. Admittedly you were kidnapped. Admittedly you did not give anyone permission to plug him into you. Nevertheless it seems to me plain you *ought* to allow him to use your kidneys for that hour—it would be indecent to refuse.

Again, suppose pregnancy lasted only an hour, and constituted no threat to life or health. And suppose that a woman becomes pregnant as a result of rape. Admittedly she did not voluntarily do anything to bring about the existence of a child. Admittedly she did nothing at all which would give the unborn person a right to the use of her body. All the same it might well be said, as in the newly emended violinist story, that she *ought* to allow it to remain for that hour—that it would be indecent in her to refuse.

Now some people are inclined to use the term "right" in such a way that it follows from the fact that you ought to allow a person to use your body for the hour he needs, that he has a right to use your body for the hour he needs, even though he has not been given that right by any person or act. They may say that it follows also that if you refuse, you act unjustly toward him. This use of the term is perhaps so common that it cannot be called wrong; nevertheless it seems to me to be an unfortunate loosening of what we would do better to keep a tight rein on. Suppose that box of chocolates I mentioned earlier had not been given to both boys jointly, but was given only to the older boy. There he sits, stolidly eating his way through the box, his small brother watching enviously. Here we are likely to say "You ought not to be so mean. You ought to give your brother some of those chocolates." My own view is that it just does not follow from the truth of this that the brother has any right to any of the chocolates. If the boy refuses to give his brother any, he is greedy, stingy, callous—but not unjust. I suppose that the people I have in mind will say it does follow that the brother has a right to some of the chocolates, and thus that the boy does act unjustly if he refuses to give his brother any. But the effect of saying this is to obscure what we should keep distinct, namely the difference between the boy's refusal in this case and the boy's refusal in the earlier case, in which the box was given to both boys jointly, and in which the small brother thus had what was from any point of view clear title to half.

A further objection to so using the term "right" that from the fact that A ought to do a thing for B, it follows that B has a right against A that A do it for him, is that it is going to make the question of whether or not a man has a right to a thing turn on how easy it is to provide him with it; and this seems not merely unfortunate, but morally unacceptable.

Take the case of Henry Fonda again. I said earlier that I had no right to the touch of his cool hand on my fevered brow, even though I needed it to save my life. I said it would be frightfully nice of him to fly in from the West Coast to provide me with it, but that I had no right against him that he should do so. But suppose he isn't on the West Coast. Suppose he has only to walk across the room, place a hand briefly on my brow—and lo, my life is saved. Then surely he ought to do it, it would be indecent to refuse. Is it to be said "Ah, well, it follows that in this case she has a right to the touch of his hand on her brow, and so it would be an injustice in him to refuse"? So that I have a right to it when it is easy for him to provide it, though no right when it's hard? It's rather a shocking idea that anyone's rights should fade away and disappear as it gets harder and harder to accord them to him.

So my own view is that even though you ought to let the violinist use your kidneys for the one hour he needs, we should not conclude that he has a right to do so—we should say that if you refuse, you are, like the boy who owns all the chocolates and will give none away, self-centered and callous, indecent in fact, but not unjust. And similarly, that even supposing a case in which a woman pregnant due to rape ought to allow the unborn person to use her body for the hour he needs, we should not conclude that he has a right to do so; we should conclude that she is self-centered, callous, indecent, but not unjust, if she refuses. The complaints are no less grave; they are just different. However, there is no need to insist on this point. If anyone does wish to deduce "he has a right" from "you ought," then all the same he must surely grant that there are cases in which it is not morally required of you that you allow that violinist to use your kidneys, and in which he does not have a right to use them, and in which you do not do him an injustice if you refuse. And so also for mother and unborn child. Except in such cases as the unborn person has a right to demand it—and we were leaving open the possibility that there may be such cases—nobody is morally *required* to make large sacrifices, of health, of all other interests and concerns, of all other duties and commitments, for nine years, or even for nine months, in order to keep another person alive.

6. We have in fact to distinguish between two kinds of Samaritan: the Good Samaritan and what we might call the Minimally Decent Samaritan. The story of the Good Samaritan, you will remember, goes like this:

A certain man went down from Jerusalem to Jericho, and fell among thieves, which stripped him of his raiment, and wounded him, and departed, leaving him half dead.

And by chance there came down a certain priest that way; and when he saw him, he passed by on the other side.

And likewise a Levite, when he was at the place, came and looked on him, and passed by on the other side.

But a certain Samaritan, as he journeyed, came where he was; and when he saw him he had compassion on him.

And went to him, and bound up his wounds, pouring in oil and wine, and set him on his own beast, and brought him to an inn, and took care of him.

And on the morrow, when he departed, he took out two pence, and gave them to the host, and said unto him, "Take care of him; and whatsoever thou spendest more, when I come again, I will repay thee."

(Luke 10:30–35)

The Good Samaritan went out of his way, at some cost to himself, to help one in need of it. We are not told what the options were, that is, whether or not the priest and the Levite could have helped by doing less than the Good Samaritan did, but assuming they could have, then the fact they did nothing at all shows they were not even Minimally Decent Samaritans, not because they were not Samaritans, but because they were not even minimally decent.

These things are a matter of degree, of course, but there is a difference, and it comes out perhaps most clearly in the story of Kitty Genovese, who, as you will remember, was murdered while thirty-eight people watched or listened, and did nothing at all to help her. A Good Samaritan would have rushed out to give direct assistance against the murderer. Or perhaps we had better allow that it would have been a Splendid Samaritan who did this, on the ground that it would have involved a risk of death for himself. But the thirty-eight not only did not do this, they did not even trouble to pick up a phone to call the police. Minimally Decent Samaritanism would call for doing at least that, and their not having done it was monstrous.

After telling the story of the Good Samaritan, Jesus said "Go, and do thou likewise." Perhaps he meant that we are morally required to act as the Good Samaritan did. Perhaps he was urging people to do more than is morally required of them. At all events it seems plain that it was not morally required of any of the thirty-eight that he rush out to give direct assistance at the risk of his own life, and that it is not morally required of anyone that he give long stretches of his life—nine years or nine months—to sustaining the life of a person who has no special right (we were leaving open the possibility of this) to demand it.

Indeed, with one rather striking class of exceptions, no one in any country in the world is *legally* required to do anywhere near as much as this for anyone else. The class of exceptions is obvious. My main concern here is not the state of the law in respect to abortion, but it is worth drawing attention to the fact that in no state in this country is any man compelled by law to be even a Minimally Decent Samaritan to any person; there is no law under which charges could be brought against the thirty-eight who stood by while Kitty Genovese died. By contrast, in most states in this country women are compelled by law to be not merely Minimally Decent Samaritans, but Good Samaritans to unborn persons inside them. This doesn't by itself settle anything one way or the other, because it may well be argued that there should be laws in this country—as there are in many European countries—compelling at least Minimally Decent Samaritanism.[8] But it does show that there is a gross injustice in the existing state of the law. And it shows also that the groups currently working against liberalization of abortion laws, in fact working toward having it declared unconstitutional for a state to permit abortion, had better start working for the adoption of Good Samaritan laws generally, or earn the charge that they are acting in bad faith.

I should think, myself, that Minimally Decent Samaritan laws would be one thing, Good Samaritan

laws quite another, and in fact highly improper. But we are not here concerned with the law. What we should ask is not whether anybody should be compelled by law to be a Good Samaritan, but whether we must accede to a situation in which somebody is being compelled—by nature, perhaps—to be a Good Samaritan. We have, in other words, to look now at third-party interventions. I have been arguing that no person is morally required to make large sacrifices to sustain the life of another who has no right to demand them, and this even where the sacrifices do not include life itself; we are not morally required to be Good Samaritans or anyway Very Good Samaritans to one another. But what if a man cannot extricate himself from such a situation? What if he appeals to us to extricate him? It seems to me plain that there are cases in which we can, cases in which a Good Samaritan would extricate him. There you are, you were kidnapped, and nine years in bed with that violinist lie ahead of you. You have your own life to lead. You are sorry, but you simply cannot see giving up so much of your life to the sustaining of his. You cannot extricate yourself, and ask us to do so. I should have thought that—in light of his having no right to the use of your body— it was obvious that we do not have to accede to your being forced to give up so much. We can do what you ask. There is no injustice to the violinist in our doing so.

7. Following the lead of the opponents of abortion, I have throughout been speaking of the fetus merely as a person, and what I have been asking is whether or not the argument we began with, which proceeds only from the fetus' being a person, really does establish its conclusion. I have argued that it does not.

But of course there are arguments and arguments, and it may be said that I have simply fastened on the wrong one. It may be said that what is important is not merely the fact that the fetus is a person, but that it is a person for whom the woman has a special kind of responsibility issuing from the fact that she is its mother. And it might be argued that all my analogies are therefore irrelevant—for you do not have that special kind of responsibility for that violinist, Henry Fonda does not have that special kind of responsibility for me. And our attention might be drawn to the fact that men and women both *are* compelled by law to provide support for their children.

I have in effect dealt (briefly) with this argument in section 4 above; but a (still briefer) recapitulation now may be in order. Surely we do not have any such "special responsibility" for a person unless we have assumed it, explicitly or implicitly. If a set of parents do not try to prevent pregnancy, do not obtain an abortion, and then at the time of birth of the child do not put it out for adoption, but rather take it home with them, then they have assumed responsibility for it, they have given it rights, and they cannot *now* withdraw support from it at the cost of its life because they now find it difficult to go on providing for it. But if they have taken all reasonable precautions against having a child, they do not simply by virtue of their biological relationship to the child who comes into existence have a special responsibility for it. They may wish to assume responsibility for it, or they may not wish to. And I am suggesting that if assuming responsibility for it would require large sacrifices, then they may refuse. A Good Samaritan would not refuse—or anyway, a Splendid Samaritan, if the sacrifices that had to be made were enormous. But then so would a Good Samaritan assume responsibility for that violinist; so would Henry Fonda, if he is a Good Samaritan, fly in from the West Coast and assume responsibility for me.

8. My argument will be found unsatisfactory on two counts by many of those who want to regard abortion as morally permissible. First, while I do argue that abortion is not impermissible, I do not argue that it is always permissible. There may well be cases in which carrying the child to term requires only Minimally Decent Samaritanism of the mother, and this is a standard we must not fall below. I am inclined to think it a merit of my account precisely that it does *not* give a general yes or a general no. It allows for and supports our sense that, for example, a sick and desperately frightened fourteen-year-old schoolgirl, pregnant due to rape, may *of course* choose abortion, and that any law which rules this out is an insane law. And it also allows for and supports our sense that in other cases resort to abortion is even positively indecent. It would be indecent in the woman to request an abortion, and indecent in a doctor to perform it, if she is in her seventh month,

and wants the abortion just to avoid the nuisance of postponing a trip abroad. The very fact that the arguments I have been drawing attention to treat all cases of abortion, or even all cases of abortion in which the mother's life is not at stake, as morally on a par ought to have made them suspect at the outset.

Secondly, while I am arguing for the permissibility of abortion in some cases, I am not arguing for the right to secure the death of the unborn child. It is easy to confuse these two things in that up to a certain point in the life of the fetus it is not able to survive outside the mother's body; hence removing it from her body guarantees its death. But they are importantly different. I have argued that you are not morally required to spend nine months in bed, sustaining the life of that violinist; but to say this is by no means to say that if, when you unplug yourself, there is a miracle and he survives, you then have a right to turn round and slit his throat. You may detach yourself even if this costs him his life; you have no right to be guaranteed his death, by some other means, if unplugging yourself does not kill him. There are some people who will feel dissatisfied by this feature of my argument. A woman may be utterly devastated by the thought of a child, a bit of herself, put out for adoption and never seen or heard of again. She may therefore want not merely that the child be detached from her, but more, that it die. Some opponents of abortion are inclined to regard this as beneath contempt—thereby showing insensitivity to what is surely a powerful source of despair. All the same, I agree that the desire for the child's death is not one which anybody may gratify, should it turn out to be possible to detach the child alive.

At this place, however, it should be remembered that we have only been pretending throughout that the fetus is a human being from the moment of conception. A very early abortion is surely not the killing of a person, and so is not dealt with by anything I have said here.

NOTES

1. I am very much indebted to James Thomson for discussion, criticism, and many helpful suggestions.
2. Daniel Callahan, *Abortion: Law, Choice and Morality* (New York, 1970), p. 373. This book gives a fascinating

survey of the available information on abortion. The Jewish tradition is surveyed in David M. Feldman, *Birth Control in Jewish Law* (New York, 1968), Part 5, the Catholic tradition in John T. Noonan, Jr., "An Almost Absolute Value in History," in *The Morality of Abortion,* ed. John T. Noonan, Jr. (Cambridge, Mass., 1970).

3. The term "direct" in the arguments I refer to is a technical one. Roughly, what is meant by "direct killing" is either killing as an end in itself, or killing as a means to some end, for example, the end of saving someone else's life. See note 6, below, for an example of its use.

4. Cf. *Encyclical Letter of Pope Pius XI on Christian Marriage,* St. Paul Editions (Boston, n.d.), p. 32: "however much we may pity the mother whose health and even life is gravely imperiled in the performance of the duty allotted to her by nature, nevertheless what could ever be a sufficient reason for excusing in any way the direct murder of the innocent? This is precisely what we are dealing with here." Noonan (*The Morality of Abortion,* p. 43) reads this as follows: "What cause can ever avail to excuse in any way the direct killing of the innocent? For it is a question of that."

5. The thesis in (4) is in an interesting way weaker than those in (1), (2), and (3): they rule out abortion even in cases in which both mother *and* child will die if the abortion is not performed. By contrast, one who held the view expressed in (4) could consistently say that one needn't prefer letting two persons die to killing one.

6. Cf. the following passage from Pius XII, *Address to the Italian Catholic Society of Midwives:* "The baby in the maternal breast has the right to life immediately from God.—Hence there is no man, no human authority, no science, no medical, eugenic, social, economic or moral 'indication' which can establish or grant a valid juridical ground for a direct deliberate disposition of an innocent human life, that is a disposition which looks to its destruction either as an end or as a means to another end perhaps in itself not illicit.—The baby, still not born, is a man in the same degree and for the same reason, as the mother" (quoted in Noonan, *The Morality of Abortion,* p. 45).

7. The need for a discussion of this argument was brought home to me by members of the Society for Ethical and Legal Philosophy, to whom this paper was originally presented.

8. For a discussion of the difficulties involved, and a survey of the European experience with such laws, see *The Good Samaritan and the Law,* ed. James M. Ratcliffe (New York, 1966).

Arguments from Bodily Rights

A Critical Analysis

FRANCIS J. BECKWITH

[Earlier] I noted that some abortion-rights advocates do not see the status of the unborn as the decisive factor in whether or not abortion is morally justified. They argue that the unborn's presence in the pregnant woman's body entails a conflict of rights if the pregnant woman does not want to be pregnant. Therefore, the unborn, regardless of whether it is fully human and has a full right to life, cannot use the body of another against her will. Hence, a pregnant woman's removal of an unborn entity from her body, even though it will probably result in that entity's death, is no more immoral than an ordinary person's refusal to donate his kidney to another in need of one, even though this refusal will probably result in the death of the prospective recipient. In this chapter we will discuss such arguments from rights.

The most famous and influential argument from rights is the one presented by philosopher Judith Jarvis Thomson. ...

ARGUMENT FROM UNPLUGGING THE VIOLINIST

In an article that by 1986 was "the most widely reprinted essay in all of contemporary philosophy," Judith Jarvis Thomson presents a philosophically sophisticated version of the argument from a woman's right to control her body. Thomson argues that even if the unborn entity is a person with a right to life, this does not mean that a woman must be forced to use her bodily organs to sustain its life. Just as one does not have a right to use another's kidney if one's kidney has failed, the unborn entity, although having a basic right to life, does not have a right to life so strong that it outweighs the pregnant woman's right to personal bodily autonomy.

It should be noted that Thomson's argument was not used in any of the landmark Supreme Court decisions that have upheld the abortion-rights position, such as *Roe v. Wade* or *Doe v. Bolton*. Recently, however, Laurence Tribe, whose influence on the Court's liberal wing is well-known, has suggested that the Court should have seriously considered Thomson's argument. Tribe writes: "[P]erhaps the Supreme Court's opinion in *Roe*, by gratuitously insisting that the fetus cannot be deemed a 'person,' needlessly insulted and alienated those for whom the view that the fetus is a person represents a fundamental article of faith or a bedrock personal commitment....The Court could instead have said: Even if the fetus is a person, our Constitution forbids compelling a woman to carry it for nine months and become a mother."

Presentation of the Argument

This argument is called "the argument from unplugging the violinist" because of a story Thomson uses to illustrate her position:

> You wake up in the morning and find yourself back to back in bed with an unconscious violinist.

A famous unconscious violinist. He has been found to have a fatal kidney ailment, and the Society of Music Lovers has canvassed all the available medical records and found that you alone have the right blood type to help. They have therefore kidnapped you, and last night the violinist's circulatory system was plugged into yours, so that your kidneys can be used to extract poisons from his blood as well as your own. The director of the hospital now tells you, "Look, we're sorry the Society of Music Lovers did this to you—we would never have permitted it if we had known. But still, they did it, and the violinist now is plugged into you. To unplug you would be to kill him. But never mind, it's only for nine months. By then he will have recovered from his ailment, and can safely be unplugged from you." Is it morally incumbent on you to accede to this situation? No doubt it would be very nice of you if you did, a great kindness. But do you *have* to accede to it? What if it were not nine months, but nine years? Or still longer? What if the director of the hospital says, "Tough luck, I agree, but you've now got to stay in bed, with the violinist plugged into you, for the rest of your life. Because remember this. All persons have a right to life, and violinists are persons. Granted you have a right to decide what happens in and to your body, but a person's right to life outweighs your right to decide what happens in and to your body. So you cannot ever be unplugged from him." I imagine that you would regard this as outrageous.

Thomson concludes that she is "only arguing that having a right to life does not guarantee having either a right to be given the use of or a right to be allowed continued use of another person's body—even if one needs it for life itself." Thomson anticipates several objections to her argument, and in the process of responding to them further clarifies it. It is not important, however, that we go over these clarifications now, for some are not germane to the pro-life position I am defending in this book, and the remaining will be dealt with in the following critique. In any event, it should not be ignored by the pro-life advocate that Thomson's argument makes some important observations which have gone virtually unnoticed by the pro-life movement. In defending the relevance of her story, Thomson points out that it is "of great interest to ask what happens if, for the sake of argument, we allow the premise [that the unborn are fully human or persons]. How, precisely, are we supposed to get from there to the conclusion that abortion is morally impermissible?" In other words, simply because a person is fully human it does not follow logically that it is *never* permissible to kill that person. Although I believe that I have and will adequately establish the premise that it is prima facie wrong to kill innocent human persons, Thomson's argument poses a special difficulty because she believes that since pregnancy constitutes an infringement on the pregnant woman's personal rights by the unborn entity, the ordinary abortion, although it results in the death of an innocent human person, is not prima facie wrong.

A Critique of Thomson's Argument

There at least nine problems with Thomson's argument. These problems can be put into three categories: ethical, legal, and ideological.

Ethical problems with Thomson's argument

1. *Thomson assumes volunteerism.* By using the story as a paradigm for all relationships, thus implying that moral obligations must be voluntarily accepted in order to have moral force, Thomson mistakenly infers that all true moral obligations to one's offspring are voluntary. But consider the following story. Suppose a couple has a sexual encounter that is fully protected by several forms of birth control short of surgical abortion (condom, the Pill, IUD), but nevertheless results in conception. Instead of getting an abortion, the mother of the conceptus decides to bring it to term, although the father is unaware of this decision. After the birth of the child, the mother pleads with the father for child support. Because he refuses, she takes legal action. Although he took every precaution to avoid fatherhood, thus showing that he did not wish to accept such a status, according to nearly all child-support laws in the United States he would still be obligated to pay support *precisely because* of his relationship to this child. As Michael Levin points out, "All child-support laws make the parental body an indirect resource for the child. If the father is a construction worker, the state will intervene unless some

of his calories he expends lifting equipment go to providing food for his children."

But this obligatory relationship is not based strictly on biology, for this would make sperm donors morally responsible for children conceived by their seed. Rather, the father's responsibility for his offspring stems from the fact that he engaged in an act, sexual intercourse, that he fully realized could result in the creation of another human being, although he took every precaution to avoid such a result. This is not an unusual way to frame moral obligations, for we hold drunk people whose driving results in manslaughter responsible for their actions, even if they did not intend to kill someone prior to becoming intoxicated. Such special obligations, although not directly undertaken voluntarily, are necessary in any civilized culture in order to preserve the rights of the vulnerable, the weak, and the young, who can offer very little in exchange for the rights bestowed upon them by the strong, the powerful, and the postuterine in Thomson's moral universe of the social contract. Thus, Thomson is wrong, in addition to ignoring in the *natural* relationship between sexual intercourse and human reproduction, when she claims that if a couple has "taken all reasonable precautions against having a child, they do not by virtue of their biological relationship to the child who comes into existence have a special responsibility for it." "Surely we do not have any such 'special responsibility' for a person unless we have assumed it, explicitly or implicitly." Hence, instead of providing reasons for rejecting any special responsibilities for one's offspring, Thomson simply dismisses the concept altogether.

2. *Thomson's argument is fatal to family morality.* It follows from the first criticism that Thomson's volunteerism is fatal to family morality, which has as one of its central beliefs that an individual has special and filial obligations to his offspring and family that he does not have to other persons. Although Thomson may not consider such a fatality as being all that terrible, since she may accept the feminist dogma that the traditional family is "oppressive" to women, a great number of ordinary men and women, who have found joy, happiness, and love in family life find Thomson's volunteerism to be counterintuitive. Philosopher Christina Sommers has come to a similar conclusion:

For it [the volunteerist thesis] means that there is no such thing as filial duty per se, no such thing as the special duty of mother to child, and generally no such thing as morality of special family or kinship relations. All of which is contrary to what people think. For most people think that we do owe special debts to our parents even though we have not voluntarily assumed our obligations to them. Most people think that what we owe to our children does not have its origin in any voluntary undertaking, explicit or implicit, that we have made to them. And "preanalytically," many people believe that we owe special consideration to our siblings even at times when we may not *feel* very friendly to them.... The idea that to be committed to an individual is to have made a voluntarily implicit or explicit commitment to that individual is generally fatal to family morality. For it looks upon the network of felt obligation and expectation that binds family members as a sociological phenomenon that is without presumptive moral force. The social critics who hold this view of family obligation usually are aware that promoting it in public policy must further the disintegration of the traditional family as an institution. But whether they deplore the disintegration or welcome it, they are bound in principle to abet it.

3. *A case can be made that the unborn does have a prima facie right to her mother's body.* Assuming that there is such a thing as a special filial obligation, a principle that does not have to be voluntarily accepted in order to have moral force, it is not obvious that the unborn entity in ordinary circumstances (that is, with the exception of when the mother's life is in significant danger) does not have a natural prima facie claim to her mother's body. There are several reasons to suppose that the unborn entity does have such a natural claim.

a. Unlike Thomson's violinist, who is artificially attached to another person in order to save his life and is therefore not naturally dependent on any particular human being, the unborn entity is a human being who by her very nature is dependent on her mother, for this is how human beings are at this stage of their development.

b. This period of a human being's natural development occurs in the womb. This is the journey which we all must take and is a necessary condition

for any human being's postuterine existence. And this fact alone brings out the most glaring difference between the violinist and the unborn: the womb is the unborn's natural environment whereas being artificially hooked up to a stranger is not the natural environment for the violinist. It would seem, then, that the unborn has a prima facie natural claim upon her mother's body.

c. This same entity, when she becomes a newborn, has a natural claim upon her parents to care for her, regardless of whether her parents wanted her (see the story of the irresponsible father). This is why we prosecute child abusers, people who throw their babies in trash cans, and parents who abandon their children. Although it should not be ignored that pregnancy and childbirth entail certain emotional, physical, and financial sacrifices on the part of the pregnant woman, these sacrifices are also endemic of parenthood in general (which ordinarily lasts much longer than nine months), and do not seem to justify the execution of troublesome infants and younger children whose existence entails a natural claim to certain financial and bodily goods that are under the ownership of their parents. If the unborn entity is fully human, as Thomson is willing to grant, why should the unborn's natural prima facie claim to her parents' goods differ before birth? Of course, a court will not force a parent to donate a kidney to her dying offspring, but this sort of dependence on the parent's body is highly unusual and is not part of the ordinary obligations associated with the natural process of human development, just as in the case of the violinist's artificial dependency on the reluctant music lover.

As Schwartz points out: "So, the very thing that makes it plausible to say that the person in bed with the violinist has no duty to sustain him; namely, that he is a stranger unnaturally hooked up to him, is precisely what is absent in the case of the mother and her child." That is to say, the mother "does have an obligation to take care of her child, to sustain her, to protect her, and especially, to let her live in the only place where she can now be protected, nourished, and allowed to grow, namely the womb."

If Thomson responds to this argument by saying that birth is the threshold at which parents become fully responsible, then she has begged the question, for her argument was supposed to show us why there is no parental responsibility before birth. That is to say, Thomson cannot appeal to birth as the decisive moment at which parents become responsible in order to prove that birth is the time at which parents become responsible.

It is evident that Thomson's violinist illustration undermines the deep natural bond between mother and child by making it seem no different from that between two strangers artificially hooked up to each other so that one can "steal" the service of the other's kidneys. Never has something so human, so natural, so beautiful, and so wonderfully demanding of our human creativity and love been reduced to such a brutal caricature. Thomson's violinist story is to motherhood what Andres Serrano's "Piss Christ" is to Good Friday.

I am not saying that the unborn entity has an absolute natural claim to her mother's body, but simply that she has a prima facie natural claim. For one can easily imagine a situation in which this natural claim is outweighed by other important prima facie values, such as when a pregnancy significantly endangers the mother's life. Since the continuation of such a pregnancy would most likely entail the death of both mother and child, and since it is better that one human should live rather than two die, terminating such a pregnancy via abortion is morally justified.

Someone may respond to the three criticisms by agreeing that Thomson's illustration may not apply in cases of ordinary sexual intercourse, but only in cases in which pregnancy results from rape or incest, although it should be noted that Thomson herself does not press this argument. She writes: "Surely the question of whether you have a right to life at all, or how much of it you have, shouldn't turn on the question of whether or not you are the product of rape."

But those who do press the rape argument may choose to argue in the following way. Just as the sperm donor is not responsible for how his sperm is used or what results from its use (e.g., it may be stolen, or an unmarried woman may purchase it, inseminate herself, and give birth to a child), the raped woman, who did not voluntarily engage in intercourse, cannot be held responsible for the unborn human who is living inside her.

But there is a problem with this analogy: The sperm donor's relinquishing of responsibility does not result in the death of a human person. The following story should help to illustrate the differences and similarities between these two cases.

Suppose that the sperm donated by the sperm donor was stolen by an unscrupulous physician and inseminated into a woman. Although he is not morally responsible for the child that results from such an insemination, the donor is nevertheless forced by an unjust court to pay a large monthly sum for child support, a sum so large that it may drive him into serious debt, maybe even bankruptcy. This would be similar to the woman who became pregnant as a result of rape. She was unjustly violated and is supporting a human being against her will at an emotional and financial cost. Is it morally right for the sperm donor to kill the child he is supporting in order to allegedly right the wrong that has been committed against him? Not at all, because such an act would be murder. Now if we assume, as does Thomson, that the raped woman is carrying a being who is fully human (or "a person"), her killing of the unborn entity by abortion, except if the pregnancy has a strong possibility of endangering her life, would be as unjust as the sperm donor killing the child he is unjustly forced to support. As the victimized man may rightly refuse to pay the child support, the raped woman may rightly refuse to bring up her child after the pregnancy has come to term. She can choose to put the child up for adoption. But in both cases, the killing of the child is not morally justified. Although neither the sperm donor nor the rape victim may have the same special obligation to their biological offspring as does the couple who voluntarily engaged in intercourse with no direct intention to produce a child, it seems that the more general obligation not to directly kill another human person does apply.

4. *Thomson ignores the fact that abortion is indeed killing and not merely the withholding of treatment.* Thomson makes an excellent point: namely, there are times when withholding and/or withdrawing medical treatment is morally justified. For instance, I am not morally obligated to donate my kidney to Fred, my next-door neighbor, simply because he needs a kidney in order to live. In other words, I am

not obligated to risk my life so that Fred may live a few years longer. Fred should not expect that of me. If, however, I donate one of my kidneys to Fred, I will have acted above and beyond the call of duty, since I will have performed a supererogatory moral act. But this case is not analogous to pregnancy and abortion.

Levin argues that there is an essential difference between abortion and the unplugging of the violinist. In the case of the violinist (as well as my relationship to Fred's welfare), "the person who withdraws [or withholds] his assistance is not completely responsible for the dependency on him of the person who is about to die, while the mother is completely responsible for the dependency of her fetus on her. When one is completely responsible for dependence, refusal to continue to aid is indeed killing." For example, "if a woman brings a newborn home from the hospital, puts it in its crib and refuses to feed it until it has starved to death, it would be absurd to say that she simply refused to assist it and had done nothing for which she should be criminally liable." In other words, just as the withholding of food kills the child after birth, in the case of abortion, the abortion kills the child. In neither case is there any ailment from which the child suffers and for which highly invasive medical treatment, with the cooperation of another's bodily organs, is necessary in order to cure this ailment and save the child's life.

Or consider the following case, which can be applied to the case of pregnancy resulting from rape or incest. Suppose a person returns home after work to find a baby at his doorstep. Suppose that no one else is able to take care of the child, but this person has only to take care of the child for nine months (after that time a couple will adopt the child). Imagine that this person, because of the child's presence, will have some bouts with morning sickness, water retention, and other minor ailments. If we assume with Thomson that the unborn child is as much a person as you or I, would "withholding treatment" from this child and its subsequent death be justified on the basis that the homeowner was only "withholding treatment" of a child he did not ask for in order to benefit himself? Is any person, born or unborn, obligated to sacrifice his life because his death would benefit another person?

Consequently, there is no doubt that such "withholding" of treatment (and it seems totally false to call ordinary shelter and sustenance "treatment") is indeed murder.

But is it even accurate to refer to abortion as the "withholding of support or treatment"? Professors Schwarz and R. K. Tacelli make the important point that although "a woman who has an abortion is indeed 'withholding support' from her unborn child…abortion is far more than that. It is the active killing of a human person by burning him, by crushing him, by dismembering him." Euphemistically calling abortion the "withholding of support or treatment" makes about as much sense as calling suffocating someone with a pillow the withdrawing of oxygen.

In summary, I agree with Professor Brody when he concludes that "Thomson has not established the truth of her claim about abortion, primarily because she has not sufficiently attended to the distinction between our duty to save X's life and our duty not to take it." But "once one attends to that distinction, it would seem that the mother, in order to regain control over her body, has no right to abort the fetus from the point at which it becomes a human being."

Legal problems with Thomson's argument

There are at least two legal problems with Thomson's argument: one has to do with tort law, and the other has to do with parental responsibility and child-welfare law.

1. *Thomson' argument ignores tort law.* Judge John T. Noonan of the U.S. Ninth Circuit Court of Appeals points out that "while Thomson focuses on this fantasy [the violinist story], she ignores a real case from which American tort law has generalized."

On a January night in Minnesota, a cattle buyer, Orlando Depue, asked a family of farmers, the Flateaus, with whom he had dined, if he could remain overnight at their house. The Flateaus refused and, although Depue was sick and had fainted, put him out of the house into the cold night. Imposing liability on the Flateaus for Depue's loss of his frostbitten fingers, the court said: "In the case at bar defendants were under no contract obligation to minister to plaintiff in his distress;

but humanity demanded they do so, if they understood and appreciated his condition.... The law as well as humanity required that he not be exposed in his helpless condition to the merciless elements." Depue was a guest for supper although not a guest after supper. The American Law Institute, generalizing, has said that it makes no difference whether the person is a guest or a trespasser. He has the privilege of staying. His host has the duty not to injure him or put him into an environment where he becomes nonviable. The obligation arises when one "understands and appreciates" the condition of the other.

Noonan concludes that "although the analogy is not exact, the case is much closer to the mother's situation than the case imagined by Thomson; and the emotional response of the Minnesota judges seems to be a truer reflection of what humanity requires."

2. *Thomson's argument ignores family law.* Thomson's argument is inconsistent with the body of well-established family law, which presupposes parental responsibility of a child's welfare. And, of course, assuming as Thomson does that the unborn are fully human, this body of law would also apply to parents' responsibility for their unborn children. According to legal scholars Dennis J. Horan and Burke J. Balche, "All 50 states, the District of Columbia, American Samoa, Guam, and the U.S. Virgin Islands have child abuse and neglect statutes which provide for the protection of a child who does not receive needed medical care." They further state that "a review of cases makes it clear that these statutes are properly applied to secure emergency medical treatment and sustenance (food or water, whether given orally or through intravenous or nasogastric tube) for children when parents, with or without the acquiescence of physicians, refuse to provide it." Evidently, "pulling the plug" on a perfectly healthy unborn entity, assuming that it is a human person, would clearly violate these statutes.

For example, in a case in New York, the court ruled that the parents' actions constituted neglect when they failed to provide medical care to a child with leukemia: "The parent...may not deprive a child of lifesaving treatment, however well-intentioned. Even when the parents' decision to decline

necessary treatment is based on constitutional grounds, such as religious beliefs, it must yield to the State's interests, as parens patriae, in protecting the health and welfare of the child." The fact of the matter is that the "courts have uniformly held that a parent has the legal responsibility of furnishing his dependent child with adequate food and medical care."

It is evident then that child-protection laws reflect our deepest moral intuitions about parental responsibility and the utter helplessness of infants and small children. And without these moral scruples—which are undoubtedly undermined by "brave new notions" of a socially contracted "voluntaristic" family (Thomson's view)—the protection of children and the natural bonds and filial obligations that are an integral part of ordinary family life will become a thing of the past. This seems too high a price for bodily autonomy.

Ideological problems with the use of Thomson's argument

There are at least three ideological problems in the use of Thomson's argument by others. The other two problems are usually found in the books, speeches, articles, or papers, of those in the feminist and/or abortion-rights movements who sometimes uncritically use Thomson's argument or ones similar to it. In fact, Thomson may very well agree with most or all of the following critique.

1. *Inconsistent use of the burden of pregnancy.* Thomson has to paint pregnancy in the most horrific of terms in order to make her argument seem plausible. Dr. Bernard Nathanson, an obstetrician/gynecologist and former abortion provider, objects "strenuously to Thomson's portrayal of pregnancy as a nine-month involuntary imprisonment in bed. This casts an unfair and wrongheaded prejudice against the consideration of the state of pregnancy and skews the argument." Nathanson points out that "pregnancy is not a 'sickness'. Few pregnant women are bedridden and many, emotionally and physically, have never felt better. For these it is a stimulating experience, even for mothers who originally did not 'want' to be pregnant." Unlike the person who is plugged into Thomson's violinist, "alpha [the unborn entity] does not hurt the mother by being 'plugged in,'...except in the case of well-defined

medical indications." And "in those few cases where pregnancy *is* a medical penalty, it is a penalty lasting nine months."

Compare and contrast Thomson's portrayal of pregnancy with the fact that researchers have recently discovered that many people believe that a pregnant woman cannot work as effectively as a nonpregnant woman who is employed to do the same job in the same workplace. This has upset a number of feminists, and rightfully so. They argue that a pregnant woman is not incapacitated or ill, but can work just as effectively as a non-pregnant woman. But why then do feminists who use Thomson's argument argue, when it comes to abortion, that pregnancy is similar to being bedridden and hooked up to a violinist for nine months? When it comes to equality in the workplace (with which I agree with the feminists) there is no problem. But in the case of morally justifying abortion rights, pregnancy is painted in the most horrific of terms. Although not logically fatal to the abortion-rights position, this sort of double-mindedness is not conducive to good moral reasoning.

2. *The libertarian principles underlying Thomson's case are inconsistent with the state-mandated agenda of radical feminism.* If Thomson's illustration works at all, it works contrary to the statist principles of radical feminism (of course, a libertarian feminist need not be fazed by this objection). Levin points out that "while appeal to an absolute right to the disposition of one's body coheres well with other strongly libertarian positions (laissez-faire in the marketplace, parental autonomy in education of their children, freedom of private association), this appeal is most commonly made by feminists who are antilibertarian on just about every other issue." For example, "feminists who advocate state-mandated quotas, state-mandated comparable worth pay scales, the censorship of 'sexist' textbooks in the public schools, laws against 'sexually harassing speech' and legal limitations on private association excluding homosexuals, will go on to advocate abortion on the basis of an absolute libertarianism at odds with every one of those policies." Although this criticism is ad hominem, as was the previous one, it serves to underscore the important political fact that many abortion-rights advocates are more than willing to hold and earnestly defend contrary

principles for the sake of legally mandating their ideological agenda.

This sort of hypocrisy is evident in abortion-rights activity throughout the United States. In the state of Nevada, those who supported an abortion-rights referendum in November of 1990 told the voting public that they wanted to "get the government off of our backs and out of the bedrooms." But when the state legislature met in January these same abortion-rights supporters, under the auspices of the Nevada Women's Lobby, proposed legislation that asked for the taxpayers of the state to fund school-based sex clinics (which will refer teenage girls to abortion services and are euphemistically called health clinics) and assorted other programs. Forgetting that many of us keep our wallets in our back pockets and place them in the evening on our dressers in our bedrooms, the members of the Nevada Women's Lobby did not hesitate to do in January what they vehemently opposed in November: to get the government *on* our backs and *in* our bedrooms.

But this proposed government intervention was not to prevent people from killing their unborn children, an intervention that is considered bad, evil, anti-choice, and intrusive. Rather, it was to take our money we earn to support our own children and use it to subsidize the killing of other people's unborn children. The libertarians of November became the social engineers of March.

3. *Thomson's argument implies a macho view of bodily control, a view inconsistent with true feminism.* Some have pointed out that Thomson's argument and/or the reasoning behind it is actually quite antifeminist. In response to a similar argument from a woman's right to control her own body, one feminist publication asks, "What kind of control are we talking about? A control that allows for violence against another human being is a macho, oppressive kind of control. Women rightly object when others try to have that kind of control over them, and the movement for women's rights asserts the moral right of women to be free from the control of others." After all, "abortion involves violence against a small, weak and dependent child. It is macho control, the very kind the feminist movement most eloquently opposes in other contexts."

Celia Wolf-Devine observes that "abortion has something…in common with the behavior ecofeminists and pacifist feminists take to be characteristically masculine; it shows a willingness to use violence in order to take control. The fetus is destroyed by being pulled apart by suction, cut in pieces, or poisoned." Wolf-Devine goes on to point out that "in terms of social thought…it is the masculine models which are most frequently employed in thinking about abortion.

Virtue Theory and Abortion

ROSALIND HURSTHOUSE

The sort of ethical theory derived from Aristotle, variously described as virtue ethics, virtue-based ethics, or neo-Aristotelianism, is becoming better known, and is now quite widely recognized as at least a possible rival to deontological and utilitarian theories. With recognition has come criticism, of varying quality. In this article I shall discuss nine separate criticisms that I have frequently encountered, most of which seem to me to betray an inadequate grasp either of the structure of virtue theory or of what would be involved in thinking about a real moral issue in its terms. In the first half I aim particularly to secure an understanding that will reveal that many of these criticisms are simply misplaced, and to articulate what I take to be the major criticism of virtue theory. I reject this criticism, but do not claim that it is necessarily misplaced. In the second half I aim to deepen that understanding and highlight the issues raised by the criticisms by illustrating what the theory looks like when it is applied to a particular issue, in this case, abortion.

VIRTUE THEORY

Virtue theory can be laid out in a framework that reveals clearly some of the essential similarities and differences between it and some versions of deontological and utilitarian theories. I begin with a rough

If masculine thought is naturally hierarchical and oriented toward power and control, then the interests of the fetus (who has no power) would naturally be suppressed in favor of the interests of the mother. But to the extent that feminist social thought is egalitarian, the question must be raised of why the mother's interests should prevail over the child's…. Feminist thought about abortion has…been deeply pervaded by the individualism which they so ardently criticize."

sketch of familiar versions of the latter two sorts of theory, not, of course, with the intention of suggesting that they exhaust the field, but on the assumption that their very familiarity will provide a helpful contrast with virtue theory. Suppose a deontological theory has basically the following framework. We begin with a premise providing a specification of right action:

P.1. An action is right iff it is in accordance with a moral rule or principle.

This is a purely formal specification, forging a link between the concepts of *right action* and *moral rule*, and gives one no guidance until one knows what a moral rule is. So the next thing the theory needs is a premise about that:

P.2. A moral rule is one that…

Historically, an acceptable completion of P.2 would have been

(i) is laid on us by God

or

(ii) is required by natural law.

From Rosalind Hursthouse, "Virtue Theory and Abortion," *The Stanford Encyclopedia of Philosophy* (Fall 2003), http://plato.stanford.edu/entries/ ethics-virtue/ (10 September 2012).

In secular versions (not, of course, unconnected to God's being pure reason, and the universality of natural law) we get such completions as

(iii) is laid on us by reason

or

(iv) is required by rationality

or

(v) would command universal rational acceptance

or

(vi) would be the object of choice of all rational beings

and so on. Such a specification forges a second conceptual link, between the concepts of *moral rule* and *rationality*.

We have here the skeleton of a familiar version of a deontological theory, a skeleton that reveals that what is essential to any such version is the links between *right action, moral rule*, and *rationality*. That these form the basic structure can be seen particularly vividly if we lay out the familiar act-utilitarianism in such a way as to bring out the contrasts.

Act-utilitarianism begins with a premise that provides a specification of right action:

P.1. An action is right iff it promotes the best consequences.

It thereby forges the link between the concepts of *right action* and *consequences*. It goes on to specify what the best consequences are in its second premise:

P.2. The best consequences are those in which happiness is maximized.

It thereby forges the link between *consequences* and *happiness*.

Now let us consider what a skeletal virtue theory looks like. It begins with a specification of right action:

P.1. An action is right iff it is what a virtuous agent would do in the circumstances.[1]

This, like the first premises of the other two sorts of theory, is a purely formal principle, giving one no guidance as to what to do, that forges the conceptual link between *right action* and *virtuous agent*. Like the other theories, it must, of course, go on to specify what the latter is. The first step toward this may appear quite trivial, but is needed to correct a prevailing tendency among many critics to define the virtuous agent as one who is disposed to act in accordance with a deontologist's moral rules.

P.1a. A virtuous agent is one who acts virtuously, that is, one who has and exercises the virtues.

This subsidiary premise lays bare the fact that virtue theory aims to provide a nontrivial specification of the virtuous agent *via* a nontrivial specification of the virtues, which is given in its second premise:

P.2. A virtue is a character trait a human being needs to flourish or live well.

This premise forges a conceptual link between *virtue* and *flourishing* (or *living well* or *eudaimonia*). And, just as deontology, in theory, then goes on to argue that each favored rule meets its specification, so virtue ethics, in theory, goes on to argue that each favored character trait meets its.

These are the bare bones of virtue theory. Following are five brief comments directed to some misconceived criticisms that should be cleared out of the way.

First, the theory does not have a peculiar weakness or problem in virtue of the fact that it involves the concept of *eudaimonia* (a standard criticism being that this concept is hopelessly obscure). Now no virtue theorist will pretend that the concept of human flourishing is an easy one to grasp. I will not even claim here (though I would elsewhere) that it is no more obscure than the concepts of *rationality* and *happiness*, since, if our vocabulary were more limited, we might, *faute de mieux*, call it (human) *rational happiness*, and thereby reveal that it has at least some of the difficulties of both. But virtue theory has never, so far as I know, been dismissed on the grounds of the *comparative* obscurity of this central concept; rather, the popular view is that it has a problem with this which deontology and utilitarianism in no way share. This, I think, is clearly false. Both *rationality* and *happiness*, as they figure in their respective theories, are rich and difficult concepts—hence all the disputes about the various tests for a rule's being an object of rational choice, and the disputes, dating back to Mill's introduction of the higher and lower pleasures, about what constitutes happiness.

Second, the theory is not trivially circular; it does not specify right action in terms of the virtuous agent and then immediately specify the virtuous agent in terms of right action. Rather, it specifies her in terms of the virtues, and then specifies these, not merely as dispositions to right action, but as the character traits (which are dispositions to feel and react as well as act in certain ways) required for *eudaimonia*.[2]

Third, it does answer the question "What should I do?" as well as the question "What sort of person should I be?" (That is, it is not, as one of the catch-phrases has it, concerned only with Being and not with Doing.)

Fourth, the theory does, to a certain extent, answer this question by coming up with rules or principles (contrary to the common claim that it does not come up with any rules or principles). Every virtue generates a positive instruction (act justly, kindly, courageously, honestly, etc.) and every vice a prohibition (do not act unjustly, cruelly, like a coward, dishonestly, etc.). So trying to decide what to do within the framework of virtue theory is not, as some people seem to imagine, necessarily a matter of taking one's favored candidate for a virtuous person and asking oneself, "What would they do in these circumstances?" (as if the raped fifteen-year-old girl might be supposed to say to herself, "Now would Socrates have an abortion if he were in my circumstances?" and as if someone who had never known or heard of anyone very virtuous were going to be left, according to the theory, with no way to decide what to do at all). The agent may instead ask herself, "If I were to do such and such now, would I be acting justly or unjustly (or neither), kindly or unkindly [and so on]?" I shall consider below the problem created by cases in which such a question apparently does not yield an answer to "What should I do?" (because, say, the alternatives are being unkind or being unjust); here my claim is only that it sometimes does—the agent may employ her concepts of the virtues and vices directly, rather than imagining what some hypothetical exemplar would do.

Fifth (a point that is implicit but should be made explicit), virtue theory is not committed to any sort of reductionism involving defining all of our moral concepts in terms of the virtuous agent. On the contrary, it relies on a lot of very significant moral

concepts. Charity or benevolence, for instance, is the virtue whose concern is the *good* of others; that concept of *good* is related to the concept of *evil* or *harm*, and they are both related to the concepts of the *worthwhile*, the *advantageous*, and the *pleasant*. If I have the wrong conception of what is worthwhile and advantageous and pleasant, then I shall have the wrong conception of what is good for, and harmful to, myself and others, and, even with the best will in the world, will lack the virtue of charity, which involves getting all this right. (This point will be illustrated at some length in the second half of this article; I mention it here only in support of the fact that no virtue theorist who takes her inspiration from Aristotle would even contemplate aiming at reductionism.)[3]

Let me now, with equal brevity, run through two more standard criticisms of virtue theory (the sixth and seventh of my nine) to show that, though not entirely misplaced, they do not highlight problems peculiar to that theory but, rather, problems that are shared by familiar versions of deontology.

One common criticism is that we do not know which character traits are the virtues, or that this is open to much dispute, or particularly subject to the threat of moral skepticism or "pluralism"[4] or cultural relativism. But the parallel roles played by the second premises of both deontological and virtue theories reveal the way in which both sorts of theory share this problem. It is at the stage at which one tries to get the right conclusions to drop out of the bottom of one's theory that, *theoretically*, all the work has to be done. Rule deontologists know that they want to get "don't kill," "keep promises," "cherish your children," and so on as the rules that meet their specification, whatever it may be. They also know that any of these can be disputed, that some philosopher may claim, of any one of them, that it is reasonable to reject it, and that at least people claim that there has been, for each rule, some culture that rejected it. Similarly, the virtue theorists know that they want to get justice, charity, fidelity, courage, and so on as the character traits needed for *eudaimonia*; and they also know that any of these can be disputed, that some philosopher will say of any one of them that it is reasonable to reject it as a virtue, and that there is said to be, for each character trait, some culture that has thus rejected it.

This is a problem for both theories, and the virtue theorist certainly does not find it any harder to argue against moral skepticism, "pluralism," or cultural relativism than the deontologist. Each theory has to stick out its neck and say, in some cases, "This person/these people/other cultures are (or would be) in error," and find some grounds for saying this.

Another criticism (the seventh) often made is that virtue ethics has unresolvable conflict built into it. "It is common knowledge," it is said, "that the requirements of the virtues can conflict; charity may prompt me to end the frightful suffering of the person in my care by killing him, but justice bids me to stay my hand. To tell my brother that his wife is being unfaithful to him would be honest and loyal, but it would be kinder to keep quiet about it. So which should I do? In such cases, virtue ethics has nothing helpful to say." (This is one version of the problem, mentioned above, that considering whether a proposed action falls under a virtue or vice term does not always yield an answer to "What should I do?")

The obvious reply to this criticism is that rule deontology notoriously suffers from the same problem, arising not only from the fact that its rules can apparently conflict, but also from the fact that, at first blush, it appears that one and the same rule (e.g., preserve life) can yield contrary instructions in a particular case.[5] As before, I agree that this is a problem for virtue theory, but deny that it is a problem peculiar to it.

Finally, I want to articulate, and reject, what I take to be the major criticism of virtue theory. Perhaps because it is *the* major criticism, the reflection of a very general sort of disquiet about the theory, it is hard to state clearly—especially for someone who does not accept it—but it goes something like this.[6] My interlocutor says:

Virtue theory can't *get* us anywhere in real moral issues because it's bound to be all assertion and no argument. You admit that the best it can come up with in the way of action-guiding rules are the ones that rely on the virtue and vice concepts, such as "act charitably," "don't act cruelly," and so on; and, as if that weren't bad enough, you admit that these virtue concepts, such as charity, presuppose concepts such as the *good*, and the *worthwhile*, and so on. But that means that any virtue theorist who writes about real moral issues must rely on her audience's agreeing with her application of all these concepts, and hence accepting all the premises in which those applications are enshrined. But some other virtue theorist might take different premises about these matters, and come up with very different conclusions, and, within the terms of the theory, there is no way to distinguish between the two. While there is agreement, virtue theory can repeat conventional wisdom, preserve the status quo, but it can't get us anywhere in the way that a normative ethical theory is supposed to, namely, by providing rational grounds for acceptance of its practical conclusions.

My strategy will be to split this criticism into two: one (the eighth) addressed to the virtue theorist's employment of the virtue and vice concepts enshrined in her rules—act charitably, honestly, and so on—and the other (the ninth) addressed to her employment of concepts such as that of the *worthwhile*. Each objection, I shall maintain, implicitly appeals to a certain *condition of adequacy* on a normative moral theory, and in each case, I shall claim, the condition of adequacy, once made explicit, is utterly implausible.

It is true that when she discusses real moral issues, the virtue theorist has to assert that certain actions are honest, dishonest, or neither; charitable, uncharitable, or neither. And it is true that this is often a very difficult matter to decide; her rules are not always easy to apply. But this counts as a criticism of the theory only if we assume, as a condition of adequacy, that any adequate action-guiding theory must make the difficult business of knowing what to do if one is to act well easy, that it must provide clear guidance about what ought and ought not to be done which any reasonably clever adolescent could follow if she chose. But such a condition of adequacy is implausible. Acting rightly *is* difficult, and *does* call for much moral wisdom, and the relevant condition of adequacy, which virtue theory meets, is that it should have built into it an explanation of a truth expressed by Aristotle,[7] namely, that moral knowledge—unlike mathematical knowledge—cannot be acquired merely by attending lectures and is not characteristically to be found in people too young to have had much experience of life. There are youthful mathematical geniuses, but rarely, if ever, youthful moral geniuses, and this tells us something significant about the sort of knowledge that moral knowledge is. Virtue ethics builds this in straight off precisely by couching its rules in terms whose application may indeed call for the most delicate and sensitive judgment.

Here we may discern a slightly different version of the problem that there are cases in which applying the virtue and vice terms does not yield an answer to "What should I do?" Suppose someone "youthful in character," as Aristotle puts it, having applied the relevant terms, finds herself landed with what is, unbeknownst to her, a case not of real but of apparent conflict, arising from a misapplication of those terms. Then she will not be able to decide what to do unless she knows of a virtuous agent to look to for guidance. But her quandary is (ex hypothesi) the result of her lack of wisdom, and just what virtue theory expects. Someone hesitating over whether to reveal a hurtful truth, for example, thinking it would be kind but dishonest or unjust to lie, may need to realize, with respect to these particular circumstances, not that kindness is more (or less) important than honesty or justice, and not that honesty or justice sometimes requires one to act unkindly or cruelly, but that one does people no kindness by concealing this sort of truth from them, hurtful as it may be. This is the *type* of thing (I use it only as an example) that people with moral wisdom know about, involving the correct application of *kind*, and that people without such wisdom find difficult.

What about the virtue theorist's reliance on concepts such as that of the *worthwhile*? If such reliance is to count as a fault in the theory, what condition of adequacy is implicitly in play? It must be that any good normative theory should provide answers to questions about real moral issues whose truth is in no way determined by truths about what is worthwhile, or what really matters in human life. Now although people are initially inclined to reject out of hand the claim that the practical conclusions of a normative moral theory have to be based on

premises about what is truly worthwhile, the alternative, once it is made explicit, may look even more unacceptable. Consider what the condition of adequacy entails. If truths about what is worthwhile (or truly good, or serious, or about what matters in human life) do *not* have to be appealed to in order to answer questions about real moral issues, then I might sensibly seek guidance about what I ought to do from someone who had declared in advance that she knew nothing about such matters, or from someone who said that, although she had opinions about them, these were quite likely to be wrong but that this did not matter, because they would play no determining role in the advice she gave me.

I should emphasize that we are talking about real moral issues and real guidance; I want to know whether I should have an abortion, take my mother off the life-support machine, leave academic life and become a doctor in the Third World, give up my job with the firm that is using animals in its experiments, tell my father he has cancer. Would I go to someone who says she has *no* views about what is worthwhile in life? Or to someone who says that, as a matter of fact, she tends to think that the only thing that matters is having a good time, but has a normative theory that is consistent both with this view and with my own rather more puritanical one, which will yield the guidance I need?

I take it as a premise that this is absurd. The relevant condition of adequacy should be that the practical conclusions of a good normative theory *must* be in part determined by premises about what is worthwhile, important, and so on. Thus I reject this "major criticism" of virtue theory, that it cannot get us anywhere in the way that a normative moral theory is supposed to. According to my response, a normative theory that any clever adolescent can apply, or that reaches practical conclusions that are in no way determined by premises about what is truly worthwhile, serious, and so on, is guaranteed to be an inadequate theory.

Although I reject this criticism, I have not argued that it is misplaced and that it necessarily manifests a failure to understand what virtue theory is. My rejection is based on premises about what an adequate normative theory must be like—what sorts of concepts it must contain, and what sort of account it must give of moral knowledge—and thereby claims, implicitly, that the "major criticism" manifests a failure to understand what an *adequate normative theory* is. But, as a matter of fact, I think the criticism is often made by people who have no idea of what virtue theory looks like when applied to a real moral issue; they drastically underestimate the variety of ways in which the virtue and vice concepts, and the others, such as that of the *worthwhile*, figure in such discussion.

As promised, I now turn to an illustration of such discussion, applying virtue theory to abortion. Before I embark on this tendentious business, I should remind the reader of the aim of this discussion. I am not, in this article, trying to solve the problem of abortion; I am illustrating how virtue theory directs one to think about it. It might indeed be said that thinking about the problem in this way "solves" it by *dissolving* it, insofar as it leads one to the conclusion that there is no single right answer, but a variety of particular answers, and in what follows I am certainly trying to make that conclusion seem plausible. But, that granted, it should still be said that I am not trying to "solve the problems" in the practical sense of telling people that they should, or should not, do this or that if they are pregnant and contemplating abortion in these or those particular circumstances.

I do not assume, or expect, that all of my readers will agree with everything I am about to say. On the contrary, given the plausible assumption that some are morally wiser than I am, and some less so, the theory has built into it that we are bound to disagree on some points. For instance, we may well disagree about the particular application of some of the virtue and vice terms; and we may disagree about what is worthwhile or serious, worthless or trivial. But my aim is to make clear how these concepts figure in a discussion conducted in terms of virtue theory. What is at issue is whether these concepts are indeed the ones that should come in, that is, whether virtue theory should be criticized for employing them. The problem of abortion highlights this issue dramatically since virtue theory quite transforms the discussion of it.

ABORTION

As everyone knows, the morality of abortion is commonly discussed in relation to just two considerations: first, and predominantly, the status of the fetus and whether or not it is the sort of thing that may or may not be innocuously or justifiably killed; and second, and less predominantly (when, that is, the discussion concerns the *morality* of abortion rather than the question of permissible legislation in a just society), women's rights. If one thinks within this familiar framework, one may well be puzzled about what virtue theory, as such, could contribute. Some people assume the discussion will be conducted solely in terms of what the virtuous agent would or would not do (cf. the third, fourth, and fifth criticisms above). Others assume that only justice, or at most justice and charity,[8] will be applied to the issue, generating a discussion very similar to Judith Jarvis Thomson's.[9]

Now if this is the way the virtue theorist's discussion of abortion is imagined to be, no wonder people think little of it. It seems obvious in advance that in any such discussion there must be either a great deal of extremely tendentious application of the virtue terms *just, charitable*, and so on or a lot of rhetorical appeal to "this is what only the virtuous agent knows." But these are caricatures; they fail to appreciate the way in which virtue theory quite transforms the discussion of abortion by dismissing the two familiar dominating considerations as, in a way, fundamentally irrelevant. In what way or ways, I hope to make both clear and plausible.

Let us first consider women's rights. Let me emphasize again that we are discussing the *morality* of abortion, not the rights and wrongs of laws prohibiting or permitting it. If we suppose that women do have a moral right to do as they choose with their own bodies, or, more particularly, to terminate their pregnancies, then it may well follow that a *law* forbidding abortion would be unjust. Indeed, even if they have no such right, such a law might be, as things stand at the moment, unjust, or impractical, or inhumane: on this issue I have nothing to say in this article. But, putting all questions about the justice or injustice of laws to one side, and supposing only that women have such a moral right, *nothing* follows from this supposition about the morality of abortion, according to virtue theory, once it is noted (quite generally, not with particular reference to abortion) that in exercising a moral right I can do something cruel, or callous, or selfish, light-minded, self-righteous, stupid, inconsiderate, disloyal, dishonest—that is, act viciously.[10] Love and friendship do not survive their parties' constantly insisting on their rights, nor do people live well when they think that getting what they have a right to is of preeminent importance; they harm others, and they harm themselves. So whether women have a moral right to terminate their pregnancies is irrelevant within virtue theory, for it is irrelevant to the question "In having an abortion in these circumstances, would the agent be acting virtuously or viciously or neither?"

What about the consideration of the status of the fetus—what can virtue theory say about that? One might say that this issue is not in the province of *any* moral theory; it is a metaphysical question, and an extremely difficult one at that. Must virtue theory then wait upon metaphysics to come up with the answer?

At first sight it might seem so. For virtue is said to involve knowledge, and part of this knowledge consists in having the *right* attitude to things. "Right" here does not just mean "morally right" or "proper" or "nice" in the modern sense; it means "accurate, true." One cannot have the right or correct attitude to something if the attitude is based on or involves false beliefs. And this suggests that if the status of the fetus is relevant to the rightness or wrongness of abortion, its status must be known, as a truth, to the fully wise and virtuous person.

But the sort of wisdom that the fully virtuous person has is not supposed to be recondite; it does not call for fancy philosophical sophistication, and it does not depend upon, let alone wait upon, the discoveries of academic philosophers.[11] And this entails the following, rather startling, conclusion: that the status of the fetus—that issue over which so much ink has been spilt—is, according to virtue theory, simply not relevant to the rightness or wrongness of abortion (within, that is, a secular morality).

Or rather, since that is clearly too radical a conclusion, it is in a sense relevant, but only in the sense that the familiar biological facts are relevant. By "the familiar biological facts" I mean the facts that most human societies are and have been familiar with—that, standardly (but not invariably), pregnancy occurs as the result of sexual intercourse, that it lasts about nine months, during which time

the fetus grows and develops, that standardly it terminates in the birth of a living baby, and that this is how we all come to be.

It might be thought that this distinction—between the familiar biological facts and the status of the fetus—is a distinction without a difference. But this is not so. To attach relevance to the status of the fetus, in the sense in which virtue theory claims it is not relevant, is to be gripped by the conviction that we must go beyond the familiar biological facts, deriving some sort of conclusion from them, such as that the fetus has rights, or is not a person, or something similar. It is also to believe that this exhausts the relevance of the familiar biological facts, that all they are relevant to is the status of the fetus and whether or not it is the sort of thing that may or may not be killed.

These convictions, I suspect, are rooted in the desire to solve the problem of abortion by getting it to fall under some general rule such as "You ought not to kill anything with the right to life but may kill anything else." But they have resulted in what should surely strike any nonphilosopher as a most bizarre aspect of nearly all the current philosophical literature on abortion, namely, that, far from treating abortion as a unique moral problem, markedly unlike any other, nearly everything written on the status of the fetus and its bearing on the abortion issue would be consistent with the human reproductive facts' (to say nothing of family life) being totally different from what they are. Imagine that you are an alien extraterrestrial anthropologist who does not know that the human race is roughly 50 percent female and 50 percent male, or that our only (natural) form of reproduction involves heterosexual intercourse, viviparous birth, and the female's (and only the female's) being pregnant for nine months, or that females are capable of childbearing from late childhood to late middle age, or that childbearing is painful, dangerous, and emotionally charged—do you think you would pick up these facts from the hundreds of articles written on the status of the fetus? I am quite sure you would not. And that, I think, shows that the current philosophical literature on abortion has got badly out of touch with reality.

Now if we are using virtue theory, our first question is not "What do the familiar biological facts show—what can be derived from them about the status of the fetus?" but "How do these facts figure in the practical reasoning, actions and passions, thoughts and reactions, of the virtuous and the nonvirtuous? What is the mark of having the right attitude to these facts and what manifests having the wrong attitude to them?" This immediately makes essentially relevant not only all the facts about human reproduction I mentioned above, but a whole range of facts about our emotions in relation to them as well. I mean such facts as that human parents, both male and female, tend to care passionately about their offspring, and that family relationships are among the deepest and strongest in our lives—and, significantly, among the longest-lasting.

These facts make it obvious that pregnancy is not just one among many other physical conditions; and hence that anyone who genuinely believes that an abortion is comparable to a haircut or an appendectomy is mistaken.[12] The fact that the premature termination of a pregnancy is, in some sense, the cutting off of a new human life, and thereby, like the procreation of a new human life, connects with all our thoughts about human life and death, parenthood, and family relationships, must make it a serious matter. To disregard this fact about it, to think of abortion as nothing but the killing of something that does not matter, or as nothing but the exercise of some right or rights one has, or as the incidental means to some desirable state of affairs, is to do something callous and light-minded, the sort of thing that no virtuous and wise person would do. It is to have the wrong attitude not only to fetuses, but more generally to human life and death, parenthood, and family relationships.

Although I say that the facts make this obvious, I know that this is one of my tendentious points. In partial support of it I note that even the most dedicated proponents of the view that deliberate abortion is just like an appendectomy or haircut rarely hold the same view of spontaneous abortion, that is, miscarriage. It is not so tendentious of me to claim that to react to people's grief over miscarriage by saying, or even thinking, "What a fuss about nothing!" would be callous and light-minded, whereas to try to laugh someone out of grief over an appendectomy scar or a botched haircut would not be. It is

hard to give this point due prominence within act-centered theories, for the inconsistency is an inconsistency in attitude about the seriousness of loss of life, not in beliefs about which acts are right or wrong. Moreover, an act-centered theorist may say, "Well, there is nothing wrong with *thinking* 'What a fuss about nothing!' as long as you do not say it and hurt the person who is grieving. And besides, we cannot be held responsible for our thoughts, only for the intentional actions they give rise to." But the character traits that virtue theory emphasizes are not simply dispositions to intentional actions, but a seamless disposition to certain actions and passions, thoughts and reactions.

To say that the cutting off of a human life is always a matter of some seriousness, at any stage, is not to deny the relevance of gradual fetal development. Notwithstanding the well-worn point that clear boundary lines cannot be drawn, our emotions and attitudes regarding the fetus do change as it develops, and again when it is born, and indeed further as the baby grows. Abortion for shallow reasons in the later stages is much more shocking than abortion for the same reasons in the early stages in a way that matches the fact that deep grief over miscarriage in the later stages is more appropriate than it is over miscarriage in the earlier stages (when, that is, the grief is solely about the loss of *this* child, not about, as might be the case, the loss of one's only hope of having a child or of having one's husband's child). Imagine (or recall) a woman who already has children; she had not intended to have more, but finds herself unexpectedly expectedly pregnant. Though contrary to her plans, the pregnancy, once established as a fact, is welcomed—and then she loses the embryo almost immediately. If this were bemoaned as a tragedy, it would, I think, be a misapplication of the concept of what is tragic. But it may still properly be mourned as a loss. The grief is expressed in such terms as "I shall always wonder how she or he would have turned out" or "When I look at the others, I shall think, 'How different their lives would have been if this other one had been part of them.'" It would, I take it, be callous and light-minded to say, or think, "Well, she has already *got* four children; what's the problem?"; it would be neither, nor arrogantly intrusive in the case of a close friend, to try to correct prolonged mourning by saying, "I know it's sad, but it's not a tragedy; rejoice in the ones you have." The application of *tragic* becomes more appropriate as the fetus grows, for the mere fact that one has lived with it for longer, conscious of its existence, makes a difference. To shrug off an early abortion is understandable just because it is very hard to be fully conscious of the fetus's existence in the early stages and hence hard to appreciate that an early abortion is the destruction of life. It is particularly hard for the young and inexperienced to appreciate this, because appreciation of it usually comes only with experience.

I do not mean "with the experience of having an abortion" (though that may be part of it) but, quite generally, "with the experience of life." Many women who have borne children contrast their later pregnancies with their first successful one, saying that in the later ones they were conscious of a new life growing in them from very early on. And, more generally, as one reaches the age at which the next generation is coming up close behind one, the counterfactuals "If I, or she, had had an abortion, Alice, or Bob, would not have been born" acquire a significant application, which casts a new light on the conditionals "If I or Alice have an abortion then some Caroline or Bill will not be born."

The fact that pregnancy is not just one among many physical conditions does not mean that one can never regard it in that light without manifesting a vice. When women are in very poor physical health, or worn out from childbearing, or forced to do very physically demanding jobs, then they cannot be described as self-indulgent, callous, irresponsible, or light-minded if they seek abortions mainly with a view to avoiding pregnancy as the physical condition that it is. To go through with a pregnancy when one is utterly exhausted, or when one's job consists of crawling along tunnels hauling coal, as many women in the nineteenth century were obliged to do, is perhaps heroic, but people who do not achieve heroism are not necessarily vicious. That they can view the pregnancy only as eight months of misery, followed by hours if not days of agony and exhaustion, and abortion only as the blessed escape from this prospect, is entirely understandable and does not manifest any lack of serious respect for human life or a shallow attitude to motherhood. What it

does show is that something is terribly amiss in the conditions of their lives, which make it so hard to recognize pregnancy and childbearing as the good that they can be.

In relation to this last point I should draw attention to the way in which virtue theory has a sort of built-in indexicality. Philosophers arguing against anything remotely resembling a belief in the sanctity of life (which the above claims clearly embody) frequently appeal to the existence of other communities in which abortion and infanticide are practiced. We should not automatically assume that it is impossible that some other communities could be morally inferior to our own; maybe some are, or have been, precisely insofar as their members are, typically, callous or light-minded or unjust. But in communities in which life is a great deal tougher for everyone than it is in ours, having the right attitude to human life and death, parenthood, and family relationships might well manifest itself in ways that are unlike ours. When it is essential to survival that most members of the community fend for themselves at a very young age or work during most of their waking hours, selective abortion or infanticide might be practiced either as a form of genuine euthanasia or for the sake of the community and not, I think, be thought callous or light-minded. But this does not make everything all right; as before, it shows that there is something amiss with the conditions of their lives, which are making it impossible for them to live really well.[13]

The foregoing discussion, insofar as it emphasizes the right attitude to human life and death, parallels to a certain extent those standard discussions of abortion that concentrate on it solely as an issue of killing. But it does not, as those discussions do, gloss over the fact, emphasized by those who discuss the morality of abortion in terms of women's rights, that abortion, wildly unlike any other form of killing, is the termination of a pregnancy, which is a condition of a woman's body and results in *her* having a child if it is not aborted. This fact is given due recognition not by appeal to women's rights but by emphasizing the relevance of the familiar biological and psychological facts and their connection with having the right attitude to parenthood and family relationships. But it may well be thought that failing to bring in women's rights still leaves some important aspects of the problem of abortion untouched.

Speaking in terms of women's rights, people sometimes say things like, "Well, it's her life you're talking about too, you know; she's got a right to her own life, her own happiness." And the discussion stops there. But in the context of virtue theory, given that we are particularly concerned with what constitutes a good human life, with what true happiness or *eudaimonia* is, this is no place to stop. We go on to ask, "And is this life of hers a good one? Is she living well?"

If we are to go on to talk about good human lives, in the context of abortion, we have to bring in our thoughts about the value of love and family life, and our proper emotional development through a natural life cycle. The familiar facts support the view that parenthood in general, and motherhood and childbearing in particular, are intrinsically worthwhile, are among the things that can be correctly thought to be partially constitutive of a flourishing human life.[14] If this is right, then a woman who opts for not being a mother (at all, or again, or now) by opting for abortion may thereby be manifesting a flawed grasp of what her life should be, and be about—a grasp that is childish, or grossly materialistic, or shortsighted, or shallow.

I said "*may* thereby": this *need* not be so. Consider, for instance, a woman who has already had several children and fears that to have another will seriously affect her capacity to be a good mother to the ones she has—she does not show a lack of appreciation of the intrinsic value of being a parent by opting for abortion. Nor does a woman who has been a good mother and is approaching the age at which she may be looking forward to being a good grandmother. Nor does a woman who discovers that her pregnancy may well kill her, and opts for abortion and adoption. Nor, necessarily, does a woman who has decided to lead a life centered around some other worthwhile activity or activities with which motherhood would compete.

People who are childless by choice are sometimes described as "irresponsible," or "selfish," or "refusing to grow up," or "not knowing what life is about." But one can hold that having children is intrinsically worthwhile without endorsing this, for we are, after all, in the happy position of there being more worthwhile things to do than can be fitted into one lifetime. Parenthood, and motherhood in particular, even if granted to be intrinsically worthwhile, undoubtedly take up a lot of one's adult life, leaving no room for some other worthwhile pursuits. But some women who choose abortion rather than have their first child, and some men who encourage their partners to choose abortion, are not avoiding parenthood for the sake of other worthwhile pursuits, but for the worthless one of "having a good time," or for the pursuit of some false vision of the ideals of freedom or self-realization. And some others who say "I am not ready for parenthood yet" are making some sort of mistake about the extent to which one can manipulate the circumstances of one's life so as to make it fulfill some dream that one has. Perhaps one's dream is to have two perfect children, a girl and a boy, within a perfect marriage, in financially secure circumstances, with an interesting job of one's own. But to care too much about that dream, to demand of life that it give it to one and act accordingly, may be both greedy and foolish, and is to run the risk of missing out on happiness entirely. Not only may fate make the dream impossible, or destroy it, but one's own attachment to it may make it impossible. Good marriages, and the most promising children, can be destroyed by just one adult's excessive demand for perfection.

Once again, this is not to deny that girls may quite properly say "I am not ready for motherhood yet," especially in our society, and, far from manifesting irresponsibility or light-mindedness, show an appropriate modesty or humility, or a fearfulness that does not amount to cowardice. However, even when the decision to have an abortion is the right decision—one that does not itself fall under a vice-related term and thereby one that the perfectly virtuous could recommend—it does not follow that there is no sense in which having the abortion is wrong, or guilt inappropriate. For, by virtue of the fact that a human life has been cut short, some evil has probably been brought about,[15] and that circumstances make the decision to bring about some evil the right decision will be a ground for guilt if getting into those circumstances in the first place itself manifested a flaw in character.

What "gets one into those circumstances" in the case of abortion is, except in the case of rape, one's sexual activity and one's choices, or the lack of them, about one's sexual partner and about contraception. The virtuous woman (which here of course does not mean simply "chaste woman" but "woman with the virtues") has such character traits as strength, independence, resoluteness, decisiveness, self-confidence, responsibility, serious-mindedness, and self-determination—and no one, I think, could deny that many women become pregnant in circumstances in which they cannot welcome or cannot face the thought of having *this* child precisely because they lack one or some of these character traits. So even in the cases where the decision to have an abortion is the right one, it can still be the reflection of a moral failing—not because the decision itself is weak or cowardly or irresolute or irresponsible or light-minded, but because lack of the requisite opposite of these failings landed one in the circumstances in the first place. Hence the common universalized claim that guilt and remorse are never appropriate emotions about an abortion is denied. They may be appropriate, and appropriately inculcated, even when the decision was the right one.

Another motivation for bringing women's rights into the discussion may be to attempt to correct the implication, carried by the killing-centered approach, that insofar as abortion is wrong, it is a wrong that only women do, or at least (given the preponderance of male doctors) that only women instigate. I do not myself believe that we can thus escape the fact that nature bears harder on women than it does on men,[16] but virtue theory can certainly correct many of the injustices that the emphasis on women's rights is rightly concerned about. With very little amendment, everything that has been said above applies to boys and men too. Although the abortion decision is, in a natural sense, the woman's decision, proper to her, boys and men are often party to it, for well or ill, and even when they are not, they are bound to have been party to the circumstances that brought it up. No less than girls and women, boys and men can, in their actions, manifest self-centeredness, callousness, and light-mindedness about life and parenthood in relation to abortion. They can be self-centered or courageous about the possibility of disability in their offspring; they need to reflect on their sexual activity and their choices, or the lack of them, about their sexual partner

and contraception; they need to grow up and take responsibility for their own actions and life in relation to fatherhood. If it is true, as I maintain, that insofar as motherhood is intrinsically worthwhile, being a mother is an important purpose in women's lives, being a father (rather than a mere generator) is an important purpose in men's lives as well, and it is adolescent of men to turn a blind eye to this and pretend that they have many more important things to do.

CONCLUSION

Much more might be said, but I shall end the actual discussion of the problem of abortion here, and conclude by highlighting what I take to be its significant features. These hark back to many of the criticisms of virtue theory discussed earlier.

The discussion does not proceed simply by our trying to answer the question "Would a perfectly virtuous agent ever have an abortion and, if so, when?"; virtue theory is not limited to considering "Would Socrates have had an abortion if he were a raped, pregnant fifteen-year-old?" nor automatically stumped when we are considering circumstances into which no virtuous agent would have got herself. Instead, much of the discussion proceeds in the virtue- and vice-related terms whose application, in several cases, yields practical conclusions (cf. the third and fourth criticisms above). These terms are difficult to apply correctly, and anyone might challenge my application of any one of them. So, for example, I have claimed that some abortions, done for certain reasons, would be callous or light-minded; that others might indicate an appropriate modesty or humility; that others would reflect a greedy and foolish attitude to what one could expect out of life. Any of these examples may be disputed, but what is at issue is, should these difficult terms be there, or should the discussion be couched in terms that all clever adolescents can apply correctly? (Cf. the first half of the "major objection" above.)

Proceeding as it does in the virtue- and vice-related terms, the discussion thereby, inevitably, also contains claims about what is worthwhile, serious and important, good and evil, in our lives. So, for example, I claimed that parenthood is intrinsically worthwhile, and that having a good time was a worthless end (in life, not on individual occasions);

that losing a fetus is always a serious matter (albeit not a tragedy in itself in the first trimester) whereas acquiring an appendectomy scar is a trivial one; that (human) death is an evil. Once again, these are difficult matters, and anyone might challenge any one of my claims. But what is at issue is, as before, should those difficult claims be there or can one reach practical conclusions about real moral issues that are in no way determined by premises about such matters? (Cf. the fifth criticism, and the second half of the "major criticism.")

The discussion also thereby, inevitably, contains claims about what life is like (e.g., my claim that love and friendship do not survive their parties' constantly insisting on their rights; or the claim that to demand perfection of life is to run the risk of missing out on happiness entirely). What is at issue is, should those disputable claims be there, or is our knowledge (or are our false opinions) about what life is like irrelevant to our understanding of real moral issues? (Cf. both halves of the "major criticism.")

Naturally, my own view is that all these concepts should be there in any discussion of real moral issues and that virtue theory, which uses all of them, is the right theory to apply to them. I do not pretend to have shown this. I realize that proponents of rival theories may say that, now that they have understood how virtue theory uses the range of concepts it draws on, they are more convinced than ever that such concepts should not figure in an adequate normative theory, because they are sectarian, or vague, or too particular, or improperly anthropocentric, and reinstate what I called the "major criticism." Or, finding many of the details of the discussion appropriate, they may agree that many, perhaps even all, of the concepts should figure, but argue that virtue theory gives an inaccurate account of the way the concepts fit together (and indeed of the concepts themselves) and that another theory provides a better account; that would be interesting to see. Moreover, I admitted that there were at least two problems for virtue theory: that it has to argue against moral skepticism, "pluralism," and cultural relativism, and that it has to find something to say about conflicting requirements of different virtues. Proponents of rival theories might argue that their favored theory provides better solutions to these problems than virtue theory can. Indeed, they might criticize virtue theory for finding problems here at all. Anyone who argued for at least one of moral skepticism, "pluralism," or cultural relativism could presumably do so (provided their favored theory does not find a similar problem); and a utilitarian might say that benevolence is the only virtue and hence that virtue theory errs when it discusses even apparent conflicts between the requirements of benevolence and some other character trait such as honesty.

Defending virtue theory against all possible, or even likely, criticisms of it would be a lifelong task. As I said at the outset, in this article I aimed to defend the theory against some criticisms which I thought arose from an inadequate understanding of it, and to improve that understanding. If I have succeeded, we may hope for more comprehending criticisms of virtue theory than have appeared hitherto.

NOTES

Versions of this article have been read to philosophy societies at University College, London, Rutgers University, and the Universities of Dundee, Edinburgh, Oxford, Swansea, and California–San Diego; at a conference of the Polish and British Academies in Cracow in 1988 on "Life, Death and the Law," and as a symposium paper at the Pacific Division of the American Philosophical Association in 1989. I am grateful to the many people who contributed to the discussions of it on these occasions, and particularly to Philippa Foot and Anne Jaap Jacobson for private discussion.

1. It should be noted that this premise intentionally allows for the possibility that two virtuous agents, faced with the same choice in the same circumstances, may act differently. For example, one might opt for taking her father off the life-support machine and the other for leaving her father on it. The theory requires that neither agent thinks that what the other does is wrong (see note 4 below), but it explicitly allows that no action is uniquely right in such a case—both are right. It also intentionally allows for the possibility that in some circumstances—those into which no virtuous agent could have got herself—no action is right. I explore this premise at greater length in "Applying Virtue Ethics," forthcoming in a *festschrift* for Philippa Foot.

2. There is, of course, the further question of whether the theory eventually describes a larger circle and winds up relying on the concept of right action in its interpretation of *eudaimonia*. In denying that the theory is trivially circular, I do not pretend to answer this intricate question. It is certainly true that virtue theory does not claim that the correct conception of *eudaimonia* can be got from "an independent 'value-free' investigation of human nature" (John McDowell, "The Role of *Eudaimonia* in Aristotle's Ethics," in *Essays on Aristotle's Ethics*, ed. Amelie Rorty [Berkeley and Los Angeles: University of California Press, 1980]). The sort of training that is required for acquiring the correct conception no doubt involves being taught from early on such things as "Decent people do this sort of thing, not that" and "To do such and such is the mark of a depraved character" (cf. *Nicomachean Ethics* 1110a22). But whether this counts as relying on the concept of right (or wrong) action seems to me very unclear and requiring much discussion.

3. Cf. Bernard Williams' point in *Ethics and the Limits of Philosophy* (London: William Collins, 1985) that we need an enriched ethical vocabulary, not a cut-down one.

4. I put *pluralism* in scare quotes to serve as a warning that virtue theory is not incompatible with all forms of it. It allows for "competing conceptions" of *eudaimonia* and the worthwhile, for instance, in the sense that it allows for a plurality of flourishing lives—the theory need not follow Aristotle in specifying the life of contemplation as the only one that truly constitutes *eudaimonia* (if he does). But the conceptions "compete" only in the sense that, within a single flourishing life, not everything worthwhile can be fitted in; the theory does not allow that two people with a correct conception of *eudaimonia* can disagree over whether the way the other is living constitutes flourishing. Moreover, the theory is committed to the strong thesis that the same set of character traits is needed for *any* flourishing life; it will not allow that, for instance, soldiers need courage but wives and mothers do not, or that judges need justice but can live well despite lacking kindness. (This obviously is related to the point made in note 1 above.) For an interesting discussion of pluralism (different interpretations thereof) and virtue theory, see Douglas B. Rasmussen, "Liberalism and Natural End Ethics," *American Philosophical Quarterly* 27 (1990): 153–61.

5. E.g., in Williams' Jim and Pedro case in J.J.C. Smart and Bernard Williams, *Utilitarianism: For and Against* (London: Cambridge University Press, 1973).

6. Intimations of this criticism constantly come up in discussion; the clearest statement of it I have found is by Onora O'Neill, in her review of Stephen Clark's *The Moral Status of Animals*, in *Journal of Philosophy* 77 (1980): 440–46. For a response I am much in sympathy with, see Cora Diamond, "Anything But Argument?" *Philosophical Investigations* 5 (1982): 23–41.

7. Aristotle, *Nicomachean Ethics* 1142a12–16.

8. It seems likely that some people have been misled by Foot's discussion of euthanasia (through no fault of hers) into thinking that a virtue theorist's discussion of terminating human life will be conducted exclusively in terms of justice and charity (and the corresponding vice terms) (Philippa Foot, "Euthanasia," *Philosophy & Public Affairs* 6, no. 2 [Winter 1977]: 85–112). But the act-category *euthanasia* is a very special one, at least as defined in her article, since such an act must be done "for the sake of the one who is to die." Building a virtuous motivation into the specification of the act in this way immediately rules out the application of many other vice terms.

9. Judith Jarvis Thomson, "A Defense of Abortion," *Philosophy & Public Affairs* 1, no. 1 (Fall 1971): 47–66. One could indeed regard this article as proto–virtue theory (no doubt to the surprise of the author) if the concepts of callousness and kindness were allowed more weight.

10. One possible qualification: if one ties the concept of justice very closely to rights, then if women do have a moral right to terminate their pregnancies it *may* follow that in doing so they do not act unjustly. (Cf. Thomson, "A Defense of Abortion.") But it is debatable whether even that much follows.

11. This is an assumption of virtue theory, and I do not attempt to defend it here. An adequate discussion of it would require a separate article, since, although most moral philosophers would be

chary of claiming that intellectual sophistication is a necessary condition of moral wisdom or virtue, most of us, from Plato onward, tend to write as if this were so. Sorting out which claims about moral knowledge are committed to this kind of elitism and which can, albeit with difficulty, be reconciled with the idea that moral knowledge can be acquired by anyone who really wants it would be a major task.

12. Mary Anne Warren, in "On the Moral and Legal Status of Abortion," *Monist* 57 (1973), sec. 1, says of the opponents of restrictive laws governing abortion that "their conviction (for the most part) is that abortion is not a *morally* serious and extremely unfortunate, even though sometimes justified, act, comparable to killing in self-defense or to letting the violinist die, but rather is closer to being a *morally neutral* act, like cutting one's hair" (italics mine). I would like to think that no one *genuinely* believes this. But certainly in discussion, particularly when arguing against restrictive laws or the suggestion that remorse over abortion might be appropriate, I have found that some people *say* they believe it (and often cite Warren's article, albeit inaccurately, despite its age). Those who allow that it is morally serious, and far from morally neutral, have to argue against restrictive laws, or the appropriateness of remorse, on a very different ground from that laid

down by the premise "The fetus is just part of the woman's body (and she has a right to determine what happens to her body and should not feel guilt about anything she does to it)."

13. For another example of the way in which "tough conditions" can make a difference to what is involved in having the right attitude to human life and death and family relationships, see the concluding sentences of Foot's "Euthanasia."

14. I take this as a premise here, but argue for it in some detail in my *Beginning Lives* (Oxford: Basil Blackwell, 1987). In this connection I also discuss adoption and the sense in which it may be regarded as "second best," and the difficult question of whether the good of parenthood may properly be sought, or indeed bought, by surrogacy.

15. I say "some evil has probably been brought about" on the ground that (human) life is (usually) a good and hence (human) death usually an evil. The exceptions would be (a) where death is actually a good or a benefit, because the baby that would come to be if the life were not cut short would be better off dead than alive, and (b) where death, though not a good, is not an evil either, because the life that would be led (e.g., in a state of permanent coma) would not be a good. (See Foot, "Euthanasia.")

16. I discuss this point at greater length in *Beginning Lives*.

ARGUMENT 3 ESSAY QUESTIONS

1. On what grounds does Beckwith reject Thomson's argument? Are his objections plausible? How do *you* respond to Thomson? On what grounds do you accept or reject it?
2. How do you think Thomson would (or could) respond to Beckwith's objections to her argument? Do you think her response would (or could) be plausible?
3. What do you think is Beckwith's strongest against Thomson's view? Is it sound? Explain.

SUGGESTIONS FOR FURTHER READING

Sidney Callahan, "A Case for Pro-Life Feminism," *Commonweal* 25, April 1986, 232–38.

Philip Devine, *The Ethics of Homicide* (Ithaca, NY: Cornell University Press, 1978).

Joel Feinberg, "Abortion," in *Matters of Life and Death*, 3rd ed., ed. Tom Regan (New York: McGraw-Hill, 1993).

Jonathan Glover, "The Sanctity of Life," in *Bioethics: An Anthology*, ed. Helga Kuhse and Peter Singer (Oxford: Blackwell, 1999), 193–202.

John Harris and Søren Holm, "Abortion," in *The Oxford Handbook of Practical Ethics* (Oxford: Oxford University Press, 2003), 112–35.

Don Marquis, "Abortion Revisited," in *The Oxford Handbook of Bioethics* (Oxford: Oxford University Press, 2007), 395–415.

Jeff McMahan, *The Ethics of Killing: Problems at the Margins of Life* (New York: Oxford University Press, 2002).

Mark Murphy, "The Natural Law Tradition in Ethics," *Stanford Encyclopedia of Philosophy*, 11 March 2008, http://plato.stanford.edu/entries/natural-law-ethics (9 June 2008).

Louis P. Pojman, *Life and Death: Grappling with the Moral Dilemmas of Our Time* (Boston: Jones and Bartlett, 1992).

Louis P. Pojman and Francis J. Beckwith, ed., *The Abortion Controversy: 25 Years After Roe v. Wade: A Reader*, 2nd ed. (Belmont, CA: Wadsworth, 1998).

James Rachels, "Killing, Letting Die, and the Value of Life," in *Can Ethics Provide Answers?* (Lanham, MD: Rowman & Littlefield, 1997).

Stephen Schwarz, *The Moral Question of Abortion* (Chicago: Loyola University Press, 1990).

Susan Sherwin, *No Longer Patient: Feminist Ethics and Health Care* (Philadelphia: Temple University Press, 1992), 108–14.

L. W. Sumner, *Abortion and Moral Theory* (Princeton, NJ: Princeton University Press, 1981).

Michael Tooley, *Abortion and Infanticide* (New York: Oxford University Press, 1983).

CHAPTER 4

Drugs and Autonomy

Few people need a batch of statistics to grasp that the United States has a drug problem (whether alcohol, nicotine, or illicit substances) and that the issue raises all sorts of pressing moral questions. But the relevant data speak volumes just the same:

- In 2010, about 22.6 million Americans aged 12 or older were illegal drug users—that is, they had used an illegal drug during the preceding month. This means that almost 9 percent of people in this age group had recently used illicit substances: marijuana or hashish, cocaine or crack, heroin, hallucinogens, inhalants, or prescription drugs used for nonmedical reasons.

- Among young adults aged 18 to 25, the rate of illegal drug use increased from 19.6 percent in 2008 to 21.5 percent in 2010, mostly because of an uptick in the use of marijuana.

- Among those aged 12 or older who used either alcohol or illicit drugs, over 22 million had problems with "substance dependence or abuse."

- In 2010, more than half of Americans in this age group were alcohol drinkers—over 131 million people. About 23 percent of these participated in binge drinking, and more than 11 percent had over the past year driven under the influence of alcohol. Excessive alcohol consumption causes about 79,000 deaths each year.

- In 2010, almost 70 million people used tobacco products; over 53 million of these were cigarette smokers. Cigarette smoking accounts for over 443,000 premature deaths each year (about one in every five deaths); another 8.6 million people have a serious illness because of smoking. Another way to state the problem: Tobacco causes more deaths each year than does the combined effects of HIV, illegal drug use, alcohol consumption, motor vehicle accidents, suicides, and murders.

- In 2009, drugs (illegal and prescription) directly caused over 37,000 deaths, many of them due to overdoses of prescription narcotics such as OxyContin and Vicodin. Illegal and prescription drugs killed more people than traffic accidents.

- The war on drugs—America's decades-old attempt to eradicate illegal drug use and trafficking—has cost billions of dollars and thousands of lives in the violence that surrounds drug dealers, drug cartels, anti-drug law enforcement, and innocents who get caught in the crossfire. In 2010, over 1,600,000 inmates were serving time in federal and state correctional facilities, and over half of the federal inmates were being held for drug violations. Largely because of zero-tolerance drug laws, many inmates were serving long sentences for possession of small amounts of marijuana. Observers from both the political left and right say the war on drugs is lost.[1]

The term **drug** can refer to a broad range of substances, most of which are legal, therapeutic, and relatively safe. In its most general sense, it means chemicals (other than food) that can affect bodily functions or structures. By this definition, alcohol and nicotine are drugs, even though most people do not think of them as such. In medicine, the word denotes chemicals that have a medical purpose, substances that can be used to prevent or treat illness or disease. But in phrases such as "drug abuse," "drug use," or "the war on drugs," *drug* generally refers to the nonmedical use of chemicals that can affect mental states. They can alter awareness, judgment, mood, perception, and behavior. Brain-altering substances (sometimes described as psychotropic) include legal drugs such as alcohol, caffeine, and nicotine, as well as illegal ones such as cocaine, heroin, and marijuana. Some legitimate medications can be misused to produce the same sort of psychotropic experiences that illegal drugs can.

The term **drug abuse** does not have a standardized medical meaning but refers to drug use that society disapproves of—namely, uses that are (1) recreational, (2) proscribed or illegal, or (3) continued because of dependence or withdrawal.[2] **Drug dependence** is a strong reliance on the effects of a drug coupled with psychological or physical distress when the drug is withdrawn. *Psychological* dependence features intense satisfaction when using a drug and a strong desire to repeat the experience or to avoid the anguish of stopping. Some substances that result mainly in psychological dependence are marijuana, LSD, amphetamine, and mescaline. *Physical* dependence causes severe physical effects when the drug is withdrawn from the user. Among the substances that can lead to harsh physical dependence are heroin, alcohol, and cocaine.

According to the National Institutes of Health, **drug addiction** is "a chronic, often relapsing brain disease that causes compulsive drug seeking and use, despite harmful consequences to the addicted individual and to those around him or her." Addiction can have a very strong hold on users, eventually weakening their self-control and their power to resist extreme cravings to take drugs. Because of brain changes, the compulsion to use drugs can be overwhelming, and quitting can be an enormous challenge. Experts disagree over the degree to which addiction impedes our autonomy. Many think that even in addiction we have a measure of free will, but others believe addiction is equivalent to slavery.

[1] Statistics from Substance Abuse and Mental Health Services Administration, "Results from the 2010 National Survey on Drug Use and Health: Summary of National Findings," NSDUH Series H-41, HHS Publication No. (SMA) 11-4658, Rockville, MD, 2011 (8 February 2012); U. S. Department of Justice, Bureau of Justice Statistics, "Prisoners in 2010," http://bjs.ojp.usdoj.gov/content/pub/pdf/p10.pdf, December 2011 (8 February 2012); National Vital Statistics Reports, "Deaths: Preliminary Data from 2010," vol. 60, no. 4, 11 January 2012 (8 February 2012); National Institute of Drug Abuse, "Trends and Statistics," http://www.drugabuse.gov/publications, 2011 (8 February 2012); National Center for Chronic Disease Prevention and Health Promotion, "Alcohol and Drug Use," 8 August 2008 (8 February 2012).
[2] *The Merck Manual*, "Overview of Drug Use and Dependence," July 2008 (8 February 2012).

PUBLIC OPINION

"Do you think the use of marijuana should be made legal, or not?"

	Legal	Not Legal	Not Sure
Oct. 6–9, 2011	50%	46%	3%
Oct. 2–7, 1969	12%	84%	4%

Gallup Poll. Oct. 6–9, 2011. *N*=1,005 adults nationwide. Margin of error ± 4.

"Do you favor, oppose or neither favor nor oppose legalizing the possession of small amounts of marijuana for personal use?"

	Favor	Oppose	Neither	Unsure
Apr. 7–10, 2010	34%	55%	11%	

"Should the regulations on marijuana be more strict than those for alcohol, the same as those for alcohol, or less strict as those for alcohol?"

	More Strict	Less Strict	The Same
Apr. 7–10, 2010	43%	44%	12%

AP-CNBC Poll conducted by GfK Roper Public Affairs & Media. April 7–12, 2010. *N*=1,001 adults nationwide. Margin of error ± 4.3.

"Keeping in mind that all of your answers in this survey are confidential, have you, yourself, ever happened to try marijuana?"

	Yes	No	Unsure/Refused
Mar. 10–14, 2010	40%	58%	2%

Pew Research Center survey. March 10–14, 2010. *N*=1,500 adults nationwide. Margin of error ± 3.

The central moral issues regarding drugs are (1) whether their nonmedical use is morally permissible and (2) whether the state may intervene to curtail such use. The first question is about the morality of individual actions; the second concerns the morality of legal restrictions or prohibitions—that is, whether government limits on a person's autonomy, or liberty, are justified.

Major moral theories provide answers to question 1. Many virtue ethicists are likely to condemn drug use because they think it hinders the development of virtues, the achievement of moral and intellectual excellence. Kantian ethics would have us never use someone—including ourselves—merely as a means to an end. But in addiction, the Kantian would say, we use ourselves to achieve the end of pleasure, emotional numbness, or oblivion. And we disrespect our personhood by degrading the capacities that make us persons—our powers of reason and our ability to make free choices. From a utilitarian perspective, however, we would be concerned with acting to maximize net pleasure or happiness, a goal that drug use may or may not help us attain.

Question 2 has become the main focus of current debates about drug use, and the key concepts that animate these discussions are *legalization, criminalization*, and *decriminalization*.[3] The disputants, however, use these terms in confusing ways, so it's important to be clear about them. Drug **legalization** makes the *production and sale of drugs* no longer a criminal offense. Legalization could come about by allowing drugs to be bought and sold in a free market without government involvement, or by giving the government a monopoly over sale and production, or by creating some other system for producing or selling drugs without criminal penalties. **Criminalization** makes the *use of drugs* a crime—that is, an act worthy of legal punishment. Currently, because of criminalization, the possession of illegal drugs—even small amounts in the case of marijuana—may be enough to earn the possessor a prison sentence. **Decriminalization** makes the use of drugs *no longer a crime*. Under a fully decriminalized system, drug users would not be subject to any legal punishment.

Some commentators take a zero-tolerance position on drugs: they oppose both legalization and decriminalization. A few insist that neither producing, selling, nor using should be a criminal offense. And others oppose legalization but advocate decriminalization. This latter view may seem contradictory, but there is no inconsistency in prohibiting the production and sale of drugs while allowing their legal use.

Decriminalization need not be an all-or-nothing affair. It can, for example, accommodate criminalization in high-risk situations. The state may decriminalize drug use generally but criminalize the use of drugs while driving, boating, flying airplanes, operating trains and buses, or working in a daycare center. Decriminalization can also be applied to some drugs and not others. Some people want to decriminalize marijuana use while making the possession of such drugs as cocaine, heroin, and Ecstasy a criminal offense. And even a comprehensive system of decriminalization does not rule out efforts by private citizens or the state to dissuade people from drug use. This work often gets done through education, advertising, taxation, private companies, nonprofit organizations, and treatment centers.

A few critics of drug use think that decriminalization amounts to an endorsement by the state of drug use—a signal from the government that there's nothing wrong with using drugs. But the absence of laws against a practice does not imply the state's approval of it, no more than the absence of laws against cheating in golf shows that the state sanctions dishonesty on the golf course.

Another kind of drug policy that has often been proposed is *harm reduction*. It focuses not on reducing the number of drug users or banishing drugs from society (which is thought to be impossible) but on decreasing the amount of harm caused by drugs or drug enforcement. Harm-reduction approaches might include decriminalizing drug use, instituting needle-exchange programs to curtail the spread of HIV-AIDS, permitting the use of marijuana for medical treatment, or allowing physicians to prescribe heroin or cocaine to addicts.

On what grounds may the state interfere with a citizen's use of drugs? What justifies a government's criminalizing the production, sale, or use of these substances? The fundamental presumption behind these questions is that persons are autonomous beings

---

[3] This discussion of terms is drawn in part from Douglas Husak in *The Legalization of Drugs* (New York: Cambridge University Press, 2005).

whose liberty cannot be curtailed without good reason. Any constraints placed on their freedom by the government must be justified. Usually the justification comes in the form of basic moral principles that purport to stipulate when it's permissible for the state to restrict liberty.

The *harm principle* says the government is justified in limiting the liberty of some to prevent harm to others. The state, for example, may decide to criminalize drug use to ensure that drug users do not cause harm to other citizens. This is the least controversial rationale for curtailing liberty, for most people understand that our liberty stops where the rights of others begin. As John Stuart Mill famously declared,

> "[T]he sole end for which mankind are warranted, individually or collectively, in interfering with the liberty of action of any of their number, is self-protection. That the only purpose for which power can be rightfully exercised over any member of a civilized community, against his will, is to prevent harm to others.... Over himself, over his own body and mind, the individual is sovereign.[4]

Many argue that drug users cause great harm to those around them, and that's reason enough to make drug use a crime. Drug users, they insist, neglect or hurt their children (prime example: "crack babies"), cheat their employers through apathy, put their coworkers at risk through their negligence, behave violently toward their family, commit crimes, and saddle taxpayers with the costs of drug treatment and incarceration. Those who favor decriminalization accuse the opposition of factual distortions and argue that many of the allegations of harm cannot be supported by empirical evidence.

Decriminalization proponents have also turned the harm argument around, contending that the war on drugs may be more harmful than the drug use it's trying to eradicate. They cite the erosion of civil liberties caused by overzealous, misguided anti-drug campaigns; the threat to public health from the unregulated sale of unsafe drugs; the corruption of law enforcement officials; the crimes committed by addicts to fund their drug habit; the damage the war on drugs has caused to our foreign relations; the waste of billions of dollars in ineffective anti-drug policies; and the overburdening of our judicial and penal systems by hundreds of thousands of people convicted of drug offenses.

Some opponents of drug laws insist that trying to justify criminalization by referring to harms caused or avoided misses the point. On this view, whether or not the state should punish someone is primarily a matter of justice and rights, not calculations of harm. After all, we tend to think that punishment for murderers and thieves should be based not on an estimate of the net advantages and disadvantages of punishment, but primarily on what justice requires—that is, on what they deserve. So any argument for criminalization appealing entirely to good and bad consequences must fail.

The *paternalism principle* says the government is justified in limiting the liberty of citizens to prevent harm to *themselves*. A person's freedom can be legitimately restricted for her own good. Clear examples of paternalistic measures are laws that require wearing seatbelts while driving and wearing helmets when riding a motorcycle. Laws barring children from using alcohol and tobacco are also paternalistic.

---

[4] John Stuart Mill, *On Liberty* (1859).

Several critics of legalization or decriminalization take a paternalistic view. According to James Q. Wilson,

> [T]he moral reason for attempting to discourage drug use is that the heavy consumption of certain drugs is destructive of human character... The dignity, autonomy, and productivity of many users, already impaired by other problems, is destroyed.[5]

Peter de Marneffe also argues a paternalistic case:

> There is only one good reason for drug prohibition, which is that some of us will be worse off if drugs are legalized. Why would any of us be worse off? With drug legalization there will be more drug abuse, and drug abuse is bad for people.[6]

Paternalism is usually thought to conflict with the exercise of personal autonomy, the rational capacity for self-determination, but some use autonomy as a starting point in paternalistic arguments. The general idea is that drugs can be addictive, and addiction can seriously diminish a person's autonomy. If this is the case, criminalization—punishment for drug use—is justified to protect or preserve autonomy.

The *legal moralism principle* says the government is justified in limiting the liberty of citizens to prevent them from committing immoral acts. Certain acts are punishable as

FACTS AND FIGURES: Drug Convictions

Number of persons under control of the U.S. criminal justice system for "drugs"[†]

	1980	1990	2009
Total	–	964,469	1,725,387
Probation	–	640,856	1,093,031
Parole	–	144,543	294,951
Federal prison	4,900	30,470	95,205
State prison	19,000	148,600	242,200

[†]The conviction of "drugs" means that possession or sales of an illegal drug was the person's most serious offense, even if he or she were convicted of multiple offenses.

Sources: Gilliard, Darrell K. and Beck, Allan J., "Prisoners in 1994," Bureau of Justice Statistics, (Washington, DC: US Department of Justice, August 1995), NCJ 151654, p. 11 & 10. **http://www.bjs.gov/content/pub/pdf/p04.pdf.** Guerino, Paul; Harrison, Paige M.; and Sabol, William J., "Prisoners in 2010," Bureau of Justice Statistics, (Washington, DC: US Department of Justice, December 2011), NCJ 236096, p. 28 & 30. **http://bjs.ojp.usdoj.gov/content/pub/pdf/p10.pdf.** Glaze, Lauren E., and Bonczar, Thomas P., "Probation and Parole in the United States, 2010," Bureau of Justice Statistics, (Washington, DC: US Department of Justice, November 2011), NCJ 236019, pp. 33 & 43. **http://bjs.ojp.usdoj.gov/content/pub/pdf/ppus10.pdf**

---

[5] James Q. Wilson, "Drugs and Crime," in *Drugs and Crime*, ed. Michael Tonry and James Q. Wilson (Chicago: Chicago University Press, 1990), 521, 523.
[6] Peter de Marneffe, in *The Legalization of Drugs* by Douglas Husak and Peter de Marneffe (New York: Cambridge University Press, 205), 109.

crimes simply because they are immoral—regardless of whether they cause harm to anyone. Many who oppose decriminalization insist that drug use is immoral, and immorality is reason enough to punish people for using illicit drugs. Wilson takes this view:

> Even now, when the dangers of drug use are well-understood, many educated people still discuss the drug problem in almost every way except the right way. They talk about the "costs" of drug use and the "socioeconomic factors" that shape that use. They rarely speak plainly—drug use is wrong because it is immoral and it is immoral because it enslaves the mind and destroys the soul.[7]

Critics of legal moralism remind us that no one believes that *all* immoral behavior should be deemed a crime and punished accordingly. Lying, breaking promises, betraying a loved one, cheating on an exam—these and many other acts are usually thought to be immoral. But who thinks they should be considered violations of criminal law and their perpetrators punished with a prison sentence? Legal moralists seem to believe that only some immoral acts should be punished as crimes. "If so," Douglas Husak says, "prohibitionists who contend that drug use should be punished because of its immorality should be pressed to explain why *this* case [drug use], unlike a case of breaking a contractual promise, should be included among those immoral behaviors the criminal law should punish."[8] Husak contends that no one has satisfactorily explained this difference, so legal moralism should be rejected as a rationale for criminalization.

A similar question arises about why taking only some drugs—but not others—should be a criminal offense because of their immorality. Critics of criminalization ask why cocaine and marijuana are thought to be immoral but alcohol and nicotine are not. Again they think no satisfactory answer has been given.

KEY TERMS

drug abuse	drug dependence	drug addiction
legalization	decriminalization	criminalization

---

[7] John Q. Wilson, in *Body Count*, by William, Bennett, John Dilulio, Jr., and John Walters (New York: Simon & Schuster, 1996), 140–141.

[8] Douglas Husak, *The Legalization of Drugs* by Douglas Husak and Peter de Marneffe (New York: Cambridge University Press, 205), 73.

4. THE HARM ARGUMENT AGAINST DRUG USE

The argument from harm says a person's use of illicit drugs harms others, and therefore it should be prohibited. That is, because of its bad effects on people other than the drug user, using drugs should be a criminal offense subject to legal punishment.

In "Against the Legalization of Drugs," James Q. Wilson argues that cocaine and heroin are extremely dangerous drugs, that their addicts cause enormous harm to the rest of society, and that criminalizing their use leads to less damage to others than decriminalizing would. (He also maintains that the use of drugs like cocaine is immoral because it debases life and "alters one's soul," and the immorality is an additional reason for making their use illegal.) The social harms of crack and heroin, says Wilson, are real and substantial, for it is not the case that "abusing drugs is a 'victimless crime.' "[9] Among the harms, he includes child neglect, fetal deformities, violent tendencies, criminal activity, and irresponsible behavior toward spouses, employers, and coworkers. These harms, he says, will probably be magnified if drug use becomes legal, because decriminalization is likely to bring a massive upsurge in drug users.

For several reasons, critics of the harm argument are skeptical that decriminalization will increase drug use, and they argue that the woes linked to drug use may be greatly outweighed by the calamities engendered by criminalization. Empirical evidence to support a firm conclusion on the effects of decriminalization is scarce or equivocal. Decriminalization advocates, however, suggest that some clues can be found in data on the decriminalization experience of other countries, especially the Netherlands. As Douglas Husak observes,

> Since the Dutch initiated the de facto legalization of marijuana in 1976, we have ample evidence about how their novel experience has worked. Overall, consumption rates in the Netherlands are probably lower than those in the United States. Recent data indicate that only 21 percent of Dutch citizens aged 12 to 18 have ever tried marijuana, compared to 38 percent of Americans that age. Nor are they more inclined to use cocaine and heroin than their American counterparts. Although there are innumerable differences between Dutch culture and that of the United States, these data are surely better than pure speculation in predicting the effects of legalization.[10]

[9] James Q. Wilson, "Against Legalization of Drugs," *Commentary*, February, 1990.
[10] Husak, 104.

Does criminalization cause more harm than decriminalization? A more manageable question is, Would the significant harm of crime increase after decriminalization? A few who support criminalization admit that crime may be caused by drug enforcement (or that the connection is not clear), but they nevertheless believe that the advantages of laws against drug use far outweigh the drawbacks. Proponents of decriminalization assert that correlations between drug use and crime are inconsistent, with some decades showing a drop in crime rates as punishment for drug use intensifies—and some decades showing the opposite effect. Moreover, they say, most drug users never commit violent acts, and it's obvious that a great deal of violence happens because drug use is illegal.

But are these utilitarian calculations of harm to the point? Some critics of criminalization insist that the heart of the matter is not the balance of good over bad consequences but the justice or injustice of punishing people for using drugs. Justice trumps reckonings of cost and benefits. The idea is that we would not think it proper to decide whether to, say, discriminate against blacks or women based on the possible advantages and disadvantages to society, for this issue is a question of justice. Libertarians argue for a strong right to liberty—the right to do as you please (including use drugs) as long as your actions do not interfere with the rights of others to act as they please. To them, no government may legitimately punish drug use or any other action without very strong justification. Non-libertarians such as Husak also think the main issue concerning criminalization and decriminalization is the moral rights of drug users. Whatever the verdict on the utility of drug laws, they say, the rights of drug users must be part of the calculation.

Against the Legalization of Drugs

JAMES Q. WILSON

In 1972, the President appointed me chairman of the National Advisory Council for Drug Abuse Prevention. Created by Congress, the Council was charged with providing guidance on how best to coordinate the national war on drugs. (Yes, we called it a war then, too.) In those days, the drug we were chiefly concerned with was heroin. When I took office, heroin use had been increasing dramatically. Everybody was worried that this increase would continue. Such phrases as "heroin epidemic" were commonplace.

That same year, the eminent economist Milton Friedman published an essay in *Newsweek* in which he called for legalizing heroin. His argument was on two grounds: as a matter of ethics, the government has no right to tell people not to use heroin (or to drink or to commit suicide); as a matter of economics, the prohibition of drug use imposes costs

on society that far exceed the benefits. Others, such as the psychoanalyst Thomas Szasz, made the same argument.

We did not take Friedman's advice. (Government commissions rarely do.) I do not recall that we even discussed legalizing heroin, though we did discuss (but did not take action on) legalizing a drug, cocaine, that many people then argued was benign. Our marching orders were to figure out how to win the war on heroin, not to run up the white flag of surrender.

That was 1972. Today, we have the same number of heroin addicts that we had then—half a million, give or take a few thousand. Having that

From James Q. Wilson, "Against the Legalization of Drugs," *Commentary*, February 1990. © Commentary, EBSCO Publishing. Note deleted.

many heroin addicts is no trivial matter; these people deserve our attention. But not having had an increase in that number for over fifteen years is also something that deserves our attention. What happened to the "heroin epidemic" that many people once thought would overwhelm us?

The facts are clear: a more or less stable pool of heroin addicts has been getting older, with relatively few new recruits. In 1976 the average age of heroin users who appeared in hospital emergency rooms was about twenty-seven; ten years later it was thirty-two. More than two-thirds of all heroin users appearing in emergency rooms are now over the age of thirty. Back in the early 1970's, when heroin got onto the national political agenda, the typical heroin addict was much younger, often a teenager. Household surveys show the same thing—the rate of opiate use (which includes heroin) has been flat for the better part of two decades. More fine-grained studies of inner-city neighborhoods confirm this. John Boyle and Ann Brunswick found that the percentage of young blacks in Harlem who used heroin fell from 8 percent in 1970–71 to about 3 percent in 1975–76.

Why did heroin lose its appeal for young people? When the young blacks in Harlem were asked why they stopped, more than half mentioned "trouble with the law" or "high cost" (and high cost is, of course, directly the result of law enforcement). Two-thirds said that heroin hurt their health; nearly all said they had had a bad experience with it. We need not rely, however, simply on what they said. In New York City in 1973–75, the street price of heroin rose dramatically and its purity sharply declined, probably as a result of the heroin shortage caused by the success of the Turkish government in reducing the supply of opium base and of the French government in closing down heroin-processing laboratories located in and around Marseilles. These were short-lived gains for, just as Friedman predicted, alternative sources of supply—mostly in Mexico—quickly emerged. But the three-year heroin shortage interrupted the easy recruitment of new users.

Health and related problems were no doubt part of the reason for the reduced flow of recruits. Over the preceding years, Harlem youth had watched as more and more heroin users died of overdoses, were poisoned by adulterated doses, or acquired hepatitis from dirty needles. The word got around: heroin can kill you. By 1974 new hepatitis cases and drug-overdose deaths had dropped to a fraction of what they had been in 1970.

Alas, treatment did not seem to explain much of the cessation in drug use. Treatment programs can and do help heroin addicts, but treatment did not explain the drop in the number of *new* users (who by definition had never been in treatment) nor even much of the reduction in the number of experienced users.

No one knows how much of the decline to attribute to personal observation as opposed to high prices or reduced supply. But other evidence suggests strongly that price and supply played a large role. In 1972 the National Advisory Council was especially worried by the prospect that U.S. servicemen returning to this country from Vietnam would bring their heroin habits with them. Fortunately, a brilliant study by Lee Robins of Washington University in St. Louis put that fear to rest. She measured drug use of Vietnam veterans shortly after they had returned home. Though many had used heroin regularly while in Southeast Asia, most gave up the habit when back in the United States. The reason: here, heroin was less available and sanctions on its use were more pronounced. Of course, if a veteran had been willing to pay enough—which might have meant traveling to another city and would certainly have meant making an illegal contact with a disreputable dealer in a threatening neighborhood in order to acquire a (possibly) dangerous dose—he could have sustained his drug habit. Most veterans were unwilling to pay this price, and so their drug use declined or disappeared.

RELIVING THE PAST

Suppose we had taken Friedman's advice in 1972. What would have happened? We cannot be entirely certain, but at a minimum we would have placed the young heroin addicts (and, above all, the prospective addicts) in a very different position from the one in which they actually found themselves. Heroin would have been legal. Its price would have been reduced by 95 percent (minus whatever we chose to recover in taxes). Now that it could be sold by the same people who make aspirin, its quality would have been assured—no poisons, no adulterants. Sterile hypodermic needles would have been readily available at the neighborhood drugstore, probably at the same counter where the heroin was sold. No need to travel to big cities or unfamiliar neighborhoods—heroin could have been purchased anywhere, perhaps by mail order.

There would no longer have been any financial or medical reason to avoid heroin use. Anybody could have afforded it. We might have tried to prevent children from buying it, but as we have learned from our efforts to prevent minors from buying alcohol and tobacco, young people have a way of penetrating markets theoretically reserved for adults. Returning Vietnam veterans would have discovered that Omaha and Raleigh had been converted into the pharmaceutical equivalent of Saigon.

Under these circumstances, can we doubt for a moment that heroin use would have grown exponentially? Or that a vastly larger supply of new users would have been recruited? Professor Friedman is a Nobel Prize-winning economist whose understanding of market forces is profound. What did he think would happen to consumption under his legalized regime? Here are his words: "Legalizing drugs might increase the number of addicts, but it is not clear that it would. Forbidden fruit is attractive, particularly to the young."

Really? I suppose that we should expect no increase in Porsche sales if we cut the price by 95 percent, no increase in whiskey sales if we cut the price by a comparable amount—because young people only want fast cars and strong liquor when they are "forbidden." Perhaps Friedman's uncharacteristic lapse from the obvious implications of price theory can be explained by a misunderstanding of how drug users are recruited. In his 1972 essay he said that "drug addicts are deliberately made by pushers, who give likely prospects their first few doses free." If drugs were legal it would not pay anybody to produce addicts, because everybody would buy from the cheapest source. But as every drug expert knows, pushers do not produce addicts. Friends or acquaintances do. In fact, pushers are usually reluctant to deal with non-users because a non-user could be an undercover cop. Drug use spreads in the same way any fad or fashion spreads: somebody who is already a user urges his friends to try, or simply shows already-eager friends how to do it.

But we need not rely on speculation, however plausible, that lowered prices and more abundant supplies would have increased heroin usage. Great Britain once followed such a policy and with almost exactly those results. Until the mid-1960's, British physicians were allowed to prescribe heroin to certain classes of addicts. (Possessing these drugs without a doctor's prescription remained a criminal offense.) For many years this policy worked well enough because the addict patients were typically middle-class people who had become dependent on opiate painkillers while undergoing hospital treatment. There was no drug culture. The British system worked for many years, not because it prevented drug abuse, but because there was no problem of drug abuse that would test the system.

All that changed in the 1960's. A few unscrupulous doctors began passing out heroin in wholesale amounts. One doctor prescribed almost 600,000 heroin tablets—that is, over thirteen pounds—in just one year. A youthful drug culture emerged with a demand for drugs far different from that of the older addicts. As a result, the British government required doctors to refer users to government-run clinics to receive their heroin.

But the shift to clinics did not curtail the growth in heroin use. Throughout the 1960's the number of addicts increased—the late John Kaplan of Stanford estimated by fivefold—in part as a result of the diversion of heroin from clinic patients to new users on the streets. An addict would bargain with the clinic doctor over how big a dose he would receive. The patient wanted as much as he could get, the doctor wanted to give as little as was needed. The patient had an advantage in this conflict because the doctor could not be certain how much was really needed. Many patients would use some of their "maintenance" dose and sell the remaining part to friends, thereby recruiting new addicts. As the clinics learned of this, they began to shift their treatment away from heroin and toward methadone, an addictive drug that, when taken orally, does not produce a "high" but will block the withdrawal pains associated with heroin abstinence.

Whether what happened in England in the 1960's was a mini-epidemic or an epidemic depends on whether one looks at numbers or at rates of change. Compared to the United States, the numbers were small. In 1960 there were 68 heroin addicts known to the British government; by 1968 there were 2,000 in treatment and many more who refused treatment. (They would refuse in part because they did not want to get methadone at a clinic if they could get heroin on the street.) Richard Hartnoll estimates that the actual number of addicts in England is five times the number officially registered. At a minimum, the number of British addicts increased by thirtyfold in ten years; the actual increase may have been much larger.

In the early 1980's the numbers began to rise again, and this time nobody doubted that a real epidemic was at hand. The increase was estimated to be 40 percent a year. By 1982 there were thought to be 20,000 heroin users in London alone. Geoffrey Pearson reports that many cities—Glasgow, Liverpool, Manchester, and Sheffield among them—were now experiencing a drug problem that once had been largely confined to London. The problem, again, was supply. The country was being flooded with cheap, high-quality heroin, first from Iran and then from Southeast Asia.

The United States began the 1960's with a much larger number of heroin addicts and probably a bigger at-risk population than was the case in Great Britain. Even though it would be foolhardy to suppose that the British system, if installed here, would have worked the same way or with the same results, it would be equally foolhardy to suppose that a combination of heroin available from leaky clinics and from street dealers who faced only minimal law-enforcement risks would not have produced a much greater increase in heroin use than we actually experienced. My guess is that if we had allowed either doctors or clinics to prescribe heroin, we would have had far worse results than were produced in Britain, if for no other reason than the vastly larger number of addicts with which we began. We would have had to find some way to police thousands (not scores) of physicians and hundreds (not dozens) of clinics. If the British civil service found it difficult to keep heroin in the hands of addicts and out of the hands of recruits when it was dealing with a few hundred people, how well would the American civil service have accomplished the same tasks when dealing with tens of thousands of people?

BACK TO THE FUTURE

Now cocaine, especially in its potent form, crack, is the focus of attention. Now as in 1972 the government is trying to reduce its use. Now as then some people are advocating legalization. Is there any more reason to yield to those arguments today than there was almost two decades ago?

I think not. If we had yielded in 1972 we almost certainly would have had today a permanent population of several million, not several hundred thousand, heroin addicts. If we yield now we will have a far more serious problem with cocaine.

Crack is worse than heroin by almost any measure. Heroin produces a pleasant drowsiness and, if hygienically administered, has only the physical side effects of constipation and sexual impotence. Regular heroin use incapacitates many users, especially poor ones, for any productive work or social responsibility. They will sit nodding on a street corner, helpless but at least harmless. By contrast, regular cocaine use leaves the user neither helpless nor harmless. When smoked (as with crack) or injected, cocaine produces instant, intense, and short-lived euphoria. The experience generates a powerful desire to repeat it. If the drug is readily available, repeat use will occur. Those people who progress to "bingeing" on cocaine become devoted to the drug and its effects to the exclusion of almost all other considerations—job, family, children, sleep, food, even sex. Dr. Frank Gawin at Yale and Dr. Everett Ellinwood at Duke report that a substantial percentage of all high-dose, binge users become uninhibited, impulsive, hypersexual, compulsive, irritable, and hyperactive. Their moods vacillate dramatically, leading at times to violence and homicide.

Women are much more likely to use crack than heroin, and if they are pregnant, the effects on their babies are tragic. Douglas Besharov, who has been following the effects of drugs on infants for twenty years, writes that nothing he learned about heroin prepared him for the devastation of cocaine. Cocaine harms the fetus and can lead to physical deformities or neurological damage. Some crack babies have for all practical purposes suffered a disabling stroke while still in the womb. The long-term consequences of this brain damage are lowered cognitive ability and the onset of mood disorders. Besharov estimates that about 30,000 to 50,000 such babies are born every year, about 7,000 in New York City alone. There may be ways to treat such infants, but from everything we now know the treatment will be long, difficult, and expensive. Worse, the mothers who are most likely to produce crack babies are precisely the ones who, because of poverty or temperament, are least able and willing to obtain such treatment. In fact, anecdotal evidence suggests that crack mothers are likely to abuse their infants.

The notion that abusing drugs such as cocaine is a "victimless crime" is not only absurd but dangerous. Even ignoring the fetal drug syndrome, crack-dependent people are, like heroin addicts, individuals who regularly victimize thier children by neglect, their spouses by improvidence, their employers by lethargy, and their coworkers by carelessness. Society is not and could never be a collection of autonomous individuals. We all have a stake in ensuring that each of us displays a minimal level of dignity, responsibility, and empathy. We cannot, of course, coerce people into goodness, but we can and should insist that some standards must be met if society itself—on which the very existence of the human personality depends—is to persist. Drawing the line that defines those standards is difficult and contentious, but if crack and heroin use do not fall below it, what does?

The advocates of legalization will respond by suggesting that my picture is overdrawn. Ethan Nadelmann of Princeton argues that the risk of legalization is less than most people suppose. Over 20 million Americans between the ages of eighteen and twenty-five have tried cocaine (according to a government survey), but only a quarter million use it daily. From this Nadelmann concludes that at most 3 percent of all young people who try cocaine develop a problem with it. The implication is clear: make the drug legal and we only have to worry about 3 percent of our youth.

The implication rests on a logical fallacy and a factual error. The fallacy is this: the percentage of occasional cocaine users who become binge users *when the drug is illegal* (and thus expensive and hard to find) tells us nothing about the percentage who will become dependent when the drug is legal (and thus cheap and abundant). Drs. Gawin and Ellinwood report, in common with several other researchers, that controlled or occasional

use of cocaine changes to compulsive and frequent use "when access to the drug increases" or when the user switches from snorting to smoking. More cocaine more potently administered alters, perhaps sharply, the proportion of "controlled" users who become heavy users.

The factual error is this: the federal survey Nadelmann quotes was done in 1985, *before* crack had become common. Thus the probability of becoming dependent on cocaine was derived from the responses of users who snorted the drug. The speed and potency of cocaine's action increases dramatically when it is smoked. We do not yet know how greatly the advent of crack increases the risk of dependency, but all the clinical evidence suggests that the increase is likely to be large.

It is possible that some people will not become heavy users even when the drug is readily available in its most potent form. So far there are no scientific grounds for predicting who will and who will not become dependent. Neither socioeconomic background nor personality traits differentiate between casual and intensive users. Thus, the only way to settle the question of who is correct about the effect of easy availability on drug use, Nadelmann or Gawin and Ellinwood, is to try it and see. But that social experiment is so risky as to be no experiment at all, for if cocaine is legalized and if the rate of its abusive use increases dramatically, there is no way to put the genie back in the bottle, and it is not a kindly genie.

HAVE WE LOST?

Many people who agree that there are risks in legalizing cocaine or heroin still favor it because, they think, we have lost the war on drugs. "Nothing we have done has worked" and the current federal policy is just "more of the same." Whatever the costs of greater drug use, surely they would be less than the costs of our present, failed efforts.

That is exactly what I was told in 1972—and heroin is not quite as bad a drug as cocaine. We did not surrender and we did not lose. We did not win, either. What the nation accomplished then was what most efforts to save people from themselves accomplish: the problem was contained and the number of victims minimized, all at a considerable cost in law enforcement and increased crime. Was the cost worth it? I think so, but others may disagree. What are the lives of would-be addicts worth? I recall some people saying to me then, "Let them kill themselves." I was appalled. Happily, such views did not prevail.

Have we lost today? Not at all. High-rate cocaine use is not commonplace. The National Institute of Drug Abuse (NIDA) reports that less than 5 percent of high-school seniors used cocaine within the last thirty days. Of course this survey misses young people who have dropped out of school and miscounts those who lie on the questionnaire, but even if we inflate the NIDA estimate by some plausible percentage, it is still not much above 5 percent. Medical examiners reported in 1987 that about 1,500 died from cocaine use; hospital emergency rooms reported about 30,000 admissions related to cocaine abuse.

These are not small numbers, but neither are they evidence of a nationwide plague that threatens to engulf us all. Moreover, cities vary greatly in the proportion of people who are involved with cocaine. To get city-level data we need to turn to drug tests carried out on arrested persons, who obviously are more likely to be drug users than the average citizen. The National Institute of Justice, through its Drug Use Forecasting (DUF) project, collects urinalysis data on arrestees in 22 cities. As we have already seen, opiate (chiefly heroin) use has been flat or declining in most of these cities over the last decade. Cocaine use has gone up sharply, but with great variation among cities. New York, Philadelphia, and Washington, D.C., all report that two-thirds or more of their arrestees tested positive for cocaine, but in Portland, San Antonio, and Indianapolis the percentage was one-third or less.

In some neighborhoods, of course, matters have reached crisis proportions. Gangs control the streets, shootings terrorize residents, and drug-dealing occurs in plain view. The police seem barely able to contain matters. But in these neighborhoods—unlike at Palo Alto cocktail parties—the people are not calling for legalization, they are calling for help. And often not much help has come. Many cities are willing to do almost anything about the drug problem except spend more money on it. The federal government cannot change that; only local voters and politicians can. It is not clear that they will.

It took about ten years to contain heroin. We have had experience with crack for only about three or four years. Each year we spend perhaps $11 billion on law enforcement (and some of that goes to deal with marijuana) and perhaps $2 billion on treatment. Large sums, but not sums that should lead anyone to say, "We just can't afford this any more."

The illegality of drugs increases crime, partly because some users turn to crime to pay for their habits, partly because some users are stimulated by certain drugs (such as crack or PCP) to act more violently or ruthlessly than they otherwise would, and partly because criminal organizations seeking to control drug supplies use force to manage their markets. These also are serious costs, but no one knows how much they would be reduced if drugs were legalized. Addicts would no longer steal to pay black-market prices for drugs, a real gain. But some, perhaps a great deal, of that gain would be offset by the great increase in the number of addicts. These people, nodding on heroin or living in the delusion-ridden high of cocaine, would hardly be ideal employees. Many would steal simply to support themselves, since snatch-and grab, opportunistic crime can be manged even by people unable to hold a regular job or plan an elaborate crime. Those British addicts who get their supplies from government clinics are not models of law-abiding decency. Most are in crime, and though their per-capita rate of criminality may be lower thanks to the cheapness of their drugs, the total volume of crime they produce may be quite large. Of course, society could decide to support all unemployable addicts on welfare, but that would mean that gains from lowered rates of crime would have to be offset by large increases in welfare budgets.

Proponents of legalization claim that the costs of having more addicts around would be largely if not entirely offset by having more money available with which to treat and care for them. The money would come from taxes levied on the sale of heroin and cocaine.

To obtain this fiscal dividend, however, legalization's supporters must first solve an economic dilemma. If they want to raise a lot of money to pay for welfare and treatment, the tax rate on the drugs will have to be quite high. Even if they themselves do not want a high rate, the politicians' love of "sin taxes" would probably guarantee that it would be high anyway. But the higher the tax, the higher the price of the drug, and the higher the price the greater the likelihood that addicts will turn to crime to find the money for it and that criminal organizations will be formed to sell tax-free drugs at below-market rates. If we managed to keep taxes (and thus prices) low, we would get that much less money to pay for welfare and treatment and more people could afford to become addicts. There may be an optimal tax rate for drugs that maximizes revenue while minimizing crime, bootlegging, and the recruitment of new addicts, but our experience with alcohol does not suggest that we know how to find it.

THE BENEFITS OF ILLEGALITY

The advocates of legalization find nothing to be said in favor of the current system except, possibly, that it keeps the number of addicts smaller than it would otherwise be. In fact, the benefits are more substantial than that.

First, treatment. All the talk about providing "treatment on demand" implies that there is a demand for treatment. That is not quite right. There are some drug-dependent people who genuinely want treatment and will remain in it if offered; they should receive it. But there are far more who want only short-term help after a bad crash; once stabilized and bathed, they are back on the street again, hustling. And even many of the addicts who enroll in a program honestly wanting help drop out after a short while when they discover that help takes time and commitment. Drug-dependent people have very short time horizons and a weak capacity for commitment. These two groups—those looking for a quick fix and those unable to stick with a long-term fix—are not easily helped. Even if we increase the number of treatment slots—as we should—we would have to do something to make treatment more effective.

One thing that can often make it more effective is compulsion. Douglas Anglin of UCLA, in common with many other researchers, has found that the longer one stays in a treatment program, the better the chances of a reduction in drug dependency. But he, again like most other researchers, has found that drop-out rates are high. He has also found, however,

that patients who enter treatment under legal compulsion stay in the program longer than those not subject to such pressure. His research on the California civil commitment program, for example, found that heroin users involved with its required drug-testing program had over the long term a lower rate of heroin use than similar addicts who were free of such constraints. If for many addicts compulsion is a useful component of treatment, it is not clear how compulsion could be achieved in a society in which purchasing, possessing, and using the drug were legal. It could be managed, I suppose, but I would not want to have to answer the challenge from the American Civil Liberties Union that it is wrong to compel a person to undergo treatment for consuming a legal commodity.

Next, education. We are now investing substantially in drug-education programs in the schools. Though we do not yet know for certain what will work, there are some promising leads. But I wonder how credible such programs would be if they were aimed at dissuading children from doing something perfectly legal. We could, of course, treat drug education like smoking education: inhaling crack and inhaling tobacco are both legal, but you should not do it because it is bad for you. That tobacco is bad for you is easily shown; the Surgeon General has seen to that. But what do we say about crack? It is pleasurable, but devoting yourself to so much pleasure is not a good idea (though perfectly legal)? Unlike tobacco, cocaine will not give you cancer or emphysema, but it will lead you to neglect your duties to family, job, and neighborhood? Everybody is doing cocaine, but you should not?

Again, it might be possible under a legalized regime to have effective drug-prevention programs, but their effectiveness would depend heavily, I think, on first having decided that cocaine use, like tobacco use, is purely a matter of practical consequences; no fundamental moral significance attaches to either. But if we believe—as I do—that dependency on certain mind-altering drugs *is* a moral issue and that their illegality rests in part on their immorality, then legalizing them undercuts, if it does not eliminate altogether, the moral message.

That message is at the root of the distinction we now make between nicotine and cocaine. Both are highly addictive; both have harmful physical effects.

But we treat the two drugs differently, not simply because nicotine is so widely used as to be beyond the reach of effective prohibition, but because its use does not destroy the user's essential humanity. Tobacco shortens one's life, cocaine debases it. Nicotine alters one's habits, cocaine alters one's soul. The heavy use of crack, unlike the heavy use of tobacco, corrodes those natural sentiments of sympathy and duty that constitute our human nature and make possible our social life. To say, as does Nadelmann, that distinguishing morally between tobacco and cocaine is "little more than a transient prejudice" is close to saying that morality itself is but a prejudice.

THE ALCOHOL PROBLEM

Now we have arrived where many arguments about legalizing drugs begin: is there any reason to treat heroin and cocaine differently from the way we treat alcohol?

There is no easy answer to that question because, as with so many human problems, one cannot decide simply on the basis either of moral principles or of individual consequences; one has to temper any policy by a common-sense judgment of what is possible. Alcohol, like heroin, cocaine, PCP, and marijuana, is a drug—that is, a mood-altering substance—and consumed to excess it certainly has harmful consequences: auto accidents, barroom fights, bedroom shootings. It is also, for some people, addictive. We cannot confidently compare the addictive powers of these drugs, but the best evidence suggests that crack and heroin are much more addictive than alcohol.

Many people, Nadelmann included, argue that since the health and financial costs of alcohol abuse are so much higher than those of cocaine or heroin abuse, it is hypocritical folly to devote our efforts to preventing cocaine or drug use. But as Mark Kleiman of Harvard has pointed out, this comparison is quite misleading. What Nadelmann is doing is showing that a *legalized* drug (alcohol) produces greater social harm than *illegal* ones (cocaine and heroin). But of course. Suppose that in the 1920's we had made heroin and cocaine legal and alcohol illegal. Can anyone doubt that Nadelmann would now be writing that it is folly to continue our ban on alcohol because cocaine and heroin are so much more harmful?

And let there be no doubt about it—widespread heroin and cocaine use are associated with all manner of ills. Thomas Bewley found that the mortality rate of British heroin addicts in 1968 was 28 times as high as the death rate of the same age group of non-addicts, even though in England at the time an addict could obtain free or low-cost heroin and clean needles from British clinics. Perform the following mental experiment: suppose we legalized heroin and cocaine in this country. In what proportion of auto fatalities would the state police report that the driver was nodding off on heroin or recklessly driving on a coke high? In what proportion of spouse-assault and child-abuse cases would the local police report that crack was involved? In what proportion of industrial accidents would safety investigators report that the forklift or drill-press operator was in a drug-induced stupor or frenzy? We do not know exactly what the proportion would be, but anyone who asserts that it would not be much higher than it is now would have to believe that these drugs have little appeal except when they are illegal. And that is nonsense.

An advocate of legalization might concede that social harm—perhaps harm equivalent to that already produced by alcohol—would follow from making cocaine and heroin generally available. But at least, he might add, we would have the problem "out in the open" where it could be treated as a matter of "public health." That is well and good, *if* we knew how to treat—that is, cure—heroin and cocaine abuse. But we do not know how to do it for all the people who would need such help. We are having only limited success in coping with chronic alcoholics. Addictive behavior is immensely difficult to change, and the best methods for changing it—living in drug-free therapeutic communities, becoming faithful members of Alcoholics Anonymous or Narcotics Anonymous—require great personal commitment, a quality that is, alas, in short supply among the very persons—young people, disadvantaged people—who are often most at risk for addiction.

Suppose that today we had, not 15 million alcohol abusers, but half a million. Suppose that we already knew what we have learned from our long experience with the widespread use of alcohol. Would we make whiskey legal? I do not know, but I suspect there would be a lively debate. The Surgeon General would remind us of the risks alcohol poses to pregnant women. The National Highway Traffic Safety Administration would point to the likelihood of more highway fatalities caused by drunk drivers. The Food and Drug Administration might find that there is a nontrivial increase in cancer associated with alcohol consumption. At the same time the police would report great difficulty in keeping illegal whiskey out of our cities, officers being corrupted by bootleggers, and alcohol addicts often resorting to crime to feed their habit. Libertarians, for their part, would argue that every citizen has a right to drink anything he wishes and that drinking is, in any event, a "victimless crime."

However the debate might turn out, the central fact would be that the problem was still, at that point, a small one. The government cannot legislate away the addictive tendencies in all of us, nor can it remove completely even the most dangerous addictive substances. But it can cope with harms when the harms are still manageable.

SCIENCE AND ADDICTION

One advantage of containing a problem while it is still containable is that it buys time for science to learn more about it and perhaps to discover a cure. Almost unnoticed in the current debate over legalizing drugs is that basic science has made rapid strides in identifying the underlying neurological processes involved in some forms of addiction. Stimulants such as cocaine and amphetamines alter the way certain brain cells communicate with one another. That alteration is complex and not entirely understood, but in simplified form it involves modifying the way in which a neurotransmitter called dopamine sends signals from one cell to another.

When dopamine crosses the synapse between two cells, it is in effect carrying a message from the first cell to activate the second one. In certain parts of the brain that message is experienced as pleasure. After the message is delivered, the dopamine returns to the first cell. Cocaine apparently blocks this return, or "reuptake," so that the excited cell and others nearby continue to send pleasure messages. When the exaggerated high produced by cocaine-influenced dopamine finally ends, the brain cells may (in ways that are still a matter of dispute) suffer from an extreme lack of dopamine, thereby making the individual unable to experience any pleasure at all. This would explain why cocaine users often feel so depressed after enjoying the drug. Stimulants may also affect the way in which other neurotransmitters, such as serotonin and noradrenaline, operate.

Whatever the exact mechanism may be, once it is identified it becomes possible to use drugs to block either the effect of cocaine or its tendency to produce dependency. There have already been experiments using desipramine, imipramine, bromocriptine, carbamazepine, and other chemicals. There are some promising results.

Tragically, we spend very little on such research, and the agencies funding it have not in the past occupied very influential or visible posts in the federal bureaucracy. If there is one aspect of the "war on drugs" metaphor that I dislike, it is its tendency to focus attention almost exclusively on the troops in the trenches, whether engaged in enforcement or treatment, and away from the research-and-development efforts back on the home front where the war may ultimately be decided.

I believe that the prospects of scientists in controlling addiction will be strongly influenced by the size and character of the problem they face. If the problem is a few hundred thousand chronic, high-dose users of an illegal product, the chances of making a difference at a reasonable cost will be much greater than if the problem is a few million chronic users of legal substances. Once a drug is legal, not only will its use increase but many of those who then use it will prefer the drug to the treatment: they will want the pleasure, whatever the cost to themselves or their families, and they will resist—probably successfully—any effort to wean them away from experiencing the high that comes from inhaling a legal substance.

IF I AM WRONG...

No one can know what our society would be like if we changed the law to make access to cocaine, heroin, and PCP easier. I believe, for reasons given, that the result would be a sharp increase in use, a more widespread degradation of the human personality, and a greater rate of accidents and violence.

I may be wrong. If I am, then we will needlessly have incurred heavy costs in law enforcement and some forms of criminality. But if I am right, and the legalizers prevail anyway, then we will have consigned millions of people, hundreds of thousands of infants, and hundreds of neighborhoods to a life of oblivion and disease. To the lives and families destroyed by alcohol we will have added countless more destroyed by cocaine, heroin, PCP, and whatever else a basement scientist can invent.

Human character is formed by society; indeed, human character is inconceivable without society,

and good character is less likely in a bad society. Will we, in the name of an abstract doctrine of radical individualism, and with the false comfort of suspect predictions, decide to take the chance that somehow individual decency can survive amid a more general level of degradation?

I think not. The American people are too wise for that, whatever the academic essayists and cocktail-party pundits may say. But if Americans today are less wise than I suppose, then Americans at some future time will look back on us now and wonder, what kind of people were they that they could have done such a thing?

A Moral Right to Use Drugs

DOUGLAS N. HUSAK

Accurate or not, the perception that drug use is out of control has triggered an enormous state response. Illegal drugs have become the single most important concern of our criminal justice system. Although estimates are imprecise, tens of billions of dollars are probably spent to enforce LAD [laws against drugs] every year, and the less direct costs of the war on drugs are several times greater. Ronald Hamowy describes this war as "the most expensive intrusion into the private lives of Americans ever undertaken in the nation's history."

About 750,000 of the 28 million illegal drug users are arrested every year. Between one-quarter and one-third of all felony charges involve drug offenses. The severity of a sentence has almost no limits for, as the Supreme Court has recently held, a term of life imprisonment without parole for the offense of possession of 677 grams of cocaine is not cruel and unusual punishment. As a result, courts have become clogged, and prison overcrowding is legendary. The U.S. Sentencing Commission has estimated that within fifteen years the Anti-Drug Abuse Act passed by Congress in 1986 will cause the proportion of inmates incarcerated for drug violations to rise from

one-third to one-half of all defendants sentenced to federal prison. The costs of punishment threaten to drain the treasury, as each prisoner requires expenditures of between $10,000 and $40,000 per year. Since the average punishment for a drug conviction has risen to seventy-seven months in prison, each new inmate will cost taxpayers approximately $109,000 for the duration of the sentence.

Law enforcement officials continue to exercise broad discretion in arresting and prosecuting drug offenders. More than three-quarters of those arrested are eventually charged with possession, typically of marijuana. Many crimes of possession involve amounts that include a presumption of intent to distribute. Sometimes the quantity of drugs that creates this presumption is small. Moreover, the means used to measure the quantity of given drugs can be peculiar. Since statutes typically refer to a "mixture or substance containing a detectable amount" of a drug, the weight of the entire mixture

From Douglas N. Husak, "A Moral Right to Use Drugs," *Drugs and Rights* (New York: Cambridge University Press, 1992).

or substance is included when calculating the quantity of a drug. If a tiny dose of LSD has been placed on a tab of paper or a cube of sugar, the weight of the tab or cube is included in the determination of the amount of the drug. The Supreme Court has recently held this practice to be constitutional.

The true extent of the war on drugs cannot be measured in quantities of dollars spent or numbers of defendants punished. The enforcement of drug laws has diminished precious civil liberties, eroding gains for which Americans have made major sacrifices for over two centuries. Increasingly common are evictions, raids, random searches, confiscations of driver's licenses, withdrawals of federal benefits such as education subsidies, and summary forfeitures of property....

First, why do so many Americans use recreational drugs? Or, more specifically, why do so many Americans use the kinds of recreational drugs of which the majority disapproves? The power of drugs per se can only be part of the explanation. Illegal drug use is less prevalent in many countries where drugs are plentiful, inexpensive, and higher in quality than those available in America. A more viable strategy to combat drugs might attempt to identify and change the conditions peculiar to America that have led to widespread use. For present purposes, I am less concerned to attempt to identify these conditions than to ask why this issue has received so little attention from drug prohibitionists. It is hard to see how a long-term solution to the drug problem can be found without knowing why so many Americans are motivated to break the law in the first place....

A second issue is typically neglected in understanding and evaluating the war on drugs: Why has war been declared on illegal drugs? The simplistic answer is that drugs pose a threat to American society comparable to that of an invading enemy. Self-protection requires the mobilization of resources equivalent to those employed in time of war. For reasons that will become clear, I do not believe that this answer can begin to explain the extraordinary efforts of the state in combating drugs. Few wars—and certainly not the war on drugs—can be understood as a purely rational response to a grave social crisis.

No one doubts that the drug problem calls for state action, but why has a militaristic response been thought appropriate? The metaphors used to describe a phenomenon constrain what will appear to be an acceptable solution to it. If we really are at war against drugs, the alternative of decriminalization can be characterized only as a shameful retreat. William von Rabb, commissioner of the U.S. Customs Service, protests that legalization would be "an unconscionable surrender in a war [in which] there can be no substitute for total victory." But what is "total victory," and why is it necessary? A policy that does not work can always be changed, but a war that is not won can only be lost....

The public fears that America is a nation in decline. Crime, poverty, poor education, corporate mismanagement, and an unproductive and unmotivated work force are cited as evidence of this deterioration. Who, or what, should be blamed? The political climate limits the range of acceptable answers. Conservatives will not allow liberals to blame institutional structures for our problems. The difficulty cannot be that government has failed to create the right social programs to help people. Nor will liberals allow conservatives to blame individuals for our problems. The difficulty cannot be that people are lazy, stupid, or egocentric. What alternative explanations remain?

Illegal drugs provide the ideal scapegoat. Drugs are alleged to be so powerful that persons cannot be blamed very much for succumbing to them, as they could be blamed for not studying or working. And drugs are so plentiful and easy to conceal that government cannot be blamed very much for failing to eliminate them. Even better, most drugs are smuggled from abroad, so Americans can attribute our decline to the influence of foreigners. In blaming drugs, politicians need not fear that they will antagonize a powerful lobby that will challenge their allegations and mobilize voters against them. Almost no organized bodies defend the interests of drug users. Illegal drugs represent a "no-lose" issue, the safest of all political crusades.

A scapegoat would be imperfect unless there were at least some plausibility in the accusations of drug prohibitionists. Perhaps illegal drug use *has* increased crime, contributed to poverty, exacerbated the decline in education, and decreased the productivity of workers. Sometimes it may have done so in dramatic ways. The stories of the most decrepit victims of drug abuse lend themselves to biographies and television docudramas that make a deep and lasting impression on viewers. Everyone has seen vivid images of persons who were driven by drugs to commit brutal crimes, abandon their children, steal from their friends, drop out of school, stop going to work, and perhaps even die. In light of these consequences, who can condone illegal drug use?

I will attempt to show that a more accurate profile of the typical adult user of illegal drugs is less negative. This picture should emerge as a result of two factors that help to keep the drug problem in perspective. First, any number of other problems that receive almost no media attention and have not been made the target of a war contribute enormously to the problems America would like to solve. Second, the terrible problems associated with drug use occur in only a very small minority of cases....

I will not further explore these two issues I believe to be significant in understanding and evaluating the war on drugs. A more detailed treatment, however important, would only reinforce the social perspective on drugs that I am anxious to replace. I am not primarily interested in showing that the disutility of drug use has been exaggerated. Instead, my position is that moral and legal questions about drug use have been approached from too narrow a perspective. In a society that boasts of its concern for moral rights, debates about drugs have tended to lose sight of individuals. Decriminalization theorists have done as much to encourage this misperception as apologists for the status quo. Both sides frame the central question in similar terms: Do drugs cause more harm than drug laws? If the answer is no, LAD should be opposed; if the answer is yes, war should be waged. But this utilitarian approach, however insightful, is not the only perspective worth adopting. I will argue that utilitarian thinking is inappropriate to apply to the act of recreational drug use unless prohibition does not infringe the moral rights of drug users. It is by the standard of moral rights that the justifiability of the war on drugs should be assessed, and it is by the standard of moral rights that the justifiability of the war on drugs is most vulnerable.

A third and final issue about the war on drugs raises a matter that I will explore in greater depth: If there is to be a war on drugs, against which drugs should it be waged?...

How is "drug" defined by those who make the effort to define it at all? The answer depends on the discipline where an answer is sought. Perhaps the most frequently cited medical definition is "any substance other than food which by its chemical nature affects the structure or function of the living organism." Undoubtedly this definition is too broad. Nonetheless, I tentatively propose to adopt it until a better alternative becomes available.

Notice that this definition refers only to the pharmacological effect of a substance and not to its legal status. For two reasons, "drugs" must not be defined as synonymous with "illegal drugs." First, it would be absurd to suppose that a non-drug could become a drug, or that a drug could become a non-drug, simply by a stroke of the pen. A legislature can change the legal classification of a substance, but not the nature of that substance; it has no more power to decide that a substance is a drug than to decide that a substance is a food. Second, a philosophical study designed to evaluate the moral rights of drug users can hardly afford to rely uncritically on the existing legal status of substances, since the legitimacy of these determinations is part of what is under investigation. To suppose that "drugs" means "illegal drugs" begs important questions and concedes much of what I will challenge. In what follows, I will use the word "drug" to refer to both legal and illegal substances that satisfy the medical definition I cited.

No doubt this usage will create confusion. Despite the desirability of distinguishing "drugs" from "illegal drugs," there is ample evidence that the public tends to equate them. Surveys indicate, for example, that whereas 95 percent of adults recognize heroin as a drug, only 39 percent categorize alcohol as a drug, and a mere 27 percent identify tobacco as a drug. This tendency is pernicious. The widespread premise that only illegal substances are drugs lulls persons into accepting unsound arguments such as the following: Drugs are illegal; whatever is illegal is bad; we drink alcohol; what we do isn't bad; therefore, alcohol is not a drug. Clear thinking about this issue is impossible unless one realizes that whether a substance is a drug is a different question from whether that substance is or should be illegal....

RECREATIONAL DRUG USE

No one pretends that drugs are good or bad per se. Trying to decide whether drugs are good or bad is like trying to decide whether fires are good or bad: It depends on the purpose(s) for which they are used. As the examination of the Controlled Substances Act demonstrates, war has not really been declared on *drugs*. War has been declared on persons who make a certain *use* of drugs. I will describe this use as *recreational*.

By "recreational use," I mean consumption that is intended to promote the pleasure, happiness, or euphoria of the user. The more specific purposes that are encompassed under this broad umbrella include sociability, relaxation, alleviation of boredom, conviviality, feelings of harmony, enhancement of sexuality, and the like. Although borderline cases are numerous, paradigm examples of recreational drug use are plentiful. Interviews with users indicate that they are most likely to consume drugs on two general occasions. First, they use drugs to attempt to improve what they anticipate will be a good time. Hence drug use is frequent during parties, concerts, and sex. Second, they use drugs to attempt to make mindless and routine chores less boring. Hence drug use is frequent during house cleaning and cooking. I regard these as paradigm examples of recreational use.

The distinction between recreational and non-recreational drug use does *not* purport to sort drugs into categories based on their pharmacological properties. Instead, this distinction sorts drug *use* into categories. The claim that a given drug is "recreational" can only mean that it is typically used for a recreational purpose. More precisely, "recreational drug" is elliptical for "drug that is used recreationally." Any drug can be, and probably has been, used for almost any purpose.

The concept of recreational use can be clarified by contrasting it with other purposes for using drugs. The most familiar nonrecreational reason to use drugs is medical. Although most drug use is either recreational or medical, these categories do not begin to exhaust the purposes for which drugs are consumed. Some persons take drugs for the explicit purpose of committing suicide. Others take drugs ceremonially, in the course of religious rituals. Still others take drugs in order to enhance their performance in competitive sports. Undoubtedly this list could be expanded, but I will make no attempt to provide a comprehensive account of the many reasons for using drugs....

Undoubtedly my focus on recreational drug use will give rise to the criticism that my approach is academic, middle class, and unresponsive to the realities of drug use in impoverished neighborhoods. Drug use in ghettos, it will be said, is not recreational. The less fortunate members of our society do not use drugs to facilitate their enjoyment at concerts but to escape from the harsh realities of their daily lives. Here, at least, gloom and despair play a central role in explaining the high incidence of drug use....

Finally, the empirical facts are ambiguous in proving that illegal drug use is a special problem for the black community. Only 20 percent of all illegal drug users are black. Whites are more likely than blacks to have tried illegal drugs, and cocaine in particular, at some time in their lives. The more drug prohibitionists succeed in portraying drug use as a ghetto phenomenon, born of frustration and despair, the easier it is to lose sight of the repudiation of liberal values that LAD entails. As I will emphasize time and time again, too much of our policy about illegal drug use is based on generalizations from worst-case scenarios that do not conform to the reality of typical drug use. I hope to undermine the inaccurate stereotypes of drug use and drug users reinforced by this objection. LAD prohibits drug use by members of all races and classes; a legal policy applicable to all should not be based on the perceived problems of a few.

THE DECRIMINALIZATION MOVEMENT

...Courts and jails have become clogged as a result of "get-tough" policies toward drug offenders. The impact of drug offenses has led a number of commentators to speak of a collapse of the criminal justice system. Federal courts have become "drug courts," where narcotics prosecutions now account for 44 percent of all criminal trials, up 229 percent in the past decade. In many jurisdictions, delays in criminal cases not involving drugs or in the adjudication of civil disputes have become intolerable. The number of Americans behind bars has recently exceeded the one million mark and sets new records every day. Prisons cannot be built fast enough to accommodate drug offenders....

Among the more serious effects of prohibition is discrimination against the poor, who increasingly consume a higher and higher percentage of illegal drugs. Although two-thirds of weekly drug users in New York State in 1987 were white, 91 percent of the persons convicted and sentenced to state prison for drug-related offenses were either black or Hispanic. Therapeutic treatment is frequently provided for middle- and upper-class users; prison is the preferred mode of "treatment" for the underprivileged....

Finally and most significantly, the war on drugs is counterproductive in making criminals of tens of millions of Americans whose behavior is otherwise lawful. Most drug users are lucky to escape detection. Others are less fortunate. Countless numbers of offenders have been forced to suffer long terms of imprisonment for violating laws that may not be morally justified. Even those who are eventually acquitted spend tremendous sums of time and money defending themselves in court....

ARGUMENTS FOR CRIMINALIZATION

Defenses of and attacks against arguments for decriminalization have become so familiar that it is easy to forget that the burden of proof should be placed on those who favor the use of criminal penalties. When arguing about criminalization, most philosophers begin with a "presumption of freedom," or liberty, which places the onus of justification on those who would interfere with what a person wants to do....

The case for or against LAD depends on which side has the better arguments; there is no need to resort to a burden of proof in assessing this controversy. In any event, a second and equally familiar presumption cuts in the opposite direction. A "presumption in favor of the status quo" allocates the burden of proof on those who oppose any change in current laws against the use of recreational drugs. No one has any clear idea about what weight to assign to these "clashing presumptions." For this reason, it is probably unproductive to worry too much about who should bear the burden of proof on this issue....

I assume without much argument that a respectable defense of criminal legislation must demonstrate that it is needed to prevent *harm*. Everyone agrees that persons lack a moral right to cause harm, so criminal laws that prohibit harmful conduct do not violate the basic principles I have described. Punishment of a person who causes harm can be justified by reference to the offender's desert. But in the absence of harm, criminal sanctions are undeserved and unjustified.

The least controversial rationale in favor of criminalization is that the conduct to be prohibited is harmful *to others*. Many legal philosophers, following the lead of Mill, believe that harm to others is a necessary condition that any criminal law must satisfy in order to be justified. This position has been defended most ably by Joel Feinberg, from whose work I will borrow extensively....A more controversial rationale in favor of criminalization is that drug use should be prohibited because it is harmful *to users* themselves. Although a number of philosophers are unsympathetic to this rationale, paternalistic arguments in favor of LAD are frequently defended....

One common complaint about my strategy is misguided. Many philosophers are quick to point out that "no man is an island" and that whatever harms oneself also harms others or at least is capable of doing so. Perhaps there are no examples of "pure" or "unmixed" paternalism, that is, of an interference with liberty that is justifiable solely on the ground that the conduct to be prohibited harms the doer. I do not maintain otherwise. I do not suppose that a given activity can harm the doer but not others. The distinction between harm to oneself and harm to others is *not* a distinction between kinds of laws, but rather it is a distinction between *rationales* for laws. Any law might be defended by more than one rationale....

My premise that the use of the criminal sanction should require harm can be questioned. Perhaps arguments can be marshaled in support of LAD that do not depend on harm, either to oneself or to others. According to *legal moralism*, the wrongfulness of conduct per se, apart from its harmful effects, is a sufficient reason to impose criminal punishment.

Many drug prohibitionists resort to legal moralism in support of LAD. Bennett replies to the cost-benefit analyses of decriminalization theorists as follows: "I find no merit in the legalizers' case. The simple fact is that drug use is wrong. And the moral argument, in the end, is the most compelling argument." There can be no doubt that popular objections to illegal recreational drug use are often couched in the strongest possible moral terms. Drug use is frequently portrayed as sinful and wicked. Even an astute commentator like Kaplan admits that "I cannot escape the feeling that drug use, aside from any harm it does, is somehow wrong."

For two reasons, however, I will have little to say about legal moralism here. First, this principle is extremely problematic. No one has presented a compelling case in favor of legal moralism; responses from philosophers have been almost entirely negative. One recurrent theme of their attack is that legal moralism might be used to enforce community prejudice. The requirement that criminal liability presupposes a *victim* who has been *harmed* helps to assure that persons will not be punished simply for doing what those with political power do not want them to do.

Second, the application of legal moralism to LAD is utterly baffling. Why would anyone believe that drug use per se is immoral, apart from any harm it might cause? David Richards is right to suggest that these beliefs are "entitled to a respectful hearing." The trick is to translate them into respectable moral arguments that can provide the basis for criminal legislation in a secular state. As long as moral reservations about drug use are presented as unsupported conclusions—or as feelings—they will prove resistant to criticism. Arguments, not conclusions, are the objects of philosophical evaluation.

What, exactly, do drug prohibitionists believe to be immoral about recreational drug use? Two alternatives are possible. Does the alleged wrong consist in the act of drug use per se, or in the alteration of consciousness that drug use produces? The former alternative seems unlikely. Suppose that the physiology of persons were altered so that a given drug no longer produced any psychological effect. Could anyone continue to believe that the use of that drug would still be immoral? In any event, contemporary Americans widely reject the view that the act of drug use is inherently wrong. Few condemn the moderate use of alcohol. The subdued moral opposition

to alcohol heard today is light years away from the level of outrage expressed by zealots during the temperance movement.

The latter alternative seems no more attractive. Why should the alteration of consciousness produced by drug use be immoral, apart from any harm that might result? Some theorists have proposed that practices such as long-distance running and meditation can trigger natural neurological reactions that alter consciousness in respects that are phenomenologically indistinguishable from the effects of drug use. No one has suggested that such practices are immoral, and for good reason. There is ample reason to doubt that harmless experiences are among the kinds of things that *can* be immoral.

Perhaps many Americans share a vague conviction that some but not all ways of altering consciousness, by the use of some but not all drugs, is immoral. If this conviction could be defended, the particular experience of alcohol intoxication might be upheld as morally permissible, whereas the experiences of intoxication produced by various illegal drugs could be condemned. As it stands, however, this conviction is a conclusion in search of an argument. Typically, persons appeal to harm, either to oneself or to others, in attempts to differentiate between intoxication from alcohol and intoxication from illegal drugs. In this guise, the argument should be taken seriously. What is less clear is how to understand a version of this argument that does *not* appeal to harm. The terrain here is so uncertain that no one should have any clear idea about how to proceed....

Moral objections to drug use might also be derived from an ideal of human excellence. Drug use might not be conducive to the attainment of a particular conception of virtue. These arguments are frequently endorsed by drug prohibitionists. According to Bennett, "Drug use degrades human character, and a purposeful, self governing society ignores its people's character at great peril." James Q. Wilson confines his virtue-based arguments to illegal drugs: "Tobacco shortens one's life, cocaine debases it. Nicotine alters one's habits, cocaine alters one's soul." What conception of virtue is employed here? The Christian tradition, for example, identifies virtue with a personal imitation of Christ, emphasizing extraordinary sacrifice in the service of others. According to this tradition, drug use, like any other recreational activity, is suspect. Recreational activities are nonaltruistic and self-indulgent....

The answer is that virtue-based arguments fail to support criminal punishment for recreational drug use. Bennett is correct that a society should not "ignore its people's character." But it does not follow that the protection of character is an appropriate objective of the criminal law. The prohibitions of the criminal law describe the minimum of acceptable behavior beneath which persons are not permitted to sink. Virtue-based considerations cannot be used to show that moderate self-indulgence, as well as any temporary impairment of rationality and autonomy brought about by most incidents of drug use, fall below this permissible level. The criminal law should not enforce a particular conception of human excellence, however attractive it may be. A theory of virtue might be applied to subject drug use to moral criticism. Opponents of LAD need not believe that drug use is beyond moral reproach. But no one should think that persons deserve to be punished as criminals because their behavior falls short of an ideal....

A MORAL RIGHT: MISINTERPRETATIONS

I have concluded that the arguments in favor of believing that adults have a moral right to use drugs recreationally are more persuasive than the arguments on the other side. This conclusion is easily misinterpreted....

First, the conclusion that adults have a moral right to use drugs recreationally does not amount to advocating drug use. The distinction between encouraging conduct and conceding that adults have a right to engage in it might seem too obvious to belabor, except that many drug prohibitionists have apparently failed to recognize it. This basic distinction is widely appreciated in most other contexts. Adults have the moral right to preach communism or to practice Buddhism. Yet no one who defends this right would be misunderstood to recommend a conversion to communism or Buddhism.

Nonetheless, one of the most widely voiced objections to the proposal to repeal LAD is that it would express the wrong symbolism about drug

use, especially among adolescents. John Lawn maintains: "Legalization of drugs would send the wrong message to our nation's youth. At a time when we have urged our young people to 'just say no' to drugs, legalization would suggest that they need only say no until they reach an appropriate age." Drug prohibitionists who emphasize the symbolic significance of LAD seldom offer a detailed account of why they believe it to be sufficiently important to justify a war on drugs. Is sending the right message about drug use intrinsically or instrumentally valuable? Perhaps this argument is just another version of the concern that a repeal of LAD would encourage drug use.

In order to dispel the impression that support for a right to use drugs is tantamount to encouraging drug use, those who reject LAD should be described as endorsing a *pro-choice* position on recreational drug use. This label has been carefully crafted by persons who uphold the right of women to terminate their pregnancies. These persons are not "pro-death," or "anti-life," as their critics would like the public to believe. Perhaps many of them would not elect abortion as their own solution to an unwanted pregnancy. Still, they believe that women have the right to make this choice for themselves. Misunderstanding would be avoided if the debate about the decriminalization of recreational drug use borrowed this terminology. The conclusion that adults have a moral right to use drugs recreationally should be described as the pro-choice position on recreational drug use....

Should the rights of adults be infringed in order to ensure that the wrong message is not received by the public (to whom this argument extends very little credit)? The main problem is that this rationale for LAD would not allow the decriminalization of *any* activity that is less than exemplary. At bottom, this argument is simply another utilitarian defense of the status quo. The rights of some adults should not be sacrificed so that others do not misinterpret a message. This injustice is multiplied when the rights of millions of Americans are at stake....

A second related but distinct misunderstanding of my position is as follows. The conclusion that the adult use of recreational drugs is protected by a moral right does not entail that drug use is beyond moral reproach. The exercise of a moral right may be subject to criticism. Perhaps all recreational drug use, legal and illegal, is morally tainted.... I remain skeptical that a virtue-based objection to all recreational drug use can be defended, although no one should be confident until some philosopher attempts to do so. In any event, some instances of recreational drug use are morally objectionable, beyond those in the special circumstances in which users create an impermissible risk of harm to others. These objectionable instances might be described by the pejorative term *drug abuse*....

If the moral right to use drugs recreationally is to be respected, the need to minimize disutility leaves society with little choice but to discourage drug abuse. The process by which this goal is reached might loosely be described as "drug education." But this process differs from drug education as it is usually conceived. Most educational programs are prevention programs. As so designed, education has generally been deemed a failure, largely because it has not been shown to achieve its objective of decreasing drug use. Yet there may be more reason for optimism if the goal of education is to decrease drug abuse.

As so construed, drug education may never have been tried. No existing educational program has attempted either to separate use from abuse or to indicate how abuse might be avoided by means other than abstinence. The introduction of scientifically respectable materials in drug education programs has been politically unacceptable....

Since I make no attempt to solve America's drug problem as a matter of social policy, I will hazard only one final observation about the prospects for success that drug education as so conceived will minimize drug abuse. To demand that recreational drug users show restraint over the time, place, and quantity of their consumption is not to require the impossible. In fact, virtually every drug user exhibits some degree of control over her consumption. The means by which users manage to avoid abuse deserve careful study and extensive publicity. Perhaps a successful educational program should seek out responsible drug users. In no other context is experience perceived as a liability, unless the experience was so devastating to the educator that he now appreciates the folly of his drug use and counsels total abstinence. Still, informal cultural controls over the use of the most dangerous drugs (such as those that exist in Peru) do not emerge quickly. To respect the moral right of adults to use recreational drugs may be painful, at least in the short run. But the protection of moral rights has a value to Americans that is not easily expressed in the utilitarian calculus of costs and benefits in which the decriminalization debate is usually cast.

ARGUMENT 4 ESSAY QUESTIONS

1. What is Wilson's harm argument against decriminalization? Is his argument sound? How might Wilson's critics criticize the argument?
2. What is Wilson's legal moralism argument? Do you accept the theory of legal moralism? Why or why not?
3. Why do some supporters of decriminalization think arguments about the harm of drug use are beside the point? Should the case for or against decriminalization be based mainly on utilitarian considerations? Why or why not?

5. THE ARGUMENT AGAINST PATERNALISM

John Stuart Mill gives us the classic statement of the case against paternalism. The state may legitimately coerce people in order to prevent harm to others, he says, but limiting people's freedom so they don't harm themselves is out of the question. Self-harm is never a valid reason to decrease personal autonomy: "[A person's] own good, either physical or moral, is not sufficient warrant."[11] He maintains that the justification for this anti-paternalism stance is utilitarian. A society that grants people liberty to do as they please as long as they do not harm others will generate more happiness for all than one that does not. On such grounds, many have urged decriminalization.

As you might expect, some use utilitarian arguments to *justify* paternalism, to make the case for criminalization. They maintain that for drug users, laws forbidding drug abuse yield more happiness, pleasure, or well-being than decriminalization does. Unrestrained use of drugs creates all sorts of woes for users; legal punishment reduces drug use and therefore minimizes the hardships.

People who call for decriminalization, however, believe that the empirical facts are on their side. They contend that many of the claims about the health hazards of drug use are exaggerated, too often based on worst-case scenarios that do not reflect typical drug use. Generalizations about drug use are frequently based on heavy users, they say, but most people who take drugs are moderate users. Those favoring decriminalization also point out a telling contrast between the way most dangerous recreational activities are regarded and the way recreational drug use is viewed. As Husak says,

> [N]o other recreational activity is singled out for severe punishment because of its risks to health. The only conceivable basis for treating illicit drugs differently from other recreational activities is that the former are more risky, by a substantial degree, than the latter. But illicit drug use is not more risky than any number of these behaviors.... [T]he use of illicit drugs is not especially high on the list of health problems in the United States today.[12]

As with the debates about harm, paternalism arguments may involve appeals to autonomy, the right of self-determination. As it turns out, the concept of autonomy has been used to bolster arguments both for and against decriminalization.

Those advocating decriminalization, of course, argue that drug laws are an assault on autonomy, an unwarranted restriction on a person's liberty to direct his or her own

---

[11] Mill, *On Liberty*.

[12] Douglas Husak and Peter de Marneffe, *The Legalization of Drugs* (New York: Cambridge University Press, 2005), 52.

life. Those favoring drug laws contend that state paternalism helps to *preserve* autonomy. They take inspiration from—strangely enough—Mill, who argued that no one should be free to willingly become a slave, for such an act would be a forfeiture of freedom. "The principle of freedom," says Mill, "cannot require that [the willing slave] should be free not to be free. It is not freedom, to be allowed to alienate his freedom."[13] So supporters of criminalization argue that paternalistic laws are necessary to prevent people from willingly giving up their autonomy—which is essentially what they do when they become addicted to drugs.

Paternalism

GERALD DWORKIN

Neither one person, nor any number of persons, is warranted in saying to another human creature of ripe years, that he shall not do with his life for his own benefit what he chooses to do with it.

—MILL

I do not want to go along with a volunteer basis. I think a fellow should be compelled to become better and not let him use his discretion whether he wants to get smarter, more healthy or more honest.

—GENERAL HERSHEY

I take as my starting point the "one very simple principle" proclaimed by Mill in *On Liberty* . . . "That principle is, that the sole end for which mankind are warranted, individually or collectively, in interfering with the liberty of action of any of their number, is self-protection. That the only purpose for which power can be rightfully exercised over any member of a civilized community, against his will, is to prevent harm to others. He cannot rightfully be compelled to do or forbear because it will be better for him to do so, because it will make him happier, because, in the opinion of others, to do so would be wise, or even right."[1]

This principle is neither "one" nor "very simple." It is at least two principles; one asserting that self-protection or the prevention of harm to others is sometimes a sufficient warrant and the other claiming that the individual's own good is *never* a sufficient warrant for the exercise of compulsion either by the society as a whole or by its individual members. I assume that no one with the possible exception of extreme pacifists or anarchists questions the correctness of the first half of the principle. This essay is an examination of the negative claim embodied in Mill's principle—the objection to paternalistic interferences with a man's liberty.

I

By paternalism I shall understand roughly the interference with a person's liberty of action justified by reasons referring exclusively to the welfare, good, happiness, needs, interests or values of the person being coerced. One is always well-advised to

---

[13] Mill, *On Liberty*.

illustrate one's definitions by examples but it is not easy to find "pure" examples of paternalistic interferences. For almost any piece of legislation is justified by several different kinds of reasons and even if historically a piece of legislation can be shown to have been introduced for purely paternalistic motives, it may be that advocates of the legislation with an anti-paternalistic outlook can find sufficient reasons justifying the legislation without appealing to the reasons which were originally adduced to support it. Thus, for example, it may be the original legislation requiring motorcyclists to wear safety helmets was introduced for purely paternalistic reasons. But the Rhode Island Supreme Court recently upheld such legislation on the grounds that it was "not persuaded that the legislature is powerless to prohibit individuals from pursuing a course of conduct which could conceivably result in their becoming public charges," thus clearly introducing reasons of a quite different kind. Now I regard this decision as being based on reasoning of a very dubious nature but it illustrates the kind of problem one has in finding examples. The following is a list of the kinds of interferences I have in mind as being paternalistic.

II

1. Laws requiring motorcyclists to wear safety helmets when operating their machines.
2. Laws forbidding persons from swimming at a public beach when lifeguards are not on duty.
3. Laws making suicide a criminal offense.
4. Laws making it illegal for women and children to work at certain types of jobs.
5. Laws regulating certain kinds of sexual conduct, e.g. homosexuality among consenting adults in private.
6. Laws regulating the use of certain drugs which may have harmful consequences to the user but do not lead to anti-social conduct.
7. Laws requiring a license to engage in certain professions with those not receiving a license subject to fine or jail sentence if they do engage in the practice.
8. Laws compelling people to spend a specified fraction of their income on the purchase of retirement annuities. (Social Security)

9. Laws forbidding various forms of gambling (often justified on the grounds that the poor are more likely to throw away their money on such activities than the rich who can afford to).
10. Laws regulating the maximum rates of interest for loans.
11. Laws against duelling.

In addition to laws which attach criminal or civil penalties to certain kinds of action there are laws, rules, regulations, decrees, which make it either difficult or impossible for people to carry out their plans and which are also justified on paternalistic grounds. Examples of this are:

1. Laws regulating the types of contracts which will be upheld as valid by the courts, e.g. (an example of Mill's to which I shall return) no man may make a valid contract for perpetual involuntary servitude.
2. Not allowing as a defense to a charge of murder or assult the consent of the victim.
3. Requiring members of certain religious sects to have compulsory blood transfusions. This is made possible by not allowing the patient to have recourse to civil suits for assault and battery and by means of injunctions.
4. Civil commitment procedures when these are specifically justified on the basis of preventing the person being committed from harming himself. (The D. C. Hospitalization of the Mentally Ill Act provides for involuntary hospitalization of a person who "is mentally ill, and because of that illness, is likely to injure *himself* or others if allowed to remain at liberty." The term injure in this context applies to unintentional as well as intentional injuries.)
5. Putting fluorides in the community water supply.

All of my examples are of existing restrictions on the liberty of individuals. Obviously one can think of interferences which have not yet been imposed. Thus one might ban the sale of cigarettes, or require that people wear safety-belts in automobiles (as opposed to merely having them installed) enforcing this by not allowing motorists to sue for injuries even when caused by other drivers if the motorist was not wearing a seat-belt at the time of the accident....

III

Bearing these examples in mind let me return to a characterization of paternalism. I said earlier that I meant by the term, roughly, interference with a person's liberty for his own good. But as some of the examples show the class of persons whose good is invoiced is not always identical with the class of persons whose freedom is restricted. Thus in the case of professional licensing it is the practitioner who is directly interfered with and it is the would-be patient whose interests are presumably being served. Not allowing the consent of the victim to be a defense to certain types of crime primarily affects the would-be aggressor but it is the interests of the willing victim that we are trying to protect. Sometimes a person may fall into both classes as would be the case if we banned the manufacture and sale of cigarettes and a given manufacturer happened to be a smoker as well.

Thus we may first divide paternalistic interferences into "pure" and "impure" cases. In "pure" paternalism the class of persons whose freedom is restricted is identical with the class of persons whose benefit is intended to be promoted by such restrictions. Examples: the making of suicide a crime, requiring passengers in automobiles to wear seat-belts, requiring a Christian Scientist to receive a blood transfusion. In the case of "impure" paternalism in trying to protect the welfare of a class of persons we find that the only way to do so will involve restricting the freedom of other persons besides those who are benefited. Now it might be thought that there are no cases of "impure" paternalism since any such case could always be justified on non-paternalistic grounds, i.e. in terms of preventing harm to others. Thus we might ban cigarette manufacturers from continuing to manufacture their product on the grounds that we are preventing them from causing illness to others in the same way that we prevent other manufacturers from releasing pollutants into the atmosphere, thereby causing danger to the members of the community. The difference is, however, that in the former but not the latter case the harm is of such a nature that it could be avoided by those individuals affected if they so chose. The incurring of the harm requires, so to speak, the active cooperation of the victim. It would be mistaken theoretically and hypocritical in practice to assert that our interference in such cases is just like our interference in standard cases of protecting others from harm. At the very least someone interfered with in this way can reply that no one is complaining about his activities. It may be that impure paternalism requires arguments or reasons of a stronger kind in order to be justified since there are persons who are losing a portion of their liberty and they do not even have the solace of having it be done "in their own interest." Of course in some sense, if paternalistic justifications are ever correct then we are protecting others, we are preventing some from injuring others, but it is important to see the differences between this and the standard case.

Paternalism then will always involve limitations on the liberty of some individuals in their own interest but it may also extend to interferences with the liberty of parties whose interests are not in question.

IV

Finally, by way of some more preliminary analysis, I want to distinguish paternalistic interferences with liberty from a related type with which it is often confused. Consider, for example, legislation which forbids employees to work more than, say, 40 hours per week. It is sometimes argued that such legislation is paternalistic for if employees desired such a restriction on their hours of work they could agree among themselves to impose it voluntarily. But because they do not the society imposes its own conception of their best interests upon them by the use of coercion. Hence this is paternalism.

Now it may be that some legislation of this nature is, in fact, paternalistically motivated. I am not denying that. All I want to point out is that there is another possible way of justifying such measures which is not paternalistic in nature. It is not paternalistic because as Mill puts it in a similar context such measures are "required not to overrule the judgment of individuals respecting their own interest, but to give effect to that judgment they being unable to give effect to it except by concert, which concert again cannot be effectual unless it receives validity and sanction from the law."[2]

The line of reasoning here is a familiar one first found in Hobbes and developed with great sophistication by contemporary economists in the last decade or so. There are restrictions which are in the interests of a class of persons taken collectively but are such that the immediate interest of each individual is furthered by his violating the rule when others adhere to it. In such cases the individuals involved may need the use of compulsion to give effect to their collective judgment of their own interest by guaranteeing each individual compliance by the others. In these cases compulsion is not used to achieve some benefit which is not recognized to be a benefit by those concerned, but rather because it is the only feasible means of achieving some benefit which *is* recognized as such by all concerned. This way of viewing matters provides us with another characterization of paternalism in general. Paternalism might be thought of as the use of coercion to achieve a good which is not recognized as such by those persons for whom the good is intended. Again while this formulation captures the heart of the matter—it is surely what Mill is objecting to in *On Liberty*—the matter is not always quite like that. For example when we force motorcyclists to wear helmets we are trying to promote a good—the protection of the person from injury—which is surely recognized by most of the individuals concerned. It is not that a cyclist doesn't value his bodily integrity; rather, as a supporter of such legislation would put it, he either places, perhaps irrationally, another value or good (freedom from wearing a helmet) above that of physical well-being or, perhaps, while recognizing the danger in the abstract, he either does not fully appreciate it or he underestimates the likelihood of its occurring. But now we are approaching the question of possible justifications of paternalistic measures and the rest of this essay will be devoted to that question.

V

I shall begin for dialectical purposes by discussing Mill's objections to paternalism and then go on to discuss more positive proposals.... The stucture of Mill's argument is as follows:

1. Since restraint is an evil the burden of proof is on those who propose such restraint.
2. Since the conduct which is being considered is purely self-regarding, the normal appeal to the protection of the interests of others is not available.
3. Therefore we have to consider whether reasons involving reference to the individual's own good, happiness, welfare, or interests are sufficient to overcome the burden of justification.
4. We either cannot advance the interests of the individual by compulsion, or the attempt to do so involves evil which outweighs the good done.
5. Hence the promotion of the individual's own interests does not provide a sufficient warrant for the use of compulsion.

Clearly the operative premise here is 4 and it is bolstered by claims about the status of the individual as judge and appraiser of his welfare, interests, needs, etc.

With respect to his own feelings and circumstances, the most ordinary man or woman has means of knowledge immeasurably surpassing those that can be possessed by any one else.[3]

He is the man most interested in his own well-being: the interest which any other person, except in cases of strong personal attachment, can have in it, is trifling, compared to that which he himself has.[4]

These claims are used to support the following generalizations concerning the utility of compulsion for paternalistic purposes.

The interferences of society to overrule his judgment and purposes in what only regards himself must be grounded in general presumptions; which may be altogether wrong, and even if right, are as likely as not to be misapplied to individual cases.[5]

But the strongest of all the arguments against the interference of the public with purely personal conduct is that when it does interfere, the odds are that it interferes wrongly and in the wrong place.[6]

All errors which the individual is likely to commit against advice and warning are far outweighed by the evil of allowing others to constrain him to what they deem his good.[7]

Performing the utilitarian calculation by balancing the advantages and disadvantages we find that:

> Mankind are greater gainers by suffering each other to live as seems good to themselves, than by compelling each other to live as seems good to the rest.[8]

From which follows the operative premise 4.

This classical case of a utilitarian argument with all the premises spelled out is not the only line of reasoning present in Mill's discussion. There are asides, and more than asides, which look quite different and I shall deal with them later. But this is clearly the main channel of Mill's thought and it is one which has been subjected to vigorous attack from the moment it appeared—most often by fellow Utilitarians. The link that they have usually seized on is, as Fitzjames Stephen put it, the absence of proof that the "mass of adults are so well acquainted with their own interests and so much disposed to pursue them that no compulsion or restraint put upon them by any others for the purpose of promoting their interest can really promote them."[9] ...

Now it is interesting to note that Mill himself was aware of some of the limitations on the doctrine that the individual is the best judge of his own interests. In his discussion of government intervention in general (even where the intervention does not interfere with liberty but provides alternative institutions to those of the market) after making claims which are parallel to those just discussed, e.g.

> People understand their own business and their own interests better, and care for them more, than the government does, or can be expected to do.[10]

He goes on to an intelligent discussion of the "very large and conspicuous exceptions" to the maxim that:

> Most persons take a juster and more intelligent view of their own interest, and of the means of promoting it than can either be prescribed to them by a general enactment of the legislature, or pointed out in the particular case by a public functionary."[11]

Thus there are things

> of which the utility does not consist in ministering to inclinations, nor in serving the daily uses of life, and the want of which is least felt where the need is greatest. This is peculiarly true of those things which are chiefly useful as tending to raise the character of human beings. The uncultivated cannot be competent judges of cultivation. Those who most need to be made wiser and better, usually desire it least, and, if they desired it, would be incapable of finding the way to it by their own lights.
>
> ... A second exception to the doctrine that individuals are the best judges of their own interest, is when an individual attempts to decide irrevocably now what will be best for his interest at some future and distant time. The presumption in favor of individual judgment is only legitimate, where the judgment is grounded on actual, and especially on present, personal experience; not where it is formed antecedently to experience, and not suffered to be reversed even after experience has condemned it.[12]

The upshot of these exceptions is that Mill does not declare that there should never be government interference with the economy but rather that

> ... in every instance, the burden of making out a strong case should be thrown not on those who resist but on those who recommend government interference. Letting alone, in short, should be the general practice: every departure from it, unless required by some great good, is a certain evil.[13]

In short, we get a presumption not an absolute prohibition. The question is why doesn't the argument against paternalism go the same way?

A consistent Utilitarian can only argue against paternalism on the grounds that it (as a matter of fact) does not maximize the good. It is always a contingent question that may be refuted by the evidence. But there is also a non-contingent argument which runs through *On Liberty*. When Mill states that "there is a part of the life of every person who has come to years of discretion, within which the individuality of that person ought to rein uncontrolled either by any other person or by the public collectively" he is saying something about what it means to be a person, an autonomous agent. It is because coercing a person for his own good denies this status as an independent entity that Mill objects to it so strongly and in such absolute terms. To be able to choose is a good that is independent of the wisdom of what is chosen. A man's "mode" of laying out his existence is the best, not because it is the best in itself, but because it is his own mode.[14]

> It is the privilege and proper condition of a human being, arrived at the maturity of his faculties, to use and interpret experience in his own way.[15]

As further evidence of this line of reasoning in Mill consider the one exception to his prohibition against paternalism.

> In this and most civilised countries, for example, an engagement by which a person should sell himself, or allow himself to be sold, as a slave, would be null and void; neither enforced by law nor by opinion. The ground for thus limiting his power of voluntarily disposing of his own lot in life, is apparent, and is very clearly seen in this extreme case. The reason for not interfering, unless for the sake of others, with a person's voluntary acts, is consideration for his liberty. His voluntary choice is evidence that what he so chooses is desirable, or at least endurable, to him, and his good is on the whole best provided for by allowing him to take his own means of pursuing it. But by selling himself for a slave, he abdicates his liberty; he foregoes any further use of it beyond that single act.
> He therefore defeats, in his own case, the very purpose which is the justification of allowing him to dispose of himself. He is no longer free; but is thenceforth in a position which has no longer the presumption in its favour, that would be afforded by his voluntarily remaining in it. The principle of freedom cannot require that he should be free not to be free. It is not freedom to be allowed to alienate his freedom.[16]

Now leaving aside the fudging on the meaning of freedom in the last line it is clear that part of this argument is incorrect. While it is true that *future* choices of the slave are not reasons for thinking that what he chooses then is desirable for him, what is at issue is limiting his immediate choice; and since this choice is made freely, the individual may be correct in thinking that his interests are best provided for by entering such a contract. But the main

consideration for not allowing such a contract is the need to preserve the liberty of the person to make future choices. This gives us a principle—a very narrow one, by which to justify some paternalistic interferences. Paternalism is justified only to preserve a wider range of freedom for the individual in question. How far this principle could be extended, whether it can justify all the cases in which we are inclined upon reflection to think paternalistic measures justified remains to be discussed. What I have tried to show so far is that there are two strains of argument in Mill—one a straightforward Utilitarian mode of reasoning and one which relies not on the goods which free choice leads to but on the absolute value of the choice itself. The first cannot establish any absolute prohibition but at most a presumption and indeed a fairly weak one given some fairly plausible assumptions about human psychology; the second while a stronger line of argument seems to me to allow on its own grounds a wider range of paternalism than might be suspected. I turn now to a consideration of these matters.

VI

We might begin looking for principles governing the acceptable use of paternalistic power in cases where it is generally agreed that it is legitimate. Even Mill intends his principles to be applicable only to mature individuals, not those in what he calls "non-age." What is it that justifies us in interfering with children? The fact that they lack some of the emotional and cognitive capacities required in order to make fully rational decisions. It is an empirical question to just what extent children have an adequate conception of their own present and future interests but there is not much doubt that there are many deficiencies. For example it is very difficult for a child to defer gratification for any considerable period of time. Given these deficiencies and given the very real and permanent dangers that may befall the child it becomes not only permissible but even a duty of the parent to restrict the child's freedom in various ways. There is however an important moral limitation on the exercise of such parental power which is provided by the notion of the child eventually coming to see the correctness of his parents interventions. Parental paternalism may be thought of as a wager by the parent on the child's subsequent recognition of the wisdom of the restrictions. There is an emphasis on what could be called future-oriented consent—on what the child will come to welcome, rather than on what he does welcome.

The essence of this idea has been incorporated by idealist philosophers into various types of "real-will" theory as applied to fully adult persons. Extensions of paternalism are argued for by claiming that in various respects, chronologically mature individuals share the same deficiencies in knowledge, capacity to think rationally, and the ability to carry out decisions that children possess. Hence in interfering with such people we are in effect doing what they would do if they were fully rational. Hence we are not really opposing their will, hence we are not really interfering with their freedom. The dangers of this move have been sufficiently exposed by Berlin in his "Two Concepts of Liberty." I see no gain in theoretical clarity nor in practical advantage in trying to pass over the real nature of the interferences with liberty that we impose on others. Still the basic notion of consent is important and seems to me the only acceptable way of trying to delimit an area of justified paternalism.

Let me start by considering a case where the consent is not hypothetical in nature. Under certain conditions it is rational for an individual to agree that others should force him to act in ways which, at the time of action, the individual may not see as desirable. If, for example, a man knows that he is subject to breaking his resolves when temptation is present, he may ask a friend to refuse to entertain his request at some later stage.

A classical example is given in the Odyssey when Odysseus commands his men to tie him to the mast and refuse all future orders to be set free because he knows the power of the Sirens to enchant men with their songs. Here we are on relatively sound ground in later refusing Odysseus' request to be set free. He may even claim to have changed his mind but since it is just such changes that he wishes to guard against we are entitled to ignore them.

A process analogous to this may take place on a social rather than individual basis. An electorate may mandate its representatives to pass legislation which when it comes time to "pay the price" may be unpalatable. I may believe that a tax increase is necessary to halt inflation though I may resent the lower pay check each month. However in both this case and that of Odysseus the measure to be enforced is specifically requested by the party involved and at some point in time there is genuine consent and agreement on the part of those persons whose liberty is infringed. Such is not the case for the paternalistic measures we have been speaking about. What must be involved here is not consent to specific measures but rather consent to a system of government, run by elected representatives, with an understanding that they may act to safeguard our interests in certain limited ways.

I suggest that since we are all aware of our irrational propensities, deficiencies in cognitive and emotional capacities and avoidable and unavoidable ignorance it is rational and prudent for us to in effect take out "social insurance policies." We may argue for and against proposed paternalistic measures in terms of what fully rational individuals would accept as forms of protection. Now, clearly since the initial agreement is not about specific measures we are dealing with a more-or-less blank check and therefore there have to be carefully defined limits. What I am looking for are certain kinds of conditions which make it plausible to suppose that rational men could reach agreement to limit their liberty even when other men's interests are not affected.

Of course as in any kind of agreement schema there are great difficulties in deciding what rational individuals would or would not accept. Particularly in sensitive areas of personal liberty, there is always a danger of the dispute over agreement and rationality being a disguised version of evaluative and normative disagreement.

Let me suggest types of situations in which it seems plausible to suppose that fully rational individuals would agree to having paternalistic restrictions imposed upon them. It is reasonable to suppose that there are "goods" such as health which any person would want to have in order to pursue his own good—no matter how that good is conceived. This is an argument that is used in connection with compulsory education for children but it seems to me that it can be extended to other goods which have this character. Then one could agree that the attainment of such goods should be promoted even when not recognized to be such, at the moment, by the individuals concerned.

An immediate difficulty that arises stems from the fact that men are always faced with competing goods and that there may be reasons why even a value such as health—or indeed life—may be overridden by competing values. Thus the problem with the Christian Scientist and blood transfusions. It may be more important for him to reject "impure substances" than to go on living. The difficult problem that must be faced is whether one can give sense to the notion of a person irrationally attaching weights to competing values.

Consider a person who knows the statistical data on the probability of being injured when not wearing seat-belts in an automobile and knows the types and gravity of the various injuries. He also insists that the inconvenience attached to fastening the belt every time he gets in and out of the car outweighs for him the possible risks to himself. I am inclined in this case to think that such a weighing is irrational. Given his life plans which we are assuming are those of the average person, his interests and commitments already undertaken, I think it is safe to predict that we can find inconsistencies in his calculations at some point. I am assuming that this is not a man who for some conscious or unconscious reasons is trying to injure himself nor is he a man who just likes to "live dangerously." I am assuming that he is like us in all the relevant respects but just puts an enormously high negative value on inconvenience—one which does not seem comprehensible or reasonable.

It is always possible, of course to assimilate this person to creatures like myself. I, also, neglect to fasten my seat-belt and I concede such behavior is not rational but not because I weigh the inconvenience differently from those who fasten the belts. It is just that having made (roughly) the same calculation as everybody else I ignore it in my actions. [Note: a much better case of weakness of the will than those usually given in ethics texts.] A plausible explanation for this deplorable habit is that athough I know in some intellectual sense what the probabilities and risks are I do not fully appreciate them in an emotionally genuine manner.

We have two distinct types of situation in which a man acts in a non-rational fashion. In one case he attaches incorrect weights to some of his values; in the other he neglects to act in accordance with his actual preferences and desires. Clearly there is a stronger and more persuasive argument for paternalism in the latter situation. Here we are really not—by assumption—imposing a good on another person. But why may we not extend our interference to what we might call evaluative delusions? After all in the case of cognitive delusions we are prepared, often, to act against the expressed will of the person involved. If a man believes that when he jumps out the window he will float upwards—Robert Nozick's example—would not we detain him, forcibly if necessary? The reply will be that this man doesn't wish to be injured and if we could convince him that he is mistaken as to the consequences of his actions he would not wish to perform the action. But part of what is involved in claiming that a man who doesn't fasten his seat-belts is attaching an irrational weight to the inconvenience of fastening them is that if he were to be involved in an accident and severely injured he would look back and admit that the inconvenience wasn't as bad as all that. So there is a sense in which if I could convince him of the consequences of his actions he also would not wish to continue his present course of action. Now the notion of consequences being used here is covering a lot of ground. In one case it's being used to indicate what will or can happen as a result of a course of action and in the other it's making a prediction about the future evaluation of the consequences—in the first sense—of a course of action. And whatever the difference between facts and values—whether it be hard and fast or soft and slow—we are genuinely more reluctant to consent to interferences where evaluative differences are the issue. Let me now consider another factor which comes into play in some of these situations which may make an important difference in our willingness to consent to paternalistic restrictions.

Some of the decisions we make are of such a character that they produce changes which are in one or another way irreversible. Situations are created in which it is difficult or impossible to return to anything like the initial stage at which the decision was made. In particular some of these changes will make it impossible to continue to make reasoned choices in the future. I am thinking specifically of decisions which involve taking drugs that are physically or psychologically addictive and those which are destructive of one's mental and physical capacities.

I suggest we think of the imposition of paternalistic interferences in situations of this kind as being a kind of insurance policy which we take out against making decisions which are far-reaching, potentially dangerous and irreversible....

A second class of cases concerns decisions which are made under extreme psychological and sociological pressure. I am not thinking here of the making of the decision as being something one is pressured into—e.g. a good reason for making duelling illegal is that unless this is done many people might have to manifest their courage and integrity in ways in which they would rather not do so—but rather of decisions such as that to commit suicide which are usually made at a point where the individual is not thinking clearly and calmly about the nature of his decision. In addition, of course, this comes under the previous heading of all-too-irrevocable decision. Now there are practical steps which a society could take if it wanted to decrease the possibility of suicide—for example not paying social security benefits to the survivors or as religious institutions do, not allowing such persons to be buried with the same status as natural deaths. I think we may count these as interferences with the liberty of persons to attempt suicide and the question is whether they are justifiable.

Using my argument schema the question is whether rational individuals would consent to such limitations. I see no reason for them to consent to an absolute prohibition but I do think it is reasonable for them to agree to some kind of enforced waiting period. Since we are all aware of the possibility of temporary states, such as great fear or depression, that are inimical to the making of well-informed and rational decisions, it would be prudent for all of us if there were some kind of institutional arrangement whereby we were restrained from making a decision which is (all too) irreversible. What this would be like in practice is difficult to envisage and it may be that if no practical arrangements were feasible then we would have to conclude that there should be no restriction at all on this kind of action. But we might have a "cooling off" period, in much

the same way that we now require couples who file for divorce to go through a waiting period. Or, more far-fetched, we might imagine a Suicide Board composed of a psychologist and another member picked by the applicant. The Board would be required to meet and talk with the person proposing to take his life, though its approval would not be required.

A third class of decisions—these classes are not supposed to be disjoint—involves dangers which are either not sufficiently understood or appreciated correctly by the persons involved. Let me illustrate, using the example of cigarette smoking, a number of possible cases.

1. A man may not know the facts—e.g. smoking between 1 and 2 packs a day shortens life expectancy 6.2 years, the cost and pain of the illness caused by smoking, etc.
2. A man may know the facts, wish to stop smoking, but not have the requisite will-power.
3. A man may know the facts but not have them play the correct role in his calculation because, say, he discounts the danger psychologically because it is remote in time and/or inflates the attractiveness of other consequences of his decision which he regards as beneficial.

In case 1 what is called for is education, the posting of warnings, etc. In case 2 there is no theoretical problem. We are not imposing a good on someone one who rejects it. We are simply using coercion to enable people to carry out their own goals. (Note: There obviously is a difficulty in that only a subclass of the individuals affected wish to be prevented from doing what they are doing.) In case 3 there is a sense in which we are imposing a good on someone since given his current appraisal of the facts he doesn't wish to be restricted. But in another sense we are not imposing a good since what is being claimed—and what must be shown or at least argued for—is that an accurate accounting on his part would lead him to reject his current course of action. Now we all know that such cases exist, that we are prone to disregard dangers that are only possibilities, that immediate pleasures are often magnified and distorted.

If in addition the dangers are severe and far-reaching we could agree to allowing the state a certain degree of power to intervene in such situations.

The difficulty is in specifying in advance, even vaguely, the class of cases in which intervention will be legitimate.

A related difficulty is that of drawing a line so that it is not the case that all ultra-hazardous activities are ruled out, e.g. mountain-climbing, bull-fighting, sports-car racing, etc. There are some risks—even very great ones—which a person is entitled to take with his life.

A good deal depends on the nature of the deprivation—e.g. does it prevent the person from engaging in the activity completely or merely limit his participation—and how important to the nature of the activity is the absence of restriction when this is weighed against the role that the activity plays in the life of the person. In the case of automobile seat-belts, for example, the restriction is trivial in nature, interferes not at all with the use or enjoyment of the activity, and does, I am assuming, considerably reduce a high risk of serious injury. Whereas, for example, making mountain climbing illegal prevents completely a person engaging in an activity which may play an important role in his life and his conception of the person he is.

In general the easiest cases to handle are those which can be argued about in the terms which Mill thought to be so important—a concern not just for the happiness or welfare, in some broad sense, of the individual but rather a concern for the autonomy and freedom of the person. I suggest that we would be most likely to consent to paternalism in those instances in which it preserves and enhances for the individual his ability to rationally consider and carry out his own decisions.

I have suggested in this essay a number of types of situations in which it seems plausible that rational men would agree to granting the legislative powers of a society the right to impose restrictions on what Mill calls "self-regarding" conduct. However, rational men knowing something about the resources of ignorance, ill-will and stupidity available to the lawmakers of a society—a good case in point is the history of drug legislation in the United States—will be concerned to limit such intervention to minimum. I suggest in closing two principles designed to achieve this end.

In all cases of paternalistic legislation there must be a heavy and clear burden of proof placed on the authorities to demonstrate the exact nature of the harmful effects (or beneficial consequences) to be avoided (or achieved) and the probability of their occurrence. The burden of proof here is two-fold—what lawyers distinguish as the burden of going forward and the burden of persuasion. That the authorities have the burden of going forward means that it is up to them to raise the question and bring forward evidence of the evils to be avoided. Unlike the case of new drugs where the manufacturer must produce some evidence that the drug has been tested and found not harmful, no citizen has to show with respect to self-regarding conduct that it is not harmful or promotes his best interests. In addition the nature and cogency of the evidence for the harmfulness of the course of action must be set at a high level. To paraphrase a formulation of the burden of proof for criminal proceedings—better 10 men ruin themselves than one man be unjustly deprived of liberty.

Finally I suggest a principle of the least restrictive alternative. If there is an alternative way of accomplishing the desired end without restricting liberty then although it may involve great expense, inconvenience, etc. the society must adopt it.

NOTES

1. J. S. Mill, *Utilitarianism* and *On Liberty* (Fontana Library Edition, ed. by Mary Warnock, London, 1962), p. 135. All further quotes from Mill are from this edition unless otherwise noted.
2. J. S. Mill, *Principles of Political Economy* (New York: P. F. Collier and Sons, 1900), p. 442.
3. Mill, *Utilitarianism* and *On Liberty*, p. 207.
4. *Ibid.*, p. 206.
5. *Ibid.*, p. 207.
6. *Ibid.*, p. 214.
7. *Ibid.*, p. 207.
8. *Ibid.*, p. 138.
9. J. F. Stephens, *Liberty, Equality, Fraternity* (New York: Henry Holt & Co., n.d.), p. 24.
10. *Ibid.*, p. 33.
11. Mill, *Principles*, II, 458.
12. *Ibid.*, II, 459.
13. *Ibid.*, II, 451.
14. Mill, *Utilitarianism* and *On Liberty*, p. 197.
15. *Ibid.*, p. 186.
16. *Ibid.*, pp. 235–236.

What Libertarianism Is

JOHN HOSPERS

The political philosophy that is called libertarianism (from the Latin *libertas*, liberty) is the doctrine that every person is the owner of his own life, and that no one is the owner of anyone else's life; and that consequently every human being has the right to act in accordance with his own choices, unless those actions infringe on the equal liberty of other human beings to act in accordance with *their* choices.

There are several other ways of stating the same libertarian thesis:

1. *No one is anyone else's master, and no one is anyone else's slave.* Since I am the one to decide how my life is to be conducted, just as you decide about yours, I have no right (even if I had the power) to make you my slave and be your master, nor have you the right to become the master by enslaving me. Slavery is *forced* servitude, and since no one owns the life of anyone else, no one has the right to enslave another. Political theories past and present have traditionally been concerned with who should be the master (usually the king, the dictator, or government bureaucracy) and who should be the slaves, and what the extent of the slavery should be. Libertarianism holds that no one has the right to use force to enslave the life of another, or any portion or aspect of that life.

2. *Other men's lives are not yours to dispose of.* I enjoy seeing operas; but operas are expensive to produce. Opera-lovers often say, "The state (or the city, etc.) should subsidize opera, so that we can all see it. Also it would be for people's betterment, cultural benefit, etc." But what they are advocating is nothing more or less than legalized plunder. They can't pay for the productions themselves, and yet they want to see opera, which involves a large number of people and their labor; so what they are saying in effect is, "Get the money through legalized force. Take a little bit more out of every worker's paycheck every week to pay for the operas we want to see." But I have no right to take by force from the workers' pockets to pay for what I want.

Perhaps it would be better if he *did* go to see opera—then I should try to convince him to go voluntarily. But to take the money from him forcibly, because in my opinion it would be good for *him*, is still seizure of his earnings, which is plunder.

Besides, if I have the right to force him to help pay for my pet projects, hasn't he equally the right to force me to help pay for his? Perhaps he in turn wants the government to subsidize rock-and-roll, or his new car, or a house in the country? If I have the right to milk him, why hasn't he the right to milk me? If I can be a moral cannibal, why can't he too?

We should beware of the inventors of utopias. They would remake the world according to their vision—with the lives and fruits of the labor of *other* human beings. Is it someone's utopian vision that others should build pyramids to beautify the landscape? Very well, then other men should provide the labor; and if he is in a position of political power, and he can't get men to do it voluntarily, then he must *compel* them to "cooperate"—i.e. he must enslave them.

A hundred men might gain great pleasure from beating up or killing just one insignificant human being; but other men's lives are not theirs to dispose of. "In order to achieve the worthy goals of the next five-year-plan, we must forcibly collectivize the peasants..."; but other men's lives are not theirs to dispose of. Do you want to occupy, rent-free, the mansion that another man has worked for twenty years to buy? But other men's lives are not yours to dispose of. Do you want operas so badly that everyone is forced to work harder to pay for their subsidization through taxes? But other men's lives are not yours to dispose of. Do you want to have free medical care at the expense of other people, whether they wish to provide it or not? But this would require them to work longer for you whether they want to or not, and other men's lives are not yours to dispose of.

From John Hospers, "What Libertarianism Is," *The Libertarian Alternative*, ed. Tibor R. Machan (Chicago: Nelson-Hall, 1974).

The freedom to engage in any type of enterprise, to produce, to own and control property, to buy and sell on the free market, is derived from the rights to life, liberty, and property... which are stated in the Declaration of Independence.... [but] when a government guarantees a "right" to an education or parity on farm products or a guaranteed annual income, it is staking a claim on the property of one group of citizens for the sake of another group. In short, it is violating one of the fundamental rights it was instituted to protect.[1]

3. *No human being should be a nonvoluntary mortgage on the life of another.* I cannot claim your life, your work, or the products of your effort as mine. The fruit of one man's labor should not be fair game for every freeloader who comes along and demands it as his own. The orchard that has been carefully grown, nurtured, and harvested by its owner should not be ripe for the plucking for any bypasser who has a yen for the ripe fruit. The wealth that some men have produced should not be fair game for looting by government, to be used for whatever purposes its representatives determine, no matter what their motives in so doing may be. The theft of your money by a robber is not justified by the fact that he used it to help his injured mother.

It will already be evident that libertarian doctrine is embedded in a view of the rights of man. Each human being has the right to live his life as he chooses, compatibly with the equal right of all other human beings to live their lives as they choose.

All man's rights are implicit in the above statement. Each man has the right to life: any attempt by others to take it away from him, or even to injure him, violates this right, through the use of coercion against him. Each man has the right to liberty: to conduct his life in accordance with the alternatives open to him without coercive action by others. And every man has the right to property: to work to sustain his life (and the lives of whichever others he chooses to sustain, such as his family) and to retain the fruits of his labor.

People often defend the rights of life and liberty but denigrate property rights, and yet the right to property is as basic as the other two; indeed, without property rights no other rights are possible.

Depriving you of property is depriving you of the means by which you live.

...All that which an individual possesses by right (including his life and property) are morally his to use, dispose of and even destroy, as he sees fit. If I own my life, then it follows that I am free to associate with whom I please and not to associate with whom I please. If I own my knowledge and services it follows that I may ask any compensation I wish for providing them for another, or I may abstain from providing them at all, if I so choose. If I own my house, it follows that I may decorate it as I please and live in it with whom I please. If I control my own business, it follows that I may charge what I please for my products or services, hire whom I please and not hire whom I please. All that which I own in fact, I may dispose of as I choose to in reality. For anyone to attempt to limit my freedom to do so is to violate my rights.

Where do my rights end? Where yours begin. I may do anything I wish with my own life, liberty and property without your consent; but I may do nothing with your life, liberty and property without your consent. If we recognize the principle of man's rights, it follows that the individual is sovereign of the domain of his own life and property, and is sovereign of no other domain. To attempt to interfere forcibly with another's use, disposal or destruction of his own property is to initiate force against him and to violate his rights.

I have no right to decide how *you* should spend your time or your money. I can make that decision for myself, but not for you, my neighbor. I may deplore your choice of life-style, and I may talk with you about it provided you are willing to listen to me. But I have no right to use force to change it. Nor have I the right to decide how you should spend the money you have earned. I may appeal to you to give it to the Red Cross, and you may prefer to go to prizefights. But that is your decision, and however much I may chafe about it I do not have the right to interfere forcibly with it, for example by robbing you in order to use the money in accordance with *my* choices. (If I have the right to rob you, have you also the right to rob me?)

When I claim a right, I carve out a niche, as it were, in my life, saying in effect, "This activity I must be able to perform without interference from others. For you and everyone else, this is off limits. And so I put up a "no trespassing" sign, which marks off the area of my right. Each individual's right is his "no trespassing" sign in relation to me and others. I may not encroach upon his domain any more than he upon mine, without my consent. Every right entails a duty, true—but the duty is only that of *forbearance*—that is, of *refraining* from violating the other person's right. If you have a right to life, I have no right to take your life; if you have a right to the products of your labor (property), I have no right to take it from you without your consent. The non-violation of these rights will not guarantee you protection against natural catastrophes such as floods and earthquakes, but it will protect you against the aggressive activities *of other men*. And rights, after all, have to do with one's relations to other human beings, not with one's relations to physical nature.

Nor were these rights created by government; governments—some governments, obviously not all—*recognize* and *protect* the rights that individuals already have. Governments regularly forbid homicide and theft: and, at a more advanced stage, protect individuals against such things as libel and breach of contract.

> *It cannot be by chance that they thus agree. They agree because the alleged creating of rights [by government] was nothing else than giving formal sanction and better definition to those assertions of claims and recognitions of claims which naturally originate from the individual desires of men who have to live in presence of one another.*
>
> *... Those who hold that life is valuable, hold, by implication, that men ought not to be prevented from carrying on life-sustaining activities.... Clearly the conception of "natural rights" originates in recognition of the truth that if life is justifiable, there must be a justification for the performance of acts essential to its preservation; and, therefore, a justification of those liberties and claims which make such acts possible.*
>
> *... To recognize and enforce the rights of individuals, is at the same time to recognize and enforce the conditions to a normal social life.*[2]

The *right to property* is the most misunderstood and unappreciated of human rights, and it is one most constantly violated by governments. "Property" of course does not mean only real estate; it includes anything you can call your own—your clothing, your car, your jewelry, your books and papers.

The right of property is not the right to just *take* it from others, for this would interfere with *their* property rights. It is rather the right to work for it, to obtain non-coercively, the money or services which you can present in voluntary exchange.

The right to property is consistently underplayed by intellectuals today, sometimes even frowned upon, as if we should feel guilty for upholding such a right in view of all the poverty in the world. But the right to property is absolutely basic. It is your hedge against the future. It is your assurance that what you have worked to earn will still be there, and be yours, when you wish or need to use it, especially when you are too old to work any longer.

Government has always been the chief enemy of the right to property. The officials of government, wishing to increase their power, and finding an increase of wealth an effective way to bring this about, seize some or all of what a person has earned—and since government has a monopoly of physical force within the geographical area of the nation, it has the power (but not the right) to do this. When this happens, of course, every citizen of that country is insecure: he knows that no matter how hard he works the government can swoop down on him at any time and confiscate his earnings and possessions. A person sees his life savings wiped out in a moment when the tax-collectors descend to deprive him of the fruits of his work; or, an industry which has been fifty years in the making and cost millions of dollars and millions of hours of time and planning, is nationalized overnight. Or the government, via inflation, cheapens the currency, so that hard-won dollars aren't worth anything any more. The effect of such actions, of course, is that people lose hope and incentive: if no matter how hard they work the government agents can take it all away, why bother to work at all, for more than today's needs? Depriving people of property is *depriving them of the means by which they live*—the freedom of the individual citizen to do what he wishes with his own life and to plan for the future. Indeed, only if property rights are respected is there any point to planning for the future and working to achieve one's goals. *Property rights are what makes long-range planning possible*—the kind of planning which is a distinctively human endeavor, as opposed to the day-by-day activity of the lion who hunts, who depends on the supply of game tomorrow but has no real insurance against starvation in a day or a week. Without the right to property, the right to life itself amounts to little: how can you sustain your life if you cannot plan ahead? and how can you plan ahead if the fruits of your labor can at any moment be confiscated by government?

> *Without property rights, no other rights are possible. If one is not free to use that which one has produced, one does not possess the right of liberty. If one is not free to make the products of one's work serve one's chosen goals, one does not possess the right to the pursuit of happiness. And—since man is not a ghost who exists in some non-material manner—if one is not free to keep and to consume the products of one's work, one does not possess the right of life. In a society where men are not free privately to own the material means of production, their position is that of slaves whose lives are at the absolute mercy of their rulers. It is relevant here to remember the statement of Trotsky: "Who does not obey shall not eat.*[3]

Indeed, the right to property may well be considered second only to the right to life. Even the freedom of speech is limited by considerations of property. If a person visiting in your home behaves in a way undesired by you, you have every right to evict him; he can scream or agitate elsewhere if he wishes, but not in your home without your consent. Does a person have a right to shout obscenities in a cathedral? No, for the owners of the cathedral (presumably the Church) have not allowed others on their property for that purpose; one may go there to worship or to visit, but not just for any purpose one wishes. Their property right is prior to your or my wish to scream or expectorate or write graffiti on their building. Or, to take the stock example, does a person have a right to shout "Fire!" falsely in a crowded theater? No, for the theater owner has permitted others to enter and use his property only for a specific purpose, that

of seeing a film or watching a stage show. If a person heckles or otherwise disturbs other members of the audience, he can be thrown out. (In fact, he can be removed for any reason the owner chooses, provided his admission money is returned.) And if he shouts "Fire!" when there is no fire, he may be endangering other lives by causing a panic or a stampede. The right to free speech doesn't give one the right to say anything anywhere; it is circumscribed by property rights.

Again, some people seem to assume that the right to free speech (including written speech) means that they can go to a newspaper publisher and demand that he print in his newspaper some propaganda or policy statement for their political party (or other group). But of course they have no right to the use of his newspaper. Ownership of the newspaper is the product of his labor, and he has a right to put into his newspaper whatever he wants, for whatever reason. If he excludes material which many readers would like to have in, perhaps they can find it in another newspaper or persuade him to print it himself (if there are enough of them, they will usually do just that). Perhaps they can even cause his newspaper to fail. But as long as he owns it, he has the right to put in it what he wishes; what would a property right be if he could not do this? They have no right to place their material in his newspaper without his consent—not for free, nor even for a fee. Perhaps other newspapers will include it, or perhaps they can start their own newspaper (in which case they have a right to put in it what they like). If not, an option open to them would be to mimeograph and distribute some handbills.

In exactly the same way, no one has a right to "free television time" unless the owner of the television station consents to give it; it is his station, he has the property rights over it, and it is for him to decide how to dispose of his time. He may not decide wisely, but it is his right to decide as he wishes. If he makes enough unwise decisions, and courts enough unpopularity with the viewing public or the sponsors, he may have to go out of business; but as he is free to make his own decisions, so is he free to face their consequences. (If the government owns the television station, then government officials will make the decisions, and there is no guarantee of *their* superior wisdom.

The difference is that when "the government" owns the station, you are forced to help pay for its upkeep through your taxes, whether the bureaucrat in charge decides to give you television time or not.)

"But why have *individual* property rights? Why not have lands and houses owned by everybody together?" Yes, this involves no violation of individual rights, as long as everybody consents to this arrangement and no one is forced to join it. The parties to it may enjoy the communal living enough (at least for a time) to overcome certain inevitable problems: that some will work and some not, that some will achieve more in an hour than others can do in a day, and still they will all get the same income. The few who do the most will in the end consider themselves "workhorses" who do the work of two or three or twelve, while the others will be "freeloaders" on the efforts of these few. But as long as they can get out of the arrangement if they no longer like it, no violation of rights is involved. They got in voluntarily, and they can get out voluntarily; no one has used force.

"But why not say that everybody owns everything? That we *all* own everything there is?"

To some this may have a pleasant ring—but let us try to analyze what it means. If everybody owns everything, then everyone has an equal right to go everywhere, do what he pleases, take what he likes, destroy if he wishes, grow crops or burn them, trample them under, and so on. Consider what it would be like in practice. Suppose you have saved money to buy a house for yourself and your family. Now suppose that the principle, "everybody owns everything," becomes adopted. Well then, why shouldn't every itinerant hippie just come in and take over, sleeping in your beds and eating in your kitchen and not bothering to replace the food supply or clean up the mess? After all, it belongs to all of us, doesn't it? So we have just as much right to it as you, the buyer, have. What happens if we *all* want to sleep in the bedroom and there's not room for all of us? Is it the strongest who wins?

What would be the result? Since no one would be responsible for anything, the property would soon be destroyed, the food used up, the facilities nonfunctional. Beginning as a house that *one*

family could use, it would end up as a house that *no one* could use. And if the principle continued to be adopted, no one would build houses any more—or anything else. What for? They would only be occupied and used by others, without remuneration.

Suppose two men are cast ashore on an island, and they agree that each will cultivate half of it. The first man is industrious and grows crops and builds a shelter, making the most of the situation with which he is confronted. The second man, perhaps thinking that the warm days will last forever, lies in the sun, picks coconuts while they last, and does a minimum of work to sustain himself. At the time of harvest, the second man has nothing to harvest, nor does he assist the first man in his labors. But later when there is a dearth of food on the island, the second man comes to the first man and demands half of the harvest as his right. But of course he has no right to the product of the first man's labors. The first man may freely choose to give part of his harvest to the second out of charity rather than see him starve; but that is just what it is—charity, not the second man's right.

How can any of man's rights be violated? Ultimately, only by the use of force. I can make suggestions to you, I can reason with you, entreat you (if you are willing to listen), but I cannot *force* you without violating your rights; only by forcing you do I cut the cord between your free decisions and your actions. Voluntary relations between individuals involve no deprivation of rights, but murder, assault, and rape do, because in doing these things I make you the unwilling victim of my actions. A man in beating his wife involves no violation of rights if she *wanted* to be beaten. *Force is behavior that requires the unwilling involvement of other persons.*

Thus the use of force need not involve the use of physical violence. If I trespass on your property or dump garbage on it, I am violating your property rights, as indeed I am when I steal your watch; although this is not force in the sense of violence, it *is* a case of your being an unwilling victim of my action. Similarly, if you shout at me so that I cannot be heard when I try to speak, or blow a siren in my ear, or start a factory next door which pollutes my land, you are again violating my rights (to free speech, to property); I am, again, an unwilling victim of your actions. Similarly, if you steal a manuscript of mine and publish it as your own, you are confiscating a piece of my property and thus violating my right to keep what is the product of my labor. Of course, if I give you the manuscript with permission to sign your name to it and keep the proceeds, no violation of rights is involved—any more than if I give you permission to dump garbage on my yard.

According to libertarianism, the role of government should be limited to the retaliatory use of force against those who have initiated its use. It should not enter into any other areas, such as religion, social organization, and economics.

GOVERNMENT

Government is the most dangerous institution known to man. Throughout history it has violated the rights of men more than any individual or group of individuals could do: it has killed people, enslaved them, sent them to forced labor and concentration camps, and regularly robbed and pillaged them of the fruits of their expended labor. Unlike individual criminals, government has the power to arrest and try; unlike individual criminals, it can surround and encompass a person totally, dominating every aspect of one's life, so that one has no recourse from it but to leave the country (and in totalitarian nations even that is prohibited). Government throughout history has a much sorrier record than any individual, even that of a ruthless mass murderer. The signs we see on bumper stickers are chillingly accurate: "Beware: the Government is Armed and Dangerous."

The only proper role of government, according to libertarians, is that of the protector of the citizen against aggression by other individuals. The government, of course, should never initiate aggression; its proper role is as the embodiment of the *retaliatory* use of force against anyone who initiates its use.

If each individual had constantly to defend himself against possible aggressors, he would have to spend a considerable portion of his life in target practice, karate exercises, and other means of self-defenses, and even so he would probably be helpless against groups of individuals who might try to kill, maim, or rob him. He would have little time for cultivating those qualities which are essential to civilized life, nor would improvements in science, medicine, and the arts be likely to occur. The function of government is to take this responsibility off his shoulders: the government undertakes to defend him against aggressors and to punish them if they attack him. When the government is effective in doing this, it enables the citizen to go about his business unmolested and without constant fear for his life. To do this, of course, government must have physical power—the police, to protect the citizen from aggression within its borders, and the armed forces, to protect him from aggressors outside. Beyond that, the government should not intrude upon his life, either to run his business, or adjust his daily activities, or prescribe his personal moral code.

Government, then, undertakes to be the individual's protector; but historically governments have gone far beyond this function. Since they already have the physical power, they have not hesitated to use it for purposes far beyond that which was entrusted to them in the first place. Undertaking initially to protect its citizens against aggression, it has often itself become an aggressor—a far greater aggressor, indeed, than the criminals against whom it was supposed to protect its citizens. Governments have done what no private citizens can do: arrest and imprison individuals without a trial and send them to slave labor camps. Government must have power in order to be effective—and yet the very means by which alone it can be effective make it vulnerable to the abuse of power, leading to managing the lives of individuals and even inflicting terror upon them.

What then should be the function of government? In a word, the *protection of human rights*.

1. *The right to life:* libertarians support all such legislation as will protect human beings against the use of force by others, for example, laws against killing, attempted killing, maiming, beating, and all kinds of physical violence.

2. *The right to liberty:* there should be no laws compromising in any way freedom of speech, of the press, and of peaceable assembly. There should be no censorship of ideas, books, films, or of anything else by government.
3. *The right to property:* libertarians support legislation that protects the property rights of individuals against confiscation, nationalization, eminent domain, robbery, trespass, fraud and misrepresentation, patent and copyright, libel and slander.

Someone has violently assaulted you. Should he be legally liable? Of course. He has violated one of your rights. He has knowingly injured you, and since he has initiated aggression against you he should be made to expiate.

Someone has negligently left his bicycle on the sidewalk where you trip over it in the dark and injure yourself. He didn't do it intentionally; he didn't mean you any harm. Should he be legally liable? Of course; he has, however unwittingly, injured you, and since the injury is caused by him and you are the victim, he should pay.

Someone across the street is unemployed. Should you be taxed extra to pay for his expenses? Not at all. You have not injured him, you are not responsible for the fact that he is unemployed (unless you are a senator or bureaucrat who agitated for further curtailing of business, which legislation passed, with the result that your neighbor was laid off by the curtailed business). You may voluntarily wish to help him out, or better still, try to get him a job to put him on his feet again; but since you have initiated no aggressive act against him, and neither purposely nor accidentally injured him in any way, you should not be legally penalized for the fact of his unemployment. (Actually, it is just such penalties that increase unemployment.)

One man, A, works hard for years and finally earns a high salary as a professional man. A second man, B, prefers not to work at all, and to spend wastefully what money he has (through inheritance), so that after a year or two he has nothing left. At the end of this time he has a long siege of illness and lots of medical bills to pay. He demands that the bills be paid by the government—that is, by the taxpayers of the land, including Mr. A.

But of course B has no such right. He chose to lead his life in a certain way—that was his voluntary decision. One consequence of that choice is that he must depend on charity in case of later need. Mr. A chose not to live that way. (And if everyone lived like Mr. B, on whom would he depend in case of later need?) Each has a right to live in the way he pleases, but each must live with the consequences of his own decision (which, as always, fall primarily on himself). He cannot, in time of need, claim A's beneficence as his right.

If a house-guest of yours starts to carve his initials in your walls and break up your furniture, you have a right to evict him, and call the police if he makes trouble. If someone starts to destroy the machinery in a factory, the factory-owner is also entitled to evict him and call the police. In both cases, persons other than the owner are permitted on the property only under certain conditions, at the pleasure of the owner. If those conditions are violated, the owner is entitled to use force to set things straight. The case is exactly the same on a college or university campus: if a campus demonstrator starts breaking windows, occupying the president's office, and setting fire to a dean, the college authorities are certainly within their rights to evict him forcibly; one is permitted on the college grounds only under specific conditions, set by the administration: study, peaceful student activity, even political activity if those in charge choose to permit it. If they do not choose to permit peaceful political activity on campus, they may be unwise, since a campus is after all a place where all sides of every issue should get discussed, and the college that doesn't permit this may soon lose its reputation and its students. All the same, the college official who does not permit it is quite within his rights; the students do not own the campus, nor do the hired trouble-makers imported from elsewhere. In the case of a privately owned college, the owners, or whoever they have delegated to administer it, have the right to make the decisions as to who shall be permitted on the campus and under what conditions. In the case of a state university or college, the ownership problem is more complex: one could say that the "government" owns the campus or that "the people" do since they are the taxpayers who support it; but in either case, the university administration has the delegated task of keeping order, and until they are removed by the state administration or the taxpayers, it is theirs to decide who shall be permitted on campus, and what non-academic activities will be permitted to their students on the premises.

Property rights can be violated by physical trespass, of course, or by anyone entering on your property for any reason without your consent. (If you *do* consent to having your neighbor dump garbage on your yard, there is no violation of your rights.) But the physical trespass of a person is only a special case of violation of property rights. Property rights can be violated by sound-waves, in the form of a loud noise, or the sounds of your neighbor's hi-fi set while you are trying to sleep. Such violations of property rights are of course the subject of action in the courts.

But there is another violation of property rights that has not thus far been honored by the courts; this has to do with the effects of *pollution* of the atmosphere.

From the beginnings of modern air pollution, the courts made a conscious decision not to protect, for example, the orchards of farmers from the smoke of nearby factories or locomotives. They said, in effect, to the farmers: yes, your private property is being invaded by this smoke, but we hold that "public policy" is more important than private property, and public policy holds factories and locomotives to be good things. These goods were allowed to override the defense of property rights with our consequent headlong rush into pollution disaster. The remedy is both "radical" and crystal clear, and it has nothing to do with multi-billion dollar palliative programs at the expense of the taxpayers which do not even meet the real issue. The remedy is simply to enjoin anyone from injecting pollutants into the air, and thereby invading the rights of persons and property. Period. The argument that such an injunction prohibition would add to the costs of industrial production is as reprehensible as the pre Civil War argument that the abolition of slavery would add to the costs of growing cotton, and therefore should

not take place. For this means that the polluters are able to impose the high costs of pollution upon those whose property rights they are allowed to invade with impunity.[4]

What about automobiles, the chief polluters of the air? One can hardly sue every automobile owner. But one can sue the manufacturers of automobiles who do not install anti-smog devices on the cars which they distribute—and later (though this is more difficult), owners of individual automobiles if they discard the equipment or do not keep it functional.

The violation of rights does not apply only to air-pollution. If someone with a factory upstream on a river pollutes the river, anyone living downstream from him, finding his water polluted, should be able to sue the owner of the factory. In this way the price of adding the anti-pollutant devices will be the owner's responsibility, and will probably be added to the cost of the products which the factory produces and thus spread around among all consumers, rather than the entire cost being borne by the users of the river in the form of polluted water, with the consequent impossibility of fishing, swimming, and so on. In each case, pollution would be stopped at the source rather than having its ill effects spread around to numerous members of the population.

What about property which you do not work to earn, but which you *inherit* from someone else? Do you have a right to that? You have no right to it until someone decides to give it to you. Consider the man who willed it to you: it was his, he had the right to use and dispose of it as *he* saw fit; and if he decided to give it to you, this is a windfall for you, but it was only the exercise of *his* right. Had the property been seized by the government at the man's death, or distributed among numerous other people designated by the government, it *would* have been a violation of his rights: for he, who worked to earn and sustain it, would not have been able to dispose of it according to his own judgment. If he doesn't have the right to determine who shall have it, who does?

What about the property status of your intellectual activity, such as inventions you may devise and books you write? These, of course, are your property also; they are the products of your mind; you worked at them, you created them. Prior to that, they did not exist. If you worked five years to write a book, and someone stole it and published it as his own, receiving royalties from its sales, he would have stolen your property just as surely as if he had robbed your home. The same is true if someone used and sold without your permission an invention which was the product of your labor and ingenuity.

The role of government with respect to this issue, at least most governments of the Western world, is a proper one: government protects the products of your labor from the moment they materialize. Copyright law protects your writings from piracy. In the United States, one's writings are protected for a period of twenty-seven years, and another twenty-seven if one applies for renewal of the copyright. In most other countries, they are protected for a period of fifty years after the author's death, permitting both himself and his surviving heirs to reap the fruits of his labor. After that they enter the "public domain"—that is, anyone may reprint them without your or your heirs' permission. Patent law protects your inventions for a limited period, which varies according to the type of invention. In no case are you forced to avail yourself of this protection; you need not apply for patent or copyright coverage if you do not wish to do so. But the protection of your intellectual property is there, in case you wish to use it.

What about the property status of the airwaves? Here the government's position is far more questionable. The government now claims ownership of the airwaves, leasing them to individuals and corporations. The government renews leases or refuses them depending on whether the programs satisfy authorities in the Federal Communications Commission. The official position is that "we all own the airwaves"; but since only one party can broadcast on a certain frequency at a certain time without causing chaos, it is simply a fact of reality that "everyone" cannot use it. In fact the government decides who shall use the airwaves, and one courts its displeasure only at the price of a revoked license. One can write without government approval, but one cannot use the airwaves without the approval of government.

What policy should have been observed with regard to the airwaves? Much the same as the policy that was followed in the case of the Homestead Act, when the lands of the American West were opening up for settlement. There was a policy of "first come, first served," with the government parcelling out a certain acreage for each individual who wanted to claim the land as his own. There was no charge for the land, but if a man had not used it and built a dwelling during the first two-year period, it was assumed that he was not homesteading and the land was given to the next man in line. The airwaves too could have been given out on a "first come, first served" basis. The first man who used a given frequency would be its owner, and the government would protect him in the use of it against trespassers. If others wanted to use the same frequency, they would have to buy it from the first man, if he was willing to sell, or try to buy another, just as one now does with land.

Laws may be classified into three types: (1) laws protecting individuals against themselves, such as laws against fornication and other sexual behavior, alcohol, and drugs; (2) laws protecting individuals against aggressions by other individuals, such as laws against murder, robbery, and fraud; (3) laws requiring people to help one another; for example, all laws which rob Peter to pay Paul, such as welfare.

Libertarians reject the first class of laws totally. Behavior which harms no one else is strictly the individual's own affair. Thus, there should be no laws against becoming intoxicated, since whether or not to become intoxicated is the individual's own decision; but there should be laws against driving while intoxicated, since the drunken driver is a threat to every other motorist on the highway (drunken driving falls into type 2). Similarly, there should be no laws against drugs (except the prohibition of sale of drugs to minors) as long as the taking of these drugs poses no threat to anyone else. Drug addiction is a psychological problem to which no present solution exists. Most of the social harm caused by addicts, other than to themselves, is the result of thefts which they perform in order to continue their habit—and then the *legal* crime is the theft, not the addiction. The actual cost of heroin is about ten cents a shot; if it were legalized, the enormous traffic in illegal sale and purchase of it would stop, as well as the accompanying proselytization to get new addicts (to make more money for the pusher) and the thefts performed by addicts who often require eighty dollars a day just to keep up the habit. Addiction would not stop, but the crimes would: it is estimated that 75 percent of the burglaries in New York City today are performed by addicts, and all these crimes could be wiped out at one stroke through the legalization of drugs. (Only when the taking of drugs could be shown to constitute a threat to *others*, should it be prohibited by law. It is only laws protecting people against *themselves* that libertarians oppose.)

Laws should be limited to the second class only: aggression by individuals against other individuals. These are laws whose function is to protect human beings against encroachment by others; and this, as we have seen, is (according to libertarianism) the sole function of government.

Libertarians also reject the third class of laws totally: no one should be forced by law to help others, not even to tell them the time of day if requested, and certainly not to give them a portion of one's weekly paycheck. Governments, in the guise of humanitarianism, have given to some by taking from others (charging a "handling fee" in the process, which, because of the government's waste and inefficiency, sometimes is several hundred percent). And in so doing they have decreased incentive, violated the rights of individuals, and lowered the standard of living of almost everyone.

All such laws constitute what libertarians call *moral cannibalism*. A cannibal in the physical sense is a person who lives off the flesh of other human beings. A *moral* cannibal is one who believes he has a right to live off the "spirit" of other human beings—who believes that he has a moral claim on the productive capacity, time, and effort expended by others.

It has become fashionable to claim virtually everything that one needs or desires as one's *right*.

Thus, many people claim that they have a right to a job, the right to free medical care, to free food and clothing, to a decent home, and so on. Now if one asks, apart from any specific context, whether it would be desirable if everyone had these things, one might well say yes. But there is a gimmick attached to each of them: *At whose expense?* Jobs, medical care, education, and so on, don't grow on trees. These are goods and services *produced only by men*. Who, then, is to provide them, and under what conditions?

If you have a right to a job, who is to supply it? Must an employer supply it even if he doesn't want to hire you? What if you are unemployable, or incurably lazy? (If you say "the government must supply it," does that mean that a job must be created for you which no employer needs done, and that you must be kept in it regardless of how much or little you work?) If the employer is forced to supply it at his expense even if he doesn't need you, then isn't *he* being enslaved to that extent? What ever happened to *his* right to conduct his life and his affairs in accordance with his choices?

If you have a right to free medical care, then, since medical care doesn't exist in nature as wild apples do, some people will have to supply it to you for free: that is, they will have to spend their time and money and energy taking care of you whether they want to or not. What ever happened to *their* right to conduct their lives as they see fit? Or do you have a right to violate theirs? Can there be a right to violate rights?

All those who demand this or that as a "free service" are consciously or unconsciously evading the fact that there is in reality no such thing as free services. All man-made goods and services are the result of human expenditure of time and effort. There is no such thing as "something for nothing" in this world. If you demand something free, you are demanding that other men give their time and effort to you without compensation. If they voluntarily choose to do this, there is no problem; but if you demand that they be *forced* to do it, you are interfering with their right not to do it if they so choose. "Swimming in this pool ought to be free!" says the indignant passerby. What he means is that others should build a pool, others should provide the materials, and still others should run it and keep it in functioning order, so that *he* can use it without fee. But what right has he to the expenditure of *their* time and effort? To expect something "for free" is to expect it *to be paid for by others* whether they choose to or not.

Many questions, particularly about economic matters, will be generated by the libertarian account of human rights and the role of government. Should government have no role in assisting the needy, in providing social security, in legislating minimum wages, in fixing prices and putting a ceiling on rents, in curbing monopolies, in erecting tariffs, in guaranteeing jobs, in managing the money supply? To these and all similar questions the libertarian answers with an unequivocal no.

"But then you'd let people go hungry!" comes the rejoinder. This, the libertarian insists, is precisely what would not happen; with the restrictions removed, the economy would flourish as never before. With the controls taken off business, existing enterprises would expand and new ones would spring into existence satisfying more and more consumer needs; millions more people would be gainfully employed instead of subsisting on welfare, and all kinds of research and production, released from the stranglehold of government, would proliferate, fulfilling man's needs

and desires as never before. It has always been so whenever government has permitted men to be free traders on a free market. But *why* this is so, and how the free market is the best solution to all problems relating to the material aspect of man's life, is another and far longer story. It is told in detail in chapters 3 to 9 of my book, *Libertarianism*.

NOTES

Professor John Hospers is Director of the School of Philosophy at the University of Southern California. He has written widely on all aspects of philosophy. His books include *Meaning and Truth in the Arts, Introduction to Philosophical Analysis, Human Conduct; An Introduction to Ethics,* and *Libertarianism.* Professor Hospers was the presidential candidate of the Libertarian Party in 1972 and received about 5,000 votes plus an electoral college vote.

1. William W. Bayes, "What Is Property?" *The Freeman,* July 1970, p. 348.
2. Herbert Spencer, *The Man vs. the State* (1884; reprint ed., Caldwell, Id.: Caxton Printers, 1940), p. 191.
3. Nathaniel Branden, *Who Is Ayn Rand?* (New York: Random House, 1962), p. 47.
4. Murray Rothbard, "The Great Ecology Issue," *The Individualist,* 2, no. 2 (Feb. 1970), p. 5.

ARGUMENT 5 ESSAY QUESTIONS

1. What is Dworkin's view on paternalism? Does he think that the state may in some circumstances limit a person's freedom? If so, in what circumstances does he think paternalism is justified? Do you agree with him? Why or why not?
2. Would Hospers countenance the kinds of narrow paternalism that Dworkin advocates? What if drug use severely disabled or killed people—would Hospers still say that government interference was unjustified? Do you agree with Hospers's libertarian views on drugs and paternalism? Why or why not?

SUGGESTIONS FOR FURTHER READING

Joel Feinberg, *Harm to Self* (Oxford: Oxford University Press, 1989).
Robert E. Goodin, "The Ethics of Smoking," *Ethics* 99, April 1989.

Douglas Husak and Peter de Marneffe, *The Legalization of Drugs* (New York: Cambridge University Press, 2005).

Douglas Husak, *Drugs and Rights* (New York: Cambridge University Press, 1992).

Daniel Shapiro, "Addiction and Drug Policy," in *Morality and Moral Controversies*, 7th ed., ed. John Arthur (Upper Saddle River, NJ: Prentice-Hall, 2004).

Thomas S. Szasz, "The Ethics of Addiction," *Harper's Magazine*, 1972.

CHAPTER 5

Euthanasia and Assisted Suicide

Almost all of the terms used to discuss the morality of killing and letting die are controversial to some degree. (Even the meaning of *death*—a seemingly straightforward concept to most people—has been a point of dispute.) Nevertheless some helpful distinctions are possible. For the sake of clarity (and neutrality), **euthanasia** can be characterized as directly or indirectly bringing about the death of another person for that person's sake.[1] The term derives from Greek words meaning "good death" and evokes the idea that causing or contributing to someone's end may bestow on that person a good. Death is usually considered an evil, perhaps the greatest evil, but many think it can be a blessing if it spares them from a slow, horrific dying or a hopeless, vegetative sleep.

Many philosophers maintain that there are two forms of euthanasia. **Active euthanasia** is said to involve performing an action that directly causes someone to die—what most people think of as "mercy killing." Giving a patient a lethal injection to end his suffering, then, is a case of active euthanasia. **Passive euthanasia** is allowing someone to die by not doing something that would prolong life. It includes removing a patient's feeding tube or respirator, failing to perform necessary surgery, and refraining from giving life-saving antibiotics. The distinction between the two is thought to be essentially this: active euthanasia is *killing*, but passive euthanasia is *letting die*.

To some people, this conceptual border between active and passive euthanasia is crucial for assessing the morality of euthanasia. They point out that whereas letting a patient die is sometimes morally permissible, deliberately and directly killing a patient is always wrong. The former practice is legal and officially endorsed by the medical profession; the latter is illegal and officially condemned. The American Medical Association blessed this dichotomy in a 1973 policy statement:

> The intentional termination of the life of one human being by another—mercy killing—is contrary to that for which the medical profession stands and is contrary to the policy of the American Medical Association.

---

[1] A definition suggested by Philippa Foot in "Euthanasia," *Philosophy & Public Affairs* 6, no. (1977), 85–112, and by Helga Kuhse in "Euthanasia," *A Companion to Ethics*, ed. Peter Singer (Oxford: Blackwell, 1993), 294–302.

… The cessation of the employment of extraordinary means to prolong the life of the body when there is irrefutable evidence that biological death is imminent is the decision of the patient and/or immediate family.[2]

So for many (including most physicians), passive euthanasia may be moral, while active euthanasia is not.

But not everyone thinks this active-passive distinction makes sense. Some argue that there is no morally significant difference between mercifully killing a patient and mercifully letting the patient die. In both situations the doctor causes the patient's death—by either intentionally doing something in the one instance or intentionally refraining from doing something in the other. Thus an act of euthanasia may be morally right or wrong, but the rightness or wrongness does not depend purely on this active-passive divide. Moreover in practice, distinguishing examples of active and passive euthanasia may not be as easy as some think. The usual view is that passive euthanasia can sometimes be performed by disconnecting a dying patient's feeding tube and respirator. But this event can also be seen as an instance of performing an action that directly causes someone to die—that is, active euthanasia.

If euthanasia in some form is morally permissible, its permissibility must be linked to the patient's consent. Thus philosophers talk about euthanasia that is voluntary, nonvoluntary, or involuntary. **Voluntary euthanasia** refers to situations in which competent patients voluntarily request or agree to euthanasia, communicating their wishes either while competent or through instructions to be followed if they become incompetent (if they fall into a persistent vegetative state, for example). Patients can indicate what is to be done in incompetence by formulating an advance directive—usually a living will or a document designating a surrogate, or proxy, to act on their behalf. **Nonvoluntary euthanasia**

LEGALITIES: Euthanasia and Assisted Suicide

1990 In *Cruzan v. Director, Missouri Department of Health*, the U.S. Supreme Court recognizes the right of patients to refuse treatment (essentially a "right to die") and finds constitutional justification for living wills and surrogates who make medical decisions for incompetent patients.

1994 Oregon passes the Death With Dignity Act, legalizing the use of physician-assisted suicide under specific conditions. It permits doctors to prescribe drugs that terminally ill patients can use to commit suicide.

1997 In separate cases—*Washington v. Glucksberg* and *Vacco v. Quill*—the Supreme Court rules that there is no constitutional right to physician-

assisted suicide but notes that each state may establish its own policy on the issue. It explicitly acknowledges a distinction between assisted suicide and the withdrawal of life-sustaining treatment.

2001 U.S. Attorney General John Ashcroft tries to thwart the Oregon right-to-die law by authorizing the Drug Enforcement Agency to act against physicians prescribing drugs for assisted suicide.

2006 The Supreme Court rules that the Justice Department (headed by Ashcroft and later Alberto Gonzales) had no authority to interfere with physicians acting under the Oregon law.

---

[2] American Medical Association, *Opinions of the Judicial Council*, Chicago, 1973.

is performed when patients are not competent to choose death for themselves and have not previously (while competent) disclosed their preferences. (Incompetent patients include not only incapacitated adults but infants and young children as well.) In these circumstances, the patient's family, physician, or other officially designated persons decide for the patient. **Involuntary euthanasia** is bringing about someone's death against her will or without asking for her consent while she is competent to decide. It is illegal and considered morally impermissible by both those who approve and disapprove of euthanasia. It is therefore generally left out of moral debates, except perhaps in slippery-slope arguments warning that voluntary or nonvoluntary euthanasia will inevitably become involuntary.

Combining the terms *active*, *passive*, *voluntary*, and *nonvoluntary*, we can identify four kinds of euthanasia that have been the main focus in ethics:

1. **Active voluntary**—Directly causing death (mercy killing) with the consent of the patient
2. **Active nonvoluntary**—Directly causing death (mercy killing) without the consent of the patient
3. **Passive voluntary**—Withholding or withdrawing life-sustaining measures with the consent of the patient
4. **Passive nonvoluntary**—Withholding or withdrawing life-sustaining measures without the consent of the patient

Legally and ethically, the starkest contrast among these is between active and passive. Active euthanasia (whether voluntary or nonvoluntary) is unlawful, but passive euthanasia (both voluntary and nonvoluntary) is legal provided certain conditions are met. Judicial rulings have firmly established a right of patients to refuse treatment—and thus to have life-sustaining treatment withheld or withdrawn—even though the patient dies as a result. Withdrawing or withholding treatment from an incompetent patient is also permitted in some circumstances if an appropriate person can be chosen to decide in the interests of the patient. Contemporary moral debate centers more on active euthanasia than on passive. There is considerable agreement about the moral rightness of allowing a patient to die, but much more controversy about the permissibility of deliberately causing a patient's death (by administering a lethal injection, for example), whether the act is considered voluntary or nonvoluntary.

Recently, disputes over euthanasia have raged alongside arguments about **physician-assisted suicide**, in which a patient takes his or her own life with the aid of a physician. In a typical scenario, a patient asks the physician for help in committing suicide, the physician assists the patient by prescribing lethal doses of drugs or explaining a method of suicide, and the patient—not the physician—performs the final act that causes death. In contrast, in active euthanasia the physician performs the final act. Many argue that this difference in the ultimate cause of death implies a difference in moral responsibility. In physician-assisted suicide, the patient is thought to bear ultimate moral responsibility for the taking of life. Others doubt that any distinction in ultimate causes can amount to a moral difference. Thus they contend that physician-assisted suicide and active voluntary euthanasia are morally equivalent. What is the moral difference, they ask, between a physician helping a patient die by (1) administering a lethal injection upon request or (2) prescribing a lethal dose of medications upon request?

Society is divided on physician-assisted suicide. The American Medical Association has denounced physician-assisted suicide as unethical and inconsistent with physicians'

PUBLIC OPINION: **Physician-Assisted Suicide**

Do you think it should be legal or illegal for doctors to help terminally ill patients end their own life by giving them a prescription for fatal drugs?

Legal	Illegal	Unsure
48%	44%	8%

If you were seriously ill with a terminal disease, would you consider ending your life, or not?

Yes	No	Probably	Maybe	Unsure
35%	55%	3%	2%	5%

Associated Press/Ipsos poll conducted by Ipsos-Public Affairs, May 22–24, 2007, 1,000 adults nationwide; margin of error = ± 3.

When a person has a disease that cannot be cured and is living in severe pain, do you think doctors should or should not be allowed by law to assist the patient to commit suicide if the patient requests it?

Should	Should Not	Unsure
56%	38%	6%

Regardless of whether or not you think it should be legal, please tell me whether you personally believe that in general doctor-assisted suicide is morally acceptable or morally wrong.

Morally Acceptable	Morally Wrong	Depends	Unsure
49%	44%	5%	2%

Gallup Poll, May 10–13, 2007, 1,003 adults nationwide; margin of error = ± 3.

Do you think a person has a moral right to end his or her own life under any of the following circumstances?

	Yes	No	Unsure
When this person has a disease that is incurable?	53%	39%	8%
When this person is suffering great pain and has no hope of improvement?	60%	34%	6%
When this person is an extremely heavy burden on his or her family?	29%	62%	9%
When this person is ready to die because living has become a burden?	33%	58%	9%

Pew Research Center survey conducted by Princeton Survey Research Associates International, November 9–27, 2005, 1,500 adults nationwide; margin of error = ± 3.

duty to promote healing and preserve life. Some surveys have suggested, however, that many doctors support the use of physician-assisted suicide,[3] and about half of adults believe it should be legal in cases of terminal illness or incurable disease with severe pain.[4] To date, it is legal only in Oregon, but the Supreme Court has ruled that states may legalize or prohibit it as they see fit.

Part of the difficulty of making everyday moral decisions about end-of-life situations is that death itself is not so easy to define. Traditionally death was understood to occur when breathing and heartbeat ceased. A person who wasn't breathing and had no heartbeat was dead. But thanks to modern medicine, machines can maintain someone's breathing and heartbeat indefinitely—even though there is permanent loss of all brain function.

---

[3] Ezekiel J. Emanuel, Diane Fairclough, Brian Clarridge, et al., "Attitudes and Practices of U.S. Oncologists Regarding Euthanasia and Physician-Assisted Suicide," *Annals of Internal Medicine*, vol. 133, issue 7, 3 October 2000, 527–532.

[4] The Harris Poll, no. 32, 27 April, 2005; Pew Research Center poll, November 2005. AP-Ipsos poll, May 22–24, 2007.

Heart and lungs keep going, but the individual is irreversibly brain-dead and can remain that way for decades. By the traditional standard, the individual is alive, but this seems counterintuitive.

We seem to need a new concept of death—an important consideration since any notion we adopt would dramatically influence our judgments about morally permissible behavior toward the living and the dead. If we judge an individual to be dead, then we would presumably think her no longer a person. If she is no longer a person, then it would seem to be permissible to disconnect all life support, harvest organs from the body for transplant, or prepare the body for burial. But if, despite appearances, she is still a person, wouldn't doing any of these things be murder? If so, those who perform these acts would be morally and legally culpable.

In 1968 a committee at Harvard Medical School formulated a new way of conceiving of death, a perspective that has since become the standard in legal and medical matters. According to this *whole brain* view of death, an individual should be judged dead when all brain functions permanently cease. Brain death means genuine death. Several experts, however, take issue with this view. They point out that some physiological processes such as respiration are partly independent of brain functions, and individuals who many would regard as dead (those in persistent vegetative states, for example) may have some residual brain activity. By the whole brain standard, an individual in a persistent vegetative state (being wakeful but lacking consciousness) is alive until all brain activity stops. To some, this consequence makes sense; to others, it seems odd. A better notion of death, some argue, is the *higher brain* view, which says that an individual should be considered dead when the higher brain operations that are responsible for consciousness permanently shut down. The thought behind this standard is that individuals are dead when they are no longer persons, regardless of what physiological activity persists, and individuals are no longer persons when consciousness permanently terminates. On the higher brain criterion, an individual in a persistent vegetative state died when the higher brain functions permanently stopped, even though other brain activity may have continued for years. Again, some would find this judgment plausible; others, bizarre.

Currently the two main hot spots in these end-of-life debates are active voluntary euthanasia and physician-assisted suicide. In most instances, arguments about the former parallel those about the latter.

KEY TERMS

euthanasia	active euthanasia	involuntary euthanasia
nonvoluntary euthanasia	passive euthanasia	
physician-assisted suicide	voluntary euthanasia	

ARGUMENTS AND READINGS

6. THE AUTONOMY ARGUMENT FOR EUTHANASIA

Probably the strongest argument for active voluntary euthanasia derives from the widely accepted principle of autonomy—the notion that persons have an inherent right of self-determination or self-governance. According to one major ethical tradition, autonomous persons have intrinsic worth precisely because they have the power to make rational decisions and moral choices. They therefore must be treated with respect, which means not violating their autonomy by ignoring or thwarting their ability to choose their own paths and make their own judgments. Proponents of euthanasia argue that respecting autonomous persons means respecting their autonomous choices—including the choice to end their lives in their own way. Their right is preeminent, its only limit marking the point where their choices bring harm to others. As one philosopher explains it,

> People have an interest in making important decisions about their lives in accordance with their own conception of how they want their lives to go. In exercising autonomy or self-determination, people take responsibility for their lives; since dying is a part of life, choices about the manner of their dying and the timing of their death are, for many people, part of what is involved in taking responsibility for their lives. Many people are concerned about what the last phase of their lives will be like, not merely because of fears that their dying might involve them in great suffering, but also because of the desire to retain dignity and as much control over their lives as possible during this phase.... There is no single, objectively correct answer as to when, if at all, life becomes a burden and unwanted. But that simply points up the importance of individuals being able to decide autonomously for themselves whether their own lives retain sufficient quality and dignity to make life worth living.[5]

In "The Philosophers' Brief," Ronald Dworkin and several other philosophers state this autonomy argument as a principle of law. They maintain that individuals have a "constitutionally protected interest" in making their own autonomous decisions regarding the meaning and value of life and death, without interference from the government. The brief asserts,

> Denying [autonomous decision making] to terminally ill patients who are in agonizing pain or otherwise doomed to an existence they regard as intolerable could only be justified on the basis of a religious or ethical conviction about the value or

---

[5] Robert Young, "Voluntary Euthanasia," *The Stanford Encyclopedia of Philosophy* (Winter 2007), ed. Edward N. Zalta, http://plato.stanford.edu/archives/win2007/entries/euthanasia-voluntary (28 January 2008).

meaning of life itself. Our Constitution forbids government to impose such convictions on its citizens.[6]

Proponents believe that this right to die, though strong, does not necessarily compel others. Almost no one who seriously urges the autonomy argument thinks that having a right to die forces a duty on others (physicians, for example) to help in the dying.

While not denying that persons have a right of self-determination, opponents of euthanasia argue against the practice in several ways. Some contend that deliberately killing a hopelessly ill person is morally wrong because such an act is inconsistent with natural law—it goes against the strong natural tendency of all humans to continue living.

Daniel Callahan argues that a person's right of self-determination does not morally justify someone else killing that person, even for mercy's sake. He maintains that even if we have a right to kill ourselves, that right cannot be transferred to someone else. John Lachs, among others, thinks Callahan's claim is implausible.

The Philosophers' Brief

RONALD DWORKIN, THOMAS NAGEL, ROBERT NOZICK, JOHN RAWLS, THOMAS SCANLON, AND

JUDITH JARVIS THOMSON

Amici are six moral and political philosophers who differ on many issues of public morality and policy. They are united, however, in their conviction that respect for fundamental principles of liberty and justice, as well as for the American constitutional tradition, requires that the decisions of the Courts of Appeals be affirmed.

INTRODUCTION AND SUMMARY OF ARGUMENT

These cases do not invite or require the Court to make moral, ethical or religious judgments about how people should approach or confront their death or about when it is ethically appropriate to hasten one's own death or to ask others for help in doing so. On the contrary, they ask the Court to recognize that individuals have a constitutionally protected interest in making those grave judgments for themselves, free from the imposition of any religious or philosophical orthodoxy by court or legislature. States have a constitutionally legitimate interest in

protecting individuals from irrational, ill-informed, pressured or unstable decisions to hasten their own death. To that end, states may regulate and limit the assistance that doctors may give individuals who express a wish to die. But states may not deny people in the position of the patient-plaintiffs in these cases the opportunity to demonstrate, through whatever reasonable procedures the state might institute—even procedures that err on the side of caution—that their decision to die is indeed informed, stable, and fully free. Denying that opportunity to terminally-ill patients who are in agonizing pain or otherwise doomed to an existence they regard as intolerable could only be justified on the basis of a religious or ethical conviction about the value or meaning of life itself. Our Constitution forbids government to impose such convictions on its citizens.

Petitioners and the amici who support them offer two contradictory arguments. Some deny that the patient-plaintiffs have any constitutionally protected liberty interest in hastening their own

---

[6] Amici curiae brief in *Washington v. Glucksberg* (1997) and *Vacco v. Quill* (1997).

deaths. But that liberty interest flows directly from this Court's previous decisions. It flows from the right of people to make their own decisions about matters "involving the most intimate and personal choices a person may make in a lifetime, choices central to personal dignity and autonomy." *Planned Parenthood v. Casey*, 505 U.S. 833, 851 (1992).

The Solicitor General, urging reversal in support of Petitioners, recognizes that the patient-plaintiffs do have a constitutional liberty interest at stake in these cases. See Brief for the United States as Amicus Curiae…[hereinafter Brief for the United States] ("The term 'liberty' in the Due Process Clause…is broad enough to encompass an interest on the part of terminally ill, mentally competent adults in obtaining relief from the kind of suffering experienced by the plaintiffs in this case, which includes not only severe physical pain, but also the despair and distress that comes from physical deterioration and the inability to control basic bodily functions."); see also id. at 13 ("*Cruzan*…supports the conclusion that a liberty interest is at stake in this case."). The Solicitor General nevertheless argues that Washington and New York properly ignored this profound interest when they required the patient-plaintiffs to live on in circumstances they found intolerable. He argues that a state may simply declare that it is unable to devise a regulatory scheme that would adequately protect patients whose desire to die might be ill-informed or unstable or foolish or not fully free and that a state may therefore fall back on a blanket prohibition. This Court has never accepted that patently dangerous rationale for denying protection altogether to a conceded fundamental constitutional interest. It would be a serious mistake to do so now. If that rationale were accepted, an interest acknowledged to be constitutionally protected would be rendered empty.

ARGUMENT

I. The Liberty Interest Asserted Here Is Protected by the Due Process Clause

The Due Process Clause of the Fourteenth Amendment protects the liberty interest asserted by the patient-plaintiffs here.

Certain decisions are momentous in their impact on the character of a person's life—decisions about religious faith, political and moral allegiance, marriage, procreation and death, for example. Such deeply personal decisions reflect controversial questions about how and why human life has value. In a free society, individuals must be allowed to make those decisions for themselves, out of their own faith, conscience and convictions. This Court has insisted, in a variety of contexts and circumstances, that this great freedom is among those protected by the Due Process Clause as essential to a community of "ordered liberty." *Palko v. Connecticut*, 302 U.S. 319, 325 (1937). In its recent decision in *Planned Parenthood v. Casey*, 505 U.S. 833, 851 (1992), the Court offered a paradigmatic statement of that principle:

> matters[] involving the most intimate and personal choices a person may make in a lifetime, choices central to a person's dignity and autonomy, are central to the liberty protected by the Fourteenth Amendment.

That declaration reflects an idea underlying many of our basic constitutional protections. As the Court explained in *West Virginia State Board of Education v. Barnette*, 319 U.S. 624, 642 (1943):

> If there is any fixed star in our constitutional constellation, it is that no official…can prescribe what shall be orthodox in politics, nationalism, religion, or other matters of opinion or force citizens to confess by word or act their faith therein.

These decisions recognize as constitutionally immune from state intrusion that realm in which individuals make "intimate and personal" decisions that define the very character of their lives. See Charles Fried, *Right and Wrong* 146–147 (1978) ("What a person is, what he wants, the determination of his life plan, of his concept of the good, are the most intimate expressions of self-determination, and by asserting a person's responsibility for the results of this self-determination, we give substance to the concept of liberty.").

A person's interest in following his own convictions at the end of life is so central a part of the more general right to make "intimate and personal choices" for himself that a failure to protect that particular interest would undermine the general right altogether. Death is, for each of us, among the most significant events of life. As the Chief Justice said in *Cruzan v. Missouri*, 497 U.S. 261, 281 (1990), "the choice between life and death is a deeply personal decision of obvious and overwhelming finality."

Most of us see death—whatever we think will follow it—as the final act of life's drama, and we want that last act to reflect our own convictions, those we have tried to live by, not the convictions of others forced on us in our most vulnerable moment.

Different people, of different religious and ethical beliefs, embrace very different convictions about which way of dying confirms and which contradicts the value of their lives. Some fight against death with every weapon their doctors can devise. Others will do nothing to hasten death even if they pray it will come soon. Still others, including the patient-plaintiffs in these cases, want to end their lives when they think that living on, in the only way they can, would disfigure rather than enhance the lives they had created. Some people make the latter choice not just to escape pain. Even if it were possible to eliminate all pain for a dying patient— and frequently that is not possible—that would not end or even much alleviate the anguish some would feel at remaining alive, but intubated, helpless and often sedated near oblivion.

None of these dramatically different attitudes about the meaning of death can be dismissed as irrational. None should be imposed, either by the pressure of doctors or relatives or by the fiat of government, on people who reject it. Just as it would be intolerable for government to dictate that doctors never be permitted to try to keep someone alive as long as possible, when that is what the patient wishes, so it is intolerable for government to dictate that doctors may never, under any circumstances, help someone to die who believes that further life means only degradation. The Constitution insists that people must be free to make these deeply personal decisions for themselves and must not be forced to end their lives in a way that appalls them, just because that is what some majority thinks proper.

II. This Court's Decisions in *Casey* and *Cruzan* Compel Recognition of a Liberty Interest Here

A. *Casey* Supports the Liberty Interest Asserted Here

In *Casey*, this Court, in holding that a State cannot constitutionally proscribe abortion in all cases,

reiterated that the Constitution protects a sphere of autonomy in which individuals must be permitted to make certain decisions for themselves. The Court began its analysis by pointing out that "at the heart of liberty is the right to define one's own concept of existence, of meaning, of the universe, and of the mystery of human life." 505 U.S. at 851. Choices flowing out of these conceptions, on matters "involving the most intimate and personal choices a person may make in a lifetime, choices central to personal dignity and autonomy, are central to the liberty protected by the Fourteenth Amendment." Id. "Beliefs about these matters," the Court continued, "could not define the attributes of personhood were they formed under compulsion of the State." Id.

In language pertinent to the liberty interest asserted here, the Court explained why decisions about abortion fall within this category of "personal and intimate" decisions. A decision whether or not to have an abortion, "originating within the zone of conscience and belief," involves conduct in which "the liberty of the woman is at stake in a sense unique to the human condition and so unique to the law." Id. at 852. As such, the decision necessarily involves the very "destiny of the woman" and is inevitably "shaped to a large extent on her own conception of her spiritual imperatives and her place in society." Id. Precisely because of these characteristics of the decision, "the State is [not] entitled to proscribe [abortion] in all instances." Id. Rather, to allow a total prohibition on abortion would be to permit a state to impose one conception of the meaning and value of human existence on all individuals. This the Constitution forbids.

The Solicitor General nevertheless argues that the right to abortion could be supported on grounds other than this autonomy principle, grounds that would not apply here. He argues, for example, that the abortion right might flow from the great burden an unwanted child imposes on its mother's life. Brief for the United States at 14–15. But whether or not abortion rights could be defended on such grounds, they were not the grounds on which this Court in fact relied. To the contrary, the Court explained at length that the right flows from the constitutional protection accorded all individuals to "define one's own concept of existence, of meaning, of the universe, and of the mystery of human life." *Casey*, 505 U.S. at 851.

The analysis in *Casey* compels the conclusion that the patient-plaintiffs have a liberty interest in this case that a state cannot burden with a blanket prohibition. Like a woman's decision whether to have an abortion, a decision to die involves one's very "destiny" and inevitably will be "shaped to a large extent on [one's] own conception of [one's] spiritual imperatives and [one's] place in society." Id. at 852. Just as a blanket prohibition on abortion would involve the improper imposition of one conception of the meaning and value of human existence on all individuals, so too would a blanket prohibition on assisted suicide. The liberty interest asserted here cannot be rejected without undermining the rationale of *Casey*. Indeed, the lower court opinions in the Washington case expressly recognized the parallel between the liberty interest in *Casey* and the interest asserted here. See *Compassion in Dying v. Washington*, 79 F.3d 790, 801 (9th Cir. 1996) (en banc) ("In deciding right-to-die cases, we are guided by the Court's approach to the abortion cases. *Casey* in particular provides a powerful precedent, for in that case the Court had the opportunity to evaluate its past decisions and to determine whether to adhere to its original judgment"), affg, 850 F. Supp. 1454, 1459 (W.D. Wash. 1994) ("The reasoning in *Casey* [is] highly instructive and almost prescriptive …"). This Court should do the same.

B. Cruzan *Supports the Liberty Interest Asserted Here*

We agree with the Solicitor General that this Court's decision in "*Cruzan*…supports the conclusion that a liberty interest is at stake in this case." Brief for the United States at 8. Petitioners, however, insist that the present cases can be distinguished because the right at issue in *Cruzan* was limited to a right to reject an unwanted invasion of one's body. But this Court repeatedly has held that in appropriate circumstances a state may require individuals to accept unwanted invasions of the body. See, e.g., *Schmerber v. California*, 384 U.S. 757 (1966) (extraction of blood sample from individual suspected of driving while intoxicated, notwithstanding defendant's objection, does not violate privilege

against self-incrimination or other constitutional rights); *Jacobson v. Massachusetts*, 197 U.S. 11 (1905) (upholding compulsory vaccination for smallpox as reasonable regulation for protection of public health). The liberty interest at stake in *Cruzan* was a more profound one. If a competent patient has a constitutional right to refuse life-sustaining treatment, then, the Court implied, the state could not override that right. The regulations upheld in *Cruzan* were designed only to ensure that the individual's wishes were ascertained correctly. Thus, if *Cruzan* implies a right of competent patients to refuse life-sustaining treatment, that implication must be understood as resting not simply on a right to refuse bodily invasions but on the more profound right to refuse medical intervention when what is at stake is a momentous personal decision, such as the timing and manner of one's death. In her concurrence, Justice O'Connor expressly recognized that the right at issue involved a "deeply personal decision" that is "inextricably intertwined" with our notion of "self-determination." 497 U.S. at 287–89.

Cruzan also supports the proposition that a state may not burden a terminally ill patient's liberty interest in determining the time and manner of his death by prohibiting doctors from terminating life support. Seeking to distinguish *Cruzan*, Petitioners insist that a state may nevertheless burden that right in a different way by forbidding doctors to assist in the suicide of patients who are not on life-support machinery. They argue that doctors who remove life support are only allowing a natural process to end in death whereas doctors who prescribe lethal drugs are intervening to cause death. So, according to this argument, a state has an independent justification for forbidding doctors to assist in suicide that it does not have for forbidding them to remove life support. In the former case though not the latter, it is said, the state forbids an act of killing that is morally much more problematic than merely letting a patient die. **This argument is based on a misunderstanding of the pertinent moral principles.** It is certainly true that when a patient does not wish to die, different acts, each of which foreseeably results in his death, nevertheless have very different moral status. When several patients need organ transplants and organs are scarce, for example, it is morally permissible for a doctor to deny an organ to one patient, even though he will die without it, in order to give it to another. But it is certainly not permissible for a doctor to kill one patient in order to use his organs to save another. The morally significant difference between those two acts is not, however, that killing is a positive act and not providing an organ is a mere omission, or that killing someone is worse than merely allowing a "natural" process to result in death. It would be equally impermissible for a doctor to let an injured patient bleed to death, or to refuse antibotics to a patient with pneumonia—in each case the doctor would have allowed death to result from a "natural" process—in order to make his organs available for transplant to others. A doctor violates his patient's rights regardless of whether the doctor acts or refrains from acting, against the patient's wishes, in a way that is designed to cause death.

When a competent patient does want to die, the moral situation is obviously different, because then it makes no sense to appeal to the patient's right not to be killed as a reason why an act designed to cause his death is impermissible. From the patient's point of view, there is no morally pertinent difference between a doctor's terminating treatment that keeps him alive, if that is what he wishes, and a doctor's helping him to end his own life by providing lethal pills he may take himself, when ready, if that is what he wishes—except that the latter may be quicker and more humane. Nor is that a pertinent difference from the doctor's point of view. If and when it is permissible for him to act with death in view, it does not matter which of those two means he and his patient choose. If it is permissible for a doctor deliberately to withdraw medical treatment in order to allow death to result from a natural process, then it is equally permissible for him to help his patient hasten his own death more actively, if that is the patient's express wish.

It is true that some doctors asked to terminate life support are reluctant and do so only in deference to a patient's right to compel them to remove unwanted invasions of his body. But other doctors, who believe that their most fundamental professional duty is to act in the patient's interests and that, in certain circumstances, it is in their patient's best interests to die, participate willingly in such decisions: they terminate life support to cause death because they know that is what their patient wants. *Cruzan* implied that

a state may not absolutely prohibit a doctor from deliberately causing death, at the patient's request, in that way and for that reason. If so, then a state may not prohibit doctors from deliberately using more direct and often more humane means to the same end when that is what a patient prefers. The fact that failing to provide life sustaining treatment may be regarded as "only letting nature take its course" is no more morally significant in this context, when the patient wishes to die, than in the other, when he wishes to live. Whether a doctor turns off a respirator in accordance with the patient's request or prescribes pills that a patient may take when he is ready to kill himself, the doctor acts with the same intention: to help the patient die.

The two situations do differ in one important respect. Since patients have a right not to have life support machinery attached to their bodies, they have, in principle, a right to compel its removal. But that is not true in the case of assisted suicide: patients in certain circumstances have a right that the state not forbid doctors to assist in their deaths, but they have no right to compel a doctor to assist them. The right in question, that is, is only a right to the help of a willing doctor.

III. State Interests Do Not Justify a Categorical Prohibition on All Assisted Suicide

The Solicitor General concedes that "a competent, terminally ill adult has a constitutionally cognizable liberty interest in avoiding the kind of suffering experienced by the plaintiffs in this case." Brief for the United States at 8. He agrees that this interest extends not only to avoiding pain, but to avoiding an existence the patient believes to be one of intolerable indignity or incapacity as well. Id. at 12. The Solicitor General argues, however, that states nevertheless have the right to "override" this liberty interest altogether, because a state could reasonably conclude that allowing doctors to assist in suicide, even under the most stringent regulations and procedures that could be devised, would unreasonably endanger the lives of a number of patients who might ask for death in circumstances when it is plainly not in their interests to die or when their consent has been improperly obtained.

This argument is unpersuasive, however, for at least three reasons. First, in *Cruzan*, this Court noted that its various decisions supported the recognition of a general liberty interest in refusing medical treatment, even when such refusal could result in death. 497 U.S. at 278–79. The various risks described by the Solicitor General apply equally to those situations. For instance, a patient kept alive only by an elaborate and disabling life support system might well become depressed, and doctors might be equally uncertain whether the depression is curable: such a patient might decide for death only because he has been advised that he will die soon anyway or that he will never live free of the burdensome apparatus, and either diagnosis might conceivably be mistaken. Relatives or doctors might subtly or crudely influence that decision, and state provision for the decision may (to the same degree in this case as if it allowed assisted suicide) be thought to encourage it.

Yet there has been no suggestion that states are incapable of addressing such dangers through regulation. In fact, quite the opposite is true. In *McKay v. Bergstedt*, 106 Nev. 808, 801 P.2d 617 (1990), for example, the Nevada Supreme Court held that "competent adult patients desiring to refuse or discontinue medical treatment" must be examined by two non-attending physicians to determine whether the patient is mentally competent, understands his prognosis and treatment options, and appears free of coercion or pressure in making his decision. Id. at 827–28, 801 P.2d at 630. See also id. (in the case of terminally-ill patients with natural life expectancy of less than six months, patient's right of self-determination shall be deemed to prevail over state interests, whereas non-terminal patient's decision to terminate life-support systems must first be weighed against relevant state interests by trial judge); *In re Farrell*, 108 N.J. 335, 354, 529 A.2d 404, 413 (1987) (terminally-ill patient requesting termination of life-support must be determined to be competent and properly informed about prognosis, available treatment options and risks, and to have made decision voluntarily and without coercion). Those protocols served to guard against precisely the dangers that the Solicitor General raises. The case law contains no suggestion that such protocols are inevitably insufficient to prevent deaths that should have been prevented.

Indeed, the risks of mistake are overall greater in the case of terminating life support. *Cruzan* implied that a state must allow individuals to make such decisions through an advance directive stipulating either that life support be terminated (or not initiated) in described circumstances when the individual was no longer competent to make such a decision himself, or that a designated proxy be allowed to make that decision. All the risks just described are present when the decision is made through or pursuant to such an advance directive, and a grave further risk is added: that the directive, though still in force, no longer represents the wishes of the patient. The patient might have changed his mind before he became incompetent, though he did not change the directive, or his proxy may make a decision that the patient would not have made himself if still competent. In *Cruzan*, this Court held that a state may limit these risks through reasonable regulation. It did not hold—or even suggest—that a state may avoid them through a blanket prohibition that, in effect, the liberty interest altogether.

Second, nothing in the record supports the conclusion that no system of rules and regulations could adequately reduce the risk of mistake. As discussed above, the experience of states in adjudicating requests to have life-sustaining treatment removed indicates the opposite. The Solicitor General has provided no persuasive reason why the same sort of procedures could not be applied effectively in the case of a competent individual's request for physician-assisted suicide.

Indeed, several very detailed schemes for regulating physician-assisted suicide have been submitted to the voters of some states and one has been enacted. In addition, concerned groups, including a group of distinguished professors of law and other professionals, have drafted and defended such schemes. See, e.g., Charles H. Baron, et al., *A Model State Act to Authorize and Regulate Physician-Assisted Suicide*, 33 Harv. J. Legis. 1 (1996). Such draft statutes propose a variety of protections and review procedures designed to insure against mistakes, and neither Washington nor New York attempted to show that such schemes would be porous or ineffective. Nor does the Solicitor General's brief: it relies instead mainly on flat and conclusory statements. It cites a New York Task Force report, written before the proposals just described were drafted, whose findings have been widely disputed and were implicitly rejected in the opinion of the Second Circuit below. See generally *Quill v. Vacco*, 80 F.3d 716 (2d Cir. 1996). The weakness of the Solicitor General's argument is signalled by his strong reliance on the experience in the Netherlands which, in effect, allows assisted suicide pursuant to published guidelines. Brief for the United States at 23–24. The Dutch guidelines are more permissive than the proposed and model American statutes, however. The Solicitor General deems the Dutch practice of ending the lives of people like neonates who cannot consent particularly noteworthy, for example, but that practice could easily and effectively be made illegal by any state regulatory scheme without violating the Constitution.

The Solicitor General's argument would perhaps have more force if the question before the Court were simply whether a state has any rational basis for an absolute prohibition; if that were the question, then it might be enough to call attention to risks a state might well deem not worth running. But, as the Solicitor General concedes, the question here is a very different one: whether a state has interests sufficiently compelling to allow it to take the extraordinary step of altogether refusing the exercise of a liberty interest of constitutional dimension. In those circumstances, the burden is plainly on the state to demonstrate that the risk of mistakes is very high, and that no alternative to complete prohibition would adequately and effectively reduce those risks. Neither of the Petitioners has made such a showing.

Nor could they. The burden of proof on any state attempting to show this would be very high. Consider, for example, the burden a state would have to meet to show that it was entitled altogether to ban public speeches in favor of unpopular causes because it could not guarantee, either by regulations short of an outright ban or by increased police protection, that such speeches would not provoke a riot that would result in serious injury or death to an innocent party. Or that it was entitled to deny those accused of crime the procedural rights that the Constitution guarantees, such as the right to a jury trial, because the security risk those rights would impose on the community would be too great. One can posit extreme circumstances in which some such argument would succeed. See, e.g., *Korematsu v. United States*, 323 U.S. 214 (1944) (permitting United States to detain individuals of Japanese ancestry during wartime). But these circumstances would be extreme indeed, and the *Korematsu* ruling has been widely and severely critized.

Third, it is doubtful whether the risks the Solicitor General cites are even of the right character to serve as justification for an absolute prohibition on the exercise of an important liberty interest. The risks fall into two groups. The first is the risk of medical mistake, including a misdiagnosis of competence or terminal illness. To be sure, no scheme of regulation, no matter how rigorous, can altogether guarantee that medical mistakes will not be made. But the Constitution does not allow a state to deny patients a great variety of important choices, for which informed consent is properly deemed necessary, just because the information on which the consent is given may, in spite of the most strenuous efforts to avoid mistake, be wrong. Again, these identical risks are present in decisions to terminate life support, yet they do not justify an absolute prohibition on the exercise of the right.

The second group consists of risks that a patient will be unduly influenced by considerations that the state might deem it not in his best interests to be swayed by, for example, the feelings and views of close family members. Brief for the United States at 20. But what a patient regards as proper grounds for such a decision normally reflects exactly the judgments of personal ethics—of why his life is important and what affects its value—that patients have a crucial liberty interest in deciding for themselves. Even people who are dying have a right to hear and, if they wish, act on what others might wish to tell or suggest or even hint to them, and it would be dangerous to suppose that a state may prevent this on the ground that it knows better than its citizens when they should be moved by or yield to particular advice or suggestion in the exercise of their right to make fateful personal decisions for themselves. It is not a good reply that some people may not decide as they really wish—as they would decide, for example, if free from the "pressure" of others.

That possibility could hardly justify the most serious pressure of all—the criminal law which tells them that they may not decide for death if they need the help of a doctor in dying, no matter how firmly they wish it.

There is a fundamental infirmity in the Solicitor General's argument. He asserts that a state may reasonably judge that the risk of "mistake" to some persons justifies a prohibition that not only risks but insures and even aims at what would undoubtedly be a vastly greater number of "mistakes" of the opposite kind—preventing many thousands of competent people who think that it disfigures their lives to continue living, in the only way left to them, from escaping that—to them—terrible injury. A state grievously and irreversibly harms such people when it prohibits that escape. The Solicitor General's argument may seem plausible to those who do not agree that individuals are harmed by being forced to live on in pain and what they regard as indignity. But many other people plainly do think that such individuals are harmed, and a state may not take one side in that essentially ethical or religious controversy as its justification for denying a crucial liberty.

Of course, a state has important interests that justify regulating physician-assisted suicide. It may be legitimate for a state to deny an opportunity for assisted suicide when it acts in what it reasonably judges to be the best interests of the potential suicide, and when its judgment on that issue does not rest on contested judgments about "matters involving the most intimate and personal choices a person may make in a lifetime, choices central to personal dignity and autonomy." *Casey,* 505 U.S. at 851. A state might assert, for example, that people who are not terminally ill, but who have formed a desire to die, are, as a group, very likely later to be grateful if they are prevented from taking their own lives. It might then claim that it is legitimate, out of concern for such people, to deny any of them a doctor's assistance. This Court need not decide now the extent to which such paternalistic interests might override an individual's liberty interest. No one can plausibly claim, however—and it is noteworthy that neither Petitioners nor the Solicitor General does claim—that any such prohibition could serve the interests of any significant number

of terminally ill patients. On the contrary, any paternalistic justification for an absolute prohibition of assistance to such patients would of necessity appeal to a widely contested religious or ethical conviction many of them, including the patient-plaintiffs, reject. Allowing that justification to prevail would vitiate the liberty interest.

Even in the case of terminally ill patients, a state has a right to take all reasonable measures to insure that a patient requesting such assistance has made an informed, competent, stable and uncoerced decision. It is plainly legitimate for a state to establish procedures through which professional and administrative judgments can be made about these matters, and to forbid doctors to assist in suicide when its reasonable procedures have not been satisfied. States may be permitted considerable leeway in designing such procedures. They may be permitted, within reason, to err on what they take to be the side of caution. But they may not use the bare possibility of error as justification for refusing to establish any procedures at all and relying instead on a flat prohibition.

CONCLUSION

Each individual has a right to make the "most intimate and personal choices central to personal dignity and autonomy." That right encompasses the right to exercise some control over the time and manner of one's death.

The patient-plaintiffs in these cases were all mentally competent individuals in the final phase of terminal illness and died within months of filing their claims. Jane Doe described how her advanced cancer made even the most basic bodily functions such as swallowing, coughing, and yawning extremely painful and that it was "not possible for [her] to reduce [her] pain to an acceptable level of comfort and to retain an alert state." Faced with such circumstances, she sought to be able to "discuss freely with [her] treating physician [her] intention of hastening [her] death through the consumption of drugs prescribed for that purpose." *Quill v. Vacco,* 80 F.2d 716, 720 (2d Cir. 1996) (quoting declaration of Jane Doe). George A. Kingsley, in advanced stages of AIDS which included, among other hardships, the attachment of a tube to an artery in his chest which made even routine functions burdensome and the development of lesions on his brain, sought advice from his doctors regarding prescriptions which could hasten his impending death. Id. Jane Roe, suffering from cancer since 1988, had been almost completely bed-ridden since 1993 and experienced constant pain which could not be alleviated by medication. After undergoing counseling for herself and her family, she desired to hasten her death by taking prescription drugs. *Compassion in Dying v. Washington*, 850 F. Supp. 1454, 1456 (1994). John Doe, who had experienced numerous AIDS-related ailments since 1991, was "especially cognizant of the suffering imposed by a lingering terminal illness because he was the primary caregiver for his long-term companion who died of AIDS" and sought prescription drugs from his physician to hasten his own death after entering the terminal phase of AIDS. Id. at 1456–57. James Poe suffered from emphysema which caused him "a constant sensation of suffocating" as well as a cardiac condition which caused severe leg pain. Connected to an oxygen tank at all times but unable to calm the panic reaction associated with his feeling of suffocation even with regular doses of morphine, Mr. Poe sought physician-assisted suicide. Id. at 1457.

A state may not deny the liberty claimed by the patient-plaintiffs in these cases without providing them an opportunity to demonstrate, in whatever way the state might reasonably think wise and necessary, that the conviction they expressed for an early death is competent, rational, informed, stable and uncoerced.

Affirming the decisions by the Courts of Appeals would establish nothing more than that there is such a constitutionally protected right in principle. It would establish only that some individuals, whose decisions for suicide plainly cannot be dismissed as irrational or foolish or premature, must be accorded a reasonable opportunity to show that their decision for death is informed and free. It is not necessary to decide precisely which patients are entitled to that opportunity. If, on the other hand, this Court reverses the decisions below, its decision could only be justified by the momentous proposition—a proposition flatly in conflict with the spirit and letter of the Court's past decisions—that an American citizen does not, after all, have the right, even in principle, to live and die in the light of his own religious and ethical beliefs, his own convictions about why his life is valuable and where its value lies.

When Self-Determination Runs Amok

DANIEL CALLAHAN

The euthanasia debate is not just another moral debate, one in a long list of arguments in our pluralistic society. It is profoundly emblematic of three important turning points in Western thought. The first is that of the legitimate conditions under which one person can kill another. The acceptance of voluntary active euthanasia would morally sanction what can only be called "consenting adult killing." By that term I mean the killing of one person by another in the name of their mutual right to be killer and killed if they freely agree to play those roles. This turn flies in the face of a longstanding

effort to limit the circumstances under which one person can take the life of another, from efforts to control the free flow of guns and arms, to abolish capital punishment, and to more tightly control warfare. Euthanasia would add a whole new category of killing to a society that already has too many excuses to indulge itself in that way.

The second turning point lies in the meaning and limits of self-determination. The acceptance of euthanasia would sanction a view of autonomy holding that individuals may, in the name of their own private, idiosyncratic view of the good life, call upon others, including such institutions as medicine, to help them pursue that life, even at the risk of harm to the common good. This works against the idea that the meaning and scope of our own right to lead our own lives must be conditioned by, and be compatible with, the good of the community, which is more than an aggregate of self-directing individuals.

The third turning point is to be found in the claim being made upon medicine: it should be prepared to make its skills available to individuals to help them achieve their private vision of the good life. This puts medicine in the business of promoting the individualistic pursuit of general human happiness and well-being. It would overturn the traditional belief that medicine should limit its domain to promoting and preserving human health, redirecting it instead to the relief of that suffering which stems from life itself, not merely from a sick body.

I believe that, at each of these three turning points, proponents of euthanasia push us in the wrong direction. Arguments in favor of euthanasia fall into four general categories, which I will take up in turn: (1) the moral claim of individual self-determination and well-being; (2) the moral irrelevance of the difference between killing and allowing to die; (3) the supposed paucity of evidence to show likely harmful consequences of legalized euthanasia; and (4) the compatibility of euthanasia and medical practice.

SELF-DETERMINATION

Central to most arguments for euthanasia is the principle of self-determination. People are presumed to have an interest in deciding for themselves, according to their own beliefs about what makes life good, how they will conduct their lives. That is an important value, but the question in the euthanasia context is, What does it mean and how far should it extend? If it were a question of suicide, where a person takes her own life without assistance from another, that principle might be pertinent, at least for debate. But euthanasia is not that limited a matter. The self-determination in that case can only

be effected by the moral and physical assistance of another. Euthanasia is thus no longer a matter only of self-determination, but of a mutual, social decision between two people, the one to be killed and the other to do the killing.

How are we to make the moral move from my right of self-determination to some doctor's right to kill me—from *my* right to *his* right? Where does the doctor's moral warrant to kill come from? Ought doctors to be able to kill anyone they want as long as permission is given by competent persons? Is our right to life just like a piece of property, to be given away or alienated if the price (happiness, relief of suffering) is right? And then to be destroyed with our permission once alienated?

In answer to all those questions, I will say this: I have yet to hear a plausible argument why it should be permissible for us to put this kind of power in the hands of another, whether a doctor or anyone else. The idea that we can waive our right to life, and then give to another the power to take that life, requires a justification yet to be provided by anyone.

Slavery was long ago outlawed on the ground that one person should not have the right to own another, even with the other's permission. Why? Because it is a fundamental moral wrong for one person to give over his life and fate to another, whatever the good consequences, and no less a wrong for another person to have that kind of total, final power. Like slavery, dueling was long ago banned on similar grounds: even free, competent individuals should not have the power to kill each other, whatever their motives, whatever the circumstances. Consenting adult killing, like consenting adult slavery or degradation, is a strange route to human dignity.

There is another problem as well. If doctors, once sanctioned to carry out euthanasia, are to be themselves responsible moral agents—not simply hired hands with lethal injections at the ready—then they must have their own *independent* moral grounds to kill those who request such services. What do I mean? As those who favor euthanasia are quick to point out, some people want it because their life has become so burdensome it no longer seems worth living.

The doctor will have a difficulty at this point. The degree and intensity to which people suffer from their diseases and their dying, and whether they find life more of a burden than a benefit, has very little directly to do with the nature or extent of their actual physical condition. Three people can have the same condition, but only one will find the suffering unbearable. People suffer, but suffering is as much a function of the values of individuals as it is of the physical causes of that suffering. Inevitably in that circumstance, the doctor will in effect be treating the patient's values. To be responsible, the doctor would have to share those values. The doctor would have to decide, on her own, whether the patient's life was "no longer worth living."

But how could a doctor possibly know that or make such a judgment? Just because the patient said so? I raise this question because, while in Holland at the euthanasia conference reported by Maurice de Wachter elsewhere in this issue, the doctors present agreed that there is no objective way of measuring or judging the claims of patients that their suffering is unbearable. And if it is difficult to measure suffering, how much more difficult to determine the value of a patient's statement that her life is not worth living?

However one might want to answer such questions, the very need to ask them, to inquire into the physician's responsibility and grounds for medical and moral judgment, points out the social nature of the decision. Euthanasia is not a private matter of self-determination. It is an act that requires two people to make it possible, and a complicit society to make it acceptable.

KILLING AND ALLOWING TO DIE

Against common opinion, the argument is sometimes made that there is no moral difference between stopping life-sustaining treatment and more active forms of killing, such as lethal injection. Instead I would contend that the notion that there is no morally significant difference between omission and commission is just wrong. Consider in its broad implications what the eradication of the distinction implies: that death from disease has been banished, leaving only the actions of physicians in terminating treatment as the cause of death. Biology, which used to bring about death, has apparently been displaced by human agency. Doctors have finally, I suppose, thus genuinely become gods, now doing what nature and the deities once did.

What is the mistake here? It lies in confusing causality and culpability, and in failing to note the way in which human societies have overlaid natural causes with moral rules and interpretations. Causality (by which I mean the direct physical causes of death) and culpability (by which I mean our attribution of moral responsibility to human actions) are confused under three circumstances.

They are confused, first, when the action of a physician in stopping treatment of a patient with an underlying lethal disease is construed as *causing* death. On the contrary, the physician's omission can only bring about death on the condition that the patient's disease will kill him in the absence of treatment. We may hold the physician morally responsible for the death, if we have morally judged such actions wrongful omissions. But it confuses reality and moral judgment to see an omitted action as having the same causal status as one that directly kills. A lethal injection will kill both a healthy person and a sick person. A physician's omitted treatment will have no effect on a healthy person. Turn off the machine on me, a healthy person, and nothing will happen. It will only, in contrast, bring the life of a sick person to an end because of an underlying fatal disease.

Causality and culpability are confused, second, when we fail to note that judgments of moral responsibility and culpability are human constructs. By that I mean that we human beings, after moral reflection, have decided to call some actions right or wrong, and to devise moral rules to deal with them. When physicians could do nothing to stop death, they were not held responsible for it. When, with medical progress, they began to have some power over death—but only its timing and circumstances, not its ultimate inevitability—moral rules were devised to set forth their obligations. Natural causes of death were not thereby banished. They were, instead, overlaid with a medical ethics designed to determine moral culpability in deploying medical power.

To confuse the judgments of this ethics with the physical causes of death—which is the connotation of the word *kill*—is to confuse nature and human action. People will, one way or another, die of some disease; death will have dominion over all of us. To say that a doctor "kills" a patient by allowing this to happen should only be understood as a moral judgment about the licitness of his omission, nothing more. We can, as a fashion of speech only, talk about a doctor *killing* a patient by omitting treatment he should have provided. It is a fashion of speech precisely because it is the underlying disease that brings death when treatment is omitted; that is its cause, not the physician's omission. It is a misuse of the word *killing* to use it when a doctor stops a treatment he believes will no longer benefit the patient—when, that is, he steps aside to allow an eventually inevitable death to occur now rather than later. The only deaths that human beings invented are those that come from direct killing—when, with a lethal injection, we both cause death and are morally responsible for it. In the case of omissions, we do not cause death even if we may be judged morally responsible for it.

This difference between causality and culpability also helps us see why a doctor who has omitted a treatment he should have provided has "killed" that patient while another doctor—performing precisely the same act of omission on another patient in different circumstances—does not kill her, but only allows her to die. The difference is that we have come, by moral convention and conviction, to classify unauthorized or illegitimate omissions as acts of "killing." We call them "killing" in the expanded sense of the term: a culpable action that permits the real cause of death, the underlying disease, to proceed to its lethal conclusion. By contrast, the doctor who, at the patient's request, omits or terminates unwanted treatment does not kill at all. Her underlying disease, not his action, is the physical cause of death; and we have agreed to consider actions of that kind to be morally licit. He thus can truly be said to have "allowed" her to die.

If we fail to maintain the distinction between killing and allowing to die, moreover, there are some disturbing possibilities. The first would be to confirm many physicians in their already too-powerful belief that, when patients die or when physicians stop treatment because of the futility of continuing it, they are somehow both morally and physically responsible for the deaths that follow. That notion needs to be abolished, not strengthened. It needlessly and wrongly burdens the physician, to whom should not be attributed the powers of the gods.

The second possibility would be that, in every case where a doctor judges medical treatment no longer effective in prolonging life, a quick and direct killing of the patient would be seen as the next, most reasonable step, on grounds of both humaneness and economics. I do not see how that logic could easily be rejected.

CALCULATING THE CONSEQUENCES

When concerns about the adverse social consequences of permitting euthanasia are raised, its advocates tend to dismiss them as unfounded and overly speculative. On the contrary, recent data about the Dutch experience suggests that such concerns are right on target. From my own discussions in Holland, and from the articles on that subject in this issue and elsewhere, I believe we can now fully see most of the *likely* consequences of legal euthanasia.

Three consequences seem almost certain, in this or any other country: the inevitability of some abuse of the law; the difficulty of precisely writing, and then enforcing, the law; and the inherent slipperiness of the moral reasons for legalizing euthanasia in the first place.

Why is abuse inevitable? One reason is that almost all laws on delicate, controversial matters are to some extent abused. This happens because not everyone will agree with the law as written and will bend it, or ignore it, if they can get away with it. From explicit admissions to me by Dutch proponents of euthanasia, and from the corroborating information provided by the Remmelink Report and the outside studies of Carlos Gomez and John Keown, I am convinced that in the Netherlands there are a substantial number of cases of nonvoluntary euthanasia, that is, euthanasia undertaken without the explicit permission of the person being killed. The other reason abuse is inevitable is that the law is likely to have a low enforcement priority in the criminal justice system. Like other laws of similar status, unless there is an unrelenting and harsh willingness to pursue abuse, violations will ordinarily be tolerated. The worst thing to me about my experience in Holland was the casual, seemingly indifferent attitude toward abuse. I think that would happen everywhere.

Why would it be hard to precisely write, and then enforce, the law? The Dutch speak about the requirement of "unbearable" suffering, but admit that such a term is just about indefinable, a highly subjective matter admitting of no objective standards. A requirement for outside opinion is nice, but it is easy to find complaisant colleagues. A requirement that a medical condition be "terminal" will run aground on the notorious difficulties of knowing when an illness is actually terminal.

Apart from those technical problems there is a more profound worry. I see no way, even in principle, to write or enforce a meaningful law that can guarantee effective procedural safeguards. The reason is obvious yet almost always overlooked. The euthanasia transaction will ordinarily take place within the boundaries of the private and confidential doctor-patient relationship. No one can possibly know what takes place in that context unless the doctor chooses to reveal it. In Holland, less than 10 percent of the physicians report their acts of euthanasia and do so with almost complete legal impunity. There is no reason why the situation should be any better elsewhere. Doctors will have their own reasons for keeping euthanasia secret, and some patients will have no less a motive for wanting it concealed.

I would mention, finally, that the moral logic of the motives for euthanasia contain within them the ingredients of abuse. The two standard motives for euthanasia and assisted suicide are said to be our right of self-determination, and our claim upon the mercy of others, especially doctors, to relieve our suffering. These two motives are typically spliced together and presented as a single justification. Yet if they are considered independently—and there is no inherent reason why they must be linked—they reveal serious problems. It is said that a competent, adult person should have a right to euthanasia for the relief of suffering. But why must the person be suffering? Does not that stipulation already compromise the principle of self-determination? How can self-determination have any limits? Whatever the person's motives may be, why are they not sufficient?

Consider next the person who is suffering but not competent, who is perhaps demented or mentally retarded. The standard argument would deny euthanasia to that person. But why? If a person is suffering but not competent, then it would seem grossly unfair to deny relief solely on the grounds of incompetence. Are the incompetent less entitled to relief from suffering than the competent? Will it only be affluent, middle-class people, mentally fit and savvy about working the medical system, who can qualify? Do the incompetent suffer less because of their incompetence?

Considered from these angles, there are no good moral reasons to limit euthanasia once the principle of taking life for that purpose has been legitimated. If we really believe in self-determination, then any competent person should have a right to be killed by a doctor for any reason that suits him. If we believe in the relief of suffering, then it seems cruel and capricious to deny it to the incompetent. There is, in short, no reasonable or logical stopping point once the turn has been made down the road to euthanasia, which could soon turn into a convenient and commodious expressway.

EUTHANASIA AND MEDICAL PRACTICE

A fourth kind of argument one often hears both in the Netherlands and in this country is that euthanasia and assisted suicide are perfectly compatible with the aims of medicine. I would note at the very outset that a physician who participates in another person's suicide already abuses medicine. Apart from depression (the main statistical cause of suicide), people commit suicide because they find life empty, oppressive, or meaningless. Their judgment is a judgment about the value of continued life, not only about health (even if they are sick). Are doctors now to be given the right to make judgments about the kinds of life worth living and to give their blessing to suicide for those they judge wanting? What conceivable competence, technical or moral, could doctors claim to play such a role? Are we to medicalize suicide, turning judgments about its worth and value into one more clinical issue? Yes, those are rhetorical questions.

Yet they bring us to the core of the problem of euthanasia and medicine. The great temptation of modern medicine, not always resisted, is to move beyond the promotion and preservation of health into the boundless realm of general human happiness and well-being. The root problem of illness and mortality is both medical and philosophical or religious. "Why must I die?" can be asked as a technical, biological question or as a question about the meaning of life. When medicine tries to respond to the latter, which it is always under pressure to do, it moves beyond its proper role.

It is not medicine's place to lift from us the burden of that suffering which turns on the meaning we assign to the decay of the body and its eventual death. It is not medicine's place to determine when lives are not worth living or when the burden of life is too great to be borne. Doctors have no conceivable way of evaluating such claims on the part of patients, and they should have no right to act in response to them. Medicine should try to relieve human suffering, but only that suffering which is brought on by illness and dying as biological phenomena, not that suffering which comes from anguish or despair at the human condition.

Doctors ought to relieve those forms of suffering that medically accompany serious illness and the threat of death. They should relieve pain, do what they can to allay anxiety and uncertainty, and be a comforting presence. As sensitive human beings, doctors should be prepared to respond to patients who ask why they must die, or die in pain. But here the doctor and the patient are at the same level. The doctor may have no better an answer to those old questions than anyone else; and certainly no special insight from his training as a physician. It would be terrible for physicians to forget this, and to think that in a swift, lethal injection, medicine has found its own answer to the riddle of life. It would be a false answer, given by the wrong people. It would be no less a false answer for patients. They should neither ask medicine to put its own vocation at risk to serve their private interests, nor think that the answer to suffering is to be killed by another. The problem is precisely that, too often in human history, killing has seemed the quick, efficient way to put aside that which burdens us. It rarely helps, and too often simply adds to one evil still another. That is what I believe euthanasia would accomplish. It is self-determination run amok.

When Abstract Moralizing Runs Amok

JOHN LACHS

Moral reasoning is more objectionable when it is abstract than when it is merely wrong. For abstractness all but guarantees error by missing the human predicament that needs to be addressed, and worse, it is a sign that thought has failed to keep faith with its mission. The function of moral reflection is to shed light on the difficult problems we face; it cannot perform its job without a clear understanding of how and why certain of our practices come to seem no longer satisfactory.

It is just this grasp of the problem that is conspicuously lacking in Daniel Callahan's assault on euthanasia in "Self-Determination Run Amok."[1] The rhetoric Callahan unleashes gives not even a hint of the grave contemporary moral problems that euthanasia and assisted suicide, a growing number of people now think, promise to resolve.

Instead, we are offered a set of abstract distinctions calculated to discredit euthanasia rather than to contribute to a sound assessment of it. Thus, Callahan informs us that suffering "brought on by illness and dying as biological phenomena"[2] is to be contrasted with suffering that comes from "anguish or despair at the human condition." The former constitutes the proper concern of medicine (so much for psychiatry!), the latter of religion and philosophy. Medication is the answer to physical pain; euthanasia can, therefore, be only a misconceived response to worries about the meaning of existence. Those who believe in it offer a "swift lethal injection" as the "answer to the riddle of life."

This way of putting the matter will come as a surprise to those who suffer from terrible diseases and who no longer find life worth living. It is grotesque to suppose that such individuals are looking for the meaning of existence and find it, absurdly, in a lethal injection. Their predicament is not intellectual but existential. They are not interested in the meaning of life but in acting on their belief that their own continued existence is, on balance, of no further benefit to them.

Those who advocate the legalization of euthanasia and the practice of assisted suicide propose them as answers to a serious and growing social problem. We now have the power to sustain the biological existence of large numbers of very sick people, and we use this power freely. Accordingly, individuals suffering from painful terminal diseases, Alzheimer's patients, and those in a persistent vegetative state are routinely kept alive long past the point where they can function as human beings. They must bear the pain of existence without the ability to perform the activities that give life meaning. Some of these people feel intensely that they are a burden to others, as well as to themselves, and that their speedy and relatively dignified departure would be a relief to all concerned. Many observers of no more than average sensitivity agree that the plight of these patients is severe enough to justify such desires.

Some of these sufferers are physically not in a position to end their lives. Others could do so if they had the necessary instruments. In our culture, however, few have a taste for blowing out their brains or jumping from high places. That leaves drugs, which almost everyone is accustomed to taking, and which everyone knows can ease one peacefully to the other side.

The medical profession has, however, acquired monopoly power over drugs. And the danger of legal entanglement has made physicians wary of helping patients hasten their deaths in the discreet, humane way that has been customary for centuries. The result is that people who want to die and for whom death has long ceased to be an evil can find no way out of their misery. Current and growing pressures on the medical profession to help such sufferers are, therefore,

due at least partly to medicine itself. People want physicians to aid in their suicides because, without such help, they cannot end their lives. This restriction of human autonomy is due to the social power of medicine; it is neither surprising nor morally wrong, therefore, to ask those responsible for this limitation to undo some of its most noxious effects. If the medical profession relinquished its hold on drugs, people could make effective choices about their future without the assistance of physicians. Even limited access to deadly drugs, restricted to single doses for those who desire them and who are certified to be of sound mind and near the end of life, would keep physicians away from dealing in death.

Unfortunately, however, there is little sensible public discussion of such policy alternatives. And these policy alternatives may, in any case, not satisfy Callahan, who appears to believe that there is something radically wrong with anyone terminating a human life. Because he plays coy, his actual beliefs are difficult to make out. He says the notion that self-determination extends to suicide "might be pertinent, at least for debate."[3] But his argument against euthanasia sidesteps this issue: he maintains that even if there is a right to kill oneself, it is not one that can be transferred. The reason for this is that doing so would lead to "a fundamental moral wrong"—that of one person giving over "his life and fate to another."

One might wonder how we know that transferring power over oneself is "a fundamental moral wrong." Callahan appears to entertain the idea with intuitive certainty, which gives him the moral and the logical high ground and entitles him to demand a justification from whoever disagrees. But such intuitions are problematic themselves: is fervent embrace of them enough to guarantee their truth? Morality would be very distant from the concerns of life if it depended on such guideposts placed here and there in the desert of facts, unrelated to each other or to anything else. Their message, moreover, makes the guideposts suspect: it comes closer to being an echo of tradition or an expression of current views than a revelation of eternal moral truths.

Most important, the very idea of a right that intrinsically *cannot* be handed on is difficult to grasp. Under normal circumstances, to have a right is to be free or to be entitled to have or to do something. I have a right, for example, to clean my teeth. No one else has the right to do that without my consent. But I can authorize another, say my sweetheart or my dental hygienist, to do it for me. Similarly, I can assign my right to my house, to my left kidney, to raising my children, to deciding when I rise, when I go to sleep, and what I do in between (by joining the Army), and by a power of attorney even to pursuing my own interest.

To be sure, the transfer of rights is not without limits. My wife and I can, for example, give over our right to our children, though we cannot do so for money. I can contract to slave away for ten hours a day cooking hamburgers, but I cannot sell myself to be, once and for all, a slave. This does not mean, however, that some rights are intrinsically non-transferable. If my right to my left kidney were non-transferable, I could neither sell it nor give it away. But I can give it away, and the only reason I cannot sell it is because sales of this sort were declared, at some point, to be against public policy. We cannot sell ourselves into slavery for the same reason: human societies set limits to this transfer of rights on account of its unacceptable costs.

The case is no different with respect to authorizing another to end my life. If I have a right to one of my kidneys, I have a right to both. And if I can tell a needy person to take one of them, I can tell two needy people to take one each. There is nothing *intrinsically* immoral about this, even though when the second helps himself I die. Yet, by dying too soon, I may leave opportunities unexplored and obligations unmet. Unscrupulous operators may take advantage of my goodwill or naiveté. The very possibility of such acts invites abuse. For these or similar reasons, we may decide that giving the first kidney is morally acceptable, but giving the second is not. The difference between the two acts, however, is not that the first is generous while the second is "a fundamental moral wrong," but that the second occurs in a context and has consequences and costs that the first does not.

Only in terms of context and cost, therefore, can we sensibly consider the issue of the morality of euthanasia. Moving on the level of abstract maxims, Callahan misses this point altogether. He declares: "There are no good moral reasons to limit euthanasia once the principle of taking life...has

been legitimated."[4] Serious moral reflection, though it takes principles into account, is little interested in legitimating *them*. Its focus is on determining the moral acceptability of certain sorts of actions performed in complex contexts of life. Consideration of the circumstances is always essential: it is fatuous, therefore, to argue that if euthanasia is ever permissible, then "any competent person should have a right to be killed by a doctor for any reason that suits him."[5]

We can achieve little progress in moral philosophy without the ability and readiness to make relevant distinctions. Why, then, does Callahan refuse to acknowledge that there are important differences between the situation of a terminally ill patient in grave pain who wants to die and that of a young father in the dental chair who wishes, for a moment, that he were dead? Callahan's reason is that he thinks all judgments about the unbearability of suffering and the worthlessness of one's existence are subjective and, as such, parts of a "private, idiosyncratic view of the good life."[6] The amount of our suffering "has very little directly to do" with our physical condition, and so the desire to end life is capricious and unreliable. If medicine honored such desires, it would "put its own vocation at risk" by serving "the private interests" of individuals.

I cannot imagine what the vocation of medicine might be if it is not to serve the private interests of individuals. It is, after all, my vision of the good life that accounts for my wish not to perish in a diabetic coma. And surgeons certainly pursue the private interests of their patients in removing cancerous growths and in providing face-lifts. Medicine does not surrender its vocation in serving the desires of individuals: since health and continued life are among our primary wishes, its career consists in just this service.

Nevertheless, Callahan is right that our judgments about the quality of our lives and about the level of our suffering have a subjective component. But so do the opinions of patients about their health and illness, yet physicians have little difficulty in placing these perceptions in a broader, objective context. Similarly, it is both possible and proper to take into account the objective circumstances that surround desires to terminate life. Physicians have developed considerable skill in relating subjective complaints to objective conditions; only by absurd exaggeration can we say that the doctor must accept either all or none of the patient's claims. The context of the young father in the dental chair makes it clear that only a madman would think of switching from novocaine to cyanide when he moans that he wants to be dead. Even people of ordinary sensitivity understand that the situation of an old person whose friends have all died and who now suffers the excruciating pain of terminal cancer is morally different.

The question of the justifiability of euthanasia, as all difficult moral questions, cannot be asked without specifying the details of context. Dire warnings of slippery slopes and of future large-scale, quietly conducted exterminations trade on overlooking differences of circumstance. They insult our sensitivity by the suggestion that a society of individuals of good will cannot recognize situations in which their fellows want and need help and cannot distinguish such situations from those in which the desire for death is rhetorical, misguided, temporary, or idiotic. It would indeed be tragic if medicine were to leap to the aid of lovelorn teenagers whenever they feel life is too much to bear. But it is just as lamentable to stand idly by and watch unwanted lives fill up with unproductive pain.

Callahan is correct in pointing out that, in euthanasia and in assisted suicide, the physician and the patient must have separate justifications for action. The patient's wish is defensible if it is the outcome of a sound reflective judgment. Such judgments take into account the current condition, pending projects, and long-term prospects of the individual and relate them to his or her permanent interests and established values. As all assessments, these can be in error. For this reason, persons soliciting help in dying must be ready to demonstrate that they are of sound mind and thus capable of making such choices, that their desire is enduring, and that both their subjective and their objective condition makes their wish sensible.

Physicians must first decide whether their personal values permit them to participate in such activities. If they do, they must diligently examine the justifiability of the patient's desire to die. Diagnosis and prognosis are often relatively easy to ascertain. But we are not without resources for a sound determination of the internal condition of individuals either: extensive questioning on multiple occasions, interviews with friends and loved ones, and exploration of the life history and values of people contribute mightily to understanding their state of mind. Physicians who are prepared to aid individuals with this last need of their lives are not, therefore, in a position where they have to believe everything they hear and act on every request. They must make independent judgments instead of subordinating themselves as unthinking tools to the passing desires of those they wish to help. This does not attribute to doctors "the powers of the gods." It only requires that they be flexible in how they aid their patients and that they do so with due caution and on the basis of sound evaluation.

Callahan is once again right to be concerned that, if allowed, euthanasia will "take place within the boundaries of the private and confidential doctor-patient relationship."[7] This does, indeed, invite abuse and permit callous physicians to take a casual attitude to a momentous decision. Callahan is wrong, however, in supposing that this constitutes an argument against euthanasia. It is only a reason not to keep euthanasia secret, but to shed on it the wholesome light of publicity. Though the decision to terminate life is intensely private, no moral consideration demands that it be kept the confidential possession of two individuals. To the contrary, the only way we can minimize wrong decisions and abuse is to require scrutiny of the decision, prior to action on it, by a suitable social body. Such examination, including at least one personal interview with the patient, should go a long distance toward relieving Callahan's concern that any law governing euthanasia would have "a low enforcement priority in the criminal justice system."[8] With formal social controls in place, there should be very little need for the involvement of courts and prosecutors.

To suppose, as Callahan does, that the principle of autonomy calls for us to stand idly by, or even to assist, whenever and for whatever reason people want to end their lives is calculated to discredit both euthanasia and autonomy. No serious moralist has ever argued that self-determination must be absolute. It cannot hold unlimited sway, as Mill and other advocates of the principle readily admit, if humans are to live in a society. And morally, it would cut no ice if murderers and rapists argued for the legitimacy of their actions by claiming that they flow naturally and solely from who they are.

The function of the principle of autonomy is to affirm *a* value and to shift the burden of justifying infringements of individual liberty to established social and governmental powers. The value it affirms is that of individual agency expressed in the belief that, through action and suffering and death, the life of each person enjoys a sort of private integrity. This means that, in the end, our lives belong to no one but ourselves. The limits to such self-determination or self-possession are set by the demands of social life. They can be discovered or decided upon in the process of moral reflection. A sensible approach to euthanasia can disclose how much weight autonomy carries in that context and

how it can be balanced against other, equally legitimate but competing values.

In the hands of its friends, the principle of self-determination does not run amok. What runs amok in Callahan's version of autonomy and euthanasia is the sort of abstract moralizing that forgets the problem it sets out to address and shuts its eye to need and suffering.

NOTES

1. D. Callahan, "Self-Determination Run Amok," *Hastings Center Report* 22 (March–April 1992): 52–55.
2. Ibid., 55.
3. Ibid., 52.
4. Ibid., 54.
5. Ibid.
6. Ibid., 52.
7. Ibid., 54.
8. Ibid.

ARGUMENT 6 ESSAY QUESTIONS

1. What is the view expressed in "The Philosophers' Brief" on the autonomy argument? Do you believe the autonomy argument is sound? Why or why not? What objections to the argument do you think critics would (or could) make?
2. What is Lachs's response to Callahan? Is it convincing? Explain.
3. Which is the better argument: the autonomy argument or the argument for the state's right to override the liberty interest in the name of patient safety? Why?

7. THE KILLING/LETTING DIE ARGUMENT

Those who oppose active voluntary euthanasia often argue from a supposed moral difference between killing and letting die, or between active and passive euthanasia. The thought is that killing a person is morally worse than letting that person die. Killing is wrong; letting die is permissible. Thus giving a patient a lethal injection is wrong, but unplugging his feeding tube or respirator may be morally acceptable. Some think that killing is morally worse because it involves a person's causing the death of another person (murder) while letting die is a matter of allowing nature do its work. In the first, a person kills; in the second, a disease kills. In any case, euthanasia is wrong because it is deliberate killing.

But critics deny that there is a morally significant difference between killing and letting die. If there is no difference, they can argue that since passive euthanasia is permissible, and it is morally equivalent to active euthanasia, active euthanasia must be permissible as well. In "Active and Passive Euthanasia," James Rachels tries to demonstrate this no-difference thesis in a famous thought experiment about parallel cases:

> In the first case, Smith stands to gain a large inheritance if anything should happen to his six-year-old cousin. One evening while the child is taking his bath, Smith sneaks into the bathroom, drowns the child, and arranges things so that it will look like an accident.
>
> In the second, Jones also stands to gain if anything should happen to his six-year-old cousin. Like Smith, Jones sneaks in, planning to drown the child in his bath. However, as he enters the bathroom Jones sees the child slip, hit his head and fall face down in the water. Jones is delighted; he stands by, ready to push the child's head back under if it is necessary, but it is not necessary. With only a little thrashing about, the child drowns all by himself, "accidentally," as Jones watches and does nothing.
>
> Now Smith killed the child, while Jones merely let the child die. That is the only difference between them. Did either man behave better, from a moral point of view?[7]

Rachels concludes that any dissimilarity between killing and letting die does not make a moral difference.

Winston Nesbitt rejects Rachels's no-difference view, arguing that the real reason Smith and Jones seem equally reprehensible is that they are both *prepared to kill*. If we assumed that Jones is ready to let his cousin die but is not prepared to kill him, we would judge Jones less harshly than Smith. If this is correct, Nesbitt says, then Rachels fails to make his case.[8]

---

[7] James Rachels, "Active and Passive Euthanasia," *New England Journal of Medicine* 292, no. 2 (9 January 1975), 79.

[8] Winston Nesbitt, "Is Killing No Worse Than Letting Die?" *Journal of Applied Philosophy* 12:1 (1995), 101–5.

Active and Passive Euthanasia

JAMES RACHELS

The distinction between active and passive euthanasia is thought to be crucial for medical ethics. The idea is that it is permissible, at least in some cases, to withhold treatment and allow a patient to die, but it is never permissible to take any direct action designed to kill the patient. This doctrine seems to be accepted by most doctors, and it is endorsed in a statement adopted by the House of Delegates of the American Medical Association on December 4, 1973:

> The international termination of the life of one human being by another—mercy killing—is contrary to that for which the medical profession stands and is contrary to the policy of the American Medical Association.
>
> The cessation of the employment of extraordinary means to prolong the life of the body when there is irrefutable evidence that biological death is imminent is the decision of the patient and/or his immediate family. The advice and judgment of the physician should be freely available to the patient and/or his immediate family.

However, a strong case can be made against this doctrine. In what follows I will set out some of the relevant arguments, and urge doctors to reconsider their views on this matter.

To begin with a familiar type of situation, a patient who is dying of incurable cancer of the throat is in terrible pain, which can no longer be satisfactorily alleviated. He is certain to die within a few days, even if present treatment is continued, but he does not want to go on living for those days since the pain is unbearable. So he asks the doctor for an end to it, and his family joins in the request.

Suppose the doctor agrees to withhold treatment, as the conventional doctrine says he may. The justification for his doing so is that the patient is in terrible agony, and since he is going to die anyway, it would be wrong to prolong his suffering needlessly. But now notice this. If one simply withholds treatment, it may take the patient longer to die, and so he may suffer more than he would if more direct action were taken and a lethal injection given. This fact provides strong reason for thinking that, once the initial decision not to prolong his agony has been made, active euthanasia is actually preferable to passive euthanasia, rather than the reverse. To say otherwise is endorse the option that leads to more suffering rather than less, and is contrary to the humanitarian impulse that prompts the decision not to prolong his life in the first place.

Part of my point is that the process of being "allowed to die" can be relatively slow and painful, whereas being given a lethal injection is relatively quick and painless. Let me give a different sort of example. In the United States about one in 600 babies is born with Down's syndrome. Most of these babies are otherwise healthy—that is, with only the usual pediatric care, they will proceed to an otherwise normal infancy. Some, however, are born with congenital defects such as intestinal obstructions that require operations if they are to live. Sometimes, the parents and the doctor will decide not to operate, and let the infant die. Anthony Shaw describes what happens then:

> When surgery is denied [the doctor] must try to keep the infant from suffering while natural forces sap the baby's life away. As a surgeon whose natural inclination is to use the scalpel to fight off death, standing by and watching a salvageable baby die is the most emotionally exhausting experience I know. It is easy at a conference, in a theoretical discussion, to decide that such infants should be allowed to die. It is altogether different to stand by in the nursery and watch as dehydration and infection wither a tiny being over hours and days. This is a terrible ordeal for me and the hospital staff—much more so than for the parents who never set foot in the nursery.[1]

I can understand why some people are opposed to all euthanasia, and insist that such infants must be

---

allowed to live. I think I can also understand why other people favor destroying these babies quickly and painlessly. But why should anyone favor letting "dehydration and infection wither a tiny being over hours and days"? The doctrine that says that a baby may be allowed to dehydrate and wither, but may not be given an injection that would end its life without suffering, seems so patently cruel as to require no further refutation. The strong language is not intended to offend, but only to put the point in the clearest possible way.

My second argument is that the conventional doctrine leads to decisions concerning life and death made on irrelevant grounds.

Consider again the case of the infants with Down's syndrome who need operations for congenital defects unrelated to the syndrome to live. Sometimes, there is no operation, and the baby dies, but when there is no such defect, the baby lives on. Now, an operation such as that to remove an intestinal obstruction is not prohibitively difficult. The reason why such operations are not performed in these cases is, clearly, that the child has Down's syndrome and the parents and doctor judge that because of that fact it is better for the child to die.

But notice that this situation is absurd, no matter what view one takes of the lives and potentials of such babies. If the life of such an infant is worth preserving, what does it matter if it needs a simple operation? Or if one thinks it better that such a baby should not live on, what difference does it make that it happens to have an unobstructed intestinal tract? In either case, the matter of life and death is being decided on irrelevant grounds. It is the Down's syndrome, and not the intestines, that is the issue. The matter should be decided, if at all, on that basis, and not be allowed to depend on the essentially irrelevant question of whether the intestinal tract is blocked.

What makes this situation possible, of course, is the idea that when there is an intestinal blockage, one can "let the baby die," but when there is no such defect there is nothing that can be done, for one must not "kill" it. The fact that this idea leads to such results as deciding life or death on irrelevant grounds is another good reason why the doctrine should be rejected.

One reason why so many people think that there is an important moral difference between active and passive euthanasia is that they think killing someone is morally worse than letting someone die. But is it? Is killing, in itself, worse than letting die? To investigate this issue, two cases may be considered that are exactly alike except that one involves killing whereas the other involves letting someone die. Then, it can be asked whether this difference makes any difference to the moral assessments. It is important that the cases be exactly alike, except for this one difference, since otherwise one cannot be confident that it is this difference and not some other that accounts for any variation in the assessments of the two cases. So, let us consider this pair of cases:

In the first, Smith stands to gain a large inheritance if anything should happen to his six-year-old cousin. One evening while the child is taking his bath, Smith sneaks into the bathroom and drowns the child, and then arranges things so that it will look like an accident.

In the second, Jones also stands to gain if anything should happen to his six-year-old cousin. Like Smith, Jones sneaks in planning to drown the child in his bath. However, just as he enters the bathroom Jones sees the child slip and hit his head, and fall face down in the water. Jones is delighted: he stands by ready to push the child's head back under if it is necessary, but it is not necessary. With only a little thrashing about, the child drowns all by himself, "accidentally," as Jones watches and does nothing.

Now Smith killed the child, whereas Jones "merely" let the child die. That is the only difference between them. Did either man behave better, from a moral point of view? If the difference between killing and letting die were in itself a morally important matter, one should say that Jones's behavior was less reprehensible than Smith's. But does one really want to say that? I think not. In the first place, both men acted from the same motive, personal gain, and both had exactly the same end in view when they acted. It may be inferred from Smith's conduct that he is a bad man, although that judgment may be withdrawn or modified if certain further facts are learned about him—for example, that he is mentally deranged. But would not the very same thing be inferred about Jones from his conduct? And would not the same further considerations also be relevant to any modification of this judgment? Moreover, suppose Jones pleaded, in his own defense, "After all, I didn't do anything except just stand there and watch the child drown. I didn't kill him: I only let him die." Again, if letting die were in itself less bad than killing, this defense should have at least some weight. But it does not. Such a "defense" can only be regarded as a grotesque perversion of moral reasoning. Morally speaking, it is no defense at all.

Now, it may be pointed out, quite properly, that the cases of euthanasia with which doctors are concerned are not like this at all. They do not involve personal gain or the destruction of normal healthy children. Doctors are concerned only with cases in which the patient's life is of no further use to him, or in which the patient's life has become or will soon become a terrible burden. However, the point is the same in these cases: the bare difference between killing and letting die does not, in itself, make a moral difference. If a doctor lets a patient die, for humane reasons, he is in the same moral position as if he had given the patient a lethal injection for humane reasons. If his decision was wrong—if, for example, the patient's illness was in fact curable—the decision would be equally regrettable no matter which method was used to carry it out. And if the doctor's decision was the right one, the method used is not in itself important.

The AMA policy statement isolates the crucial issue very well: the crucial issue is "the intentional termination of the life of one human being by another." But after identifying this issue, and forbidding "mercy killing," the statement goes on to deny that the cessation of treatment is the intentional termination of a life. This is where the mistake comes in, for what is the cessation of treatment, in these circumstances, if it is not "the intentional termination of the life of one human being by another?" Of course it is exactly that, and if it were not, there would be no point to it.

Many people will find this judgment hard to accept. One reason, I think, is that it is very easy to conflate the question of whether killing is, in itself, worse than letting die, with the very different question of whether most actual cases of killing are more reprehensible than most actual cases of letting die. Most actual cases of killing are clearly terrible (think, for example, of all the murders reported in the newspapers), and one hears of such cases every day. On the other hand, one hardly ever hears of a case of letting die except for the actions of doctors who are motivated by humanitarian reasons. So one learns to think of killing in a much worse light than of letting die. But this does not mean that there is something about killing that makes it in itself worse than letting die, for it is not the bare difference between killing and letting die that makes the difference in these cases. Rather, the other factors—the murderer's motive of personal gain, for example, contrasted with the doctor's humanitarian motivation—account for different reactions to the different cases.

I have argued that killing is not in itself any worse than letting die: if my contention is right, it follows that active euthanasia is not any worse than passive euthanasia. What arguments can be given on the other side? The most common, I believe, is the following:

"The important difference between active and passive euthanasia is that, in passive euthanasia, the doctor does not do anything to bring about the patient's death. The doctor does nothing, and the patient dies of whatever ills already afflict him. In active euthanasia, however, the doctor does something to bring about the patient's death: he kills him. The doctor who gives the patient with cancer a lethal injection has himself caused his patient's death; whereas if he merely ceases treatment, the cancer is the cause of the death."

A number of points need to be made here. The first is that it is not exactly correct to say that in passive euthanasia the doctor does nothing, for he does do one thing that is very important; he lets the patient die. "Letting someone die" is certainly different, in some respects, from other types of action—mainly in that it is a kind of action that one may perform by way of not performing certain other actions. For example, one may let a patient die by way of not giving medication, just as one may insult someone by way of not shaking his hand. But for any purpose of moral assessment, it is a type of action nonetheless. The decision to let a patient die is subject to moral appraisal in the same way that a decision to kill him would be subject to moral appraisal: it may be assessed as wise or unwise, compassionate or sadistic, right or wrong. If a doctor deliberately let a patient die who was suffering from a routinely curable illness, the doctor would certainly be to blame for what he had done, just as he would be to blame if he had needlessly killed the patient. Charges against him would then be appropriate. If so, it would be no defense at all for him to insist that he didn't "do anything." He would have done something very serious indeed, for he let his patient die.

Fixing the cause of death may be very important from a legal point of view, for it may determine whether criminal charges are brought against the doctor. But I do not think that this notion can be used to show a moral difference between active and passive euthanasia. The reason why it is considered bad to be the cause of someone's death is that death is regarded as a great evil—and so it is. However, if it has been decided that euthanasia—even passive euthanasia—is desirable in a given case, it has also been decided that in this instance death is no greater an evil than the patient's continued existence. And if this is true, the usual reason for not wanting to be the cause of someone's death simply does not apply.

Finally, doctors may think that all of this is only of academic interest—the sort of thing that philosophers may worry about but that has no practical bearing on their own work. After all, doctors must be concerned about the legal consequences of what they do, and active euthanasia is clearly forbidden by the law. But even so, doctors should also be concerned with the fact that the law is forcing upon them a moral doctrine that may well be indefensible, and has a considerable effect on their practices. Of course most doctors are not now in the position of being coerced in this matter, for they do not regard themselves as merely going along with what the law requires. Rather, in statements such as the AMA policy statement that I have quoted, they are endorsing this doctrine as a central point of medical ethics. In that statement, active euthanasia is condemned not merely as illegal but as "contrary to that for which the medical profession stands," whereas passive euthanasia is approved. However, the preceding considerations suggest that there is really no moral difference between the two, considered in themselves (there may be important moral differences in some cases in their *consequences*, but, as I pointed out, these differences may make active euthanasia, and not passive euthanasia, the morally preferable option). So, whereas doctors may have to discriminate between active and passive euthanasia to satisfy the law, they should not do any more than that. In particular, they should not give the distinction any added authority and weight by writing it into official statements of medical ethics.

NOTE

1. Shaw A: 'Doctor, Do We Have a Choice?' *The New York Times Magazine*, January 30, 1972, p 54.

Is Killing No Worse Than Letting Die?

WINSTON NESBITT

I want in this paper to consider a kind of argument sometimes produced against the thesis that it is worse to kill someone (that is, to deliberately take action that results in another's death) than merely to allow someone to die (that is, deliberately to fail to take steps which were available and which would have saved another's life). Let us, for brevity's sake, refer to this as the "difference thesis," since it implies that there is a moral difference between killing and letting die.

One approach commonly taken by opponents of the difference thesis is to produce examples of cases in which an agent does not kill, but merely lets someone die, and yet would be generally agreed to be just as morally reprehensible as if he had killed. This kind of appeal to common intuitions might seem an unsatisfactory way of approaching the issue. It has been argued[1] that what stance one takes concerning the difference thesis will depend on the ethical theory one holds, so that we cannot decide what stance is correct independently of deciding what is the correct moral theory. I do not, however, wish to object to the approach in question on these grounds. It may be true that different moral theories dictate different stances concerning the difference thesis, so that a theoretically satisfactory defence or refutation of the thesis requires a satisfactory defence of a theory which entails its soundness or unsoundness. However, the issue of its soundness or otherwise is a vital one in the attempt to decide some pressing moral questions[2], and we cannot wait for a demonstration of the correct moral theory before taking up any kind of position with regard to it. Moreover, decisions on moral questions directly affecting practice are rarely derived from ethical first principles, but are usually based at some level on common intuitions, and it is arguable that at least where the question is one of public policy, this is as it should be.

2

It might seem at first glance a simple matter to show at least that common moral intuitions favour the difference thesis. Compare, to take an example of John Ladd's[3], the case in which I push someone who I know cannot swim into a river, thereby killing her, with that in which I come across someone drowning and fail to rescue her, although I am able to do so, thereby letting her die. Wouldn't most of us agree that my behaviour is morally worse in the first case?

However, it would be generally agreed by those involved in the debate that nothing of importance for our issue, not even concerning common opinion, can be learned through considering such an example. As Ladd points out, without being told any more about the cases mentioned, we are inclined to assume that there are other morally relevant differences between them, because there usually would be.

We assume, for example, some malicious motive in the case of killing, but perhaps only fear or indifference in the case of failing to save. James Rachels and Michael Tooley, both of whom argue against the difference thesis, make similar points[4], as does Raziel Abelson, in a paper defending the thesis[5]. Tooley, for example, notes that as well as differences in motives, there are also certain other morally relevant differences between typical acts of killing and typical acts of failing to save which may make us judge them differently. Typically, saving someone requires more effort than refraining from killing someone. Again, an act of killing necessarily results in someone's death, but an act of failing to save does not—someone else may come to the rescue. Factors such as these, it is suggested, may account for our tendency to judge failure to save (i.e., letting die) less harshly than killing. Tooley concludes that if one wishes to appeal to intuitions here, "One must be careful to confine one's attention to pairs of cases that do not differ in these, or other significant respects"[6].

Accordingly, efforts are made by opponents of the difference thesis to produce pairs of cases which do not differ in morally significant respects (other than in one being a case of killing while the other is a case of letting die or failing to save). In fact, at least the major part of the case mounted by Rachels and Tooley against the difference thesis consists of the production of such examples. It is suggested that when we compare a case of killing with one which differs from it *only in* being a case of letting die, we will agree that either agent is as culpable as the other; and this is then taken to show that any inclination we ordinarily have to think killing worse than letting die is attributable to our tending, illegitimately, to think of typical cases of killing and of letting die, which differ in other morally relevant respects. I want now to examine the kind of example usually produced in these contexts.

3

I will begin with the examples produced by James Rachels in the article mentioned earlier, which is fast becoming one of the most frequently reprinted articles in the area[7]. Although the article has been the subject of a good deal of discussion, as far as I know the points which I will make concerning it have not been previously made. Rachels asks us to compare the following two cases. The first is that of Smith, who will gain a large inheritance should his six-year-old cousin die. With this in mind, Smith one evening sneaks into the bathroom where his nephew is taking a bath, and drowns him. The other case, that of Jones, is identical, except that as Jones is about to drown his nephew, the child slips, hits his head, and falls, face down and unconscious, into the bath water. Jones, delighted at his good fortune, watches as his nephew drowns.

Rachels assumes that we will readily agree that Smith, who kills his nephew, is no worse, morally speaking, than Jones, who merely lets his nephew die. Do we really want to say, he asks, that either behaves better from the moral point of view than the other? It would, he suggests, be a "grotesque perversion of moral reasoning" for Jones to argue, "After all, I didn't do anything except just stand and watch the child drown. I didn't kill him; I only let him die."[8] Yet, Rachels says, if letting die were in itself less bad than killing, this defence would carry some weight.

There is little doubt that Rachels is correct in taking it that we will agree that Smith behaves no worse in his examples than does Jones. Before we are persuaded by this that killing someone is in itself morally no worse than letting someone die, though, we need to consider the examples more closely. We concede that Jones, who merely let his nephew die, is just as reprehensible as Smith, who killed his nephew. Let us ask, however, just what is the ground of our judgement of the agent in each case. In the case of Smith, this seems to be adequately captured by saying that Smith drowned his nephew for motives of personal gain. But can we say that the grounds on which we judge Jones to be reprehensible, and just as reprehensible as Smith, are that he let his nephew drown for motives of personal gain? I suggest not—for this neglects to mention a crucial fact about Jones, namely that he was fully prepared to kill his nephew, and would have done so had it proved necessary. It would be generally accepted, I think, quite independently of the present debate, that someone who is fully prepared to perform a reprehensible action, in the expectation of certain circumstances, but does not do so because the expected circumstances do not eventuate, is just as reprehensible as someone who actually performs that action in those circumstances. Now this alone is sufficient to account for our judging Jones as harshly as Smith. He was fully prepared to do what Smith did, and would have done so if circumstances had not turned out differently from those in Smith's case. Thus, though we may agree that he is just as reprehensible as Smith, this cannot be taken as showing that his letting his nephew die is as reprehensible as Smith's killing his nephew— for we would have judged him just as harshly, given what he was prepared to do, even if he had not let his nephew die. To make this clear, suppose that we modify Jones' story along the following lines— as before, he sneaks into the bathroom while his nephew is bathing, with the intention of drowning the child in his bath. This time, however, just before he can seize the child, *he* slips and hits his head on the bath, knocking himself unconscious. By the time he regains consciousness, the child, unaware of his intentions, has called his parents, and the opportunity is gone. Here, Jones neither kills his nephew *nor* lets him die—yet I think it would be agreed that given his preparedness to kill the child for personal gain, he is as reprehensible as Smith.

The examples produced by Michael Tooley, in the book referred to earlier, suffer the same defect as those produced by Rachels. Tooley asks us to consider the following pair of scenarios, as it happens also featuring Smith and Jones. In the first, Jones is about to shoot Smith when he sees that Smith will be killed by a bomb unless Jones warns him, as he easily can. Jones does not warn him, and he is killed by the bomb—i.e., Jones lets Smith die. In the other, Jones wants Smith dead, and shoots him—i.e., he kills Smith.

Tooley elsewhere[9] produces this further example: two sons are looking forward to the death of their wealthy father, and decide independently to poison him. One puts poison in his father's whiskey, and is discovered doing so by the other, who was just about to do the same. The latter then allows his father to drink the poisoned whiskey, and refrains from giving him the antidote, which he happens to possess.

Tooley is confident that we will agree that in each pair of cases, the agent who kills is morally no worse than the one who lets die. It will be clear, however, that his examples are open to criticisms parallel to those just produced against Rachels. To take first the case where Jones is saved the trouble of killing Smith by the fortunate circumstance of a bomb's being about to explode near the latter: it is true that we judge Jones to be just as reprehensible as if he had killed Smith, but since he was fully prepared to kill him had he not been saved the trouble by the bomb, we would make the same judgement even if he had neither killed Smith nor let him die (even if, say, no bomb had been present, but Smith suffered a massive and timely heart attack). As for the example of the like-minded sons, here too the son who didn't kill was prepared to do so, and given this, would be as reprehensible as the other even if he had not let his father die (if, say, he did not happen to possess the antidote, and so was powerless to save him).

Let us try to spell out more clearly just where the examples produced by Rachels and Tooley fail. What both writers overlook is that what determines whether someone is reprehensible or not is not simply what he in fact does, but what he is prepared to do, perhaps as revealed by what he in fact does. Thus, while Rachels is correct in taking it that we will be inclined to judge Smith and Jones in his examples equally harshly, this is not surprising, since both are judged reprehensible for precisely the same reason, namely that they were fully prepared to kill for motives of personal gain. The same, of course, is true of Tooley's examples. In each example he gives of an agent who lets another die, the agent is fully prepared to kill (though in the event, he is spared the necessity). In their efforts to ensure that the members of each pair of cases they produce do not differ in any morally relevant respect (except that one is a case of killing and the other of letting die), Rachels and Tooley make them *too* similar—not only do Rachels' Smith and Jones, for example, have identical motives, but both are guilty of the same moral offence.

4

Given the foregoing account of the failings of the examples produced by Rachels and Tooley, what modifications do they require if they are to be legitimately used to gauge our attitudes towards killing and letting die, respectively? Let us again concentrate on Rachels' examples. Clearly, if his argument is to avoid the defect pointed out, we must stipulate that though Jones was prepared to let his nephew die once he saw that this would happen unless he

intervened, he was not prepared to kill the child. The story will now go something like this: Jones stands to gain considerably from his nephew's death, as before, but he is not prepared to kill him for this reason. However, he happens to be on hand when his nephew slips, hits his head, and falls face down in the bath. Remembering that he will profit from the child's death, he allows him to drown. We need, however, to make a further stipulation, regarding the explanation of Jones's not being prepared to kill his nephew. It cannot be that he fears untoward consequences for himself, such as detection and punishment, or that he is too lazy to choose such an active course, or that the idea simply had not occurred to him. I think it would be common ground in the debate that if the only explanation of his not being prepared to kill his nephew was one of these kinds, he would be morally no better than Smith, who differed only in being more daring, or more energetic, whether or not fate then happened to offer him the opportunity to let his nephew die instead. In that case, we must suppose that the reason Jones is prepared to let his nephew die, but not to kill him, is a moral one—not intervening to save the child, he holds, is one thing, but actually bringing about his death is another, and altogether beyond the pale.

I suggest, then, that the case with which we must compare that of Smith is this: Jones happens to be on hand when his nephew slips, hits his head, and falls unconscious into his bath water. It is clear to Jones that the child will drown if he does not intervene. He remembers that the child's death would be greatly to his advantage, and does not intervene. Though he is prepared to let the child die however, and in fact does so, he would not have been prepared to kill him, because, as he might put it, wicked though he is, he draws the line at killing for gain.

I am not entirely sure what the general opinion would be here as to the relative reprehensibility of Smith and Jones. I can only report my own, which is that Smith's behaviour is indeed morally worse than that of Jones. What I do want to insist on, however, is that, for the reasons I have given, we cannot take our reactions to the examples provided by Rachels and Tooley as an indication of our intuitions concerning the relative heinousness of killing and of letting die.

So far, we have restricted ourselves to discussion of common intuitions on our question, and made no attempt to argue for any particular answer. I will conclude by pointing out that, given the fairly common view that the raison d'être of morality is to make it possible for people to live together in reasonable peace and security, it is not difficult to provide a rationale for the intuition that in our modified version of Rachels' examples, Jones is less reprehensible than Smith. For it is clearly preferable to have Jones-like persons around rather than Smith-like ones. We are not threatened by the former—such a person will not save me if my life should be in danger, but in this he is no more dangerous than an incapacitated person, or for that matter, a rock or tree (in fact he may be better, for he *might* save me as long as he doesn't think he will profit from my death). Smith-like persons, however, *are* a threat—if such a person should come to believe that she will benefit sufficiently from my death, then not only must I expect no help from her if my life happens to be in danger, but I must fear positive attempts on my life. In that case, given the view mentioned of the point of morality, people prepared to behave as Smith does are clearly of greater concern from the moral point of view than those prepared only to behave as Jones does; which is to say that killing is indeed morally worse than letting die.

NOTES

1. See, for example, John Chandler (1990). Killing and letting die—putting the debate in context, *Australasian Journal of Philosophy* 68, no. 4, 1990, pp. 420–431.
2. It underlies, or is often claimed to underlie, for example, the Roman Catholic position on certain issues in the abortion debate, and the view that while 'passive' euthanasia may sometimes be permissible, 'active' euthanasia never is. It also seems involved in the common view that even if it is wrong to fail to

give aid to the starving of the world, thereby letting them die, it is not as wrong as dropping bombs on them, thereby killing them.
3. John Ladd (1985). Positive and negative euthanasia, in James E. White (ed.), *Contemporary Moral Problems* (St Paul, West Publishing Co), pp. 58–68.
4. James Rachels (1979). Active and passive euthanasia, in James Rachels (ed.), *Moral Problems* (NY, Harper and Row), pp. 490–497; Michael Tooley (1983). *Abortion and Infanticide* (Oxford, Clarendon Press), pp. 187–188.
5. Raziel Abelson (1982). There is a moral difference, in Raziel Abelson and Marie-Louise Friquegnon (eds.), *Ethics for Modern Life* (New York, St Martin's Press), pp. 73–83.
6. Tooley, op. cit., p. 189.
7. Apart from the anthology cited in footnote 4, it appears, for example, in James E. White (ed.) (1991). *Contemporary Moral Problems* (St Paul, West Publishing Co), pp. 103–107; Bonnte Steinbock (ed.) (1980). *Killing and Letting Die* (Englewood Cliffs, NJ, Prentice-Hall), pp. 63–68; Tom L. Beauchamp and Leroy Walters (eds.) (1982). *Contemporary Issues in Bioethics* (Belmont, Wadsworth Publishing Co), pp. 313–316; Robert F. Weir (ed.) (1986). *Ethical Issues in Death and Dying* (NY, Columbia University Press), pp. 249–256; Ronald Munson (ed.) (1992). *Interventions and Reflections* (Belmont, Wadsworth Publishing Co), pp. 163–166; John Arras and Nancy Rhoden (eds.) (1989). *Ethical Issues in Modern Medicine* (Calif, Mayfield Publishing Co), pp. 241–244; and in Thomas A. Mappes and Jane S. Zembaty (eds.) (1977). *Social Ethics* (NY, McGraw-Hill), pp. 62–66.
8. Rachels, op. cit., p. 494.
9. (1980) An irrelevant consideration: killing and letting die, in Bonnte Steinbock (ed.), *Killing and Letting Die* (Englewood Cliffs, NJ, Prentice-Hall), pp. 56–62.

ARGUMENT 7 ESSAY QUESTIONS

1. Does Nesbitt successfully counter Rachels's argument? Explain.
2. What would be the implications for the euthanasia debate if the killing/letting die distinction were bogus? If it were legitimate?
3. Do you think there is in fact a morally significant difference between killing and letting die? Why or why not?

8. THE SLIPPERY-SLOPE ARGUMENT AGAINST EUTHANASIA

Probably the most straightforward arguments against active euthanasia and physician-assisted suicide are appeals to bad consequences. They make their case at the policy level, asking us to consider the ramifications of legalizing or widely accepting these practices. Often their logical shape is the slippery slope: allowing active euthanasia or physician-assisted suicide will inevitably lead to dangerous extensions or perversions of the original practices. In "Why Doctors Must Not Kill," Leon R. Kass argues (1) that legalization [of physician-assisted suicide] will lead quickly from active voluntary euthanasia to active nonvoluntary euthanasia to outright involuntary forms of killing, (2) that physicians or families will start pushing unwilling or unsure patients toward assisted suicide or voluntary euthanasia, and (3) that physicians and nurses will become increasingly willing to give lethal injections to people who are elderly, mentally ill, chronically ill, uninsured, and disabled.

One critic of euthanasia describes the treacherous slide like this:

> [E]uthanasia as a policy is a slippery slope. A person apparently hopelessly ill may be allowed to take his own life. Then he may be permitted to deputize others to do it for him should he no longer be able to act. The judgment of others then becomes the ruling factor. Already at this point euthanasia is not personal and voluntary, for others are acting "on behalf of" the patient as they see fit. This may well incline them to act on behalf of other patients who have not authorized them to exercise their judgment. It is only a short step, then, from voluntary euthanasia (self-inflicted or authorized), to directed euthanasia administered to a patient who has given no authorization, to involuntary euthanasia conducted as part of a social policy.[9]

The general argument, as applied to active voluntary euthanasia, says that if the general acceptance or approval of active voluntary euthanasia leads to widespread abuses (unjustified killing), then the practice is morally wrong—and the general acceptance or approval *will in fact* lead to widespread abuses. In such an argument, the latter assertion is the sticking point, an empirical claim that is often difficult to assess. Much of the debate therefore has centered on whether any good empirical evidence supports such a premise.

Unfortunately, relevant scientific research has been scant, with most of it focused on the Netherlands, where physician-assisted suicide and active voluntary euthanasia have been legal since 2002. (There is even less data on Oregon, where a law permitting physician-assisted suicide was passed by Oregon voters in 1994 but not green-lighted until

---

[9] J. Gay-Williams, "The Wrongfulness of Euthanasia," in *Intervention and Reflection: Basic Issues in Medical Ethics*, ed. Ronald Munson, 7th ed. (Belmont, CA: Wadsworth, 2004), 710–11.

the Supreme Court decision of 2006.) Thus both those who favor and those who oppose euthanasia and assisted suicide try to make their case with data from the Dutch experience. One question they want the research to answer is whether legalization of voluntary euthanasia has expanded the use of nonvoluntary euthanasia, for a significant expansion would seem to support slippery-slope arguments. Opponents of legalization point to all the instances of Dutch physicians performing active euthanasia without the patient's consent (approximately one thousand per year, or about 0.8 percent of all deaths nationwide). Proponents reply that most of those patients were already near death or had become incompetent after initially asking for euthanasia, or that the euthanasia was passive, consisting of withholding or withdrawing treatment. Most of all, they emphasize that the few studies done so far provide no evidence that legalization has significantly multiplied the cases of nonvoluntary euthanasia.

Most parties in this dispute recognize the need for better evidence to assess the slipperiness of the slippery slope. But they also understand that the *mere possibility* of abuses arising from allowing euthanasia or assisted suicide is not in itself a good reason to ban the practices. If merely possible dangers or abuses justified prohibiting a practice, then we would have good reason to disallow advance directives, surrogate decision making, and any kind of voluntary passive euthanasia. For a slippery-slope argument to work, there must be good evidence that the bad consequences of taking the first step are probable and serious.

Why Doctors Must Not Kill

LEON R. KASS

Do you want your doctor licensed to kill? Should he or she be permitted or encouraged to inject or prescribe poison? Shall the mantle of privacy that protects the doctor-patient relationship, in the service of life and wholeness, now also cloak decisions for death? Do you want *your* doctor deciding, on the basis of his own private views, when you still deserve to live and when you now deserve to die? And what about the other fellow's doctor—that shallow technician, that insensitive boor who neither asks nor listens, that unprincipled money-grubber, that doctor you used to go to until you got up the nerve to switch: do you want *him* licensed to kill? Speaking generally, shall the healing profession become also the euthanizing profession?

Common sense has always answered, "No." For more than two millennia, the reigning medical ethic, mindful that the power to cure is also the power to kill, has held as an inviolable rule, "Doctors must not kill." Yet this venerable taboo is now under attack. Proponents of euthanasia and physician-assisted suicide would have us believe that it is but an irrational vestige of religious prejudice, alien to a true ethic of medicine, which stands in the way of a rational and humane approach to suffering at the end of life. Nothing could be further from the truth. The taboo against doctors killing patients (even on request) is the very embodiment of reason and wisdom. Without it, medicine will have trouble doing its proper work; without it, medicine will have lost its claim to be an ethical and trustworthy profession; without it, all of us will suffer—yes, more

From "Why Doctors Must Not Kill" by Leon R. Kass, *Commonweal*, 14 Supplement (9 August 1991), 472–475. © Commonweal Magazine.

than we now suffer because some of us are not soon enough released from life.

Consider first the damaging consequences for the doctor-patient relationship. The patient's trust in the doctor's whole-hearted devotion to the patient's best interests will be hard to sustain once doctors are licensed to kill. Imagine the scene: you are old, poor, in failing health, and alone in the world; you are brought to the city hospital with fractured ribs and pneumonia. The nurse or intern enters late at night with a syringe full of yellow stuff for your intravenous drip. How soundly will you sleep? It will not matter that your doctor has never yet put anyone to death; that he is legally entitled to do so will make a world of difference.

And it will make a world of psychic difference too for conscientious physicians. How easily will they be able to care whole-heartedly for patients when it is always possible to think of killing them as a "therapeutic option"? Shall it be penicillin and a respirator one more time, or, perhaps, this time just an overdose of morphine? Physicians get tired of treating patients who are hard to cure, who resist their best efforts, who are on their way down—"gorks," "gomers," and "vegetables" are only some of the less than affectionate names they receive from the house officers. Won't it be tempting to think that death is the best "treatment" for the little old lady "dumped" again on the emergency room by the nearby nursing home?

It is naive and foolish to take comfort from the fact that the currently proposed change in the law provides "aid-in-dying" only to those who request it. For we know from long experience how difficult it is to discover what we truly want when we are suffering. Verbal "requests" made under duress rarely reveal the whole story. Often a demand for euthanasia is, in fact, an angry or anxious plea for help, born of fear of rejection or abandonment, or made in ignorance of available alternatives that could alleviate pain and suffering. Everyone knows how easy it is for those who control the information to engineer requests and to manipulate choices, especially in the vulnerable. Paint vividly a horrible prognosis, and contrast it with that "gentle, quick release": which will the depressed or frightened patient choose, especially in the face of a spiraling hospital bill or children who visit grudgingly? Yale Kamisar asks the right questions: "Is this the kind of choice,

assuming that it can be made in a fixed and rational manner, that we want to offer a gravely ill person? Will we not sweep up, in the process, some who are not really tired of life, but think others are tired of them; some who do not really want to die, but who feel that they should not live on, because to do so when there looms the legal alternative of euthanasia is to do a selfish or cowardly act? Will not some feel an obligation to have themselves 'eliminated' in order that funds allocated for their terminal care might be better used by their families or, financial worries aside, in order to relieve their families of the emotional strain involved?"

Euthanasia, once legalized, will not remain confined to those who freely and knowingly elect it—and the most energetic backers of euthanasia do not really want it thus restricted. Why? Because the vast majority of candidates who merit mercy-killing cannot request it for themselves: adults with persistent vegetative state or severe depression or senility or aphasia or mental illness or Alzheimer's disease; infants who are deformed; and children who are retarded or dying. All incapable of requesting death, they will thus be denied our new humane "assistance-in-dying." But not to worry. The lawyers and the doctors (and the cost-containers) will soon rectify this injustice. The enactment of a law legalizing mercy killing (or assisted suicide) on voluntary request will certainly be challenged in the courts under the equal-protection clause of the Fourteenth Amendment. Why, it will be argued, should the comatose or the demented be denied the right to such a "dignified death" or such a "treatment" just because they cannot claim it for themselves? With the aid of court-appointed proxy consenters, we will quickly erase the distinction between the right to choose one's own death and the right to request someone else's—as we have already done in the termination-of-treatment cases.

Clever doctors and relatives will not need to wait for such changes in the law. Who will be around to notice when the elderly, poor, crippled, weak, powerless, retarded, uneducated, demented, or gullible are mercifully released from the lives their doctors, nurses, and next of kin deem no longer worth living? In Holland, for example, a recent survey of 300 physicians (conducted by an author who supports euthanasia) disclosed that over 40 percent had performed euthanasia *without the patient's request,* and over 10 percent had done so in more than five cases. Is there any reason to believe that the average American physician is, in his private heart, more committed than his Dutch counterpart to the equal worth and dignity of every life under his care? Do we really want to find out what he is like, once the taboo is broken?

Even the most humane and conscientious physician psychologically needs protection against himself and his weaknesses, if he is to care fully for those who entrust themselves to him. A physician-friend who worked many years in a hospice caring for dying patients explained it to me most convincingly: "Only because I knew that I could not and would not kill my patients was I able to enter most fully and intimately into caring for them as they lay dying." The psychological burden of the license to kill (not to speak of the brutalization of the physician-killers) could very well be an intolerably high price to pay for the physician-assisted euthanasia.

The point, however, is not merely psychological: it is also moral and essential. My friend's horror at the thought that he might be tempted to kill his patients, were he not enjoined from doing so, embodies a deep understanding of the medical ethic and its intrinsic limits. We move from assessing consequences to looking at medicine itself.

The beginning of ethics regarding the use of power generally lies in nay-saying. The wise setting of limits on the use of power is based on discerning the excesses to which the power, unrestrained, is prone. Applied to the professions, this principle would establish strict outer boundaries—indeed, inviolable taboos—against those "occupational hazards" to which each profession is especially prone. *Within* these outer limits, no fixed rules of conduct apply; instead, prudence—the wise judgment of the man-on-the-spot—finds and adopts the best course of action in the light of the circumstances. But the outer limits themselves are fixed, firm, and nonnegotiable.

What are those limits for medicine? At least three are set forth in the venerable Hippocratic Oath: no breach of confidentiality; no sexual relations with patients; no dispensing of deadly drugs. These unqualified, self-imposed restrictions are readily understood in terms of the temptations to

which the physician is most vulnerable, temptations in each case regarding an area of vulnerability and exposure that the practice of medicine requires of patients. Patients necessarily divulge and reveal private and intimate details of their personal lives; patients necessarily expose their naked bodies to the physician's objectifying gaze and investigating hands; patients necessarily expose and entrust the care of their very lives to the physician's skill, technique, and judgment. The exposure is, in all cases, one-sided and asymmetric: the doctor does not reveal his intimacies, display his nakedness, offer up his embodied life to the patient. Mindful of the meaning of such nonmutual exposure, the physician voluntarily sets limits on his own conduct, pledging not to take advantage of or to violate the patient's intimacies, naked sexuality, or life itself.

The prohibition against killing patients, the first negative promise of self-restraint sworn to in the Hippocratic Oath, stands as medicine's first and most abiding taboo: "I will neither give a deadly drug to anybody if asked for it, nor will I make a suggestion to this effect.... In purity and holiness I will guard my life and my art." In forswearing the giving of poison, the physician recognizes and restrains a god-like power he wields over patients, mindful that his drugs can both cure and kill. But in forswearing the giving of poison, *when asked for it,* the Hippocratic physician rejects the view that the patient's choice for death can make killing him—or assisting his suicide—right. For the physician, at least, human life in living bodies commands respect and reverence—*by its very nature.* As its respectability does not depend upon human agreement or patient consent, revocation of one's consent to live does not deprive one's living body of respectability. The deepest ethical principle restraining the physician's power is not the autonomy or freedom of the patient; neither is it his own compassion or good intention. Rather, it is the dignity and mysterious power of human life itself, and, therefore, also what the oath calls the purity and holiness of the life and art to which he has sworn devotion. A person can choose to be a physician, but he cannot simply choose what physicianship means.

The central meaning of physicianship derives not from medicine's powers but from its goal, not from its means but from its end: to benefit the sick by the activity of healing. The physician as physician serves only the sick. He does not serve the relatives or the hospital or the national debt inflated due to Medicare costs. Thus he will never sacrifice the well-being of the sick to the convenience or pocketbook or feelings of the relatives or society. Moreover, the physician serves the sick not because they have rights or wants or claims, but because they are sick. The healer works with and for those who need to be healed, in order to help make them whole. Despite enormous changes in medical technique and institutional practice, despite enormous changes in nosology and therapeutics, the center of medicine has not changed: it is as true today as it was in the days of Hippocrates that the ill desire to be whole; that wholeness means a certain well-working of the enlivened body and its unimpaired powers to sense, think, feel, desire, move, and maintain itself; and that the relationship between the healer and the ill is constituted, essentially even if only tacitly, around the desire of both to promote the wholeness of the one who is ailing.

Can wholeness and healing ever be compatible with intentionally killing the patient? Can one benefit the patient as a whole by making him dead? There is, of course, a logical difficulty: how can any good exist for a being that is not? But the error is more than logical: to intend and to act for someone's good requires his continued existence to receive the benefit.

To be sure, certain attempts to benefit may in fact turn out, unintentionally, to be lethal. Giving adequate morphine to control pain might induce respiratory depression leading to death. But the intent to relieve the pain of the living presupposes that the living still live to be relieved. This must be the starting point in discussing all medical benefits: no benefit without a beneficiary.

Against this view, someone will surely bring forth the hard cases: patients so ill-served by their bodies that they can no longer bear to live, bodies riddled with cancer and racked with pain, against which their "owners" protest in horror and from which they insist on being released. Cannot the person "in the body" speak up against the rest, and request death for "personal" reasons?

However sympathetically we listen to such requests, we must see them as incoherent. Such person-body dualism cannot be sustained. "Personhood" is manifest on earth only in living bodies; our highest mental functions are held up by, and are inseparable from, lowly metabolism, respiration, circulation, excretion. There may be blood without consciousness, but there is never consciousness without blood. Thus one who calls for death in the service of personhood is like a tree seeking to cut its roots for the sake of growing its highest fruit. No physician, devoted to the benefit of the sick, can serve the patient as person by denying and thwarting his personal embodiment.

To say it plainly, to bring nothingness is incompatible with serving wholeness: one cannot heal—or comfort—by making nil. The healer cannot annihilate if he is truly to heal. The physician-euthanizer is a deadly self-contradiction.

But we must acknowledge a difficulty. The central goal of medicine—health—is, in each case, a perishable good: inevitably, patients get irreversibly sick, patients degenerate, patients die. Healing the sick is *in principle* a project that must at some point fail. And here is where all the trouble begins: How does one deal with "medical failure"? What does one seek when restoration of wholeness—or "much" wholeness—is by and large out of the question?

Contrary to the propaganda of the euthanasia movement, there is, in fact, much that can be done. Indeed, by recognizing finitude yet knowing that we will not kill, we are empowered to focus on easing and enhancing the *lives* of those who are dying. First of all, medicine can follow the lead of the hospice movement and—abandoning decades of shameful mismanagement—provide truly adequate (and now technically feasible) relief of pain and discomfort. Second, physicians (and patients and families) can continue to learn how to withhold or withdraw those technical interventions that are, in truth, merely burdensome or degrading medical additions to the unhappy end of a life—including, frequently, hospitalization itself. Ceasing treatment and allowing death to occur when (and if) it will seem to be quite compatible with the respect life itself commands for itself. Doctors may and must allow to die, even if they must not intentionally kill.

Ceasing medical intervention, allowing nature to take its course, differs fundamentally from mercy killing. For one thing, death does not necessarily follow the discontinuance of treatment;

Karen Ann Quinlan lived more than ten years after the court allowed the "life-sustaining" respirator to be removed. Not the physician, but the underlying fatal illness becomes the true cause of death. More important morally, in ceasing treatment the physician need not *intend* the death of the patient, even when the death follows as a result of his omission. His intention should be to avoid useless and degrading medical *additions* to the already sad end of a life. In contrast, in active, direct mercy killing the physician must, necessarily and indubitably, intend *primarily* that the patient be made dead. And he must knowingly and indubitably cast himself in the role of the agent of death. This remains true even if he is merely an assistant in suicide. A physician who provides the pills or lets the patient plunge the syringe after he leaves the room is *morally* no different from one who does the deed himself. "I will neither give a deadly drug to anybody if asked for it, nor will I make a suggestion to this effect."

Once we refuse the technical fix, physicians and the rest of us can also rise to the occasion: we can learn to act humanly in the presence of finitude. Far more than adequate morphine and the removal of burdensome machinery, the dying need our presence and our encouragement. Dying people are all too easily reduced ahead of time to "thinghood" by those who cannot bear to deal with the suffering or disability of those they love. Withdrawal of contact, affection, and care is the greatest single cause of the dehumanization of dying. Not the alleged humaneness of an elixir of death, but the humanness of connected living-while-dying is what medicine—and the rest of us—most owe the dying. The treatment of choice is company and care.

The euthanasia movement would have us believe that the physician's refusal to assist in suicide or perform euthanasia constitutes an affront to human dignity. Yet one of their favorite arguments seems to me rather to prove the reverse. Why, it is argued, do we put animals out of their misery but insist on compelling fellow human beings to suffer to the bitter end? Why, if it is not a contradiction for the veterinarian, does the medical ethic absolutely rule out mercy killing? Is this not simply inhumane?

Perhaps *inhumane*, but not thereby *inhuman*. On the contrary, it is precisely because animals are not human that we must treat them (merely) humanely. We put dumb animals to sleep because they do not know that they are dying, because they can make nothing of their misery or mortality, and, therefore, because they cannot live deliberately—i.e., humanly—in the face of their own suffering and dying. They cannot live out a fitting end. Compassion for their weakness and dumbness is our only appropriate emotion, and given our responsibility for their care and well-being, we do the only humane thing we can. But when a conscious human being asks us for death, by that very action he displays the presence of something that precludes our regarding him as a dumb animal. Humanity is owed humanity, not humaneness. Humanity is owed the bolstering of the human, even or especially in its dying moments, in resistance to the temptation to ignore its presence in the sight of suffering.

What humanity needs most in the face of evils is courage, the ability to stand against fear and pain and thoughts of nothingness. The deaths we most admire are those of people who, knowing that they are dying, face the fact frontally and act accordingly: they set their affairs in order, they arrange what could be final meetings with their loved ones, and yet, with strength of soul and a small reservoir of hope, they continue to live and work and love as much as they can for as long as they can. Because such conclusions of life require courage, they call for our encouragement—and for the many small speeches and deeds that shore up the human spirit against despair and defeat.

Many doctors are in fact rather poor at this sort of encouragement They tend to regard every dying or incurable patient as a failure, as if an earlier diagnosis or a more vigorous intervention might have avoided what is, in truth, an inevitable collapse. The enormous successes of medicine these past fifty years have made both doctors and laymen less prepared than ever to accept the fact of finitude. Doctors behave, not without some reason, as if they have godlike powers to revive the moribund; laymen expect an endless string of medical miracles. Physicians today are not likely to be agents of encouragement once their technique begins to fail.

It is, of course, partly for these reasons that doctors will be pressed to kill—and many of them will, alas, be willing. Having adopted a largely technical approach to healing, having medicalized so much of the end of life, doctors are being asked—often with thinly veiled anger—to provide a final technical solution for the evil of human finitude and for their own technical failure: If you cannot cure me, kill me. The last gasp of autonomy or cry for dignity is asserted against a medicalization and institutionalization of the end of life that robs the old and the incurable of most of their autonomy and dignity: intubated and electrified, with bizarre mechanical companions, once proud and independent people find themselves cast in the roles of passive, obedient, highly disciplined children. People who care for autonomy and dignity should try to reverse this dehumanization of the last stages of life, instead of giving dehumanization its final triumph by welcoming the desperate goodbye-to-all—that contained in one final plea for poison.

The present crisis that leads some to press for active euthanasia is really an opportunity to learn the limits of the medicalization of life and death and to recover an appreciation of living with and against mortality. It is an opportunity for physicians to recover an understanding that there remains a residual human wholeness—however precarious—that can be cared for even in the face of incurable and terminal illness. Should doctors cave in, should doctors become technical dispensers of death, they will not only be abandoning their posts, their patients, and their duty to care; they will set the worst sort of example for the community at large—teaching technicism and so-called humaneness where encouragement and humanity are both required and sorely lacking. On the other hand, should physicians hold fast, should doctors learn that finitude is no disgrace and that human wholeness can be cared for to the very end, medicine may serve not only the good of its patients, but also, by example, the failing moral health of modern times.

Voluntary Active Euthanasia

DAN W. BROCK

Since the case of Karen Quinlan first seized public attention fifteen years ago, no issue in biomedical ethics has been more prominent than the debate about forgoing life-sustaining treatment. Controversy continues regarding some aspects of that debate, such as forgoing life-sustaining nutrition and hydration, and relevant law varies some from state to state. Nevertheless, I believe it is possible to identify an emerging consensus that competent patients, or the surrogates of incompetent patients, should be permitted to weigh the benefits and burdens of alternative treatments, including the alternative of no treatment, according to the patient's values, and either to refuse any treatment or to select from among available alternative treatments. This consensus is reflected in bioethics scholarship, in reports of prestigious bodies such as the President's Commission for the Study of Ethical Problems in Medicine, The Hastings Center, and the American Medical Association, in a large body of judicial decisions in courts around the country, and finally in the beliefs and practices of health care professionals who care for dying patients.

More recently, significant public and professional attention has shifted from life-sustaining treatment to euthanasia—more specifically, voluntary active euthanasia—and to physician-assisted suicide. Several factors have contributed to the increased interest in euthanasia. In the Netherlands, it has been openly practiced by physicians for several years with the acceptance of the country's highest court. In 1988 there was an unsuccessful attempt to get the question of whether it should be made legally permissible on the ballot in California. In November 1991 voters in the state of Washington defeated a widely publicized referendum proposal to legalize both voluntary active euthanasia and physician-assisted suicide. Finally, some cases of this kind, such as "It's Over, Debbie," described in *the Journal of the American Medical Association*, the "suicide machine" of Dr. Jack Kevorkian, and the cancer patient "Diane" of Dr. Timothy Quill, have captured wide public and professional attention. Unfortunately, the first two of these cases were sufficiently problematic that even most supporters of euthanasia or assisted suicide did not defend the physicians' actions in them. As a result, the subsequent debate they spawned has often shed more heat than light. My aim is to increase the light, and perhaps as well to reduce the heat, on this important subject by formulating and evaluating the central ethical arguments for and against voluntary active euthanasia and physician-assisted suicide. My evaluation of the arguments leads me, with reservations to be noted, to support permitting both practices. My primary aim, however, is not to argue for euthanasia, but to identify confusions in some common arguments, and problematic assumptions and claims that need more defense or data in others. The issues are considerably more complex than either supporters or opponents often make out; my hope is to advance the debate by focusing attention on what I believe the real issues under discussion should be.

In the recent bioethics literature some have endorsed physician-assisted suicide but not euthanasia. Are they sufficiently different that the moral arguments for one often do not apply to the other? A paradigm case of physician-assisted suicide is a patient's ending his or her life with a lethal dose of a medication requested of and provided by a physician for that purpose. A paradigm case of voluntary active euthanasia is a physician's administering the lethal dose, often because the patient is unable to do so. The only difference that need exist between the two is the person who actually administers the lethal dose—the physician or the patient. In each, the physician plays an active and necessary causal role.

In physician-assisted suicide the patient acts last (for example, Janet Adkins herself pushed the button after Dr. Kevorkian hooked her up to his suicide machine), whereas in euthanasia the physician acts last by performing the physical equivalent of pushing the button. In both cases, however, the choice rests fully with the patient. In both the patient acts last in the sense of retaining the right to change his or her mind until the point at which the lethal process becomes irreversible. How could there be a substantial moral difference between the two based only on this small difference in the part played by the physician in the causal process resulting in death? Of course, it might be held that the moral difference is clear and important—in euthanasia the physician kills the patient whereas in physician-assisted suicide the patient kills him- or herself. But this is misleading at best. In assisted suicide the physician and patient together kill the patient. To see this, suppose a physician supplied a lethal dose to a patient with the knowledge and intent that the patient will wrongfully administer it to another. We would have no difficulty in morality or the law recognizing this as a case of joint action to kill for which both are responsible.

If there is no significant, intrinsic moral difference between the two, it is also difficult to see why public or legal policy should permit one but not the other; worries about abuse or about giving anyone dominion over the lives of others apply equally to either. As a result, I will take the arguments evaluated below to apply to both and will focus on euthanasia.

My concern here will be with *voluntary* euthanasia only—that is, with the case in which a clearly competent patient makes a fully voluntary and persistent request for aid in dying. Involuntary euthanasia, in which a competent patient explicitly refuses or opposes receiving euthanasia, and nonvoluntary euthanasia, in which a patient is incompetent and unable to express his or her wishes about euthanasia, will be considered here only as potential unwanted side-effects of permitting voluntary euthanasia. I emphasize as well that I am concerned with *active* euthanasia, not with holding or withdrawing life-sustaining treatment, which some commentators characterize as "passive euthanasia." Finally, I will be concerned with euthanasia where the motive of those who perform it is to respect the wishes of the patient and to provide the patient with a "good death," though one important issue is whether a change in legal policy could restrict the performance of euthanasia to only those cases.

A last introductory point is that I will be examining only secular arguments about euthanasia, though of course many people's attitudes to it are inextricable from their religious views. The policy issue is only whether euthanasia should be permissible, and no one who has religious objections to it should be required to take any part in it, though of course this would not fully satisfy some opponents.

THE CENTRAL ETHICAL ARGUMENT FOR VOLUNTARY ACTIVE EUTHANASIA

The central ethical argument for euthanasia is familiar. It is that the very same two fundamental ethical values supporting the consensus on patient's rights to decide about life-sustaining treatment also support the ethical permissibility of euthanasia. These values are individual self-determination or autonomy and individual well-being. By self-determination as it bears on euthanasia, I mean people's interest in making important decisions about their lives for themselves according to their own values or conceptions of a good life, and in being left free to act on those decisions. Self-determination is valuable because it permits people to form and live in accordance with their own conception of a good life, at least within the bounds of justice and consistent with others doing so as well. In exercising self-determination people take responsibility for their lives and for the kinds of persons they become. A central aspect of human dignity lies in people's capacity to direct their lives in this way. The value of exercising self-determination presupposes some minimum of decision-making capacities or competence, which thus limits the scope of euthanasia supported by self-determination; it cannot justifiably be administered, for example, in cases of serious dementia or treatable clinical depression.

Does the value of individual self-determination extend to the time and manner of one's death? Most people are very concerned about the nature of the last stage of their lives. This reflects not just a fear of experiencing substantial suffering when dying, but also a desire to retain dignity and control during this last period of life. Death is today increasingly preceded by a long period of significant physical and mental decline, due in part to the technological interventions of modern medicine. Many people adjust to these disabilities and find meaning and value in new activities and ways. Others find the impairments and burdens in the last stage of their lives at some point sufficiently great to make life no longer worth living. For many patients near death, maintaining the quality of one's life, avoiding great suffering, maintaining one's dignity, and insuring that others remember us as we wish them to become of paramount importance and outweigh merely extending one's life. But there is no single, objectively correct answer for everyone as to when, if at all, one's life becomes all things considered a burden and unwanted. If self-determination is a fundamental value, then the great variability among people on this question makes it especially important that individuals control the manner, circumstances, and timing of their dying and death.

The other main value that supports euthanasia is individual well-being. It might seem that individual well-being conflicts with a person's self-determination when the person requests euthanasia. Life itself is commonly taken to be a central good for persons, often valued for its own sake, as well as necessary for pursuit of all other goods within a life. But when a competent patient decides to forgo all further life-sustaining treatment then the patient, either explicitly or implicitly, commonly decides that the best life possible for him or her with treatment is of sufficiently poor quality that it is worse than no further life at all. Life is no longer considered a benefit by the patient, but has now become a burden. The same judgment underlies a request for euthanasia: continued life is seen by the patient as no longer a benefit, but now a burden. Especially in the often severely compromised and debilitated states of many critically ill or dying patients, there is no objective standard, but only the competent patient's judgment of whether continued life is no longer a benefit.

Of course, sometimes there are conditions, such as clinical depression, that call into question whether the patient has made a competent choice, either to forgo life-sustaining treatment or to seek euthanasia, and then the patient's choice need not be evidence that continued life is no longer a benefit for him or her. Just as with decisions about treatment, a determination of incompetence can warrant not honoring the patient's choice; in the case of treatment, we then transfer decisional authority to a surrogate, though in the case of voluntary active euthanasia a determination that the patient is incompetent means that choice is not possible.

The value or right of self-determination does not entitle patients to compel physicians to act contrary to their own moral or professional values. Physicians are moral and professional agents whose own self-determination or integrity should be respected as well. If performing euthanasia became legally permissible, but conflicted with a particular physician's reasonable understanding of his or her moral or professional responsibilities, the care of a patient who requested euthanasia should be transferred to another.

Most opponents do not deny that there are some cases in which the values of patient self-determination and well-being support euthanasia. Instead, they commonly offer two kinds of arguments against it that on their view outweigh or override this support. The first kind of argument is that in any individual case where considerations of the patient's self-determination and well-being do support euthanasia, it is nevertheless always ethically wrong or impermissible. The second kind of argument grants that in some individual cases euthanasia may *not* be ethically wrong, but maintains nonetheless that public and legal policy should never permit it. The first kind of argument focuses on features of any individual case of euthanasia, while the second kind focuses on social or legal policy. In the next section I consider the first kind of argument.

EUTHANASIA IS THE DELIBERATE KILLING OF AN INNOCENT PERSON

The claim that any individual instance of euthanasia is a case of deliberate killing of an innocent person is, with only minor qualifications, correct. Unlike forgoing life-sustaining treatment, commonly understood as allowing to die, euthanasia is clearly killing, defined as depriving of life or causing the death of a living being. While providing morphine for pain relief at doses where the risk of respiratory depression and an earlier death may be a foreseen but unintended side effect of treating the patient's pain, in a case of euthanasia the patient's death is deliberate or intended even if in both the physician's ultimate end may be respecting the patient's wishes. If the deliberate killing of an innocent person is wrong, euthanasia would be nearly always impermissible.

In the context of medicine, the ethical prohibition against deliberately killing the innocent derives some of its plausibility from the belief that nothing in the currently accepted practice of medicine is deliberate killing. Thus, in commenting on the "It's Over, Debbie" case, four prominent physicians and bioethicists could entitle their paper "Doctors Must Not Kill." The belief that doctors do not in fact kill requires the corollary belief that forgoing life-sustaining treatment, whether by not starting or by stopping treatment, is allowing to die, not killing. Common though this view is, I shall argue that it is confused and mistaken.

Why is the common view mistaken? Consider the case of a patient terminally ill with ALS disease. She is completely respirator dependent with no hope of ever being weaned. She is unquestionably competent but finds her condition intolerable and persistently requests to be removed from the respirator and allowed to die. Most people and physicians would agree that the patient's physician should respect the patient's wishes and remove her from the respirator, though this will certainly cause the patient's death. The common understanding is that the physician thereby allows the patient to die. But is that correct?

Suppose the patient has a greedy and hostile son who mistakenly believes that his mother will never decide to stop her life-sustaining treatment and that even if she did her physician would not remove her from the respirator. Afraid that his inheritance will be dissipated by a long and expensive hospitalization, he enters his mother's room while she is sedated, extubates her, and she dies. Shortly thereafter the medical staff discovers what he has done and confronts the son. He replies, "I didn't kill her, I merely allowed her to die. It was her ALS disease that caused her death." I think this would rightly be dismissed as transparent sophistry—the son went into his mother's room and deliberately killed her. But, of course, the son performed just the same physical actions, did just the same thing, that the physician would have done. If that is so, then doesn't the physician also kill the patient when he extubates her?

I underline immediately that there are important ethical differences between what the physician and the greedy son do. First, the physician acts with the patient's consent whereas the son does not. Second, the physician acts with a good motive—to respect the patient's wishes and self-determination—whereas the son acts with a bad motive—to protect his own inheritance. Third, the physician acts in a social role through which he is legally authorized to carry out the patient's wishes regarding treatment whereas the son has no such authorization. These and perhaps other ethically important differences show that what the physician did was morally justified whereas what the son did was morally wrong. What they do *not* show, however, is that the son killed while the physician allowed to die. One can either kill or allow to die with or without consent, with a good or bad motive, within or outside of a social role that authorizes one to do so.

The difference between killing and allowing to die that I have been implicitly appealing to here is roughly that between acts and omissions resulting in death. Both the physician and the greedy son act in a manner intended to cause death, do cause death, and so both kill. One reason this conclusion is resisted is that on a different understanding of the distinction between killing and allowing to die, what the physician does is allow to die. In this account, the mother's ALS is a lethal disease whose normal progression is being held back or blocked by the life-sustaining respirator treatment. Removing this artificial intervention is then viewed as standing aside and allowing the patient to die of her underlying disease. I have argued elsewhere that this alternative account is deeply problematic, in part because it commits us to accepting that what the greedy son does is to allow to die, not kill. Here, I want to note two other reasons why the conclusion that stopping life support is killing is resisted.

The first reason is that killing is often understood, especially within medicine, as unjustified causing of death; in medicine it is thought to be done only accidentally or negligently. It is also increasingly widely accepted that a physician is ethically justified in stopping life support in a case like that of the ALS patient. But if these two beliefs are correct, then what the physician does cannot be killing, and so must be allowing to die. Killing patients is not, to put it flippantly, understood to be part of physicians' job description. What is mistaken in this line of reasoning is the assumption that all killings are *unjustified* causings of death. Instead, some killings are ethically justified, including many instances of stopping life support.

Another reason for resisting the conclusion that stopping life support is often killing is that it is psychologically uncomfortable. Suppose the physician had stopped the ALS patient's respirator and had made the son's claim, "I didn't kill her, I merely allowed her to die. It was her ALS disease that caused her death." The clue to the psychological role here is how naturally the "merely" modifies "allowed her to die." The characterization as allowing to die is meant to shift felt responsibility away from the agent—the physician—and to the lethal disease process. Other language common in death and dying contexts plays a similar role; "letting nature take its course" or "stopping prolonging the dying process" both seem to shift responsibility from the physician who stops life support to the fatal disease process. However psychologically helpful these conceptualizations may be in making the difficult responsibility of a physician's role in the patient's death bearable, they nevertheless are confusions. Both physicians and family members can instead be helped to understand that it is the patient's decision and consent to stopping treatment that limits their responsibility for the patient's death and that shifts that responsibility to the patient.

Many who accept the difference between killing and allowing to die as the distinction between acts and omissions resulting in death have gone on to argue that killing is not in itself morally different from allowing to die. In this account, very roughly, one kills when one performs an action that causes the death of a person (we are in a boat, you cannot swim, I push you overboard, and you drown), and one allows to die when one has the ability and opportunity to prevent the death of another, knows this, and omits doing so, with the result that the person dies (we are in a boat, you cannot swim, you fall overboard, I don't throw you an available life ring, and you drown). Those who see no moral difference between killing and allowing to die typically employ the strategy of comparing cases that differ in these and no other potentially morally important respects. This will allow people to consider whether the mere difference that one is a case of killing and the other of allowing to die matters morally, or whether instead it is other features that make most cases of killing worse than most instances of allowing to die. Here is such a pair of cases:

Case 1. A very gravely ill patient is brought to a hospital emergency room and sent up to the ICU. The patient begins to develop respiratory failure that is likely to require intubation very soon. At that point the patient's family members and long-standing physician arrive at the ICU and inform the ICU staff that there had been extensive discussion about future care with the patient when he was unquestionably competent. Given his grave and terminal illness, as well as his state of debilitation, the patient had firmly rejected being placed on a respirator under any circumstances, and the family and physician produce the patient's advance directive to that effect. The ICU staff do not intubate the patient, who dies of respiratory failure.

Case 2. The same as Case 1 except that the family and physician are slightly delayed in traffic and arrive shortly after the patient has been intubated and placed on the respirator. The ICU staff extubate the patient, who dies of respiratory failure.

In Case 1 the patient is allowed to die, in Case 2 he is killed, but it is hard to see why what is done in Case 2 is significantly different morally than what is done in Case 1. It must be other factors that make most killings worse than most allowings to die, and if so, euthanasia cannot be wrong simply because it is killing instead of allowing to die.

Suppose both my arguments are mistaken. Suppose that killing is worse than allowing to die and that withdrawing life support is not killing, although euthanasia is. Euthanasia still need not for that reason be morally wrong. To see this, we need to determine the basic principle for the moral evaluation of killing persons. What is it that makes paradigm cases of wrongful killing wrongful? One very plausible answer is that killing denies the victim something that he or she values greatly—continued life or a future. Moreover, since continued life is necessary for pursuing any of a person's plans and purposes, killing brings the frustration of all of these plans and desires as well. In a nutshell, wrongful killing deprives a person of a valued future, and of all the person wanted and planned to do in that future.

A natural expression of this account of the wrongness of killing is that people have a moral right not to be killed. But in this account of the wrongness of killing, the right not to be killed, like other rights, should be waivable when the person makes a competent decision that continued life is no longer wanted or a good, but is instead worse than no further life at all. In this view, euthanasia is properly understood as a case of a person having waived his or her right not to be killed.

This rights view of the wrongness of killing is not, of course, universally shared. Many people's moral views about killing have their origins in religious views that human life comes from God and cannot be justifiably destroyed or taken away, either by the person whose life it is or by another. But in a pluralistic society like our own with a strong commitment to freedom of religion, public policy should not be grounded in religious beliefs which many in that society reject. I turn now to the general evaluation of public policy on euthanasia.

WOULD THE BAD CONSEQUENCES OF EUTHANASIA OUTWEIGH THE GOOD?

The argument against euthanasia at the policy level is stronger than at the level of individual cases, though even here I believe the case is ultimately unpersuasive, or at best indecisive. The policy level is the place where the main issues lie, however, and where moral considerations that might override arguments in favor of euthanasia will be found, if they are found anywhere. It is important to note two kinds of disagreement about the consequences for public policy of permitting euthanasia. First, there is empirical or factual disagreement about what the consequences would be. This disagreement is greatly exacerbated by the lack of firm data on the issue. Second, since on any reasonable assessment there would be both good and bad consequences, there are moral disagreements about the relative importance of different effects. In addition to these two sources of disagreement, there is also no single, well-specified policy proposal for legalizing euthanasia on which policy assessments can focus. But without such specification, and especially without explicit procedures for protecting against well-intentioned misuse and ill-intentioned abuse, the consequences for policy are largely speculative. Despite these difficulties, a preliminary account of the main likely good and bad consequences is possible. This should help clarify where better data or more moral analysis and argument are needed, as well as where policy safeguards must be developed.

Potential Good Consequences of Permitting Euthanasia

What are the likely good consequences? First, if euthanasia were permitted it would be possible to respect the self-determination of competent patients who want it, but now cannot get it because of its illegality. We simply do not know how many such patients and people there are. In the Netherlands, with a population of about 14.5 million (in 1987), estimates in a recent study were that about 1,900 cases of voluntary active euthanasia or physician-assisted suicide occur annually. No straightforward extrapolation to the United States is possible for many reasons, among them, that we do not know how many people here who want euthanasia now get it, despite its illegality. Even with better data on the number of persons who want euthanasia but cannot get it, significant moral disagreement would remain about how much weight should be given to any instance of failure to respect a person's self-determination in this way.

One important factor substantially affecting the number of persons who would seek euthanasia is the extent to which an alternative is available. The widespread acceptance in the law, social policy, and medical practice of the right of a competent patient to forgo life-sustaining treatment suggests that the number of competent persons in the United States who would want euthanasia if it were permitted is probably relatively small.

A second good consequence of making euthanasia legally permissible benefits a much larger group. Polls have shown that a majority of the American public believes that people should have a right to obtain euthanasia if they want it. No doubt the vast majority of those who support this right to euthanasia will never in fact come to want euthanasia for themselves. Nevertheless, making it legally permissible would reassure many people that if they ever do want euthanasia they would be able to obtain it. This reassurance would supplement the broader control over the process of dying given by the right to decide about life-sustaining treatment. Having fire insurance on one's house benefits all who have it, not just those whose houses actually burn down, by reassuring them that in the unlikely event of their house burning down, they will receive the money needed to rebuild it. Likewise, the legalization of euthanasia can be thought of as a kind of insurance policy against being forced to endure a protracted dying process that one has come to find burdensome and unwanted, especially when there is no life-sustaining treatment to forgo. The strong concern about losing control of their care expressed by many people who face serious illness likely to end in death suggests that they give substantial importance to the legalization of euthanasia as a means of maintaining this control.

A third good consequence of the legalization of euthanasia concerns patients whose dying is filled with severe and unrelievable pain or suffering. When there is a life-sustaining treatment that, if forgone, will lead relatively quickly to death, then doing so can bring an end to these patients' suffering without recourse to euthanasia. For patients receiving no such treatment, however, euthanasia may be the only release from their otherwise prolonged suffering and agony. This argument from mercy has always been the strongest argument for euthanasia in those cases to which it applies.

The importance of relieving pain and suffering is less controversial than is the frequency with which patients are forced to undergo untreatable agony that only euthanasia could relieve. If we focus first on suffering caused by physical pain, it is crucial to distinguish pain that *could* be adequately relieved with modern methods of pain control, though it in fact is not, from pain that is relievable only by death. For a variety of reasons, including some physicians' fear of hastening the patient's death, as well as the lack of a publicly accessible means for assessing the amount of the patient's pain, many patients suffer pain that could be, but is not, relieved.

Specialists in pain control, as for example the pain of terminally ill cancer patients, argue that there are very few patients whose pain could not be adequately controlled, though sometimes at the cost of so sedating them that they are effectively unable to interact with other people or their environment. Thus, the argument from mercy in cases of physical pain can probably be met in a large majority of cases by providing adequate measures of pain relief. This should be a high priority, whatever our legal policy on euthanasia—the relief of pain and suffering has long been, quite properly, one of the central goals of medicine. Those cases in which pain could be effectively relieved, but in fact is not, should only count significantly in favor of legalizing euthanasia if all reasonable efforts to change pain management techniques have been tried and have failed.

Dying patients often undergo substantial psychological suffering that is not fully or even principally the result of physical pain. The knowledge about how to relieve this suffering is much more limited than in the case of relieving pain, and efforts to do so are probably more often unsuccessful. If the argument from mercy is extended to patients experiencing great and unrelievable psychological suffering, the numbers of patients to which it applies are much greater.

One last good consequence of legalizing euthanasia is that once death has been accepted, it is often more humane to end life quickly and peacefully, when that is what the patient wants. Such a death will often be seen as better than a more prolonged one. People who suffer a sudden and unexpected death, for example by dying quickly or in their sleep from a heart attack or stroke, are often considered lucky to have died in this way. We care about how we die in part because we care about how others remember us, and we hope they will remember us as we were in "good times" with them and not as we might be when disease has robbed us of our dignity as human beings. As with much in the treatment and care of the dying, people's concerns differ in this respect, but for at least some people, euthanasia will be a more humane death than what they have often experienced with other loved ones and might otherwise expect for themselves.

Some opponents of euthanasia challenge how much importance should be given to any of these good consequences of permitting it, or even whether some would be good consequences at all. But more frequently, opponents cite a number of bad consequences that permitting euthanasia would or could produce, and it is to their assessment that I now turn.

Potential Bad Consequences of Permitting Euthanasia

Some of the arguments against permitting euthanasia are aimed specifically against physicians, while others are aimed against anyone being permitted to perform it. I shall first consider one argument of the former sort. Permitting physicians to perform euthanasia, it is said, would be incompatible with their fundamental moral and professional commitment as healers to care for patients and to protect life. Moreover, if euthanasia by physicians became common, patients would come to fear that a medication was intended not to treat or care, but instead to kill, and would thus lose trust in their physicians. This position was forcefully stated in a paper by Willard Gaylin and his colleagues:

> The very soul of medicine is on trial...This issue touches medicine at its moral center; if this moral center collapses, if physicians become killers or are even licensed to kill, the profession—and, therewith, each physician—will never again be worthy of trust and respect as healer and comforter and protector of life in all its frailty.

These authors go on to make clear that, while they oppose permitting anyone to perform euthanasia, their special concern is with physicians doing so:

> We call on fellow physicians to say that they will not deliberately kill. We must also say to each of our fellow physicians that we will not tolerate killing of patients and that we shall take disciplinary action against doctors who kill. And we must say to the broader community that if it insists on tolerating or legalizing active euthanasia, it will have to find nonphysicians to do its killing.

If permitting physicians to kill would undermine the very "moral center" of medicine, then almost certainly physicians should not be permitted to perform euthanasia. But how persuasive is this claim? Patients should not fear, as a consequence of permitting *voluntary* active euthanasia, that their physicians will substitute a lethal injection for what patients want and believe is part of their care. If active euthanasia is restricted to cases in which it is truly voluntary, then no patient should fear getting it unless she or he has voluntarily requested it. (The fear that we might in time also come to accept non-voluntary, or even involuntary, active euthanasia is a slippery slope worry I address below.) Patients' trust of their physicians could be increased, not eroded, by knowledge that physicians will provide aid in dying when patients seek it.

Might Gaylin and his colleagues nevertheless be correct in their claim that the moral center of medicine would collapse if physicians were to become killers? This question raises what at the deepest level should be the guiding aims of medicine, a question that obviously cannot be fully explored here. But I do want to say enough to indicate the direction that I believe an appropriate response to this challenge should take. In spelling out above what I called the positive argument for voluntary active euthanasia, I suggested that two principal values—respecting patients' self-determination and promoting their well-being—underlie the consensus that competent patients, or the surrogates of incompetent patients, are entitled to refuse any life-sustaining treatment and to choose from among available alternative treatments. It is the commitment to these two values in guiding physicians' actions as healers, comforters, and protectors of their patients' lives that should be at the "moral center" of medicine, and these two values support physicians' administering euthanasia when their patients make competent requests for it.

What should not be at that moral center is a commitment to preserving patients' lives as such, without regard to whether those patients want their lives preserved or judge their preservation a benefit to them. Vitalism has been rejected by most physicians, and despite some statements that suggest it, is almost certainly not what Gaylin and colleagues intended. One of them, Leon Kass, has elaborated elsewhere the view that medicine is a moral profession whose proper aim is "the naturally given end of health," understood as the wholeness and well-working of the human being; "for the physician, at least, human life in living bodies commands respect and reverence—*by its very nature*." Kass continues, "the deepest ethical principle restraining the physician's power is not the autonomy or freedom of the patient; neither is it his own compassion or good intention. Rather, it is the dignity and mysterious power of human life itself." I believe Kass is in the end mistaken about the proper account of the aims of medicine and the limits on physicians' power, but this difficult issue will certainly be one of the central themes in the continuing debate about euthanasia.

A second bad consequence that some foresee is that permitting euthanasia would weaken society's commitment to provide optimal care for dying patients. We live at a time in which the control of health care costs has become, and is likely to continue to be, the dominant focus of health care policy. If euthanasia is seen as a cheaper alternative to adequate care and treatment, then we might become less scrupulous about providing sometimes costly support and other services to dying patients. Particularly if our society comes to embrace deeper and more explicit rationing of health care, frail, elderly, and dying patients will need to be strong and effective advocates for their own health care and other needs, although they are hardly in a position to do this. We should do nothing to weaken their ability to obtain adequate care and services.

This second worry is difficult to assess because there is little firm evidence about the likelihood of the feared erosion in the care of dying patients. There are at least two reasons, however, for skepticism about this argument. The first is that the same worry could have been directed at recognizing patients' or surrogates' rights to forgo life-sustaining treatment, yet there is no persuasive evidence that recognizing the right to refuse treatment has caused a serious erosion in the quality of care of dying patients. The second reason for skepticism about this worry is that only a very small proportion of deaths would occur from euthanasia if it were permitted. In the Netherlands, where euthanasia under specified circumstances is permitted by the courts, though not authorized by statute, the best estimate of the proportion of overall deaths that result from it is about 2 percent. Thus, the vast majority of critically ill and dying patients will not request it, and so will still have to be cared for by physicians, families, and others. Permitting euthanasia should not diminish people's commitment and concern to maintain and improve the care of these patients.

A third possible bad consequence of permitting euthanasia (or even a public discourse in which strong support for euthanasia is evident) is to threaten the progress made in securing the rights of patients or their surrogates to decide about and to refuse life-sustaining treatment. This progress has been made against the backdrop of a clear and firm legal prohibition of euthanasia, which has provided a relatively bright line limiting the dominion of others over patients' lives. It has therefore been an important reassurance to concerns about how the authority to take steps ending life might be misused, abused, or wrongly extended.

Many supporters of the right of patients or their surrogates to refuse treatment strongly oppose euthanasia, and if forced to choose might well withdraw their support of the right to refuse treatment rather than accept euthanasia. Public policy in the last fifteen years has generally let life-sustaining treatment decisions be made in health care settings between physicians and patients or their surrogates, and without the involvement of the courts. However, if euthanasia is made legally permissible greater involvement of the courts is likely, which could in turn extend to a greater court involvement in life-sustaining treatment decisions. Most agree, however, that increased involvement of the courts in these decisions would be undesirable, as it would make sound decision making more cumbersome and difficult without sufficient compensating benefits.

As with the second potential bad consequence of permitting euthanasia, this third consideration too is speculative and difficult to assess. The feared erosion of patients' or surrogates' rights to decide about life-sustaining treatment, together with greater court involvement in those decisions, are both possible. However, I believe there is reason to discount this general worry. The legal rights of competent patients and, to a lesser degree, surrogates of incompetent patients to decide about treatment are very firmly embedded in a long line of informed consent and life-sustaining treatment cases, and are not likely to be eroded by a debate over, or even acceptance of, euthanasia. It will not be accepted without safeguards that reassure the public about abuse, and if that debate shows the need for similar safeguards for some life-sustaining treatment decisions they should be adopted there as well. In neither case are the only possible safeguards greater court involvement, as the recent growth of institutional ethics committees shows. . . .

This final potential bad consequence is the central concern of many opponents of euthanasia and, I believe, is the most serious objection to a legal policy permitting it. According to this "slippery slope" worry, although active euthanasia may be morally permissible in cases in which it is unequivocally voluntary and the patient finds his or her condition unbearable, a legal policy permitting euthanasia would inevitably lead to active euthanasia being performed in many other cases in which it would be morally wrong. To prevent those other wrongful cases of euthanasia we should not permit even morally justified performance of it.

Slippery slope arguments of this form are problematic and difficult to evaluate. From one perspective, they are the last refuge of conservative defenders of the status quo. When all the opponent's objections to the wrongness of euthanasia itself have been met, the opponent then shifts ground and acknowledges both that it is not in itself wrong and that a legal policy which resulted only in its being performed would not be bad. Nevertheless, the opponent maintains, it should still not be permitted because doing so would result in its being performed in other cases in which it is not voluntary and would be wrong. In this argument's most extreme form, permitting euthanasia is the first and fateful step down the slippery slope to Nazism. Once on the slope we will be unable to get off.

Now it cannot be denied that it is *possible* that permitting euthanasia could have these fateful consequences, but that cannot be enough to warrant prohibiting it if it is otherwise justified. A similar *possible* slippery slope worry could have been raised to securing competent patients' rights to decide about life support, but recent history shows such a worry would have been unfounded. It must be relevant how likely it is that we will end with horrendous consequences and an unjustified practice of euthanasia. How *likely* and *widespread* would the abuses and unwarranted extensions of permitting it be?

By abuses, I mean the performance of euthanasia that fails to satisfy the conditions required for voluntary active euthanasia, for example, if the patient has been subtly pressured to accept it. By unwarranted extensions of policy, I mean later changes in legal policy to permit not just voluntary euthanasia, but also euthanasia in cases in which, for example, it need not be fully voluntary. Opponents of voluntary euthanasia on slippery slope grounds have not provided the data or evidence necessary to turn their speculative concerns into well-grounded likelihoods. ...

ARGUMENT 8 ESSAY QUESTIONS

1. What is Kass's argument against permitting doctors to perform euthanasia?
2. Is Kass's slippery-slope argument cogent? Explain.
3. What is Brock's assessment of slippery-slope concerns? Do you think it is correct? Explain.

SUGGESTIONS FOR FURTHER READING

Margaret Pabst Battin, *Ending Life: Ethics and the Way We Die* (New York: Oxford University Press, 2005).

Tom L. Beauchamp, ed., *Intending Death: The Ethics of Assisted Suicide and Euthanasia* (Upper Saddle River, NJ: Prentice-Hall, 1996).

R.B. Brandt, "The Morality and Rationality of Suicide," in *A Handbook for the Study of Suicide*, ed. Seymour Perlin (New York: Oxford University Press, 1975).

Dan W. Brock, "Medical Decisions at the End of Life," in *A Companion to Bioethics* (Malden, MA: Blackwell, 2001) 231–41.

Gerald Dworkin, R. Frey, and S. Bok, *Euthanasia and Physician-Assisted Suicide* (Cambridge, England: Cambridge University Press, 1998).

Gerald Dworkin, "Physician-Assisted Death: The State of the Debate," in *The Oxford Handbook of Bioethics*, ed. Bonnie Steinbock (Oxford: Oxford University Press, 2007), 375–392.

Philippa Foot, "Euthanasia," *Philosophy & Public Affairs*, vol. 6, no. 2 (1977).

Walter Glannon, "Medical Decisions at the End of Life," in *Biomedical Ethics* (New York: Oxford University Press, 2005.

Jonathan Glover, "The Sanctity of Life," in *Bioethics: An Anthology*, ed. Helga Kuhse and Peter Singer (Oxford: Blackwell, 1999), 193–202.

Leon Kass, "Is There a Right to Die?" *Hastings Center Report*, vol. 23, no. 1 (1993), 34–43.

Mark Murphy, "The Natural Law Tradition in Ethics," *Stanford Encyclopedia of Philosophy*, 11 March 2008, http://plato.stanford.edu/entries/natural-law-ethics (9 June 2008).

New York State Task Force on Life and the Law, *When Death Is Sought: Assisted Suicide and Euthanasia in the Medical Context*, April 1997.

Louis P. Pojman, "Euthanasia," in *Life and Death* (Belmont, CA: Wadsworth, 2000), 85–94.

The President's Commission for the Study of Ethical Problems in Medicine and Biomedical and Behavioral Research, *Defining Death* (Washington, DC: U.S. Government Printing Office, 1981).

Peter Singer, "Voluntary Euthanasia: A Utilitarian Perspective," *Bioethics*, vol. 17, nos. 5–6 (2003).

Bonnie Steinbock and Alastair Norcross, ed., *Killing and Letting Die*, 2nd ed. (New York: Fordham University Press, 1994).

CHAPTER 6

Genetic Engineering and Cloning

In recent years, world-shaking developments in genetics and biotechnology have sent tremors through ethics. These fields have once again outpaced conventional moral understanding and inserted a host of raw, hard issues into our lives. Among the more troubling questions are: Is it "playing God" to alter someone's genes to treat diseases or prevent them in future generations? Should genetic technology be used to select a child's gender or other attributes such as eye and hair color and musical or athletic ability? Should eugenics be employed? That is, should genetic knowledge be applied to whole populations in an attempt to improve the human genome? Is human cloning morally impermissible? Would cloning be wrong even if it were the only way for an infertile couple to have a child with whom they are genetically related? Or the only way to avoid passing on a genetic disease to their children?

GENE THERAPY

Cells are the fundamental components of every living thing, and DNA (deoxyribonucleic acid) makes up the chemical coding that directs their construction, development, and operation. For nearly all organisms, DNA is the language of the genetic software that runs the cells and ensures the inheritance of traits from one generation to the next. Whether in ants, worms, gazelles, or humans, DNA consists of the same chemical ingredients and has the same molecular architecture: double, parallel strands linked together by chemical crossbars and twisted like a spiral staircase—the classic double helix. Each crossbar is formed by a matching pair of chemical bases, called a base pair. There are only four bases—adenine (A), guanine (G), cytosine (C), and thymine (T)—yet they constitute the entire "alphabet" of the genetic code. Their order (the DNA sequence) along the strands (ATTCCGGA, for example) encodes all the instructions required for making and maintaining an organism. As it "reads" the code, a cell constructs, according to the precise specifications, various proteins, which carry out most biological processes and provide almost all of the material for building cells.

An organism's entire complement of DNA is known as its **genome**. The human genome consists of about three billion base pairs, and there is a complete genome in nearly every human cell. (A mouse genome has 2.6 billion base pairs; a fruit fly, 137 million; and an *E. coli* bacterium, 4.6 million.) In a typical human cell, the DNA strands total about six feet, coiled and crammed efficiently into an incredibly small space.

A cell does not "read" the 3 billion base pairs as one long stream of letters but as separate segments, or "words," of the stream, each segment providing instructions to the cell for manufacturing a customized protein or small group of proteins. These words of genetic code are **genes**, the fundamental units of biological inheritance. The human genome contains 20,000 to 25,000 genes, which vary in the length of their instructions from hundreds of DNA bases up to 2 million. Each gene has a duplicate, with one copy inherited from the male parent, and one from the female parent.

In the cell's nucleus, the genes are neatly organized—bundled into forty-six string-like molecules known as **chromosomes**. These bundles are arranged into twenty-three pairs, with twenty-two of the pairs appearing the same for both males and females, and the twenty-third pair—the sex chromosomes—differing for males and females. Males have both an X and Y chromosome while females have two X chromosomes.

Through the workings of all this genetic machinery, a human organism is produced and sustained, and a vast share of its characteristics is determined. (Genes have their say, but not necessarily the final say, on how a person turns out, for he or she is also affected by the incredibly complex interactions between genetic systems and environmental factors.) When the machinery operates properly, the organism thrives. But flaws in the system—mistakes in the genes' coded instructions—can sometimes lead to devastating disease or disability. Mistakes (mutations or alterations) can arise when the order of bases in a DNA sequence is wrong, or bases have been added, deleted, or duplicated. Occasionally extra genes or chromosomes are added, or essential ones are left out.

Some genetic mutations are acquired—they happen in people randomly or because of exposure to noxious agents such as radiation, chemicals, or cigarette smoke. The exposure disorders can "run in families" not because they are hereditary but because family members are exposed to the same harmful environmental factors. But many mutations are indeed hereditary and are transmitted through families, triggering the same genetic disease in subsequent generations. The genetic errors are responsible for more than four thousand hereditary diseases.

Unfortunately, the relation between genetic flaws and genetic disease is usually anything but simple. In most cases, genetic diseases arise not from a single gene defect but from many mutations in one or more genes, coupled with a person's lifestyle habits and environmental influences. Researchers believe that many common disorders such as heart disease, cancer, and diabetes are in this category.

Nevertheless, after deciphering the vast codex of the human genome and peering into the rich patterning of genes, humans have taken the next, seemingly inevitable, step: to try to repair the genetic flaws they see. This incredible repair work is known as **gene therapy** (also referred to as genetic engineering), the manipulation of someone's genetic material to prevent or treat disease. It is an attempt to alter the workings of cells by, among other things, (1) replacing a missing or defective gene with a normal one, (2) repairing a faulty gene so it will function properly, or (3) activating or deactivating a gene (switching it on or off).

To date, most uses of gene therapy have been of the first kind, the insertion of a normal copy of a gene into cells to do the job that defective or absent genes should be doing. But delivering a gene to a cell is tricky and usually must be done with a carrier, or vector, such as a virus. Viruses can seek out particular cells and transfer pieces of DNA into them. Scientists put this natural talent of viruses to work by inactivating their harmful characteristics and modifying them to carry particular genes into designated cells. The genes can then induce the production of the proteins needed for normal functioning. A good example of this approach is the treatment of hemophilia (hemophilia A and B), a disorder that puts people at risk of bleeding to death because of impaired blood-clotting. The problem is caused by mutations in the genes that manufacture the proteins necessary for clotting (called blood-clotting factors), resulting in deficiencies of the proteins. In both animals and humans, scientists have used viruses to transfer normal copies of these genes into cells, enabling the genes to start producing the blood-clotting factors. The therapy has worked in animals and has shown promise in humans.

Gene therapy is of two types: somatic cell and germ-line cell. The former involves altering genes in a person's somatic (body) cells, such as liver or muscle cells, to treat an existing disorder. The alterations can help the person suffering from the disease but are not inheritable—they cannot be passed on to the person's offspring. They affect the person's genome but not the genomes of subsequent generations. The other type of gene therapy entails modifying genes in germ-line cells (egg and sperm cells) and zygotes— and these alterations are inheritable. Currently the scientific focus is on somatic-cell gene therapy, with most research evaluating treatments for cancer, heart disease, and infectious diseases. Gene therapy in germ-line cells is not yet feasible. But the ability to manipulate germ-line cells evokes both the dream of eradicating mutations from future generations (and thus permanently banishing particular disorders) and the nightmare of fabricating "designer" babies or introducing horrible errors into the human genome.

For scientists, physicians, and policy makers, the potential of gene therapy to effect cures is too great to ignore, so research will likely continue (and expand) indefinitely. But devising effective gene therapies is extremely difficult, and they can pose risks to patients. To develop any kind of effective gene therapy, scientists have to solve several technical problems. Chief among them are the difficulty of controlling viruses to accurately deliver genes to cells, the risk of virus carriers causing disease or provoking a harmful immune system response, and the complexity of treating disorders generated by multiple genes (such as diabetes, arthritis, heart diseases, and Alzheimer's). For these and other reasons, the field is still experimental, with hundreds of gene therapy studies in progress all over the world but few or no therapies approved for routine use. So far, scientific studies demonstrating success in using gene therapy have been intriguing and encouraging but preliminary. But there is little doubt among experts that safe and effective gene therapies (at least the somatic-cell kind) will be devised in the next few years.

In 1990 researchers conducted the first federally approved study of gene therapy, treating a four-year-old girl suffering from adenosine deaminase (ADA) deficiency, a life-shortening disorder of severely weakened immunity. A normal gene generates ADA, an enzyme crucial to a healthy immune system, but in the girl the gene was missing, leaving her without any defense against life-threatening infections. Using a virus carrier, the researchers delivered the normal ADA gene to the girl's immune cells, hoping that it would produce the needed enzyme. The treatment worked. Her immune system soon began to function normally and did so for years.

Since that promising experiment, there have also been disappointments—and lessons to learn about the risks involved in gene therapy. In 1999 eighteen-year-old Jesse Gelsinger experienced multiple organ failures and died during gene therapy to treat ornithine transcarboxylase deficiency (OTCD). The ultimate cause of death was traced back to his immune system's devastating reaction to the virus carrier. A few years later scientists used gene therapy to treat children with severe combined immunodeficiency (SCID), an intractable disorder that usually results in death by the age of one. Amazingly, most of the children were cured. But two of them developed a condition like leukemia, so in 2003 the Food and Drug Administration (FDA) temporarily suspended clinical trials using these

---

TIME LINE: Gene Therapy Research

- **March 2009** The School of Pharmacy in London is testing a treatment in mice that delivers genes wrapped in nanoparticles to cancer cells to target and destroy hard-to-reach cancer cells.
- **April 2008** UK researchers from the UCL Institute of Ophthalmology and Moorfields Eye Hospital NIHR Biomedical Research Centre have announced results from the world's first clinical trial to test a revolutionary gene therapy treatment for a type of inherited blindness. The results, published in the *New England Journal of Medicine*, show that the experimental treatment is safe and can improve sight. The findings are a landmark for gene therapy technology and could have a significant impact on future treatments for eye disease.
- **May 2007** A team of British doctors from Moorfields Eye Hospital and University College in London conduct first human gene therapy trials to treat Leber's congenital amaurosis, a type of inherited childhood blindness caused by a single abnormal gene. The procedure has already been successful at restoring vision for dogs. This is the first trial to use gene therapy in an operation to treat blindness in humans.
- **January 2007** A combination of two tumor-suppressing genes delivered in lipid-based nanoparticles drastically reduces the number and size of human lung cancer tumors in mice during trials conducted by researchers from the University of Texas M. D. Anderson Cancer Center and the University of Texas Southwestern Medical Center.
- **August 2006** Researchers at the National Cancer Institute (NCI), part of the National Institutes of Health, successfully reengineer immune cells, called lymphocytes, to target and attack cancer cells in patients with advanced

metastatic melanoma. This is the first time that gene therapy is used to successfully treat cancer in humans.
- **March 2006** Gene therapy is effectively used to treat two adult patients for a disease affecting nonlymphocytic white blood cells called myeloid cells. Myeloid disorders are common and include a variety of bone marrow failure syndromes, such as acute myeloid leukemia. The study is the first to show that gene therapy can cure diseases of the myeloid system.
- **February 2005** Gene therapy cures deafness in guinea pigs. Each animal had been deafened by destruction of the hair cells in the cochlea that translate sound vibrations into nerve signals. A gene, called Atoh1, which stimulates the hair cells' growth, was delivered to the cochlea by an adenovirus. The genes triggered regrowth of the hair cells, and many of the animals regained up to 80% of their original hearing thresholds. This study, which may pave the way to human trials of the gene, was the first to show that gene therapy can repair deafness in animals.
- **March 2003** University of California, Los Angeles, research team gets genes into the brain using liposomes coated in a polymer called polyethylene glycol (PEG). The transfer of genes into the brain is a significant achievement because viral vectors are too big to get across the "blood-brain barrier." This method has potential for treating Parkinson's disease.

Excerpted from Office of Science, U.S. Department of Energy, "Gene Therapy," *Human Genome Project Information*, 6 August 2007, http://www.ornl.gov/sci/techresources/Human_Genome/medicine/genetherapy.shtml (31 December 2007).

procedures. Later the trials resumed with closer FDA oversight and a greater appreciation among scientists generally of the inherent risks and the curative possibilities of gene therapy.

As you might suspect, many moral questions about gene therapy center on its potential for harm and help. In somatic-cell gene therapy, the risks and benefits of using the technology have become the primary moral concern, spurred on by much soul-searching after the early clinical mistakes. Regulatory agencies and review boards have sprung up to oversee clinical trials and to ensure an acceptable balance of risks and benefits for study subjects. The prevailing view is that if such steps are taken to minimize harm, and if the potential benefits are substantial, somatic-cell therapy is morally permissible.

Germ-line therapy is a different matter. The safety concerns surrounding the technology are so worrisome that, at least in its current immature stage, it is generally thought to be morally unacceptable. The main problem is that scientists do not yet fully understand the likely ramifications of refashioning the genetic machinery of germ-line cells. The addition or modification of genes might make a condition worse or prevent one disease but cause others that are more severe. The result could be catastrophic or fatal to a child born of such engineering, and the calamities could happen at birth or years later. Worse, the resulting disorders could be passed on to future children. The nightmare scenario is that the genetic changes are inherited by many people, and the human genome itself is altered for the worse. These unknowns have compelled scientists not to renounce this research but to proceed with extreme caution and to forgo clinical trials until the genetics of germ-line cells is better understood.

Many moral arguments for and against gene therapy—perhaps the most controversial ones—do not appeal to the possibility of harm from the procedure itself, or they work from the assumption that the safety and effectiveness of gene therapy will eventually be established. Those arguments in favor of applying gene therapy (in either form) work along these lines: if it is within our power to correct genetic flaws and thereby prevent or cure diseases, aren't we obligated to do so? If gene therapy offers us the chance to prevent harm to future people, don't we have a duty to try? If the principle of autonomy (or reproductive liberty) grants us the freedom to reproduce or not reproduce, doesn't it also give us the right to decide whether our offspring will have a disability or disease?

Opponents of gene therapy insist that reproductive freedom has limits, that germ-line therapy crosses the line, that the manipulation or destruction of embryos that may occur in germ-line therapy shows disrespect for human life, or that gene therapy (especially germ-line) disrespects or discriminates against people with disabilities.

REPRODUCTIVE CLONING

Clones, in the sense used by biologists, are genetically identical entities, whether cells, DNA molecules, plants, animals, or humans. **Cloning** is the asexual production of a genetically identical entity from an existing one. In animals and humans, since the genetic blueprint for an individual is in each of its cells (mostly in the nucleus), all the cells of a clone contain the same blueprint as all the cells of the clone's progenitor. An animal or human clone is not a perfect copy of an individual—not like a photocopy of an original document—but a living thing that shares a set of genetic instructions with another.

In agriculture, cloning to propagate plant strains is commonplace, and for years scientists have been cloning human and animal cells for research purposes. Molecular biologists often clone fragments of DNA for study. Among animals and humans, clones appear naturally in the form of identical twins, individuals with identical sets of DNA. Scientists have managed to duplicate this process in a form of cloning known as *twinning*. Through in vitro fertilization they produce an embryo (zygote), and when it consists of two to four identical cells, they separate them and let them grow into discrete but genetically identical organisms.

The cloning that has provoked the most public consternation and media attention is the creation of a genetic duplicate of an adult animal or human, what has often been called **reproductive cloning**. The aim of this work is the live birth of an individual. (Cloning for other purposes is called **therapeutic**, or **research**, **cloning**.) This kind of cloning suddenly became front-page news in 1997 when scientists announced that they had managed to clone an adult sheep, resulting in the birth of an apparently healthy clone called Dolly. She was the genetic twin of her adult "parent" and the first mammal so cloned. After her, scientists cloned additional animals in similar fashion—cattle, goats, pigs, cats, rabbits, mice, and more—and are working on others.

The primary cloning method for producing live-birth mammals, and the one most likely to be considered for human cloning, is known as somatic cell nuclear transfer (SCNT). The usual steps are:

1. Extract the DNA-packed nucleus from an egg cell (creating an enucleated egg).
2. Replace the egg's nucleus with the donor nucleus of an ordinary body (somatic) cell from the adult individual to be cloned. (It's also possible to use cells from existing embryos.)
3. Stimulate the reconfigured cell with chemicals or electricity to start cell division and growth to the embryo stage.
4. Transfer the cloned embryo to a host uterus for development and birth.

The egg and somatic nucleus can come from two different individuals or the same individual. If from two different ones, the largest portion of the clone's DNA will be from the nucleus donor since almost all DNA resides in the nucleus, with only a tiny amount located outside the nucleus in the cell's mitochondria. If from the same individual, the clone will get its entire complement of DNA from the nucleus and mitochondria of the same individual.

To date, no human has been successfully cloned, and for technical and moral reasons none is likely to be cloned any time soon. At this stage of the technology, both scientists and policy makers have serious concerns about the safety and ethics of human reproductive cloning.

A typical response to the prospect of human cloning is moral outrage—which too often is based on misunderstandings. Chief among these is the notion that a human clone would be identical to an existing person, the clone's "parent." This idea has led to a host of silly fantasies played out in movies, literature, and the popular mind: an army of Hitler clones spawned from one of the führer's cells, a laboratory of Albert Einsteins discovering the secrets of the universe, the perfect team of Hank Aaron or Michael Jordan clones, a houseful of identical children who are exact copies of a rich, eccentric egotist. The underlying fallacy is that genes make the person, that genetics ordains all of an individual's characteristics. This view is known as *genetic determinism*, and it is a myth. The National Academy of Sciences explains:

> Even if clones are genetically identical with one another, they will not be identical in physical or behavioral characteristics, because DNA is not the only determinant of these characteristics. A pair of clones will experience different environments

TIME LINE: Cloning

1970 British developmental biologist John Gurdon clones a frog.

1978 Louise Brown is born, the first baby conceived through IVF.

1980 The U.S. Supreme Court holds that a genetically engineered life form—a bacterium—can be patented.

1996 Through the work of Ian Wilmut and his colleagues, the first animal cloned from adult cells—a sheep named Dolly—is born.

1997 President Bill Clinton declares a five-year moratorium on federal funding for research into human cloning.

1997 Wilmut and his colleagues create Polly, a sheep with a human gene in each of its cells.

2001 Scientists in Massachusetts clone the first human embryo.

2002 The President's Council on Bioethics recommends a ban on reproductive cloning.

2003 In South Korea, human embryonic stems are cloned.

2003 Dolly, aged six years, is euthanized when she is found to have lung disease.

2004 A company called Genetics Savings and Clone says it will clone people's cats for them for $50,000 per cat.

2005 The creator of Dolly is licensed to clone human embryos for medical research.

and nutritional inputs while in the uterus, and they would be expected to be subject to different inputs from their parents, society, and life experience as they grow up. If clones derived from identical nuclear donors and identical mitochondrial donors are born at different times, as is the case when an adult is the donor of the somatic cell nucleus, the environmental and nutritional differences would be expected to be more pronounced than for monozygotic (identical) twins. And even monozygotic twins are not fully identical genetically or epigenetically because mutations, stochastic [random] developmental variations, and varied imprinting effects (parent-specific chemical marks on the DNA) make different contributions to each twin.[1]

Einstein's clone would have Einstein's genes but would not and could not be Einstein. The clone would be unique and probably not much like his famous progenitor at all.

At this stage of scientific knowledge, human cloning seems likely to result in high rates of serious birth defects.[2] Under these circumstances, most commentators agree that cloning should not be attempted. (A few question this conclusion, noting that now even parents who are certain to conceive and bear children with terrible genetic disorders are permitted to do so.) Nevertheless, since 1997 the dispute over the moral permissibility of cloning has raged on, fueled by the thought that, given the usual pace of scientific progress, the problem of congenital malformations will be solved and the efficient cloning of human beings will soon be technologically feasible.

---

[1] National Academy of Sciences, Committee on Science, Engineering, and Public Policy, *Scientific and Medical Aspects of Human Reproductive Cloning* (Washington, DC: National Academy Press, 2002), 26.

[2] Human Genome Project Information, "Cloning Fact Sheet," *Genomics.Energy.Gov*, 29 August 2006, www.ornl.gov/sci/techsources/Human_Genome/elsi/cloning.shtml (15 June 2008).

As we would expect, many of those who favor the use of cloning rest their case on its likely benefits. For some people, their only hope of having a child with whom they are genetically related would be through cloning. Some men have no sperm; some women, no eggs; cloning could get around the problem. For couples who value this genetic connection and who also want to avoid passing on a genetic disease or health risk to their child, cloning would be an attractive option—perhaps the only option. Parents whose only child dies could have her cloned from a cell harvested from her body, ensuring that some part of her would live on. A boy who needs an organ transplant to live could be cloned so his clone could provide the needed organ, perfectly matched to avoid transplant rejection.

Many claim a moral right to use cloning, arguing that people have a basic right of reproductive liberty and that cloning is covered by that right. They deny that this right to cloning is absolute (overriding all other considerations) but believe that it carries great weight nonetheless. As one writer puts it:

> [I]t is reasonable to hold that the freedom of infertile couples to use cloning is a form of procreative freedom. Procreative freedom is worthy of respect in part because freedom in general is worthy of respect. But more than this, procreative freedom is an especially important freedom because of the significance that procreative decisions can have for persons' lives. For these reasons, the freedom of infertile couples to use cloning is worthy of respect.[3]

A common objection to cloning and other reproductive technologies holds that they replace natural procreation with the artificial *manufacture* of children as products—a demeaning process that erodes our respect for human beings. Cloning is thus profoundly dehumanizing. "Human nature," says Leon Kass, "becomes merely the last part of nature to succumb to the technological project, which turns all of nature into raw material at human disposal."[4]

Why assume cloning is dehumanizing? Dan Brock says that we should not:

> It would be a mistake, however, to conclude that a human being created by human cloning is of less value or is less worthy of respect than one created by sexual reproduction. It is the nature of a being, not how it is created, that is the source of its value and makes it worthy of respect.[5]

KEY TERMS

chromosome	eugenics	genome
gene	gene therapy	cloning
cloning, reproductive	cloning, therapeutic or research	

---

[3] Carson Strong, "The Ethics of Human Reproductive Cloning," *Ethics, Law and Moral Philosophy of Reproductive Biomedicine*, vol. 1, no. 1, March 2005: 45–49.
[4] Leon R. Kass, "The Wisdom of Repugnance," *The New Republic*, 2 June 1997, 17–26.
[5] Brock, "Cloning Human Beings."

9. THE BENEFICENCE ARGUMENT FOR GENETIC ENHANCEMENT

Some argue that gene therapy should not be permitted because it amounts to **eugenics**, the deliberate attempt to improve the genetic makeup of humans by manipulating reproduction. The word calls up images of the Nazi drive to racial purity through mandatory sterilization of undesirables, as well as the early twentieth-century programs in the United States to forcibly sterilize criminals, "imbeciles," and other "defective persons." Such misdeeds are morally objectionable for several reasons, most notably because they violate people's autonomy, the central transgression of state-sponsored coercion. But the term *eugenics* is broad, covering a range of practices that are not necessarily coercive and that have been called eugenics of either a *negative* or *positive* kind. Negative eugenics is thought to involve the prevention or treatment of diseases through methods such as genetic testing, abortion of defective embryos, and germ-line therapy. By this definition, prenatal screening—which is a matter of public policy and generally considered morally permissible—is a type of negative eugenics. Positive eugenics is said to include attempts to improve on normal functions. It seeks not repair, but enhancement. Theoretically through germ-lime therapy, parents could produce children who are smarter, taller, or more resistant to certain diseases than normal children are. Such enhancements are controversial, even though they may not be technically possible for many years.

The idea of a distinction between repair and enhancement is prominent in moral debates because some argue that the former is morally obligatory while the latter is not. That is, we may have a duty to use gene therapy to treat Tay-Sachs disease or cystic fibrosis, but not to give a child an abnormally long life or a super immune system.

Several philosophers reject this view, denying the distinction and appealing to the moral principle of beneficence. They argue, in effect, If we have the power to make someone's life better, isn't it morally right to do so? In "Is Gene Therapy a Form of Eugenics?" John Harris puts forth such an argument:

> [S]uppose genes coding for repair enzymes which would not only repair radiation damage or damage by other environmental pollutants but would also prolong healthy life expectancy could be inserted into humans. Again, would it be permissible to let people continue suffering such damage when they could be protected against it? Would it in short be OK to let them suffer?
>
> It is not normal for the human organism to be self-repairing in this way; this must be eugenic if anything is. But if available, its use would surely, like penicillin before it, be more than merely [permissible].

.... There is in short no moral difference between attempts to cure dysfunction and attempts to enhance function where the enhancement protects life or health.[6]

Probably the strongest objection to genetic enhancement is that it would lead to the most flagrant kind of social injustice. As Walter Glannon argues,

The main moral concern about genetic enhancement of physical and mental traits is that it would give some people an unfair advantage over others with respect to competitive goods like beauty, sociability, and intelligence.... Enhancement would be unfair because only those who could afford the technology would have access to it, and many people are financially worse off than others through no fault of their own. Insofar as the possession of these goods gives some people an advantage over others in careers, income, and social status, the competitive nature of these goods suggests that there would be no limit to the benefits that improvements to physical and mental capacities would yield to those fortunate enough to avail themselves of the technology.[7]

Is Gene Therapy a Form of Eugenics?

JOHN HARRIS

Eugenic A. *adj.* Pertaining or adapted to the production of fine offspring. **B.** *sh.* in *pl.* The science which treats of this.

(*The Shorter Oxford English Dictionary* Third Edition 1965).

It has now become a serious necessity to better the breed of the human race. The average citizen is too base for the everyday work of modern civilization. Civilised man has become possessed of vaster powers than in old times for good or ill but has made no corresponding advance in wits and goodness to enable him to conduct his conduct rightly.

(*Sir Francis Gallon*)

If, as I believe, gene therapy is in principle ethically sound except for its possible connection with eugenics then there are two obvious ways of giving a simple and straightforward answer to a question such as this. The first is to say "yes it is, and so what?" The second is to say "no it isn't so we shouldn't worry." If we accept the first of the above definitions we might well be inclined to give the

[6] John Harris, "Is Gene Therapy a Form of Eugenics?" in *Bioethics: An Anthology*, ed. Helga Kuhse and Peter Singer (Oxford: Blackwell Publishers, 1999), 165–170.
[7] Walter Glannon, *Genes and Future People: Philosophical Issues in Human Genetics* (Boulder, CO: Westview Press, 2001), 94–101.

first of our two answers. If on the other hand, we accept the sort of gloss that Ruth Chadwick gives on Galton's account, "those who are genetically weak should simply be discouraged from reproducing," either by incentives or compulsory measures, we get a somewhat different flavour, and one which might incline a decent person who favours gene therapy towards the second answer.

The nub of the problem turns on how we are to understand the objective of producing "fine children." Does "fine" mean "as fine as children normally are," or does it mean "as fine as a child can be"? Sorting out the ethics of the connection between gene therapy and eugenics seems to involve the resolution of two morally significant issues. The first is whether or not there is a relevant moral distinction between attempts to remove or repair dysfunction on the one hand and measures designed to enhance function on the other, such that it would be coherent to be in favour of curing dysfunction but against enhancing function? The second involves the question of whether gene therapy as a technique involves something specially morally problematic.

THE MORAL CONTINUUM
Is it morally wrong to wish and hope for a fine baby girl or boy? Is it wrong to wish and hope that one's child will not be born disabled? I assume that my feeling that such hopes and wishes are not wrong is shared by every sane decent person. Now consider whether it would be wrong to wish and hope for the reverse? What would we think of someone who hoped and wished that their child would be born with disability? Again I need not spell out the answer to these questions.

But now let's bridge the gap between thought and action, between hopes and wishes and their fulfilment. What would we think of someone who, hoping and wishing for a fine healthy child, declined to take the steps necessary to secure this outcome when such steps were open to them?

Again I assume that unless those steps could be shown to be morally unacceptable our conclusions would be the same.

Consider the normal practice at I.V.F. clinics where a woman who has had, say, five eggs fertilised in vitro, wishes to use some of these embryos

to become pregnant. Normal practice would be to insert two embryos or at most three. If pre-implantation screening had revealed two of the embryos to possess disabilities of one sort or another, would it be right to implant the two embryos with disability rather than the others? Would it be right to choose the implantation embryos randomly? Could it be defensible for a doctor to override the wishes of the mother and implant the disabled embryos rather than the healthy ones—would we applaud her for so doing?[1]

The answer that I expect to all these rhetorical questions will be obvious. It depends however on accepting that disability is somehow disabling and therefore undesirable. If it were not, there would be no motive to try to cure or obviate disability in health care more generally. If we believe that medical science should try to cure disability where possible, and that parents would be wrong to withhold from their disabled children cures as they become available, then we will be likely to agree on our answers to the rhetorical questions posed.

WHAT IS DISABILITY?
It is notoriously hard to give a satisfactory definition of disability although I believe we all know pretty clearly what we mean by it. A disability is surely a physical or mental condition we have a strong rational preference not to be in; it is, more importantly, a condition which is in some sense a "harmed condition."[2] I have in mind the sort of condition in which if a patient presented with it unconscious in the casualty department of a hospital and the condition could be easily and immediately reversed, but not reversed unless the doctor acts without delay, a doctor would be negligent were she not to attempt reversal. Or, one which, if a pregnant mother knew that it affected her fetus and knew also she could remove the condition by simple dietary adjustment, then to fail to do so would be to knowingly harm her child.[3]

To make clearer what's at issue here let's imagine that as a result of industrial effluent someone had contracted a condition that she felt had disabled or harmed her in some sense. How might she convince a court, say, that she had suffered disability or injury?

The answer is obvious but necessarily vague. Whatever it would be plausible to say in answer to such a question is what I mean (and what is clearly meant) by disability and injury. It is not possible to stipulate exhaustively what would strike us as plausible here, but we know what injury is and we know what disability or incapacity is. If the condition in question was one which set premature limits on their lifespan—made their life shorter than it would be with treatment, or was one which rendered her specially vulnerable to infection, more vulnerable than others, we would surely recognise that she had been harmed and perhaps to some extent disabled. At the very least such events would be plausible candidates for the description "injuries" or "disabilities."

Against a background in which many people are standardly protected from birth or before against pollution hazards and infections and have their healthy life expectancy extended, it would surely be plausible to claim that failure to protect in this way constituted an injury and left them disabled. Because of their vulnerability to infection and to environmental pollutants there would be places it was unsafe for them to go and people with whom they could not freely consort. These restrictions on liberty are surely at least prima facie disabling as is the increased relative vulnerability.

These points are crucial because it is sometimes said that while we have an obligation to cure disease—to restore normal functioning—we do not have an obligation to enhance or improve upon a normal healthy life, that enhancing function is permissive but could not be regarded as obligatory. But, what constitutes a normal healthy life is determined in part by technological and medical and other advances (hygiene, sanitation etc.). It is normal now for example to be protected against tetanus; the continued provision of such protection is not merely permissive. If the AIDS pandemic continues unabated and the only prospect, or the best prospect, for stemming its advance is the use of gene therapy to insert genes coding for antibodies to AIDS, I cannot think that it would be coherent to regard making available such therapy as permissive rather than mandatory.[4]

If this seems still too like normal therapy to be convincing, suppose genes coding for repair enzymes which would not only repair radiation damage or damage by other environmental pollutants but

would also prolong healthy life expectancy could be inserted into humans. Again, would it be permissible to let people continue suffering such damage when they could be protected against it? Would it in short be O.K. to let them suffer?

It is not normal for the human organism to be self-repairing in this way; this must be eugenic if anything is. But if available, its use would surely, like penicillin before it, be more than merely permissive.

Of course, there will be unclarity at the margins but at least this conception of disability captures and emphasises the central notion that a disability is disabling in some sense, that it is a harm to those who suffer it, and that to knowingly disable another individual or leave them disabled when we could remove the disability is to harm that individual.[5]

This is not an exhaustive definition of disability but it is a way of thinking about it which avoids certain obvious pitfalls. First it does not define disability in terms of any conception or normalcy. Secondly it does not depend on post hoc ratification by the subject of the condition—it is not a prediction about how the subject of the condition will feel. This is important because we need an account of disability we can use for the potentially self-conscious, gametes, embryos, fetuses and neonates, and for the temporarily unconscious, which does not wait upon subsequent ratification by the person concerned.

With this account in mind we can extract the sting from at least one dimension of the charge that attempts to produce fine healthy children might be wrongful. Two related sorts of wrongfulness are often alleged here. One comes from some people and groups of people with disability or from their advocates. The second comes from those who are inclined to label such measures as attempts at eugenic control.

It is often said by those with disability or by their supporters[6] that abortion for disability, or failure to keep disabled infants alive as long as possible, or even positive infanticide for disabled neonates, constitutes discrimination against the disabled as a group, that it is tantamount to devaluing them as persons, to devaluing them in some existential sense. Alison Davis identifies this view with utilitarianism and comments further that "(i)t would also justify using me as a donor bank for someone more physically perfect (I am confined to a wheelchair due to spina bifida) and, depending on our view of relative worth, it would justify using any of us as a donor if someone of the status of Einstein or Beethoven, or even Bob Geldof, needed one of our organs to survive."[7] This is a possible version of utilitarianism of course, but not I believe one espoused by anyone today. On the view assumed here and which I have defended in detail elsewhere,[8] all persons share the same moral status whether disabled or not. To decide not to keep a disabled neonate alive no more constitutes an attack on the disabled than does curing disability. To set the badly broken legs of an unconscious casualty who cannot consent does not constitute an attack on those confined to wheelchairs. To prefer to remove disability where we can is not to prefer non-disabled individuals as persons. To reiterate, if a pregnant mother can take steps to cure a disability affecting her fetus she should certainly do so, for to fail to do so is to deliberately handicap her child. She is not saying that she prefers those without disability as persons when she says she would prefer not to have a disabled child.

The same is analogously true of charges of eugenics in related circumstances. The wrong of practising eugenics is that it involves the assumption that "those who are genetically weak should be discouraged from reproducing" or are less morally important than other persons and that compulsory measures to prevent them reproducing might be defensible.

It is not that the genetically weak should be discouraged from reproducing but that everyone should be discouraged from reproducing children who will be significantly harmed by their genetic constitution.[9]

Indeed, gene therapy offers the prospect of enabling the genetically weak to reproduce and give birth to the genetically strong. It is to this prospect and to possible objections to it that we must now turn.

In so far as gene therapy might be used to delete specific genetic disorders in individuals or repair damage that had occurred genetically or in any other way it seems straightforwardly analogous to any other sort of therapy and to fail to use it would be deliberately to harm those individuals whom its use would protect.

It might thus, as we have just noted, enable individuals with genetic defects to be sure of having healthy rather than harmed children and thus liberate them from the terrible dilemma of whether or not to risk having children with genetic defects.

Suppose now that it becomes possible to use gene therapy to introduce into the human genome genes coding for antibodies to major infections like AIDS, hepatitis B, malaria and others, or coding for repair enzymes which could correct the most frequently occurring defects caused by radiation damage, or which could retard the ageing process and so lead to greater healthy longevity, or which might remove predispositions to heart disease, or which would destroy carcinogens or maybe permit human beings to tolerate other environmental pollutants?[10]

I have called individuals who might have these protections built into their germ line a "new breed."[11] It might be possible to use somatic cell therapy to make the same changes. I am not here interested in the alleged moral differences between germ line and somatic line therapy, though elsewhere I have argued strongly that there is no morally relevant difference.[12] The question we must address is whether it would be wrong to fail to protect individuals in ways like these which would effectively enhance their function rather than cure dysfunction, which would constitute improvements in human individuals or indeed to the human genome, rather than simple (though complex in another sense and sophisticated) repairs? I am assuming of course that the technique is tried, tested and safe.

To answer this question we need to know whether to fail to protect individuals whom we could protect in this way would constitute a harm to them.[13] The answer seems to be clearly that it would. If the gene therapy could enhance prospects for healthy longevity then just as today, someone who had a life expectancy of fifty years rather than one of seventy would be regarded as at a substantial disadvantage, so having one of only seventy when others were able to enjoy ninety or so would be analogously disadvantageous. However, even if we concentrate on increased resistance, or reduced susceptibility, to disease there would still be palpable harms involved. True, to be vulnerable is not necessarily to suffer the harm to which one is vulnerable, although even this may constitute some degree of psychological damage. However, the right analogy seems here to be drawn from aviation.

Suppose aircraft manufacturers could easily build in safety features which would render an aircraft immune to, or at least much less susceptible to, a wide range of aviation hazards. If they failed to do so we would regard them as culpable whether or not a particular aircraft did in fact succumb to any of these hazards in the course of its life. They would in short be like a parent who failed to protect her children from dangerous diseases via immunization or our imagined parent who fails to protect through gene therapy.

I hope enough has been said to make clear that where gene therapy will effect improvements to human beings or to human nature that provide protections from harm or the protection of life itself in the form of increases in life expectancy ("death postponing" is after all just "life saving" redescribed) then call it what you will, eugenics or not, we ought to be in favour of it. There is in short no moral difference between attempts to cure dysfunction and attempts to enhance function where the enhancement protects life or health.

WHAT SORTS OF ENHANCEMENT PROTECT HEALTH?

I have drawn a distinction between attempts to protect life and health and other uses of gene therapy. I have done so mostly for the sake of brevity and to avoid the more contentious area of so-called cosmetic or frivolous uses of gene therapy. Equally and for analogous reasons I have here failed to distinguish between gene therapy on the germ line and gene therapy on the somatic line. I avoid contention here not out of distaste for combat but simply because to deploy the arguments necessary to defend cosmetic uses of gene therapy would take up more space than I have available now. Elsewhere I have deployed these arguments.[14] However, the distinction between preservation of life and health or normal medical uses and other uses of gene therapy is difficult to draw and it is worth here just illustrating this difficulty.

The British Government's "Committee on the Ethics of Gene Therapy" in its report to Parliament attempted to draw this distinction. The report, known by the surname of its chairman as *The Clothier Report* suggested "in the current state of knowledge it would not be acceptable to attempt to change traits not associated with disease."[15] This was an attempt to rule out so-called cosmetic uses of gene therapy which would include attempts to manipulate intelligence.[16]

Imagine two groups of mentally handicapped or educationally impaired children. In one the disability is traceable to a specific disease state or injury, in the other it has no obvious cause. Suppose now that gene therapy offered the chance of improving the intelligence of children generally and those in both these groups in particular. Those who think that using gene therapy to improve intelligence is wrong because it is not a dimension of health care would have to think that neither group of children should be helped and those, like Clothier, who are marginally more enlightened would have to think that it might be ethical to help children in the first group but not those in the second.[17]

I must now turn to the question of whether or not gene therapy as a technique is specially morally problematic.

WHAT'S WRONG WITH GENE THERAPY?

Gene therapy may of course be scientifically problematic in a number of ways and in so far as these might make the procedure unsafe we would have some reason to be suspicious of it. However, these problems are ethically uninteresting and I shall continue to assume that gene therapy is tried and tested from a scientific perspective. What else might be wrong with it?

One other ethical problem for gene therapy has been suggested and it deserves the small space left. Ruth Chadwick has given massive importance to the avoidance of doubt over one's genetic origins. Chadwick suggests that someone:

> who discovers that her parents had an extra gene or genes added...may suffer from what today in the "problem pages" is called an "identity crisis"...Part of this may be an uncertainty about her genetic history. We have stressed the importance of this knowledge, and pointed out that when one does not know where 50 per cent of one's genes come from, it can cause unhappiness.[18]

Chadwick then asks whether this problem can be avoided if only a small amount of genetic make-up is involved. Her answer is equivocal but on balance she seems to feel that "we must be cautious about producing a situation where children feel they do not really belong anywhere, because their genetic history is confused."[19] This sounds mild enough until we examine the cash value of phrases like "can cause unhappiness" or "be cautious" as Chadwick uses them.

In discussing the alleged unhappiness caused by ignorance of 50 per cent of one's genetic origin, Chadwick argued strongly that such unhappiness was so serious that "it seems wise to restrict artificial reproduction to methods that do not involve donation of genetic material. This rules out AID, egg donation, embryo donation and partial surrogacy."[20]

In elevating doubt about one's genetic origin to a cause of unhappiness so poignant that it would be better that a child who might experience it had never been born, Chadwick ignores entirely the (in fact false) truism that while motherhood is a fact paternity is always merely a hypothesis. It is a wise child indeed that knows her father and since such doubt might reasonably cloud the lives of a high proportion of the population of the world, we have reason to be sceptical that its effects are so terrible that people should be prevented from reproducing except where such doubt can be ruled out.

The effect of Chadwick's conclusion is to deny gay couples and single people the possibility of reproducing. Chadwick denies this, suggesting "they are not being denied the opportunity to have children. If they are prepared to take the necessary steps ('the primitive sign of wanting is trying to get') their desire to beget can be satisfied." What are we to make of this? It seems almost self-consciously mischievous. In the first place gay couples and single women resorting to what must, *ex hypothesi*, be distasteful sex with third parties merely for procreational purposes, are unlikely to preserve the identity of their sexual partners for the benefit of their offspring's alleged future peace of mind. If this is right then doubt over genetic origin will not be removed. Since Chadwick is explicitly addressing public policy issues she should in consistency advocate legislation against such a course of action rather than recommend it.

But surely, if we are to contemplate legislating against practices which give rise to doubt about genetic origins we would need hard evidence not only that such practices harm the resulting children but that the harm is of such high order that not only would it have been better that such children had never been born but also better that those who want such children should suffer the unhappiness consequent on a denial of their chance to have children using donated genetic material.

Where such harm is not only unavoidable but is an inherent part of sexual reproduction and must affect to some degree or other a high percentage of all births, it is surely at best unkind to use the fear of it as an excuse for discriminating against already persecuted minorities in the provision of reproductive services.

Where, as in the case of gene therapy, such donated[21] material also protects life and health or improves the human condition we have an added reason to welcome it.

NOTES

1. The argument here follows that of my paper "Should We Attempt to Eradicate Disability" to be published in the Proceedings of the Fifteenth International Wittgenstein Symposium.
2. See my discussion of the difference between harming and wronging in my *Wonderwoman & Superman; The Ethics of Human Biotechnology.* Oxford, 1992. Chapter 4.
3. This goes for relatively minor conditions like the loss of a finger or deafness and also for disfiguring conditions right through to major disability like paraplegia.
4. In this sense the definition of disability is like that of "poverty."
5. See my more detailed account of the relationship between harming and wronging in my *Wonderwoman & Superman*, Oxford University Press, Oxford, 1992. Chapter 4.
6. Who should of course include us all.
7. Davis 1988, p. 150.
8. See my *The Value of Life*, Routledge, London, 1985 & 1990, Ch. 1, and my "Not all babies should be kept alive as long as possible" in Raanan Gillon and Anne Lloyd, Eds. *Principles of Health Care Ethics*, John Wiley & Sons, Chichester, in press, publication 1993.
9. I use the term "weak" here to echo Chadwick's use of the term. I take "genetically weak" to refer to those possessing a debilitating genetic condition or those

who will inevitably pass on such a condition. All of us almost certainly carry some genetic abnormalities and are not thereby rendered "weak".

10. Here I borrow freely from my *Wonderwoman & Superman: The Ethics of Human Biotechnology*, Oxford University Press, 1992, Chapter 9, where I discuss all these issues in greater depth than is possible here.

11. Ibid.

12. Ibid, Chapter 8.

13. For an elaboration on the importance of this distinction see my discussion of "the wrong of wrongful life" in *Wonderwoman & Superman*, Chapter 4.

14. Ibid, Chapter 7.

15. *Report of the Committee on the Ethics of Gene Therapy*, presented to Parliament by Command of Her Majesty, January 1992. London, HMSO, para.4.22.

16. In fact intelligence is unlikely to prove responsive to such manipulation because of its multifactorial nature.

17. There would be analogous problems about attempts to block the use of gene therapy to change things like physical stature and height since it might be used in the treatment of achondroplasia or other forms of dwarfism.

18. Ruth Chadwick, *Ethics, Reproduction and Genetic Control*, Routledge, London, 1987, page 126.

19. Ibid, page 127.

20. Ibid, page 39.

21. I use the term "donated" here but I do not mean to rule out commerce in such genetic material. See *My Wonderwoman & Superman*, Chapter 6.

Genetic Enhancement

WALTER GLANNON

Gene therapy must be distinguished from genetic enhancement. The first is an intervention aimed at treating disease and restoring physical and mental functions and capacities to an adequate baseline. The second is an intervention aimed at improving functions and capacities that already are adequate. Genetic enhancement augments functions and capacities "that without intervention would be considered entirely normal."[1] Its goal is to "amplify 'normal' genes in order to make them better."[2] In chapter 1 I cited Norman Daniels's definitions of health and disease as well as what the notion of just health care entailed. This involved maintaining or restoring mental and physical functions at or to normal levels, which was necessary to ensure fair equality of opportunity for all citizens. Insofar as this aim defines the goal of medicine, genetic enhancement falls outside this goal. Furthermore, insofar as this type of intervention is not part of the goal of medicine and has no place in a just health care system, there are no medical or moral reasons for genetically enhancing normal human functions and capacities.

Some have argued that it is mistaken to think that a clean line of demarcation can be drawn between treatment and enhancement, since certain forms of enhancement are employed to prevent disease. Leroy Walters and Julie Gage Palmer refer to the immune system as an example to make this point:

In current medical practice, the best example of a widely accepted health-related physical enhancement is immunization against infectious disease.

Reprinted with permission of the publisher from *Genes and Future People: Philosophical Issues in Human Genetics* by Walter Glannon (Boulder, CO: Westview Press, 2001, pp. 94–101.) Copyright © by Westview Press, a Member of the Perseus Books Group.

With immunizations against diseases like polio and hepatitis B, what we are saying is in effect, "The immune system that we inherited from our parents may not be adequate to ward off certain viruses if we are exposed to them. Therefore, we will enhance the capabilities of our immune system by priming it to fight against these viruses."

From the current practice of immunizations against particular diseases, it would seem to be only a small step to try to enhance the general function of the immune system by genetic means.... In our view the genetic enhancement of the immune system would be morally justifiable if this kind of enhancement assisted in preventing disease and did not cause offsetting harms to the people treated by the technique.[3]

Nevertheless, because the goal of the technique would be to prevent disease, it would not, strictly speaking, be enhancement, at least not in terms of the definitions given at the outset of this section. Genetically intervening in the immune system as described by Walters and Palmer is a means of maintaining it in proper working order so that it will be better able to ward off pathogens posing a threat to the organism as a whole. Thus, it is misleading to call this intervention "enhancement." When we consider what is normal human functioning, we refer to the whole human organism consisting of immune, endocrine, nervous, cardiovascular, and other systems, not to these systems understood as isolated parts. The normal functioning in question here pertains to the ability of the immune system to protect the organism from infectious agents and thus ensure its survival. Any preventive genetic intervention in this system would be designed to maintain the normal functions of the organism, not to restore them or raise them above the norm. It would be neither therapy not enhancement but instead a form of maintenance. Therefore, the alleged ambiguity surrounding what Walters and Palmer call "enhancing" the immune system does not impugn the distinction between treatment and enhancement.

If enhancement could make adequately functioning bodily systems function even better, then presumably there would be no limit to the extent to which bodily functions can be enhanced. Yet, beyond a certain point, heightened immune sensitivity to infectious agents can lead to an overly aggressive response, resulting in autoimmune disease that can damage healthy cells, tissues, and organs. In fact, there would be a limit to the beneficial effects of genetic intervention in the immune system, a limit beyond which the equilibrium between humoral and cellular response mechanisms would be disturbed.[4] If any intervention ensured that the equilibrium of the immune system was maintained in proper working order, then it would be inappropriate to consider it as a form of enhancement.

To further support the treatment-enhancement distinction, consider a nongenetic intervention, the use of a bisphosphonate such as alendronate sodium. Its purpose is to prevent postmenopausal women from developing osteoporosis, or to rebuild bone in women or men who already have osteoporosis. Some might claim that, because it can increase bone density, it is a form of enhancement. But its more general purpose is to prevent bone fractures and thus maintain proper bone function so that one can have normal mobility and avoid the morbidity resulting from fractures. In terms of the functioning of the entire organism, therefore, it would be more accurate to consider the use of bisphosphonates as prevention, treatment, or maintenance rather than enhancement.

Some might raise a different question. Suppose that the parents of a child much shorter than the norm for his age persuaded a physician to give him growth hormone injections in order to increase his height. Suppose further that the child's shortness was not due to an iatrogenic cause, such as radiation to treat a brain tumor. Would this be treatment or enhancement? The question that should be asked regarding this issue is not whether the child's height is normal for his age group. Rather, the question should be whether his condition implies something less than normal physical functioning, such that he would have fewer opportunities for achievement and a decent minimum level of well-being over his lifetime. Diminutive stature alone does not necessarily imply that one's functioning is or will be so limited as to restrict one's opportunities for achievement. Of course, being short might limit one's opportunities if one wanted to become a professional basketball player. But most of us are quite flexible when it comes to formulating and carrying out life plans. Robert Reich, the treasury secretary in President Clinton's first administration, is just one example of how one can achieve very much in life despite diminutive stature. If a child's stature significantly limited his functioning and opportunities, then growth-hormone injections should be considered therapeutic treatment. If his stature were not so limiting, then the injections should be considered enhancement.

Admittedly, there is gray area near the baseline of adequate functioning where it may be difficult to distinguish between treatment and enhancement. Accordingly, we should construe the baseline loosely or thickly enough to allow for some minor deviation above or below what would be considered normal functioning. An intervention for a condition near the baseline that would raise one's functioning clearly above the critical level should be considered an enhancement. An intervention for a condition making one's functioning fall clearly below the baseline, with the aim of raising one's functioning to the critical level, should be considered a treatment. For example, an athlete with a hemoglobin level slightly below the norm for people his age and mildly anemic may want to raise that level significantly in order to be more competitive in his sport. To the extent that his actual hemoglobin level does not interfere with his ordinary physical functioning, an intervention to significantly raise that level would be an instance of enhancement. In contrast, for a child who has severe thalassemia and severe anemia, with the risk of bone abnormalities and heart failure, an intervention to correct the disorder would be an instance of treatment.

The main moral concern about genetic enhancement of physical and mental traits is that it would give some people an unfair advantage over others with respect to competitive goods like beauty, sociability, and intelligence. Unlike the cognitively disabled individual considered earlier, we can assume that their mental states would not be so different and that they would retain their identity. Enhancement would be unfair because only those who could afford the technology would have access to it, and many people are financially worse off than others through no fault of their own. Insofar as the possession of these goods gives some people an advantage over others in careers, income, and social status, the competitive nature of these goods suggests that there would be no limit to the benefits that improvements to physical and mental capacities

would yield to those fortunate enough to avail themselves of the technology. This is altogether different from the example of immune-system enhancement. There would be no diminishing marginal value in the degree of competitive advantage that one could have over others for the social goods in question and presumably no limit to the value of enhancing the physical and mental capacities that would give one this advantage. Not having access to the technology that could manipulate genetic traits in such a way as to enhance these capacities would put one at a competitive disadvantage relative to others who would have access to it.

Advancing an argument similar to the one used by those who reject the treatment-enhancement distinction, one might hold that competitive goods collapse the categorical distinction between correcting deficient capacities and improving normal ones. This is because competitive goods are continuous, coming in degrees, and therefore the capacities that enable one to achieve these goods cannot be thought of as either normal or deficient.[5] Nevertheless, to the extent that any form of genetic intervention is motivated by the medical and moral aim to enable people to have adequate mental and physical functioning and fair equality of opportunity for a decent minimum level of well-being, the goods in question are not *competitive* but *basic*. In other words, the aim of any medical intervention by genetic means is to make people better off than they were before by raising or restoring them to an absolute baseline of normal physical and mental functioning, not to make them comparatively better off than others. Competitive goods above the baseline may be continuous; but the basic goods that enable someone to reach or remain at the baseline are not. Given that these two types of goods are distinct, and that they result from the distinct aims and practices of enhancement and treatment, we can affirm that enhancement and treatment can and should be treated separately. We can uphold the claim that the purpose of any genetic intervention should be to treat people's abnormal functions and restore them to a normal level, not to enhance those functions that already are normal.

As I have mentioned, genetic enhancement that gave some people an advantage over others in possessing competitive goods would entail considerable unfairness. A likely scenario would be one in which parents paid to use expensive genetic technology to raise the cognitive ability or improve the physical beauty of their children. This would give them an advantage over other children with whom they would compete for education, careers, and income. Children of parents who could not afford to pay for the technology would be at a comparative disadvantage. Even if the goods in question fell above the normal functional baseline, one still could maintain that such an advantage would be unfair. It would depend on people's ability to pay, and inequalities in income are unfair to the extent that they result from some factors beyond people's control.

We could not appeal to the notion of a genetic lottery to resolve the problem of fairness regarding genetic enhancement. For, as I argued in the last section, such a lottery is better suited to meeting people's needs than their preferences, and enhancements correspond to people's preferences. Moreover, a lottery might only exacerbate the problem by reinforcing the perception of unfairness, depending on how losers in the lottery interpreted the fact that others won merely as a result of a random selection. One suggestion for resolving the fairness problem (short of banning the use of the technology altogether) would be to make genetic enhancement available to all. Of course, how this system could be financed is a question that admits of no easy answer. But the more important substantive point is that universal access to genetic enhancement would not be a solution. Indeed, the upshot of such access would provide a reason for prohibiting it.

Universal availability of genetic enhancement would mean that many competitive goods some people had over others would be canceled out collectively. The idea of a competitive advantage gradually would erode, and there would be more equality among people in their possession of goods. There would not be complete equality, however. Differing parental attitudes toward such goods as education could mean differences in the extent to which cognitive enhancement was utilized. Some parents would be more selective than others in sending their children to better schools or arranging for private tutors. So, there still would be some inequality in the general outcome of the enhancement. But quite apart from this, the process of neutralizing competitive goods could end up being self-defeating on a collective level.[6] More specifically, one probable side-

effect of boosting children's mental capacity on a broad scale would be some brain damage resulting in cognitive and affective impairment in some of the children who received the genetic enhancement. The net social cost of using the technology would outweigh any social advantage of everyone using it. If no one is made better off than they were before in terms of their goods, but some people are made worse off than they were before in terms of their mental functioning, then the net social disadvantage would provide a reason for prohibiting collective genetic enhancement.

There is another moral aspect of enhancement that should be considered. I have maintained that inequalities above the baseline of normal physical and mental functioning are of no great moral importance and may be neutral on the question of fairness. Although equality and fairness are closely related, one does not necessarily imply the other. Again, fairness pertains to meeting people's needs. Once these needs have been met, inequalities in the possession of goods relating to preferences are not so morally significant. Thus, if the idea of an absolute baseline implies that people's basic physical and mental needs have been met, and if people who are comparatively better or worse off than others all have functioning at or above the baseline, then any inequalities in functioning above this level should not matter very much morally. If this is plausible, then it seems to follow that there would be nothing unfair and hence nothing morally objectionable about enhancements that made some people better off than others above the baseline. Nevertheless, this could undermine our belief in the importance of the fundamental equality of all people, regardless of how well off they are in absolute terms. Equality is one of the social bases of self-respect, which is essential for social harmony and stability.[7] Allowing inequalities in access to and possession of competitive goods at any level of functioning or welfare might erode this basis and the ideas of harmony and stability that rest on it. Although it would be difficult to measure, this type of social cost resulting from genetic enhancement could constitute another reason for prohibiting it.

Yet, suppose that we could manipulate certain genes to enhance our noncompetitive virtuous traits, such as altruism, generosity, and compassion.[8] Surely, these would contribute to a stable, well-ordered society and preserve the principle of fair equality of opportunity. Nothing in this program would be incompatible with the goal of medicine as the prevention and treatment of disease. But it would threaten the individual autonomy essential to us as moral agents who can be candidates for praise and blame, punishment and reward. What confers moral worth on our actions, and indeed on ourselves as agents, is our capacity to cultivate certain dispositions leading to actions. This cultivation involves the exercise of practical reason and a process of critical self-reflection, whereby we modify, eliminate, or reinforce dispositions and thereby come to identify with them as our own. Autonomy consists precisely in this process of reflection and identification. It is the capacity for reflective self-control that enables us to take responsibility for our mental states and the actions that issue from them. Given the importance of autonomy, it would be preferable to have fewer virtuous dispositions that we can identify with as our own than to have more virtuous dispositions implanted in us through genetic enhancement. These would threaten to undermine our moral agency because they would derive from an external source.[9] Even if our genes could be manipulated in such a way that our behavior always conformed to an algorithm for the morally correct course of action in every situation, it is unlikely that we would want it. Most of us would rather make autonomous choices that turned out not to lead to the best courses of action. This is because of the intrinsic importance of autonomy and the moral growth and maturity that come with making our own choices under uncertainty. The dispositions with which we come to identify, imperfect as they may be, are what make us autonomous and responsible moral agents. Enhancing these mental states through artificial means external to our own exercise of practical reason and our own process of identification would undermine our autonomy by making them alien to us.

In sum, there are four reasons why genetic enhancement would be morally objectionable. First, it would give an unfair advantage to some people over others because some would be able to pay for expensive enhancement procedures while others would not. Second, if we tried to remedy the first problem by making genetic enhancement universally accessible, then it would be collectively self-

defeating. Although much competitive unfairness at the individual level would be canceled out at the collective level, there would be the unacceptable social cost of some people suffering from adverse cognitive or emotional effects of the enhancement. Third, inequalities resulting from enhancements above the baseline of normal physical and mental functioning could threaten to undermine the conviction in the fundamental importance of equality as one of the bases of self-respect, and in turn social solidarity and stability. Fourth, enhancement of noncompetitive dispositions would threaten to undermine the autonomy and moral agency essential to us as persons.

NOTES

1. Jon Gordan, "Genetic Enhancement in Humans," *Science* 283 (March 26, 1999): 2023–2024.

2. Eric Juengst, "Can Enhancement Be Distinguished from Prevention in Genetic Medicine?" *Journal of Medicine and Philosophy* 22 (1997): 125–142, and "What Does Enhancement Mean?" in Erik Parens, ed., *Enhancing Human Traits: Ethical and Social Implications* (Washington, DC: Georgetown University Press, 1998): 27–47, at 27. Also, Dan Brock, "Enhancements of Human Function: Some Distinctions for Policymakers," Ibid., 48–69.

3. *The Ethics of Human Gene Therapy*, 110. Instead of distinguishing between treatments and enhancements, Walters and Palmer distinguish between health-related and non-health-related enhancements. But I do not find this distinction to be very helpful.

4. Brock points this out in "Enhancements of Human Function," 59. Marc Lappe makes a more compelling case for the same point in *The Tao of Immunology*.

5. Kavka develops and defends the idea that competitive goods are continuous. in "Upside Risks," 164–165.

6. Kavka, "Upside Risks," 167. Also, Brock, "Enhancements of Human Function" 60; and Buchanan et al., *From Chance to Choice*, chap. 8.

7. Rawls makes this point in *A Theory of Justice*, 7–11, and in "Social Unity and Primary Goods," 162. See also Daniels. *Just Health Care*.

8. Walters and Palmer present this thought-experiment in *The Ethics of Human Gene Therapy*, 123–128. As they note, Jonathan Glover introduced this idea in *What Sort of People Should Them Be?* (Harmondsworth: Penguin, 1984).

9. Drawing on the work of Lionel Trilling and Charles Taylor, Carl Elliott discusses cognitive and affective

enhancement that undermine what he calls the "ethics of authenticity" in "The Tyranny of Happiness: Ethics and Cosmetic Psychopharmacology," in Parens, *Enhancing Human Traits*, 177–188. Also

ARGUMENT 9 ESSAY QUESTIONS

1. Do you think that Harris is right to deny a distinction between repair and enhancement? Why or why not?
2. Who makes the stronger case regarding genetic enhancement—Harris or Glannon? Explain.
3. Do you think that genetic enhancement should be permitted? Give reasons for your answer.

relevant to this issue is Harry Frankfurt, "Identification and Externality," in Frankfurt, *The Importance of What We Care About* (New York: Cambridge University Press, 1989):58–68.

10. THE OPEN-FUTURE ARGUMENT AGAINST CLONING

Some critics of human cloning have charged that it violates the rights of the resulting clone—specifically, the right to a unique identity. A clone by definition is not genetically unique; his genome is iterated in his "parent." Aside from doubts about whether such a right exists, the strongest reply to this worry is that genetic uniqueness is neither necessary nor sufficient for personal uniqueness:

> What is the sense of identity that might plausibly be each person has a right to have uniquely, which constitutes the special uniqueness of each individual? Even with the same genes, two individuals, for example homozygous twins, are numerically distinct and not identical, so what is intended must be the various properties and characteristics that make each individual qualitatively unique and different than others. Does having the same genome as another person undermine that unique qualitative identity? Only in the crudest genetic determinism.... But there is no reason whatever to believe in that kind of genetic determinism, and I do not think that anyone does.[8]

A similar rights argument, however, has seemed more persuasive to some cloning opponents. It says that cloning would be wrong because it violates what has been called a "right

---

[8] Dan W. Brock, "Cloning Human Beings: An Assessment of the Ethical Issues Pro and Con," paper prepared for the National Bioethics Advisory Commission, 1997.

to ignorance" or a "right to an open future." Consider a situation in which a clone begins his life many years after his older twin does. The younger twin seems to re-live the life of the older one, thinking—correctly or incorrectly—that his genetically identical sibling has already lived the life that he (the younger twin) has barely started. He believes that his future is already set. His sense of personal freedom and of a future of possibilities is diminished. In this way, the argument goes, his right to an open-ended life story has been violated.

In "A Life in the Shadow: One Reason Why We Should Not Clone Humans," Søren Holm echoes this argument, calling the predicament of a clone a "life in the shadow":

> What is wrong with living your life as a clone in the shadow of the life of the original? It diminishes the clone's possibility of living a life that is in a full sense of that word his or her life. The clone is forced to be involved in an attempt to perform a complicated partial re-enactment of the life of somebody else (the original).[9]

But some think this argument is built on flimsy assumptions:

> [A]ll of these concerns are not only quite speculative, but are directly related to certain specific cultural values. Someone created through the use of somatic cell nuclear transfer techniques may or may not believe that their future is relatively constrained. Indeed, they may believe the opposite. In addition, quite normal parenting usually involves many constraints on a child's behavior that children may resent.[10]

Cloning Human Beings
An Assessment of the Ethical Issues Pro and Con

DAN W. BROCK

The world of science and the public at large were both shocked and fascinated by the announcement in the journal *Nature* by Ian Wilmut and his colleagues that they had successfully cloned a sheep from a single cell of an adult sheep (Wilmut, 1997). But many were troubled or apparently even horrified at the prospect that cloning of adult humans by the same process might be possible as well. The response of

most scientific and political leaders to the prospect of human cloning, indeed of Dr. Wilmut as well, was of immediate and strong condemnation.

---

[9] Søren Holm, "A Life in the Shadow: One Reason Why We Should Not Clone Humans," *Cambridge Quarterly of Healthcare Ethics*, vol. 7, no. 2 (Spring 1998): 160–62.
[10] National Bioethics Advisory Commission, *Cloning Human Beings: Report and Recommendations*, June 1997, 67.

A few more cautious voices were heard both suggesting some possible benefits from the use of human cloning in limited circumstances and questioning its too quick prohibition, but they were a clear minority. A striking feature of these early responses was that their strength and intensity seemed far to outrun the arguments and reasons offered in support of them—they seemed often to be "gut level" emotional reactions rather than considered reflections on the issues. Such reactions should not be simply dismissed, both because they may point us to important considerations otherwise missed and not easily articulated, and because they often have a major impact on public policy. But the formation of public policy should not ignore the moral reasons and arguments that bear on the practice of human cloning—these must be articulated in order to understand and inform people's more immediate emotional responses. This essay is an effort to articulate, and to evaluate critically, the main moral considerations and arguments for and against human cloning. Though many people's religious beliefs inform their views on human cloning, and it is often difficult to separate religious from secular positions, I shall restrict myself to arguments and reasons that can be given a clear secular formulation.

On each side of the issue there are two distinct kinds of moral arguments brought forward. On the one hand, some opponents claim that human cloning would violate fundamental moral or human rights, while some proponents argue that its prohibition would violate such rights. While moral and even human rights need not be understood as absolute, they do place moral restrictions on permissible actions that an appeal to a mere balance of benefits over harms cannot justify overriding; for example, the rights of human subjects in research must be respected even if the result is that some potentially beneficial research is more difficult or cannot be done. On the other hand, both opponents and proponents also cite the likely harms and benefits, both to individuals and to society, of the practice. I shall begin with the arguments in support of permitting human cloning, although with no implication that it is the stronger or weaker position.

MORAL ARGUMENTS IN SUPPORT OF HUMAN CLONING

Is There a Moral Right to Use Human Cloning?

What moral right might protect at least some access to the use of human cloning? A commitment to individual liberty, such as defended by J. S. Mill, requires that individuals be left free to use human cloning if they so choose and if their doing so does not cause significant harms to others, but liberty is too broad in scope to be an uncontroversial moral right (Mill, 1859; Rhodes, 1995). Human cloning is a means of reproduction (in the most literal sense) and so the most plausible moral right at stake in its use is a right to reproductive freedom or procreative liberty (Robertson, 1994a; Brock, 1994), understood to include both the choice not to reproduce, for example, by means of contraception or abortion, and also the right to reproduce.

The right to reproductive freedom is properly understood to include the right to use various assisted reproductive technologies (ARTs), such as in vitro fertilization (IVF), oocyte donation, and so forth. The reproductive right relevant to human cloning is a negative right, that is, a right to use ARTs without interference by the government or others when made available by a willing provider. The choice of an assisted means of reproduction should be protected by reproductive freedom even when it is not the only means for individuals to reproduce, just as the choice among different means of preventing conception is protected by reproductive freedom. However, the case for permitting the use of a particular means of reproduction is strongest when it is necessary for particular individuals to be able to procreate at all, or to do so without great burdens or harms to themselves or others. In some cases human cloning could be the only means for individuals to procreate while retaining a biological tie to their child, but in other cases different means of procreating might also be possible.

It could be argued that human cloning is not covered by the right to reproductive freedom because whereas current ARTs and practices covered by that right are remedies for inabilities to reproduce sexually, human cloning is an entirely new means of reproduction; indeed, its critics see it as more a means of manufacturing humans than of reproduction. Human cloning is a different means of reproduction than sexual reproduction, but it is a means that can serve individuals' interest in reproducing. If it is not protected by the moral right to reproductive freedom, I believe that must be not because it is a new means of reproducing, but instead because it has other objectionable or harmful features; I shall evaluate these other ethical objections to it later.

When individuals have alternative means of procreating, human cloning typically would be chosen because it replicates a particular individual's genome. The reproductive interest in question then is not simply reproduction itself, but a more specific interest in choosing what kind of children to have. The right to reproductive freedom is usually understood to cover at least some choice about the kind of children one will have. Some individuals choose reproductive partners in the hope of producing offspring with desirable traits. Genetic testing of fetuses or preimplantation embryos for genetic disease or abnormality is done to avoid having a child with those diseases or abnormalities. Respect for individual self-determination, which is one of the grounds of a moral right to reproductive freedom, includes respecting individuals' choices about whether to have a child with a condition that will place severe burdens on them, and cause severe burdens to the child itself.

The less a reproductive choice is primarily the determination of one's own life, but primarily the determination of the nature of another, as in the case of human cloning, the more moral weight the interests of that other person, that is the cloned child, should have in decisions that determine its nature (Annas, 1994). But even then parents are typically accorded substantial, but not unlimited, discretion in shaping the persons their children will become, for example, through education and other childrearing decisions. Even if not part of reproductive freedom, the right to raise one's children as one sees fit, within limits mostly determined by the interests of the children, is also a right to determine within limits what kinds of persons one's children will become. This right includes not just preventing

certain diseases or harms to children, but selecting and shaping desirable features and traits in one's children. The use of human cloning is one way to exercise that right.

Public policy and the law now permit prospective parents to conceive, or to carry a conception to term, when there is a significant risk or even certainty that the child will suffer from a serious genetic disease. Even when others think the risk or certainty of genetic disease makes it morally wrong to conceive, or to carry a fetus to term, the parents' right to reproductive freedom permits them to do so. Most possible harms to a cloned child are less serious than the genetic harms with which parents can now permit their offspring to be conceived or born.

I conclude that there is good reason to accept that a right to reproductive freedom presumptively includes both a right to select the means of reproduction, as well as a right to determine what kind of children to have, by use of human cloning. However, the specific reproductive interest of determining what kind of children to have is less weighty than are other reproductive interests and choices whose impact falls more directly and exclusively on the parents rather than the child. Even if a moral right to reproductive freedom protects the use of human cloning, that does not settle the moral issue about human cloning, since there may be other moral rights in conflict with this right, or serious enough harms from human cloning to override the right to use it; this right can be thought of as establishing a serious moral presumption supporting access to human cloning.

What Individual or Social Benefits Might Human Cloning Produce?

Largely Individual Benefits

The literature on human cloning by nuclear transfer or by embryo splitting contains a few examples of circumstances in which individuals might have good reasons to want to use human cloning. However, human cloning seems not to be the unique answer to any great or pressing human need and its benefits appear to be limited at most. What are the principal possible benefits of human cloning that might give individuals good reasons to want to use it?

1. Human cloning would be a new means to relieve the infertility some persons now experience. Human cloning would allow women who have no ova or men who have no sperm to produce an offspring that is biologically related to them (Eisenberg, 1976; Robertson, 1994b, 1997; LaBar, 1984). Embryos might also be cloned, by either nuclear transfer or embryo splitting, in order to increase the number of embryos for implantation and improve the chances of successful conception (NABER, 1994). The benefits from human cloning to relieve infertility are greater the more persons there are who cannot overcome their infertility by any other means acceptable to them. I do not know of data on this point, but the numbers who would use cloning for this reason are probably not large.

The large number of children throughout the world possibly available for adoption represents an alternative solution to infertility only if we are prepared to discount as illegitimate the strong desire of many persons, fertile and infertile, for the experience of pregnancy and for having and raising a child biologically related to them. While not important to all infertile (or fertile) individuals, it is important to many and is respected and met through other forms of assisted reproduction that maintain a biological connection when that is possible; that desire does not become illegitimate simply because human cloning would be the best or only means of overcoming an individual's infertility.

2. Human cloning would enable couples in which one party risks transmitting a serious hereditary disease to an offspring to reproduce without doing so (Robertson, 1994b). By using donor sperm or egg donation, such hereditary risks can generally be avoided now without the use of human cloning. These procedures may be unacceptable to some couples, however, or at least considered less desirable than human cloning because they introduce a third party's genes into their reproduction instead of giving their offspring only the genes of one of them. Thus, in some cases human cloning could be a reasonable means of preventing genetically transmitted harms to offspring. Here too, we do not know how many persons would want to use human cloning instead of other means of avoiding the risk of genetic transmission of a disease or of accepting the risk of transmitting the disease, but the numbers again are probably not large.

3. Human cloning to make a later twin would enable a person to obtain needed organs or tissues for transplantation (Robertson, 1994b, 1997; Kahn, 1989; Harris, 1992). Human cloning would solve the problem of finding a transplant donor whose organ or tissue is an acceptable match and would eliminate, or drastically reduce, the risk of transplant rejection by the host. The availability of human cloning for this purpose would amount to a form of insurance to enable treatment of certain kinds of medical conditions. Of course, sometimes the medical need would be too urgent to permit waiting for the cloning, gestation, and development that is necessary before tissues or organs can be obtained for transplantation. In other cases, taking an organ also needed by the later twin, such as a heart or a liver, would be impermissible because it would violate the later twin's rights.

Such a practice can be criticized on the ground that it treats the later twin not as a person valued and loved for his or her own sake, as an end in itself in Kantian terms, but simply as a means for benefiting another. This criticism assumes, however, that only this one motive defines the reproduction and the relation of the person to his or her later twin. The well-known case some years ago in California of the Ayalas, who conceived in the hopes of obtaining a source for a bone marrow transplant for their teenage daughter suffering from leukemia, illustrates the mistake in this assumption. They argued that whether or not the child they conceived turned out to be a possible donor for their daughter, they would value and love the child for itself, and treat it as they would treat any other member of their family. That one reason they wanted it, as a possible means to saving their daughter's life, did not preclude their also loving and valuing it for its own sake; in Kantian terms, it was treated as a possible means to saving their daughter, but not *solely as a means*, which is what the Kantian view proscribes.

Indeed, when people have children, whether by sexual means or with the aid of ARTs, their motives and reasons for doing so are typically many and complex, and include reasons less laudable than obtaining lifesaving medical treatment, such as having someone who needs them, enabling them to live on their own, qualifying for government benefit programs, and so forth. While these are not admirable motives for having children and may not bode well for the child's upbringing and future, public policy does not assess prospective parents' motives and reasons for procreating as a condition of their doing so.

4. *Human cloning would enable individuals to clone someone who had special meaning to them, such as a child who had died* (Robertson, 1994b). There is no denying that if human cloning were available, some individuals would want to use it for this purpose, but their desire usually would be based on a deep confusion. Cloning such a child would not replace the child the parents had loved and lost, but would only create a different child with the same genes. The child they loved and lost was a unique individual who had been shaped by his or her environment and choices, not just his or her genes, and more importantly who had experienced a particular relationship with them. Even if the later cloned child could not only have the same genes but also be subjected to the same environment, which of course is impossible, it would remain a different child than the one they had loved and lost because it would share a different history with them (Thomas, 1974). Cloning the lost child might help the parents accept and move on from their loss, but another already existing sibling or a new child that was not a clone might do this equally well; indeed, it might do so better since the appearance of the cloned later twin would be a constant reminder of the child they had lost. Nevertheless, if human cloning enabled some individuals to clone a person who had special meaning to them and doing so gave them deep satisfaction, that would be a benefit to them even if their reasons for wanting to do so, and the satisfaction they in turn received, were based on a confusion. ...

MORAL ARGUMENTS AGAINST HUMAN CLONING

Would the Use of Human Cloning Violate Important Moral Rights?

Many of the immediate condemnations of any possible human cloning following Wilmut's cloning of Dolly claimed that it would violate moral or human rights, but it was usually not specified precisely, or often even at all, what rights would be violated (WHO, 1997). I shall consider two possible candidates for such a right: a right to have a unique identity and a right to ignorance about one's future or to an open future. Claims that cloning denies individuals a unique identity are common, but I shall argue that even if there is a right to a unique identity, it could not be violated by human cloning. The right to ignorance or to an open future has only been explicitly defended, to my knowledge, by two commentators, and in the context of human cloning, only by Hans Jonas; it supports a more promising, but in my view ultimately unsuccessful, argument that human cloning would violate an important moral or human right.

Is there a moral or human right to a unique identity, and if so would it be violated by human cloning? For human cloning to violate a right to a unique identity, the relevant sense of identity would have to be genetic identity, that is, a right to a unique unrepeated genome. This would be violated by human cloning, but is there any such right? It might be thought that cases of identical twins show there is no such right because no one claims that the moral or human rights of the twins have been violated. However, this consideration is not conclusive (Kass, 1985; NABER, 1994). Only human actions can violate others' rights; outcomes that would constitute a rights violation if deliberately caused by human action are not a rights violation if a result of natural causes. If Arthur deliberately strikes Barry on the head so hard as to cause his death, he violates Barry's right not to be killed; if lightning strikes Cheryl, causing her death, her right not to be killed has not been violated. Thus, the case of twins does not show that there could not be a right to a unique genetic identity.

What is the sense of identity that might plausibly be what each person has a right to have uniquely that constitutes the special uniqueness of each individual (Macklin 1994; Chadwick 1982)? Even with the same genes, homozygous twins are numerically distinct and not identical, so what is intended must be the various properties and characteristics that make each individual qualitatively unique and different from others. Does having the same genome as another person undermine that unique qualitative identity? Only on the crudest genetic determinism, according to which an individual's genes completely and decisively determine everything else about the individual, all his or her other nongenetic features and properties, together with the entire history or biography that constitutes his or her life. But there is no reason whatever to believe that kind of genetic determinism. Even with the same genes, differences in genetically identical twins' psychological and personal characteristics develop over time together with differences in their life histories, personal relationships, and life choices; sharing an identical genome does not prevent twins from developing distinct and unique personal identities of their own.

We need not pursue whether there is a moral or human right to a unique identity—no such right is found among typical accounts and enumerations of moral or human rights—because even if there is such a right, sharing a genome with another individual as a result of human cloning would not violate it. The idea of the uniqueness, or unique identity, of each person historically predates the development of modern genetics. A unique genome thus could not be the ground of this long-standing belief in the unique human identity of each person.

I turn now to whether human cloning would violate what Hans Jonas called a right to ignorance, or what Joel Feinberg called a right to an open future (Jonas, 1974; Feinberg, 1980). Jonas argued that human cloning in which there is a substantial time gap between the beginning of the lives of the earlier and later twin is fundamentally different from the simultaneous beginning of the lives of homozygous twins that occur in nature. Although contemporaneous twins begin their lives with the same genetic inheritance, they do so at the same time, and so in ignorance of what the other who shares the same genome will by his or her choices make of his or her life.

A later twin created by human cloning, Jonas argues, knows, or at least believes she knows, too much about herself. For there is already in the world another person, her earlier twin, who from the same genetic starting point has made the life choices that are still in the later twin's future. It will seem that her life has already been lived and played out by

another, that her fate is already determined; she will lose the sense of human possibility in freely and spontaneously creating her own future and authentic self. It is tyrannical, Jonas claims, for the earlier twin to try to determine another's fate in this way.

Jonas's objection can be interpreted so as not to assume either a false genetic determinism, or a belief in it. A later twin might grant that he is not determined to follow in his earlier twin's footsteps, but nevertheless the earlier twin's life might always haunt him, standing as an undue influence on his life, and shaping it in ways to which others' lives are not vulnerable. But the force of the objection still seems to rest on the false assumption that having the same genome as his earlier twin unduly restricts his freedom to create a different life and self than the earlier twin's. Moreover, a family environment also importantly shapes children's development, but there is no force to the claim of a younger sibling that the existence of an older sibling raised in that same family is an undue influence on the younger sibling's freedom to make his own life for himself in that environment. Indeed, the younger twin or sibling might gain the benefit of being able to learn from the older twin's or sibling's mistakes.

A closely related argument can be derived from what Joel Feinberg has called a child's right to an open future. This requires that others raising a child not so close off the future possibilities that the child would otherwise have as to eliminate a reasonable range of opportunities for the child autonomously to construct his or her own life. One way this right might be violated is to create a later twin who will believe her future has already been set for her by the choices made and the life lived by her earlier twin.

The central difficulty in these appeals to a right either to ignorance or to an open future is that the right is not violated merely because the later twin is likely to *believe* that his future is already determined, when that belief is clearly false and supported only by the crudest genetic determinism. If we know the later twin will falsely believe that his open future has been taken from him as a result of being cloned, even though in reality it has not, then we know that cloning will cause the twin psychological distress, but not that it will violate his right. Jonas's right to ignorance, and Feinberg's right of a child to an open future, are not violated by human cloning, though they do point to psychological harms that a later twin may be likely to experience and that I will take up later.

Neither a moral or human right to a unique identity, nor one to ignorance and an open future, would be violated by human cloning. There may be other moral or human rights that human cloning would violate, but I do not know what they might be. I turn now to consideration of the harms that human cloning might produce.

What Individual or Social Harms Might Human Cloning Produce?

There are many possible individual or social harms that have been posited by one or another commentator and I shall only try to cover the more plausible and significant of them.

Largely Individual Harms

1. *Human cloning would produce psychological distress and harm in the later twin.* No doubt knowing the path in life taken by one's earlier twin might often have several bad psychological effects (Callahan, 1993; LaBar, 1984; Macklin, 1994; McCormick, 1993; Studdard, 1978; Rainer, 1978; Verhey, 1994). The later twin might feel, even if mistakenly, that her fate has already been substantially laid out, and so have difficulty freely and spontaneously taking responsibility for and making her own fate and life. The later twin's experience or sense of autonomy and freedom might be substantially diminished, even if in actual fact they are diminished much less than it seems to her. She might have a diminished sense of her own uniqueness and individuality, even if once again these are in fact diminished little or not at all by having an earlier twin with the same genome. If the later twin is the clone of a particularly exemplary individual, perhaps with some special capabilities and accomplishments, she might experience excessive pressure to reach the very high standards of ability and accomplishment of the earlier twin (Rainer, 1978). These various psychological effects might take a heavy toll on the later twin and be serious burdens to her.

While psychological harms of these kinds from human cloning are certainly possible, and perhaps even likely in some cases, they remain at this point only speculative since we have no experience with human cloning and the creation of earlier and later twins. Nevertheless, if experience with human cloning confirmed that serious and unavoidable psychological harms typically occurred to the later twin, that would be a serious moral reason to avoid the practice. Intuitively at least, psychological burdens and harms seem more likely and more serious for a person who is only one of many identical later twins cloned from one original source, so that the clone might run into another identical twin around every street corner. This prospect could be a good reason to place sharp limits on the number of twins that could be cloned from any one source. ...

Largely Social Harms

3. *Human cloning would lessen the worth of individuals and diminish respect for human life.* Unelaborated claims to this effect were common in the media after the announcement of the cloning of Dolly. Ruth Macklin explored and criticized the claim that human cloning would diminish the value we place on, and our respect for, human life because it would lead to persons being viewed as replaceable (Macklin, 1994). As I have argued concerning a right to a unique identity, only on a confused and indefensible notion of human identity is a person's identity determined solely by his or her genes, and so no individual could be fully replaced by a later clone possessing the same genes. Ordinary people recognize this clearly. For example, parents of a child dying of a fatal disease would find it insensitive and ludicrous to be told they should not grieve for their coming loss because it is possible to replace him by cloning him; it is *their child who is dying* whom they love and value, and that child and his importance to them is not replaceable by a cloned later twin. Even if they would also come to love and value a later twin as much as they now love and value their child who is dying, that would be to love and value that *different child* for its own sake, not as a replacement for the child they lost. Our relations of love and friendship are with distinct, historically situated individuals with whom over time we have shared experiences and our lives, and whose loss to us can never be replaced.

A different version of this worry is that human cloning would result in persons' worth or value seeming diminished because we would come to see persons as able to be manufactured or "handmade." This demystification of the creation of human life would reduce our appreciation and awe of human life and of its natural creation. It would be a mistake, however, to conclude that a person created by human cloning is of less value or is less worthy of respect than one created by sexual reproduction. At least outside of some religious contexts, it is the nature of a being, not how it is created, that is the source of its value and makes it worthy of respect. For many people, gaining a scientific understanding of the truly extraordinary complexity of human reproduction and development increases, instead of decreases, their awe of the process and its product. ...

4. Human cloning might be used by commercial interests for financial gain. Both opponents and proponents of human cloning agree that cloned embryos should not be able to be bought and sold. In a science fiction frame of mind, one can imagine commercial interests offering genetically certified and guaranteed embryos for sale, perhaps offering a catalogue of different embryos cloned from individuals with a variety of talents, capacities, and other desirable properties. This would be a fundamental violation of the equal moral respect and dignity owed to all persons, treating them instead as objects to be differentially valued, bought, and sold in the marketplace. Even if embryos are not yet persons at the time they would be purchased or sold, they would be being valued, bought, and sold for the persons they will become. The moral consensus against any commercial market in embryos, cloned or otherwise, should be enforced by law whatever the public policy ultimately is on human cloning. ...

CONCLUSION

Human cloning has until now received little serious and careful ethical attention because it was typically dismissed as science fiction, and it stirs deep, but difficult to articulate, uneasiness and even revulsion in many people. Any ethical assessment of human cloning at this point must be tentative and provisional. Fortunately, the science and technology of human cloning are not yet in hand, and so a public and professional debate is possible without the need for a hasty, precipitate policy response.

The ethical pros and cons of human cloning, as I see them at this time, are sufficiently balanced and uncertain that there is not an ethically decisive case either for or against permitting it or doing it. Access to human cloning can plausibly be brought within a moral right to reproductive freedom, but its potential legitimate uses appear few and do not promise substantial benefits. It is not a central component of the moral right to reproductive freedom and it does not uniquely serve any major or pressing individual or social needs. On the other hand, contrary to the pronouncements of many of its opponents, human cloning seems not to be a violation of moral or human rights. But it does risk some significant individual or social harms, although most are based on common public confusions about genetic determinism, human identity, and the effects of human cloning. Because most potential harms feared from human cloning remain speculative, they seem insufficient to warrant at this time a complete legal prohibition of either research on or later use of human cloning, if and when its safety and efficacy are established, Legitimate moral concerns about the use and effects of human cloning, however, underline the need for careful public oversight of research on its development, together with a wider public and professional debate and review before cloning is used on human beings.

REFERENCES

Annas, G. J. (1994). "Regulatory Models for Human Embryo Cloning: The Tree Market, Professional Guidelines, and Government Restrictions." *Kennedy Institute of Ethics Journal* 4,3:235–249.

Brock, D. W. (1994). "Reproductive Freedom: Its Nature, Bases and Limits," in *Health Care Ethics: Critical Issues for Health Professionals*, eds. D. Thomasma and J. Monagle. Gaithersburg, MD: Aspen Publishers.

Brock, D. W. (1995). "The Non-Identity Problem and Genetic Harm." *Bioethics* 9:269–275.

Callahan, D. (1993). "Perspective on Cloning: A Threat to Individual Uniqueness," *Los Angeles Times.* November 11, 1993:B7.

Chadwick, R. F. (1982). "Cloning." *Philosophy* 57:201–209.

Eisenberg, L. (1976). "The Outcome as Cause: Predestination and Human Cloning." *The Journal of Medicine and Philosophy* 1:318–331.

Feinberg, J. (1980). "The Child's Right to an Open Future," in *Whose Child? Children's Rights, Parental Authority, and State Power*, eds. W. Aiken and H. LaFollette. Totowa, NJ: Rowman and Littlefield.

Harris, J. (1992). *Wonderwoman and Superman: The Ethics of Biotechnology*. Oxford: Oxford University Press.

Huxley, A. (1932). *Brave New World*. London: Chalto and Winders.

Jonas, H. (1974), Philosophical Essays: *From Ancient Creed to Technological Man*. Englewood Cliffs, NJ: Prentice-Hall.

Kahn, C. (1989). "Can We Achieve Immortality?" *Free Inquiry* 9:14–18.

Kass, L. (1985). *Toward a More Natural Science*. New York: The Free Press.

LaBar, M. (1984). "The Pros and Cons of Human Cloning." *Thought* 57:318–333.

Lederberg, J. (1966), "Experimental Genetics and Human Evolution," *The American Naturalist* 100: 519–531.

Levin, I. (1976). *The Boys from Brazil*. New York: Random House.

Macklin, R. (1994). "Splitting Embryos on the Slippery Slope: Ethics and Public Policy." *Kennedy Institute of Ethics Journal* 4:209–226.

McCormick, R. (1993). "Should We Clone Humans?" *Christian Century* 110:1148–1149.

McKinnell, R. (1979). *Cloning: A Biologist Reports*. Minneapolis, MN: University of Minnesota Press.

Mill, J. S. (1859). *On Liberty*. Indianapolis, IN: Bobbs-Merrill Publishing.

NABER (National Advisory Board on Ethics in Reproduction) (1994). "Report on Human Cloning Through Embryo Splitting: An Amber Light." *Kennedy Institute of Ethics Journal* 4:151–282.

Parfit, D. (1984). *Reasons and Persons*. Oxford: Oxford University Press.

Rainer, J. D. (1978). "Commentary." *Man and Medicine: The Journal of Values and Ethics in Health Care* 3:115–117.

Rhodes, R. (1995). "Clones, Harms, and Rights." *Cambridge Quarterly of Healthcare Ethics* 4:285–290.

Robertson, J. A. (1994a). *Children of Choice: Freedom and the New Reproductive Technologies*. Princeton, NJ: Princeton University Press.

Robertson, J. A. (1994b). "The Question of Human Cloning." *Hastings Center Report* 24:6–14.

Robertson, J. A. (1997). "A Ban on Cloning and Cloning Research is Unjustified." Testimony Presented to the National Bioethics Advisory Commission, March 1997.

Smith, G. P. (1983). "Intimations of Immortality: Clones, Cyrons and the Law." *University of New South Wales Law Journal* 6:119–132.

Studdard, A. (1978). "The Lone Clone." *Man and Medicine: The Journal of Values and Ethics in Health Care* 3:109–114.

Thomas, L. (1974). "Notes of a Biology Watcher: On Cloning a Human Being." *New England Journal of Medicine* 291:1296–1197.

Verhey, A. D. (1994). "Cloning: Revisiting an Old Debate." *Kennedy Institute of Ethics Journal* 4:227–234.

Walters, W. A. W. (1982). "Cloning, Ectogenesis, and Hybrids: Things to Come?" in *Test-Tube Babies*, eds. W. A. W. Walters and P. Singer. Melbourne: Oxford University Press.

Weiss, R. (1997). "Cloning Suddenly Has Government's Attention." *International Herald Tribune*, March 7, 1997.

WHO (World Health Organization Press Office). (March 11, 1997). "WHO Director General Condemns Human Cloning." World Health Organization, Geneva, Switzerland.

Wilmut, I., et al. (1997). "Viable Offspring Derived from Fetal and Adult Mammalian Cells." *Nature* 385:810–813.

A Life in the Shadow
One Reason Why We Should Not Clone Humans

SØREN HOLM

INTRODUCTION

One of the arguments that is often put forward in the discussion of human cloning is that it is in itself wrong to create a copy of a human being.

This argument is usually dismissed by pointing out that a) we do not find anything wrong in the existence of monozygotic twins even though they are genetically identical, and b) the clone would not be an exact copy of the original even in those cases where it is an exact genetic copy since it would have experienced a different environment that would have modified its biological and psychological development.

In my view both these counterarguments are valid, but nevertheless I think that there is some core of truth in the assertion that it is wrong deliberately to try to create a copy of an already existing human being. It is this idea that I will briefly try to explicate here.

THE LIFE IN THE SHADOW ARGUMENT

When we see a pair of monozygotic twins who are perfectly identically dressed some of us experience a slight sense of unease, especially in the cases where the twins are young children. This unease is exacerbated when people establish competitions where the winners are the most identical pair of twins. The reason for this uneasiness is, I believe, that the identical clothes could signal a reluctance on the part of the parents to let each twin develop his or her individual and separate personality or a reluctance to let each twin lead his or her own life. In the extreme case each twin is constantly compared with the other and any difference is counteracted.

In the case of cloning based on somatic cells we have what is effectively a set of monozygotic twins with a potentially very large age difference. The original may have lived all his or her life and may

even have died before the clone is brought into existence. Therefore, there will not be any direct day-by-day comparison and identical clothing, but then a situation that is even worse for the clone is likely to develop. I shall call this situation "a life in the shadow" and I shall develop an argument against human cloning that may be labeled the "life in the shadow argument."

Let us try to imagine what will happen when a clone is born and its social parents have to begin rearing it. Usually when a child is born we ask hypothetical questions like "How will it develop?" or "What kind of person will it become?" and we often answer them with reference to various psychological traits we think we can identify in the biological mother or father or in their families, for instance "I hope that he won't get the kind of temper you had when you were a child!"

In the case of the clone we are, however, likely to give much more specific answers to such questions. Answers that will then go on to affect the way the child is reared. There is no doubt that the common public understanding of the relationship between genetics and psychology contains substantial strands of genetic essentialism, i.e., the idea that the genes determine psychology and personality.[1] This public idea is reinforced every time the media report the finding of new genes for depression, schizophrenia, etc. Therefore, it is likely that the parents of the clone will already have formed in their minds a quite definite picture of how the clone will develop, a picture that is based on the actual development of the original. This picture will control the way they rear the child. They will try to prevent some developments, and try to promote others. Just imagine how a clone of Adolf Hitler or Pol Pot would be reared, or how a clone of Albert Einstein,

Ludwig van Beethoven, or Michael Jordan would be brought up. The clone would in a very literal way live his or her life in the shadow of the life of the original. At every point in the clone's life there would be someone who had already lived that life, with whom the clone could be compared and against whom the clone's accomplishments could be measured.

That there would in fact be a strong tendency to make the inference from genotype to phenotype and to let the conclusion of such an inference affect rearing can perhaps be seen more clearly if we imagine the following hypothetical situation:

In the future new genetic research reveals that there are only a limited number of possible human genotypes, and that genotypes are therefore recycled every 300 years (i.e., somebody who died 300 years ago had exactly the same genotype as me). It is further discovered that there is some complicated, but not practically impossible, method whereby it is possible to discover the identity of the persons who 300, 600, 900, etc. years ago instantiated the genotype that a specific fetus now has.

I am absolutely certain that people would split into two sharply disagreeing camps if this became a possibility. One group, perhaps the majority, would try to identify the previous instantiations of their child's genotype. Another group would emphatically not seek this information because they would not want to know and would not want their children to grow up in the shadow of a number of previously led lives with the same genotype. The option to remain in ignorance is, however, not open to social parents of contemporary clones.

If the majority would seek the information in this scenario, firms offering the method of identification would have a very brisk business, and it could perhaps even become usual to expect of prospective parents that they make use of this new possibility. Why would this happen? The only reasonable explanation, apart from initial curiosity, is that people would believe that by identifying the previous instantiation of the genotype they would thereby gain valuable knowledge about their child. But knowledge is in general only valuable if it can be converted into new options for action, and the

most likely form of action would be that information about the previous instantiations would be used in deciding how to rear the present child. This again points to the importance of the public perception of genetic essentialism, since the environment must have changed considerably in the 300-year span between each instantiation of the genotype.

WHAT IS WRONG ABOUT A LIFE IN THE SHADOW?

What is wrong with living your life as a clone in the shadow of the life of the original? It diminishes the clone's possibility of living a life that is in a full sense of that word his or her life. The clone is forced to be involved in an attempt to perform a complicated partial re-enactment of the life of somebody else (the original). In our usual arguments for the importance of respect for autonomy or for the value of self-determination we often affirm that it is the final moral basis for these principles that they enable persons to live their lives the way they themselves want to live these lives. If we deny part of this opportunity to clones and force them to live their lives in the shadow of someone else we are violating some of our most fundamental moral principles and intuitions. Therefore, as long as genetic essentialism is a common cultural belief there are good reasons not to allow human cloning.

FINAL QUALIFICATIONS

It is important to note that the 'life in the shadow argument' does not rely on the false premise that we can make an inference from genotype to (psychological or personality) phenotype, but only on the true premise that there is a strong public tendency to make such an inference. This means that the conclusions of the argument only follow as long as this empirical premise remains true. If ever the public relinquishes all belief in genetic essentialism the 'life in the shadow argument' would fail, but such a development seems highly unlikely.

In conclusion I should perhaps also mention that I am fully aware of two possible counterarguments to the argument presented above. The first points out that even if a life in the shadow of the original is perhaps problematic and not very good, it is the only life the clone can have, and that it is therefore in the clone's interest to have this life as long as it is not worse than having no life at all. The 'life in the shadow argument' therefore does not show that cloning should be prohibited. I am unconvinced by this counterargument, just as I am by all arguments involving comparisons between existence and non-existence, but it is outside the scope of the present short paper to show decisively that the counterargument is wrong.

The second counterargument states that the conclusions of the 'life in the shadow argument' can be avoided if all clones are anonymously put up for adoption, so that no knowledge about the original

is available to the social parents of the clone. I am happy to accept this counterargument, but I think that a system where I was not allowed to rear the clone of myself would practically annihilate any interest in human cloning. The attraction in cloning for many is exactly in the belief that I can recreate myself. The cases where human cloning solves real medical or reproductive problems are on the fringe of the area of cloning.

NOTE

1. Nelkin D, Lindee MS. *The DNA Mystique: The Gene as a Cultural Icon.* New York: W.H. Freeman and Company, 1995.

ARGUMENT 10 ESSAY QUESTIONS

1. What is Brock's response to the notion of a right to a unique identity? Do you find his arguments convincing? Why or why not?
2. What is your assessment of Holm's "life in the shadow" argument?
3. Do you think that any open-future arguments against cloning are plausible? Why or why not?

SUGGESTIONS FOR FURTHER READING

Dan W. Brock, "Genetic Engineering," in *A Companion to Applied Ethics*, ed. R.G. Frey and Christopher Heath Wellman (Oxford: Blackwell Publishing, 2003), 356–357, 361–367.

Ruth Chadwick, "Gene Therapy," in *A Companion to Bioethics*, ed. Helga Kuhse and Peter Singer (Oxford: Blackwell Publishing, 2001), 189–197.

Angus Clarke, "Genetic Screening and Counseling," in *A Companion to Bioethics* (Oxford: Blackwell Publishing, 2001), 215–228.

Walter Glannon, *Genes and Future People: Philosophical Issues in Human Genetics* (Boulder, CO: Westview Press, 2001).

Jonathan Glover, "Future People, Disability, and Screening," in *Justice Between Age Groups and Generations*, ed. J. Fishkin and P. Laslett (New Haven, CT: Yale University Press, 1992).

Jonathan Glover, *Choosing Children: The Ethical Dilemmas of Genetic Intervention* (Oxford: Oxford University Press, 2006).

Human Genome Program, U.S. Department of Energy, *Genomics and Its Impact on Science and Society: A 2003 Primer*, 2003.

National Bioethics Advisory Commission, *Cloning Human Beings*, June 1997, http://bioethics. georgetown.edu (14 July 2007).

John A. Robertson, "Extending Preimplantation Genetic Diagnosis: Medical and Non-Medical Uses," *Journal of Medical Ethics*, vol. 29, August 2003, 213–216.

President's Council on Bioethics, *Human Cloning and Human Dignity: An Ethical Inquiry*, 2002, www.bioethics.gov (14 July 2007).

Bonnie Steinbock and Ron McClamrock, "When Is Birth Unfair to the Child?" *Hastings Center Report*, vol. 24, no. 6, November 1994.

U.S. National Library of Medicine, *Handbook: Help Me Understand Genetics*, *Genetics Home Reference*, 26 November 2007, http:ghr.nlm.nih.gov (3 December 2007).

LeRoy Walters and Julie Gage Palmer, *The Ethics of Human Gene Therapy* (New York: Oxford University Press, 1997).

CHAPTER 7

The Death Penalty

Is it permissible for a society to put one of its members to death for committing a serious crime? This is the central ethical issue in debates over **capital punishment**—officially sanctioned punishment by death for very grievous (capital) crimes. On one side of this dispute are the **abolitionists**, those who want to do away with capital punishment, who believe the death penalty is *never* justified. On the other side are the **retentionists**, those who want to retain the death penalty as part of a system of legal punishment, who believe that sometimes capital punishment *is* warranted.

Despite their stark difference of opinion, both abolitionists and retentionists are likely to agree that legal punishment is a legitimate function of society. They also generally concur on the importance of preserving life, respecting the inherent value of persons, and ensuring that punishment is fair and reasonable. Beyond these broad areas of harmony, they part company on many points.

In 2008, 37 people were executed in the United States (down from 42 in 2007), marking a fourteen-year low. The number of new death sentences in 2008 was 111 (as of 5 December 2008), and 115 in 2007, the lowest numbers since 1976.[1] Forty-one of the 2007 executions were by lethal injection; one was by electrocution.[2] Since 1976, 1,136 people have been executed, over half of them in Texas, Virginia, and Oklahoma.[3]

In 2007, all those executed were men, 28 were white, and 14 were black. The death row population stood at 3,350 (56 of whom were women). Of that number, 1,804 were white; 1,345 black; 26 American Indian; 35 Asian; and 10 of unknown race. At year's end, the youngest inmate on death row was 19; the oldest, 92.[4]

Ninety-five percent of the executions in 2008 were carried out in southern states: 18 in Texas; 4 in Virginia; 3 each in Georgia and South Carolina; 2 each in Florida, Mississippi, and Oklahoma; and 1 in Kentucky. (There were two executions in Ohio.) Thirty-six states

---

[1] Death Penalty Information Center, "The Death Penalty in 2008: Year End Report," 5 December 2008, http://www.deathpenaltyinfo.org/ (1 January 2009).

[2] Bureau of Justice Statistics, Department of Justice, "Capital Punishment Statistics: Summary Findings," December 2008, http://www.ojp.usdoj.gov/bjs/cp.htm# findings (31 December 2008).

[3] Death Penalty Information Center.

[4] Bureau of Justice Statistics.

FACTS AND FIGURES: Capital Punishment

- In 2010, 46 inmates were executed; in 2008, 37; and in 2007, 42.
- In 2011, 43 inmates were executed. The executions happened in 13 states—13 in Texas; 6 in Alabama; 5 in Ohio; 4 in Georgia; 4 in Arizona; and the remaining 11 in 8 other states.
- Of those inmates on death row in 2010, 55 percent were white and 42 percent were black. Ninety-eight percent were male, and 2 percent were female.
- Of the 46 executions in 2010, 28 were white; 13, black; and 5, Hispanic.
- At the end of 2010, the death penalty was authorized by 36 states.
- At the end of 2010, all 36 of the death-penalty states authorized lethal injection as their execution

method. Sixteen states authorized other execution methods (in addition to lethal injection): hanging, electrocution, firing squad, or lethal gas.
- By the end of 2010, the number of prisoners under sentence of death had decreased for the fifth straight year to 104.
- At the end of 2010, 3,158 inmates were on death row in the United States.
- In 2010, the average elapsed time from sentence of death to execution was 178 months.

From The Bureau of Justice Statistics, Department of Justice, "Capital Punishment, 2010—Statistical Tables," December 2011, http://www.bjs.gov/content/pub/pdf/cp10st.pdf (23 February 2012).

plus the federal government and the U.S. military have death penalty statutes; fourteen states and the District of Columbia do not.[5]

Polls indicate substantial public backing for capital punishment for the crime of murder. In 2008, 64 percent of Americans supported the death penalty; in 2007, 69 percent. The high-water mark of support was 80 percent in 1994. These numbers dropped steeply, however, when alternative punishments such as life in prison without parole were included in the surveys.[6]

On the issue of the death penalty, the contrast between the United States and most of the rest of the planet is stark. By December 2008, the death penalty had been eliminated by law or practice in one hundred thirty-eight countries—two-thirds of the world. Canada, Mexico, Australia, United Kingdom, Western Europe, Central and South America, and most countries in Africa have eliminated the practice. In 2007, only twenty-four countries executed someone. Meanwhile the United Nations General Assembly voted to abolish capital punishment.[7]

According to the latest figures, just five countries account for 88 percent of all known executions: China, Iran, Saudi Arabia, Pakistan, and the United States. China is thought

[5] Death Penalty Information Center.
[6] Death Penalty Information Center.
[7] Amnesty International USA, "Death Penalty Statistics," 2008, http://www.amnestyusa.org/death-penalty/death-penalty-facts/page.do?id=1101088 (1 January 2009).

to have executed at least 470 people in 2007, while Saudi Arabia had the most executions per capita (143).[8]

Despite having many opportunities to rule that legal punishment by execution is unconstitutional, the Supreme Court has never done so, although it has several times objected to how the death penalty is administered. In the 1972 case *Furman v. Georgia*, the Court held that a punishment amounted to "cruel and unusual" treatment when it was applied arbitrarily or when it did not fit the crime. Using this standard, the Court declared that Georgia's death penalty statute was unconstitutional because it allowed juries to hand out death sentences without restraint or guidance—that is, arbitrarily. The decision invalidated the existing death penalty statutes in many states, effectively suspending all executions throughout the land.

States quickly passed new death penalty statutes, in some instances trying to correct the arbitrariness problem of previous laws by *requiring* death sentences for some capital crimes. But in 1976 the Court ruled in *Woodson v. North Carolina* that mandatory capital punishment is unconstitutional.

Other states enacted statutes establishing guidelines for judges and juries deciding whether to sentence someone to death. The Court accepted this approach, holding in the 1976 case *Gregg v. Georgia* that the sentencing-guideline statutes of Georgia, Florida, and Texas are constitutional. The ruling allowed executions to resume, and the first one came in Utah on 17 January 1977 when Gary Gilmore was put to death by firing squad.

Since *Gregg*, the Court has further constrained the use of capital punishment. In 1986 it prohibited the execution of people judged insane (*Ford v. Wainwright*). In 2002 it ruled that the execution of mentally retarded persons is forbidden by the Eighth Amendment's prohibition against cruel and unusual punishment (*Atkins v. Virginia*). And in 2005 the Court held that executing juvenile offenders is unconstitutional for the same reason (*Roper v. Simmons*). From 1976 to 2005, twenty-two people were put to death for crimes they committed as juveniles.

Arguments for and against the death penalty are of two kinds: consequentialist and deontological. The consequentialist (usually utilitarian) arguments appeal to the good or bad consequences of capital punishment. The deontological arguments appeal to moral principles that hold independently of the consequences.

Many retentionists take the consequentialist path by arguing that the death penalty has positive effects on society—specifically that it either *prevents* criminals from harming others again or *deters* would-be offenders from capital crimes. Executing hardened murders, say retentionists, is the best way to prevent them from killing other inmates or escaping and killing innocent people. Abolitionists respond that life in prison without parole (and with appropriate security measures) is as effective as execution in preventing inmates from repeating their crimes. To make their arguments stick, both sides in this dispute have to support their nonmoral claims with empirical evidence, but definitive evidence for the effectiveness of the two prevention strategies is hard to come by. Each side can challenge the other to produce evidence to back their assertions.

---

[8] Amnesty International USA.

LEGALITIES: Capital Punishment

1968—*Witherspoon v. Illinois.* Dismissing potential jurors solely because they express opposition to the death penalty held unconstitutional.

June 1972—*Furman v. Georgia.* Supreme Court effectively voids 40 death penalty statutes and suspends the death penalty.

1976—*Gregg v. Georgia.* Guided discretion statutes approved. Death penalty reinstated.

January 17, 1977—Ten-year moratorium on executions ends with the execution of Gary Gilmore by firing squad in Utah.

1986—*Ford v. Wainwright.* Execution of insane persons banned.

1987—*McCleskey v. Kemp.* Racial disparities not recognized as a constitutional violation of "equal protection of the law" unless intentional racial discrimination against the defendant can be shown.

1988—*Thompson v. Oklahoma.* Executions of offenders age fifteen and younger at the time of their crimes is unconstitutional.

1989—*Stanford v. Kentucky,* and *Wilkins v. Missouri.* Eighth Amendment does not prohibit the death penalty for crimes committed at age sixteen or seventeen.

1989—*Penry v. Lynaugh.* Executing persons with mental retardation is not a violation of the Eighth Amendment.

2002—*Atkins v. Virginia.* the execution of mentally retarded defendants violates the Eighth Amendment's ban on cruel and unusual punishment.

March 2005—In *Roper V. Simmons,* the United States Supreme Court ruled that the death penalty for those who had committed their crimes under 18 years of age was cruel and unusual punishment.

Death Penalty Information Center, "Introduction to the Death Penalty," *Death Penalty Information Center,* 2008, http://www.deathpenaltyinfo.org/ (1 January 2009).

Retentionists often maintain that the most powerful deterrent against murders is the threat of the ultimate punishment, death. Several sociological studies seem to support this claim, but they have been the subject of a good deal of critical scrutiny and debate, a fact that abolitionists are quick to point out. Some retentionists argue that common sense tells us that the death penalty is a better deterrent than life in prison. It seems obvious, they say, that the more severe the punishment, the more it deters potential offenders. Abolitionists reply that there are reasons to think the commonsense view is mistaken.

Some retentionists take the deontological path through **retributivism**, the doctrine that people should be punished simply because they *deserve* it and that the punishment should be *proportional* to the crime. Retributivism is not revenge: revenge arises from a desire to retaliate by inflicting suffering; retributivism is an ethical stance concerning justice or desert. Retributivists who favor the death penalty argue that sometimes people deserve to be executed, that the only just and fitting punishment is death.

Many abolitionists reject the retributivist theory of punishment and thus reject the retentionist argument that it supports. But some of them accept it, arguing that although offenders should get the punishment they deserve, no one deserves the death penalty.

Like retentionists, abolitionists also try to make their case on consequentialist grounds. They may contend that life in prison for murderers results in greater overall happiness or goodness for society than sentencing them to death. For one thing, if human life has great value, then preserving it by forgoing the death penalty must maximize the good. Abolitionists also insist that the death penalty brings with it some drawbacks that life sentences avoid. They may assert that the monetary costs involved in capital punishment exceed the costs of life sentences without parole, that the chances of unintentionally executing the innocent are great, or that the execution of offenders may actually provoke murders or have an overall dehumanizing effect on society. Retentionists may dispute these claims by questioning the evidence for them, or they may take a retributivist line by arguing that the consequences are beside the point.

Taking a deontological tack, many abolitionists argue from plausible moral principles. Against the death penalty, they affirm that: (1) human beings have inherent value and dignity, (2) all persons have a right to life, (3) punishment should be fair (and the use of capital punishment discriminates against minorities and the poor), or (4) the punishment should fit the crime (and the death penalty is unjust because it does not fit the crime). Typically retentionists counter that executing the guilty actually respects their dignity by treating them as autonomous persons who can be held accountable. Moreover, by taking someone's life, the offender forfeits his own right to life. Punishment, says the retentionist, should indeed be fairly administered and proportional to the crime. But discriminatory use of the death penalty does not show that the punishment itself is unjust, and execution for the crime of murder is in fact a fitting penalty.

KEY TERMS
capital punishment   abolitionist   retentionist
retributivism

ARGUMENTS AND READINGS

II. KANT'S RETRIBUTIVISM ARGUMENT FOR THE DEATH PENALTY

In opposition to utilitarian views of punishment, Immanuel Kant (1724–1804) holds to retributivism and strongly endorses the death penalty for murder. In "The Right of Punishing," he declares that legal punishment should never be administered merely for the good of society or the offender but "must in all cases be imposed only because the individual on whom it is inflicted has committed a crime."[9] Criminals should be punished

[9] Immanuel Kant, *The Philosophy of Law*, trans. W. Hastie (Edinburgh: Clark, 1887), 195.

because they deserve to be punished, because they must receive their just deserts. And murderers, he argues, deserve death, and a just society will punish them accordingly :

> Even if a civil society resolved to dissolve itself with the consent of all its members...the last murderer lying in prison ought to be executed before the resolution was carried out. This ought to be done in order that every one may realize the desert of his deeds, and that blood-guiltiness may not remain on the people; for otherwise they will all be regarded as participants in the murder as a public violation of justice.[10]

As a retributivist, Kant believes that the punishment must fit the crime. But unlike many contemporary retributivists, he believes that the punishment must also *resemble* the crime. He subscribes to the doctrine of *lex talionis*, the "eye for an eye" notion of punishment in which society does to the criminal what he has done to his victim. As Kant says,

> But what is the mode and measure of punishment which public justice takes as its principle and standard? It is just the principle of equality, by which the pointer of the scale of justice is made to incline no more to the one side than the other. It may be rendered by saying that the undeserved evil which any one commits on another, is to be regarded as perpetrated on himself. "...if you strike another, you strike yourself; if you kill another, you kill yourself." This is the right of retaliation (justalionis)...whoever has committed murder must die.[11]

Many death-penalty retributivists (and all abolitionists), however, reject the idea of punishment resembling the crime, for it implies that bombers should be bombed, torturers should be tortured, and rapists should be raped. They instead take the view that punishment should fit the crime in degree of seriousness but not in kind. For them, murder is so heinous a crime that it merits the severest penalty, capital punishment. Paul G. Cassell expresses this point:

> Capital punishment is proportionate to the offense of the intentional and unjustified taking of an innocent person's life. Murder does not simply differ in magnitude from other crimes like robbery and burglary; it differs in kind. As a result, the available punishments for premeditated murder must also differ in kind. The available punishment must reflect the inviolability of human life.[12]

A common criticism of retentionist views is that the death penalty violates the moral principle of respect for persons (a Kantian idea), constituting a denial of human dignity and a rejection of the notion of persons as ends-in-themselves. But Kant and other retentionists actually appeal to the respect-for-persons principle to bolster their case. Kant's view is that by executing a murderer, we give full recognition to the murderer as a person,

---

[10] Kant, *Philosophy of Law*, 198.

[11] Kant, *Philosophy of Law*, 194–98.

[12] Paul G. Cassell, "In Defense of the Death Penalty," in *Debating the Death Penalty*, ed. Hugo Bedau and Paul Cassell (New York: Oxford University Press, 2004), 199.

as a rational, moral agent who chooses freely and can be held responsible for his or her actions. To fail to hold offenders responsible is to treat them like nonpersons, like animals. Other retentionists argue that executing murderers is the only way to recognize the dignity and worth of the victims. As one of them puts it:

> It's because I have so much regard for human life that I favor capital punishment. Murder is the most terrible crime there is. Anything less than the death penalty is an insult to the victim and society. It says, in effect, that we don't value the victim's life enough to punish the killer fully.[13]

One abolitionist answer to such retentionist arguments is that even when persons commit horrible crimes, they still retain some rights. Stephen Nathanson argues for this position:

> According to the view I am defending, people do not lose all of their rights when they commit terrible crimes. They still deserve some level of decent treatment simply because they remain living, functioning human beings. This level of moral desert need not be earned, and it cannot be forfeited. This view may sound controversial, but in fact everyone who believes that cruel and unusual punishment should be forbidden implicitly agrees with it. That is, they agree that even after someone has committed a terrible crime, we do not have the right to do anything whatsoever to him.
>
> What I am suggesting is that by renouncing the use of death as a punishment, we express and reaffirm our belief in the inalienable, unforfeitable core of human dignity.[14]

The Right of Punishing

IMMANUEL KANT

The Right of administering Punishment, is the Right of the Sovereign as the Supreme Power to inflict pain upon a Subject on account of a Crime committed by him. The Head of the State cannot therefore be punished; but his supremacy may be withdrawn from him. Any Transgression of the public law which makes him who commits it incapable of being a Citizen, constitutes a *Crime*, either simply as a private Crime (*crimen*), or also as a *public* Crime (*crimen publicum*). Private crimes are dealt with by a Civil Court; Public Crimes by

From *The Philosophy of Law* by Immanuel Kant, trans. W. Hastie, pp. 90–92 (Edinburgh: Clark, 1887).

---

[13] Mike Royko, *Chicago Sun-Times*, September 1983.
[14] Stephen Nathanson, from *An Eye for an Eye?* (Lanham, MD: Rowman and Littlefield, 2001).

a Criminal Court.—Embezzlement or peculation of money or goods entrusted in trade, Fraud in purchase or sale, if done before the eyes of the party who suffers, are Private Crimes. On the other hand, Coining false money or forging Bills of Exchange, Theft, Robbery, etc., are Public Crimes, because the Commonwealth, and not merely some particular individual, is endangered thereby. Such Crimes may be divided into those of a *base* character (*indolis abjectae*) and those of a *violent* character (*indolis violentiae*).

Judicial or Juridical Punishment, (*paena forensis*) is to be distinguished from Natural Punishment (*paena naturalis*), in which Crime as Vice punishes itself, and does not as such come within the cognizance of the Legislator. Juridical Punishment can never be administered merely as a means for promoting another Good either with regard to the Criminal himself or to Civil Society, but must in all cases be imposed only because the individual on whom it is inflicted *has committed a Crime.* For one man ought never to be dealt with merely as a means subservient to the purpose of another, nor be mixed up with the subjects of Real Right. Against such treatment his Inborn Personality has a Right to protect him, even although he may be condemned to lose his Civil Personality. He must first be found guilty and *punishable*, before there can be any thought of drawing from his Punishment any benefit for himself or his fellow-citizens. The Penal Law is a Categorical Imperative; and woe to him who creeps through the serpent-windings of Utilitarianism to discover some advantage that may discharge him from the Justice of Punishment, or even from the due measure of it, according to the Pharisaic maxim: 'It is better that *one* man should die than that the whole people should perish.' For if Justice and Righteousness perish, human life would no longer have any value in the world.—What, then, is to be said of such a proposal as to keep a Criminal alive who has been condemned to death, on his being given to understand that if he agreed to certain dangerous experiments being performed upon him, he would be allowed to survive if he came happily through them? It is argued that Physicians might thus obtain new information that would

be of value to the Commonweal. But a Court of Justice would repudiate with scorn any proposal of this kind if made to it by the Medical Faculty; for Justice would cease to be Justice, if it were bartered away for any consideration whatever.

But what is the mode and measure of Punishment which Public Justice takes as its Principle and Standard? It is just the Principle of Equality, by which the pointer of the Scale of Justice is made to incline no more to the one side than the other. It may be rendered by saying that the undeserved evil which any one commits on another, is to be regarded as perpetrated on himself. Hence it may be said: 'If you slander another, you slander yourself; if you steal from another, you steal from yourself; if you strike another, you strike yourself; if you kill another, you kill yourself.' This is the Right of RETALIATION (*jus talionis*); and properly understood, it is the only Principle which in regulating a Public Court, as distinguished from mere private judgment, can definitely assign both the quality and the quantity of a just penalty. All other standards are wavering and uncertain; and on account of other considerations involved in them, they contain no principle conformable to the sentence of pure and strict Justice. It may appear, however, that difference of social status would not admit the application of the Principle of Retaliation, which is that of 'Like with Like.' But although the application may not in all cases be possible according to the letter, yet as regards the effect it may always be attained in practice, by due regard being given to the disposition and sentiment of the parties in the higher social sphere. Thus a pecuniary penalty on account of a verbal injury, may have no direct proportion to the injustice of slander; for one who is wealthy may be able to indulge himself in this offence for his own gratification. Yet the attack committed on the honour of the party aggrieved may have its equivalent in the pain inflicted upon the pride of the aggressor, especially if he is condemned by the judgment of the Court, not only to retract and apologize, but to submit to some meaner ordeal, as kissing the hand of the injured person. In like manner, if a man of the highest rank has violently assaulted an innocent citizen of the lower orders, he may be condemned not only to apologize but to undergo a solitary and painful imprisonment, whereby, in addition to the discomfort endured, the vanity of the offender would be painfully affected, and the very shame of his position would constitute an adequate Retaliation after the principle of 'Like with Like.' But how then would we render the statement: 'If you *steal* from another, you steal from yourself'? In this way, that whoever steals anything makes the property of all insecure; he therefore robs himself of all security in property, according to the Right of Retaliation. Such a one has nothing, and can acquire nothing, but he has the Will to live; and this is only possible by others supporting him. But as the State should not do this gratuitously, he must for this purpose yield his powers to the State to be used in penal labour; and thus he falls for a time, or it may be for life, into a condition of slavery.—But whoever has committed Murder, must *die*. There is, in this case, no juridical substitute or surrogate, that can be given or taken for the satisfaction of Justice. There is no *Likeness* or proportion between Life, however painful, and Death; and therefore there is no Equality between the crime of Murder and the retaliation of it but what is judicially accomplished by the execution of the Criminal. His death, however, must be kept free from all maltreatment that would make the humanity suffering in his Person loathsome or abominable. Even if a Civil Society resolved to dissolve itself with the consent of all its members—as might be supposed in the case of a People inhabiting an island resolving to separate and scatter themselves throughout the whole world—the last Murderer lying in the prison ought to be executed before the resolution was carried out. This ought to be done in order that every one may realize the desert of his deeds, and that bloodguiltiness may not remain upon the people; for otherwise they might all be regarded as participators in the murder as a public violation of Justice.

A Life for a Life

IGOR PRIMORATZ

The conclusion of the preceding section is not in the least binding on those retentionists who approach the problem of the moral basis of punishment in general from the retributive standpoint. According to the retributive theory, consequences of punishment, however important from the practical point of view, are irrelevant when it comes to its justification; *the* moral consideration is its justice. Punishment is morally justified insofar as it is meted out as retribution for the offense committed. When someone has committed an offense, he deserves to be punished: it is just, and consequently justified, that he be punished. The offense is the sole ground of the state's right and duty to punish. It is also the measure of legitimate punishment; the two ought to be proportionate. So the issue of capital punishment within the retributive approach comes down to the question, Is this punishment ever proportionate retribution for the offense committed, and thus deserved, just, and justified?

The classic representatives of retributivism believed that it was, and that it was the only proportionate and hence appropriate punishment, if the offense was *murder*—that is, criminal homicide, perpetrated voluntarily and intentionally. In other cases, the demand for proportionality between offense and punishment can be satisfied by fines or prison terms; the crime of murder, however, is an exception in this respect, and calls for the literal interpretation of the *lex talionis*. The uniqueness of this crime has to do with the uniqueness of the value which has been deliberately destroyed. We come across this idea as early as the original formulation of the retributive view—the biblical teaching on punishment: "You shall accept no ransom for the life of a murderer who is guilty of death; but he shall be put to death." The rationale of this command— one that clearly distinguishes the biblical conception of the criminal law from contemporaneous criminal law systems in the Middle East—is that man was not only created *by* God, like every other creature, but also, alone among all the creatures, *in the image of God:*

> That man was made in the image of God...is expressive of the peculiar and supreme worth of man. Of all creatures, Genesis 1 relates, he alone possesses this attribute, bringing him into closer relation to God than all the rest and conferring upon him the highest value....This view of the uniqueness and supremacy of human life...places life beyond the reach of other values. The idea that life may be measured in terms of money or other property...is excluded. Compensation of any kind is ruled out. The guilt of the murderer is infinite because the murdered life is invaluable; the kinsmen of the slain man are not competent to say when he has paid for. An absolute wrong has been committed, a sin against God which is not subject to human discussion....Because human life is invaluable, to take it entails the death penalty.

This view that the value of human life is not commensurable with other values, and that consequently there is only one truly equivalent punishment for murder, namely death, does not necessarily presuppose a theistic outlook. It can be claimed that, simply because we have to be alive if we are to experience and realize any other value at all, there is nothing equivalent to the murderous destruction of a human life except the destruction of the life of the murderer. Any other retribution, no matter how severe, would still be less than what is proportionate, deserved, and just. As long as the murderer is alive, no matter how bad the conditions of his life may be, there are always at least *some* values he can

experience and realize. This provides a plausible interpretation of what the classical representatives of retributivism as a philosophical theory of punishment, such as Kant and Hegel, had to say on the subject.

It seems to me that this is essentially correct. With respect to the larger question of the justification of punishment in general, it is the retributive theory that gives the right answer. Accordingly, capital punishment ought to be retained where it obtains, and reintroduced in those jurisdictions that have abolished it, although we have no reason to believe that, as a means of deterrence, it is any better than a very long prison term. It ought to be retained, or reintroduced, for one simple reason: that justice be done in cases of murder, that murderers be punished according to their deserts.

There are a number of arguments that have been advanced against this rationale of capital punishment.

Two of these arguments have to do, in different ways, with the idea of the right to life. The first is the famous argument of Beccaria that the state cannot have the right to take away the life of its citizen, because its rights in relation to him are based on the social contract, and it cannot be assumed that he has transferred his right to life to the state and consented to be executed.

> By what right can men presume to slaughter their fellows? Certainly not that right which is the foundation of sovereignty and the laws. For these are nothing but the sum of the smallest portions of each man's own freedom; they represent the general will which is the aggregate of the individual wills. Who has ever willingly given up to others the authority to kill him? How on earth can the minimum sacrifice of each individual's freedom involve handing over the greatest of all goods, life itself? And even if that were so, how can it be reconciled with the other principle which denies that a man is free to commit suicide, which he must be, if he is able to transfer that right to others or to society as a whole?

The most obvious way of attacking Beccaria's argument would be to call into question its philosophical basis, the social contract theory of political obligation. This is what Hegel does, for instance;

he conceives of the nature and grounds of political obligation in a completely different manner, so he can do away with Beccaria with a single sentence: "The state is not a contract at all." I shall not argue along these lines, however. This is not the place to take up the problem of political obligation and to assess the social contract theory as a solution to it. What Beccaria is saying here can in any case be refuted even within the framework of that theory.

Both steps in his argument are wrong, and for the same reason. The act of consenting to be executed if one commits murder is presented as a kind of suicide. Against the background of this conflation, it seems convincing to claim that it would be utterly unreasonable to do that, and the case appears to be strengthened even further by the appeal to the moral prohibition of suicide. This latter prohibition is, of course, rather controversial, to say the least; it was controversial in Beccaria's time as well. But his argument fails even if we grant him this point. For by consenting to be executed if I murder someone, I do not commit a kind of suicide—I do not "sacrifice the greatest of all goods" I have, my own life. My consent could be described in these terms if it were unconditional, if it implied that others were entitled to do with my life whatever they chose, quite independently of my own choices and actions. In order to show that capital punishment is legitimate from the standpoint of the contract theory of political obligation, however, we need not assume that citizens have agreed to *that*. All that is needed is the assumption of a conditional consent—consent to be executed *if* one commits murder; and it is, of course, up to everyone to choose whether to commit such a crime or not. To agree to this, obviously, is not the same as to sacrifice one's life, to commit a suicide of sorts. And it is not so unreasonable to assume that citizens have agreed to this if, against the background of the social contract theory, we grant, first, that the laws, including criminal laws, ought to be just; and second, that the only proportionate and hence just punishment for murder is capital punishment.

The second abolitionist argument makes use of the idea of a right to life in a more straightforward manner: it simply says that capital punishment is illegitimate because it violates the right to life, which is a fundamental, absolute, sacred right belonging to each and every human being, and therefore ought to be respected even in a murderer.

If any rights are fundamental, the right to life is certainly one of them; but to claim that it is absolute, inviolable under any circumstances and for any reason, is a different matter. If an abolitionist wants to argue her case by asserting an absolute right to life, she will also have to deny moral legitimacy to taking human life in war, revolution, and self-defense. This kind of pacifism is a consistent but farfetched and hence implausible position.

I do not believe that the right to life (nor, for that matter, any other right) is absolute. I have no general theory of rights to fall back upon here; instead, let me pose a question. Would we take seriously the claim to an absolute, sacred, inviolable right to life—coming from the mouth of a *confessed murderer*? I submit that we would not, for the obvious reason that it is being put forward by the person who confessedly denied another human being this very right. But if the murderer cannot plausibly claim such a right for himself, neither can *anyone else* do that in his behalf. This suggests that there is an element of reciprocity in our general rights, such as the right to life or property. I can convincingly claim these rights only so long as I acknowledge and respect the same rights of others. If I violate the rights of others, I thereby lose the same rights. If I am a murderer, I have no *right* to live.

Some opponents of capital punishment claim that a criminal law system which includes this punishment is contradictory: "It seems absurd to me," says Beccaria, "that the laws, which are the expression of the public will, and which hate and punish murder, should themselves commit one, and that to deter citizens from murder, they should decree a public murder."

This seems to be one of the more popular arguments against the death penalty, but it is not a good one. If it were valid, it would prove too much. Exactly the same might be claimed of other kinds of punishment: of prison terms, that they are "contradictory" to the legal protection of liberty; of fines, that they are "contradictory" to the legal protection of property. Fortunately enough, it is not valid, for it begs the question at issue. In order to be able to talk of the state as "murdering" the person it executes, one has to use the word "murder" in the very same sense—that is, in the usual sense, which implies the idea of the *wrongful* taking the life of another—both when speaking of what the murderer has done to the victim and of what the state is doing to him by way of punishment. But this is precisely the question at issue: whether capital punishment *is* "murder," whether it is wrongful or morally justified and right.

The next two arguments attack the retributive rationale of capital punishment by questioning the claim that it is only this punishment that satisfies the demand for proportion between offense and punishment in the case of murder. The first points out that any two human lives are different in many important respects, such as age, health, physical and mental capability, so that it does not make much sense to consider them equally valuable. What if the murdered person was very old, practically at the very end of her natural life, while the murderer is young, with most of his life still ahead of him, for instance? Or if the victim was gravely and incurably ill, and thus doomed to live her life in suffering and hopelessness, without being able to experience almost anything that makes a human life worth living, while the murderer is in every respect capable of experiencing and enjoying things life has to offer? Or the other way round? Would not the death penalty in such cases amount either to taking a more valuable life as a punishment for destroying a less valuable one, or *vice versa*? Would it not be either too much, or too little, and in both cases disproportionate, and thus unjust and wrong, from the standpoint of the retributive theory itself?

Any plausibility this argument might appear to have is the result of a conflation of differences between, and value of, human lives. No doubt, any two human lives are *different* in innumerable ways, but this does not entail that they are not *equally valuable*. I have no worked-out general theory of equality to refer to here, but I do not think that one is necessary in order to do away with this argument. The modern humanistic and democratic tradition in ethical, social, and political thought is based on the idea that all human beings are equal. This finds its legal expression in the principle of equality of people under the law. If we are not willing to give up this principle, we have to stick to the assumption that, all differences notwithstanding, any two

human lives, *qua* human lives, are equally valuable. If, on the other hand, we allow that, on the basis of such criteria as age, health, or mental or physical ability, it can be claimed that the life of one person is more or less valuable than the life of another, and we admit such claims in the sphere of law, including criminal law, we shall thereby give up the principle of equality of people under the law. In all consistency, we shall not be able to demand that property, physical and personal integrity, and all other rights and interests of individuals be given equal consideration in courts of law either—that is, we shall have to accept systematic discrimination between individuals on the basis of the same criteria across the whole field. I do not think anyone would seriously contemplate an overhaul of the whole legal system along these lines.

The second argument having to do with the issue of proportionality between murder and capital punishment draws our attention to the fact that the law normally provides for a certain period of time to elapse between the passing of a death sentence and its execution. It is a period of several weeks or months; in some cases it extends to years. This period is bound to be one of constant mental anguish for the condemned. And thus, all things considered, what is inflicted on him is disproportionately hard and hence unjust. It would be proportionate and just only in the case of "a criminal who had warned his victim of the date at which he would inflict a horrible death on him and who, from that moment onward, had confined him at his mercy for months."

The first thing to note about this argument is that it does not support a full-fledged abolitionist stand; if it were valid, it would not show that capital punishment is *never* proportionate and just, but only that it is *very rarely* so. Consequently, the conclusion would not be that it ought to be abolished outright, but only that it ought to be restricted to those cases that would satisfy the condition cited above. Such cases do happen, although, to be sure, not very often; the murder of Aldo Moro, for instance, was of this kind. But this is not the main point. The main point is that the argument actually does not hit at capital punishment itself, although it is presented with that aim in view. It hits at something else: a particular way of carrying out this punishment, which is widely adopted in our time. Some hundred years ago and more, in the Wild West, they frequently hanged the man convicted to die almost immediately after pronouncing the sentence. I am not arguing here that we should follow this example today; I mention this piece of historical fact only in order to show that the interval between sentencing someone to death and carrying out the sentence is not a *part* of capital punishment itself. However unpalatable we might find those Wild West hangings, whatever objections we might want to voice against the speed with which they followed the sentencing, surely we shall not deny them the *description* of "executions." So the implication of the argument is not that we ought to do away with capital punishment altogether, nor that we ought to restrict it to those cases of murder where the murderer had warned the victim weeks or months in advance of what he was going to do to her, but that we ought to reexamine the procedure of carrying out this kind of punishment. We ought to weigh the reasons for having this interval between the sentencing and executing, against the moral and human significance of the repercussions such an interval inevitably carries with it.

These reasons, in part, have to do with the possibility of miscarriages of justice and the need to rectify them. Thus we come to the argument against capital punishment which, historically, has been the most effective of all: many advances of the abolitionist movement have been connected with discoveries of cases of judicial errors. Judges and jurors are only human, and consequently some of their beliefs and decisions are bound to be mistaken. Some of their mistakes can be corrected upon discovery; but precisely those with most disastrous—those which result in innocent people being executed—can never be rectified. In all other cases of mistaken sentencing we can revoke the punishment, either completely or in part, or at least extend compensation. In addition, by exonerating the accused we give moral satisfaction. None of this is possible after an innocent person has been executed; capital punishment is essentially different from all other penalties by being completely irrevocable and irreparable. Therefore, it ought to be abolished.

A part of my reply to this argument goes along the same lines as what I had to say on the previous one. It is not so far-reaching as abolitionists assume; for it would be quite implausible, even fanciful, to claim that there have *never* been cases of murder which left no room whatever for reasonable doubt as to the guilt and full responsibility of the accused. Such cases may not be more frequent than those others, but they do happen. Why not retain the death penalty at least for them?

Actually, this argument, just as the preceding one, does not tell against capital punishment itself, but against the existing procedures for trying capital cases. Miscarriages of justice result in innocent people being sentenced to death and executed, even in the criminal-law systems in which the greatest care is taken to ensure that it never comes to that. But this does not stem from the intrinsic nature of the institution of capital punishment; it results from deficiencies, limitations, and imperfections of the criminal law procedures in which this punishment is meted out. Errors of justice do not demonstrate the need to do away with capital punishment; they simply make it incumbent on us to do everything possible to improve even further procedures of meting it out.

To be sure, this conclusion will not find favor with a diehard abolitionist. "I shall ask for the abolition of Capital Punishment until I have the infallibility of human judgement demonstrated to me," that is, as long as there is even the slightest possibility that innocent people may be executed because of judicial errors, Lafayette said in his day. Many an opponent of this kind of punishment will say the same today. The demand to do away with capital punishment altogether, so as to eliminate even the smallest chance of that ever happening— the chance which, admittedly, would remain even after everything humanly possible has been done to perfect the procedure, although then it would be very slight indeed—is actually a demand to give a privileged position to murderers as against all other offenders, big and small. For if we acted on this demand, we would bring about a situation in which proportionate penalties would be meted out for all offenses, *except* for murder. Murderers would not be receiving the only punishment truly proportionate to their crimes, the punishment of death, but some other, lighter, and thus disproportionate penalty. All other offenders would be punished according to their deserts; only murderers would be receiving less than *they* deserve. In all other cases justice would be done in full; only in cases of the gravest of offenses, the crime of murder, justice would not be carried out in full measure. It is a great and tragic miscarriage of justice when an innocent person is mistakenly sentenced to death and executed, but systematically giving murderers advantage over all other offenders would also be a grave injustice. Is the fact that, as long as capital punishment is retained, there is a possibility that over a number of years, or even decades, an injustice of the first kind may be committed, unintentionally and unconsciously, reason enough to abolish it altogether, and thus end up with a system of punishments in which injustices of the second kind are perpetrated daily, consciously, and inevitably?

There is still another abolitionist argument that actually does not tell against capital punishment itself, but against something else. Figures are sometimes quoted which show that this punishment is much more often meted out to the uneducated and poor than to the educated, rich, and influential people; in the United States, much more often to African Americans than to whites. These figures are adduced as a proof of the inherent injustice of this kind of punishment. On account of them, it is claimed that capital punishment is not a way of doing justice by meting out deserved punishment to murderers, but rather a means of social discrimination and perpetuation of social injustice.

I shall not question these findings, which are quite convincing, and anyway, there is no need to do that in order to defend the institution of capital punishment. For there seems to be a certain amount of discrimination and injustice not only in sentencing people to death and executing them, but also in meting out other penalties. The social structure of the death rows in American prisons, for instance, does not seem to be basically different from the general social structure of American penitentiaries. If this argument were valid, it would call not only for abolition of the penalty of death, but for doing away with other penalties as well.

But it is not valid; as Burton Leiser has pointed out,

this is not an argument, either against the death penalty or against any other form of punishment.

It is an argument against the unjust and inequitable distribution of penalties. If the trials of wealthy men are less likely to result in convictions than those of poor men, then something must be done to reform the procedure in criminal courts. If those who have money and standing in the community are less likely to be charged with serious offenses than their less affluent fellow citizens, then there should be a major overhaul of the entire system of criminal justice…But the maldistribution of penalties is no argument against any particular form of penalty.

There is, finally, the argument that the moral illegitimacy of capital punishment is obvious from the widespread contempt for those who carry it out: "Logically, if the Death Penalty *were* morally justified, the executioner's calling would be considered an honourable one. The fact that even its keenest supporters shrink from such a man with loathing and exclude him from their circle, is in itself an indication that Capital Punishment stands morally condemned."

This is also a poor argument, for several reasons. The contempt for the executioner and the accompanying social ostracism is by no means a universal phenomenon in history; on the contrary, it is a comparatively modern one. In earlier ages, the person who carried out capital punishment—whether the professional executioner or, before this became an occupation in its own right, the judge, or some other high-ranking official, sometimes even the ruler himself, or a relative of the murdered person—was always regarded with respect. Quite apart from this, the so-called common moral consciousness to which the argument appeals is not to be seen as some kind of supreme tribunal in moral matters. Among reasons of general nature for this is that it would be an unreliable, inconsistent, confused, and confusing tribunal. On the one hand, when viewed historically, it hardly seems a very good guide to the moral status of various occupations, for in earlier ages it used to condemn very resolutely and strongly the merchant, the banker, the actor, which no one would think of disparaging today, abolitionists included. On the other hand, it has proved itself quite inconsistent on the issue of the moral basis of punishment in general, voicing incompatible views, now retributive, now utilitarian. It is not at all surprising that both advocates and opponents of capital punishment have claimed its support for their views. But if it supports both sides in this more restricted dispute as well, then it actually supports neither.

There is still another facet of this illogical, irrational streak inherent to the common moral consciousness that comes to the fore in connection with this dispute. If the contempt for the executioner is really rooted in the belief that what he carries out is morally reprehensible, then it is surely heaped upon the wrong person. For he merely carries out

decisions on which he has no say whatsoever. Those who are responsible are, in the first instance, the judge and members of the jury. They, on their part, act as they do against the background of criminal laws for which responsibility lies at a further remove still—with the legislators. These, again, legislate in the name of the people, if the political system is a representative one. But for some reason the common moral consciousness has never evinced contempt of any of these.

An Eye for an Eye?

STEPHEN NATHANSON

Suppose we leave behind institutional frameworks, then, and try to determine what people deserve from a strictly moral point of view. How shall we proceed?

The most usual suggestion is that we look at a person's actions because what someone deserves would appear to depend on what he or she does. A person's actions, it seems, provide not only a basis for a moral appraisal of the person but also a guide to how he should be treated. According to the *lex talionis* or principle of "an eye for an eye," we ought to treat people as they have treated others. What people deserve as recipients of rewards or punishments is determined by what they do as agents.

This is a powerful and attractive view, one that appears to be backed not only by moral common sense but also by tradition and philosophical thought. The most famous statement of philosophical support for this view comes from Immanuel Kant, who linked it directly with an argument for the death penalty. Discussing the problem of punishment, Kant writes,

> What kind and what degree of punishment does legal justice adopt as its principle and standard? None other than the principle of equality…the principle of not treating one side more favorably than the other. Accordingly, any undeserved evil

that you inflict on someone else among the people is one that you do to yourself. If you vilify, you vilify yourself; if you steal from him, you steal from yourself; if you kill him, you kill yourself. Only the law of retribution (*jus talionis*) can determine exactly the kind and degree of punishment.

Kant's view is attractive for a number of reasons. First, it accords with our belief that what a person deserves is related to what he does. Second, it appeals to a moral standard and does not seem to rely on any particular legal or political institutions. Third, it seems to provides a measure of appropriate punishment that can be used as a guide to creating laws and instituting punishments. It tells us that the punishment is to be identical with the crime. Whatever the criminal did to the victim is to be done in turn to the criminal.

In spite of the attractions of Kant's view, it is deeply flawed. When we see why, it will be clear that the whole "eye for an eye" perspective must be rejected.

PROBLEMS WITH THE EQUAL PUNISHMENT PRINCIPLE

There are two main problems with this view. First, appearances to the contrary, it does not actually

From *An Eye for an Eye?*, 2nd ed., by Stephen Nathanson. © Rowman and Littlefield, Lanham, MD, 2001.

provide a measure of moral desert. Second, it does not provide an adequate criterion for determining appropriate levels of punishment.

Let us begin with the second criticism, the claim that Kant's view fails to tell us how much punishment is appropriate for particular crimes. We can see this, first, by noting that for certain crimes, Kant's view recommends punishments that are not morally acceptable. Applied strictly, it would require that we rape rapists, torture torturers, and burn arsonists whose acts have led to deaths. In general, where a particular crime involves barbaric and inhuman treatment, Kant's principle tells us to act barbarically and inhumanly in return. So, in some cases, the principle generates unacceptable answers to the question of what constitutes appropriate punishment.

This is not its only defect. In many other cases, the principle tells us nothing at all about how to punish. While Kant thought it obvious how to apply his principle in the case of murder, his principle cannot serve as a general rule because it does not tell us how to punish many crimes. Using the Kantian version or the more common "eye for an eye" standard, what would we decide to do to embezzlers, spies, drunken drivers, airline hijackers, drug users, prostitutes, air polluters, or persons who practice medicine without a license? If one reflects on this question, it becomes clear that there is simply no answer to it. We could not in fact design a system of punishment simply on the basis of the "eye for an eye" principle.

In order to justify using the "eye for an eye" principle to answer our question about murder and the death penalty, we would first have to show that it worked for a whole range of cases, giving acceptable answers to questions about amounts of punishment. Then, having established it as a satisfactory general principle, we could apply it to the case of murder. It turns out, however, that when we try to apply the principle generally, we find that it either gives wrong answers or no answers at all. Indeed, I suspect that the principle of "an eye for an eye" is no longer even a principle. Instead, it is simply a metaphorical disguise for expressing belief in the death penalty. People who cite it do not take it seriously. They do not believe in a kidnapping for a kidnapping, a theft for a theft, and so on. Perhaps "an eye for an eye" once was a genuine principle, but now it is merely a slogan. Therefore, it gives us no guidance in deciding whether murderers deserve to die.

In reply to these objections, one might defend the principle by saying that it does not require that punishments be strictly identical with crimes. Rather, it requires only that a punishment produce an amount of suffering in the criminal which is equal to the amount suffered by the victim. Thus, we don't have to hijack airplanes belonging to airline hijackers, spy on spies, etc. We simply have to reproduce in them the harm done to others.

Unfortunately, this reply really does not solve the problem. It provides no answer to the first objection, since it would still require us to behave barbarically in our treatment of those who are guilty of barbaric crimes. Even if we do not reproduce their actions exactly, any action which caused equal suffering would itself be barbaric. Second, in trying to produce equal amounts of suffering, we run into many problems. Just how much suffering is produced by an airline hijacker or a spy? And how do we apply this principle to prostitutes or drug users, who may not produce any suffering at all? We have rough ideas about how serious various crimes are, but this may not correlate with any clear sense of just how much harm is done.

Furthermore, the same problem arises in determining how much suffering a particular punishment would produce for a particular criminal. People vary in their tolerance of pain and in the amount of unhappiness that a fine or a jail sentence would cause them. Recluses will be less disturbed by banishment than extroverts. Nature lovers will suffer more in prison than people who are indifferent to natural beauty. A literal application of the principle would require that we tailor punishments to individual sensitivities, yet this is at best impractical. To a large extent, the legal system must work with standardized and rather crude estimates of the negative impact that punishments have on people.

The move from calling for a punishment that is identical to the crime to favoring one that is equal in the harm done is no help to us or to the defense of the principle. "An eye for an eye" tells us neither what people deserve nor how we should treat them when they have done wrong.

PROPORTIONAL RETRIBUTIVISM

The view we have been considering can be called "equality retributivism," since it proposes that we repay criminals with punishments equal to their crimes. In the light of problems like those I have cited, some people have proposed a variation on this view, calling not for equal punishments but rather for punishments which are proportional to the crime. In defending such a view as a guide for setting criminal punishments, Andrew von Hirsch writes:

> If one asks how severely a wrongdoer deserves to be punished, a familiar principle comes to mind: Severity of punishment should be commensurate with the seriousness of the wrong. Only grave wrongs merit severe penalties; minor misdeeds deserve lenient punishments. Disproportionate penalties are undeserved—severe sanctions for minor wrongs or vice versa. This principle has variously been called a principle of "proportionality" or "just deserts"; we prefer to call it commensurate deserts.

Like Kant, von Hirsch makes the punishment which a person deserves depend on that person's actions, but he departs from Kant in substituting proportionality for equality as the criterion for setting the amount of punishment.

In implementing a punishment system based on the proportionality view, one would first make a list of crimes, ranking them in order of seriousness. At one end would be quite trivial offenses like parking meter violations, while very serious crimes such as murder would occupy the other. In between, other crimes would be ranked according to their relative gravity. Then a corresponding scale of punishments would be constructed, and the two would be correlated. Punishments would be proportionate to crimes so long as we could say that the more serious the crime was, the higher on the punishment scale was the punishment administered.

This system does not have the defects of equality retributivism. It does not require that we treat those guilty of barbaric crimes barbarically. This is because we can set the upper limit of the punishment scale so as to exclude truly barbaric punishments. Second, unlike the equality principle, the proportionality view is genuinely general, providing a way of handling all crimes. Finally, it does justice to our ordinary belief that certain punishments are unjust because they are too severe or too lenient for the crime committed.

The proportionality principle does, I think, play a legitimate role in our thinking about punishments. Nonetheless, it is no help to death penalty advocates, because it does not require that murderers be executed. All that it requires is that if murder is the most serious crime, then murder should be punished by the most severe punishment on the scale. The principle does not tell us what this punishment should be, however, and it is quite compatible with the view that the most severe punishment should be a long prison term.

This failure of the theory to provide a basis for supporting the death penalty reveals an important gap in proportional retributivism. It shows that while the theory is general in scope, it does not yield any specific recommendations regarding punishment. It tells us, for example, that armed robbery should be punished more severely than embezzling and less severely than murder, but it does not tell us how much to punish any of these. This weakness is, in effect, conceded by von Hirsch, who admits that if we want to implement the "commensurate deserts" principle, we must supplement it with information about what level of punishment is needed to deter crimes. In a later discussion of how to "anchor" the punishment system, he deals with this problem in more depth, but the factors he cites as relevant to making specific judgments (such as available prison space) have nothing to do with what people deserve. He also seems to suggest that a range of punishments may be appropriate for a particular crime. This runs counter to the death penalty supporter's sense that death alone is appropriate for some murderers.

Neither of these retributive views, then, provides support for the death penalty. The equality principle fails because it is not in general true that the appropriate punishment for a crime is to do to the criminal what he has done to others. In some cases this is immoral, while in others it is impossible. The proportionality principle may be correct, but by itself it cannot determine specific punishments for specific crimes. Because of its flexibility and open-endedness, it is compatible with a great range of different punishments for murder.

A MORE SERIOUS OBJECTION

So far, in looking at these versions of retributivism, I have tried to show that they do not help us to determine the appropriate punishment for specific crimes. That is, they do not really tell us what sort of treatment is deserved by people who have acted in certain ways.

There is a more serious defect of both versions of the theory, however. Neither one succeeds in basing punishment on what a person morally deserves. Why is this? Because both theories focus solely on the action that a person has performed, and this action is not the proper basis for determining moral desert. We cannot tell what a person deserves simply by examining what he has done.

While it may sound odd to say that a person's degree of moral desert is not determined by his actions, the point is actually a matter of common sense morality. We can see this by considering the following examples, all of which are cases of rescuing a drowning person.

1. A and B have robbed a bank, but B has hidden the money from A. A finds B at the beach and sees that he is drowning. A drags B from the water, revives him, finds out the location of the money, and then shoots him, leaving him for dead. The shot, however, is not fatal. A has saved B's life.

2. C recognizes D, a wealthy businessman, at the beach. Later, she sees D struggling in the water and, hoping to get a reward, she saves him. C would not have saved D if she had not thought that a reward was likely.

3. E is drowning at the beach and is spotted by F, a poor swimmer. F leaps into the water and, at great risk to her own life, manages to save E.

4. G is drowning at the beach but is spotted by Superman, who rescues him effortlessly.

In each of these cases, the very same act occurs. One person saves another from drowning. Yet, if we attempt to assess what each rescuer morally deserves, we will arrive at very different answers for each case. This is because judgments of desert are moral judgments about people and not just about their actions or how they should be treated. Our moral judgments about A, C, F, and Superman in the examples above are quite different, in spite of the similarity of their actions. From a moral point of view, we would not rate A as being praiseworthy at all because he had no concern for B's well-being and in fact wished him dead. C, the rescuer motivated by the prospect of a reward, wished D no harm but is also less praiseworthy because her act was not motivated by genuine concern for D's well-being. Finally, while F, the poor swimmer, and Superman both acted from benevolent motives, F is more deserving of praise because of the greater risk which she took and the greater difficulties she faced in accomplishing the rescue.

What these cases make clear is that there is no direct connection between what a person does and his or her degree of moral desert. To make judgments of moral desert, we need to know about a person's intentions, motivations, and circumstances, not just about the action and its result. Since both Kant and von Hirsch base their judgments concerning appropriate punishments simply on the act that has been committed, they do not succeed in basing their recommended punishments on what a person morally deserves, for what a person deserves depends on factors which they do not consider.

It is quite ironic that Kant overlooks this and provides an exclusively act-oriented account of assessing people in his discussion of punishment. In other writings, Kant insists that the fact that an action is harmful or helpful does not by itself tell us how to assess the moral value of the agent's performing it. He lays great stress on the significance of motivation, claiming that the moral value of actions depends entirely on whether they are done from a moral motive.

"PAYBACK" RETRIBUTIVISM

With this criticism in mind, it is instructive to look back at the passage from Kant about the need to execute murderers. What is striking about the passage is that Kant does not talk about desert at all. He does not say that a person deserves to die because he has killed and therefore that he ought to be executed. Rather, he says that a person should be executed simply because he has killed.

The lack of any reference to moral desert in this passage is more than just a linguistic oversight by Kant. It reflects the existence of a form of retributivism that is related to but different from the view that I have been discussing. I have assumed that the central retributivist ideal is that people ought to get what they deserve. But there is another view of retribution, according to which justice is done when a person is paid back for what he does. In this famous passage, Kant expresses the "payback" version of retributivism rather than a form of the view that focuses on moral desert. Why this is I do not know, but in any case, Kant is not alone in thinking that retribution has been achieved when a person has been treated as he has treated others.

Although retribution is often cited as a goal of the criminal law, this "payback" conception is weak and unattractive. First, it provides no justification for punishment. We want to know why it is morally permissible to punish someone who has committed a crime, and the answer of the "payback" retributivist is simply that it is permissible to pay people back for their deeds by doing to them what they have done to others. This reply begs the question by offering no independent reason for punishing. By contrast, one who justifies punishment by saying that the person being punished deserves this treatment appears to be offering a substantive, independent reason for punishing, making this view much more attractive than the "payback" conception. He is pointing to some feature of the person which makes the punishment appropriate.

Second, the "payback" retributivist defines the actions people have committed by reference to the results of those actions. If we consider this view, however, it is easy to generate conclusions that the retributivist himself would find unacceptable. When people who believe in "an eye for an eye" say that those who kill must be killed in turn, this cannot possibly be their final word on the matter. If it were, then they would be committed to the view that those who kill accidentally must be killed. More absurdly, they would have to hold that whenever the death penalty is imposed, the executioner of the murderer would in turn have to be killed because he has killed, as would the executioner of the executioner and so on.

These absurd conclusions can, of course, be avoided by describing actions in more sophisticated ways. Doing this makes it possible to deny that accidental and intentional killings are the same. It allows us to distinguish the intentional killing done by the original murderer from the intentional killing performed by the executioner. Having done this, we can call one of these acts murder, a second accidental homicide, and the third a legal execution. Furthermore, we then say that it is only murderers—and not those who commit accidental homicide or perform legal executions—who should be paid back for their deeds. Once we do this, however, we have moved away from the "payback" version of retributivism and its simple focus on the results of actions. In distinguishing these various killings, we have been forced to look at motives, intentions, and circumstances and not just to consider actions and results. To do this is to leave behind "payback" retributivism and to return to the more complex "giving people what they deserve" version of the theory. Indeed, this is the most plausible version of the theory. Retributivism without desert is simply too crude a view to be plausible.

Any reasonable principle, then, will recognize that not all killings are murders and hence that not all who kill deserve to die. This is, in fact, the view of common sense morality, which sanctions some types of killing (for example, killing in self-defense) and thus allows that one who kills may even be morally blameless. Furthermore, even among those killings that are illegitimate and that we want to classify as murder, not all are equally reprehensible. This is reflected in the Supreme Court's judgment that mandatory death sentences for murder are unconstitutional. Though the Court often speaks the language of retribution, its decisions depart from the simplicity of "payback" retributivism.

CONCLUSIONS

In this chapter, I have examined some of the arguments that might be used to defend the view that murderers deserve to die. I have tried to show why these arguments fail. The traditional versions of retributivism do not justify death as a specific punishment for murder. Moreover, in their usual forms, they omit factors that are essential to determining what a person deserves. Paradoxically, one cannot tell what a person deserves simply by knowing what he has done. In particular, it is not enough to know that someone has killed someone else or even that

he has done so unjustifiably. The examples of the various rescuers show that we must consider more than a person's deeds to determine what he or she deserves.

Capital Attrition: Error Rates in Capital Cases, 1973–1995

JAMES S. LIEBMAN, JEFFREY FAGAN, VALERIE WEST, AND JONATHAN LLOYD

I. INTRODUCTION

Americans seem to be of two minds about the death penalty. In the last several years, the overall number of executions has risen steeply, reaching a fifty-year high this year. Although two-thirds of the public support the penalty, this figure represents a sharp decline from the four-fifths of the population that endorsed the death penalty only six years ago, leaving support for capital punishment at a twenty-year low. When life without parole is offered as an alternative, support for the penalty drops even more—often below a majority. Grants of executive clemency reached a twenty-year high in 1999.

In 1999 and 2000, governors, attorneys general and legislators in Alabama, Arizona, Florida, and Tennessee fought high-profile campaigns to increase the speed and number of executions. In the same period, however:

- The Republican Governor of Illinois, with support from a majority of the electorate, declared a moratorium on executions in that state.
- The Nebraska Legislature attempted to enact a similar moratorium. Although the Governor vetoed the legislation, the legislature appropriated money for a comprehensive study of the even-handedness of the state's exercise of capital punishment.
- Similar studies have been ordered in Illinois by the Chief Justice, task forces of both houses of the state legislature, and the governor. Indiana, Maryland, and the Attorney General of the United States have followed suit.

- Serious campaigns to abolish the death penalty are under way in New Hampshire and (with the support of the governor and a popular former Republican senator) in Oregon.
- The Florida Supreme Court and Mississippi Legislature recently acted to improve the quality of counsel in capital cases, and bills with bipartisan sponsorship aiming to do the same and to improve capital prisoners' access to DNA evidence have been introduced in both houses of the United States Congress.

Observers in the *Wall Street Journal, New York Times Magazine, Salon,* and on *ABC This Week* see "a tectonic shift in the politics of the death penalty."

In April 2000 alone, George Will and Reverend Pat Robertson—both strong death penalty supporters—expressed doubts about the manner in which government officials carry out the penalty in the United States, and Robertson subsequently advocated a moratorium, on *Meet the Press.* In response, Reverend Jerry Falwell called for continued—even swifter—execution of death sentences.

Fueling these competing initiatives are two beliefs about the death penalty: One is that death sentences move too slowly from imposition to execution, undermining deterrence and retribution, subjecting our criminal laws and courts to ridicule, and increasing the agony of victims. The other is that death sentences are fraught with error, causing

justice too often to miscarry, and subjecting innocent and other undeserving defendants—mainly,
racial minorities and the poor—to execution.

Some observers attribute these seemingly conflicting events and opinions to "America's own
schizophrenia.... We believe in the death penalty,
but shrink from it as applied." These views may
not conflict, however, and Americans who hold
both may not be irrational. It may be that capital sentences spend too much time under review
and that they are fraught with disturbing amounts
of error. Indeed, it may be that capital sentences
spend so much time under judicial review precisely *because* they are persistently and systematically fraught with alarming amounts of error, and
that the expanding production of death sentences
may compound the production of error. We are
led to this conclusion by a study of all 4,578 capital sentences that were finally reviewed by state
direct appeal courts and all 599 capital sentences
that were finally reviewed by federal habeas corpus courts between 1973 and 1995.

II. SUMMARY OF CENTRAL FINDINGS

In *Furman v. Georgia* in 1972, the Supreme Court
reversed all existing capital statutes and death sentences. The modern death-sentencing era began the
next year with the implementation of new capital
statutes designed to satisfy *Furman*. In order to collect information about capital sentences imposed
and reviewed after 1973 (no central repository exists),
we conducted a painstaking search, beginning in
1995, of all published state and federal judicial opinions in the United States conducting direct and
habeas review of capital judgments, and many of the
available opinions conducting state post-conviction
review of those judgments. We then (1) checked and
catalogued all cases the opinions revealed, (2) collected hundreds of items of information about each
case from the published decisions and the NAACP
Legal Defense Fund's quarterly death row census,
(3) tabulated the results, and (4) (still in progress)
conducted multivariate statistical analyses to identify factors that may contribute to those results.

Six years in the making, our central findings
thus far are these:

- Between 1973 and 1995, approximately 5,760
  death sentences were imposed in the United

States. Only 313 (5.4%; one in 19) of those
resulted in an execution during the period.

- Of the 5,760 death sentences imposed in the
  study period, 4,578 (79%) were finally reviewed
  on "direct appeal" by a state high court. Of
  those, 1,885 (41%) were thrown out on the basis
  of "serious error" (error that substantially
  undermines the reliability of the outcome).

- Most of the remainder of the death sentences
  were then inspected by state post-conviction
  courts. Although incomplete, our data (reported in *A Broken System*) reveal that state post-
  conviction review is an important source
  of review in some states, including Florida,
  Georgia, Indiana, Maryland, Mississippi, and
  North Carolina. In Maryland, for example, at
  least 52% of capital judgments reviewed in state
  post-conviction proceedings during the study
  period were overturned due to serious error;
  the same was true for at least 25% of the capital judgments that were similarly reviewed in
  Indiana, and at least 20% of those reviewed in
  Mississippi.

- Of the death sentences that survived state
  direct and post-conviction review, 599 were
  finally reviewed on a first habeas corpus petition during the 23-year study period. Of those
  599, 237 (40%) were overturned due to serious
  error.

- The "overall success rate" of capital judgments
  undergoing judicial inspection, and its converse, the "overall error rate," are crucial factors in assessing the efficiency of our capital
  punishment system. The "overall *success* rate"
  is the proportion of capital judgments that
  underwent, and *passed*, the three-stage judicial
  inspection process during the study period.
  The "overall *error* rate" is the frequency with
  which capital judgments that underwent full
  inspection were *overturned* at one of the three
  stages due to serious error. Nationally, over the
  entire 1973–1995 period, the overall error rate
  in our capital punishment system was 68%.

- Because "serious error" is error that substantially undermines the reliability of the guilt
  finding or death sentence imposed at trial,
  each instance of that error warrants public
  concern. The most common errors found at
  the state post-conviction stage (where our data

are most complete) are (1) egregiously incompetent defense lawyering (accounting for 37% of the state post-conviction reversals), and (2) prosecutorial suppression of evidence that the defendant is innocent or does not deserve the death penalty (accounting for another 16%—or 19%, when all forms of law enforcement misconduct are considered). These two violations count as "serious," and thus warrant reversal, *only* when there is a "reasonable probability" that, but for the responsible lawyer's miscues, the outcome of the trial would have been different.

The result of very high rates of serious, reversible error among capital convictions and sentences, and very low rates of capital reconviction and resentencing, is the severe attrition of capital judgments....

For every 100 death sentences imposed and reviewed during the study period, 41 were turned back at the state direct appeal phase because of serious error. Of the 59 that got through that phase to the second, state post-conviction stage, at least 10%—six more of the original 100—were turned back due to serious flaws. And, of the 53 that got through that stage to the third, federal habeas checkpoint, 40%—an additional 21 of the original 100— were turned back because of serious error. Overall, at least 68 of the original 100 were thrown out because of serious flaws, compared to only 32 (or less) that were found to have passed muster—after an average of 9–10 years had passed.

And for each such 68 individuals whose death sentences were overturned for serious error, 82% (56) were found on retrial *not* to have deserved the death penalty, including 7% (5) who were *cleared of the capital offense.*

• The seriousness of these errors is also revealed by what happens on retrial when the errors are supposed to be cured. In our state post-conviction sub-study where the post-reversal outcome is known, over four-fifths (56 out of 68) of the capital judgments that were reversed were replaced on retrial with a sentence less than death, or no sentence at all. In the latter regard, fully 7% of the reversals for serious error resulted in a determination on retrial that the defendant was *not guilty* of the offense for which he previously was sentenced to die.

• High error rates pervade American capital-sentencing jurisdictions, and are geographically dispersed. Among the twenty-six death-sentencing jurisdictions in which at least one case has been reviewed in both the state and federal courts and in which information about all three judicial inspection stages is available:

1. 24 (92%) have overall error rates of 52% or higher;
2. 22 (85%) have overall errors rates of 60% or higher;
3. 15 (61%) have overall error rates of 70% or higher.
4. Among other states, Georgia, Alabama, Mississippi, Indiana, Oklahoma, Wyoming, Montana, Arizona, and California have overall error rates of 75% or higher.

It is sometimes suggested that Illinois, whose governor declared a moratorium on executions in January 2000 because of the spate of death row exonerations there, generates less reliable death sentences than other states. Our data do not support this hypothesis: The overall rate of error found to infect Illinois capital sentences (66%) is slightly *lower* than the rate in capital-sentencing states as a whole (68%).

• High error rates have persisted for decades. More than 50% of all cases reviewed were found seriously flawed in 20 of the 23 study years, including in 17 of the last 19 years. In half of the years studied, the error rate was over 60%. Although error rates detected on state direct appeal and federal habeas corpus dropped modestly in the early 1990s, they went back up in 1995. The amount of error detected on state post-conviction has risen sharply throughout the 1990s.

• The 68% rate of *capital* error found by the three-stage inspection process is much higher than the < 15% rate of error those same three inspections evidently discover in *noncapital* criminal cases.

• Appointed federal judges are sometimes thought to be more likely to overturn capital sentences than elected state judges. In fact, state judges are the first and most important line of defense against erroneous death sentences. Elected state judges found serious error in and reversed 90% (2,133 of 2,370) of the capital sentences that were overturned during the study period.

- Under current state and federal law, capital prisoners have a legal right to one round of direct appellate, state post-conviction, and federal habeas corpus review. The high rates of error found at *each* stage, and at the *last* stage, and the persistence of high error rates over time and across the nation, confirm the need for multiple judicial inspections. Without compensating changes at the front-end of the process, the contrary policy of cutting back on judicial inspection would seem to make no more sense than responding to the impending insolvency of the Social Security System by forbidding it to be audited.

- Finding this much error takes time. Calculating the amount of time using information in published decisions is difficult. Only a small percentage of direct appeals decisions report the sentence date. By the end of the habeas stage, however, a much larger proportion of sentencing dates is reported in some decision in the case. It accordingly is possible to get an accurate sense of timing for the 599 cases that were finally reviewed on habeas corpus. Among those cases:

1. It took an average of 7.6 years after the defendant was sentenced to die to complete federal habeas corpus consideration in the 40% of habeas cases in which reversible error was found.

2. In the cases in which no error was detected at the third inspection stage and an execution occurred, the average time between sentence and execution was nine years.

...[H]igh rates of error frustrate the goals of the death penalty system.... In general, where the overall error rate reaches 55% or above (as is true for the vast majority of the states), the percentage of death sentences carried out drops below 7%.

...The pattern of capital outcomes for the State of Virginia is clearly an outlier—the State's high execution rate is nearly *double* that of the next nearest state and *five times* the national average, and its low rate of capital reversals is nearly *half* that of the next nearest state and less than *one-fourth* the national average. A sharp discrepancy between Virginia and other capital-sentencing jurisdictions characterizes most of our analyses. That discrepancy presents an important question for further study: Are Virginia capital judgments in fact half as prone to serious error as the next lowest state and four times less than the national average? Or, on the other hand, are its courts more tolerant of serious error? Or, have Virginia's legislature and courts censored opportunities to inspect verdicts and detect error by procedurally constraining the definition of error and the time within which errors can be identified? We will address this issue below and in a subsequent report.

The rising number of executions nationally does not render these patterns obsolete. Instead of indicating improvement in the *quality* of death sentences under review, the rising number of executions may simply reflect how many *more* sentences have piled up awaiting review. If the error-induced pile-up of cases on death row is the *cause* of rising executions, their rise provides no proof that a cure has been found for disturbingly high and persistent error rates. The rising execution rate and the persistent error rate increase the likelihood of an increase in the incidence of wrongful executions. To see why this is true, consider a factory that produced 100 toasters in a year, only 32 of which worked. The factory's production problem would not be deemed fixed if the company simply raised its production run to 200 the next year in order to double the number of working toasters to 66. Thus, the real question isn't the *number* of death sentences carried out each year, but the *proportion*.

...[I]n contrast to the annual *number* of executions...the *proportion* of death row inmates executed each year...has remained remarkably stable—and extremely low.

...Since post-*Furman* executions began in earnest in 1984, the nation has executed only an average of about 1.3% of its death row inmates each year; in no year has it carried out more than 2.6%—or one in thirty-nine—of death sentences exposed to full review.

...[T]he rising number of executions...is *not* caused by any improvement in the quality of capital judgments, but instead by the inexorable pile-up of people on death row...as judges struggle to exercise a degree of quality control over decade upon decade of error-prone capital judgments.

III. CONFIRMATION FROM A PARALLEL STUDY

Results from a parallel study by the U.S. Department of Justice suggest that our 32% figure for valid death sentences actually overstates the chance of execution. The 1998 Justice Department study includes a report showing the outcome of the 263 death sentences imposed in 1989. A final disposition of only 103 of the 263 death sentences had been reached nine years later. Of those 103, 78 (76%) had been overturned by a state or federal court. Only thirteen death sentences had been carried out. So, for every one member of the death row class of 1989 whose case was finally reviewed and who was executed as of 1998, six members of the class had their cases overturned in the courts. Because of the intensive review needed to catch so much error, 160 (61%) of the 263 death sentences imposed in 1989 were still under scrutiny nine years later.

The approximately 3500 people on death row today have been waiting an average of 7.4 years for a final declaration that their capital verdict is error free—or, far more probably, that it is the product of serious error. Of the 6700 people sentenced to die between 1973 and 1999, only 598—less than one in eleven—were executed. About three times as many had their capital judgments overturned or gained clemency.

IV. IMPLICATIONS OF CENTRAL FINDINGS

To help appreciate these findings, consider a scenario that might unfold any of the nearly 300 times a year that a death sentence is imposed in the United States. Suppose the defendant, or a relative of the victim, asks a lawyer or the judge, "What now?" Based on almost a quarter century of experience in thousands of cases in 28 death-sentencing states in the United States between 1973 and 1995, a responsible answer would be: "The capital conviction or sentence will probably be overturned due to serious errors. It'll take about nine years to find out, given how many other capital cases being reviewed for likely error are lined up ahead of this one. If the judgment is overturned, a lesser conviction or sentence will probably be imposed."

As any person hearing this statement would likely conclude as a matter of common sense, these reversals due to serious error, and the time it takes to expose them, are costly. Capital trials and sentences cost more than noncapital ones. Each time they have to be done over—as happens 68% of the time—some or all of that difference is doubled. The error-detection system all this capital error requires is itself a huge expense—evidently *millions of dollars* per case.

When retrial demonstrates that nearly four-fifths of the capital judgments in which serious error is found are more appropriately handled as non-capital cases (and in a sizeable number of instances, as non-murder or even *non-criminal* cases), it is hard to escape the conclusion that most of the resources the capital system currently consumes are not buying the public, or victims, the valid death sentences for egregious offenses that a majority support. Rather, those resources are being wasted on the trial and review of cases that for the most part are not capital and are seriously flawed.

Public faith in the courts and the criminal justice system is another casualty of high capital error rates. When the vast majority of capital sentencing jurisdictions carry out fewer than 6% of the death sentences they impose, and when the nation as a whole never executes more than 3% of its death population in a year, the retributive and deterrent credibility of the death penalty is low.

When condemned inmates turn out to be *innocent*, the error is different in its consequences, but *not* evidently different in its causes, from the other serious error discussed here. There is no accounting for this cost to the wrongly convicted; to the family of the victim, whose search for justice and closure has been in vain; to later victims whose lives are threatened—and even taken—because the real killers remain at large; and to the wrongly *executed*, should justice miscarry at trial, and should reviewing judges, harried by the amount of capital error they are asked to catch, miss one.

If the issue was the fabrication of toasters (to return to our prior example), or the licensing of automobile drivers, or the conduct of any other private or public sector activity, neither the consuming public nor managers and investors would tolerate the error rates and attendant costs that dozens of states and the nation as a whole have tolerated in their capital punishment systems over the course of decades. Any system with this much error and expense would be halted immediately, examined, and either reformed or scrapped. We ask taxpayers, public managers, and policymakers whether that same response is warranted here, when the issue is not the content and quality of tomorrow's breakfast but whether society has a swift and sure response to murder and whether thousands of men and women condemned for that crime in fact deserve to die.

ARGUMENT 11 ESSAY QUESTIONS

1. What are Nathanson's arguments against the retributivist position on capital punishment?
2. What are Primoratz's criticisms of common abolitionist arguments? Do you think them cogent? Explain.
3. What is the right-to-life argument against the death penalty? How have retentionists tried to rebut it?

12. THE DISCRIMINATION ARGUMENT AGAINST THE DEATH PENALTY

Abolitionists contend that the death penalty is imposed unfairly—that equals are not treated equally—so it is unjust and should be abolished. The usual way of framing the argument is that the death penalty is biased against minorities (primarily African Americans) and the poor, and since any discriminatory system of punishment is unjust, the death penalty is unjust. One of the more blunt statements of the charge of unfairness comes from the abolitionist Bryan Stevenson:

> The legacy of racial apartheid, racial bias, and ethnic discrimination is unavoidably evident in the administration of capital punishment in America. Death sentences are imposed in a criminal justice system that treats you better if you are rich and guilty than if you are poor and innocent.[15]

[15] Bryan Stevenson, "Close to Death: Reflections on Race and Capital Punishment in America," in *Debating the Death Penalty*, ed. Hugo Bedau and Paul Cassell (New York: Oxford University Press, 2004), 97.

Applied to African Americans, the empirical claim in the argument says that the imposition of the death penalty discriminates against them—or more concretely, that blacks are much more likely to be sentenced to death than whites are for the same crime. In "Administrative Objections," Paul G. Cassell backs up this assertion like this:

> when compared to their percentage in the overall population African Americans are overrepresented on death row. For example, while 12 percent of the population is African American, about 43 percent of death row inmates are African American, and 38 percent of prisoners executed since 1977 are African American.[16]

While agreeing that we should try to root out any discriminatory practices in the justice system and that the overrepresentation of blacks on death row is a serious concern, retentionists generally deny that statistics support the empirical claim. For example, they maintain that statistical comparisons like those just mentioned are faulty:

> The relevant population for comparison is not the general population, but rather the population of murderers. If the death penalty is administered without regard to race, the percentage of African American death row inmates found at the end of the process should not exceed the percentage of African American defendants charged with murder at the beginning. The available statistics indicate that is precisely what happens. The Department of Justice found that while African Americans constituted 48 percent of adults charged with homicide, they were only 41 percent of those admitted to prison under sentence of death. In other words, once arrested for murder, blacks are actually less likely to receive a capital sentence than are whites.[17]

Sometimes abolitionists support the discrimination charge with data that seem to suggest that the chances of blacks getting the death penalty for murder increase significantly if the victims are white. Retentionists dispute this claim, contending that abolitionists overlook or misinterpret the relevant data.

Retentionists also have a more fundamental criticism of the abolitionist argument: unjust administration of the death penalty does not make the death penalty itself unjust. As Louis Pojman says,

> First of all, it is not true that a law applied in a discriminatory manner is unjust. Unequal justice is no less justice, however uneven its application. The discriminatory application, not the law itself, is unjust. A just law is still just, even if it is not applied consistently.... The discriminatory practice should be reformed, and in many cases it can be. But imperfect practices in themselves do not entail that the laws engendering these practices are themselves unjust.[18]

Many abolitionists reject this distinction, maintaining that the death penalty and how it is administered are unavoidably intertwined.

---

[16] Paul G. Cassell, *Debating the Death Penalty*, 201.

[17] Paul G. Cassell, *Debating the Death Penalty*, 201.

[18] Louis P. Pojman, *Life and Death* (Belmont, CA: Wadsworth, 2000), 146.

Administrative Objections

PAUL G. CASSELL

Because their general objections to the death penalty have found so little support, abolitionists have largely abandoned these claims. Even if the death penalty *is* justified in principle, they maintain, in practice it is unfairly administered. The collection of essays here is typical of the modern debate. Three of the four abolitionist chapters (by Governor Ryan, Bright, and Stevenson) rest almost exclusively on administrative challenges to the penalty.

The abolitionists most frequently raise three particular administrative challenges to the death penalty: first, that it is infected with racism; second, that innocent persons have been executed; and finally, that capital defendants do not receive effective assistance of legal counsel. This section explains why each of these objections cannot justify nationwide abolition of the penalty. But before turning to the details of these objections, an opening observation is in order.

No responsible supporter of the death penalty holds any brief for inadequate defense attorneys, racist prosecutors, or inattentive judges. If problems arise in a particular case, they should be corrected. And, indeed, in many of the cases cited by the abolitionists here, the problems in particular cases were in fact corrected. The issue debated in this volume, however, is whether such problems are sufficiently widespread to justify completely depriving the federal government and 38 states of the option of imposing a capital sentence on a justly convicted offender. These are global questions that cannot be resolved by reciting isolated instances of abuse in a single jurisdiction (e.g., Alabama, where Bryan Stephenson conducts most of his work, or Illinois, where Governor Ryan conducted a review). Rather, these questions are appropriately resolved by examining the data about the system as a whole. With the big picture in view, it is clear that the administrative objections provide no grounds for abolishing capital punishment.

Capital punishment in America is racist, its opponents claim. The arguments about racism come in two forms: a "mass market" version and a "specialist" form. Both versions are seriously flawed.

In the "mass market" version, we are told that the death penalty discriminates against African American defendants. For instance, the Reverend Jesse Jackson, in his book *Legal Lynching*, argues that "[n]umerous researchers have shown conclusively that African American defendants are far more likely to receive the death penalty than are white defendants charged with the same crime." The support for this claim is said to be the undisputed fact that when compared to their percentage in the overall population African Americans are overrepresented on death row. For example, while 12 percent of the population is African American, about 43 percent of death row inmates are African American, and 38 percent of prisoners executed since 1977 [have been] African American.

Such simple statistics of overrepresentation fail to prove racial bias. The relevant population for comparison is not the general population, but rather the population of murderers. If the death penalty is administered without regard to race, the percentage of African American death row inmates found at the end of the process should not exceed the percentage of African American defendants charged with murder at the beginning. The available statistics indicate that is precisely what happens. The Department of Justice found that while African Americans constituted 48 percent of adults charged with homicide, they were only 41 percent of those admitted to prison under sentence of death. In other words, once arrested for murder, blacks are actually less likely to receive a capital sentence than are whites.

Critics of these data might argue that police may be more likely to charge African Americans than whites with murder at the outset of the process. No

From "Administrative Objections" by Paul G. Cassell in *Debating the Death Penalty*, ed. Hugo Bedau and Paul Cassell, 200–205. © 2004 New York: Oxford University Press.

such claim is advanced in the abolitionist chapters of this book and in any event, the data do not support it. One way of investigating this claim is to analyze crime victim reports of the race of those who commit crimes against them. While it is obviously impossible to talk to murder victims, it is possible to talk to victims of armed robberies, who are reasonable surrogates. When victim reports for armed robbery are compared with criminal justice processing, there is no evidence of racial discrimination in charging decisions.

The overrepresentation of African Americans on death row to which Reverend Jackson refers is, indisputably, of great public concern. Policy makers must certainly examine the causes of that overrepresentation—for example, differences in economic or educational opportunities—and address them. But given such societal factors, racial bias cannot be inferred from such simplistic calculations.

To confirm or dispel concern about black defendants being singled out for the death penalty, one must conduct more sophisticated social science research. Various researchers (often of an abolitionist bent) have set out to prove such racial discrimination. They have been disappointed. The studies of the post-*Furman* death penalty in America have generally found that African American defendants are not more likely than white defendants to receive the death penalty. Summarizing all the data in 1990, the General Accounting Office concluded that evidence that blacks were discriminated against was "equivocal." Similarly, in a comprehensive study Professor Baldus and his colleagues reported that "regardless of the methodology used" studies show "no systematic race-of-defendant" effect.

This ought to be treated as good news of progress in the American criminal justice system. One could draw the following conclusion: That while African American defendants in capital cases were previously treated unfairly (especially in the South), modern statistics reveal considerable progress. This conclusion, of course, is anathema to the agenda of abolitionists. Thus, when pressed by someone who is familiar with the social science data finding no discrimination against African American offenders, more sophisticated abolitionists often abandon the mass market version of their racism argument and shift to the specialist

version. In his chapter in this book, for example, Bryan Stevenson argues that data demonstrate the existence of "racial bias in Georgia's use of the death penalty"—by which he means statistics suggesting that blacks who kill whites are more likely to receive a death penalty than are other victim/offender combinations.

These specialist statistics are no less misleading than the mass market statistics. But before turning to them, it is important to note the implications of this retreat to a race-of-the-victim claim. It seems implausible, to say the least, that a racist criminal justice system would look past minority defendants and discriminate solely on the more attenuated basis of the race of their victims. If racists are running the system, why wouldn't they just discriminate directly against minority defendants?

In any event, the race-of-the-victim claim cannot withstand close scrutiny. It is first important to understand that the claim cannot be proven by the kind of seat-of-the-pants anecdotes recounted here at considerable length by Bryan Stevenson and Stephen Bright. Of necessity, a race-of-the-victim claim involves comparison—that is, comparing the facts of comparable cases in different victim and offender combinations to see whether unexplainable disparities emerge. Thus, the anecdotes tell us little; the question belongs in the realm of statistical analysis.

Statisticians Stanley Rothman and Stephen Powers have offered the best review of the relevant data. As they explain, the vast majority of homicides (no less than other offenses) are intraracial: about 95 percent do not cross racial lines. The small minority of inter-racial homicides have vastly different characteristics. Black-on-black homicides and white-on-white homicides are most likely to occur during altercations between persons who know one another—circumstances often viewed as inappropriate for the death penalty. On the other hand, black-on-white homicides are much more often committed during the course of a serious felony—a classic case for the death penalty. For example, in Georgia, only 7 percent of the black-defendant-kills-black-victim cases involve armed robbery, compared to 67 percent of the black-defendant-kills-white-victim cases. Similarly, black-defendant-kills-white-victim cases more often involve the murder of a law enforcement officer, kidnaping and rape, mutilation, execution-style killing, and torture—all quintessential aggravating factors—than do other combinations. Finally, white-defendant-kills-black-victim cases are so rare that it is difficult to draw meaningful statistical conclusions from them.

Given these obvious differences between, on the one hand, intraracial homicides and, on the other, black-on-white homicides, the simple comparison of the percentage of death sentences within each classification reported in this volume by Bryan Stevenson and Stephen Bright is unilluminating. To put the point in more precise statistical terms, an alleged race-of-the-victim effect will be an obvious "spurious" correlation. To cite but one example, a significant number of death penalty cases involve murder of law enforcement officers, about 85 percent of whom are white. Unless there are statistical controls for this fact, it is virtually certain that a simple eyeballing of statistics will show a race-of-the-victim effect that is instead immediately explainable by this fact (among many others).

The issue about spurious correlations and the alleged race-of-the-victim effect was put on trial in 1984 before United States District Court Judge J. Owen Forrester. Judge Forrester took testimony from Professor Baldus and other statisticians who purported to have identified a genuine race-of-the-victim effect in Georgia. In an opinion that spans 65 pages in the federal reporter, Judge Forrester squarely rejected the claim. Judge Forrester first observed that Baldus found no race-of-the-*defendant* effect—that is, black defendants were not directly discriminated against. With respect to the race-of-the-*victim*, only his "summary" models (i.e., models including just a few control variables) purported to demonstrate the effect. The effect in fact disappeared entirely as additional control variables were added. When Baldus ran his regression equations with all the 430 control variables

for which he had collected data, no statistically significant evidence of discrimination remained. Judge Forrester accordingly held: "The best models which Baldus was able to devise which account to any significant degree for the major non-racial variables ... produce no statistically significant evidence that races play a part in either [the prosecution's or the jury's capital decisions]."

Judge Forrester's carefully reasoned and detailed opinion should have put an end to race-of-the-victim claims: It is, after all, the only review of the claim by a neutral decision maker. Moreover, Judge Forrester's findings about the Baldus study—that a purported race of the victim effect in "summary" models gradually disappears as more control variables are added into the equations—apply equally to the other race-of-the-victim studies cited in this volume. Without exception, the studies purporting to demonstrate a race-of-the-victim effect control for only a few relevant variables (nowhere approaching the 430 variables ultimately analyzed by Judge Forrester), producing a spurious correlation rather than any causal connection. But abolitionists—including all of the contributors to this volume—never discuss his findings. Instead, they refer to the later U.S. Supreme Court decision reviewing Judge Forrester's opinion. The Supreme Court, perhaps unwilling to dive into the statistical subtleties of multiple regression analysis, decided to proceed on the "assumption" that the Baldus race-of-the-victim figures were *factually* accurate. The Court found that the figures were nonetheless *legally* insufficient to establish a cognizable claim of discrimination. Because it proceeded on this assumption, the Supreme Court could affirm Judge Forrester without needing to reach the statistical question of whether a race-of-the-victim effect actually existed. But Judge Forrester's opinion might well serve as an emblematic example of abolitionist claims: When put to the test before a fair-minded observer, they cannot withstand scrutiny.

Capital Punishment and the Legacy of Racial Bias in America

BRYAN STEVENSON

At the end of 2002, there were 3,692 people on death row in the United States. Thirty-eight of the 50 states have death penalty statutes. Since the death penalty was resurrected in 1976, there have been over 800 executions, 89 percent of which have occurred in the American South. Women, juveniles, and the mentally ill are among the hundreds who have been shot, electrocuted, asphyxiated, hanged, and injected with lethal poisons by state governments in America. Most of these executions have taken place in the last ten years, as support for capital punishment has acquired greater political resonance and as federal courts have retreated from the degree of oversight and review that existed in the early 1980s. In the last year of the twentieth century, the world's "leading democracy" executed close to 100 of its residents. All of the executed were poor, a disproportionately high number were racial minorities convicted of killing white victims, many of the executed were mentally ill, and some were juveniles at the time their crimes occurred. There is no meaningful assurance that all of the executed were guilty.

Injustices such as those that occurred in Walter McMillian's case unfortunately are far from rare. In recent years, there has been a steady drumroll of exonerations of erroneously convicted criminal defendants. These revelations have served to focus attention on the various actions of judges, prosecutors, and police officers that may cause or contribute to erroneous convictions or improper death sentences. Instances where exculpatory evidence has been withheld by the police or prosecutors, reliance on jailhouse informants or snitches, erroneous jury instructions, bias on the part of judges or jurors, incompetent or corrupt forensic "experts," and ineffective assistance from defense counsel have all been documented as causing innocent people to be wrongly convicted and sentenced to death.

Closer scrutiny of the operation of the death penalty has also resulted in greater awareness of some of the capital punishment system's other abuses. These include the imposition of capital punishment on the most vulnerable offenders—the mentally retarded, the mentally ill, juveniles and foreign nationals. Although the Supreme Court declared in June 2002 that execution of mentally retarded persons violates the Eighth Amendment, the United States remains among the small number of nations that permit the execution of individuals who were under the age of 18 at the time of the crime. Most of my practice has been in Alabama, which has the largest number of death-sentenced juveniles per capita in the country. I have frequently dealt with the especially troubling issues generated by legal representation of 16- and 17-year-old children who have been sentenced to death. At present, 7 percent of Alabama's death row—14 people—were sentenced for crimes they were convicted of committing at the age of 16 or 17. In Texas, 6 percent of death row is made up of juveniles. Alabama and Texas have 51 percent of all juveniles currently sentenced to death in America. A less examined but equally troubling aspect of the juvenile death penalty are the hundreds of even younger children, many 13 and 14 years of age, who have been prosecuted for capital crimes and "mercifully spared of the death penalty" and sentenced to life imprisonment without parole. It is only in a country in which the juvenile death penalty exists that a sentence of life imprisonment without parole for a 14-year-old could be considered "lenient."

Serious problems plague the administration of the death penalty in the United States. The inability of the poor to receive adequate legal representation is the core problem surrounding capital punishment. However, the pervasive and indelible taint

From "Capital Punishment and the Legacy of Racial Bias" by Bryan Stevenson in *Debating the Death Penalty*, ed. Hugo Bedau and Paul Cassell, 82, 84–88.

of racial discrimination also reveals a fundamental problem endemic to capital punishment that implicates American society in a significant way that transcends the administration of criminal justice. Although the capital punishment system's other systemic problems are certainly worthy of discussion as well, the endemic racial bias issues provide a particularly useful vehicle for demonstrating that the death penalty should be abandoned in this country.

The most glaringly obvious symptom of the dysfunctions of the American criminal justice process, readily apparent to even the most casual observer, is the stark overrepresentation of people of color (primarily African Americans and Latinos) in the ranks of those who are prosecuted for crimes in the United States. One out of three African American men between the ages of 18 and 35 is in jail, in prison, on probation, or on parole in the United States. Evidence of disparate treatment of racial minorities becomes more pronounced at each juncture of the criminal justice process (arrest, filing of charges, pretrial detention, conviction, and incarceration) as systemic decision makers (police officers, prosecutors, and judges), who tend to be predominantly white, frequently exercise their discretion in ways that disfavor people of color. Even though there is evidence of disproportionately high involvement by African Americans and Latinos in some criminal offense categories, the disparities in arrest, sentencing, and incarceration persist even when offender rates are racially proportionate. For example, people of color are disproportionately represented among those arrested, prosecuted, convicted, and sentenced to prison for drug offenses. While African Americans make up 13 percent of the nation's monthly drug users, they represent 35 percent of those arrested for drug possession, 53 percent of those convicted of drug offenses, and 75 percent of those sentenced to prison in this offense category.

When the Supreme Court struck down the use of capital punishment in 1972 in *Furman v. Georgia*, some of the Justices frankly acknowledged the existence of racial bias in this country's administration of the death penalty. When the Court thereafter upheld the constitutionality of capital punishment in 1976 in *Gregg v. Georgia* and

its companion cases, the Court refused to presume that historic racial bias could not be remedied. On being presented with the relevant empirical data in *McCleskey v. Kemp* in 1987—data that documented the existence of racial bias in Georgia's use of the death penalty—the Court did not deny the taint of racial bias. Indeed, the Court freely admitted that race-based sentencing disparities are "an inevitable part of our criminal justice system." Expressing the concern that responding to racial bias in death penalty cases might necessarily require confronting racial bias in other criminal cases, the Court concluded that the Constitution does not place such "totally unrealistic conditions" on the use of capital punishment or the administration of criminal justice.

It seems unimaginable that the Supreme Court of the United States, an institution vested with the responsibility to achieve "equal justice under the law," could issue an opinion that condones the existence of racial bias in the criminal justice system, particularly in the application of a penalty as grave and irrevocable as capital punishment. However, it is precisely this acceptance of bias and the tolerance of racial discrimination that has come to define America's criminal justice system, including the administration of the death penalty.

In the years since the *McCleskey* decision was issued in 1987, the evidence of racial bias in the capital punishment system has continued to mount. A report by the United States General Accounting Office in 1990 concluded that 82 percent of the empirically valid studies on the subject show that the race of the victim has an impact on capital charging decisions or sentencing verdicts or both. A 1998 study by David Baldus, whose earlier data had been presented to the Court in *McCleskey*, found—on the basis of data from 27 of the 37 states that have employed the death penalty since the *Furman* decision in 1972—that more than 90 percent of these jurisdictions exhibit patterns of racial bias in capital charging or sentencing of defendants accused of killing white victims. In 2000, a review of the federal death penalty revealed similar racial disparities in sentencing and charging decisions. President Clinton and Attorney General Janet Reno concluded that a moratorium on federal executions was necessary to conduct a further study of the problem. That study was abandoned in 2001 by newly appointed Attorney General John Ashcroft, who asserted that a supplemental study showed "no evidence of racial bias in the administration of the federal death penalty" and who declared that the Department of Justice would not suspend executions on the basis of doubts about racial fairness.

In some capital cases, the existence of racial bias is overt and graphic. The Supreme Court vacated the death sentence of Victor Saldano in 2000 after the attorney general of Texas conceded that the "prosecution's introduction of race as a factor for determining 'future dangerousness' constituted a violation of the appellant's right to equal protection and due process." At trial, the state's expert testified at the penalty phase that one of the factors associated with a defendant's future dangerousness was his race or ethnicity. The state's "expert" identified the Argentinean defendant as Hispanic and relied on the overrepresentation of black and brown people in prison to support his assumption about the correlation between race and dangerousness. After the United States Supreme Court vacated the sentence based on the Texas attorney general's confession of error, the Texas Court of Criminal Appeals reinstated the death sentence. The Texas court concluded that the attorney general had no authority to confess error in a death penalty case appealed to a federal court.

Many appellate courts have shown a willingness to excuse overt racial bias in death penalty cases. Anthony Ray Peek, an African American, was wrongly convicted of capital murder and

sentenced to death in Florida after a white trial judge improperly admitted evidence and expedited the penalty phase proceedings by stating from the bench, "Since the nigger mom and dad are here anyway, why don't we go ahead and do the penalty phase today instead of having to subpoena them back at cost to the state." Mr. Peek was sentenced to death. On appeal, the Florida Supreme Court reversed Mr. Peek's conviction on evidentiary grounds not directly related to the racist comments made by the judge. With regard to the defendant's arguments concerning the racial bigotry exhibited by the judge, the court, in a one-paragraph analysis, merely admonished state trial court judges to "convey the image of impartiality." Mr. Peek was retried in front of a different judge and acquitted.

In 1989, a federal judge found that Wilburn Dobbs was tried by a state court judge who had spent his life and career defending racial segregation and who would only refer to Mr. Dobbs at trial as "colored" or "colored boy." Dobbs was convicted by a jury, some of whom later revealed that they believed that the Ku Klux Klan did good things in the community and that black people are more violent than whites. Mr. Dobbs was defended by an attorney whose racist views included a belief that black people are morally inferior, less intelligent, and biologically destined to steal. The District Court and the Eleventh Circuit nevertheless affirmed Mr. Dobbs's conviction and death sentence. The lower court rulings eventually were reversed by the United States Supreme Court on other grounds.

ARGUMENT 12 ESSAY QUESTIONS

1. Does Stevenson's argument show that the death penalty itself is unjust? Why or why not?

2. Do you think the death penalty is imposed unfairly on minorities? If so, what are your reasons? If not, why not?

3. Cassell argues that statistics do not support the charge that the death penalty is administered unfairly against blacks. How does he support this claim? Do you agree with him? Explain.

13. THE DETERRENCE ARGUMENT FOR THE DEATH PENALTY

Many retentionists argue that the death penalty is morally justified because it deters capital crimes (namely, first-degree murders). Since it dissuades would-be killers from taking innocent lives, it is justified on utilitarian grounds, by its enormous benefit to society.

To support the deterrence claim, retentionists typically cite relevant scientific research. For example:

> [Researchers] of the Department of Economics at Emory University have recently [2001] published the most comprehensive analysis of the American death penalty data.... The Emory researchers analyzed data for 3,054 American counties over the period 1977 to 1996, controlling for such variables as police and judicial resources devoted to crime, economic indicators, and other potentially confounding influences on the murder rate. The Emory researchers found that, in general, murder rates fell as more murderers were arrested, sentenced, and—most important for present purposes—executed. In particular, they concluded that each additional execution during this period of time resulted, on average, in 18 fewer murders.[19]

Controlling all the variables in such research, however, is difficult, and abolitionists (and some retentionists) believe that the results so far have been inconclusive.

In "On Deterrence and the Death Penalty," Ernest van den Haag admits that the deterrence value of the death penalty is difficult to assess. Nevertheless he argues that our most prudent and moral option is to bet that the death penalty does indeed dissuade murderers. Reasoning in a utilitarian vein, he says we have only two choices—to apply the death penalty or not to apply it. To apply it is to risk killing murderers but save innocent people who would be the murderers' victims; not to apply it (to abolish capital punishment) is to risk the deaths of the innocent victims but spare the lives of the killers. Van den Haag argues that if we must risk lives either way, we should risk the lives of murderers rather than the lives of innocents. Therefore, we should continue to use capital punishment against murderers.

Many proponents of the death penalty believe that even without indisputable scientific evidence, a good case can be made for deterrence by appealing to common sense. Louis Pojman lays out a commonsense argument like this:

1. What people (including potential criminals) fear more will have a greater deterrent effect on them.
2. People (including potential criminals) fear death more than they do any other humane punishment.
3. The death penalty is a humane punishment.

---

[19]   Paul G. Cassell, *Debating the Death Penalty*, 195.

4. Therefore, people (including criminals) will be deterred more by the death penalty than by any other humane punishment.[20]

Pojman thinks several obvious facts support the second premise:

… [A] great deal of crime is committed on a cost-benefit schema, wherein the criminal engages in some form of risk assessment as to his or her chances of getting caught and punished in some manner. If he or she estimates the punishment mild, the crime becomes inversely attractive, and vice versa. The fact that those who are condemned to death do everything in their power to get their sentences postponed or reduced to long-term prison sentences, in the way *lifers* do not, shows that they fear death more than life in prison.[21]

But abolitionists have their own commonsense reasons for doubting that the death penalty deters as well as retentionists think. For one thing, as Hugo Adam Bedau says, "A punishment can be an effective deterrent only if it is consistently and promptly employed. Capital punishment cannot be administered to meet these conditions."[22] Few first-degree murderers are sentenced to death, few of these are actually executed, and all executions occur many months or years after the crime is committed. In addition, most murders are committed by people who do not calculate the risks and benefits of their actions. They kill in the heat of the moment. And from the fact that would-be killers fear the death penalty more than life in prison, we cannot conclude that the death penalty deters better.

On Deterrence and the Death Penalty

ERNEST VAN DEN HAAG

I

If rehabilitation and the protection of society from unrehabilitated offenders were the only purposes of legal punishment the death penalty could be abolished: it cannot attain the first end, and is not needed for the second. No case for the death penalty can be made unless "doing justice," or "deterring others," are among our penal aims.[1] Each of these purposes can justify capital punishment by itself; opponents, therefore, must show that neither actually does, while proponents can rest their case on either.

Although the argument from justice is intellectually more interesting, and, in my view, decisive enough, utilitarian arguments have more appeal: the claim that capital punishment is useless because it does not deter others, is most persuasive. I shall, therefore, focus on this claim. Lest the argument be thought

From "On Deterrence and the Death Penalty" by Ernest Van Den Haag in *Journal of Criminal Law, Criminology, and Police Science*, vol. 60, no. 2, (June 1969), 141–147. © Northwestern School of Law.

---

[20] Louis P. Pojman, "Why the Death Penalty Is Morally Permissible," in *Debating the Death Penalty*, ed. Hugo Bedau and Paul Cassell (New York: Oxford University Press, 2004), 60.

[21] Louis P. Pojman, *Debating the Death Penalty*, 61.

[22] Hugo Adam Bedau, "The Case Against the Death Penalty," ACLU, 1997.

to be unduly narrow, I shall show, nonetheless, that some claims of injustice rest on premises which the claimants reject when arguments for capital punishment are derived therefrom; while other claims of injustice have no independent standing: their weight depends on the weight given to deterrence.

II

Capital punishment is regarded as unjust because it may lead to the execution of innocents, or because the guilty poor (or disadvantaged) are more likely to be executed than the guilty rich.

Regardless of merit, these claims are relevant only if "doing justice" is one purpose of punishment. Unless one regards it as good, or, at least, better, that the guilty be punished rather than the innocent, and that the equally guilty be punished equally,[2] unless, that is, one wants penalties to be just, one cannot object to them because they are not. However, if one does include justice among the purposes of punishment, it becomes possible to justify any one punishment—even death—on grounds of justice. Yet, those who object to the death penalty because of its alleged injustice, usually deny not only the merits, or the sufficiency, of specific arguments based on justice, but the propriety of justice as an argument: they exclude "doing justice" as a purpose of legal punishment. If justice is not a purpose of penalties, injustice cannot be an objection to the death penalty, or to any other; if it is, justice cannot be ruled out as an argument for any penalty.

Consider the claim of injustice on its merits now. A convicted man may be found to have been innocent; if he was executed, the penalty cannot be reversed. Except for fines, penalties never can be reversed. Time spent in prison cannot be returned. However, a prison sentence may be remitted once the prisoner serving it is found innocent; and he can be compensated for the time served (although compensation ordinarily cannot repair the harm). Thus, though (nearly) all penalties are irreversible, the death penalty, unlike others, is irrevocable as well.

Despite all precautions, errors will occur in judicial proceedings: the innocent may be found guilty;[3] or the guilty rich may more easily escape conviction, or receive lesser penalties than the guilty poor. However, these injustices do not reside in the penalties inflicted but in their maldistribution. It is not the

penalty—whether death or prison—which is unjust when inflicted on the innocent, but its imposition on the innocent. Inequity between poor and rich also involves distribution, not the penalty distributed.[4] Thus injustice is not an objection to the death penalty but to the distributive process—the trial. Trials are more likely to be fair when life is at stake—the death penalty is probably less often unjustly inflicted than others. It requires special consideration not because it is more, or more often, unjust than other penalties, but because it is always irrevocable.

Can any amount of deterrence justify the possibility of irrevocable injustice? Surely injustice is unjustifiable in each actual individual case; it must be objected to whenever it occurs. But we are concerned here with the process that may produce injustice, and with the penalty that would make it irrevocable—not with the actual individual cases produced, but with the general rules which may produce them. To consider objections to a general rule (the provision of any penalties by law) we must compare the likely net result of alternative rules and select the rule (or penalty) likely to produce the least injustice. For however one defines justice, to support it cannot mean less than to favor the least injustice. If the death of innocents because of judicial error is unjust, so is the death of innocents by murder. If some murders could be avoided by a penalty conceivably more deterrent than others—such as the death penalty—then the question becomes: which penalty will minimize the number of innocents killed (by crime and by punishment)? It follows that the irrevocable injustice sometimes inflicted by the death penalty would not significantly militate against it, if capital punishment deters enough murders to reduce the total number of innocents killed so that fewer are lost than would be lost without it.

In general, the possibility of injustice argues against penalization of any kind only if the expected usefulness of penalization is less important than the probable harm (particularly to innocents) and the probable inequities. The possibility of injustice argues against the death penalty only inasmuch as the added usefulness (deterrence) expected from irrevocability is thought less important than the added harm. (Were my argument specifically concerned with justice, I could compare the injustice inflicted by the courts with the injustice—outside the courts—avoided by the judicial process. I.e., "important" here may be used to include everything to which importance is attached.)

We must briefly examine now the general use and effectiveness of deterrence to decide whether the death penalty could add enough deterrence to be warranted.

III

Does any punishment "deter others" at all? Doubts have been thrown on this effect because it is thought to depend on the incorrect rationalistic psychology of some of its 18th and 19th century proponents. Actually deterrence does not depend on rational calculation, on rationality or even on capacity for it; nor do arguments for it depend on rationalistic psychology. Deterrence depends on the likelihood and on the regularity—not on the rationality—of human responses to danger; and further on the possibility of reinforcing internal controls by vicarious external experiences.

Responsiveness to danger is generally found in human behavior; the danger can, but need not, come from the law or from society; nor need it be explicitly verbalized. Unless intent on suicide, people do not jump from high mountain cliffs, however tempted to fly through the air; and they take precautions against falling. The mere risk of injury often restrains us from doing what is otherwise attractive; we refrain even when we have no direct experience, and usually without explicit computation of probabilities, let alone conscious weighing of expected pleasure against possible pain. One abstains from dangerous acts because of vague, inchoate, habitual and, above all, pre-conscious fears. Risks and rewards are more often felt than calculated; one abstains without accounting to oneself, because "it isn't done," or because one literally does not conceive of the action one refrains from. Animals as well refrain from painful or injurious experiences presumably without calculation; and the threat of punishment can be used to regulate their conduct.

Unlike natural dangers, legal threats are constructed deliberately by legislators to restrain actions which may impair the social order. Thus legislation transforms social into individual dangers. Most people further transform external into internal danger: they acquire a sense of moral obligation, a conscience, which threatens them, should they do what is wrong. Arising originally from the external authority of rulers and rules, conscience is internalized and becomes independent of external forces. However, conscience is constantly reinforced in those whom it controls by the coercive imposition of external authority on recalcitrants and on those who have not acquired it. Most people refrain from offenses because they feel an obligation to behave lawfully. But this obligation would scarcely be felt if those who do not feel or follow it were not to suffer punishment.

Although the legislators may calculate their threats and the responses to be produced, the effectiveness of the threats neither requires nor depends on calculations by those responding. The predictor (or producer) of effects must calculate; those whose responses are predicted (or produced) need not. Hence, although legislation (and legislators) should be rational, subjects, to be deterred as intended, need not be: they need only be responsive.

Punishments deter those who have not violated the law for the same reasons—and in the same degrees (apart from internalization: moral obligation) as do natural dangers. Often natural dangers—all dangers not deliberately created by legislation (e.g., injury of the criminal inflicted by the crime victim) are insufficient. Thus, the fear of injury (natural danger) does not suffice to control city traffic; it must be reinforced by the legal punishment meted out to those who violate the rules. These punishments keep most people observing the regulations. However, where (in the absence of natural danger) the threatened punishment is so light that the advantage of violating rules tends to exceed the disadvantage of being punished (divided by the risk), the rule is violated (i.e., parking fines are too light). In this case the feeling of obligation tends to vanish as well. Elsewhere punishment deters.

To be sure, not everybody responds to threatened punishment. Non-responsive persons may be a) self-destructive or b) incapable of responding to threats, or even of grasping them. Increases in the size, or certainty, of penalties would not affect these two groups. A third group c) might respond to more certain or more severe penalties.[5] If the punishment threatened for burglary, robbery, or rape were a $5 fine in North Carolina, and 5 years in prison in South Carolina, I have no doubt that the North Carolina treasury would become quite opulent until vigilante justice would provide the deterrence not provided by law. Whether to increase penalties (or improve enforcement), depends on the importance of the rule to society, the size and likely reaction of the group that did not respond before, and the acceptance of the added punishment and enforcement required to deter it. Observation would have to locate the points—likely to differ in different times and places—at which diminishing, zero, and negative returns set in. There is no reason to believe that all present and future offenders belong to the *a priori* non-responsive groups, or that all penalties have reached the point of diminishing, let alone zero returns.

IV

Even though its effectiveness seems obvious, punishment as a deterrent has fallen into disrepute. Some ideas which help explain this progressive heedlessness were uttered by Lester Pearson, then Prime Minister of Canada, when, in opposing the death penalty, he proposed that instead "the state seek to eradicate the causes of crime—slums, ghettos and personality disorders."[6]

"Slums, ghettos and personality disorders" have not been shown, singly or collectively, to be "the causes" of crime.

(1) The crime rate in the slums is indeed higher than elsewhere; but so is the death rate in hospitals. Slums are no more "causes" of crime, than hospitals are of death; they are locations of crime, as hospitals are of death. Slums and hospitals attract people selectively; neither is the "cause" of the condition (disease in hospitals, poverty in slums) that leads to the selective attraction.

As for poverty which draws people into slums, and, sometimes, into crime, any relative disadvantage may lead to ambition, frustration, resentment and, if insufficiently restrained, to crime. Not all relative disadvantages can be eliminated; indeed very few can be, and their elimination increases the resentment generated by the remaining ones; not even relative poverty can be removed altogether. (Absolute poverty—whatever that may be—hardly affects crime.) However, though contributory, relative disadvantages are not a necessary or sufficient cause of crime: most poor people do not commit crimes, and some rich people do. Hence,

"eradication of poverty" would, at most, remove one (doubtful) cause of crime.

In the United States, the decline of poverty has not been associated with a reduction of crime. Poverty measured in dollars of constant purchasing power, according to present government standards and statistics, was the condition of 1/2 of all our families in 1920; of 1/5th in 1962; and of less than 1/6 in 1966. In 1967, 5.3 million families out of 49.8 million were poor—1/9 of all families in the United States. If crime has been reduced in a similar manner, it is a well kept secret.

Those who regard poverty as a cause of crime often draw a wrong inference from a true proposition: the rich will not commit certain crimes—Rockefeller never riots; nor does he steal. (He mugs, but only on T.V.) Yet while wealth may be the cause of not committing (certain) crimes, it does not follow that poverty (absence of wealth) is the cause of committing them. Water extinguishes or prevents fire; but its absence is not the cause of fire. Thus, if poverty could be abolished, if everybody had all "necessities" (I don't pretend to know what this would mean), crime would remain, for, in the words of Aristoteles "the greatest crimes are committed not for the sake of basic necessities but for the sake of superfluities." Superfluities cannot be provided by the government; they would be what the government does not provide.

(2) Negro ghettos have a high, Chinese ghettos have a low crime rate. Ethnic separation, voluntary or forced, obviously has little to do with crime; I can think of no reason why it should.[7]

(3) I cannot see how the state could "eradicate" personality disorders even if all causes and cures were known and available. (They are not.) Further, the known incidence of personality disorders within the prison population does not exceed the known incidence outside—though our knowledge of both is tenuous. Nor are personality disorders necessary, or sufficient causes for criminal offenses, unless these be identified by means of (moral, not clinical) definition with personality disorders. In this case, Mr. Pearson would have proposed to "eradicate" crime by eradicating crime—certainly a sound, but not a helpful idea.

Mr. Pearson's views are part as well of the mental furniture of the former U.S. Attorney General, Ramsey Clark, who told a congressional committee that "…only the elimination of the causes of crime can make a significant and lasting difference in the incidence of crime." Uncharitably interpreted, Mr. Clark revealed that only the elimination of causes eliminates effects—a sleazy cliche and wrong to boot. Given the benefit of the doubt, Mr. Clark probably meant that the causes of crime are social; and that therefore crime can be reduced "only" by non-penal (social) measures.

This view suggests a fireman who declines fire-fighting apparatus by pointing out that "in the long run only the elimination of the causes" of fire "can make a significant and lasting difference in the incidence" of fire, and that fire-fighting equipment does not eliminate "the causes"—except that such a fireman would probably not rise to fire chief. Actually, whether fires are checked, depends on equipment and on the efforts of the firemen using it no less than on the presence of "the causes": inflammable materials. So with crimes. Laws, courts and police actions are no less important in restraining them, than "the causes" are in impelling them. If firemen (or attorneys general) pass the buck and refuse to use the means available, we may all be burned while waiting for "the long run" and "the elimination of the causes."

Whether any activity—be it lawful or unlawful—takes place depends on whether the desire for it, or for whatever is to be secured by it, is stronger than the desire to avoid the costs involved. Accordingly people work, attend college, commit crimes, go to the movies—or refrain from any of these activities. Attendance at a theatre may be high because the show is entertaining and because the price of admission is low. Obviously the attendance depends on both—on the combination of expected gratification and cost. The wish, motive or impulse for doing anything—the experienced, or expected, gratification—is the cause of doing it; the wish to avoid the cost is the cause of not doing it. One is no more and no less "cause" than the other. (Common speech supports this use of "cause" no less than logic: "Why did you go to Jamaica?" "*Because* it is such a beautiful place." "Why didn't you go to Jamaica?" "*Because* it is too expensive."—"Why do you buy this?" "*Because* it is so cheap." "Why don't you buy that?" "*Because* it is too expensive.") Penalties (costs) are causes of lawfulness, or (if too low or uncertain) of unlawfulness, of crime. People do commit crimes because, given their conditions, the desire for the

satisfaction sought prevails. They refrain if the desire to avoid the cost prevails. Given the desire, low cost (penalty) causes the action, and high cost restraint. Given the cost, desire becomes the causal variable. Neither is intrinsically more causal than the other. The crime rate increases if the cost is reduced or the desire raised. It can be decreased by raising the cost or by reducing the desire.

The cost of crime is more easily and swiftly changed than the conditions producing the inclination to it. Further, the costs are very largely within the power of the government to change, whereas the conditions producing propensity to crime are often only indirectly affected by government action, and some are altogether beyond the control of the government. Our unilateral emphasis on these conditions and our undue neglect of costs may contribute to an unnecessarily high crime rate.

V

The foregoing suggests the question posed by the death penalty: is the deterrence added (return) sufficiently above zero to warrant irrevocability (or other, less clear, disadvantages)? The question is not only whether the penalty deters, but whether it deters more than alternatives and whether the difference exceeds the cost of irrevocability. (I shall assume that the alternative is actual life imprisonment so as to exclude the complication produced by the release of the unrehabilitated.)

In some fairly infrequent but important circumstances the death penalty is the only possible deterrent. Thus, in case of acute *coups d'état*, or of acute substantial attempts to overthrow the government, prospective rebels would altogether discount the threat of any prison sentence. They would not be deterred because they believe the swift victory of the revolution will invalidate a prison sentence and turn it into an advantage. Execution would be the only deterrent because, unlike prison sentences, it cannot be revoked by victorious rebels. The same reasoning applies to deterring spies or traitors in wartime. Finally, men who, by virtue of past acts, are already serving, or are threatened, by a life sentence, could be deterred from further offenses only by the threat of the death penalty.[8]

What about criminals who do not fall into any of these (often ignored) classes? Prof. Thorsten Sellin has made a careful study of the available statistics: he concluded that they do not yield evidence for the deterring effect of the death penalty.[9] Somewhat surprisingly, Prof. Sellin seems to think that this lack of evidence for deterrence is evidence for the lack of deterrence. It is not. It means that deterrence has not been demonstrated statistically—not that non-deterrence has been.

It is entirely possible, indeed likely (as Prof. Sellin appears willing to concede), that the statistics used, though the best available, are nonetheless too slender a reed to rest conclusions on. They indicate that the homicide rate does not vary greatly between similar areas with or without the death penalty, and in the same area before and after abolition. However, the similar areas are not similar enough; the periods are not long enough; many social differences and changes, other than the abolition of the death penalty, may account for the variation (or lack of) in homicide rates with and without, before and after abolition; some of these social differences and changes are likely to have affected homicide rates. I am unaware of any statistical analysis which adjusts for such changes and differences. And logically, it is quite consistent with the postulated deterrent effect of capital punishment that there be less homicide after abolition: with retention there might have been still less.

Homicide rates do not depend exclusively on penalties any more than do other crime rates. A number of conditions which influence the propensity to crime, demographic, economic or generally social, changes or differences—even such matters as changes of the divorce laws or of the cotton price—may influence the homicide rate. Therefore variation or constancy cannot be attributed to variations or constancy of the penalties, unless we know that no other factor influencing the homicide rate has changed. Usually we don't. To believe the death penalty deterrent does not require one to believe that the death penalty, or any other, is the only, or the decisive causal variable; this would be as absurd as the converse mistake that "social causes" are the only, or always the decisive factor. To favor capital punishment, the efficacy of neither variable need be denied. It is enough to affirm that the severity of the penalty may influence some potential criminals, and that the added severity of the death penalty adds to deterrence, or may do so. It is quite possible that such a deterrent effect may be offset (or intensified) by non-penal factors which affect propensity; its presence or absence therefore may be hard, and perhaps impossible to demonstrate.

Contrary to what Prof. Sellin et al. seem to presume, I doubt that offenders are aware of the absence or presence of the death penalty state by state or period by period. Such unawareness argues against the assumption of a calculating murderer. However, unawareness does not argue against the death penalty if by deterrence we mean a preconscious, general response to a severe, but not necessarily specifically and explicitly apprehended, or calculated threat. A constant homicide rate, despite abolition, may occur because of unawareness and not because of lack of deterrence: people remain deterred for a lengthy interval by the severity of the penalty in the past, or by the severity of penalties used in similar circumstances nearby.

I do not argue for a version of deterrence which would require me to believe that an individual shuns murder while in North Dakota, because of the death penalty, and merrily goes to it in South Dakota since it has been abolished there; or that he will start the murderous career from which he had hitherto refrained, after abolition. I hold that the generalized threat of the death penalty may be a deterrent, and the more so, the more generally applied. Deterrence will not cease in the particular areas of abolition or at the particular times of abolition. Rather, general deterrence will be somewhat weakened, through local (partial) abolition. Even such weakening will be hard to detect owing to changes in many offsetting, or reinforcing, factors.

For all of these reasons, I doubt that the presence or absence of a deterrent effect of the death penalty is likely to be demonstrable by statistical means. The statistics presented by Prof. Sellin et al. show only that there is no statistical proof for the deterrent effect of the death penalty. But they do not show that there is no deterrent effect. Not to demonstrate presence of the effect is not the same as to demonstrate its absence; certainly not when there are plausible explanations for the non-demonstrability of the effect.

It is on our uncertainty that the case for deterrence must rest.[10]

VI

If we do not know whether the death penalty will deter others, we are confronted with two uncertainties. If we impose the death penalty, and achieve no deterrent effect thereby, the life of a convicted murderer has been expended in vain (from a deterrent viewpoint). There is a net loss. If we impose the death sentence and thereby deter some future murderers, we spared the lives of some future victims (the prospective murderers gain too; they are spared punishment because they were deterred). In this case, the death penalty has led to a net gain, unless the life of a convicted murderer is valued more highly than that of the unknown victim, or victims (and the non-imprisonment of the deterred non-murderer).

The calculation can be turned around, of course. The absence of the death penalty may harm no one and therefore produce a gain—the life of the convicted murderer. Or it may kill future victims of murderers who could have been deterred, and thus produce a loss—their life.

To be sure, we must risk something certain—the death (or life) of the convicted man, for something uncertain—the death (or life) of the victims of murderers who may be deterred. This is in the nature of uncertainty—when we invest, or gamble, we risk the money we have for an uncertain gain. Many human actions, most commitments—including marriage and crime—share this characteristic with the deterrent purpose of any penalization, and with its rehabilitative purpose (and even with the protective).

More proof is demanded for the deterrent effect of the death penalty than is demanded for the deterrent effect of other penalties. This is not justified by the absence of other utilitarian purposes such as protection and rehabilitation; they involve no less uncertainty than deterrence.[11]

Irrevocability may support a demand for some reason to expect more deterrence than revocable penalties might produce, but not a demand for more proof of deterrence, as has been pointed out above. The reason for expecting more deterrence lies in the greater severity, the terrifying effect inherent in finality. Since it seems more important to spare victims than to spare murderers, the burden of proving that the greater severity inherent in irrevocability adds nothing to deterrence lies on those who oppose capital punishment. Proponents of the death penalty need show only that there is no more uncertainty about it than about greater severity in general.

The demand that the death penalty be proved more deterrent than alternatives cannot be satisfied any more than the demand that six years in prison be proved to be more deterrent than three. But the uncertainty which confronts us favors the death penalty as long as by imposing it we might save future victims of murder. This effect is as plausible as the general idea that penalties have deterrent effects which increase with their severity. Though we have no proof of the positive deterrence of the penalty, we also have no proof of zero, or negative effectiveness. I believe we have no right to risk additional future victims of murder for the sake of sparing convicted murderers; on the contrary, our moral obligation is to risk the possible ineffectiveness of executions. However rationalized, the opposite view appears to be motivated by the simple fact that executions are more subjected to social control than murder. However, this applies to all penalties and does not argue for the abolition of any.

NOTES

1. Social solidarity or "community feeling" (here to be ignored) might be dealt with as a form of deterrence.
2. Certainly a major meaning of *suum cuique tribue*.
3. I am not concerned here with the converse injustice, *which I regard as no less grave*.
4. Such inequity, though likely, has not been demonstrated. Note that, since there are more poor than rich, there are likely to be more guilty poor; and, if poverty contributes to crime, the proportion of the poor who are criminals also should be higher than that of the rich.
5. I neglect those motivated by civil disobedience or, generally, moral or political passion. Deterring them depends less on penalties than on the moral support they receive, though penalties play a role. I also neglect those who may belong to all three groups listed, some successively, some even simultaneously, such as drug addicts. Finally, I must altogether omit the far from negligible role problems of apprehension and conviction play in deterrence—beyond saying that by reducing the government's ability to

apprehend and convict, courts are able to reduce the risks of offenders.

6. *N.Y. Times*, Nov. 24, 1967, at 22. The actual psychological and other factors which bear on the disrepute—as distinguished from the rationalizations—cannot be examined here.

7. Mixed areas, incidentally, have higher crime rates than segregated ones. See, e.g., Ross & Van Den Haag, *The Fabric of Society*, 102–4 (1957). Because slums are bad (morally) and crime is, many people seem to reason that "slums spawn crime"—which confuses some sort of moral with a causal relation.

8. Cautious revolutionaries, uncertain of final victory, might be impressed by prison sentences—but not in the acute stage, when faith in victory is high. And one can increase even the severity of a life sentence in prison. Finally, harsh punishment of rebels can intensify rebellious impulses. These points, though they qualify it, hardly impair the force of the argument.

9. Prof. Sellin considered mainly homicide statistics. His work may be found in his *Capital Punishment* (1967), or, most conveniently, in Bedau, *The Death Penalty in America* (1964), which also offers other material, mainly against the death penalty.

10. In view of the strong emotions aroused (itself an indication of effectiveness to me: might murderers not be as upset over the death penalty as those who wish to spare them?) and because I believe penalties must reflect community feeling to be effective, I oppose mandatory death sentences and favor optional recommendations by juries after their finding of guilt. The opposite course risks the non-conviction of guilty defendants by juries who do not want to see them executed.

11. Rehabilitation or protection are of minor importance in our actual penal system (though not in our theory). We confine many people who do not need rehabilitation and against whom we do not need protection (e.g., the exasperated husband who killed his wife); we release many unrehabilitated offenders against whom protection is needed. Certainly rehabilitation and protection are not, and deterrence is, the main actual function of legal punishment, if we disregard non-utilitarian purposes.

Capital Punishment and Social Defense

HUGO ADAM BEDAU

THE ANALOGY WITH SELF-DEFENSE

Capital punishment, it is sometimes said, is to the body politic what self-defense is to the individual. If the latter is not morally wrong, how can the former be? To assess the strength of this analogy, we need first to inspect the morality of self-defense.

Except for absolute pacifists, who believe it is morally wrong to use violence even to defend themselves or others from undeserved aggression, most of us believe that it is not morally wrong and may even be our moral duty to use violence to prevent aggression directed against either ourselves or innocent third parties. The law has long granted persons the right to defend themselves against the unjust aggressions of others, even to the extent of using lethal force to kill an assailant. It is very difficult to think of any convincing argument that would show it is never rational to risk the death of another to prevent death or grave injury to oneself. Certainly self-interest dictates the legitimacy of self-defense. So does concern for the well-being of others. So also does justice. If it is unfair for one person to inflict undeserved violence on another, then it is hard to see how morality could require the victim to acquiesce in the attempt by another to do so, even if resistance involves risks or injury to the assailant.

From "Capital Punishment and Social Defense" by Hugo Adam Bedau in *Matters of Life and Death*, 3rd ed., ed. Tom Regan, 177–185. © 1993 New York: McGraw-Hill.

The foregoing account assumes that the person acting in self-defense is innocent of any provocation of the assailant. It also assumes that there is no alternative to victimization except resistance. In actual life, both assumptions—especially the second—are often false, because there may be a third alternative: escape, or removing oneself from the scene of imminent aggression. Hence, the law imposes on us the "duty to retreat." Before we use violence to resist aggression, we must try to get out of the way, lest unnecessary violence be used to resist aggression. Now suppose that unjust aggression is imminent, and there is no path open for escape. How much violence may justifiably be used to ward off aggression? The answer is: No more violence than is necessary to prevent the aggressive assault. Violence beyond that is unnecessary and therefore unjustified. We may restate the principle governing the use of violence in self-defense by reference to the concept of "deadly force" by the police in the discharge of their duties. The rule is this: Use of deadly force is justified only to prevent loss of life in immediate jeopardy where a lesser use of force cannot reasonably be expected to save the life that is threatened.

In real life, violence in self-defense in excess of the minimum necessary to prevent aggression, even though it is not justifiable, is often excusable. One cannot always tell what will suffice to deter an aggressor and avoid becoming a victim; thus the law looks with a certain tolerance upon the frightened and innocent would-be victim who in self-protection turns upon a vicious assailant and inflicts a fatal injury even though a lesser injury would have been sufficient. What is not justified is deliberately using more violence than is necessary to avoid becoming a victim. It is the deliberate, not the impulsive or the unintentional, use of violence that is relevant to the death-penalty controversy, since the death penalty is enacted into law and carried out in each case deliberately—with ample time to weigh alternatives. Notice that we are assuming that the act of self-defense is to protect oneself or a third party. The reasoning outlined here does not extend to the defense of one's property. Shooting a thief to prevent one's automobile from being stolen cannot be excused or justified in the way that shooting an assailant charging with a knife pointed at one's face can be. Our criterion must be that deadly force is never justified to prevent crimes against property or other violent crimes not immediately threatening the life of an innocent person.

The rationale for self-defense as set out above illustrates two moral principles of great importance to our discussion (recall §13). One is that if a life is to be risked, then it is better that it be the life of someone who is guilty (in this context, the initial assailant) rather than the life of someone who is not (the innocent potential victim). It is not fair to expect the innocent prospective victim to run the added risk of severe injury or death in order to avoid using violence in self-defense to the extent of possibly killing his or her assailant. Rather, fairness dictates that the guilty aggressor ought to be the one to run the risk.

The other principle is that taking life deliberately is not justified so long as there is any feasible alternative. One does not expect miracles, of course, but in theory, if shooting a burglar through the foot will stop the burglary and enable one to call the police for help, then there is no reason to shoot to kill. Likewise, if the burglar is unarmed, there is no reason to shoot at all. In actual life, of course, a burglar is likely to be shot at by an aroused householder who does not know whether the burglar is armed, and prudence may seem to dictate the assumption that he or she is. Even so, although the burglar has no right to commit a felony against a person or a person's property, the attempt does not give the victims the right to respond in whatever way they please, and then to excuse or justify such conduct on the ground that they were "only acting in self-defense." In these ways the law shows a tacit regard for the life even of a felon and discourages the use of unnecessary violence even by the innocent; morality can hardly do less.

DETERRENCE, INCAPACITATION, AND CRIME PREVENTION

The analogy with self-defense leads naturally to the empirical and the conceptual questions surrounding the death penalty as a method of crime prevention. Notice first that crimes can be prevented without recourse to punishment; we do that when we take weapons from offenders, protect targets by bolts and alarms, and educate the public to be less vulnerable to victimization. As for punishment, it prevents crimes by *incapacitation* and by *deterrence*. The two are theoretically independent because they achieve prevention very differently. Executing a murderer prevents crimes by means of *incapacitation* to the extent that the murderer would have committed further crimes if not executed. Incapacitating a murderer will not have any preventive benefits, however, unless the murderer would otherwise have committed some further crimes. (In fact relatively few murderers turn out to be homicidal recidivists.) Nor is killing persons the only way to incapacitate them; isolation and restraints will suffice. Executing a murderer prevents crimes by means of *deterrence* to the extent that others are frightened into not committing any capital crimes by the knowledge that convicted offenders are executed. Thus, successful deterrence is prevention by a psychologically effective threat; incapacitation, if it prevents crimes at all, does so by physically disabling the offender.

THE DEATH PENALTY AND INCAPACITATION

Capital punishment is unusual among penalties because its incapacitative effects limit its deterrent effects. The death penalty can never deter an executed person from further crimes. At most, it incapacitates the executed person from committing them. (Popular discussions of the death penalty are frequently confused because they so often assume that the death penalty is a perfect and infallible deterrent so far as the executed criminal is concerned.) Even more important, it is also wrong to think that in every execution the death penalty has proved to be an infallible crime preventive. True, once an offender has been executed, it is physically impossible for that person to commit any further crimes, since the punishment is totally incapacitative. But incapacitation is not identical with prevention. Prevention by means of incapacitation occurs only if the executed criminal would have committed other crimes if he or she had not been executed and had been punished only in some less incapacitative way (e.g., by imprisonment).

What evidence is there that the incapacitative results of the death penalty are an effective crime preventive? From the study of imprisonment, parole, and release records, this much is clear: If the murderers and other criminals who have been executed are like the murderers who were convicted but not executed, then (1) executing all convicted murderers would have prevented many crimes, including some murders; and (2) convicted murderers, whether inside prison or outside after release, have as good a record of no further criminal activity as any other class of convicted felon.

These facts show that the general public tends to overrate the danger and threat to public safety constituted by the failure to execute every murderer who is caught and convicted. While it would be quite wrong to say that there is no risk such criminals will repeat their crimes—or similar ones—if they are not executed, it would be nearly as erroneous to say that executing every convicted murderer would prevent many horrible crimes. All we know is that such executions would prevent a few such crimes from being committed; we do not know how many or by whom they would have been committed. (Obviously, if we did know we would have tried to prevent them!) This is the nub of the problem. There is no way to know in advance which if any of the incarcerated or released murderers will kill again. It is useful in this connection to remember that the only way to guarantee that no horrible crimes ever occur is to execute *everyone* who might conceivably commit such a crime. Similarly, the only way to guarantee that no convicted murderer ever commits another murder is to execute them all. No modern society has ever done this, and for two hundred years Western societies have been moving steadily in the opposite direction.

These considerations show that our society has implicitly adopted an attitude toward the risk of murder rather like the attitude it has adopted toward the risk of fatality from other causes, such as automobile accidents, lung cancer, or drowning. Since no one knows when or where or upon whom any of these lethal events will fall, it would be too great an invasion of freedom to undertake the severe restrictions that alone would suffice to prevent any such deaths from occurring. It is better to take the risks and keep our freedom than to try to eliminate the risks altogether and lose our freedom in the process. Hence, we have lifeguards at the beach, but swimming is not totally prohibited; smokers are warned, but cigarettes are still legally sold; pedestrians may have the right of way in a crosswalk, but marginally competent drivers are still allowed to operate motor vehicles. Some risk is thereby imposed on the innocent; in the name of our right to freedom, we do not insist on having society protect us at all costs.

THE DEATH PENALTY AND DETERRENCE

Determining whether the death penalty is an effective deterrent is even more difficult than determining its effectiveness as a crime preventive. In general, our knowledge about how penalties deter crimes and whether in fact they do—whom they deter, from which crimes, and under what conditions—is distressingly inexact. Most people nevertheless are convinced that punishments do deter, and that the more severe a punishment is the better it will deter. For half a century, social scientists have studied the questions whether the death penalty is a deterrent and whether it is a better deterrent than the alternative of imprisonment. Their verdict, while not unanimous, is nearly so. Whatever may be true about the deterrence of lesser crimes by other penalties, the deterrence achieved by the death penalty for murder is not measurably any greater than the deterrence achieved by long-term imprisonment. In the nature of the case, the evidence is quite indirect. No one can identify for certain any crimes that did not occur because the would-be offender was deterred by the threat of the death penalty and could not have been deterred by a less severe threat. Likewise, no one can identify any crimes that did occur because the offender was not deterred by the threat of prison even though he or she could have been deterred by the threat of death. Nevertheless, such evidence as we have fails to show that the more severe penalty (death) is really a better deterrent than the less severe penalty (imprisonment) for such crimes as murder.

If the death penalty and long-term imprisonment are equally effective (or ineffective) as deterrents to murder, then the argument for the death penalty on grounds of deterrence is seriously weakened. One of the moral principles identified earlier now comes into play: Unless there is a good reason for choosing a more rather than a less severe punishment for a crime, the less severe penalty is to be preferred. This principle obviously commends itself to anyone who values human life and who concedes that, all other things being equal, less pain and suffering is always

better than more. Human life is valued in part to the degree that it is free of pain, suffering, misery, and frustration, and in particular to the extent that it is free of such experiences when they serve no known purpose. If the death penalty is not a more effective deterrent than imprisonment, then its greater severity amounts to nothing less than gratuitous suffering and deprivation. Accordingly, we must reject it in favor of some less severe alternative, unless we can identify some more weighty moral principle that the death penalty serves better and that any less severe mode of punishment ignores. Whether there is any such principle is unclear.

A COST/BENEFIT ANALYSIS OF THE DEATH PENALTY

A full study of the costs and benefits involved in the practice of capital punishment would not be confined solely to the question of whether it is a better deterrent or preventive of murder than imprisonment. Any thoroughgoing utilitarian approach to the death-penalty controversy would need to examine carefully other costs and benefits as well, because maximizing the balance of all the social benefits over all the social costs is the sole criterion of right and wrong according to utilitarianism (recall §8). Let us consider, therefore, some of the other costs and benefits to be calculated. Clinical psychologists have presented evidence to suggest that the death penalty actually incites some persons of unstable mind to murder others, either because they are afraid to take their own lives and hope that society will punish them for murder by putting them to death, or because they fancy that they, too, are killing with justification analogously to the lawful and presumably justified killing involved in capital punishment. If such evidence is sound, capital punishment can serve as a counter-preventive or even an incitement to murder; such incited murders become part of its social cost. Imprisonment, however, has not been known to incite any murders or other crimes of violence in a comparable fashion. (A possible exception might be found in the imprisonment of terrorists, which has inspired other terrorists to take hostages as part of a scheme to force the authorities to release their imprisoned comrades.) The risks of executing the innocent are also part of the social cost. The historical record is replete with innocent persons arrested, indicted, convicted, sentenced, and occasionally legally executed for crimes they did not commit. This is quite apart from the guilty persons unfairly convicted, sentenced to death, and executed on the strength of perjured testimony, fraudulent evidence, subornation of jurors, and other violations of the civil rights and liberties of the accused. Nor is this all. The high costs of a capital trial and of the inevitable appeals, the costly methods of custody most prisons adopt for convicts on "death row," are among the straightforward economic costs that the death penalty incurs. Conducting a valid cost/benefit analysis of capital punishment would be extremely difficult; nevertheless, on the basis of the evidence we have, it is quite possible that such a study would show that abolition of all death penalties is much less costly than their retention.

WHAT IF EXECUTIONS DID DETER?

From the moral point of view, it is quite important to determine what one should think about capital punishment if the evidence were clearly to show that the death penalty is a distinctly superior method of social defense by comparison with less severe alternatives. Kantian moralists, as we have seen (in §5), would have no use for such knowledge, because their entire case for the morality of the death penalty rests on the way it is thought to provide just retribution, not on the way it is thought to provide superior social defense. For a utilitarian, however, such knowledge would be conclusive. Those who follow Locke's reasoning would also be gratified, because they defend the morality of the death penalty both on the ground that it is retributively just and on the ground that it provides needed social defense.

What about the opponents of the death penalty, however? To oppose the death penalty in the face of incontestable evidence that it is an effective method of social defense violates the moral principle that where grave risks are to be run, it is better that they be run by the guilty than by the innocent. Consider in this connection an imaginary world in which executing the murderer would invariably restore the murder victim to life, whole and intact, as though no murder had ever occurred. In such a miraculous world, it is hard to see how anyone could

oppose the death penalty on moral grounds. Why shouldn't a murderer die if that will infallibly bring the innocent victim back to life? What could possibly be morally wrong with taking the murderer's life under such conditions? The death penalty would be an instrument of perfect restitution, and it would give a new and better meaning to *lex talionis*, "a life for a life." The whole idea is fanciful, of course, but it shows as nothing else can how opposition to the death penalty cannot be both moral and wholly unconditional. If opposition to the death penalty is to be morally responsible, then it must be conceded that there are conditions (however unlikely) under which that opposition should cease.

But even if the death penalty were known to be a uniquely effective social defense, we could still imagine conditions under which it would be reasonable to oppose it. Suppose that in addition to being a slightly better preventive and deterrent than imprisonment, executions also have a slight incitive effect (so that for every ten murders an execution prevented or deterred, another murder was incited). Suppose also that the administration of criminal justice in capital cases was inefficient and unequal, and tended to secure convictions and death sentences only for murderers who least "deserved" to be sentenced to death (including some death sentences and a few executions of the innocent). Under such conditions, it would be reasonable to oppose the death penalty, because on the facts supposed more (or not fewer) innocent lives would be threatened and lost by using the death penalty than would be risked by abolishing it. It is important to remember throughout our evaluation of the deterrence controversy that we cannot ever apply the principle (recall §13) that advises us to risk the lives of the guilty to save the lives of the innocent. Instead, we must rely on a weaker principle: Weigh the risk for the general public against the execution of those who are *found* guilty by an imperfect system of criminal justice. These hypothetical factual assumptions illustrate the contingencies upon which the morality of opposition to the death penalty rests. And not only the morality of opposition; the morality of any defense of the death penalty rests on the same contingencies. This should help us understand why, in resolving the morality of capital punishment one way or the other, it is so important to know, as well as we can, whether the death penalty really does prevent or incite crime, whether the innocent really are ever executed, and how likely is the occurrence of these things in the future.

HOW MANY GUILTY LIVES IS ONE INNOCENT LIFE WORTH?

The great unanswered question that utilitarians must face concerns the level of social defense that executions should be expected to achieve before it is justifiable to carry them out. Consider three possible situations: (1) At the level of a hundred executions per year, each additional execution of a convicted murderer reduces the number of murder victims by ten. (2) Executing every convicted murderer reduces the number of murders to 5,000 victims annually, whereas executing only one out of ten reduces the number to 5,001. (3) Executing every convicted murderer reduces the murder rate no more than does executing one in a hundred and no more than does a random pattern of executions.

Many people contemplating situation (1) would regard this as a reasonable trade-off: The execution of each additional guilty person saves the lives of ten innocent ones. (In fact, situation (1) or something like it may be taken as a description of what most of those who defend the death penalty on grounds of social defense believe is true.) But suppose that, instead of saving 10 lives, the number dropped to 0.5, i.e., one victim avoided for each two additional executions. Would that be a reasonable price to pay? We are on the road toward the situation described in (2), where a drastic 90 percent reduction in the number of persons executed causes the level of social defense to drop by only 0.0002 percent. Would it be worth it to execute so many more murderers to obtain such a slight increase in social defense? How many guilty lives is one innocent life worth? (Only those who think that guilty lives are worthless—or of worth equal to that of the innocent—can avoid facing this problem.) In situation (3), of course, there is no basis for executing all convicted murderers, since there is no gain in social defense to show for each additional execution after the first out of each hundred has been executed.

How, then, should we determine which out of each hundred convicted murderers is the unlucky one to be put to death?

If a complete and thoroughgoing cost/benefit analysis of the death penalty were possible, we might be able to answer such questions. But an appeal merely to the moral principle that if lives are to be risked then let it be the lives of the guilty rather than of the innocent will not suffice. (We have already noticed, in §23, that this abstract principle is of little use in the actual administration of criminal justice, because the police and the courts do not deal with the guilty as such but only with those *judged* guilty.) Nor will it suffice to agree that society deserves all the crime prevention and deterrence it can get as a result of inflicting severe punishments. These principles are consistent with too many different policies. They are too vague by themselves to resolve the choice on grounds of social defense when one is confronted with hypothetical situations like those proposed above.

Since no adequate cost/benefit analysis of the death penalty exists, there is no way to resolve these questions from that standpoint at this time. Moreover, it can be argued that we cannot have such an analysis without already establishing in some way or other the relative value of innocent lives versus guilty lives. Far from being a product of cost/benefit analysis, a comparative evaluation of lives would have to be available to us before we undertook any such analysis. Without it, no cost/benefit analysis of this problem can get off the ground. Finally, it must be noted that our knowledge at present does not indicate that we are in anything like the situation described above in (1). On the contrary, from the evidence we do have it seems we achieve about the same deterrent and preventive effects whether we punish murder by death or by imprisonment (recall §21). Something like the situation in (2) or in (3) may therefore be correct. If so, this shows that the choice between the two policies of capital punishment and life imprisonment for murder will probably have to be made on some basis other than social defense; on that basis alone, the two policies are equivalent and therefore equally acceptable.

ARGUMENT 13 ESSAY QUESTIONS

1. What is van den Haag's argument for the deterrence value of capital punishment? Does he prove his case? Explain.
2. What reasons does Bedau give for denying that the death penalty prevents or deters crime? Are his reasons convincing? Why or why not?
3. Do you think that capital punishment deters crime? If so, does the deterrence justify using the death penalty? If not, do you think capital punishment can be justified in other ways? Explain.

SUGGESTIONS FOR FURTHER READING

Hugo Adam Bedau and Paul Cassell, eds., *Debating the Death Penalty* (New York: Oxford University Press, 2004).

Sidney Hook, "The Death Sentence," *The New Leader*, vol. 44 (April 3, 1961).

Burton Leiser, "The Death Penalty Is Permissible," in *Liberty, Justice and Morals* (New York: Macmillan, 1986).

Stephen Nathanson, *An Eye for an Eye?* (Lanham, MD: Rowman & Littlefield, 1987).

Opinion in *Gregg v. Georgia*, United States Supreme Court, 428 U.S. 153 (1976).

Igor Primoratz, "A Life for a Life," from *Justifying Legal Punishment* (Atlantic Highlands, NJ: Humanities Press International, 1989).

Jeffrey H. Reiman, "Justice, Civilization, and the Death Penalty," *Philosophy & Public Affairs*, vol. 14, no. 2 (Spring 1985).

Jeffrey H. Reiman, "Common Sense, the Deterrent Effect of the Death Penalty, and the Best Bet Argument," in Louis P. Pojman and Jeffrey Reiman, The *Death Penalty: For and Against* (Lanham, MD: Rowman and Littlefield, 1998), 102–107.

Ernest van den Haag, "On Deterrence and the Death Penalty," *Journal of Criminal Law, Criminology, and Police Science*, vol. 60, no. 2 (1969).

Ernest van den Haag, "The Ultimate Punishment: A Defense," *Harvard Law Review*, 99 (1986).

CHAPTER 8

War, Terrorism, and Torture

Is war ever morally justified? Can it be reconciled with our commonsense moral proscriptions against killing? Is terrorism morally permissible? Can it be squared with our strong prohibitions against taking the lives of innocents? Can torture ever be right? Can it be permissible even though it conflicts with the bedrock moral principle of respect for persons?

These questions sting, in large part, because they ask us whether we are ever morally justified in knowingly doing horrible evil. War, terrorism, and torture are great evils—that is, they are inherently bad in the same way that pain or starvation is inherently bad, and their badness seems grievous. Can it ever be right to deliberately cause such terrible evil? Aren't people who cause evil, evil? Yet tragic events in the first decade of the twenty-first century have forced thoughtful people to consider whether they, who consider themselves basically good persons, could in some cases be morally right to participate in or condone the evils of war, terrorism, or torture.

WAR

We can identify three main positions on the ethical justification of war: (1) realism, (2) antiwar pacifism, and (3) just war theory. **Realism**, or moral nihilism, regarding war is the view that morality does not apply to warfare, that the categories of right and wrong are irrelevant to actions occurring in war. The only legitimate concerns are the aims and interests of the state and whether war furthers those interests. It makes no sense to say that a war is immoral, only that it does or does not advance state interests. Thus, no means are excluded; no amount of devastation is barred; all's fair in love and war.

Realism can arise from skepticism about morality generally or from the idea that moral standards pertain only to persons and not to states. Nonrealists reject moral skepticism, and they find implausible the notion that morality is irrelevant to states. Commonsense morality, they say, suggests that moral standards and judgments apply even to the chaos and savagery of war. We seem to straightforwardly apply moral norms to warfare and believe that there are some things that should not be done to people even in wartime. The wanton slaughter of children, genocide, mass rape—we generally condemn such horrors regardless of what ends they may serve.

According to **antiwar pacifism**, war is never morally justified. All wars are wrong. For these pacifists, even a war to defend themselves against deadly aggression is impermissible.

Some of them may be absolute pacifists who reject all violence and all killing, and some may allow that using violence in personal self-defense or law enforcement is acceptable. But they all hold that war is always immoral.

Antiwar pacifists may argue that war is wrong because it violates people's right to life or because the bad consequences of war always outweigh whatever good can be gained. Critics charge that the right-to-life view is contradictory: it says people have a right to life and therefore must not be killed, yet it forbids them from defending that right against those who try to violate it. Presumably, having a right not to be harmed implies a right to defend against harm. A typical response to the pacifist's consequentialist argument is that not all wars result in more bad than good. Some wars—perhaps very few—may in the long run prevent the loss of more lives than are lost in the wars themselves. Perhaps a short war against the murderous regime of Pol Pot in Cambodia could have prevented his slaughter of a million innocent people. Maybe a war causing a few hundred casualties could have stopped the genocide in Rwanda that left a million people dead.

Just war theory is the dominant approach to the ethics of war. Systematically expounded by Thomas Aquinas (1225–1274) and elaborated in later centuries by many other thinkers, the theory says that war may be justified provided that certain conditions are met. The doctrine tries to answer two separate questions: When is resorting to war morally permissible (issues known formally as *jus ad bellum*, or "the justice of war")? And what actions are morally permissible in the conduct of war (issues of *jus in bello*, or "justice in war")? Just war theory acknowledges that though war is a terrible evil, we are sometimes morally justified in participating in this evil.

According to principles of *jus ad bellum*, going to war can be justified only if:

1. *The conflict is endorsed by legitimate or competent authority.* This condition is usually understood to refer to the officials of governments or nation-states, but theorists point out that "competent authority" may also apply to revolutionaries, parties to a civil war, and other non-state groups. In any case, private citizens cannot declare war, and spontaneous uprisings do not count as legitimate authority. But the distinction between revolutionaries and organized criminals can be difficult to draw, and the legitimacy of state authority is often in dispute. Do autocracies like those in Africa and the Middle East have legitimate authority? Are only democracies legitimate? What about democracies like the United States whose leaders have often been elected by a minority of its citizens or by less than a majority of the total votes?

2. *The cause is just.* A war is permissible only if it is waged for morally acceptable reasons. Chief among these is self-defense, in which a state fights to protect itself from physical attack by another state. For many theorists, self-defense also includes defending other states or peoples against violent external aggression. More controversial is the view that a just cause for war includes *humanitarian intervention*, the intervening of a state in another state's internal affairs to protect people from their government's violent attacks. There is widespread agreement, however, about the injustice of some causes—most notably, religious persecution or conversion, genocide, and empire expansion.

Over the centuries (and particularly in recent years), people have differed dramatically in their understanding of self-defense in war and therefore of their justifications for war. For many, self-defense means simply a response to an attack that has actually occurred (or is occurring), so only a real aggression by another state can justify a war of self-defense. For others, self-defense has a broader meaning; it includes military action against another state that is clearly preparing to launch an attack soon. Here the threat is both immediate and imminent. Such a war of self-defense—a *preemptive war*—is thought to be justified even though it is not a reaction to an actual military strike. Still some people favor an even more inclusive view of self-defense, asserting a right to attack another state if they merely fear the state is a threat—a doctrine of *preventive war*. The danger may be real but more distant and uncertain.

Scholars and much of the international community recognize a right to wage a preemptive war, but not a preventive one. The distinction is also subject to various interpretations and, recently, to heated debate. The administration of George W. Bush, for example, provoked controversy with its change in American war policy, one that critics denounced as a perilous switch to a doctrine of preventive war.

3. *The war is waged with rightful intentions.* Wars should be fought not only for a just cause and with proper authority, but with morally good motives—that is, as Aquinas says, a "rightful intention" to effect the "advancement of good, or the avoidance of evil."[1] Bad motives include hatred, greed, vengeance, bloodlust, and persecution.

4. *The war is a last resort.* Mass violence is permissible only if all reasonable alternatives have been vigorously pursued first, including diplomacy and nonviolent pressure.

5. *The good accomplished by going to war is proportional to the evil that the conflict causes.* The war's just cause should be worth the high costs that will result from the conflict. This requirement rules out wars fought for trivial reasons or for insignificant political objectives. Pacifists take issue with this principle, arguing that the evils of war always greatly outweigh any resulting good.

6. *There is a reasonable possibility of success.* Since a war involves vast destruction and considerable loss of life, launching a futile war—one sure to cause great loss without any reasonable chance of gain—is unjust.

In just war theory, the distinction between *jus ad bellum* and *jus in bello* allows us to make separate moral assessments of the resort to war and its conduct. Thus actions in a just war can be morally wrong; actions in an unjust war, morally right. So we may plausibly claim (as do some just war theorists) that World War II was a just war, but that the tactic of bombing German cities was immoral.

The principles of *jus in bello* embody the so-called "rules of war" and typically include:

1. *Discrimination between warriors and innocents.* The most fundamental rule of war is the prohibition against deliberately harming noncombatants—usually meaning unarmed women, children, and the injured. These are said to have *noncombatant immunity*, which means that combatants must never intentionally target them. The killing and wounding of innocents in war, though inevitable, must be unintended.

But in modern warfare, discriminating between those who should and should not be targeted is often difficult and morally problematic. Sometimes combatants dress like civilians, hide among them, and use them as human shields. Civilians may support the combatants' cause and provide them with food, shelter, medicine, and weapons. Combatants may use women and children as suicide bombers or even enlist them as armed fighters.

Some writers insist that the duty of discrimination is so strong that soldiers are obliged to put their own lives at risk to shield noncombatants from harm. Others think such a policy asks too much of soldiers. They believe it permissible for soldiers in battle to kill a noncombatant if killing him is the only way to save the lives of other noncombatants or soldiers.

[1] Thomas Aquinas, *Summa Theologica* in *Basic Writings of St. Thomas Aquinas*, trans. A.C. Pegis (New York: Random House, 1945), Second Part of the Second Part, Question 40, Article 1.

FACTS AND FIGURES: America's Wars

American Revolution (1775–1783)—4,435 battle deaths; 6,188 nonmortal woundings

War of 1812 (1812–1815)—2,260 battle deaths; 4,505 nonmortal woundings

Indian Wars (1817–1898)—1,000 battle deaths

Mexican War (1846–1848)—1,733 battle deaths; 4,152 nonmortal woundings

Civil War (1861–1865)—(Union) 140,414 battle deaths; 281,881 nonmortal woundings (Confederate) 74,524 battle deaths; unknown nonmortal woundings

Spanish-American War (1898–1902)—4,385 battle deaths; 1,662 nonmortal woundings

World War I (1917–1918)—53,402 battle deaths; 204,002 nonmortal woundings

World War II (1941–1945)—291,557 battle deaths; 671,846 nonmortal woundings

Korean War (1950–1953)—33,741 battle deaths; 103,284 nonmortal woundings

Vietnam War (1964–1975)—47,425 battle deaths; 153,303 nonmortal woundings[*]

Gulf War (1990–1991)—147 battle deaths; 467 nonmortal woundings

War in Afghanistan (2001–)—1,987 battle deaths; 17,519 wounded in action[†]

U.S.–Iraq War (2003–2010)—4,409 battle deaths; 31,925 wounded in action[‡]

[*] Covers period 11/1/55–5/15/75.

[†] Covers period from 2001–September 2012.

[‡] Covers period 2003–September 2012. From Department of Defense. http://www.defense.gov/RegisteredSites/RegisteredSites.aspx

---

2. *The proportional use of force.* The level of violence used should not exceed what is needed to achieve the mission. The number of casualties and degree of damage should be just enough and no more. As many just war theorists see it, this principle forbids mistreatment of innocents and prisoners, wanton destruction of resources ("scorched earth" tactics), pillage, rapes, massacres, and nuclear strikes.

TERRORISM

Most of us think we know terrorism when we see it. We would likely say these are clear-cut examples of terrorist acts: the 1988 bombing of Pan Am flight 103 over Lockerbie, Scotland, killing all 259 passengers and crew; the 1995 bombing of the federal building in Oklahoma City by Timothy McVeigh, killing 166 people; the September 11, 2001, attacks on the United States by agents of Al-Qaida, killing 3,025 people, both Americans and other nationals; the 2004 bombing of commuter trains in Madrid by radical Islamists, killing 191 and injuring over 1,500; the July 7, 2005, bombing in London of a bus and subway trains by jihadists, killing fifty-two passengers; and the 2008 three-day rampage in Mumbai, India, of armed militants who roamed the city killing randomly over 170 people. Yet defining terrorism is both tricky and controversial. We must distinguish it from ordinary crimes and acts of war while giving logic and common usage their due. Developing a plausible definition is important because, for one thing, our ethical judgments about terrorism in general and particular terrorist incidents depend on our understanding the nature of the beast.

Some definitions are too broad; they imply that crimes such as bank robbery are terrorist acts or that any use of violence to achieve a political end through fear constitutes terrorism. Other definitions fail because they are not neutral—they smuggle in judgments about the morality of terrorism. This question-begging complicates our efforts to evaluate the rightness or wrongness of the actions in question. And some definitions restrict terrorism to violence committed against noncombatants by entities *other than governments*—"subnational groups" or "nonstate agents."[2] According to these views, the mass killings of September 11 and the London bombings of 2005 were terrorist acts, but the mass killings of civilians in Hiroshima and Dresden during World War II were not. The latter were merely acts of war. But some reject these more restrictive definitions, claiming that the deliberate killing of civilians for political ends is terrorism whether done by individuals or states. The implication is that the horrors of Hiroshima and Dresden were the result of terrorism perpetrated by terrorist governments.

Fortunately, the many conflicting definitions of terrorism contain common elements. As one philosopher explains,

> Despite its notorious vagueness and looseness, some overlap among the multiplicity of the word's definitions and characterizations exists. Quite a number of definitions in the literature, as well as characterizations in the media and in everyday discourse, include the idea that terrorism is the threat or the actual use of violence—the unlawful use of force—directed against civilians (e.g. noncombatants in wartime) *and they alone*, sometimes with the addition of the words, "*for political* purposes."[3]

For our discussion, then, we can characterize **terrorism** as the deliberate use or threat of physical violence against noncombatants to advance political, religious, or ideological aims.

Terrorism in this sense has been with us for at least two millennia. Its first manifestations were religiously inspired, a form that brought fear and death to many for hundreds of years. Among the more notable perpetrators were the Jewish Zealots, the Muslim Assassins, and the Hindu Thugees. Religious terrorism mainly receded by the middle of the nineteenth century and did not appear again until the latter part of the twentieth, taking an increasing toll in lives to the present day.

Secular terrorism (and the term *terrorism* itself) was born of the French Revolution's Reign of Terror, the murderous program of the new regime to cut down thousands of "traitors" and protect the state. The nineteenth century saw the rise of terrorist attacks by anarchists and nationalists in Russia, Ireland, the Balkans, and the United States (where the Civil War spawned terrorism on both sides, and an anarchist assassinated President William McKinley).

In the twentieth century, nationalist terrorism continued throughout the world while variations on the terrorist's trade emerged. The new threats were state-sponsored terrorism (by Serbia, Bulgaria, Iran, Libya, and Syria, for example); state-run terrorism (by Nazi Germany, Stalinist Russia, Fascist Italy, and brutal regimes in South America and Africa); and ideological or ethnic terrorism (by the Provisional Irish Republican Army, the Palestinian Liberation Organization, the Italian Red Brigades, and others).[4]

Probably the most troubling and basic ethical question about terrorism is whether it can be morally permissible. On various grounds, some theorists assert that the answer is yes. They

---

[2] See for example, U.S. Department of State, *Patterns of Global Terrorism 2003* (Washington, D.C., April 2004), xii.

[3] Haig Khatchadourian, *The Morality of Terrorism* (New York: Peter Lang, 1998), 2.

[4] This historical sketch is drawn from Mark Burgess, "A Brief History of Terrorism," *Center for Defense Information*, 2 July 2003, http://www.cdi.org/program/index.cfm?programid=39 (21 January 2009).

may take a consequentialist line and argue that the good to be achieved through terrorist acts often outweighs the evil that the acts entail. In this calculation, the innocence of the victims is not a major concern; the net balance of good over bad matters far more. Others argue in a deontological vein that terrorism may sometimes be justified in the name of justice or rights for an aggrieved group. They may claim, for example, that some terrorist violence can be justified because it passes the ethical tests laid down by just war theory. As Andrew Valls says,

> My conclusion, then, is that if just war theory can justify violence committed by states, then terrorism committed by nonstate actors can also, under certain circumstances, be justified by it as well.[5]

Many philosophers reject this appeal to just war theory, contending that in fact terrorism conflicts with just war requirements. Michael Walzer, for example, argues that terrorism, by deliberately attacking the innocent, violates the principle of discrimination. Moreover, he says, the terrorists' common excuses for their actions—that terrorism is a last resort and that it achieves its goals—are groundless. The upshot is that, "every act of terrorism is a wrongful act."[6] Haig Khatchadourian contends that terrorism not only tramples on the just war principles of discrimination and proportionality, but also violates its victims' right to life. "[A]ll types and forms of terrorism I have distinguished," he says, "seriously violate the human rights of their immediate victims and the victimized as moral persons."[7]

TORTURE

Torture, like terrorism, is easier to identify than to define. Most people would probably agree that

> Torture includes such practices as searing with hot irons, burning at the stake, electric shock treatment to the genitals, cutting out parts of the body, e.g., tongue, entrails or genitals, severe beatings, suspending by the legs with arms tied behind back, applying thumbscrews, inserting a needle under the fingernails, drilling through an unanesthetized tooth, making a person crouch for hours in the "Z" position, waterboarding (submersion in water or dousing to produce the sensation of drowning), and denying food, water or sleep for days or weeks on end.[8]

A rough characterization of **torture** is an act of intentionally inflicting severe pain or suffering on a person for purposes of coercion, punishment, intimidation, or extraction of information. Torture as an instrument of government authority has been a part of Western civilization for hundreds of years. Beginning in late medieval times, torture was legally and regularly used in Europe by judges to acquire evidence. The practice, called judicial torture, was long known to be an unreliable method of uncovering truth but was

---

[5] Andrew Valls, "Can Terrorism Be Justified?" in *Ethics in International Affairs*, ed. Andrew Valls (Lanham, MD: Rowman & Littlefield, 2003), 65–79.

[6] Michael Walzer, "Terrorism: A Critique of Excuses," in *Problems of International Justice*, ed. Steven Luper-Foy (Boulder, CO: Westview Press, 1988), 237–47.

[7] Haig Khatchadourian, "The Morality of Terrorism," in *The Morality of Terrorism* (New York: Peter Lang, 1998), 31.

[8] Seumas Miller, "Torture," in *The Stanford Encyclopedia of Philosophy*, Fall 2008 edition, ed. Edward N. Zalta, http://plato.stanford.edu/archives/fall2008/entries/torture/ (22 January 2009).

TIME LINE: Terrorist Attacks

Notable terrorist incidents, 1998–2011:

U.S. Embassy Bombings in East Africa, August 7, 1998: A bomb exploded at the rear entrance of the U.S. Embassy in Nairobi, Kenya, killing 12 U.S. citizens, 32 Foreign Service Nationals (FSNs), and 247 Kenyan citizens. Approximately 5,000 Kenyans, 6 U.S. citizens, and 13 FSNs were injured. The U.S. Embassy building sustained extensive structural damage. Almost simultaneously, a bomb detonated outside the U.S. Embassy in Dar es Salaam, Tanzania, killing 7 FSNs and 3 Tanzanian citizens and injuring 1 U.S. citizen and 76 Tanzanians. The explosion caused major structural damage to the U.S. Embassy facility. The U.S. Government held Usama Bin Laden responsible.

Hamas Restaurant Bombing, August 9, 2001: A Hamas-planted bomb detonated in a Jerusalem pizza restaurant, killing 15 people and wounding more than 90. The Israeli response included occupation of Orient House, the Palestine Liberation Organization's political headquarters in East Jerusalem.

Terrorist Attacks on U.S. Homeland, September 11, 2001: Two hijacked airliners crashed into the twin towers of the World Trade Center. Soon thereafter, the Pentagon was struck by a third hijacked plane. A fourth hijacked plane, suspected to be bound for a high-profile target in Washington, crashed into a field in southern Pennsylvania. The attacks killed 3,025 U.S. citizens and other nationals. President Bush and Cabinet officials indicated that Usama Bin Laden was the prime suspect and that they considered the United States in a state of war with international terrorism. In the aftermath of the attacks, the United States formed the Global Coalition Against Terrorism.

Car Bomb Explosion in Bali, October 12, 2002: A car bomb exploded outside the Sari Club Discotheque in Denpasar, Bali, Indonesia, killing 202 persons and wounding 300 more. Most of the casualties, including 88 of the dead, were Australian tourists. Seven Americans were among the dead. Al-Qaida claimed responsibility.

Chechen Rebels Seize a Moscow Theater, October 23–26, 2002: Fifty Chechen rebels led by Movsar Barayev seized the Palace of Culture Theater in Moscow, Russia, to demand an end to the war in Chechnya. They seized more than 800 hostages from 13 countries and threatened to blow up the theater. During a three-day siege, they killed a Russian policeman and five Russian hostages. On October 26, Russian Special Forces pumped an anesthetic gas through the ventilation system and then stormed the theater. All the rebels were killed, but 94 hostages (including one American) also died, many from the effects of the gas. A group led by Chechen warlord Shamil Basayev claimed responsibility.

Night Club Bombing in Colombia, February 7, 2003: A car bomb exploded outside a night club in Bogota, Colombia, killing 32 persons and wounding 160. No group claimed responsibility, but Colombian officials suspected the Colombian Revolutionary Armed Forces (FARC) of committing the worst terrorist attack in the country in a decade.

Truck Bomb Attacks in Saudi Arabia, May 12, 2003: Suicide bombers attacked three residential compounds for foreign workers in Riyadh, Saudi Arabia. The 34 dead included 9 attackers, 7 other Saudis, 9 U.S. citizens, and 1 citizen each from the United Kingdom, Ireland, and the Philippines. Another American died on June 1. It was the first major attack on U.S. targets in Saudi Arabia since the end of the war in Iraq. Saudi authorities arrested 11 Al-Qaida suspects on May 28.

Bombing of the UN Headquarters in Baghdad, August 19, 2003: A truck loaded with surplus Iraqi ordnance exploded outside the United Nations Headquarters in Baghdad's Canal Hotel. A hospital across the street was also heavily damaged. The 23 dead included UN Special Representative Sergio Viera de Mello. More than 100 persons were wounded. It was not clear whether the bomber was a Baath Party loyalist or a foreign Islamic militant. An Al-Qaida branch called the Brigades of the Martyr Abu Hafz al-Masri later claimed responsibility.

Bombing in Madrid, Spain, March 11, 2004: Islamic extremists killed 191 civilians and wounded 1,841 others in bomb attacks.

Bombing in London, July 7, 2005: Fifty-two civilians were killed and 700 others were injured in suicide bomb attacks by Islamic extremists.

Bomb attack in Turkey, July 27, 2008: In Istanbul 5 children and 12 civilians were killed and 154 civilians were wounded in a bomb attack by suspected KGK.

Shooting spree in Mumbai, India, 2008: Over the course of several days, Pakistan-based militants killed 174 people, shooting innocent civilians at random.

Bombing attack in the North-West Frontier, Pakistan, March 2009: A suicide bomber entered a mosque during Friday prayers and detonated the improvised explosive device (IED) strapped to his body, killing at least 55 civilians (28 Pakistani; 27 Afghan),

16 soldiers, and 11 children (6 Pakistani; 5 Afghan), and injuring at least 100 civilians (50 Pakistani; 50 Afghan), 55 children (30 Pakistani; 25 Afghan), and at least 25 soldiers.

Assault in Pakistan, May 28, 2010: At least seven assailants armed with firearms and hand grenades, three of whom were suicide bombers wearing IEDs, near-simultaneously attacked two Ahmadi-sect places of worship, killing 79 civilians (78 Pakistani and one British), children, police, and one reporter, and injuring 118 civilians.

Bombing and Shooting in Norway, 2011. Over the course of one day, an alleged Christian right-wing extremist detonated a bomb in Oslo, Norway, killing eight people, then later shot and killed 69 others at a nearby island youth camp.

Excerpted and compiled from U.S. Department of State, "Significant Terrorist Incidents, 1961–2003: A Brief Chronology," *U.S. Department of State*, March 2004, http://www.state.gov/r/pa/ho/pubs/fs/5902.htm (18 January 2009); National Counterterrorism Center, "Worldwide Incidents Tracking system," *National Counterterrorism Center*, http://wits.nctc.gov/Main.do (18 January 2009); and *National Counterterrorism Center, Report on Terrorism 2009 and 2010* (23 February 2012).

not abolished until the eighteenth century. From 1540 to 1640, England experimented with official torture to investigate crimes, issuing warrants that allowed its use. It was an extralegal tool of the state, applied mainly to ferret out traitors.[9]

Today torture is condemned throughout the world—but still used by many regimes, including those that disavow it. It is also contrary to international law. An absolute ban on torture was set forth in the United Nations Convention Against Torture and Other Cruel, Inhuman or Degrading Treatment or Punishment, which took effect in 1987 and has been ratified by most nations, including the United States. The Convention is unequivocal, declaring that

No exceptional circumstances whatsoever, whether a state of war or a threat of war, internal instability or any other public emergency, may be invoked as a justification of torture.[10]

[9] John H. Langbein, "The Legal History of Torture," in *Torture: A Collection*, ed. Sanford Levinson (Oxford: Oxford University Press, 2004), 93–103.
[10] United Nations, "Convention Against Torture and Other Cruel, Inhuman or Degrading Treatment or Punishment," *Office of the High Commissioner for Human Rights*, 26 June 1987, http://www.unhchr.ch/html/menu3/b/h_cat39.htm (30 January 2009).

Torture is also banned by the Universal Declaration of Human Rights (1948), the International Covenant on Civil and Political Rights (1966), and the Geneva Conventions.

Officially, the United States government has always rejected the use of torture, but after the terrorist attacks of September 11, 2001, the Bush administration was widely criticized for allowing harsh interrogation methods to be employed against suspected terrorists—methods considered by many critics (including some administration officials) to be torture. Officials in the Justice Department defined torture so that severe interrogation techniques would be considered lawful, and a department memorandum specifically authorized some of them, including exposure to freezing temperatures and simulated drowning ("waterboarding"). Abusive and inhumane treatment of detainees has occurred in several U.S.-run facilities, including Guantánamo Bay naval base and Abu Ghraib prison in Iraq. In 2009 President Barack Obama signed an executive order mandating that all interrogations be conducted humanely according to guidelines set out by the U.S. *Army Field Manual.*

Contemporary debates about torture usually concern its use in getting information from suspects (often suspected terrorists) regarding future attacks, the identity of the suspects' associates, the operations of terrorist cells, and the like. How effective torture is for this purpose is in dispute, mostly because of a lack of scientific evidence on the question. We are left with a lot of anecdotal accounts, some of which suggest that torture works, and some that it doesn't. People who are tortured often lie, saying anything that will make the torturers stop. On the other hand, in a few instances torture seems to have gleaned from the tortured some intelligence that helped thwart a terrorist attack.

Almost everyone involved in the torture debates begins with the assumption that torture is a ghastly evil. The fact that torture is a very bad thing is not in dispute. The bigger question is whether we are ever justified in inflicting this evil on anyone, whether torture is a *necessary* evil. Sometimes people are justified in causing evil to prevent a greater evil, as when a surgeon amputates a limb to save a life. Sometimes they are forced to choose between the lesser of two evils, as when someone must decide whether to abort a fetus to save the mother's life or let them both die. Is torture an evil that we are sometimes morally justified in allowing?

In this single query, two questions lurk. The first asks whether in any particular instance it could be morally permissible to torture a person. The second asks whether state-administered torture should be legalized or institutionalized. The questions are distinct, for we may coherently claim that in some cases torture is justified and should be legalized, or that it is sometimes justified but should not be legalized. Of course, we can also argue that torture is never morally permissible and therefore should not be legalized.

In answer to the first question, many people have asserted that in rare situations torture is indeed justified. They typically present scenarios in which torturing a terrorist is the only way to prevent the deaths of hundreds or thousands of people. Consider: In Washington, D.C., a terrorist has planted a bomb set to detonate soon and kill a half million people. FBI agents capture him and realize that the only way to disarm the bomb in time is for the terrorist to tell them where it is, and the only way to get him to talk is to torture him. Is it morally permissible then to stick needles under his fingernails or waterboard him? For many, moral common sense suggests that the answer must be yes. When they weigh the temporary agony of a terrorist against the deaths of thousands of innocents, the ethical answer seems obvious.

Critics of this view insist that such cases are not realistic, that these "ticking bomb" scenarios could not happen. Others take a much stronger stand against torture, contending that it is always and everywhere wrong. For them, "do not torture" is a moral absolute, admitting no exceptions.

Those who agree that in extreme situations torture can be morally right differ dramatically on the part it should play in our institutions (the second question mentioned above). Many think that legalizing or institutionalizing torture would corrupt society and liberal democracy. Others believe that torture should be an official tool of the state but applied only according to strict rules and with maximum accountability.

A few argue that torture should not be an official function of government but should be used unofficially out of the public eye. Alan Dershowitz describes this view, calling it hypocritical:

> In my debates with two prominent civil libertarians, Floyd Abrams and Harvey Silvergate, both have acknowledged that they would want nonlethal torture to be used if it could prevent thousands of deaths, but they did not want torture to be officially recognized by our legal system. As Abrams put it: "In a democracy sometimes it is necessary to do things off the books and below the radar screen."[11]

KEY TERMS

realism	antiwar pacifism	just war theory
terrorism	torture	

ARGUMENTS AND READINGS

14. THE PACIFIST ARGUMENT AGAINST WAR

An important argument for antiwar pacifism is that wars are always wrong because they violate a fundamental right to life. In "Pacifism," Douglas P. Lackey explains:

> [T]he antiwar pacifist does not take the killing of soldiers for granted. Everyone has a right to life, and the killing of soldiers in war is intentional killing, a deliberate violation of the right to life. According to the standard interpretation of basic rights, it is never morally justifiable to violate a basic right in order to produce some

---

[11] Alan M. Dershowitz, "Should the Ticking Bomb Terrorist Be Tortured?", *Why Terrorism Works: Understanding the Threat, Responding to the Challenge* (New Haven, CT: Yale University Press, 2002).

good; the end, in such cases, does not justify the means. How, then, can the killing of soldiers in war be morally justified—or even excused?[12]

Because everyone has a right to life, it is not permissible to kill others in war even to defend against deadly, unprovoked attacks.

Jan Narveson, however, sees a confusion here:

What this all adds up to, then, is that *if* we have any rights at all, we have a right to use force to prevent the deprivation of the thing to which we are said to have a right. But the pacifist, of *all* people, is the one most concerned to insist that we do have some rights, namely, the right not to have violence done to us....If [pacifists] attempt to formulate their position using our standard concepts of rights, their position involves a contradiction: Violence is wrong, *and* it is wrong to resist it. But the right to resist is precisely what having a right of safety of person is, if it is anything at all.[13]

A pacifist argument related to the right-to-life version says that all wars are immoral because they inevitably involve the killing of innocents. As Lackey says,

[W]hat about the deaths of civilians that are the unavoidable results of military operations directed to some *other* result? The pacifist classifies such killings as immoral, whereas most nonpacifists call them regrettable but unavoidable deaths, not murders. But why are they not murder, if the civilians are innocent, and if it is known in advance that some civilians will be killed? Isn't this an intentional killing of the innocent, which is the traditional definition of murder?[14]

Some accuse those who use this argument of faulty reasoning. The argument says that since the killing of innocents is wrong, and war involves the killing of innocents, war on the whole is wrong. But, these critics insist, from the fact that some aspects of war are immoral, it does not follow that war as a whole is immoral—no more than abuses of power in religion or government prove that religion or government overall is corrupt or evil.

---

[12] Douglas P. Lackey, "Pacifism," *The Ethics of War and Peace*, 6–24.

[13] Jan Narveson, "Pacifism: A Philosophical Analysis," *Ethics* 75:4 (1965), 623–70.

[14] Douglas P. Lackey, "Pacifism."

Pacifism

DOUGLAS P. LACKEY

1. VARIETIES OF PACIFISM

Everyone has a vague idea of what a pacifist is, but few realize that there are many kinds of pacifists. (Sometimes the different kinds quarrel with each other!) One task for the student of international ethics is to distinguish the different types of pacifism and to identify which types represent genuine moral theories.

Most of us at some time or other have run into the "live and let live" pacifist, the person who says, "I am absolutely opposed to killing and violence—but I don't seek to impose my own code on anyone else. If other people want to use violence, so be it. They have their values and I have mine." For such a person, pacifism is one life-style among others, a life-style committed to gentleness and care, and opposed to belligerence and militarism. Doubtless, many people who express such commitments are sincere and are prepared to live by their beliefs. At the same time, it is important to see why "live and let live" pacifism does not constitute a moral point of view.

When someone judges that a certain action, A, is morally wrong, that judgment entails that no one should do A. Thus, there is no way to have moral values without believing that these values apply to other people. If a person says that A is morally wrong but that it doesn't matter if other people do A, then that person either is being inconsistent or doesn't know what the word "moral" means. If a person believes that killing, in certain circumstances, is morally wrong, that belief implies that no one should kill, at least in those circumstances. If a pacifist claims that killing is wrong in *all* circumstances, but that it is permissible for other people to kill on occasion, then he has not understood the universal character of genuine moral principles. If pacifism is to be a moral theory, it must be prescribed for all or prescribed for none.

Once one recognizes this "universalizing" character of genuine moral beliefs, one will take moral commitments more seriously than those who treat a moral code as a personal life-style. Since moral principles apply to everyone, we must take care that our moral principles are correct, checking that they are not inconsistent with each other, developing and adjusting them so that they are detailed and subtle enough to deal with a variety of circumstances, and making sure that they are defensible against the objections of those who do not accept them. Of course many pacifists do take the business of morality seriously and advance pacifism as a genuine moral position, not as a mere life-style. All such serious pacifists believe that *everyone* ought to be a pacifist, and that those who reject pacifism are deluded or wicked. Moreover, they do not simply endorse pacifism; they offer arguments in its defense.

We will consider four types of pacifist moral theory. First, there are pacifists who maintain that the central idea of pacifism is the immorality of killing. Second, there are pacifists who maintain that the essence of pacifism is the immorality of violence, whether this be violence in personal relations or violence in relations between nation-states. Third, there are pacifists who argue that personal violence is always morally wrong but that political violence is sometimes morally right: for example, that it is sometimes morally permissible for a nation to go to war. Fourth and finally, there are pacifists who believe that personal violence is sometimes morally permissible but that war is always morally wrong.

Albert Schweitzer, who opposed all killing on the grounds that life is sacred, was the first sort of pacifist. Mohandas Gandhi and Leo Tolstoy, who opposed not only killing but every kind of coercion and violence, were pacifists of the second sort: I will call such pacifists "universal pacifists." St. Augustine, who condemned self-defense but endorsed wars against heretics, was a pacifist of the third sort. Let us call him a "private pacifist," since he condemned only violence in the private sphere. Pacifists of the fourth sort, increasingly common in

From *The Ethics of War and Peace* by Douglas P. Lackey, 6–11, 18–24. © 1989, Reprinted by permission of Pearson Education, Inc, Upper Saddle River, NJ.

the modern era of nuclear and total war, I will call "antiwar pacifists."

2. THE PROHIBITION AGAINST KILLING

(a) The Biblical Prohibition

One simple and common argument for pacifism is the argument that the Bible, God's revealed word, says to all people "Thou shalt not kill" (Exod. 20:13). Some pacifists interpret this sentence as implying that no one should kill under any circumstances, unless God indicates that this command is suspended, as He did when He commanded Abraham to slay Isaac. The justification for this interpretation is the words themselves, "Thou shalt not kill," which are presented in the Bible bluntly and without qualification, not only in Exodus but also in Deuteronomy (5:17).

This argument, however, is subject to a great many criticisms. The original language of Exodus and Deuteronomy is Hebrew, and the consensus of scholarship says that the Hebrew sentence at Exodus 20:13, "Lo Tirzach," is best translated as "Thou shalt do no murder," not as "Thou shalt not kill." If this translation is correct, then Exodus 20:13 does not forbid all killing but only those killings that happen to be murders. Furthermore, there are many places in the Bible where God commands human beings to kill in specified circumstances. God announces 613 commandments in all, and these include "Thou shalt not suffer a witch to live" (Exod. 22:18); "He that blasphemeth the name of the Lord…shall surely be put to death, and all the congregation shall stone him" (Lev. 24:16); "He that killeth any man shall surely be put to death" (Lev. 24:17); and so forth. It is difficult to argue that these instructions are like God's specific instructions to Abraham to slay Isaac: these are general commandments to be applied by many people, to many people, day in and day out. They are at least as general and as divinely sanctioned as the commandment translated "Thou shalt not kill."

There are other difficulties for pacifists who pin their hopes on prohibitions in the Hebrew Bible. Even if the commandment "Thou shalt not kill," properly interpreted, did prohibit all types of killing, the skeptic can ask whether this, by itself, proves that all killing is immoral. First, how do we know that the statements in the Hebrew Bible really are God's word,

and not just the guesses of ancient scribes? Second, even if the commandments in the Bible do express God's views, why are we morally bound to obey divine commands? (To say that we will be punished if we do not obey is to appeal to fear and self-interest, not to moral sentiments.) Third, are the commandments in the Old Testament laws for all people, or just laws for the children of Israel? If they are laws for all people, then all people who do not eat unleavened bread for Passover are either deluded or wicked. If they are laws only for the children of Israel, they are religious laws and not moral laws, since they lack the universality that all moral laws must have.

Finally, the argument assumes the existence of God, and philosophers report that the existence of God is not easy to demonstrate. Even many religious believers are more confident of the truth of basic moral judgments, such as "Small children should not be tortured to death for purposes of amusement," than they are confident of the existence of God. For such people, it would seem odd to try to justify moral principles by appeals to religious principles, since the evidence for those religious principles is weaker than the evidence for the moral principles they are supposed to justify.

(b) The Sacredness of Life

There are, however, people who oppose all killing but do not seek justification in divine revelation. Many of these defend pacifism by appeal to the sacredness of life. Almost everyone is struck with wonder when watching the movements and reactions of a newborn baby, and almost everyone can be provoked to awe by the study of living things, great or small. The complexity of the mechanisms found in living bodies, combined with the efficiency with which they fulfill their functions, is not matched by any of the processes in nonliving matter. People who are particularly awestruck by the beauty of living things infer from these feelings that life is sacred, that all killing is morally wrong.

Different versions of pacifism have been derived from beliefs about the sacredness of life. The most extreme version forbids the killing of any living thing. This view was allegedly held by Pythagoras, and is presently held by members of the Jain religion in India. (Those who think that such pacifists must soon starve to death should note that a life-sustaining diet can easily be constructed from milk, honey, fallen fruit and vegetables, and other items that are consumable without prior killing.) A less extreme view sanctions the killing of plants but forbids the killing of animals. The most moderate view prohibits only the killing of fellow human beings.

There is deep appeal in an argument that connects the sacredness of life with the wrongfulness of taking life. Even people who are not pacifists are often revolted by the spectacle of killing, and most Americans would be unable to eat meat if they had to watch how the animals whose flesh they consume had been slaughtered, or if they had to do the slaughtering themselves. Most people sense that they do not own the world they inhabit and recognize that they are not free to do with the world as they will, that the things in it, most especially living things, are worthy of respect and care. Seemingly nothing could violate the respect living things deserve more than killing, especially since much of the taking of human and nonhuman life is so obviously unnecessary.

But with the introduction of the word "unnecessary" a paradox arises. Sometimes—less often than we think, but sometimes—the taking of some lives will save other lives. Does the principle that life is sacred and ought to be preserved imply that nothing should ever be killed, or does it imply that as much life should be preserved as possible? Obviously pacifists take the former view; nonpacifists the latter.

The view that killing is wrong because it destroys what is sacred seems to imply that killing is wrong because killing diminishes the amount of good in the world. It seems to follow that if a person can save more lives by killing than by refusing to kill, arguments about the sacredness of life would not show that killing in these circumstances is wrong. (It might be wrong for other reasons.) The more lives saved, the greater the quantity of good in the world.

The difficulty that some killing might, on balance, save lives, is not the only problem for pacifism based on the sacredness of life. If preserving life is the highest value, a value not comparable with other, non-life-preserving goods, it follows that any acts which place life at risk are immoral. But many admirable actions have been undertaken in the face of death, and many less heroic but morally

impeccable actions—driving on a road at moderate speed, authorizing a commercial flight to take off, and so forth—place life at risk. In cases of martyrdom in which people choose death over religious conversion, life is just as much destroyed as it is in a common murder. Yet, on the whole, automobile drivers, air traffic controllers, and religious martyrs are not thought to be wicked. Likewise, people on life-sustaining machinery sometimes request that the machines be turned off, on the grounds that quality of life matters more than quantity of life. We may consider such people mistaken, but we hardly think that they are morally depraved.

In answering this objection, the pacifist may wish to distinguish between *killing other people and getting oneself killed*, arguing that only the former is immoral. But although there is a genuine distinction between killing and getting killed, the distinction does not entail that killing other people destroys life but getting oneself killed does not. If life is sacred, life, including one's own life, must be preserved at all cost. In many cases, people consider the price of preserving their own lives simply to be too high.

(c) The Right to Life

Some pacifists may try to avoid the difficulties of the "sacredness of life" view by arguing that the essential immorality of killing is that it violates the *right to life* that every human being possesses. If people have a right to life, then it is never morally permissible to kill some people in order to save others, since according to the usual interpretation of rights, it is never permissible to violate a right in order to secure some good.

A discussion of the logic of rights in general and the right to life in particular is beyond the scope of this book. But a number of students of this subject are prepared to argue that the possession of any right implies the permissibility of defending that right against aggression: if this were not so, what would be the point of asserting the existence of rights? But if the possession of a right to life implies the permissibility of defending that right against aggression—a defense that may require killing the aggressor—then the existence of a right to life cannot by itself imply the impermissibility of killing. On this view, the right to life implies the right to self-defense, including violent self-defense. It does not imply pacifism.

.....

3. ANTIWAR PACIFISM

Most people who believe in the right to personal self-defense also believe that some wars are morally justified. In fact, the notion of self-defense and the notion of just war are commonly linked: just wars are said to be defensive wars, and the justice of defensive war is inferred from the right of personal self-defense, projected from the individual to the national level. But some people reject this projection: they endorse the validity of personal self-defense, but they deny that war can be justified by appeal to self-defense or any other right. On the contrary, they argue that war always involves an inexcusable violation of rights. For such anti-war pacifists, all participation in war is morally wrong.

(a) The Killing of Soldiers

One universal and necessary feature of wars is that soldiers get killed in them. Most people accept such killings as a necessary evil, and judge the killing of soldiers in war to be morally acceptable. If the war is fought for a just cause, the killing of enemy soldiers is justified as necessary to the triumph of right. If the war is fought for an unjust cause, the killing of enemy soldiers is acceptable because it is considered an honorable thing to fight for one's country, right or wrong, provided that one fights well and cleanly. But the antiwar pacifist does not take the killing of soldiers for granted. Everyone has a right to life, and the killing of soldiers in war is intentional killing, a deliberate violation of the right to life. According to the standard interpretation of basic rights, it is never morally justifiable to violate a basic right in order to produce some good; the end, in such cases, does not justify the means. How, then, can the killing of soldiers in war be morally justified—or even excused?

Perhaps the commonest reply to the challenge of antiwar pacifism is that killing in war is a matter of self-defense, *personal* self-defense, the right to which is freely acknowledged by the antiwar pacifist. In war, the argument goes, it is either kill or be killed—and that type of killing is killing in

self-defense. But though the appeal to self-defense is natural, antiwar pacifists believe that it is not successful. First of all, on the usual understanding of "self-defense," those who kill can claim the justification of self-defense only if (a) they had no other way to save their lives or preserve themselves from physical harm except by killing, and (b) they did nothing to provoke the attack to which they are subjected. Antiwar pacifists point out that soldiers on the battlefield do have a way of saving themselves from death or harm without killing anyone: they can surrender. Furthermore, for soldiers fighting for an unjust cause—for example, German soldiers fighting in the invasion of Russia in 1941—it is difficult to argue that they "did nothing to provoke" the deadly force directed at them. But if the German army provoked the Russians to stand and fight on Russian soil, German soldiers cannot legitimately claim self-defense as a moral justification for killing Russian soldiers.

To the nonpacifist, these points might seem like legalistic quibbles. But the antiwar pacifist has an even stronger argument against killing soldiers in war. The vast majority of soldiers who die in war do not die in "kill or be killed" situations. They are killed by bullets, shells, or bombs directed from safe launching points—"safe" in the sense that those who shoot the bullets or fire the shells or drop the bombs are in no immediate danger of death. Since those who kill are not in immediate danger of death, they cannot invoke "self-defense" to justify the deaths they cause.

Some other argument besides self-defense, then, must explain why the killing of soldiers in war should not be classified as murder. Frequently, nonpacifists argue that the explanation is found in the doctrine of "assumption of risk," the idea, common in civil law, that persons who freely assume a risk have only themselves to blame if the risk is realized. When a soldier goes to war, he is well aware that one risk of his trade is getting killed on the battlefield. If he dies on the field, the responsibility for his death lies with himself, not with the man who shot him. By assuming the risk—so the argument goes—he waived his right to life, at least on the battlefield.

One does not have to be a pacifist to see difficulties in this argument. First of all, in all substantial modern wars, most of the men on the line are not volunteers, but draftees. Only a wealthy nation like the United States can afford an all-volunteer army, and most experts believe that the American volunteer ranks will have to be supplemented by draftees should the United States become involved in another conflict on the scale of Korea or Vietnam. Second, in many cases in which a risk is realized, responsibility for the bad outcome lies not with the person who assumed the risk but with the person who created it. If an arsonist sets fire to a house and a parent rushes in to save the children, dying in the rescue attempt, responsibility for the parent's death lies not with the parent who assumed the risk but with the arsonist who created it. So if German armies invade Russia, posing the risk of death in battle, and if Russian soldiers assume this risk and fight back, the deaths of Russians are the fault of German invaders, not the fault of the defenders who assumed the risk.

These criticisms of German foot soldiers will irritate many who served in the armed forces and who know how little political and military decision making is left to the men on the front lines, who seem to be the special target of these pacifist arguments. But antiwar pacifists will deny that their aim is to condemn the men on the battlefield. Most antiwar pacifists feel that soldiers in war act under considerable compulsion and are excused for that reason from responsibility for the killing they do. But to say that battlefield killings are *excusable* is not to say that they are morally *justified*. On the contrary, if such killings are excusable, it must be that there is some immorality to be excused.

(b) The Killing of Civilians

In the chronicles of ancient wars, conflict was total and loss in battle was frequently followed by general slaughter of men, women, and children on the losing side. It has always been considered part of the trend toward civilization to confine the destruction of war to the personnel and instruments of war, sparing civilians and their property as much as possible. This civilizing trend was conspicuously reversed in World War II, in which the ratio of civilian deaths to total war deaths was perhaps the highest it had been since the wars of religion in the seventeenth century. A very high ratio of civilian deaths to total deaths was also characteristic of the war in Vietnam. Given the immense firepower of

modern weapons and the great distances between the discharges of weapons and the explosions of bullets or shells near the targets, substantial civilian casualties are an inevitable part of modern land war. But it is immoral to kill civilians, the antiwar pacifist argues, and from this it follows that modern land warfare is necessarily immoral.

Few nonpacifists will argue that killing enemy civilians is justifiable when such killings are avoidable. Few will argue that killing enemy civilians is justifiable when such killings are the *primary* objective of a military operation. But what about the deaths of civilians that are the unavoidable results of military operations directed to some *other* result? The pacifist classifies such killings as immoral, whereas most nonpacifists call them regrettable but unavoidable deaths, not murders. But why are they not murder, if the civilians are innocent, and if it is known in advance that some civilians will be killed? Isn't this an intentional killing of the innocent, which is the traditional definition of murder?

The sophisticated nonpacifist may try to parry this thrust with analogies to policies outside the arena of war. There are, after all, many morally acceptable policies that, when adopted, have the effect of killing innocent persons. If the Congress decides to set a speed limit of 55 miles per hour on federal highways, more people will die than if Congress sets the speed limit at 45 miles per hour. Since many people who die on the highway are innocent, the Congress has chosen a policy that knowingly brings death to the innocent, but no one calls it murder. Or suppose, for example, that a public health officer is considering a national vaccination program to forestall a flu epidemic. He knows that if he does not implement the vaccination program, many people will die from the flu. On the other hand, if the program is implemented, a certain number of people will die from allergic reactions to the vaccine. Most of the people who die from allergic reactions will be people who would not have died of the flu if the vaccination program had not been implemented. So the vaccination program will kill innocent people who would otherwise be saved if the program were abandoned. If the public health officer implements such a program, we do *not* think that he is a murderer.

Nonpacifists argue that what makes the action of Congress and the action of the public health officer morally permissible in these cases is that the deaths of the innocent, although foreseen, are not the intended goal of these policies. Congress does not want people to die on the highways; every highway death is a regrettable death. The purpose of setting the speed limit at 55 miles per hour is not to kill people but to provide a reasonable balance between safety and convenience. Likewise, it is not the purpose of the public health officer to kill people by giving them vaccine. His goal is to save lives on balance, and every death from the vaccine is a regrettable death. Likewise, in war, when civilians are killed as a result of necessary military operations, the deaths of the civilians are not the intended goal of the military operation. They are foreseen, but they are always regretted. If we do not accuse the Congress of murder and the Public Health Service of murder in these cases, consistency requires that we not accuse military forces of murder when they cause civilian deaths in war, especially if every attempt is made to keep civilian deaths to a minimum.

Antiwar pacifists do not condemn the Congress and the Public Health Service in cases like these. But they assert that the case of war is different in a morally relevant way. To demonstrate the difference, antiwar pacifists provide an entirely different analysis of the moral justification for speed limits and vaccination programs. In their opinion, the facts that highway deaths and vaccination deaths are "unintended" and "regretted" is morally irrelevant. The real justification lies in the factor of consent. In the case of federal highway regulations, the rules are decided by Congress, which is elected by the people, the same people who use the highways. If Congress decides on a 55-mile-an-hour speed limit, this is a regulation that, in some sense, highway drivers have imposed upon themselves. Those people who die on the highway because of a higher speed limit have, in a double sense, assumed the risks generated by that speed limit: they have, through the Congress, created the risk, and by venturing onto the highway, have freely exposed themselves to the risk. The responsibility for these highway deaths, then, lies either on the drivers themselves or on the people who crashed into them—not on the Congress.

Likewise, in the case of the vaccination program, if people are warned in advance of the risks of vaccination, and if they nevertheless choose to be vaccinated, they are responsible for their own deaths should the risks be realized. According to the antiwar pacifist, it is this consent given by drivers and vaccination volunteers that justifies these policies, and it is precisely this element of consent that is absent in the case of the risks inflicted on enemy civilians in time of war.

Consider the standard textbook example of allegedly justifiable killing of civilians in time of war. Suppose that the destruction of a certain bridge is an important military objective, but if the bridge is bombed, it is very likely that civilians living close by will be killed. (The civilians cannot be warned without alerting the enemy to reinforce the bridge.) If the bridge is bombed and some civilians are killed, the bombing victims are not in the same moral category as highway victims or victims of vaccination. The bombing victims did not order the bombing of themselves through some set of elected representatives. Nor did the bombing victims freely consent to the bombing of their bridge. Nor was the bombing in any way undertaken as a calculated risk in the interest of the victims. For all these reasons, the moral conclusions regarding highway legislation and vaccination programs do not carry over to bombing of the bridge.

Nonpacifists who recognize that it will be very difficult to fight wars without bombing bridges may argue that the victims of this bombing in some sense assumed the risks of bombardment by choosing to live close to a potential military target. Indeed, it is occasionally claimed that all the civilians in a nation at war have assumed the risks of war, since they could avoid the risks of war simply by moving to a neutral country. But such arguments are strained and uncharitable, even for those rare warring nations that permit freedom of emigration. Most people consider it a major sacrifice to give up their homes, and an option that requires such a sacrifice cannot be considered an option open for free choice. The analogy between the unintended victims of vaccination and the unintended civilian victims of war seems to have broken down.

(c) The Balance of Good and Evil in War

It is left to the nonpacifist to argue that the killing of soldiers and civilians in war is in the end justifiable in order to obtain great moral goods that can be obtained only by fighting for them. Civilians have rights to life, but those rights can be outweighed by the national objectives, provided those objectives are morally acceptable and overwhelmingly important. Admittedly, this argument for killing civilians is available only to the just side in a war, but if the argument is valid, it proves that there can *be* a just side, contrary to the arguments of antiwar pacifism.

Antiwar pacifists have two lines of defense. First, they can continue to maintain that the end does not justify the means, if the means be murderous. Second, they can, and will, go on to argue that it is a tragic mistake to believe that there are great moral goods that can be obtained only by war. According to antiwar pacifists, the amount of moral good produced by war is greatly exaggerated. The Mexican War, for example, resulted in half of Mexico being transferred to American rule. This was a great good for the United States, but not a great moral good, since the United States had little claim to the ceded territory, and no great injustice would have persisted if the war had not been fought at all.

The Revolutionary War in America is widely viewed as a war that produced a great moral good; but if the war had not been fought, the history of the United States would be similar to the history of Canada (which remained loyal)—and no one feels that the Canadians have suffered or are suffering great injustices that the American colonies avoided by war. Likewise, it is difficult to establish the goods produced by World War I or the moral losses that would have ensued if the winning side, "our side," had lost. Bertrand Russell imagined the results of a British loss in World War I as follows:

> The greatest sum that foreigners could possibly exact would be the total economic rent of the land and natural resources of England. [But] the working classes, the shopkeepers, manufacturers, and merchants, the literary men and men of science— all the people that make England of any account in the world—have at most an infinitesimal and accidental share in the rental of England. The men who have a share use their rents in luxury, political

corruption, taking the lives of birds, and depopulating and enslaving the rural districts. It is this life of the idle rich that would be curtailed if the Germans exacted tribute from England. (*Justice in War Time*, pp. 48–49)

But multiplying examples of wars that did little moral good will not establish the pacifist case. The pacifist must show that *no* war has done enough good to justify the killing of soldiers and the killing of civilians that occurred in the war. A single war that produces moral goods sufficient to justify its killings will refute the pacifist claim that *all* wars are morally unjustifiable. Obviously this brings the antiwar pacifist head to head with World War II.

It is commonly estimated that 35 million people died as a result of World War II. It is difficult to imagine that any cause could justify so much death, but fortunately the Allies need only justify their share of these killings. Between 1939 and 1945 Allied forces killed about 5.5 million Axis soldiers and about 1 million civilians in Axis countries. Suppose that Britain and the United States had chosen to stay out of World War II and suppose that Stalin had, like Lenin, surrendered to Germany shortly after the invasion. Does avoiding the world that would have resulted from these decisions justify killing 6.5 million people?

If Hitler and Tojo had won the war, doubtless they would have killed a great many people both before and after victory, but it is quite likely that the total of *additional* victims, beyond those they killed in the war that *was* fought, would have been less than 6.5 million and, at any rate, the responsibility for those deaths would fall on Hitler and Tojo, not on Allied nations. If Hitler and Tojo had won the war, large portions of the world would have fallen under foreign domination, perhaps for a very long time. But the antiwar pacifist will point out that the main areas of Axis foreign domination—China and Russia—were not places in which the citizens enjoyed a high level of freedom *before the war began*. Perhaps the majority of people in the conquered areas would have worked out a *modus vivendi* with their new rulers, as did the majority of French citizens during the German occupation. Nor can it be argued that World War II was necessary to save six million Jews from annihilation in the Holocaust, since in fact the war did *not* save them.

The ultimate aims of Axis leaders are a matter for historical debate. Clearly the Japanese had no intention of conquering the United States, and some historians suggest that Hitler hoped to avoid war with England and America, declaring war with England reluctantly, and only after the English declared it against him. Nevertheless, popular opinion holds that Hitler intended to conquer the world, and if preventing the conquest of a Russia and China could not justify six and one-half million killings, most Americans are quite confident that preventing the conquest of England and the United States does justify killing on this scale.

The antiwar pacifist disagrees. Certainly German rule of England and the United States would have been a very bad thing. At the same time, hatred of such German rule would be partially fueled by hatred of foreigners, and hatred of foreigners, as

such, is an irrational and morally unjustifiable passion. After all, if rule by foreigners were, by itself, a great moral wrong, the British, with their great colonial empire, could hardly consider themselves the morally superior side in World War II.

No one denies that a Nazi victory in World War II would have had morally frightful results. But, according to antiwar pacifism, killing six and one-half million people is also morally frightful, and preventing one moral wrong does not obviously outweigh committing the other. Very few people today share the pacifists' condemnation of World War II, but perhaps that is because the dead killed by the Allies cannot speak up and make sure that their losses are properly counted on the moral scales. Antiwar pacifists speak on behalf of the enemy dead, and on behalf of all those millions who would have lived if the war had not been fought. On this silent constituency they rest their moral case.

Pacifism: A Philosophical Analysis

JAN NARVESON

Several different doctrines have been called "pacifism," and it is impossible to say anything cogent about it without saying which of them one has in mind. I must begin by making it clear, then, that I am limiting the discussion of pacifism to a rather narrow band of doctrines, further distinctions among which will be brought out below. By "pacifism," I do *not* mean the theory that violence is evil. With appropriate restrictions, this is a view that every person with any pretensions to morality doubtless holds: Nobody thinks that we have a right to inflict pain wantonly on other people. The pacifist goes a very long step further. *His* belief is not only that violence is evil but also that it is morally wrong to use force to resist, punish, or prevent violence. This further step makes pacifism a radical moral doctrine. What I shall try to establish

below is that it is in fact, more than merely radical—it is actually incoherent because self-contradictory in its fundamental intent. I shall also suggest that several moral attitudes and psychological views which have tended to be associated with pacifism as I have defined it do not have any necessary connection with that doctrine. Most proponents of pacifism, I shall argue, have tended to confuse these different doctrines, and that confusion is probably what accounts for such popularity as pacifism has had.

It is next in order to point out that the pacifistic attitude is a matter of degree and this in two respects.

From "Pacifism: A Philosophical Analysis" by Jan Narveson in *Ethics*, 75:4, 1965, 259–271. © University of Chicago Press. Notes deleted.

In the first place, there is the question: How much violence should not be resisted, and what degree of force is one not entitled to use in resisting, punishing, or preventing it? Answers to this question will make a lot of difference. For example, everyone would agree that there are limits to the kind and degree of force with which a particular degree of violence is to be met: we do not have a right to kill someone for rapping us on the ribs, for example, and yet there is no tendency toward pacifism in this. We might go further and maintain, for example, that capital punishment, even for the crime of murder, is unjustified without doing so on pacifist grounds. Again, the pacifist should say just what sort of a reaction constitutes a forcible or violent one. If somebody attacks me with his fists and I pin his arms to his body with wrestling holds which restrict him but cause him no pain, is that all right in the pacifist's book? And again, many non-pacifists could consistently maintain that we should avoid, to the extent that it is possible, inflicting a like pain on those who attempt to inflict pain on us. It is unnecessary to be a pacifist merely in order to deny the moral soundness of the principle, "an eye for an eye and a tooth for a tooth." We need a clarification, then, from the pacifist as to just how far he is and is not willing to go. But this need should already make us pause, for surely the pacifist cannot draw these lines in a merely arbitrary manner. It is his reasons for drawing the ones he does that count, and these are what I propose to discuss below.

The second matter of degree in respect of which the pacifist must specify his doctrine concerns the question: Who ought not to resist violence with force? For example, there are pacifists who would only claim that they themselves ought not to. Others would say that only pacifists ought not to, or that all persons of a certain type, where the type is not specified in terms of belief or non-belief in pacifism, ought not to resist violence with force. And, finally, there are those who hold that everyone ought not to do so. We shall see that considerations about this second variable doom some forms of pacifism to contradiction.

My general program will be to show that (1) only the doctrine that everyone ought not to resist violence with force is of philosophical interest among those doctrines known as "pacifism"; (2) that doctrine, if advanced as a moral doctrine, is logically untenable; and (3) the reasons for the popularity of pacifism rest on failure to see exactly what the doctrine is. The things which pacifism wishes to accomplish, insofar as they are worth accomplishing, can be managed on the basis of quite ordinary and conservative moral principles.

Let us begin by being precise about the kind of moral force the principle of pacifism is intended to have. One good way to do this is to consider what it is intended to deny. What would non-pacifists, which I suppose includes most people, say of a man who followed Christ's suggestion and when unaccountably slapped simply turned the other cheek? They might say that such a man is either a fool or a saint. Or they might say, "It's all very well for him to do that, but it's not for me"; or they might simply shrug their shoulders and say, "Well, it takes all kinds, doesn't it?" But they would *not* say that a man who did that ought to be punished in some way; they would not even say that he had done anything wrong. In fact, as I have mentioned, they would more likely than not find something admirable about it. The point, then, is this: The non-pacifist does *not* say that it is your *duty* to resist violence with force. The non-pacifist is merely saying that there's nothing wrong with doing so, that one has every right to do so if he is so inclined. Whether we wish to add that a person would be foolish or silly to do so is quite another question, one on which the non-pacifist does not *need* to take any particular position.

Consequently, a genuine pacifist cannot merely say that we may, if we wish, prefer not to resist violence with force. Nor can he merely say that there is something admirable or saintly about not doing so, for, as pointed out above, the non-pacifist could perfectly well agree with that. He must say, instead, that, for whatever class of people he thinks it applies to, there is something positively wrong about meeting violence with force. He must say that, insofar as the people to whom his principle applies resort to force, they are committing a breach of moral duty— a very serious thing to say. Just how serious, we shall ere long see.

Next, we must understand what the implications of holding pacifism as a moral principle are, and the first such implication requiring our attention concerns the matter for the size of the class of people to which it is supposed to apply. It will be of interest to discuss two of the four possibilities previously listed, I think. The first is that in which the pacifist says that only pacifists have the duty of pacifism. Let us see what this amounts to.

If we say that the principle of pacifism is the principle that all and only pacifists have a duty of not opposing violence with force, we get into a very odd situation. For suppose we ask ourselves, "Very well, which people are the pacifists then?" The answer will have to be "All those people who believe that pacifists have the duty not to meet violence with force." But surely one could believe that a certain class of people, whom we shall call "pacifists" have the duty not to meet violence with force without believing that one ought not, oneself, to meet violence with force. That is to say, the "principle" that pacifists ought to avoid, meeting violence with force, is circular: It presupposes that one already knows who the pacifists are. Yet this is precisely what that statement of the principle is supposed to answer! We are supposed to be able to say that anybody who believes that principle is a pacifist; yet, as we have seen, a person could very well believe that a certain class of people called "pacifists" ought not to meet violence with force without believing that he himself ought not to meet violence with force. Thus everyone could be a "pacifist" in the sense of believing that statement and yet no one believe that he *himself* (or anyone in particular) ought to avoid meeting violence with force. Consequently, pacifism cannot be specified in that way. A pacifist must be a person who believes either that he himself (at least) ought not to meet force with force or that some larger class of persons, perhaps everyone, ought not to meet force with force. He would then be believing something definite, and we are then in a position to ask why.

Incidentally, it is worth mentioning that when people say things such as "Only pacifists have the duty of pacifism," "Only Catholics have the duties of Catholicism," and, in general, "Only X-ists have the duties of X-ism" they probably are falling into a trap which catches a good many people. It is, namely, the mistake of supposing that what it *is* to have a certain duty is to *believe* that you have a certain duty. The untenability of this is parallel to the untenability of the previously mentioned attempt to say what pacifism is. For if having a duty is believing that you have a certain duty, the question arises,

"*What* does such a person believe?" The answer that must be given if we follow this analysis would then be, "He believes that he believes that he has a certain duty"; and so on, ad infinitum.

On the other hand, one might believe that having a duty does not consist in believing that one has and yet believe that only those people really have the duty who believe that they have it. But in that case, we would, being conscientious, perhaps want to ask the question, "Well, *ought* I to believe that I have that duty, or oughtn't I?" If you say that the answer is "Yes," the reason cannot be that you already do believe it, for you are asking whether you *should*. On the other hand, the answer "No" or "It doesn't make any difference—it's up to you," implies that there is really no reason for doing the thing in question at all. In short, asking whether I ought to believe that I have a duty to do *x*, is equivalent to asking whether I should do *x*. A person might very well believe that he ought to do *x* but be wrong. It might be the case that he really ought *not* to do *x*; in that case the fact that he believes he ought to do *x*, far from being a reason why he ought to do it, is a reason for us to point out his error. It also, of course, presupposes that he has some reason other than his belief for thinking it is his duty to do *x*.

Having cleared this red herring out of the way, we must consider the view of those who believe that they themselves have a duty of pacifism and ask ourselves the question: What general kind of reason must a person have for supposing a certain type of act to be *his* duty, in a moral sense? Now, one answer he might give is that pacifism as such is a duty, that is, that meeting violence with force is, as such, wrong. In that case, however, what he thinks is not merely that *he* has this duty, but that *everyone* has this duty.

Now he might object, "Well, but no; I don't mean that everyone has it. For instance, if a man is defending, not himself, but *other* people, such as his wife and children, then he has a right to meet violence with force." Now this, of course, would be a very important qualification to his principle and one of a kind which we will be discussing in a moment. Meanwhile, however, we may point out that he evidently still thinks that, if it weren't for certain more important duties, everyone would have a duty to avoid meeting violence with force. In other words, he then believes that, other things being equal, one ought not to meet violence with force. He believes, to put it yet another way, that if one does meet violence with force, one must have a special excuse or justification of a moral kind; then he may want to give some account of just which excuses and justifications would do. Nevertheless, he is now holding a general principle.

Suppose, however, he holds that no one *else* has this duty of pacifism, that only he himself ought not to meet force with force, although it is quite all right for others to do so. Now if this is what our man feels, we may continue to call him a "pacifist," in a somewhat attenuated sense, but he is then no longer holding pacifism as a *moral* principle or, indeed, as a principle at all. For now his disinclination for violence is essentially just a matter of taste. I like pistachio ice cream, but I wouldn't dream of saying that other people have a duty to eat it; similarly, this man just doesn't *like* to meet force with force, although he wouldn't dream of insisting that others act as he does. And this is a secondary sense of "pacifism," first, because pacifism has always been advocated on moral grounds and, second, because non-pacifists can easily have this same feeling. A person might very well feel squeamish, for example, about using force, even in self-defense, or he might not be able to bring himself to use it even if he wants to. But none of these has anything to do with asserting pacifism to be a duty. Moreover, a mere attitude could hardly license a man to refuse military service if it were required of him, or to join ban-the-bomb crusades, and so forth. (I fear, however, that such attitudes have sometimes caused people to do those things.)

And, in turn, it is similarly impossible to claim that your support of pacifism is a moral one if your position is that a certain selection of people, but no one else, ought not to meet force with force, even though you are unprepared to offer any reason whatever for this selection. Suppose, for example, that you hold that only the Arapahoes, or only the Chinese, or only people more than six feet high have this "duty." If such were the case, and no reasons offered at all, we could only conclude that you had a very peculiar attitude toward the Arapahoes, or whatever, but we would hardly want to say that you had a moral principle. Your "principle" amounts to

saying that these particular individuals happen to have the duty of pacifism just because they are the individuals they are, and this, as Bentham would say, is the "negation of all principles." Of course, if you meant that somehow the property of being over six feet tall *makes* it your duty not to use violence, then you have a principle, all right, but a very queer one indeed unless you can give some further reasons. Again, it would not be possible to distinguish this from a sheer attitude.

Pacifism, then, must be the principle that the use of force to meet force is wrong *as such*, that is, that nobody may do so unless he has a special justification.

There is another way in which one might advocate a sort of "pacifism," however, which we must also dispose of before getting to the main point. One might argue that pacifism is desirable as a tactic: that, as a matter of fact, some good end, such as the reduction of violence itself, is to be achieved by "turning the other cheek." For example, if it were the case that turning the other cheek caused the offender to break down and repent, then that would be a very good reason for behaving "pacifistically." If unilateral disarmament causes the other side to disarm, then certainly unilateral disarmament would be a desirable policy. But note that its desirability, if this is the argument, is due to the fact that peace is desirable, a moral position which anybody can take, pacifist or no, plus the purely contingent fact that this policy causes the other side to disarm, that is, it brings about peace.

And, of course, that's the catch. If one attempts to support pacifism because of its probable effects, then one's position depends on what the effects are. Determining what they are is a purely empirical matter, and, consequently, one could not possibly be a pacifist as a matter of pure principle if his reasons for supporting pacifism are merely tactical. One must, in this case, submit one's opinions to the governance of fact.

It is not part of my intention to discuss matters of fact, as such, but it is worthwhile to point out that the general history of the human race certainly offers no support for the supposition that turning the other cheek always produces good effects on the aggressor. Some aggressors, such as the Nazis, were apparently just "egged on" by the "pacifist" attitude of their victims. Some of the S.S. men apparently became curious to see just how much torture the victim would put up with before he began to resist. Furthermore, there is the possibility that, while pacifism might work against some people (one might cite the British, against whom pacifism in India was apparently rather successful—but the British are comparatively nice people), it might fail against others (e.g., the Nazis).

A further point about holding pacifism to be desirable as a tactic is that this could not easily support the position that pacifism is a *duty*. The question whether we have no *right* to fight back can hardly be settled by noting that not to fight back might cause the aggressor to stop fighting. To prove that a policy is a desirable one because it works is not to prove that it is *obligatory* to follow it. We surely need considerations a good deal less tenuous than this to prove such a momentous contention as that we have no *right* to resist.

It appears, then, that to hold the pacifist position as a genuine, full-blooded moral principle is to hold that nobody has a right to fight back when attacked, that fighting back is inherently evil, as such. It means that we are all mistaken in supposing that we have a right of self-protection. And, of course, this is an extreme and extraordinary position in any case. It appears to mean, for instance, that we have no right to punish criminals, that all of our machinery of criminal justice is, in fact, unjust. Robbers, murderers, rapists, and miscellaneous delinquents ought, on this theory, to be let loose.

Now, the pacifist's first move, upon hearing this, will be to claim that he has been misrepresented. He might say that it is only one's *self* that one has no right to defend, and that one may legitimately fight in order to defend other people. This qualification cannot be made by those pacifists who qualify as conscientious objectors, however, for the latter are refusing to defend their fellow citizens and not merely themselves. But this is comparatively trivial when we contemplate the next objection to this amended version of the theory. Let us now ask ourselves what it is about attacks on *other* people which could possibly justify *us* in defending them, while we are not justified in defending ourselves? It cannot be the mere fact that they are other people than ourselves, for, of course, everyone is a different

person from everyone else, and if such a consideration could ever of itself justify anything at all it could also justify anything whatever. That mere difference of person, as such, is of no moral importance, is a presupposition of anything that can possibly pretend to be a moral theory.

Instead of such idle nonsense, then, the pacifist would have to mention some specific characteristic which every *other* person has which we lack and which justifies us in defending them. But this, alas, is impossible, for, while there may be some interesting difference between *me,* on the one hand, and everyone else, on the other, the pacifist is not merely addressing himself to me. On the contrary, as we have seen, he has to address himself to everyone. He is claiming that each person has no right to defend himself, although he does have a right to defend other people. And, therefore, what is needed is a characteristic which distinguishes *each* person from everyone else, and not just *me* from everyone else—which is plainly self-contradictory.

If the reader does not yet see why the "characteristic" of being identical with oneself cannot be used to support a moral theory, let him reflect that the proposition "Everyone is identical with himself" is a trivial truth—as clear an example of an analytic proposition as there could possibly be. But a statement of moral principle is not a trivial truth; it is a substantive moral assertion. But non-tautologous statements, as everyone knows, cannot logically be derived from tautologies, and, consequently, the fact that everyone is identical with himself cannot possibly be used to prove a moral position.

Again, then, the pacifist must retreat in order to avoid talking idle nonsense. His next move, now, might be to say that we have a right to defend all those who are not able to defend themselves. Big, grown-up men who are able to defend themselves ought not to do so, but they ought to defend mere helpless children who are unable to defend themselves.

This last, very queer theory could give rise to some amusing logical gymnastics. For instance, what about groups of people? If a group of people who cannot defend themselves singly can defend themselves together, then when it has grown to that size ought it to stop defending itself? If so, then every time a person *can* defend someone else, he would form with the person being defended a "defensive unit" which was able to defend itself, and thus would by his very presence debar himself from making the defense. At this rate, no one will ever get defended, it seems: The defenseless people by definition cannot defend themselves, while those who can defend them would enable the group consisting of the defenders and the defended to defend themselves, and hence they would be obliged not to do so.

Such reflections, however, are merely curious shadows of a much more fundamental and serious logical problem. This arises when we begin to ask: But why should even defenseless people be defended? If resisting violence is inherently evil, then how can it suddenly become permissible when we use it on behalf of other people? The fact that they are defenseless cannot possibly account for this, for it follows from the theory in question, that everyone ought to put himself in the position of people who are defenseless by refusing to defend himself. This type of pacifist, in short, is using the very characteristic (namely, being in a state of not defending oneself) which he wishes to encourage in others as a reason for denying it in the case of those who already have it (namely, the defenseless). This is indeed self-contradictory.

To attempt to be consistent, at least, the pacifist is forced to accept the characterization of him at which we tentatively arrived. He must indeed say that no one ought ever to be defended against attack. The right of self-defense can be denied coherently only if the right of defense, in general, is denied. This in itself is an important conclusion.

It must be borne in mind, by the way, that I have not said anything to take exception to the man who simply does not wish to defend himself. So long as he does not attempt to make his pacifism into a principle, one cannot accuse him of any inconsistency, however much one might wish to say that he is foolish or eccentric. It is solely with moral principles that I am concerned here.

We now come to the last and most fundamental problem of all. If we ask ourselves what the point of pacifism is, what gets it going, so to speak, the answer is, of course, obvious enough: opposition to violence. The pacifist is generally thought of as the man who is so much opposed to violence that he will not even use it to defend himself or anyone else. And it is precisely this characterization which

I wish to show is far from being plausible, morally inconsistent.

To begin with, we may note something which at first glance may seem merely to be a matter of fact, albeit one which should worry the pacifist, in our latest characterization of him. I refer to the commonplace observation that, generally speaking, we measure a man's degree of opposition to something by the amount of effort he is willing to put forth against it. A man could hardly be said to be dead set against something if he is not willing to lift a finger to keep it from going on. A person who claims to be completely opposed to something yet does nothing to prevent it would ordinarily be said to be a hypocrite.

As facts, however, we cannot make too much of these. The pacifist could claim to be willing to go to any length, short of violence, to prevent violence. He might, for instance, stand out in the cold all day long handing out leaflets (as I have known some to do), and this would surely argue for the sincerity of his beliefs.

But would it really?

Let us ask ourselves, one final time, what we are claiming when we claim that violence is morally wrong and unjust. We are, in the first place, claiming that a person *has no right* to indulge in it, as such (meaning that he has no right to indulge in it, *unless* he has an overriding justification). But what do we mean when we say that he has no right to indulge in it? Violence, of the type we are considering, is a two-termed affair: one does violence *to* somebody, one cannot simply "do violence." It might be oneself, of course, but we are not primarily interested in those cases, for what makes it wrong to commit violence is that it harms the people to whom it is done. To say that it is wrong is to say that those to whom it is done have a right *not* to have it done to them. (This must again be qualified by pointing out that this is so only if they have done nothing to merit having that right abridged.)

Yet what could that right to their own security, which people have, possibly consist in, if not a right at least to defend themselves from whatever violence might be offered them? But lest the reader think that this is a gratuitous assumption, note carefully the reason why having a right involves having a right to be defended from breaches of that right. It is because the prevention of infractions of that right is precisely what one has a right to when one has a right at all. A right just *is* a status justifying preventive action. To say that you have a right to *X* but that no one has any justification whatever for preventing people from depriving you of it, is self-contradictory. If you claim a right to *X,* then to describe some action as an act of depriving you of *X,* is logically to imply that its absence is one of the things that you have a right to.

Thus far it does not follow logically that we have a right to use force in our own or anyone's defense. What does follow logically is that one has a right to whatever may be necessary to prevent infringements of his right. One might at first suppose that the universe *could* be so constructed that it is never necessary to use force to prevent people who are bent on getting something from getting it.

Yet even this is not so, for when we speak of "force" in the sense in which pacifism is concerned with it, we do not mean merely physical "force." To call an action a use of force is not merely to make a reference to the laws of mechanics. On the contrary, it is to describe whatever is being done as being a means to the infliction on somebody of something (ordinarily physical) which he does not want done to him; and the same is true for "force" in the sense in which it applies to war, assault and battery, and the like.

The proper contrary of "force" in this connection is "rational persuasion." Naturally, one way there *might* be of getting somebody not to do something he has no right to do is to convince him he ought not to do it or that it is not in his interest to do it. But it is inconsistent, I suggest, to argue that rational persuasion is the only morally permissible method of preventing violence. A pragmatic reason for this is easy enough to point to: Violent people are too busy being violent to be reasonable. We cannot engage in rational persuasion unless the enemy is willing to sit down and talk; but what if he isn't? One cannot contend that every human being can be persuaded to sit down and talk before he strikes, for this is not something we can determine just by reasoning: it is a question of observation, certainly. But these points are not strictly relevant anyway, for our question is not the empirical question of whether there is some handy way which can always be used to get a person to sit down and discuss moral philosophy when he is about to murder you. Our question is: *If* force is the only way to prevent violence in a given case, is

its use justified *in that case?* This is a purely moral question which we can discuss without any special reference to matters of fact. And, moreover, it is precisely this question which we should have to discuss with the would-be violator. The point is that if a person can be rationally persuaded that he ought not to engage in violence, then precisely what he would be rationally persuaded of if we were to succeed would be the proposition that the use of force is justifiable to prevent him from doing so. For note that if we were to argue that only rational persuasion is permissible as a means of preventing him, we would have to face the question: Do we mean *attempted* rational persuasion, or *successful* rational persuasion, that is, rational persuasion which really does succeed in preventing him from acting? Attempted rational persuasion might fail (if only because the opponent is unreasonable), and then what? To argue that we have a right to use rational persuasion which also succeeds (i.e., we have a right to its success as well as to its use) is to imply that we have a right to prevent him from performing the act. But this, in turn, means that, if attempts at rational persuasion fail, we have a right to the use of force. Thus what we have a right to, if we ever have a *right* to anything, is not merely the use of rational persuasion to keep people from depriving you of the thing to which you have the right. We do indeed have a right to that, but we also have a right to anything else that might be necessary (other things being equal) to prevent the deprivation from occurring. And it is a logical truth, not merely a contingent one, that what *might* be necessary is *force.* (If merely saying something could miraculously deprive someone of the ability to carry through a course of action, then those speech-acts would be called a type of force, if a very mysterious one. And we could properly begin to oppose their use for precisely the same reasons as we now oppose violence.)

What this all adds up to, then, is that *if* we have any rights at all, we have a right to use force to prevent the deprivation of the thing to which we are said to have a right. But the pacifist, of *all* people, is the one most concerned to insist that we do have some rights, namely, the right not to have violence done to us. This is logically implied in asserting it to be a duty on everyone's part to avoid violence. And this is why the pacifist's position is self-contradictory. In saying that violence is wrong, one is at the same time saying that people have a right to its prevention, by force if necessary. Whether and to what extent it may be necessary is a question of fact, but, since it is a question of fact only, the *moral* right to use force on some possible occasions is established....

The true test of the pacifist comes, of course, when he is called upon to assist in the protection of the safety of other persons and not just of himself. For while he is, as I have said, surely entitled to be pacific about his own person if he is so inclined, he is not entitled to be so about the safety of others. It is here that the test of principles comes out. People have a tendency to brand conscientious objectors as cowards or traitors, but

this is not quite fair. They are acting as if they were cowards or traitors, but claiming to do so on principle. It is not surprising if a community should fail to understand such "principles," for the test of adherence to a principle is willingness to act on it, and the appropriate action, if one believes a certain thing to be grossly wrong, is to take steps to prevent or resist it. Thus people who assess conscientious objection as cowardice or worse are taking an understandable step: from an intuitive feeling that the pacifist does not really believe what he is saying they infer that his actions (or inaction) must be due to cowardice. What I am suggesting is that this is not correct: The actions are due, not to cowardice, but to confusion....

ARGUMENT 14 ESSAY QUESTIONS

1. Do you agree with Narveson that there is a contradiction in the pacifist's position? Why or why not?
2. What are Lackey's arguments for pacifism? Do you think they are sound? Suppose you are not an anti-war pacifist. What would be your strongest argument *against* the position?
3. Suppose you an anti-war pacifist. What would be your strongest argument *for* the position?

15. THE SELF-DEFENSE ARGUMENT FOR WAR

Probably the strongest justification for the resort to war is self-defense. In "The Legalist Paradigm," Michael Walzer argues that we all have a right of self-defense, a right to defend ourselves and possibly others from an aggressor, and if we have such a right, we may be justified in taking a life to exercise it, both in personal self-defense and in a war of self-defense. In particular, Walzer contends, the right of self-defense in war is based on an analogy with personal self-defense. As another philosopher puts it, "if it's moral to defend your family, friends, or innocent people from an assailant by killing the assailant, then it's moral to defend your country or another friendly country from being taken over by an aggressor by attacking that aggressor."[15]

---

[15] Louis P. Pojman, "War," *Life and Death* (Belmont, CA: Wadsworth, 2000), 191.

Some pacifists may be willing to accept half of this argument—that is, to agree that personal self-defense may be justified but to reject self-defense in war. Your resisting the assault of a crazed killer may be permissible, but going to war to defend against Hitler's brutal blitzkrieg is not. Some observers, however, think this view is incoherent. For example:

> It is doubtful, however, that an *absolute* rejection of war can be coherently grounded on anything other than an absolute prohibition of certain types of act necessarily involved in war—e.g. intentional violence and killing. And any prohibition of certain types of action that will rule out war in all instances will almost certainly rule out the use of violence in individual self-defence.[16]

Pacifists have a tough response to one version of the self-defense argument. Some nonpacifists view self-defense in war as *personal* self-defense, as a matter of kill or be killed. In such a situation, they say, killing is surely justified. But pacifists can then charge that this kind of self-defense does not obtain in war:

> First of all, on the usual understanding of "self-defense," those who kill can claim the justification of self-defense only if (a) they had no other way to save their lives or preserve themselves from physical harm except by killing, and (b) they did nothing to provoke the attack to which they are subjected. Antiwar pacifists point out that soldiers on the battlefield do have a way of saving themselves from death or harm without killing anyone: they can surrender. Furthermore, for soldiers fighting for an unjust cause—for example, German soldiers fighting in the invasion of Russia in 1941—it is difficult to argue that they "did nothing to provoke" the deadly force directed at them. But if the German army provoked the Russians to stand and fight on Russian soil, German soldiers cannot legitimately claim self-defense as a moral justification for killing Russian soldiers.[17]

The Legalist Paradigm

MICHAEL WALZER

If states actually do possess rights more or less as individuals do, then it is possible to imagine a society among them more or less like the society of individuals. The comparison of international to civil order is crucial to the theory of aggression. I have already been making it regularly. Every reference to aggression as the international equivalent of armed robbery

"The Legalist Paradigm" by Michael Walzer in *Just and Unjust Wars*, 58–63. © 1977 New York: Basic Books.

---

[16] Jeff McMahan, "War and Peace," in *A Companion to Ethics*, ed. Peter Singer (Oxford: Blackwell, 1993), 386.

[17] Douglas P. Lackey, "Pacifism."

or murder, and every comparison of home and country or of personal liberty and political independence, relies upon what is called the *domestic analogy*. Our primary perceptions and judgments of aggression are the products of analogical reasoning. When the analogy is made explicit, as it often is among the lawyers, the world of states takes on the shape of a political society the character of which is entirely accessible through such notions as crime and punishment, self-defense, law enforcement, and so on.

These notions, I should stress, are not incompatible with the fact that international society as it exists today is a radically imperfect structure. As we experience it, that society might be likened to a defective building, founded on rights; its superstructure raised, like that of the state itself, through political conflict, cooperative activity, and commercial exchange; the whole thing shaky and unstable because it lacks the rivets of authority. It is like domestic society in that men and women live at peace within it (sometimes), determining the conditions of their own existence, negotiating and bargaining with their neighbors. It is unlike domestic society in that every conflict threatens the structure as a whole with collapse. Aggression challenges it directly and is much more dangerous than domestic crime, because there are no policemen. But that only means that the "citizens" of international society must rely on themselves and on one another. Police powers are distributed among all the members. And these members have not done enough in the exercise of their powers if they merely contain the aggression or bring it to a speedy end—as if the police should stop a murderer after he has killed only one or two people and send him on his way. The rights of the member states must be vindicated, for it is only by virtue of those rights that there is a society at all. If they cannot be upheld (at least sometimes), international society collapses into a state of war or is transformed into a universal tyranny.

From this picture, two presumptions follows. The first, which I have already pointed out, is the presumption in favor of military resistance once aggression has begun. Resistance is important so that rights can be maintained and future aggressors deterred. The theory of aggression restates the old doctrine of the just war: it explains when fighting is a crime and when it is permissible, perhaps even morally desirable.[1] The victim of aggression fights in self-defense,

but he isn't only defending himself, for aggression is a crime against society as a whole. He fights in its name and not only in his own. Other states can rightfully join the victim's resistance; their war has the same character as his own, which is to say, they are entitled not only to repel the attack but also to punish it. All resistance is also law enforcement. Hence the second presumption: when fighting breaks out, there must always be some state against which the law can and should be enforced. Someone must be responsible, for someone decided to break the peace of the society of states. No war, as medieval theologians explained, can be just on both sides.

There are, however, wars that are just on neither side, because the idea of justice doesn't pertain to them or because the antagonists are both aggressors, fighting for territory or power where they have no right. The first case I have already alluded to in discussing the voluntary combat of aristocratic warriors. It is sufficiently rare in human history that nothing more need be said about it here. The second case is illustrated by those wars that Marxists call "imperialist," which are not fought between conquerors and victims but between conquerors and conquerors, each side seeking dominion over the other or the two of them competing to dominate some third party. Thus Lenin's description of the struggles between "have" and "have-not" nations in early twentieth-century Europe: "...picture to yourselves a slave-owner who owned 100 slaves warring against a slave-owner who owned 200 slaves for a more 'just' distribution of slaves. Clearly, the application of the term 'defensive' war in such a case...would be sheer deception..." But it is important to stress that we can penetrate the deception only insofar as we can ourselves distinguish justice and injustice: the theory of imperialist war presupposes the theory of aggression. If one insists that all wars on all sides are acts of conquest or attempted conquest, or that all states at all times would conquer if they could, then the argument for justice is defeated before it begins and the moral judgments we actually make are derided as fantasies. Consider the following passage from Edmund Wilson's book on the American Civil War:

> I think that it is a serious deficiency on the part of historians...that they so rarely interest themselves

in biological and zoological phenomena. In a recent...film showing life at the bottom of the sea, a primitive organism called a sea slug is seen gobbling up small organisms through a large orifice at one end of its body; confronted with another sea slug of an only slightly lesser size, it ingurgitates that, too. Now the wars fought by human beings are stimulated as a rule...by the same instincts as the voracity of the sea slug.

There are no doubt wars to which that image might be fit, though it is not a terribly useful image with which to approach the Civil War. Nor does it account for our ordinary experience of international society. Not all states are sea-slug states, gobbling up their neighbors. There are always groups of men and women who would live if they could in peaceful enjoyment of their rights and who have chosen political leaders who represent that desire. The deepest purpose of the state is not ingestion but defense, and the least that can be said is that many actual states serve that purpose. When their territory is attacked or their sovereignty challenged, it makes sense to look for an aggressor and not merely for a natural predator. Hence we need a theory of aggression rather than a zoological account.

The theory of aggression first takes shape under the aegis of the domestic analogy. I am going to call that primary form of the theory the *legalist paradigm,* since it consistently reflects the conventions of law and order. It does not necessarily reflect the arguments of the lawyers, though legal as well as moral debate has its starting point here. Later on, I will suggest that our judgments about the justice and injustice of particular wars are not entirely determined by the paradigm. The complex realities of international society drive us toward a revisionist perspective, and the revisions will be significant ones. But the paradigm must first be viewed in its unrevised form; it is our baseline, our model, the fundamental structure for the moral comprehension of war. We begin with the familiar world of individuals and rights, of crimes and punishments. The theory of aggression can then be summed up in six propositions.

1. *There exists an international society of independent states.* States are the members of this society, not private men and women. In the absence of

a universal state, men and women are protected and their interests represented only by their own governments. Though states are founded for the sake of life and liberty, they cannot be challenged in the name of life and liberty by any other states. Hence the principle of non-intervention, which I will analyze later on. The rights of private persons can be recognized in international society, as in the UN Charter of Human Rights, but they cannot be enforced without calling into question the dominant values of that society: the survival and independence of the separate political communities.

2. *This international society has a law that establishes the rights of its members—above all, the rights of territorial integrity and political sovereignty.* Once again, these two rest ultimately on the right of men and women to build a common life and to risk their individual lives only when they freely choose to do so. But the relevant law refers only to states, and its details are fixed by the intercourse of states, through complex processes of conflict and consent. Since these processes are continuous, international society has no natural shape; nor are rights within it ever finally or exactly determined. At any given moment, however, one can distinguish the territory of one people from that of another and say something about the scope and limits of sovereignty.

3. *Any use of force or imminent threat of force by one state against the political sovereignty or territorial integrity of another constitutes aggression and is a criminal act.* As with domestic crime, the argument here focuses narrowly on actual or imminent boundary crossings: invasions and physical assaults. Otherwise, it is feared, the notion of resistance to aggression would have no determinate meaning. A state cannot be said to be forced to fight unless the necessity is both obvious and urgent.

4. *Aggression justifies two kinds of violent response: a war of self-defense by the victim and a war of law enforcement by the victim and any other member of international society.* Anyone can come to the aid of a victim, use necessary force against an aggressor, and even make whatever is the international equivalent of a "citizen's arrest." As in domestic society, the obligations of bystanders are not easy to make out, but it is the tendency of the theory to undermine the right of neutrality and to require widespread participation in the business of

law enforcement. In the Korean War, this participation was authorized by the United Nations, but even in such cases the actual decision to join the fighting remains a unilateral one, best understood by analogy to the decision of a private citizen who rushes to help a man or woman attacked on the street.

5. *Nothing but aggression can justify war.* The central purpose of the theory is to limit the occasions for war. "There is a single and only just cause for commencing a war," wrote Vitoria, "namely, a wrong received." There must actually have been a wrong, and it must actually have been received (or its receipt must be, as it were, only minutes away). Nothing else warrants the use of force in international society—above all, not any difference of religion or politics. Domestic heresy and injustice are never actionable in the world of states: hence, again, the principle of nonintervention.

6. *Once the aggressor state has been militarily repulsed, it can also be punished.* The conception of just war as an act of punishment is very old, though neither the procedures nor the forms of punishment have ever been firmly established in customary or positive international law. Nor are its purposes entirely clear: to exact retribution, to deter other states, to restrain or reform this one?

When War Is Unjust
Being Honest in Just-War Thinking

JOHN HOWARD YODER

MAKING THE TRADITION CREDIBLE
The preceding review of the ups and downs of history should have made it clear that the just-war tradition is not a simple formula ready to be applied in a self-evident and univocal way. It is rather a set of very broad assumptions whose implications demand—if they are to be respected as morally honest—that they be spelled out in some detail and then tested for their ability to throw serious light

All three figure largely in the literature, though it is probably fair to say that deterrence and restraint are most commonly accepted. When people talk of fighting a war against war, this is usually what they have in mind. The domestic maxim is, punish crime to prevent violence; its international analogue is, punish aggression to prevent war. Whether the state as a whole or only particular persons are the proper objects of punishment is a harder question, for reasons I will consider later on. But the implication of the paradigm is clear: if states are members of international society, the subjects of rights, they must also be (somehow) the objects of punishment.

NOTE
1. I shall say nothing here of the argument for nonviolent resistance to aggression, according to which fighting is neither desirable nor necessary. This argument has not figured much in the development of the conventional view. Indeed, it poses a radical challenge to the conventions: if aggression can be resisted, and at least sometimes successfully resisted, without war, it may be a less serious crime than has commonly been supposed. I will take up this possibility and its moral implications in the Afterword.

on real situations and on the decisions of persons and institutions regarding those situations. We therefore turn to the effort to itemize the resources that would be needed if such authentic implementation were to become a reality.

From *When War Is Unjust: Being Honest in Just-War Thinking*, 1996, by John Howard Yoder, 71–80. Used with permission of Anne Marie Yoder.

Intention

Beginning from the inside, we would need to clarify whether in the minds and the hearts of the people using this language there has been a conscious commitment to make the sacrifices required to apply the doctrine negatively. At some time, if the doctrine is not a farce, there would be cases where an intrinsically just cause would have to go undefended militarily because there would be no authority legitimated to defend it. Or an intrinsically just cause defended by a legitimate authority would have to be forsaken because the only way to defend it would be by unjust means. That would be the setting for testing whether citizens or leaders were able in principle to conceive of the sacrifice of that value as morally imperative. Is it something citizens would press on their leaders? Is it reason for the draftee to refuse to serve, or reason for a statesman to negotiate peace?

There is no strong evidence for believing that most people using just-war language are ready, either psychically or intellectually, for that serious choice. In popular language—which translates "negotiated peace" as "surrender," proclaims that there is "no substitute for victory," and loosely uses the military language of "necessity" to cover almost any infraction of the laws of war—we have seen the evidence not merely of the high value attributed uncritically to one's own nation or to the righteousness of its cause, but also a profound psychodynamic avoidance mechanism. By refusing to face real options, that avoidance makes it highly unlikely that in undesirable situations there will be any chance of making the hard moral choice.

Last Resort

What constitutes a situation of last resort is not something that can be decided only at the last minute or only by one party. What is decisive to determine whether efforts to resolve political conflicts by means less destructive than war have been adequate will largely depend on whether there was any disposition or plan to attempt to use such prior means in the first place.

During the first decade after Hiroshima the United States could count on its nuclear monopoly to enforce its view of peace around the world; there were not sufficient non-nuclear military means available for effective use in smaller conflicts, so

that disproportionate nuclear means threatened to become not the last but the only resort. Similarly, any preoccupation with projecting an image of strength tempts the strong party to leapfrog up the scale past the less destructive recourses.

The United States has been less willing than some other nations to accept in principle the authority of agencies of international arbitration, with the Connally Amendment[1] actually undercutting in a formal way the possibility of recourse to agencies like The Hague International Court of Justice. Even less have we invested in means of conflict resolution on lower levels. We spent forty years sharing with the Soviet Union and China the strategy of escalating local conflicts into surrogates for superpower confrontation, rather than seeking to maximize the authentic independence of non-aligned nations or mediating institutions.

The economic patterns dominating our country have militated against the use of economic and cultural sanctions (positive and negative) to foster international goals, although there have been more efforts (mostly ad hoc, clumsy, and often counterproductive) to use means short of war in some cases.[2] Our international aid agencies hardly have the expertise to administer positive reinforcement in such a way as to diminish recourse to military sanctions without falling prey to new forms of dependency, corruption, and so on. When a government abroad raises any questions about our national interests, we have agencies like the CIA that contribute to escalating rather than diminishing tensions. If we sought to be honest about the restraint on violence implied in the just-war tradition, we would have a nonviolent alternative to the CIA. This would be a creative, non-threatening, information-gathering instrument, which instead of destabilizing regimes it considers unfriendly would find positive means of fostering interdependent development.

Strategies of Nonviolence

Recourse to international agencies of arbitration and mediation as a factor in evaluating when a situation of "last resort" exists is an old idea becoming increasingly pertinent. More attention needs to be given, and has only begun to be given, to a newer development, namely, the rise of aggressive nonviolent strategies for social conflict and change. The impact of Gandhi and King is only the tip of the iceberg. Besides, beyond, and since them, there have also been:

a) Numerous spontaneous phenomena of non-cooperation with injustice, which have achieved sometimes the desired social change and sometimes a more powerful witness of martyrdom than lashing out with firearms would have done[3];

b) A growing circle of leaders, using similar tactics in their most varied circumstances, most notably and recently:

- the change of government in Manila in February 1986;
- changes of government in Eastern Europe in the fall of 1989 and in Madagascar in 1991; sometimes the recourse to nonviolence was thought through and sometimes it was spontaneous;

c) A growing body of political science literature projecting the serious possibility of attaining without military violence some of the objectives it has previously been claimed could only be attained by war.[4] Nonviolent action on behalf of justice is no automatic formula for success, but neither is war. Most people who go to war for some cause they deem worthy are defeated.[5]

A careful reading of history can find far greater reason than many have previously recognized for expecting nonviolent strategies to be effective. Both anecdotal evidence and social-science analysis have made good beginnings toward projecting and evaluating possible nonmilitary means for defending those values which military means can no longer defend, whether that "no longer" is taken morally or practically.

It is not our task to review that body of literature. If there is available a body of thought and a set of tools of analysis and projection that can respond seriously to the question, How can we defend ourselves if war can no longer do it?, then the situation called last resort cannot be held to obtain. Most of these thinkers are not doctrinaire pacifists.[6] For their arguments to hold water it suffices to agree that war is not justified when it does not achieve its stated aims and when it does more harm than good.

If there are more nonviolent resources available than people have thought about, and if there would

be still more available if they *were* thought about, then the conclusion is unavoidable that the notion of last resort—one of the classical criteria of the just-war tradition—must exercise more restraint than it did before.

Authority

The next logical test of the mental readiness of people to live within the limits of honest just-war thinking is at the institutional level. Our government invests millions of staff hours and billions of taxpayers' dollars in developing contingency plans for all possible situations in which the legitimate military prosecution of hostilities would be effective. Where is the contingency planning, where are the thought exercises and training maneuvers for continuing the defense of our values in those situations where military means will not be appropriate? In the 1960s Stephen King-Hall projected the case for defense in a nuclear age needing to be, at least in some cases, nonmilitary.[7] Since then many others have spelled out these possibilities. It cannot be said that the failure of military scientists or political ethicists to respond to King-Hall's challenge is due to the author's not being competent and respected or his argument not being cogent. Whether the avoidance mechanisms that refuse to face this challenge are best analyzed in budgetary, psychodynamic, or political terms, they tend to count against the credibility of those who refuse to respond to the practically formulated challenges of King-Hall, Sharp, and the others. Thereby they tend to compromise the credibility of their *pro forma* adherence to the laws of war, and thereby in turn they tend to discredit the coherence of the just-war system itself.

The last few sentences made a backhanded argument. Now I should state the affirmation that corresponds to it. The legitimate authority, which claims the right and the duty to defend the legitimate interests of its citizens (or its allies) by the disciplined and proportionate use of military violence, will be morally credible only when and as it gives evidence of a proportionate investment of creativity and foresight in arrangements to defend those same values by alternate means, in those other contexts in which military means would *not* be morally or legally or technically appropriate. If they are not making those contingency plans, then both their claim that they have the right and duty to use war and their claim that they will do it within the moral limits of the just-war heritage and the legal limits of the laws of war lose credibility.

This awareness that contingency planning for alternative strategies would be a proof of sincerity yields another benefit for our conversation. It tells us that in the measurement of what constitutes last resort, it is not morally sufficient for politicians and strategists to shrug their shoulders and say "we could not think of anything else to do." At least in our times we have the social-science instruments and the intellectual discipline for thinking of alternatives. Last resort can only be claimed when other recourses short of the last have been tested seriously.

Proportion

The reasoning process required by the just-war tradition calls for the evil likely to be caused by warfare to be measured against the evil it hopes to prevent. The critics of the tradition have always wondered what kind of reasoning is going on when one measures various kinds of goods and evils against each other: for example, lives against freedom, or institutions against architecture. We are now trying to wager on the credibility of the tradition. Those who believe that this thought pattern is reliable owe it to their own integrity (and to their potential victims) to possess reliable and verifiable measures of the evil they claim to be warding off and the lesser evil they are willing to commit, albeit reluctantly and without "direct intention."

Such calculation must properly seek to take account not only of specific deeds that one is immediately aware of choosing, but also of the potential for escalation and proliferation which a first step across the threshold of violence can let loose. One would have to factor in the greater or lesser degree of uncertainty with which one can predict both kinds of evils and their causal connection so as to promise just-cause results. Certainly decisions based upon the claimed ability to bring about less evil results, and to do so at the cost of the lives and values of others, need for the sake of one's own integrity to stand up to testing. Such reckoning of proportionality can never be fully certain, but the burden of proof lies with the party who says that it

is probable enough to justify intervening by causing some certain lethal evil in order to reduce other projected evils.[8]

Moral Leverage

Thus far I have been describing what institutional instruments would be needed to make the doctrine credible in the sense of applicable. There are however other questions which might come first logically from the perspective of religious moral commitment. Are there people who affirm that their own uncoerced allegiance as believers gives them strength and motivation to honor the restraints of the just-war tradition and to help one another to do so? This might be the only angle from which the development of the needed institutions could be fostered. Would believers commit themselves, and commit themselves to press each other, to be willing to enter the political opposition, or to resign public office, or to espouse selective objection? Does any church teach future soldiers and citizens in such a way that they will know beyond what point they cannot support an unjust war or use an unjust weapon?

Since the capacity to reach an independent judgment concerning the legality and morality of what is being done by one's rulers depends on information, which by the nature of the case must be contested, does the religious community provide alternative resources for gathering and evaluating information concerning the political causes for which their governments demand their violent support? What are the preparations being made to obtain and verify an adequately independent and reliable source of facts and of analytical expertise, enabling honest dissent to be so solidly founded as to be morally convincing? Is every independent thinker on his or her own, or will the churches support agencies to foster dissent when called for?

Neither the pacifist nor the crusader needs to study in depth the facts of politics in order to make a coherent decision. The person claiming to respect just-war rationality must do so, however, and therefore must have a reliable independent source of information. I have stated this as a question about the church, but it also applies to the society. Is there free debate? Are the information media free? Is opposition legitimate? Does the right of conscientious objection have legal recognition?

Are soldiers when assigned a mission given sufficient information to determine whether this is an order they should obey? If a person under orders is convinced he or she must disobey, will the command structure, the society, and the church honor that dissent? It is reported that in the case of the obliteration bombing of Dresden the pilots were not informed that it could hardly be considered a military target. For most of the rest of the just-war criteria factual knowledge is similarly indispensable.

Until today church agencies on any level have invested little effort in literature or other educational means to teach the just-war limitations. The few such efforts one sees are in no way comparable to the way in which the churches teach their young people about other matters concerning which they believe morality is important, such as sexuality. The understanding of the just-war logic that led American young men to refuse to serve in Vietnam came to them not primarily from the ecclesiastical or academic interpreters of the tradition but rather from the notions of fair play presupposed in our popular culture.[9]

A Fair Test

Those who conclude, either deliberately or rapidly, that in a given situation of injustice there are no nonviolent options available, often do so in a way that avoids responsibility for any intensive search for such options. The military option for which they so quickly reach has involved a long lead time in training and equipping the forces. It demands the preparation of a special class of leadership, for which most societies have special schools and learning experiences. It demands costly special resources dependent on abundant government funding, and it demands broad alliances. It includes the willingness to lose lives and to take lives, to sacrifice other cultural values for a generation or more, and the willingness of families to be divided.

Yet the decision that nonviolent means will not work for comparable ends is made without any comparable investment of time or creativity, without comparable readiness to sacrifice, and without serious projection of comparable costs. The American military forces would not "work" if we did not invest billions of dollars in equipping, planning,

and training. Why should it be fair to measure the moral claims of an alternative strategy by setting up the debate in such a way that that other strategy should have to promise equivalent results with far less financial investment and less planning on every level? The epigram of the 1960s—People give nonviolence two weeks to solve their problems and then say it has failed; they've gone on with violence for centuries, and it seems never to have failed—is not a pacifist argument. It is a sober self-corrective within just-war reasoning.

In sum, the challenge should be clear. If the tradition which claims that war may be justified does not also admit that in particular cases it may *not* be justified, the affirmation is not morally serious. A Christian who prepares the case for a justifiable war without being equally prepared for the negative case has not soberly weighed the *prima facie* presumption that any violence is wrong until the case for the exception has been made. We honor the moral seriousness of the nonpacifist Christian when we spell out the criteria by which the credibility of that commitment, shaped in the form of the just-war system, must be judged.

NOTES

1. In 1946 the United States Senate passed Resolution 196 concerning the submission of United States international affairs to the jurisdiction of the International Court of Justice. Senator Connally's amendment consisted of six words: "as determined by the United States." That is, we get to determine what is domestic and to be controlled by our courts, and what is not domestic and hence controlled by international justice. In 1984–85 the United States ruled that the mining of harbors in Nicaragua was domestic.

2. The cynic observing the reluctance of U.S. legislators and administrators to commit troops in overseas interventions (e.g., Somalia, Bosnia, Haiti) would suggest that it was the product not of just-war scruples but of unwillingness to run risks where strong economic "national interests" would not be served.

3. Some of these stories are told by Ronald J. Sider, *Nonviolence: The Invincible Weapon?* (Dallas: Word Books, 1989).

4. See John Howard Yoder, "The Power of Nonviolence," available from the Joan B. Kroc Institute for

International Peace Studies, Notre Dame, IN 46556 (document 6:WP:2).

5. Logically speaking, one side in every war is defeated. Often the "victor" is also worse off than before. The classical just-war criterion of probable success is one of the most difficult to honor; it is one of the points where holy or macho reflexes most easily override rational restraint.

6. See King-Hall, *Defense in a Nuclear Age.* Sir Stephen King-Hall served as instructor in military science in the war colleges of the United Kingdom during World War II. Gene Sharp's numerous publications are based on political realism.

7. King-Hall, *Defense in a Nuclear Age.*

8. "If you have the choice between a real evil and a hypothetical evil, always take the hypothetical one" (Joan Baez, "Three Cheers for Grandma!" *Daybreak* [New York: Dial, 1968] and *Atlantic Monthly* [August 1968], cited in J. Yoder, ed., *What Would You Do?* [Scottdale, Penn.: Herald Press, 1992], 63).

9. Like the morality plays of medieval Europe, the police thriller and the western in our culture are the primary instruments of moral education. That the good guy does not shoot first, that innocents should not be killed, and that the good guy wins in the end even though (or even because) he fights by the rules, are staples of that narrative moral instruction.

ARGUMENT 15 ESSAY QUESTIONS

1. Do you believe that the analogy of personal self-defense provides an adequate justification for going to war in self-defense? Why or why not?

2. What is Walzer's view on war and self-defense? Does he show that some wars are morally permissible? Explain.

3. Do you think some wars are morally justified? If so, on what grounds? If not, why not?

16. THE JUST WAR ARGUMENT AGAINST TERRORISM

Some argue that terrorism is immoral for the same reason that some wars are immoral: it violates principles of just war theory. Haig Khatchadourian, for example, contends that terrorism is always morally wrong because it falls short of the just war requirements of discrimination, proportionality, and necessity.

He distinguishes four types of terrorism and asserts that they all run afoul of the *jus in bello* principle of discrimination (the prohibition against deliberately harming noncombatants):

In many acts of terrorism some or all of the immediate victims and/or victimized are innocent persons, in no way morally connected with or in any degree responsible for the wrong moralistic terrorism is intended to help rectify, hence for the physical or mental harm that the terrorists inflict on them. In predatory terrorism the immediate victims and the victimized are, almost without exception, innocent persons. That is also often true of retaliatory terrorism, at least as far as the immediate victims are concerned.... In political and political-moralistic terrorism, whether in wartime or in time of peace, some of the immediate victims or some of the victimized are likely to be innocent persons; but some may be noninnocents, such as members (especially high-ranking members) of the military, who are morally responsible for the real or imagined wrong that triggers the terrorism.[18]

He maintains that terrorism violates both the *jus ad bellum* and *jus in bello* forms of the principle of proportionality (the requirement to balance the good achieved through violence with the resulting evil). Regarding *jus ad bellum* proportionality, he argues that:

[T]he preceding types of terrorism are indeed in serious violation of the political principle of proportion. For the result of tallying the evils of terrorist acts in human pain and suffering, death and destruction, against the nonexistent overall benefits leaves a huge surplus of unmitigated evil on the negative side. I refer not only to the evil inflicted by the terrorists upon their victims and the victimized but also the evil they draw upon themselves and their families by risking loss of life, limb, or liberty in ultimately futile pursuit of their dangerous and violent objectives.[19]

Andrew Valls also thinks that just war theory can help us evaluate the morality of terrorism, but he argues, contrary to Khatchadourian, that *jus ad bellum* and *jus in bello* principles can actually justify some terrorist acts:

Though stateless, some groups can nevertheless have a just cause when their right of self-determination is frustrated. Under such circumstances, a representative organization can be a morally legitimate authority to carry out violence as a last resort to defend the group's rights. Such violence must conform to the other criteria, especially discrimination, but terrorism, I have argued can do so.... I have little doubt that most terrorist acts do not satisfy all of the criteria of just war theory and that many of them fall far short. In such cases we are well justified in condemning them.[20]

---

[18] Haig Khatchadourian, "The Morality of Terrorism," 24.
[19] Haig Khatchadourian, "The Morality of Terrorism," 28.
[20] Andrew Valls, "Can Terrorism Be Justified?" in *Ethics in International Affairs*, ed. Andrew Valls (Lanham, MD: Rowman and Littlefield, 2000), 65–79.

The Morality of Terrorism

HAIG KHATCHADOURIAN

I

Although the literature on terrorism is constantly growing, very little has been written about the morality of terrorism; perhaps because the writers take it for granted that terrorism is a scourge, always morally reprehensible and wrong: note for instance the common equation of terrorism with murder. Only a mere handful of articles by Anglo-American philosophers (some of which will be referred to in this chapter) and only one book to date by a philosopher, Burleigh Taylor Wilkins' *Terrorism and Collective Responsibility*[1] deals with it at all. The same is true of books on terrorism by nonphilosophers. Only two books I know of are devoted to the subject: *The Morality of Terrorism: Religious and Secular Justifications,* edited by David C. Rapaport and Yonah Alexander,[2] and *Political Murder* by Franklin Lord[3] (note the title). Paul Wilkinson includes a short section entitled "Terrorism and Criminality" in his *Terrorism and the Liberal State.*[4] He begins by noting[5] that

> Because terrorists, by definition, follow a systematic policy of terror…their acts are analogous to crimes….In most legal systems the typical acts of terrorist groups (such as bombings, murders, kidnaping, wounding and blackmail) constitute serious offences under the prevailing codes. Without exception murder is punishable under the legal code of all states. As terrorism involves systematic cold-blooded murder it is particularly repugnant to the Judaeo-Christian tradition and to all societies which are deeply infused with human values.

This is not a very auspicious beginning for a moral evaluation of terrorism. From the fact that terrorist acts, including the killing of immediate victims, are prohibited in many if not all municipal legal systems, it does not follow that some or all such acts are *morally* wrong. Calling terrorist killings "murder" begs the complex ethical issues involved, even if one subscribes to the traditional Natural Law theory of law or to a contemporary form of that

theory: that is if one supposes that a putative law is law proper only if it is just or moral. Even then the putative immorality of terrorist acts must first be established for the Natural Law legal philosopher or jurist to accept the municipal laws that outlaw terrorist acts as *bona fide* laws rather than (in Aquinas' graphic description) "violence."[6]

Wilkinson distinguishes four "special cases of exception" to the still widely held "divine injunction" against murder. These special cases or exceptions, according to him, are: "(i) murder committed in the course of a just war on behalf of one's country…, (ii) judicial execution in punishment for the crimes of murder or treason…, (iii) murder committed in the course of a just rebellion against tyrannical rule or foreign conquest; and (iv) in self-defense against violent attack."[7] He adds: "Clearly there is a world of difference between justification for specific acts of murder and justification for a systematic policy of indiscriminate murder as a means to a political end."[8] (We can add "predatory," "retaliatory" and "moralistic/religious" to "political end.")

Whether at a minimum some terrorist acts committed in the course of a just war or rebellion are morally justified is an important question and will be discussed in this chapter in relation to just war theory, as well as in relation to Liberationist revolutionary movements. But no terrorist killings or other forms of violence against the immediate victims can fall under—and so can be justified as—"self-defense"; and clearly, terrorist killing cannot be normally regarded as "judicial execution in punishment for the crimes of murder or treason." Wilkinson is therefore right that terrorist killings cannot be morally justified as falling under exceptions (i) and (iii). I am assuming for the sake of argument that in certain circumstances killing in self-defense and in judicial execution are morally justifiable.

From *The Morality of Terrorism* by Haig Khatchadourian, 17–34. © 1998 New York: Peter Lang.

I say that no act of terrorist killing can be *normally* considered as judicial execution because a terrorist *state* that practices terrorism from above against its own citizens may conceivably execute its victims "judicially." That is, if such "execution" is in accord with the country's municipal law. Even then such executions would be murder unless one adopts a radical legal positivist theory of law.[9] On a Natural Law theory of jurisprudence the execution *would* be murder, hence unlawful, if terrorism from above is immoral. Thus we come back to the fundamental question of the morality of terrorism, in this case terrorism from above.

Executions by kangaroo courts, whose victims are framed or otherwise denied the rights and protections of a just penal system, are clearly reprehensible and must be automatically eliminated from the present inquiry into the morality of terrorism. Two examples of such horrible miscarriages of justice in living memory are Joseph Stalin's infamous purges in the 1930s, and the "disappearances" of thousands of people in South American countries during the 1970s. But the "judicial" executions practiced even by a terrorist state cannot be dismissed *en masse*, as cold blooded murder, without examination.[10] Assuming that capital punishment is morally justifiable, it is just conceivable—though unlikely in the extreme—that the courts in a terrorist state may on occasion justly execute properly convicted murderers.

In the book referred to above, Wilkinson condemns the "deliberate choice of systematic and indiscriminate murder as their [the terrorists'] sole or principal means of struggle,"[11] even if they claim, "as they commonly do, that they are waging a just war or just rebellion in terms of the classical criteria laid down by theologians and moral philosophers."[12] He adds that it is "a logical absurdity to try to justify terrorism in terms of an ethic founded on the sanctity of individual human life."[13]

Wilkinson next considers the supposed "higher 'revolutionary morality' which transvalues everything in terms of the revolutionary struggle," according to which terrorists claim to act.[14] His point is that terrorism is "a moral crime, a crime against humanity, an attack not only on our security, our rule of law, and the safety of the state, but on civilized society itself."[15] Once again he rests his conclusion on "Western Judaeo-Christian, liberal and humanist values, and the ethical and legal systems that have been shaped by this tradition."[16]

Finally, Wilkinson notes the existence of what he calls "revolutionary crimes against humanity. Revolutionary terrorists are those who choose to devote themselves to the macabre specialisms of revolutionary criminality."[17]

Since the central thesis of this chapter and a main thesis of this book is that all types and forms of terrorism are always wrong, I wholeheartedly agree with Wilkinson and all others who condemn terrorism. But Wilkinson's highly suggestive arguments are too sketchy as they stand. What is required are more systematic arguments, particularly as the view that terrorism is always wrong is not universally accepted. True, some who practice or who defend what their critics call terrorism refuse to consider it so at all. They call it "freedom fighting,"[18] implying that terrorism is either universally wrong or wrong in certain instances. On the other hand some philosophers, including some moral philosophers, either defend certain forms of terrorism, or terrorism in certain special circumstances.

TERRORISM AND JUST WAR THEORY

The traditional conditions of a just war are of two sorts: conditions of justified going to war (*jus ad bellum*) and conditions of the just prosecution of a war in progress (*jus in bello*). One of the fundamental conditions of the latter kind is that

> The destruction of life and property, even enemy life and property, is inherently bad. It follows that military forces should cause no more destruction than is strictly necessary to achieve their objectives. (Notice that the principle does not say that whatever is necessary is permissible, but that everything permissible must be necessary.) This is the principle of necessity: that *wanton* destruction is forbidden. More precisely, the principle of necessity specifies that a military operation is forbidden if there is some alternative operation that causes less destruction but has the same probability of producing a successful military result.[19]

Another fundamental condition is the principle of discrimination or noncombatant immunity, which prohibits the deliberate harming—above all the killing—of innocent persons. In "Just War Theory" William O'Brien defines that condition as the principle that "prohibits direct intentional attacks on non-combatants and nonmilitary targets,"[20] and Douglas Lackey, in *The Ethics of War and Peace,* characterizes it as "the idea that...civilian life and property should not be subjected to military force: military force must be directed only at military objectives."[21] A third fundamental condition is the principle of proportion, as "applied to discrete military ends."[22] That condition is defined by O'Brien as "requiring proportionality of means to political and military ends."[23] Or as Lackey states it, it is the idea that "the amount of destruction permitted in pursuit of a military objective must be proportionate to the importance of the objective. This is the *military* principle of proportionality (which must be distinguished from the *political* principle of proportionality in the *jus ad bellum*)."[24]

My contention, which I shall justify, is that these three principles, duly modified or adapted, are analogically applicable to all the types of terrorism already distinguished and that they are flagrantly violated by them. Indeed, all but the moralistic/religious type of terrorism violate a further condition of just war theory. I refer to the first and most important condition of *jus ad bellum* and one of the most important conditions of a just war in general: the condition of just cause. This condition is defined by Lackey as the rule "...that the use of military force requires a just cause," that is, a "wrong received."[25] As he notes regarding discussions held since the U.N. Charter was framed, "Members of the United Nations have continued to assume that just cause consists only in self-defense, but 'self-defense' has come to be understood as a response to "aggression."[26] The definition of "aggression" adopted by the General Assembly on December 14, 1974, consists of seven articles. These articles, Lackey points out, count as aggression "only military acts that might substantially affect the physical security of the nation suffering aggression. The only violation of rights that merits the unilateral use of force by nations is the physically threatening use of force by another state." Lackey observes that the definition excludes "attacks on citizens abroad, assaults on nonmilitary ships and aircraft on the high seas, and the seizure of property of aliens."[27]

Of the four main types of terrorism, predatory, retaliatory and nonmoralistic/religious terrorism clearly run afoul of the just cause condition, understood—in a nutshell—as the self-defensive use of force. Conceivably only some acts of moralistic and moralistic/religious terrorism can satisfy that condition. It is clear that the former three types of terrorism violate that condition.

Let us begin with predatory terrorism, terrorism motivated by greed. Like "ordinary" acts of armed robbery, of which it is the terrorist counterpart, predatory terrorism is a crime and is morally wrong. Both cause terror and indiscriminately hurt whoever happens to be where they strike. Indeed, hostage-taking by armed robbers in hopes of escaping unscathed by forcing the authorities to give them a getaway car or plane is an additional similarity to terrorism. It can even be regarded as predatory terrorism itself, particularly if it is systematic and not a one-time affair, since both political and moralistic terrorism tend to be systematic, as Wilkinson notes in relation to political terrorism. Even then, armed robbery involving hostage-taking, must be distinguished from the kind of armed robbery that political or moralistic terrorists may indulge in to raise money for their particular political/moralistic/religious ends.

Nonetheless, bona fide predatory (and even retaliatory) terrorism is often unsystematic; like ordinary armed robbery, it may also be a one-time thing. Some well-known terrorist airplane hijackings in the United States for monetary gain have been one-time incidents, although in all but one instance I know of, that was simply because the hijackers were apprehended!

Like predatory terrorism, retaliatory terrorism may or may not be systematic. International terrorism usually includes a systematic policy of retaliation against a hated, enemy state or its citizens. A notorious example a few years ago was the retaliatory terrorism against the United States and its interests, sponsored by Libya, Syria, and/or Iran.

More important for the present discussion, retaliatory terrorism violates, among other moral rules, the just cause condition and the principles of justice, and is consequently wrong. For what is retaliation but another (more euphemistic?) word for revenge, which is incompatible with self-defense as well as due process. That is no less true in war, if retaliatory terrorism is practiced by a country in its efforts to defend itself against aggression. For example, if an attempt is made on the life of the aggressor country's head of state by agents of the victim state in retaliation for attacks on its territory, the assassination attempt would be (a) an act of *terrorism* if it is *intended* to pressure the aggressor's military to end the aggression. But despite its *goal* and the victim's perception of it as part of its national self-defense, it remains (b) an act of retaliation, not an act of self-defense.

What I have said about predatory and retaliatory terrorism in relation to just cause applies to non-moralistic political terrorism, to terrorism whose political goals are *not* moral. An example is when a revolutionary group commits acts of terrorism against a legitimate, democratically elected government it wants to overthrow out of lust for power.

By definition, moralistic terrorism satisfies just cause if "just cause" is interpreted broadly to mean a morally justifiable cause, for example, political terrorism strictly as part of a national liberation movement against a foreign occupier or indigenous oppressive regime. It *may* also satisfy the condition of right intention. Consequently, I shall turn to the other two conditions of just war I mentioned earlier, to ascertain whether even such terrorism can be morally justifiable.

Principle of Necessity and Terrorism

The principle of necessity states that "*wanton destruction* [in war] is forbidden. More precisely, the principle…specifies that a military operation is forbidden if there is some alternative operation that causes less destruction but has the same probability of producing a successful military result."[28] *Pace* Lackey, who regards it as a more precise form of the condition, it is distinct from, although closely related to, the principle that wanton destruction is forbidden in war. If a war *is* a last resort, it would follow that the destruction of life and property is necessary, not wanton. And if it is necessary, it *is* a last resort.

It is clear that predatory terrorism is always a wanton destruction of life or property, and the same

is true of retaliatory terrorism; however, the concept of "last resort" is inapplicable to them. If Iran had chosen to sue the United States for compensation or reparation at the International Court of Justice at the Hague, for shooting down an Iranian airbus during the Iraq-Iran war, that would have constituted a peaceful, nonviolent *alternative* to any terrorist retaliation against the United States Iran may have sponsored in its aftermath, such as the destruction of Pan Am flight 103 over Lockerbie, Scotland, which some believe was instigated and financed by Iran and implemented by a notorious Palestinian terrorist. (The United States has steadfastly held Libya, and possibly Syria, responsible for that atrocity.) Logically, retaliation on the one hand and reparation, compensation, or restitution, or other peaceful ways of undoing or rectifying a wrong, are horses of very different colors.

Principle of Discrimination and Terrorism

In many acts of terrorism some or all of the immediate victims and/or victimized are innocent persons, in no way morally connected with or in any degree responsible for the wrong moralistic terrorism is intended to help rectify, hence for the physical or mental harm that the terrorists inflict on them. In predatory terrorism the immediate victims and the victimized are, almost without exception, innocent persons. That is also often true of retaliatory terrorism, at least as far as the immediate victims are concerned. Two very tragic examples in recent memory are the hijacking of the *Achille Lauro*, and the destruction of the Pan Am plane over Lockerbie. In political and political-moralistic terrorism, whether in wartime or in time of peace, some of the immediate victims or some of the victimized are likely to be innocent persons; but some may be noninnocents, such as members (especially high-ranking members) of the military, who are morally responsible for the real or imagined wrong that triggers the terrorism.

The problem of distinguishing innocent and noninnocent persons in relation to different types and forms of terrorism, except terrorism in war, is on the whole less difficult than the much-vexed corresponding problem in relation to war. My position, *mutatis mutandis* in relation to war, simply stated, is this: (1) "Innocence" and "noninnocence" refer to *moral* innocence and noninnocence, relative to the particular acts, types, or forms of terrorism *T*. (2) Innocence and noninnocence are a matter of degree. (3) A perfectly innocent person is one who has no moral responsibility, *a fortiori*, no causal responsibility at all, for any wrong that gave rise to *T*. A paradigmatically noninnocent person is someone who has an appreciable degree of moral, hence direct or indirect causal responsibility for the wrong, triggering *T*.[29] Between that extreme and paradigmatic noninnocents there would be, theoretically, cases of decreasing moral responsibility corresponding to decreasing degrees of causal responsibility. Here the targets would be noninnocent in some but lesser degree than in paradigmatic cases of noninnocence. (4) Moral responsibility may be direct or indirect, by virtue of a person's direct or indirect role in *T*'s causation—where *T* is triggered or has its root cause(s) in some real injustice or wrong. The degree of a person's innocence may therefore also vary in that way. Everyone whose actions are a proximate cause of the wrong is noninnocent in a higher degree than those whose responsibility for it is indirect. In particular cases it is always possible in principle to ascertain whether an individual is, causally, directly involved. Generally it is also actually possible, although often quite difficult, to do so in practice. Ascertaining who is indirectly responsible and who is not at all responsible is another matter. Since we are mainly concerned with the theoretical problem of the morality of terrorism, that is not too disquieting. But it is of the essence from the point of view of would-be terrorists and that of the law—unless the terrorists happen to be deranged and target innocent individuals or groups they imagine to be morally responsible for the grievances they are out to avenge or redress. Further, the very life of some individuals may depend on the potential terrorists' ability to distinguish innocent from noninnocent persons or groups. Political, retaliatory, or moralistic terrorists, driven by passion or paranoia, often baselessly enlarge, sometimes to a tragically absurd extent, the circle of alleged noninnocent persons. They sometimes target individuals, groups or whole nations having only a tenuous relation, often of a completely innocent kind, to those who have wronged their compatriots or ancestors, stolen their

land, and so on. The example given earlier of terrorists striking at the high-ranking officials of governments whose predecessors committed crimes against their people, illustrates this. Another example is terrorism targeting innocent persons presumed to be guilty by association, simply because they happen to be of the same race, nationality, or religion, or enjoy the same ethnic heritage as those deemed responsible for the hurt.

An extreme, horrifying kind of justification of the targeting of completely innocent persons was brought to my attention by Anthony O'Heare.[30] It involves the justification one sometimes hears of the killing of holidaymakers, travelers, and others, in Israel and other terrorist targets, "on the ground that...the very fact that they were contributing to the economy and morale of the targeted country [unwittingly] implicated them." As O'Heare comments, that defense is "a disgusting piece of casuistry." Its implications, I might add, are so far-reaching as to be positively frightening. If the travelers or holidaymakers were guilty of a crime against, say, the Palestinian people, as is claimed, then by parity of reasoning all individuals, institutions, groups or peoples, all countries or nations that have any kind of economic dealings with Israel and so contribute to its economy would likewise be guilty of a crime against the Palestinian people and so may be justifiably targeted! But then why exempt those *Arabs* who live in Israel and even those *Palestinians* residing in the West Bank or in the Gaza Strip who are employed in Israel—indeed, all those who spend any amount of money there—from guilt?

Finally, to be able to protect individuals against terrorism, law enforcement agencies as well as governments in general need to be able to protect individuals against terrorism, need to make reliable predictions about who is a likely target of known terrorist organizations. Yet in few other kinds of coercion or other uses of force is the element of unpredictability and surprise greater or the strikes more impelled by emotion and passion than in terrorism. This problem will be later taken up again in a discussion of responses to terrorism.

Principles of Proportion and Terrorism

In addition to its violation of the moral principles considered above, terrorism may appear to violate two other principles of just war theory: (1) the *political* principle of proportion of *jus ad bellum* and (2) the *military* principle of proportion of *jus in bello*. The former is stated by William O'Brien as requiring that "the good to be achieved by the realisation of the war aims be proportionate to the evil resulting from the war."[31] And "the calculus of proportionality in just cause [that is, the political purpose, *raison d'etat*, "the high interests of the state"] is to the total good to be expected if the war is successful balanced against the evil the war is likely to cause."[32] Lackey describes the political principle of proportionality as stipulating that "a war cannot be just unless the evil that can reasonably be expected to ensue from the war is less than the evil that can reasonably be expected to ensue if the war is not fought."[33]

The military counterpart of the political principle is described by Lackey as the idea that "the amount of destruction permitted in pursuit of a military objective must be proportionate to the importance of the objective. It follows from the military principle of proportionality that certain objectives should be ruled out of consideration on the ground that too much destruction would be caused in obtaining them."[34]

As in the case of war, the main problem facing any attempt to apply the *political* principle of proportion to terrorism is the difficulty of reaching even the roughest estimate of the total expected good *vis-a-vis* the total evil likely to be caused by a series of connected acts of political or *moralistic/religious* terrorism. The crudest estimates of the expected good of some political-moralistic/religious cause against the suffering or death of even one victim or victimized person are exceedingly difficult to come by. And if we turn from isolated acts of political-moralistic/religious terrorism to a whole series of such acts extending over a period of years or decades, as with Arab or IRA terrorism, the task becomes utterly hopeless. For how can we possibly measure the expected good resulting from the creation of, for example, an independent Catholic Northern Ireland or a Catholic Northern Ireland united with the Irish Republic, and compare it with the overall evil likely to be the lot of the Ulster Protestants in such an eventuality or on different scenarios of their eventual fate—then add the latter evil to the evils consisting in and consequent

upon all the acts of terrorism that are supposed to help realise the desired good end? I see no possible way in which these factors can be quantified, hence added or subtracted.[35]

It seems then that we cannot ascertain whether political or moralistic/religious terrorism sometimes or always violates the political principle of proportion. However, it is a patent fact that no political or moralistic/religious terrorist movement in this century—whether Palestinian, Lebanese, Libyan, Syrian, Iranian, Irish, or Algerian—has succeeded in realizing its ultimate or overall political or moralistic objectives. Moreover, these movements have no more chance of success in the future than they have had so far. Palestinian terrorism is typical. Since, in Israel and the West, terrorism is almost synonymous with murder, it is not surprising that instead of helping the eminently just Palestinian cause, Palestinian acts of terrorism (as distinguished from Palestinian resistance, e.g. the intifada) from the very start have hurt that cause almost beyond repair. Not only has terrorism failed to win the Palestinians their human and other rights or brought them any closer to self-determination: it has created strong public sympathy in the West for Israel and turned public attitudes strongly against the Palestinians, or at least their leadership, and has further increased Israeli security concerns.[36] This does enable us, I think, to conclude after all that the preceding types of terrorism are indeed in serious violation of the political principle of proportion. For the result of tallying the evils of terrorist acts in human pain and suffering, death and destruction, against the nonexistent overall benefits leaves a huge surplus of unmitigated evil on the negative side. I refer not only to the evil inflicted by the terrorists upon their victims and the victimized but also the evil they draw upon themselves and their families by risking loss of life, limb, or liberty in ultimately futile pursuit of their dangerous and violent objectives.

We now turn to the military principle of proportionality—in O'Brien's words, the principle that "a discrete military means...when viewed independently on the basis of its intermediate military end (*raison de guerre*), must...be proportionate...to that military end for which it was used, irrespective of the ultimate end of the war at the level of *raison* d'etat."[37] This principle, applied to discrete military means, O'Brien observes, is in line with the law of Nuremberg, which judged the "legitimacy of discrete acts of the German forces,...inter alia, in terms of their proportionality to intermediate military goals, *raison de guerre.*...It was a reasonable way to evaluate the substance of the allegations that war crimes had occurred."[38]

The present form of the principle *can* be applied, *mutatis mutandis*, to discrete acts of terrorism provided that their probable intermediate results can be roughly assessed. For example, in evaluating the morality of the *Achille Lauro* seajacking, the short-term and intermediate "political" gains the terrorists expected to receive must be weighed, if possible, against the killing of an innocent passenger and the terrorism visited on the other passengers on board. It can be safely said that apart from the damage the seajacking did to the PLO and to the Middle East peace process as a whole, whatever benefit the seajackers expected to reap from their acts,[39] such as publicity and the dramatization of the plight of the Palestinians under Israeli military rule in the occupied territories, was vastly outweighed by the evils the seajacking resulted in.[40] More important still, the actual and not (as in O'Brien's formulation of the principle) merely the expected outcome of acts of terrorism, good and bad, must be weighed, if possible, against each other. That is, actual proportionality must obtain if, in retrospect, the acts are to be objectively evaluated. But to do so is precisely to assess the outcomes of the acts in terms of consequentialist criteria, and so will be left for later consideration.

The same general factors need to be weighted for the evaluation of other discrete acts of terrorism in relation to the military principle of proportionality; for example, the assassination of members of the Israeli Olympic team in Munich in 1972, the hijacking of TWA flight 847 in Athens, Greece, in 1985, the downing of Pan Am flight 103 over Lockerbie, Scotland, in 1989, and so on.

Terrorism and Human Rights

It can be safely said that the belief that all human beings have a (an equal) human right to life, at least in the minimal sense of a negative right to life—a right not to be unjustly or wrongly killed—is held by anyone who believes in the existence of human rights at all. That idea is also found in the United Nations *Universal Declaration of Human Rights*. Thus, Article 3 states, among other things, that "Everyone has the right to life." The importance of our acknowledging such a universal human right is evident: the protection of human life is the sine qua non of the individual's capacity to realize anything and everything—any and all values—a human being is capable of realizing in relation to himself or herself and others. But even if one does not acknowledge a distinct human right, a right to life as such, I believe that one is forced to acknowledge the existence of some protective norms, such as other human rights and/or principles of fairness and justice, that prohibit, except in very special circumstances, the taking of human life. For instance, justice prohibits the execution of an innocent person for a crime he or she has not committed. Or the moral protection of human life can be placed under the protective umbrella of, for example, a human right to be treated as a moral person rather than be used as an "object."

The special exceptional circumstances I have in mind are those in which the right to life is overridden by stronger moral or other axiological claims. They may include the protection of the equal rights of others, including others' right to life itself (such as in the case of soldiers sent by their country to war, to defend the lives and freedoms of their countrymen against an aggressor nation); or situations where a certain act is (1) the lesser or two evils and (2) violates no one's equal human or other moral rights, or the principles of fairness and justice. For instance, in some instances of passive or active euthanasia, or assisted suicide, such as in the case of terminal patients who are suffering unbearable physical pain [condition (1)] and the euthanasia or assisted suicide fulfils the patient's devout wish and desire to die [condition (2)]. Except in such or similar exceptional cases, the deliberate or the knowing killing of innocent persons is morally wrong.

Elsewhere[41] I have argued that we must acknowledge a fundamental human right of all individuals to be treated as moral persons. Further, that that right includes an equal right of all to be free to satisfy their needs and interests, and to actualize their potentials: that is, to seek to realize themselves and their well-being.[42] In addition, I have argued that all human beings have an equal right to equal opportunity and treatment, to help enable them to realize the aforementioned values, either as part of or as implied by the right to be treated as a moral person.

A universal negative human right to life,[43] hence a right to one's physical and mental security and integrity, can be readily derived from the right to equal treatment and opportunity as a premise, if such a right is acknowledged,[44] as a condition of the very possibility of exercising that right at all or any other moral, legal, or other kind of right or rights, including the right to be treated as a moral person as a whole. The rights to equal treatment and opportunity would be empty or meaningless in practice if not in theory if one's security is not protected. Indeed, given Thomas Hobbes' three principal causes of quarrel in human nature—competition, "diffidence" or desire for safety, and the desire for glory in the absence of the protective norm of the equal human right to life and its reinforcement by law, human existence would tend to exemplify Hobbes' State of Nature. There would be "no arts; no letters; no society; and which is worst of all, continual fear, and danger of violent death; and the life of man, solitary, poor, nasty, brutish, and short."[45]

It is clear that if a negative right to life is assumed, terrorists' killings of their immediate victims—unless they satisfy conditions (1) and (2) above—are always morally wrong. In reality, condition (1) may perhaps be sometimes satisfied, but condition (2) cannot ever be satisfied. In fact all types and forms of terrorism I have distinguished seriously violate the human rights of their immediate victims and the victimized as moral persons.

Treating people as moral persons means treating them with consideration in two closely related ways. First, it means respecting their autonomy as individuals with their own desires and interests, plans and projects, commitments and goals. That autonomy is clearly violated if they are humiliated, coerced and terrorized, taken hostage or kidnapped, and above all killed. Second, consideration involves "a certain cluster of attitudes, hence certain ways of acting toward, reacting to and thinking and feeling about" people.[46] It includes sensitivity to and consideration of their feelings and desires, aspirations, projects, and goals. That in turn is an integral part

of treating their life as a whole—including their relationships and memories—as a thing of value. Finally, it includes respecting their "culture or ethnic, religious or racial identity or heritage."[47] These things are the very antithesis of what terrorism does to its victims and the victimized.

NOTES

1. Burleigh Taylor Wilkins, *Terrorism and Collective Responsibility* (New York, 1992). Wilkins' arguments are examined below.
2. David C. Rappaport and Yonah Alexander, eds., *The Morality of Terrorism: Religious and Secular Justifications* (New York, 1983).
3. Franklin Lord, *Political Murder* (Cambridge, MA, 1985).
4. Paul Wilkinson, *Terrorism and the Liberal State*, 2nd ed. (London, 1986).
5. Ibid., 65–66.
6. The same is even more obvious in relation to legal positivism, including the somewhat attenuated form of it advocated by H.L.A. Hart, since for legal positivism the validity of a law is logically or conceptually independent of its morality, its moral goodness or badness.
7. Wilkinson, *Terrorism and the Liberal State*, 66. The word "killing" should be substituted for "murder" in (i)–(iv), since—as the word is normally used—murder includes the concept of unlawfulness and moral wrongness.
8. Ibid.
9. I say "radical legal positivist theory" since H.L.A. Hart, for example, the leading positivist in the Anglo-American world today, accepts what he calls "the core of good sense in the doctrine of Natural Law"—what he calls "the minimum [moral] content of natural law." Hart, *The Concept of Law* (New York, 1961), ch. 9.
10. The way in which particular terrorist states used or may use their municipal legal systems as instruments of terrorism against their own peoples or against segments of them, deserves serious attention. But it is beyond the scope of the present work.
11. Wilkinson, *Terrorism and the Liberal State*, 66.
12. Ibid.
13. Ibid. Despite its alleged absurdity, such an attempt will be considered in order to ascertain whether

a rule-utilitarian justification of *any* form of political-moralistic/religious terrorism is possible.

14. A striking similarity may be noted between this claim—to the extent that terrorists in fact do make the claim—and Raskolnikov's theory of crime in Dostoevsky's *Crime and Punishment*. On that theory the "extraordinary," Napoleonic or "bronze" man is that rare individual who is above and beyond conventional morality and law, for whom "everything"—all that is conventionally considered to be crime—is permitted. For these "crimes"—if they can be considered crimes—are committed solely for the benefit of humankind.

15. Wilkinson, *Terrorism and the Liberal State*, 66.
16. Ibid.
17. Ibid., 67.
18. See Chapter 5.
19. Douglas P. Lackey, *The Ethics of War and Peace* (Englewood Cliffs, NJ, 1989), 59. Italics in original.
20. William O'Brien, "Just-War Theory," in Burton M. Leiser, *Liberty, Justice, and Morals,* 2nd ed. (New York, 1979), 39. This section is in large measure reproduced from sections III–V of Haig Khatchadourian, "Terrorism and Morality," *Journal of Applied Philosophy*, 5, no. 2(1958): 134–143.
21. Lackey, *Ethics*, 59.
22. Ibid., 37.
23. Ibid., 30.
24. Ibid., 59. Italics in original.
25. Ibid., 33.
26. Ibid., 34.
27. Ibid., 35.
28. Lackey, *Ethics*, 59. Italics in original.
29. What constitutes an "appreciable degree" of moral responsibility would of course be a matter of controversy.
30. Private communication to the author.
31. O'Brien, "Just-War Theory," 37.
32. Ibid.
33. Lackey, *Ethics*, 40.
34. Ibid., 59.
35. For the special significance of this in relation to revolutionary terrorism, see Chapter 4.
36. A personal note: My own moral condemnation of terrorism and my conviction that it was bound to

hurt rather than help the Palestinian cause led me, soon after the first Palestinian skyjacking, to send an open letter to the PLO leadership. In the letter I pointed these things out and pleaded that the PLO put an end to such acts. For rather obvious reasons the Beirut publication to which I sent the letter could not publish it.

37. O'Brien, "Just-War Theory," 37.
38. Ibid., 38.
39. One of the seajackers stated after being captured that the original objective was a suicide mission in Israel. That objective, of course, was not realized.
40. Note that the question whether the capture, trial, and almost certain punishment of the seajackers and others implicated in the act is to be judged a good or an evil to be added to one or the other side of the balance sheet, partly depends for its answer on the evaluation of the act itself as morally justified or unjustified. I say "partly depends" because the legal implications of the act are also relevant.
41. Haig Khatchadourian, "Toward a Foundation for Human Rights," *Man and World*, 18 (1985): 219–240, and "The Human Right to be Treated as a Person," *Journal of Value Inquiry*, 19 (1985): 183–195.
42. Khatchadourian, "The Human Right," passim.
43. As distinguished from a positive human right to life, which includes—over and above the right not to be physically hurt or killed—a right to a minimum standard of welfare.
44. Such a right can also be derived from John Rawls' first and second principles of justice in *A Theory of Justice* (Cambridge, MA, 1971). *Indeed, the right to equal opportunity is part of his first principle.*
45. Thomas Hobbes, "Self-Interest," in *Great Traditions in Ethics,* 5th ed., Ethel M. Albert et al., eds. (Belmont, CA, 1984), 134. Reprinted from *Leviathan*. I should add that Hobbes himself regarded self-preservation as the first law of (human) nature, and that his social contract, the creation of the "Leviathan" of civil and political society, is intended to provide, inter alia, safety and security.
46. Khatchadourian, "The Human Right," 192.
47. Ibid.

Terrorism

A Critique of Excuses

MICHAEL WALZER

No one these days advocates terrorism, not even those who regularly practice it. The practice is indefensible now that it has been recognized, like rape and murder, as an attack upon the innocent. In a sense, indeed, terrorism is worse than rape and murder commonly are, for in the latter cases the victim has been chosen for a purpose; he or she is the direct object of attack, and the attack has some reason, however twisted or ugly it may be. The victims of a terrorist attack are third parties, innocent bystanders; there is no special reason for attacking them; anyone else within a large class of (unrelated) people will do as well. The attack is directed indiscriminately against the entire class. Terrorists are like killers on a rampage, except that their rampage is not just expressive of rage or madness; the rage is purposeful and programmatic. It aims at a general vulnerability: Kill these people in order to terrify those. A relatively small number of dead victims makes for a very large number of living and frightened hostages.

This, then, is the peculiar evil of terrorism—not only the killing of innocent people but also the intrusion of fear into everyday life, the violation of private purposes, the insecurity of public spaces, the endless coerciveness of precaution. A crime wave might, I suppose, produce similar effects, but no one plans a crime wave; it is the work of a thousand individual decisionmakers, each one independent of the others, brought together only by the invisible hand. Terrorism is the work of visible hands; it is an organizational project, a strategic choice, a conspiracy to murder and intimidate...you and me. No wonder the conspirators have difficulty defending, in public, the strategy they have chosen.

The moral difficulty is the same, obviously, when the conspiracy is directed not against you and me but against *them*—Protestants, say, not Catholics; Israelis, not Italians or Germans; blacks, not whites. These "limits" rarely hold for long; the logic of terrorism steadily expands the range of vulnerability. The more hostages they hold, the stronger the terrorists are. No one is safe once whole populations have been put at risk. Even if the risk were contained, however, the evil would be no different. So far as individual Protestants or Israelis or blacks are concerned, terrorism is random, degrading, and frightening. That is its hallmark, and that, again, is why it cannot be defended.

But when moral justification is ruled out, the way is opened for ideological excuse and apology. We live today in a political culture of excuses. This is far better than a political culture in which terrorism is openly defended and justified, for the excuse at least acknowledges the evil. But the improvement is precarious, hard won, and difficult to sustain. It is not the case, even in this better world, that terrorist organizations are without supporters. The support is indirect but by no means ineffective. It takes the form of apologetic descriptions and explanations, a litany of excuses that steadily undercuts our knowledge of the evil. Today that knowledge is insufficient unless it is supplemented and reinforced by a systematic critique of excuses. That is my purpose in this chapter. I take the principle for granted: that every act of terrorism is a wrongful act. The wrongfulness of the excuses, however, cannot be taken for granted; it has to be argued. The excuses themselves are familiar enough, the stuff of contemporary political debate. I shall state them in stereotypical form. There is no need to attribute them to this or that writer, publicist, or commentator; my readers can make their own attributions.[1]

THE EXCUSES FOR TERRORISM

The most common excuse for terrorism is that it is a last resort, chosen only when all else fails. The image

"Terrorism: A Critique of Excuses" by Michael Walzer in *Problems of International Justice*, ed. Steven Luper-Foy, 237–247 (Boulder, CO: Westview Press, 1988). Reprinted with permission of the author.

is of people who have literally run out of options. One by one, they have tried every legitimate form of political and military action, exhausted every possibility, failed everywhere, until no alternative remains but the evil of terrorism. They must be terrorists or do nothing at all. The easy response is to insist that, given this description of their case, they should do nothing at all; they have indeed exhausted their possibilities. But this response simply reaffirms the principle, ignores the excuse; this response does not attend to the terrorists' desperation. Whatever the cause to which they are committed, we have to recognize that, given the commitment, the one thing they cannot do is "nothing at all."

But the case is badly described. It is not so easy to reach the "last resort." To get there, one must indeed try everything (which is a lot of things) and not just once, as if a political party might organize a single demonstration, fail to win immediate victory, and claim that it was now justified in moving on to murder. Politics is an art of repetition. Activists and citizens learn from experience, that is, by doing the same thing over and over again. He is by no means clear when they run out of options, but even under conditions of oppression and war, citizens have a good run short of that. The same argument applies to state officials who claim that they have tried "everything" and are now compelled to kill hostages or bomb peasant villages. Imagine such people called before a judicial tribunal and required to answer the question, What exactly did you try? Does anyone believe that they could come up with a plausible list? "Last resort" has only a notional finality; the resort to terror is ideologically last, not last in an actual series of actions, just last for the sake of the excuse. In fact, most state officials and movements militants who recommend a policy of terrorism recommend it as a first resort; they are for it from the beginning, although they may not get their way at the beginning. If they are honest, then, they must make other excuses and give up the pretense of the last resort.

The second excuse is designed for national liberation movements struggling against established and powerful states. Now the claim is that nothing else is possible, that no other strategy is available except terrorism. This is different from the first excuse because it does not require would-be terrorists to run through all the available options. Or, the second excuse requires terrorist to run through all the options in their heads, not in the world; notional finality is enough. Movement strategists consider their options and conclude that they have no alternative to terrorism. They think that they do not have the political strength to try anything else, and thus they do not try anything else. Weakness is their excuse.

But two very different kinds of weakness are commonly confused here: the weakness of the movement vis-à-vis the opposing state and the movement's weakness vis-à-vis its own people. This second kind of weakness, the inability of the movement to mobilize the nation, makes terrorism the "only" option because it effectively rules out all the others: nonviolent resistance, general strikes, mass demonstrations, unconventional warfare, and so on.

These options are only rarely ruled out by the sheer power of the state, by the pervasiveness and intensity of oppression. Totalitarian states may be immune to nonviolent or guerrilla resistance, but all the evidence suggests that they are also immune to terrorism. Or, more exactly, in totalitarian states state terror dominates every other sort. Where terrorism is a possible strategy for the oppositional movement (in liberal and democratic states, most obviously), other strategies are also possible if the movement has some significant degree of popular support. In the absence of popular support, terrorism may indeed be the one available strategy, but it is hard to see how its evils can then be excused. For it is not weakness alone that makes the excuse, but the claim of the terrorists to represent the weak; and the particular form of weakness that makes terrorism the only option calls that claim into question.

One might avoid this difficulty with a stronger insistence on the actual effectiveness of terrorism. The third excuse is simply that terrorism works (and nothing else does); it achieves the ends of the oppressed even without their participation. "When the act accuses, the result excuses."[2] This is a consequential argument, and given a strict understanding of consequentialism, this argument amounts to a justification rather than an excuse. In practice, however, the argument is rarely pushed so far. More often, the argument begins with an acknowledgment of the terrorists' wrongdoing. Their hands are dirty, but we must make a kind of peace with them because they have acted effectively for the sake of people who could not act for themselves. But, in fact, have the terrorists' actions been effective? I doubt that terrorism has ever achieved national liberation—no nation that I know of owes its freedom to a campaign of random murder—although terrorism undoubtedly increases the power of the terrorists within the national liberation movement. Perhaps terrorism is also conducive to the survival and notoriety (the two go together) of the movement, which is now dominated by terrorists. But even if we were to grant some means-end relationship between terror and national liberation, the third excuse does not work unless it can meet the further requirements of a consequentialist argument. It must be possible to say that the desired end could not have been achieved through any other, less wrongful, means. The third excuse depends, then, on the success of the first or second, and neither of these look likely to be successful.

The fourth excuse avoids this crippling dependency. This excuse does not require the apologist to defend either of the improbable claims that terrorism is the last resort or that it is the only possible resort. The fourth excuse is simply that terrorism is the universal resort. All politics is (really) terrorism. The appearance of innocence and decency is always a piece of deception, more or less convincing in accordance with the relative power of the deceivers. The terrorist who does not bother with appearances is only doing openly what everyone else does secretly.

This argument has the same form as the maxim "All's fair in love and war." Love is always fraudulent, war is always brutal, and political action is always terrorist in character. Political action works (as Thomas Hobbes long ago argued) only by generating fear in innocent men and women. Terrorism is the politics of state officials and movement militants alike. This argument does not justify either the officials or the militants, but it does excuse them all. We hardly can be harsh with people who act the way everyone else acts. Only saints are likely to act differently, and sainthood in politics is supererogatory, a matter of grace, not obligation.

But this fourth excuse relies too heavily on our cynicism about political life, and cynicism only sometimes answers well to experience. In fact, legitimate states do not need to terrorize their citizens,

and strongly based movements do not need to terrorize their opponents. Officials and militants who live, as it were, on the margins of legitimacy and strength sometimes choose terrorism and sometimes do not. Living in terror is not a universal experience. The world the terrorists create has its entrances and exits.

If we want to understand the choice of terror, the choice that forces the rest of us through the door, we have to imagine what in fact always occurs, although we often have no satisfactory record of the occurrence: A group of men and women, officials or militants, sits around a table and argues about whether or not to adopt a terrorist strategy. Later on, the litany of excuses obscures the argument. But at the time, around the table, it would have been no use for defenders of terrorism to say, "Everybody does it," because there they would be face to face with people proposing to do something else. Nor is it historically the case that the members of this last group, the opponents of terrorism, always lose the argument. They can win, however, and still not be able to prevent a terrorist campaign; the would-be terrorists (it does not take very many) can always split the movement and go their own way. Or, they can split the bureaucracy or the police or officer corps and act in the shadow of state power. Indeed, terrorism often has its origin in such splits. The first victims are the terrorists' former comrades or colleagues. What reason can we possibly have, then, for equating the two? If we value the politics of the men and women who oppose terrorism, we must reject the excuses of their murderers. Cynicism at such a time is unfair to the victims.

The fourth excuse can also take, often does take, a more restricted form. Oppression, rather than political rule more generally, is always terroristic in character, and thus, we must always excuse the opponents of oppression. When they choose terrorism, they are only reacting to someone else's previous choice, repaying in kind the treatment they have long received. Of course, their terrorism repeats the evil—innocent people are killed, who were never themselves oppressors—but repetition is not the same as initiation. The oppressors set the terms of the struggle. But if the struggle is fought on the oppressors' terms, then the oppressors are likely to win. Or, at least, oppression is likely to win, even if it takes on a new face. The whole point of a liberation movement or a popular mobilization is to change the terms. We have no reason to excuse the terrorism reactively adopted by opponents of oppression unless we are confident of the sincerity of their opposition, the seriousness of their commitment to a nonoppressive politics. But the choice of terrorism undermines that confidence.

We are often asked to distinguish the terrorism of the oppressed from the terrorism of the oppressors. What is it, however, that makes the difference? The message of the terrorist is the same in both cases: a denial of the peoplehood and humanity of the groups among whom he or she finds victims. Terrorism anticipates, when it does not actually enforce, political domination. Does it matter if one dominated group is replaced by another? Imagine a slave revolt whose protagonists dream only of enslaving in their turn the children of their masters. The dream is understandable, but the fervent desire of the children that the revolt be repressed is equally understandable. In neither case does understanding make for excuse—not, at least, after a politics of universal freedom has become possible. Nor does an understanding of oppression excuse the terrorism of the oppressed, once we have grasped the meaning of "liberation."

These are the four general excuses for terror, and each of them fails. They depend upon statements about the world that are false, historical arguments for which there is no evidence, moral claims that turn out to be hollow or dishonest. This is not to say that there might not be more particular excuses that have greater plausibility, extenuating circumstances in particular cases that we would feel compelled to recognize. As with murder, we can tell a story (like the story that Richard Wright tells in *Native Son*, for example) that might lead us, not to justify terrorism, but to excuse this or that individual terrorist. We can provide a personal history, a psychological study, of compassion destroyed by fear, moral reason by hatred and rage, social inhibition by unending violence—the product, an individual driven to kill or readily set on a killing course by his or her political leaders.[3] But the force of this story will not depend on any of the four general excuses, all of which grant what the storyteller will have to deny: that terrorism is

the deliberate choice of rational men and women. Whether they conceive it to be one option among others or the only one available, they nevertheless argue and choose. Whether they are acting or reacting, they have made a decision. The human instruments they subsequently find to plant the bomb or shoot the gun may act under some psychological compulsion, but the men and women who choose terror as a policy act "freely." They could not act in any other way, or accept any other description of their action, and still pretend to be the leaders of the movement or the state. We ought never to excuse such leaders.

THE RESPONSE TO TERRORISM

What follows from the critique of excuses? There is still a great deal of room for argument about the best way of responding to terrorism. Certainly, terrorists should be resisted, and it is not likely that a purely defensive resistance will ever be sufficient. In this sort of struggle, the offense is always ahead. The technology of terror is simple; the weapons are readily produced and easy to deliver. It is virtually impossible to protect people against random and indiscriminate attack. Thus, resistance will have to be supplemented by some combination of repression and retaliation. This is a dangerous business because repression and retaliation so often take terroristic forms and there are a host of apologists ready with excuses that sound remarkably like those of the terrorists themselves. It should be clear by now, however, that counterterrorism cannot be excused merely because it is reactive. Every new actor, terrorist or counterterrorist, claims to be reacting to someone else, standing in a circle and just passing the evil along. But the circle is ideological in character; in fact, every actor is a moral agent and makes an independent decision.

Therefore, repression and retaliation must not repeat the wrongs of terrorism, which is to say that repression and retaliation must be aimed systematically at the terrorists themselves, never at the people for whom the terrorists claim to be acting. That claim is in any case doubtful, even when it is honestly made. The people do not authorize the terrorists to act in their name. Only a tiny number actually participate in terrorist activities; they are far more likely to suffer than to benefit from the terrorist program. Even if they supported the program and hoped to benefit from it, however, they would still be immune from attack—exactly as civilians in time of war who support the war effort but are not themselves part of it are subject to the same immunity. Civilians may be put at risk by attacks on military targets, as by attacks on terrorist targets, but the risk must be kept to a minimum, even at some cost to the attackers. The refusal to make ordinary people into targets, whatever their nationality or even their politics, is the only way to say no to terrorism. Every act of repression and retaliation has to be measured by this standard.

But what if the "only way" to defeat the terrorists is to intimidate their actual or potential supporters? It is important to deny the premise of this question: that terrorism is a politics dependent on mass support. In fact, it is always the politics of an elite, whose members are dedicated and fanatical and more than ready to endure, or to watch others endure, the devastations of a counterterrorist campaign. Indeed, terrorists will welcome counterterrorism; it makes the terrorists' excuses more plausible and is sure to bring them, however many people are killed or wounded, however many are terrorized, the small number of recruits needed to sustain the terrorist activities.

Repression and retaliation are legitimate responses to terrorism only when they are constrained by the same moral principles that rule out terrorism itself. But there is an alternative response that seeks to avoid the violence that these two entail. The alternative is to address directly, ourselves, the oppression the terrorists claim to oppose. Oppression, they say, is the cause of terrorism. But that is merely one more excuse. The real cause of terrorism is the decision to launch a terrorist campaign, a decision made by that group of people sitting around a table whose deliberations I have already described. However, terrorists do exploit oppression, injustice, and human misery generally and look to these at least for their excuses. There can hardly be any doubt that oppression strengthens their hand. Is that a reason for us to come to the defense of the oppressed? It seems to me that we have our own reasons to do that, and do not need this one, or should not, to prod us into action. We might imitate those movement militants who argue against

the adoption of a terrorist strategy—although not, as the terrorists say, because these militants are prepared to tolerate oppression. They already are opposed to oppression and now add to that opposition, perhaps for the same reasons, a refusal of terror. So should we have been opposed before, and we should now make the same addition.

But there is an argument, put with some insistence these days, that we should refuse to acknowledge any link at all between terrorism and oppression—as if any defense of oppressed men and women, once a terrorist campaign has been launched, would concede the effectiveness of the campaign. Or, at least, a defense of oppression would give terrorism the appearance of effectiveness and so increase the likelihood of terrorist campaigns in the future. Here we have the reverse side of the litany of excuses; we have turned over the record. First oppression is made into an excuse for terrorism, and then terrorism is made into an excuse for oppression. The first is the excuse of the far left; the second is the excuse of the neoconservative right.[4] I doubt that genuine conservatives would think it a good reason for defending the status quo that it is under terrorist attack; they would have independent reasons and would be prepared to defend the status quo against any attack. Similarly, those of us who think that the status quo urgently requires change have our own reasons for thinking so and need not be intimidated by terrorists or, for that matter, antiterrorists.

If one criticizes the first excuse, one should not neglect the second. But I need to state the second more precisely. It is not so much an excuse for oppression as an excuse for doing nothing (now) about oppression. The claim is that the campaign against terrorism has priority over every other political activity. If the people who take the lead in this campaign are the old oppressors, then we must make a kind of peace with them—temporarily, of course, until the terrorists have been beaten. This is a strategy that denies the possibility of a two-front war. So long as the men and women who pretend to lead the fight against oppression are terrorists, we can concede nothing to their demands. Nor can we oppose their opponents.

But why not? It is not likely in any case that terrorists would claim victory in the face of a serious effort to deal with the oppression of the people they claim to be defending. The effort would merely expose the hollowness of their claim, and the nearer it came to success, the more they would escalate their terrorism. They would still have to be defeated, for what they are after is not a solution to the problem but rather the power to impose their own solution. No decent end to the conflict in Ireland, say, or in Lebanon, or in the Middle East generally, is going to look like a victory for terrorism—if only because the different groups of terrorists are each committed, by the strategy they have adopted, to an indecent end.[5] By working for our own ends, we expose the indecency.

OPPRESSION AND TERRORISM

It is worth considering at greater length the link between oppression and terror. To pretend that there is no link at all is to ignore the historical record, but the record is more complex than any of the excuses acknowledge. The first thing to be read out of it, however, is simple enough: Oppression is not so much the cause of terrorism as terrorism is one of the primary means of oppression. This was true in ancient times, as Aristotle recognized, and it is still true today. Tyrants rule by terrorizing their subjects; unjust and illegitimate regimes are upheld through a combination of carefully aimed and random violence.[6] If this method works in the state, there is no reason to think that it will not work, or that it does not work, in the liberation movement. Wherever we see terrorism, we should look for tyranny and oppression. Authoritarian states, especially in the moment of their founding, need a terrorist apparatus—secret police with unlimited power, secret prisons into which citizens disappear, death squads in unmarked cars. Even democracies may use terror, not against their own citizens, but at the margins, in their colonies, for example, where colonizers also are likely to rule tyrannically. Oppression is sometimes maintained by a steady and discriminate pressure, sometimes by intermittent and random violence—what we might think of as terrorist melodrama—designed to render the subject population fearful and passive.

This latter policy, especially if it seems successful, invites imitation by opponents of the state. But terrorism does not spread only when it is imitated. If it can be invented by state officials, it can also be invented by movement militants. Neither one need take lessons from the other; the circle has no single or necessary starting point. Wherever it starts, terrorism in the movement is tyrannical and oppressive in exactly the same way as is terrorism in the state. The terrorists aim to rule, and murder is their method. They have their own internal police, death squads, disappearances. They begin by killing or intimidating those comrades who stand in their way, and they proceed to do the same, if they can, among the people they claim to represent. If terrorists are successful, they rule tyrannically, and their people bear, without consent, the costs of the terrorists' rule. (If the terrorists are only partly successful, the costs to the people may be even greater: What they have to bear now is a war between rival terrorist gangs.) But terrorists cannot win the ultimate victory they seek without challenging the established regime or colonial power and the people it claims to represent, and when terrorists do that, they themselves invite imitation. The regime may then respond with its own campaign of aimed and random violence. Terrorist tracks terrorist, each claiming the other as an excuse.

The same violence can also spread to countries where it has not yet been experienced; now terror is reproduced not through temporal succession but through ideological adaptation. State terrorists wage bloody wars against largely imaginary enemies: army colonels, say, hunting down the representatives of "international communism." Or movement terrorists wage bloody wars against enemies with whom, but for the ideology, they could readily negotiate and compromise: nationalist fanatics committed to a permanent irredentism. These wars, even if they are without precedents, are likely enough to become precedents, to start the circle of terror and counterterror, which is endlessly oppressive for the ordinary men and women whom the state calls its citizens and the movement its "people."

The only way to break out of the circle is to refuse to play the terrorist game. Terrorists in the state and the movement warn us, with equal vehemence, that any such refusal is a sign of softness and naiveté. The self-portrait of the terrorists is always the same. They are tough-minded and realistic; they know their enemies (or privately invent them for ideological purposes); and they are ready to do what must be done for victory. Why then do terrorists turn around and around in the same circle? It is true: Movement terrorists win support because they pretend to deal energetically and effectively with the brutality of the state. It also is true: State terrorists win support because they pretend to deal energetically and effectively with the brutality of the movement. Both feed on the fears of brutalized and oppressed people. But there is no way of overcoming brutality with terror. At most, the burden is shifted from these people to those; more likely, new burdens are added for everyone. Genuine liberation can come only through a politics that mobilizes the victims of brutality and takes careful aim at its agents, or by a politics that surrenders the hope of victory and domination and deliberately seeks a compromise settlement. In either case, once tyranny is repudiated, terrorism is no longer an option. For what lies behind all the excuses, of officials and militants alike, is the predilection for a tyrannical politics.

NOTES

1. I cannot resist a few examples: Edward Said, "The Terrorism Scam," *The Nation,* June 14, 1986; and (more intelligent and circumspect) Richard Falk,

"Thinking About Terrorism," *The Nation,* June 28, 1986.

2. Machiavelli, *The Discourses* I:ix. As yet, however, there have been no results that would constitute a Machiavellian excuse.

3. See, for example, Daniel Goleman, "The Roots of Terrorism Are Found in Brutality of Shattered Childhood," *New York Times,* September 2, 1986, pp. C1, 8. Goleman discusses the psychic and social history of particular terrorists, not the roots of terrorism.

4. The neoconservative position is represented, although not as explicitly as I have stated it here, in Benjamin Netanyahu, ed., *Terrorism: How the West Can Win* (New York: Farrar, Straus & Giroux, 1986).

5. The reason the terrorist strategy, however indecent in itself, cannot be instrumental to some decent political purpose is because any decent purpose must somehow accommodate the people against whom the terrorism is aimed, and what terrorism expresses is precisely the refusal of such an accommodation, the radical devaluing of the Other. See my argument in *Just and Unjust Wars* (New York: Basic Books, 1977), pp. 197–206, especially 203.

6. Aristotle, *The Politics* 1313–1314a.

Can Terrorism Be Justified?

ANDREW VALLS

[As other chapters] amply demonstrate, just war theory, despite its ambiguities, provides a rich framework with which to assess the morality of war. But interstate war is only the most conventional form of political violence. The question arises, Is it the only form of political violence that may ever be justified? If not, how are we to assess the morality of other cases of political violence, particularly those involving nonstate actors? In short, does just war theory apply to terrorism, and, if so, can terrorism satisfy its criteria?

In the public and scholarly reactions to political violence, a double standard often is at work. When violence is committed by states, our assessment tends to be quite permissive, giving states a great benefit of the doubt about the propriety of their violent acts. However, when the violence is committed by nonstate actors, we often react with horror,

"Can Terrorism Be Justified?" by Andrew Valls in *Ethics in International Affairs*, ed. Andrew Valls, 65–79. © 2000 Lanham, MD: Rowman and Littlefield.

and the condemnations cannot come fast enough. Hence, terrorism is almost universally condemned, whereas violence by states, even when war has not been declared, is seen as legitimate, if not always fully justified. This difference in assessments remains when innocent civilians are killed in both cases and sometimes when such killing is deliberate. Even as thoughtful a commentator as Michael Walzer, for example, seems to employ this double standard. In his *Just and Unjust Wars*, Walzer considers whether "soldiers and statesmen [can] override the rights of innocent people for the sake of their own political community" and answers "affirmatively, though not without hesitation and worry" (1992, 254). Walzer goes on to discuss a case in point, the Allied bombing of German cities during World War II, arguing that, despite the many civilians who deliberately were killed, the bombing was justified. However, later in the book, Walzer rejects out of hand the possibility that terrorism might sometimes be justified, on the grounds that it involves the deliberate killing of innocents (1992, chapter 12). He never considers the possibility that stateless communities might confront the same "supreme emergency" that justified, in his view, the bombing of innocent German civilians. I will have more to say about Walzer's position below, but for now I wish to point out that, on the face of it at least, his position seems quite inconsistent.

From a philosophical point of view, this double standard cannot be sustained. As Coady (1985) argues, consistency requires that we apply the same standards to both kinds of political violence, state and nonstate. Of course, it may turn out that there are simply some criteria that states can satisfy that nonstate actors cannot, so that the same standard applied to both inevitably leads to different conclusions. There may be morally relevant features of states that make their use of violence legitimate and its use by others illegitimate. However, I will argue that this is not the case. I argue that, on the most plausible account of just war theory, taking into account the ultimate moral basis of its criteria, violence undertaken by nonstate actors can, in principle, satisfy the requirements of a just war.

To advance this view, I examine each criterion of just war theory in turn, arguing in each case that terrorism committed by nonstate actors can satisfy the criterion. The most controversial parts of my argument will no doubt be those regarding just cause, legitimate authority, and discrimination, so I devote more attention to these than to the others. I argue that, once we properly understand the moral basis for each of these criteria, it is clear that some nonstate groups may have the same right as states to commit violence and that they are just as capable of committing that violence within the constraints imposed by just war theory. My conclusion, then, is that if just war theory can justify violence committed by states, then terrorism committed by nonstate actors can also, under certain circumstances, be justified by it as well. But before commencing the substantive argument, I must attend to some preliminary matters concerning the definition of *terrorism*.

DEFINITIONAL ISSUES

There is little agreement on the question of how *terrorism* is best defined. In the political arena, of course, the word is used by political actors for political purposes, usually to paint their opponents as monsters. Scholars, on the other hand, have at least attempted to arrive at a more detached position, seeking a definition that captures the essence of terrorism. However, there is reason, in addition to the lack of consensus, to doubt whether much progress has been made.

Most definitions of terrorism suffer from at least one of two difficulties. First, they often define terrorism as murder or otherwise characterize it as intrinsically wrong and unjustifiable. The trouble with this approach is that it prejudges the substantive moral issue by a definitional consideration. I agree with Teichman, who writes that "we ought not to begin by *defining* terrorism as a bad thing" (1989, 507). Moral conclusions should follow from moral reasoning, grappling with the moral issues themselves. To decide a normative issue by definitional considerations, then, ends the discussion before it begins.

The second shortcoming that many definitions of terrorism exhibit is being too revisionist of its meaning in ordinary language. As I have noted, the word is often used as a political weapon, so ordinary language will not settle the issue. Teichman (1989, 505) again is correct that any definition will necessarily be stipulative to some extent. But ordinary language does, nevertheless, impose some constraints on the stipulative definition that we can accept. For example, Carl Wellman defines *terrorism* as "the use or attempted use of terror as a means of coercion" (1979, 251) and draws the conclusion that when he instills terror in his students with threats of grade penalties on late papers, he commits terrorism. Clearly this is not what most of us have in mind when we speak of terrorism, so Wellman's definition, even if taken as stipulative, is difficult to accept.

Some definitions of terrorism suffer from both of these shortcomings to some degree. For example, those that maintain that terrorism is necessarily random or indiscriminate seem both to depart markedly from ordinary usage—there are lots of acts we call terrorist that specifically target military facilities and personnel—and thereby to prejudge the moral issue. (I will argue below that terrorism need not be indiscriminate at all.) The same can be said of definitions that insist that the aim of terrorism must be to terrorize, that it targets some to threaten many more (see, for example, Khatchadourian 1998). As Virginia Held has argued, "We should probably not construe either the intention to spread fear or the intention to kill noncombatants as necessary for an act of political violence to be an act of terrorism" (1991, 64). Annette Baier adds that "the terrorist may be ill named" because what she sometimes wants is not to terrorize but "the shocked attention of her audience population" (1994, 205).

With all of this disagreement, it would perhaps be desirable to avoid the use of the term *terrorism* altogether and simply to speak instead of political violence. I would be sympathetic to this position were it not for the fact that *terrorism* is already too much a part of our political vocabulary to be avoided. Still, we can with great plausibility simply define *terrorism* as a form of political violence, as Held does: "I [see] terrorism as a form of violence to achieve political goals, where creating fear is usually high among the intended effects" (1991, 64). This is a promising approach, though I would drop as nonessential the stipulation that terrorism is usually intended to spread fear. In addition, I would make two stipulations of my own. First, "violence" can include damage to property as well as harm to people. Blowing up a power plant can surely be an act of

terrorism, even if no one is injured. Second, for the purposes of this chapter, I am interested in violence committed by nonstate actors. I do not thereby deny the existence of state terrorism. Indeed, I endorse Gordon and Lopez's discussion of it in their chapter. However, for the purposes of my present argument, I assume that when a state commits terrorism against its own citizens, this is a matter for domestic justice, and that when it commits violence outside of its own borders, just war theory can, fairly easily, be extended to cover these cases. The problem for international ethics that I wish to address here is whether just war theory can be extended to nonstate actors. So my stipulative definition of *terrorism* in this chapter is simply that it is violence committed by nonstate actors against persons or property for political purposes. This definition appears to leave open the normative issues involved and to be reasonably consistent with ordinary language.

JUS AD BELLUM

It is somewhat misleading to speak of just war *theory*, for it is not a single theory but, rather, a tradition within which there is a range of interpretation. That is, just war theory is best thought of as providing a framework for discussion about whether a war is just, rather than as providing a set of unambiguous criteria that are easily applied. In what follows I rely on what I believe is the most plausible and normatively appealing version of just war theory, one that is essentially the same as the one articulated and developed by the preceding chapters. I begin with the *jus ad bellum* criteria, concerning the justice of going to war, and then turn to *jus in bello* criteria, which apply to the conduct of the war.

Just Cause

A just cause for a war is usually a defensive one. That is, a state is taken to have a just cause when it defends itself against aggression, where *aggression* means the violation or the imminent threat of the violation of its territorial integrity or political independence (Walzer 1992). So the just cause provision of just war theory holds, roughly, that the state has a right to defend itself against the aggression of other states.

But on what is this right of the state based? Most students of international ethics maintain that any right that a state enjoys is ultimately based on the rights of its citizens. States in and of themselves have value only to the extent that they serve some good for the latter. The moral status of the state is therefore derivative, not foundational, and it is derivative of the rights of the individuals within it. This, it seems, is the dominant (liberal) view, and only an exceedingly statist perspective would dispute it (Beitz 1979b; Walzer 1992).

The right that is usually cited as being the ground for the state's right to defend itself is the right of self-determination. The state is the manifestation of, as well as the arena for, the right of a people to determine itself. It is because aggression threatens the common life of the people within a state, as well as threatening other goods they hold dear, that the state can defend its territory and independence. This is clear, for example, from Walzer's (1992, chapter 6) discussion of intervention. Drawing on John Stuart Mill (1984), Walzer argues that states generally ought not to intervene in the affairs of other states because to do so would be to violate the right of self-determination of the community within the state. However, once the right of self-determination is recognized, its implications go beyond a right against intervention or a right of defense. Walzer makes this clear as well, as his discussion of Mill's argument for nonintervention is followed immediately by exceptions to the rule, one of which is secession. When a secessionist movement has demonstrated that it represents the will of its people, other states may intervene to aid the secession because, in this case, secession reflects the self-determination of that people.

In the twenty years since Walzer presented this argument, a great deal of work has been done on nationalism, self-determination, and secession. Despite the range of views that has developed, it is fair to say that something of an overlapping consensus has formed, namely, that under certain circumstances, certain kinds of groups enjoy a right of self-determination that entitles them to their own state or at least to some autonomy in a federal arrangement within an existing state. The debate is mostly over what these circumstances are and what kinds of groups enjoy the right. For example, Allen Buchanan, in his important book *Secession* (1991), argues that the circumstances must include a historical injustice before a group is entitled to secede.

Others are more permissive. Christopher Wellman (1995) and Daniel Philpott (1995) argue that past injustice is not required to entitle a group to secession and, indeed, that any group within a territory may secede, even if it is not plausibly seen as constituting a nation.

The modal position in the debate is, perhaps, somewhere between these positions, holding that certain groups, even absent a history of injustice, have a right to self-determination but that this applies not to just any group but only to "peoples" or "nations." This is essentially the position taken by Kymlicka (1995), Tamir (1993), Miller (1995), and Margalit and Raz (1990). There are, of course, important differences among these authors. Kymlicka argues that groups with "societal cultures" have a right to self-government but not necessarily secession. Margalit and Raz advance a similar argument, and their notion of an "encompassing group" is very close to Kymlicka's "societal culture." Tamir emphasizes that, in her view, the right to self-determination is a cultural right, not a political one, and does not necessarily support a right to political independence. Miller does interpret the right of self-determination as a right to a state, but he hesitates to call it a right, for it may not always be achievable due to the legitimate claims of others. (His concern would perhaps be alleviated by following Philpott in speaking of a "prima facie" right.)

For the purposes of my present argument, I need not enter this important debate but only point out that any one of these views can support the weak claim I wish to make. The claim is that under some circumstances, some groups enjoy a right to self-determination. The circumstances may include—or, following Buchanan, even be limited to—cases of injustice toward the group, or, in a more permissive view, it may not. This right may be enjoyed only by nations or by any group within a territory. It may be that the right of self-determination does not automatically ground a right to political independence, but if some form of self-determination cannot be realized within an existing state, then it can, under these circumstances, ground such a right. For the sake of simplicity, in the discussion that follows I refer to nations or peoples as having a right of self-determination, but this does not commit me to the view that other kinds of groups do not enjoy this right. Similarly, I will sometimes fail to distinguish between a right of self-determination and a right to a state, despite realizing that the former does not necessarily entail the latter. I will assume that in some cases—say, when a federal arrangement cannot be worked out—one can ground the right to a state on the right to self-determination.

My conclusion about the just cause requirement is obvious. Groups other than those constituted by the state in which they live can have a just cause to defend their right of self-determination. While just war theory relies on the rights of the citizens to ground the right of a state to defend itself, other communities within a state may have that same right. When the communal life of a nation is seriously threatened by a state, that nation has a just cause to defend itself. In the case in which the whole nation is within a single state, this can justify secession. In a case in which the community is stateless, as with colonial rule, it is probably less accurate to speak of secession than national liberation.

This is not a radical conclusion. Indeed, it is recognized and endorsed by the United Nations, as Khatchadourian points out: "The UN definition of 'just cause' recognizes the rights of peoples as well as states," and in Article 7 of the definition of *aggression*, the United Nations refers to "the right to self-determination, freedom, and independence, as derived from the Charter, of *peoples* forcibly deprived of that right" (1998, 41). So both morally and legally, "peoples" or "nations" enjoy a right to self-determination. When that right is frustrated, such peoples, I have argued, have the same just cause that states have when the self-determination of their citizens is threatened.

Legitimate Authority

The legitimate authority requirement is usually interpreted to mean that only states can go to war justly. It rules out private groups waging private wars and claiming them to be just. The state has a monopoly on the legitimate use of force, so it is a necessary condition for a just war that it be undertaken by the entity that is uniquely authorized to wield the sword. To allow other entities, groups, or agencies to undertake violence would be to invite chaos. Such violence is seen as merely private violence, crime.

The equation of legitimate authority with states has, however, been criticized by a number of philosophers—and with good reason. Gilbert has argued that "the equation of proper authority with a lawful claim to it should be resisted" (1994, 29). Tony Coates (1997, chapter 5) has argued at some length and quite persuasively that to equate legitimate authority with state sovereignty is to rob the requirement of the moral force that it historically has had. The result is that the principle has become too permissive by assuming that any de facto state may wage war. This requirement, then, is too easily and quickly "checked off": If a war is waged by a state, this requirement is satisfied. This interpretation has meant that "the criterion of legitimate authority has become the most neglected of all the criteria that have been traditionally employed in the moral assessment of war" (Coates 1997, 123). Contrary to this tendency in recent just war thinking, Coates argues that we must subject to close scrutiny a given state's claim to represent the interests and rights of its people.

When we reject the view that all states are legitimate authorities, we may also ask if some nonstates may be legitimate authorities. The considerations just adduced suggest that being a state is not sufficient for being a legitimate authority. Perhaps it is not necessary either. What matters is the plausibility of the claim to represent the interests and rights of a people. I would like to argue that some nonstate entities or organizations may present a very plausible case for being a people's representative. Surely it is sufficient for this that the organization is widely seen as their representative by the members of the nation itself. If an organization claims to act on behalf of a people and is widely seen by that people as legitimately doing so, then the rest of us should look on that organization as the legitimate authority of the people for the purposes of assessing its entitlement to engage in violence on their behalf.

The alternative view, that only states may be legitimate authorities, "leads to political quietism [and is] conservative and uncritical" (Coates 1997, 128). Once we acknowledge that stateless peoples may have the right to self-determination, it would render that right otiose to deny that the right could be defended and vindicated by some nonstate entity. As Dugard (1982, 83) has pointed out, in the case of colonial domination, there is no victim state, though there is a victim people. If we are to grant that a colonized people has a right to self-determination, it seems that we must grant that a nonstate organization—a would-be state, perhaps—can act as a legitimate authority and justly engage in violence on behalf of the people. Examples are not difficult to find. Coates cites the Kurds and the Marsh Arabs in Iraq and asks, "Must such persecuted communities be denied the right of collective self-defense simply because, through some historical accident, they lack the formal character of states?" (1997, 128).

It must be emphasized that the position advocated here requires that the organization not only claim representative status but be perceived to enjoy that status by the people it claims to represent. This is a rather conservative requirement because it rules out "vanguard" organizations that claim representative status despite lack of support among the people themselves. The position defended here is also more stringent than that suggested by Wilkins, who writes that it might "be enough for a terrorist movement simply to claim to represent the aspirations or the moral rights of a people" (1992, 71). While I agree that "moral authority may be all that matters" (Wilkins 1992, 72), I would argue that moral authority requires not merely claiming to represent a people but also being seen by the people themselves as their representative.

How do we know whether this is the case? No single answer can be given here. Certainly the standard should not be higher than that used for states. In the case of states, for example, elections are not required for legitimacy, as understood in just war theory. There are many members of the international community in good standing that are not democratic regimes, authorized by elections. In the case of nonstate entities, no doubt a number of factors will weigh in, either for or against the claim to representativeness, and, in the absence of legal procedures (or public opinion polls), we may have to make an all-things-considered judgment. No doubt there will be some disagreement in particular cases, but all that is required for the present

argument is that, in principle, nonstate organizations may enjoy the moral status of legitimate authorities.

Right Intention

If a national group can have a just cause, and if a nonstate entity can be a legitimate authority to engage in violence on behalf of that group, it seems unproblematic that those engaging in violence can be rightly motivated by that just cause. Hence, if just cause and legitimate authority can be satisfied, there seems to be no reason to think that the requirement of right intention cannot be satisfied. This is not to say, of course, that if the first two are satisfied, the latter is as well, but only that if the first two requirements are met, the latter can be. All that it requires is that the relevant actors be motivated by the just cause and not some other end.

Last Resort

Can terrorist violence, undertaken by the representatives of a stateless nation to vindicate their right of self-determination, be a last resort? Some have doubted that it can. For example, Walzer refers to the claim of last resort as one of the "excuses" sometimes offered for terrorism. He suggests that terrorism is usually a first resort, not a last one, and that to truly be a last resort, "one must indeed try everything (which is a lot of things), and not just once....Politics is an art of repetition" (1988, 239). Terrorists, according to Walzer, often claim that their resort to violence is a last resort but in fact it never is and never can be.

Two problems arise concerning Walzer's position. First, related to the definitional issues discussed above and taken up again below when discrimination is treated, Walzer takes terrorism to be "an attack upon the innocent," and he "take[s] the principle for granted: that every act of terrorism is a wrongful act" (1988, 238). Given the understanding of terrorism as murder, it can never be a justified last resort. But as Fullinwider (1988) argues in his response to Walzer, it is puzzling both that Walzer construes terrorism this way, for not all terrorism is random murder, and that Walzer simply takes it for granted that nothing can justify terrorism. Walzer's position is undermined by a prejudicial definition of *terrorism* that begs the substantive moral questions, reflected in the fact that he characterizes arguments in defense of terrorism as mere "excuses."

The second problem is that again Walzer appears to use a double standard. While he does not say so explicitly in the paper under discussion, Walzer elsewhere clearly endorses the resort to war by states. Here, however, he argues that, because "politics is an art of repetition," the last resort is never arrived at for nonstate actors contemplating violence. But why is it that the territorial integrity and political independence of, say, Britain, justify the resort to violence—even violence that targets civilians—but the right of self-determination of a stateless nation never does? Why can states arrive at last resort, while stateless nations cannot? Walzer never provides an answer to this question.

The fact is that judgment is called for by all political actors contemplating violence, and among the judgments that must be made is whether last resort has been. This is a judgment about whether all reasonable nonviolent measures have been tried, been tried a reasonable number of times, and been given a reasonable amount of time to work. There will always be room for argument about what *reasonable* means here, what it requires in a particular case, but I see no justification for employing a double standard for what it means, one for states, another for nonstate actors. If states may reach the point of deciding that all nonviolent measures have failed, then so too can nonstate actors.

Probability of Success

Whether terrorism ever has any probability of success, or enough probability of success to justify embarking on a terrorist campaign, depends on a number of factors, including the time horizon one has in mind. Whether one considers the case of state actors deciding to embark on a war or nonstate actors embarking on terrorism, a prospective judgment is required, and prospective judgments are liable to miscalculations and incorrect estimations of many factors. Still, one must make a judgment, and if one judges that the end has little chance of being achieved through violence, the probability of success criterion requires that the violence not be commenced.

Does terrorism ever have any probability of success? There are differing views of the historical

record on this question. For example, Walzer thinks not. He writes, "No nation that I know of owes its freedom to a campaign of random murder" (1988, 240). Again, we find that Walzer's analysis is hindered by his conception of what terrorism is, and so it is of little help to us here. To those who have a less loaded notion of terrorism, the evidence appears more ambiguous. Held provides a brief, well-balanced discussion of the issue. She cites authors who have argued on both sides of the question, including one who uses the bombing of the U.S. Marines' barracks in Beirut in 1982 (which prompted an American withdrawal) as an example of a successful terrorist attack. Held concludes that "it may be impossible to predict whether an act of terrorism will in fact have its intended effect" but notes that in this it is no different from other prospective judgments (1991, 71). Similarly, Teichman concludes that the historical evidence on the effectiveness of terrorism is "both ambiguous and incomplete" (1989, 517). And Baier suggests that, at the least, "the prospects for the success of a cause do not seem in the past to have been reduced by resort to unauthorized force, by violent demonstrations that cost some innocent lives" (1994, 208). Finally, Wilkins (1992, 39) believes that some terrorist campaigns have indeed accomplished their goal of national independence and cites Algeria and Kenya as examples.

I am not in a position to judge all of the historical evidence that may be relevant to this issue. However, it seems clear that we cannot say that it is never the case that terrorism has some prospect of success. Perhaps in most cases—the vast majority of them, even—there is little hope of success. Still, we cannot rule out that terrorism can satisfy the probability of success criterion.

Proportionality

The proportionality criterion within *jus ad bellum* also requires a prospective judgment—whether the overall costs of the violent conflict will be outweighed by the overall benefits. In addition to the difficulties inherent in prospective judgments, this criterion is problematic in that it seems to require us to measure the value of costs and benefits that may not be amenable to measurement and seems to assume that all goods are commensurable, that their value can be compared. As a result, there is probably no way to make these kinds of judgments with any great degree of precision.

Still, it seems clear that terrorism can satisfy this criterion at least as well as conventional war. Given the large scale of destruction that often characterizes modern warfare, and given that some very destructive wars are almost universally considered just, it appears that just war theory can countenance a great deal of violence if the end is of sufficient value. If modern warfare is sometimes justified, terrorism, in which the violence is usually on a far smaller scale, can be justified as well. This is especially clear if the end of the violence is the same or similar in both cases, such as when a nation wishes to vindicate its right to self-determination.

JUS IN BELLO

Even if terrorism can meet all the criteria of *jus ad bellum*, it may not be able to meet those of *jus in bello*, for terrorism is often condemned, not so much for who carries it out and why but for how it is carried out. Arguing that it can satisfy the requirements of *jus in bello*, then, may be the greatest challenge facing my argument.

Proportionality

The challenge, however, does not come from the proportionality requirement of *jus in bello*. Like its counterpart in *jus ad bellum*, the criterion requires proportionality between the costs of an action and the benefits to be achieved, but now the requirement is applied to particular acts within the war. It forbids, then, conducting the war in such a way that it involves inordinate costs, costs that are disproportionate to the gains.

Again, there seems to be no reason to believe that terrorist acts could not satisfy this requirement. Given that the scale of the death and destruction usually involved in terrorist acts pales in comparison with that involved in wars commonly thought to be just, it would seem that terrorism would satisfy this requirement more easily than war (assuming that the goods to be achieved are not dissimilar). So if the means of terrorism is what places it beyond the moral pale for many people, it is probably not because of its disproportionality.

Discrimination

The principle of discrimination holds that in waging a war we must distinguish between legitimate and illegitimate targets of attack. The usual way of making this distinction is to classify persons according to their status as combatants and noncombatants and to maintain that only combatants may be attacked. However, there is some disagreement as to the moral basis of this distinction, which creates disagreement as to where exactly this line should be drawn. While usually based on the notion of moral innocence, noncombatant status, it can be argued, has little to do with innocence, for often combatants are conscripts, while those truly responsible for aggression are usually not liable (practically, not morally) to attack. Moreover, many who provide essential support to the war effort are not combatants.

For the moment, though, let us accept the conventional view that discrimination requires that violence be directed at military targets. Assuming the line can be clearly drawn, two points can be made about terrorism and discrimination. The first is that, a priori, it is possible for terrorism to discriminate and still be terrorism. This follows from the argument presented above that, as a matter of definition, it is implausible to define terrorism as intrinsically indiscriminate. Those who define terrorism as random or indiscriminate will disagree and maintain that "discriminate terrorism" is an oxymoron, a conceptual impossibility. Here I can only repeat that this position departs substantially from ordinary language and does so in a way that prejudges the moral issues involved. However, if my argument above does not convince on this question, there is little more to be said here.

Luckily, the issue is not a purely a priori one. The fact is that terrorists, or at least those called terrorists by almost everyone, in fact do often discriminate. One example, cited above, is the bombing of the barracks in Beirut, which killed some 240 American soldiers. Whatever one wants to say to condemn the attack, one cannot say that it was indiscriminate. Fullinwider cites the example of the kidnapping, trail, and killing of Aldo Moro by the Italian Red Brigades in 1978 and argues that, whatever else one might want to say about it, "there was nothing indiscriminate about the taking of Aldo Moro" (1988, 250). Coady (1985, 63) cites another example, that of an American diplomat in Uruguay who was targeted and killed in 1970 because of the assistance he was providing to the authoritarian regime. These may be the exceptions rather than the rule, but it clearly is not accurate to say that terrorists—and there was never any doubt that these were acts of terrorism—never discriminate.

It might be useful to look, one last time, at Walzer's position on this issue because, from the point of view I have developed, he errs on both the conceptual and the empirical question. Walzer maintains that "terrorism in the strict sense, the random murder of innocent people, emerged...only in the period after World War II" (1992, 198). Previously, nonstate actors, especially revolutionaries, who committed violence did discriminate. Walzer gives several examples of this in which Russian revolutionaries, the Irish Republican Army, and the Stern Gang in the Middle East went to great lengths to not kill civilians. He also notes that these people were called terrorists. Yet he refuses to say that they *were* terrorists, insisting instead that they were not, really, and using scare quotes when he himself calls them terrorists. This is tortured analysis indeed. Why not simply acknowledge that these earlier terrorists were indeed terrorists while also maintaining, if evidence supports it, that today more terrorists are more indiscriminate than in the past? I suspect that Walzer and I would agree in our moral assessment of particular acts. Our main difference is that he believes that calling an act terrorism (without the scare quotes) settles the question.

All of this is consistent with the assumption that a clear line can be drawn between combatants and noncombatants. However, the more reasonable view may be that combatancy status, and therefore liability to attack, are matters of degree. This is suggested by Holmes (1989, 187), and though Holmes writes as a pacifist critic of just war theory, his suggestion is one that just war theorists may nevertheless want to endorse. Holmes conceives of a

spectrum along which we can place classes of individuals, according to their degree of responsibility for an aggressive war. At one end he would place political leaders who undertake the aggression, followed by soldiers, contributors to the war, supporters, and, finally, at the other end of the spectrum, noncontributors and nonsupporters. This view does indeed better capture our moral intuitions about liability to attack and avoids debates (which are probably not resolvable) about where the absolute line between combatants and noncombatants is to be drawn.

If correct, this view further complicates the question of whether and when terrorism discriminates. It means we must speak of more and less discriminate violence, and it forces us to ask questions like, To what *extent* were the targets of violence implicated in unjust aggression? Children, for example, would be clearly off-limits, but nonmilitary adults who actively take part in frustrating a people's right to self-determination may not be. With terrorism, as with war, the question to ask may not be, Was the act discriminate, yes or no? but, rather, How discriminate was the violence? Our judgment on this matter, and hence our moral appraisal of the violence, is likely to be more nuanced if we ask the latter question than if we assume that a simple yes or no settles the matter. After all, is our judgment really the same—and ought it be—when a school bus is attacked as when gun-toting citizens are attacked? Terrorism, it seems, can be more discriminate or less so, and our judgments ought to reflect the important matters of degree involved.

One final issue is worth mentioning, if only briefly. Even if one were to grant that terrorism necessarily involves the killing of innocents, this alone does not place it beyond the scope of just war theory, for innocents may be killed in a just war. All that just war theory requires is that innocents not be *targeted*. The basis for this position is the principle of double effect, which holds, roughly, that innocents may be killed as long as their deaths are not the intended effects of violence but, rather, the unintended (though perhaps fully foreseen) side effects of violence. So the most that can be said against my position, even granting that terrorism involves the killing of innocents, is that the difference between (just) war and terrorism is that in the former innocents are not targeted but (routinely) killed while in the latter they are targeted and killed. Whether this is a crucial distinction is a question that would require us to go too far afield at this point. Perhaps it is enough to say that if there are reasons to reject the principle of double effect, such as those offered by Holmes (1989, 193–200), there is all the more basis to think that terrorism and war are not so morally different from each other.

CONCLUSION

I have argued that terrorism, understood as political violence committed by nonstate actors, can be assessed from the point of view of just war theory and that terrorist acts can indeed satisfy the theory's criteria. Though stateless, some groups can nevertheless have a just cause when their right to self-determination is frustrated. Under such circumstances, a representative organization can be a morally legitimate authority to carry out violence as a last resort to defend the group's rights. Such violence must conform to the other criteria, especially discrimination, but terrorism, I have argued, can do so.

The argument has taken place entirely within the just war tradition but can be endorsed from other perspectives as well. For example, Annette Baier, though no just war theorist, comes to a very similar conclusion:

> It is fairly easy to say that the clearer it is that the terrorist's group's case is *not* being listened to in decision making affecting it and that the less violent ways to get attention have been tried in vain, the more excuse the terrorist has; that his case is better the more plausible his claim to represent his group's sense of injustice or wrong, not just his own; that the more limited, the less indiscriminate, his violence, the less outrage will we feel for his inhumanity. Those are not daring conclusions. [1994, 217]

Indeed they are not daring conclusions, and mine certainly are not. I have avoided consequentialist arguments that might, on utilitarian grounds, justify violence for the greater good to be achieved. I have not endorsed the notion of collective guilt, which, in my view, goes too far in eroding the distinction between combatants and noncombatants (see Wilkins 1992). My argument would not support the violence of a vanguard party, committing

violence in the hope of winning the support of those it claims to already represent. Hence, the argument presented here places real, stringent moral limits on violence committed by nonstate actors.

Indeed, placing limits on violence is what just war theory is all about. As Coates argues in his contribution the main purpose of just war theory is to constrain violence. Coates emphasizes that just war theory should not convince perpetrators of violence of their own righteousness but, rather, is meant to instill a sense of limits and restraint. If we assume that terrorism is beyond the pale, however, we deprive ourselves of the capacity to impose some moral limits. If terrorists are monsters, then there is no reasoning with them. However, if we take their claims seriously, if we assess their violence by the same standards used to assess the violence of states, we at least have a chance that just war theory will impose some restraint on them, as it does (or at least is supposed to) with states.

It is important to be clear about what I have not argued here. I have not defended terrorism in general, nor certainly have I defended any particular act of violence. It follows from my argument not that terrorism can be justified but that if war can be justified, then terrorism can be as well. I wish to emphasize the conditional nature of the conclusion. I have not established just war theory as the best or the only framework within which to think about the moral issues raised by political violence. Instead I have relied on it because it is the most developed and widely used in thinking about violence carried out by states. I have done so because the double standard that is often used in assessing violence committed by states and nonstate actors seems indefensible. Applying just war theory to both, I believe, is a plausible way to bring both kinds of violence under one standard.

I have little doubt that most terrorist acts do not satisfy all of the criteria of just war theory and that many of them fall far short. In such cases we are well justified in condemning them. But the condemnation must follow, not precede, examination of the case and is not settled by calling the act terrorism and its perpetrators terrorists. I agree with Fullinwider that, while terrorism often fails to be morally justified, "this failure is contingent, not necessary. We cannot define terrorism into a moral corner where we do not have to worry any more about justification" (1988, 257). Furthermore, failure to satisfy the requirements of just war theory is not unique to acts of terrorism. The same could be said of wars themselves. How many wars, after all, are undertaken and waged within the constraints imposed by the theory?

The conditional nature of the conclusion, if the above argument is sound, forces a choice. Either both interstate war and terrorism can be justified or neither can be. For my part, I must confess to being sorely tempted by the latter position, that neither war nor terrorism can be justified. This temptation

is bolstered by pacifist arguments, such as that presented by Holmes (1989, chapter 6), that the killing of innocents is a perfectly predictable effect of modern warfare, the implication of which is that no modern war can be just. That is, even if we can imagine a modern just war, it is not a realistic possibility. Though the pacifist position is tempting, it also seems clear that some evils are great enough to require a response, even a violent response. And once we grant that states may respond violently, there seems no principled reason to deny that same right to certain nonstate groups that enjoy a right to self-determination.

ARGUMENT 16 ESSAY QUESTIONS

1. Who makes the stronger case—Khatchadourian or Valls? Why do you think so?
2. Does Walzer successfully counter Valls's view? Why or why not?
3. Do you think terrorism is ever justified? Explain your reasoning.

17. THE TICKING BOMB ARGUMENT FOR TORTURE

In "The Case for Torturing the Ticking Bomb Terrorist," Alan M. Dershowitz puts forth a popular form of the ticking bomb argument for torture. It could happen, he contends, that the only way to prevent a thousand innocent people from being killed by a nuclear bomb planted by a terrorist is to torture the terrorist until he reveals the location of the bomb. Considering the many innocent lives that could be saved, it would be morally permissible—even morally obligatory—to torture the terrorist. Thus torture is sometimes morally justified. And if that's so, legalizing or institutionalizing torture is also morally justified.

Charles Krauthammer also uses a ticking bomb argument:

> [T]here is no denying the monstrous evil that is any form of torture. And there is no denying how corrupting it can be to the individuals and society that practice it. But elected leaders, responsible above all for the protection of their citizens, have the obligation to tolerate their own sleepless nights by doing what is necessary—and

only what is necessary, nothing more—to get information that could prevent mass murder.[21]

The crux of the argument is, of course, that a ticking bomb scenario could actually occur that would justify torture. Many accept this premise, as Krauthammer does, and some reject it, insisting that in the real world such a state of affairs would simply not happen or that even if it would, torture is an absolute moral wrong. Those who think that a ticking bomb situation could be actual try to make their case by providing possible scenarios that seem completely realistic.

Critics who reject an absolute prohibition of torture may argue that if killing people is not an absolute wrong (since killing seems sometimes permissible in, for example, self-defense and in war), and if killing people is worse than torturing them, then it makes no sense to maintain that torture is an absolute moral wrong. If killing a person is not absolutely impermissible, then neither is torture.

It seems clear that whether or not the ticking bomb premise is true, the conclusion of the argument—that legalizing or institutionalizing torture is morally justified—does not follow from it. As we have seen, whether an instance of torturing someone is morally justified is a separate question from whether torture should be adopted by our institutions.

Thus many who agree that torture is sometimes morally permissible argue against making it an official or unofficial part of our law or institutions. They contend that legalizing or institutionalizing torture would (1) create a "culture of torture" in which torturing people would become routine, morally corrupting, and eradicable; (2) contradict and undermine democratic institutions (as Seumas Miller observes, "It would be equivalent to a liberal democracy legalizing and institutionalizing slavery on the grounds, say, of economic necessity."[22]); and (3) permit the practice of torture to become more widespread and more brutal.

Dershowitz takes a different view. He believes that torture is being used today by the United States and would almost certainly be used in any real-life ticking bomb scenario. If this is correct, he says,

> [T]hen it is important to ask the following question: if torture is being or will be practiced, is it worse to close our eyes to it and tolerate its use by low-level law enforcement officials without accountability, or instead to bring it to the surface by requiring that a warrant of some kind be required as a precondition to the infliction of any type of torture under any circumstances?[23]

Dershowitz therefore favors a form of legalization in which agents of the state may torture someone if they first obtain judicial permission in the form of "torture warrants" similar to the judicial warrants required for the police to legally tap someone's phone. Such a warrant system, he says, would "decrease the amount of physical violence directed against suspects" and "the rights of the suspect would be better protected with a warrant requirement."[24]

[21] Charles Krauthammer, "The Truth about Torture," *The Weekly Standard*, 5 December 2005.
[22] Seumas Miller, "Torture," *The Stanford Encyclopedia of Philosophy*.
[23] Alan M. Dershowitz, "Tortured Reasoning," in *Torture: A Collection*, ed. Sanford Levinson (Oxford: Oxford University Press, 2004), 257.
[24] Alan M. Dershowitz, "Should the Ticking Bomb Terrorist Be Tortured?"

The Case for Torturing the Ticking Bomb Terrorist

ALAN M. DERSHOWITZ

The arguments in favor of using torture as a last resort to prevent a ticking bomb from exploding and killing many people are both simple and simple-minded. Bentham constructed a compelling hypothetical case to support his utilitarian argument against an absolute prohibition on torture:

> Suppose an occasion were to arise, in which a suspicion is entertained, as strong as that which would be received as a sufficient ground for arrest and commitment as for felony—a suspicion that at this very time a considerable number of individuals are actually suffering, by illegal violence inflictions equal in intensity to those which if inflicted by the hand of justice, would universally be spoken of under the name of torture. For the purpose of rescuing from torture these hundred innocents, should any scruple be made of applying equal or superior torture, to extract the requisite information from the mouth of one criminal, who having it in his power to make known the place where at this time the enormity was practising or about to be practised, should refuse to do so? To say nothing of wisdom, could any pretence be made so much as to the praise of blind and vulgar humanity, by the man who to save one criminal, should determine to abandon 100 innocent persons to the same fate?

If the torture of one guilty person would be justified to prevent the torture of a hundred innocent persons, it would seem to follow—certainly to Bentham—that it would also be justified to prevent the murder of thousands of innocent civilians in the ticking bomb case. Consider two hypothetical situations that are not, unfortunately, beyond the realm of possibility. In fact, they are both extrapolations on actual situations we have faced.

Several weeks before September 11, 2001, the Immigration and Naturalization Service detained Zacarias Moussaoui after flight instructors reported suspicious statements he had made while taking flying lessons and paying for them with large amounts of cash. The government decided not to seek a warrant to search his computer. Now imagine that they had, and that they discovered he was part of a plan to destroy large occupied buildings, but without any further details. They interrogated him, gave him immunity from prosecution, and offered him large cash rewards and a new identity. He refused to talk. They then threatened him, tried to trick him, and employed every lawful technique available. He still refused. They even injected him with sodium pentothal and other truth serums, but to no avail. The attack now appeared to be imminent, but the FBI still had no idea what the target was or what means would be used to attack it. We could not simply evacuate all buildings indefinitely. An FBI agent proposes the use of nonlethal torture—say, a sterilized needle inserted under the fingernails to produce unbearable pain without any threat to health or life, or the method used in the film *Marathon Man*, a dental drill through an unanesthetized tooth.

The simple cost-benefit analysis for employing such nonlethal torture seems overwhelming: it is surely better to inflict nonlethal pain on one guilty terrorist who is illegally withholding information needed to prevent an act of terrorism than to permit a large number of innocent victims to die. Pain is a lesser and more remediable harm than death; and the lives of a thousand innocent people should be valued more than the bodily integrity of one guilty person. If the variation on the Moussaoui case is not sufficiently compelling to make this point, we can always raise the stakes. Several weeks after September 11, our government received reports that a ten-kiloton nuclear weapon may have been stolen from Russia and was on its way to New York City, where it would be detonated and kill hundreds of thousands of people. The reliability of the source, code named Dragonfire, was

From *Why Terrorism Works: Understanding the Threat, Responding to the Challenge* by Alan M. Dershowitz. Copyright © 2002 Yale University Press. Reprinted with permission of the publisher.

uncertain, but assume for purposes of this hypothetical extension of the actual case that the source was a captured terrorist—like the one tortured by the Philippine authorities—who knew precisely how and where the weapon was being bought into New York and was to be detonated. Again, everything short of torture is tried, but to no avail. It is not absolutely certain torture will work, but it is our last, best hope for preventing a cataclysmic nuclear devastation in a city too large to evacuate in time. Should nonlethal torture be tried? Bentham would certainly have said yes.

The strongest argument against any resort to torture, even in the ticking bomb case, also derives from Bentham's utilitarian calculus. Experience has shown that if torture, which has been deemed illegitimate by the civilized world for more than a century, were now to be legitimated—even for limited use in one extraordinary type of situation—such legitimation would constitute an important symbolic setback in the worldwide campaign against human rights abuses. Inevitably, the legitimation of torture by the world's leading democracy would provide a welcome justification for its more widespread use in other parts of the world. Two Bentham scholars, W. L. Twining and P. E. Twining, have argued that torture is unacceptable even if it is restricted to an extremely limited category of cases:

> There is at least one good practical reason for drawing a distinction between justifying an isolated act of torture in an extreme emergency of the kind postulated above and justifying the *institutionalisation* of torture as a regular practice. The circumstances are so extreme in which most of us would be prepared to justify resort to torture, if at all, the conditions we would impose would be so stringent, the practical problems of devising and enforcing adequate safeguards so difficult and the risks of abuse so great that it would be unwise and dangerous to entrust any government, however enlightened, with such a power. Even an out-and-out utilitarian can support an absolute prohibition against institutionalised torture on the ground that no government in the world can be trusted not to abuse the power and to satisfy in practice the conditions he would impose.

Bentham's own justification was based on *case* or *act* utilitarianism—a demonstration that in a *particular case*, the benefits that would flow from the limited use of torture would outweigh its costs. The argument against any use of torture would derive from *rule* utilitarianism—which considers the implications of establishing a precedent that would inevitably be extended beyond its limited case utilitarian justification to other possible evils of lesser magnitude. Even terrorism itself could be justified by a case utilitarian approach. Surely one could come up with a singular situation in which the targeting of a small number of civilians could be thought necessary to save thousands of other civilians—blowing up a German kindergarten by the relatives of inmates in a Nazi death camp, for example, and threatening to repeat the targeting of German children unless the death camps were shut down.

The reason this kind of single-case utilitarian justification is simple-minded is that it has no inherent limiting principle. If nonlethal torture of one person is justified to prevent the killing of many important people, then what if it were necessary to use lethal torture—or at least torture that posed a substantial risk of death? What if it were necessary to torture the suspect's mother or children to get him to divulge the information? What if it took threatening to kill his family, his friends, his entire village? Under a simple-minded quantitative case utilitarianism, anything goes as long as the number of people tortured or killed does not exceed the number that would be saved. This is morality by numbers, unless there are other constraints on what we can properly do. These other constraints can come from *rule* utilitarianisms or other principles of morality, such as the prohibition against deliberately punishing the innocent. Unless we are prepared to impose some limits on the use of torture or other barbaric tactics that might be of some use in preventing terrorism, we risk hurtling down a slippery slope into the abyss of amorality and ultimately tyranny. Dostoevsky captured the complexity of this dilemma in *The Brothers Karamazov* when he had Ivan pose the following question to Alyosha: "Imagine that you are creating a fabric of human destiny with the object of making men happy in the end, giving them peace at least, but that it was essential and inevitable to torture to death only one tiny creature—that baby beating its breast with its fist, for instance—and to found that edifice on its unavenged tears, would you consent to be the architect on those conditions? Tell me the truth."

A willingness to kill an innocent child suggests a willingness to do anything to achieve a necessary result. Hence the slippery slope.

It does not necessarily follow from this understandable fear of the slippery slope that we can never consider the use of nonlethal infliction of pain, if its use were to be limited by acceptable principles of morality. After all, imprisoning a witness who refuses to testify after being given immunity is designed to be punitive—that is painful. Such imprisonment can, on occasion, produce more pain and greater risk of death than nonlethal torture. Yet we continue to threaten and use the pain of imprisonment to loosen the tongues of reluctant witnesses.

It is commonplace for police and prosecutors to threaten recalcitrant suspects with prison rape. As one prosecutor put it: "You're going to be the boyfriend of a very bad man." The slippery slope is an argument of caution, not a debate stopper, since virtually every compromise with an absolutist approach to rights carries the risk of slipping further. An appropriate response to the slippery slope is to build in a principled break. For example, if nonlethal torture were legally limited to convicted terrorists who had knowledge of future massive terrorist acts, were given immunity, and still refused to provide the information, there might still be objections to the use of torture, but they would have to go beyond the slippery slope argument.

The case utilitarian argument for torturing a ticking bomb terrorist is bolstered by an argument from analogy—an *a fortiori* argument. What moral principle could justify the death penalty for past individual murders and at the same time condemn nonlethal torture to prevent future mass murders? Bentham posed this rhetorical question as support for his argument. The death penalty is, of course, reserved for convicted murderers. But again, what if torture was limited to convicted terrorists who refused to divulge information about future terrorism? Consider as well the analogy to the use of deadly force against suspects fleeing from arrest for dangerous felonies of which they have not yet been convicted. Or military retaliations that produce the predictable and inevitable collateral killing of some

innocent civilians. The case against torture, if made by a Quaker who opposes the death penalty, war, self-defense, and the use of lethal force against fleeing felons, is understandable. But for anyone who justifies killing on the basis of a cost-benefit analysis, the case against the use of nonlethal torture to save multiple lives is more difficult to make. In the end, absolute opposition to torture—even nonlethal torture in the ticking bomb case—may rest more on historical and aesthetic considerations than on moral or logical ones.

In debating the issue of torture, the first question I am often asked is, "Do you want to take us back to the Middle Ages?" The association between any form of torture and gruesome death is powerful in the minds of most people knowledgeable of the history of its abuses. This understandable association makes it difficult for many people to think about nonlethal torture as a technique for *saving* lives.

The second question I am asked is, "What kind of torture do you have in mind?" When I respond by describing the sterilized needle being shoved under the fingernails, the reaction is visceral and often visible—a shudder coupled with a facial gesture of disgust. Discussions of the death penalty on the other hand can be conducted without these kinds of reactions, especially now that we literally put the condemned prisoner "to sleep" by laying him out on a gurney and injecting a lethal substance into his body. There is no breaking of the neck, burning of the brain, bursting of internal organs, or gasping for breath that used to accompany hanging, electrocution, shooting, and gassing. The executioner has been replaced by a paramedical technician, as the aesthetics of death have become more acceptable. All this tends to cover up the reality that death is forever while nonlethal pain is temporary. In our modern age death is underrated, while pain is overrated.

I observed a similar phenomenon several years ago during the debate over corporal punishment that was generated by the decision of a court in Singapore to sentence a young American to medically supervised lashing with a cane. Americans who support the death penalty and who express little concern about inner-city prison conditions were outraged by the specter of a few welts on the buttocks of an American. It was an utterly irrational display of hypocrisy and double standards. Given a choice between a medically administered whipping and one month in a typical state lockup or prison, any rational and knowledgeable person would choose the lash. No one dies of welts or pain, but many inmates are raped, beaten, knifed, and otherwise mutilated and tortured in American prisons. The difference is that we don't see—and we don't want to see—what goes on behind their high walls. Nor do we want to think about it. Raising the issue of torture makes Americans think about a brutalizing and unaesthetic phenomenon that has been out of our consciousness for many years.

·····

The debate over the use of torture goes back many years, with Bentham supporting it in a limited category of cases, Kant opposing it as part of his categorical imperative against improperly using people as means for achieving noble ends, and Voltaire's views on the matter being "hopelessly confused." The modern resort to terrorism has renewed the debate over how a rights-based society should respond to the prospect of using nonlethal torture in the ticking bomb situation. In the late 1980s the Israeli government appointed a commission headed by a retired Supreme Court justice to look into precisely that situation. The commission concluded that there are "three ways for solving this grave dilemma between the vital need to preserve the very existence of the state and its citizens, and maintain its character as a law-abiding state." The first is to allow the security services to continue to fight terrorism in "a twilight zone which is outside the realm of law." The second is "the way of the hypocrites: they declare that they abide by the rule of law, but turn a blind eye to what goes on beneath the surface." And the third, "the truthful road of the rule of law," is that the "law itself must insure a proper framework for the activity" of the security services in seeking to prevent terrorist acts.

There is of course a fourth road: namely to forgo any use of torture and simply allow the preventable terrorist act to occur. After the Supreme Court of Israel outlawed the use of physical pressure, the Israeli security services claimed that, as a result of the Supreme Court's decision, at least one preventable act of terrorism had been allowed to take

place, one that killed several people when a bus was bombed. Whether this claim is true, false, or somewhere in between is difficult to assess. But it is clear that if the preventable act of terrorism was of the magnitude of the attacks of September 11, there would be a great outcry in any democracy that had deliberately refused to take available preventive action, even if it required the use of torture. During numerous public appearances since September 11, 2001, I have asked audiences for a show of hands as to how many would support the use of nonlethal torture in a ticking bomb case. Virtually every hand is raised. The few that remain down go up when I ask how many believe that torture would actually be used in such a case.

Law enforcement personnel give similar responses. This can be seen in reports of physical abuse directed against some suspects that have been detained following September 11, reports that have been taken quite seriously by at least one federal judge. It is confirmed by the willingness of U.S. law enforcement officials to facilitate the torture of terrorist suspects by repressive regimes allied with our intelligence agencies. As one former CIA operative with thirty years of experience reported: "A lot of people are saying we need someone at the agency who can pull fingernails out. Others are saying, 'Let others use interrogation methods that we don't use.' The only question then is, do you want to have CIA people in the room?" The real issue, therefore, is not whether some torture would or would not be used in the ticking bomb case—it would. The question is whether it would be done openly, pursuant to a previously established legal procedure, or whether it would be done secretly, in violation of existing law.

Several important values are pitted against each other in this conflict. The first is the safety and security of a nation's citizens. Under the ticking bomb scenario this value may require the use of torture, if that is the only way to prevent the bomb from exploding and killing large numbers of civilians. The second value is the preservation of civil liberties and human rights. This value requires that we not accept torture as a legitimate part of our legal system. In my debates with two prominent civil libertarians, Floyd Abrams and Harvey Silverglate, both have acknowledged that they would want nonlethal torture to be used if it could prevent thousands of deaths, but they did not want torture to be officially recognized by our legal system. As Abrams put it: "In a democracy sometimes it is necessary to do things off the books and below the radar screen." Former presidential candidate Alan Keyes took the position that although torture might be *necessary* in a given situation it could never be *right*. He suggested that a president *should* authorize the torturing of a ticking bomb terrorist, but that this act should not be legitimated by the courts or incorporated into our legal system. He argued that wrongful and indeed unlawful acts might sometimes be necessary to preserve the nation, but that no aura of legitimacy should be placed on these actions by judicial imprimatur.

This understandable approach is in conflict with the third important value: namely, open accountability and visibility in a democracy. "Off-the-book actions below the radar screen" are antithetical to the theory and practice of democracy. Citizens cannot approve or disapprove of governmental actions of which they are unaware. We have learned the lesson of history that off-the-book actions can produce terrible consequences. Richard Nixon's creation of a group of "plumbers" led to Watergate, and Ronald Reagan's authorization of an off-the-books foreign policy in Central America led to the Iran-Contra scandal. And these are only the ones we know about!

Perhaps the most extreme example of such a hypocritical approach to torture comes—not surprisingly—from the French experience in Algeria. The French army used torture extensively in seeking to prevent terrorism during a brutal colonial war from 1955 to 1957. An officer who supervised this torture, General Paul Aussaresses, wrote a book recounting what he had done and seen, including the torture of dozens of Algerians. "The best way to make a terrorist talk when he refused to say what he knew was to torture him," he boasted. Although the book was published decades after the war was over, the general was prosecuted—but not for what he had done to the Algerians. Instead, he was prosecuted for *revealing* what he had done, and seeking to justify it.

In a democracy governed by the rule of law, we should never want our soldiers or our president to take any action that we deem wrong or illegal. A good test of whether an action should or should not be done is whether we are prepared to have it disclosed—perhaps not immediately, but certainly after some time has passed. No legal system operating under the rule of law should ever tolerate an "off-the-books" approach to necessity. Even the defense of necessity must be justified lawfully. The road to tyranny has always been paved with claims of necessity made by those responsible for the security of a nation. Our system of checks and balances requires that all presidential actions, like all legislative or military actions, be consistent with governing law. If it is necessary to torture in the ticking bomb case, then our governing laws must accommodate this practice. If we refuse to change our law to accommodate any particular action, then our government should not take that action.

Only in a democracy committed to civil liberties would a triangular conflict of this kind exist. Totalitarian and authoritarian regimes experience no such conflict, because they subscribe to neither the civil libertarian nor the democratic values that come in conflict with the value of security. The hard question is: which value is to be preferred when an inevitable clash occurs? One or more of these values must inevitably be compromised in making the tragic choice presented by the ticking bomb case. If we do not torture, we compromise the security and safety of our citizens. If we tolerate torture, but keep it off the books and below the radar screen, we compromise principles of democratic accountability. If we create a legal structure for limiting and controlling torture, we compromise our principled opposition to torture in all circumstances and create a potentially dangerous and expandable situation.

In 1678, the French writer François de La Rochefoucauld said that "hypocrisy is the homage that vice renders to virtue." In this case we have two vices: terrorism and torture. We also have two virtues: civil liberties and democratic accountability. Most civil libertarians I know prefer hypocrisy, precisely because it appears to avoid the conflict between security and civil liberties, but by choosing the way of the hypocrite these civil libertarians compromise the value of democratic accountability. Such is the nature of tragic choices in a complex world. As Bentham put it more than two centuries ago: "Government throughout is but a choice of evils." In a democracy, such choices must be made, whenever possible, with openness and democratic accountability, and subject to the rule of law.

Consider another terrible choice of evils that could easily have been presented on September 11, 2001—and may well be presented in the future: a hijacked passenger jet is on a collision course with a densely occupied office building; the only way to prevent the destruction of the building and the killing of its occupants is to shoot down the jet, thereby killing its innocent passengers. This choice now seems easy, because the passengers are certain to die anyway and their somewhat earlier deaths will save numerous lives. The passenger jet must be shot down. But what if it were only *probable*, not certain, that the jet would crash into the building? Say, for example, we know from cell phone transmissions that passengers are struggling to regain control of the hijacked jet, but it is unlikely they will succeed in time. Or say we have no communication with the jet and all we know is that it is off course and heading toward Washington, D.C., or some other densely populated city. Under these more questionable circumstances, the question becomes *who* should make this life and death choice between evils—a decision that may turn out tragically wrong?

No reasonable person would allocate this decision to a fighter jet pilot who happened to be in the area or to a local airbase commander—unless of course there was no time for the matter to be passed up the chain of command to the president or the secretary of defense. A decision of this kind should be made at the highest level possible, with visibility and accountability.

Why is this not also true of the decision to torture a ticking bomb terrorist? Why should that choice of evils be relegated to a local policeman, FBI agent, or CIA operative, rather than to a judge, the attorney general, or the president?

There are, of course, important differences between the decision to shoot down the plane and the decision to torture the ticking bomb terrorist. Having to shoot down an airplane, though tragic, is not likely to be a recurring issue. There is no slope down which to slip. Moreover, the jet to be shot down is filled with our fellow citizens—people with whom we can identity. The suspected terrorist we may choose to torture is a "they"—an enemy with whom we do not identify but with whose potential victims we do identify. The risk of making the wrong decision, or of overdoing the torture, is far greater, since we do not care as much what happens to "them" as to "us." Finally, there is something different about torture—even nonlethal torture—that sets it apart from a quick death. In addition to the horrible history associated with torture, there is also the aesthetic of torture. The very idea of deliberately subjecting a captive human being to excruciating pain violates our sense of what is acceptable. On a purely rational basis, it is far worse to shoot a fleeing felon in the back and kill him, yet every civilized society authorizes shooting such a suspect who poses dangers of committing violent crimes against the police or others. In the United States we execute convicted murderers, despite compelling evidence of the unfairness and ineffectiveness of capital punishment. Yet many of us recoil at the prospect of shoving a sterilized needle under the finger of a suspect who is refusing to divulge information that might prevent multiple deaths. Despite the irrationality of these distinctions, they are understandable, especially in light of the sordid history of torture.

We associate torture with the Inquisition, the Gestapo, the Stalinist purges, and the Argentine colonels responsible for the "dirty war." We recall it as a prelude to death, an integral part of a regime of gratuitous pain leading to a painful demise. We find it difficult to imagine a benign use of nonlethal torture to save lives.

Yet there was a time in the history of Anglo-Saxon law when torture was used to save life, rather than to take it, and when the limited administration of nonlethal torture was supervised by judges, including some who are well remembered in history. This fascinating story has been recounted by Professor John Langbein of Yale Law School, and it is worth summarizing here because it helps inform the debate over whether, if torture would in fact be used in a ticking bomb case, it would be worse to make it part of the legal system, or worse to have it done off the books and below the radar screen.

In his book on legalized torture during the sixteenth and seventeenth centuries, *Torture and the Law of Proof,* Langbein demonstrates the trade-off between torture and other important values.

Torture was employed for several purposes. First, it was used to secure the evidence necessary to obtain a guilty verdict under the rigorous criteria for conviction required at the time—either the testimony of two eyewitnesses or the confession of the accused himself. Circumstantial evidence, no matter how compelling, would not do. As Langbein concludes, "no society will long tolerate a legal system in which there is no prospect in convicting unrepentant persons who commit clandestine crimes. Something had to be done to extend the system to those cases. The two-eyewitness rule was hard to compromise or evade, but the confession invited 'subterfuge.'" The subterfuge that was adopted permitted the use of torture to obtain confessions from suspects against whom there was compelling circumstantial evidence of guilt. The circumstantial evidence, alone, could not be used to convict, but it was used to obtain a torture warrant. That torture warrant was in turn used to obtain a confession, which then had to be independently corroborated—at least in most cases (witchcraft and other such cases were exempted from the requirement of corroboration).

Torture was also used against persons already convicted of capital crimes, such as high treason, who were thought to have information necessary to prevent attacks on the state.

Langbein studied eighty-one torture warrants, issued between 1540 and 1640, and found that in many of them, especially in "the higher cases of treasons, torture is used for discovery, and not for evidence." Torture was "used to protect the state" and "mostly that meant preventive torture to identify and forestall plots and plotters." It was only when the legal system loosened its requirement of proof (or introduced the "black box" of the jury system) and when perceived threats against the state diminished that torture was no longer deemed necessary to convict guilty defendants against whom there had previously been insufficient evidence, or to secure preventive information.

The ancient Jewish system of jurisprudence came up with yet another solution to the conundrum of convicting the guilty and preventing harms to the community in the face of difficult evidentiary barriers. Jewish law required two witnesses and a specific advance warning before a guilty person could be convicted. Because confessions were disfavored,

torture was not an available option. Instead, the defendant who had been seen killing by one reliable witness, or whose guilt was obvious from the circumstantial evidence, was formally acquitted, but he was then taken to a secure location and fed a concoction of barley and water until his stomach burst and he died. Moreover, Jewish law permitted more flexible forms of self-help against those who were believed to endanger the community.

Every society has insisted on the incapacitation of dangerous criminals regardless of strictures in the formal legal rules. Some use torture, others use informal sanctions, while yet others create the black box of a jury, which need not explain its commonsense verdicts. Similarly, every society insists that, if there are steps that can be taken to prevent effective acts of terrorism, these steps should be taken, even if they require some compromise with other important principles.

In deciding whether the ticking bomb terrorist should be tortured, one important question is whether there would be less torture if it were done as part of the legal system, as it was in sixteenth- and seventeenth-century England, or off the books, as it is in many countries today. The Langbein study does not definitively answer this question, but it does provide some suggestive insights. The English system of torture was more visible and thus more subject to public accountability, and it is likely that torture was employed less frequently in England than in France. "During these years when it appears that torture might have become routinized in English criminal procedure, the Privy Council kept the torture power under careful control and never allowed it to fall into the hands of the regular law enforcement officers," as it had in France. In England "no law enforcement officer...acquired the power to use torture without special warrant." Moreover, when torture warrants were abolished, "the English experiment with torture left no traces." Because it was under centralized control, it was easier to abolish than it was in France, where it persisted for many years.

It is always difficult to extrapolate from history, but it seems logical that a formal, visible, accountable, and centralized system is somewhat easier to control than an ad hoc, off-the-books, and under-the-radar-screen nonsystem. I believe, though I certainly cannot prove, that a formal requirement of a judicial warrant as a prerequisite to nonlethal torture would decrease the amount of physical violence directed against suspects. At the most obvious level, a double check is always more protective than a single check. In every instance in which a warrant is requested, a field officer has already decided that torture is justified and, in the absence of a warrant requirement, would simply proceed with the torture. Requiring that decision to be approved by a judicial officer will result in fewer instances of torture even if the judge rarely turns down a request. Moreover, I believe that most judges would require compelling evidence before they would authorize so extraordinary a departure from our constitutional norms, and law enforcement officials would be reluctant to seek a warrant unless they had compelling evidence that the suspect had information needed to prevent an imminent terrorist attack. A record would be kept of every warrant granted, and although it is certainly possible that some individual agents might torture without a warrant, they would have no excuse, since a warrant procedure would be available. They could not claim "necessity," because the decision as to whether the torture is indeed necessary has been taken out of their hands and placed in the hands of a judge. In addition, even if torture were deemed totally illegal without any exception, it would still occur, though the public would be less aware of its existence.

I also believe that the rights of the suspect would be better protected with a warrant requirement. He would be granted immunity, told that he was now compelled to testify, threatened with imprisonment if he refused to do so, and given the option of providing the requested information. Only if he refused to do what he was legally compelled to do—provide necessary information, which could not incriminate him because of the immunity—would he be threatened with torture. Knowing that such a threat was authorized by the law, he might well provide the information. If he still refused to, he would be subjected to judicially monitored physical measures designed to cause excruciating pain without leaving any lasting damage.

Let me cite two examples to demonstrate why I think there would be less torture with a warrant requirement than without one. Recall the case of the alleged national security wiretap placed on the phones of Martin Luther King by the Kennedy administration in the early 1960s. This was in the days when the attorney general could authorize a national security wiretap without a warrant. Today no judge would issue a warrant in a case as flimsy as that one. When Zacarias Moussaoui was detained after raising suspicions while trying to learn how to fly an airplane, the government did not even seek a national security wiretap because its lawyers believed that a judge would not have granted one. If Moussaoui's computer could have been searched without a warrant, it almost certainly would have been.

It should be recalled that in the context of searches, our Supreme Court opted for a judicial check on the discretion of the police, by requiring a search warrant in most cases. The Court has explained the reason for the warrant requirement as follows: "The informed and deliberate determinations of magistrates…are to be preferred over the hurried action of officers." Justice Robert Jackson elaborated:

The point of the Fourth Amendment, which often is not grasped by zealous officers, is not that it denies law enforcement the support of the usual inferences which reasonable men draw from evidence. Its protection consists in requiring that those inferences be drawn by a neutral and detached magistrate instead of being judged by the officer engaged in the often competitive enterprise of ferreting out crime. Any assumption that evidence sufficient to support a magistrate's disinterested determination to issue a search warrant will justify the officers in making a search without a warrant would reduce the Amendment to nullity and leave the people's homes secure only in the discretion of police officers.

Although torture is very different from a search, the policies underlying the warrant requirement are relevant to the question whether there is likely to be more torture or less if the decision is left entirely to field officers, or if a judicial officer has to approve a request for a torture warrant. As Abraham Maslow once observed, to a man with a hammer, everything looks like a nail. If the man with the hammer must get judicial approval before he can use it, he will probably use it less often and more carefully.

There are other, somewhat more subtle, considerations that should be factored into any decision regarding torture. There are some who see silence as a virtue when it comes to the choice among such horrible evils as torture and terrorism. It is far better, they argue, not to discuss or write about issues of this sort, lest they become legitimated. And legitimation is an appropriate concern. Justice Jackson, in his opinion in one of the cases concerning the detention of Japanese-Americans during World War II, made the following relevant observation:

> Much is said of the danger to liberty from the Army program for deporting and detaining these citizens of Japanese extraction. But a judicial construction of the due process clause that will sustain this order is a far more subtle blow to liberty than the promulgation of the order itself. A military order, however unconstitutional, is not apt to last longer than the military emergency. Even during that period a succeeding commander may revoke it all. But once a judicial opinion rationalizes such an order to show that it conforms to the Constitution, or rather rationalizes the Constitution to show that the Constitution sanctions such an order, the Court for all time has validated the principle of racial discrimination in criminal procedure and of transplanting American citizens. The principle then lies about like a loaded weapon ready for the hand of any authority that can bring forward a plausible claim of an urgent need. Every repetition imbeds that principle more deeply in our law and thinking and expands it to new purposes. All who observe the work of courts are familiar with what Judge Cardozo described as "the tendency of a principle to expand itself to the limit of its logic." A military commander may overstep the bounds of constitutionality, and it is an incident. But if we review and approve, that passing incident becomes the doctrine of the Constitution. There it has a generative power of its own, and all that it creates will be in its own image.

A similar argument can be made regarding torture: if an agent tortures, that is "an incident," but if the courts authorize it, it becomes a precedent. There is, however, an important difference between the detention of Japanese-American citizens and torture. The detentions were done openly and with presidential accountability; torture would be done secretly, with official deniability. Tolerating an off-the-book system of secret torture can also establish a dangerous precedent.

A variation on this "legitimation" argument would postpone consideration of the choice between authorizing torture and forgoing a possible tactic necessary to prevent an imminent act of terrorism until after the choice—presumably the choice to torture—has been made. In that way, the discussion would not, in itself, encourage the use of torture. If it were employed, then we could decide whether it was justified, excusable, condemnable, or something in between. The problem with that argument is that no FBI agent who tortured a suspect into disclosing information that prevented an act of mass terrorism would be prosecuted—as the policemen who tortured the kidnapper into disclosing the whereabouts of his victim were not prosecuted. In the absence of a prosecution, there would be no occasion to judge the appropriateness of the torture.

I disagree with these more passive approaches and believe that in a democracy it is always preferable to decide controversial issues in advance, rather than in the heat of battle. I would apply this rule to other tragic choices as well, including the possible use of a nuclear first strike, or retaliatory strikes—so long as the discussion was sufficiently general to avoid giving our potential enemies a strategic advantage by their knowledge of our policy.

Even if government officials decline to discuss such issues, academics have a duty to raise them and submit them to the marketplace of ideas. There may be danger in open discussion, but there is far greater danger in actions based on secret discussion, or no discussion at all.

Whatever option our nation eventually adopts—no torture even to prevent massive terrorism, no torture except with a warrant authorizing nonlethal torture, or no "officially" approved torture but its selective use beneath the radar screen—the choice is ours to make in a democracy. We do have a choice, and we should make it—before local FBI agents make it for us on the basis of a false assumption that we do not really "have a choice." We have other choices to make as well, in balancing security with liberty. It is to these choices that we now turn.

ARGUMENT 17 ESSAY QUESTIONS

1. What does Dershowitz say about the policy of officially making torture illegal but using it anyway "below the radar"?
2. Do you think torture is ever morally permissible? Why or why not? Should it be legal or illegal?

SUGGESTIONS FOR FURTHER READING

G. E. M. Anscombe, "War and Murder," in *Nuclear Weapons: A Catholic Response*, ed. Walter Stein (New York: Sheed & Ward, 1961).

Thomas Aquinas, *Summa Theologica*, Questions XL, LXIV, and LXIX.

Joseph M. Boyle, Jr., "Just War Doctrine and the Military Response to Terrorism," *The Journal of Political Philosophy*, vol. 11, no. 2 (2003), 153–70.

Paul Christopher, *The Ethics of War and Peace* (Upper Saddle River, NJ: Prentice-Hall, 2004).

Carl von Clausewitz, *On the Art of War* (1832), Chap. 1, J. J. Graham, trans. (London: Penguin Books, 1968).

Martin L. Cook, "Ethical Issues in Counterterrorism Warfare," in *Contemporary Moral Issues*, Lawrence M. Hinman (Upper Saddle River, NJ: Pearson/Prentice-Hall, 2006), 184–88.

R. G. Frey and Christopher W. Morris, "Terrorism," in *Violence, Terrorism, and Justice*, ed. R. G. Frey and Christopher W. Morris (New York: Cambridge University Press, 1991), 1–11.

Robert Fullinwider, "Terrorism, Innocence, and War," in *War After September 11*, ed. Verna V. Gehring (Lanham, MD: Rowman & Littlefield, 2003).

Robert Fullinwider, "Understanding Terrorism," in *Problems of International Justice*, ed. Steven Luper-Foy (Boulder, CO: Westview Press, 1988), 248–59.

Hugo Grotius, *On the Law of War and Peace* (De Jure Belli ac Pacis), Bks. I, II, and III.

James Turner Johnson, "Threats, Values, and Defense: Does the Defense of Values by Force Remain a Moral Possibility?" *Parameters* (Spring 1985).

Haig Khatchadourian, *The Morality of Terrorism* (New York: Peter Lang, 1998).

Charles Krauthammer, "The Truth about Torture," *The Weekly Standard*, 5 December 2005.

John H. Langbein, "The Legal History of Torture," in *Torture: A Collection*, ed. Sanford Levinson (Oxford: Oxford University Press, 2004), 93–103.

Burton M. Leiser, "The Case for Iraq War II," in *Morality in Practice*, 7th ed., ed. James P. Sterba (Belmont, CA: Wadsworth, 2004), 619–26.

Sanford Levinson, ed., *Torture: A Collection* (Oxford: Oxford University Press, 2004).

David Luban, "The War on Terrorism and the End of Human Rights," *Philosophy & Public Policy Quarterly*, vol. 22, no. 3 (Summer 2002).

Larry May, Eric Rovie, and Steve Viner, ed., *The Morality of War: Classical and Contemporary Readings* (Upper Saddle River, NJ: Prentice-Hall, 2006).

Jeff McMahan, "War and Peace," in *A Companion to Ethics* (Cambridge, MA: Basil Blackwell, 1993), 384–95.

Seumas Miller, "Torture," in *The Stanford Encyclopedia of Philosophy*, Fall 2008 edition, ed. Edward N. Zalta, http://plato.stanford.edu/archives/fall2008/entries/torture/ (22 January 2009).

Thomas Nagel, "War and Massacre," *Philosophy and Public Affairs* (1972).

Jan Narveson, "Pacifism: A Philosophical Analysis," *Ethics*, 75: 4 (1965), 623–70.

Brian Orend, "War," in *The Stanford Encyclopedia of Philosophy*, Winter 2005 edition, ed. Edward N. Zalta, http://plato.stanford.edu/archives/win2005/entries/war/ (20 December 2005).

Gabriel Palmer-Fernandez, "Terrorism, Innocence, and Justice," *Philosophy & Public Policy Quarterly,* vol. 25, no. 3 (Summer 2005).

Louis P. Pojman, "The Moral Response to Terrorism and the Cosmopolitan Imperative," in *Terrorism and International Justice,* ed. James P. Sterba (New York: Oxford University Press, 2003).

Igor Primoratz, ed., *Terrorism: The Philosophical Issues* (New York: Palgrave Macmillan, 2004).

David Rodin, "Terrorism Without Intention," *Ethics,* July 2004.

Henry Shue, "War," in *The Oxford Handbook of Practical Ethics* (Oxford: Oxford University Press, 2003, 734–61.

James P. Sterba, "Iraqi War II: A Blatantly Unjust War," in *Morality in Practice,* 7th ed., ed. James P. Sterba (Belmont, CA: Wadsworth, 2004), 626–35.

Andrew Sullivan, "The Abolition of Torture," *The New Republic,* 2005.

Charles Townshend, *Terrorism: A Very Short Introduction* (Oxford: Oxford University Press, 2002).

United Nations, "Convention Against Torture and Other Cruel, Inhuman or Degrading Treatment or Punishment," *Office of the High Commissioner for Human Rights,* 26 June 1987, http://www.unhchr.ch/html/menu3/b/h_cat39.htm (30 January 2009).

Michael Walzer, *Just and Unjust Wars,* 2nd ed. (New York: Basic Books, 1992).

Michael Walzer, "The Argument about Humanitarian Intervention," *Dissent,* vol. 49, no. 1 (Winter 2002).

Michael Walzer, "Moral Judgment in Time of War," *Dissent,* vol. 14, no. 3 (1967), 284–92.

Richard A. Wasserstrom, "On the Morality of War," *Stanford Law Review* 21, no. 6 (June 1969), 1627–56.

CHAPTER 9

Pornography and Free Speech

Whenever pornography exists for public consumption, a clash of interests and values occurs, and when pornography is plentiful and the public appetite is large, the clash can be ferocious.

Today both the supply of and demand for pornography have reached historic levels—and the history of pornography is long, stretching back thousands of years. Porn is now delivered to an avid and curious audience via videotape, cable TV, video and computer games, magazines, DVDs, photographs, and film (both live action and animation). It is also, of course, always just a mouse click or ring tone away. In 2006 the porn industry's revenues topped $13 billion. (Yet the porn revenues in other countries were even greater: for example, China, $27.4 billion; South Korea, $25.73 billion; and Japan, $19.98 billion.) Twelve percent of all websites (4.2 million) were pornographic; 42.7 percent of Internet users viewed porn; and visitors to porn websites were 72 percent male, 28 percent female.[1]

The definition of **pornography** is itself a subject of debate, but to help us approach the moral issues with minimal confusion, we may define it as sexually explicit words or images intended to provoke sexual arousal. By this standard, some sexually explicit materials—say, pictures in a medical textbook—are not pornographic. (For many people, of course, this neutral definition will not do, for to them the term *pornography* refers to materials that are somehow inherently objectionable or bad.)

What's bad about pornography, some argue, is that it is obscene. **Obscenity** is a property that is thought to render sexually explicit words or images morally or legally illicit. As you might expect, people have different ideas about what precisely this property is:

The obscenity might be taken to be intrinsic to the content of the material itself (for example, that it depicts deviant sexual acts that are immoral in themselves) or it may lie in contingent effects that the material has (for example, that it tends

---

[1] Jerry Ropelato, "Internet Pornography Statistics," *TopTen Reviews*, 2006, http://www.internet-filter-review.toptenreviews.com/internet-pornography-statistics.html (9 February 2009).

to offend "reasonable" people, or to deprave and corrupt viewers, or to erode traditional family and religious values). If all sexually explicit material is obscene by whichever of these standards is chosen, then all sexually explicit material will be pornography on this definition. This is the definition of pornography that moral conservatives typically favour.[2]

Obscenity is also an important concept in law, providing the chief legal grounds for exempting sexually explicit materials from the Constitution's guarantee of free speech. Generally when sexually candid words or images are banned (a rare event), it's because they were found to be legally obscene.

In the 1973 case of *Miller v. California*, the U.S. Supreme Court established a set of standards for legal obscenity, the so-called "Miller test." To determine if pornographic materials are obscene, the courts must ask

(a) whether "the average person, applying contemporary community standards" would find that the work, taken as a whole, appeals to the prurient interest [unwholesome sexual desire] . . . (b) whether the work depicts or describes, in a patently offensive way, sexual conduct specifically defined by the applicable state law, and (c) whether the work, taken as a whole, lacks serious literary, artistic, political, or scientific value.[3]

Since *Miller*, the Court has ruled in many obscenity and indecency cases, addressing some legal questions on pornography and clarifying the Miller test. The Court has held, for example, that child pornography is not protected by the First Amendment (1982); that municipalities cannot ban adult theaters but may place zoning restrictions on them (1986); and that federal laws designed to control Internet pornography are unconstitutional (1997, 2007).

The main ethical questions about pornography are (1) whether producing, publishing, or using it is morally permissible and (2) whether any of these activities should be legally prohibited. This latter issue, the subject of this chapter, typically reduces to whether the state should try through censorship to prevent consenting adults from viewing or reading pornography. The common ground in the debate is that child pornography should be banned and that laws prohibiting the exposure of children and nonconsenting adults to pornography may be justified.

Many who support censorship argue that pornography should be banned because it is an affront to traditional morality: creating and using pornography is inherently immoral; pornography is offensive to many who hold traditional or religious beliefs; it promotes immoral acts (adultery, premarital intercourse, and deviant sex, for example); and it undermines morality generally. Moreover pornography corrupts and subverts character, traditional family values, religious life, and communities.

The assumption underlying this procensorship stance is **legal moralism**, the view that a community's basic moral standards should be enshrined in law and enforced by the state. Legal moralists contend that a legitimate role of government is protecting the moral

[2] Caroline West, "Pornography and Censorship," *The Stanford Encyclopedia of Philosophy,* Fall 2008 edition, http://plato.stanford.edu/entries/pornography-censorship/#Oth (9 February 2009).
[3] United States Supreme Court, *Miller v. California*, 413 U.S. 15 (1973).

FACTS AND FIGURES: Pornography

In 2006:

- The pornography industry's revenues exceeded **$13 billion** (more than the combined revenues of ABC, CBS, and NBC).
- **12** percent of all websites (4.2 million) were pornographic; 42.7 percent of Internet users viewed porn.
- **25** percent of daily search-engine requests (68 million) were pornographic.
- **100,000** websites offered illegal child pornography.

- **20** percent of men accessed pornography at work.
- **13** percent of women accessed pornography at work.
- The largest consumer of Internet pornography was the **35–49 age group**.
- **40 million** adults in the United States were regular visitors to pornography websites.

From TopTen Reviews, "Internet Pornography Statistics," *TopTen Reviews*, 2006, http://www.internet-filter-review. toptenreviews.com/internet-pornography-statistics.html (9 February 2009).

well-being of society or preventing people from behaving in ways that offend the sensibilities of the community. Many reject legal moralism in the name of individual liberty, declaring that the state has no business imposing the moral choices of the majority on individuals.

Some proponents of censorship appeal not to traditional morality but to the likelihood of harmful consequences. Specifically they argue that pornography should be censored because it leads to rape or other sexual violence against women. To be credible, this claim must be supported by solid empirical evidence, but so far the relevant data have been contradictory and subject to much disagreement. Official investigations have concluded both that scientific evidence does not substantiate the claim and that only violent or degrading pornography may lead to sexual violence.[4] Studies have uncovered correlations between violent pornography and aggressive attitudes toward women, and between degrading pornography and insensitive or distorted views about rape. But these findings are far from establishing cause-and-effect relationships.

Some feminist writers argue that censorship is justified because pornography harms women in an insidious but profound way. Pornography, they say, is sexually explicit material that degrades or subordinates women while sanctioning such pernicious attitudes. They contrast pornography with **erotica**, sexually explicit material that does not demean women but depicts them as consenting, equal partners in sexual activity. As Helen E. Longino says,

> What is wrong with pornography, then, is its degrading and dehumanizing portrayal of women (and *not* its sexual content). Pornography, by its very nature,

---

[4] President's Commission on Obscenity and Pornography, *Report of The Commission on Obscenity and Pornography* (Washington, D. C.: U. S. Government Printing Office, 1970); Bernard Williams, *Obscenity and Film Censorship : An Abridgement of The Williams Report* (New York : Cambridge University Press, 1981); United States Attorney General's Commission on Pornography, *Final Report* (Washington: U.S. Department of Justice, 1986).

PUBLIC OPINION: Pornography

48 percent of adults believe that "pornography is demeaning towards women."

48 percent believe that pornography "changes men's expectations of how women should behave." (Fifty-eight percent of women believe this; 37 percent of men.)

40 percent believe that pornography "harms relationships between men and women."

22 percent think that pornography "improves the sex life of people who look at it." Thirty-six

percent disagree (29 percent of men; 43 percent of women).

23 percent believe that "whether one likes it or not people should have full access to pornography under the Constitution's First Amendment."

42 percent believe that "the government needs to regulate Internet pornography specifically so that children cannot access X-rated material."

Harris Interactive Inc. survey, conducted online September 20–26, 2004; 2,555 adults nationwide.

requires that women be subordinate to men and mere instruments for the fulfillment of male fantasies.... [I] have argued that [pornography] is defamatory and libelous toward women, that it condones crimes against women, and that it invites tolerance of the social, economic, and cultural oppression of women.[5]

The main argument against censorship is an appeal to individual liberty: as autonomous persons, we are entitled to freedom of speech or expression, freedom of conscience, a right to privacy, and the right to choose our own life plans as we see fit. As long as we do no harm to others, we are entitled to exercise our liberty—to create or use pornography if we choose to—without interference from the broader community. Only for very weighty reasons may the state restrict our freedom to partake of pornography, and preventing offense to the community is not one of them.

KEY TERMS

pornography   obscenity   legal moralism
erotica

---

[5] Helen E. Longino, "Pornography, Oppression, and Freedom: A Closer Look," in *Take Back the Night: Women on Pornography*, ed. Laura Lederer (New York: William Morrow, 1980).

ARGUMENTS AND READINGS

18. THE LIBERTY ARGUMENT AGAINST CENSORSHIP

A typical version of the liberty argument against censoring pornography says that persons possess a fundamental right of autonomy, or self-determination, the freedom to decide and choose according to their own lights. This freedom includes, above all, freedom of speech or expression, which must not be curtailed except for the weightiest of reasons and certainly not just because others think it offensive, unwise, or disadvantageous. Since pornography is a form of speech or expression, people have a right to create or publish it, however detested or unsavory the material is to many. It can be legitimately constrained or controlled by the state only if it causes significant harm to others and if there is very strong evidence of such harm.

In *On Liberty* John Stuart Mill probably makes the most memorable case for individual liberty and thus provides the inspiration for many contemporary liberty arguments against censorship:

> [T]he only purpose for which power can be rightfully exercised over any member of a civilized community, against his will, is to prevent harm to others. His own good, either physical or moral, is not a sufficient warrant. He cannot rightfully be compelled to do or forbear because it will be better for him to do so, because it will make him happier, because, in the opinion of others, to do so would be wise or even right. These are good reasons for remonstrating with him, or reasoning with him, or persuading him, or entreating him, but not for compelling him, or visiting him with any evil in case he do otherwise. To justify that, the conduct from which it is desired to deter him, must be calculated to produce evil to someone else. The only part of the conduct of any one for which he is amenable to society, is that which concerns others. In the part which merely concerns himself, his independence is, of right, absolute.... The only freedom which deserves the name, is that of pursuing our own good in our own way, so long as we do not attempt to deprive others of theirs, or impede their efforts to obtain it.[6]

Ronald Dworkin agrees. Like many others who oppose censorship, he finds pornography repellent but still insists that, in general, revulsion is no grounds for overriding the principle of individual liberty:

---

[6] John Stuart Mill, from *On Liberty*, chap. 1, 1859.

Pornography is often grotesquely offensive; it is insulting, not only to women but to men as well. But we cannot consider that a sufficient reason for banning it without destroying the principle that the speech we hate is as much entitled to protection as any other. The essence of negative liberty [not having our actions interfered with] is freedom to offend, and that applies to the tawdry as well as the heroic.[7]

Legal moralists, of course, reject the liberty argument against censorship. They believe that the harm done to traditional moral or religious values by pornography provides reason enough to ban it. Many others accept the principle of liberty but contend that the great harm done by certain kinds of pornography may justify censorship. For some of these critics, the harm of most concern is sexual violence against women. For others, the harm is thought to come from pornography's power to promote systematic discrimination against, and inequality of, women. In all cases, the presumption is that liberty rights may be restricted and pornography forbidden because of its moral, physical, or social harmfulness.

On Liberty

JOHN STUART MILL

The time, it is to be hoped, is gone by, when any defence would be necessary of the 'liberty of the press' as one of the securities against corrupt or tyrannical government. No argument, we may suppose, can now be needed, against permitting a legislature or an executive, not identified in interest with the people, to prescribe opinions to them, and determine what doctrines or what arguments they shall be allowed to hear. This aspect of the question, besides, has been so often and so triumphantly enforced by preceding writers, that it needs not be specially insisted on in this place. Though the law of England, on the subject of the press, is as servile to this day as it was in the time of the Tudors, there is little danger of its being actually put in force against political discussion, except during some temporary panic, when fear of insurrection

drives ministers and judges from their propriety;[1] and, speaking generally, it is not, in constitutional countries, to be apprehended, that the government, whether completely responsible to the people or not, will often attempt to control the expression of opinion, except when in doing so it makes itself the organ of the general intolerance of the public. Let us suppose, therefore, that the government is entirely at one with the people, and never thinks of exerting any power of coercion unless in agreement with what it conceives to be their voice. But I deny the right of the people to exercise such coercion, either by themselves or by their government. The power itself is illegitimate. The best government

From *On Liberty* (London: Longmore, Roberts, & Green, 1869).

---

[7]   Ronald Dworkin, "Liberty and Pornography," *The New York Review of Books*, October 21, 1993.

has no more title to it than the worst. It is as noxious, or more noxious, when exerted in accordance with public opinion, than when in opposition to it. If all mankind minus one, were of one opinion, and only one person were of the contrary opinion, mankind would be no more justified in silencing that one person, than he, if he had the power, would be justified in silencing mankind. Were an opinion a personal possession of no value except to the owner; if to be obstructed in the enjoyment of it were simply a private injury, it would make some difference whether the injury was inflicted only on a few persons or on many. But the peculiar evil of silencing the expression of an opinion is, that it is robbing the human race; posterity as well as the existing generation; those who dissent from the opinion, still more than those who hold it. If the opinion is right, they are deprived of the opportunity of exchanging error for truth: if wrong, they lose, what is almost as great a benefit, the clearer perception and livelier impression of truth, produced by its collision with error.

It is necessary to consider separately these two hypotheses, each of which has a distinct branch of the argument corresponding to it. We can never be sure that the opinion we are endeavouring to stifle is a false opinion; and if we were sure, stifling it would be an evil still.

First: the opinion which it is attempted to suppress by authority may possibly be true. Those who desire to suppress it, of course deny its truth; but they are not infallible. They have no authority to decide the question for all mankind, and exclude every other person from the means of judging. To refuse a hearing to an opinion, because they are sure that it is false, is to assume that *their* certainty is the same thing as *absolute* certainty. All silencing of discussion is an assumption of infallibility. Its condemnation may be allowed to rest on this common argument, not the worse for being common.

Unfortunately for the good sense of mankind, the fact of their fallibility is far from carrying the weight in their practical judgement, which is always allowed to it in theory; for while every one well knows himself to be fallible, few think it necessary to take any precautions against their own fallibility, or admit the supposition that any opinion, of which

they feel very certain, may be one of the examples of the error to which they acknowledge themselves to be liable. Absolute princes, or others who are accustomed to unlimited deference, usually feel this complete confidence in their own opinions on nearly all subjects. People more happily situated, who sometimes hear their opinions disputed, and are not wholly unused to be set right when they are wrong, place the same unbounded reliance only on such of their opinions as are shared by all who surround them, or to whom they habitually defer: for in proportion to a man's want of confidence in his own solitary judgement, does he usually repose, with implicit trust, on the infallibility of 'the world' in general. And the world, to each individual, means the part of it with which he comes in contact; his party, his sect, his church, his class of society: the man may be called, by comparison, almost liberal and large-minded to whom it means anything so comprehensive as his own country or his own age. Nor is his faith in this collective authority at all shaken by his being aware that other ages, countries, sects, churches, classes, and parties have thought, and even now think, the exact reverse. He devolves upon his own world the responsibility of being in the right against the dissentient worlds of other people; and it never troubles him that mere accident has decided which of these numerous worlds is the object of his reliance, and that the same causes which make him a Churchman in London, would have made him a Buddhist or a Confucian in Pekin. Yet it is as evident in itself, as any amount of argument can make it, that ages are no more infallible than individuals; every age having held many opinions which subsequent ages have deemed not only false but absurd; and it is as certain that many opinions, now general, will be rejected by future ages, as it is that many, once general, are rejected by the present.

The objection likely to be made to this argument would probably take some such form as the following. There is no greater assumption of infallibility in forbidding the propagation of error, than in any other thing which is done by public authority on its own judgement and responsibility. Judgement is given to men that they may use it. Because it may be used erroneously, are men to be told that they ought not to use it at all? To prohibit what they think pernicious, is not claiming exemption from error, but fulfilling the duty incumbent on them, although fallible, of acting on their conscientious conviction. If we were never to act on our opinions, because those opinions may be wrong, we should leave all our interests uncared for, and all our duties unperformed. An objection which applies to all conduct, can be no valid objection to any conduct in particular. It is the duty of governments, and of individuals, to form the truest opinions they can; to form them carefully, and never impose them upon others unless they are quite sure of being right. But when they are sure (such reasoners may say), it is not conscientiousness but cowardice to shrink from acting on their opinions, and allow doctrines which they honestly think dangerous to the welfare of mankind, either in this life or in another, to be scattered abroad without restraint, because other people, in less enlightened times, have persecuted opinions now believed to be true. Let us take care, it may be said, not to make the same mistake: but governments and nations have made mistakes in other things, which are not denied to be fit subjects for the exercise of authority: they have laid on bad taxes, made unjust wars. Ought we therefore to lay on no taxes, and, under whatever provocation, make no wars? Men, and governments, must act to the best of their ability. There is no such thing as absolute certainty, but there is assurance sufficient for the purposes of human life. We may, and must, assume our opinion to be true for the guidance of our own conduct: and it is assuming no more when we forbid bad men to pervert society by the propagation of opinions which we regard as false and pernicious.

I answer, that it is assuming very much more. There is the greatest difference between presuming an opinion to be true, because, with every opportunity for contesting it, it has not been refuted, and assuming its truth for the purpose of not permitting its refutation. Complete liberty of contradicting and disproving our opinion, is the very condition which justifies us in assuming its truth for purposes of action; and on no other terms can a being with human faculties have any rational assurance of being right.

When we consider either the history of opinion, or the ordinary conduct of human life, to what is

it to be ascribed that the one and the other are no worse than they are? Not certainly to the inherent force of the human understanding; for, on any matter not self-evident, there are ninety-nine persons totally incapable of judging of it, for one who is capable; and the capacity of the hundreth person is only comparative; for the majority of the eminent men of every past generation held many opinions now known to be erroneous, and did or approved numerous things which no one will now justify. Why is it, then, that there is on the whole a preponderance among mankind of rational opinions and rational conduct? If there really is this preponderance—which there must be unless human affairs are, and have always been, in an almost desperate state—it is owing to a quality of the human mind, the source of everything respectable in man either as an intellectual or as a moral being, namely, that his errors are corrigible. He is capable of rectifying his mistakes, by discussion and experience. Not by experience alone. There must be discussion, to show how experience is to be interpreted. Wrong opinions and practices gradually yield to fact and argument: but facts and arguments, to produce any effect on the mind, must be brought before it. Very few facts are able to tell their own story, without comments to bring out their meaning. The whole strength and value, then, of human judgement, depending on the one property, that it can be set right when it is wrong, reliance can be placed on it only when the means of setting it right are kept constantly at hand. In the case of any person whose judgement is really deserving of confidence, how has it become so? Because he has kept his mind open to criticism of his opinions and conduct. Because it has been his practice to listen to all that could be said against him; to profit by as much of it as was just, and expound to himself, and upon occasion to others, the fallacy of what was fallacious. Because he has felt, that the only way in which a human being can make some approach to knowing the whole of a subject, is by hearing what can be said about it by persons of every variety of opinion, and studying all modes in which it can be looked at by every character of mind. No wise man ever acquired his wisdom in any mode but this; nor is it in the nature of human intellect to become wise in any other manner. The steady habit of correcting and completing his own opinion by collating it with those of others, so far from causing doubt and hesitation in carrying it into practice, is the only stable foundation for a just reliance on it: for, being cognisant of all that can, at least obviously, be said against him, and having taken up his position against all gainsayers—knowing that he has sought for objections and difficulties, instead of avoiding them, and has shut out no light which can be thrown upon the subject from any quarter—he has a right to think his judgement better than that of any person, or any multitude, who have not gone through a similar process.

It is not too much to require that what the wisest of mankind, those who are best entitled to trust their own judgement, find necessary to warrant their relying on it, should be submitted to by that miscellaneous collection of a few wise and many foolish individuals, called the public. The most intolerant of churches, the Roman Catholic Church, even at the canonization of a saint, admits, and listens patiently to, a 'devil's advocate'. The holiest of men, it appears, cannot be admitted to posthumous honours, until all that the devil could say against him is known and weighed. If even the Newtonian philosophy were not permitted to be questioned, mankind could not feel as complete assurance of its truth as they now do. The beliefs which we have most warrant for, have no safeguard to rest on, but a standing invitation to the whole world to prove them unfounded. If the challenge is not accepted, or is accepted and the attempt fails, we are far enough from certainty still; but we have done the best that the existing state of human reason admits of; we have neglected nothing that could give the truth a chance of reaching us: if the lists are kept open, we may hope that if there be a better truth, it will be found when the human mind is capable of receiving it; and in the meantime we may rely on having attained such approach to truth, as is possible in our own day. This is the amount of certainty attainable by a fallible being, and this the sole way of attaining it.

Strange it is, that men should admit the validity of the arguments for free discussion, but object to their being 'pushed to an extreme'; not seeing that unless the reasons are good for an extreme case, they are not good for any case. Strange that they

should imagine that they are not assuming infallibility, when they acknowledge that there should be free discussion on all subjects which can possibly be *doubtful*, but think that some particular principle or doctrine should be forbidden to be questioned because it is so *certain*, that is, because *they are certain* that it is certain. To call any proposition certain, while there is any one who would deny its certainty if permitted, but who is not permitted, is to assume that we ourselves, and those who agree with us, are the judges of certainty, and judges without hearing the other side.

In the present age—which has been described as "destitute of faith, but terrified at scepticism"—which people feel sure, not so much that their opinions are true, as that they should not know what to do without them—the claims of an opinion to be protected from public attack are rested not so much on its truth, as on its importance to society. There are, it is alleged, certain beliefs, so useful, not to say indispensable to well-being, that it is as much the duty of governments to uphold those beliefs, as to protect any other of the interests of society. In a case of such necessity, and so directly in the line of their duty; something less than infallibility may, it is maintained, warrant, and even bind, governments, to act on their own opinion, confirmed by the general opinion of mankind. It is also often argued, and still oftener thought, that none but bad men would desire to weaken these salutary beliefs; and there can be nothing wrong, it is thought, in restraining bad men, and prohibiting what only such men would wish to practise. This mode of thinking makes the justification of restraints on discussion not a question of the truth of doctrines, but of their usefulness; and flatters itself by that means to escape the responsibility of claiming to be an infallible judge of opinions. But those who thus satisfy themselves, do not perceive that the assumption of infallibility is merely shifted from one point to another. The usefulness of an opinion is itself matter of opinion: as disputable, as open to discussion, and requiring discussion as much, as the opinion itself. There is the same need of an infallible judge of opinions to decide an opinion to be noxious, as to decide it to be false, unless the opinion condemned has full opportunity of defending itself. And it will not do to say that the heretic may be allowed to maintain the utility or harmlessness of his opinion, though forbidden to maintain its truth. The truth of an opinion is part of its utility. If we would know whether or not it is desirable that a proposition should be believed, is it possible to exclude the consideration of whether or not it is true? In the opinion, not of bad men, but of the best men, no belief which is contrary to truth can be really useful: and can you prevent such men from urging that plea, when they are charged with culpability for denying some doctrine which they are told is useful, but which they believe to be false? Those who are on the side of received opinions, never fail to take all possible advantage of this plea; you do not find them handling the question of utility as if it could be completely abstracted from that of truth: on the contrary, it is, above all, because their doctrine is the "truth," that the knowledge or the belief of it is held to be so indispensable. There can be no fair discussion of the question of usefulness, when an argument so vital may be employed on one side, but not on the other. And, in point of fact, when law or public feeling do not permit the truth of an opinion to be disputed, they are just as little tolerant of a denial of its usefulness. The utmost they allow is an extenuation of its absolute necessity, or of the positive guilt of rejecting it.

In order more fully to illustrate the mischief of denying a hearing to opinions because we, in our own judgement, have condemned them, it will be desirable to fix down the discussion to a concrete case; and I choose, by preference, the cases which are least favourable to me—in which the argument against freedom of opinion, both on the score of truth and on that of utility, is considered the strongest. Let the opinions impugned be the belief in a God and in a future state, or any of the commonly received doctrines of morality. To fight the battle on such ground, gives a great advantage to an unfair antagonist; since he will be sure to say (and many who have no desire to be unfair will say it internally), are these the doctrines which you do not deem sufficiently certain to be taken under the protection of law? Is the belief in a God one of the opinions, to feel sure of which, you hold to be assuming infallibility? But I must be permitted to observe, that it is not the feeling sure of a doctrine (be it what it may) which I call an assumption of infallibility. It is the undertaking to decide that question *for others*,

without allowing them to hear what can be said on the contrary side. And I denounce and reprobate this pretension not the less, if put forth on the side of my most solemn convictions. However positive any one's persuasion may be, not only of the falsity but of the pernicious consequences—not only of the pernicious consequences, but (to adopt expressions which I altogether condemn) the immorality and impiety of an opinion; yet if, in pursuance of that private judgement, though backed by the public judgement of his country or his contemporaries, he prevents the opinion from being heard in its defence, he assumes infallibility. And so far from the assumption being less objectionable or less dangerous because the opinion is called immoral or impious, this is the case of all others in which it is most fatal. These are exactly the occasions on which the men of one generation commit those dreadful mistakes, which excite the astonishment and horror of posterity. It is among such that we find the instances memorable in history, when the arm of the law has been employed to root out the best men and the noblest doctrines; with deplorable success as to the men, though some of the doctrines have survived to be (as if in mockery) invoked, in defence of similar conduct towards those who dissent from *them*, or from their received interpretation.

Mankind can hardly be too often reminded, that there was once a man named Socrates, between whom and the legal authorities and public opinion of his time, there took place a memorable collision. Born in an age and country abounding in individual greatness, this man has been handed down to us by those who best knew both him and the age, as the most virtuous man in it; while *we* know him as the head and prototype of all subsequent teachers of virtue, the source equally of the lofty inspiration of Plato and the judicious utilitarianism of Aristotle, "*i maëstri di color che sanno*,"[2] the two headsprings of ethical as of all other philosophy. This acknowledged master of all the eminent thinkers who have since lived—whose fame, still growing after more than two thousand years, all but outweights the whole remainder of the names which make his native city illustrious—was put to death by his countrymen, after a judicial conviction, for impiety and immorality. Impiety, in denying the gods recognized by the State; indeed his accuser asserted (see the *Apologia*) that he believed in no gods at all. Immorality, in being, by his doctrines and instructions, a "corruptor of youth." Of these charges the tribunal, there is every ground for believing, honestly found him guilty, and condemned the man who probably of all then born had deserved best of mankind, to be put to death as a criminal.

NOTES

1. These words had scarcely been written, when, as if to give them an emphatic contradiction, occurred the Government Press Prosecutions of 1858. That ill-judged interference with the liberty of public discussion has not, however, induced me to alter a single word in the text, nor has it at all weakened my conviction that, moments of panic excepted, the era of pains and penalties for political discussion has, in our own country, passed away. For, in the first place, the prosecutions were not persisted in; and, in the second, they were never, properly speaking, political prosecutions. The offence charged was not that of criticizing institutions, or the acts or persons of rulers, but of circulating what was deemed an immoral doctrine, the lawfulness of Tyrannicide.

If the arguments of the present chapter are of any validity, there ought to exist the fullest liberty of professing and discussing, as a matter of ethical conviction, any doctrine, however immoral it may be considered. It would, therefore, be irrelevant and out of place to examine here, whether the doctrine of Tyrannicide deserves that title. I shall content myself with saying that the subject has been at all times one of the open questions of morals; that the act of a private citizen in striking down a criminal, who, by raising himself above the law, has placed himself beyond the reach of legal punishment or control, has been accounted by whole nations, and by some of the best and wisest of men, not a crime, but an act of exalted virtue; and that, right or wrong, it is not of the nature of assassination, but of civil war. As such, I hold that the instigation to it, in a specific case, may be a proper subject of punishment, but only if an overt act has followed, and at least a probable connexion can be established between the act and the instigation. Even then, it is not a foreign government, but the very government assailed, which alone, in the exercise of self-defence, can legitimately punish attacks directed against its own existence.

2. "The master of Those who Know."

Hate Speech and Pornography

Do We Have to Choose Between Freedom of Speech and Equality?

NADINE STROSSEN

I. INTRODUCTION

Two important current controversies about free speech have been the focus of academic and public policy debates. Both involve unpopular types of speech that are said to cause harm to particular individuals and societal groups, but have been protected under traditional First Amendment principles. Recently, however, these two types of speech have been the focus of new arguments for suppression and have prompted calls for a re-examination and revision of traditional free speech principles.

The first of these two closely related categories of allegedly harmful speech is commonly called "hate speech." It conveys hatred or prejudice based on race, religion, gender, or some other social grouping. Advocates of suppressing hate speech claim that it

"Hate Speech and Pornography: Do We Have to Choose Between Freedom and Equality?" by Nadine Strossen, *Case Western Reserve Law Review*, vol. 46, no. 2 (Winter 1996), 449–478. (Notes deleted.) © Case Western Reserve University/School of Law.

promotes discrimination and violence against those it describes.

The second, related type of controversial speech is a category of sexually explicit speech that some prominent feminist scholars call for censoring on the theory that it is, in essence, hate speech against women, promoting discrimination and violence against us. Specifically, they want to suppress sexually explicit expression that is "subordinating" or "degrading" to women. They label this expression "pornography" to distinguish it from the subset of sexual speech that the Supreme Court currently deems constitutionally unprotected, and hence subject to banning under the label "obscenity." In contrast to the sexist harms that some feminists attribute to the pornography they want to ban, the alleged harm targeted by anti-obscenity laws is the undermining of the general moral tone of society.

A central feature of U.S. free speech law, which distinguishes it from the law of other countries, is the protection of controversial and unpopular speech, including hate speech and pornography. Probably the best known case that reaffirmed this strong free speech concept was *Village of Skokie v. National Socialist Party of America*. In *Skokie*, the American Civil Liberties Union (ACLU) argued that free speech rights extended even to neo-Nazis seeking to stage a peaceful demonstration in Skokie, Illinois. Skokie had a large Jewish population, including many Holocaust survivors, who were profoundly upset by the prospect of the proposed demonstration. The courts agreed with the ACLU that this demonstration was constitutionally protected expression.

More recently, the ACLU has been the prime opponent of a new incarnation of anti-hate speech laws that has become popular: codes adopted by colleges and universities that prohibit hate speech on their campuses. In these cases, too, we have been uniformly successful in challenging the codes on First Amendment grounds.

The concept of suppressible pornography that some feminists advocate—pornography as a type of hate speech—was enacted into two municipal laws. The ACLU participated in lawsuits successfully challenging both of them.

In the face of all these judicial rulings, there are intense pressures to re-examine and reformulate the traditional American approach to hate speech and pornography. Recently, some prominent legal scholars and liberal activists have joined forces with political and religious conservatives to renew their arguments for suppressing one or both types of speech. In light of the changing political climate throughout this country and the many recent personnel changes on the U.S. Supreme Court, it is not clear whether our legal system will continue to protect both hate speech and pornography.

The United States saw just a hint of possible changes in this area only two days after the historic 1994 national elections. On November 10, 1994, the Clinton Administration filed a brief in the Supreme Court in *United States v. Knox*, asserting a broad view of the government's power to suppress pornography. This was the Clinton Administration's second Supreme Court brief in the *Knox* case, which had first come before the Supreme Court a year earlier. In its first brief, the Administration had advocated a narrow construction of the anti-pornography statute at issue. As an anti-pornography activist noted, this about-face on the pornography issue "'is the first indication of how the…Clinton Administration will react in [the new, post-election] conservative world.'"

II. OVERVIEW

I will first explain the traditional U.S. constitutional approach to hate speech and pornography. Under this approach, such speech is protected by a grand vision of the First Amendment that was initially set out in the early decades of this century by Supreme Court Justices Oliver Wendell Holmes and Louis Brandeis. This "free speech tradition" has been carried forward by more recent Supreme Court Justices including, preeminently, Hugo Black, William O. Douglas, and William J. Brennan, Jr.

After outlining this traditional free speech approach, I will address the new arguments that some prominent legal scholars have advanced for altering it. Although I ultimately reject these arguments, they are important and worthy of serious consideration. These arguments are based on another fundamental right under the U.S. Constitution, which is of equivalent importance to the free speech right: the right to equality before the law. The ACLU certainly takes the new equality-based arguments for restricting hate speech and pornography very seriously. We have always been in the forefront of defending equality rights, including women's rights. As I explain in Part IV, though, censoring hate speech and pornography would not effectively advance equality for women or other disempowered groups, but to the contrary, could well undermine their equality.

III. TRADITIONAL U.S. FREE SPEECH PRINCIPLES REGARDING HATE SPEECH AND PORNOGRAPHY

Before discussing the recent equality-based arguments for and against censoring hate speech and pornography, this Article will first outline the traditional First Amendment tenets that underlie our courts' current protection of these types of speech. While I welcome recent calls to re-examine these principles, my re-examination convinces me of their enduring soundness.

Our law's traditional protection of all types of hate speech, including misogynistic speech, reflects two cardinal principles at the core of our free speech jurisprudence. The first specifies what is *not* a sufficient justification for restricting speech, and the second prescribes what *is* a sufficient justification.

A. Viewpoint Neutrality Requirement

The first basic principle requires "viewpoint neutrality." It holds that government may never limit speech just because any listener—or even the majority of the community—disagrees with or is offended by its content or the viewpoint it conveys. The Supreme Court has called this the "bedrock principle" of the proud free speech tradition under American law.

In three recent cases, the Court enforced this basic principle to protect speech with a viewpoint deeply offensive to many, if not most, Americans. The first two involved burning an American flag in political demonstrations against national policies and the third involved burning a cross near the home of an African-American family that had recently moved into a previously all-white neighborhood.

The viewpoint-neutrality principle reflects the philosophy that, in a free society, the appropriate response to speech with which one disagrees is not censorship but counterspeech—more speech, not less. Rejecting this philosophy, the movements to censor hate speech and pornography target speech precisely because of its viewpoint, specifically, its discriminatory viewpoint. For this reason, Seventh Circuit Judge Frank Easterbrook struck

down an anti-pornography ordinance that the City of Indianapolis had adopted at the behest of some feminists. Stressing that the law's fatal First Amendment flaw was its viewpoint discrimination, Judge Easterbrook explained that, under the ordinance,

> Speech treating women in the approved way—in sexual encounters "premised on equality"—is lawful no matter how sexually explicit. Speech treating women in the disapproved way—as submissive in matters sexual or as enjoying humiliation—is unlawful no matter how significant the literary, artistic, or political qualities of the work taken as a whole. The state may not ordain preferred viewpoints in this way.

B. "Clear and Present Danger" Requirement

Any laws restricting hate speech or pornography would also violate the second core principle of U.S. free speech law: namely, that a restriction on speech can be justified only when necessary to prevent actual or imminent harm, such as violence or injury to others. This is often summarized as the "clear and present danger" requirement. To satisfy this requirement, the restricted speech must pose an "imminent danger." It may not just have a "bad tendency," that is, a more speculative, attenuated connection to potential future harm.

If we banned the expression of all ideas that might lead individuals to actions that may adversely impact even important interests such as national security or public safety, then scarcely any idea would be safe, and surely no idea that challenged the status quo would be. This point was emphasized by Judge Easterbrook when he struck down the Indianapolis anti-pornography ordinance. For the sake of argument, Judge Easterbrook assumed the correctness of the law's cornerstone assumption that "depictions of [women's] subordination tend to perpetuate subordination." Even so, he concluded, the law was unconstitutional. Judge Easterbrook explained,

> If pornography is what pornography does, so is other speech.... Efforts to suppress communist speech in the United States were based on the belief that the public acceptability of such ideas would increase the likelihood of totalitarian government....

Racial bigotry, anti-Semitism, violence on television, reporters' biases—these and many more influence the culture and shape our socialization....Yet all is protected as speech, however insidious. Any other answer leaves the government in control of all of the institutions of culture, the great censor and director of which thoughts are good for us.

Sexual responses often are unthinking responses, and the association of sexual arousal with the subordination of women therefore may have a substantial effect. But almost all cultural stimuli provoke unconscious responses. Religious ceremonies condition their participants. Teachers convey messages by selecting what not to cover; the implicit message about what is off limits or unthinkable may be more powerful than the messages for which they present rational argument....If the fact that speech plays a role in a process of conditioning were enough to permit governmental regulation, that would be the end of freedom of speech.

C. Re-examination and Reaffirmation

As earlier stated, I have accepted the call by current advocates of restricting hate speech and pornography to re-examine the landmark free speech rulings that set forth the foregoing two core principles concerning viewpoint neutrality and "clear and present danger." That re-examination has left me more impressed than ever with the universal, timeless force of these rulings. They remain relevant and persuasive, specifically in the context of the current hate speech and pornography debates.

For example, consider the powerful concurring opinion of Justice Brandeis in *Whitney v. California*. The *Whitney* majority upheld a long prison sentence that had been imposed on a woman because she was a member of the Communist Labor Party, whose platform advocated the violent overthrow of the United States government. Brandeis rejected the majority's approach in an opinion that a later Supreme Court endorsed. While Brandeis was sympathetic to fears about potential speech-induced harms, he eloquently explained that the United States constitutional philosophy reflects and requires not fear, but rather courage, in the realm of ideas. He also anticipated and responded to the concerns about the relatively powerless status of certain members of our society, including women,

expressed by those who now advocate restricting hate speech and pornography. Brandeis astutely warned that any fear-based repression will be used *against* precisely those who are relatively weak.

His words are familiar, but well worth considering again, as if they were answering current arguments:

> Those who won our independence...believed liberty to be the secret of happiness and courage to be the secret of liberty.... They recognized the risks to which all human institutions are subject. But they knew that...it is hazardous to discourage thought, hope and imagination; that fear breeds repression; that repression breeds hate; that hate menaces stable government; that the path of safety lies in the opportunity to discuss freely supposed grievances and proposed remedies; and that the fitting remedy for evil counsels is good ones....
>
> Fear of serious injury cannot alone justify suppression of free speech.... Men feared witches and burned women....
>
> Those who won our independence by revolution were not cowards.... They did not exalt order at the cost of liberty.... Only an emergency can justify repression.

These themes were eloquently echoed several decades later by Justice Hugo Black, carrying forward the brave Brandeisian free speech tradition for new generations. For example, in a McCarthy-era case concerning laws restricting Communist ideas and speech, Justice Black made a statement that applies to all restrictions on any unpopular speech, including the current proposals to restrict hate speech and pornography:

> Ultimately all the questions...really boil down to one—whether we as a people will try fearfully and futilely to preserve democracy by adopting totalitarian methods, or whether in accordance with our traditions and our Constitution we will have the confidence and courage to be free.

IV. CENSORING HATE SPEECH AND PORNOGRAPHY WOULD UNDERMINE, RATHER THAN ADVANCE, EQUALITY GOALS

As previously noted, before the government may restrict expression, it must show not only that the expression threatens imminent serious harm, but also that the restriction is necessary to avert the harm.

Undeniably, the interests that advocates of censoring hate speech and pornography seek to promote—namely, the equality and safety of minority groups and women—are compellingly important. However, advocates of suppressive laws cannot even show that these laws would effectively promote the safety and equality of minority groups and women, let alone that they are the necessary means for doing so. To the contrary, from an equality perspective, these censorship measures would be at best ineffective, and at worst counterproductive.

For precisely this reason, Justice Black dissented from a 1952 Supreme Court decision that upheld an anti-hate-speech statute. Fortunately, this decision is no longer good law. Alluding to the concept of a "pyrrhic victory," Black presciently wrote, "If there be minority groups who hail this holding as their victory, they might consider . . . this ancient remark: 'Another such victory and I am undone.'"

As an overview, this Article will first list the many reasons for concluding that suppressing hate speech and pornography would do more harm than good, specifically in terms of equality values. It will then elaborate on several.

The reasons why suppressing hate speech does not promote, and may well undermine, racial and other forms of equality include the following. Because the pornography concept advocated by some feminists is a type of hate speech, these points apply to it as well.

- Censoring hate speech increases attention to, and sympathy for, bigots.
- It drives bigoted expression and ideas underground, thus making response more difficult.
- It is inevitably enforced disproportionately against speech by and on behalf of minority group members themselves.
- It reinforces paternalistic stereotypes about minority group members, suggesting that they need special protection from offensive speech.
- It increases resentment towards minority group members, the presumed beneficiaries of the censorship.

- Censoring racist expression undermines a mainstay of the civil rights movement, which has always been especially dependent on a robust concept of constitutionally protected free speech.
- An anti-hate-speech policy curbs the candid intergroup dialogue concerning racism and other forms of bias, which is an essential precondition for reducing discrimination.
- Positive intergroup relations will more likely result from education, free discussion, and the airing of misunderstandings and insensitivity, rather than from legal battles; anti-hate-speech rules will continue to generate litigation and other forms of controversy that increase intergroup tensions.
- Finally, censorship is diversionary; it makes it easier to avoid coming to grips with less convenient and more expensive, but ultimately more meaningful, strategies for combating discrimination. Censoring discriminatory expression diverts us from the essential goals of eradicating discriminatory attitudes and conduct.

The following list outlines the specific reasons why suppressing pornography does not promote, and may well undermine, the critically important goals of reducing discrimination and violence against women. Many of these parallel my analysis of anti-hate-speech laws:

- Censoring pornography would suppress many works that are especially valuable to women and feminists.
- Any pornography censorship scheme would be enforced in a way that discriminates against the least popular, least powerful groups in our society, including feminists and lesbians.
- It would perpetuate demeaning stereotypes about women, including that sex is bad for us.
- It would perpetuate the disempowering notion that women are essentially victims.
- It would distract us from constructive approaches to countering discrimination and violence against women.
- It would harm women who voluntarily work in the sex industry.

- It would harm women's efforts to develop their own sexuality.
- It would strengthen the power of the right wing, whose patriarchal agenda would curtail women's rights.
- By undermining free speech, censorship would deprive feminists of a powerful tool for advancing women's equality.
- Finally, since sexual freedom and freedom for sexually explicit expression are essential aspects of human freedom, censoring such expression would undermine human rights more broadly.

Before I elaborate on a few of the common reasons for concluding that censoring both hate speech and pornography undermines equality goals, I would like to quote Seventh Circuit Judge Richard Posner (since he, too, was one of your Canary Lecturers), who has recently supported one of the specific points I just listed concerning pornography. Specifically, Judge Posner concurs in my conclusion that censoring pornography would do more harm than good to the women who earn their living in the pornography business. As even censorship advocates recognize, any censorship scheme would not prevent the production of all pornography, but rather, would drive that production underground. However, this development would be devastating to the women who would continue to work in the pornography business, as Judge Posner explained, from his law and economics perspective:

> When an economic activity is placed outside the protection of the law—as we know from Prohibition, prostitution, the campaign against drugs and the employment of illegal immigrants—the participants in that activity will resort to threats and violence in lieu of the contractual and other legal remedies denied them. The pimp is an artifact of the illegality of prostitution, and the exploitation of pornographic actresses and models by their employers is parallel to the exploitation of illegal immigrant labor by their employers. These women would be better off if all pornography were legal.

I will now expand upon several of the common reasons why censoring hate speech or pornography would be as dangerous for equality rights as for free speech rights.

A. Free Speech Is Especially Important to People Who Have Traditionally Suffered from Discrimination

First and foremost, all groups who seek equal rights and freedom have an especially important stake in securing free speech. Throughout history, free speech consistently has been the greatest ally of those seeking equal rights for groups that have been subject to discrimination. For example, the Civil Rights Movement during the 1950s and 1960s depended on the vigorous enforcement of free speech rights by the U.S. Supreme Court under the leadership of Chief Justice Earl Warren. This essential interrelationship was forcefully described in a 1965 book by University of Chicago law professor Harry Kalven, entitled *The Negro and the First Amendment*.

Only strong principles of free speech and association could—and did—protect the drive for desegregation. These principles allowed protestors to carry their messages to audiences that found such messages highly offensive and threatening to their most deeply cherished views of themselves and their way of life. Martin Luther King, Jr. wrote his historic letter from a Birmingham jail, but the Warren Court later struck down the Birmingham parade ordinance that King and other demonstrators had violated, holding that it had breached their First Amendment rights.

The more disruptive, militant forms of civil rights protest—such as marches, sit-ins, and kneel-ins—were especially dependent on the Warren Court's generous constructions of the First Amendment. Notably, many of these speech-protective interpretations initially had been formulated in cases brought on behalf of opponents of civil rights. The insulting and often racist language that some militant black activists hurled at police officers and other government officials was also protected under the same principles and precedents.

The foregoing history does not prove conclusively that free speech is an essential precondition for equality, as some respected political philosophers argue. But it does belie the central contention of those who claim an incompatibility between free speech and equality: that equality is an essential precondition for free speech. This history also shows the positive, symbiotic interrelationship between free speech and equality. As stated by Benjamin

Hooks, former Executive Director of the NAACP, "The civil rights movement would have been vastly different without the shield and spear of the First Amendment."

Like the Civil Rights Movement, the women's rights movement also has always depended on a vibrant free speech guarantee. This point was made by the lower federal court judge who initially struck down the Indianapolis anti-pornography law, in the ruling Judge Easterbrook affirmed in *American Booksellers Ass'n v. Hudnut.* Interestingly, this federal district court judge was a woman, Sara Evans Barker. She emphasized that advocates of women's rights have far more to lose than to gain from suppressing expression: "It ought to be remembered by…all…who would support [this anti-pornography law] that, in terms of altering sociological patterns, much as alteration may be necessary and desirable, free speech, rather than being the enemy, is a long-tested and worthy ally."

B. Censorship Has Especially Victimized Members of Politically Powerless Groups, Including Racial Minorities and Women

Just as free speech has always been the strongest weapon to *advance* equal rights causes, censorship has always been the strongest weapon to *thwart* them. Ironically, the explanation for this pattern lies in the very analysis of those who want to curb hate speech and pornography. They contend that racial minorities and women are relatively disempowered and marginalized.

I agree with that analysis of the problem and am deeply committed to working toward solving it. However, I strongly disagree that censorship is a solution. To the contrary, precisely because women and minorities are relatively powerless, it makes no sense to hand the power structure yet another tool that it can use to further suppress them, in both senses of the word.

Consistent with the analysis of the censorship advocates themselves, the government will inevitably wield this tool, along with others, to the particular disadvantage of already disempowered groups. This conclusion is confirmed by the enforcement record of all censorship measures, around the world, and throughout history. The pattern of

disempowered groups being disproportionately targeted under censorship measures extends even to measures that are allegedly designed for their benefit. This is clearly illustrated by the enforcement record in the many countries that have outlawed hate speech, and the one country that has outlawed pornography as defined by some contemporary feminists.

First, consider the historical enforcement record of anti-hate-speech laws. The first individuals prosecuted under the British Race Relations Act of 1965, which criminalized the intentional incitement of racial hatred, were black power leaders. Rather than curbing speech offensive to minorities, this British law instead has been used regularly to curb the speech of blacks, trade unionists, and anti-nuclear activists. In perhaps the ultimate irony, this statute, which was intended to restrain the neo-Nazi National Front, instead has barred expression by the Anti-Nazi League.

The British experience is typical. Although French law then criminalized group libel, no one who made anti-Semitic statements against Captain Alfred Dreyfus was ever prosecuted, despite the tragic impact of these statements. In contrast, Emile Zola was prosecuted for libeling the French clergy and military in his classic letter deploring the anti-Semitic vendetta against Dreyfus, "J'Accuse," and had to flee to England to escape punishment. A similar enforcement pattern resulted under the German Criminal Code of 1871, which punished offenses against personal honor. According to Professor Eric Stein, "[T]he German Supreme Court…consistently refused to apply this article to insults against Jews as a group—although it gave the benefit of its protection to such groups as 'Germans living in Prussian provinces, large landowners, all Christian clerics, and German officers….'"

In 1990, Canada's Supreme Court upheld an anti-hate-speech law against a challenge under the free speech provision in Canada's Constitution. Under this law, in 1993, Canadian customs officials detained at the U.S.-Canadian border a shipment of fifteen hundred copies of a book called *Black Looks: Race and Representations,* by the black feminist professor bell hooks. These books had been en route to several Canadian universities. Indeed, because Canada's anti-hate-speech law had previously been used to suppress important expression—including that on behalf of minority group rights—three Canadian Supreme Court Justices dissented from the Court's 1990 decision upholding such laws, leading to a closely split 4–3 ruling. As the dissent explained,

Although the [law] is of relatively recent origin, it has [already] provoked many questionable actions on the part of the authorities.... [T]he record amply demonstrates that intemperate statements about identifiable groups, particularly if they represent an unpopular viewpoint, may attract state involvement or calls for police action. Novels such as Leon Uris' pro-Zionist novel, *The Haj*, face calls for banning.... Other works, such as Salman Rushdie's *Satanic Verses*, are stopped at the border.... Films may be temporarily kept out, as happened to a film entitled "Nelson Mandela," ordered as an educational film by Ryerson Polytechnical Institute.... Arrests are even made for distributing pamphlets containing the words "Yankee Go Home."

The foregoing examples simply illustrate a longstanding, ongoing global pattern. That was made clear in a book published in 1992 by Article XIX, the London-based International Centre Against Censorship, which takes its name from the free speech guarantee in the Universal Declaration of Human Rights, Article 19.

Two conclusions clearly emerged from this book's comparative analysis. First, the enforcement of anti-hate-speech laws does not correlate at all with successful national experiences in countering discrimination or promoting equality and tolerance among different racial, ethnic, and religious groups. Second, the enforcement of such laws often undermines the goals of promoting intergroup harmony and societal equality, for several reasons, including their disproportionate enforcement against minority group speakers.

The general international pattern of disproportionate enforcement of legal measures curbing hate speech against minority group members also holds true on university and college campuses, where such measures have recently been most vigorously advocated in the United States. In 1974, in a move aimed at the neo-Nazi National Front, the British National Union of Students (NUS) resolved that "representatives of 'openly racist and fascist organizations' were

to be prevented from speaking on college campuses 'by whatever means necessary (including disruption of the meeting).'" A major motivation for the rule was to stem an increase in campus anti-Semitism. Ironically, though, following the United Nations' cue, some British students deemed Zionism a form of racism beyond the bounds of permitted discussion. Accordingly, in 1975, British students invoked the NUS resolution to disrupt speeches by Israelis and Zionists, including the Israeli ambassador to England. The intended target of the NUS resolution, the National Front, applauded this result. The NUS itself, though, became disenchanted by this and other unintended consequences of its resolution and repealed it in 1977.

The British experience under its campus anti-hate-speech rule parallels the more recent U.S. experience. The U.S. campus hate speech code about which we have the most enforcement data is one that was in effect at the University of Michigan from April 1988 until October 1989. Because the ACLU brought a lawsuit to challenge the code, the University was forced to disclose information, which otherwise would have been unavailable to the public, about how the code had been enforced.

During the year and a half that the University of Michigan rule was in effect, there were more than twenty cases of whites charging blacks with racist speech. The only two instances in which the rule was used to punish racist speech, as opposed to other forms of hate speech, involved the punishment of speech by black students. The only student who was subjected to a full-fledged disciplinary hearing under the Michigan rule was an African-American student accused of homophobic and sexist expression. In seeking clemency from the punishment that was imposed on him after this hearing, the student said that he had received such harsh treatment in large part because of his race.

Others who were punished at Michigan included several Jewish students accused of anti-Semitic expression and an Asian-American student accused of making an anti-black comment. The Jewish students wrote graffiti, including a swastika, on a classroom blackboard, saying they intended it as a practical joke. The Asian-American student's allegedly hateful remark was to ask why black people feel discriminated against; he said he raised this question because the black students in his dormitory tended to socialize together, making him feel isolated.

The available information indicates that other campus hate speech codes are subject to the same enforcement patterns. For example, the ACLU successfully represented the student who challenged the University of Connecticut's hate speech code. This student, who had been penalized for an allegedly homophobic remark, was Asian-American. She claimed that other students had engaged in similar expression but that she had been singled out for punishment because of her ethnic background.

C. Censorship of Sexual Expression Has Particularly Harmed Women and Women's Rights Advocates

What lesson do we learn from the anti-hate-speech enforcement record that I have outlined? It is this: If you belong to a group that has traditionally suffered discrimination, including women, restrictions on hate speech are especially likely to be wielded against your speech. In fact, all forms of censorship have consistently been used to suppress speech by, about, and for women. Of particular importance for the current pornography debate, laws permitting the suppression of sexually-oriented information have often been used to suppress information essential for women's rights, including reproductive freedom.

In the United States, anti-obscenity laws consistently have been used to suppress information about contraception and abortion. The first federal anti-obscenity statute in this country, the "Comstock Law" enacted in 1873, was repeatedly used to prosecute pioneering feminists and birth control advocates early in this century. Its targets included Margaret Sanger, the founder of Planned Parenthood.

Sanger also had the dubious distinction of being one of the first victims of a new form of censorship that was applied to a then-new medium early in this century. The U.S. Supreme Court had ruled in 1915 that movies were not protected "speech" under the First Amendment. One of the first films banned under that decision was *Birth Control*, a 1917 picture produced by and featuring Margaret Sanger.

The banning of films concerning birth control and other sexually-oriented subjects of particular interest to feminists continued in the United States into the second half of this century. This fact was stressed by UCLA Law Professor Kenneth Karst when he urged pro-censorship feminists to think twice about arguing that pornography should not be constitutionally protected speech. Karst noted that, until the 1950s, censors routinely banned films that treated sexual themes of particular concern to women, including pregnancy, birth control, abortion, illegitimacy, prostitution, and divorce.

We now have actual experience with a feminist-style anti-pornography law in one country: Canada. In 1992, the Canadian Supreme Court incorporated the pro-censorship feminists' definition of pornography into Canada's obscenity law in *Butler v. The Queen*. The court held that, henceforth, the obscenity law would bar sexual materials that are "degrading" or "dehumanizing" to women.

Alas for women, though, the enforcement record under this law has followed the familiar pattern; it has harmed the very groups that it was supposed to help. The particular victims of Canada's new censorship regime have been the writings and bookstores of women, feminists, lesbians, and gay men. Within the first two and a half years after the *Butler* decision, approximately two-thirds of all Canadian feminist bookstores had materials confiscated or detained by customs. *Butler's* supposed rationale is to protect women from works that harm them; it is hard to understand how the feminist writings that have been seized under this decision would harm women.

Ironically, some feminist material has been suppressed under *Butler* on the ground that it is allegedly degrading and harmful not to women, but to men. In the ultimate irony, two books written by a leading U.S. anti-pornography feminist, the New York writer Andrea Dworkin, were seized at the U.S.-Canada border. According to Canadian customs officials, they illegally "eroticized pain and bondage."

Although the primary targets of Canada's post-*Butler* enforcement efforts have been feminist, lesbian, and gay materials, *Butler* has also emboldened customs officials to seize other works, including serious mainstream books. Canadian Customs has seized books by critically acclaimed authors such as Kathy Acker, Ambrose Bierce, Marguerite Duras, Langston

Hughes, Zora Neale Hurston, David Leavitt, Audre Lorde, Anne Rice, Gertrude Stein, and Oscar Wilde.

D. Restricting Sexual Expression Undermines Human Rights More Broadly

I will now turn to one final example of the adverse impacts on equality goals that follow from censoring any hate speech, including pornography. Recall that the pro-censorship feminists' conception of suppressible pornography is sexually explicit sexist expression. To highlight the dangers of this concept, I would like to underscore the positive role that sexual expression plays in advancing human freedom.

Sexual expression is an integral aspect of human freedom. Hence, governments that repress human rights in general have always suppressed sexual speech. Correspondingly, laws against sexual speech have always targeted views that challenge the prevailing political, religious, cultural, or social orthodoxy.

Sexually explicit speech has been banned by the most repressive regimes, including Communism in the former Soviet Union, Eastern bloc countries, and China, apartheid in South Africa, and fascist or clerical dictatorships in Chile, Iran, and Iraq. Conversely, recent studies of Russia have correlated improvements in human rights, including women's rights, with the rise of free sexual expression.

In places where real pornography is conspicuously absent, tellingly, political dissent is labeled as such. The Communist government of the former Soviet Union suppressed political dissidents under obscenity laws. In 1987, when the Chinese Communist government dramatically increased its censorship of books and magazines with Western political and literary messages, it condemned them as "obscene," "pornographic," and "bawdy." The white supremacist South African government harmed black writing as "pornographically immoral." In Nazi Germany and the former Soviet Union, Jewish writings were reviled as "pornographic," as were any works that criticized the Nazi or Communist party, respectively.

Even in societies that generally respect human rights, including free speech, the terms "obscenity" and "pornography" tend to be used as epithets to stigmatize expression that is politically or socially unpopular. Obscenity laws have been enforced against individuals who have expressed disfavored ideas about political or religious subjects. One of the earliest British obscenity prosecutions, in the eighteenth century, was brought by the Tory government to imprison its leading Whig opponent, John Wilkes. In early American history, anti-obscenity laws targeted speech that was offensive to the prevailing religious orthodoxy.

The pattern holds today. Obscenity laws in the United States regularly have been used to suppress expression of those who are relatively unpopular or disempowered, whether because of their ideas or because of their membership in particular societal groups. Recent major obscenity prosecutions have targeted expressions by or about members of groups that are powerless and unpopular, including rap music of young African-American men and homoerotic photographs and other works by gay and lesbian artists. Likewise, the National Endowment for the Arts (NEA) has been subject to many political attacks for its funding of art exploring feminist or homoerotic themes. This point was recognized by the federal district court judge in the "NEA Four" case, in which the ACLU represented four artists whose NEA grants were cut off because of their works' controversial political and sexual themes. He wrote, "The NEA has been the target of congressional critics…for funding works…that express women's anger over male dominance in the realm of sexuality or which endorse equal legitimacy for homosexual and heterosexual practices."

One recent obscenity prosecution in Ohio vividly displayed the characteristic hallmarks of such prosecutions—specifically, the targeting of expression with an unpopular political message and the persecution of gays and lesbians. During the summer of 1994, the City of Cincinnati brought obscenity charges against a gay and lesbian bookstore, the Pink Pyramid, and its owner, its manager, and its clerk. These individuals, who were arrested and handcuffed, faced sentences of up to six months' imprisonment and fines of up to $1,000.

Their "crime"? They had rented out a video of the film "Salo, 120 Days of Sodom," by Pier Paolo Pasolini, a world-renowned Italian filmmaker, novelist, and poet. The film's sexual-political subject is the dark aspect of sexuality that had served Italian fascism. According to film critic Peter Bondanella, *Salo* "is a desperate…attack against…a society dominated by manipulative and sadistic power."

Just as the allegedly obscene video itself had a deeply political message, so too did the charges against those who rented it out. These prosecutions were announced on the opening day of a federal lawsuit brought by the ACLU and Lambda Legal Defense & Education Fund challenging a referendum that had overturned gay and lesbian civil rights legislation. As the National Coalition Against Censorship commented, "At best, the timing suggests indifference to the possibility that these prosecutions would exacerbate already existing prejudices and intolerance." At worst, given the frivolous nature of obscenity charges based on a film of such indisputably serious value, the prosecution was a calculated act of harassment. Accordingly, the ACLU filed a brief on behalf of an impressive array of individuals and organizations from the worlds of film, art, and academia, urging the court to dismiss these charges before subjecting the defendants to a pointless and chilling criminal trial. The Judge rejected this argument.

The historical and ongoing enforcement record of laws against sexual speech make clear that what is at stake is more than freedom of sexual expression, important as that is. Even beyond that, the freedom to produce or consume anything called "pornography" is an essential aspect of the freedom to defy prevailing political and social mores. As Stanford University Law Professor Kathleen Sullivan wrote, "In a world where sodomy may still be made a crime, gay pornography is the samizdat of the oppressed." Furthermore, just as gay pornography is the samizdat of individuals who are oppressed or dissident sexually, pornography in general is the samizdat of those who are oppressed or dissident in any respect.

UCLA Law Professor Kenneth Karst provides intriguing insights into the link between sexual freedom, including free sexual expression, and freedom from discrimination:

> The suppression of Unreason is rooted in the same fears that produce group subordination: men's fear of the feminine, whites' fear of blackness, heterosexuals' anxiety about sexual orientation. Historically,

all these fears have been closely connected with the fear of sexuality. It is no accident that the 1960s, a period of sexual "revolution," also saw the acceleration of three movements that sought major redefinitions of American's social boundaries: the civil rights movement, the gay liberation movement, and the women's movement.

For the reasons Professor Karst articulates, free sexual expression is intimately connected with equality—hardly at odds with it, as argued by the anti-pornography feminists. Indeed, free sexual expression is an integral aspect of all human freedom, even beyond freedom from discrimination. This vital interconnection was eloquently stated by Dr. Gary Mongiovi, who teaches at St. John's University in New York:

> Sexual expression is perhaps the most fundamental manifestation of human individuality. Erotic material is subversive in the sense that it celebrates, and appeals to, the most uniquely personal aspects of an individual's emotional life. Thus, to allow freedom of expression and freedom of thought in this realm is to…promote diversity and nonconformist behavior in general.…
>
> It is no coincidence that one of the first consequences of democratization and political liberalization in the former Soviet Union, Eastern Europe and China was a small explosion of erotic publications.… Suppression of pornography is not just a free-speech issue: Attempts to stifle sexual expression are part of a larger agenda directed at the suppression of human freedom and individuality more generally.

V. CONCLUSION

I would like to close by quoting a powerful, timeless statement by former Supreme Court Justice Black. Significantly, Black is as justly remembered for his heroic championship of equality rights as for his staunch free speech absolutism. In this 1951 statement, Justice Black was specifically referring to the ideology of Communism, which was then seen as especially harmful, and hence especially worthy of suppression. However, Justice Black's wise words apply equally to the ideologies of racism and sexism, which are now seen as especially harmful, and hence especially worthy of suppression.

With twenty-twenty hindsight, we now see how exaggerated our earlier fears were that Communist authoritarianism would defeat individual liberty. I fervently hope that, in the near future, we will have a similar view about current concerns that racism and sexism could triumph over individual equality. In both cases, free speech plays a vital role in defeating doctrines at odds with human rights. Thus, as Supreme Court Justices such as Brandeis and Black repeatedly reminded us, in the very situations when it seems we have the most to fear in *defending* free

speech—then, above all, do we actually have even more to fear in *not* defending free speech. As Justice Black wrote,

> Fears of [certain] ideologies have frequently agitated the nation and inspired legislation aimed at suppressing…those ideologies. At such times the fog of public excitement obscures the ancient landmarks set up in our Bill of Rights. Yet then, of all times, should [we] adhere most closely to the course they mark.

Pornography, Oppression, and Freedom

HELEN E. LONGINO

I. INTRODUCTION

The much-touted sexual revolution of the 1960's and 1970's not only freed various modes of sexual behavior from the constraints of social disapproval, but also made possible a flood of pornographic material. According to figures provided by WAVPM (Women Against Violence in Pornography and Media), the number of pornographic magazines available at newsstands has grown from zero in 1953 to forty in 1977, while sales of pornographic films in Los Angeles alone have grown from $15 million in 1969 to $85 million in 1976.

Traditionally, pornography was condemned as immoral because it presented sexually explicit material in a manner designed to appeal to "prurient interests" or a "morbid" interest in nudity and sexuality, material which furthermore lacked any redeeming social value and which exceeded "customary limits of candor." While these phrases, taken from a definition of "obscenity" proposed in the 1954 American Law Institute's *Model Penal Code*, require some criteria of application to eliminate vagueness, it seems that what is objectionable is the explicit description or representation of bodily parts or sexual behavior for the purpose of inducing sexual stimulation or pleasure on the part of the

reader or viewer. This kind of objection is part of a sexual ethic that subordinates sex to procreation and condemns all sexual interactions outside of legitimated marriage. It is this code which was the primary target of the sexual revolutionaries in the 1960's, and which has given way in many areas to more open standards of sexual behavior.

One of the beneficial results of the sexual revolution has been a growing acceptance of the distinction between questions of sexual mores and questions of morality. This distinction underlies the old slogan, "Make love, not war," and takes harm to others as the defining characteristic of immorality. What is immoral is behavior which causes injury to or violation of another person or people. Such injury may be physical or it may be psychological. To cause pain to another, to lie to another, to hinder another in the exercise of her or his rights, to exploit another, to degrade another, to misrepresent and slander another are instances of immoral behavior. Masturbation or engaging

"Pornography, Oppression, and Freedom: A Closer Look" by Helen E. Longino in *Take Back the Night: Women on Pornography*, ed. Laura Lederer, 40–52. © 1980 William Morrow and Company, Inc.

voluntarily in sexual intercourse with another consenting adult of the same or the other sex, as long as neither injury nor violation of either individual or another is involved, are not immoral. Some sexual behavior is morally objectionable, but not because of its sexual character, Thus, adultery is immoral not because it involves sexual intercourse with someone to whom one is not legally married, but because it involves breaking a promise (of sexual and emotional fidelity to one's spouse). Sadistic, abusive, or forced sex is immoral because it injures and violates another.

The detachment of sexual chastity from moral virtue implies that we cannot condemn forms of sexual behavior merely because they strike us as distasteful or subversive of the Protestant work ethic, or because they depart from standards of behavior we have individually adopted. It has thus seemed to imply that no matter how offensive we might find pornography, we must tolerate it in the name of freedom from illegitimate repression. I wish to argue that this is not so, that pornography is immoral because it is harmful to people.

II. WHAT IS PORNOGRAPHY?

I define pornography as *verbal or pictorial explicit representations of sexual behavior that,* in the words of the Commission on Obscenity and Pornography, *have as a distinguishing characteristic "the degrading and demeaning portrayal of the role and status of the human female...as a mere sexual object to be exploited and manipulated sexually."* In pornographic books, magazines, and films, women are represented as passive and as slavishly dependent upon men. The role of female characters is limited to the provision of sexual services to men. To the extent that women's sexual pleasure is represented at all, it is subordinated to that of men and is never an end in itself as is the sexual pleasure of men. What pleases women is the use of their bodies to satisfy male desires. While the sexual objectification of women is common to all pornography, women are the recipients of even worse treatment in violent pornography, in which women characters are killed, tortured, gang-raped, mutilated, bound, and otherwise abused, as a means of providing sexual stimulation or pleasure to the male characters. It is this development which has attracted the attention of feminists and been the stimulus to an analysis of pornography in general.

Not all sexually explicit material is pornography, nor is all material which contains representations of sexual abuse and degradation pornography.

A representation of a sexual encounter between adult persons which is characterized by mutual respect is, once we have disentangled sexuality and morality, not morally objectionable. Such a representation would be one in which the desires and experiences of each participant were regarded by the other participants as having a validity and a subjective importance equal to those of the individual's own desire and experiences. In such an encounter, each participant acknowledges the other participant's basic human dignity and personhood. Similarly, a representation of a nude human body (in whole or in part) in such a manner that the person shown maintains self-respect—e.g., is not portrayed in a degrading position—would not be morally objectionable. The educational films of the National Sex Forum, as well as a certain amount of erotic literature and art, fall into this category. While some erotic materials are beyond the standards of modesty held by some individuals, they are not for this reason immoral.

A representation of a sexual encounter which is not characterized by mutual respect, in which at least one of the parties is treated in manner beneath her or his dignity as a human being, is no longer simple erotica. That a representation is of degrading behavior does not in itself, however, make it pornographic. Whether or not it is pornographic is a function of contextual features. Books and films may contain descriptions or representations of a rape in order to explore the consequences of such an assault upon its victim. What is being shown is abusive or degrading behavior which attempts to deny the humanity and dignity of the person assaulted, yet the context surrounding the representation, through its exploration of the consequences of the act, acknowledges and reaffirms her dignity. Such books and films, far from being pornographic, are (or can be) highly moral, and fall into the category of moral realism.

What makes a work a work of pornography, then, is not simply its representation of degrading and abusive sexual encounters, but its implicit, if not explicit, approval and recommendation of sexual behavior that is immoral, i.e., that physically or psychologically violates the personhood of one of the participants. Pornography, then, is verbal or pictorial material which represents or describes sexual behavior that is degrading or abusive to one or more of the participants *in such a way as to endorse the degradation.* The participants so treated in virtually all heterosexual pornography are women or children, so heterosexual pornography is, as a matter of fact, material which endorses sexual behavior that is degrading and/or abusive to women and children. As I use the term "sexual behavior," this includes sexual encounters between persons, behavior which produces sexual stimulation or pleasure for one of the participants, and behavior which is preparatory to or invites sexual activity. Behavior that is degrading or abusive includes physical harm or abuse, and physical or psychological coercion. In addition, behavior which ignores or devalues the real interests, desires, and experiences of one or more participants in any way is degrading. Finally, that a person has chosen or consented to be harmed, abused, or subjected to coercion does not alter the degrading character of such behavior.

Pornography communicates its endorsement of the behavior it represents by various features of the pornographic context: the degradation of the female characters is represented as providing pleasure to the participant males and, even worse, to the participant females, and there is no suggestion that this sort of treatment of others is inappropriate to their status as human beings. These two features are together sufficient to constitute endorsement of the represented behavior. The contextual features which make material pornographic are intrinsic to the material. In addition to these, extrinsic features, such as the purpose for which the material is presented—i.e., the sexual arousal/pleasure/satisfaction of its (mostly) male consumers—or an accompanying text, may reinforce or make explicit the endorsement. Representations which in and of themselves do not show or endorse degrading behavior may be put into a pornographic context by juxtaposition with others that are degrading, or by a text which invites or recommends degrading behavior toward the subject represented. In such a case the whole complex—the series of representations or representations with text—is pornographic.

The distinction I have sketched is one that applies most clearly to sequential material—a verbal or pictorial (filmed) story—which represents an action and provides a temporal context for it. In showing the before and after, a narrator or film-maker has plenty of opportunity to acknowledge the dignity of the person violated or clearly to refuse to do so. It is somewhat more difficult to apply the distinction to single still representations. The contextual features cited above, however, are clearly present in still photographs or pictures that glamorize degradation and sexual violence. Phonograph album covers and advertisements offer some prime examples of such glamorization. Their representations of women in chains (the Ohio Players), or bound by ropes and black and blue (the Rolling Stones) are considered high-quality commercial "art" and glossily prettify the violence they represent. Since the standard function of prettification and glamorization is the communication of desirability, these albums and ads are communicating the desirability of violence against women. Representations of women bound or chained, particularly those of women bound in such a way as to make their breasts, or genital or anal areas vulnerable to any passerby, endorse the scene they represent by the absence of any indication that this treatment of women is in any way inappropriate.

To summarize: Pornography is not just the explicit representation or description of sexual behavior, nor even the explicit representation or description of sexual behavior which is degrading and/or abusive to women. Rather, it is material that explicitly represents or describes degrading and abusive sexual behavior so as to endorse and/or recommend the behavior as described. The contextual features, moreover, which communicate such endorsement are intrinsic to the material; that is, they are features whose removal or alteration would change the representation or description.

This account of pornography is underlined by the etymology and original meaning of the word "pornography." *The Oxford English Dictionary* defines pornography as "Description of the life, manners, etc. of prostitutes and their patrons [from πόρνη (porne) meaning "harlot" and γράφειν (graphein) meaning "to write"]; hence the expression or suggestion of obscene or unchaste subjects in literature or art."

Let us consider the first part of the definition for a moment. In the transactions between prostitutes and their clients, prostitutes are paid, directly or indirectly, for the use of their bodies by the client for sexual pleasure.[1] Traditionally males have obtained from female prostitutes what they could not or did not wish to get from their wives or women friends, who, because of the character of their relation to the male, must be accorded some measure of human respect. While there are limits to what treatment is seen as appropriate toward women as wives or women friends, the prostitute as prostitute exists to provide sexual pleasure to males. The female characters of contemporary pornography also exist to provide pleasure to males, but in the pornographic context no pretense is made to regard them as parties to a contractual arrangement. Rather, the anonymity of these characters makes each one Everywoman, thus suggesting not only that all women are appropriate subjects for the enactment of the most bizarre and demeaning male sexual fantasies, but also that this is their primary purpose. The recent escalation of violence in pornography—the presentation of scenes of bondage, rape, and torture of women for the sexual stimulation of the male characters or male viewers—while shocking in itself, is from this point of view merely a more vicious extension of a genre whose success depends on treating women in a manner beneath their dignity as human beings.

III. PORNOGRAPHY: LIES AND VIOLENCE AGAINST WOMEN

What is wrong with pornography, then, is its degrading and dehumanizing portrayal of women (and *not* its sexual content). Pornography, by its very nature, requires that women be subordinate to men and mere instruments for the fulfillment of male fantasies. To accomplish this, pornography must lie. Pornography lies when it says that our sexual life is or ought to be subordinate to the service of men, that our pleasure consists in pleasing men and not ourselves, that we are depraved, that we are fit subjects for rape, bondage, torture, and murder. Pornography lies explicitly about women's sexuality, and through such lies fosters more lies about our humanity, our dignity, and our personhood.

Moreover, since nothing is alleged to justify the treatment of the female characters of pornography save their womanhood, pornography depicts all women as fit objects of violence by virtue of their sex alone. Because it is simply being female that, in the pornographic vision, justifies being violated, the lies of pornography are lies about all women. Each work of pornography is on its own libelous and defamatory, yet gains power through being reinforced by every other pornographic work. The sheer number of pornographic productions expands the moral issue to include not only assessing the morality or immorality of individual works, but also the meaning and force of the mass production of pornography.

The pornographic view of women is thoroughly entrenched in a booming portion of the publishing, film, and recording industries, reaching and affecting not only all who look to such sources for sexual stimulation, but also those of us who are forced into an awareness of it as we peruse magazines at newsstands and record albums in record stores, as we check the entertainment sections of city newspapers, or even as we approach a counter to pay for groceries. It is not necessary to spend a great deal of time reading or viewing pornographic material to absorb its male-centered definition of women. No longer confined within plain brown wrappers, it jumps out from billboards that proclaim "Live X-rated Girls!" or "Angels in Pain" or "Hot and Wild," and from magazine covers displaying a woman's genital area being spread open to the viewer by her own fingers.[2] Thus, even men who do not frequent pornographic shops and movie houses are supported in the sexist objectification of women by their environment. Women, too, are crippled by internalizing as self-images those that are presented to us by pornographers. Isolated from one another and with no source of support for an alternative view of female sexuality, we may not always find the strength to resist a message that dominates the common cultural media.

The entrenchment of pornography in our culture also gives it a significance quite beyond its explicit sexual messages. To suggest, as pornography does, that the primary purpose of women is to provide sexual pleasure to men is to deny that women are independently human or have a status equal to that of men. It is, moreover, to deny our equality at one of the most intimate levels of human experience. This denial is especially powerful in a hierarchical, class society such as ours, in which individuals feel good about themselves by feeling superior to others. Men in our society have a vested interest in maintaining their belief in the inferiority of the female sex, so that no matter how oppressed and exploited by the society in which they live and work, they can feel that they are at least superior to someone or some category of individuals—a woman or women. Pornography, by presenting women as wanton, depraved, and made for the sexual use of men, caters directly to that interest.[3] The very intimate nature of sexuality which makes pornography so corrosive also protects it from explicit public discussion. The consequent lack of any explicit social disavowal of the pornographic image of women enables this image to continue fostering sexist attitudes even as the society publicly proclaims its (as yet timid) commitment to sexual equality.

In addition to finding a connection between the pornographic view of women and the denial to us of our full human rights, women are beginning to connect the consumption of pornography with commiting rape and other acts of sexual violence against women. Contrary to the findings of the Commission on Obscenity and Pornography a growing body of research is documenting (1) a correlation between exposure to representations of violence and the committing of violent acts generally, and (2) a correlation between exposure to pornographic materials and the committing of sexually abusive or violent acts against women. While more study is needed to establish precisely what the causal relations are, clearly so-called hard-core pornography is not innocent.

From "snuff" films and miserable magazines in pornographic stores to *Hustler*, to phonograph album covers and advertisements, to *Vogue*, pornography has come to occupy its own niche in the communications and entertainment media and to acquire a quasi-institutional character (signaled by the use of diminutives such as "porn" or "porno" to refer to pornographic material, as though such familiar naming could take the hurt out). Its acceptance by the mass media, whatever the motivation, means a cultural endorsement of its message. As much as the materials themselves, the social tolerance of these degrading and distorted images of women in such quantities is harmful to us, since it

indicates a general willingness to see women in ways incompatible with our fundamental human dignity and thus to justify treating us in those ways.[4] The tolerance of pornographic representations of the rape, bondage, and torture of women helps to create and maintain a climate more tolerant of the actual physical abuse or women.[5] The tendency on the part of the legal system to view the victim of a rape as responsible for the crime against her is but one manifestation of this.

In sum, pornography is injurious to women in at least three distinct ways:

1. Pornography, especially violent pornography, is implicated in the committing of crimes of violence against women.
2. Pornography is the vehicle for the dissemination of a deep and vicious lie about women. It is defamatory and libelous.
3. The diffusion of such a distorted view of women's nature in our society as it exists today supports sexist (i.e., male-centered) attitudes, and thus reinforces the oppression and exploitation of women.

Society's tolerance of pornography, especially pornography on the contemporary massive scale, reinforces each of these modes of injury: By not disavowing the lie, it supports the male-centered myth that women are inferior and subordinate creatures. Thus, it contributes to the maintenance of a climate tolerant of both psychological and physical violence against women.

IV. PORNOGRAPHY AND THE LAW

Congress shall make no law respecting the establishment of religion, or prohibiting the free exercise thereof; or abridging the freedom of speech, or of the press; or the right of the people peaceably to assemble, and to petition the Government for a redress of grievances.

First Amendment, Bill of Rights of the United States Constitution

Pornography is clearly a threat to women. Each of the modes of injury cited above offers sufficient reason at least to consider proposals for the social and legal control of pornography. The almost universal response from progressives to such proposals is that constitutional guarantees of freedom of speech and privacy preclude recourse to law. While I am concerned about the erosion of constitutional rights and also think for many reasons that great caution must be exercised before undertaking a legal campaign against pornography, I find objections to such a campaign that are based on appeals to the First Amendment or to a right to privacy ultimately unconvincing.

Much of the defense of the pornographer's right to publish seems to assume that, while pornography may be tasteless and vulgar, it is basically an entertainment that harms no one but its consumers, who may at worst suffer from the debasement of their taste; and that therefore those who argue for its control are demanding an unjustifiable abridgment of the rights to freedom of speech of those who make and distribute pornographic materials and of the rights to privacy of their customers. The account of pornography given above shows that the assumptions of this position are false. Nevertheless, even some who acknowledge its harmful character feel that it is granted immunity from social control by the First Amendment, or that the harm that would ensue from its control outweighs the harm prevented by its control.

There are three ways of arguing that control of pornography is incompatible with adherence to constitutional rights. The first argument claims that regulating pornography involves an unjustifiable interference in the private lives of individuals. The second argument takes the First Amendment as a basic principle constitutive of our form of government, and claims that the production and distribution of pornographic material, as a form of speech, is an activity protected by that amendment. The third argument claims not that the pornographer's rights are violated, but that others' rights will be if controls against pornography are instituted.

The privacy argument is the easiest to dispose of. Since the open commerce in pornographic materials is an activity carried out in the public sphere, the publication and distribution of such materials, unlike their use by individuals, is not protected by rights to privacy. The distinction between the private consumption of pornographic material and the production and distribution of, or open commerce in, it is sometimes blurred by defenders of

pornography. But I may entertain, in the privacy of my mind, defamatory opinions about another person, even though I may not broadcast them. So one might create without restraint—as long as no one were harmed in the course of preparing them—pornographic materials for one's personal use, but be restrained from reproducing and distributing them. In both cases what one is doing—in the privacy of one's mind or basement—may indeed be deplorable, but immune from legal proscription. Once the activity becomes public, however—i.e., once it involves others—it is no longer protected by the same rights that protect activities in the private sphere.[6]

In considering the second argument (that control of pornography, private or public, is wrong in principle), it seems important to determine whether we consider the right to freedom of speech to be absolute and unqualified. If it is, then obviously all speech, including pornography, is entitled to protection. But the right is, in the first place, not an unqualified right: There are several kinds of speech not protected by the First Amendment, including the incitement to violence in volatile circumstances, the solicitation of crimes, perjury and misrepresentation, slander, libel, and false advertising.[7] That there are forms of proscribed speech shows that we accept limitations on the right to freedom of speech if such speech, as do the forms listed, impinges on other rights. The manufacture and distribution of material which defames and threatens all members of a class by its recommendation of abusive and degrading behavior toward some members of that class simply in virtue of their membership in it seems a clear candidate for inclusion on the list. The right is therefore not an unqualified one.

Nor is it an absolute or fundamental right, underived from any other right: If it were there would not be exceptions or limitations. The first ten amendments were added to the Constitution as a way of guaranteeing the "blessings of liberty" mentioned in its preamble, to protect citizens against the unreasonable usurpation of power by the state. The specific rights mentioned in the First Amendment—those of religion, speech, assembly, press, petition—reflect the recent experiences of the makers of the Constitution under colonial government as well as a sense of what was and is required generally to secure liberty.

It may be objected that the right to freedom of speech is fundamental in that it is part of what we mean by liberty and not a right that is derivative from a right to liberty. In order to meet this objection, it is useful to consider a distinction explained by Ronald Dworkin in his book *Taking Rights Seriously*. As Dworkin points out, the word "liberty" is used in two distinct, if related, senses: as "license," i.e., the freedom from legal constraints to do as one pleases, in some contexts; and as "independence," i.e., "the status of a person as independent and equal rather than subservient," in others. Failure to distinguish between these senses in discussions of rights and freedoms is fatal to clarity and understanding.

If the right to free speech is understood as a partial explanation of what is meant by liberty, then liberty is perceived as license: The right to do as one pleases includes a right to speak as one pleases. But license is surely not a condition the First Amendment is designed to protect. We not only tolerate but require legal constraints on liberty as license when we enact laws against rape, murder, assault, theft, etc. If everyone did exactly as she or he pleased at any given time, we would have chaos if not lives, as Hobbes put it, that are "nasty, brutish, and short." We accept government to escape, not to protect, this condition.

If, on the other hand, by liberty is meant independence, then freedom of speech is not necessarily a part of liberty; rather, it is a means to it. The right to freedom of speech is not a fundamental, absolute right, but one derivative from, possessed in virtue of, the more basic right to independence. Taking this view of liberty requires providing arguments showing that the more specific rights we claim are necessary to guarantee our status as persons "independent and equal rather than subservient." In the context of government, we understand independence to be the freedom of each individual to participate as an equal among equals in the determination of how she or he is to be governed. Freedom of speech in this context means that an individual may not only entertain beliefs concerning government privately, but may express them publicly. We express our opinions about taxes, disarmament, wars, social-welfare programs, the function of the police, civil rights, and so on. Our right to freedom of speech includes the right to criticize the government and to protest against various forms of injustice and the abuse of power. What we wish to protect is the free expression of ideas even when they are unpopular. What we do not always remember is that speech has functions other than the expression of ideas.

Regarding the relationship between a right to freedom of speech and the publication and distribution of pornographic materials, there are two points to be made. In the first place, the latter activity is hardly an exercise of the right to the free expression of ideas as understood above. In the second place, to the degree that the tolerance of material degrading to women supports and reinforces the attitude that women are not fit to participate as equals among equals in the political life of their communities, and that the prevalence of such an attitude effectively prevents women from so participating, the absolute and fundamental right of women to liberty (political independence) is violated.

This second argument against the suppression of pornographic material, then, rests on a premise that must be rejected, namely, that the right to freedom of speech is a right to utter anything one wants. It thus fails to show that the production and distribution of such material is an activity protected by the First Amendment. Furthermore, an examination of the issues involved leads to the conclusion that tolerance of this activity violates the rights of women to political independence.

The third argument (which expresses concern that curbs on pornography are the first step toward political censorship) runs into the same ambiguity that besets the arguments based on principle. These arguments generally have as an underlying assumption that the maximization of freedom is a worthy social goal. Control of pornography diminishes freedom—directly the freedom of pornographers, indirectly that of all of us. But again, what is meant by "freedom"? It cannot be that what is to be maximized is license—as the goal of a social group whose members probably have at least some incompatible interests, such a goal would be internally inconsistent. If, on the other hand, the maximization of political independence is the goal, then that is in no way enhanced by, and may be endangered by, the tolerance of pornography. To argue that the control of pornography would create a precedent for suppressing political speech is thus to confuse license with political independence. In addition, it ignores a crucial basis for the control of pornography, i.e., its character as libelous speech. The prohibition of such speech is justified by the need for protection from the injury (psychological as well as physical or economic) that results from libel. A very different kind of argument would be required to justify curtailing the right to speak our minds about the institutions which govern us. As long as such distinctions are insisted upon, there is little danger of the government's using the control of pornography as precedent for curtailing political speech.

In summary, neither as a matter of principle nor in the interests of maximizing liberty can it be supposed that there is an intrinsic right to manufacture and distribute pornographic material.

The only other conceivable source of protection for pornography would be a general right to do what we please as long as the rights of others are respected. Since the production and distribution of pornography violates the rights of women—to respect and to freedom from defamation, among others—this protection is not available.

V. CONCLUSION

I have defined pornography in such a way as to distinguish it from erotica and from moral realism, and have argued that it is defamatory and libelous toward women, that it condones crimes against women, and that it invites tolerance of the social, economic, and cultural oppression of women. The production and distribution of pornographic material is thus a social and moral wrong. Contrasting both the current volume of pornographic production and its growing infiltration of the communications media with the status of women in this culture makes clear the necessity for its control. Since the goal of controlling pornography does not conflict with constitutional rights, a common obstacle to action is removed.

Appeals for action against pornography are sometimes brushed aside with the claim that such action is a diversion from the primary task of feminists—the elimination of sexism and of sexual inequality. This approach focuses on the enjoyment rather than the manufacture of pornography, and sees it as merely a product of sexism which will disappear when the latter has been overcome and the sexes are socially and economically equal. Pornography cannot be separated from sexism in this way: Sexism is not just a set of attitudes regarding the inferiority of women but the behaviors and social and economic rules that manifest such attitudes. Both the manufacture and distribution of pornography and the enjoyment of it are instances of sexist behavior. The enjoyment of pornography on the part of individuals will presumably decline as such individuals begin to accord women their status as fully human. A cultural climate which tolerates the degrading representation of women is not a climate which facilitates the development of respect for women. Furthermore, the demand for pornography is stimulated not just by the sexism of individuals but by the pornography industry itself. Thus, both as a social phenomenon and in its effect on individuals, pornography, far from being a mere product, nourishes sexism. The campaign against it is an essential component of women's struggle for legal, economic, and social equality, one which requires the support of all feminists.

NOTES

1. In talking of prostitution here, I refer to the concept of, rather than the reality of prostitution. The same is true of my remarks about relationships between women and their husbands or men friends.
2. This was a full-color magazine cover seen in a rack at the check-out counter of a corner delicatessen.
3. Pornography thus becomes another tool of capitalism. One feature of some contemporary pornography—the use of Black and Asian women in both still photographs and films—exploits the racism as well as the sexism of its white consumers. For a discussion of the interplay between racism and sexism under capitalism as it relates to violent crimes against women, see Angela Y. Davis, "Rape, Racism, and the Capitalist Setting," *The Black Scholar*, Vol. 9, No. 7, April 1978.
4. This tolerance has a linguistic parallel in the growing acceptance and use of nonhuman nouns such as "chick," "bird," "filly," "fox," "doll," "babe," "skirt," etc., to refer to women, and of verbs of harm such as "fuck," "screw," "bang" to refer to sexual intercourse. See Robert Baker and Frederick Elliston. "'Pricks' and 'Chicks': A Plea for Persons," *Philosophy and Sex* (Buffalo, N.Y.: Prometheus Books, 1975).
5. This is supported by the fact that in Denmark the number of rapes committed has increased while the number of rapes reported to the authorities has decreased over the past twelve years. See *WAVPM Newspage*, Vol. II, No. 5, June, 1978, quoting M. Harry, "Denmark Today—The Causes and Effects of Sexual Liberty" (paper presented to The

Responsible Society, London, England, 1976). See also Eysenck and Nias, *Sex, Violence and the Media* (New York: St. Martin's Press, 1978), pp. 120–124.

6. Thus, the right to use such materials in the privacy of one's home, which has been upheld by the United States Supreme Court (*Stanley* v. *Georgia*, 394 U.S. 557), does not include the right to purchase them or to have them available in the commercial market. See also *Paris Adult Theater I* v. *Slaton*, 431 U.S. 49.

7. The Supreme Court has also traditionally included obscenity in this category. As not everyone agrees it should be included, since as defined by statutes, it is a highly vague concept, and since the grounds accepted by the Court for including it miss the point, I prefer to omit it from this list.

Sticks and Stones

JOHN ARTHUR

A recent *New York Times* article described the intense controversy surrounding a German court's decision that a bumper-sticker proclaiming "soldiers are murderers" is constitutionally protected, just as it would be under the First Amendment to the United States Constitution. Chancellor Helmut Kohl characterized himself as "outraged" at the court's decision, saying that "We cannot and must not stand by while our soldiers are placed on the same level with criminals." A leading German newspaper editorialized that "In a democracy, criticism of war and the military is naturally not forbidden. But among reasonable people, it must be done in a civilized way and not with brutal insults like 'murderers.'" And the judge in the case, who said he regretted having to decide as he did, complained that earlier decisions of the Constitutional Court "are steadily placing freedom of speech ahead of the protection of people's honor" (*New York Times*, January 15, 1996, p. A-5). As this event shows, hate speech occurs in a wide array of contexts; it can also be directed at many different targets, not just racial groups. It is also unclear, of course, whether and in what form hate speech should be censored.

Proponents of limiting hate speech on college campuses and elsewhere have generally taken one of two approaches. One is to pass a "speech code" that identifies which words or ideas are banned, the punishment that may be imposed, and (as at the University of Michigan) an interpretive "Guide" meant to explain how the rules will be applied. The other approach has been to treat hate speech as a form of harassment. Here the censorship is justified on anti-discrimination grounds: hate speech, it is argued, subjects its victims to a "hostile" work environment, which courts have held constitutes job discrimination (*Meritor Savings Bank* v. *Vinson*, 1986).

Advocates of banning hate speech do not usually include all expressions of hatred, however devastating and humiliating they may be. Few would ban such criticism of the military, for example. And words directed at another person because of what he has done are also not normally included: "You bastard, you murdered my father!" is not thought of as "hate speech," nor is an attack on a person simply for being stupid or incompetent. Rather than censoring all expressions of hatred, advocates of banning hate speech use the term narrowly, to refer to speech directed at people *in virtue of their membership in a (usually historically disadvantaged) racial, religious, ethnic, sexual or other group.*

Such a conception can be criticized, of course, on the ground that it arbitrarily narrows the field to one form of hate speech. Perhaps, however, there

From John Arthur, "Sticks and Stones," *Ethics in Practice: An Anthology*, ed. H. LaFollette (Blackwell, 1997).

is reason to focus on a limited problem: if it turns out, for example, that hate speech directed against such groups is especially harmful, then it may seem reasonable to have created this special usage of the term. In this paper I consider some of the important issues surrounding hate speech and its regulation: the political and legal importance of free speech; the types of harm that might be attributed to it; and whether, even if no harm results, causing emotional distress and offense is by itself sufficient to warrant censorship.

1 WHY PROTECT FREEDOM OF SPEECH?

Respecting freedom of speech is important for a variety of reasons. First, as J. S. Mill argued long ago, free and unfettered debate is vital for the pursuit of truth. If knowledge is to grow, people must be free to put forth ideas and theories they deem worthy of consideration, and others must be left equally free to criticize them. Even false ideas should be protected, Mill argued, so that the truth will not become mere dogma, unchallenged and little understood. "However true [an opinion] may be," he wrote, "if it is not fully, frequently, and fearlessly discussed, it will be held as a dead dogma, not a living truth" (Mill, 1978, p. 34). It helps, of course, if the competition among ideas is fair and all sides have an equal opportunity to have their ideas expressed. Censorship is therefore only one of the dangers to the marketplace of ideas; unequal access to the media is another.

Free speech is also an essential feature of democratic, efficient and just government. Fair, democratic elections cannot occur unless candidates are free to debate and criticize each other's policies, nor can government be run efficiently unless corruption and other abuses can be exposed by a free press. But beyond that, there is an important sense in which freedom of speech provides a necessary precondition for the protection of other rights and therefore for justice. Free and open debate about the nature and limits of other rights to privacy, religion, equal treatment and the rest is vital if society is to reach sound and fair decisions about when and how those other rights must be defined and respected. We cannot expect sound political deliberation, including deliberation about rights themselves, without first securing freedom of speech.

A third value, individual autonomy, is also served by free speech. In chapter III of *On Liberty*, "Of Individuality, as One of the Elements of Well Being," Mill writes that "He who lets the world, or his own portion of it, choose his plan of life for him, has no need of any other faculty than the ape-like one of imitation.... Among the works of man, which human life is rightly employed in perfecting and beautifying, the first in importance surely is man himself" (Mill, 1978, p. 56). Mill's suggestion is that the best life does not result from being forced to live a certain way, but instead is freely chosen without coercion from outside. But if Mill is right, then freedom of speech as well as action are important to achieve a worthwhile life. Free and open discussion helps people exercise their capacities of reasoning and judgment, capacities that are essential for autonomous and informed choices.

Besides these important social advantages of respecting free speech, including learning the truth, securing efficient, democratic and just government, and promoting individual autonomy, freedom of expression is important for its own sake, because it is a basic human right. Not only does free speech *promote* autonomy, as Mill argued, but it is also a *reflection* of individual autonomy and of human equality. Censorship denigrates our status as equal, autonomous persons by saying, in effect, that some people simply cannot be trusted to make up their own minds about what is right or true. Because of the ideas they hold or the subjects they find interesting, they need not be treated with the same respect as other citizens with whom they disagree; only we, not they, are free to believe as we wish. Viewed that way, denying free speech is much like establishing an official religion: it says to some citizens that because of their beliefs they are less than equal members of society. So, unlike the previous arguments, which see speech as an instrument to realize other important values, here the claim is that free speech must be protected out of respect for the fact that each adult in the community is entitled to be treated as an equal among others (Dworkin, 1996, ch. 8).

Because it serves important social goals, and also must be respected in the name of equal citizenship, the right to speak and write freely is perhaps the most important of all rights. But beyond that, two further points also need to be stressed. Free speech is fragile, in two respects. The first is the chilling effect that censorship poses. Language banning hate speech will inevitably be vague and indeterminate, at least to some extent: words like "hate" and "denigrate" and "victimize," which often occur in such rules, are not self-defining. When such bans bring strict penalties, as they sometimes do, they risk sweeping too broadly, capturing valuable speech in their net along with the speech they seek to prohibit. Criminal or civil penalties therefore pose a threat to speech generally, and the values underlying it, as people consider the potential risks of expressing their opinions while threatened by legal sanctions. Censorship risks having a chilling effect.

The second danger of censorship, often referred to as the "slippery slope," begins with the historical observation that unpopular minorities and controversial ideas are always vulnerable to political repression, whether by authoritarian regimes hoping to remain in power, or elected officials desiring to secure reelection by attacking unpopular groups or silencing political opponents. For that reason, it is important to create a high wall of constitutional protection securing the right to speak against attempts to limit it. Without strong, politically resistant constraints on governmental efforts to restrict speech, there is constant risk—demonstrated by historical experience—that what begins as a minor breech in the wall can be turned by governmental officials and intolerant majorities into a large, destructive exception.

Protecting speech is essential if society is to protect truth, autonomy, efficiency, democracy, and justice; it also must be protected if we are to show equal respect for others with whom we differ. Censorship is also risky, I have argued, given the dangers of chilling effects and slippery slopes. Given all this, it is not surprising that the United States Supreme Court has sought ways to protect freedom of speech. So before considering hate-speech regulations, it will be helpful to look briefly at how the US Supreme Court has understood the First Amendment's guarantee of freedom of speech.

2 FREE SPEECH AND THE CONSTITUTION

The Supreme Court has not always interpreted the First Amendment's free speech and press clauses

in a manner consistent with speech's importance. Early in the twentieth century people were often jailed, and their convictions upheld, for expressing unpopular political views, including distributing pamphlets critical of American military intervention in the Russian revolution (*Abrams* v. *United States*, 1919). Then, in the McCarthy era of the 1950s, government prosecuted over a hundred people for what was in effect either teaching Marxism or belonging to the Communist Party (*Dennis* v. *United States*, 1951). Beginning in the 1960s, however, the US Supreme Court changed direction, interpreting the Constitution's command that government not restrict freedom of speech as imposing strict limits on governmental power to censor speech and punish speakers.

Pursuing this goal, the first defined "speech" broadly, to include not just words but other forms of expression as well. Free speech protection now extends to people who wear arm bands, burn the flag, and peaceably march. The Court has also made a critically important distinction, between governmental regulations aimed at the *content* or *ideas* a person wishes to convey and content-neutral restrictions on the *time, place, and manner* in which the speech occurs. Thus, government is given fairly wide latitude to curtail speakers who use bullhorns at night, spray-paint their ideas on public buildings, or invade private property in order to get their messages across. But when governmental censors object not to how or where the speech occurs, but instead to the content itself, the Constitution is far more restrictive. Here, the Supreme Court has held, we are at the very heart of the First Amendment and the values it protects. Indeed, said the Court, there is "no such thing as a false idea" under the US Constitution (*Gertz.* v. *Robert Welch, Inc.*, 1974).

Wary of the chilling effect and the slippery slope, the Supreme Court has therefore held that government cannot regulate the content of speech unless it falls within certain narrowly defined categories. These constitutionally "unprotected categories" include libel (but criticisms of public officials must not only be false but uttered "maliciously" to be libelous), incitement to lawlessness (if the incitement is "immanent," such as yelling "Let's kill the capitalist!" in front of an angry mob), obscenity (assuming that the speech also lacks substantial social value), and "fighting words" (like "fascist pig" that are uttered in a face-to-face context likely to injure or provoke immediate, hostile reaction). In that way, each of these unprotected categories is precisely defined so as not to endanger free expression in general. Like Ulysses tying himself to the mast, the Supreme Court uses the unprotected-categories approach to reduce the chance that we will return to a time when constitutional protections were vaguely defined and government was left free to issue vaguely worded sedition statutes, stifle dissent and lock up critics. Harmless advocacy of revolution, for example, is now constitutionally protected, as is virtually all criticism of public officials.

Applying these principles, the Supreme Court held in 1989 that a "flag desecration" is constitutionally protected (*Texas* v. *Johnson*, 1989). Texas's statute had defined "desecration" in terms of the tendency to "offend" someone who was likely to know of the act. But, said the Court in striking down the statute, not only does flag burning involve ideas, the statute is not viewpoint neutral. Because it singled out one side of a debate—those who are critical of government—the law must serve an especially clear and important purpose. Mere "offense," the justices concluded, was insufficiently important to warrant intrusion into free expression.

In light of this constitutional history, it is not surprising that attempts to ban hate speech have fared poorly in American courts. Responding to various acts of racist speech on its campus, the University of Michigan passed one of the most far-reaching speech codes ever attempted at an American university; it prohibited "stigmatizing or victimizing" either individuals or groups on the basis of "race, ethnicity, religion, sex, sexual orientation, creed, national origin, ancestry, age, marital status, handicap or Vietnam-era veteran status." According to a "Guide" published by the University to help explain the code's meaning, conduct that violates the code would include a male student who "makes remarks in class like 'Women just aren't as good in this field as men,' thus creating a hostile learning atmosphere for female classmates." Also punishable under the code were "derogatory" comments about a person's or group's "physical appearance or sexual orientation, or their cultural origins, or religious beliefs" (*Doe* v. *University of*

Michigan, 1989, pp. 857–8). To almost nobody's surprise, the Michigan Code was rejected as unconstitutional, on grounds that it violated rights both to free speech and to due process of law. The case was brought by a psychology instructor who feared that his course in developmental psychology, which discussed biological differences between males and females, might be taken by some to be "stigmatizing and victimizing." The Court agreed with the professor, holding that the Michigan code was both "over-broad" and "unconstitutionally vague." A second code at the University of Wisconsin soon met a similar fate, even though it banned only slurs and epithets (*UMV Post* v. *Board of Regents of the University of Wisconsin*, 1991).

Confirming these lower court decisions, the Supreme Court in 1992 ruled unconstitutional a city ordinance making it a misdemeanor to place on public or private property any "symbol, object, appellation, characterization or graffiti" that the person knows or has reasonable grounds for knowing will arouse "anger, alarm or resentment" on the basis of race, color, creed, religion or gender (*R.A.V.* v. *City of St. Paul*, 1992, p. 2541). In overturning a juvenile's conviction for placing a burning cross on a black family's lawn, the majority held that even if the statute were understood very narrowly, to limit only "fighting words," it was nonetheless unconstitutional because it punished only some fighting words and not others. In so doing, argued one justice, the law violated the important principle of content neutrality: it censored some uses of fighting words, namely those focusing on race, color, creed, religion or gender, but not others. It prescribed political orthodoxy. Other justices emphasized that no serious harm had been identified that could warrant restrictions on speech. The law, wrote Justice White, criminalizes conduct that "causes only hurt feelings, offense, or resentment, and is protected by the First Amendment" (*R.A.V.* v. *City of St. Paul*, 1992, p. 2559).

Perhaps, however, the Court has gone too far in protecting hate speech. Advocates of banning hate speech commonly claim it harms its victims. "There is a great difference," writes Charles Lawrence, "between the offensiveness of words that you would rather not hear because they are labelled dirty, impolite, or personally demeaning and the injury [of hate speech]" (Lawrence, 1990, p. 74). Elsewhere he describes hate speech as "aimed at an entire group with the effect of causing significant *harm* to individual group members" (Lawrence, 1990, p. 57, emphasis added). Richard Delgado similarly claims that it would be rare for a white who is called a "dumb honkey" to be in a position to claim legal redress since, unlike a member of an historically oppressed group, it would be unlikely that a white person would "suffer *harm* from such an insult" (Delgado, 1982, p. 110, emphasis added).

But are these writers correct that various forms of hate speech cross the boundary from the distressing and offensive to the genuinely harmful? To weigh their claim, we will first ask how we are to understand the concept of harm. Once that is clear, we can then proceed to the question of whether hate speech is in fact harmful, and then to whether it should be banned on other grounds.

3 HARM AND OFFENSE

To claim that someone has been harmed is different from claiming she has been wronged. I can break into your house undetected, do no damage, and leave. While I have wronged you, I might not have harmed you, especially if you didn't know about it and I didn't take anything.

What then must be the case for wronging somebody to also constitute a harm? First, to be harmed is not merely to experience a minor irritation or hurt, nor is it simply to undergo an unwanted experience. Though unwanted, the screech of chalk on the blackboard, an unpleasant smell, a pinch or slap, a brief but frightening experience, and a revolting sight are not harms. Harms are significant events. Following Joel Feinberg, I will assume that harms occur not when we are merely hurt or offended, but when our "interests" are frustrated, defeated or set back (Feinberg, 1984, pp. 31–51). By interests he means something in which we have a stake—just as we may have a "stake" in a company. So while many of our interests are obviously tied to our wants and desires, a mere want does not constitute an interest. A minor disappointment is not a frustration of interests in the relevant sense. Feinberg thus emphasizes the "directional" nature of interests that are "set back" when one is harmed, pointing out that the interests are

"ongoing concerns" rather than temporary wants. Genuine harms thus impede or thwart people's future objectives or options, which explains why the unpleasant memory or smell and the bite's itch are not harms while loss of a limb, of freedom, and of health are. Harms can therefore come from virtually any source: falling trees, disease, economic or romantic competitors, and muggers are only a few examples.

It seems clear therefore why government is concerned about harm and its prevention. Whether caused by other people or by nature, to be harmed is never trivial; it involves a setback or frustration of an interest of a person. For government to ignore genuinely harmful acts requires justification; sometimes such a justification is easy to see, as when competition causes economic harm or a person injures another in self-defense. But, absent such a justification, there is a *prima facie* case that harmful actions should not be allowed.

We now turn to the question of whether hate speech causes harm. In discussing this, we will consider various types of harm that might result, as well as making important distinctions between group and individual harm, between cumulative and individual harm and between direct and indirect harm.

4 GROUP HARM

One typical form of hate speech is directed not at any particular individual but at a group: fliers attacking racial and religious minorities are typical examples. But why might it be thought that attacks on groups are harmful? Here are some possibilities.

Larry May argues that attacks on groups harm people "vicariously." Because people care about others in their group, an attack on any one of them is in effect an attack on them all. He terms this state "solidarity." "If people are in a state of solidarity," he writes, "in which they identify the interests of others as their own interests, then…vicarious harm is possible" (May, 1987, p. 115). But that seems wrong: even assuming people are in a state of solidarity and identify strongly with the interests of others in the group, and also assuming that the hate speech harms the interests of its specific subject in some way, it still does not follow that others in the group are harmed by such an attack. Even such an attack on a family member might not result in such vicarious *harm*, though it could surely cause distress, anger, and resentment. Attacks on group members cause harm only if they also frustrate others' interests, understood as limiting ongoing objectives or options. But group "solidarity" is not normally like that; no doubt other group members are often distressed, but to suffer distress is not, by itself, a harm.

Perhaps, however, the harm caused by attacks aimed at a racial or other group is to the group itself rather than to any particular individual. But what sense can be made of such a claim, that the group itself is somehow harmed? It may seem that groups are not the sort of thing that *can* be harmed, only individual members. But consider corporations. Not only do they have duties and rights (they can sue and be sued, be held legally liable, and be fined) but they also have goals and objectives (namely to make a profit or to achieve some charitable goal if they are not-for-profit corporations). Nor is the corporation's goal reducible to the interests of its members: individuals involved with the corporation may care little or nothing about whether the corporation makes a profit, worrying instead about their salary, job security, work conditions, status among others, or whatever. So because corporations have independent goals, it seems that corporations can also be harmed. Exxon Corporation, for example, was probably harmed by the Alaskan oil spill, and certainly US auto makers were harmed by competition from the Japanese in the 1980s.

It is far from clear, however, how the analogy with corporations can be extended to religious, racial, or other groups. Consider the group of people on board an airplane. *Individuals* on the airplane can be harmed, of course, but it makes little sense to ask after a crash whether, in addition to all the deaths, the *group* itself was harmed. One reason that some groups, like corporations, can be harmed while others, such as people on airplanes, cannot is that corporations exist in a legal environment that provides them with their own, independent goal: both their charter and the legal context in which they function define their purpose as making profits for shareholders. A second point, besides legally defined purpose, is that corporations have an organizational structure whose purpose is to achieve the goal. For these reasons, sense can be made of a corporation being harmed in its pursuit of its goals. The situation is different, however, for racial, religious, ethnic, or cultural groups. These groups are socially, not legally created, and obviously do not have a charter defining their goals; nor do they have the organizational structures that allowed us to make sense of a corporation's goals. Lacking a purpose, they therefore cannot be harmed in its pursuit.

It might be argued in response, however, that at least some groups, like religious ones, *can* have defined goals: The goal of the Jewish people, it is sometimes said, is to be a "light unto the nations," and that of Evangelical Christians, to preach salvation. But again it is unclear how to make sense of these "group" goals without assuming there is somebody else, God, who has established the purpose for the groups. But then it would be God, and not the group itself, that has the goal. On the other hand, if God has not established such a purpose then it seems reasonable to think of the goal as residing in individual members, not in the group itself. Similarly, a people or nation are sometimes said to have goals such as creating "socialist man" or achieving "manifest destiny," but again this depends on an organizational structure, usually a government, that represents the people and pursues the objective. Take that structure away, and the "group" goal dissolves.

The claim that hate speech harms a racial, religious, or ethnic group is therefore best not taken literally. Group harm is best understood as a shorthand way of suggesting individual members have been harmed. What sort of harm is then at issue, exactly? And how might hate speech cause it?

5 CUMULATIVE VS. INDIVIDUAL HARM

To give this argument its due, we must first distinguish between harms flowing from *individual* actions and *cumulative* harms. Often what is a singly harmless act can be damaging when added to other similar acts. One person walking across a lawn does little damage, but constant walking will destroy the lawn. Indeed the single act might be entirely without negative effect. Pollution, for instance, is often harmful only cumulatively, not singly. Though one car battery's lead may do no harm to those who drink the water downstream, when added to the pollution of many others the cumulative harm can be disastrous.

Further, the fact that it was singly harmless is no justification for performing the act. The complete response to a person who insists that he had a right to pollute since his action did no damage is that if everyone behaved that way great harm would follow: once a legal scheme protecting the environment is in place, criminal law is rightly invoked even against individually harmless acts on grounds of cumulative harm.

It might then be argued that even if individual hate speech acts do not cause harm, it should still be banned because of its cumulatively harmful effects. What might that harm consist in? Defending hate speech codes, Mari J. Matsuda writes that "As much as one may try to resist a piece of hate propaganda, the effect on one's self-esteem and sense of personal security is devastating. To be hated, despised, and alone is the ultimate fear of all human beings.... [R]acial inferiority is planted in our minds as an idea that may hold some truth" (Matsuda, 1989, p. 25). Besides the distress caused by the hate speech, Matsuda is suggesting, hate speech victims may also be harmed in either of two ways: reduced self-esteem or increased risk of violence and discrimination. I will begin with self-esteem, turning to questions of violence and discrimination in the next section.

6 CUMULATIVE HARM TO SELF-ESTEEM

What then is self-esteem? Following Rawls, let us assume that by "self-esteem" or "self-respect" we mean the sense both that one's goals and life-plan are worthwhile and that one has talents and other characteristics sufficient to make their accomplishment possible (Rawls, 1971, pp. 440–6). Loss of self-esteem might therefore constitute harm because it reduces motivation and willingness to put forth effort. If hate-speech victims believe they have little or no chance of success, their future options will be reduced, rather as former slaves are sometimes said to have had their futures foreclosed as a result of the attitudes they inherited from slavery.

Assuming loss of self-esteem is a harm, how plausible is Matsuda's suggestion that hate speech

has the (cumulative) effect of reducing it? Many factors can reduce self-esteem. Demeaning portrayals of one's group in the media, widespread antisocial behavior of others in the group, family breakdown, poor performance in school and on the job, drugs, and even well intended affirmative action programs all may lessen self-esteem. Indeed, I suggest that, absent those other factors, simply being subject to hate speech would not significantly reduce self-esteem. An otherwise secure and confident person might be made angry (or fearful) by racial or other attacks, feeling the speaker is ignorant, rude, or stupid. But without many other factors it is hard to see that hate speech by itself would have much impact on self-esteem. Gerald Gunther, who as a Jew was subjected to some of the worst hate speech imaginable, nevertheless opposes speech codes. While writing eloquently of the distress such speech caused, there is no suggestion that the speech had an impact on the self-esteem of an otherwise self-confident person (Gunther, 1990).

But even assuming hate speech does reduce self-esteem to some degree, notice how far the argument has strayed from the original, robust claim that hate speech should be banned because it causes harm. First each individual act must be added to other acts of hate speech, but then it must also be added to the many other, more important factors that together reduce self-esteem. Given the importance of protecting speech I discussed earlier, and the presumption it creates against censorship, Matsuda's argument that it reduces self-esteem seems far too speculative and indirect to warrant criminalizing otherwise protected speech.

7 DISCRIMINATION AND VIOLENCE AS INDIRECT HARMS

But surely, it may be objected, the real issue is simply this: hate speech should be banned because it increases racial or other forms of hatred, which in turn leads to increased violence and discrimination—both of which are obviously harmful. That is a serious claim, and must be taken seriously. Notice first, however, that this effect of hate speech, if it exists, is only indirect; hate speech is harmful only because of its impact on others who are then led in turn to commit acts of violence or discrimination. The claim is not that the speech itself directly caused the harm, but instead that it encouraged attitudes in people who then, on their own, acted wrongly and harmed others.

There are important problems with this as an argument for banning hate speech. One, epistemological problem is whether we really know that the link exists between hate speech, increased hatred, and illegal acts. Suppose we discovered a close correlation between reading hate speech and committing acts of violence—what have we proved? Not, as might be thought, that hate speech causes violence. Rather, we would only know that *either* (A) reading such material increases hatred and violence, *or* (B) those who commit hate crimes also tend to like reading hate speech. The situation with respect to hate speech mirrors arguments about violence and pornography: the observation that rapists subscribe in greater proportion to pornographic magazines than do non-rapists does not show we can reduce rape by banning pornography. Maybe people who rape just tend also to like pornography. Similarly, reduction in hate speech might, or might not, reduce hate-related crime, even assuming that those who commit hate crimes are avid readers of hate literature.

Nor is it clear that hate speech has the effect on people's attitudes that the argument assumes. Consider an example reported recently in Missoula, Montana, where a vandal threw a brick through a window of the house of a Jewish family that had put a Menorah in their window to celebrate Hanukkah. In response, much of that overwhelmingly Christian city simply put pictures of a Menorah in their own windows, published in the local newspaper. Far from encouraging anti-Jewish hatred, this act seemed to have the opposite effect. Indeed it seems clear that members of groups whom hate-speech regulations are aimed to protect are themselves aware that hate speech can sometimes be beneficial. At my university alone, we have had two incidents in which acts of hate speech were perpetrated by members of the attacked group itself. Evidently, those students believed that rather than increasing hatred they could use hate speech to call attention to problems of racism and anti-Semitism and increase people's sympathy, just as occurred in Missoula. We cannot assume, therefore, that censoring hate speech would reduce hatred. The reaction in Missoula, to meet racist speech with more speech, not only

avoided censorship but also allowed people to make a powerful statement of their feelings about the importance of respecting the rights of others in their community.

It is unclear, I am suggesting, that regulating hate speech really would reduce hatred, let alone reduce hate crimes. And that uncertainty matters in the case of speech. Pollution, walking on the grass, and other activities that are less important than speech, and less threatened by governmental regulation, can be restricted without clear demonstration of their harmful effects. We need not wait to see for certain that a product is toxic to ban it; sometimes only a reasonable suspicion is enough if the product is relatively unimportant and the risks it may pose are significant. But speech, I have argued, is not like that. Freedom of expression is of great social value, enjoys the status as a basic right, and is in real danger due to slippery slopes and chilling effects.

There is a further problem, in addition to the epistemological one we have been discussing, with the argument that, by increasing hatred, hate speech in turn leads to more violence and discrimination. Any accused criminal, including one whose acts were motivated by racial or group hatred, must be shown to have *mens rea* or "guilty mind" in order to be convicted. That means, roughly, that the accused must have been aware of the nature of the act, aware that it was illegal or wrong, and was *able to have complied with the law*. But if the person could have complied with the law, then it follows that despite having read or heard the hate speech, and (we are now assuming) thereby had his hatred increased, he must still have been able to ask himself whether he wished to *act* on the basis of that attitude. Between the desire and the action comes the decision. Criminals are not zombies, controlled by their desires and unable to reflect on the nature and quality of their actions. It is no excuse that the criminal acted on a strong desire, whether it was to be wealthy without earning money, have sex without another's consent, or express hatred of a group through violent acts or discrimination.

This means, then, that we have on hand two different ways of dealing with acts of violence and discrimination motivated by hatred: by using government censorship in an effort at thought control, trying to eliminate hatred and prejudice, or by insisting that whether people like somebody or not they cannot assault them or discriminate against them. My suggestion is that passing and vigorously enforcing laws against violence and discrimination themselves is a better method of preventing indirect harm than curtailing speech. Government should not be in the business of making people like each other; it should, however, insist that we treat each other fairly and respect each other's rights. Indeed, using the power of government to persuade people how they should live and whom they should like seem quite incompatible with Mill's claim, discussed earlier, that individual autonomy and freedom are part of the valuable life. Even if we could, through government, force people to share our attitudes it is not clear we should try.

8 OFFENSIVE EXPRESSION AND EPITHETS

I have argued that hate speech should not be banned on the ground of preventing harm. But government often restricts behavior that is not strictly speaking harmful: it prevents littering, for instance, and limits how high we build our buildings, the drugs we take and the training our doctors receive, to mention only a few examples. Some of these restrictions are controversial, of course, especially ones that seem designed only to keep us from harming ourselves. But others, for example limiting alterations of historic buildings and preventing littering, are rarely disputed. Government also limits various forms of public behavior that are grossly offensive, revolting or shocking. An assault on the sense of smell and hearing, unusual or even common sexual activities in public, extreme provocations of anger, or threats that generate great anxiety or fear, are generally regarded as examples of behavior that can be restricted although they do not cause genuine harm.

Charles Lawrence suggests that this argument also applies to hate speech. The experience of being called "nigger," "spic," "Jap," or "kike," he writes, "is like receiving a slap in the face. The injury is instantaneous" (Lawrence, 1990, pp. 68–9). He describes the experience of a student who was called a "faggot" on a subway: "He found himself in a state of semi-shock, nauseous, dizzy, unable to muster the witty, sarcastic, articulate rejoinder he was accustomed to making" (Lawrence, 1990, p. 70).

Sometimes, of course, hate speech can be banned, even speech about important public issues. A Nazi yelling about the virtues of Fascism in a public bus or library, for example, can be asked to stop by a policeman. But that is not *content* regulation, unless somebody yelling just as loudly about the virtues of patriotism or of the Republican Party would be permitted to remain. Neutral regulations that prevent people from disturbing others, without regard to what is being said, do not raise the same constitutional and political issues as does content regulation of political speech.

But because of speech's critical importance and government's tendency to regulate and limit political discussion to suit its own ends, I have argued, it is important to limit governmental censorship to narrowly and precisely defined unprotected categories. This provides a more secure protection of speech than allowing officials to balance, case by case, the relative costs and benefits of individual laws government might wish to pass limiting free speech. Assuming that we might wish to keep this unprotected-categories approach, how might offensive hate speech be regulated? One possibility is to allow government to ban speech that "causes substantial distress and offense" to those who hear it. Were we to adopt such a principle, however, we would effectively gut the First Amendment. All kinds of political speech, including much that we would all think must be protected, is offensive to somebody somewhere. "Fuck the draft" is but one of many examples of constitutionally protected offensive speech (*Cohen* v. *California*, 1971); burning the American Flag is another (*Texas* v. *Johnson*, 1989).

Nor would it work to limit the unprotected category to all speech that is distressing and offensive to members of historically stigmatized groups, for that too would sweep far too broadly. Speech critical of peoples, nations, and religious institutions and practices often offends group members, as do discussions of differences between the races and sexes. Social and biological scientists sometimes find themselves confronted by people who have been deeply wounded by their words, as the instructor who got in trouble at the University of Michigan over his comments about sex-linked abilities illustrates. Or what about psychologists who wish to do research into group IQ differences? Should only those who reach conclusions that are not offensive be allowed to publish? Or should we perhaps simply ban research into any topic that offends? Such examples can be repeated endlessly, of course; it is virtually impossible to predict what might be taken as offensive. Even Malcolm X's auto-biography might be punishable; he says at one point that "I'd had too much experience that women were only tricky, deceitful, untrustworthy flesh" (Malcolm X, 1964, p. 226).

Others, however, have suggested another, less sweeping approach: why not at least ban racial or other *epithets* since they are a unique form of "speech act" that does not deserve protection. Unlike other forms of protected speech, it is claimed that epithets and name calling are constitutionally useless; they constitute acts of "subordination" that treat others as "moral inferiors" (Altmann, 1993). Racial, religious and ethnic epithets are therefore a distinct type of speech act in which the speaker is subordinating rather than claiming, asserting, requesting, or any of the other array of actions we accomplish with language. So (it is concluded) while all the other types of speech acts deserve protection, mere epithets and slurs do not.

The problem with this argument, however, is that epithets are *not* simply acts of subordination, devoid of social and political significance or meaning, any more than burning a flag is simply an act of heating cloth. Besides "subordinating" another, epithets can also express emotion (anger or hatred, for example) or defiance of authority. And like burning or refusing to salute the flag (both protected acts), epithets also can be seen to express a political message, such as that another person or group is less worthy of moral consideration or is receiving underserved preferences. That means, then, that however objectionable the content of such epithets is they go well beyond mere acts of "subordination" and therefore must be protected.

It is worth emphasizing, however, that although people have a political and constitutional *right* to use such language, it does not follow that they *should* use it or that they are behaving decently or morally when they exercise the right. A wrong remains a wrong, even if government may for good

reason choose not to punish it. I am therefore in no way defending on moral grounds those who utter hate speech—an impossible task, in my view—but instead have tried to show why meeting hatred with more speech, as was done in Missoula, is a better response than governmental censorship. Nor is it correct to think that because government allows people to speak it is thereby condoning either the speech or the speaker. Government doesn't condone Christians, Jews, Muslims and atheists by merely allowing them to exercise their religious freedom, as it would if it established and financed one religion. In religious matters, as well as in the case of speech, government's job is to remain neutral.

What, finally, should be said when a university is seeking to prevent harassment by limiting speech that creates a "hostile" environment for faculty and students? Clearly, a university could on aesthetic grounds prevent people from hanging banners or other material from their windows and doors, or pasting billboards on public walls. But again such a regulation must be content neutral; a state university cannot ban some messages while leaving other students, with different, less controversial and offensive views, to express themselves. (Private universities, since they are not run by government and therefore not bound by the First Amendment, are free to impose whatever orthodoxy they choose.)

More than most places, a university is committed to scholarship and the pursuit of knowledge. Freedom of inquiry is its life-blood. That means, however, that nobody can be guaranteed never to be offended or upset. (How often are students in a religion class deeply offended by what they hear? Or conservative Christians by openly gay, or pro-choice speech?) Being forced to confront people with widely different views and attitudes, including those whom we dislike and who dislike us, is rarely easy or pleasant; but it can also be an important part of acquiring an education. Once it is admitted that for purposes of regulating speech *content* there is no such thing as a false idea, Nazi marches have as much constitutional value as civil rights marches, swastikas as much value as anti-war or Israeli symbols, and emotionally charged speeches by members of the Klan as much value as Martin Luther King's "I Have a Dream" speech. Indeed, it is rare that hate speech is merely expressive and does not have at least some political or social content. However offensive and stupid Louis Farrakhan's description of Jews as "blood-sucking" may be, it is more than contentless expression of emotion.

None of this implies, however, that genuine harassment, whether in the workplace or university, should be protected. But harassment is not hate speech. For one thing, to suffer harassment requires more than hearing an offensive remark. Genuine harassment requires a pattern of behavior, not just a single event, and must occur in a context in which its intended victim(s) are made to feel sufficiently intimidated or distressed that their ability to perform is impeded. Nor would verbal harassment be limited to "hate speech" directed at women and racial or ethnic minorities. Vulgar, sexually explicit language directed at a religiously conservative white male could be part of a pattern of harassment of him, for example, as could verbal attacks aimed at people for being short, or in a fraternity, or long haired, or even (a personal concern of mine) being bald. Nor, finally, are acts of harassment limited to speech; other actions (making late-night noise or dumping litter, for example) would also have to be included under a genuine anti-harassment regulation. The point, then, is not that people have a free speech right to harass others. Rather, it is that a ban on harassment would be both broader and narrower than a ban on hate speech. To avoid the charge that they are disguised censorship, harassment regulations must ban more than hate speech as well as avoid treating hate speech per se as harassment.

But how, then, should others respond to those, on a university or off, who are offended and distressed when others exercise their right to speak? When children call each other names and cruelly tease each other, the standard adult response is to work on both sides of the problem. Teasers are encouraged to be more sensitive to others' feelings, and victims are encouraged to ignore the remarks. "Sticks and stones can break my bones, but names can never hurt me" was a commonplace on the playground when I was a child. A minimum of self-assurance and toughness can be expected of people, including students at college.

Like the sexual freedoms of homosexuals, freedom of speech is often the source of great distress to others. I have argued, however, that because of the risks and costs of censorship there is no alternative to accepting those costs, or more precisely to imposing the costs on those who find themselves distressed and offended by the speech. Like people who are offended by homosexuality or interracial couples, targets of hate speech can ask why *they* should have to suffer distress. The answer is the same in each case: nobody has the right to demand that government protect them against distress when doing so would violate others' rights. Many of us believe that racists would be better people and lead more worthwhile lives if they didn't harbor hatred, but that belief does not justify restricting their speech, any more than the Puritans' desire to save souls would warrant religious intolerance, or Catholics' moral disapproval of homosexuality justify banning homosexual literature.

REFERENCES

Abrams v. *United States*, 250 US 616 (1919).

Altmann, A. (1993) "Liberalism and Campus Hate Speech," *Ethics* 103.

Cohen v. *California*, 403 US 15 (1971).

Delgado, R. (1982) "Words that Wound: A Tort Action for Racial Insults, Epithets, and Name Calling," 17, *Harvard Civil Rights - Civil Liberties Law Review* 133 (1982); reprinted in Matsuda et al. (1993).

Dennis v. *United States*, 341 US 494 (1951).

Doe v. *University of Michigan*, 721 F. Supp. 852 (E. D. Mich. 1989).

Dworkin, R. (1996) *Freedom's Law: The Moral Reading of the American Constitution.* Cambridge, MA: Harvard University Press.

Feinberg, J. (1984) *The Moral Limits of the Criminal Law*, Volume I: *Harm to Others.* New York: Oxford University Press.

———(1985) *The Moral Limits of the Criminal Law*, Volume II: *Offense to Others.* New York: Oxford University Press.

Gertz. v. *Robert Welch, Inc.*, 418 US 323, 339 (1974).

Gunther, G. (1990) "Good Speech, Bad Speech – No," *Stanford Lawyer*, 24.

Lawrence, C. (1990) "If He Hollers Let Him Go: Regulating Racist Speech on Campus," *Duke Law Journal*, 431; reprinted in Matsuda et al. (1993).

Malcolm X, and Haley, A. (1964) *The Autobiography of Malcolm X.* New York: Grove Press.

Matsuda, M. (1989) "Public Response to Racist Speech: Considering the Victim's Story," *Michigan Law Review*, 87, reprinted in Matsuda et al. (1993).

Matsuda, M., Lawrence, C. R., Delgado, R., and Crenshaw, K. W. (1993) *Words that Wound: Critical Race Theory, Assaultive Speech, and the First Amendment*, Boulder, CO: Westview Press.

May, L. (1987) *The Morality of Groups: Collective Responsibility, Group-Based Harm, and Corporate Rights*. Notre Dame: University of Notre Dame Press.

Meritor Savings Bank v. *Vinson*, 477 US 57 (1986).

Mill, J. S. (1978) *On Liberty*, Indianapolis, IN: Hackett.

R. A. V. v. *City of St. Paul*, 50 US 377 (1992).

Rawls, J. (1971) *A Theory of Justice*, Cambridge, MA: Harvard University Press.

Texas v. *Johnson*, 491 US 397 (1989).

UMV Post v. *Board of Regents of the University of Wisconsin*, 774 F. supp. 1163 (1991).

ARGUMENT 18 ESSAY QUESTIONS

1. Who makes the stronger case—Strossen or Longino? Explain.
2. How does Strossen rebut the kind of harm-to-women arguments that Longino makes?
3. Are you a legal moralist? Give reasons for your answer.

19. MACKINNON'S HARM-TO-WOMEN ARGUMENT FOR CENSORSHIP

In "Pornography, Civil Rights, and Speech," the feminist Catharine MacKinnon argues that pornography should be censored because it does women great harm—it literally violates their civil rights. It does so by degrading and subordinating women through sexually explicit portrayals and simultaneously endorsing this demeaning view. Thus pornography defines women as inferior, and pornography's audience is conditioned to view and treat women accordingly. As MacKinnon says,

> Pornography is integral to attitudes and behaviors of violence and discrimination that define the treatment and status of half the population.... Pornography is a practice of discrimination on the basis of sex, on one level because of its role in creating and maintaining sex as a basis for discrimination. It harms many women one at a time and helps keep all women in an inferior status by defining our subordination as our sexuality and equating that with our gender. It is also sex discrimination because its victims, including men, are selected for victimization on the basis of their gender. But for their sex, they would not be so treated.[8]

---

[8] Catharine MacKinnon, "Pornography, Civil Rights, and Speech," *Harvard Civil Rights/Civil Liberties Law Review*, 20, 1985, 22, 27.

Critics of MacKinnon's view (including other feminists) have argued that pornography does not cause the harm she alleges, that banning offensive viewpoints violates bedrock principles of free speech, and that antipornography censorship itself causes harm to women.

Ronald Dworkin, for example, rejects MacKinnon's charge that pornography denies women their liberty by defining, or "reconstructing," them for society according to male fantasies:

> We must notice, first, that [MacKinnon's contention] remains a causal argument. It claims not that pornography is a consequence or symptom or symbol of how the identity of women has been reconstructed by men, but an important cause or vehicle of that reconstruction.
>
> That seems strikingly implausible. Sadistic pornography is revolting, but it is not in general circulation, except for its milder, soft-porn manifestations. It seems unlikely that it has remotely the influence over how women's sexuality or character or talents are conceived by men, and indeed by women, that commercial advertising and soap operas have.[9]

Nadine Strossen argues that censorship of pornography runs counter to, among other things, the fundamental "viewpoint neutrality" principle of free speech:

> [This principle] holds that government may never limit speech just because any listener—or even the majority of the community—disagrees with or is offended by its content or the viewpoint it conveys....
>
> The viewpoint-neutrality principle reflects the philosophy that, in a free society, the appropriate response to speech with which one disagrees is not censorship but counterspeech—more speech, not less. Rejecting this philosophy, the movements to censor hate speech and pornography target speech precisely because of its viewpoint, specifically, its discriminatory viewpoint.[10]

Wendy Kaminer, also a strong defender of free speech, maintains that censorship would likely have little effect on the prevalence of pornography and sexual violence but could end up hurting women and feminist causes instead:

> The history of antiporn campaigns in this country is partly a history of campaigns against reproductive choice and changing roles for men and women. The first federal obscenity legislation, known as the Comstock law, passed in 1873, prohibited the mailing of not only dirty pictures but also contraceptives and information about abortion. Early in this century [the pioneering feminist and birth control advocate] Margaret Sanger and the sex educator Mary Ware Dennett were prosecuted for obscenity violations....In Canada a landmark Supreme Court ruling...[that] adopted a feminist argument against pornography was first used to prohibit distribution of a small lesbian magazine, which a politically correct feminist would be careful to label erotica.[11]

---

[9] Ronald Dworkin, "Liberty and Pornography."

[10] Nadine Strossen, "Hate Speech and Pornography: Do We Have to Choose Between Freedom of Speech and Equality?" *Case Western Reserve Law Review* 46, no. 2 (Winter 1996).

[11] Wendy Kaminer, "Feminists Against the First Amendment," *The Atlantic Monthly,* November 1992.

Pornography, Civil Rights, and Speech

CATHARINE A. MACKINNON

There is a belief that this is a society in which women and men are basically equals. Room for marginal corrections is conceded, flaws are known to exist, attempts are made to correct what are conceived as occasional lapses from the basic condition of sex equality. Sex discrimination law has centered most of its focus on these occasional lapses. It is difficult to overestimate the extent to which this belief in equality is an article of faith to most people, including most women, who wish to live in self-respect in an internal universe, even (perhaps especially) if not in the world. It is also partly an expression of natural law thinking: If we are inalienably equal, we can't "really" be degraded.

This is a world in which it is worth trying. In this world of presumptive equality, people make money based on their training or abilities or diligence or qualifications. They are employed and advanced on the basis of merit. In this world of just deserts, if someone is abused, it is thought to violate the basic rules of the community. If it doesn't, that person is seen to have done something she could have chosen to do differently, by exercise of will or better judgment. Maybe such people have placed themselves in a situation of vulnerability to physical abuse. Maybe they have done something provocative. Or maybe they were just unusually unlucky. In such a world, if such a person has an experience, there are words for it. When they speak and say it, they are listened to. If they write about it, they will be published. If there are certain experiences that are never spoken, or certain people or issues seldom heard from, it is supposed that silence has been chosen. The law, including much of the law of sex discrimination and the first amendment, operates largely within the realm of these beliefs.

Feminism is the discovery that women do not live in this world, that the person occupying this realm is a man, so much more a man if he is white and wealthy. This world of potential credibility, authority, security, and just rewards, recognition of one's identity and capacity, is a world that some people do inhabit as a condition of birth, with variations *among them*. It is not a basic condition accorded humanity in this society, but a prerogative of status, a privilege, among other things, of gender.

I call this a discovery because it has not been an assumption. Feminism is the first theory, the first practice, the first movement, to take seriously the situation of all women from the point of view of all women, both on our situation and on social life as a whole. The discovery has therefore been made that the implicit social content of humanism, as well as the standpoint from which legal method has been designed and injuries have been defined, has not been women's standpoint. Defining feminism in a way that connects epistemology with power as the politics of women's point of view, this discovery can be summed up by saying that women live in another world: specifically, a world of *not* equality, a world of inequality.

Looking at the world from this point of view, a whole shadow world of previously invisible silent abuse has been discerned. Rape, battery, sexual harassment, forced prostitution, and the sexual abuse of children emerge as common and systematic. We find rape happens to women in all contexts, from the family, including rape of girls and babies, to students and women in the workplace, on the streets, at home, in their own bedrooms by men that they do not know, and by men that they do know, by men they are married to, men they have had a social conversation with, or, least often, men they have never seen before. Overwhelmingly, rape is something that men do or attempt to do to women (forty-four percent according to a recent study) at some point in our lives. Sexual harassment

"Pornography, Civil Rights, and Speech" by Catharine MacKinnon, *Harvard Civil Rights/Civil Liberties Law Review*, vol. 20, no.; 9–22, 25–31, 50–68. (Notes deleted.) © 1985 CR/CLL Review.

of women by men is common in workplaces and educational institutions. Up to eighty-five percent of women in one study report it, many in physical forms. Between a quarter and a third of women are battered in their homes by men. Thirty-eight percent of little girls are sexually molested inside or outside the family. Until women listened to women, this world of sexual abuse was *not spoken* of. It was the unspeakable. What I am saying is, if you *are* the tree falling in the epistemological forest, your demise doesn't make a sound if no one is listening. Women did not "report" these events, and overwhelmingly do not today, because no one is listening, because no one believes us. This silence does not mean nothing happened, and it does not mean consent. It is the silence of women of which Adrienne Rich has written, "Do not confuse it with any kind of absence."

Believing women who say we are sexually violated has been a radical departure, both methodologically and legally. The extent and nature of rape, marital rape, and sexual harassment itself, were discovered in this way. Domestic battery as a syndrome, almost a habit, was discovered through refusing to believe that when a woman is assaulted by a man to whom she is connected, that is not an assault. The sexual abuse of children was uncovered, Freud notwithstanding, by believing that children were not making up all this sexual abuse. Now what is striking is that when each discovery is made, and somehow made real in the world, the response has been: It happens to men too. If women are hurt, men are hurt. If women are raped, men are raped. If women are sexually harassed, men are sexually harassed. If women are battered, men are battered. Symmetry must be reasserted. Neutrality must be reclaimed. Equality must be reestablished.

The only places where the available evidence supports this, where anything like what happens to women also happens to men, are with children—little boys are sexually abused—and in prison. The liberty of prisoners is restricted, their freedom restrained, their humanity systematically diminished, their bodies and emotions confined, defined, and regulated. If paid at all, they are paid starvation wages. They can be tortured at will, and it is passed off as discipline or as means to an end. They become compliant. They can be raped at will, at any

moment, and nothing will be done about it. When they scream, nobody hears. To be a prisoner means to be defined as a member of a group for whom the rules of what can be done to you, of what is seen as abuse of you, are reduced as part of the definition of your status. To be a woman is also that kind of definition and has that kind of meaning.

Men *are* damaged by sexism. (By men, I am referring to the status of masculinity which is accorded to males on the basis of their biology, but is not itself biological.) But whatever the damage of sexism is to men, the condition of being a man is not defined as subordinate to women by force. Looking at the facts of the abuses of women all at once, you see that a woman is socially defined as a person who, whether or not she is or has been, *can at any time* be treated in these ways by men, and little, if anything, will be done about it. This is what it means when feminists say that maleness is a form of power and femaleness is a form of powerlessness.

In this context, what all of this "men too" stuff is about, is that people don't really seem to believe that the things I have just said are true, though there really is little question about their empirical accuracy. The data are extremely simple, like women's fifty-nine cent on the dollar pay figure. People don't really seem to believe that either. Yet there is no question of its empirical validity. This is the workplace story: What women do is seen as not worth much or what is not worth much is seen as something for women to do. *Women* are not seen as worth much, is the thing. Now why are these basic realities of the subordination of women to men, such that for example only 7.8 percent of women have never been sexually assaulted, not effectively believed, not perceived as real in the face of all this evidence? Why don't women believe our own experiences? In the face of all this evidence, especially of systematic sexual abuse—subjection to violence with impunity is one extreme expression, although not the only expression, of a degraded status—the view that basically the sexes are equal in this society remains unchallenged and unchanged. The day I got this was the day I understood its real message, its real coherence: *This is equality for us.*

I could describe this but I couldn't explain it until I started studying a lot of pornography. In pornography, there it is, in one place, all of the abuses that women had to struggle so long even to begin to artic-ulate, all the *unspeakable* abuse: the rape, the bat-tery, the sexual harassment, the prostitution, and the sexual abuse of children. Only in the pornography it is called something else: sex, sex, sex, sex, and sex, respectively. Pornography sexualizes rape, battery, sexual harassment, prostitution, and child sexual abuse; it thereby celebrates, promotes, authorizes, and legitimizes them. More generally, it eroticizes the dominance and submission that is the dynamic common to all. It makes hierarchy sexy and calls that "the truth about sex" or just a mirror of reality. Through this process, pornography constructs what a woman is as what men want from sex. This is what the pornography means. (I will talk about the way it works behaviorally, with the evidence on it, when I talk about the ordinance itself.)

Pornography constructs what a woman is in terms of its view of what men want sexually, such that acts of rape, battery, sexual harassment, prosti-tution, and sexual abuse of children become acts of sexual equality. Pornography's world of equality is a harmonious and balanced place. Men and women are perfectly complementary and perfectly bipo-lar. Women's desire to be fucked by men is equal to men's desire to fuck women. All the ways men love to take and violate women, women love to be taken and violated. The women who most love this are most men's equals, the most liberated; the most participatory child is the most grown-up, the most equal to an adult. Their consent merely expresses or ratifies these preexisting facts.

The content of pornography is one thing. There, women substantively desire dispossession and cru-elty. We desparately want to be bound, battered, tortured, humiliated, and killed. Or, to be fair to the soft core, merely taken and used. This is erotic to the male point of view. Subjection itself with self-determination ecstatically relinquished is the content of women's sexual desire and desirabil-ity. Women are there to be violated and possessed, men to violate and possess us either on screen or by camera or pen on behalf of the consumer. On a simple descriptive level, the inequality of hierarchy, of which gender is the primary one, seems neces-sary for the sexual arousal to work. Other added inequalities identify various pornographic genres or sub-themes, although they are always added

through gender: age, disability, homosexuality, ani-mals, objects, race (including anti-semitism), and so on. Gender is never irrelevant.

What pornography *does* goes beyond its con-tent: It eroticizes hierarchy, it sexualizes inequality. It makes dominance and submission sex. Inequality is its central dynamic; the illusion of freedom com-ing together with the reality of force is central to its working. Perhaps because this is a bourgeois culture, the victim must look free, appear to be freely acting. Choice is how she got there. Willing is what she is when she is being equal. It seems equally important that then and there she actually be forced and that forcing be communicated on some level, even if only through still photos of her in postures of receptivity and access, available for penetration. Pornography in this view is a form of forced sex, a practice of sex-ual politics, an institution of gender inequality.

From this perspective, pornography is neither harmless fantasy nor a corrupt and confused mis-representation of an otherwise natural and healthy sexual situation. It institutionalizes the sexuality of male supremacy, fusing the erotization of domi-nance and submission with the social construction of male and female. To the extent that gender is sex-ual, pornography is part of constituting the meaning of that sexuality. Men treat women as who they see women as being. Pornography constructs who that is. Men's power over women means that the way men see women defines who women can be. Pornography is that way. Pornography is not imagery in some relation to a reality elsewhere constructed. It is not a distortion, reflection, projection, expression, fan-tasy, representation, or symbol either. It is a sexual reality.

In Andrea Dworkin's definitive work on pornog-raphy, sexuality itself is a social construct gendered to the ground. Male dominance here is not an artificial overlay upon an underlying inalterable substratum of uncorrupted essential sexual being. Dworkin's *Pornography: Men Possessing Women* presents a sex-ual theory of gender inequality of which pornog-raphy is a constitutive practice. The way in which pornography produces its meaning constructs and defines men and women as such. Gender has no basis in anything other than the social reality its hegemony constructs. Gender is what gender means. The process that gives sexuality its male supremacist meaning is the same process through which gender inequality becomes socially real.

In this approach, the experience of the (overwhelmingly) male audiences who consume pornography is therefore not fantasy or simulation or catharsis but sexual reality, the level of reality on which sex itself largely operates. Understanding this dimension of the problem does not require noticing that pornography models are real women to whom, in most cases, something real is being done; nor does it even require inquiring into the systematic infliction of pornography and its sexuality upon women, although it helps. The way in which the pornography itself provides what those who consume it want matters. Pornography *participates* in its audience's eroticism through creating an accessible sexual object, the possession and consumption of which *is* male sexuality, as socially constructed; to be consumed and possessed as which, *is* female sexuality, as socially constructed; and pornography is a process that constructs it that way.

The object world is constructed according to how it looks with respect to its possible uses. Pornography defines women by how we look according to how we can be sexually used. Pornography codes how to look at women, so you know what you can do with one when you see one. Gender is an assignment made visually, both originally and in everyday life. A sex object is defined on the basis of its looks, in terms of its usability for sexual pleasure, such that both the looking—the quality of the gaze, including its point of view—and the definition according to use become eroticized as part of the sex itself. This is what the feminist concept "sex object" means. In this sense, sex in life is no less mediated than it is in art. One could say men have sex with *their image* of a woman. It is not that life and art imitate each other; in this sexuality, they *are* each other.

To give a set of rough epistemological translations, to defend pornography as consistent with the equality of the sexes is to defend the subordination of women to men as sexual equality. What in the pornographic view is love and romance looks a great deal like hatred and torture to the feminist. Pleasure and eroticism become violation. Desire appears as lust for dominance and submission. The vulnerability of women's projected sexual availability, that acting we are allowed (i.e. asking to be acted upon),

is victimization. Play conforms to scripted roles. Fantasy expresses ideology, is not exempt from it. Admiration of natural physical beauty becomes objectification. Harmlessness becomes harm. Pornography is a harm of male supremacy made difficult to see because of its pervasiveness, potency, and, principally, because of its success in making the world a pornographic place. Specifically, its harm cannot be discerned, and will not be addressed, if viewed and approached neutrally, because it *is* so much of "what is." In other words, to the extent pornography succeeds in constructing social reality, it becomes invisible as harm. If we live in a world that pornography creates through the power of men in a male dominated situation the issue is not what the harm of pornography is, but how that harm is to become visible.

Obscenity law provides a very different analysis and conception of the problem. In 1973, the legal definition of obscenity became that which

the average person, applying contemporary community standards, would find that, taken as a whole, appeals to the prurient interest; that which depicts and describes in a patently offensive way [You feel like you're a cop reading someone's *Miranda* rights] sexual conduct as defined by the applicable state law; and that which, taken as a whole, lacks serious literary, artistic, political or scientific value.

Feminism doubts whether the average gender-neutral person exists; has more questions about the content and process of defining what community standards are than it does about deviations from them; wonders why prurience counts but powerlessness does not, and why sensibilities are better protected from offense than women are from exploitation; defines sexuality, and thus its violation and expropriation, more broadly than does state law; and questions why a body of law which has not in practice been able to tell rape from intercourse should, without further guidance, be entrusted with telling pornography from anything less. Taking the work "as a whole" ignores that which the victims of pornography have long known: Legitimate settings diminish the injury perceived to be done to those whose trivialization and objectification it contextualizes. Besides, and this is a heavy one, if a woman is subjected, why should it matter that the work has other value? Maybe what redeems the work's value is what enhances its injury to women, not to mention that existing standards of literature, art, science, and politics, examined in a feminist light, are remarkably consonant with pornography's mode, meaning, and message. And finally—first and foremost, actually—although the subject of these materials is overwhelmingly women, their contents almost entirely comprised of women's bodies, our invisibility has been such, our equation as a sex *with* sex has been such, that the law of obscenity has never even considered pornography a woman's issue.

Obscenity, in this light, is a moral idea; an idea about judgments of good and bad. Pornography, by contrast, is a political practice, a practice of power and powerlessness. Obscenity is ideational and abstract; pornography is concrete and substantive. The two concepts represent two entirely different things. Nudity, excess of candor, arousal or excitement, prurient appeal, illegality of the acts depicted, and unnaturalness or perversion are all qualities that bother obscenity law when sex is depicted or portrayed. Sex forced on real women so that it can be sold at a profit to be forced on other real women; women's bodies trussed and maimed and raped and made into things to be hurt and obtained and accessed and this presented as the nature of women in a way that is acted on and acted out over and over; the coercion that is visible and the coercion that has become invisible—this and more bothers feminists about pornography. Obscenity as such probably does little harm. Pornography is integral to attitudes and behaviors of violence and discrimination which define the treatment and status of half the population.

At the request of the city of Minneapolis, Andrea Dworkin and I conceived and designed a local human rights ordinance in accordance with our approach to the pornography issue. We define pornography as a practice of sex discrimination, a violation of women's civil rights, the opposite of sexual equality. Its point is to hold accountable, to those who are injured, those who profit from and benefit from that injury. It means that women's injury—our damage, our pain, our enforced inferiority—should outweigh their pleasure and their profits, or sex equality is meaningless.

We define pornography as the graphic sexually explicit subordination of women through pictures or words that also includes women dehumanized as sexual objects, things, or commodities, enjoying pain or humiliation or rape, being tied up, cut up, mutilated, bruised, or physically hurt, in postures of sexual submission or servility or display, reduced to body parts, penetrated by objects or animals, or presented in scenarios of degradation, injury, torture, shown as filthy or inferior, bleeding, bruised, or hurt in a context that makes these conditions sexual. Erotica, defined by distinction as not this, might be sexually explicit materials premised on equality. We also provide that the use of men, children or transsexuals in the place of women is pornography. The definition is substantive in that it is sex-specific, but it covers everyone in a sex-specific way, so is gender neutral in overall design.

......

This law aspires to guarantee women's rights consistent with the first amendment by making visible a conflict of rights between the equality guaranteed to all women and what, in some legal sense, is now the freedom of the pornographers to make and sell, and their consumers to have access to, the materials this ordinance defines. Judicial resolution of this conflict, if they do for women what they have done for others, is likely to entail a balancing of the rights of women arguing that our lives and opportunities, including our freedom of speech and action, are constrained by—and in many cases, flatly precluded by, in, and through—pornography, against those who argue that the pornography is harmless, or harmful only in part but not in the whole of the definition; or that it is more important to preserve the pornography than it is to prevent or remedy whatever harm it does.

In predicting how a court would balance these interests, it is important to understand that this ordinance cannot now be said to be either conclusively legal or illegal under existing law or precedent, although I think the weight of authority is on our side. This ordinance enunciates a new form of the previously recognized governmental interest in sex equality. Many laws make sex equality a governmental interest. Our law is designed to further the equality of the sexes, to help make sex equality real. Pornography is a practice of discrimination on the basis of sex, on one level because of its role in creating and maintaining sex as a basis for discrimination. It harms many women one at a time and helps keep all women in an inferior status by defining our subordination as our sexuality and equating that with our gender. It is also sex discrimination because its victims, including men, are selected for victimization on the basis of their gender. But for their sex, they would not be so treated.

The harm of pornography, broadly speaking, is the harm of the civil inequality of the sexes made invisible as harm because it has become accepted as the sex difference. Consider this analogy with race: If you see Black people as different, there is no harm to segregation; it is merely a recognition of that difference. To neutral principles, separate but equal was equal. The injury of racial separation to Blacks arises "solely because [they] choose to put that construction upon it." Epistemologically translated: How you see it is not the way it is. Similarly, if you see women as just different, even or especially if you don't know that you do, subordination will not look like subordination at all, much less like harm. It will merely look like an appropriate recognition of the sex difference.

Pornography does treat the sexes differently, so the case for sex differentiation can be made here. Men as a group do not tend to be (although some individuals may be) treated like women are treated in pornography. But as a social group, men are not hurt by pornography the way women as a social group are. Their social status is not defined as *less* by it. So the major argument does not turn on mistaken differentiation, particularly since women's treatment according to pornography's dictates makes it all too often accurate. The salient quality of a distinction between the top and the bottom in a hierarchy is not difference, although top is certainly different from bottom; it is power. So the major argument is: Subordinate but equal is not equal.

Particularly since this is a new legal theory, a new law, and "new" facts, perhaps the situation of women it newly exposes deserves to be considered on its own terms. Not to mention, why the problems of fifty-three percent of the population have to look like somebody else's problems before they can be recognized as existing, but then can't be addressed if they do look like other people's problems, about which something might have to be done

if something is done about these, is a construction of things that truly deserves inquiry. Limiting the justification for this law to the situation of women would serve to limit the precedential value of a favorable ruling. Its particularity to one side, the *approach to* the injury is supported by a whole array of prior decisions that have justified exceptions to first amendment guarantees, when something that matters is seen to be directly at stake. What unites many cases where speech interests are raised and implicated but not, on balance, protected, is harm, harm that counts. In some existing exceptions, the definitions are much more open-ended than ours. In some, the sanctions are more severe, or potentially more so. For instance, ours is a civil law; most others are criminal, although not all.

Almost none show as many people directly affected. Evidence of harm in other cases tends to be vastly less concrete and more conjectural, which is not to say that there is necessarily less of it. None of the previous cases addresses a problem of this scope or magnitude—for instance, an $8 billion a year industry. Nor do other cases address an abuse, the practice of which has such widespread legitimacy. Courts have seen harm in other cases. The question is, will they see it here, especially given that the pornographers got there first. I will confine myself here to arguing from cases on harm to people, on the supposition that, the pornographers notwithstanding, women are not flags.

· · · · ·

To reach the magnitude of this problem on the scale it exists, our law makes trafficking in pornography—production, sale, exhibition, or distribution—actionable. Under the obscenity rubric, much legal and psychological scholarship has centered on a search for the elusive link between pornography defined as obscenity and harm. They have looked high and low—in the mind of the male consumer, in society or in its "moral fabric," in correlations between variations in levels of anti-social acts and liberalization of obscenity laws. The only harm they have found has been one they have attributed to "the social interest in order and morality." Until recently, no one looked very persistently for harm to women, particularly harm to women through men.

The rather obvious fact that the sexes *relate* has been overlooked in the inquiry into the male consumer and his mind. The pornography doesn't just drop out of the sky, go into his head and stop there. Specifically, men rape, batter, prostitute, molest, and sexually harass women. Under conditions of inequality, they also hire, fire, promote, and grade women, decide how much or whether or not we are worth paying and for what, define and approve and disapprove of women in ways that count, that determine our lives.

If women are not just born to be sexually used, the fact that we are seen and treated as though that is what we are born for becomes something in need of explanation. If we see that men relate to women in a pattern of who they see women as being, and that forms a pattern of inequality, it becomes important to ask where that view came from or, minimally, how it is perpetuated or escalated. Asking this requires asking different questions about pornography than the ones obscenity law made salient.

Now I'm going to talk about causality in its narrowest sense. Recent experimental research on pornography shows that the materials covered by our definition cause measurable harm to women through increasing men's attitudes and behaviors of discrimination in both violent and nonviolent forms. Exposure to some of the pornography in our definition increases normal men's immediately subsequent willingness to aggress against women under laboratory conditions. It makes normal men more closely resemble convicted rapists attitudinally, although as a group they don't look all that different from them to start with. It also significantly increases attitudinal measures known to correlate with rape and self-reports of aggressive acts, measures such as hostility toward women, propensity to rape, condoning rape, and predicting that one would rape or force sex on a woman if one knew one would not get caught. This latter measure, by the way, begins with rape at about a third of all men and moves to half with "forced sex."

As to that pornography covered by our definition in which normal research subjects seldom perceive violence, long-term exposure still makes them see women as more worthless, trivial, non-human, and object-like, i.e., the way those who are discriminated against are seen by those who discriminate

against them. Crucially, all pornography by our definition acts dynamically over time to diminish one's ability to distinguish sex from violence. The materials work behaviorally to diminish the capacity of both men and women to perceive that an account of a rape is an account of a rape. X-only materials, in which subjects perceive no force, also increase perceptions that a rape victim is worthless and decrease the perception she was harmed. The overall direction of current research suggests that the more expressly violent materials accomplish on less exposure what the less overtly violent—that is, the so-called "sex only materials"—accomplish over the longer term. Women are rendered fit for use and targeted for abuse. The only thing that the research cannot document is which individual women will be next on the list. (This cannot be documented experimentally because of ethics constraints on the researchers—constraints which do not operate in life.) Although the targeting is systematic on the basis of sex, it targets individuals at random. They are selected on the basis of roulette. Pornography can no longer be said to be just a mirror. It does not just reflect the world or some people's perceptions. It *moves* them. It increases attitudes that are lived out, circumscribing the status of half the population.

What the experimental data predict would happen, actually does happen in women's real lives. You know, it's fairly frustrating that women have known that these things do happen for some time. As Ed Donnerstein, an experimental researcher in this area, often puts it, "we just quantify the obvious." It is women, primarily, to whom the research results have been the obvious, because we live them. But not until a laboratory study predicts that these things *would* happen, do people begin to believe you when you say they *did* happen to you. There is no—*not any*—inconsistency between the patterns the laboratory studies predict and the data on what actually happens to real women. Show me an abuse of women in society, I'll show it to you made sex in the pornography. If you want to know who is being hurt in this society, go see what is being done and to whom in pornography and then go look for them other places in the world. You will find them being hurt in just that way. We did in our hearings.

In our hearings, women spoke, to my knowledge for the first time in history in public, about the damage pornography does to them. We learned that pornography is used to break women, to train women to sexual submission, to season women, to terrorize women, and to silence their dissent. It is this that has previously been termed "having no effect." Men inflict on women the sex that they experience through the pornography in a way that gives women no choice about seeing the pornography or doing the sex. Asked if anyone ever tried to inflict sex acts on them they did not want that they knew came from pornography, ten percent of women in a recent random study said yes. Twenty-four percent of married women said yes. That is a lot of women. A lot more don't know. Some of those who do testified in Minneapolis. One wife said of her ex-husband: "He would read from the pornography like a text book, like a journal. In fact when he asked me to be bound, when he finally convinced me to do it, he read in the magazine how to tie the knots.... Another woman said of her boyfriend: "[H]e went to this party, saw pornography, got an erection, got me...to inflict his erection on.... There is a direct causal relationship there." One women who said her husband had rape and bondage magazines all over the house, discovered two suitcases full of Barbie dolls with rope tied on their arms and legs and with tape across their mouths. Now think about the silence of women. She said, "He used to tie me up and he tried those things on me." A therapist in private practice reported:

> Presently or recently I have worked with clients who have been sodomized by broom handles, forced to have sex with over 20 dogs in the backseat of their car, tied up and then electrocuted on their genitals. These are children, [all] in the ages of 14 to 18, all of whom [have been directly affected by pornography,] [e]ither where the perpetrator has read the manuals and manuscripts at night and used these as recipe books by day or had the pornography present at the time of the sexual violence.

One woman, testifying that all the women in a group of ex-prostitutes were brought into prostitution as children through pornography, characterized their collective experience: "[I]n my experience there was not one situation where a client was not using pornography while he was using me or that he had not just watched pornography or that it was

verbally referred to and directed me to pornography." "Men," she continued, "witness the abuse of women in pornography constantly and if they can't engage in that behavior with their wives, girlfriends or children, they force a whore to do it."

Men also testified about how pornography hurts them. One young gay man who had seen *Playboy* and *Penthouse* as a child said of heterosexual pornography:

> It was one of the places I learned about sex and it showed me that sex was violence. What I saw there was a specific relationship between men and women.... [T]he woman was to be used, objectified, humiliated and hurt; the man was in a superior position, a position to be violent. In pornography I learned that what it meant to be sexual with a man or to be loved by a man was to accept his violence.

For this reason, when he was battered by his first lover, which he described as "one of the most profoundly destructive experiences of my life," he accepted it.

Pornography also hurts men's capacity to relate to women. One young man spoke about this in a way that connects pornography—not the prohibition on pornography—with fascism. He spoke of his struggle to repudiate the thrill of dominance, of his difficulty finding connection with a woman to whom he is close. He said:

> My point is that if women in a society filled by pornography must be wary for their physical selves, a man, even a man of good intentions, must be wary for his mind.... I do not want to be a mechanical, goose stepping follower of the Playboy bunny, because that is what I think it is...[T]hese are the experiments a master race perpetuates on those slated for extinction."

The woman he lives with is Jewish. There was a very brutal rape near their house. She was afraid; she tried to joke. It didn't work. "She was still afraid. And just as a well-meaning German was afraid in 1933, I am also very much afraid."

Pornography stimulates and reinforces, it does not cathect or mirror, the connection between one-sided freely available sexual access to women and masculine sexual excitement and sexual satisfaction. The catharsis hypothesis is fantasy. The fantasy theory is fantasy. Reality is: Pornography conditions male orgasm to female subordination. It tells men what sex means, what a real woman is, and codes them together in a way that is behaviorally reinforcing. This is a real five-dollar sentence but I'm going to say it anyway: Pornography is a set of hermeneutical equivalences that work on the epistemological level. Substantively, pornography defines the meaning of what a woman is by connecting access to her sexuality with masculinity through orgasm. The behavioral data show that what pornography means *is* what it does.

So far, opposition to our ordinance centers on the trafficking provision. This means not only that it is difficult to comprehend a group injury in a liberal culture—that what it *means* to be a woman is defined by this and that it is an injury for all women, even if not for all women equally. It is not only that the pornography has got to be accessible, which is the bottom line of virtually every objection to this law. It is also that power, as I said, is when you say something, it is taken for reality. If you talk about rape, it will be agreed that rape is awful. But rape is a conclusion. If a victim describes the facts of a rape, maybe she was asking for it, or enjoyed it, or at least consented to it, or the man might have thought she did, or maybe she had had sex before. It is now agreed that there is something wrong with sexual harassment. But describe what happened to you, and it may be trivial or personal or paranoid, or maybe you should have worn a bra that day. People are against discrimination. But describe the situation of a real woman, and they are not so sure she wasn't just unqualified. In law, all these disjunctions between women's perspective on our injuries and the standards we have to meet go under dignified legal rubrics like burdens of proof, credibility, defenses, elements of the crime, and so on. These standards all contain a definition of what a woman is in terms of what sex is and the low value placed on us through it. They reduce injuries done to us to authentic expressions of who we are. Our silence is written all over them. So is the pornography.

By contrast, we have as yet encountered comparatively little objection to the coercion, force, or assault provisions of our ordinance. I think that's partly because the people who make and approve laws may not yet see what they do as that. They *know*

they use the pornography as we have described it in this law, and our law defines that, the reality of pornography, as a harm to women. If they suspect that they might on occasion engage in or benefit from coercion or force or assault, they may think that the victims won't be able to prove it—and they're right. Women who charge men with sexual abuse are not believed. The pornographic view of them is: They want it; they all want it. When women bring charges of sexual assault, motives such as veniality or sexual repression must be invented, because we cannot really have been hurt. Under the trafficking provision, women's lack of credibility cannot be relied upon to negate the harm. There's no woman's story to destroy, no credibility-based decision on what happened. The hearings establish the harm. The definition sets the standard. The grounds of reality definition are authoritatively shifted. Pornography is bigotry, *period*. We are now—*in* the world pornography has decisively defined—having to meet the burden of proving, once and for all, for all of the rape and torture and battery, all of the sexual harassment, all of the child sexual abuse, all of the forced prostitution, *all* of it that the pornography is part of and that is part of the pornography, that the harm does happen and that when it happens it looks like this. Which may be why all this evidence never seems to be enough.

It is worth considering what evidence has been enough when other harms involving other purported speech interests have been allowed to be legislated against. By comparison to our trafficking section, analytically similar restrictions have been allowed under the first amendment, with a legislative basis far less massive, detailed, concrete, and conclusive. Our statutory language is more ordinary, objective, and precise, and covers a harm far narrower than its legislative record substantiates. Under *Miller,* obscenity was allowed to be made criminal in the name of the "danger of offending the sensibilities of unwilling recipients, or exposure to juveniles." Under our law, we have direct evidence of harm, not just a conjectural danger, that unwilling women in considerable numbers are not simply offended in their sensibilities, but are violated in their persons and restricted in their options. Obscenity law also suggests that the applicable standard for legal adequacy in measuring such connections may not be statistical certainty. The Supreme Court has said that it is not their job to resolve empirical uncertainties that underlie state obscenity legislation. Rather, it is for them to determine whether a legislature could reasonably have determined that a connection might exist between the prohibited material and harm of a kind in which the state has legitimate interest. Equality should be such an area. The Supreme Court recently recognized that prevention of sexual exploitation and abuse of children is, in their words, "a governmental objective of surpassing importance." This might also be the case for sexual exploitation and abuse of women, although I think a civil remedy is initially more appropriate to the goal of empowering adult women than a criminal prohibition would be.

Other rubrics provide further support for the argument that this law is narrowly tailored to further a legitimate governmental interest consistent with the interests underlying the first amendment. Exceptions to the first amendment—you may have gathered from this—exist. The reason they exist is that the harm done by some speech outweighs its expressive value, if any. In our law, a legislature recognizes that pornography, as defined and made actionable, undermines sex equality. One can say—and I have—that pornography is a causal factor in violations of women; one can also say that women will be violated so long as pornography exists; but one can also say simply that pornography violates women. Perhaps this is what the woman had in mind who testified at our hearings that whether or not pornography causes violent acts to be perpetrated against some women is not her only issue. "Porn is already a violent act against women. It is our mothers, our daughters, our sisters, and our wives that are for sale for pocket change at the newsstands in this country." *Chaplinsky v. New Hampshire* recognizes the ability to restrict as "fighting words" speech which, "by [its] very utterance inflicts injury…." Perhaps the only reason that pornography has not been "fighting words"—in the sense of words which by their utterance tend to incite immediate breach of the peace—is that women have seldom fought back, yet.

Some concerns close to those of this ordinance underlie group libel laws, although the differences are equally important. In group libel law, as Justice Frankfurter's opinion in *Beauharnais* illustrates, it has been understood that individuals' treatment and alternatives in life may depend as much on the reputation of the group to which such a person belongs as on their own merit. Not even a partial analogy can be made to group libel doctrine without examining the point made by Justice Brandeis, and recently underlined by Larry Tribe: Would more speech, rather than less, remedy the harm? In the end, the answer may be yes, but not under the abstract system of free speech, which only enhances the power of the pornographers while doing nothing substantively to guarantee the free speech of women, for which we need civil equality. The situation in which women presently find ourselves with respect to the pornography is one in which more *pornography* is inconsistent with rectifying or even counterbalancing its damage through speech, because so long as the pornography exists in the way it does there *will not be more speech by women*. Pornography strips and devastates women of credibility, from our accounts of sexual assault to our everyday reality of sexual subordination. We are deauthoritized and reduced and devalidated and silenced. Silenced here means that the purposes of the first amendment, premised upon conditions presumed and promoted by protecting free speech, do not pertain to women because they are not our conditions. Consider them: individual self-fulfillment—how does pornography promote our individual self-fulfillment? How does sexual inequality even permit it? Even if she can form words, who listens to a woman with a penis in her mouth? Facilitating consensus—to the extent pornography does so, it does so one-sidedly by silencing protest over the injustice of sexual subordination. Participation in civic life—central to Professor Meiklejohn's theory—how does pornography enhance women's participation in civic life? Anyone who cannot walk down the street or even lie down in her own bed without keeping her eyes cast down and her body clenched against assault is unlikely to have much to say about the issues of the day, still less will she become Tolstoy. Facilitating change—*this law* facilitates the change the existing first amendment theory has been used to throttle. Any system of freedom of expression that does not address a problem where the free speech of men silences the free speech of women, a real conflict between speech interests as well as between people, is not serious about securing freedom of expression in this country.

For those of you who still think pornography is only an idea, consider the possibility that obscenity law got one thing right. Pornography is more act-like than thought-like. The fact that pornography, in a feminist view, furthers the idea of the sexual inferiority of women, which is a political idea, doesn't make the pornography itself into a political idea. One can express the idea a practice embodies. That does not make that practice into an idea. Segregation expresses the idea of the inferiority of one group to another on the basis of race. That does not make segregation an idea. A sign that says "Whites Only" is only words. Is it therefore protected by the first amendment? Is it not an act, a practice, of segregation because of the inseparability of what it means from what it does? *Law* is only words.

The issue here is whether the fact that the central link in the cycle of abuse that I have connected is words and pictures will immunize that entire cycle, about which we cannot do anything without doing something about the pornography. As Justice Stewart said in *Ginsburg*, "When expression occurs in a setting where the capacity to make a choice is absent, government regulation of that expression may coexist with and *even implement* First Amendment guarantees." I would even go so far as to say that the pattern of evidence we have closely approaches Justice Douglas' requirement that "freedom of expression can be suppressed if, and to the extent that, it is so closely brigaded with illegal action as to be an inseparable part of it." Those of you who have been trying to separate the acts from the speech—that's an act, that's an act, there's a law against that act, regulate that act, don't touch the *speech—notice here* that the fact that the acts involved are illegal doesn't mean that the speech that is "brigaded with" it, *cannot* be regulated. It is when it *can* be.

I take one of two penultimate points from Andrea Dworkin, who has often said that pornography is not speech for women, it is the silence of women. Remember the mouth taped, the woman gagged, "Smile I can get a lot of money for that." The smile is not her expression. It is her silence, and it is not her expression not because it didn't happen, but because it *did* happen. The screams of the women in pornography are silence, like Kitty Genovese's screams, whose plight was misinterpreted by some onlookers as a lovers' quarrel. The flat expressionless voice of the woman in the New Bedford gang rape, testifying, is the silence of women. She was raped as men cheered and watched like they do in and with the pornography. When women resist and men say, "Like this you stupid bitch, here is how to do it" and shove their faces into the pornography, this "truth of sex" is the silence of women. When they say, "If you love me, you'll try," the enjoyment we fake, the enjoyment we learn, is silence. Women who submit because there is more dignity in it than in losing the fight over and over live in silence. Having to sleep with your publisher or director to get access to what men call speech is silence. Being humiliated on the basis of your appearance, whether by approval or disapproval, because you have to look a certain way for a certain job, whether you get the job or not, is silence. The absence of a woman's voice, everywhere that it cannot be heard, is silence. And anyone who thinks that what women say in pornography is women's speech—the "Fuck me, do it to me, harder," all of that—has never heard the sound of a woman's voice.

The most basic assumption underlying first amendment adjudication is that, socially, speech is free. The first amendment says Congress shall not abridge the freedom of speech. Free speech, get it, *exists*. Those who wrote the first amendment *had* speech—they wrote the Constitution. *Their* problem was to keep it free from the only power that realistically threatened it: the federal government. They designed the first amendment to prevent government from constraining that which if unconstrained by government was free, meaning *accessible to them*. At the same time, we can't tell much about the intent of the Framers with regard to the question of women's speech, because I don't think we crossed their minds. It is consistent with this analysis that their posture to freedom of speech tends to presuppose that whole segments of the population are not systematically silenced, socially, prior to government action. If everyone's power were equal to theirs, if this were a non-hierarchical society, that might make sense. But the place of pornography in the inequality of the sexes makes the assumption of equal power untrue.

This is a hard question. It involves risks. Classically, opposition to censorship has involved keeping government off the backs of people. Our law is about getting some people off the backs of other people. The risks that it will be misused have to be measured against the risks of the status quo. Women will never have that dignity, security,

Women and Pornography

RONALD DWORKIN

1

People once defended free speech to protect the rights of firebrands attacking government, or dissenters resisting an established church, or radicals campaigning for unpopular political causes. Free speech was plainly worth fighting for, and it still is in many parts of the world where these rights hardly exist. But in America now, free-speech partisans find themselves defending mainly racists shouting "nigger" or Nazis carrying swastikas or—most often—men looking at pictures of naked women with their legs spread open.

Conservatives have fought to outlaw pornography in the United States for a long time: for decades the Supreme Court has tried, though without much success, to define a limited category of "obscenity" that the Constitution allows to be banned. But the campaign for outlawing all forms of pornography has been given new and fiercer form, in recent years, by the feminist movement. It might seem odd that feminists have devoted such energy to that campaign: other issues, including abortion and the fight for women's equality in employment and politics, seem so much more important. No doubt mass culture is in various ways an obstacle to sexual equality, but the most popular forms of that culture—the view of women presented in soap operas and commercials, for example—are much greater obstacles to that equality than the dirty films watched by a small minority.

compensation that is the promise of equality so long as the pornography exists as it does now. The situation of women suggests that the urgent issue of our freedom of speech is not primarily the avoidance of state intervention as such, but getting affirmative access to speech for those to whom it has been denied.

But feminists' concentration on pornography nevertheless seems easy to explain. Pornographic photographs, films, and videos are the starkest possible expression of the idea feminists most loathe: that women exist principally to provide sexual service to men. Advertisements, soap operas, and popular fiction may actually do more to spread that idea in our culture, but pornography is the rawest, most explicit symbol of it. Like swastikas and burning crosses, pornography is deeply offensive in itself, whether or not it causes any other injustice or harm. It is also particularly vulnerable politically: the religious right supports feminists on this issue, though on few others, so feminists have a much greater chance to win political campaigns for censorship than any of the other campaigns they fight.

And pornography seems vulnerable on principle as well. The conventional explanation of why freedom of speech is important is Mill's theory that truth is most likely to emerge from a "marketplace" of ideas freely exchanged and debated. But most pornography makes no contribution at all to political or intellectual debate: it is preposterous to think that we are more likely to reach truth about anything at all because pornographic videos are available. So liberals defending a right to pornography find themselves

"Women and Pornography" by Ronald Dworkin in *The New York Review of Books*, vol. 40, no. 17, October 21, 1993. © The New York Review of Books.

triply on the defensive: their view is politically weak, deeply offensive to many women, and intellectually doubtful. Why, then, should we defend pornography? Why should we care if people can no longer watch films of people copulating for the camera, or of women being whipped and enjoying it? What would we lose, except a repellent industry?

Professor Catharine MacKinnon's new book of three short essays, *Only Words,* offers a sharp answer to the last of these questions: society would lose nothing if all pornography were banned, she says, except that women would lose their chains. MacKinnon is the most prominent of the feminists against pornography. She believes that men, want to subordinate women, to turn them into sexual devices, and that pornography is the weapon they use to achieve that result. In a series of highly charged articles and speeches, she has tried to talk or shock other women into that view. In 1986, she wrote that

> Pornography constructs what a woman is as what men want from sex. This is what pornography means.... It institutionalizes the sexuality of male supremacy, fusing the eroticization of dominance and submission with the social construction of male and female.... Pornography is a harm of male supremacy made difficult to see because of its pervasiveness, potency, and principally, because of its success in making the world a pornographic place.[1]

Only Words is full of language apparently intended to shock. It refers repeatedly to "penises slamming into vaginas," offers page after page of horrifying descriptions of women being whipped, tortured, and raped, and begins with this startling passage:

> You grow up with your father holding you down and covering your mouth so that another man can make a horrible, searing pain between your legs. When you are older, your husband ties you to the bed and drips hot wax on your nipples and brings in other men to watch and makes you smile through it. Your doctor will not give you drugs he has addicted you to unless you suck his penis.

The book offers arguments as well as images, however, and these are presented as a kind of appeal, to the general public, from a judicial decision MacKinnon lost. In 1983, she and a feminist colleague, Andrea Dworkin, drafted an ordinance that outlawed or attached civil penalties to all pornography, defined as the "graphic sexually explicit subordination of women through pictures and/or words" that meet one or more of a series of tests (some of which are impossibly vague) including: "women are presented dehumanized as sexual object, things, or commodities"; or "women are presented as sexual objects experiencing sexual pleasure in rape, incest, or other sexual assaults"; or "in positions of sexual submission, servility, or display"; or "women's body parts—including but not limited to vaginas, breasts, or buttocks—are exhibited such that women are reduced to those parts."

In 1984, largely through their efforts, a similar ordinance was adopted by the Indianapolis legislature. The ordinance included no exception for literary or artistic value, and it could plausibly be interpreted to outlaw not only classic pornography like John Cleland's *Memoirs of a Woman of Pleasure,* but a great deal else, including, for example, D.H. Lawrence's novels and Titian's *Danae.* In 1985, the Seventh Circuit Court of Appeals held the ordinance unconstitutional on the grounds that it violated the First Amendment's guarantees of free speech and press, and in 1986, the Supreme Court declined to overrule the Seventh Circuit's decision.[2]

Only Words offers several arguments in favor of the Indianapolis ordinance and against the Seventh Circuit's ruling, though some of these are run together and must be disentangled to make sense. Some of MacKinnon's arguments are old ones that I have already considered in these pages.[3] But she devotes most of the book to a different and striking claim. She argues that even if the publication of literature degrading to women is protected by the First Amendment, as the Seventh Circuit declared, such material offends another, competing constitutional value: the ideal of equality embedded in the equal protection clause of the Fourteenth Amendment, which declares that no state may deprive any person of the equal protection of the laws. If so, she says, then the courts must balance the two constitutional values, and since pornography contributes nothing of any importance to political debate, they should resolve the conflict in favor of equality and censorship.

Unlike MacKinnon's other arguments, this claim has application far beyond the issue of pornography. If her analysis is right, national and state governments have much broader constitutional powers than most lawyers think to prohibit or censor any "politically incorrect" expression that might reasonably be thought to sustain or exacerbate the unequal positions of women or of racial, ethnic, or other minorities. I shall therefore concentrate on this new argument, but I shall first comment briefly on MacKinnon's more conventional points.

2

In *Only Words,* she repeats the now familiar claim that pornography significantly increases the number of rapes and other sexual crimes. If that claim could be shown to be even probable, through reliable research, it would provide a very strong though not necessarily decisive argument for censorship. But in spite of MacKinnon's fervent declarations, no reputable study has concluded that pornography is a significant cause of sexual crime: many of them conclude, on the contrary, that the causes of violent personality lie mainly in childhood, before exposure to pornography can have had any effect, and that desire for pornography is a symptom rather than a cause of deviance.[4] MacKinnon tries to refute these studies, and it is important to see how weak her arguments are. One of them, though repeated several times, is only a metaphysical sleight-of-hand. She several times insists that pornography is not "only words" because it is a "reality." She says that because it is used to stimulate a sexual act—masturbation—it is sex, which seems to suggest that a film or description of rape is itself a kind of rape. But obviously that does not help to show that pornography causes rape in the criminal sense, and it is only the latter claim that can count as a reason for outlawing it.

Sometimes MacKinnon relies on breathtaking hyperbole disguised as common sense. "Sooner or later," she declares, "in one way or another, the consumers want to live out the pornography further in three dimensions. Sooner or later, in one way or another, they do. *It* does make them want to; when they believe they can, when they feel they can get away, *they* do." (Confronted with the fact that many men who read pornography commit no rapes, she suggests that their rapes are unreported.)[5] Elsewhere she appeals to doubtful and unexamined correlations: In a recent article, for example, she declares that "pornography saturated Yugoslavia

before the war," and suggests that pornography is therefore responsible for the horrifying and widely reported rapes of Croatian and Muslim women by Serbian soldiers.[6] But, as George Kennan has noted in these pages, rape was also "ubiquitous" in the Balkan wars of 1913, well before any "saturation" by pornography had begun.[7]

Her main arguments, however, are anecdotal: she cites examples of rapists and murderers who report themselves as having been consumers of pornography, like Thomas Shiro, who was sentenced to death in 1981 in Indiana for raping and then killing a young woman (and copulating with her corpse) and who pleaded that he was not responsible because he was a lifelong pornography reader. Such evidence is plainly unreliable, however, not just because it is so often selfserving, but because, as the feminists Deborah Cameron and Elizabeth Fraser have pointed out, criminals are likely to take their views about their own motives from the folklore of their community, whether it is sound or not, rather than from serious analysis of their motives. (Cameron and Fraser, who favor banning pornography on other grounds, concede that "arguments that pornography 'causes' violent acts are, indeed, inadequate.")[8]

MacKinnon's second argument for censorship is a radically different one: that pornography should be banned because it "silences" women by making it more difficult for them to speak and less likely that others will understand what they say. Because of pornography, she says,

> You learn that language does not belong to you.... You learn that speech is not what you say but what your abusers do to you.... You develop a self who is ingratiating and obsequious and imitative and aggressively passive and silent.[9]

In an earlier work she put the point even more graphically:

> Who listens to a woman with a penis in her mouth?...Anyone who cannot walk down the street or even lie down in her own bed without keeping her eyes cast down and her body clenched against assault is unlikely to have much to say about the issues of the day....Any system of freedom of expression that does not address a problem where

the free speech of men silences the free speech of women is…not serious about securing freedom of expression."[10]

On this view, which has been argued more elaborately by others,[11] it is women not pornographers who need First Amendment protection, because pornography humiliates or frightens them into silence and conditions men to misunderstand what they say. (It conditions them to think, for example—as some stupid judges have instructed juries in rape trials—that when a woman says no she sometimes means yes.) Because this argument cites the First Amendment as a reason for banning, not for protecting, pornography, it has the appeal of paradox. But it is premised on an unacceptable proposition: that the right to free speech includes a right to circumstances that encourage one to speak, and a right that others grasp and respect what one means to say.

These are obviously not rights that any society can recognize or enforce. Creationists, flat-earthers, and bigots, for example, are ridiculed in many parts of America now; that ridicule undoubtedly dampens the enthusiasm many of them have for speaking out and limits the attention others pay to what they say. Many political and constitutional theorists, it is true, insist that if freedom of speech is to have any value, it must include some right to the opportunity to speak: they say that a society in which only the rich enjoy access to newspapers, television, or other public media does not accord a genuine right to free speech. But it goes far beyond that to insist that freedom of speech includes not only opportunity to speak to the public but a guarantee of a sympathetic or even competent understanding of what one says.

MacKinnon's third argument centers on the production rather than the distribution or consumption of pornography: she argues that women who act in pornographic films suffer actual, direct sexual subordination, compounded by the fact that their degradation is recorded for posterity. She points out that some women are coerced or tricked into making pornographic films, and mentions the notorious "snuff" films which are said to record the actual murder of women. But of course all these crimes can be prosecuted without banning pornography, and, as MacKinnon herself concedes, it would be

wrong to "rely on the fact that some pornography is made through coercion as a legal basis for restricting all of it." Laws banning child pornography are indeed justified on the grounds that children may be damaged by appearing in pornographic films. But these laws, like many others that treat children differently, suppose that they are not competent to understand and consent to acts that may well be against their present and future interests.

It would plainly be a mistake to assume that women (or men) who appear in pornographic films do so unwillingly. Our economic system does, it is true, make it difficult for many women to find satisfactory, fulfilling employment, and may well encourage some of them to accept roles in pornographic films they would otherwise reject. The system, as MacKinnon grimly notes, works to the benefit of the pornographers. But it also works to the benefit of many other employers—fast-food chains, for example—who are able to employ women at low wages. There is great economic injustice in America, but that is no reason for depriving poor women of an economic opportunity some of them may prefer to the available alternatives.

I should mention a fourth consideration that MacKinnon puts forward, though it is difficult to find an argument in it. She says that much pornography is not just speech—it is not "only words"—because it produces erections in men and provides them with masturbatory fantasies. (She warns her readers never to "underestimate the power of an erection.") Her view of the psychology of sexual arousal is mechanical—she thinks men who read pornography "are sexually habituated to its kick, a process that is largely unconscious and works as primitive conditioning, with pictures and words as sexual stimuli." In any case, she thinks that pornography's physiological power deprives it of First Amendment protection: "An orgasm is not an argument," she says, "and cannot be argued with. Compared with a thought, it raises far less difficult speech issues, if it raises any at all." But that seems a plain non sequitur: a piece of music or a work of art or poetry does not lose whatever protection the First Amendment affords it when some people find it sexually arousing, even if that effect does not depend on its argumentative or aesthetic merits, or whether it has any such merits at all.

3

The continued popularity of bad arguments such as those in *Only Words* testifies to the strength of the real but hidden reason why so many people despise pornography and want to ban it. The sado-masochistic genre of pornography, particularly, is so comprehensibly degrading that we are appalled and shamed by its existence. Contrary to MacKinnon's view, almost all men, I think, are as disgusted by it as almost all women.

Because those who want to forbid pornography know that offensiveness alone does not justify censorship, however, they disguise their repulsion as concern that pornography will cause rape, or silence women, or harm the women who make it.

In the most interesting parts of *Only Words*, MacKinnon offers a new argument that is also designed to transcend mere repulsion. She says that the way in which pornography is offensive—that it portrays women as submissive victims who enjoy torture and mutilation—contributes to the unequal opportunities of women in American society, and therefore contradicts the values meant to be protected by the equal protection clause. She concedes, for the sake of this argument, that in spite of its minimal contribution to intellectual or political debate, pornography is protected under the First Amendment. But that First Amendment protection must be balanced, she says, against the Fourteenth Amendment's requirement that people be treated equally. "The law of equality and the law of freedom of speech are on a collision course in this country," she says, and she argues that the balance, which has swung too far toward liberty, must now be redressed.

The censorship of pornography, she says, should be regarded as like other kinds of government action designed to create genuine equality of opportunity. It is now accepted by almost everyone that government may properly prohibit discrimination against blacks and women in employment and education, for example. But such discrimination may take the form, not merely of refusing them jobs or university places, but of subjecting those who do manage to find jobs or places to an environment of insult and prejudice that makes work or education less attractive or even impossible. Government prohibits racial or sexual harassment at work—it punishes employers who subject blacks to racial insult or women to sexual pressures, in spite of the fact that these objectionable practices are carried out through speech—and many universities have adopted "speech codes" that prohibit racial insults in classrooms or on campus.

Banning or punishing pornography, MacKinnon suggests, should be regarded as a more general remedy of the same kind. If pornography contributes to the general subordination of women by picturing them as sexual or servile objects, as she believes it does, then eliminating pornography can also be defended as serving equality of opportunity even though it restricts liberty.[12] The "egalitarian" argument for censorship is in many ways like the "silencing" argument I described earlier: it supposes not that pornography significantly increases sexual crimes of violence, but that it works more insidiously to damage the standing and power of women within the community. But the "egalitarian" argument is in two ways different and apparently more cogent.

First, it claims not a new and paradoxical conflict within the idea of liberty, as the silencing argument does, but a conflict between liberty and equality, two ideals that many political philosophers think are often in conflict. Second, it is more limited in its scope. The "silencing" argument supposes that everyone—the bigot and the creationist as well the social reformer—has a right to whatever respectful attention on the part of others is necessary to encourage him to speak his mind and to guarantee that he will be correctly understood; and that is absurd. The "egalitarian" argument, on the contrary, supposes only that certain groups—those that are victims of persisting disadvantage in our society—should not be subjected to the kind of insult, harassment, or abuse that has contributed to that disadvantage.

But the "egalitarian" argument is nevertheless much broader and more dangerous in its scope than might first appear. The analogies MacKinnon proposes—to sexual harassment laws and university speech codes—are revealing, because though each of these forms of regulation might be said to serve a general egalitarian purpose, they are usually defended on much more limited and special grounds. Laws against sexual harassment are designed to protect women not from the diffuse effects of whatever derogatory opinions about them are part of the general culture, but from direct sexual taunts and other degrading language in the workplace.[13] University speech codes are defended on a different ground: they are said to serve an educational purpose by preserving the calm and reflective atmosphere of mutual respect and of appreciation for a diversity of cultures and opinions that is essential for effective teaching and research.

I do not mean that such regulations raise no problems about free speech. They do. Even if university speech codes, for example, are enforced fairly and scrupulously (and in the charged atmosphere of university politics they often are not) they sometimes force teachers and students to compromise or suppress their opinions by erring on the side of safety, and some speech codes may actually be unconstitutional. I mean only that constraints on speech at work and on the campus can be defended without appealing to the frightening principle that considerations of equality require that some people not be free to express their tastes or convictions or preferences anywhere. MacKinnon's argument for banning pornography from the community as a whole does presuppose this principle, however, and accepting her argument would therefore have devastating consequences.

Government could then forbid the graphic or visceral or emotionally charged expression of any opinion or conviction that might reasonably offend a disadvantaged group. It could outlaw performances of The Merchant of Venice, or films about professional women who neglect their children, or caricatures or parodies of homosexuals in nightclub routines. Courts would have to balance the value of such expression, as a contribution to public debate or learning, against the damage it might cause to the standing or sensibilities of its targets. MacKinnon thinks that pornography is different from other forms of discriminatory or hostile speech. But the argument she makes for banning it would apply to much else. She pointedly declares that freedom of speech is respected too much by Americans and that the Supreme Court was right in 1952 when it sustained a prosecution of anti-Semitic literature—a decision it has since abandoned[14]—and wrong in 1978 when it struck down an ordinance banning a Nazi march in Illinois.[15]

So if we must make the choice between liberty and equality that MacKinnon envisages—if the two constitutional values really are on a collision course—we should have to choose liberty because the alternative would be the despotism of thought-police.

But is she right that the two values do conflict in this way? Can we escape despotism only by cheating on the equality the Constitution also guarantees? The most fundamental egalitarian command of the Constitution is for equality throughout the political process. We can imagine some compromises of political equality that would plainly aid disadvantaged groups—it would undoubtedly aid blacks and women, for example, if citizens who have repeatedly expressed racist or sexist or bigoted views were denied the vote altogether. That would be unconstitutional, of course; the Constitution demands that everyone be permitted to play an equal part in the formal process of choosing a president, a Congress, and other officials, that no one be excluded on the ground that his opinions or tastes are too offensive or unreasonable or despicable to count.

Elections are not all there is to politics, however. Citizens play a continuing part in politics between elections, because informal public debate and argument influences what responsible officials—and officials anxious for re-election—will do. So the First Amendment contributes a great deal to political equality: it insists that just as no one may be excluded from the vote because his opinions are despicable, so no one may be denied the right to speak or write or broadcast because what he will say is too offensive to be heard.

That amendment serves other goals as well, of course: free speech helps to expose official stupidity and corruption, and it allows vigorous public debate that sometimes generates new ideas and refutes old ones. But the First Amendment's egalitarian role is independent of these other goals: it forbids censoring cranks or neo-Nazis not because anyone thinks that their contributions will prevent corruption or improve public debate, but just because equality demands that everyone, no matter how eccentric or despicable, have a chance to influence policies as well as elections. Of course it does not follow that government will in the end respect everyone's opinion equally, or that official decisions will be equally congenial to all groups.

Equality demands that everyone's opinion be given a chance for influence, not that anyone's opinion will triumph or even be represented in what government eventually does.

The First Amendment's egalitarian role is not confined, however, to political speech. People's lives are affected not just by their political environment—not just by what their presidents and legislators and other public officials do—but even more comprehensively by what we might call their moral environment. How others treat me—and my own sense of identity and self-respect—are determined in part by the mix of social conventions, opinions, tastes, convictions, prejudices, life styles, and cultures that flourish in the community in which I live. Liberals are sometimes accused of thinking that what people say or or think in private has no impact on anyone except themselves, and that is plainly wrong. Someone to whom religion is of fundamental importance, for example, will obviously lead a very different and perhaps more satisfying life in a community in which most other people share his convictions than in a dominant secular society of atheists for whom his beliefs are laughable superstitions. A woman who believes that explicit sexual material degrades her will likely lead a very different, and no doubt more satisfying, life among people who also despise pornography than in a community where others, including other women, think it liberating and fun.

Exactly because the moral environment in which we all live is in good part created by others, however, the question of who shall have the power to help shape that environment, and how, is of fundamental importance, though it is often neglected in political theory. Only one answer is consistent with the ideals of political equality: that no one may be prevented from influencing the shared moral environment, through his own private choices, tastes, opinions, and example, just because these tastes or opinions disgust those who have the power to shut him up or lock him up. Of course, the ways in which anyone may exercise that influence must be limited in order to protect the security and interests of others. People may not try to mold the moral climate by intimidating women with sexual demands or by burning a cross on a black family's lawn, or by refusing to hire women or blacks at all, or by

making their working conditions so humiliating as to be intolerable.

But we cannot count, among the kinds of interests that may be protected in this way, a right not to be insulted or damaged just by the fact that others have hostile or uncongenial tastes, or that they are free to express or indulge them in private. Recognizing that right would mean denying that some people—those whose tastes these are—have any right to participate in forming the moral environment at all. Of course it should go without saying that no one has a right to *succeed* in influencing others through his own private choices and tastes. Sexists and bigots have no right to live in a community whose ideology or culture is even partially sexist or bigoted: they have no right to any proportional representation for their odious views. In a genuinely egalitarian society, however, those views cannot be locked out, in advance, by criminal or civil law: they must instead be discredited by the disgust, outrage, and ridicule of other people.

MacKinnon's "egalitarian" argument for censorship is important mainly because it reveals the most important reason for resisting her suggestions, and also because it allows us to answer her charge that liberals who oppose her are crypto-pornographers themselves. She thinks that people who defend the right to pornography are acting out of self-interest, not principle—she says she has been driven to the conclusion that "speech *will* be defined so that men can have their pornography." That charge is based on the inadequacy of the conventional explanation, deriving from John Stuart Mill, that pornography must be protected so that truth may emerge. What is actually at stake in the argument about pornography, however, is not society's chance to discover truth, but its commitment to the very ideal of equality that MacKinnon thinks underrated in the American community. Liberals defend pornography, though most of them despise it, in order to defend a conception of the First Amendment that includes, as at least one of its purposes, protecting equality in the processes through which the moral as well as the political environment is formed. First Amendment liberty is not equality's enemy, but the other side of equality's coin.

MacKinnon is right to emphasize the connection between the fight over pornography and the larger, more general and important, argument about the freedom of Americans to say and teach what others think politically incorrect. She and her followers regard freedom of speech and thought as an elitist, inegalitarian ideal that has been of almost no value to women, blacks, and others without power; they say America would be better off if it demoted that ideal as many other nations have. But most of her constituents would be appalled if this denigration of freedom should escape from universities and other communities where their own values about political correctness are now popular and take root in the more general political culture. Local majorities may find homosexual art or feminist theater just as degrading to women as the kind of pornography MacKinnon hates, or radical or separatist black opinion just as inimical to racial justice as crude racist epithets.

That is an old liberal warning—as old as Voltaire—and many people have grown impatient with it. They are willing to take that chance, they say, to advance a program that seems overwhelmingly important now. Their impatience may prove fatal for that program rather than essential to it, however. If we abandon our traditional understanding of equality for a different one that allows a majority to define some people as too corrupt or offensive or radical to join in the informal moral life of the nation, we will have begun a process that ends, as it has in so many other parts of the world, in making equality something to be feared rather than celebrated, a mocking, "correct" euphemism for tyranny.

NOTES

1. Catharine MacKinnon, "Pornography, Civil Rights and Speech," reprinted in Catherine Itzin, editor, *Pornography: Women, Violence and Civil Liberties, A Radical View* (Oxford University Press, 1992), page 456. (Quotations are from 461–463.)
2. *American Booksellers Ass'n v. Hudnut, 771 F.2d 323 (1985), aff'd 475 US 1001 (1986).* In a decision that MacKinnon discusses at length, a Canadian court upheld a similar Canadian statute as consistent with that nation's Charter of Rights and Freedoms. I discuss that decision in "The Coming Battle over Free Speech," *The New York Review*, June 11, 1992.
3. "Two Concepts of Liberty," in *Isaiah Berlin: A Celebration*, edited by Edna and Avishai Margalit

(University of Chicago Press, 1991), and printed in *The New York Review of Books*, August 15, 1991.
4. Among the prestigious studies denying the causal link MacKinnon claims are the 1970 report of the National Commission on Obscenity and Pornography, appointed by Lyndon Johnson to consider the issue, the 1979 report of the Williams Commission in Britain, and a recent year-long British study which concluded that "the evidence does not point to pornography as a cause of deviant sexual orientation in offenders. Rather it seems to be used as part of that deviant sexual orientation." MacKinnon and other feminists cite the voluminous, two-volume report of the infamous Meese Commission, which was appointed by Reagan to contradict the findings of the earlier Johnson-appointed group and was headed by people who had made a career of opposing pornography. The Meese Commission duly declared that although the scientific evidence was inconclusive, it believed that pornography (vast tracts of which were faithfully reprinted in its report) did indeed cause crime. But the scientists on whose work the report relied protested, immediately after its publication, that the commission had misunderstood and misused their work. For a thorough analysis of all these and other studies, see Marcia Pally, *Sense and Censorship: The Vanity of Bonfires* (Americans for Constitutional Freedom, 1991). MacKinnon also appeals to legal authority: she says, citing the Seventh Circuit opinion holding her antipornography statute unconstitutional, that "not even courts equivocate over [pornography's] carnage anymore." But this is disingenuous: that opinion assumed that pornography is a significant cause of sexual crime only for the sake of the argument it made, and it cited, among other material, the Williams Commission report, as support for the Court's own denial of any such demonstrated causal connection.
5. In "Pornography, Civil Rights and Speech," MacKinnon said, "It does not make sense to assume that pornography has no role in rape simply because little about its use or effects distinguishes convicted rapists from other men, when we know that a lot of those other men *do* rape women; they just never get caught" (page 475).
6. "Turning Rape Into Pornography: Postmodern Genocide," *Ms.*, July/August 1993, p. 28.
7. "The Balkan Crisis: 1913 and 1993," *The New York Review*, July 15, 1993.

8. Catherine Itzin, editor, *Pornography: Women, Violence and Civil Liberties*, p. 359. At one point MacKinnon offers a surprisingly timid formulation of her causal thesis: she says that "there is no evidence that pornography does no harm." The same negative claim can be made, of course, about any genre of literature. Ted Bundy, the serial murderer who said he had read pornography since his youth, and whom feminists often cite for that remark, also said that he had studied Dostoevski's *Crime and Punishment*. Even MacKinnon's weak statement is controversial, moreover. Some psychologists have argued that pornography, by providing a harmless outlet for violent tendencies, may actually reduce the amount of such crime. See Patricia Gillian, "Therapeutic Uses of Obscenity," and other articles reprinted and cited in *Censorship and Obscenity*, edited by Rajeev Dhavan and Christie Davies (Rowman and Littlefield, 1978). And it is at least relevant that nations with the most permissive laws about pornography are among those with the least sexual crime, (see Marjorie Heins; *Sex, Sin, and Blasphemy*, New Press, 1993, p. 152) though of course that fact might be explained in other ways.

9. MacKinnon's frequent rhetorical use of "you" and "your," embracing all female readers, invites every woman to see herself as a victim of the appalling sexual crimes and the abuses she describes, and reinforces an implicit suggestion that women are, in pertinent ways, all alike: all passive, innocent, and subjugated.

10. Reprinted in Catherine Itzin, editor, *Pornography: Women, Violence and Civil Liberties*, p. 483–484.

11. See Frank L. Michelman, "Conceptions of Democracy in American Constitutional Argument: The Case of Pornography Regulation," *Tennessee Law Review* Vol. 56, No. 2. (1989), pp. 303–304.

12. Not all feminists agree that pornography contributes to the economic or social subordination of women. Linda Williams, for example, in the Fall, 1993 issue of the *Threepenny Review*, claims that "the very fact that today a variety of different pornographies are now on the scene in mass market videos is good for feminism, and that to return to the time of repressing pornographic sexual representations would mean the resurgence of at least some elements of an underground tradition…of misogyny."

13. See Barbara Presley Noble, "New Reminders on Harassment," *The New York Times*, August 15, 1993, p. 25.

14. *Beauharnais v. Illinois*, 343 US 250 (1952), abandoned in *New York Times* v. *Sullivan*, 376 US 254 (1964) at 268–269.

15. See *Smith* v. *Coffins*, 439 US 916 (1978).

Feminists Against the First Amendment

WENDY KAMINER

Despite efforts to redevelop it, New York's Forty-second Street retains its underground appeal, especially for consumers of pornography. What city officials call "sex-related uses"—triple-X video (formerly book) stores, peep shows, and topless bars—have declined in number since their heyday in the 1970s, and much of the block between Seventh and Eighth avenues is boarded up, a hostage to development. New sex businesses—yuppie topless bars and downscale lap-dancing joints (don't ask)—are prospering elsewhere in Manhattan. But Peepland (MULTIVIDEO BOOTHS! NUDE DANCING GIRLS!) still reigns, and Show World, a glitzy sex emporium, still anchors the west end of the block, right around the corner from The New York Times.

In the late 1970s I led groups of suburban women on tours through Show World and other Forty-second Street hot spots, exposing them, in the interests of consciousness-raising, to pornography's various genres: Nazi porn, nurse porn, lesbian porn, bondage porn—none of it terribly imaginative. The women didn't exactly hold hands as they ventured down the street with me, but they did stick close together; traveling en masse, they were not so conspicuous as individuals. With only a little less discomfort than resolve, they dutifully viewed the pornography.

This was in the early days of the feminist anti-porn movement, when legislative strategies against pornography were mere gleams in the eye of the feminist writer Andrea Dworkin, when it seemed possible to raise consciousness about pornography without arousing demands for censorship. That period of innocence did not last long. By 1981 the New Right had mounted a nationwide censorship campaign to purge schools and public libraries of sex education and other secular-humanist forms of "pornography." Sex education was "filth and perversion," Jerry Falwell announced in a fund-raising letter that included, under the label "Adults Only. Sexually Explicit Material," excerpts from a college health text. By the mid-1980s right-wing advocates of traditional family values had co-opted feminist anti-porn protests—or, at least, they'd co-opted feminist rhetoric. The feminist attorney and law professor Catharine MacKinnon characterized pornography as the active subordination of women, and Phyllis Schlafly wrote, "Pornography really should be defined as the degradation of women. Nearly all porn involves the use of women involves subordinate, degrading poses for the sexual, exploitative, and even sadistic and violent pleasures of men." Just like a feminist, Schlafly worried about how pornography might "affect a man who is already prone to violence against women." President Ronald Reagan deplored the link between pornography and violence against women.

PORNOGRAPHY AS SEX DISCRIMINATION

Of course, while feminists blamed patriarchy for pornography, moral majoritarians blamed feminism and other humanist rebellions. The alliance between feminists and the far right was not

ideological but political. In 1984 antiporn legislation devised by Andrea Dworkin and Catharine MacKinnon, defining pornography as a violation of women's civil rights, was introduced in the Indianapolis city council by an anti-ERA activist, passed with the support of the right, and signed into law by the Republican mayor, William Hudnut.

With the introduction of this bill, a new legislative front opened in the war against pornography, alienating civil-libertarian feminists from their more censorious sisters, while appealing to populist concerns about declining moral values. By calling for the censorship of pornography, some radical feminists found their way into the cultural mainstream—and onto the margins of First Amendment law.

The legislation adopted in Indianapolis offered a novel approach to prohibiting pornography which had all the force of a semantic distinction: pornography was not simply speech, Catharine MacKinnon suggested, but active sex discrimination, and was therefore not protected by the First Amendment. (In her 1989 book *Toward a Feminist Theory of the State*, MacKinnon characterized pornography as "a form of forced sex.") Regarding pornography as action, defining it broadly as any verbal or visual sexually explicit material (violent or not) that subordinates women, presuming that the mere existence of pornography oppresses women, the Indianapolis ordinance gave any woman offended by any arguably pornographic material the right to seek an order prohibiting it, along with damages for the harm it presumably caused. In other words, any woman customer browsing in a bookstore or patrolling one, glancing at a newsstand or a triple-X video store, was a potential plaintiff in a sex-discrimination suit. Given all the literature, films, and videos on the mass market that could be said to subordinate women, this ordinance would have created lots of new business for lawyers—but it did not stand. Within a year of its enactment the Dworkin-MacKinnon law was declared unconstitutional by a federal appeals court, in a decision affirmed by the U.S. Supreme Court.

The feminist anti-porn movement retreated from the legislative arena and passed out of public view in the late 1980s, only to re-emerge with renewed strength on college campuses. College professors following fashions in post-structuralism asserted that legal principles, like those protecting speech, were mere rhetorical power plays: without any objective, universal merit, prevailing legal ideals were simply those privileged by the mostly white male ruling class. The dominant poststructural dogma of the late 1980s denied the First Amendment the transcendent value that the liberal belief in a marketplace of ideas has always awarded it.

MASSACHUSETTS MISCHIEF

This unlikely convergence of first amendment critiques from multiculturalists, post-structuralists, and advocates of traditional family values, recently combined with high-profile rape and harassment cases and women's abiding concern with sexual violence, buoyed the feminist anti-porn movement. This year it re-emerged on the national and local scene with renewed legislative clout. The presumption that pornography oppresses women and is a direct cause of sexual violence is the basis for bills introduced in the U.S. Senate and the Massachusetts legislature. Last June the Senate Judiciary Committee passed the Pornography Victims' Compensation Act, which would make producers, distributors, exhibitors, and retailers convicted of disseminating material adjudged obscene liable for damages to victims of crimes who could claim that the material caused their victimization. The Massachusetts legislature held hearings on a much broader anti-porn bill, closely modeled on the Indianapolis ordinance. Disarmingly titled "An Act to Protect the Civil Rights of Women and Children," the Massachusetts bill would not only make purveyors of pornography liable for crimes committed by their customers; it would also allow any woman, whether or not she has been the victim of a crime, to sue the producers, distributors, exhibitors, or retailers of any sexually explicit visual material that subordinates women. (The exclusion of verbal "pornography" from the anti-trafficking provision would protect the likes of Norman Mailer, whom many feminists consider a pornographer, so long as his works are not adapted for the screen.) What this bill envisions is that the First Amendment would protect only that speech considered sexually correct.

The feminist case against pornography is based on the presumption that the link between pornography and sexual violence is clear, simple, and inexorable. The argument is familiar: censorship

campaigns always blame unwanted speech for unwanted behavior: Jerry Falwell once claimed that sex education causes teenage pregnancy, just as feminists claim that pornography causes rape. One objection to this assertion is that it gives rapists and batterers an excuse for their crimes, and perhaps even a "pornography made me do it" defense.

The claim that pornography causes rape greatly oversimplifies the problem of sexual violence. We can hardly say that were it not for pornography, there would be no rape or battering. As feminists opposed to anti-porn legislation have pointed out, countries in which commercial pornography is illegal—Saudi Arabia, for example—are hardly safe havens for women.

This is not to deny that there probably is some link between violence in the media and violence in real life, but it is complicated, variable, and difficult to measure. Not all hate speech is an incantation; not all men are held spellbound by pornography. Post-structural feminists who celebrate subjectivism should be among the first to admit that different people respond to the same images differently. All we can confidently claim is that the way women are imagined is likely to have a cumulative effect on the way they're treated, but that does not mean any single image is the clear and simple cause of any single act.

The Dworkin-MacKinnon bill, however, did more than assume that pornography causes sex discrimination and other crimes against women. It said that pornography is violence and discrimination: the active subordination of women (and it assumed that we can all agree on what constitutes subordination). MacKinnon and her followers deny that prohibiting pornography is censorship, because they effectively deny that pornography is speech—and that is simply Orwellian. The line between speech and behavior is sometimes blurred: dancing nude down a public street is one way of expressing yourself which may also be a form of disorderly conduct. But if pornography is sex discrimination, then an editorial criticizing the President is treason.

Most feminists concerned about pornography are probably not intent on suppressing political speech, but the legislation they support, like the Massachusetts anti-porn bill, is so broad, and its definition of pornography so subjective, that it would be likely to jeopardize sex educators and artists more than it would hard-core pornographers, who are used to operating outside the law. Feminist legislation makes no exception for "pornography" in which some might find redeeming social value; it could, for example, apply in the case of a woman disfigured by a man who had seen too many paintings by Willem de Kooning. "If a woman is subjected," Catharine MacKinnon writes, "why should it matter that the work has other value?"

With this exclusive focus on prohibiting material that reflects incorrect attitudes toward women, anti-porn feminists don't deny the chilling effect of censorship; they embrace it. Any speech that subordinates women—any pornography—is yelling "Fire!" in a crowded theater, they say, falling back on a legal canard. But that's true only if, just as all crowds are deemed potential mobs, all men are deemed potential abusers whose violent impulses are bound to be sparked by pornography. It needs to be said, by feminists, that efforts to censor pornography reflect a profound disdain for men. Catharine MacKinnon has written that "pornography works as a behavioral conditioner, reinforcer and stimulus, not as idea or advocacy. It is more like saying "kill" to a trained guard dog—and also the training process itself." That's more a theory of sexuality than of speech: pornography is action because all men are dogs on short leashes.

This bleak view of male sexuality condemns heterosexuality for women as an exercise in wish fulfillment (if only men weren't all dogs) or false consciousness (such as male-identified thinking). True feminism, according to MacKinnon, unlike liberal feminism, "sees sexuality as a social sphere of male power of which forced sex is paradigmatic." With varying degrees of clarity, MacKinnon and Dworkin suggest that in a context of pervasive, institutionalized inequality, there can be no consensual sex between men and women: we can never honestly distinguish rape from intercourse.

AN ESOTERIC DEBATE

A modified version of the message may well have particular appeal to some women today, who make up an important constituency for the anti-porn movement. In their late teens and early twenties, these women are still learning to cope with sexuality, in a violent and unquestionably misogynistic world. Feminism on campus tends to focus on

issues of sexuality, not of economic equity. Anxiety about date rape is intense, along with anxiety about harassment and hate speech. Understanding and appreciation of the First Amendment is a lot less evident and concern about employment discrimination seems somewhat remote. It's not hard to understand why: college women, in general, haven't experienced overt repression of opinions and ideas, or many problems in the workplace, but from childhood they've known what it is to fear rape. In the age of AIDS, the fear can be crippling.

Off campus the anti-porn feminist critique of male sexuality and heterosexuality for women has little appeal, but it is not widely known. MacKinnon's theoretical writings are impenetrable to readers who lack familiarity with poststructural jargon and the patience to decode sentences like this: "If objectivity is the epistemological stance of which women's sexual objectification is the social process, its imposition the paradigm of power in the male form, then the state will appear most relentless in imposing the male point of view when it comes closest to achieving its highest formal criterion of distanced aperspectivity." Dworkin is a much more accessible polemicist, but she is also much less visible outside feminist circles. Tailored, with an air of middle-class respectability and the authority of a law professor, MacKinnon looks far less scary to mainstream Americans than her theories about sexuality, which drive the anti-porn movement, might sound.

If anti-pornography crusades on the right reflect grassroots concern about changing sexual mores and the decline of the traditional family, anti-pornography crusades on the feminist left reflect the concerns and perceptions of an educated elite. In the battle for the moral high ground, anti-porn feminists claim to represent the interests of a racially diverse mixture of poor and working-class women who work in the pornography industry—and they probably do represent a few. But many sex-industry workers actively oppose anti-porn legislation (some feminists would say they've been brainwashed by patriarchy or actually coerced), and it's not at all clear that women who are abused in the making of pornography would be helped by forcing it deeper underground; working conditions in an illegal business are virtually impossible to police. It's hard to know how many other alleged victims of pornography feel represented by the anti-porn movement, and I know of no demographic study of the movement's active members.

Leaders of the feminist anti-porn movement, however, do seem more likely to emerge from academia and the professions than from the streets or battered-women's shelters. Debra Robbin, a former director of the New Bedford Women's Center, one of the first shelters in Massachusetts, doesn't believe that "women on the front lines," working with victims of sexual violence, will "put much energy into a fight against pornography." Activists don't have time: "They can barely leave their communities to go to the statehouses to fight for more funding." The poor and working-class women they serve would say, "Yeah, pornography is terrible, but I don't have food on my table." Carolin Ramsey, the executive director of the Massachusetts Coalition of Battered Women Service Groups, says that the pornography debate "doesn't have a lot to do with everyday life for me and the women I'm serving." She explains, "Violence in the home and the streets that directly threatens our lives and our families is more pressing than a movie. Keeping my kids away from drugs is more important than keeping them away from literature."

Ramsey is sympathetic to anti-porn feminists ("there's room in the movement for all of us"), and she believes that "violence in the media contributes to violence in real life." Still, she considers the pornography debate "esoteric" and "intellectual" and feels under no particular pressure from her constituents to take a stand against pornography.

If censoring pornography is the central feminist issue for Catharine MacKinnon, it is a peripheral issue for activists like Robbin and Ramsey. Robbin in particular does not believe that eliminating pornography would appreciably lessen the incidence of sexual abuse. David Adams, a co-founder and the executive director of Emerge, a Boston counseling center for male batterers, believes that only a minority of his clients (perhaps 10 to 20 percent) use hard-core pornography. He estimates that half may have substance-abuse problems, and adds that alcohol seems more directly involved in abuse than pornography. Adams agrees with feminists that pornography is degrading to women but does not support legislation regulating it, because "the

legislation couldn't work and would only open the door to censorship."

What might work instead? Emerge conducts programs in Boston and Cambridge public schools on violence, aimed at both victims and perpetrators. "There's a lot of violence in teen relationships," Adams observes. Debra Robbin wishes that women in the anti-porn movement would "channel their energies into funding battered women's shelters and rape-crisis centers."

Reforming the criminal-justice system is also a priority for many women concerned about sexual violence. Anti-stalking laws could protect many more women than raids on pornographic video stores are ever likely to; so could the efficient processing of cases against men who abuse women.

SENSATIONALISM AS AN ORGANIZING TOOL

Why do some women channel their energies into a fight against pornography? Antiporn legislation has the appeal of a quick fix, as Robbin notes. And, she adds, "there's notoriety to be gained from protesting pornography." The "harder work"—promoting awareness and understanding of sexual violence, changing the way children are socialized, and helping women victims of violence—is less sensationalist and less visible.

Sensationalism, however, is an organizing tool for antiporn feminists. If questions about the effects of pornography seem intellectual to some women involved in social-service work, the popular campaign against pornography is aggressively anti-intellectual. Although advocates of First Amendment freedoms are stuck with intellectual defenses of the marketplace of ideas, anti-porn feminists whip up support for their cause with pornographic slide shows comprising hard-core pictures of women being tortured, raped, and generally degraded. Many feminists are equally critical of the soft-core porn movies available at local video stores and on cable TV, arguing that the violence in pornography is often covert (and they include mainstream advertising images in their slide shows). But hard-core violence is what works on the crowd. Feminist rhetoric often plays on women's worst fears about men: "Pornography tells us that there but for the grace of God go us," Gail Dines, a sociology professor at Wheelock

College, exclaimed during her recent slide show at Harvard, as she presented photographs of women being brutalized.

Dines's porn show was SRO, its audience some three hundred undergraduates who winced and gasped at the awful slides and cheered when Dines pointed to a pornographic picture of a woman and said, "When I walk down the street, what they know about me is what they know about her!" She warned her mostly female audience that pornographers have "aggressively targeted college men." She seemed preoccupied with masturbation. Part of the problem of pornography, she suggested, is that men use it to masturbate, and "women weren't put on this world to facilitate masturbation." She advised a student concerned about the presence of Playboy in the college library that library collections of pornography aren't particularly worrisome, because men are not likely to masturbate in libraries.

In addition to condemnations of male sexuality, Dines offered questionable horror stories about pornography's atrocities, like this: Rape vans are roaming the streets of New York. Women are dragged into the vans and raped on camera; when their attackers sell the rape videos in commercial outlets, the women have no legal recourse.

A story like this is impossible to disprove (how do you prove a negative?), but it should probably not be taken at face value, as many students in Dines's audience seemed to take it. William Daly, the director of New York City's Office of Midtown Enforcement, which is responsible for monitoring the sex industry in New York, has never heard of rape vans; almost anything is possible on Forty-second Street, but he is skeptical that rape vans are a problem. Part of Dines's story, however, is simply untrue: under New York State privacy law, says Nan Hunter, a professor of law at Brooklyn Law School, women could seek damages for the sale of the rape videos, and also an injunction against their distribution.

It would be difficult even to raise questions about the accuracy of the rape-van story, however, in the highly emotional atmosphere of a slide show; you'd be accused of "not believing the women." Just as slides of bloody fetuses pre-empt rational debate about abortion, pornographic slide shows pre-empt argumentative questions and rational consideration of First Amendment freedoms, the probable effect of efforts to censor pornography, and the actual relationship between pornography and violence.

A PORNOGRAPHIC CULTURE

Does pornography cause violence against women, as some feminists claim? Maybe, in some cases, under some circumstances involving explicitly violent material. Readers interested in the social-science debate should see both the report of the Attorney General's Commission on Pornography, which found a link between pornography and violence against women, and the feminist writer Marcia Pally's "Sense and Censorship," published by Americans for Constitutional Freedom and the Freedom to Read Foundation. In addition to the equivocal social-science data, however, we have the testimony of women who claim to have been brutalized by male consumers of pornography. Anti-porn feminists generally characterize pornography as a "how to" literature on abusing women, which men are apparently helpless to resist. But evidence of this is mainly anecdotal: At a hearing last March on the anti-porn bill in the Massachusetts legislature, several women told awful, lurid tales of sexual abuse, said to have been inspired by pornography. Like a TV talk show, the Attorney General's commission presented testimony from pornography's alleged victims, which may or may not have been true. It's difficult to cross-examine a sobbing self-proclaimed victim; you either take her testimony at face value or you don't.

Still, many people don't need reliable, empirical evidence about a link between pornography and behavior to believe that one exists. When feminists talk about pornography, after all, they mean a wide range of mainstream media images—Calvin Klein ads, Brian De Palma films, and the endless stream of TV shows about serial rapist stranglers and housewives who moonlight as hookers. How could we not be affected by the routine barrage of images linking sex and violence and lingerie? The more broadly pornography is defined, the more compelling are assertions about its inevitable effect on behavior, but the harder it is to control. How do we isolate the effects of any particular piece of pornography if we live in a pornographic culture?

Narrowly drawn anti-porn legislation, which legislators are most likely to pass and judges most likely to uphold, would not begin to address the larger cultural problem of pornography. Feminists themselves usually claim publicly that they're intent on prohibiting only hard-core pornography, although on its face their legislation applies to a much broader range of material. But if you accept the feminist critique of sexism in the media, hard-core porn plays a relatively minor role in shaping attitudes and behavior. If feminists are right about pornography, it is a broad social problem, not a discrete legal one—that is, pornography is not a problem the law can readily solve, unless perhaps we suspend the First Amendment entirely and give feminists the power to police the mainstream media, the workplace, and the schools.

The likelihood that feminists would not be the ones to police Forty-second Street should anti-porn legislation pass is one reason that many feminists oppose the anti-porn campaign. If society is as sexist as Andrea Dworkin and Catharine MacKinnon claim, it is not about to adopt a feminist agenda when it sets out to censor pornography. The history of anti-porn campaigns in this country is partly a history of campaigns against reproductive choice and changing roles for men and women. The first federal obscenity legislation, known as the Comstock Law, passed in 1873, prohibited the mailing of not only dirty pictures but also contraceptives and information about abortion. Early in this century Margaret Sanger and the sex educator Mary Ware Dennett were prosecuted for obscenity violations. Recently the New Right campaign against socially undesirable literature has focused on sex education in public schools. Anti-porn activists on the right consider feminism and homosexuality (which they link) to be threats to traditional family life (which, in fact, they are). In Canada a landmark Supreme Court ruling this year which adopted a feminist argument against pornography was first used to prohibit distribution of a small lesbian magazine, which politically correct feminists would be careful to label erotica.

Gay and lesbian groups, as well as advocates of sex education and the usual array of feminist and nonfeminist civil libertarians, actively oppose anti-pornography legislation. Some state chapters of the National Organization for Women—New York, California, and Vermont—have taken strong anti-censorship stands, but at the national level NOW has not taken a position in the pornography debate. Its president, Patricia Ireland, would like to see pornography become socially unacceptable, "like smoking," but is wary of taking legal action against it, partly because she's wary of "giving people like Jesse Helms the power to decide what we read and see." But for major, national feminist organizations, like NOW and the NOW Legal Defense and Education Fund, the pornography debate is a minefield to be carefully avoided. Pornography is probably the most divisive issue feminists have faced since the first advocates of the ERA, in the 1920s, squared off against advocates of protective labor legislation for women. Feminists for and against anti-porn legislation are almost as bitterly divided as pro-choice activists and members of Operation Rescue.

Renewed concern about abortion rights may drain energy from the anti-porn movement. Feminists may awaken to the danger that anti-pornography laws will be used against sex educators and advocates of choice. (The imposition of a gag rule on family-planning clinics may have made some feminists more protective of the First Amendment.) Politicians courting women voters may find that anti-porn legislation alienates more feminists than it pleases. Still, censorship campaigns will always have considerable appeal. Like campaigns to reinstate the death penalty, they promise panaceas for profound social pathologies. They make their case by exploiting the wrenching anecdotal testimony of victims: politicians pushing the death penalty hold press conferences flanked by mothers of murdered children, just as feminists against pornography spotlight raped and battered women.

Rational argument is no match for highly emotional testimony. But it may be wishful thinking to believe that penalizing the production and distribution of hard-core pornography would have much effect on sexual violence. It would probably have little effect even on pornography, given the black market. It would, however, complicate campaigns to distribute information about AIDS, let alone condoms, in the public schools. It would distract us from the harder, less popular work of reforming sexual stereotypes and roles, and addressing actual instead of metaphorical instruments of violence. The promise of the anti-porn movement is the promise of a world in which almost no one can buy pornography and almost anyone can buy a gun.

ARGUMENT 19 ESSAY QUESTIONS

1. What are Dworkin's arguments against MacKinnon's view?
2. Do Dworkin and Kaminer successfully refute MacKinnon's case against pornography? Why or why not?
3. Are you more in agreement with MacKinnon or Dworkin and Kaminer? What are your reasons?

SUGGESTIONS FOR FURTHER READING

Ronald Dworkin, "Do We Have a Right to Pornography?" in *A Matter of Principle* (Boston: Harvard University Press, 1985).

Ann Garry, "Sex, Lies, and Pornography," in *Ethics in Practice*, 2nd ed., ed. Hugh LaFollette (Malden, MA: Blackwell, 2001).

Wendy McElroy, "A Feminist Defense of Pornography," in *Sexual Correctness: The Gender-Feminist Attack on Women* (Jefferson, NC: McFarland, 1996).

John Stuart Mill, Chapter I from *On Liberty* (1859).

President's Commission on Obscenity and Pornography, *Report of The Commission on Obscenity and Pornography* (Washington, D.C.: U.S. Government Printing Office, 1970).

United States Attorney General's Commission on Pornography, *Final Report* (Washington: U.S. Department of Justice, 1986).

Caroline West, "Pornography and Censorship," in *The Stanford Encyclopedia of Philosophy* (Fall 2008 edition), ed. Edward N. Zalta, http://plato.stanford.edu/entries/pornography-censorship/, (2 February 2009).

Mark R. Wicclair, "Feminism, Pornography, and Censorship," in *Social Ethics: Morality and Social Policy* (New York: McGraw-Hill, 2002), 233–239.

Ellen Willis, "Feminism, Moralism, and Pornography," in *Beginning to See the Light* (Hanover: Wesleyan University Press, 1992).

CHAPTER 10

Economic Justice: Health Care

In public and private life, in the cold workings of the state and in the common struggles of ordinary persons, questions of justice inexorably intrude. In its broadest sense, *justice* refers to people getting what is fair or what is their due. Justice that concerns the fair meting out of punishment for wrongdoing is known as *retributive justice*. In this sphere, some argue that justice is served only when people are punished for past wrongs, when they get their just deserts. Others insist that justice demands that people be punished not because they deserve punishment, but because the punishment will deter further unacceptable behavior. **Distributive justice** concerns the fair distribution of society's advantages and disadvantages: such things as jobs, income, taxes, rights, welfare aid, and—today's hotly debated social good—health care.

The problem of justice in health care arises because the current system for allocating it is widely believed to be not only unjust, but also ineffective and unsustainable. These concerns raise ethical questions of the most basic kind: To what are the less fortunate entitled, and what is society obligated to give? Are the needy due only the health care they can afford to buy for themselves, even if they can afford nothing? Or is society obligated to provide more? Is it obliged to provide everyone with access to health care regardless of ability to pay? Or is the claim on society's resources even stronger: do people have a right to health care? If so, to what exactly are they entitled? To a guarantee of a state of well-being equal to that of everyone else? To an equal share of health care resources? To the best health care available? Or to something more modest—a decent minimum amount of health care? And what, exactly, is a decent minimum?

The central issue is: who should get health care, who should provide it, and who should pay for it? In other words, what is just? In the painful, complicated task of dividing up society's health care resources (including medical treatment, disease prevention, emergency care, and public health measures), what does justice demand?

Whatever answer is devised, it must take into account some hard realities. No system can provide maximum health care for everyone; there are limits—sometimes severe—to what any system can provide. Costs restrict how much health care can be delivered and how much can be obtained, and they can rise rapidly enough to destroy the best-laid plans for fair access. Moreover, a society's finite resources must be allocated to satisfy many needs besides health care—education, defense, transportation, law enforcement, and others. Some kinds of health care can increase the well-being of more people to a greater degree than others, so considerations of efficiency will have to shape the allocation of resources. And somehow these quantitative factors must be reconciled with freedom of choice. In a free society, this value is paramount and cannot be entirely discarded for the sake of a more rational distribution of health care.

Most careful thinkers on the subject believe that a just apportioning of health care is possible. But how?

SYSTEM FAILURES

Almost everyone agrees that all citizens should somehow have access to health care. But many people go without. Health care is so expensive that few can afford it unless they have some type of health insurance, which is itself expensive—so expensive in fact that the high cost is the main reason for lack of coverage. In 2007, about 45 million people under the age of 65 were uninsured, and millions of those were children. Nearly a third of the under-65 population—almost 90 million people—had no health insurance for at least part of 2006 or 2007. The number of people without health insurance rose by almost 9 million from 2000 to 2006.[1]

The consequences of going without health coverage are just what you might expect. The uninsured are less likely than the insured to get needed medical treatment, prescription drugs, preventive tests (Pap smears and prostate exams, for example), and follow-up care when they do mange to see a doctor. Not surprisingly, researchers have estimated that the risk of death is 25 percent higher for the uninsured than the insured, resulting in about 18,000 more deaths in 2000 among those age 25 to 64.[2]

Traditionally most people under age 65 got health coverage as a benefit of employment, but a smaller percentage of them are now obtaining insurance this way—69 percent in 2000 down to 60 percent in 2007. Fewer employers are offering this benefit (one-third of companies do not), and even when they do, many employees are either not eligible for it or cannot afford to pay their portion of the insurance premium. Over 80 percent of the uninsured are members of families with full-time workers.[3]

People who are age 65 and older and some adults under 65 with permanent disabilities are covered by the public health insurance program known as Medicare. Medicare collects payroll taxes from workers during their employment years and provides coverage when they turn 65, paying many health care expenses, including physician and hospital services and prescription drugs. Medicaid, another publicly supported program, covers some under-65 low-income people, including children and the disabled. But coverage varies from state to state and, because of eligibility rules, does not extend to 37 percent of people below the federal poverty level. Together, all public health insurance programs—including Medicare, Medicaid, and other kinds of state insurance—cover 16 percent of people under age 65.[4]

[1] The Kaiser Commission on Medicaid and the Uninsured, *The Uninsured: A Primer*, The Kaiser Family Foundation, October 2007, http://www.kff.org/uninsured/7451.cfm (21 March 2008); The National Coalition on Health Care, "Health Insurance Coverage," 2008, http://www.nchc.org/facts/coverage.shtml (21 March 2008).
[2] Institute of Medicine, "Insuring America's Health: Principles and Recommendations," The National Academy Press, 2004, http://www.nap.edu/catalog.php?record_id=10874#toc (21 March 2008).
[3] The Kaiser Commission, *The Uninsured: A Primer*.
[4] Ibid.

FACTS AND FIGURES: **U.S. Health Care**

- In 2010, 49.1 million Americans had no health insurance—18.5 percent of people under age 65.
- Nearly 90 million were without health coverage for part of 2006 or 2007.
- About 77 percent of the uninsured were members of working families.
- In 2010, 20 percent of workers were uninsured.
- In 2010, there were nearly 8 million uninsured children—10 percent of all children.
- According to data published in 2007, per capita spending on health care in the United States was $6,102; in Canada, $3,326; and in the United Kingdom, $2,724.
- The average infant mortality in the U.S. was 7 deaths per 1,000 live births, higher than that of Canada, the United Kingdom, Western European nations, and many other developed countries.

- Almost half of the health care that people receive in the U.S. does not meet established standards of recommended care.

The Kaiser Commission on Medicaid and the Uninsured, "Health Insurance Coverage in America, 2007," The Kaiser Family Foundation, 6 February 2009, http://facts.kff.org/chartbook.aspx?cb=55 (20 February 2009); The National Coalition on Health Care, "Health Insurance Coverage," The National Coalition on Health Care, 2008, http://www.nchc.org/facts/coverage.shtml (21 March 2008); Organization for Economic Cooperation and Development, OECD Health Data 2007, July 2007, http://www.oecd.org (27 March 2008); E.A. McGlynn, et al, "The Quality of Health Care Delivered in the United States," *The New England Journal of Medicine*, 2003: 348(26): 2635–2645; S. Asch, et al, "Who Is at Greatest Risk for Receiving Poor-Quality Health Care?" *The New England Journal of Medicine*, 2006: 354(11): 1147–1156; United Nations, Department of Economic and Social Affairs, *World Population Prospects, the 2010 Revision* 28 June 2011 (23 February 2012).

Critics of the U.S. health care system point to discrepancies between the huge expenditures for health care and surprisingly low grades on standard measures of national health. According to recent data, the country's per capita spending on health care was $6,102—more than twice as much as the average amount spent by the richest nations in the world. (The list of the richest comprises thirty democracies in the Organization for Economic Cooperation and Development, including France, Germany, Switzerland, Denmark, Canada, the United Kingdom, Norway, and Japan.) The country coming closest to that level of spending was Luxembourg at $5,352; Canada spent $3,326; the United Kingdom, $2,724; and Japan, $2,358. Yet in the United States, life expectancy at birth (77.8 years) was lower than the average for the OECD countries (78.6 years) and lower than that of other economically advanced nations such as Canada, France, Japan, the United Kingdom, Switzerland, Iceland, Australia, and Spain. The infant mortality rate in the United States was also higher than the OECD average—6.8 deaths per 1,000 live births compared to 5.4. In fact, it was higher than the rate of any of the other developed countries.[5]

Though the United States spends more on health care than any other country, the quality of the care is not obviously better overall than that of other countries. The U.S. system outshines them in some ways, but lags behind in others. For example, it excels in the development and use of medical technologies and has lower wait times for nonemergency surgeries. But it also has higher death rates from medical errors and fewer physicians per capita, and Americans have more trouble getting treated on nights and weekends and

---

[5] Organization for Economic Cooperation and Development, *OECD Health Data 2007*, July 2007, http://www.oecd.org (27 March 2008).

obtaining same-day appointments with doctors.[6] Research shows that for almost half of the people who do receive care, that care is inadequate—that is, it does not meet established standards of recommended care.[7]

In the United States most health care is allocated through **managed care**, a system for providing care to a particular group of patients (members of the system) using regulatory restraints to control costs and increase efficiency. People who enroll in a managed care plan—such as a health maintenance organization (HMO) or a preferred provider organization (PPO)—get health care at discounted prices from the plan's network of providers (physicians, hospitals, etc.). Managed care plans try to control costs by influencing the kind and amount of care that providers offer and by restricting the choices that members have. Though cost control and efficiency are laudable goals, many critics worry that they are at odds with patient welfare. The concern is that for the sake of economical medicine, providers may cut corners, decide not to order necessary tests, pay less attention to patients' needs, or refuse to treat certain serious health problems. Some charge that managed care as it's currently practiced forces physicians to try to serve both the patient and organizational efficiency, an impossible task that weakens the patient's trust in the physician.

WHAT IS JUST?

Debates about ethical allocations of health care resources rely heavily on general theories of justice. To justify a particular scheme of allocation, philosophers, politicians, and others may appeal to a theory of justice, and those who criticize the scheme may do so by arguing against that underlying theory or by offering an alternative theory they believe to be superior. At the heart of any plausible justice theory is the principle that *equals should be treated equally*—that people should be treated the same unless there is a morally relevant reason for treating them differently. Disagreements among theorists have generally not been about the legitimacy of this principle, but about how it should be interpreted. Different theories of justice try to explain *in what respects* equals should be treated equally.

According to **libertarian theories of justice**, the benefits and burdens of society should be distributed through the fair workings of a free market and the exercise of liberty rights of noninterference. The role of government is to protect the rights of individuals to freely pursue their own interests in the economic marketplace without violations of their liberty through coercion, manipulation, or fraud. Government may use coercion, but only to preserve liberty. Beyond these protections, the government has no obligation to adjust the distribution of benefits and burdens among people; the distribution is the responsibility of free and autonomous individuals. People may have equal rights or equal worth, but that does not entitle them to an equal distribution of society's benefits. The government acts unjustly if it coercively redistributes those benefits.

On this view, no one has a right to health care, and a government program using tax dollars to provide universal health care or even health care only for low-income families

[6] Congressional Research Service, *CRS Report for Congress: U.S. Health Care Spending: Comparison with Other OECD Countries*, 17 September 2007.

[7] E. A. McGlynn, et al., "The Quality of Health Care Delivered in the United States," *New England Journal of Medicine*, 2003: 348(26): 2635–45; S. Asch, et al., "Who Is at Greatest Risk for Receiving Poor-Quality Health Care?" *New England Journal of Medicine*, 2006: 354(11): 1147–56.

would be unjust. Such a program would be a coercive violation of people's right to use their resources as they see fit. The libertarian would accept a system of health care only if it is freely endorsed and financed by those who participate in it. So health insurance acquired through free choice by a group of private citizens to meet their own health care needs is acceptable. State-supported health insurance financed by taxes is not. But none of this would rule out voluntary charity by well-off citizens to provide health care for the poor.

In **utilitarian theories of justice**, a just distribution of benefits and burdens is one that maximizes the net good (utility) for society. Some allocations (or principles of allocation) of society's resources are more beneficial overall than others, and these are what utilitarian justice demands. A utilitarian may grant some principles of allocation the status of rights—rules that can be enforced by society and that can override considerations of utility in specific situations. But the ultimate justification of the rules is utilitarian (actually, rule-utilitarian): consistently following the rules may maximize utility generally, although rule adherence in some instances may not produce a net good.

On a utilitarian view, a just allocation of health care can take several forms, depending on the facts about society's resources and needs and the likely effects of various allocation policies and programs. Thus, depending on calculations of net benefits, a utilitarian might endorse a system of universal health care insurance, or a qualified right to health

---

PUBLIC OPINION: Obtaining Adequate Health Care

"Overall, how would you rate the quality of health care in this country—as excellent, good, only fair, or poor?"

Excellent	Good	Only fair	Poor	Unsure
20%	39%	29%	11%	1%

"Overall, how would you rate health care coverage in this country—as excellent, good, only fair, or poor?"

Excellent	Good	Only fair	Poor	Unsure
6%	27%	41%	24%	2%

"Are you generally satisfied or dissatisfied with the total cost of health care in this country?"

Satisfied	Dissatisfied	Unsure
20%	78%	2%

"Which of these statements do you think best describes the U.S. health care system today? It is in a state of crisis. It has major problems. It has minor problems. OR, It does not have any problems."

State of Crisis	Major Problems	Minor Problems	No Problems	Unsure
16%	57%	24%	1%	1%

"Do you think it is the responsibility of the federal government to make sure all Americans have health care coverage, or is that not the responsibility of the federal government?"

Is	Is not	Unsure
50%	46%	4%

Gallup Poll. Nov. 3–6, 2011. N=1,012 adults nationwide. Margin of error ± 4

care, or a two-tiered plan (like the U.S. arrangement) in which government-supported health insurance is combined with the option of privately purchased health coverage for those who can afford it.

Egalitarian theories of justice affirm that important benefits and burdens of society should be distributed equally. To achieve greater equality, the egalitarian (unlike the libertarian) would not be averse to mandating changes to the distribution of society's goods or to interfering in the workings of a free market. And the egalitarian (unlike the utilitarian) would not allow utility to be the ultimate overriding consideration in a system of distribution. From egalitarian premises, theorists have derived several schemes for allocating health care, including systems that give equal access to all legitimate forms of health care, that offer a guaranteed minimal level of health care for everyone, or that provide care only to those most in need.

Between strict libertarian and egalitarian views of justice lie some theories that try to achieve a plausible fusion of both perspectives. With a nod toward libertarianism, these theories may exhibit a healthy respect for individual liberty and limit governmental interference in economic enterprises. But leaning toward egalitarianism, they may also mandate that the basic needs of the least well off citizens be met.

A RIGHT TO HEALTH CARE

No matter what theory of justice people accept, they are likely to agree that it would be good for everyone to have adequate health care, or that beneficence may justify society's providing health care to the neediest, or that making particular kinds of health care available to certain groups may produce a net benefit for society. But some assert a much stronger claim: people have a moral *right* to health care. A right is an entitlement, a bona fide claim, to something. A person's rights impose duties on others—either (1) duties not to interfere with that person's obtaining something or (2) duties to help that person in her efforts to get something. Rights entailing the former obligations are called negative rights; those entailing the latter are called positive rights. People who insist that an individual has a right to health care are referring to a positive right and are claiming that society has an obligation to provide that benefit in some way.

Libertarians are likely to deny that there is a right to health care, for generally they accept negative rights and disallow positive rights. Utilitarians can admit a right to health care, though it would be what some have called a *derivative right*, a rule ultimately justified by assessments of utility. Others, including egalitarians, can accommodate a right to health care and interpret it in the strong sense of being an entitlement that ultimately outweighs calculations of maximized utility.

A pivotal question that confronts every serious advocate of a moral right to health care is what health care resources it includes. Some have thought the right encompasses universal equal access to all available health care resources. But this arrangement is not technically or economically feasible; a right to health care, it seems, must have limits. Recognizing this, many have argued for a weaker right to a "decent minimum" level of health care. On this view, everyone would have access to a minimal, basic array of health care resources. This tier of care would be universally available, publically supported, and guaranteed for all in need. A second tier of additional health care services (elective or nonessential therapies, for example) would be available in the free marketplace for those who can afford them.

Allen Buchanan rejects the idea of a right to a decent minimum of care, but he understands its attractions:

> First, the notion that people have a right to a decent minimum or adequate level, rather than to *all* health care that produces any net benefit, clearly acknowledges that, because not all health care is of equal importance, allocational priorities must be set within health care and that resources must also be allocated to goods other than health care. Second, this [decent minimum] position is also consonant with the intuitively plausible conviction that our obligations to the less fortunate, although fundamental enough to be expressed in the language of rights, are nonetheless *not unlimited*. Third, the decent minimum is a floor beneath which no one should be allowed to fall, not a ceiling above which the better-off are prohibited from purchasing services if they wish.[8]

But the implications of the decent-minimum standard have been extremely difficult to specify in a plausible way. What is, after all, a *decent minimum* of health care? We may assume it includes such things as immunizations, annual physical exams, and "routine" medical care. Should it also include heart transplants, treatments for rare or orphan diseases, cosmetic surgery, expensive but marginally effective care for very elderly or dying patients, costly life-long therapies for mentally impaired persons who will never reach "normal" functioning?

Buchanan believes that although there is no right to a decent minimum of health care, there are good reasons for supposing that society should nevertheless provide the kind and amount of health care that a decent-minimum right would demand. That is, there is no individual right, but there may be a societal duty. Among these reasons are arguments that people have special rights (as opposed to universal rights) to health care—rights of restitution to certain groups for past wrongs, rights of compensation for "those who have suffered unjust harm or who have been unjustly exposed to health risks by the assignable actions of private individuals or corporations," and rights to health care for honorable service to society (for wounded soldiers, for instance). There are also prudential arguments, Buchanan says, such as that "the availability of certain basic forms of health care make for a more productive labor force or improve the fitness of the citizenry for national defense." Arguments for what he calls "enforced beneficence" can also be made out. To maximize the practical effect of our moral obligations of charity or beneficence regarding health care for those in need, "an enforced decent minimum principle is needed to achieve coordinated joint effort."[9] Thus, for example, the government could levy taxes to provide health care to the poor—not in the name of egalitarian justice, but for the sake of beneficence.

RATIONING
Rationing has been a dirty word in debates about health care, laden as it is with images of extreme measures of last resort for managing a dearth of resources. But in health care, rationing—in the broad sense of parceling out important limited goods—has always been

---

[8] Allen Buchanan, "Health-Care Delivery and Resource Allocation," in *Medical Ethics*, ed. Robert M. Veatch (Boston: Jones and Bartlett Publishers, 1997), 351.
[9] Ibid.

with us and probably always will be. People's health care needs are virtually boundless, yet the supply of health care resources is ever limited. So we ration: Medicare and Medicaid allot health care to the elderly and the poor; HMOs limit medical procedures, tests, and access to doctors to control costs; hospitals restrict the use of ICUs, cardiac surgical teams, emergency departments, hospital beds, and expensive drugs; organ transplants are doled out to the few because of shortages of useable organs; and the health care system as a whole rations a great deal of care by people's ability to pay for it.

Thus the tough choices of rationing fall hard upon us, and we are forced to ask: who should get what share of limited health care goods and services? In countless troubling instances, the question reduces to this: who should live and who must die? In nearly the same breath we have to ask: on what ethical grounds do we make these choices? The fundamental issue of the proper allocation of insufficient resources troubles several levels at once. It arises both on the scale of the total health care system (concerning what portion of society's resources should go to health care and how this allotment should be used—so-called *macroallocation*) and on the scale of individual patients and providers (regarding who should receive specific resources—known as *microallocation*).

Let's consider just a few of the smaller scale (microallocation) questions raised by one of our scarcest life-saving resources—organ transplants. Transplant operations are incredibly expensive, organs are in very short supply, and transplants are desperately needed by far more people than can be accommodated. The waiting list for transplants is long, and many die while marking time.

Rationing organ transplants is like dispensing a meager supply of air to desperate humans on an airless planet: thousands will live or die by the rules of distribution. Screening committees at transplant centers decide whether someone should be placed on the waiting list and what ranking they should receive. They use various criteria to make these decisions, some explicit, some informal or unspoken, some plausible (such as the patient's need and likelihood of benefit), and some controversial (such as ability to pay, social worthiness, and health habits).

But what criteria *should* be used? What rationing policy for transplants is morally justified? Many proposed criteria are utilitarian, concerned with maximizing benefits to the patient and society. Many are egalitarian, focusing on justice and the moral equality of persons. Some philosophers propose rationing policies that emphasize one or the other, while some try systematically to accommodate both.[10] No policy is completely satisfactory, but some seem to capture our moral intuitions better than others.

One utilitarian approach to rationing care to patients is to measure objectively the benefits that a treatment is likely to give each patient, then selectively treat particular patients or conditions to maximize total benefits. The objective measure of benefits that has often been used in such calculations is known as QALY, or quality-adjusted life year. One QALY is equivalent to one year of life in good health, and a year of life in poor health is equal to less than 1 QALY. The lower the quality of life for a person in poor health, the lower the QALY value. A transplant operation that allows a patient to live seven years without disability or suffering is worth 7 QALYs; if it results in the patient's living seven years burdened by severe pain, it is worth less than 7 QALYs. Thus QALYs gauge a treatment's impact by,

---

[10] I owe this distinction to Tom L. Beauchamp and James F. Childress, *Principles of Biomedical Ethics*, 5th ed. (New York: Oxford University Press, 2001), 264–65.

plausibly, trying to take into account both the length of life and its quality. Intuitively this seems right because both quality of life and length of life matter to people. Most would probably rather enjoy a few years of good health than suffer through many years of terrible illness or disability. Suppose, then, that three people are awaiting heart transplants, without which they will die within six months, and only two transplants are possible. Two of the potential recipients are young, so a transplant for either one of them would yield 10 QALYs. The third person is much older; a transplant for her would yield only 5 QALYs. So a transplant selection committee using the QALY standard alone would likely allocate the available transplants to the two younger patients, maximizing total benefits.

The utilitarian purpose behind using QALYs is to do the most good with the resources available. But critics have charged that relying on QALYs to allocate or ration health care can lead to morally unacceptable decisions. John Harris argues, for example, that QALYs discriminate against older people:

> Maximizing QALYs involves an implicit and comprehensive ageist bias. For saving the lives of younger people is, other things being equal, always likely to be productive of more QALYs than saving older people. Thus on the QALY arithmetic we always have a reason to prefer, for example, neonatal or paediatric care to all 'later' branches of medicine. This is because any calculation of the life-years generated for a particular patient by a particular therapy, must be based on the life expectancy of that patient. The older a patient is when treated, the fewer the life-years that can be achieved by the therapy.[11]

QALYs, he says, are also unfair to the disabled:

> Suppose for example that if an accident victim were treated, he would survive, but with paraplegia. This might always cash out at fewer QALYs than a condition which with treatment would give a patient perfect remission for about five years after which the patient would die. Suppose that both candidates wanted to go on living as long as they could and so both wanted, equally fervently, to be given the treatment that would save their lives. Is it clear that the candidate with most QALYs on offer should always and inevitably be the one to have priority? To judge so would be to count the paraplegic's desire to live the life that was available to him as of less value than his rival's.[12]

Harris and others contend that a crucial failing of QALYs is that these objective measurements cannot accommodate the subjective nature of people's assessments of the value of their own lives. A paraplegic may value his life and think its quality extremely high despite his disability. A perfectly healthy person may think her life miserable despite a lack of physical ailments. The subjective valuation seems to be the important one; the objective measurement seems to be beside the point.

Policies for rationing transplants to a particular group of patients generally try to take into account the probability of transplant success or the urgency of the patients' needs. Both factors can be morally relevant. Regarding the former, because transplants are a

---

[11] John Harris, "QALYfying the Value of Life," *Journal of Medical Ethics*, vol. 13:117–22, 1987.
[12] Ibid.

scarce resource, fairness seems to demand that they be given to those who are likely to benefit from them—otherwise the resource will be wasted, and people will be deprived of a treatment that could have saved them. Regarding the latter, giving transplants to those who cannot survive for much longer without them fulfills a duty to preserve lives.

Nevertheless some maintain that allocating resources in light of one of these considerations while disregarding the other is a mistake:

> For example, although heart-transplant surgeons sometimes list their patients as urgent priority candidates for an available heart because the patients will soon die if they do not receive a transplant, some of these patients are virtually certain to die even if they do receive the heart. High quality candidates are passed over in the process. A classification and queuing system that permits urgent need to determine priority exclusively is as unjust as it is inefficient.[13]

Neither probability of success nor urgent need seems to be as controversial as another kind of criterion: the *social value* of people's lives. Here the question is which potential recipients—if given the chance to live—are expected to contribute most to the good of society? To state the issue concretely: all things being equal, should the medical student get the transplant instead of the poet or the prostitute? Nicholas Rescher thinks this question of social utility important and morally relevant:

> In "choosing to save" one life rather than another, "the society," through the mediation of the particular medical institution in question—which should certainly look upon itself as a trustee for the social interest—is clearly warranted in considering the likely pattern of future *services to be rendered* by the patient (adequate recovery assumed), considering his age, talent, training, and past record of performance. In its allocations of [exotic life-saving therapy], society "invests" a scarce resource in one person as against another and is thus entitled to look to the probable prospective "return" on its investment.[14]

Others reject this line altogether, arguing from an egalitarian or Kantian perspective that all persons have equal worth. Morally, the medical student is not worth more than the poet or prostitute, and vice versa. Education, achievement, occupation, and the like are not morally relevant.

Nevertheless, while generally taking this view, some philosophers maintain that in very rare cases, social worth can outweigh egalitarian concerns. It seems reasonable that in a natural disaster involving mass casualties, injured physicians or nurses should be treated first if they can aid the other survivors. We can imagine analogous situations involving organ transplants, says Walter Glannon:

> Suppose that Nelson Mandela needed a liver transplant in 1992. This was the time when he was leading the transition from apartheid to democracy in South Africa. The transition turned out to be peaceful; but the political situation was potentially

---

[13] Tom L. Beauchamp and James F. Childress, *Principles of Biomedical Ethics*, 5th ed. (New York: Oxford University Press, 2001), 266.

[14] Nicholas Rescher, "The Allocation of Exotic Medical Lifesaving Therapy," *Ethics* 79 (April 1969).

volatile. Mandela was essential to maintaining social stability. Suppose further that a younger individual also needed a liver and would have at least as good an outcome with a transplant. In the light of the political and social circumstances, Mandela should have been given priority over the younger patient in receiving a liver. His survival would have ensured the social stability of the country. It would have ensured that many people would not suffer a loss of welfare or life from the social instability that might have resulted otherwise. Mandela's social worth was a function of the dependence of many people's welfare and lives on his survival. That worth would have been a decisive factor in giving the organ to him rather than to another person with the same need.[15]

KEY TERMS

distributive justice	egalitarian theories of justice
libertarian theories of justice	managed care
utilitarian theories of justice	

ARGUMENTS AND READINGS

---

20. DANIELS'S ARGUMENT FOR A RIGHT TO HEALTH CARE

The state should provide health care to people for the simple reason that they have a moral right to it. That, anyway, is a widely held view of the matter—and the conclusion of an influential argument.

In "Is There a Right to Health Care and, if so, What Does It Encompass?" Norman Daniels, taking an egalitarian path, asserts that a right to health care can be derived from one of the principles of justice articulated by John Rawls, specifically the right to "fair equality of opportunity."[16] Rawls maintains that everyone is entitled to an equal chance to obtain the basic goods of society, though there is no guarantee of an equal share of them (see Chapter 2). A just society would ensure equal opportunities to its citizens. Daniels argues that disease and disability diminish people's "normal species functioning" and thus restrict the range of opportunities open to them. But "health care in all its forms, whether public health or medical, preventive or acute or chronic, aims to keep people functioning as

---

[15] Walter Glannon, *Biomedical Ethics* (New York: Oxford University Press, 2005), 158–59.

[16] John Rawls, *A Theory of Justice*, rev. ed. (Cambridge: Harvard University Press, 1999).

close to normally as possible.... Health care thus preserves for us the range of opportunities we would have, were we not ill or disabled, given our talents and skills."[17] Since people are entitled to fair equality of opportunity, and adequate health care can protect or restore their normal range of opportunities, they have a positive right to adequate health care.

For Daniels, then, a right to health care is a positive right:

> [A] right to health care imposes an obligation on others to assist the right-bearers in obtaining needed and appropriate services. Specifically, claiming a right to health care includes these other claims: society has the duty to its members to allocate an adequate share of its total resources to health-related needs; society has the duty to provide a just allocation of different types of health care services, taking into account the competing claims of different types of health-care needs; each person is entitled to a fair share of such services, where a "fair share" includes an answer to the question, who should pay for the services? Health-care rights thus form a part of a broader family of positive "welfare" rights that includes rights to education and to income support.[18]

Daniels's argument has its detractors, especially among libertarian critics. H. Tristram Engelhardt, Jr., for example, declares that "A basic human secular moral right to health care does not exist—not even to a 'decent minimum of health care.'"[19] The very notion of such a right, he says, has major problems:

> The difficulty with supposed rights to health care, as well as with many claims regarding justice or fairness in access to health care, should be apparent. Since the secular moral authority for common action is derived from permission or consent, it is difficult (indeed, for a large-scale society, materially impossible) to gain moral legitimacy for the thoroughgoing imposition on health care of one among the many views of beneficence and justice. There are, after all, as many accounts of beneficence, justice, and fairness as there are major religions.
>
> Most significantly, there is a tension between the foundations of general secular morality and the various particular positive claims founded in particular visions of beneficence and justice. It is materially impossible both to respect the freedom of all and to achieve their long-range best interests.[20]

In his view, justice requires that we distinguish between losses that people suffer because of bad fortune and those due to unfairness. The former do not establish a duty of aid to the unfortunate (there is no moral right to such aid), but the latter may constitute claims on others. Out of compassion or benevolence, society may freely consent to help those in need, but there is no forced obligation to do so.

---

[17] Norman Daniels, "Is There a Right to Health Care and, If So, What Does It Encompass?" in *A Companion to Bioethics*, ed. Helga Kuhse and Peter Singer (Oxford: Blackwell Publishers, 1998), 316–25.

[18] Ibid.

[19] H. Tristram Engelhardt, Jr., *Foundations of Bioethics*, 2nd ed. (New York: Oxford University Press, 1996), 375–410.

[20] Ibid.

Is There a Right to Health Care and, if so, What Does It Encompass?

NORMAN DANIELS

IS THERE A RIGHT TO HEALTH CARE?

Legal vs Moral Rights to Health Care

One way to answer this question is to adopt the stance of legal positivists, who claim that there are no rights except those that are embodied in actual institutions through law. We would then be able to reply that in nearly every advanced industrial democracy in the world, there is a right to health care, since institutions exist in them that assure everyone access to needed services regardless of ability to pay. The notable exception is the United States, where many poor and near poor people have no insurance coverage for, and thus no assured access to, medically necessary services, although by law they cannot be denied emergency services.

The legal right to health care is embodied in a wide variety of types of health care systems. These range from national health services, where the government is the provider of services, as in Great Britain, to public insurance schemes, where the government finances services, as in Canada, to mixed public and private insurance schemes, as in Germany and the Netherlands. Despite these differences in the design of systems, there is a broad overlap in the scope or content of the legal right to health care in these countries. Most cover 'medically necessary' services, including a broad range of preventive, curative, rehabilitative and long-term care for physical and mental diseases, disorders and disabilities. Most exclude uses of medical technologies that enhance otherwise normal functioning or appearance, such as purely cosmetic surgery. The legal rights vary in significant ways, however, for example in the degree to which they cover new reproductive technologies, or in the types of mental health and long-term care services that are offered.

In the context of rising costs and the rapid dissemination of new technologies, there is growing debate in many countries about how to set limits on the scope of a right to health care. This debate about the scope of rights to health care pushes moral deliberation about such a right into the forefront, even where a legal right is recognized. Legal entitlements, most people believe, should reflect what society is morally obliged to provide by way of medical services. What, then, is the basis and scope of a moral right to health care?

Positive vs Negative Rights

A right to health care is a *positive* as opposed to a *negative* right. Put quite simply, a positive right requires others to do something beneficial or enabling for right-bearers, whereas a negative right requires others to refrain from doing something usually harmful or restrictive, to right-bearers. To say that others are required to do something or to refrain from doing something is to say they must so act or refrain even if they could produce more good or improve the world by not doing so (Thomson, 1990). For example, a negative right to free expression requires others to refrain from censuring the expression of the right-bearer even if censuring this speech would make a better world. Some public-health measures that protect people against interference with their health, such as environmental protections that protect people against polluters of air, water and food sources, might be construed as requirements of a negative right. More generally, however, a right to health care imposes an obligation on others to assist the right-bearers in obtaining needed and appropriate services. Specifically, claiming a right to health care includes these other claims: society has the duty to its members to allocate an adequate share of its total resources to health-related needs; society has the duty to provide a just allocation of different types of health care services, taking into account the

---

"Is There a Right to Health Care and, If So, What Does It Encompass?" by Norman Daniels in *A Companion to Bioethics*, ed. Helga Kuhse and Peter Singer, 316–325. Oxford: Blackwell Publishers, 1998.

competing claims of different types of health-care needs: each person is entitled to a fair share of such services, where a "fair share" includes an answer to the question, who should pay for the services? (Daniels, 1985). Health-care rights thus form a part of a broader family of positive "welfare" rights that includes rights to education and to income support. Because positive rights require other people to contribute their resources or skills to benefit right-bearers, rather than merely refraining from interfering with them, they have often been thought more difficult to justify than negative rights, and their scope and limits have been harder to characterize.

Theories of Justice and Rights to Health Care

If we are to think of a right to health care as a requirement of justice, then we should look to more general theories of justice as a way to specify the scope and limits of that right. On some theories of justice, however, there is little basis for requiring people to assist others by meeting their health care or other needs. Libertarians, for example, believe that fundamental rights to property, including rights to personal assets, such as talents and skills, are violated if society coerces individuals into providing "needed" resources or skills (Nozick, 1974). Libertarians generally recognize an "imperfect" duty to act beneficently or charitably, but this duty involves discretion. It can be discharged in different ways that are matters of choice. People denied charity have no right to it and have no complaint against people who act charitably in other ways. Though some have argued that the difficulty of coordinating the delivery of charitable assistance might justify coercive measures (Buchanan, 1984), and others have tried to show that even libertarians must recognize some forms of welfare rights (Sterba, 1985), most libertarians resist any weakening of the property rights at the core of their view (Brennan and Friedman, 1981).

A spectre sometimes raised by libertarians against the idea of a right to health care is that such a right is a "bottomless pit." Since new technologies continuously expand the scope of "medical needs," a right to health care would give rise to unlimited claims on the resources of others (Fried, 1969; Engelhardt, 1986). Protecting such an expansive

right to health care would thus not be compatible with the function of a libertarian 'minimal state' to assure the non-violation of rights to liberty and property.

Though there remains controversy about whether utilitarians can provide a basis for recognizing true moral rights, there are strong utilitarian arguments in favour of governments assuring access to at least some broad range of effective medical services. Preventing or curing disease or disability reduces suffering and enables people to function in ways that contribute to aggregate welfare. In addition, knowing that health-care services are available increases personal security and strengthens the ties of community. Utilitarians can also justify redistributing the burden of delivering these benefits to society as a whole, citing the decreasing marginal utility of money to support progressive financing of health-care services (Brandt, 1979).

Beneath these quite general arguments, however, there lies a more specific controversy about the scope of utilitarian entitlements to health care. There seems to be little utilitarian justification for investing resources in health care if those resources would produce more net welfare when invested in other things, yet many people believe they have moral obligations to assist others with their health-care needs even at a net cost in utility. For example, some highly expensive and effective medical treatments that most people believe should be offered to people might not be "cost beneficial" and thus not defensible on utilitarian grounds. Similarly, many forms of long-term care, especially for those who cannot be restored to productive social activity, are also difficult to defend on utilitarian grounds, yet we insist our health-care systems are obliged to provide such services.

Lack of moral acceptance of the distributive implications of utilitarianism makes many uncomfortable with the use of methods, such as cost-effectiveness analysis, that are intended to guide decisions about resource allocation in health care. For example, an assumption of cost-effectiveness analysis is that a unit of health benefit, such as a quality-adjusted life year (QALY), is of equal value or importance regardless of where it is distributed. But this assumption does not capture the concerns many people have about how much priority to give to the sickest patients, or when aggregating modest benefits to large numbers of people it outweighs the moral importance of delivering more significant benefits to fewer people (Nord, 1993; Daniels, 1993).

Two points about a utilitarian framework for a right to health care are worth noting. Recognizing a right to health care is compatible with recognizing limits on entitlements that result from resource scarcity and the fact that there are competing uses of those resources. Consequently, recognizing a right to health care need not open a bottomless pit. Second, just what entitlements to services follow from a right to health care cannot be specified outside the context of a *system* properly designed to deliver health care in a way that promotes aggregate utility. For the utilitarian, entitlements are *system-relative*. The same two points apply to other accounts of the foundations and limits of a right to health care.

Because many people reject the utilitarian rationales for health care (and other welfare) rights, theorists have explored other ways to ground such rights. Some claim that these rights are presupposed as enabling conditions for the exercise of other rights or liberties, or as practical presuppositions of all views of justice (Braybrooke, 1987) or as a way of avoiding vulnerability and exploitation (Goodin, 1988). One approach that has been developed in some detail views a right to health care as a special case of a right to equality of opportunity (Daniels, 1985). This approach shows how the most important contractarian theory of justice, Rawls' (1971) account of justice as fairness, can be extended to the problem of health care, since that theory gives prominence to a principle protecting equality of opportunity (Rawls, 1993). Without endorsing that account here, we shall use it to illustrate further the complexity surrounding the concept of a right to health care.

Equal Opportunity and a Right to Health Care

The central observation underlying this account of a right to health care is that disease and disability restrict the range of opportunities that would otherwise be open to individuals. This is true whether they shorten our lives or impair our ability to function, including through pain and suffering. Health care in all its forms, whether public health or medical, preventive or acute or chronic, aims to keep people functioning as close to normally as possible. Since we are complex social creatures, our normal functional capabilities include our capabilities for emotional and cognitive functioning and not just physical capabilities. Health care thus preserves for us the range of opportunities we would have, were we not ill or disabled, given our talents and skills.

The significant contribution health care makes to protecting the range of opportunities open to individuals is nevertheless *limited* in two important ways. It is *limited* because other things, such as the distribution of wealth and income and education, also profoundly affect equality of opportunity. It is also limited because health care, by restricting its aim to protecting normal functioning, leaves the normal distribution of talents and skills unmodified. It aims to help us function as 'normal' competitors, not strictly equal ones.

Some argue that an equal opportunity account of health care should abandon the limit set by a focus on normal functioning (see Arneson, 1988: G. A. Cohen, 1989; Sen, 1992). They claim our concerns about equality, including equality of opportunity, require us to use health-care technologies whenever doing so would equalize opportunity for welfare or equalize capabilities. For example, if through medical intervention we can 'enhance' the otherwise normal capabilities of those who are at a competitive disadvantage, then our commitment to equality of opportunity requires us to do so. Obviously, this version of an equal opportunity account would vastly expand the moral requirements on medicine, yielding a right to health care much more expansive than any now embodied in actual systems and, arguably, one that would make administration of a health-care system unwieldy (Sabin and Daniels, 1994).

This expansive version of the appeal to equal opportunity ignores an important fact about justice: our concern for equality must be reconciled with considerations of liberty and efficiency in arriving at the overall requirements of justice (see Sen, 1992; Cohen, 1995; Daniels, 1996). Such a reconciliation seems to underlie the limits we commonly accept when we appeal to equality of opportunity. We generally believe that rights to equal opportunity are violated only if unfair social practices or preventable or curable diseases or disabilities interfere with the pursuit of reasonable plans of life within our society by making us lose competitive advantage. We accept, however, the fact that the natural distribution of talents and skills, working in an efficient market for them, will both enhance the social product and lead to inequalities in social outcomes. A just society will try to mitigate the effects of these inequalities in competitive advantage in other ways than by eliminating all eliminable differences in capabilities. For example, on Rawls' account, transfers that make the worst off as well off as they can be mitigate the effects on equality of allowing the natural distribution of talents and skills to enhance productivity. In what follows, the account of a right to health care rests on a more limited appeal to equal opportunity, one that takes the maintenance of normal functioning as a reasonable limit.

WHAT DOES A RIGHT TO HEALTH CARE INCLUDE?

System-relative Entitlements

By making the right to health care a special case of rights to equality of opportunity, we arrive at a reasonable, albeit incomplete and imperfect, way of restricting its scope while still recognizing its importance. The account does not give individuals a basic right to have all of their health-care needs met. At the same time, there are social obligations to design a health-care system that protects opportunity through an appropriate set of health-care services. If social obligations to provide appropriate health care are not met, then individuals are definitely wronged. For example, if people are denied access—because of discrimination or inability to pay—to a basic tier of services adequate to protect normal functioning, injustice is done to them. If the basic tier available to people omits important categories of services without consideration of their effects on normal functioning, for example, whole categories of mental health or long-term care or preventive services, their rights are violated.

Still, not every medical need gives rise to an entitlement to services. The scope and limits of rights to health care, that is, the entitlements they actually carry with them, will be relative to certain facts about a given system. For example, a health-care system can protect opportunity only within the limits imposed by resource scarcity and technological development within a society. We cannot make a direct inference from the fact that an individual has a right to health care to the conclusion that this person is entitled to some specific health-care service, even if the service would meet a health-care need. Rather the individual is entitled to a specific service only if, in the light of facts about a society's technological capabilities and resource limitations, it should be a part of a system that appropriately protects fair equality of opportunity. The equal opportunity account of a right to health care, like the utilitarian account, makes entitlements to health care system-relative.

Effective Treatment of Disease and Disability

The health care we have strongest claim to is care that effectively promotes normal functioning by reducing the impact of disease and disability, thus protecting the range of opportunities that would otherwise be open to us. Just what counts as "effective," however? And what should we do about hard cases on the boundary between treatment of disease or disability and enhancement of capabilities?

It is a common feature of public and private insurance systems to limit care to treatments that are not "experimental" and have some "proven effectiveness." Unfortunately, many services that count as standard treatment have little direct evidence about outcomes to support their use (Hadorn, 1992). They are often just customary treatment. Furthermore, it is often controversial just when new treatments or technologies should count as "safe and efficacious." What counts as "reasonably effective" is then a matter of judgement and depends on the kind of condition and the consequences of not correcting it. We might, for example, want to lower our standards for effectiveness when we face a treatment of last resort, or raise them if resource scarcity is very great. On the other hand, we do not owe people a chance to obtain miracles through whatever unproven procedures they prefer to try.

By focusing a right to health care on the maintenance of normal functioning, a line is drawn between uses of medical technologies that count as legitimate "treatments" and those that we may want but which do not meet our "health-care needs." Although we may want medical services that can enhance our appearance, like cosmetic (as opposed to reconstructive) plastic surgery, or that can optimize our otherwise normal functioning, like some forms of counselling or some uses of Prozac, we do not truly need these services to maintain normal functioning. We are obliged to help others achieve normal functioning, but we do not "owe" each other whatever it takes to make us more beautiful or strong or completely happy (Daniels, 1985).

Though this line is widely used in both public and private insurance practices, it leaves us with hard cases. Some of the hardest issues involve reproductive technologies. Abortion, where there is no preventive or therapeutic need, does not count as 'treatment' because an unwanted pregnancy is not a disease or disability. Some nevertheless insist that requirements of justice, including a right to control one's body, means that non-therapeutic abortion should be included as an entitlement in a health-care system. Some national health-insurance schemes do not cover infertility services. Yet infertility is a departure from normal functioning, even if some people never want to bear children. Controversy may remain about how much social obligation we have to correct this form of impaired opportunity, especially where the costs of some interventions, such as *in vitro* fertilization, are high and their effectiveness is modest. Different societies will judge this question differently, in part because they may place different values on the rearing of biologically related children or on the experience of child-bearing.

Hard cases involve non-reproductive technologies as well. In the United States, for example, many insurers will cover growth hormone treatment only for children deficient in growth hormone, not for those who are equally short but without any pathology. Yet the children denied therapy will suffer just as much as those who are eligible. Similar difficulties are involved in drawing a line between covered and non-covered uses of mental health services (Sabin and Daniels, 1994). As in the cases of reproductive technologies, there is room for different societies to "construct"

the concept of mental disorder somewhat differently, with resulting variation in decisions about insurance coverage.

Rights and Limits on Effective Treatments

Even when some health-care service is reasonably effective at meeting a medical need, not all such needs are equally important. When a disease or disability has little impact on the range of opportunities open to someone, it is not as morally important to treat as other conditions that more seriously impair opportunity. The effect on opportunity thus gives us some guidance in thinking about resource allocation priorities.

Unfortunately, the impact on our range of opportunities gives only a crude and incomplete measure of the importance or priority we should give to a need or service. In making decisions about priorities for purposes of resource allocation in health care, we face difficult questions about distributive fairness that are not answered by this measure of importance. For example, we must sometimes make a choice between investing in a technology that delivers a significant benefit to few people or one that delivers a more modest benefit to a larger number of people. Sometimes we must make a choice between investing in a service that helps the sickest, most impaired patients or one that helps those whose functioning is less impaired. Sometimes we must decide between the fairness of giving a scarce resource to those who derive the largest benefit or giving a broader range of people some chance at getting a benefit. In all of these cases, we lack clear principles for deciding how to make our choices, and the account of a right to health care we are discussing does not provide those principles either (Daniels, 1993). Some methodologies, like cost-effectiveness analysis, are intended to help us make appropriate resource allocation decisions in these kinds of cases. But these methodologies may themselves embody controversial moral assumptions about distributive fairness. This means they cannot serve as decision procedures for making these choices and can at best serve as aids to decision-makers who must be explicit about the moral reasoning that determines the distributive choices they make (Gold et al., 1996).

In any health-care system, then, some choices will have to be made by a fair, publicly accountable, decision-making process. Just what constitutes a fair decision-making procedure for resolving moral disputes about health care entitlements is itself a matter of controversy. It is a problem that has been addressed little in the literature. Our rights are not violated, however, if the choices that are made through fair decision-making procedures turn out to be ones that do not happen to meet our personal needs, but instead meet needs of others that are judged more important (Daniels and Sabin, 1997).

How Equal Must Our Rights to Health Care Be?

How equal must our rights to health care be? Specifically, must everyone receive exactly the same kinds of health-care services and coverage, or is fairness in health care compatible with a 'tiered' system? Around the world, even countries that offer universal health insurance differ in their answers to this question. In Canada and Norway, for example, no supplementary insurance is permitted. Everyone is served solely by the national health-insurance schemes, though people who seek additional services or more rapid service may go elsewhere, as some Canadians do by crossing the border. In Britain, supplementary private insurance allows about 10 per cent of the population to gain quicker access to services for which there is extensive queuing in the public system. Basing a right to health care on an obligation to protect equality of opportunity is compatible with the sort of tiering the British have, but it does not require it, and it imposes some constraints on the kind of tiering allowed.

The primary social obligation is to assure everyone access to a tier of services that effectively promotes normal functioning and thus protects equality of opportunity. Since health care is not the only important good, resources to be invested in the basic tier are appropriately and reasonably limited, for example, by democratic decisions about how much to invest in education or job training as opposed to health care. Because of their very high "opportunity costs," there will be some beneficial medical services that it will be reasonable not to provide in the basic tier, or to

provide only on a limited basis, for example, with queuing. To say that these services have "high opportunity costs" means that providing them consumes resources that would produce greater health benefits and protect opportunity more if used in other ways.

In a society that permits significant income and wealth inequalities, some people will want to buy coverage for these additional services. Why not let them? After all, we allow people to use their after-tax income and wealth as they see fit to pursue the "quality of life" and opportunities they prefer. The rich can buy special security systems for their homes. They can buy safer cars. They can buy private schooling for their children. Why not allow them to buy supplementary health care for their families?

One objection to allowing a supplementary tier is that its existence might undermine the basic tier either economically or politically. It might attract better-quality providers away from the basic tier, or raise costs in the basic tier, reducing the ability of society to meet its social obligations. The supplementary tier might undermine political support for the basic tier, for example, by undercutting the social solidarity needed if people are to remain committed to protecting opportunity for all. These objections are serious, and where a supplementary tier undermines the basic tier in either way, economically or politically, priority must be given to protecting the basic tier. In principle, however, it seems possible to design a system in which the supplementary tier does not undermine the basic one. If that can be done, then a system that permits tiering avoids restricting liberty in ways that some find seriously objectionable.

A second objection is not to tiering itself but to the structure of inequality that results. Compare two scenarios. In one, most people are adequately served by the basic tier and only the best-off groups in society have the means and see the need to purchase supplementary insurance. That is the case in Great Britain. In the other, the basic tier serves only the poorest groups in society and most other people buy supplementary insurance. The Oregon plan to expand Medicaid eligibility partly through rationing the services it covers has aspects of this structure of inequality, since most people are covered by plans that avoid these restrictions (Daniels, 1991). The first scenario seems preferable to the second on grounds of fairness. In the second, the poorest groups can complain that they are left behind by others in society even in the protection of their health. In the first, the majority has less grounds for reasonable resentment or regret.

If the basic tier is not undermined by higher tiers, and if the structure of the inequality that results is not objectionable, then it is difficult to see why some tiering should not be allowed. There is a basic conflict here between concerns about equality and concerns about liberty, between wanting to make sure everyone is treated properly with regard to health care and wanting to give people the liberty to use their resources (after tax) to improve their lives as they see fit. In practice, the crucial constraint on the liberty we allow people seems to depend on the magnitude of the benefit available in the supplementary tier and unavailable in the basic tier. Highly visible forms of saving lives and improving function would be difficult to exclude from the basic tier while we make them available in a supplementary tier. In principle, however, some forms of tiering will not be unfair even when they involve medical benefits not available to everyone.

REFERENCES

Arneson, Richard (1988). Equality and equal opportunity for welfare. *Philosophical Studies*, 54. 79–95.

Brandt, Richard (1979). *A Theory of the Good and the Right*. Oxford: Oxford University Press.

Braybrooke, David (1987). *Meeting Needs*. Princeton, NJ: Princeton University Press.

Brennan, Geoffrey and Friedman, David (1981). A libertarian perspective on welfare. In Peter G. Brown, Conrad Johnson and Paul Vernier (eds). *Income Support: Conceptual and Policy Issues*. Totowa, NJ: Rowman and Littlefield.

Buchanan, Allen (1984). The right to a decent minimum of health care. *Philosophy and Public Affairs*, 13, 55–78.

Cohen, G. A. (1989). On the currency of egalitarian justice *Ethics*, 99, 906–44.

Cohen, Joshua (1995). Amartya Sen: Inequality Reexamined. *Journal of Philosophy*, 92/5, 275–88.

Daniels, M. (1985). *Just Health Care*. Cambridge: Cambridge University Press.

——— (1991). Is the Oregon rationing plan fair? *Journal of the American Medical Association*, 265, 2232–5.

——— (1993). Rationing fairly: programmatic considerations. *Bioethics*, 7, 224–33.

——— (1996). *Justice and Justification: Reflective Equilibrium in Theory and Practice*. Cambridge: Cambridge University Press.

Daniels, N. and Sabin, J. (1997). Limits to health care: fair procedures, democratic deliberation, and the legitimacy problem for insurers. *Philosophy and Public Affairs*, 26/4, 303–50.

Engelhardt, H. Tristram (1986). *The Foundations of Bioethics*. Oxford: Oxford University Press.

Fried, Charles (1969). *An Anatomy of Value*. Cambridge, MA: Harvard University Press.

Gold, Marthe, Siegel, Joanna, Russell, Louise and Weinstein, Milton (eds) (1996). *Cost-Effectiveness in Health and Medicine: Recommendations of the Panel on Cost-Effectiveness in Health and Medicine*. New York: Oxford University Press.

Goodin, Robert (1988). *Reasons for Welfare*. Princeton. NJ: Princeton University Press.

Hadorn, David (ed.) (1992). *Basic Benefits and Clinical Guidelines*. Boulder. CO: Westview Press.

Nord, Eric (1993). The relevance of health state alter treatment in prioritizing between different patients. *Journal of Medical Ethics*, 19, 37–42.

Nozick, R. (1974). *Anarchy, State, and Utopia*. New York: Basic Books.

Rawls, J. (1971). *A Theory of Justice*. Cambridge, MA: Harvard University Press.

——— (1993). *Political Liberalism*. New York: Columbia University Press.

Sabin, James and Daniels, Norman (1994). Determining 'medical necessity' in mental health practice. *Hastings Center Report*, 24/6, 5–13.

Sen, Amartya (1992). *Inequality Reexamined*. Cambridge, MA: Harvard University Press.

Sterba, James (1985). From liberty to welfare. *Social Theory and Practice*, 11, 285–305.

Thomson, Judith (1990). *The Realm of Rights*. Cambridge, MA: Harvard University Press.

The Right to a Decent Minimum of Health Care

ALLEN E. BUCHANAN

The force of the objections to the claim that there is an egalitarian right to health care helps to explain the popularity of the view that although there is a right to health care, it is a limited right, a right to a decent minimum or adequate level of care. Such a position has several attractions (President's Commission 1983, 20). First, the notion that people have a right to a decent minimum or adequate level, rather than to *all* health care that produces any net benefit, clearly acknowledges that, because not all health care is of equal importance, allocational priorities must be set within health care and that resources must also be allocated to goods other than health care. Second, this position is also consonant with the intuitively plausible conviction that our obligations to the less fortunate, although fundamental enough to be expressed in the language of rights, are nonetheless *not unlimited*. Third, the decent minimum is a floor beneath which no one should be allowed to fall, not a ceiling above which the better-off are prohibited from purchasing services if they wish. Thus, this position avoids the troublesome interferences with individual liberty, which an egalitarian right requires (President's Commission 1983, 20).

The chief objection to this way of understanding the right to health care is that it is virtually devoid of content. The chief import of the claim—that the right to health care is the right to a decent minimum or adequate level of care—is negative. It indicates only that neither a right to all care that is of any net benefit nor to only all technically possible care is appropriate. Beyond this cautionary function, little is conveyed, unless a reasonable way of filling out the content is supplied.

Although it acknowledges the inadequacies of various ad hoc proposals for specifying the adequate level of care, the President's Commission offers little by way of a concrete alternative. At one point, the report offers the apparently plausible suggestion that

the fundamental idea behind the notion of an adequate level is the belief that everyone is to have access to "...enough care to achieve sufficient welfare, opportunity, information, and evidence of interpersonal concern to facilitate a reasonably full and satisfying life" (President's Commission 1983, 20). Unfortunately, this statement, in effect, takes back much of what was said about the obligation being a limited one because some individuals are so badly off that enormous amounts of resources could be spent in attempting to ensure them of "... a reasonably full and satisfying life." Further, there may be considerable disagreement over what counts as a "reasonably full and satisfying life." This is simply the notion of quality of life that crops up elsewhere in medical ethics—a mask for sharply conflicting values.

In an attempt to provide practical content to the notion of a decent minimum of care while avoiding an unlimited obligation that would raise the specter of the black holes problem, Alan Gibbard has proposed a seemingly simple but ingenious hypothetical choice procedure or thought experiment (Gibbard 1983, 153–178). To determine which health-care services should be included in the decent minimum, Gibbard asks us to think of a person as choosing among different lifetime health-care insurance policies, each of which represents a different mix of preventive and curative services, medical and nonmedical services, and so forth. Because different persons would choose different policies tailored to their own particular health-care needs if they could predict them, it is necessary to impose a veil of ignorance—a set of informational constraints—upon the choosers. Gibbard suggests that it would be necessary to think of a person as

From "Health-Care Delivery and Resources Allocation" by Allen Buchanan in *Medical Ethics*, ed. Robert M. Veatch, 351–353. Boston: Jones and Bartlett Publishers, 1997.

choosing among policies before his or her own conception because, from conception on, our health-care prospects diverge. Granted this restriction, the rational choice of an insurance policy would be based on general statistical information about overall morbidity and mortality rates for one's society.

Before a determinate choice could be made, however, another parameter of the choice situation must be specified—the chooser must know his or her budget, what his or her total disposable wealth is. The choice of a particular health-care insurance policy will then depend not only on one's estimate of the comparative health-care benefits of the different policies, but also on how much one values the health-care benefits in question relative to benefits that could be obtained by using one's resources on goods and services other than health care.

The fundamental limitation on this strategy for specifying the ethically required decent minimum, of course, is not simply that it yields a determinate outcome if a fixed budget for the individual is assumed, but what that budget should be is itself an ethical question. Gibbard frankly acknowledges this when he describes his thought experiment as a way of giving content to the guaranteed decent minimum of health care once we know what the appropriate guaranteed income share is. In other words, until we know what individuals have a right to, by way of the allocation of income, we cannot determine how health-care resources ought to be allocated. So it seems that we have merely substituted the problem of specifying one kind of decent minimum for another. Further, there is also a problem of circularity—whether something is a fair income share (or an adequate level of income) depends on whether it would be sufficient for providing adequate levels of various important goods, including health care. Both these objections point to the conclusion that

the rational health-care insurance chooser approach cannot settle the most fundamental ethical issues concerning the allocation of health-care resources and fails to provide a fully satisfying response to the objection that the notion of a right to a decent minimum or adequate level of care is too vague to be of much practical value (Baily, 1986).

Indeed, once the problem of vagueness is appreciated, it may even become difficult to distinguish between the decent minimum view and the egalitarian view that its proponents reject. Those who believe that there is an egalitarian right to health care but who are not committed to across-the-board egalitarianism presumably hold that there is something special about health care that requires it to be distributed equally even if (some) other goods need not be. But if health care means all forms of health care, then this is a most implausible position, because, at best, only some of the most important forms of health care could have this special status. Consequently, the claim that there is an egalitarian right to health care should be understood as meaning that everyone is to have equal access to some especially important subset of health-care services and resources. Until these are specified, and until it is determined whether they exceed those included in a decent minimum, it will not be possible to distinguish between the egalitarian view and the decent minimum view. After all, the right to a decent minimum is an egalitarian right—everyone is to have equal access to whatever it is that constitutes the decent minimum. Without a clearer specification of what the decent minimum includes, it is possible to distinguish between it and the claim that there is an egalitarian right to health care only if the latter is taken in an unrestricted sense, as meaning that everyone is to have equal access to all beneficial forms of health care that anyone else is getting (assuming equal need).

ARGUMENT 20 ESSAY QUESTIONS

1. Does Daniels successfully establish a positive right to health care? Explain.
2. Does Buchanan agree with Daniels that there is a positive right to health care? Explain.
3. How does Buchanan try to establish that the government has a duty to provide a decent minimum of health care?

21. THE ARGUMENT FOR RATIONING BY MORAL WORTHINESS

What criteria would you use to decide who should get—and who should not get—scarce, expensive, life-saving organ transplants? In making your decision, would you consider not just medical factors but *moral* ones? That is, would you think it fair to decide the fate of transplant candidates by taking into account their moral worthiness? Some people would say yes. They argue, for example, that alcoholics who need liver transplants (because their heavy drinking caused severe liver damage) should be penalized for their condition or even automatically rejected as transplant candidates. These alcoholics, by their own bad behavior, caused their liver disease. They are therefore morally blameworthy and are less deserving of new livers than nonalcoholics.

On some views, this argument works even if alcoholism is, as several experts claim, a disease, not a moral fault:

> Even if it is true that alcoholics suffer from a somatic disorder, many people will argue that this disorder results in deadly liver disease only when coupled with a weakness of will—a weakness for which part of the blame must fall on the alcoholic. This consideration underlies the conviction that the alcoholic needing a transplanted liver, unlike a nonalcoholic needing the same liver, is at least partly responsible for his or her need. Therefore, some conclude, the alcoholic's personal failing is rightly considered in deciding upon his or her entitlement to this very scarce resource.[21]

But other writers reject this view. In "Alcoholics and Liver Transplantation," Carl Cohen and his colleagues argue that we would be justified in denying alcoholics new livers on moral grounds only if we assume there is some kind of moral test for receiving an organ transplant. But there is no agreement on what such a test would entail, and even if there was agreement, applying the test fairly would involve inquiries into the morality of patients' private lives—inquiries "universally thought repugnant."[22] More importantly, in deliberations about transplant candidates, we do not use a moral test; we keep moral evaluations out of it:

> We do not seek to determine whether a particular transplant candidate is an abusive parent or a dutiful daughter, whether candidates cheat on their income taxes or their spouses, or whether potential recipients pay their parking tickets or routinely lie when they think it is in their best interests.... If alcoholics should be penalized

---

[21] Carl Cohen, Martin Benjamin, et al., "Alcoholics and Liver Transplantation," *Journal of the American Medical Association*, 13 March 1991, vol. 265, 1299–1301.

[22] Ibid.

because of their moral fault, then all others who are equally at fault in causing their own medical needs should be similarly penalized.[23]

Some people may concede this point but offer another argument against liver transplants for alcoholics: because of the alcoholic's bad habits, he or she would not do well after a transplant, and the scarce resource would be wasted—a result we are morally obligated to avoid.

Others doubt that alcoholics will always fare worse than other transplant groups. And they point out that even if this claim were true, it would not be fair to reject alcoholics on that score. After all, we do not reject other groups just because of a poor prognosis.

Fault and the Allocation of Spare Organs

BRIAN SMART

There has been much useful discussion over the allocation of spare resources between patients who are not at fault for the scarcity of healthy organs. The debate here has been over the criteria for the fair distribution of such resources. Should the choice between those who are to receive spare organs and those who are not to receive them be made by lot, by social usefulness, by quality-adjusted life years, (QALY) or by appeal to the "good innings" criterion (1)? For our present purposes I shall assume that we have an answer in the "distributive justice criterion" (DJC). The DJC gives us an order of priority between innocent parties. The question is: should the DJC be restricted to allocations involving innocent parties or should it apply to those responsible for the scarcity too? Should the allocation of spare organs ignore all questions of fault, or should considerations of rectificatory justice enter when at least one of the patients in need is responsible for the scarcity? Rectificatory justice covers both punishment and reparation for wrongs, and in law is to be found both in the criminal and civil law, for example in torts and contract (2).

HISTORICAL FAULT

There are those who hold that the DJC should command all allocation simply on the ground that the question of responsibility never arises. Michael Lockwood, for example, expresses scepticism about free will: "…we are all of us victims of our genetic inheritance, upbringing and so forth, and…it is not true that people who bring certain kinds of health care need on themselves—for example by driving dangerously, overeating, smoking or abusing drugs or alcohol—really *could*, in the final analysis, have acted any differently" (3). This is not the place to discuss the issue of free will and responsibility. But, whether we believe in free will or not, we need to discuss its *implications*, and Lockwood has not addressed these. Our everyday practice of morality and law certainly does distinguish between people who are at fault and those who are not. The cloth out of which that everyday practice weaves culpability is made up of intention and foresight, knowledge of right and wrong, rationality, control over

Reproduced from *Journal of Medical Ethics*, vol. 20, 1994, 26–30 with permission from BMJ Publishing Group Ltd.

---

[23] Ibid.

one's actions and emotions, beliefs about the circumstances of the action and a capacity to exercise reasonable care about others. For those who wish to reserve judgement on free will our question still stands: *if* a person is responsible for a shortage of healthy organs, should their access be determined wholly by distributive criteria or should rectificatory justice (punishment or reparation) be involved?

In a recent article proposing a complete criterion of allocation, Michael J. Langford distinguishes between past fault, which his proposed criterion excludes as ground for allocation, and a present or future condition, for example alcoholism, which could ground allocation "if it rendered the medical prognosis poor" (4). However, he does not provide any reason why past fault should be excluded. Now for our purposes it may just be the case that Langford has successfully delineated *the* DJC. Indeed, exclusion of historical fault would be definitionally required, for it would exclude questions of rectificatory justice. But it would plainly beg the question arbitrarily to exclude rectificatory criteria from a complete criterion of allocation: that requires argument.

It is, however, possible to reconstruct a line of reasoning that may have influenced Langford. He believes that a principle of equality should govern his criterion, and he claims "that certainly looks like a deontological principle" (4), by which he means "one that relates to rights and duties that are alleged to apply regardless of the consequences" (5). However, it emerged that he is not defending a deontological principle since he is elaborating a principle to which deontologists, utilitarians (who are interested in only the consequences) and those uncommitted to an ethical theory may subscribe (4). But there is no such neutral principle. It is only utilitarianism which, at base, wholly rejects the moral significance of the past. It is only utilitarianism which would find no possible role for historical fault in a complete principle of allocation: deontology and ordinary morality commonly base judgements of desert, entitlement and liability on past fault of one of the parties involved.

It might also be the case that Langford believes that including rectificatory criteria turns scarce resource allocation into punishment. To that argument I now turn.

A NON-PUNITIVE PRINCIPLE OF RESTITUTION

The idea that historical fault should play a key role in the allocation of health care is vigorously rejected by John Harris. He writes:

> "We all, of course, have a duty to encourage and promote morality, but to do so by choosing between candidates for treatment on moral grounds is to arrogate to ourselves not simply the promotion of morality but the punishment of immorality. And to choose to let one person rather than another die on the grounds of some moral defect in their behaviour or character is to take upon ourselves the right not simply to punish, but capitally to punish, offenders against morality" (6).

We need to distinguish here between at least two different ways of choosing between people for treatment on moral grounds. The first way is where we give preference to one on grounds of her superior moral character or behaviour, but where neither party is in any way responsible for the scarcity of resources. To decide in this way is to include morality in the DJC: it is not addressed to rectifying any wrong, for the problem of scarcity is neither party's fault. Harris may be right not to include morality in the DJC, but that is another matter. The second way of choosing between people for treatment on moral grounds is where the need to choose is the fault of one of the parties in need of treatment. However, the most obvious cases of such choices are not cases of punishment at all, but cases of self-defence and other-defence.

Consider a case of other-defence in which an unprovoked attack has been launched on Kurt by Charles. Kurt cannot retreat or restrain Charles but you have the power, at no risk to yourself, of intervening by killing Charles. Suppose you do this on the ground that Charles is at fault for causing the dilemma. There is a scarcity of resources, since you do not have the power to save *both* Kurt *and* Charles, only the power to save *either* Kurt *or* Charles. A just case of other-defence would be one in which you choose between these two on moral grounds, not on grounds of general character blemishes but on the ground that Charles is at fault for causing the scarcity of resources and so should bear the cost. This ground needs elaboration. Kurt is not at fault, and so not only should he not have to bear the cost, but Charles *should be forced to make restitution* to Kurt: in other words, Charles should be forced to restore Kurt to the position he rightfully enjoyed before Charles's attack endangered his life (7).

Here we have all the ingredients of a preferential choice between lives on moral grounds. But does it constitute the punishment of immorality, or, in this case, capital punishment? I suggest not. First of all, there is no account of punishment which licenses the treatment justified by self-defence. If Charles is killed for launching an unsuccessful attempt on Kurt's life, that is not because it is a suitable punishment but because it is the minimal reasonable force to defend Kurt: as punishment it would exceed even the harsh limits imposed by the *lex talionis* (an eye for an eye...). If all that was needed to defend Kurt was for you to give Charles a slap on the cheek or a harsh frown then that would hardly be a punishment to fit the crime of attempted murder, but it would be all that would be licensed by other-defence. In cases of self-defence and other-defence where the aggressor survives, we can distinguish more clearly between the treatment licensed by defence and the treatment licensed by punishment: the question of punishment obviously does arise in cases of unsuccessful murder even when the aggressor has received the harm that was minimally necessary for a successful defence of the victim.

SELF-INFLICTED HARM IS NOT A CRIME

A second reason for rejecting preferential treatment as punishment lies in the fact that self-inflicted harm is not a crime. Damaging one's own heart or lungs by smoking is not forbidden by law: it would be legal paternalism if it were. So the justification, if there is one, for discriminating against a smoker when only one healthy spare set of heart and lungs is available must be non-punitive. And that justification lies in restitution. For suppose that what the smoker who is at fault must do is to restore to others what was rightfully theirs before the commission of the fault. True, the smoker has inflicted harm on only himself. But this ceases to be true if he does not forfeit equality of entitlement to a spare set of

heart and lungs. For example, if there is no forfeiture of equality, then the one non-smoker in need of a transplant has a 1/2 chance of acquiring the spare set rather than a 1/1 chance. Without differential treatment according to fault the non-smoker would be denied his rightful opportunity. By forfeiting his own right to equality the smoker restores the non-smoker to her rightful status quo.

Interestingly, much of this argument applies to someone who damages another's healthy heart or who vandalises one of the two healthy spare sets of organs available (8). The obvious difference is that a crime has now been committed—harm to the person or damage to property: punishment is a matter for the criminal courts. But, in addition to the crime, we have the same kind of situation that arose with self-inflicted harm: there is a scarcity of resources. By harming another's heart, or by vandalising a spare set of organs on their way to the theatre, the person at fault has forfeited his right to equal priority with the innocent patient. The innocent patient is owed restitution of his 1/1 chance of access to healthy organs that he possessed before the fault occurred. Restitution and reparation is a matter either for the civil courts or may be settled out of court.

It might be thought that self- and other-defence are sufficiently unlike choice between lives caused by a shortage of resources to provide a useful insight into the nature of that choice. After all, self- and other-defence involve an aggressor who is a current threat to the victim. For this reason, Langford's distinction between historical fault and current condition might explain why he could justify self- and other-defence. And it might also explain why Harris might want to assimilate preferential treatment against a patient at fault to punishment: for it would involve an historical and not an ongoing fault.

THE THREAT MAY BE CURRENT

But historical fault may be found in self-defence. The threat may be current, but the fault may be historical (9). Imagine the aggressor has pushed his trolley to the crest of the hill and has now tied himself in it so that he cannot jump out: you are tied to the track down which the trolley is heading and fortunately you can operate by remote control a bulldozer which, at the flick of the switch, will straddle the track, protect you but kill the aggressor when his trolley smashes into it. The fault is historical in the sense that after the trolley has crested the hill, the aggressor can do nothing more about it, and flight or effective threats are not open to the victim. This is unlike the current fault of an aggressor who is trying to strangle you and in whose power it is to desist right up to the moment of the victim's death. In this case both the threat and the fault are current. But the burden of restitution is the same in both cases. Indeed, it is not inappropriate to ask, in the present tense, "Who is responsible?" in both cases of historical and current fault.

We now have a non-punitive principle of restitution. It properly belongs to rectificatory, not distributive justice, since it requires those at fault to restore those endangered or harmed to their rightful status quo. It is not punishment, since it is like paying damages in a civil libel suit.

PRIORITY OF NON-SMOKERS OVER SMOKERS IN ACCESS TO SPARE ORGANS?

What are the implications of this principle of restitution? Should medical practitioners supplement the DJC with a fault criterion that prioritises the innocent? Notoriously in ethics, as in economics and physics, there is a large gap between the enunciation of a sound principle and its practical application.

First of all, it is unclear who should apply the DJC supplemented by a rule of restitution. We have ruled out criminal courts since forfeiting priority of access to scarce resources is not a matter for punishment. But the application of the principle does introduce a dimension not covered by the DJC: assessing degrees of culpability. So expertise for assessing fault is required on any panel that is involved in the allocation: assessing fault is not a medical skill. It is to be hoped that the composition of any panel would, like juries, introduce more democracy and in some way involve consultation with those needing a transplant or with their representatives. One crucial reason for this is that if restitution is owed to another party, it does not follow that the restitution

has to be made. For it is always open to the person who has the right to restitution *to waive* that right. This is not peculiar to debts of restitution, but a more general feature of obligations. After all, I do not have to pay you back the £10 I promised to repay you if you waive your right to repayment. You are morally sovereign over whether I will be held to that promise or not.

If, as law and ordinary morality suggests, it is an empirical matter whether individuals are at fault, there are undoubtedly difficulties in identifying particular cases. For example, the problem with many cases of self-inflicted heart or lung disease is that it may be caused by addiction to nicotine. Addiction as such does not rule out fault. For someone may have taken up smoking or drinking quite freely, but foreseen that he would not be able to give it up once he was addicted (10). On the other hand, a large proportion of smokers become addicted in their early teens and so, because of immaturity, are not responsible for their addiction. Nor should we ignore the stress-related conditions that might cause much smoking in adults: unemployment, inability to keep up mortgage repayments and broken relationships are familiar examples of such causes. Fault is either negated or much reduced by such causes. But it would be a mistake to exaggerate the difficulties of assessing culpability. Let us grant that many complex cases are impossible to resolve and that many others may be resolvable only by the rarified skills of trained lawyers. Because of the constraints of time such cases would be beyond the scope of the allocation of scarce medical resources. Such cases may be contrasted with those in which the relevant histories of the parties are known and which present good, and non-conflicting, evidence of the culpability of one of them. We would insist on this if other-defence were to be justified.

We must now distinguish between being responsible for a condition and being at fault or culpable for that condition arising. For there to be a fault there must be a wrong committed as well as there being responsibility for that wrong. A miner or fireman chooses freely to subject himself to greater risk of harm or disease than is met with in most occupations. And, on the special assumption that if he were not to make that choice nobody would fill his place, it may be true that he causes a short-fall in spare healthy organs. But, because of the social value placed upon such occupations, we are not tempted to say that such a shortfall is the *fault* of the miner or the fireman. Since there is no fault there can be no case for saying that miners should have less priority than those who have no responsibility for their condition. But why should the social value of the occupations involving these risks mean that no fault occurs? The justification lies in fairness. In this case the value is one of social need: the society needs firemen and miners for its welfare. To ask people to take an extra risk (which may be rewarded by danger money) and then to give them lower medical priority than any ordinary member of the public would simply be unfair: indeed there is a case for giving them a higher medical priority in addition to danger money.

One qualification should be made here. The society asks people in dangerous occupations to take only the risks that are reasonable in the circumstances. Negligence can incur harm that was reasonably avoidable. Society did not ask the miner to harm himself in that way.

DANGEROUS SPORTS

Dangerous sports such as rock-climbing and para-gliding are not pursued out of social necessity since they do not contribute to social welfare. Society does not ask people to engage in rock-climbing or paragliding. If people freely engage in these sports should they not pay all the extra costs such activities risk and so receive a lower priority in access to spare organs? The argument with smoking is that it is unfair to spread the extra risks of this self-indulgence to those who prefer not to impose an extra risk on themselves. Should not the same apply to dangerous sports? A strong case can be made here for the social value of such sports, providing they are not too dangerous, and providing they are practised non-negligently. The value does not belong to social welfare, it is not socially necessary as has been stated. But these sports do enhance lives as well as endanger them. Their value is both intrinsic and extrinsic. Intrinsically, skills of a very high order can be acquired, with an accompanying feeling of achievement; but even beginners find the activity exciting and challenging. Yet it is also a spectator sport, in the sense that it can be followed with binoculars or cameras and be read about. Extrinsically, the activity is character-forming as well as being able to provide the best exponents with a living. Activities of this kind thus become a part of our culture and their value contributes to a worthwhile life. After all, social welfare is not an end in itself: it simply enables us to choose and pursue a worthwhile life.

MORAL COMPLICITY

Do dangerous sports differ in important respects from smoking or hard drinking? I think it is easy to show that our society delivers a mixed message on this issue. On the one hand, it permits advertising and sponsorship which may target children, and which presents smoking and drinking as appendages to a glamorous life-style. And, on the whole, it does not restrict smoking very seriously in public places, even when the dangers of passive smoking are well known. Such a policy seems to countenance the sharing of risks between smokers and the general public. On the other hand, government health warnings are compulsory on packets and advertisements. I think the upshot of this is that our society may be charged with moral complicity in the tobacco companies' operations and in the smokers' self-infliction of harm. Part of the message is that there is no fault: the other part of the message is that the activity is dangerous. When combined, these messages are compatible with the claim that smoking is a valuable (chic, cool) way of living in which it would be fair that we should all, smokers and non-smokers alike, bear the costs equally in the case of access to medical care: it would be unjust if non-smokers were given priority.

The claim that smoking is socially valuable should be challenged. One familiar way of doing this is to point out that its value is an illusion created by advertisers, an illusion which can affect young people at an impressionable and vulnerable phase in their lives. We have remarked on how it can be seen as a part of stylish living: this claim might be sustainable if we could substitute a substance that had no deleterious effects on our health. But in the light of its probable effects, the illusion can be sustained only by screening off or ignoring those probable effects. Also, safer remedies are available for removing the stress that smoking can remove (for example exercise or alcohol in moderate quantities). It may be rightly claimed that smoking causes private pleasure while not harming anyone else if practised privately. But that is a reason why people's right to smoke in private should be defended, provided they are aware of the risks. It is not a reason why those risks should be shared with the general public and so reduced for the participants themselves: if the activity lacks social value then the risks should be borne by the participants alone.

So far as smoking is concerned this paper is deliberately hedged about with qualifications. A society which banned the advertising of tobacco and attached no social value to smoking would share no fault with those who smoked of their own free will. In such circumstances, it would be fair to give a lower priority to smokers in the allocation of spare organs.

The argument for this conclusion has been deontological and has been based on a principle of restitution for an historical fault. Yet deontological thinking is only part of our moral thought: we must be sensitive to the consequences of our actions. It is therefore worth remarking that it is likely that the consequences of introducing a restitutive principle would be beneficial. Now that might appear doubtful if we consider Michael Lockwood's observation about one likely consequence of adopting a rule of priority according to fault:

"...there might be good welfarist reasons for according the claims of [smokers] on health care resources a relatively low priority, if the fact were to be widely publicized and could act as an effective deterrent to such irresponsible behaviour. But I doubt whether it would. Someone who is undeterred by the prospect of seriously damaging his health is hardly likely, in my opinion, to be deterred by the prospect of less than ideal health care thereafter" (11).

Lockwood may be right about this particular consequence, at least in the vast majority of cases. Few are likely to be made *more responsible* by a rectificatory response to their fault. But he ignores the possibility that a system of equal access for all alike might induce many to become *more irresponsible* about

their health. This is a phenomenon that occurs in the field of safety measures (12). For example, if seat-belts are made compulsory there is a tendency for drivers to drive faster and so restore the former accident rates.

To conclude: rectificatory but non-punitive justice has in principle a role to play in the allocation of scarce medical resources. However, this would be just only within a framework of robust preventive medicine: this would mean effective health education and the elimination of cigarette advertising and sponsorship.

REFERENCES AND NOTES

1. For the most recent account of a sophisticated allocative criterion see Langford MJ. Who should get the kidney machine? *Journal of Medical Ethics* 1992; 18: 12–17.
2. For the introduction of this distinction see Aristotle, *The Nicomachean Ethics* bk 5: 1130a 22–1132a 27.
3. Lockwood M. Quality of life and resource allocation. In: Bell JM, Mendus S, eds. *Philosophy and Medical Welfare*. Royal Institute of Philosophy, Lecture Series 23. Cambridge: Cambridge University Press, 1988: 49.
4. See reference (1) 13.
5. See reference (1) 16.
6. Harris J. *The Value of Life*. London: Routledge and Kegan Paul, 1985: 108.
7. For a detailed account see Smart BJ. Understanding and justifying self-defence. *International Journal of Moral and Social Studies* 1989; 4, 3: 231–244.
8. For such a hypothetical see Wasserman D. Justifying self-defense. *Philosophy and Public Affairs* 1987; 16, 4: 367, fn 29.
9. David Wasserman wrongly attempts to dissociate an aggressor from his current threat where the fault is historical and the point of no return has been passed. See reference (8) 371–372. For a fault principle characterised as distributive rather than retributive or restitutive see Montague P. The morality of self-defense. *Philosophy and Public Affairs* 1989; 18, 1:88.
10. See reference (2): bk 3: 1114a 15–21.
11. See reference (3): 49.
12. See Trammell RL et al. Utility and survival. *Philosophy* 1977; 52: 336.

Alcoholics and Liver Transplantation

CARL COHEN, MARTIN BENJAMIN, AND THE ETHICS AND SOCIAL IMPACT COMMITTEE OF THE

TRANSPLANT AND HEALTH POLICY CENTER, ANN ARBOR, MICHIGAN

Alcoholic cirrhosis of the liver—severe scarring due to the heavy use of alcohol—is by far the major cause of end-stage liver disease.[1] For persons so afflicted, life may depend on receiving a new, transplanted liver. The number of alcoholics in the United States needing new livers is great, but the supply of available livers for transplantation is small. *Should those whose end-stage liver disease was caused by alcohol abuse be categorically excluded from candidacy for liver transplantation?* This question, partly medical and partly moral, must now be confronted forthrightly. Many lives are at stake.

Reasons of two kinds underlie a widespread unwillingness to transplant livers into alcoholics: First, there is a common conviction—explicit or tacit—that alcoholics are morally blameworthy, their condition the result of their own misconduct, and that such blameworthiness disqualifies alcoholics in unavoidable competition for organs with others equally sick but blameless. Second, there is a common belief that because of their habits, alcoholics will not exhibit satisfactory survival rates after transplantation, and that, therefore, good stewardship of a scarce lifesaving resource requires that alcoholics not be considered for liver transplantation. We examine both of these arguments.

THE MORAL ARGUMENT

A widespread condemnation of drunkenness and a revulsion for drunks lie at the heart of this public policy issue. Alcoholic cirrhosis—unlike other causes of end-stage liver disease—is brought on by a person's conduct, by heavy drinking. Yet if the dispute here were only about whether to treat someone who is seriously ill because of personal conduct, we would not say—as we do not in cases of other serious diseases resulting from personal conduct—that such conduct disqualifies a person from receiving desperately needed medical attention. Accident victims injured because they were not wearing seat belts are treated

without hesitation; reformed smokers who become coronary bypass candidates partly because they disregarded their physicians' advice about tobacco, diet, and exercise are not turned away because of their bad habits. But new livers are a scarce resource, and transplanting a liver into an alcoholic may, therefore, result in death for a competing candidate whose liver disease was wholly beyond his or her control. Thus we seem driven, in this case unlike in others, to reflect on the weight given to the patient's personal conduct. And heavy drinking—unlike smoking, or overeating, or failing to wear a seat belt—is widely regarded as morally wrong.

Many contend that alcoholism is not a moral failing but a disease. Some authorities have recently reaffirmed this position, asserting that alcoholism is "best regarded as a chronic disease."[2] But this claim cannot be firmly established and is far from universally believed. Whether alcoholism is indeed a disease, or a moral failing, or both, remains a disputed matter surrounded by intense controversy.[3-9]

Even if it is true that alcoholics suffer from a somatic disorder, many people will argue that this disorder results in deadly liver disease only when coupled with a weakness of will—a weakness for which part of the blame must fall on the alcoholic. This consideration underlies the conviction that the alcoholic needing a transplanted liver, unlike a nonalcoholic competing for the same liver, is at least partly responsible for his or her need. Therefore, some conclude, the alcoholic's personal failing is rightly considered in deciding upon his or her entitlement to this very scarce resource.

Is this argument sound? We think it is not. Whether alcoholism is a moral failing, in whole or

"Alcoholics and Liver Transplantation" by Carl Cohen, et al, *Journal of the American Medical Association*, 13 March 1991, vol. 265, 1299–1301.

in part, remains uncertain. But even if we suppose that it is, it does not follow that we are justified in categorically denying liver transplants to those alcoholics suffering from end-stage cirrhosis. We could rightly preclude alcoholics from transplantation only if we assume that qualification for a new organ requires some level of moral virtue or is canceled by some level of moral vice. But there is absolutely no agreement—and there is likely to be none—about what constitutes moral virtue and vice and what rewards and penalties they deserve. The assumption that undergirds the moral argument for precluding alcoholics is thus unacceptable. Moreover, even if we could agree (which, in fact, we cannot) upon the kind of misconduct we would be looking for, the fair weighting of such a consideration would entail highly intrusive investigations into patients' moral habits—investigations universally thought repugnant. Moral evaluation is wisely and rightly excluded from all deliberations of who should be treated and how.

Indeed, we do exclude it. We do not seek to determine whether a particular transplant candidate is an abusive parent or a dutiful daughter, whether candidates cheat on their income taxes or their spouses, or whether potential recipients pay their parking tickets or routinely lie when they think it is in their best interests. We refrain from considering such judgments for several good reasons: (1) We have genuine and well-grounded doubts about comparative degrees of voluntariness and, therefore, *cannot pass judgment fairly.* (2) Even if we could assess degrees of voluntariness reliably, we *cannot know what penalties different degrees of misconduct deserve.* (3) *Judgments of this kind could not be made consistently in our medical* system—and a fundamental requirement of a fair system in allocating scarce resources is that it treat all in need of certain goods on the same standard, without unfair discrimination by group.

If alcoholics should be penalized because of their moral fault, then all others who are equally at fault in causing their own medical needs should be similarly penalized. To accomplish this, we would have to make vigorous and sustained efforts to find out whose conduct has been morally weak or sinful and to what degree. That inquiry, as a condition for medical care or for the receipt of goods in short supply, we certainly will not and should not undertake.

The unfairness of such moral judgments is compounded by other accidental factors that render moral assessment especially difficult in connection with alcoholism and liver disease. Some drinkers have a greater predisposition for alcohol abuse than others. And for some who drink to excess, the predisposition to cirrhosis is also greater; many grossly intemperate drinkers do not suffer grievously from liver disease. On the other hand, alcohol consumption that might be considered moderate for some may cause serious liver disease in others. It turns out, in fact, that the disastrous consequences of even low levels of alcohol consumption may be much more common in women than in men.[10] Therefore, penalizing cirrhotics by denying them transplant candidacy would have the effect of holding some groups arbitrarily to a higher standard than others and would probably hold women to a higher standard of conduct than men.

Moral judgments that eliminate alcoholics from candidacy thus prove unfair and unacceptable. The alleged (but disputed) moral misconduct of alcoholics with end-stage liver disease does not justify categorically excluding them as candidates for liver transplantation.

MEDICAL ARGUMENT

Reluctance to use available livers in treating alcoholics is due in some part to the conviction that, because alcoholics would do poorly after transplant as a result of their bad habits, good stewardship of organs in short supply requires that alcoholics be excluded from consideration.

This argument also fails, for two reasons: First, it fails because the premise—that the outcome for alcoholics will invariably be poor relative to other groups—is at least doubtful and probably false. Second, it fails because, even if the premise were true, it could serve as a good reason to exclude alcoholics only if it were an equally good reason to exclude other groups having a prognosis equally bad or worse. But equally low survival rates have not excluded other groups; fairness therefore requires that this group not be categorically excluded either.

In fact, the data regarding the post-transplant histories of alcoholics are not yet reliable. Evidence gathered in 1984 indicated that the 1-year survival rate for patients with alcoholic cirrhosis was well below the survival rate for other recipients of liver transplants, excluding those with cancer.[11] But a 1988 report, with a larger (but still small) sample number, shows remarkably good results in alcoholics receiving transplants: 1-year survival is 73.2%—and of 35 carefully selected (and possibly non-representative) alcoholics who received transplants and lived 6 months or longer, only two relapsed into alcohol abuse.[12] Liver transplantation, it would appear, can be a very sobering experience. Whether this group continues to do as well as a comparable group of non-alcoholic liver recipients remains uncertain. But the data, although not supporting the broad inclusion of alcoholics, do suggest that medical considerations do not now justify categorically excluding alcoholics from liver transplantation.

A history of alcoholism is of great concern when considering liver transplantation, not only because of the impact of alcohol abuse upon the entire system of the recipient, but also because the life of an alcoholic tends to be beset by general disorder. Returning to heavy drinking could ruin a new liver, although probably not for years. But relapse into heavy drinking would quite likely entail the inability to maintain the routine of multiple medication, daily or twice-daily, essential for immunosuppression and survival. As a class, alcoholic cirrhotics may therefore prove to have substantially-lower survival rates after receiving transplants. All such matters should be weighed, of course. But none of them gives any solid reason to exclude alcoholics from consideration categorically.

Moreover, even if survival rates for alcoholics selected were much lower than normal—a supposition now in substantial doubt—what could fairly be concluded from such data? Do we exclude from transplant candidacy members of other groups known to have low survival rates? In fact we do not. Other things being equal, we may prefer not to transplant organs in short supply into patients afflicted, say, with liver cell cancer, knowing that such cancer recurs not long after a new liver is implanted.[13,14] Yet in some individual cases we do it. Similarly, some transplant recipients have other malignant neoplasms or other conditions that suggest low survival probability. Such matters are weighed in selecting recipients, but they are insufficient grounds to categorically exclude an entire group. This shows that the argument for excluding alcoholics based on survival probability rates alone is simply not just.

THE ARGUMENTS DISTINGUISHED

In feet, the exclusion of alcoholics from transplant candidacy probably results from an intermingling, perhaps at time confusion, of the moral and medical arguments. But if the moral argument indeed does not apply, no combination of it with probable survival rates can make it applicable. Survival data, carefully collected and analyzed, deserve to be weighed in selecting candidates. These data do not come close to precluding alcoholics from consideration. Judgments of blameworthiness, which ought to be excluded generally, certainly should be excluded when weighing the impact of those survival rates. Some people with a strong antipathy to alcohol abuse and abusers may, without realizing it, be relying on assumed unfavorable data to support a fixed moral judgment. The arguments must be untangled. Actual results with transplanted alcoholics must be considered without regard to moral antipathies.

The upshot is inescapable: there are no good grounds at present—moral or medical—to disqualify a patient with end-stage liver disease from consideration for liver transplantation simply because of a history of heavy drinking.

SCREENING AND SELECTION OF LIVER TRANSPLANT CANDIDATES

In the initial evaluation of candidates for any form of transplantation, the central questions are whether patients (1) are sick enough to need a new organ and (2) enjoy a high enough probability of benefiting from this limited resource. At this stage the criteria should be non-comparative.[15,16] Even the initial screening of patients must, however, be done individually and with great care.

The screening process for those suffering from alcoholic cirrhosis must be especially rigorous—not for moral reasons, but because of factors affecting survival, which are themselves influenced by a history of heavy drinking—and even more by its resumption. Responsible stewardship of scarce organs requires that the screening for candidacy take into consideration the manifold impact of heavy drinking on long-term transplant success. Cardiovascular problems brought on by alcoholism and other systematic contraindications must be looked for. Psychiatric and social evaluation is also in order, to determine whether patients understand and have come to terms with their condition and whether they have the social support essential for continuing immunosuppression and follow-up care.

Precisely which factors should be weighed in this screening process have not been firmly established. Some physicians have proposed a specified period of alcohol abstinence as an "objective" criterion for selection—but the data supporting such a criterion are far from conclusive, and the use of this criterion to exclude a prospective recipient is at present medically and morally arbitrary.[17,18]

Indeed, one important consequence of overcoming the strong presumption against considering alcoholics for liver transplantation is the research opportunity it presents and the encouragement it gives to the quest for more reliable predictors of medical success. As that search continues, some defensible guidelines for case-by-case determination have been devised, based on factors associated with sustained recovery from alcoholism and other considerations related to liver transplantation success in general. Such guidelines appropriately include (1) refined diagnosis by those trained in the treatment of alcoholism, (2) acknowledgment by the patient of a serious drinking problem, (3) social and familial stability, and (4) other factors experimentally associated with long-term sobriety.[19]

The experimental use of guidelines like these, and their gradual refinement over time, may lead to more reliable and more generally applicable predictors. But those more refined predictors will never be developed until prejudices against considering alcoholics for liver transplantation are overcome.

Patients who are sick because of alleged self-abuse ought not be grouped for discriminatory treatment—unless we are prepared to develop a detailed calculus of just deserts for health care based on good conduct. Lack of sympathy for those who bring serious disease upon themselves is understandable, but the temptation to institutionalize that emotional response must be tempered by our inability to apply such considerations justly and by our duty *not* to apply them unjustly. In the end, some patients with alcoholic cirrhosis may be judged, after careful evaluation, as good risks for a liver transplant.

OBJECTION AND REPLY

Providing alcoholics with transplants may present a special "political" problem for transplant centers. The public perception of alcoholics is generally negative. The already low rate of organ donation, it may be argued, will fall even lower when it becomes known that donated organs are going to alcoholics. Financial support from legislatures may also suffer. One can imagine the effect on transplantation if the public were to learn that the liver of a teenager killed by a drunken driver had been transplanted into an alcoholic patient. If selecting even a few alcoholics as transplant candidates reduces the number of lives saved overall, might that not be good reason to preclude alcoholics categorically?

No. The fear is understandable, but excluding alcoholics cannot be rationally defended on that basis. Irresponsible conduct attributable to alcohol abuse should not be defended. No excuses should be made for the deplorable consequences of drunken behavior, from highway slaughter to familial neglect and abuse. But alcoholism must be distinguished from those consequences; not all alcoholics are morally irresponsible, vicious, or neglectful drunks. If there is a general failure to make this distinction, we must strive to overcome that failure, not pander to it.

Public confidence in medical practice in general, and in organ transplantation in particular, depends on the scientific validity and moral integrity of the policies adopted. Sound policies will prove publicly defensible. Shaping present health care policy on the basis of distorted public perceptions or prejudices will, in the long run, do more harm than good to the process and to the reputation of all concerned.

Approximately one in every 10 Americans is a heavy drinker, and approximately one family in every three has at least one member at risk for alcoholic cirrhosis.[3] 'The care of alcoholics and the just treatment of them when their lives are at stake are matters a democratic polity may therefore be expected to act on with concern and reasonable judgment over the long run. The allocation of organs in short supply does present vexing moral problems; if thoughtless or shallow moralizing would cause some to respond very negatively to transplanting livers into alcoholic cirrhotics, that cannot serve as good reason to make such moralizing the measure of public policy.

We have argued that there is now no good reason, either moral or medical, to preclude alcoholics categorically from consideration for liver transplantation. We further conclude that it would therefore be unjust to implement that categorical preclusion simply because others might respond negatively if we do not.

NOTES

1. Consensus conference on liver transplantation, NIH. *JAMA.* 1983;250:2961–2964.
2. Klerman FL. Treatment of alcoholism. *N Engl J Med.* 1989;320:394–396.
3. Vaillant GE. *The Natural History of Alcoholism.* Cambridge, Mass: Harvard University Press; 1983.
4. Jellinek EM. *The Disease Concept of Alcoholism.* New Haven, Conn: College and University Press; 1960.
5. Rose RM, Barret JE, eds. *Alcoholism: Origins and Outcome.* New York, NY: Raven Press; 1988.
6. *Alcohol and Health: Sixth Special Report to the Congress.* Washington, DC: US Dept of Health and Human Services; 1987. DHHS publication ADM87-1519.
7. Fingarette H. Alcoholism: the mythical disease. *Public Interest.* 1988;91:3–22.
8. Madsen W. Thin thinking about heavy drinking. *Public Interest.* 1989;95:112–118.
9. Fingarette H. A rejoinder to Madsen. *Public Interest.* 1989;95:118–121.
10. Berglund M. Mortality in alcoholics related to clinical state at first admission: a study of 637 deaths. *Acta Psychiatr Scand.* 1984;70:407–416.
11. Scharschmidt BF. Human liver transplantation: analysis of data on 540 patients from four centers. *Hepatology.* 1984;4:95–111.
12. Starzl TE, Van Thiel D, Tzakis AG, et al. Orthotopic liver transplantation for alcoholic cirrhosis. *JAMA* 1988;260:2542–2544.
13. Gordon RD, Iwatsuki S, Tazkis AG, et al. The Denver-Pittsburgh Liver Transplant Series. In: Terasaki PI, ed. *Clinical Transplants.* Los Angeles, Calif: UCLA Tissue-Typing Laboratory; 1987:43–49.
14. Gordon ED, Iwatsuki S, Esquivel CO. Liver transplantation. In: Cerilli GJ, ed. *Organ Transplantation and Replacement.* Philadelphia Lippincott; 1988:511–534.
15. Childress JF. Who shall live when not all can live? *Soundings.* 1970;53:339–362.
16. Stanzl TE, Gordon RD, Tzakis S, et al. Equitable allocation of extrarenal organs: with special reference to the liver. *Transplant Proc.* 1988;20:131–138.
17. Schenker S, Perkins HS, Sorrell MF. Should patients with end-stage alcoholic liver disease have a new liver? *Hepatology.* 1990;11:314–319.
18. *Allen v Mansour A,* US District Court for the Eastern District of Michigan, Southern Division. 1986:86-73429.
19. Beresford TP, Turcotte JG, Merion R, et al. A rational approach to liver transplantation for the alcoholic patient. *Psychosomatics.* 1990;31:241–254.

ARGUMENT 21 ESSAY QUESTIONS

1. What are Cohen's arguments against using a moral test for choosing transplant recipients? Do you agree with them? Explain.
2. What is Smart's view on using moral fault to allocate spare organs?
3. Do you think a person's moral worthiness should be a factor in deciding whether he or she gets a life-saving transplant? What are your reasons?

SUGGESTIONS FOR FURTHER READING

Michael Boylan, "The Universal Right to Health Care," in *Medical Ethics*, ed. Michael Boylan (Upper Saddle River, NJ: Prentice-Hall, 2000), 391–402.

Allen Buchanan, "Justice: A Philosophical Review," in *Justice and Health Care*, ed. Earl Shelp (Dordrecht: D. Reidel Publishing, 1981), 3–21.

Allen Buchanan, "Health-Care Delivery and Resource Allocation," in *Medical Ethics*, ed. Robert M. Veatch (Sudbury, MA: Jones and Bartlett, 1997), 321–61.

Tom L. Beauchamp and James F. Childress, "Justice," in *Principles of Biomedical Ethics*, 5th ed. (New York: Oxford University Press, 2001), 225–82.

Norman Daniels, "Health-Care Needs and Distributive Justice," in *Justice and Justification* (Cambridge: Cambridge University Press, 1996).

Norman Daniels, *Just Health Care* (Cambridge: Cambridge University Press, 1985).

Walter Glannon, "Allotting Scarce Medical Resources," in *Biomedical Ethics* (Oxford: Oxford University Press, 2005), 143–66.

The Kaiser Commission on Medicaid and the Uninsured, *The Uninsured: A Primer*, The Kaiser Family Foundation, October 2007, http://www.kff.org/uninsured/7451.cfm (21 March 2008).

Louis P. Pojman and Owen McLeod, *What Do We Deserve? A Reader on Justice and Desert* (New York: Oxford University Press, 1999).

Rosamond Rhodes, Margaret P. Battin, and Anita Silvers, ed., *Medicine and Social Justice* (New York: Oxford University Press, 2002).

Lewis Vaughn, *Bioethics: Principles, Issues, and Cases* (New York: Oxford University Press, 2010).

CHAPTER 11

Animal Rights and Environmental Duty

Once upon a time, eons ago, humans scratched a living from what must have seemed like a boundless, eternal planet of limitless abundance. Every tree and root, every elk and salmon, every drop of water and breath of air seemed a human birthright, ready for the taking. To much of humankind, the whole earth appeared waiting to be plundered.

Those times are long gone—and those delusions with them. In the twenty-first century, we are reminded every day that Mother Earth is finite, fragile, and sick. The planet and its inhabitants are threatened now as never before by global warming, climate change, pollution, ozone depletion, deforestation, population pressures, world hunger, famine, diminishing resources, and species extinction. These woes have prompted many people urgently to ask questions both practical and ethical: (1) how can we solve these problems? and (2) what moral values should we embrace in the solving? Or, to put the ethical query more concretely, what are our moral obligations to the environment and to the nonhuman animals that inhabit it?

The practical questions are scientific, technological, and political. The ethical questions are of a different kind, but they are just as important and pressing because the answers we give to them determine how we approach the practical concerns. Do we have moral duties to nonhuman animals? Is it morally permissible to use them in any way at all to advance human interests—to eat them, hunt them, experiment on them, kill them by the millions in slaughterhouses, and torment them in factory farms? Or do we owe them a measure of moral respect that would restrict what we can do to them? Or are our obligations to them even stronger—do they have *rights*? If so, do all nonhuman animals have rights—or just those that are sentient (capable of having experiences)? If we think an ape deserves moral consideration, should we have equal regard for a fox, a turtle, a bacterium? And what of the rest of the natural world: does it, in whole or in part, have moral value in its own right, regardless of whether it serves human interests? Does a tree have rights? a species of tree? a forest? And if the environment has intrinsic moral value, how should we weigh this value against the interests of people? For example, is it morally right to put a thousand lumbermen out of work to save a grove of trees or a species of mulberry or a single majestic redwood? Are we obligated to transform our way of life to prevent animal suffering or environmental ruin—to become vegetarians, lower our standard of living, or abandon our voracious consumer culture?

PUBLIC OPINION: Animal Rights and Environmental Concerns

Which of these statements comes closest to your view about the treatment of animals? Animals deserve the exact same rights as people to be free from harm and exploitation. Animals deserve some protection from harm and exploitation, but it is still appropriate to use them for the benefit of humans. OR, Animals don't need much protection from harm and exploitation since they are just animals.

Same Rights As People	They Are Just Animals	Unsure
25%	Some Protection 72%	3%	1%

Gallup Poll. May 8–11, 2008. N = 1,017 adults nationwide. MoE ± 3.

Next, I'm going to read you a list of issues. Regardless of whether or not you think it should be legal, for each one, please tell me whether you personally believe that in general it is morally acceptable or morally wrong. How about…?

	Morally Acceptable	Morally Wrong
Medical testing on animals	59%	37%
Buying and wearing clothing made of animal fur	58%	38%
Cloning animals	36%	59%

Gallup Poll. May 10–13, 2007. N = 1,003 adults nationwide. MoE ± 3.

How would you rate the condition of the natural environment in the world today: excellent, good, fair, poor, or very poor?

Excellent	Good	Fair	Poor	Very Poor
3%	21%	38%	28%	9%

You may have heard about the idea that the world's temperature may have been going up slowly over the past 100 years. What is your personal opinion on this? Do you think this has probably been happening, or do you think it probably has not been happening?

Has Been	Hasn't Been	Unsure
80%	18%	2%

ABC News/Planet Green/Stanford University poll. July 23–28, 2008. N = 1,000 adults nationwide. MoE ± 3. Fieldwork by TNS.

With which one of these statements about the environment and the economy do you most agree? Protection of the environment should be given priority, even at the risk of curbing economic growth. OR, Economic growth should be given priority, even if the environment suffers to some extent.

Environment Given Priority	Economic Growth Given Priority	Both Equally	Unsure
49%	44%	6%	1%

CNN/Opinion Research Corporation Poll. June 26–29, 2008. N = 1,026 adults nationwide. MoE ± 3.

Disputes on these issues often focus on **moral status**, or moral considerability. An entity has moral status if it is eligible for moral concern or respect regardless of its relationship to others. Such an entity is entitled to moral consideration in its own right, not because it is a means to something else or because it is useful to someone. If a being has moral status, we cannot view it in the same way we would a hammer, a doll, or a windup toy. However we behave toward it, we must consider its moral standing. Normal humans are presumed to have moral status and are expected to be treated accordingly. If, as many people believe, a dog has some sort of moral status, then intentionally inflicting pain on it for fun would be wrong. Deliberately causing it pain would be permissible only if done for good reasons.

In the Western world, the traditional view for hundreds of years has been that animals have no moral status at all. They are merely dumb, expendable instruments to be used for human purposes. This attitude prevailed in much of Judeo-Christian thought and was affirmed by some eminent philosophers and scientists. The book of Genesis exhorts humans to subdue the earth and to "have dominion" over all its creatures, using them for the good of mankind. The great philosophers Thomas Aquinas, René Descartes, and Immanuel Kant declare that people may use animals in any way they please, for animals are nothing more than raw materials or disposable, edible machines. Aquinas insists that cruelty to animals is not wrong in itself but should be avoided because it might make humans callous toward one another. Descartes voiced the common opinion of his day that animals are insensible mechanisms that can no more experience pain or pleasure than a clock. Kant says that we should always treat persons as ends in themselves, never merely as a means to an end—but an animal is not a person, so we have no moral duties to it.

Today the traditional view lives on, although almost everyone accepts that many animals are sentient (they can feel pain, pleasure, and an array of emotions) and that causing them unnecessary pain is morally unacceptable. The basic argument against animals having moral status is that they lack an essential property that qualifies them for that status. Humans have this property, but animals do not. Animals may have value but only in relation to human needs and desires. Traditionalists disagree about the nature of this crucial property, but the candidates include (1) possessing a soul, (2) having the capacity for humanlike family relationships, (3) being human (having human DNA), (4) being able to enter into social contracts, (5) being a person or moral agent, and (6) being able to reason and to act autonomously.

The first two possibilities have their supporters but face several strong criticisms. The soul view (an article of faith for some) has been called into question by philosophical considerations, and the family-relationships idea has been undermined by scientific evidence (research shows that some animal species maintain complex and enduring family ties).

To many, a much more plausible claim is that being a member of the human species automatically gives one moral status. That is, having human DNA is a necessary and sufficient condition for moral considerability; nonhuman animals therefore lack moral status. But some detractors contend that even though all normal, adult humans have moral status, not all beings that possess it have to be human. It seems possible, they say, that there could exist intelligent, rational, autonomous beings (creatures from other planets?) that obviously have moral status—but are not human. If this state of affairs is possible, then having human DNA is not necessary for moral respect.

Properties (4), (5), and (6) seem plausible because we normally think that any individual that can participate in social contracts, is a moral agent, or makes rational, autonomous choices deserves our moral respect. But critics ask why these criteria should matter for moral status. They say that from the fact that animals lack any of these properties, it does not follow that animals lack moral status. Animals may derive their moral considerability from something else, perhaps their capacity for having interests, such as interests in surviving or in not suffering. Those who make this argument also point out that the status-granting properties can cut both ways. As criteria, they exclude nonhuman animals from moral considerability but also leave out some humans—babies, young children, the mentally impaired, and individuals in comas. This implication is worrisome because people generally treat these humans with moral respect despite their lack of cognitive abilities.

In recent years, philosophers have launched vigorous rebuttals to the traditional attitude toward animals. Peter Singer is the most prominent among them, credited with forcefully challenging the old ideas and setting in motion the animal rights movement. He argues that sentient animals have moral status for the same reason that humans do—they can experience pain and pleasure. Any creature that can suffer has moral standing. Moreover humans and animals merit equal moral consideration because they are capable of comparable suffering; equal suffering must be given equal moral weight. The pain of a pig is just as important as the like pain of a human being.

As a utilitarian, Singer thinks that our moral duty is to maximize utility for all concerned, and *all concerned* should include human and nonhuman animals alike. On Singer's theory, our brutal methods of meat production and our scientific experimentation on animals are immoral. He argues on utilitarian grounds that the enormous suffering these practices cause to animals greatly outweighs the trivial pleasures of meat eating and the marginal gains in scientific knowledge.

Singer asserts that people who refuse to see humans and animals as moral equals are guilty of **speciesism**, a close cousin of racism. A speciesist discriminates against animals purely because of their species, just as a racist discriminates against other people merely because of their race.

Some philosophers make even stronger claims on behalf of animals. Tom Regan, for example, argues for **animal rights**—moral status that cannot be easily overridden. (Many people also use *animal rights* in a weaker sense to refer to moral status.) Animal rights are analogous to rights for persons: if a person has a bona fide right to free speech, then she is entitled to exercise it even if her words offend or embarrass others, even if the rest of the world would be happier if she were silenced. Only in rare cases and for the strongest of reasons can her right be legitimately rescinded. Regan argues that all conscious beings (actually all mature mammals, humans included) have rights. All have inherent value—and all have it equally. "[A]ll have an equal right to be treated with respect," Regan says, "to be treated in ways that do not reduce them to the status of things, as if they exist

FACTS AND FIGURES: The Treatment of Animals

- In 2008, 154 million cattle, calves, hogs, sheep, and lambs were slaughtered for food.
- Also in 2008, 9.37 billion chickens, turkeys, and ducks were slaughtered.
- In 2007, the media reported 1,880 cases of animal cruelty (many more cases go unreported).
- Forty-five states have felony laws for animal cruelty. Arkansas, Idaho, Mississippi, North Dakota, and South Dakota are the exceptions.
- In 2004, approximately 8 percent of large animals used in research were subjected to unrelieved

"pain or distress." This percentage does not include smaller animals such as mice and rats, which are used in about 90 percent of animal research.

U.S. Department of Agriculture, National Agricultural Statistical Services, *Livestock Slaughter: 2008 Annual Summary*, March 2009; *Poultry Slaughter: 2008 Annual Summary*, March 2009; The Humane Society of the United States, "Animal Cruelty Facts, Statistics, and Trends," 2009, http://www.hsus.org/acf/, (8 March 2009);

as resources for others."[1] If so, this doctrine is a sweeping indictment of all the rights-denying practices inherent in the meat industry, sport hunting and trapping, and animal experimentation.

Alongside the debates about animals, disputes over the moral status of the rest of nature have raged among philosophers, environmental activists, and policymakers. Once again, the key questions are, Which entities—if any—have moral considerability and how much do they have? And once more the basic positions of the disputants take familiar form.

The traditional view is **anthropocentrism**, the doctrine that humans alone have moral status. Like traditionalists regarding animals, anthropocentrists claim that the environment has value only as it relates to human interests. All of nature—the animals, habitats, plants, and ecosystems—is a resource to be used in the service of humankind. If nature is to be protected or preserved, the justification is that the actions are for the good of humans. If it is to be degraded or used up, the rationale is the same. Why do humans deserve this preferential treatment? Because, the anthropocentrist says, humans have souls, or the power of reason, or the capacity for moral agency, or some other essential characteristic—and nature does not.

Biocentrism veers sharply away from the anthropocentric view, affirming the principle that *all living things* have some degree of moral status. The biocentrist enlarges the circle of moral considerability to encompass both the sentient and the nonsentient—from zebras to oaks to lichens to bacteria. This view implies that human interactions with the natural world must not be based solely on utilitarian factors; the moral status of living entities must be taken into account. Some biocentrists (the egalitarians) insist that all living things have equal moral standing. A man has the same moral worth as an elephant or a tulip. Others (the nonegalitarians) believe that the moral standing of living things comes in degrees; some species deserve more moral respect than others. An ape may have greater moral standing than a rabbit, and a rabbit more than a rose.

Those who believe that all animals or all living things have moral status disagree about whether the individual entity or the whole species or community of entities should be the focus of moral concern. Ecological individualists maintain that the individual matters as much as, or more than, the species or ecosystem. They give priority to protecting or saving the individual members. Killing individual gnus for the good of the African plains, then, is prima facie wrong. Ecological holists, however, say that the good of entire species or ecosystems is more important than the fate of individuals. They believe it morally permissible, even obligatory, to sacrifice individuals to preserve the well-being and beauty of the whole. Thus we may be justified in killing a few elephants to preserve a grassland habitat or in allowing hunters to decimate a species of duck to maintain biological balance in an ecosystem.

KEY TERMS

animal rights	moral status	speciesism
anthropocentrism	biocentrism	

---

[1] Tom Regan, "The Case for Animal Rights," in *In Defense of Animals*, ed. Peter Singer (Oxford: Blackwell, 1985), 21.

ARGUMENTS AND READINGS

22. SINGER'S "ALL ANIMALS ARE EQUAL" ARGUMENT

According to Peter Singer, we need a revolution in the way we humans view and treat other species, specifically nonhuman animals. We need, in fact, to recognize animals as our moral equals. This attitude, he says, is demanded of us by the most fundamental tenet of ethics itself: the principle of equal consideration of interests.

In *Practical Ethics*, he argues that the principle requires that in our moral deliberations, we give equal weight "to the like interests of all those affected by our actions."[2] This means, for example, that if two people are suffering the same degree of intense pain, they both have an interest in relief of pain, and their interests warrant the same level of respect from others. This equality of consideration derives solely from the interests involved, not from the characteristics or abilities of those concerned. As Singer says,

> The principle of equal consideration of interests acts like a pair of scales, weighing interests impartially. True scales favour the side where the interest is stronger or where several interests combine to outweigh a smaller number of similar interests; but they take no account of whose interests they are weighing.[3]

Singer argues that the principle cannot be limited to humans but must be extended beyond our own species to nonhuman animals. The crucial property that entitles a being to equal consideration, he says, is the capacity for suffering:

> If a being suffers, there can be no moral justification for refusing to take that suffering into consideration. No matter what the nature of the being, the principle of equality requires that its suffering be counted equally with the like suffering—in so far as rough comparisons can be made—of any other being. If a being is not capable of suffering, or of experiencing enjoyment or happiness, there is nothing to be taken into account.[4]

But equality of consideration for relevant interests, he says, does not entail equality of treatment. It means only that when humans and animals have comparable interests (interests in not being killed or in avoiding pain, for example), we should give their interests equal consideration. When the interests are not alike, we need not treat humans and animals the same. A man may suffer if deprived of the opportunity to create art or to express

---

[2] Peter Singer, *Practical Ethics*, 2nd ed. (Cambridge: Cambridge University Press, 1993), 21.
[3] Singer, 22.
[4] Singer, 57.

his ideas freely, but a horse cannot suffer in this way. So we would give moral weight to the man's interests and treat him accordingly, but we need not treat the horse similarly because it has no comparable interests. As Singer says, a human dying from cancer may suffer more than a mouse dying of cancer because of the human's greater understanding of his situation. On the other hand, sometimes animals may suffer more because of their lack of understanding of what's happening to them.

Arguments against Singer's position are numerous, many of them positing some property—ability to reason, use of language, or autonomy, for example—that distinguish humans from animals and thus justify greater moral consideration for the former. Singer's response is that if we use these properties to show that animals have a lower moral status than humans, then intellectually disabled humans would have the same low moral status as animals.

Singer's utilitarian view has also been criticized for not being truly egalitarian. Singer advocates equal consideration of interests, but some critics maintain that on this view individuals have no value in their own right. Individuals, they say, are entitled to something more—to equal inherent value.

All Animals Are Equal

PETER SINGER

RACISM AND SPECIESISM

[I've given] reasons for believing that the fundamental principle of equality, on which the equality of all human beings rests, is the principle of equal consideration of interests. Only a basic moral principle of this kind can allow us to defend a form of equality that embraces all human beings with all the differences that exist between them. I shall now contend that while this principle does provide an adequate basis for human equality, it provides a basis that cannot be limited to humans. In other words I shall suggest that, having accepted the principle of equality as a sound moral basis for relations with others of our own species, we are also committed to accepting it as a sound moral basis for relations with those outside our own species—the non-human animals.

This suggestion may at first seem bizarre. We are used to regarding discrimination against members of racial minorities, or against women, as among the most important moral and political issues facing the world today. These are serious matters, worthy of the time and energy of any concerned person.

But animals? Isn't the welfare of animals in a different category altogether, a matter for people who are dotty about dogs and cats? How can anyone waste their time on equality for animals when so many humans are denied real equality?

This attitude reflects a popular prejudice against taking the interests of animals seriously—a prejudice no better founded than the prejudice of white slave-owners against taking the interests of their African slaves seriously. It is easy for us to criticise the prejudices of our grandfathers, from which our fathers freed themselves. It is more difficult to distance ourselves from our own views, so that we can dispassionately search for prejudices among the beliefs and values we hold. What is needed now is a willingness to follow the arguments where they lead, without a prior assumption that the issue is not worth our attention.

The argument for extending the principle of equality beyond our own species is simple, so simple that it amounts to no more than a clear understanding of the nature of the principle of equal consideration of interests. We have seen that this principle implies that our concern for others ought not to depend on what they are like, or what abilities they possess (although precisely what this concern requires us to do may vary according to the characteristics of those affected by what we do). It is on this basis that we are able to say that the fact that some people are not members of our race does not entitle us to exploit them, and similarly the fact that some people are less intelligent than others does not mean that their interests may be disregarded. But the principle also implies that the fact that beings are not members of our species does not entitle us to exploit them, and similarly the fact that other animals are less intelligent than we are does not mean that their interests may be disregarded.

We saw previously that many philosophers have advocated equal consideration of interests, in some form or other, as a basic moral principle. Only a few have recognised that the principle has applications beyond our own species, one of the few being Jeremy Bentham, the founding father of modern utilitarianism. In a forward-looking passage, written at a time when African slaves in the British dominions were still being treated much as we now treat nonhuman animals, Bentham wrote:

> The day may come when the rest of the animal creation may acquire those rights which never could have been withholden from them but by the hand of tyranny. The French have already discovered that the blackness of the skin is no reason why a human being should be abandoned without redress to the caprice of a tormentor. It may one day come to be recognised that the number of the legs, the villosity of the skin or the termination of the *os sacrum,* are reasons equally insufficient for abandoning a sensitive being to the same fate. What else is it that should trace the insuperable line? Is it the faculty of reason, or perhaps the faculty of discourse? But a fullgrown horse or dog is beyond comparison a more rational, as well as a more conversable animal, than an infant of a day, or a week, or even a month, old. But suppose they were otherwise, what would it avail? The question is not, Can they *reason?* nor Can they *talk*? But, *Can they suffer?*

In this passage Bentham points to the capacity for suffering as the vital characteristic that entitles a being to equal consideration. The capacity for suffering—or more strictly, for suffering and/or enjoyment or happiness—is not just another characteristic like the capacity for language, or for higher mathematics. Bentham is not saying that those who try to mark "the insuperable line" that determines whether the interests of a being should be considered happen to have selected the wrong characteristic. The capacity for suffering and enjoying things is a prerequisite for having interests at all, a condition that must be satisfied before we can speak of interest in any meaningful way. It would be nonsense to say that it was not in the interests of a stone to be kicked along the road by a schoolboy. A stone does not have interests because it cannot suffer. Nothing that we can do to it could possibly make any difference to its welfare. A mouse, on the other hand, does have an interest in not being tormented, because mice will suffer if they are treated in this way.

If a being suffers, there can be no moral justification for refusing to take that suffering into consideration. No matter what the nature of the being, the principle of equality requires that the suffering be counted equally with the like suffering—in so far as rough comparisons can be made—of any other being. If a being is not capable of suffering, or of experiencing enjoyment or happiness, there is nothing to be taken into account. This is why the limit of sentience (using the term as a convenient, if not strictly accurate, shorthand for the capacity to suffer or experience enjoyment or happiness) is the only defensible boundary of concern for the interests of others. To mark this boundary by some characteristic like intelligence or rationality would be to mark it in an arbitrary way. Why not choose some other characteristic, like skin colour?

Racists violate the principle of equality by giving greater weight to the interests of members of their own race when there is a clash between their interests and the interests of those of another race. Racists of European descent typically have not accepted that pain matters as much when it is felt by Africans, for example, as when it is felt by Europeans. Similarly those I would call "speciesists" give greater weight to the interests of members of their own species when there is a clash between their interests and the interests of those of other species. Human speciesists do not accept that pain is as bad when it is felt by pigs or mice as when it is felt by humans.

That, then, is really the whole of the argument for extending the principle of equality to nonhuman animals; but there may be some doubts about what this equality amounts to in practice. In particular, the last sentence of the previous paragraph may prompt some people to reply "Surely pain felt by a mouse just is not as bad as pain felt by a human. Humans have much greater awareness of what is happening to them, and this makes their suffering worse. You can't equate the suffering of, say, a person dying slowly from cancer, and a laboratory mouse undergoing the same fate."

I fully accept that in the case described the human cancer victim normally suffers more than the nonhuman cancer victim. This in no way undermines the extension of equal consideration of interests to nonhumans. It means, rather, that we must take care when we compare the interests of different species. In some situations a member of one species will suffer more than a member of another species. In this case we should still apply the principle of equal consideration of interests but the result of so doing is, of course, to give priority to relieving the greater suffering. A simpler case may help to make this clear.

If I give a horse a hard slap across its rump with my open hand, the horse may start, but it presumably feels little pain. Its skin is thick enough to protect it against a mere slap. If I slap a baby in the same way, however, the baby will cry and presumably does feel pain, for the baby's skin is more sensitive. So it is worse to slap a baby than a horse, if both slaps are administered with equal force. But there must be some kind of blow—I don't know exactly what it would be, but perhaps a blow with a heavy stick— that would cause the horse as much pain as we cause a baby by a simple slap. That is what I mean by "the same amount of pain" and if we consider it wrong to inflict that much pain on a baby for no good reason then we must, unless we are speciesists, consider it equally wrong to inflict the same amount of pain on a horse for no good reason.

There are other differences between humans and animals that cause other complications. Normal adult human beings have mental capacities that will,

in certain circumstances, lead them to suffer more than animals would in the same circumstances. If, for instance, we decided to perform extremely painful or lethal scientific experiments on normal adult humans, kidnapped at random from public parks for this purpose, adults who entered parks would become fearful that they would be kidnapped. The resultant terror would be a form of suffering additional to the pain of the experiment. The same experiments performed on nonhuman animals would cause less suffering since the animals would not have the anticipatory dread of being kidnapped and experimented upon. This does not mean, of course, that it would be *right* to perform the experiment on animals, but only that there is a reason, and one that is not speciesist, for preferring to use animals rather than normal adult humans, if the experiment is to be done at all. Note, however, that this same argument gives us a reason for preferring to use human infants—orphans perhaps—or severely intellectually disabled humans for experiments, rather than adults, since infants and severely intellectually disabled humans would also have no idea of what was going to happen to them. As far as this argument is concerned, nonhuman animals and infants and severely intellectually disabled humans are in the same category; and if we use this argument to justify experiments on nonhuman animals we have to ask ourselves whether we are also prepared to allow experiments on human infants and severely intellectually disabled adults. If we make a distinction between animals and these humans, how can we do it, other than on the basis of a morally indefensible preference for members of our own species?

There are many areas in which the superior mental powers of normal adult humans make a difference: anticipation, more detailed memory, greater knowledge of what is happening, and so on. These differences explain why a human dying from cancer is likely to suffer more than a mouse. It is the mental anguish that makes the human's position so much harder to bear. Yet these differences do not all point to greater suffering on the part of the normal human being. Sometimes animals may suffer more because of their more limited understanding. If, for instance, we are taking prisoners in wartime we can explain to them that while they must submit to capture, search, and confinement they will not otherwise be harmed and will be set free at the conclusion of hostilities. If we capture wild animals, however, we cannot explain that we are not threatening their lives. A wild animal cannot distinguish an attempt to overpower and confine from an attempt to kill; the one causes as much terror as the other.

It may be objected that comparisons of the sufferings of different species are impossible to make, and that for this reason when the interests of animals and humans clash, the principle of equality gives no guidance. It is true that comparisons of suffering between members of different species cannot be made precisely. Nor, for that matter, can comparisons of suffering between different human beings be made precisely. Precision is not essential. As we shall see shortly, even if we were to prevent the infliction of suffering on animals only when the interests of humans will not be affected to anything like the extent that animals are affected, we would be forced to make radical changes in our treatment of animals that would involve our diet, the farming methods we use, experimental procedures in many fields of science, our approach to wildlife and to hunting, trapping and the wearing of furs, and areas of entertainment like circuses, rodeos, and zoos. As a result, the total quantity of suffering caused would be greatly reduced; so greatly that it is hard to imagine any other change of moral attitude that would cause so great a reduction in the total sum of suffering in the universe.

So far I have said a lot about the infliction of suffering on animals, but nothing about killing them. This omission has been deliberate. The application of the principle of equality to the infliction of suffering is, in theory at least, fairly straightforward. Pain and suffering are bad and should be prevented or minimised, irrespective of the race, sex, or species of the being that suffers. How bad a pain is depends on how intense it is and how long it lasts, but pains of the same intensity and duration are equally bad, whether felt by humans or animals. When we come to consider the value of life, we cannot say quite so confidently that a life is a life, and equally valuable, whether it is a human life or an animal life. It would not be speciesist to hold that the life of a self-aware being, capable of abstract thought, of planning for the future, of complex acts of communication, and

so on, is more valuable than the life of a being without these capacities. (I am not saying whether this view is justifiable or not; only that it cannot simply be rejected as speciesist, because it is not on the basis of species itself that one life is held to be more valuable than another.) The value of life is a notoriously difficult ethical question, and we can only arrive at a reasoned conclusion about the comparative value of human and animal life after we have discussed the value of life in general. This is a topic for a separate chapter. Meanwhile there are important conclusions to be derived from the extension beyond our own species of the principle of equal consideration of interests, irrespective of our conclusions about the value of life.

SPECIESIM IN PRACTICE

Animals as Food

For most people in modem, urbanised societies, the principal form of contact with nonhuman animals is at meal times. The use of animals for food is probably the oldest and the most widespread form of animal use. There is also a sense in which it is the most basic form of animal use, the foundation stone on which rests the belief that animals exist for our pleasure and convenience.

If animals count in their own right, our use of animals for food becomes questionable—especially when animal flesh is a luxury rather than a necessity. Eskimos living in an environment where they must kill animals for food or starve might be justified in claiming that their interest in surviving overrides that of the animals they kill. Most of us cannot defend our diet in this way. Citizens of industrialised societies can easily obtain an adequate diet without the use of animal flesh. The overwhelming weight of medical evidence indicates that animal flesh is not necessary for good health or longevity. Nor is animal production in industrialised societies an efficient way of producing food, since most of the animals consumed have been fattened on grains and other foods that we could have eaten directly. When we feed these grains to animals, only about 10 per cent of the nutritional value remains as meat for human consumption. So, with the exception of animals raised entirely on grazing land unsuitable for crops, animals are eaten neither for health, nor to increase our food supply. Their flesh is a luxury, consumed because people like its taste.

In considering the ethics of the use of animal flesh for human food in industrialised societies, we are considering a situation in which a relatively minor human interest must be balanced against the lives and welfare of the animals involved. The principle of equal consideration of interests does not allow major interests to be sacrificed for minor interests.

The case against using animals for food is at its strongest when animals are made to lead miserable lives so that their flesh can be made available to humans at the lowest possible cost. Modern forms of intensive farming apply science and technology to the attitude that animals are objects for us to use. In order to have meat on the table at a price that people can afford, our society tolerates methods of meat production that confine sentient animals in cramped, unsuitable conditions for the entire duration of their lives. Animals are treated like machines that convert fodder into flesh, and any innovation that results in a higher "conversion ratio" is liable to be adopted. As one authority on the subject has said, "Cruelty is acknowledged only when profitability ceases." To avoid speciesism we must stop these practices. Our custom is all the support that factory farmers need. The decision to cease giving them that support may be difficult, but it is less difficult than it would have been for a white Southerner to go against the traditions of his society and free his slaves; if we do not change our dietary habits, how can we censure those slaveholders who would not change their own way of living?

These arguments apply to animals who have been reared in factory farms—which means that we should not eat chicken, pork, or veal, unless we know that the meat we are eating was not produced by factory farm methods. The same is true of beef that has come from cattle kept in crowded feedlots (as most beef does in the United States). Eggs will come from hens kept in small wire cages, too small even to allow them to stretch their wings, unless the eggs are specifically sold "free range" (or unless one lives in a relatively enlightened country like Switzerland, which has prohibited the cage system of keeping hens).

These arguments do not take us all the way to a vegetarian diet, since some animals, for instance sheep, and in some countries cattle, still graze freely outdoors. This could change. The American pattern of fattening cattle in crowded feedlots is spreading to other countries. Meanwhile, the lives of free-ranging animals are undoubtedly better than those of animals reared in factory farms. It is still doubtful if using them for food is compatible with equal consideration of interests. One problem is, of course, that using them as food involves killing them—but this is an issue to which, as I have said, we shall return when we have discussed the value of life. Apart from taking their lives there are also many other things done to animals in order to bring them cheaply to our dinner table. Castration, the separation of mother and young, the breaking up of herds, branding, transporting, and finally the moments of slaughter—all of these are likely to involve suffering and do not take the animals' interests into account. Perhaps animals could be reared on a small scale without suffering in these ways, but it does not seem economical or practical to do so on the scale required for feeding our large urban populations. In any case, the important question is not whether animal flesh *could* be produced without suffering, but whether the flesh we are considering buying was produced without suffering. Unless we can be confident that it was, the principle of equal consideration of interests implies that it was wrong to sacrifice important interests of the animal in order to satisfy less important interests of our own; consequently we should boycott the end result of this process.

For those of us living in cities where it is difficult to know how the animals we might eat have lived and died, this conclusion brings us close to a vegetarian way of life. I shall consider some objections to it in the final section of this chapter.

Experimenting on Animals

Perhaps the area in which speciesism can most clearly be observed is the use of animals in experiments. Here the issue stands out starkly, because experimenters often seek to justify experimenting on animals by claiming that the experiments lead us to discoveries about humans; if this is so, the experimenter must agree that human and nonhuman animals are similar in crucial respects. For instance, if forcing a rat to choose between starving to death and crossing an electrified grid to obtain food tells us anything about the reactions of humans to stress, we must assume that the rat feels stress in this kind of situation.

People sometimes think that all animal experiments serve vital medical purposes, and can be justified on the grounds that they relieve more suffering than they cause. This comfortable belief is mistaken. Drug companies test new shampoos and cosmetics they are intending to market by dripping concentrated solutions of them into the eyes of rabbits, in a test known as the Draize test. (Pressure from the animal liberation movement has led several cosmetic companies to abandon this practice. An alternative test, not using animals, has now been found. Nevertheless, many companies, including some of the largest, still continue to perform the Draize test.) Food additives, including artificial colourings and preservatives, are tested by what is known as the LD50—a test designed to find the "lethal dose," or level of consumption that will make 50 per cent of a sample of animals die. In the process nearly all of the animals are made very sick before some finally die and others pull through. These tests are not necessary to prevent human suffering: even if there were no alternative to the use of animals to test the safety of the products, we already have enough shampoos and food colourings. There is no need to develop new ones that might be dangerous.

In many countries, the armed forces perform atrocious experiments on animals that rarely come to light. To give just one example: at the U.S. Armed Forces Radiobiology Institute, in Bethesda, Maryland, rhesus monkeys have been trained to run inside a large wheel. If they slow down too much, the wheel slows down, too, and the monkeys get an electric shock. Once the monkeys are trained to run for long periods, they are given lethal doses of radiation. Then, while sick and vomiting, they are forced to continue to run until they drop. This is supposed to provide information on the capacities of soldiers to continue to fight after a nuclear attack.

Nor can all university experiments be defended on the grounds that they relieve more suffering than they inflict. Three experimenters at Princeton University kept 256 young rats without food or water until they died. They concluded that young rats under conditions of fatal thirst and starvation are much more active than normal adult rats given food and water. In a well-known series of experiments that went on for more than fifteen years, H. F. Harlow of the Primate Research Center, Madison, Wisconsin, reared monkeys under conditions of maternal deprivation and total isolation. He found that in this way he could reduce the monkeys to a state in which, when placed among normal monkeys, they sat huddled in a corner in a condition of persistent depression and fear. Harlow also produced monkey mothers so neurotic that they smashed their infant's face into the floor and rubbed it back and forth. Although Harlow himself is no longer alive, some of his former students at other U.S. universities continue to perform variations on his experiments.

In these cases, and many others like them, the benefits to humans are either nonexistent or uncertain, while the losses to members of other species are certain and real. Hence the experiments indicate a failure to give equal consideration to the interests of all beings, irrespective of species.

In the past, argument about animal experimentation has often missed this point because it has been put in absolutist terms: would the opponent of experimentation be prepared to let thousands die from a terrible disease that could be cured by experimenting on one animal? This is a purely hypothetical question, since experiments do not have such dramatic results, but as long as its hypothetical nature is clear, I think the question should be answered affirmatively—in other words, if one, or even a dozen animals had to suffer experiments in order to save thousands, I would think it right and in accordance with equal consideration of interests that they should do so. This, at any rate, is the answer a utilitarian must give. Those who believe in absolute rights might hold that it is always wrong to sacrifice one being, whether human or animal, for the benefit of another. In that case the experiment should not be carried out, whatever the consequences.

To the hypothetical question about saving thousands of people through a single experiment on an animal, opponents of speciesism can reply with a hypothetical question of their own: would experimenters be prepared to perform their experiments on orphaned humans with severe and irreversible brain damage if that were the only way to save thousands? (I say "orphaned" in order to avoid the complication of the feelings of the human parents.) If experimenters are not prepared to use orphaned humans with severe and irreversible brain damage, their readiness to use nonhuman animals seems to discriminate on the basis of species alone, since apes, monkeys, dogs, cats, and even mice and rats are more intelligent, more aware of what is happening to them, more sensitive to pain, and so on, than many severely brain-damaged humans barely surviving in hospital wards and other institutions. There seems to be no morally relevant characteristic that such humans have that nonhuman animals lack. Experimenters, then, show bias in favour of their own species whenever they carry out experiments on nonhuman animals for purposes that they would not think justified them in using human beings at an equal or lower level of sentience, awareness, sensitivity, and so on. If this bias were eliminated, the number of experiments performed on animals would be greatly reduced. . . . .

SOME OBJECTIONS

I first put forward the views outlined in this chapter in 1973. At that time there was no animal liberation or animal rights movement. Since then a movement has sprung up, and some of the worst abuses of animals, like the Draize and LD50 tests, are now less widespread, even though they have not been eliminated. The fur trade has come under attack, and as a result fur sales have declined dramatically in countries like Britain, the Netherlands, Australia, and the United States. Some countries are also starting to phase out the most confining forms of factory farming. As already mentioned, Switzerland has prohibited the cage system of keeping laying hens. Britain has outlawed the raising of calves in individual stalls, and is phasing out individual stalls for pigs. Sweden, as in other areas of social reform, is in the lead here, too: in 1988 the Swedish Parliament passed a law that will, over a ten-year period, lead to the elimination of all systems of factory farming that confine animals for long periods and prevent them carrying out their natural behaviour.

Despite this increasing acceptance of many aspects of the case for animal liberation, and the slow but tangible progress made on behalf of animals, a variety of objections have emerged, some straightforward and predictable, some more subtle and unexpected. In this final section of the chapter I shall attempt to answer the most important of these objections. I shall begin with the more straightforward ones.

How Do We Know That Animals Can Feel Pain?

We can never directly experience the pain of another being, whether that being is human or not. When I see my daughter fall and scrape her knee, I know that she feels pain because of the way she behaves—she cries, she tells me her knee hurts, she rubs the sore spot, and so on. I know that I myself behave in a somewhat similar—if more inhibited—way when I feel pain, and so I accept that my daughter feels something like what I feel when I scrape my knee.

The basis of my belief that animals can feel pain is similar to the basis of my belief that my daughter can feel pain. Animals in pain behave in much the same way as humans do, and their behaviour is sufficient justification for the belief that they feel pain. It is true that, with the exception of those apes who have been taught to communicate by sign language, they cannot actually say that they are feeling pain—but then when my daughter was very young she could not talk, either. She found other ways to make her inner states apparent, thereby demonstrating that we can be sure that a being is feeling pain even if the being cannot use language.

To back up our inference from animal behaviour, we can point to the fact that the nervous systems of all vertebrates, and especially of birds and mammals, are fundamentally similar. Those parts of the human nervous system that are concerned with feeling pain are relatively old, in evolutionary terms. Unlike the cerebral cortex, which developed fully only after our ancestors diverged from other mammals, the basic nervous system evolved in more distant ancestors common to ourselves and the other 'higher' animals. This anatomical parallel makes it likely that the capacity of animals to feel is similar to our own.

It is significant that none of the grounds we have for believing that animals feel pain hold for plants. We cannot observe behaviour suggesting pain—sensational claims to the contrary have not been substantiated—and plants do not have a centrally organised nervous system like ours.

Animals Eat Each Other, So Why Shouldn't We Eat Them?

This might be called the Benjamin Franklin Objection. Franklin recounts in his *Autobiography* that he was for a time a vegetarian but his abstinence from animal flesh came to an end when he was watching some friends prepare to fry a fish they had just caught. When the fish was cut open, it was found to have a smaller fish in its stomach. "Well," Franklin said to himself, "if you eat one another, I don't see why we may not eat you" and he proceeded to do so.

Franklin was at least honest. In telling this story, he confesses that he convinced himself of the validity of the objection only after the fish was already in the frying pan and smelling "admirably well", and he remarks that one of the advantages of being a "reasonable creature" is that one can find a reason for whatever one wants to do. The replies that can be made to this objection are so obvious that Franklin's acceptance of it does testify more to his love of fried fish than to his powers of reason.

For a start, most animals who kill for food would not be able to survive if they did not, whereas we have no need to eat animal flesh. Next, it is odd that humans, who normally think of the behaviour of animals as "beastly" should, when it suits them, use an argument that implies that we ought to look to animals for moral guidance. The most decisive point, however, is that nonhuman animals are not capable of considering the alternatives open to them or of reflecting on the ethics of their diet. Hence it is impossible to hold the animals responsible for what they do, or to judge that because of their killing they "deserve" to be treated in a similar way. Those who read these lines, on the other hand, must consider the justifiability of their dietary habits. You cannot evade responsibility by imitating beings who are incapable of making this choice.

Sometimes people point to the fact that animals eat each other in order to make a slightly different point. This fact suggests, they think, not that animals deserve to be eaten, but rather that there is a natural law according to which the stronger prey upon the weaker, a kind of Darwinian 'survival of the fittest' in which by eating animals we are merely playing our part.

This interpretation of the objection makes two basic mistakes, one a mistake of fact and the other an error of reasoning. The factual mistake lies in the assumption that our own consumption of animals is part of the natural evolutionary process. This might be true of a few primitive cultures that still hunt for food, but it has nothing to do with the mass production of domestic animals in factory farms.

Suppose that we did hunt for our food, though, and this was part of some natural evolutionary process. There would still be an error of reasoning in the assumption that because this process is natural it is right. It is, no doubt, "natural" for women to produce an infant every year or two from puberty to menopause, but this does not mean that it is wrong to interfere with this process. We need to know the natural laws that affect us in order to estimate the consequences of what we do; but we do not have to assume that the natural way of doing something is incapable of improvement.

Differences Between Humans and Animals

That there is a huge gulf between humans and animals was unquestioned for most of the course of Western civilisation. The basis of this assumption has been undermined by Darwin's discovery of our animal origins and the associated decline in the credibility of the story of our Divine Creation, made in the image of God with an immortal soul. Some have found it difficult to accept that the differences between us and the other animals are differences of degree rather than kind. They have searched for ways of drawing a line between humans and animals. To date these boundaries have been shortlived. For instance, it used to be said that only humans used tools. Then it was observed that the Galapagos woodpecker used a cactus thorn to dig insects out of crevices in trees. Next it was suggested that even if other animals used tools, humans are the only toolmaking animals. But Jane Goodall found that chimpanzees in the jungles of Tanzania chewed up leaves to make a sponge for sopping up water, and trimmed the leaves off branches to make tools for catching insects. The use of language was another boundary line—but now chimpanzees, gorillas, and an orangutan have learnt Ameslan, the sign language of the deaf, and there is some evidence suggesting that whales and dolphins may have a complex language of their own.

If these attempts to draw the line between humans and animals had fitted the facts of the situation, they would still not carry any moral weight. As Bentham pointed out, the fact that a being does not use language or make tools is hardly a reason for ignoring its suffering. Some philosophers have claimed that there is a more profound difference. They have claimed that animals cannot think or reason, and that accordingly they have no conception of themselves, no self-consciousness. They live from instant to instant, and do not see themselves as distinct entities with a past and a future. Nor do they have autonomy, the ability to choose how to live one's life. It has been suggested that autonomous, self-conscious beings are in some way much more valuable, more morally significant, than beings who live from moment to moment, without the capacity to see themselves as distinct beings with a past and a future. Accordingly, on this view, the interests of autonomous, self-conscious beings ought normally to take priority over the interests of other beings.

I shall not now consider whether some nonhuman animals are self-conscious and autonomous. The reason for this omission is that I do not believe that, in the present context, much depends on this question. We are now considering only the application of the principle of equal consideration of interests. When we discuss questions about the value of life, we shall see that there are reasons for holding that self-consciousness is crucial in debates about whether a being has a right to life; and we shall then investigate the evidence for self-consciousness in nonhuman animals. Meanwhile the more important issue is: does the fact that a being is self-conscious entitle that being to some kind of priority of consideration?

The claim that self-conscious beings are entitled to prior consideration is compatible with the principle of equal consideration of interests if it amounts to no more than the claim that something that happens to self-conscious beings can be contrary to their interests while similar events would not be contrary to the interests of beings who were not self-conscious. This might be because the self-conscious creature has greater awareness of what is happening, can fit the event into the overall framework of a longer time period, has different desires, and so on. But this is a point I granted, at the start of this chapter, and provided that it is not carried to ludicrous extremes—like insisting that if I am self-conscious and a veal calf is not, depriving me of veal causes more suffering than depriving the calf of his freedom to walk, stretch and eat grass—it is not denied by the criticisms I made of animal experimentation and factory farming.

It would be a different matter if it were claimed that, even when a self-conscious being did not suffer more than a being that was merely sentient, the suffering of the self-conscious being is more important because these are more valuable types of being. This introduces nonutilitarian claims of value—claims that do not derive simply from taking a universal standpoint in the manner described. Since the argument for utilitarianism developed was admittedly tentative, I cannot use that argument to rule out all nonutilitarian values. Nevertheless we are entitled to ask *why* self-conscious beings should be considered more valuable and in particular why the alleged greater value of a self-conscious being should result in preferring the lesser interests of a self-conscious being to the greater interests of a merely sentient being, even where the self-consciousness of the former being is not itself at stake. This last point is an important one, for we are not now considering cases in which the lives of self-conscious beings are at risk but cases in which self-conscious beings will go on living, their faculties intact, whatever we decide. In these cases, if the existence of self-consciousness does not affect the nature of the interests under comparison, it is not clear why we should drag self-consciousness into the discussion at all, any more than we should drag species, race or sex into similar discussions. Interests are interests, and ought to be given equal consideration whether they are the interests of human or non-human animals, self-conscious or non-self-conscious animals.

There is another possible reply to the claim that self-consciousness, or autonomy, or some similar characteristic, can serve to distinguish human from nonhuman animals: recall that there are intellectually disabled humans who have less claim to be regarded as self-conscious or autonomous than many non-human animals. If we use these characteristics to place a gulf between humans and other animals, we place these less able humans on the other side of the gulf; and if the gulf is taken to mark a difference in moral status, then these humans would have the moral status of animals rather than humans.

This reply is forceful, because most of us find horrifying the idea of using intellectually disabled humans in painful experiments, or fattening them for gourmet dinners. But some philosophers have argued that these consequences would not really follow from the use of a characteristic like self-consciousness or autonomy to distinguish humans from other animals. I shall consider three of these attempts.

The first suggestion is that severely intellectually disabled humans who do not possess the capacities that mark the normal human off from other animals should nevertheless be treated as if they did possess these capacities, since they belong to a species, members of which normally do possess them. The suggestion is, in other words, that we treat individuals not in accordance with their actual qualities, but in accordance with the qualities normal for their species.

It is interesting that this suggestion should be made in defence of treating members of our species better than members of another species, when it would be firmly rejected if it were used to justify treating members of our race or sex better than members of another race or sex. When discussing the impact of possible differences in IQ between members of different ethnic groups, I made the obvious point that whatever the difference between the *average* scores for different groups, some members of the group with the lower average score will do better than some members of groups with the higher average score, and so we ought to treat people as individuals and not according to the average score for their ethnic group, whatever the explanation of that average might be. If we accept this we cannot consistently accept the suggestion that when dealing with severely intellectually disabled humans

we should grant them the status or rights normal for their species. For what is the significance of the fact that this time the line is to be drawn around the species rather than around the race or sex? We cannot insist that beings be treated as individuals in the one case, and as members of a group in the other. Membership of a species is no more relevant in these circumstances than membership of a race or sex.

A second suggestion is that although severely intellectually disabled humans may not possess higher capacities than other animals, they are nonetheless human beings, and as such we have special relations with them that we do not have with other animals. As one reviewer of *Animal Liberation* put it: "Partiality for our own species, and within it for much smaller groupings is, like the universe, something we had better accept...The danger in an attempt to eliminate partial affections is that it may remove the source of all affections."

This argument ties morality too closely to our affections. Of course some people may have a closer relationship with the most profoundly intellectually disabled human than they do with any non-human animal, and it would be absurd to tell them that they should not feel this way. They simply do, and as such there is nothing good or bad about it. The question is whether our moral obligations to a being should be made to depend on our feelings in this manner. Notoriously, some human beings have a closer relationship with their cat than with their neighbours. Would those who tie morality to affections accept that these people are justified in saving their cats from a fire before they save their neighbours? And even those who are prepared to answer this question affirmatively would, I trust, not want to go along with racists who could argue that if people have more natural relationships with, and greater affection towards, others of their own race, it is all right for them to give preference to the interests of other members of their own race. Ethics does not demand that we eliminate personal relationships and partial affections, but it does demand that when we act we assess the moral claims of those affected by our actions with some degree of independence from our feelings for them.

The third suggestion invokes the widely used "slippery slope" argument. The idea of this argument is that once we take one step in a certain direction we shall find ourselves on a slippery slope and shall slither further than we wished to go. In the present context the argument is used to suggest that we need a clear line to divide those beings we can experiment upon, or fatten for dinner, from those we cannot. Species membership makes a nice sharp dividing line, whereas levels of self-consciousness, autonomy, or sentience do not. Once we allow that an intellectually disabled human being has no higher moral status than an animal, the argument goes, we have begun our descent down a slope, the next level of which is denying rights to social misfits, and the bottom of which is a totalitarian government disposing of any groups it does not like by classifying them as subhuman.

The slippery slope argument may serve as a valuable warning in some contexts, but it cannot bear too much weight. If we believe that, as I have argued in this chapter, the special status we now give to humans allows us to ignore the interests of billions of sentient creatures, we should not be deterred from trying to rectify this situation by the mere possibility that the principles on which we base this attempt will be misused by evil rulers for their own ends. And it is no more than a possibility. The change I have suggested might make no

difference to our treatment of humans, or it might even improve it.

In the end, no ethical line that is arbitrarily drawn can be secure. It is better to find a line that can be defended openly and honestly. When discussing euthanasia we shall see that a line drawn in the wrong place can have unfortunate results even for those placed on the higher, or human side of the line.

It is also important to remember that the aim of my argument is to elevate the status of animals rather than to lower the status of any humans. I do not wish to suggest that intellectually disabled humans should be force-fed with food colourings until half of them die—although this would certainly give us a more accurate indication of whether the substance was safe for humans than testing it on rabbits or dogs does. I would like our conviction that it would be wrong to treat intellectually disabled humans in this way to be transferred to nonhuman animals at similar levels of self-consciousness and with similar capacities for suffering. It is excessively pessimistic to refrain from trying to alter our attitudes on the grounds that we might start treating intellectually disabled humans with the same lack of concern we now have for animals, rather than give animals the greater concern that we now have for intellectually disabled humans. ...

The Case for the Use of Animals in Biomedical Research

CARL COHEN

Using animals as research subjects in medical investigations is widely condemned on two grounds: first, because it wrongly violates the *rights* of animals,[1] and second, because it wrongly imposes on sentient creatures much avoidable *suffering*.[2] Neither of these arguments is sound. The first relies on a mistaken understanding of rights; the second relies on a mistaken calculation of consequences. Both deserve definitive dismissal.

WHY ANIMALS HAVE NO RIGHTS

A right, properly understood, is a claim, or potential claim, that one party may exercise against another. The target against whom such a claim may

"The Case for the Use of Animals in Biomedical Research" by Carl Cohen, *The New England Journal of Medicine*, vol. 315, no. 14, 2 Oct. 1986, 865–870. © 1986. Massachusetts Medical Society.

be registered can be a single person, a group, a community, or (perhaps) all humankind. The content of rights claims also varies greatly: repayment of loans, nondiscrimination by employers, noninterference by the state, and so on. To comprehend any genuine right fully, therefore, we must know *who* holds the right, *against whom* it is held, and *to what* it is a right.

Alternative sources of rights add complexity. Some rights are grounded in constitution and law (e.g., the right of an accused to trial by jury); some rights are moral but give no legal claims (e.g., my right to your keeping the promise you gave me); and some rights (e.g., against theft or assault) are rooted both in morals and in law.

The differing targets, contents, and sources of rights, and their inevitable conflict, together weave a tangled web. Notwithstanding all such complications, this much is clear about rights in general: they are in every case claims, or potential claims, within a community of moral agents. Rights arise, and can be intelligibly defended, only among beings who actually do, or can, make moral claims against one another. Whatever else rights may be, therefore, they are necessarily human; their possessors are persons, human beings.

The attributes of human beings from which this moral capability arises have been described variously by philosophers, both ancient and modern: the inner consciousness of a free will (Saint Augustine[3]); the grasp, by human reason, of the binding character of moral law (Saint Thomas[4]); the self-conscious participation of human beings in an objective ethical order (Hegel[5]); human membership in an organic moral community (Bradley[6]); the development of the human self through the consciousness of other moral selves (Mead[7]); and the underivative, intuitive cognition of the rightness of an action (Prichard[8]). Most influential has been Immanuel Kant's emphasis on the universal human possession of a uniquely moral will and the autonomy its use entails.[9] Humans confront choices that are purely moral; humans—but certainly not dogs or mice—lay down moral laws, for others and for themselves. Human beings are self-legislative, morally *auto-nomous.*

Animals (that is, nonhuman animals, the ordinary sense of that word) lack this capacity for free moral judgment. They are not beings of a kind capable of exercising or responding to moral claims. Animals therefore have no rights, and they can have none. This is the core of the argument about the alleged rights of animals. The holders of rights must have the capacity to comprehend rules of duty, governing all including themselves. In applying such rules, the holders of rights must recognize possible conflicts between what is in their own interest and what is just. Only in a community of beings capable of self-restricting moral judgments can the concept of a right be correctly invoked.

Humans have such moral capacities. They are in this sense self-legislative, are members of communities governed by moral rules, and do possess rights. Animals do not have such moral capacities. They are not morally self-legislative, cannot possibly be members of a truly moral community, and therefore cannot possess rights. In conducting research on animal subjects, therefore, we do not violate their rights, because they have none to violate.

To animate life, even in its simplest forms, we give a certain natural reverence. But the possession of rights presupposes a moral status not attained by the vast majority of living things. We must not infer, therefore, that a live being has, simply in being alive, a "right" to its life. The assertion that all animals, only because they are alive and have interests, also possess the "right to life"[10] is an abuse of that phrase, and wholly without warrant.

It does not follow from this, however, that we are morally free to do anything we please to animals. Certainly not. In our dealings with animals, as in our dealings with other human beings, we have obligations that do not arise from claims against us based on rights. Rights entail obligations, but many of the things one ought to do are in no way tied to another's entitlement. Rights and obligations are not reciprocals of one another, and it is a serious mistake to suppose that they are.

Illustrations are helpful. Obligations may arise from internal commitments made: physicians have obligations to their patients not grounded merely in their patients' rights. Teachers have such obligations to their students, shepherds to their dogs, and cowboys to their horses. Obligations may arise from differences of status: adults owe special care when playing with young children, and children owe special care when playing with young pets. Obligations may arise from special relationships: the payment of my son's college tuition is something to which he may have no right, although it may be my obligation to bear the burden if I reasonably can; my dog has no right to daily exercise and veterinary care, but I do have the obligation to provide these things for her. Obligations may arise from particular acts or circumstances: one may be obliged to another for a special kindness done, or obliged to put an animal out of its misery in view of its condition—although neither the human benefactor nor the dying animal may have had a claim of right.

Plainly, the grounds of our obligations to humans and to animals are manifold and cannot be formulated simply. Some hold that there is a general obligation to do no gratuitous harm to sentient creatures (the principle of nonmaleficence); some hold that there is a general obligation to do good to sentient creatures when that is reasonably within one's power (the principle of beneficence). In our dealings with animals, few will deny that we are at least obliged to act humanely—that is, to treat them with the decency and concern that we owe, as sensitive human beings, to other sentient creatures. To treat animals humanely, however, is not to treat them as humans or as the holders of rights.

A common objection, which deserves a response, may be paraphrased as follows:

> If having rights requires being able to make moral claims, to grasp and apply moral laws, then many humans—the brain-damaged, the comatose, the senile—who plainly lack those capacities must be without rights. But that is absurd. This proves [the critic concludes] that rights do not depend on the presence of moral capacities.[1,10]

This objection fails; it mistakenly treats an essential feature of humanity as though it were a screen for sorting humans. The capacity for moral judgment that distinguishes humans from animals is not a test to be administered to human beings one by one. Persons who are unable, because of some disability, to perform the full moral functions natural to human beings are certainly not for that reason ejected from the moral community. The issue is one of kind. Humans are of such a kind that they may be the subject of experiments only with their voluntary consent. The choices they make freely must be respected. Animals are of such a kind that it is impossible for them, in principle, to give or withhold voluntary consent or to make a moral choice. What humans retain when disabled, animals have never had.

A second objection, also often made, may be paraphrased as follows:

> Capacities will not succeed in distinguishing humans from the other animals. Animals also reason; animals also communicate with one another; animals also care passionately for their young; animals also exhibit desires and preferences.[11, 12] Features of moral relevance—rationality, interdependence, and love—are not exhibited uniquely by human beings. Therefore [this critic concludes], there can be no solid moral distinction between humans and other animals.[10]

This criticism misses the central point. It is not the ability to communicate or to reason, or dependence on one another, or care for the young, or the exhibition of preference, or any such behavior that marks the critical divide. Analogies between human families and those of monkeys, or between human communities and those of wolves, and the like, are entirely beside the point. Patterns of conduct are not at issue. Animals do indeed exhibit remarkable behavior at times. Conditioning, fear, instinct, and intelligence all contribute to species survival. Membership in a community of moral agents nevertheless remains impossible for them. Actors subject to moral judgment must be capable of grasping the generality of an ethical premise in a practical syllogism. Humans act immorally often enough, but only they—never wolves or monkeys—can discern, by applying some moral rule to the facts of a case, that a given act ought or ought not to be performed. The moral restraints imposed by humans on themselves are thus highly abstract and are often in conflict with the self-interest of the agent. Communal behavior among animals, even when most intelligent and most endearing, does not approach autonomous morality in this fundamental sense.

Genuinely moral acts have an internal as well as an external dimension. Thus, in law, an act can be criminal only when the guilty deed, the actus reus, is done with a guilty mind, mens rea. No animal can ever commit a crime: bringing animals to criminal trial is the mark of primitive ignorance. The claims of moral right are similarly inapplicable to them. Does a lion have a right to eat a baby zebra? Does a baby zebra have a right not to be eaten? Such questions, mistakenly invoking the concept of right where it does not belong, do not make good sense. Those who condemn biomedical research because it violates 'animal rights' commit the same blunder.

IN DEFENSE OF "SPECIESISM"
Abandoning reliance on animal rights, some critics resort instead to animal sentience—their feelings of pain and distress. We ought to desist from the imposition of pain insofar as we can. Since all or nearly all experimentation on animals does impose pain and could be readily forgone, say these critics, it should be stopped. The ends sought may be worthy, but those ends do not justify imposing agonies on humans, and by animals the agonies are felt no less. The laboratory use of animals (these critics conclude) must therefore be ended—or at least very sharply curtailed.

Argument of this variety is essentially utilitarian, often expressly so[13]; it is based on the calculation of the net product, in pains and pleasures, resulting from experiments on animals. Jeremy Bentham, comparing horses and dogs with other sentient creatures, is thus commonly quoted: 'The question is not, Can they reason? nor Can they talk? but, Can they suffer?'[14]

Animals certainly can suffer and surely ought not to be made to suffer needlessly. But in inferring, from these uncontroversial premises, that biomedical research causing animal distress is largely (or wholly) wrong, the critic commits two serious errors.

The first error is the assumption, often explicitly defended, that all sentient animals have equal moral standing. Between a dog and a human being, according to this view, there is no moral difference; hence the pains suffered by dogs must be weighed no differently from the pains suffered by humans. To deny such equality, according to this critic, is to give unjust preference to one species over another; it is "speciesism." The most influential statement of this moral equality of species was made by Peter Singer:

The racist violates the principle of equality by giving greater weight to the interests of members of his own race when there is a clash between their interests and the interests of those of another race. The sexist violates the principle of equality by favoring the interests of his own sex. Similarly the speciesist allows the interests of his own species to override the greater interests of members of other species. The pattern is identical in each case.[2]

This argument is worse than unsound; it is atrocious. It draws an offensive moral conclusion from a deliberately devised verbal parallelism that is utterly specious. Racism has no rational ground whatever. Differing degrees of respect or concern for humans for no other reason than that they are members of different races is an injustice totally without foundation in the nature of the races themselves. Racists, even if acting on the basis of mistaken factual beliefs, do grave moral wrong precisely because there is no morally relevant distinction among the races. The supposition of such differences has led to outright horror. The same is true of the sexes, neither sex being entitled by right to greater respect or concern than the other. No dispute here.

Between species of animate life, however—between (for example) humans on the one hand and cats or rats on the other—the morally relevant differences are enormous, and almost universally appreciated. Humans engage in moral reflection; humans are morally autonomous; humans are members of moral communities, recognizing just claims against their own interest. Human beings do have rights; theirs is a moral status very different from that of cats or rats.

I am a speciesist. Speciesism is not merely plausible; it is essential for right conduct, because those who will not make the morally relevant distinctions among species are almost certain, in consequence, to misapprehend their true obligations. The analogy between speciesism and racism is insidious. Every sensitive moral judgment requires that the differing natures of the beings to whom obligations are owed be considered. If all forms of animate life—or vertebrate animal life?—must be treated equally, and if therefore in evaluating a research program the pains of a rodent count equally with the pains of a human, we are forced to conclude (1) that neither humans nor rodents possess rights, or (2) that rodents possess all the rights that humans possess. Both alternatives are absurd. Yet one or the other must be swallowed if the moral equality of all species is to be defended.

Humans owe to other humans a degree of moral regard that cannot be owed to animals. Some humans take on the obligation to support and heal others, both humans and animals, as a principal duty in their lives; the fulfillment of that duty may require the sacrifice of many animals. If biomedical investigators abandon the effective pursuit of their professional objectives because they are convinced that they may not do to animals what the service of humans requires, they will fail, objectively, to do their duty. Refusing to recognize the moral differences among species is a sure path to calamity. (The largest animal rights group in the country is People for the Ethical Treatment of Animals; its codirector, Ingrid Newkirk, calls research using animal subjects "fascism" and "supremacism." "Animal liberationists do not separate out the *human* animal," she says, "so there is no rational basis for saying that a human being has special rights. A rat is a pig is a dog is a boy. They're all mammals."[15])

Those who claim to base their objection to the use of animals in biomedical research on their reckoning of the net pleasures and pains produced make a second error, equally grave. Even if it were true—as it is surely not—that the pains of all animate beings must be counted equally, a cogent utilitarian calculation requires that we weigh all the consequences of the use, and of the nonuse, of animals in laboratory research. Critics relying (however mistakenly) on animal rights may claim to ignore the beneficial results of such research, rights being trump cards to which interest and advantage must give way. But an argument that is explicitly framed in terms of interest and benefit for all over the long run must attend also to the disadvantageous consequences of not using animals in research, and to all the achievements attained and attainable only through their use. The sum of the benefits of their use is utterly beyond quantification. The elimination of horrible disease, the increase of longevity, the avoidance of great pain, the saving of lives, and the improvement of the quality of lives (for humans and for animals) achieved through research using animals is so incalculably great that the argument

of these critics, systematically pursued, establishes not their conclusion but its reverse: to refrain from using animals in biomedical research is, on utilitarian grounds, morally wrong.

When balancing the pleasures and pains resulting from the use of animals in research, we must not fail to place on the scales the terrible pains that would have resulted, would be suffered now, and would long continue had animals not been used. Every disease eliminated, every vaccine developed, every method of pain relief devised, every surgical procedure invented, every prosthetic device implanted—indeed, virtually every modern medical therapy is due, in part or in whole, to experimentation using animals. Nor may we ignore, in the balancing process, the predictable gains in human (and animal) well-being that are probably achievable in the future but that will not be achieved if the decision is made now to desist from such research or to curtail it.

Medical investigators are seldom insensitive to the distress their work may cause animal subjects. Opponents of research using animals are frequently insensitive to the cruelty of the results of the restrictions they would impose.[2] Untold numbers of human beings—real persons, although not now identifiable—would suffer grievously as the consequence of this well-meaning but shortsighted tenderness. If the morally relevant differences between humans and animals are borne in mind, and if all relevant considerations are weighed, the calculation of long-term consequences must give overwhelming support for biomedical research using animals.

CONCLUDING REMARKS

Substitution

The humane treatment of animals requires that we desist from experimenting on them if we can accomplish the same result using alternative methods—in vitro experimentation, computer simulation, or others. Critics of some experiments using animals rightly make this point.

It would be a serious error to suppose, however, that alternative techniques could soon be used in most research now using live animal subjects. No other methods now on the horizon—or perhaps ever to be available—can fully replace the testing of a drug, a procedure, or a vaccine, in live organisms. The flood of new medical possibilities being opened by the successes of recombinant DNA technology will turn to a trickle if testing on live animals is forbidden. When initial trials entail great risks, there may be no forward movement whatever without the use of live animal subjects. In seeking knowledge that may prove critical in later clinical applications, the unavailability of animals for inquiry may spell complete stymie. In the United States, federal regulations require the testing of new drugs and other products on animals, for efficacy and safety, before human beings are exposed to them.[16, 17] We would not want it otherwise.

Every advance in medicine—every new drug, new operation, new therapy of any kind—must sooner or later be tried on a living being for the first time. That trial, controlled or uncontrolled, will be an experiment. The subject of that experiment, if it is not an animal, will be a human being. Prohibiting the use of live animals in biomedical research, therefore, or sharply restricting it, must result either in the blockage of much valuable research or in the replacement of animal subjects with human subjects. These are the consequences—unacceptable to most reasonable persons—of not using animals in research.

Reduction

Should we not at least reduce the use of animals in biomedical research? No, we should increase it, to avoid when feasible the use of humans as experimental subjects. Medical investigations putting human subjects at some risk are numerous and greatly varied. The risks run in such experiments are usually unavoidable, and (thanks to earlier experiments on animals) most such risks are minimal or moderate. But some experimental risks are substantial.

When an experimental protocol that entails substantial risk to humans comes before an institutional review board, what response is appropriate? The investigation, we may suppose, is promising and deserves support, so long as its human subjects are protected against unnecessary dangers. May not the investigators be fairly asked, Have you done all that you can to eliminate risk to humans by the extensive testing of that drug, that procedure, or that device on animals? To achieve maximal safety

for humans we are right to require thorough experimentation on animal subjects before humans are involved.

Opportunities to increase human safety in this way are commonly missed; trials in which risks may be shifted from humans to animals are often not devised, sometimes not even considered. Why? For the investigator, the use of animals as subjects is often more expensive, in money and time, than the use of human subjects. Access to suitable human subjects is often quick and convenient, whereas access to appropriate animal subjects may be awkward, costly, and burdened with red tape. Physician-investigators have often had more experience working with human beings and know precisely where the needed pool of subjects is to be found and how they may be enlisted. Animals, and the procedures for their use, are often less familiar to these investigators. Moreover, the use of animals in place of humans is now more likely to be the target of zealous protests from without. The upshot is that humans are sometimes subjected to risks that animals could have borne, and should have borne, in their place. To maximize the protection of human subjects, I conclude, the wide and imaginative use of live animal subjects should be encouraged rather than discouraged. This enlargement in the use of animals is our obligation.

Consistency

Finally, inconsistency between the profession and the practice of many who oppose research using animals deserves comment. This frankly ad hominem observation aims chiefly to show that a coherent position rejecting the use of animals in medical research imposes costs so high as to be intolerable even to the critics themselves.

One cannot coherently object to the killing of animals in biomedical investigations while continuing to eat them. Anesthetics and thoughtful animal husbandry render the level of actual animal distress in the laboratory generally lower than that in the abattoir. So long as death and discomfort do not substantially differ in the two contexts, the consistent objector must not only refrain from all eating of animals but also protest as vehemently against others eating them as against others experimenting on them. No less vigorously must the critic object to the wearing of animal hides in coats and shoes, to employment in any industrial enterprise that uses animal parts, and to any commercial development that will cause death or distress to animals.

Killing animals to meet human needs for food, clothing, and shelter is judged entirely reasonable by most persons. The ubiquity of these uses and the virtual universality of moral support for them confront the opponent of research using animals with an inescapable difficulty. How can the many common uses of animals be judged morally worthy, while their use in scientific investigation is judged unworthy?

The number of animals used in research is but the tiniest fraction of the total used to satisfy assorted human appetites. That these appetites, often base and satisfiable in other ways, morally justify the far larger consumption of animals, whereas the quest for improved human health and understanding cannot justify the far smaller, is wholly implausible. Aside from the numbers of animals involved, the distinction in terms of worthiness of use, drawn with regard to any single animal, is not defensible. A given sheep is surely not more justifiably used to put lamb chops on the supermarket counter than to serve in testing a new contraceptive or a new prosthetic device. The needless killing of animals is wrong; if the common killing of them for our food or convenience is right, the less common but more humane uses of animals in the service of medical science are certainly not less right.

Scrupulous vegetarianism, in matters of food, clothing, shelter, commerce, and recreation, and in all other spheres, is the only fully coherent position the critic may adopt. At great human cost, the lives of fish and crustaceans must also be protected, with equal vigor, if speciesism has been forsworn. A very few consistent critics adopt this position. It is the reductio ad absurdum of the rejection of moral distinctions between animals and human beings.

Opposition to the use of animals in research is based on arguments of two different kinds—those relying on the alleged rights of animals and those relying on the consequences for animals. I have argued that arguments of both kinds must fail. We surely do have obligations to animals, but they

have, and can have, no rights against us on which research can infringe. In calculating the consequences of animal research, we must weigh all the long-term benefits of the results achieved—to animals and to humans—and in that calculation we must not assume the moral equality of all animate species.

NOTES

1. Regan T. *The case for animal rights*. Berkeley, Calif.: University of California Press, 1983.
2. Singer P. *Animal liberation*. New York: Avon Books, 1977.
3. St. Augustine. *Confessions*. Book Seven. 397 A.D. New York: Pocket-books, 1957:104–26.
4. St. Thomas Aquinas. *Summa theologica*. 1273 A.D. New York: Oxford University Press, 1960:353–66.
5. Hegel GWF. *Philosophy of right*. 1821. London: Oxford University Press, 1952:105–10.
6. Bradley FH. Why should I be moral? 1876. In: Melden AI, ed. *Ethical theories*. New York: Prentice-Hall, 1950: 345–59.
7. Mead GH. The genesis of the self and social control. 1925. In: Reck AJ, ed. *Selected writings*. Indianapolis: Bobbs-Merrill, 1964:26–93.
8. Pilchard HA. Does moral philosophy rest on a mistake? 1912. In: Cellars W, Hospers J, eds. *Readings in ethical theory*. New York: Appleton-Century-Crofts, 1952:149–63.
9. Kant I. *Fundamental principles of the metaphysic of morals*. 1785. New York: Liberal Arts Press, 1949.
10. Rollin BE. *Animal rights and human morality*. New York: Prometheus Books, 1981.
11. Hoff C. Immoral and moral uses of animals. *N Engl J Med* 1980; 302:115–8.
12. Jamieson D. Killing persons and other beings. In: Miller HB, Williams WH, eds. *Ethics and animals*. Clifton, N.J.: Humana Press. 1983: 135–46.
13. Singer P. Ten years of animal liberation. *New York Review of Books*. 1985; 31:46–52.
14. Bentham J. *Introduction to the principles of morals and legislation*. London: Athlone Press, 1970.
15. McCabe K. Who will live, who will die? *Washingtonian Magazine*. August 1986:115.
16. U.S. Code of Federal Regulations. Title 21. Sect. 505(i). Food, drug, and cosmetic regulations.
17. U.S. Code of Federal Regulations, Title 16. Sect. 1500.40–2. Consumer product regulations.

Our Duties to Animals

IMMANUEL KANT

Baumgarten speaks of duties towards being which are beneath us and beings which are above us. But so far as animals are concerned, we have no direct duties. Animals are not self-conscious and are there merely as a means to an end. That end is man. We can ask, "Why do animals exist?" But to ask, "Why does man exist?" is a meaningless question. Our duties towards animals are merely indirect duties towards humanity. Animal nature has analogies to human nature, and by doing our duties to animals in respect of manifestations which correspond to manifestations of human nature, we indirectly do our duty towards humanity. Thus, if a dog has served his master long and faithfully, his service, on the analogy of human service, deserves reward, and when the dog has grown too old to serve, his master ought to keep him until he dies. Such action helps to support us in our duties towards human beings, where they are bounden duties. If then any acts of animals are analogous to human acts and spring from the same principles, we have duties towards the animals because thus we cultivate the corresponding duties towards human beings. If a man shoots his dog because the animal is no longer capable of service, he does not fail in his duty to the dog, for the dog cannot judge, but his act is inhuman and damages in himself that humanity which it is his duty to show towards mankind. If he is not to stifle his human feelings, he must practise kindness towards animals, for he who is cruel to animals becomes hard also in his dealings with men. We can judge the heart of a man by his treatment of animals. Hogarth depicts this in his engravings. He shows how cruelty grows and develops. He shows the child's cruelty to animals, pinching the tail of a dog or a cat; he then depicts the grown man in his cart running over a child; and lastly, the culmination of cruelty in murder. He thus brings home to us in a terrible fashion the rewards of cruelty, and this should be an impressive lesson to children. The more we come in contact with animals and observe their behaviour, the more we love them, for we see how great is their care for their young. It is then difficult for us to be cruel in thought even to a wolf. Leibnitz used a tiny worm for purposes of observation, and then carefully replaced it with its leaf on the tree so that it should not come to harm through any act of his. He would have been sorry—a natural feeling for a humane man—to destroy such a creature for no reason. Tender feelings towards dumb animals develop humane feelings towards mankind. In England butchers and doctors do not sit on a jury because they are accustomed to the sight of death and hardened. Vivisectionists, who use living animals for their experiments, certainly act cruelly, although their aim is praiseworthy, and they can justify their cruelty, since animals must be regarded as man's instruments; but any such cruelty for sport cannot be justified. A master who turns out his ass or his dog because the animal can no longer earn its keep manifests a small mind. The Greeks' ideas in this respect were highminded, as can be seen from the fable of the ass and the bell of ingratitude. Our duties towards animals, then, are indirect duties towards mankind.

Our duties towards immaterial beings are purely negative. Any course of conduct which involves dealings with spirits is wrong. Conduct of this kind makes men visionaries and fanatics, renders them superstitious, and is not in keeping with the dignity of mankind; for human dignity cannot subsist without a healthy use of reason, which is impossible for those who have commerce with spirits. Spirits may exist or they may not; all that is said of them may be true; but we know them not and can have no intercourse with them. This applies to good and to evil spirits alike. Our Ideas of good and evil are coordinate, and as we refer all evil to hell so we refer all good to heaven. If we personify the perfection of evil, we have the Idea of the devil. If we believe that evil spirits can have an influence upon us, can appear and haunt us at night, we become a prey to phantoms and incapable of using our powers in a reasonable way. Our duties towards such beings must, therefore, be negative.

"Duties to Animals and Spirits" by Immanuel Kant, *Lectures on Ethics*, trans. Louis Infield, 239–241. © 1930 London: Methuen.

ARGUMENT 22 ESSAY QUESTIONS

1. What are Cohen's arguments against Singer's position? Do you find them convincing? Explain.
2. What is Kant's view on animal rights? Do you agree with him? Explain.
3. Do you think all animals are equal in Singer's sense? Why or why not?

23. REGAN'S ARGUMENT FOR ANIMAL RIGHTS

In "The Case for Animal Rights," Tom Regan argues that nonhuman animals possess more than minimal moral status; they have *moral rights*. He maintains that any sensitive being capable of experiences—a being he calls an "experiencing subject of a life"—has inherent moral worth regardless of its interests, biological properties, or cognitive abilities. Moreover, all who have inherent moral worth have it equally. Human beings obviously possess such worth: "[W]e are each of us [humans] the experiencing subjects of a life, a conscious creature having an individual welfare that has importance to us whatever our usefulness to others."[5] Since animals are also experiencing subjects of a life, they too have inherent worth, and their inherent worth must be equal to our own. Because this moral status cannot be easily overridden by utilitarian or practical concerns, it rises to the level of rights.

This theory (called the rights view) implies that whatever would be wrong to do to humans would also be wrong to do to animals. We should not eat, hunt, dissect, and abuse humans; likewise we may not do such things to animals. The implications for animal research and commercial farming, says Regan, are "clear and uncompromising":

> In the case of the use of animals in science, the rights view is categorically abolitionist.…Because these animals are treated routinely, systematically as if their value were reducible to their usefulness to others, they are routinely, systematically treated with a lack of respect, and thus are their rights routinely, systematically violated.…As for commercial animal agriculture, the rights view takes a similar abolitionist position.… [The abuses] are symptoms and effects of the deeper, systematic wrong that allows these animals to be viewed and treated as lacking independent value, as resources for us—as, indeed, a renewable resource.[6]

Like Singer, Regan has a ready response to the claim that only humans have such moral worth due to their intelligence, autonomy, or reason: "But there are many, many

---

5 Tom Regan, "The Case for Animal Rights," 22.
6 Tom Regan, 24–25.

humans who fail to meet these standards and yet are reasonably viewed as having value above and beyond their usefulness to others."[7]

Perhaps the most formidable arguments against Regan's view are those that acknowledge that animals have rights but insist that these rights are less robust than the rights of humans. For example, Mary Anne Warren draws a distinction between the *content* of a right (the activities covered by the right) and the *strength* of a right (the weight of the reasons needed to override it). In content, she says, a human's right can be more extensive than an animal's right:

> Consider, for instance, the right to liberty. The *human* right to liberty precludes imprisonment without due process of law, even if the prison is spacious and the conditions of confinement cause no obvious physical suffering. But it is not so obviously wrong to imprison animals, especially when the area to which they are confined provides a fair approximation of the conditions of their natural habitat, and a reasonable opportunity to pursue the satisfactions natural to their kind. Such conditions.... need not frustrate the needs or interests of animals in any significant way, and thus do not clearly violate their rights.[8]

As for the strength of a right, Warren says that the rights of humans can be stronger than those of animals because humans' interests are often weightier than animals' interests. The right to life, for example, is stronger for humans than for animals: "Human lives, one might say, have greater intrinsic value, because they are worth more *to their possessors.*"

The Case for Animal Rights

TOM REGAN

I regard myself as an advocate of animal rights—as a part of the animal rights movement. That movement, as I conceive it, is committed to a number of goals, including:

- the total abolition of the use of animals in science;
- the total dissolution of commercial animal agriculture;

- the total elimination of commercial and sport hunting and trapping.

There are, I know, people who profess to believe in animal rights but do not avow these goals. Factory

---

"The Case for Animal Rights" by Tom Regan, in *In Defense of Animals*, ed. Peter Singer. Copyright © 1995 Oxford: Basil Blackwell. Reproduced with permission of Blackwell Publishing Ltd.

---

[7] Tom Regan, "The Case for Animal Rights," 22.

[8] Mary Anne Warren, "The Rights of the Nonhuman World," in *Environmental Philosophy: A Collection of Readings*, ed. Robert Elliot and Arran F. Gare (Queensland: Queensland University Press, 1983).

farming, they say, is wrong—it violates animals' rights—but traditional animal agriculture is all right. Toxicity tests of cosmetics on animals violates their rights, but important medical research—cancer research, for example—does not. The clubbing of baby seals is abhorrent, but not the harvesting of adult seals. I used to think I understood this reasoning. Not any more. You don't change unjust institutions by tidying them up.

What's wrong—fundamentally wrong—with the way animals are treated isn't the details that vary from case to case. It's the whole system. The forlornness of the veal calf is pathetic, heart wrenching; the pulsing pain of the chimp with electrodes planted deep in her brain is repulsive; the slow, tortuous death of the racoon caught in the leg-hold trap is agonizing. But what is wrong isn't the pain, isn't the suffering, isn't the deprivation. These compound what's wrong. Sometimes—often—they make it much, much worse. But they are not the fundamental wrong.

The fundamental wrong is the system that allows us to view animals as *our resources*, here for *us*—to be eaten, or surgically manipulated, or exploited for sport or money. Once we accept this view of animals—as our resources—the rest is as predictable as it is regrettable. Why worry about their loneliness, their pain, their death? Since animals exist for us, to benefit us in one way or another, what harms them really doesn't matter—or matters only if it starts to bother us, makes us feel a trifle uneasy when we eat our veal escalope, for example. So, yes, let us get veal calves out of solitary confinement, give them more space, a little straw, a few companions. But let us keep our veal escalope.

But a little straw, more space and a few companions won't eliminate—won't even touch—the basic wrong that attaches to our viewing and treating these animals as our resources. A veal calf killed to be eaten after living in close confinement is viewed and treated in this way: but so, too is another who is raised (as they say) "more humanely." To right the wrong of our treatment of farm animals requires more than making rearing methods "more humane"; it requires the total dissolution of commercial animal agriculture.

How we do this, whether we do it or, as in the case of animals in science, whether and how we abolish their use—these are to a large extent political

questions. People must change their beliefs before they change their habits. Enough people, especially those elected to public office, must believe in change—must want it—before we will have laws that protect the rights of animals. This process of change is very complicated, very demanding, very exhausting, calling for the efforts of many hands in education, publicity, political organization and activity, down to the licking of envelopes and stamps. As a trained and practising philosopher, the sort of contribution I can make is limited but, I like to think, important. The currency of philosophy is ideas—their meaning and rational foundation—not the nuts and bolts of the legislative process, say, or the mechanics of community organization. That's what I have been exploring over the past ten years or so in my essays and talks and, most recently, in my book. *The Case for Animal Rights.* I believe the major conclusions I reach in the book are true because they are supported by the weight of the best arguments. I believe the idea of animal rights has reason, not just emotion, on its side.

In the space I have at my disposal here I can only sketch, in the barest outline, some of the main features of the book. Its main themes—and we should not be surprised by this—involve asking and answering deep, foundational moral questions about what morality is, how it should be understood and what is the best moral theory, all considered. I hope I can convey something of the shape I think this theory takes. The attempt to do this will be (to use a word a friendly critic once used to describe my work) cerebral, perhaps too cerebral. But this is misleading. My feelings about how animals are sometimes treated run just as deep and just as strong as those of my more volatile compatriots. Philosophers do—to use the jargon of the day—have a right side to their brains. If it's the left side we contribute (or mainly should), that's because what talents we have reside there.

How to proceed? We begin by asking how the moral status of animals has been understood by thinkers who deny that animals have rights. Then we test the mettle of their ideas by seeing how well they stand up under the heat of fair criticism. If we start our thinking in this way, we soon find that some people believe that we have no duties directly to animals, that we owe nothing to them, that we can do nothing that wrongs them. Rather, we can do wrong acts that involve animals, and so we have duties regarding them, though none to them. Such views may be called indirect duty views. By way of illustration: suppose your neighbour kicks your dog. Then your neighbour has done something wrong. But not to your dog. The wrong that has been done is a wrong to you. After all, it is wrong to upset people, and your neighbour's kicking your dog upsets you. So you are the one who is wronged, not your dog. Or again: by kicking your dog your neighbour damages your property. And since it is wrong to damage another person's property, your neighbour has done something wrong—to you, of course, not to your dog. Your neighbour no more wrongs your dog than your car would be wronged if the windshield were smashed. Your neighbour's duties involving your dog are indirect duties to you. More generally, all of our duties regarding animals are indirect duties to one another—to humanity.

How could someone try to justify such a view? Someone might say that your dog doesn't feel anything, and so isn't hurt by your neighbour's kick, doesn't care about the pain since none is felt, is as unaware of anything as is your windshield. Someone might say this, but no rational person will, since, among other considerations, such a view will commit anyone who holds it to the position that no human being feels pain either—that human beings also don't care about what happens to them. A second possibility is that though both humans and your dog are hurt when kicked, it is only human pain that matters. But, again, no rational person can believe this. Pain is pain wherever it occurs. If your neighbour's causing you pain is wrong because of the pain that is caused, we cannot rationally ignore or dismiss the moral relevance of the pain that your dog feels.

Philosophers who hold indirect duty views—and many still do—have come to understand that they must avoid the two defects just noted: that is, both the view that animals don't feel anything as well as the idea that only human pain can be morally relevant. Among such thinkers the sort of view now favoured is one or other form of what is called *contractarianism*.

Here, very crudely, is the root idea: morality consists of a set of rules that individuals voluntarily agree to abide by, as we do when we sign a contract (hence the name contractarianism). Those who understand and accept the terms of the contract are covered directly; they have rights created and recognized by, and protected in, the contract. And these contractors can also have protection spelled out for others who, though they lack the ability to understand morality and so cannot sign the contract themselves, are loved or cherished by those who can. Thus young children, for example, are unable to sign contracts and lack rights. But they are protected by the contract none the less because of the sentimental interests of others, most notably their parents. So we have, then, duties involving these children, duties regarding them, but no duties to them. Our duties in their case are indirect duties to other human beings, usually their parents.

As for animals, since they cannot understand contracts, they obviously cannot sign; and since they cannot sign, they have no rights. Like children, however, some animals are the objects of the sentimental interest of others. You, for example, love your dog or cat. So those animals that enough people care about (companion animals, whales, baby seals, the American bald eagle), though they lack rights themselves, will be protected because of the sentimental interests of people. I have, then, according to contractarianism, no duty directly to your dog or any other animal, not even the duly not to cause them pain or suffering; my duty not to hurt them is a duty I have to those people who care about what happens to them. As for other animals, where no or little sentimental interest is present—in the case of farm animals, for example, or laboratory rats—what duties we have grow weaker and weaker, perhaps to vanishing point. The pain and death they endure, though real, are not wrong if no one cares about them.

When it comes to the moral status of animals contractarianism could be a hard view to refute if it were an adequate theoretical approach to the moral status of human beings. It is not adequate in this latter respect, however, which makes the question of its adequacy in the former case, regarding animals, utterly moot. For consider: morality, according to the (crude) contractarian position before us, consists of rules that people agree to abide by. What people? Well, enough to make a difference—enough, that is, *collectively* to have the power to enforce the rules that are drawn up in the contract. That is very well and good for the signatories but not so good for anyone who is not asked to sign. And there is nothing in contractarianism of the sort we are discussing that guarantees or requires that everyone will have a chance to participate equally in framing the rules of morality. The result is that this approach to ethics could sanction the most blatant forms of social, economic, moral and political injustice, ranging from a repressive caste system to systematic racial or sexual discrimination. Might, according to this theory, does make right. Let those who are the victims or injustice suffer as they will. It matters not so long as no one else—no contractor, or too few of them—cares about it. Such a theory takes one's moral breath away ... as if, for example, there would be nothing wrong with apartheid in South Africa, if few white South Africans were upset by it. A theory with so little to recommend it at the level of the ethics of our treatment of our fellow humans cannot have anything more to recommend it when it comes to the ethics of how we treat our fellow animals.

The version of contractarianism just examined is, as I have noted, a crude variety, and in fairness to those of a contractarian persuasion it must be noted that much more refined, subtle and ingenious varieties are possible. For example, John Rawls, in his *A Theory of Justice*, sets forth a version of contractarianism that forces contractors to ignore the accidental features of being a human being—for example, whether one is white or black, male or female, a genius or of modest intellect. Only by ignoring such features, Rawls believes, can we ensure that the principles of justice that contractors would agree upon are not based on bias or prejudice. Despite the improvement a view such as Rawls's represents over the cruder forms of contractarianism, it remains deficient: it systematically denies that we have direct duties to those human beings who do not have a sense of justice—young children, for instance, and many mentally retarded humans. And yet it seems reasonably certain that, were we to torture a young child or a retarded elder, we would be doing something that wronged him or her, not something that would be wrong if (and only if) other humans with a sense of justice were upset. And since this is true in the case of these humans, we cannot rationally deny the same in the case of animals.

Indirect duty views, then, including the best among them, fail to command our rational assent.

Whatever ethical theory we should accept rationally, therefore, it must at least recognize that we have some duties directly to animals, just as we have some duties directly to each other. The next two theories I'll sketch attempt to meet this requirement.

The first I call the cruelty-kindness view. Simply stated, this says that we have a direct duty to be kind to animals and a direct duty not to be cruel to them. Despite the familiar, reassuring ring of these ideas, I do not believe that this view offers an adequate theory. To make this clearer, consider kindness. A kind person acts from a certain kind of motive—compassion or concern, for example. And that is a virtue. But there is no guarantee that a kind act is a right act. If I am a generous racist, for example, I will be inclined to act kindly towards members of my own race, favouring their interests above those of others. My kindness would be real and, so far as it goes, good. But I trust it is too obvious to require argument that my kind acts may not be above moral reproach—may, in fact, be positively wrong because rooted in injustice. So kindness, notwithstanding its status as a virtue to be encouraged, simply will not carry the weight of a theory of right action.

Cruelty fares no better. People or their acts are cruel if they display either a lack of sympathy for or, worse, the presence of enjoyment in another's suffering. Cruelty in all its guises is a bad thing, a tragic human failing. But just as a person's being motivated by kindness does not guarantee that he or she does what is right, so the absence of cruelty does not ensure that he or she avoids doing what is wrong. Many people who perform abortions, for example, are not cruel, sadistic people. But that fact alone does not settle the terribly difficult question of the morality of abortion. The case is no different when we examine the ethics of our treatment of animals. So, yes, let us be for kindness and against cruelty. But let us not suppose that being for the one and against the other answers questions about moral right and wrong.

Some people think that the theory we are looking for is utilitarianism. A utilitarian accepts two moral principles. The first is that of equality: everyone's interests count, and similar interests must be counted as having similar weight or importance. White or black, American or Iranian, human or animal—everyone's pain or frustration matter, and matter just as much as the equivalent pain or frustration of anyone else. The second principle a utilitarian accepts is that of utility: do the act that will bring about the best balance between satisfaction and frustration for everyone affected by the outcome.

As a utilitarian, then, here is how I am to approach the task of deciding what I morally ought to do: I must ask who will be affected if I choose to do one thing rather than another, how much each individual will be affected, and where the best results are most likely to lie—which option, in other words, is most likely to bring about the best results, the best balance between satisfaction and frustration. That option, whatever it may be, is the one I ought to choose. That is where my moral duty lies.

The great appeal of utilitarianism rests with its uncompromising *egalitarianism:* everyone's interests count and count as much as the like interests of everyone else. The kind of odious discrimination that some forms of contractarianism can justify—discrimination based on race or sex, for example—seems disallowed in principle by utilitarianism, as is speciesism, systematic discrimination based on species membership.

The equality we find in utilitarianism, however, is not the sort an advocate of animal or human rights should have in mind. Utilitarianism has no room for the equal moral rights of different individuals because it has no room for their equal inherent value or worth. What has value for the utilitarian is the satisfaction of an individual's interests, not the individual whose interests they are. A universe in which you satisfy your desire for water, food and warmth is, other things being equal, better than a universe in which these desires are frustrated. And the same is true in the case of an animal with similar desires. But neither you nor the animal have any value in your own right. Only your feelings do.

Here is an analogy to help make the philosophical point clearer: a cup contains different liquids, sometimes sweet, sometimes bitter, sometimes a mix of the two. What has value are the liquids: the sweeter the better, the bitterer the worse. The cup, the container, has no value. It is what goes into it, not what they go into, that has value. For the utilitarian you and I are like the cup; we have no value as individuals and thus no equal value. What has value

is what goes into us, what we serve as receptacles for; our feelings of satisfaction have positive value, our feelings of frustration negative value.

Serious problems arise for utilitarianism when we remind ourselves that it enjoins us to bring about the best consequences. What does this mean? It doesn't mean the best consequences for me alone, or for my family or friends, or any other person taken individually. No, what we must do is, roughly, as follows: we must add up (somehow!) the separate satisfactions and frustrations of everyone likely to be affected by our choice, the satisfactions in one column, the frustrations in the other. We must total each column for each of the options before us. That is what it means to say the theory is aggregative. And then we must choose that option which is most likely to bring about the best balance of totalled satisfactions over totalled frustrations. Whatever act would lead to this outcome is the one we ought morally to perform—it is where our moral duty lies. And that act quite clearly might not be the same one that would bring about the best results for me personally, or for my family or friends, or for a lab animal. The best aggregated consequences for everyone concerned are not necessarily the best for each individual.

That utilitarianism is an aggregative theory—different individuals' satisfactions or frustrations are added, or summed, or totalled—is the key objection to this theory. My Aunt Bea is old, inactive, a cranky, sour person, though not physically ill. She prefers to go on living. She is also rather rich. I could make a fortune if I could get my hands on her money, money she intends to give me in any event, after she dies, but which she refuses to give me now. In order to avoid a huge tax bite, I plan to donate a handsome sum of my profits to a local children's hospital. Many, many children will benefit from my generosity, and much joy will be brought to their parents, relatives and friends. If I don't get the money rather soon, all these ambitions will come to naught. The once-in-a-lifetime opportunity to make a real killing will be gone. Why, then, not kill my Aunt Bea? Oh, of course I *might* get caught. But I'm no fool and, besides, her doctor can be counted on to co-operate (he has an eye for the same investment and I happen to know a good deal about his shady past). The deed can be done...professionally, shall we say. There is *very* little chance of getting caught. And as for my conscience being guilt-ridden, I am a resourceful sort of fellow and will take more than sufficient comfort—as I lie on the beach at Acapulco—in contemplating the joy and health I have brought to so many others.

Suppose Aunt Bea is killed and the rest of the story comes out as told. Would I have done anything wrong? Anything immoral? One would have thought that I had. Not according to utilitarianism. Since what I have done has brought about the best balance between totalled satisfaction and frustration for all those affected by the outcome, my action is not wrong. Indeed, in killing Aunt Bea the physician and I did what duty required.

This same kind of argument can be repeated in all sorts of cases, illustrating, time after time, how the utilitarian's position leads to results that impartial people find morally callous. It *is* wrong to kill my Aunt Bea in the name of bringing about the best results for others. A good end does not justify an evil means. Any adequate moral theory will have to explain why this is so. Utilitarianism fails in this respect and so cannot be the theory we seek.

What to do? Where to begin anew? The place to begin, I think, is with the utilitarian's view of the value of the individual—or, rather, lack of value. In its place, suppose we consider that you and I, for example, do have value as individuals—what we'll call *inherent value*. To say we have such value is to say that we are something more than, something different from, mere receptacles. Moreover, to ensure that we do not pave the way for such injustices as slavery or sexual discrimination, we must believe that all who have inherent value have it equally, regardless of their sex, race, religion, birthplace and so on. Similarly to be discarded as irrelevant are one's talents or skills, intelligence and wealth, personality or pathology, whether one is loved and admired or despised and loathed. The genius and the retarded child, the prince and the pauper, the brain surgeon and the fruit vendor, Mother Teresa and the most unscrupulous used-car salesman—all have inherent value, all possess it equally, and all have an equal right to be treated with respect, to be treated in ways that do not reduce them to the status of things, as if they existed as resources for others. My value as an individual is independent of my usefulness to you. Yours is not dependent on your usefulness to me.

For either of us to treat the other in ways that fail to show respect for the other's independent value is to act immorally, to violate the individual's rights.

Some of the rational virtues of this view—what I call the rights view—should be evident. Unlike (crude) contractarianism, for example, the rights view *in principle* denies the moral tolerability of any and all forms of racial, sexual or social discrimination; and unlike utilitarianism, this view *in principle* denies that we can justify good results by using evil means that violate an individual's rights—denies, for example, that it could be moral to kill my Aunt Bea to harvest beneficial consequences for others. That would be to sanction the disrespectful treatment of the individual in the name of the social good, something the rights view will not—categorically will not—ever allow.

The rights view, I believe, is rationally the most satisfactory moral theory. It surpasses all other theories in the degree to which it illuminates and explains the foundation of our duties to one another—the domain of human morality. On this score it has the best reasons, the best arguments, on its side. Of course, if it were possible to show that only human beings are included within its scope, then a person like myself, who believes in animal rights, would be obliged to look elsewhere.

But attempts to limit its scope to humans only can be shown to be rationally defective. Animals, it is true, lack many of the abilities humans possess. They can't read, do higher mathematics, build a bookcase or make *baba ghanoush*. Neither can many human beings, however, and yet we don't (and shouldn't) say that they (these humans) therefore have less inherent value, less of a right to be treated with respect, than do others. It is the *similarities* between those human beings who most clearly, most non-controversially have such value (the people reading this, for example), not our differences, that matter most. And the really crucial, the basic similarity is simply this: we are each of us the experiencing subject of a life, a conscious creature having an individual welfare that has importance to us whatever our usefulness to others. We want and prefer things, believe and feel things, recall and expect things. And all these dimensions of our life, including our pleasure and pain, our enjoyment and suffering, our satisfaction and frustration, our continued existence or our untimely death—all make a difference to the quality of our life as lived, as experienced, by us as individuals. As the same is true of those animals that concern us (the ones that are eaten and trapped, for example), they too must be viewed as the experiencing subjects of a life, with inherent value of their own.

Some there are who resist the idea that animals have inherent value. "Only humans have such value," they profess. How might this narrow view be defended? Shall we say that only humans have the requisite intelligence, or autonomy, or reason? But there are many, many humans who fail to meet these standards and yet are reasonably viewed as having value above and beyond their usefulness to others. Shall we claim that only humans belong to the right species, the species *Homo sapiens*? But this is blatant speciesism. Will it be said, then, that all—and only—humans have immortal souls? Then our opponents have their work cut out for them. I am myself not ill-disposed to the proposition that there are immortal souls. Personally, I profoundly hope I have one. But I would not want to rest my position on a controversial ethical issue on the even more controversial question about who or what has an immortal soul. That is to dig one's hole deeper, not to climb out. Rationally, it is better to resolve moral issues without making more controversial assumptions than are needed. The question of who has inherent value is such a question, one that is resolved more rationally without the introduction of the idea of immortal souls than by its use.

Well, perhaps some will say that animals have some inherent value, only less than we have. Once again, however, attempts to defend this view can be shown to lack rational justification. What could be the basis of our having more inherent value than animals? Their lack of reason, or autonomy, or intellect? Only if we are willing to make the same judgement in the case of humans who are similarly deficient. But it is not true that such humans—the retarded child, for example, or the mentally deranged—have less inherent value than you or I. Neither, then, can we rationally sustain the view that animals like them in being the experiencing subjects of a life have less inherent value. *All* who have inherent value have it *equally*, whether they be human animals or not.

Inherent value, then, belongs equally to those who are the experiencing subjects of a life. Whether it belongs to others—to rocks and rivers, trees and glaciers, for example—we do not know and may never know. But neither do we need to know, if we are to make the case for animal rights. We do not need to know, for example, how many people are eligible to vote in the next presidential election before we can know whether I am. Similarly, we do not need to know how many individuals have inherent value before we can know that some do. When it comes to the case for animal rights, then, what we need to know is whether the animals that, in our culture, are routinely eaten, hunted and used in our laboratories, for example, are like us in being subjects of a life. And we do know this. We do know that many—literally, billions and billions—of these animals are the subjects of a life in the sense explained and so have inherent value if we do. And since, in order to arrive at the best theory of our duties to one another, we must recognize our equal inherent value as individuals, reason—not sentiment, not emotion—reason compels us to recognize the equal inherent value of these animals and, with this, their equal right to be treated with respect.

That, *very* roughly, is the shape and feel of the case for animal rights. Most of the details of the supporting argument are missing. They are to be found in the book to which I alluded earlier. Here, the details go begging, and I must, in closing, limit myself to four final points.

The first is how the theory that underlies the case for animal rights shows that the animal rights movement is a part of, not antagonistic to, the human rights movement. The theory that rationally grounds the rights of animals also grounds the rights of humans. Thus those involved in the animal rights movement are partners in the struggle to secure respect for human rights—the rights of women, for example, or minorities, or workers. The animal rights movement is cut from the same moral cloth as these.

Second, having set out the broad outlines of the rights view, I can now say why its implications for farming and science, among other fields, are both clear and uncompromising. In the case of the use of animals in science, the rights view is categorically abolitionist. Lab animals are not our tasters; we are not their kings. Because these animals are treated routinely, systematically as if their value were reducible to their usefulness to others, they are routinely, systematically treated with a lack of respect, and thus are their rights routinely, systematically violated. This is just as true when they are used in trivial, duplicative, unnecessary or unwise research as it is when they are used in studies that hold out real promise of human benefits. We can't justify harming or killing a human being (my Aunt Bea, for example) just for these sorts of reason. Neither can we do so even in the case of so lowly a creature as a laboratory rat. It is not just refinement or reduction that is called for, not just larger, cleaner cages, not just more generous use of anaesthetic or the elimination of multiple surgery, not just tidying up the system. It is complete replacement. The best we can do when it comes to using animals in science is—not to use them. That is where our duty lies, according to the rights view.

As for commercial animal agriculture, the rights view takes a similar abolitionist position. The fundamental moral wrong here is not that animals are kept in stressful close confinement or in isolation, or that their pain and suffering, their needs and preferences are ignored or discounted. All these *are* wrong, of course, but they are not the fundamental wrong. They are symptoms and effects of the deeper, systematic wrong that allows these animals to be viewed and treated as lacking independent value, as resources for us—as, indeed, a renewable resource. Giving farm animals more space, more natural environments, more companions does not right the fundamental wrong, any more than giving lab animals more anaesthesia or bigger, cleaner cages would right the fundamental wrong in their case. Nothing less than the total dissolution of commercial animal agriculture will do this, just as, for similar reasons I won't develop at length here, morality requires nothing less than the total elimination of hunting and trapping for commercial and sporting ends. The rights view's implications, then, as I have said, are clear and uncompromising.

My last two points are about philosophy, my profession. It is, most obviously, no substitute for political action. The words I have written here and in other places by themselves don't change a thing. It is what we do with the thoughts that the words express—our acts, our deeds—that changes things. All that philosophy can do, and all I have attempted, is to offer a vision of what our deeds should aim at. And the why. But not the how.

Finally, I am reminded of my thoughtful critic, the one I mentioned earlier, who chastised me for being too cerebral. Well, cerebral I have been: indirect duty views, utilitarianism, contractarianism—hardly the stuff deep passions are made of. I am also reminded, however, of the image another friend once set before me—the image of the ballerina as expressive of disciplined passion. Long hours of sweat and toil; of loneliness and practice, of doubt and fatigue: those are the discipline of her craft. But the passion is there, too, the fierce drive to excel, to speak through her body, to do it right, to pierce our minds. That is the image of philosophy I would leave with you, not "too cerebral" but *disciplined passion*. Of the discipline enough has been seen. As for the passion: there are times, and these not infrequent, when tears come to my eyes when I see, or read, or hear of the wretched plight of animals in the hands of humans. Their pain, their suffering, their loneliness, their innocence, their death. Anger. Rage. Pity. Sorrow. Disgust. The whole creation groans under the weight of the evil we humans visit upon these mute, powerless creatures. It *is* our hearts, not just our heads, that call for an end to it all, that demand of us that we overcome, for them, the habits and forces behind their systematic oppression. All great movements, it is written, go through three stages: ridicule, discussion, adoption. It is the realization of this third stage, adoption, that requires both our passion and our discipline, our hearts and our heads. The fate of animals is in our hands. God grant we are equal to the task.

The Rights of the Nonhuman World

MARY ANNE WARREN

Western philosophers have typically held that human beings are the only proper objects of human moral concern. Those who speak of *duties* generally hold that we have duties only to human beings (or perhaps to God), and that our apparent duties towards animals, plants and other nonhuman entities in nature are in fact indirect duties to human beings. Those who speak of moral *rights* generally ascribe such rights only to human beings.

This strictly homocentric (human-centered) view of morality is currently challenged from two seemingly disparate directions. On the one hand, environmentalists argue that because humanity is only one part of the natural world, an organic species in the total, interdependent, planetary biosystem, it is necessary for consistency to view all of the elements of that system, and not just its human elements, as worthy of moral concern in themselves, and not only because of their usefulness to us. The ecologist Aldo Leopold was one of the first and most influential exponents of the view that not only human beings, but plants, animals and natural habitats, have moral rights. We need, Leopold argued, a new ethical system that will deal with our relationships not only with other human individuals and with human society, but also with the land, and its nonhuman inhabitants. Such a "land ethic" would seek to change "the role of *Homo sapiens* from conqueror of the land community to plain member and citizen of it." It would judge our interaction with the nonhuman world as "right when it tends to preserve the integrity, stability, and beauty of the biotic community", and "wrong when it tends otherwise."

On the other hand, homocentric morality is attacked by the so-called animal liberationists, who have argued, at least as early as the eighteenth century (in the Western tradition), that insofar as (some) nonhuman animals are sentient beings, capable of experiencing pleasure and pain, they are worthy in their own right of our moral concern. On the surface at least, the animal liberationist ethic appears to be quite different from that of ecologists such as Leopold. The land ethic is *wholistic* in its emphasis: it treats the good of the biotic *community* as the ultimate measure of the value of individual organisms or species, and of the rightness or wrongness of human actions. In contrast, the animal-liberationist ethic is largely inspired by the utilitarianism of Jeremy Bentham and John Stuart Mill. The latter tradition is individualist in its moral focus, in that it treats the needs and interests of individual sentient beings as the ultimate basis for conclusions about right and wrong.

These differences in moral perspective predictably result in differences in the emphasis given to specific moral issues. Thus, environmentalists treat the protection of endangered species and habitats as matters for utmost concern, while, unlike many of the animal liberationists, they generally do not object to hunting, fishing or rearing animals for food, so long as these practices do not endanger the survival of certain species or otherwise damage the natural environment. Animal liberationists, on the other hand, regard the inhumane treatment or killing of animals which are raised for meat, used in scientific experimentation and the like, as just as objectionable as the killing or mistreatment of "wild" animals. They oppose such practices not only because they may sometimes lead to environmental damage, but because they cause suffering or death to sentient beings.

Contrasts such as these have led some philosophers to conclude that the theoretical foundations of the Leopoldian land ethic and those of the

Excerpted from "The Rights of the Nonhuman World" by Mary Anne Warren in *Environmental Philosophy: A Collection of Readings*, ed. Robert Elliot and Arran Gare, 1983. Notes deleted.

animal-liberationist movement are fundamentally incompatible, or that there are "intractable practical differences" between them. I shall argue on the contrary, that a harmonious marriage between these two approaches is possible, provided that each side is prepared to make certain compromises. In brief, the animal liberationists must recognize that although animals do have significant moral rights, these rights are not precisely the same as those of human beings; and that part of the difference is that the rights of animals may sometimes be overriden, for example, for environmental or utilitarian reasons, in situations where it would not be morally acceptable to override human rights for similar reasons. For their part, the environmentalists must recognize that while it may be acceptable, as a legal or rhetorical tactic, to speak of the rights of trees or mountains, the logical foundations of such rights are quite different from those of the rights of human and other sentient beings. The issue is of enormous importance for moral philosophy, for it centres upon the theoretical basis for the the ascription of moral rights, and hence bears directly upon such disputed cases as the rights of (human) foetuses, children, the comatose, the insane, etc. Another interesting feature is the way in which utilitarians and deontologists often seem to exchange sides in the battle—the former insist upon the universal application of the principle that to cause unnecessary pain is wrong, while the latter refuse to apply that principle to other than human beings, unless there are utilitarian reasons for doing so.

In section I I will examine the primary line of argument presented by the contemporary animal-rights advocates, and suggest that their conclusions must be amended in the way mentioned above. In section II I will present two arguments for distinguishing between the rights of human beings and those of (most) nonhuman animals. In section III I will consider the animal liberationists' objection that any such distinction will endanger the rights of certain "nonparadigm" human beings, for example, infants and the mentally incapacitated. In section IV I will reply to several current objections to the attempt to found basic moral rights upon the sentience, or other psychological capacities, of the entity involved.

I

Why (Some) Animals Have (Some) Moral Rights

Peter Singer is the best known contemporary proponent of animal liberation. Singer maintains that all sentient animals, human or otherwise, should be regarded as morally equal; that is, that their interests should be given equal consideration. He argues that sentience, the capacity to have conscious experiences such as pain or pleasure, is "the only defensible boundary of concern for the interests of others." In Bentham's often-quoted words, "the question is not, Can they reason? nor, Can they talk? but Can they suffer?" To suppose that the interests of animals are outside the scope of moral concern is to commit a moral fallacy analogous to sexism or racism, a fallacy which Singer calls *speciesism*. True, women and members of "minority" races are more *intelligent* than (most) animals—and almost certainly no less so than white males—but that is not the point. The point does not concern these complex capabilities at all. For, Singer says, "The claim to equality does not depend on intelligence, moral capacity, physical strength, or similar matters of fact."

As a utilitarian, Singer prefers to avoid speaking of moral *rights*, at least insofar as these are construed as claims which may sometimes override purely utilitarian considerations. There are, however, many other advocates of animal liberation who do maintain that animals have moral rights, rights which place limitations upon the use of utilitarian justifications, for killing animals or causing them to suffer. Tom Regan, for example, argues that if all or most human beings have a right to life, then so do at least some animals. Regan points out that unless we hold that animals have a right to life, we may not be able to adequately support many of the conclusions that most animal liberationists think are important, for example, that it is wrong to kill animals painlessly to provide human beings with relatively trivial forms of pleasure.

This disagreement between Singer and Regan demonstrates that there is no single well-defined theory of the moral status of animals which can be identified as *the* animal liberationist position. It is clear, however, that neither philosopher is committed to the claim that the moral status of animals is completely identical to that of humans. Singer points out that his basic principle of equal *consideration* does not imply identical *treatment*. Regan holds only that animals have *some* of the same moral rights as do human beings, not that *all* of their rights are necessarily the same.

Nevertheless, none of the animal liberationists have thus far provided a clear explanation of how and why the moral status of (most) animals differs from that of (most) human beings; and this is a point which must be clarified if their position is to be made fully persuasive. That there is such a difference seems to follow from some very strong moral intuitions which most of us share. A man who shoots squirrels for sport may or may not be acting reprehensibly; but it is difficult to believe that his actions should be placed in *exactly* the same moral category as those of a man who shoots women, or black children, for sport. So too it is doubtful that the Japanese fishermen who slaughtered dolphins because the latter were thought to be depleting the local fish populations were acting quite *as* wrongly as if they had slaughtered an equal number of their human neighbours for the same reason.

Can anything persuasive be said in support of these intuitive judgments? Or are they merely evidence of unreconstructed speciesism? To answer these questions we must consider both certain similarities and certain differences between ourselves and other animals, and then decide which of these are relevant to the assignment of moral rights. To do this we must first ask just what it means to say than an entity possesses a certain moral right.

There are two elements of the concept of a moral right which are crucial for our present purposes. To say that an entity, X, has a moral right to Y (some activity, benefit or satisfaction) is to imply at least the following:

1. that it would be morally wrong for any moral agent to intentionally deprive X of Y without some sufficient justification;
2. that this would be wrong, at least in part, *because of the (actual or potential) harm which it would do to the interests of X.*

On this (partial) definition of a moral right, to ask whether animals have such rights is to ask whether there are some ways of treating them which are morally objectionable because of the harm done to the animals themselves, and not merely because of some *other* undesirable results, such as damaging the environment or undermining the moral character of human beings. As Regan and other animal liberationists have pointed out, the arguments for ascribing at least some moral rights to sentient nonhuman animals are very similar to the arguments for ascribing those same rights to sentient human beings. If we argue that human beings have rights not to be tortured, starved or confined under inhumane conditions, it is usually by appealing to our knowledge that they will suffer in much the same ways that we would under like circumstances. A child must learn that other persons (and animals) can experience, for example, pain, fear or anger, on the one hand; pleasure or satisfaction, on the other, in order to even begin to comprehend why some ways of behaving towards them are morally preferable to others.

If these facts are morally significant in the case of human beings, it is attractive to suppose that they should have similar significance in the case of animals. Everything that we know about the behaviour, biology and neurophysiology of, for instance, nonhuman mammals, indicates that they are capable of experiencing the same basic types of physical suffering and discomfort as we are, and it is reasonable to suppose that their pleasures are equally real and approximately as various. Doubts about the sentience of other animals are no more plausible than doubts about that of other human beings. True, most animals cannot use human language to *report* that they are in pain, but the vocalizations and "body language" through which they *express* pain, and many other psychological states, are similar enough to our own that their significance is generally clear.

But to say this is not yet to establish that animals have moral rights. We need a connecting link between the premise that certain ways of treating animals cause them to suffer, and the conclusion that such actions are *prima facie* morally wrong, that is, wrong unless proven otherwise. One way to make this connection is to hold that it is a *self-*

evident truth that the unnecessary infliction of suffering upon any sentient being is wrong. Those who doubt this claim may be accused (perhaps with some justice) of lacking empathy, the ability to "feel with" other sentient beings, to comprehend the reality of their experience. It may be held that it is possible to regard the suffering of animals as morally insignificant only to the extent that one suffers from blindness to "the ontology of animal reality"; that is, from a failure to grasp the fact that they are centres of conscious experience, as we are.

This argument is inadequate, however, since there may be those who fully comprehend the fact that animals are sentient beings, but who still deny that their pains and pleasures have any direct moral significance. For them, a more persuasive consideration may be that our moral reasoning will gain in clarity and coherence if we recognize that the suffering of a nonhuman being is an evil of the same general sort as that of a human being. For if we do not recognize that suffering is an intrinsic evil, something which ought not to be inflicted deliberately without just cause, then we will not be able to fully understand why treating *human beings* in certain ways is immoral.

Torturing human beings, for example, is not wrong merely because it is illegal (where it is illegal), or merely because it violates some implicit agreement amongst human beings (though it may). Such legalistic or contractualistic reasons leave us in the dark as to why we *ought* to have, and enforce, laws and agreements against torture. The essential reason for regarding torture as wrong is that it *hurts*, and that people greatly prefer to avoid such pain— as do animals. I am not arguing, as does Kant, that cruelty to animals is wrong because it causes cruelty to human beings, a position which consequentalists often endorse. The point, rather, is that unless we view the deliberate infliction of needless pain as inherently wrong we will not be able to understand the moral objection to cruelty of *either* kind.

It seems we must conclude, therefore, that sentient nonhuman animals have certain basic moral rights, rights which they share with all beings that are psychologically organized around the pleasure/pain axis. Their capacity for pain gives them the right that pain not be intentionally and needlessly inflicted upon them. Their capacity for pleasure

gives them the right not to be prevented from pursuing whatever pleasures and fulfillments are natural to creatures of their kind. Like human rights, the rights of animals may be overriden if there is a morally sufficient reason for doing so. What *counts* as a morally significant reason, however, may be different in the two cases.

II

Human and Animal Rights Compared

There are two dimensions in which we may find differences between the rights of human beings and those of animals. The first involves the *content* of those rights, while the second involves their strength; that is, the strength of the reasons which are required to override them.

Consider, for instance, the right to liberty. The *human* right to liberty precludes imprisonment without due process of law, even if the prison is spacious and the conditions of confinement cause no obvious physical suffering. But it is not so obviously wrong to imprison animals, especially when the area to which they are confined provides a fair approximation of the conditions of their natural habitat, and a reasonable opportunity to pursue the satisfactions natural to their kind. Such conditions, which often result in an increased lifespan, and which may exist in wildlife sanctuaries or even well-designed zoos, need not frustrate the needs or interests of animals in any significant way, and thus do not clearly violate their rights. Similarly treated human beings, on the other hand (e.g., native peoples confined to prison-like reservations), do tend to suffer from their loss of freedom. Human dignity and the fulfillment of the sorts of plans, hopes and desires which appear (thus far) to be uniquely human, require a more extensive freedom of movement than is the case with at least many nonhuman animals. Furthermore, there are aspects of human freedom, such as freedom of thought, freedom of speech and freedom of political association, which simply do not apply in the case of animals.

Thus, it seems that the human right to freedom is more extensive; that is, it precludes a wider range of specific ways of treating human beings than does the corresponding right on the part of animals. The argument cuts both ways, of course. *Some* animals, for example, great whales and migratory birds, may require at least as much physical freedom as do human beings if they are to pursue the satisfactions natural to their kind, and this fact provides a moral argument against keeping such creatures imprisoned. And even chickens may suffer from the extreme and unnatural confinement to which they are subjected on modern "factory farms." Yet it seems unnecessary to claim for *most* animals a right to a freedom quite as broad as that which we claim for ourselves.

Similar points may be made with respect to the right to life. Animals, it may be argued, lack the cognitive equipment to value their lives in the way that human beings do. Ruth Cigman argues that animals have *no* right to life because death is no misfortune for them. In her view, the death of an animal is not a misfortune, because animals have no desires which are *categorical*; that is which do not "merely presuppose being alive (like the desire to eat when one is hungry), but rather answer the question whether one wants to remain alive." In other words, animals appear to lack the sorts of long-range hopes, plans, ambitions and the like, which give human beings such a powerful interest in continued life. Animals, it seems, take life as it comes and do not specifically desire that it go on. True, squirrels store nuts for the winter and deer run from wolves; but these may be seen as instinctive or conditioned responses to present circumstances, rather than evidence that they value life as such.

These reflections probably help to explain why the death of a sparrow seems less tragic than that of a human being. Human lives, one might say, have greater intrinsic value, because they are worth more *to their possessors*. But this does not demonstrate that no nonhuman animal has *any* right to life. Premature death may be a less *severe* misfortune for sentient nonhuman animals than for human beings, but it is a misfortune nevertheless. In the first place, it is a misfortune in that it deprives them of whatever pleasures the future might have held for them, regardless of whether or not they ever *consciously anticipated* those pleasures. The fact that they are not here afterwards, to *experience* their loss, no more shows that they have not lost anything than it does in the case of humans. In the second place, it is (possibly) a misfortune in that it frustrates

whatever future-oriented desires animals *may* have, unbeknownst to us. Even now, in an age in which apes have been taught to use simplified human languages and attempts have been made to communicate with dolphins and whales, we still know very little about the operation of nonhuman minds. We know much too little to assume that nonhuman animals never consciously pursue relatively distant future goals. To the extent that they do, the question of whether such desires provide them with *reasons for living* or merely *presuppose* continued life, has no satisfactory answer, since they cannot contemplate these alternatives—or, if they can, we have no way of knowing what their conclusions are. All we know is that the more intelligent and psychologically complex an animal is, the more *likely* it is that it possesses specifically future-oriented desires, which would be frustrated even by *painless* death.

For these reasons, it is premature to conclude from the apparent intellectual inferiority of nonhuman animals that they have no right to life. A more plausible conclusion is that animals do have a right to life but that it is generally somewhat weaker than that of human beings. It is, perhaps, weak enough to enable us to justify killing animals when we have no other ways of achieving such vital goals as feeding or clothing ourselves, or obtaining knowledge which is necessary to save human lives. Weakening their right to life in this way does not render meaningless the assertion that they have such a right. For the point remains that *some* serious justification for the killing of sentient nonhuman animals is always necessary; they may not be killed merely to provide amusement or minor gains in convenience.

If animals' rights to liberty and life are somewhat weaker than those of human beings, may we say the same about their right to *happiness*; that is, their right not to be made to suffer needlessly or to be deprived of the pleasures natural to their kind? If so, it is not immediately clear why. There is little reason to suppose that pain or suffering are any less unpleasant for the higher animals (at least) than they are for us. Our large brains *may* cause us to experience pain more intensely than do most animals, and *probably* cause us to suffer more from the anticipation or remembrance of pain. These facts might tend to suggest that pain is, on the whole, a worse experience for us than for them. But it may also be argued that pain may be *worse* in some respects for nonhuman animals, who are presumably less able to distract themselves from it by thinking of something else, or to comfort themselves with the knowledge that it is temporary. Brigid Brophy points out that "pain is likely to fill the sheep's whole capacity for experience in a way it seldom does in us, whose intellect and imagination can create breaks for us in the immediacy of our sensations."

The net result of such contrasting considerations is that we cannot possibly claim to know whether pain is, on the whole, worse for us than for animals, or whether their pleasures are any more or any less intense than ours. Thus, while we may justify assigning them a somewhat weaker right to life or liberty, on the grounds that they desire these goods less intensely than we do, we cannot discount their rights to freedom from needlessly inflicted pain or unnatural frustration on the same basis. There may, however, be *other* reasons for regarding all of the moral rights of animals as somewhat less stringent than the corresponding human rights.

A number of philosophers who deny that animals have moral rights point to the fact that nonhuman animals evidently lack the capacity for moral autonomy. Moral autonomy is the ability to act as a moral agent; that is, to act on the basis of an understanding of, and adherence to, moral rules or principles. H. J. McCloskey, for example, holds that "it is the capacity for moral autonomy...that is basic to the possibility of possessing a right." McCloskey argues that it is inappropriate to ascribe moral rights to any entity which is not a moral agent, or *potentially* a moral agent, because a right is essentially an entitlement granted to a moral agent, licensing him or her to *act* in certain ways and to *demand* that other moral agents refrain from interference. For this reason, he says, "Where there is no possibility of [morally autonomous] action, potentially or actually...and where the being is not a member of a kind which is normally capable of [such] action, we withhold talk of rights."

If moral autonomy—or being *potentially* autonomous, or a member of a kind which is *normally* capable of autonomy—is a necessary condition for having moral rights, then probably no nonhuman animal can qualify. For moral autonomy requires such probably uniquely human traits as "the capacity

to be critically self-aware, manipulate concepts, use a sophisticated language, reflect, plan, deliberate, choose, and accept responsibility for acting."

But why, we must ask, should the capacity for autonomy be regarded as a precondition for possessing moral rights? Autonomy is clearly crucial for the *exercise* of many human moral or legal rights, such as the right to vote or to run for public office. It is less clearly relevant, however, to the more basic human rights, such as the right to life or to freedom from unnecessary suffering. The fact that animals, like many human beings, cannot *demand* their moral rights (at least not in the words of any conventional human language) seems irrelevant. For, as Joel Feinberg points out, the interests of non-morally autonomous human beings may be defended by others, for example, in legal proceedings; and it is not clear why the interests of animals might not be represented in a similar fashion.

It is implausible, therefore, to conclude that because animals lack moral autonomy they should be accorded *no moral rights whatsoever.* Nevertheless, it may be argued that the moral autonomy of (most) human beings provides a second reason, in addition to their more extensive interests and desires, for according somewhat *stronger* moral rights to human beings. The fundamental insight behind contractualist theories of morality is that, for morally autonomous beings such as ourselves, there is enormous mutual advantage in the adoption of a moral system designed to protect each of us from the harms that might otherwise be visited upon us by others. Each of us ought to accept and promote such a system because, to the extent that others also accept it, we will all be safer from attack by our fellows, more likely to receive assistance when we need it, and freer to engage in individual as well as cooperative endeavours of all kinds.

Thus, it is the possibility of *reciprocity* which motivates moral agents to extend *full and equal* moral rights, in the first instance, only to other moral agents. I respect your rights to life, liberty and the pursuit of happiness in part because you are a sentient being, whose interests have intrinsic moral significance. But I respect them as *fully equal to my own* because I hope and expect that you will do the same for me. Animals, insofar as they lack the degree of rationality necessary for moral autonomy, cannot agree to respect our interests as equal in moral importance to their own, and neither do they expect or demand each respect from us. Of course, domestic animals may expect to be fed, etc. But they do not, and cannot, expect to be treated as moral equals, for they do not understand that moral concept or what it implies. Consequently, it is neither pragmatically feasible nor morally obligatory to extend to them the same *full and equal* rights which we extend to human beings.

Is this a speciesist conclusion? Defenders of a more extreme animal rights position may point out that this argument, from the lack of moral autonomy, has exactly the same form as that which has been used for thousands of years to rationalize denying equal moral rights to women and members of "inferior" races. Aristotle, for example, argued that women and slaves are naturally subordinate beings, because they lack the capacity for moral autonomy and self-direction; and contemporary versions of this argument, used to support racist or sexist conclusions, are easy to find. Are we simply repeating Aristotle's mistake, in a different context?

The reply to this objection is very simple: animals, unlike women and slaves, really *are* incapable of moral autonomy, at least to the best of our knowledge. Aristotle certainly *ought* to have known that women and slaves are capable of morally autonomous action; their capacity to use moral language alone ought to have alerted him to this likelihood. If comparable evidence exists that (some) nonhuman animals are moral agents we have not yet found it. The fact that some apes (and, possibly, some cetaceans) are capable of learning radically simplified human languages, the terms of which refer primarily to objects and events in their immediate environment, in no way demonstrates that they can understand abstract moral concepts, rules or principles, or use this understanding to regulate their own behaviour.

On the other hand, this argument implies that if we *do* discover that certain nonhuman animals are capable of moral autonomy (which is certainly not impossible), then we ought to extend full and equal moral rights to those animals. Furthermore, if we someday encounter extraterrestrial beings, or build robots, androids or supercomputers which function as self-aware moral agents, then we must extend full and equal moral rights to these as well. Being a member of the human species is not a necessary condition for the possession of full "human" rights. Whether it is nevertheless a *sufficient* condition is the question to which we now turn.

III

The Moral Rights of Nonparadigm Humans

If we are justified in ascribing somewhat different, and also somewhat stronger, moral rights to human beings than to sentient but non-morally autonomous animals, then what are we to say of the rights of human beings who happen not to be capable of moral autonomy, perhaps not even potentially? Both Singer and Regan have argued that if any of the superior intellectual capacities of normal and mature human beings are used to support a distinction between the moral status of *typical*, or paradigm, human beings, and that of animals, then consistency will require us to place certain "nonparadigm" humans, such as infants, small children and the severely retarded or incurably brain damaged, in the same inferior moral category. Such a result is, of course, highly counterintuitive.

Fortunately, no such conclusion follows from the autonomy argument. There are many reasons for extending strong moral rights to non-paradigm humans; reasons which do not apply to most nonhuman animals. Infants and small children are granted strong moral rights in part because of their *potential* autonomy. But *potential* autonomy, as I have argued elsewhere, is not in itself a sufficient reason for the ascription of full moral rights; if it were, then not only human foetuses (from conception onwards) but even ununited human sperm-egg pairs would have to be regarded as entities with a right to life the equivalent of our own—thus making not only abortion, but any intentional failure to procreate, the moral equivalent of murder. Those who do not find this extreme conclusion acceptable must appeal to reasons other than the *potential* moral autonomy of infants and small children to explain the strength of the latter's moral rights.

One reason for assigning strong moral rights to infants and children is that they possess not just *potential* but *partial* autonomy, and it is not clear how much of it they have at any given moment. The fact that, unlike baby chimpanzees, they are already learning the things which will enable them to *become* morally autonomous, makes it likely that their minds have more subtleties than their speech (or the lack of it) proclaims. Another reason is simply that most of us tend to place a very high value on the lives and well-being of infants. Perhaps we are to some degree "programmed" by nature to love and protect them; perhaps our reasons are somewhat egocentric; or perhaps we value them for their potential. Whatever the explanation, the fact that we do feel this way about them is in itself a valid reason for extending to them stronger moral and legal protections than we extend to nonhuman animals, even those which may have just as well or better-developed psychological capacities. A third, and perhaps the most important, reason is that if we did *not* extend strong moral rights to infants, far too few of them would ever *become* responsible, morally autonomous adults; too many would be treated "like animals" (i.e., in ways that it is generally wrong to treat even animals), and would consequently become socially crippled, antisocial or just very unhappy people. If any part of our moral code is to remain intact, it seems that infants and small children *must* be protected and cared for.

Analogous arguments explain why strong moral rights should also be accorded to other nonparadigm humans. The severely retarded or incurably senile, for instance, may have no potential for moral autonomy, but there are apt to be friends, relatives or other people who care what happens to them. Like children, such individuals may have more mental capacities than are readily apparent. Like children, they are more apt to achieve, or return to moral autonomy if they are valued and well cared for. Furthermore, any one of us may someday become mentally incapacitated to one degree or another, and we would all have reason to be anxious about our own futures if such incapacitation were made the basis for denying strong moral rights.

There are, then, sound reasons for assigning strong moral rights even to human beings who lack the mental capacities which justify the general distinction between human and animal rights. Their rights are based not only on the value which they

themselves place upon their lives and well-being, but also on the value which other human beings place upon them.

But is this a valid basis for the assignment of moral rights? Is it consistent with the definition presented earlier, according to which X may be said to have a moral right to Y only if depriving X of Y is *prima facie* wrong *because of the harm done to the interests of X*, and not merely because of any further consequences? Regan argues that we cannot justify the ascription of stronger rights to nonparadigm humans than to nonhuman animals in the way suggested, because "what underlies the ascription of rights to any given X is that X has value independently of anyone's valuing X." After all, we do not speak of expensive paintings or gemstones as having rights, although many people value them and have good reasons for wanting them protected.

There is, however, a crucial difference between a rare painting and a severely retarded or senile human being; the latter not only has (or may have) value for other human beings but *also* has his or her own needs and interests. It may be this which leads us to say that such individuals have intrinsic value. The sentience of nonparadigm humans, like that of sentient nonhuman animals, gives them a place in the sphere of rights holders. So long as the moral rights of all sentient beings are given due recognition, there should be no objection to providing some of them with *additional* protections, on the basis of our interests as well as their own. Some philosophers speak of such additional protections, which are accorded to X on the basis of interests other than X's own, as *conferred* rights, in contrast to *natural* rights, which are entirely based upon the properties of X itself. But such "conferred" rights are not necessarily any weaker or less binding upon moral agents than are "natural" rights. Infants, and most other nonparadigm humans have the *same* basic moral rights that the rest of us do, even though the reasons for ascribing those rights are somewhat different in the two cases.

IV

Other Objections to Animal Rights

We have already dealt with the primary objection to assigning *any* moral rights to nonhuman animals;

that is, that they lack moral autonomy, and various other psychological capacities which paradigm humans possess. We have also answered the animal liberationists' primary objection to assigning somewhat *weaker*, or less-extensive rights to animals; that is, that this will force us to assign similarly inferior rights to nonparadigm humans. There are two other objections to animal rights which need to be considered. The first is that the claim that animals have a right to life, or other moral rights, has absurd consequences with respect to the natural relationships *among* animals. The second is that to accord rights to animals on the basis of their (differing degrees of) sentience will introduce intolerable difficulties and complexities into our moral reasoning.

Opponents of animal rights often accuse the animal liberationists of ignoring the realities of nature, in which many animals survive only by killing others. Callicott, for example, maintains that, whereas environmentally aware persons realize that natural predators are a vital part of the biotic community, those who believe that animals have a right to life are forced to regard all predators as "merciless, wanton, and incorrigible murderers of their fellow creatures." Similarly, Ritchie asks whether, if animals have rights, we are not morally obligated to "protect the weak among them against the strong? Must we not put to death blackbirds and thrushes because they feed on worms, or (if capital punishment offends our humanitarianism) starve them slowly by permanent captivity and vegetarian diet?"

Such a conclusion would of course be ridiculous, as well as wholly inconsistent with the environmental ethic. However, nothing of the sort follows from the claim that animals have moral rights. There are two independently sufficient reasons why it does not. In the first place, nonhuman predators are not moral agents, so it is absurd to think of them as wicked, or as *murdering* their prey. But this is not the most important point. Even if wolves and the like *were* moral agents, their predation would still be morally acceptable, given that they generally kill only to feed themselves, and generally do so without inflicting prolonged or unnecessary suffering. If we have the right to eat animals, in order to avoid starvation, then why shouldn't animals have the right to eat one another, for the same reason?

This conclusion is fully consistent with the lesson taught by the ecologists, that natural predation is essential to the stability of biological communities. Deer need wolves, or other predators, as much as the latter need them; without predation they become too numerous and fall victim to hunger and disease, while their overgrazing damages the entire ecosystem. Too often we have learned (or failed to learn) this lesson the hard way, as when the killing of hawks and other predators produces exploding rodent populations—which must be controlled, often in ways which cause further ecological damage. The control of natural predators may *sometimes* be necessary, for example, when human pressures upon the populations of certain species become so intense that the latter cannot endure continued *natural* predation. (The controversial case of the wolves and caribou in Alaska and Canada may or may not be one of this sort.) But even in such cases it is preferreable, from an environmentalist perspective, to reduce human predation enough to leave room for natural predators as well.

Another objection to assigning moral rights to sentient nonhuman animals is that it will not only complicate our own moral system, but introduce seemingly insoluble dilemmas. As Ritchie points out, "Very difficult questions of casuistry will...arise because of the difference in grades of sentience." For instance, is it morally worse to kill and eat a dozen oysters (which are at most minimally sentient) or one (much more highly sentient) rabbit? Questions of this kind, considered in isolation from any of the practical circumstances in which they might arise, are virtually unanswerable. But this ought not to surprise us, since similarly abstract questions about the treatment of human beings are often equally unanswerable. (For instance, would it be worse to kill one child or to cause a hundred to suffer from severe malnutrition?)

The reason such questions are so difficult to answer is not just that we lack the skill and knowledge to make such precise comparisons of interpersonal or interspecies utility, but also that these questions are posed in entirely unrealistic terms. Real moral choices rarely depend entirely upon the comparison of two abstract quantities of pain or pleasure deprivation. In deciding whether to eat molluscs or mammals (or neither or both) a human society must consider *all* of the predictable consequences of each option, for example, their respective impacts on the ecology or the economy, and not merely the individual interests of the animals involved.

Of course, other things being equal, it would be morally preferable to refrain from killing *any* sentient animal. But other things are never equal. Questions about human diet involve not only the rights of individual animals, but also vital environmental and human concerns. On the one hand, as Singer points out, more people could be better fed if food suitable for human consumption were not fed to meat-producing animals. On the other hand, a mass conversion of humanity to vegetarianism would represent "an increase in the efficiency of the conversion of solar energy from plant to human biomass," with the likely result that the human

population would continue to expand and, in the process, to cause greater environmental destruction than might occur otherwise. The issue is an enormously complex one, and cannot be solved by any simple appeal to the claim that animals have (or lack) certain moral rights.

In short, the ascription of moral rights to animals does not have the absurd or environmentally damaging consequences that some philosophers have feared. It does not require us to exterminate predatory species, or to lose ourselves in abstruse speculations about the relative degrees of sentience of different sorts of animals. It merely requires us to recognize the interests of animals as having intrinsic moral significance; as demanding some consideration, regardless of whether or not human or environmental concerns are also involved. . . .

The Moral Status of Animals

ROGER SCRUTON

The account of moral reasoning that I have sketched offers an answer, even if not a fully reasoned answer, to the question of animals. In developing this answer, I shall use the term "animal" to mean those animals that lack the distinguishing features of the moral being—rationality, self-consciousness, personality, and so on. If there are non-human animals who are rational and self-conscious, then they, like us, are persons, and should be described and treated accordingly. If *all* animals are persons, then there is no longer a problem as to how we should treat them. They would be full members of the moral community, with rights and duties like the rest of us. But it is precisely because there are animals who are not persons that the moral problem exists. And to treat these non-personal animals as persons is not to grant to them a privilege nor to raise their chances of contentment. It is to ignore what they essentially are and so to fall out of relation with them altogether.

The concept of the person belongs to the ongoing dialogue which binds the moral community. Creatures who are by nature incapable of entering into this dialogue have neither rights nor duties nor personality. If animals had rights, then we should require their consent before taking them into captivity, training them, domesticating them or in any way putting them to our uses. But there is no conceivable process whereby this consent could be delivered or withheld. Furthermore, a creature with rights is duty-bound to respect the rights of others. The fox would be duty-bound to respect the right to life of the chicken and whole species would be condemned out of hand as criminal by nature. Any law which compelled persons to respect the rights of

"The Moral Status of Animals" in *Animal Rights and Wrongs* by Roger Scruton, 51–56, 79–83 (Continuum, 2007). © Demos Medical Publishing.

non-human species would weigh so heavily on the predators as to drive them to extinction in a short while. Any morality which really attributed rights to animals would therefore constitute a gross and callous abuse of them.

Those considerations are obvious, but by no means trivial. For they point to a deep difficulty in the path of any attempt to treat animals as our equals. By ascribing rights to animals, and so promoting them to full membership of the moral community, we tie them in obligations that they can neither fulfil nor comprehend. Not only is this senseless cruelty in itself; it effectively destroys all possibility of cordial and beneficial relations between us and them. Only by refraining from personalising animals do we behave towards them in ways that they can understand. And even the most sentimental animal lovers know this, and confer "rights" on their favourites in a manner so selective and arbitrary as to show that they are not really dealing with the ordinary moral concept. When a dog savages a sheep no one believes that the dog, rather than its owner, should be sued for damages. Sei Shonagon, in *The Pillow Book*, tells of a dog breaching some rule of court etiquette and being horribly beaten, as the law requires. The scene is most disturbing to the modern reader. Yet surely, if dogs have rights, punishment is what they must expect when they disregard their duties.

But the point does not concern rights only. It concerns the deep and impassable difference between personal relations, founded on dialogue, criticism and the sense of justice, and animal relations, founded on affections and needs. The moral problem of animals arises because they cannot enter into relations of the first kind, while we are so much bound by those relations that they seem to tie us even to creatures who cannot themselves be bound by them.

Defenders of "animal liberation" have made much of the fact that animals suffer as we do: they feel pain, hunger, cold and fear and therefore, as Singer puts it, have "interests" which form, or ought to form, part of the moral equation. While this is true, it is only part of the truth. There is more to morality than the avoidance of suffering: to live by no other standard than this one is to avoid life, to forgo risk and adventure, and to sink into a state of

cringing morbidity. Moreover, while our sympathies ought to be—and unavoidably will be—extended to the animals, they should not be indiscriminate. Although animals have no rights, we still have duties and responsibilities towards them, or towards some of them. These will cut across the utilitarian equation, distinguishing the animals who are close to us and who have a claim on our protection from those towards whom our duties fall under the broader rule of charity.

This is important for two reasons. Firstly, we relate to animals in three distinct situations, which define three distinct kinds of responsibility: as pets, as domestic animals reared for human purposes and as wild creatures. Secondly, the situation of animals is radically and often irreversibly changed as soon as human beings take an interest in them. Pets and other domestic animals are usually entirely dependent on human care for their survival and well-being; and wild animals, too, are increasingly dependent on human measures to protect their food supplies and habitats.

Some shadow version of the moral law therefore emerges in our dealings with animals. I cannot blithely count the interests of my dog as on a par with the interests of any other dog, wild or domesticated, even though they have an equal capacity for suffering and an equal need for help. My dog has a special claim on me, not wholly dissimilar from the claim of my child. I caused it to be dependent on me precisely by leading it to expect that I would cater for its needs.

The situation is further complicated by the distinction between species. Dogs form life-long attachments and a dog brought up by one person may be incapable of living comfortably with another. A horse may be bought or sold many times, with little or no distress, provided it is properly cared for by each of its owners. Sheep maintained in flocks are every bit as dependent on human care as dogs and horses; but they do not notice it and regard their shepherds and guardians as little more than aspects of the environment, which rise like the sun in the morning and depart like the sun at night.

For these reasons, we must consider our duties towards animals in three separate ways: as pets, as animals reared for our purposes and as creatures of the wild.

ARGUMENT 23 ESSAY QUESTIONS
1. What are Warren's criticisms of Regan's animal rights position? Are they credible?
2. How does Scruton's view differ from Regan's?
3. Which view of animal rights do you think is more plausible, Regan's or Warren's? Explain.

24. THE SUFFERING ARGUMENT FOR VEGETARIANISM

In "The Moral Argument for Vegetarianism," James Rachels makes a case for vegetarianism by appealing to the wrongness of causing unnecessary suffering. He argues that causing suffering is wrong unless there is a justifying reason; the raising and slaughtering of animals for food causes them enormous suffering; the pleasure we derive from eating meat does not justify this misery; therefore, we should not participate in this great wrong; we should stop eating meat (become vegetarians).[9]

A typical reply to this line is "My personal eating habits cannot possibly affect the suffering of animals in the meat industry. So how could my meat eating be wrong?" James Rachels thinks this reasoning is flawed: "If one really thinks that a social practice is immoral, that is sufficient grounds for refusing to participate in it."[10] Presumably, by eating meat, we are participating, however indirectly, in the animals' immoral treatment.

Some have pointed out that the argument from suffering does not show that meat eating itself is immoral, only that the treatment animals receive as they are turned into food is immoral. As R.G. Frey says,

> What the arguments [for vegetarianism] make out to be morally wrong is not actually eating animals but violating their alleged moral rights or killing them or making them suffer. Do none of these things, and the wrongness of eating meat vanishes. Here, then, are vegetarians of whom vegetarianism is only demanded if animals are treated one way rather than another.[11]

Can we conclude from this that we don't necessarily have to stop eating animals? Rachels says no: "This sounds plausible until we realize that it would be impossible to treat animals decently and still produce meat in sufficient quantities to make it a normal part of our diets."[12]

---

[9] James Rachels, *Can Ethics Provide Answers?* (Lanham, MD: Rowman & Littlefield, 1997).
[10] James Rachels, 107.
[11] R.G. Frey, *Rights, Killing, and Suffering* (Oxford: Blackwell Publishers, 1983), 31.
[12] James Rachels, 102.

Other philosophers, however, are not as pessimistic as Rachels about the possibility of more ethical methods of meat production. Frey, for instance, insists that there are already millions of animals being "farmed but not factory-farmed," that not all animals suffer as much as veal calves do, and that animal farming methods that cause less suffering than those used in intensive factory-farming (traditional farming methods, for example) are possible.

The Moral Argument for Vegetarianism

JAMES RACHELS

The idea that it is morally wrong to eat meat may seem faintly ridiculous. After all, eating meat is a normal, well-established part of our lives; people have always eaten meat; and many find it difficult even to conceive of what an alternative diet would be like. So it is not easy to take seriously the possibility that it might be wrong. Moreover, vegetarianism is commonly associated with Eastern religions whose tenets we do not accept and with extravagant, unfounded claims about health. A quick perusal of vegetarian literature might confirm the impression that it is all a crackpot business; tracts have titles like "Victory through Vegetables" and promise that if we will only keep to a meatless diet, we will have perfect health and be filled with wisdom. Of course we can ignore this kind of nonsense. However, there are other arguments for vegetarianism that must be taken seriously. The most powerful argument appeals to the principle that it is wrong to cause unnecessary suffering.

The wrongness of cruelty to animals is often explained in terms of its effects on human beings. The idea seems to be that although the animals themselves are not morally important, cruelty has bad consequences for humans, and so it is wrong for that reason. In legal writing, cruelty to animals has been included among the "victimless crimes," and the problem of justifying legal prohibitions has been viewed as comparable to justifying the prohibition of other behavior, such as prostitution or the distribution of pornography, where no one is hurt. In

1963 the distinguished legal scholar Louis Schwartz wrote that, in prohibiting the torturing of animals, "It is not the mistreated dog who is the ultimate object of concern....Our concern is for the feelings of other human beings, a large proportion of whom, although accustomed to the slaughter of animals for food, readily identify themselves with a tortured dog or horse and respond with great sensltivity to its sufferings."[1]

Philosophers have also adopted this attitude. Kant, for example, held that we have no direct duties to nonhuman animals. "The Categorical Imperative," the ultimate principle of morality, applies only to our dealings with people: "The practical imperative, therefore, is the following: Act so that you treat humanity, whether in your own person or in that of another, always as an end and never as a means only."[2] And of other animals, Kant says: "But so far as animals are concerned, we have no direct duties. Animals are not self-conscious, and are there merely as means to an end. That end is man."[3] He adds that we should not be cruel to animals only because "he who is cruel to animals becomes hard also in his dealings with men."[4]

Surely, this is unacceptable. Cruelty to animals ought to be opposed, not only because of the ancillary effects on humans, but also because of the direct

"The Moral Argument for Vegetarianism" by James Rachels in Can Ethics Provide Answers?, 99–107. © 1997 Lanham, MD: Rowman and Littlefield.

effects on the animals themselves. Animals that are tortured suffer, just as tortured humans suffer, and that is the primary reason it is wrong. We object to torturing humans on a number of grounds, but the main one is that the victims suffer so. Insofar as nonhuman animals also suffer, we have the same reason to oppose torturing them, and it is indefensible to take the one suffering but not the other as grounds for objection.

Although cruelty to animals is wrong, it does not follow that we are never justified in inflicting pain on an animal. Sometimes we are justified in doing this, just as we are sometimes justified in inflicting pain on humans. It does follow, however, that there must be a good reason for causing the suffering, and if the suffering is great, the justifying reason must be correspondingly powerful. As an example, consider the treatment of the civet cat, a highly intelligent and sociable animal. Civet cats are trapped and placed in small cages inside darkened sheds, where fires keep the temperature up to 110 degrees Fahrenheit.[5] They are confined in this way until they die. What justifies this extraordinary mistreatment? These animals have the misfortune to produce a substance that is useful in the manufacture of perfume. Musk, which is scraped from their genitals once a day for as long as they can survive, makes the scent of perfume last a bit longer after each application. (The heat increases their "production" of musk.) Here Kant's rule—"Animals are merely means to an end; that end is man"—is applied with a vengeance. To promote one of the most trivial interests we have, animals are tormented for their whole lives.

It is usually easy to persuade people that this use of animals is not justified and that we have a moral duty not to support such cruelties by consuming their products. The argument is simple: Causing suffering is not justified unless there is a good reason; the production of perfume made with musk causes suffering; our enjoyment of this product is not a good enough reason to justify causing that suffering; therefore, the use of animals in this way is wrong. Once people learn the facts about musk production, they come to regard using such products as morally objectionable. They are surprised to discover, however, that an exactly analogous argument can be given in connection with the use of animals as food. Animals that are raised and slaughtered

for food also suffer, and our enjoyment of the way they taste is not a sufficient justification for mistreating them.

Most people radically underestimate the amount of suffering that is caused to animals who are raised and slaughtered for food.[6] They believe, in a vague way, that slaughterhouses are cruel and perhaps that methods of slaughter ought to be made more humane. But after all, the visit to the slaughterhouse is a relatively brief episode in the animal's life; and beyond that, people imagine that the animals are treated well enough. Nothing could be further from the truth. Today the production of meat is big business, and the helpless animals are treated more as machines in a factory than as living creatures.

Veal calves, for example, spend their lives in pens too small to allow them to turn around or even to lie down comfortably—exercise toughens the muscles, which reduces the quality of the meat; and besides, allowing the animals adequate living space would be prohibitively expensive. In these pens the calves cannot perform such basic actions as grooming themselves, which they naturally desire to do, because there is not room for them to twist their heads around. It is clear that the calves miss their mothers, and like human infants they want something to suck; they can be seen trying vainly to suck the sides of their stalls. In order to keep their meat pale and tasty, they are fed a liquid diet deficient in iron and roughage. Naturally, they develop cravings for these things, because they need them. The calf's craving for iron is so strong that if it is allowed to turn around, it will lick at its own urine, although calves normally find this repugnant. The tiny stall, which prevents the animal from turning, solves this problem. The craving for roughage is especially strong since without it the animal cannot form a cud to chew. It cannot be given any straw for bedding, since the animal would be driven to eat it and that would spoil the meat. For these animals the slaughterhouse is not an unpleasant end to an otherwise contented life. As terrifying as the process of slaughter is, for them it may actually be a merciful release.

Similar stories can be told about the treatment of other animals on which we dine. In order to produce animals by the millions, it is necessary to keep them crowded together in small spaces. Chickens are commonly kept four or five to a space smaller than a newspaper page. Unable to walk around or even stretch their wings—much less build a nest—the birds become vicious and attack one another. The problem is exacerbated because the birds are so crowded that because they are unable to move, their feet sometimes grow around the wire floors of the cages, anchoring them to the spot. An anchored bird cannot escape attack no matter how desperate it becomes. Mutilation of the animals is an efficient solution. To minimize the damage they can do to one another, poultry farmers cut off their beaks. The mutilation is painful but probably not as painful as other sorts of mutilations that are routinely practiced. Cows are castrated, not to prevent the unnatural "vices" to which overcrowded chickens are prone, but because castrated cows put on more weight and there is less danger of meat being tainted by male hormones.

> In Britain an anesthetic must be used, unless the animal is very young, but in America anesthetics are not in general use. The procedure is to pin the animal down, take a knife and slit the scrotum, exposing the testides. You then grab each testicle in turn and pull on it, breaking the cord that attaches it; on older animals it may be necessary to cut the cord.[7]

It must be emphasized that such treatment is not out of the ordinary. It is typical of the way that animals raised for food are treated, now that meat production is big business. As Peter Singer puts it, these are the sorts of things that happened to your dinner when it was still an animal.

What accounts for such cruelties? As for the meat producers, there is no reason to think they are unusually cruel people. They simply accept the common attitude expressed by Kant: "Animals are merely means to an end; that end is man." The cruel practices are adopted not because they are cruel but because they are efficient, given that one's only concern is to produce meat (and eggs) for humans as cheaply as possible. But clearly this use of animals is immoral if anything is. Since we can nourish ourselves very well without eating them, our only reason for doing all this to the animals is our enjoyment of the way they taste. And this will not even come close to justifying the cruelty.

Does this mean that we should stop eating meat? It is tempting to say: "What is objectionable is not *eating* the animals, but only making them suffer. Perhaps we ought to protest the way they are treated and even work for better treatment of them. But it doesn't follow that we must stop eating them." This sounds plausible until we realize that it would be impossible to treat the animals decently and still produce meat in sufficient quantities to make it a normal part of our diets. Cruel methods are used in the meat-production industry because such methods are economical; they enable the producers to market a product that people can afford. Humanely produced chicken, beef, and pork would be so expensive that only the very rich could afford them. (Some of the cruelties might be eliminated without too much expense—the cows could be given an anesthetic before castration, for example, even though this alone would mean a slight increase in the cost of beef. But others, such as overcrowding, could not be eliminated without really prohibitive cost.) So to work for better treatment for the animals would be to work for a situation in which most of us would have to adopt a vegetarian diet.

Still, there remains the interesting theoretical question: If meat could be produced humanely, without mistreating the animals before killing them painlessly, would there be anything wrong with it? The question has only theoretical interest, because the actual choice we face in the supermarket is whether to buy the remains of animals that were not treated humanely. Still, the question has some interest, and we may take a quick look at it.

First, it is a vexing issue whether animals have a "right to life" that is violated when we kill them for trivial purposes; but we should not simply assume until it is proved otherwise that they don't have such a right. We assume that humans have a right to life—it would be wrong to murder a normal, healthy human even if it were done painlessly—and it is hard to think of any plausible rationale for granting this right to humans that does not also apply to other animals. Other animals live in communities, as do humans; they communicate with one another and have ongoing social relationships; killing them disrupts lives that are perhaps not as complex emotionally and intellectually as our own but that are nevertheless quite complicated. They suffer and are capable of happiness as well as fear and distress, as we are. So what could be the rational basis for saying that we have a right to life but that they don't? Or even more pointedly, what could be the rational basis for saying that a severely retarded human, who is inferior in every important respect to an intelligent animal, has a right to life but that the animal doesn't? Philosophers often treat such questions as "puzzles," assuming that there must be answers even if we are not clever enough to find them. But perhaps there are no acceptable answers to this question. If it seems, intuitively, that there must be some difference between us and the other animals that confers on us, but not on them, a right to life, perhaps this intuition is mistaken. At the very least, the difficulty of answering such questions should make us hesitant about asserting that it is all right to kill animals so long as we don't make them suffer, unless we are also willing to take seriously the possibility that it is all right to kill people so long as we don't make them suffer.

But let me make a more definite suggestion about this. If we want to know whether animals have a right to life, we should start by asking why humans have such a right. What is it about humans that gives them a right to life? If humans have a right to life, but plants, say, do not, then there must be some difference between them that explains why one has a right the other lacks. There must be characteristics possessed by humans but not by plants that qualify the humans for this right. Therefore, one way to approach our question is by trying to identify those characteristics. Then we can ask whether any non-human animals have those characteristics.

With respect to the characteristics that qualify one for a right to life, my suggestion is that an individual has a right to life if that individual has a life. Like many philosophical ideas, this one is more complicated than it first appears.

Having a life is different from merely being alive. The latter is a biological notion—to be alive is just to be a functioning biological organism. It is the opposite of being dead. But "a life," in the sense that concerns us here, is a notion of biography rather than of biology. "The life of Babe Ruth" will be concerned not with the biological facts of Ruth's existence—he had a heart and liver and blood and kidneys—but with facts about his history, beliefs, actions, and relationships:

He was born George Herman Ruth in Baltimore in 1895, the troubled child of a poor family. He was sent to live at St. Mary's School when he was eight; he learned baseball there and started pitching for the Red Sox at nineteen. Babe was an outstanding pitcher for six seasons before switching to the Yankee outfield and going on to become the most idolized slugger in the history of the game. He hit 60 home runs in a single season and 714 overall. He was the beer-guzzling friend of Lou Gehrig and was married to Claire. He died of cancer at age fifty-three.

These are some of the facts of his life. They are not biological facts.

Death is an evil when it puts an end not simply to being alive but to a life. Some humans, tragically, do not have lives and never will. An infant with Tay-Sachs disease will never develop beyond about six months of age, there may be some regression at that point, and it will die. Suppose such an infant contracts pneumonia; the decision might be made not to treat the pneumonia and to allow the baby to die. The decision seems justified because in the absence of any possibility of a life in the biographical sense, life in the biological sense has little value. The same sort of consideration explains why it seems so pointless to maintain persons in irreversible coma. The families of such patients are quick to realize that merely being alive is unimportant. The mother of a man who died after six years in a coma told a newspaper reporter, "My son died at age 34 after having lived for 28 years."[8] It was a melodramatic remark, and on the surface a paradoxical one—how can one die at 34 and have lived only 28 years?—yet what she meant is clear enough. The man's life was over when he entered the coma, even though he was alive for 6 years longer. The temporal boundaries of one's being alive need not be the same as the temporal boundaries of one's life.

Therefore, it is unwise to insist that any animal, human or nonhuman, has a right to life simply because it is a living being. The doctrine of the sanctity of life, interpreted as applying merely to biological life, has little to recommend it. My suggestion about the right to life is that an individual has a right to life if that individual has a life in the biographical sense. By this criterion, at least some nonhuman animals would have such a right. Monkeys, to take the most obvious example, have lives that are quite complex. They are remarkably intelligent, they have families and live together in social groups, and they apparently have forward-looking and backward-looking attitudes. Their lives do not appear to be as emotionally or intellectually complex as the lives of humans; but the more we learn about them, the more impressed we are with the similarities between them and us.

Of course we do not know a great deal about the lives of the members of most other species. To make intelligent judgments about them, we need the sort of information that could be gained by observing animals in their natural homes rather than in the laboratory—although laboratory-acquired information can be helpful. When baboons, dogs, and wolves have been studied in the wild, it has been found that the lives of individual animals, carried out within pack societies, are surprisingly diverse. But we are only beginning to appreciate the richness of the animal kingdom.

In our present state of semi-ignorance about other species, the situation seems to be this. When we consider the mammals with which we are most familiar, it is reasonable to believe that they do have lives in the biographical sense. They have emotions and cares and social systems and the rest, although perhaps not in just the way that humans do. Then the further down the old phylogenetic scale we go, the less confidence we have that there is anything resembling a life. When we come to bugs, or shrimp, the animals pretty clearly lack the mental capacities necessary for a life, although they certainly are alive. Most of us already have an intuitive sense of the importance of these gradations—we think that killing a human is worse than killing a monkey, but we also think that killing a monkey is a more morally serious matter than swatting a fly. And when we come to plants, which are alive but to which the notion of a biographical life is not applicable at all, our moral qualms about killing vanish altogether. If my suggestion about the right to life is correct, these feelings have a rational basis: insofar as we have reason to view other creatures as having lives, as we do, we have reason to view them as having a right to life, if we do.

Finally, it is important to see the slaughter of animals for food as part of a larger pattern that characterizes our whole relationship with the non-human world. Animals are taken from their natural homes to be made objects of our entertainment in zoos, circuses, and rodeos. They are used in laboratories, not only for experiments that are themselves morally questionable, but also in testing everything from shampoo to chemical weapons. They are killed so that their heads can be used as wall decorations or their skins as ornamental clothing or rugs. Indeed, simply killing them for the fun of it is thought to be sport. This pattern of cruel exploitation flows naturally from the Kantian attitude that animals are nothing more than things to be used for our purposes. It is this whole attitude that must be opposed, and not merely its manifestation in our willingness to hurt the animals we eat. Once one rejects this attitude and no longer regards the animals as disposable at one's whim, one ceases to think it all right to kill them, even painlessly, just for a snack.

But for those of us who do not live on old-fashioned family farms, the question of whether it would be permissible to eat humanely treated, painlessly slaughtered animals is merely theoretical. The meat available to us at the supermarket was not produced by humane methods. To provide this meat, animals were abused in ways similar to the ones we have described; and millions of other animals are being treated in these ways now, with their flesh to appear soon in the markets. The practical issue is, should we support such practices by purchasing and consuming their products?

It is discouraging to realize that no animals will actually be helped simply by one person ceasing to eat meat. One consumer's behavior, by itself, cannot have a noticeable impact on an industry as vast as the meat business. However, it is important to see one's behavior in a larger context. There are already millions of vegetarians, and because they don't eat meat, there *is* less cruelty than there otherwise would be. The question is whether one ought to side with that group or with the people whose practices cause the suffering. Compare the position of someone thinking about whether to buy slaves in 1820. He might reason as follows: "The whole practice of slavery is immoral, but I cannot help any of the poor slaves by keeping clear of it. If I don't buy these slaves, someone else will. One person's decision can't by itself have any impact on such a vast business. So I may as well own slaves like everyone else." The first thing we notice is that this fellow was too pessimistic about the possibilities of a successful movement; but beyond that, there is something else wrong with his reasoning. If one really thinks that a social practice is immoral, that is sufficient grounds for refusing to participate in it. In 1848 Henry David Thoreau remarked that even if someone did not want to devote himself to the abolition movement and actively oppose slavery, "it is his duty, at least, to wash his hands of it, and if he gives it no thought longer, not to give it practically his support."[9] In the case of slavery, this seems clear. If it seems less clear in the case of the cruel exploitation of nonhuman animals, perhaps it is because the Kantian attitude has so tenacious a hold on us.

NOTES

1. Louis B. Schwartz, "Morals Offenses and the Model Penal Code," in *Philosophy of Law*, ed. Joel Feinberg

and Hyman Gross (Encino, Calif.: Dickenson, 1975), 156. First published in *Columbia Law Review* 63 (1963): 669–84.

2. Immanuel Kant, *Foundations of the Metaphysics of Morals*, trans. Lewis White Beck (Indianapolis: Bobbs-Merrill, 1959), 47.
3. Immanuel Kant, *Lectures on Ethics*, trans. Louis Infield (New York: Harper, 1963), 239.
4. Kant, *Lectures on Ethics*, 240.
5. Muriel the Lady Dowding, "Furs and Cosmetics: Too High a Price?" in *Animals, Men, and Morals*, ed. Stanley Godlovitch, Roslind Godlovitch, and John Harris (New York: Taplinger, 1972), 36.
6. The best account is chap. 3 of Peter Singer's *Animal Liberation* (New York: New York Review Books, 1975). I have drawn on Singer's work for the factual material in the following two paragraphs.
7. Singer, *Animal Liberation*, 152.
8. *Miami Herald*, 26 August 1972, sec. A, p. 3.
9. Henry David Thoreau, *Walden and Civil Disobedience*, ed. Owen Thomas (New York: W. W. Norton & Co., 1966), 229–30. First published in 1848.

Moral Vegetarianism and the Argument from Pain and Suffering

R. G. FREY

This argument, championed by Peter Singer in *Animal Liberation* and *Practical Ethics*, by Stephen Clark in *The Moral Status of Animals*, and by many others, moves either directly or indirectly to moral vegetarianism from the pain and suffering which animals undergo in being bred, raised, and slaughtered for food. (Perhaps the most common way the argument moves from pain and suffering to moral vegetarianism indirectly is via the notion of interests. This requires that animals have interests, and one aim of my *Interests and Rights* was to deny that they do, at least in a sense that enables the argument to work.)

The argument from pain and suffering, of course, has a past; its use by Singer and others is but the most recent among several. The significance it has come to have, especially under the stimulus of *Animal Liberation*, stems from its application to intensive methods of food production, to factory or commercial farming. What Singer, amongst others, has done is to give the argument new and important life, by describing how some aspects of intensive

"Moral Vegetarianism and the Argument from Pain and Suffering" in *Rights, Killing, and Suffering* by R. G. Frey, 21–23, 27, 30–35. © 1983 Blackwell Publishers.

farming involve animal suffering and then using the argument to combat these farming practices.

I do not believe it betrays undue sensitivity to find certain practices employed on factory farms profoundly disturbing. To put no finer point on the matter, there are practices afoot on them, pre-eminently in the cases of laying hens and veal calves, of which we cannot be proud. Even if such practices are necessary to sustain the level of profits by which farmers, their families, the meat industry as a whole, and, through it, a very great many others prosper, we still do well not to be proud of having to resort to them. Some might suggest that the great pleasure human beings receive from consuming veal more than outweighs the suffering (no grain, no straw-bedding, no exercise, perpetual confinement in tiny slatted stalls, little muscle-growth, induced iron-deficiency and anemia, almost no daylight, tethered to prevent seeking iron and exercise) which these calves undergo in reaching the table. Even so, treatment such as this is not the sort of thing in which, morally, we take pride; and if it is something required in order to sustain a level or style of life to which we have become accustomed, we still do well to be disturbed that this is so.

As information about the treatment of, for example, veal calves has been more widely disseminated, more people have come to see this treatment as wrong. But this is by no means the end or even the essence of the matter for Singer; for it is central to his position—in fact, it seems the main feature of his position—that moral vegetarianism is *the means by which each of us* can move directly to eliminate the pains of food animals. Once we come to see our treatment of veal calves as wrong, vegetarianism is seen by Singer as the means by which each of us can do something about this treatment. This emerges very clearly from the central argument of *Animal Liberation*.

Animals can suffer, and since they can suffer, they have interests. In view of this fact, the moral principle of the equal consideration of interests applies to them, and this means that we are not morally justified in setting aside, ignoring, or otherwise devaluing their interests. This, however, is precisely what some factory farming practices, with their accompaniment of animal suffering, appear to involve, and the immorality which this represents

is, if anything, accentuated by the fact that we do not need meat in order to survive and to lead healthy lives.

We can, on the other hand, do something about this situation: by boycotting meat, we can draw down market forces upon the head of the factory farmer and so reduce or eliminate the suffering of food animals. When demand slackens, prices fall; when prices fall, profits diminish; and when profits diminish, the factory farmer has less capital to re-invest in food stock. (The same is true for farmers who employ traditional methods of farming.) By becoming a vegetarian, then, each of us hits directly and immediately at factory farming; for in giving up meat, we reduce the number of food animals bred and raised for market and thereby total animal suffering. Accordingly, a genuine concern for the interests of animals and so with a diminution in their suffering requires that we cease rearing animals for food and cease eating them.

The picture one carries away from Singer's book, then, is that becoming a moral vegetarian is the means by which each of us can reduce animal suffering and so help in the effort to right a wrong. Once we have identified certain farming practices as wrong, we can use vegetarianism as the tool, as the direct and immediate means for eliminating or mitigating those practices. What is more, this means is relatively painless on us, given that there are wholesome and nutritious alternatives to meat readily available.

This picture is enormously appealing and has contributed in no small measure, I think, to the impact of Singer's book. Later, in considering some aspects of the argument from pain and suffering, I shall challenge this picture of the effects of one's becoming a moral vegetarian; indeed, Singer himself, partly in response to my arguments, which he saw in earlier draft, has returned to it in his recent paper "Utilitarianism and vegetarianism" and has tried partially to redraw it, and I shall have something to say as well about these more recent remarks. Here, however, I am concerned only to make plain the contrast between this animal-based argument from pain and suffering and human-based arguments for moral vegetarianism.

·····

By moral vegetarianism, then, I have in mind those cases for vegetarianism which locate the moral basis for boycotting meat in our treatment of animals in rearing and converting them into food.

Modern proponents of vegetarianism on this basis have relied principally upon three arguments to show that eating meat is wrong.

The argument from moral rights. This is the view that our present treatment of animals in converting them into food violates their moral right to life and/ or freedom from unnecessary suffering. It is wrong to eat meat, then, because animals' moral rights have been violated in the course of their reaching our tables.

The argument from killing. This is the view that it is wrong to kill animals or to kill them for food, except, if at all, under conditions which few of us can pretend to be in. It is wrong to eat meat because animals have undergone the irretrievable wrong of being killed, in the course of becoming food for human consumption.

The argument from pain and suffering. This is the view, to repeat, that it is wrong to eat meat, because factory-farmed (and perhaps even some traditionally-farmed) animals have suffered a good deal and, thus, been wrongly treated, in the course of being turned into food.

. . . . .

There is a curious feature of the arguments from moral rights, killing, and pain and suffering that I am sure many readers have noticed. It consists in the fact that, even if we were to regard the arguments as completely successful, they would by no means bar or eliminate all meat-eating. In this can be found the basis for distinguishing two very different conceptions of the status of vegetarianism.

PARTIAL AND ABSOLUTE EXCLUSIONS

When I first arrived at Oxford from Virginia, I became friendly with a mathematician from Calcutta. He was a vegetarian and abstained from all meat. Meals in college were very unpleasant for him, since they invariably featured meat dishes, and what vegetables there were were unappetizing, always the same, and—the great English gastronomic failure—overcooked. He regarded eating meat as an abomination; there were no circumstances—apart,

perhaps from direst necessity, and even this was uncertain—in which he would allow it to be right. Eating meat was simply excluded from consideration, and there was an end to it.

The arguments from moral rights, killing, and pain and suffering do not have the same absolutely dismissive effect. The reason is that the objections which they severally pose are not actually to eating animals but to the treatment animals receive in the course of being converted into food. The result is obvious: to animals which have not undergone the treatment in question, the arguments do not apply. Thus, since the argument from moral rights makes the wrongness of violating animals' moral rights crucial, it places no objection in the way of eating meat from animals whose rights have not been violated. Someone who is a vegetarian solely on the basis of this argument, then, has no reason per se to abstain from such meat, any more than someone who is a vegetarian on the basis of the argument from pain and suffering has any reason per se to abstain from eating the flesh of animals who have not been cruelly treated in being turned into food. This does not mean, of course, that these individuals will eat the meat in question, only that they must have one more shot in their lockers, if they are going to abstain on principle from this meat as well.

To my Indian friend, this situation would appear very strange indeed. For here are purported vegetarians who, prima facie, have no reason not to eat this meat. *He* does not eat meat at all; eating meat is quite excluded from consideration, whether the animal has had its rights violated or been killed or been made to suffer, or whether it has simply fallen from the heavens at one's feet or miraculously appeared in one's cooking pot. To him, it would be exceedingly peculiar to think that his vegetarianism required him to look carefully into the question of whether this chicken has had its rights violated, or had dropped dead from heart seizure, or had not suffered at some point in the past, as if one as opposed to some other answer would make it right for him to eat meat. The plain fact is that, so far as *his* vegetarianism is concerned, such questions are beside the point. Conversely, to the proponents of the three arguments, these questions are very much to the point, and their vegetarianism is conditioned by the responses given in their respective cases.

To this Indian, then, proponents of the three arguments appear more exercised by rights, killing, and suffering than by eating animals. What the arguments make out to be morally wrong is not actually eating animals but violating their alleged moral rights or killing them or making them suffer. Do none of these things, and the wrongness of eating meat vanishes. Here, then, are vegetarians of whom vegetarianism is only demanded if animals are treated one way rather than another. (In the case of the argument from pain and suffering, this result gives rise to a view which prima facie seems very strange. For there seems something odd indeed about a view which says in effect that when animals are (treated in such a way as to be) miserable they may not be eaten but when they are (treated in such a way as to be) happy and content they may be eaten. One's natural inclination would be to say the opposite, that when animals are contented, their lives are a benefit to them and that then, if ever, vegetarianism is demanded of us. I shall return to this point later, in connection with claims about the replaceability of animals.)

CONDITIONAL AND UNCONDITIONAL CONCEPTIONS

If we think of the position of this Indian mathematician as unconditional vegetarianism and that of the proponents of the three arguments as conditional vegetarianism, then how might we characterize the essential difference between these two conceptions of vegetarianism?

In his paper "Utilitarianism and vegetarianism," Peter Singer objects to Cora Diamond's claim[1] that his position yields the curious result that it is perfectly permissible to eat animals which are accident victims:

Why is this curious? It is only curious on the assumption that vegetarians must think it *always* wrong to eat meat. No doubt some vegetarians are moral absolutists, just as there are absolute pacifists, absolute anti-abortionists and absolute truth-tellers who would never tell a lie. I reject all these forms of moral absolutism.[2]

Doubtless Singer would regard unconditional vegetarians as absolutists, and doubtless there is a significant difference between my Indian friend and

Singer on this score. But the suggestion of the above passage—that some people think it always wrong to eat meat, whereas others, including Singer, think it only sometimes wrong—is not quite explicit as to the full difference between them.

If we think in terms of a distinction between unconditional and conditional vegetarianism, then the point I was making earlier can be put this way: when conditions of food animal treatment are one way rather than another, conditional vegetarianism ceases to have a ground, the result of which is, in the circumstances, to remove from conditional vegetarians their reason for abstaining from meat. When conditions are one way rather than another, vegetarianism is pointless; for the whole point of conditional vegetarianism is to improve the conditions in which animals are bred, raised, and slaughtered for food, and if conditions are already of the appropriate sort, then there is no point in adopting vegetarianism as the tactic by which to make them of that sort. Here, it seems to me, is encapsulated the essence of conditional vegetarianism: it is a tactic by means of which one hopes to improve the treatment of food animals. This is especially clear in the case of Singer, who regards vegetarianism based upon the argument from pain and suffering as the means by which to combat the pains of factory-farmed animals.

At the core of conditional vegetarianism, then, is a conception of vegetarianism as a tactic for combating the treatment or pains of food animals. But tactics are appropriate to circumstances, and a change in circumstances can, as we have seen, render one's tactics pointless. In the case of a conditional vegetarian, to persist in abstaining from meat, even when circumstances are of the desired sort, becomes a needless gesture.

Accordingly, to say merely that what separates my Indian friend from Singer is a form of absolutism, to say merely that conditional vegetarianism is limited (or applies only in respect of some animals) whereas unconditional vegetarianism is unlimited, leaves out any mention of the tactical conception of vegetarianism, which essentially defines the conditional position. This omission is of the utmost importance; for no one even remotely in sympathy with the views of my Indian friend could accept such a conception of vegetarianism. To this Indian, vegetarianism is something quite different: it represents a decision about how he will live in the world, a decision tantamount in part to the adoption of a way of life, for a world which contains a multiplicity of creatures and things, each as much a part of the whole as he is. It represents an attempt to live in harmony with the creatures and things he finds around him and to encroach on them as little as they on the whole encroach on him. It represents an effort to see himself as part of the world, and not a world—and law—unto himself. So far as I can see, nothing could be further from a tactical conception of vegetarianism than this conception of how we shall live in a world where we are but part of the whole, of which conception vegetarianism is a constituent.

(Someone armed with such a conception of vegetarianism is very likely to find Singer's emphasis upon pain rather puzzling. For though my Indian friend is not indifferent to the pains of animals, it is not by virtue of the fact that they can feel pain that he thinks they warrant and obtain his respect. If asked whether it was because animals can feel pain that he tries to live in harmony with them, as one part of nature with another, he would, I think, view both the question and the questioner with deep puzzlement, not least because many portions of the whole of which he sees himself as a part *cannot* feel pain. In time, I believe he would come to think that only someone with a particular theory would seize upon pain in this way and elevate it or its avoidance to supreme importance in ethics.)[3]

I myself am as much opposed to moral absolutisms as is Singer and, I suspect, for many of the same reasons. I have used the example of this Indian mathematician simply in order to bring out the tactical conception of vegetarianism, which lies at the heart of conditional vegetarianism, especially that of Singer.

COUNTER-ARGUMENT AND COMPETING TACTICS

Apart from the fact that, as we have seen, some vegetarians reject the tactical conception of vegetarianism, this conception is exposed to counter-arguments of a specific type. If we stick with Singer as our example, then these counter-arguments stem directly from the literature on utilitarianism.

The specific type of counter-argument is this: if vegetarianism is a tactic for combating the pains of food animals, then this tactic ceases to have any point whatever, if we develop ways of breeding, raising, and slaughtering animals painlessly. In this

eventuality, we could eat all the meat we liked, and Singer would have no ground for complaint.

It will be claimed, however, that there is no meat available from animals which have not, in particular, been reared by painful methods. To this, there are three responses.

First, it is factually false; there are millions upon millions of animals presently being farmed but not factory-farmed. It is both tempting to argue and not obviously wrong to suggest that because traditional farming methods are held, even by vegetarians, to be vastly less painful than intensive ones, the argument from pain and suffering does not provide a reason for abstaining from the flesh of traditionally-farmed animals. (As we shall see, in connection with his views on killing, Singer himself appears prepared to accept this point about traditional farming.)

Second, not all intensively farmed animals suffer to anything like the degree of veal calves, or have the same methods of production used upon them. To give but a single example, in the United States, dairy cows are commercially farmed, and when their days as milk-producers come to an end, they are sent to slaughter. However, their lives are by no means as miserable as those of veal calves.

Third, if we focus solely upon factory-farmed animals, then we can see clearly to what the tactical conception of vegetarianism finally exposes Singer. For just as not eating meat is a tactic for dealing with the pains of food animals, so, too, is the package involving, among other things, maintaining and expanding traditional farming techniques, progressivly eliminating painful practices in intensive farming, and funding research into and developing pain-killing drugs. As tactics, both are on all fours; one is not *per se* more morally correct than the other. Moreover, the latter tactic has two further attractions: first, it enables us not only to deal with animal pain but also to retain our present, meat-based diet intact, and second, it enables us to meet the claim that the heavy demand for meat today can only be satisfied by intensive methods of production.

In this way, vegetarianism, Singer's tactic, is confronted with competition. That is, we are confronted with different tactics for combating the pains of food animals, and the central issue between them becomes simply the degree of effectiveness in achieving this end. The determination of which of two tactics is more effective in lessening animal pain is not a piece of theory but a matter of fact. If technological developments succeed in the encompassing way the one tactic envisages, then it may well be, on grounds of effectiveness, the preferred one, as new and better pain-killers, administered painlessly, reach more and more animals. This very real possibility cannot be eliminated a priori through any theoretical considerations. This is especially true for utilitarians such as Singer, for whom it must always remain a contingent affair whether the implementation of one policy has consequences which, in comparison with those of the implementation of another, make it the preferred or right policy. Effectiveness, then, is everything, and vegetarianism must confront and defeat (or at least not be defeated by) one after another competitor on this score; it by no means is *obviously* the most effective tactic for reducing the pains of food animals, so that all potential competitors can be ignored *ab initio*. (Later, I shall argue that the view that vegetarianism

is the most effective step one can take to reduce and eliminate food animal suffering is false.)

To my Indian friend, of course, all this squabbling over effectiveness is beside the point; for whether it is Singer or his opponent who has the more effective means for coming to grips with animal pain, eating meat remains an abomination, and that is that.

NOTES

1. Cora Diamond, "Eating meat and eating people," *Philosophy*, vol. 53, 1978, pp. 465–79.
2. Singer, "Utilitarianism and vegetarianism," pp. 327–8; italics in original.
3. It is not accidental that many of those concerned to develop an environmental ethic, especially if they have been influenced by the work of Aldo Leopold, are hostile to the use of pain to confer moral standing. See ch. 14. See also Frey, *Interests and Rights*, ch.4.

ARGUMENT 24 ESSAY QUESTIONS

1. Do you agree with Frey that the argument from suffering does not show that eating meat itself is immoral? Why or why not?
2. Is ethical meat production virtually impossible as Rachels says? Or is Frey right that more ethical methods are available? Explain.
3. Is Rachels' argument for vegetarianism sound? If not, where does it fail?

25. TAYLOR'S ARGUMENT FOR THE EQUALITY OF ALL LIFE

Biocentrists hold that all living things have moral status: all are entitled to be treated with respect that we would not render nonliving objects. Some of them say that life forms can vary in their degree of moral considerability, but other biocentrists claim that all living entities possess *equal* moral status and therefore deserve equal respect.

In "The Ethics of Respect for Nature," Paul Taylor defends this equality-of-life view with a striking argument: (1) humans are "members of the Earth's community of life" in the same way and on the same terms as all the nonhuman members, (2) humans and all other species are interdependent elements in a complex web of biological existence, (3) each organism is an individual striving toward "its own good in its own way" (it is a "teleological center of life"), (4) the claim that humans are superior to other species is unfounded. (5) Therefore, all living beings have equal inherent worth and are entitled to equal respect (biocentric egalitarianism).[13]

This argument is not valid (it is not the case that if the premises are true, the conclusion must also be true). But Taylor believes that if we accept the first three premises, it would be reasonable to accept the fourth (no superiority of humans over other species). And if we accept the fourth, it would be reasonable to accept the final conclusion (all living things have equal inherent worth).

Yet critics demur, pointing out that even if we accept the first four premises, we can still reasonably reject the conclusion. As David Schmidtz says,

> Having accepted that our form of life is not superior, we might choose instead to regard it as inferior. More plausibly, we might view our form of life as noncomparable. We simply do not have the same kind of value as nonhumans. The question of how we compare to nonhumans has a simple answer: we do not compare to them. We are not equal. We are not unequal. We are simply different.[14]

Schmidtz also thinks that the species egalitarianism of Taylor and others rests on the same kind of arbitrariness that anthropocentrism is thought to harbor:

> ...Taylor defines anthropocentrism as giving exclusive or primary consideration to human interests above the good of other species. So, when we acknowledge the ability to think as a valuable capacity, and acknowledge that some but not all living things possess this valuable capacity, are we giving exclusive or primary consideration to human interests?...Put it this way: if biocentrism involves resolving to ignore

---

[13] Paul W. Taylor, "The Ethics of Respect for Nature," *Environmental Ethics* 3 (1981).
[14] David Schmidtz, "Are All Species Equal?" *Journal of Applied Philosophy* 15 (1998):57–67.

the fact that cognitive capacity is something we value—if biocentrism amounts to a resolution to value only those capacities that all living things share—then biocentrism is at least as arbitrary and question-begging as anthropocentrism.[15]

More fundamentally, biocentric egalitarianism has been accused of conflicting dramatically with our moral intuitions. It implies that an onion, a rat, a panda, and a man have equal inherent worth and deserve equal respect. But this suggests that killing the onion is just as bad as killing the rat or the panda, which is just as bad as killing the man. It suggests that experimenting on the man is no worse than experimenting on the onion or the rat. It suggests that if one species must be sacrificed to ensure the survival of the planet, there can be no moral reason for preferring to destroy onions or rats instead of humans.

The Ethics of Respect for Nature

PAUL W. TAYLOR

I. HUMAN-CENTERED AND LIFE-CENTERED SYSTEMS OF ENVIRONMENTAL ETHICS

In this paper I show how the taking of a certain ultimate moral attitude toward nature, which I call "respect for nature," has a central place in the foundations of a life-centered system of environmental ethics. I hold that a set of moral norms (both standards of character and rules of conduct) governing human treatment of the natural world is a rationally grounded set if and only if, first, commitment to those norms is a practical entailment of adopting the attitude of respect for nature as an ultimate moral attitude, and second, the adopting of that attitude on the part of all rational agents can itself be justified. When the basic characteristics of the attitude of respect for nature are made clear, it will be seen that a life-centered system of environmental ethics need not be holistic or organicist in its conception of the kinds of entities that are deemed the appropriate objects of moral concern and consideration. Nor does such a system require that the

concepts of ecological homeostasis, equilibrium, and integrity provide us with normative principles from which could be derived (with the addition of factual knowledge) our obligations with regard to natural ecosystems. The "balance of nature" is not itself a moral norm, however important may be the role it plays in our general outlook on the natural world that underlies the attitude of respect for nature. I argue that finally it is the good (well-being, welfare) of individual organisms, considered as entities having inherent worth, that determines our moral relations with the Earth's wild communities of life.

In designating the theory to be set forth as life-centered, I intend to contrast it with all anthropocentric views. According to the latter, human actions affecting the natural environment and

Excerpted from "The Ethics of Respect for Nature" by Paul W. Taylor, *Environmental Ethics*, vol. 3, no. 3 (Fall 1981), 197–218. Published by Environmental Philosophy, Inc. © Paul W. Taylor. Notes deleted.

---

[15] David Schmidtz, "Are All Species Equal?"

its nonhuman inhabitants are right (or wrong) by either of two criteria: they have consequences which are favorable (or unfavorable) to human well-being, or they are consistent (or inconsistent) with the system of norms that protect and implement human rights. From this human-centered standpoint it is to humans and only to humans that all duties are ultimately owed. We may have responsibilities *with regard to* the natural ecosystems and biotic communities of our planet, but these responsibilities are in every case based on the contingent fact that our treatment of those ecosystems and communities of life can further the realization of human values and/or human rights. We have no obligation to promote or protect the good of nonhuman living things, independently of this contingent fact.

A life-centered system of environmental ethics is opposed to human-centered ones precisely on this point. From the perspective of a life-centered theory, we have prima facie moral obligations that are owed to wild plants and animals themselves as members of the Earth's biotic community. We are morally bound (other things being equal) to protect or promote their good for *their* sake. Our duties to respect the integrity of natural ecosystems, to preserve endangered species, and to avoid environmental pollution stem from the fact that these are ways in which we can help make it possible for wild species populations to achieve and maintain a healthy existence in a natural state. Such obligations are due those living things out of recognition of their inherent worth. They are entirely additional to and independent of the obligations we owe to our fellow humans. Although many of the actions that fulfill one set of obligations will also fulfill the other, two different grounds of obligation are involved. Their well-being, as well as human well-being, is something to be realized *as an end in itself.*

If we were to accept a life-centered theory of environmental ethics, a profound reordering of our moral universe would take place. We would begin to look at the whole of the Earth's biosphere in a new light. Our duties with respect to the "world" of nature would be seen as making prima facie claims upon us to be balanced against our duties with respect to the "world" of human civilization. We could no longer simply take the human point of view and consider the effects of our actions exclusively from the perspective of our own good.

II. THE GOOD OF A BEING AND THE CONCEPT OF INHERENT WORTH

What would justify acceptance of a life-centered system of ethical principles? In order to answer this it is first necessary to make clear the fundamental moral attitude that underlies and makes intelligible the commitment to live by such a system. It is then necessary to examine the considerations that would justify any rational agent's adopting that moral attitude.

Two concepts are essential to the taking of a moral attitude of the sort in question. A being which does not "have" these concepts, that is, which is unable to grasp their meaning and conditions of applicability, cannot be said to have the attitude as part of its moral outlook. These concepts are, first, that of the good (well-being, welfare) of a living thing, and second, the idea of an entity possessing inherent worth. I examine each concept in turn.

(1) Every organism, species population, and community of life has a good of its own which moral agents can intentionally further or damage by their actions. To say that an entity has a good of its own is simply to say that, without reference to any *other* entity, it can be benefited or harmed. One can act in its overall interest, or contrary to its overall interest, and environmental conditions can be good for it (advantageous to it) or bad for it (disadvantageous to it). What is good for an entity is what "does it good" in the sense of enhancing or preserving its life and well-being. What is bad for an entity is something that is detrimental to its life and well-being.

We can think of the good of an individual nonhuman organism as consisting in the full development of its biological powers. Its good is realized to the extent that it is strong and healthy. It possesses whatever capacities it needs for successfully coping with its environment and so preserving its existence throughout the various stages of the normal life cycle of its species. The good of a population or community of such individuals consists in the population or community maintaining itself from generation to generation as a coherent system of genetically and ecologically related organisms whose average good is at an optimum level for the given environment. (Here *average good* means that the degree of realization of the good of *individual organisms* in the population or community is, on average, greater than would be the case under any other ecologically functioning order of interrelations among those species populations in the given ecosystem.)

The idea of a being having a good of its own, as I understand it, does not entail that the being must have interests or take an interest in what affects its life for better or for worse. We can act in a being's interest or contrary to its interest without its being interested in what we are doing to it in the sense of wanting or not wanting us to do it. It may, indeed, be wholly unaware that favorable and unfavorable events are taking place in its life. I take it that trees, for example, have no knowledge or desires or feelings. Yet is is undoubtedly the case that trees can be harmed or benefited by our actions. We can crush their roots by running a bulldozer too close to them. We can see to it that they get adequate nourishment and moisture by fertilizing and watering the soil around them. Thus we can help or hinder them in the realization of their good. It is the good of trees themselves that is thereby affected. We can similarly act so as to further the good of an entire tree population of a certain species (say, all the redwood trees in a California valley) or the good of a whole community of plant life in a given wilderness area, just as we can do harm to such a population or community.

When construed in this way, the concept of a being's good is not coextensive with sentience or the capacity for feeling pain. William Frankena has argued for a general theory of environmental ethics in which the ground of a creature's being worthy of moral consideration is its sentience. I have offered some criticisms of this view elsewhere, but the full refutation of such a position, it seems to me, finally depends on the positive reasons for accepting a life-centered theory of the kind I am defending in this essay.

It should be noted further that I am leaving open the question of whether machines—in particular, those which are not only goal-directed, but also self-regulating—can properly be said to have a good of their own. Since I am concerned only with human treatment of wild organisms, species populations,

and communities of life as they occur in our planet's natural ecosystems, it is to those entities alone that the concept "having a good of its own" will here be applied. I am not denying that other living things, whose genetic origin and environmental conditions have been produced, controlled, and manipulated by humans for human ends, do have a good of their own in the same sense as do wild plants and animals. It is not my purpose in this essay, however, to set out or defend the principles that should guide our conduct with regard to their good. It is only insofar as their production and use by humans have good or ill effects upon natural ecosystems and their wild inhabitants that the ethics of respect for nature comes into play.

(2) The second concept essential to the moral attitude of respect for nature is the idea of inherent worth. We take that attitude toward wild living things (individuals, species populations, or whole biotic communities) when and only when we regard them as entities possessing inherent worth. Indeed, it is only because they are conceived in this way that moral agents can think of themselves as having validly binding duties, obligations, and responsibilities that are *owed* to them as their *due*. I am not at this juncture arguing why they *should* be so regarded; I consider it at length below. But so regarding them is a presupposition of our taking the attitude of respect toward them and accordingly understanding ourselves as bearing certain moral relations to them. This can be shown as follows:

What does it mean to regard an entity that has a good of its own as possessing inherent worth? Two general principles are involved: the principle of moral consideration and the principle of intrinsic value.

According to the principle of moral consideration, wild living things are deserving of the concern and consideration of all moral agents simply in virtue of their being members of the Earth's community of life. From the moral point of view their good must be taken into account whenever it is affected for better or worse by the conduct of rational agents. This holds no matter what species the creature belongs to. The good of each is to be accorded some value and so acknowledged as having some weight in the deliberations of all rational agents. Of course, it may be necessary for such agents to act in ways contrary to the good of this or that particular organism or group of organisms in order to further the good of others, including the good of humans. But the principle of moral consideration prescribes that, with respect to each being an entity having its own good, every individual is deserving of consideration.

The principle of intrinsic value states that, regardless of what kind of entity it is in other respects, if it is a member of the Earth's community of life, the realization of its good is something *intrinsically* valuable. This means that its good is prima facie worthy of being preserved or promoted as an end in itself and for the sake of the entity whose good it is. Insofar as we regard any organism, species population, or life community as an entity having inherent worth, we believe that it must never be treated as if it were a mere object or thing whose entire value lies in being instrumental to the good of some other entity. The well-being of each is judged to have value in and of itself.

Combining these two principles, we can now define what it means for a living thing or group of living things to possess inherent worth. To say that it possesses inherent worth is to say that its good is deserving of the concern and consideration of all moral agents, and that the realization of its good has intrinsic value, to be pursued as an end in itself and for the sake of the entity whose good it is.

The duties owed to wild organisms, species populations, and communities of life in the Earth's natural ecosystems are grounded on their inherent worth. When rational, autonomous agents regard such entities as possessing inherent worth, they place intrinsic value on the realization of their good and so hold themselves responsible for performing actions that will have this effect and for refraining from actions having the contrary effect. ...

.... The attitude we take toward living things in the natural world depends on the way we look at them, on what kind of beings we conceive them to be, and on how we understand the relations we bear to them. Underlying and supporting our attitude is a certain *belief system* that constitutes a particular world view or outlook on nature and the place of human life in it. To give good reasons for adopting the attitude of respect for nature, then, we must first articulate the belief system which underlies and supports that attitude. If it appears that the belief system is internally coherent and well-ordered, and if, as far as we can now tell, it is consistent with all known scientific truths relevant to our knowledge of the object of the attitude (which in this case includes the whole set of the Earth's natural ecosystems and their communities of life), then there remains the task of indicating why scientifically informed and rational thinkers with a developed capacity of reality awareness can find it acceptable as a way of conceiving of the natural world and our place in it. To the extent we can do this we provide at least a reasonable argument for accepting the belief system and the ultimate moral attitude it supports.

I do not hold that such a belief system can be *proven* to be true, either inductively or deductively. As we shall see, not all of its components can be stated in the form of empirically verifiable propositions. Nor is its internal order governed by purely logical relationships. But the system as a whole, I contend, constitutes a coherent, unified, and rationally acceptable "picture" or "map" of a total world. By examining each of its main components and seeing how they fit together, we obtain a scientifically informed and well-ordered conception of nature and the place of humans in it.

This belief system underlying the attitude of respect for nature I call (for want of a better name) "the biocentric outlook on nature." Since it is not wholly analyzable into empirically confirmable assertions, it should not be thought of as simply a compendium of the biological sciences concerning our planet's ecosystems. It might best be described as a philosophical world view, to distinguish it from a scientific theory or explanatory system. However, one of its major tenets is the great lesson we have learned from the science of ecology: the interdependence of all living things in an organically unified order whose balance and stability are necessary conditions for the realization of the good of its constituent biotic communities. ...

V. THE BIOCENTRIC OUTLOOK ON NATURE

The biocentric outlook on nature has four main components. (1) Humans are thought of as members of the Earth's community of life, holding that membership on the same terms as apply to all the nonhuman members. (2) The Earth's natural ecosystems as a totality are seen as a complex web of interconnected elements, with the sound biological functioning of each being dependent on the sound biological functioning of the others. (This is the component referred to above as the great lesson that the science of ecology has taught us). (3) Each individual organism is conceived of as a teleological center of life, pursuing its own good in its own way. (4) Whether we are concerned with standards of merit or with the concept of inherent worth, the claim that humans by their very nature are superior to other species is a groundless claim and, in the light of elements (1), (2), and (3) above, must be rejected as nothing more than an irrational bias in our own favor.

The conjunction of these four ideas constitutes the biocentric outlook on nature. In the remainder of this paper I give a brief account of the first three components, followed by a more detailed analysis of the fourth. I then conclude by indicating how this outlook provides a way of justifying the attitude of respect for nature.

VI. HUMANS AS MEMBERS OF THE EARTH'S COMMUNITY OF LIFE

We share with other species a common relationship to the Earth. In accepting the biocentric outlook we take the fact of our being an animal species to be a fundamental feature of our existence. We consider it an essential aspect of "the human condition." We do not deny the differences between ourselves and other species, but we keep in the forefront of our consciousness the fact that in relation to our planet's natural ecosystems we are but one species population among many. Thus we acknowledge our origin in the very same evolutionary process that gave rise to all other species and we recognize ourselves to be confronted with similar environmental challenges to those that confront them. The laws of genetics, of natural selection, and of adaptation apply equally to all of us as biological creatures. In this light we consider ourselves as one with them, not set apart from them. We, as well as they, must face certain basic conditions of existence that impose requirements on us for our survival and well-being. Each animal and plant is like us in having a good of its own. Although our human good (what is of true value in human life, including the exercise of individual

autonomy in choosing our own particular value systems) is not like the good of a nonhuman animal or plant, it can no more be realized than their good can without the biological necessities for survival and physical health.

When we look at ourselves from the evolutionary point of view, we see that not only are we very recent arrivals on Earth, but that our emergence as a new species on the planet was originally an event of no particular importance to the entire scheme of things. The Earth was teeming with life long before we appeared. Putting the point metaphorically, we are relative newcomers, entering a home that has been the residence of others for hundreds of millions of years, a home that must now be shared by all of us together.

The comparative brevity of human life on Earth may be vividly depicted by imagining the geological time scale in spatial terms. Suppose we start with algae, which have been around for at least 600 million years. (The earliest protozoa actually predated this by several *billion* years.) If the time that algae have been here were represented by the length of a football field (300 feet), then the period during which sharks have been swimming in the world's oceans and spiders have been spinning their webs would occupy three quarters of the length of the field; reptiles would show up at about the center of the field; mammals would cover the last third of the field; hominids (mammals of the family *Hominidae*) the last two feet; and the species *Homo sapiens* the last six inches.

Whether this newcomer is able to survive as long as other species remains to be seen. But there is surely something presumptuous about the way humans look down on the "lower" animals, especially those that have become extinct. We consider the dinosaurs, for example, to be biological failures, though they existed on our planet for 65 million years. One writer has made the point with beautiful simplicity:

> We sometimes speak of the dinosaurs as failures; there will be time enough for that judgment when we have lasted even for one tenth as long....

The possibility of the extinction of the human species, a possibility which starkly confronts us in the contemporary world, makes us aware of another respect in which we should not consider ourselves privileged beings in relation to other species. This is the fact that the well-being of humans is dependent upon the ecological soundness and health of many plant and animal communities, while their soundness and health does not in the least depend upon human well-being. Indeed, from their standpoint the very existence of humans is quite unnecessary. Every last man, woman, and child could disappear from the face of the Earth without any significant detrimental consequence for the good of wild animals and plants. On the contrary, many of them would be greatly benefited. The destruction of their habitats by human "developments" would cease. The poisoning and polluting of their environment would come to an end. The Earth's land, air, and water would no longer be subject to the degradation they are now undergoing as the result of large-scale technology and uncontrolled population growth. Life communities in natural ecosystems would gradually return to their former healthy state. Tropical forests, for example, would again be able to make their full contribution to a life-sustaining atmosphere for the whole planet. The rivers, lakes, and oceans of the world would (perhaps) eventually become clean again. Spilled oil, plastic trash, and even radioactive waste might finally, after many centuries, cease doing their terrible work. Ecosystems would return to their proper balance, suffering only the disruptions of natural events such as volcanic eruptions and glaciation. From these the community of life could recover, as it has so often done in the past. But the ecological disasters now perpetrated on it by humans—disasters from which it might never recover—these it would no longer have to endure.

If, then, the total, final, absolute extermination of our species (by our own hands?) should take place and if we should not carry all the others with us into oblivion, not only would the Earth's community of life continue to exist, but in all probability its well-being would be enhanced. Our presence, in short, is not needed. If we were to take the standpoint of the community and give voice to its true interest, the ending of our six-inch epoch would most likely be greeted with a hearty "Good riddance!"

VII. THE NATURAL WORLD AS AN ORGANIC SYSTEM

To accept the biocentric outlook and regard ourselves and our place in the world from its perspective is to see the whole natural order of the Earth's biosphere as a complex but unified web of interconnected organisms, objects, and events. The ecological relationships between any community of living things and their environment form an organic whole of functionally interdependent parts. Each ecosystem is a small universe itself in which the interactions of its various species populations comprise an intricately woven network of cause-effect relations. Such dynamic but at the same time relatively stable structures as food chains, predator-prey relations, and plant succession in a forest are self-regulating, energy-recycling mechanisms that preserve the equilibrium of the whole.

As far as the well-being of wild animals and plants is concerned, this ecological equilibrium must not be destroyed. The same holds true of the well-being of humans. When one views the realm of nature from the perspective of the biocentric outlook, one never forgets that in the long run the integrity of the entire biosphere of our planet is essential to the realization of the good of its constituent communities of life, both human and nonhuman.

Although the importance of this idea cannot be overemphasized, it is by now so familiar and so widely acknowledged that I shall not further elaborate on it here. However, I do wish to point out that this "holistic" view of the Earth's ecological systems does not itself constitute a moral norm. It is a factual aspect of biological reality, to be understood as a set of causal connections in ordinary empirical terms. Its significance for humans is the same as its significance for nonhumans, namely, in setting basic conditions for the realization of the good of living things. Its ethical implications for our treatment of the natural environment lie entirely in the fact that our *knowledge* of these causal connections is an essential *means* to fulfilling the aims we set for ourselves in adopting the attitude of respect for nature. In addition, its theoretical implications for the ethics of respect for nature lie in the fact that it (along with the other elements of the biocentric outlook) makes the adopting of that attitude a rational and intelligible thing to do.

VIII. INDIVIDUAL ORGANISMS AS TELEOLOGICAL CENTERS OF LIFE

As our knowledge of living things increases, as we come to a deeper understanding of their life cycles, their interactions with other organisms, and the manifold ways in which they adjust to the environment, we become more fully aware of how each of them is carrying out its biological functions according to the laws of its species-specific nature. But besides this, our increasing knowledge and understanding also develop in us a sharpened awareness of the uniqueness of each individual organism. Scientists who have made careful studies of particular plants and animals, whether in the field or in laboratories, have often acquired a knowledge of their subjects as identifiable individuals. Close observation over extended periods of time has led them to an appreciation of the unique "personalities" of their subjects. Sometimes a scientist may come to take a special interest in a particular animal or plant, all the while remaining strictly objective in the gathering and recording of data. Nonscientists may likewise experience this development of interest when, as amateur naturalists, they make accurate observations over sustained periods of close acquaintance with an individual organism. As one becomes more and more familiar with the organism and its behavior, one becomes fully sensitive to the particular way it is living out its life cycle. One may become fascinated by it and even experience some involvement with its good and bad fortunes (that is, with the occurrence of environmental conditions favorable or unfavorable to the realization of its good). The organism comes to mean something to one as a unique, irreplaceable individual. The final culmination of this process is the achievement of a genuine understanding of its point of view and, with that understanding, an ability to "take" that point of view. *Conceiving of it as a center of life, one is able to look at the world from its perspective.*

This development from objective knowledge to the recognition of individuality, and from the recognition of individuality to full awareness of an organism's standpoint, is a process of heightening our consciousness of what it means to be an individual living thing. We grasp the particularity of the organism as a teleological center of life, striving to preserve itself and to realize its own good in its own unique way.

It is to be noted that we need not be falsely anthropomorphizing when we conceive of individual plants and animals in this manner. Understanding them as teleological centers of life does not necessitate "reading into" them human characteristics. We need not, for example, consider them to have consciousness. Some of them may be aware of the world around them and others may not. Nor need we deny that different kinds and levels of awareness are exemplified when consciousness in some form is present. But conscious or not, all are equally teleological centers of life in the sense that each is a unified system of goal-oriented activities directed toward their preservation and well-being.

When considered from an ethical point of view, a teleological center of life is an entity whose "world" can be viewed from the perspective of *its* life. In looking at the world from that perspective we recognize objects and events occurring in its life as being beneficent, maleficent, or indifferent. The first are occurrences which increase its powers to preserve its existence and realize its good. The second decrease or destroy those powers. The third have neither of these effects on the entity. With regard to our human role as moral agents, we can conceive of a teleological center of life as a being whose standpoint we can take in making judgments about what events in the world are good or evil, desirable or undesirable. In making those judgments it is what promotes or protects the being's own good, not what benefits moral agents themselves, that sets the standard of evaluation. Such judgments can be made about anything that happens to the entity which is favorable or unfavorable in relation to its good. As was pointed out earlier, the entity itself need not have any (conscious) *interest* in what is happening to it for such judgments to be meaningful and true.

It is precisely judgments of this sort that we are disposed to make when we take the attitude of respect for nature. In adopting that attitude those judgments are given weight as reasons for action in our practical deliberation. They become morally relevant facts in the guidance of our conduct.

IX. THE DENIAL OF HUMAN SUPERIORITY

This fourth component of the biocentric outlook on nature is the single most important idea in establishing the justifiability of the attitude of respect for nature. Its central role is due to the special relationship it bears to the first three components of the outlook. This relationship will be brought out after the concept of human superiority is examined and analyzed.

In what sense are humans alleged to be superior to other animals? We are different from them in having certain capacities that they lack. But why should these capacities be a mark of superiority? From what point of view are they judged to be signs of superiority and what sense of superiority is meant? After all, various nonhuman species have capacities that humans lack. There is the speed of a cheetah, the vision of an eagle, the agility of a monkey. Why should not these be taken as signs of *their* superiority over humans?

One answer that comes immediately to mind is that these capacities are not as *valuable* as the human capacities that are claimed to make us superior. Such uniquely human characteristics as rational thought, aesthetic creativity, autonomy and self-determination, and moral freedom, it might be held, have a higher value than the capacities found in other species. Yet we must ask: valuable to whom, and on what grounds?

The human characteristics mentioned are all valuable to humans. They are essential to the preservation and enrichment of our civilization and culture. Clearly it is from the human standpoint that they are being judged to be desirable and good. It is not difficult here to recognize a begging of the question. Humans are claiming human superiority from a strictly human point of view, that is, from a point of view in which the good of humans is taken as the standard of judgment. All we need to do is to look at the capacities of nonhuman animals (or plants, for that matter) from the standpoint of *their* good to find a contrary judgment of superiority. The speed of the cheetah, for example, is a sign of its superiority to humans when considered from the standpoint of the good of its species. If it were as slow a runner as a human, it would not be able to survive. And so for all the other abilities of nonhumans which further their good but which are lacking in humans. In each case the claim to human superiority would be rejected from a nonhuman standpoint.

When superiority assertions are interpreted in this way, they are based on judgments of *merit*. To judge the merits of a person or an organism one must apply grading or ranking standards to it. (As I show below, this distinguishes judgments of merit from judgments of inherent worth.) Empirical investigation then determines whether it has the "good-making properties" (merits) in virtue of which it fulfills the standards being applied. In the case of humans, merits may be either moral or nonmoral. We can judge one person to be better than (superior to) another from the moral point of view by applying certain standards to their character and conduct. Similarly, we can appeal to nonmoral criteria in judging someone to be an excellent piano player, a fair cook, a poor tennis player, and so on. Different social purposes and roles are implicit in the making of such judgments, providing the frame of reference for the choice of standards by which the nonmoral merits of people are determined. Ultimately such purposes and roles stem from a society's way of life as a whole. Now a society's way of life may be thought of as the cultural form given to the realization of human values. Whether moral or nonmoral standards are being applied, then, all judgments of people's merits finally depend on human values. All are made from an exclusively human standpoint.

The question that naturally arises at this juncture is: why should standards that are based on human values be assumed to be the only valid criteria of merit and hence the only true signs of superiority? This question is especially pressing when humans are being judged superior in merit to nonhumans. It is true that a human being may be a better mathematician than a monkey, but the monkey may be a better tree climber than a human being. If we humans value mathematics more than tree climbing, that is because our conception of civilized life makes the development of mathematical ability more desirable than the ability to climb trees. But is it not unreasonable to judge nonhumans by the values of human civilization, rather than by values connected with what it is for a member of *that* species to live a good life? If all living things have a good of their own, it at least makes sense to judge the merits of nonhumans by standards derived from *their* good. To use only standards based on human values is already to commit oneself to holding that humans are superior to nonhumans, which is the point in question.

A further logical flaw arises in connection with the widely held conviction that humans are *morally* superior beings because they possess, while others lack, the capacities of a moral agent (free will, accountability, deliberation, judgment, practical reason). This view rests on a conceptual confusion. As far as moral standards are concerned, only beings that have the capacities of a moral agent can properly be judged to be *either* moral (morally good) *or* immoral (morally deficient). Moral standards are simply not applicable to beings that lack such capacities. Animals and plants cannot therefore be said to be morally inferior in merit to humans. Since the only beings that can have moral merits *or be deficient in such merits* are moral agents, it is conceptually incoherent to judge humans as superior to nonhumans on the ground that humans have moral capacities while nonhumans don't.

Up to this point I have been interpreting the claim that humans are superior to other living things as a grading or ranking judgment regarding their comparative merits. There is, however, another way of understanding the idea of human superiority. According to this interpretation, humans are superior to nonhumans not as regards their merits but as regards their inherent worth. Thus the claim of human superiority is to be understood as asserting that all humans, simply in virtue of their humanity, have *a greater inherent worth* than other living things.

The inherent worth of an entity does not depend on its merits. To consider something as possessing inherent worth, we have seen, is to place intrinsic value on the realization of its good. This is done regardless of whatever particular merits it might have or might lack, as judged by a set of grading or ranking standards. In human affairs, we are all familiar with the principle that one's worth as a person does not vary with one's merits or lack of merits. The same can hold true of animals and plants. To regard such entities as possessing inherent worth entails disregarding their merits and deficiencies, whether they are being judged from a human standpoint or from the standpoint of their own species.

The idea of one entity having more merit than another, and so being superior to it in merit, makes perfectly good sense. Merit is a grading or ranking concept, and judgments of comparative merit are based on the different degrees to which things satisfy a given standard. But what can it mean to talk about one thing being superior to another in inherent worth? In order to get at what is being asserted in such a claim it is helpful first to look at the social origin of the concept of degrees of inherent worth.

The idea that humans can possess different degrees of inherent worth originated in societies having rigid class structures. Before the rise of modern democracies with their egalitarian outlook, one's membership in a hereditary class determined one's social status. People in the upper classes were looked up to, while those in the lower classes were looked down upon. In such a society one's social superiors and social inferiors were clearly defined and easily recognized.

Two aspects of these class-structured societies are especially relevant to the idea of degrees of inherent worth. First, those born into the upper classes were deemed more worthy of respect than those born into the lower orders. Second, the superior worth of upper class people had nothing to do with their merits nor did the inferior worth of those in the lower classes rest on their lack of merits. One's superiority or inferiority entirely derived from a social position one was born into. The modern concept of a meritocracy simply did not apply. One could not advance into a higher class by any sort of moral or nonmoral achievement. Similarly, an aristocrat held his title and all the privileges that went with it just because he was the eldest son of a titled nobleman. Unlike the bestowing of knighthood in contemporary Great Britain, one did not earn membership in the nobility by meritorious conduct.

We who live in modern democracies no longer believe in such hereditary social distinctions. Indeed, we would wholeheartedly condemn them on moral grounds as being fundamentally unjust. We have come to think of class systems as a paradigm of social injustice, it being a central principle of the democratic way of life that among humans there are no superiors and no inferiors. Thus we have rejected the whole conceptual framework in which people are judged to have different degrees of inherent worth. That idea is incompatible with our notion of human equality based on the doctrine that all humans, simply in virtue of their humanity, have the same inherent worth. (The belief in universal human rights is one form that this egalitarianism takes.)

The vast majority of people in modern democracies, however, do not maintain an egalitarian outlook when it comes to comparing human beings with other living things. Most people consider our own species to be superior to all other species and this superiority is understood to be a matter of inherent worth, not merit. There may exist thoroughly vicious and depraved humans who lack all merit. Yet because they are human they are thought to belong to a higher class of entities than any plant or animal. That one is born into the species *Homo sapiens* entitles one to have lordship over those who are one's inferiors, namely, those born into other species. The parallel with hereditary social classes is very close. Implicit in this view is a hierarchical conception of nature according to which an organism has a position of superiority or inferiority in the Earth's community of life simply on the basis of its genetic background. The "lower" orders of life are looked down upon and it is considered perfectly proper that they serve the interests of those belonging to the highest order, namely humans. The intrinsic value we place on the well-being of our fellow humans reflects our recognition of their rightful position as our equals. No such intrinsic value is to be placed on the good of other animals, unless we choose to do so out of fondness or affection for them. But their well-being imposes no moral requirement on us. In this respect there is an absolute difference in moral status between ourselves and them.

This is the structure of concepts and beliefs that people are committed to insofar as they regard humans to be superior in inherent worth to all other species. I now wish to argue that this structure of concepts and beliefs is completely groundless. If we accept the first three components of the biocentric outlook and from that perspective look at the major philosophical traditions which have supported that structure, we find it to be at bottom nothing more than the expression of an irrational bias in our own favor. The philosophical traditions themselves rest on very questionable assumptions or else simply beg the question. I briefly consider three of the main traditions to substantiate the point. These are classical Greek humanism, Cartesian dualism, and the Judeo-Christian concept of the Great Chain of Being.

The inherent superiority of humans over other species was implicit in the Greek definition of man as a rational animal. Our animal nature was identified with "brute" desires that need the order and restraint of reason to rule them (just as reason is the special virture of those who rule in the ideal state). Rationality was then seen to be the key to our superiority over animals. It enables us to live on a higher plane and endows us with a nobility and worth that other creatures lack. This familiar way of comparing humans with other species is deeply ingrained in our Western philosopical outlook. The point to consider here is that this view does not actually provide an argument *for* human superiority but rather makes explicit the framework of thought that is implicitly used by those who think of humans as inherently superior to nonhumans. The Greeks who held that humans, in virtue of their rational capacities, have a kind of worth greater than that of any nonrational being, never looked at rationality as but one capacity of living things among many others. But when we consider rationality from the standpoint of the first three elements of the ecological outlook, we see that its value lies in its importance for *human* life. Other creatures achieve their species-specific good without the need of rationality, although they often make use of capacities that humans lack. So the humanistic outlook of classical Greek thought does not give us a neutral (nonquestion-begging) ground on which to construct a scale of degrees of inherent worth possessed by different species of living things.

The second tradition, centering on the Cartesian dualism of soul and body, also fails to justify the claim to human superiority. That superiority is supposed to derive from the fact that we have souls while animals do not. Animals are mere automata and lack the divine element that makes us spiritual beings. I won't go into the now familiar criticisms of this two-substance view. I only add the point that, even if humans are composed of an immaterial, unextended soul and a material, extended body, this in itself is not a reason to deem them of greater worth than entities that are only bodies.

Why is a soul substance a thing that adds value to its possessor? Unless some theological reasoning is offered here (which many, including myself, would find unacceptable on epistemological grounds), no logical connection is evident. An immaterial something which thinks is better than a material something which does not think only if thinking itself has value, either intrinsically or instrumentally. Now it is intrinsically valuable to humans alone, who value it as an end in itself, and it is instrumentally valuable to those who benefit from it, namely humans.

For animals that neither enjoy thinking for its own sake nor need it for living the kind of life for which they are best adapted, it has no value. Even if "thinking" is broadened to include all forms of consciousness, there are still many living things that can do without it and yet live what is for their species a good life. The anthropocentricity underlying the claim to human superiority runs throughout Cartesian dualism.

A third major source of the idea of human superiority is the Judeo-Christian concept of the Great Chain of Being. Humans are superior to animals and plants because their Creator has given them a higher place on the chain. It begins with God at the top, and then moves to the angels, who are lower than God but higher than humans, then to humans, positioned between the angels and the beasts (partaking of the nature of both), and then on down to the lower levels occupied by nonhuman animals, plants, and finally inanimate objects. Humans, being "made in God's image," are inherently superior to animals and plants by virtue of their being closer (in their essential nature) to God.

The metaphysical and epistemological difficulties with this conception of a hierarchy of entities are, in my mind, insuperable. Without entering into this matter here, I only point out that if we are unwilling to accept the metaphysics of traditional Judaism and Christianity, we are again left without good reasons for holding to the claim of inherent human superiority.

The foregoing considerations (and others like them) leave us with but one ground for the assertion that a human being, regardless of merit, is a higher kind of entity than any other living thing. This is the mere fact of the genetic makeup of the species *Homo sapiens*. But this is surely irrational and arbitrary. Why should the arrangement of genes of a certain type be a mark of superior value, especially when this fact about an organism is taken by itself, unrelated to any other aspect of its life? We might just as well refer to any other genetic makeup as a ground of superior value. Clearly we are confronted here with a wholly arbitrary claim that can only be explained as an irrational bias in our own favor.

That the claim is nothing more than a deep-seated prejudice is brought home to us when we look at our relation to other species in the light of the first three elements of the biocentric outlook. Those elements taken conjointly give us a certain overall view of the natural world and of the place of humans in it. When we take this view we come to understand other living things, their environmental conditions, and their ecological relationships in such a way as to awake in us a deep sense of our kinship with them as fellow members of the Earth's community of life. Humans and nonhumans alike are viewed together as integral parts of one unified whole in which all living things are functionally interrelated. Finally, when our awareness focuses on the individual lives of plants and animals, each is seen to share with us the characteristic of being a teleological center of life striving to realize its own good in its own unique way.

As this entire belief system becomes part of the conceptual framework through which we understand and perceive the world, we come to see ourselves as bearing a certain moral relation to nonhuman forms of life. Our ethical role in nature takes on a new significance. We begin to look at other species as we look at ourselves, seeing them as beings which have a good they are striving to realize just as we have a good we are striving to realize. We accordingly develop the disposition to view the world from the standpoint of their good as well as from the standpoint of our own good. Now if the groundlessness of the claim that humans are inherently superior to other species were brought clearly before our minds, we would not remain intellectually neutral toward that claim but would reject it as being fundamentally at variance with our total world outlook. In the absence of any good reasons for holding it, the assertion of human superiority would then appear simply as the expression of an irrational and self-serving prejudice that favors one particular species over several million others.

Rejecting the notion of human superiority entails its positive counterpart: the doctrine of species impartiality. One who accepts that doctrine regards all living things as possessing inherent worth—the *same* inherent worth, since no one species has been shown to be either "higher" or "lower" than any other. Now we saw earlier that, insofar as one thinks of a living thing as possessing inherent worth, one considers it to be the appropriate object of the attitude of respect and believes that attitude to be the only fitting or suitable one for all moral agents to take toward it.

Here, then, is the key to understanding how the attitude of respect is rooted in the biocentric outlook on nature. The basic connection is made through the denial of human superiority. Once we reject the claim that humans are superior either in merit or in worth to other living things, we are ready to adopt the attitude of respect. The denial of human superiority is itself the result of taking the perspective on nature built into the first three elements of the biocentric outlook.

Now the first three elements of the biocentric outlook, it seems clear, would be found acceptable to any rational and scientifically informed thinker who is fully "open" to the reality of the lives of nonhuman organisms. Without denying our distinctively human characteristics, such a thinker can acknowledge the fundamental respects in which we are members of the Earth's community of life and in which the biological conditions necessary for the realization of our human values are inextricably linked with the whole system of nature. In addition, the conception of individual living things as teleological centers of life simply articulates how a scientifically informed thinker comes to understand them as the result of increasingly careful and detailed observations. Thus, the biocentric outlook recommends itself as an acceptable system of concepts and beliefs to anyone who is clear-minded, unbiased, and factually enlightened, and who has a developed capacity of reality awareness with regard to the lives of individual organisms. This, I submit,

is as good a reason for making the moral commitment involved in adopting the attitude of respect for nature as any theory of environmental ethics could possibly have.

X. MORAL RIGHTS AND THE MATTER OF COMPETING CLAIMS

I have not asserted anywhere in the foregoing account that animals or plants have moral rights. This omission was deliberate. I do not think that the reference class of the concept, bearer of moral rights, should be extended to include nonhuman living things. My reasons for taking this position, however, go beyond the scope of this paper. I believe I have been able to accomplish many of the same ends which those who ascribe rights to animals or plants wish to accomplish. There is no reason, moreover, why plants and animals, including whole species populations and life communities, cannot be accorded *legal* rights under my theory. To grant them legal protection could be interpreted as giving them legal entitlement to be protected, and this, in fact, would be a means by which a society that subscribed to the ethics of respect for nature could give public recognition to their inherent worth.

There remains the problem of competing claims, even when wild plants and animals are not thought of as bearers of moral rights. If we accept the biocentric outlook and accordingly adopt the attitude of respect for nature as our ultimate moral attitude, how do we resolve conflicts that arise from our respect for persons in the domain of human ethics and our respect for nature in the domain of environmental ethics? This is a question that cannot adequately be dealt with here. My main purpose in this paper has been to try to establish a base point from which we can start working toward a solution to the problem. I have shown why we cannot just begin with an initial presumption in favor of the interests of our own species. It is after all within our power as moral beings to place limits on human population and technology with the deliberate intention of sharing the Earth's bounty with other species. That such sharing is an ideal difficult to realize even in an approximate way does not take away its claim to our deepest moral commitment.

Are All Species Equal?

DAVID SCHMIDTZ

I. RESPECT FOR NATURE

Species egalitarianism is the view that all species have equal moral standing[1]. To have moral standing is, at a minimum, to command respect, to be something more than a mere thing. Is there any reason to believe that all species have moral standing in even this most minimal sense? If so—that is, if all species command respect—is there any reason to believe they all command *equal* respect?

The following sections summarise critical responses to the most famous philosophical argument for species egalitarianism. I then try to explain why other species command our respect but also why they do not command equal respect. The intuition that we should have respect for nature is part of what motivates people to embrace species egalitarianism, but one need not be a species egalitarian to have respect for nature. I close by questioning whether species egalitarianism is even compatible with respect for nature.

II. THE GROUNDING OF SPECIES EGALITARIANISM

According to Paul Taylor, anthropocentrism "gives either exclusive or primary consideration to human interests above the good of other species" [2]. The alternative to anthropocentrism is biocentrism, and it is biocentrism that, in Taylor's view, grounds species egalitarianism:

The beliefs that form the core of the biocentric outlook are four in number:

(a) The belief that humans are members of the Earth's Community of life in the same sense and on the same terms in which other living things are members of that community.

(b) The belief that the human species, along with all other species, are integral elements in a system of interdependence.

(c) The belief that all organisms are teleological centres of life in the sense that each is a unique individual pursuing its own good in its own way.

(d) The belief that humans are not inherently superior to other living beings[3].

Taylor concludes, "Rejecting the notion of human superiority entails its positive counterpart: the doctrine of species impartiality. One who accepts that doctrine regards all living things as possessing inherent worth—the *same* inherent worth, since no one species has been shown to be either higher or lower than any other."[4]

Taylor does not claim that this is a valid argument, but he thinks that if we concede (a), (b), and (c), it would be unreasonable not to move to (d), and then to his egalitarian conclusion. Is he right? For those who accept Taylor's three premises (and who thus interpret those premises in terms innocuous enough to render them acceptable), there are two responses. First, we may go on to accept (d), following Taylor, but then still deny that there is any warrant for moving from there to Taylor's egalitarian conclusion. Having accepted that our form of life is not superior, we might choose instead to regard it as inferior. More plausibly, we might view our form of life as noncomparable. We simply do not have the same kind of value as nonhumans. The question of how we compare to nonhumans has a simple answer: we do not compare to them.

Alternatively, we may reject (d) and say humans are indeed inherently superior but our superiority is a moot point. Whether we are inherently superior (that is, superior as a form of life) does not matter much. Even if we are superior, the fact remains that within the web of ecological interdependence mentioned in premises (a) and (b), it would be a mistake to ignore the needs and the telos of the other species referred to in premise (c). Thus, there are two ways of rejecting Taylor's argument for species egalitarianism. Each, on its face, is compatible with the respect for nature that motivates Taylor's egalitarianism in the first place.

Taylor's critics, such as James Anderson and William French, have taken the second route. They reject (d). After discussing their arguments, and building on some while rejecting others, I explore some of our reasons to have respect for nature and ask whether they translate into reasons to be species egalitarians.

III. IS SPECIES EGALITARIANISM HYPOCRITICAL?

Paul Taylor and Arne Naess[5] are among the most intransigent of species egalitarians, yet they allow that human needs override the needs of nonhumans. William C. French argues that they cannot have it both ways[6]. French perceives a contradiction between the egalitarian principles that Taylor and Naess officially endorse and the unofficial principles they offer as the real principles by which we should live. Having proclaimed that we are all equal, French asks, what licenses Taylor and Naess to say that, in cases of conflict, nonhuman interests can legitimately be sacrificed to vital human interests?

French has a point. James C. Anderson [7] makes a similar point. Yet, somehow the inconsistency of Taylor and Naess is too obvious. Perhaps their position is not as blatantly inconsistent as it appears. Let me suggest how Taylor and Naess could respond to French. Suppose I find myself in a situation of mortal combat with an enemy soldier. If I kill my enemy to save my life, that does not entail that I regard my enemy as inherently inferior (i.e., as an inferior form of life). Likewise, if I kill a bear to save my life, that does not entail that I regard the bear as inherently inferior. Therefore, Taylor and Naess can, without hypocrisy, deny that species egalitarianism requires a radically self-effacing pacifism.

What, then, does species egalitarianism require? It requires us to avoid mortal combat whenever we can, not just with other humans but with living things in general. On this view, we ought to regret finding ourselves in kill-or-be-killed situations that we could have avoided. There is no point in regretting the fact that we must kill in order to eat, though, for there is no avoiding that. Species egalitarianism is compatible with our having a limited license to kill.

What seems far more problematic for species egalitarianism is that it seems to suggest that it makes no difference *what* we kill. Vegetarians typically think it is worse to kill a cow than to kill a potato. Are they wrong?[8] Yes they are, according to species egalitarianism. In this respect, species egalitarianism cannot be right. I do believe we have reason to respect nature. But we fail to give nature due respect if we say we should have no more respect for a cow than for a potato.

IV. IS SPECIES EGALITARIANISM ARBITRARY?

Suppose interspecies comparisons are possible. Suppose the capacities of different species, and whatever else gives species moral standing, are commensurable. In that case, it could turn out that all species are equal, but that would be quite a fluke.

Taylor says a being has intrinsic worth if and only if it has a good of its own. Anderson does not disagree, but he points out that if we accept Taylor's idea of a thing having a good of its own, then that licenses us to notice differences among the various kinds of "good of its own." (We can notice differences without being committed to ranking them.) For example, we can distinguish, along Aristotelian lines, vegetative, animal, and cognitive goods of one's own. To have a vegetative nature is to be what Taylor, in premise (c), calls a teleological centre of life. A being with an animal nature is a teleological centre of life, and more. A being with a cognitive as well as animal nature is a teleological centre of life, and more still. Cognitive nature may be something we share with whales, dolphins, and higher primates. It is an empirical question. Anderson's view is that so long as we do not assume away this possibility, valuing cognitive capacity is not anthropocentric. The question is what would make *any* species superior to another (p. 348).

As mentioned earlier, Taylor defines anthropocentrism as giving exclusive or primary consideration to human interests above the good of other species. So, when we acknowledge that cognitive capacity is one valuable capacity among others, are we giving exclusive or primary considerations to human interests? Anderson thinks not, and surely he is right. Put it this way: if biocentrism involves resolving to ignore the fact that cognitive capacity is something we value—if biocentrism amounts to a resolution to value only those capacities that all living things share—then biocentrism is at least as arbitrary and question-begging as anthropocentrism.

It will not do to defend species egalitarianism by singling out a property that all species possess, arguing that this property is morally important, and then concluding that all species are therefore of equal moral importance. The problem with this sort of argument is that, where there is one property that provides a basis for moral standing, there might be others. Other properties might be possessed by some but not all species, and might provide bases for different kinds or degrees of moral standing.

V. THE MULTIPLE BASES OF MORAL STANDING

Taylor is aware of the Aristotelian classification scheme, but considers its hierarchy of capacities to be question-begging. Taylor himself assumes that human rationality is on a par with a cheetah's foot-speed[9]. In this case, though, perhaps it is Taylor who begs the question. It hardly seems unreasonable to see the difference between the foot-speed of chimpanzees and cheetahs as a difference of degree, while seeing the difference between the sentience of a chimpanzee and the nonsentience of a tree as a difference in kind.

Anthropocentrists might argue that the good associated with cognitive capacity is superior to the good associated with vegetative capacity. Could they be wrong? Let us suppose they are wrong. For argument's sake, let us suppose *vegetative* capacity is the superior good. Even so, the exact nature of the good associated with an organism's vegetative capacity will depend upon the organism's other capacities. For example, Anderson (p. 358) points out that even if health in a human and health in a tree are instances of the same thing, they need not have the same moral standing. Why not? Because health in a human has an instrumental value that health in a tree lacks. John Stuart Mill's swine can take pleasure in its health but trees cannot. Animals have a plant's capacities plus more. In turn, humans (and possibly dolphins, apes, and so on) have an animal's capacities plus more. The comparison between Socrates and swine therefore is less a matter of comparing swine to non-swine

and more a matter of comparing swine to "swine-plus" (Anderson, p. 361). Crucially, Anderson's argument for the superiority of Socrates over swine does not presume that one capacity is higher than another. We do not need to make any assumptions about the respective merits of animal or vegetative versus cognitive capacities in order to conclude that the capacities of "swine-plus" are superior to those of swine.

We may of course conclude that *one* of the grounds of our moral standing (i.e., our vegetative natures) is something we share with all living things. Beyond that, nothing about equality even suggests itself. In particular, it begs no questions to notice that there are grounds for moral standing that we do not share with all living things.

VI. IN PRAISE OF SPECIESISM

William French invites us to see species rankings not "as an assessment of some inherent superiority, but rather as a considered moral recognition of the fact that greater ranges of vulnerability are generated by broader ranges of complexity and capacities" (p. 56). One species outranks another not because it is a superior form of life but rather because it is a more vulnerable form of life. French, if I understand correctly, interprets vulnerability as a matter of having *more* to lose. This interpretation is problematic. It implies that a millionaire, having more to lose than a pauper, is by that fact more vulnerable than the pauper. Perhaps this interpretation is forced upon French, though. If French had instead chosen a more natural interpretation—if he had chosen to interpret vulnerability as a matter of *probability* of loss—then a ranking by vulnerability would not be correlated to complex capacities in the way he wants. Ranking by probability of loss would change on a daily basis, and the top-ranked species often would be an amphibian.

If we set aside questions about how to interpret vulnerability, there remains a problem with French's proposal. If having complex capacities is not itself morally important, then being in danger of losing them is not morally important either. Vulnerability, on any interpretation, is essentially of derivative importance; any role it could play in ranking species must already be played by the capacities themselves.

Yet, although I reject French's argument, I do not reject his inegalitarian conclusion. The conclusion that mice are the moral equals of chimpanzees is about as insupportable as a conclusion can be. Suppose that, for some reason, we take an interest in how chimpanzees rank compared to mice. Perhaps we wonder what we would do in an emergency where we could save a drowning chimpanzee or a drowning mouse but not both. More realistically, we might wonder whether, other things equal, we have any reason to use mice in our medical experiments rather than chimpanzees. Species egalitarianism seems to say not.

Suppose we decide upon reflection that, from our human perspective, chimpanzees are superior to mice and humans are superior to chimpanzees. Would the perceived superiority of our form of life give us reason to think we have no obligations whatsoever to mice, or to chimpanzees? Those who believe we have fewer obligations to inferior species might be pressed to say whether they also would allow that we have fewer obligations to inferior human beings. Lawrence Johnson, for example, rhetorically asks whether it is worse to cause a person pain if the person is a Nobel Prize winner[10]. Well, why not? Echoing Peter Singer[11], Johnson argues that if medical researchers had to choose between harvesting the organs of a chimpanzee or a brain-damaged human baby, "one thing we cannot justify is trying to have it both ways. If rationality is what makes the basic moral difference, then we cannot maintain that the brain-damaged infant ought to be exempt from utilisation just because it is human while at the same time allowing that the animal can be used if utility warrants" (p. 52).

Does this seem obvious? It should not. Johnson presumes that rationality is relevant to justification at the *token* level when speciesists (i.e., those who believe some species, the human species in particular, are superior to others) presumably would invoke rationality as a justification at the *type* level. One can say rationality makes a moral difference at the type level without thereby taking any position on whether rationality makes a moral difference at the token level. A speciesist could say humanity's characteristic rationality mandates respect for humanity, not merely for particular humans who exemplify human rationality. Similarly, once we

note that chimpanzees have characteristic cognitive capacities that mice lack, we do not need to compare individual chimpanzees and mice on a case by case basis in order to have a moral justification for planning to use a mouse rather than a chimpanzee in an experiment.

Of course, some chimpanzees lack the characteristic features in virtue of which chimpanzees command respect as a species, just as some humans lack the characteristic features in virtue of which humans command respect as a species. It is equally obvious that some chimpanzees have cognitive capacities (for example) that are superior to the cognitive capacities of some humans. But whether every human being is superior to every chimpanzee is beside the point. The point is that we can, we do, and we should make decisions on the basis of our recognition that mice, chimpanzees, and humans are relevantly different types. We can have it both ways after all. Or so a speciesist could argue.

VII. EQUALITY AND TRANSCENDENCE

Even if speciesists are right to see a nonarbitary distinction between humans and other species, though, the fact remains that, as Anderson (p. 362) points out, claims of superiority do not easily translate into justifications of domination[12]. We can have reasons to treat nonhuman species with respect, regardless of whether we consider them to be on a moral par with *homo sapiens*.

What kind of reasons do we have for treating other species with respect? We might have respect for chimpanzees or even mice on the grounds that they are sentient. Even mice have a rudimentary point of view and rudimentary hopes and dreams, and we might well respect them for that. But what about plants? Plants, unlike mice and chimpanzees, do not care what happens to them. It is literally true that they could not care less. So, why should we care? Is it even possible for us to have any good reason, other than a purely instrumental reason, to care what happens to plants?

When we are alone in a forest wondering whether it would be fine to chop down a tree for fun, our perspective on what happens to the tree is, so far as we know, the only perspective there is. The tree does not have its own. Thus, explaining why we have reason to care about trees requires us to explain caring from our point of view, since that (we are supposing) is all there is. In that case, we do not have to satisfy *trees* that we are treating them properly; rather, we have to satisfy *ourselves*. So, again, can we have noninstrumental reasons for caring about trees—for treating them with respect?

One reason to care (not the only one) is that gratuitous destruction is a failure of self-respect. It is a repudiation of the kind of self-awareness and self-respect that we can achieve by repudiating wantonness. So far as I know, no one finds anything puzzling in the idea that we have reason to treat our lawns or living rooms with respect. Lawns and living rooms have instrumental value, but there is more to it than that. Most of us have the sense that taking reasonable care of our lawns and living rooms is somehow a matter of self-respect, not merely a matter of preserving their instrumental value. Do we have similar reasons to treat forests with respect? I think we do. There is an aesthetic involved, the repudiation of which would be a failure of self-respect. (Obviously, not everyone feels the same way about forests. Not everyone feels the same way about lawns and living rooms, either. But the point here is to make sense of respect for nature, not to argue that respect for nature is in fact universal or that failing to respect nature is irrational[13].) If and when we identify with a Redwood, in the sense of being inspired by it, having respect for its size and age and so on, then as a psychological fact, we really do face moral questions about how we ought to treat it. If and when we come to see a Redwood in that light, subsequently turning our backs on it becomes a kind of self-effacement. The values that we thereby fail to take seriously are *our* values, not the tree's.

A related way of grounding respect for nature is suggested by Jim Cheney's remark that "moral regard is appropriate wherever we are *able* to manage it—in light of our sensibilities, knowledge, and cultural/personal histories...The limits of moral regard are set only by the limitations of one's own (or one's species' or one's community's) ability to respond in a caring manner."[14] Should we believe Cheney's rather startling proposal that moral regard is appropriate whenever we can manage it? One reason to take it very seriously is that exercising our capacity for moral regard is a way of expressing respect for that capacity. Developing that capacity is a form of self-realization.

Put it this way. I am arguing that the attitude we take toward gazelles (for example) raises issues of self-respect insofar as we see ourselves as relevantly like gazelles. My reading of Cheney suggests a different and complementary way of looking at the issue. Consider that lions owe nothing to gazelles. Therefore, if we owe it to gazelles not to hunt them, it must be because we are *unlike* lions, not (or not only) because we are *like* gazelles.

Unlike lions, we have a choice about whether to hunt gazelles, and we are capable of deliberating about that choice in a reflective way. We are capable of caring about the gazelle's pain, the gazelle's beauty, the gazelle's hopes and dreams (such as they are), and so forth. And if we do care, then in a more or less literal way, something is wrong with us—we are less than fully human—if we cannot adjust our behaviour in the light of what we care about. If we do not care, then we are missing something. For a human being, to lack a broad respect for living things and beautiful things and well-functioning things is to be stunted in a way.

Our coming to see other species as commanding respect is itself a way of transcending our animal natures. It is ennobling. It is part of our animal natures unthinkingly to see ourselves as superior, and to try to dominate accordingly; our capacity to see ourselves as equal is one of the things that makes us different. Thus, our capacity to see ourselves as equal may be one of the things that makes us superior. Coming to see all species as equal may not be the best way of transcending our animal natures—it does not work for me—but it is one way. Another way of transcending our animal natures and expressing due respect for nature is simply to not worry so much about ranking species. This latter way is, I think, better. It is more respectful of our own reflective natures. It does not dwell on rankings. It does not insist on seeing equality where a more reflective being simply would see what is there to be seen and would not shy away from respecting the differences as well as the commonalities. The whole idea of ranking species, even as equals, sometimes seems like a child's game. It seems beneath us.

VIII. RESPECT FOR EVERYTHING

Thus, a broad respect for living or beautiful or well-functioning things need not translate into equal respect. It need not translate into universal respect, either. I can appreciate mosquitoes to a degree. My wife (a biochemist who studies mosquito immune systems) even finds them beautiful, or so she says. My own appreciation, by contrast, is thin and grudging and purely intellectual. In neither degree nor kind is it anything like the appreciation I have for my wife, or for human beings in general, or even for the rabbits I sometimes find eating my flowers in the morning. Part of our responsibility as moral agents is to be somewhat choosy about what we respect and how we respect it. I can see why people shy away from openly accepting that responsibility, but they still have it.

Johnson says speciesism is as arbitrary as racism unless we can show that the differences are morally relevant (p. 51). This is, to be sure, a popular sentiment among radical environmentalists and animal liberationists[15]. But are we really like racists when we think it is worse to kill a dolphin than to kill a tuna? The person who says there is a relevant similarity between speciesism and racism has the burden of proof: go ahead and identify the similarity. Is seeing moral significance in biological differences between chimpanzees and potatoes anything like seeing moral significance in biological differences between races? I think not.

Is it true that we need good reason to *exclude* plants and animals from the realm of things we regard as commanding respect? Or do we need reason to *include* them? Should we be trying to identify properties in virtue of which a thing forfeits presumptive moral standing? Or does it make more sense to be trying to identify properties in virtue of which a thing commands respect? The latter seems more natural to me, which suggests the burden of proof lies with those who claim we should have respect for other species.

I would not say, though, that this burden is unbearable. One reason to have regard for other species has to do with self-respect. (As I said earlier, when we mistreat a tree that we admire, the values we fail to respect are our values, not the tree's.) A second reason has to do with self-realisation. (As I said, exercising our capacity for moral regard is a form of self-realisation.) Finally, at least some species seem to share with human beings precisely those cognitive and affective characteristics that lead us to see human life as especially worthy of esteem. Johnson describes experiments in which rhesus monkeys show extreme reluctance to obtain food by means that would subject monkeys in neighbouring cages to electric shock (p. 64n). He describes the case of Washoe, a chimpanzee who learned sign language. Anyone who has tried to learn a foreign language ought to be able to appreciate how astonishing an intellectual feat it is that an essentially nonlinguistic creature could learn a language—a language that is not merely foreign but the language of another species.

Johnson believes Washoe has moral standing (p. 27–31), but he does not believe that the moral standing of chimpanzees, and indeed of all living creatures, implies that we must resolve never to kill (p. 136). Thus, Johnson supports killing introduced animal species (feral dogs, rabbits, and so forth) to prevent the extermination of Australia's native species, including native plant species (p. 174).

Is Johnson guilty of advocating the speciesist equivalent of ethnic cleansing? Has he shown himself to be no better than a racist? I think not. Johnson is right to want to take drastic measures to protect Australia's native flora, and the idea of respecting trees is intelligible. Certainly one thing I feel in the presence of Redwoods is something like a feeling of respect. But I doubt that what underlies Johnson's willingness to kill feral dogs is mere respect for Australia's native plants. I suspect that his approval of such killings turns on the needs and aesthetic sensibilities of human beings, not just the interests of plants[16]. For example, if the endangered native species happened to be a malaria-carrying mosquito, I doubt that Johnson would advocate wiping out an exotic but minimally intrusive species of amphibian in order to save the mosquitoes.

Aldo Leopold[17] urged us to see ourselves as plain citizens of, rather than conquerors of, the biotic community, but there are some species with whom we can never be fellow citizens. The rabbits eating my flowers in the back yard are neighbours, and I cherish their company, minor frictions notwithstanding. I feel no sense of community with mosquitoes, though, and not merely because they are not warm and furry. Some mosquito species are so adapted to making human beings miserable that mortal combat is not accidental; rather, combat is a natural state. It is how such creatures live. Recall Cheney's remark that the limits of moral regard are set by the limits of our ability to respond in a caring manner. I think it is fair to say human beings are not able to respond to malaria-carrying mosquitoes in a caring manner. At very least, most of us would think less of a person who did respond to them in a caring manner. We would regard the person's caring as a parody of respect for nature.

The conclusion that *all* species have moral standing is unmotivated. For human beings, viewing apes as having moral standing is a form of self-respect. Viewing viruses as having moral standing is not. It is good to have a sense of how amazing living things are, but being able to marvel at living things is not the same as thinking all species have moral standing. Life as such commands respect only in the limited but nonetheless important sense that for self-aware and reflective creatures who want to act in ways that make sense, deliberately killing something is an act that does not make sense unless we have good reason to do it. Destroying something for no good reason is (at best) the moral equivalent of vandalism.

IX. THE HISTORY OF THE DEBATE

There is an odd project in the history of philosophy that equates what seem to be three distinct projects:

1. determining our essence;
2. specifying how we are different from all other species;
3. specifying what makes us morally important.

Equating these three projects has important ramifications. Suppose for the sake of argument that what makes us morally important is that we are capable of suffering. If what makes us morally important is necessarily the same property that constitutes our essence, then our essence is that we are capable of suffering. And if our essence necessarily is what makes us different from all other species, then we can deduce that dogs are not capable of suffering.

Likewise with rationality. If rationality is our essence, then rationality is what makes us

morally important and also what makes us unique. Therefore, we can deduce that chimpanzees are not rational. Alternatively, if some other animal becomes rational, does that mean our essence will change? Is that why some people find Washoe, the talking chimpanzee, threatening?

The three projects, needless to say, should not be conflated in the way philosophy seems historically to have conflated them, but we can reject species equality without conflating them [18]. If we like, we can select a property with respect to which all species are the same, then argue that that property confers moral standing, then say all species have moral standing. To infer that all species have the same standing, though, would be to ignore the possibility that there are other morally important properties with respect to which not all species are equal.

There is room to wonder whether species egalitarianism is even compatible with respect for nature. Is it true that we should have no more regard for dolphins than for tuna? Is it true that the moral standing of chimpanzees is no higher that that of mosquitoes? I worry that these things are not only untrue, but also disrespectful. Dolphins and chimpanzees command more respect than species egalitarianism allows.

There is no denying that it demeans us to destroy species we find beautiful or otherwise beneficial. What about species in which we find neither beauty nor benefit? It is, upon reflection, obviously in our interest to enrich our lives by finding them beautiful or beneficial, if we can. By and large, we must agree with Leopold that it is too late for conquering the biotic community. Our most pressing task now is to find ways of fitting in. Species egalitarianism is one way of trying to understand how we fit in. In the end, it is not an acceptable way. Having respect for nature and being a species egalitarian are two different things.

NOTES

1. A species egalitarian may or may not believe that individual living things all have equal moral standing. A species egalitarian may think a given whooping crane matters more than a given bald eagle because the cranes are endangered, despite believing that the differences between the two species qua species are

not morally important. I thank Stephen Clark for this observation.

2. Paul W. Taylor (1983). In defense of biocentrism, *Environmental Ethics*, 5: 237–43, here p. 240. Taylor takes pains to distinguish anthropocentrism from the trivial and unobjectionable position that human beings make judgments from a human point of view.

3. Paul Taylor (1986). *Respect for Nature* (Princeton: Princeton University Press), p. 99ff. See also Taylor (1994). The ethics of respect for nature, *Planet in Peril*, edited by Dale & Fred Westphal (Orlando, Harcourt Brace), 15–37.

4. Taylor (1994), op. cit., p. 35.

5. Arne Naess (1973). The shallow and the deep, long-range ecology movement: a summary. *Inquiry*, 16: 95–100.

6. William C. French (1995). Against biospherical egalitarianism, *Environmental Ethics*, 17: 39–57, here pp. 44ff.

7. James C. Anderson (1993). Species equality and the foundations of moral theory, *Environmental Values*, 2: 347–65, here p. 350.

8. I thank Austin Dacey for raising this question.

9. Taylor (1994), op. cit., p. 33.

10. Lawrence Johnson (1991). *A Morally Deep World* (New York, Cambridge University Press), p. 52.

11. Peter Singer (1990). *Animal Liberation*, 2nd edition (New York, Random House), pp. 1–23.

12. James Sterba evidently thinks otherwise, for he considers it true by *definition* that "To treat humans as superior overall to other living beings is to aggress against them by sacrificing their basic needs to meet the nonbasic needs of humans (definition)." James P. Sterba (1995). From biocentric individualism to biocentric pluralism, *Environmental Ethics*, 17: 191–207, here p. 194.

Sterba does not say whether regarding chimpanzees as superior to mice is, by definition, a way of aggressing against mice.

13. Thus, the objective is to explain how a rational agent could have respect for trees, not to argue that a rational agent could not fail to have respect. In utilitarian terms, a person whose utility function leaves no room to derive pleasure from respecting trees is not irrational for failing to respect trees, but people whose utility functions include a potential for deriving pleasure from respecting trees have reason (other things equal) to enrich their lives by realising that potential.

14. Jim Cheney (1987). Eco-feminism and deep ecology, *Environmental Ethics* 9: 115–45, here p. 144.

15. See Peter Singer (1994). All animals are equal, in Dale & Fred Westphal, eds, *Planet in Peril* (Orlando: Harcourt Brace), 175–94, here p. 189.

16. Johnson believes ecosystems as such have moral standing and that, consequently, "we should always stop short of entirely destroying or irreparably degrading any ecosystem" (p. 276). "Chopping some trees is one thing, then, but destroying a forest is something else" (p. 276). But this is impossible to square with his remark that there "is an ecosystem in a tiny puddle of water in a rotting stump" (p. 265). Thus, when Johnson says ecosystems should never be destroyed, he does not mean ecosystems per se. Rather he means forests, deserts, marshes, and so on—ecosystems that are recognisable as habitat either for humans or for species that humans care about.

17. Leopold Aldo (1966, first published in 1949). *Sand County Almanac* (New York, Oxford University Press), p. 240.

18. Will Kymlicka notes that Mary Midgley makes a similar point in a critique of Karl Marx. *Contra* Marx, Midgley says, what constitutes a good life for a human being is not a question "about biological classification." It is a question in moral philosophy. And we do not help ourselves at all in answering it if we decide in advance that the answer ought to be a single, simple characteristic, unshared by other species, such as the differentia is meant to be. Mary Midgley (1978). *Beast and Man: The roots of human nature* (New York, New American Library), p. 204.

Reverence for Life

ALBERT SCHWEITZER

The ethic of reverence for life shows its truth also in that it includes in itself the different elements of ethics in their natural connection. Hitherto no system of ethics has been able to present in their parallelism and their interaction the effort after self-perfecting, in which man acts upon himself without outward deeds, and activist ethics. The ethics of reverence for life can do this, and indeed in such a way that they not only answer academic questions, but also produce a deepening of ethical insight.

Ethics are reverence for the will-to-live within me and without me. From the former comes first the profound life-affirmation of resignation. I apprehend my will-to-live as not only something which can live itself out in happy occurrences, but also something which has experience of itself. If I refuse to let this self-experience disappear in thoughtlessness, and persist in feeling it to be valuable, I begin to learn the secret of spiritual self-realization; I win an unsuspected freedom from the various destinies of life. At moments when I had expected to find myself shattered, I find myself exalted in an inexpressible and surprising happiness of freedom from the world, and I experience therein a clarification of my life-view. Resignation is the vestibule through which we enter ethics. Only he who in deepened devotion to his own will-to-live experiences inward freedom from outward occurrences, is capable of devoting himself in profound and steady fashion to the life of others.

Just as in reverence for my own will-to-live I struggle for freedom from the destinies of life, so I struggle too for freedom from myself. Not only in face of what happens to me, but also with regard to the way in which I concern myself with the world, I practise the higher self-maintenance. Out of reverence for my own existence I place myself under the compulsion of veracity towards myself. Everything I might acquire would be purchased too dearly by action in defiance of my convictions. I fear that if I were untrue to myself, I should be wounding my will-to-live with a poisoned spear.

The fact that Kant makes, as he does, sincerity towards oneself the central point of his ethics, testifies to the depth of his ethical feeling. But because in his search for the essential nature of the ethical he fails to find his way through to reverence for life, he cannot comprehend the connection between veracity towards oneself and activist ethics.

As a matter of fact, the ethics of sincerity towards oneself passes imperceptibly into that of devotion to others. Such sincerity compels me to actions which manifest themselves as self-devotion in such a way that ordinary ethics derive them from devotion.

Why do I forgive anyone? Ordinary ethics say, because I feel sympathy with him. They allow men, when they pardon others, to seem to themselves wonderfully good, and allow them to practise a style of pardoning which is not free from humiliation of the other. They thus make forgiveness a sweetened triumph of self-devotion.

The ethics of reverence for life do away with this crude point of view. All acts of forbearance and of pardon are for them acts forced from one by sincerity towards oneself. I must practise unlimited forgiveness because, if I did not, I should be wanting in sincerity to myself, for it would be acting as if I myself were not guilty in the same way as the other has been guilty towards me. Because my life is so liberally spotted with falsehood, I must forgive falsehood which has been practised upon me; because I myself have been in so many cases wanting in love, and guilty of hatred, slander, deceit, or arrogance, I must pardon any want of love, and all hatred, slander, deceit, or arrogance which have been directed against myself. I must forgive quietly and unostentatiously; in fact I do not really pardon at all, for I do not let things develop to any such act of judgement. Nor is this any eccentric proceeding; it is only a necessary widening and refining of ordinary ethics.

From *Civilization and Ethics* by Albert Schweitzer, trans. A. Naish, 247–254. © London: Black, 1923.

We have to carry on the struggle against the evil that is in mankind, not by judging others, but by judging ourselves. Struggle with oneself and veracity towards oneself are the means by which we influence others. We quietly draw them into our efforts to attain the deep spiritual self-realization which springs from reverence for one's own life. Power makes no noise. It is there, and works. True ethics begin where the use of language ceases.

The innermost element then, in activist ethics, even if it appears as self-devotion, comes from the compulsion to sincerity towards oneself, and obtains therein its true value. The whole ethics of being other than the world flow pure only when they come from this source. It is not from kindness to others that I am gentle, peaceable, forbearing, and friendly, but because by such behaviour I prove my own profoundest self-realization to be true. Reverence for life which I apply to my own existence, and reverence for life which keeps me in a temper of devotion to other existence than my own, interpenetrate each other.

* * *

Because ordinary ethics possess no basic principle of the ethical, they must engage at once in the discussion of conflicting duties. The ethics of reverence for life have no such need for hurry. They take their own time to think out in all directions their own principle of the moral. Knowing themselves to be firmly established, they then settle their position with regard to these conflicts.

They have to try conclusions with three adversaries: these are thoughtlessness, egoistic self-assertion, and society.

To the first of these they usually pay insufficient attention, because no open conflicts arise between them. This adversary does, nevertheless, obstruct them imperceptibly.

There is, however, a wide field of which our ethics can take possession without any collision with the troops of egoism. Man can accomplish much that is good, without having to require of himself any sacrifice. And if there really goes with it a bit of his life, it is so insignificant that he feels it no more than if he were losing a hair or a flake of dead skin.

Over wide stretches of conduct the inward liberation from the world, the being true to oneself, the being different from the world, yes, and even self-devotion to other life, is only a matter of giving attention to this particular relationship. We fall short so much, because we do not keep ourselves up to it. We do not stand sufficiently under the pressure of any inward compulsion to be ethical. At all points the steam hisses out of the boiler that is not tightly closed. In ordinary ethics the resulting losses of energy are as high as they are because such ethics have at their disposal no single basic principle of the moral which acts upon thought. They cannot tighten the lid of the boiler, indeed, they do not ever even examine it. But reverence for life being something which is ever present to thought, penetrates unceasingly and in all directions a man's observation, reflection, and resolutions. He can keep himself clear of it as little as the water can prevent itself from being coloured by the dye-stuff which is dropped into it. The struggle with thoughtlessness is started, and is always going on.

But what is the position of the ethics of reverence for life in the conflicts which arise between inward compulsion to self-sacrifice, and the necessary upholding of the ego?

I too am subject to division of my will-to-life against itself. In a thousand ways my existence stands in conflict with that of others. The necessity to destroy and to injure life is imposed upon me. If I walk along an unfrequented path, my foot brings destruction and pain upon the tiny creatures which populate it. In order to preserve my own existence, I must defend myself against the existence which injures it. I become a persecutor of the little mouse which inhabits my house, a murderer of the insect which want to have its nest there, a mass-murderer of the bacteria which may endanger my life. I get my food by destroying plants and animals. My happiness is built upon injury done to my fellow-men.

How can ethics be maintained in face of the horrible necessity to which I am subjected through the division of my will-to-live against itself?

Ordinary ethics seek compromises. They try to dictate how much of my existence and of my happiness I must sacrifice, and how much I may preserve at the cost of the existence and happiness of other lives. With these decisions they produce experimental, relative ethics. They offer as ethical what is in reality not ethical but a mixture of non-ethical necessity and ethics. They thereby bring about a huge confusion, and allow the starting of an ever-increasing obscuration of the conception of the ethical.

The ethics of reverence for life know nothing of a relative ethic. They make only the maintenance and promotion of life rank as good. All destruction of and injury to life, under whatever circumstances they take place, they condemn as evil. They do not keep in store adjustments between ethics and necessity all ready for use. Again and again and in ways that are always original they are trying to come to terms in man with reality. They do not abolish for him all ethical conflicts, but compel him to decide for himself in each case how far he can remain ethical and how far he must submit himself to the necessity for destruction of and injury to life, and therewith incur guilt. It is not by receiving instruction about agreement between ethical and necessary, that a man makes progress in ethics, but only by coming to hear more and more plainly the voice of the ethical, by becoming ruled more and more by the longing to preserve and promote life, and by becoming more and more obstinate in resistance to the necessity for destroying or injuring life.

In ethical conflicts man can arrive only at subjective decisions. No one can decide for him at what point, on each occasion, lies the extreme limit of possibility for his persistence in the preservation and furtherance of life. He alone has to judge this issue, by letting himself be guided by a feeling of the highest possible responsibility towards other life.

We must never let ourselves become blunted. We are living in truth, when we experience these conflicts more profoundly. The good conscience is an invention of the devil.

* * *

What does reverence for life say about the relations between man and the animal world?

Whenever I injure life of any sort, I must be quite clear whether it is necessary. Beyond the unavoidable, I must never go, not even with what seems insignificant. The farmer, who has mown down a thousand flowers in his meadow as fodder for his cows, must be careful on his way home not to strike off in wanton pastime the head of a single flower by the roadside, for he thereby commits a wrong against life without being under the pressure of necessity.

Those who experiment with operations or the use of drugs upon animals, or inoculate them with diseases, so as to be able to bring help to mankind with the results gained, must never quiet any misgivings they feel with the general reflection that their cruel proceedings aim at valuable result. They must first have considered in each individual case whether there is a real necessity to force upon any animal this sacrifice for the sake of mankind. And they must take the most anxious care to mitigate as much as possible the pain inflicted. How much wrong is committed in scientific institutions through neglect of anaesthetics, which to save time or trouble are not administered! How much, too, through animals being subjected to torture merely to demonstrate to students generally known phenomena! By the very fact that animals have been subjected to experiments, and have by their pain won such valuable results for suffering humanity, a new and special relation of solidarity has been established between them and us. From that springs for each one of us a compulsion to do to every animal all the good we possibly can. By helping an insect when it is in difficulties, I am only attempting to cancel part of man's ever new debt to the animal world. Whenever an animal is in any way forced into the service of man, every one of us must be concerned with the sufferings which for that reason it has to undergo. None of us must allow to take place any suffering for which he himself is not responsible, if he can hinder it in any way. He must not soothe his conscience with the reflection that he would be mixing himself up in something which does not concern him. No one must shut his eyes and regard as non-existent the sufferings of which he spares himself the sight. Let no one regard as light the burden of his responsibility. While so much ill-treatment of animals goes on, while the moans of thirsty animals in railway trucks sound unheard, while so much brutality prevails in our slaughter-houses, while animals have to suffer in our kitchens painful death from unskilled hands, while animals have to endure intolerable treatment from heartless men, or are left to the cruel play of children, we all share the guilt.

We are afraid of making ourselves conspicuous, if we let it be noticed how we feel for the sufferings which man brings upon the animals. At the same time we think that others have become more "rational" than we are, and regard what we are excited about as usual and a matter of course. Yet suddenly they will let slip a word which shows us that they too have not yet learnt to acquiesce. And now, though they were strangers, they are quite near us. The mask in which we deceived each other falls off. We know now, from one another, that we feel alike about being unable to escape from the gruesome proceedings that are taking place unceasingly around us. What a making of a new acquaintance!

The ethics of reverence for life guard us from letting each other believe through our silence that we no longer experience what, as thinking men, we must experience. They prompt us to keep each other sensitive to what distresses us, and to talk and to act together, just as the responsibility we feel moves us, and without any feeling of shyness. They make us join in keeping on the look-out for opportunities of bringing some sort of help to animals, to make up for the great misery which men inflict on them, and thus to step for a moment out of the incomprehensible horror of existence.

* * *

In the matter also of our relation to other men, the ethics of reverence for life throw upon us a responsibility so unlimited as to be terrifying.

Here again they offer us no rules about the extent of the self-maintenance which is allowable; again, they bid us in each case to thrash the question out with the absolute ethics of self-devotion. I have to decide in accordance with the responsibility of which I am conscious, how much of my life, my possessions, my rights, my happiness, my time, and my rest I must devote to others, and how much I may keep for myself.

In the question of possessions, the ethics of reverence for life are outspokenly individualist in the sense that wealth acquired or inherited should be placed at the service of the community, not through any measures taken by society, but through the absolutely free decision of the individual. They expect everything from a general increase in the feeling of responsibility. Wealth they regard as the property of society left in the sovereign control of the individual. One man serves society by carrying on a business in which a number of employees earn their living; another by giving away his wealth in order to help his fellows. Between these two extreme kinds of service, let each decide according to the responsibility which he finds determined for him by the circumstances of his life. Let no man judge his neighbour. The one thing that matters is that each shall value what he possesses as means to action. Whether this is accomplished by his keeping and increasing his wealth, or by surrender of it, matters little. Wealth must reach the community in the most varied ways, if it is to be of the greatest benefit to all.

People or Penguins
The Case for Optimal Pollution

WILLIAM F. BAXTER

I start with the modest proposition that, in dealing with pollution, or indeed with any problem, it is helpful to know what one is attempting to accomplish. Agreement on how and whether to pursue a particular objective, such as pollution control, is not possible unless some more general objective has been identified and stated with reasonable

precision. We talk loosely of having clean air and clean water, of preserving our wilderness areas, and

From *People or Penguins: The Case for Optimal Pollution* by William Baxter, © 1974 Columbia University Press. Reprinted with the permission of the publisher. Notes deleted.

so forth. But none of these is a sufficiently general objective: each is more accurately viewed as a means rather than as an end.

With regard to clean air, for example, one may ask, "how clean?" and "what does clean mean?" It is even reasonable to ask, "why have clean air?" Each of these questions is an implicit demand that a more general community goal be stated—a goal sufficiently general in its scope and enjoying sufficiently general assent among the community of actors that such "why" questions no longer seem admissible with respect to that goal.

If, for example, one states as a goal the proposition that "every person should be free to do whatever he wishes in contexts where his actions do not interfere with the interests of other human beings," the speaker is unlikely to be met with a response of "why." The goal may be criticized as uncertain in its implications or difficult to implement, but it is so basic a tenet of our civilization—it reflects a cultural value so broadly shared, at least in the abstract—that the question "why" is seen as impertinent or imponderable or both.

I do not mean to suggest that everyone would agree with the "spheres of freedom" objective just stated. Still less do I mean to suggest that a society could subscribe to four or five such general objectives that would be adequate in their coverage to serve as testing criteria by which all other disagreements might be measured. One difficulty in the attempt to construct such a list is that each new goal added will conflict, in certain applications, with each prior goal listed; and thus each goal serves as a limited qualification on prior goals.

Without any expectation of obtaining unanimous consent to them, let me set forth four goals that I generally use as ultimate testing criteria in attempting to frame solutions to problems of human organization. My position regarding pollution stems from these four criteria. If the criteria appeal to you and any part of what appears hereafter does not, our disagreement will have a helpful focus: which of us is correct, analytically, in supposing that his position on pollution would better serve these general goals. If the criteria do not seem acceptable to you, then it is to be expected that our more particular judgements will differ, and the task will then be yours to identify the basic set of criteria upon which your particular judgments rest.

My criteria are as follows:

1. The spheres of freedom criterion stated above.
2. Waste is a bad thing. The dominant feature of human existence is scarcity—our available resources, our aggregate labors, and our skill in employing both have always been, and will continue for some time to be, inadequate to yield to every man all the tangible and intangible satisfactions he would like to have. Hence, none of those resources, or labors, or skills, should be wasted—that is, employed so as to yield less than they might yield in human satisfactions.
3. Every human being should be regarded as an end rather than as a means to be used for the betterment of another. Each should be afforded dignity and regarded as having an absolute claim to an even-handed application of such rules as the community may adopt for its governance.
4. Both the incentive and the opportunity to improve his share of satisfactions should be preserved to every individual. Preservation of incentive is dictated by the "no-waste" criterion and enjoins against the continuous, totally egalitarian redistribution of satisfactions, or wealth; but subject to that constraint, everyone should receive, by continuous redistribution if necessary, some minimal share of aggregate wealth so as to avoid a level of privation from which the opportunity to improve his situation becomes illusory.

The relationship of these highly general goals to the more specific environmental issues at hand may not be readily apparent, and I am not yet ready to demonstrate their pervasive implications. But let me give one indication of their implications. Recently scientists have informed us that use of DDT in food production is causing damage to the penguin population. For the present purposes let us accept that assertion as an indisputable scientific fact. The scientific fact is often asserted as if the correct implication—that we must stop agricultural use of DDT—followed from the mere statement of the fact of penguin damage. But plainly it does not follow if my criteria are employed.

My criteria are oriented to people, not penguins. Damage to penguins, or sugar pines, or geological marvels is, without more, simply irrelevant. One must go further, by my criteria, and say: Penguins are important because people enjoy seeing them walk about rocks; and furthermore, the well-being of people would be less impaired by halting use of DDT than by giving up penguins. In short, my observations about environmental problems will be people-oriented, as are my criteria. I have no interest in preserving penguins for their own sake.

It may be said by way of objection to this position, that it is very selfish of people to act as if each person represented one unit of importance and nothing else was of any importance. It is undeniably selfish. Nevertheless I think it is the only tenable starting place for analysis for several reasons. First, no other position corresponds to the way most people really think and act—i.e., corresponds to reality.

Second, this attitude does not portend any massive destruction of nonhuman flora and fauna, for people depend on them in many obvious ways, and they will be preserved because and to the degree that humans do depend on them.

Third, what is good for humans is, in many respects, good for penguins and pine trees—clean air for example. So that humans are, in these respects, surrogates for plant and animal life.

Fourth, I do not know how we could administer any other system. Our decisions are either private or collective. Insofar as Mr. Jones is free to act privately, he may give such preferences as he wishes to other forms of life: he may feed birds in winter and do less with himself, and he may even decline to resist an advancing polar bear on the ground that the bear's appetite is more important than those portions of himself that the bear may choose to eat. In short my basic premise does not rule out private altruism to competing life-forms. It does rule out, however, Mr. Jones' inclination to feed Mr. Smith to the bear, however hungry the bear, however despicable Mr. Smith.

Insofar as we act collectively on the other hand, only humans can be afforded an opportunity to participate in the collective decisions. Penguins cannot vote now and are unlikely subjects for the franchise—pine trees more unlikely still. Again each individual is free to cast his vote so as to benefit sugar pines if that is his inclination. But many of the more extreme assertions that one hears from some conservationists amount to tacit assertions that they are specially appointed representatives of sugar pines, and hence that their preferences should be weighted more heavily than the preferences of other humans who do not enjoy equal rapport with "nature." The simplistic assertion that agricultural use of DDT must stop at once because it is harmful to penguins is of that type.

Fifth, if polar bears or pine trees or penguins, like men, are to be regarded as ends rather than means, if they are to count in our calculus of social organization, someone must tell me how much each one counts, and someone must tell me how these life-forms are to be permitted to express their preferences, for I do not know either answer. If the answer is that certain people are to hold their proxies, then I want to know how those proxy-holders are to be selected: self-appointment does not seem workable to me.

Sixth, and by way of summary of all the foregoing, let me point out that the set of environmental issues under discussion—although they raise very complex technical questions of how to achieve any objective—ultimately raise a normative question: what *ought* we to do. Questions of *ought* are unique to the human mind and world—they are meaningless as applied to a nonhuman situation.

I reject the proposition that we *ought* to respect the "balance of nature" or to "preserve the environment" unless the reason for doing so, express or implied, is the benefit of man.

I reject the idea that there is a "right" or "morally correct" state of nature to which we should return. The word "nature" has no normative connotation. Was it "right" or "wrong" for the earth's crust to heave in contortion and create mountains and seas? Was it "right" for the first amphibian to crawl up out of the primordial ooze? Was it "wrong" for plants to reproduce themselves and alter the atmospheric composition in favor of oxygen? For animals to alter the atmosphere in favor of carbon dioxide both by breathing oxygen and eating plants? No answers can be given to these questions because they are meaningless questions.

All this may seem obvious to the point of being tedious, but much of the present controversy over environment and pollution rests on tacit normative assumptions about just such nonnormative phenomena: that it is "wrong" to impair penguins with DDT, but not to slaughter cattle for prime rib roasts. That it is wrong to kill stands of sugar pines with industrial fumes, but not to cut sugar pines and build housing for the poor. Every man is entitled to his own preferred definition of Walden Pond, but there is no definition that has any moral superiority over another, except by reference to the selfish needs of the human race.

From the fact that there is no normative definition of the natural state, it follows that there is no normative definition of clean air or pure water—hence no definition of polluted air—or of pollution—except by reference to the needs of man. The "right" composition of the atmosphere is one which has some dust in it and some lead in it and some hydrogen sulfide in it—just those amounts that attend a sensibly organized society thoughtfully and knowledgeably pursuing the greatest possible satisfaction for its human members.

The first and most fundamental step toward solution of our environmental problems is a clear recognition that our objective is not pure air or water but rather some optimal state of pollution. That step immediately suggests the question: How do we define and attain the level of pollution that will yield the maximum possible amount of human satisfaction?

Low levels of pollution contribute to human satisfaction but so do food and shelter and education and music. To attain ever lower levels of pollution, we must pay the cost of having less of these other things. I contrast that view of the cost of pollution control with the more popular statement that pollution control will "cost" very large numbers of dollars. The popular statement is true in some senses, false in others; sorting out the true and false senses is of some importance. The first step in that sorting process is to achieve a clear understanding of the difference between dollars and resources. Resources are the wealth of our nation; dollars are merely claim checks upon those

resources. Resources are of vital importance; dollars are comparatively trivial.

Four categories of resources are sufficient for our purposes: At any given time a nation, or a planet if you prefer, has a stock of labor, of technological skill, of capital goods, and of natural resources (such as mineral deposits, timber, water, land, etc.). These resources can be used in various combinations to yield goods and services of all kinds—in some limited quantity. The quantity will be larger if they are combined efficiently, smaller if combined inefficiently. But in either event the resource stock is limited, the goods and services that they can be made to yield are limited; even the most efficient use of them will yield less than our population, in the aggregate, would like to have.

If one considers building a new dam, it is appropriate to say that it will be costly in the sense that it will require x hours of labor, y tons of steel and concrete, and z amount of capital goods. If these resources are devoted to the dam, then they cannot be used to build hospitals, fishing rods, schools, or electric can openers. That is the meaningful sense in which the dam is costly.

Quite apart from the very important question of how wisely we can combine our resources to produce goods and services, is the very different question of how they get distributed—who gets how many goods? Dollars constitute the claim checks which are distributed among people and which control their share of national output. Dollars are nearly valueless pieces of paper except to the extent that they do represent claim checks to some fraction of the output of goods and services. Viewed as claim checks, all the dollars outstanding during any period of time are worth, in the aggregate, the goods and services that are available to be claimed with them during that period—neither more nor less.

It is far easier to increase the supply of dollars than to increase the production of goods and services—printing dollars is easy. But printing more dollars doesn't help because each dollar then simply becomes a claim to fewer goods, i.e., becomes worth less.

The point is this: many people fall into error upon hearing the statement that the decision to build a dam, or to clean up a river, will cost $X million. It is regrettably easy to say: "It's only money. This is a wealthy country, and we have lots of money." But you cannot build a dam or clean a river with $X million—unless you also have a match, you can't even make a fire. One builds a dam or cleans a river by diverting labor and steel and trucks and factories from making one kind of goods to making another. The cost in dollars is merely a shorthand way of describing the extent of the diversion necessary. If we build a dam for $X million, then we must recognize that we will have $X million less housing and food and medical care and electric can openers as a result.

Similarly, the costs of controlling pollution are best expressed in terms of the other goods we will have to give up to do the job. This is not to say the job should not be done. Badly as we need more housing, more medical care, and more can openers, and more symphony orchestras, we could do with somewhat less of them, in my judgment at least, in exchange for somewhat cleaner air and rivers. But that is the nature of the trade-off, and analysis of the problem is advanced if that unpleasant reality is kept in mind. Once the trade-off relationship is clearly perceived, it is possible to state in a very general way what the optimal level of pollution is. I would state it as follows:

People enjoy watching penguins. They enjoy relatively clean air and smog-free vistas. Their health is improved by relatively clean water and air. Each of these benefits is a type of good or service. As a society we would be well advised to give up one washing machine if the resources that would have gone into that washing machine can yield greater human satisfaction when diverted into pollution control. We should give up one hospital if the resources thereby freed would yield more human satisfaction when devoted to elimination of noise in our cities. And so on, trade-off by trade-off, we should divert our productive capacities from the production of existing goods and services to the production of a cleaner, quieter, more pastoral nation up to—and no further than—the point at which we value more highly the next washing machine or hospital that we would have to do without than we value the next unit of environmental improvement that the diverted resources would create.

Now this proposition seems to me unassailable but so general and abstract as to be unhelpful—at least unadministerable in the form stated. It assumes we can measure in some way the incremental units of human satisfaction yielded by very different types of goods....But I insist that the proposition stated describes the result for which we should be striving—and again, that it is always useful to know what your target is even if your weapons are too crude to score a bull's eye.

ARGUMENT 25 ESSAY QUESTIONS

1. Does Taylor's biocentric egalitarianism conflict with our moral intuitions? If so, how? How much weight should our moral intuitions carry on this issue?
2. Who makes the stronger case—Taylor or Schmidtz? Explain.
3. Are you a biocentric egalitarianism? If so, why? If not, what is your view on the equality of all life?

SUGGESTIONS FOR FURTHER READING

J. Baird Callicott, "The Search for an Environmental Ethic," in *Matters of Life and Death* (New York: Random House, 1986).
Carl Cohen, "The Case Against Animal Rights," in the *New England Journal of Medicine*, 1986.

David DeGrazia, *Animal Rights: A Very Short Introduction* (Oxford: Oxford University Press, 2002).

Robert Elliot, "Environmental Ethics," in *A Companion to Ethics*, ed. Hugh LaFollette (Oxford: Blackwell, 1993), 284–93.

R. G. Frey, "Animals," in *The Oxford Handbook of Practical Ethics*, ed. Hugh LaFollette (New York: Oxford University Press, 2003), 161–87.

R. G. Frey, *Rights, Killing, and Suffering* (Oxford: Blackwell, 1983).

Lori Gruen, "Animals," in *A Companion to Ethics*, ed. Hugh LaFollette (Oxford: Blackwell, 1993), 343–53.

Garrett Hardin, "The Tragedy of the Commons," *Science* 162:1243–48, 13 December 1968.

Robert Heilbroner, "What Has Posterity Ever Done for Me?" *New York Times Magazine*, January 19, 1975.

Aldo Leopold, "The Land Ethic," in *A Sand County Almanac: And Sketches Here and There* (New York: Oxford University Press, 1981), 237–65.

Mary Midgley, *Animals and Why They Matter* (Harmondsworth, UK: Penguin, 1984).

James Rachels, *Created from Animals: The Moral Implications of Darwinism* (Oxford: Oxford University Press, 1990).

Tom Regan and Peter Singer, eds. *Animal Rights and Human Obligations*, 2nd ed. (Englewood Cliffs, NJ: Prentice-Hall, 1989).

Tom Regan, *The Case for Animal Rights* (Berkeley: University of California Press, 1983).

Holmes Rolston, III, "Values in and Duties to the Natural World," in *Ecology, Economics, Ethics: The Broken Circle* (New Haven, CT: Yale University Press, 1991), 73–96.

Roger Scruton, *Animal Rights and Wrongs* (London: Metro Publishing, 1998).

Peter Singer, *Animal Liberation*, 2nd ed. (New York: New York Review of Books, 1990).

Bonnie Steinbock, "Speciesism and the Idea of Equality," *Philosophy*, vol. 53, no. 204 (April 1978): 247–56.

Christopher D. Stone, "Should Trees Have Standing? Toward Legal Rights for Natural Objects" in *Should Trees Have Standing? Toward Legal Rights for Natural Objects* (Los Altos, CA: William Kaufman, 1974).

Cass R. Sunstein and Martha C. Nussbaum, eds., *Animal Rights* (New York: Oxford University Press, 2004).

Mary Anne Warren, "The Rights of the Nonhuman World," in *Environmental Philosophy*, eds. Robert Elliot and Arran Gare (State College: Pennsylvania State University Press, 1983).

Lynn White, Jr., "The Historical Roots of Our Ecological Crisis," *Science*, vol. 155 (1967).

CHAPTER 12

Economic Justice and Global Obligations

For millennia, the people of the world have been segregated into the haves and the have-nots, the well off and the painfully poor, the well fed and the slowly starving. In our era these separate and unequal domains persist as if they were ordained by laws of nature. Almost half the planet's population subsists on less than $2.50 a day. Of the earth's 6 billion inhabitants, 1 billion are hungry, and 2 billion are undernourished. Each day 25,000 adults and children die from hunger and related causes. Some 80 percent of the world's wealth (measured by gross domestic product) belongs to 17 percent of its people, the citizens of the relatively rich, developed nations. Twenty percent of the wealth is divided among the rest of humankind, the people of developing countries.[1]

What gives these facts ethical import is that the affluent—both individuals and nations—have the wherewithal to ease the suffering of the poor and hungry. Whatever the causes of the gulf between the haves and the have-nots, the haves can do much to bridge it, or at least pull many unfortunates from the brink. What, then, are the moral duties of the rich regarding the needy of the world? What are we—the secure and comfortable denizens of the West—obligated to do for the impoverished, starving, and dying of the Third World?

We can sort those who offer answers to these questions into three groups. Some argue that we have very strong duties to aid the poor and hungry in other countries, duties that demand substantial sacrifices from us. Others deny that we have any such obligations. And many take a middle path, holding that we should help the needy but not if the burden is excessive.

Those in the first group include strong egalitarians who argue that since all persons have equal moral worth, they are all entitled to equal portions of the world's essential goods such as food and water. We are therefore obligated to share the earth's resources with all

---

[1] Statistics from World Bank Development Research Group, "The Developing World Is Poorer Than We Thought," Worldbank.org, August 2008, http://www.worldbank.org/ (11 April 2009); UNICEF, "The State of the World's Children, 2005," UNICEF, 2005, http://www.unicef.org/sowc05/english/sowc05.pdf (11 April 2009); World Bank, "World Development Indicators 2008," Worldbank.org, 2008, http://www.worldbank.org/ (11 April 2009); United Nations Department of Public Information, "Millennium Development Goals: Fact Sheet," 25 September 2008.

FACTS AND FIGURES: World Hunger and Poverty

- It is estimated that 1 billion people go hungry, and 2 billion are undernourished.
- Almost half the world's children—1 billion—live in poverty.
- Each day, 30,000 children die due to poverty.
- Each year 10.9 million children under age five die in developing countries.
- In developing countries, nearly one quarter of the children are underweight and at risk for long-term health problems due to undernourishment.
- 1.4 billion people survive on $1.25 or less per day.
- Worldwide, 15 million children have been orphaned by HIV/AIDS.

- In 2005, the wealthiest 20 percent of the world was responsible for nearly 75 percent of consumption.

World Bank Development Research Group, "The Developing World Is Poorer Than We Thought," *Worldbank.org*, August 2008, http://www.worldbank.org/ (11 April 2009); UNICEF, "The State of the World's Children, 2005," *UNICEF*, 2005, http://www.unicef.org/sowc05/english/sowc05.pdf (11 April 2009); World Bank, "World Development Indicators 2008," *Worldbank.org*, 2008, http://www.worldbank.org/ (11 April 2009); United Nations Department of Public Information, "Millennium Development Goals: Fact Sheet," 25 September 2008; Global Issues, "Poverty Around the World," 12 November 2011, http://www.globalissues.org/article/4/poverty-around-the-world#WorldBanksPovertyEstimatesRevised (24 February 2012).

those in need. The resulting distribution may lower our standard of living, impoverish us, or threaten our survival, but share we must, in the name of equality.

This view, of course, is built on deontological, or nonconsequentialist, premises (see Chapter 2), but other positions urging strong duties to the needy are utilitarian. Peter Singer offers the most widely discussed argument of this kind as he presses for radical changes in how we the affluent live and how we think about aid to the needy. He contends that if we have the power to prevent a very bad thing from occurring, and if we can prevent it without "sacrificing anything morally significant," then we have a moral duty to do it.[2] Luxuries such as new clothes, for example, are not morally significant, so we should forgo them and give the money to famine relief. This principle, Singer says, establishes a person's obligation to help needy people even if they are far away and regardless of whether the person is the only one giving aid or one among many.

People in the second group hold that we have no duty to feed the hungry in distant lands and, in fact, have a duty *not* to feed them. Like Singer, many of them argue from a utilitarian perspective, but they reach a contrary conclusion. As they see it, the problems of poverty and starvation are due to uncontrolled population growth. In any inhabited area, the human population naturally increases over time and, if unchecked, eventually outpaces the food supply—the "carrying capacity" of the environment. The result is famine, a decimation of the inhabitants, and a return to a proper balance between population and carrying capacity. This tragic cycle thus "solves" the problem of famine and starvation. Giving the hungry inhabitants food will make the situation much worse by artificially enlarging the population still more, causing it to outstrip the carrying capacity even further. When the inevitable famine finally comes, it will be an even bigger catastrophe—causing an even greater loss of life—than before the food aid arrived. The conclusion to be drawn is that we should not give food to needy countries where population growth is unrestrained. Doing so leads to suffering and death on a vast scale.

[2] Peter Singer, "Famine, Affluence, and Morality," *Philosophy and Public Affairs* 1 (1972).

Others in the second group appeal to a restricted notion of rights. A right is a bona fide claim to something, an entitlement that imposes obligations on others. Rights can be either positive or negative. If a person has **negative rights**, then others have a duty *not to interfere* with her getting something. If she has **positive rights**, then others have a duty *to help her* get something. Most people assume that we have both negative and positive rights, but some assert that all our rights are negative. A person has no positive rights, they say, and therefore others are not obligated to help him or her acquire anything. Those who take this view would insist that we have no duty to aid poor or starving people in other countries. We of course should not do anything to harm them or to make their plight worse, but we are not obliged to send them food or medicine.

This negative-rights approach to aiding the needy does not, however, rule out charitable acts. Out of the goodness of our hearts, we might decide to help needy, distant people. But, the argument goes, we have no obligation to do so. If we refuse to send aid, we do no wrong.

People in the third group think we should make a reasonable, not exhaustive, effort to aid the needy. They generally recognize a **duty of beneficence**—the moral obligation to do good to others and avoid harming them—but hold that this duty must be weighed against other obligations or rights.

John Arthur, for example, contends that our moral code urges us to help others in need and to respect their rights, but we must also take into account our own rights. Suppose, he says, you meet someone who is blind or in need of a kidney, and you can prevent a great evil (blindness or death) by giving him one of your eyes or kidneys. Must you relinquish it? The answer is no:

> If anything is clear, however, it is that our code does not *require* such heroism; you are entitled to keep your second eye and kidney... The reason for this is often expressed in terms of rights; it's your body, you have a right to it, and that weighs against whatever duty you have to help. To sacrifice a kidney for a stranger is to do more than is required, it's heroic.... [O]ur code expects us to help people in need as well as to respect negative and positive rights. But we are entitled to invoke our own rights as justification for not giving to distant strangers or when the cost to us is substantial, as when we give an eye or kidney.[3]

Robert van Wyk argues in a Kantian vein that individuals have a duty to do their fair share to feed the hungry but that there are limits to personal beneficence. To relieve the suffering of others by providing them with the basic necessities of life is to treat them as ends in themselves. But a duty to devote your whole life to providing these necessities would require you to treat yourself as a mere means to an end:

> Of course a person might choose to make the rescuing of those in distress her special vocation, and it may be noble for her to do so, but to claim that if the needs of others are great enough she has a duty to surrender any choice about the direction of her own life is to claim that a person has a duty to be purely the means to meeting the needs of others, and so in fact a duty to love others not as oneself, but instead of oneself.[4]

---

[3] John Arthur, "World Hunger and Obligation: The Case Against Singer," in *Equality, Entitlements, and Distribution of Income* (1984).

[4] Robert N. van Wyk, "Perspectives on World Hunger and the Extent of Our Positive Duties," *Public Affairs Quarterly*, vol. 2, no. 2 (April 1988).

KEY TERMS

negative rights   positive rights   duty of beneficence

ARGUMENTS AND READINGS

---

26. HARDIN'S LIFEBOAT ARGUMENT AGAINST AIDING THE POOR

In "Living on a Lifeboat," Garrett Hardin argues that the affluent should not aid the poor and starving people of the world because doing so will only lead to disaster for everyone, rich and poor. Helping desperately needy, overpopulated countries is morally wrong. He makes his case using several metaphors, the "lifeboat" being the most memorable.

Imagine, he says, that the affluent nations are lifeboats carrying rich people in a sea dotted with the desperately poor, many of them trying to clamber aboard or seize some of the passengers' supplies. Each lifeboat has a limited carrying capacity, just as each rich nation does. For safety's sake, a lifeboat should carry fewer passengers than it can actually accommodate, just as a country should have a population small enough to guarantee excess carrying capacity to offset emergencies such as droughts or crop failures. No lifeboat can take on more passengers or give handouts without risking disaster for everyone. If all those trying to climb aboard are taken into a boat, it will capsize and everyone will drown. If only some of the poor people are let on board—enough to fill the craft to maximum capacity—the safety factor is eliminated and the boat will sink sooner or later. The third option, unthinkable to some, is to turn away all the poor. Many will perish, but the lucky few already on board will survive. Given these cruel realities, the morally right course for affluent nations is clear: do not aid the people of desperately poor, overpopulated countries.

Hardin bolsters his argument with another metaphor, "the tragedy of the commons." The commons is any land or resource that is open to all to exploit. In any arrangement based on a commons system—such as a public field where all shepherds can freely graze their sheep, or a social system in which all goods are shared alike—it is in each member's self-interest to use the system's resources to the maximum. It is in each shepherd's interest, for example, to graze as many sheep as possible to support his family. There is no incentive for him to think about the common good, to act responsibly so the field is not overgrazed and ruined for everyone. The result is disaster; the field is destroyed. This is the tragedy of the commons: "mutual ruin" from a well-meaning system of sharing.

Hardin claims that in a world where all resources are shared and reproduction in the impoverished countries is uncontrolled, the tragedy of the commons is inevitable. The catastrophe will come when rich countries let the poor inundate their lifeboats or when a world food bank becomes an international commons that shares the earth's food reserves. "For the foreseeable future," Hardin says, "survival demands that we govern our actions by the ethics of a lifeboat. Posterity will be ill served if we do not."[5]

Hardin's lifeboat ethics has many detractors. Some accuse his analysis of being simplistic. For one thing, they say, the metaphor implies that the rich lifeboats barely interact with the poor, but in the real world the rich countries have greatly affected the poor ones, and often for the worse. As some critics say,

> [B]y colonization and actual wars of commerce, and through the international marketplace, rich nations have arranged an exchange of goods that has maintained and even increased the economic imbalance between rich and poor nations.[6]

Others question Hardin's assertion that aiding the poor will inevitably increase their suffering:

> Granted, we can make things worse by merely giving food handouts....However, intelligent ways exist to aid, such as providing agricultural instruction and technological know-how to nations committed to responsible population policies, promoting mutually beneficial international trade agreements, and seeking ways to eradicate conditions that cause famine and malnutrition....But to dismiss these options out of hand and simply advocate pushing people off our lifeboat is as oversimplistic as it is cruel.[7]

Living on a Lifeboat

GARRETT HARDIN

Susanne Langer (1942) has shown that it is probably impossible to approach an unsolved problem save through the door of metaphor. Later, attempting to meet the demands of rigor, we may achieve some success in cleansing theory of metaphor, though our success is limited if we are unable to avoid using common language, which is shot through and

through with fossil metaphors. (I count no less than five in the preceding two sentences.)

From *Bioscience*, by Garrett Hardin. Copyright © 1974 by American Institute of Biological Sciences (AIBS). Reproduced with permission of American Institute of Biological Sciences.

---

[5] Garrett Hardin, "Living on a Lifeboat," *Science* 24 (1974).
[6] William W. Murdoch and Allan Oaten, "Population and Food: Metaphors and the Reality," *Bioscience* 25 (1975).
[7] Louis Pojman, 174.

Since metaphorical thinking is inescapable it is pointless merely to weep about our human limitations. We must learn to live with them, to understand them, and to control them. "All of us," said George Eliot in *Middlemarch*, "get our thoughts entangled in metaphors, and act fatally on the strength of them." To avoid unconscious suicide we are well advised to pit one metaphor against another. From the interplay of competitive metaphors, thoroughly developed, we may come closer to metaphor-free solutions to our problems.

No generation has viewed the problem of the survival of the human species as seriously as we have. Inevitably, we have entered this world of concern through the door of metaphor. Environmentalists have emphasized the image of the earth as a spaceship—Spaceship Earth. Kenneth Boulding (1966) is the principal architect of this metaphor. It is time, he says, that we replace the wasteful "cowboy economy" of the past with the frugal "spaceship economy" required for continued survival in the limited world we now see ours to be. The metaphor is notably useful in justifying pollution control measures.

Unfortunately, the image of a spaceship is also used to promote measures that are suicidal. One of these is a generous immigration policy, which is only a particular instance of a class of policies that are in error because they lead to the tragedy of the commons (Hardin 1968). These suicidal policies are attractive because they mesh with what we unthinkingly take to be the ideals of "the best people." What is missing in the idealistic view is an insistence that rights and responsibilities must go together. The "generous" attitude of all too many people results in asserting inalienable rights while ignoring or denying matching responsibilities.

For the metaphor of a spaceship to be correct the aggregate of people on board would have to be under unitary sovereign control (Ophuls 1974). A true ship always has a captain. It is conceivable that a ship could be run by a committee. But it could not possibly survive if its course were determined by bickering tribes that claimed rights without responsibilities.

What about Spaceship Earth? It certainly has no captain, and no executive committee. The United Nations is a toothless tiger, because

the signatories of its charter wanted it that way. The spaceship metaphor is used only to justify spaceship demands on common resources without acknowledging corresponding spaceship responsibilities.

An understandable fear of decisive action leads people to embrace "incrementalism"—moving toward reform by tiny stages. As we shall see, this strategy is counterproductive in the area discussed here if it means accepting rights before responsibilities. Where human survival is at stake, the acceptance of responsibilities is a precondition to the acceptance of rights, if the two cannot be introduced simultaneously.

LIFEBOAT ETHICS

Before taking up certain substantive issues let us look at an alternative metaphor, that of a lifeboat. In developing some relevant examples the following numerical values are assumed. Approximately two-thirds of the world is desperately poor, and only one-third is comparatively rich. The people in poor countries have an average per capita GNP (Gross National Product) of about $200 per year; the rich, of about $3,000. (For the United States it is nearly $5,000 per year.) Metaphorically, each rich nation amounts to a lifeboat full of comparatively rich people. The poor of the world are in other, much more crowded lifeboats. Continuously, so to speak, the poor fall out of their lifeboats and swim for a while in the water outside, hoping to be admitted to a rich lifeboat, or in some other way to benefit from the "goodies" on board. What should the passengers on a rich lifeboat do? This is the central problem of "the ethics of a lifeboat."

First we must acknowledge that each lifeboat is effectively limited in capacity. The land of every nation has a limited carrying capacity. The exact limit is a matter for argument, but the energy crunch is convincing more people every day that we have already exceeded the carrying capacity of the land. We have been living on "capital"—stored petroleum and coal—and soon we must live on income alone.

Let us look at only one lifeboat—ours. The ethical problem is the same for all, and is as follows. Here we sit, say 50 people in a lifeboat. To be generous, let us assume our boat has a capacity of 10 more, making 60. (This, however, is to violate the engineering principle of the "safety factor." A new plant disease or a bad change in the weather may decimate our population if we don't preserve some excess capacity as a safety factor.)

The 50 of us in the lifeboat see 100 others swimming in the water outside, asking for admission to the boat, or for handouts. How shall we respond to their calls? There are several possibilities.

One. We may be tempted to try to live by the Christian ideal of being "our brother's keeper," or by the Marxian ideal (Marx 1875) of "from each according to his abilities, to each according to his needs." Since the needs of all are the same, we take all the needy into our boat, making a total of 150 in a boat with a capacity of 60. The boat is swamped, and everyone drowns. Complete justice, complete catastrophe.

Two. Since the boat has an unused excess capacity of 10, we admit just 10 more to it. This has the disadvantage of getting rid of the safety factor, for which action we will sooner or later pay dearly. Moreover, *which* 10 do we let in? "First come, first served?" The best 10? The neediest 10? How do we *discriminate*? And what do we say to the 90 who are excluded?

Three. Admit no more to the boat and preserve the small safety factor. Survival of the people in the lifeboat is then possible (though we shall have to be on our guard against boarding parties).

The last solution is abhorrent to many people. It is unjust, they say. Let us grant that it is.

"I feel guilty about my good luck," say some. The reply to this is simple: *Get out and yield your place to others.* Such a selfless action might satisfy the conscience of those who are addicted to guilt but it would not change the ethics of the lifeboat. The needy person to whom a guilt-addict yields his place will not himself feel guilty about his sudden good luck. (If he did he would not climb aboard.) The net result of conscience-stricken people relinquishing their unjustly held positions is the elimination of their kind of conscience from the lifeboat. The lifeboat, as it were, purifies itself of guilt. The ethics of the lifeboat persist, unchanged by such momentary aberrations.

This then is the basic metaphor within which we must work out our solutions. Let us enrich the image step by step with substantive additions from the real world.

REPRODUCTION

The harsh characteristics of lifeboat ethics are heightened by reproduction, particularly by reproductive differences. The people inside the lifeboats of the wealthy nations are doubling in numbers every 87 years; those outside are doubling every 35 years, on the average. And the relative difference in prosperity is becoming greater.

Let us, for a while, think primarily of the U.S. lifeboat. As of 1973 the United States had a population of 210 million people, who were increasing by 0.8% per year, that is, doubling in number every 87 years.

Although the citizens of rich nations are outnumbered two to one by the poor, let us imagine an equal number of poor people outside our lifeboat—a mere 210 million poor people reproducing at a quite different rate. If we imagine these to be the combined populations of Colombia, Venezuela, Ecuador, Morocco, Thailand, Pakistan, and the Philippines, the average rate of increase of the people "outside" is 3.3% per year. The doubling time of this population is 21 years.

Suppose that all these countries, and the United States, agreed to live by the Marxian ideal, "to each according to his needs," the ideal of most Christians as well. Needs, of course, are determined by population size, which is affected by reproduction. Every nation regards its rate of reproduction as a sovereign right. If our lifeboat were big enough in the beginning it might be possible to live *for a while* by Christian-Marxian ideals. *Might.*

Initially, in the model given, the ratio of non-Americans to Americans would be one to one. But consider what the ratio would be 87 years later. By this time Americans would have doubled to a population of 420 million. The other group (doubling every 21 years) would now have swollen to 3,540 million. Each American would have more than eight people to share with. How could the lifeboat possibly keep afloat?

All this involves extrapolation of current trends into the future, and is consequently suspect. Trends may change. Granted: but the change will not necessarily be favorable. If—as seems likely—the rate of population increase falls faster in the ethnic group presently inside the lifeboat than it does among those now outside, the future will turn out to be even worse than mathematics predicts, and sharing will be even more suicidal.

RUIN IN THE COMMONS

The fundamental error of the sharing ethics is that it leads to the tragedy of the commons. Under a system of private property the man (or group of men) who own property recognize their responsibility to care for it, for if they don't they will eventually suffer. A farmer, for instance, if he is intelligent, will allow no more cattle in a pasture than its carrying capacity justifies. If he overloads the pasture, weeds take over, erosion sets in, and the owner loses in the long run.

But if a pasture is run as a commons open to all, the right of each to use it is not matched by an operational responsibility to take care of it. It is no use asking independent herdsmen in a commons to act responsibly, for they dare not. The considerate herdsman who refrains from overloading the commons suffers more than a selfish one who says his needs are greater. (As Leo Durocher says, "Nice guys finish last.") Christian-Marxian idealism is counterproductive. That it *sounds* nice is no excuse. With distribution systems, as with individual morality, good intentions are no substitute for good performance.

A social system is stable only if it is insensitive to errors. To the Christian-Marxian idealist a selfish person is a sort of "error." Prosperity in the system of the commons cannot survive errors. If *everyone* would only restrain himself, all would be well; but it takes *only one less than everyone* to ruin a system of voluntary restraint. In a crowded world of less than perfect human beings—and we will never know any other—mutual ruin is inevitable in the commons. This is the core of the tragedy of the commons.

One of the major tasks of education today is to create such an awareness of the dangers of the commons that people will be able to recognize its many varieties, however disguised. There is pollution of the air and water because these media are treated as commons. Further growth of population and growth in the per capita conversion of natural resources into pollutants require that the system of the commons be modified or abandoned in the disposal of "externalities."

The fish populations of the oceans are exploited as commons, and ruin lies ahead. No technological invention can prevent this fate: in fact, all improvements in the art of fishing merely hasten the day of complete ruin. Only the replacement of the system of the commons with a responsible system can save oceanic fisheries.

The management of western range lands, though nominally rational, is in fact (under the steady pressure of cattle ranchers) often merely a government-sanctioned system of the commons, drifting toward ultimate ruin for both the rangelands and the residual enterprisers.

WORLD FOOD BANKS

In the international arena we have recently heard a proposal to create a new commons, namely an international depository of food reserves to which nations will contribute according to their abilities, and from which nations may draw according to their needs. Nobel laureate Norman Borlaug has lent the prestige of his name to this proposal.

A world food bank appeals powerfully to our humanitarian impulses. We remember John Donne's celebrated line, "Any man's death diminishes me." But before we rush out to see for whom the bell tolls let us recognize where the greatest political push for international granaries comes from, lest we be disillusioned later. Our experience with Public Law 480 clearly reveals the answer. This was the law that moved billions of dollars worth of U.S. grain to food-short, population-long countries during the past two decades. When P.L. 480 first came into being, a headline in the business magazine *Forbes* (Paddock and Paddock 1970) revealed the power behind it: "Feeding the World's Hungry Millions: How it will mean billions for U.S. business."

And indeed it did. In the years 1960 to 1970 a total of $7.9 billion was spent on the "Food for Peace" program, as P.L. 480 was called. During the years 1948 to 1970 an additional $49.9 billion were extracted from American taxpayers to pay for other economic aid programs, some of which went for food and food-producing machinery. (This figure does *not* include military aid.) That P.L. 480 was a give-away program was concealed. Recipient countries went through the motions of paying for P.L. 480 food—with IOU's. In December 1973 the charade was brought to an end as far as India was concerned when the United States "forgave"

India's $3.2 billion debt (Anonymous 1974). Public announcement of the cancellation of the debt was delayed for two months: one wonders why.

"Famine—1974!" (Paddock and Paddock 1970) is one of the few publications that points out the commercial roots of this humanitarian attempt. Though all U.S. taxpayers lost by P.L. 480, special interest groups gained handsomely. Farmers benefited because they were not asked to contribute the grain—it was bought from them by the taxpayers. Besides the direct benefit there was the indirect effect of increasing demand and thus raising prices of farm products generally. The manufacturers of farm machinery, fertilizers, and pesticides benefited by the farmers' extra efforts to grow more food. Grain elevators profited from storing the grain for varying lengths of time. Railroads made money hauling it to port, and shipping lines by carrying it overseas. Moreover, once the machinery for P.L. 480 was established an immense bureaucracy had a vested interest in its continuance regardless of its merits.

Very little was ever heard of these selfish interests when P.L. 480 was defended in public. The emphasis was always on its humanitarian effects. The combination of multiple and relatively silent selfish interests with highly vocal humanitarian apologists constitutes a powerful lobby for extracting money from taxpayers. Foreign aid has become a habit that can apparently survive in the absence of any known justification. A news commentator in a weekly magazine (Lansner 1974), after exhaustively going over all the conventional arguments for foreign aid—self-interest, social justice, political advantage, and charity—and concluding that none of the known arguments really held water, concluded: "So the search continues for some logically compelling reasons for giving aid … " In other words. *Act now, Justify later*—if ever. (Apparently a quarter of a century is too short a time to find the justification for expending several billion dollars yearly.)

The search for a rational justification can be short-circuited, by interjecting the word "emergency." Borlaug uses this word. We need to look sharply at it. What is an "emergency?" It is surely something like an accident, which is correctly defined as *an event that is certain to happen, though with a low frequency* (Hardin 1972a). A well-run organization prepares for everything that is certain, including accidents and emergencies. It budgets for them. It saves for them. It expects them—and mature decision-makers do not waste time complaining about accidents when they occur.

What happens if some organizations budget for emergencies and others do not? If each organization is solely responsible for its own well-being, poorly managed ones will suffer. But they should be able to learn from experience. They have a chance to mend their ways and learn to budget for infrequent but certain emergencies. The weather, for instance, always varies and periodic crop failures are certain. A wise and competent government saves out of the production of the good years in anticipation of bad years that are sure to come. This is not a new idea. The Bible tells us that Joseph taught this policy to Pharaoh in Egypt more than 2,000 years ago. Yet it is literally true that the vast majority of the governments of the world today have no such policy. They lack either the wisdom or the competence, or both. Far more difficult than the transfer of wealth from one country to another is the transfer of wisdom between sovereign powers or between generations.

"But it isn't their fault! How can we blame the poor people who are caught in an emergency? Why must we punish them?" The concepts of blame and punishment are irrelevant. The question is, what are the operational consequences of establishing a world food bank? If it is open to every country every time a need develops, slovenly rulers will not be motivated to take Joseph's advice. Why should they? Others will bail them out whenever they are in trouble.

Some countries will make deposits in the world food bank and others will withdraw from it: there will be almost no overlap. Calling such a depository-transfer unit a "bank" is stretching the metaphor of *bank* beyond its elastic limits. The proposers, of course, never call attention to the metaphorical nature of the word they use.

THE RATCHET EFFECT

An "international food bank" is really, then, not a true bank but a disguised one-way transfer device for moving wealth from rich countries to poor. In the absence of such a bank, in a world inhabited by individually responsible sovereign nations, the population of each nation would repeatedly go through a cycle. P2 is greater than P1, either in absolute numbers or because a deterioration of the food supply has removed the safety factor and produced a dangerously low ratio of resources to population. P2 may be said to represent a state of overpopulation, which becomes obvious upon the appearance of an "accident," e.g., a crop failure. If the "emergency" is not met by outside help, the population drops back to the "normal" level—the "carrying capacity" of the environment—or even below. In the absence of population control by a sovereign, sooner or later the population grows to P2 again and the cycle repeats. The long-term population curve (Hardin 1966) is an irregularly fluctuating one, equilibrating more or less about the carrying capacity.

A demographic cycle of this sort obviously involves great suffering in the restrictive phase, but such a cycle is normal to any independent country with inadequate population control. The third century theologian Tertullian (Hardin 1969a) expressed what must have been the recognition of many wise men when he wrote: 'The scourges of pestilence, famine, wars, and earthquakes have come to be regarded as a blessing to overcrowded nations, since they serve to prune away the luxuriant growth of the human race."

Only under a strong and farsighted sovereign—which theoretically could be the people themselves, democratically organized—can a population equilibrate at some set point below the carrying capacity, thus avoiding the paints normally caused by periodic and unavoidable disasters. For this happy state to be achieved it is necessary that those in power be able to contemplate with equanimity the "waste" of surplus food in times of bountiful harvests. It is essential that those in power resist the temptation to convert extra food into extra babies. On the public relations level it is necessary that the phrase "surplus food" be replaced by "safety factor."

But wise sovereigns seem not to exist in the poor world today. The most anguishing problems are created by poor countries that are governed by rulers insufficiently wise and powerful. If such countries can draw on a world food bank in times of "emergency," the population *cycle*...will be replaced by the population *escalator*...The input of food from a food bank acts as the pawl of a ratchet, preventing the population from retracing its steps to a lower level. Reproduction pushes the population upward, inputs from the world bank prevent its moving downward. Population size escalates, as does the absolute magnitude of "accidents" and "emergencies." The process is brought to an end only by the total collapse of the whole system, producing a catastrophe of scarcely imaginable proportions.

Such are the implications of the well-meant sharing of food in a world of irresponsible reproduction.

I think we need a new word for systems like this. The adjective "melioristic" is applied to systems that produce continual improvement; the English word is derived from the Latin *meliorare,* to become or make better. Parallel with this it would be useful to bring in the word *pejoristic* (from the Latin *pejorare,* to become or make worse). This word can be applied to those systems which, by their very nature, can be relied upon to make matters worse. A world food bank coupled with sovereign state irresponsibility in reproduction is an example of a pejoristic system.

This pejoristic system creates an unacknowledged commons. People have more motivation to draw from than to add to the common store. The license to make such withdrawals diminishes whatever motivation poor countries might otherwise have to control their populations. Under the guidance of this ratchet, wealth can be steadily moved in one direction only, from the slowly-breeding rich to the rapidly-breeding poor, the process finally coming to a halt only when all countries are equally and miserably poor.

All this is terribly obvious once we are acutely aware of the pervasiveness and danger of the commons. But many people still lack this awareness and the euphoria of the "benign demographic transition" (Hardin 1973) interferes with the realistic appraisal of pejoristic mechanisms. As concerns public policy, the deductions drawn from the benign demographic transition are these:

1) If the per capita GNP rises the birth rate will fall; hence, the rate of population increase will fall, ultimately producing ZPG (Zero Population Growth).

2) The long-term trend all over the world (including the poor countries) is of a rising per capita GNP (for which no limit is seen).

3) Therefore, all political interference in population matters is unnecessary; all we need to do is foster economic "development"—*note the metaphor*—and population problems will solve themselves.

Those who believe in the benign demographic transition dismiss the population escalator in the belief that each input of food from the world outside fosters development within a poor country, thus resulting in a drop in the rate of population increase. Foreign aid has proceeded on this assumption for more than two decades. Unfortunately it has produced no indubitable instance of the asserted effect. It has, however, produced a library of excuses. The air is filled with plaintive calls for more massive foreign aid appropriations so that the hypothetical melioristic process can get started.

The doctrine of demographic laissez-faire implicit in the hypothesis of the benign demographic transition is immensely attractive. Unfortunately there is more evidence against the melioristic system than there is for it (Davis 1963). On the historical side there are many counter-examples. The rise in per capita GNP in France and Ireland during the past century has been accompanied by a rise in population growth. In the 20 years following the Second World War the same positive correlation was noted almost everywhere in the world. Never in world history before 1950 did the worldwide population growth reach 1% per annum. Now the average population growth is over 2% and shows no signs of slackening.

On the theoretical side, the denial of the [population escalator] probably springs from the hidden acceptance of the "cowboy economy" that Boulding castigated. Those who recognize the limitations of a spaceship, if they are unable to achieve population control at a safe and comfortable level, accept the necessity of the corrective feedback of the population cycled....No one who knew in his bones that he was living on a true spaceship would countenance political support of the population escalator....

ECO-DESTRUCTION VIA THE GREEN REVOLUTION

The demoralizing effect of charity on the recipient has long been known. "Give a man a fish and he will eat for a day: teach him how to fish and he will eat for the rest of his days." So runs an ancient Chinese proverb. Acting on this advice the Rockefeller and Ford Foundations have financed a multipronged program for improving agriculture in the hungry nations. The result, known as the "Green Revolution," has been quite remarkable. "Miracle wheat" and "miracle rice" are splendid technological achievements in the realm of plant genetics.

Whether or not the Green Revolution can increase food production is doubtful (Harris 1972, Paddock 1970, Wilkes 1972), but in any event not particularly important. What is missing in this great and well-meaning humanitarian effort is a firm grasp of fundamentals. Considering the importance of the Rockefeller Foundation in this effort it is ironic that the late Alan Gregg, a much-respected vice-president of the Foundation, strongly expressed his doubts of the wisdom of all attempts to increase food production some two decades ago. (This was before Borlaug's work—supported by Rockefeller—had resulted in the development of "miracle wheat.") Gregg (1955) likened the growth and spreading of humanity over the surface of the earth to the metastasis of cancer in the human body, wryly remarking that "Cancerous growths demand food; but, as far as I know, they have never been cured by getting it."

"Man does not live by bread alone"—the scriptural statement has a rich meaning even in the material realm. Every human being born constitutes a draft on all aspects of the environment—food, air, water, unspoiled scenery, occasional and optional solitude, beaches, contact with wild animals, fishing, hunting—the list is long and incompletely known. Food can, perhaps, be significantly increased: but what about clean beaches, unspoiled forests, and solitude? If we satisfy the need for food in a growing population we necessarily decrease the supply of other goods, and thereby increase the difficulty of equitably allocating scarce goods (Hardin 1969b, 1972b).

The present population of India is 600 million, and it is increasing by 15 million per year. The environmental load of this population is already great. The forests of India are only a small fraction of what they were three centuries ago. Soil erosion, floods, and the psychological costs of crowding are serious. Every one of the net 15 million lives added each year stresses the Indian environment more severely. *Every life saved this year in a poor country diminishes the quality of life for subsequent generations.*

Observant critics have shown how much harm we wealthy nations have already done to poor nations through our well-intentioned but misguided attempts to help them (Paddock and Paddock 1973). Particularly reprehensible is our failure to carry out post-audits of these attempts (Farvar and Milton 1972), Thus have we shielded our tender consciences from knowledge of the harm we have done. Must we Americans continue to fail to monitor the consequences of our external "do-gooding?" If, for instance, we thoughtlessly make it possible for the present 600 million Indians to swell to 1,200 millions by the year 2001—as their present growth rate promises—will posterity in India thank *us* for facilitating an even greater destruction of *their* environment? Are good intentions ever a sufficient excuse for bad consequences?

IMMIGRATION CREATES A COMMONS
I come now to the final example of a commons in action, one for which the public is least prepared for rational discussion. The topic is at present enveloped by a great silence which reminds me of a comment made by Sherlock Holmes in A. Conan Doyle's story, "Silver Blaze." Inspector Gregory had asked, "Is there any point to which you would wish to draw my attention?" To this Holmes responded:

"To the curious incident of the dog in the night-time."

"The dog did nothing in the nighttime," said the Inspector.

"That was the curious incident," remarked Sherlock Holmes.

By asking himself what would repress the normal barking instinct of a watch dog Holmes realized that it must be the dog's recognition of his master as the criminal trespasser. In a similar way we should ask ourselves what repression keeps us from discussing something as important as immigration?

It cannot be that immigration is numerically of no consequence. Our government acknowledges a *net* inflow of 400,000 a year. Hard data are understandably lacking on the extent of illegal entries, but a not implausible figure is 600,000 per year

(Buchanan 1973). The natural increase of the resident population is now about 1.7 million per year. This means that the yearly gain from immigration is at least 19%, and may be 37%, of the total increase. It is quite conceivable that educational campaigns like that of Zero Population Growth, Inc., coupled with adverse social and economic factors—inflation, housing shortage, depression, and loss of confidence in national leaders—may lower the fertility of American women to a point at which all of the yearly increase in population would be accounted for by immigration. Should we not at least ask if that is what we want? How curious it is that we so seldom discuss immigration these days!

Curious, but understandable—as one finds out the moment he publicly questions the wisdom of the status quo in immigration. He who does so is promptly charged with *isolationism, bigotry, prejudice, ethnocentrism, chauvinism,* and *selfishness.* These are hard accusations to bear. It is pleasanter to talk about other matters, leaving immigration policy to wallow in the cross-currents of special interests that take no account of the good of the whole—*or of the interests of posterity.*

We Americans have a bad conscience because of things we said in the past about immigrants. Two generations ago the popular press was rife with references to *Dagos, Wops, Pollacks, Japs, Chinks,* and *Krauts*—all pejorative terms which failed to acknowledge our indebtedness to Goya, Leonardo, Copernicus, Hiroshige, Confucius, and Bach. Because the implied inferiority of foreigners was *then* the justification for keeping them out, it is *now* thoughtlessly assumed that restrictive policies can only be based on the assumption of immigrant inferiority. *This is not so.*

Existing immigration laws exclude idiots and known criminals; future laws will almost certainly continue this policy. But should we also consider the quality of the average immigrant, as compared with the quality of the average resident? Perhaps we should, perhaps we shouldn't. (What is "quality" anyway?) But the quality issue is not our concern here.

From this point on, *it will be assumed that immigrants and native-born citizens are of exactly equal quality,* however quality may be defined. The focus is only on quantity. The conclusions reached depend on nothing else, so all charges of ethnocentrism are irrelevant.

World food banks move food to the people, thus facilitating the exhaustion of the environment of the poor. By contrast, unrestricted immigration moves people to the food, thus speeding up the destruction of the environment in rich countries. Why poor people should want to make this transfer is no mystery: but why should rich hosts encourage it? This transfer, like the reverse one, is supported by both selfish interests and humanitarian impulses.

The principal selfish interest in unimpeded immigration is easy to identify: it is the interest of the employers of cheap labor, particularly that needed for degrading jobs. We have been deceived about the forces of history by the lines of Emma Lazarus inscribed on the Statue of Liberty:

> Give me your tired, your poor
> Your huddled masses yearning to
>   breathe free,
> The wretched refuse of your teeming
>   shore,
> Send these, the homeless, tempest-
>   tossed, to me:
> I lift my lamp beside the golden door.

The image is one of an infinitely generous earth-mother, passively opening her arms to hordes of immigrants who come here on their own initiative. Such an image may have been adequate for the early days of colonization, but by the time these lines were written (1886) the force for immigration was largely manufactured inside our own borders by factory and mine owners who sought cheap labor not to be found among laborers already here. One group of foreigners after another was thus enticed into the United States to work at wretched jobs for wretched wages.

At present, it is largely the Mexicans who are being so exploited. It is particularly to the advantage of certain employers that there be many illegal immigrants. Illegal immigrant workers dare not complain about their working conditions for fear of being repatriated. Their presence reduces the bargaining power of all Mexican-American laborers. Cesar Chavez has repeatedly pleaded with congressional committees to close the doors to more Mexicans so that those here can negotiate effectively for higher wages and decent working conditions. Chavez understands the ethics of a lifeboat.

The interests of the employers of cheap labor are well served by the silence of the intelligentsia of the country. WASPS—White Anglo-Saxon Protestants—are particularly reluctant to call for a closing of the doors to immigration for fear of being called ethnocentric bigots. It was, therefore, an occasion of pure delight for this particular WASP to be present at a meeting when the points he would like to have made were made better by a non-WASP speaking to other non-WASPS. It was in Hawaii, and most of the people in the room were second-level Hawaiian officials of Japanese ancestry. All Hawaiians are keenly aware of the limits of their environment, and the speaker had asked how it might be practically and constitutionally possible to close the doors to more immigrants to the islands. (To Hawaiians, immigrants from the other 49 states are as much of a threat as those from other nations. There is only so much room in the islands, and the islanders know it. Sophistical arguments that imply otherwise do not impress them.)

Yet the Japanese-Americans of Hawaii have active ties with the land of their origin. This point was raised by a Japanese-American member of the audience who asked the Japanese-American speaker: "But how can we shut the doors now? We have many friends and relations in Japan that we'd like to bring to Hawaii some day so that they can enjoy this beautiful land."

The speaker smiled sympathetically and responded slowly: "Yes, but we have children now and someday we'll have grandchildren. We can bring more people here from Japan only by giving away some of the land that we hope to pass on to our grandchildren some day. What right do we have to do that?"

To be generous with one's own possessions is one thing; to be generous with posterity's is quite another. This, I think, is the point that must be gotten across to those who would, from a commendable love of distributive justice, institute a ruinous system of the commons, either in the form of a world food bank or that of unrestricted immigration. Since every speaker is a member of some ethnic group it is always possible to charge him with ethnocentrism. But even after purging an argument of ethnocentrism the rejection of the commons is still valid and necessary if we are to save at least some parts of the world from environmental ruin. Is it not desirable that at least some of the grandchildren of people now living should have a decent place in which to live?

THE ASYMMETRY OF DOOR-SHUTTING

We must now answer this telling point: "How can you justify slamming the door once you're inside? You say that immigrants should be kept out. But aren't we all immigrants, or the descendants of immigrants? Since we refuse to leave, must we not, as a matter of justice and symmetry, admit all others?"

It is literally true that we Americans of non-Indian ancestry are the descendants of thieves. Should we not, then, "give back" the land to the Indians; that is, give it to the now-living Americans of Indian ancestry? As an exercise in pure logic I see no way to reject this proposal. Yet I am unwilling to live by it; and I know no one who is. Our reluctance to embrace pure justice may spring from pure selfishness. On the other hand, it may arise from an unspoken recognition of consequences that have not yet been clearly spelled out.

Suppose, becoming intoxicated with pure justice, we "Anglos" should decide to turn our land over to the Indians. Since all our other wealth has also been derived from the land, we would have to give that to the Indians, too. Then what would we non-Indians do? Where would we go? There is no open land in the world on which men without capital can make their living (and not much unoccupied land on which men with capital can either). Where would 209 million putatively justice-loving, non-Indian, Americans go? Most of them—in the persons of their ancestors—came from Europe, but they wouldn't be welcomed back there. Anyway, Europeans have no better title to their land than we to ours. They also would have to give up their homes. (But to whom? And where would *they* go?)

Clearly, the concept of pure justice produces an infinite regress. The law long ago invented statutes of limitations to justify the rejection of pure justice, in the interest of preventing massive disorder. The law zealously defends property rights—but only

recent property rights. It is as though the physical principle of exponential decay applies to property rights. Drawing a line in time may be unjust, but any other action is practically worse.

We are all the descendants of thieves, and the world's resources are inequitably distributed, but we must begin the journey to tomorrow from the point where we are today. We cannot remake the past. We cannot, without violent disorder and suffering, give land and resources back to the "original" owners—who are dead anyway.

We cannot safely divide the wealth equitably among all present peoples, so long as people reproduce at different rates, because to do so would guarantee that our grandchildren—everyone's grandchildren—would have only a ruined world to inhabit.

MUST EXCLUSION BE ABSOLUTE?

To show the logical structure of the immigration problem I have ignored many factors that would enter into real decisions made in a real world. No matter how convincing the logic may be it is probable that we would want, from time to time, to admit a few people from the outside to our lifeboat. Political refugees in particular are likely to cause us to make exceptions: We remember the Jewish refugees from Germany after 1933, and the Hungarian refugees after 1956. Moreover, the interests of national defense, broadly conceived, could justify admitting many men and women of unusual talents, whether refugees or not. (This raises the quality issue, which is not the subject of this essay.)

Such exceptions threaten to create runaway population growth inside the lifeboat, i.e., the receiving country. However, the threat can be neutralized by a population policy that includes immigration. An effective policy is one of flexible control.

Suppose, for example, that the nation has achieved a stable condition of ZPG, which (say) permits 1.5 million births yearly. We must suppose that an acceptable system of allocating birth-rights to potential parents is in effect. Now suppose that an inhumane regime in some other part of the world creates a horde of refugees, and that there is a widespread desire to admit some to our country. At the same time, we do not want to sabotage our population control system. Clearly, the rational path to pursue is the following. If we decide to admit 100,000 refugees this year we should compensate for this by reducing the allocation of birth-rights in the following year by a similar amount, that is downward to a total of 1.4 million. In that way we could achieve both humanitarian and population control goals. (And the refugees would have to accept the population controls of the society that admits them. It is not inconceivable that they might be given proportionately fewer rights than the native population.)

In a democracy, the admission of immigrants should properly be voted on. But by whom? It is not obvious. The usual rule of a democracy is votes for all. But it can be questioned whether a universal franchise is the most just one in a case of this sort. Whatever benefits there are in the admission of immigrants presumably accrue to everyone. But the costs would be seen as falling most heavily on potential parents, some of whom would have to postpone or forego having their (next) child because of the influx of immigrants. The double question *Who benefits? Who pays?* suggests that a restriction of the usual democratic franchise would be appropriate and just in this case. Would our particular quasi-democratic form of government be flexible enough to institute such a novelty? If not, the majority might, out of humanitarian motives, impose an unacceptable burden (the foregoing of parenthood) on a minority, thus producing political instability.

Plainly many new problems will arise when we consciously face the immigration question and seek rational answers. No workable answers can be found if we ignore population problems. And—if the argument of this essay is correct—so long as there is no true world government to control reproduction everywhere it is impossible to survive in dignity if we are to be guided by Spaceship ethics. Without a world government that is sovereign in reproductive matters mankind lives, in fact, on a number of sovereign lifeboats. For the foreseeable future survival demands that we govern our actions by the ethics of a lifeboat. Posterity will be ill served if we do not.

REFERENCES

Anonymous. 1974. *Wall Street Journal* 19 Feb.

Borlaug, N. 1973. Civilization's future: a call for international granaries. *Bull. At. Sci.* 29: 7–15.

Boulding, K. 1966. The economics of the coming Spaceship earth. *In* H. Jarrett, ed. *Environmental Quality in a Growing Economy.* Johns Hopkins Press, Baltimore.

Buchanan, W. 1973. Immigration statistics. *Equilibrium* 1(3): 16–19.

Davis, K. 1963. Population. *Sci. Amer.* 209(3): 62–71.

Farvar, M. T., and J. P. Milton. 1972. *The Careless Technology.* Natural History Press, Garden City, N.Y.

Gregg, A. 1955. A medical aspect of the population problem. *Science* 121:681–682.

Hardin, G. 1966. Chap. 9 in *Biology: Its Principles and Implications,* 2nd ed. Freeman, San Francisco.

———. 1968. The tragedy of the commons. *Science* 162:1243–1248.

———. 1969a Page 18 in *Population, Evolution, and Birth Control,* 2nd ed. Freeman, San Francisco.

———. 1969b. The economics of wilderness. *Nat. Hist.* 78(6): 20–27.

———. 1972a. Pages 81–82 in *Exploring New Ethics for Survival: The Voyage of the Spaceship Beagle.* Viking, N.Y.

———. 1972b. Preserving quality on Spaceship Earth. *In* J. B. Trefethen, ed. Transactions of the Thirty-Seventh North American Wildlife and Natural Resources Conference. Wildlife Management Institute, Washington, D.C.

———. 1973. Chap. 23 in *Stalking the Wild Taboo.* Kaufmann, Los Altos, Calif.

Harris, M. 1972. How green the revolution. *Nat Hist.* 81(3): 28–30.

Langer, S. K. 1942. *Philosophy in a New Key.* Harvard University Press, Cambridge.

Lansner, K. 1974. Should foreign aid begin at home? *Newsweek,* 11 Feb., p. 32.

Marx, K. 1875. Critique of the Gotha program. Page 388 in R. C. Tucker, ed. *The Marx-Engels Reader.* Norton, N.Y., 1972.

Ophuls, W. 1974. The scarcity society. *Harpers* 248(1487): 47–52.

Paddock, W. C. 1970. How green is the green revolution? *BioScience* 20: 897–902.

Paddock, W., and E. Paddock. 1973. *We Don't Know How.* Iowa State University Press, Ames, Iowa.

Paddock, W., and P. Paddock. 1967. *Famine—1975!* Little, Brown, Boston.

Wilkes, H. G. 1972. The green revolution. *Environment* 14(8): 32–39.

A Critique of Lifeboat Ethics

WILLIAM W. MURDOCH AND ALLAN OATEN

Should rich countries provide food, fertilizers, technical assistance, and other aid to poor countries? The obvious answer is "yes." It is natural to want to fight poverty, starvation, and disease, to help raise living standards and eliminate suffering.

Yet, after 25 years of aid, diets and living standards in many poor countries have improved little, owing partly to the population explosion that occurred during these same years. Death rates in poor countries dropped sharply in the 1940's and 1950's, to around 14/1,000 at present, while their birth rates declined very little, remaining near 40/1,000. Some populations are now growing faster than their food supply.

As a result an apparently powerful argument against aid is increasingly heard. Its premise is simply stated. "More food means more babies" (Hardin 1969). Our benevolence leads to a spiral that can result only in disaster: aid leads to increased populations, which require more aid, which leads.... This premise mandates a radically new policy: rich countries can perhaps provide contraceptives to poor countries, but they should not provide food, help increase food production, or help combat poverty or disease.

This policy would result in the agonizing deaths, by starvation and disease, of millions of people. Consequently, one expects its advocates to have arrived at it reluctantly, forced to suppress their humanitarian feelings by inexorable logic and the sheer weight of evidence. Its apparent brutality seems a sure guarantee of its realism and rationality.

We believe that this allegedly realistic "nonhelp" policy is in fact mistaken as well as callous; that the premise on which it is based is at best a half-truth; and that the arguments adduced in its support are not only erroneous, but often exhibit indifference to both the complexities of the problem and much of the available data. We also believe that the evidence shows better living standards and lower population growth rates to be complementary, not contradictory; that aid programs carefully designed to

benefit the poorest people can help to achieve both of these ends; and that such programs, though difficult to devise and carry out, are not beyond either the resources or the ingenuity of the rich countries.

In the next two sections, we analyze some of the standard arguments in support of nonhelp policies, by focusing first on the article "Living on a Lifeboat" (Hardin 1974) and then on "The Tragedy of the Commons" (Hardin 1968). We will consider the long-term effects of nonhelp policies and some possible reasons for their widespread appeal. Then we will summarize some of the evidence about birth rates that is available and seems relevant. This evidence suggests that if we are serious about halting the food-population spiral and minimizing deaths from starvation and disease (in the long-term as well as the short), then it may be more rational to help than to stand back and watch. Finally, we will estimate the costs of some aid and discuss some difficulties in achieving reduced birth rates.

MISLEADING METAPHORS

The "lifeboat" article actually has two messages. The first is that our immigration policy is too generous. This will not concern us here. The second, and more important, is that by helping poor nations we will bring disaster to rich and poor alike:

> Metaphorically, each rich nation amounts to a lifeboat full of comparatively rich people. The poor of the world are in other, much more crowded lifeboats. Continuously, so to speak, the poor fall out of their lifeboats and swim for a while in the water outside, hoping to be admitted to a rich lifeboat, or in some other way to benefit from the "goodies" on board. What should the passengers on a rich lifeboat do? This is the central problem of "the ethics of a lifeboat." (Hardin 1974, p. 561)

"Population and Food: Metaphors and the Reality" by William W. Murdoch and Allen Oaten, *Bioscience*, #25, 1975, 561–567. © American Institute of Biological Sciences.

Among these so-called "goodies" are food supplies and technical aid such as that which led to the Green Revolution. Hardin argues that we should withhold such resources from poor nations on the grounds that they help to maintain high rates of population increase, thereby making the problem worse. He foresees the continued supplying and increasing production of food as a process that will be "brought to an end only by the total collapse of the whole system, producing a catastrophe of scarcely imaginable proportions" (p. 564).

Turning to one particular mechanism for distributing these resources, Hardin claims that a world food bank is a commons—people have more motivation to draw from it than to add to it; it will have a ratchet or escalator effect on population because inputs from it will prevent population declines in over-populated countries. Thus "wealth can be steadily moved in one direction only, from the slowly-breeding rich to the rapidly-breeding poor, the process finally coming to a halt only when all countries are equally and miserably poor" (p. 565). Thus our help will not only bring ultimate disaster to poor countries, but it will also be suicidal for us.

As for the "benign demographic transition" to low birth rates, which some aid supporters have predicted, Hardin states flatly that the weight of evidence is against this possibility.

Finally, Hardin claims that the plight of poor nations is partly their own fault: "wise sovereigns seem not to exist in the poor world today. The most anguishing problems are created by poor countries that are governed by rulers insufficiently wise and powerful." Establishing a world food bank will exacerbate this problem: "slovenly rulers" will escape the consequences of their incompetence—"Others will bail them out whenever they are in trouble"; "Far more difficult than the transfer of wealth from one country to another is the transfer of wisdom between sovereign powers or between generations" (p. 563).

What arguments does Hardin present in support of these opinions? Many involve metaphors: lifeboat, commons, and ratchet or escalator. These metaphors are crucial to his thesis, and it is, therefore, important for us to examine them critically.

The lifeboat is the major metaphor. It seems attractively simple, but it is in fact simplistic and obscures important issues. As soon as we try to use it to compare various policies, we find that most relevant details of the actual situation are either missing or distorted in the lifeboat metaphor. Let us list some of these details.

- Most important, perhaps, Hardin's lifeboats barely interact. The rich lifeboats may drop some handouts over the side and perhaps repel a boarding party now and then, but generally they live their own lives. In the real world, nations interact a great deal, in ways that affect food supply and population size and growth, and the effect of rich nations on poor nations has been strong and not always benevolent.

First, by colonization and actual wars of commerce, and through the international marketplace, rich nations have arranged an exchange of goods that has maintained and even increased the economic imbalance between rich and poor nations. Until recently we have taken or otherwise obtained cheap raw material from poor nations and sold them expensive manufactured goods that they cannot make themselves. In the United States, the structure of tariffs and internal subsidies discriminates selectively against poor nations. In poor countries, the concentration on cash crops rather than on food crops, a legacy of colonial times, is now actively encouraged by western multinational corporations (Barraclough 1975). Indeed, it is claimed that in famine-stricken Sahelian Africa, multinational agribusiness has recently taken land out of food production for cash crops (Transnational Institute 1974). Although we often self-righteously take the "blame" for lowering the death rates of poor nations during the 1940's and 1950's, we are less inclined to accept responsibility for the effects of actions that help maintain poverty and hunger. Yet poverty directly contributes to the high birth rates that Hardin views with such alarm.

Second, U.S. foreign policy, including foreign aid programs, has favored "pro-Western" regimes, many of which govern in the interests of a wealthy elite and some of which are savagely repressive. Thus, it has often subsidized a gross maldistribution of income and has supported political leaders who have opposed most of the social changes that can lead to reduced birth rates. In this light, Hardin's pronouncements on the alleged wisdom gap between poor leaders and our own, and the difficulty of filling it, appear as a grim joke: our response to leaders with the power and wisdom Hardin yearns for has often been to try to replace them or their policies as soon as possible. Selective giving and withholding of both military and nonmilitary aid has been an important ingredient of our efforts to maintain political leaders we like and to remove those we do not. Brown (1974b), after noting that the withholding of U.S. food aid in 1973 contributed to the downfall of the Allende government in Chile, comments that "although Americans decry the use of petroleum as a political weapon, calling it 'political blackmail,' the United States has been using food aid for political purposes for twenty years—and describing this as 'enlightened diplomacy.'"

- Both the quantity and the nature of the supplies on a lifeboat are fixed. In the real world, the quantity has strict limits, but these are far from having been reached (University of California Food Task Force 1974). Nor are we forced to devote fixed proportions of our efforts and energy to automobile travel, pet food, packaging, advertising, corn-fed beef, "defense," and other diversions, many of which cost far more than foreign aid does. The fact is that enough food is now produced to feed the world's population adequately. That people are malnourished is due to distribution and to economics, not to agricultural limits (United Nations Economic and Social Council 1974).
- Hardin's lifeboats are divided merely into rich and poor, and it is difficult to talk about birth rates on either. In the real world, however, there are striking differences among the birth rates of the poor countries and even among the birth rates of different parts of single countries. These differences appear to be related to social conditions (also absent from lifeboats) and may guide us to effective aid policies.
- Hardin's lifeboat metaphor not only conceals facts, but misleads about the effects of his proposals. The rich lifeboat can raise the ladder and sail away. But in real life, the problem will not

necessarily go away just because it is ignored. In the real world, there are armies, raw materials in poor nations, and even outraged domestic dissidents prepared to sacrifice their own and others' lives to oppose policies they regard as immoral.

No doubt there are other objections. But even this list shows the lifeboat metaphor to be dangerously inappropriate for serious policy making because it obscures far more than it reveals. Lifeboats and "lifeboat ethics" may be useful topics for those who are shipwrecked; we believe they are worthless—indeed detrimental—in discussions of food-population questions.

The ratchet metaphor is equally flawed. It, too, ignores complex interactions between birth rates and social conditions (including diets), implying as it does that more food will simply mean more babies. Also, it obscures the fact that the decrease in death rates has been caused at least as much by developments such as DDT, improved sanitation, and medical advances, as by increased food supplies, so that cutting out food aid will not necessarily lead to population declines.

The lifeboat article is strangely inadequate in other ways. For example, it shows an astonishing disregard for recent literature. The claim that we can expect no "benign demographic transition" is based on a review written more than a decade ago (Davis 1963). Yet, events and attitudes are changing rapidly in poor countries: for the first time in history, most poor people live in countries with birth control programs; with few exceptions, poor nations are somewhere on the demographic transition to lower birth rates (Demeny 1974); the population-food squeeze is now widely recognized, and governments of poor nations are aware of the relationship. Again, there is a considerable amount of evidence that birth rates can fall rapidly in poor countries given the proper social conditions (as we will discuss later); consequently, crude projections of current population growth rates are quite inadequate for policy making.

THE TRAGEDY OF THE COMMONS

Throughout the lifeboat article, Hardin bolsters his assertions by reference to the "commons" (Hardin 1968). The thesis of the commons, therefore, needs critical evaluation.

Suppose several privately owned flocks, comprising 100 sheep altogether, are grazing on a public commons. They bring in an annual income of $1.00 per sheep. Fred, a herdsman, owns only one sheep. He decides to add another. But 101 is too many: the commons is overgrazed and produces less food. The sheep lose quality and income drops to 90¢ per sheep. Total income is now $90.90 instead of $100.00. Adding the sheep has brought an overall loss. But Fred has gained: *his* income is $1.80 instead of $1.00. The gain from the additional sheep, which is his alone, outweighs the loss from overgrazing, which he shares. Thus he promotes his interest at the expense of the community.

This is the problem of the commons, which seems on the way to becoming an archetype. Hardin, in particular, is not inclined to underrate its importance: "One of the major tasks of education today is to create such an awareness of the dangers of the commons that people will be able to recognize its many varieties, however disguised" (Hardin 1974, p. 562) and "All this is terribly obvious once we are acutely aware of the pervasiveness and danger of the commons. But many people still lack this awareness…" (p. 565).

The "commons" affords a handy way of classifying problems: the lifeboat article reveals that sharing, a generous immigration policy, world food banks, air, water, the fish populations of the ocean, and the western range lands are, or produce, a commons. It is also handy to be able to dispose of policies one does not like as "only a particular instance of a class of policies that are in error because they lead to the tragedy of the commons" (p. 561).

But no metaphor, even one as useful as this, should be treated with such awe. Such shorthand can be useful, but it can also mislead by discouraging thought and obscuring important detail. To dismiss a proposal by suggesting that "all you need to know about this proposal is that it institutes a commons and is, therefore, bad" is to assert that the proposed commons is worse than the original problem. This might be so if the problem of the commons were, indeed, a tragedy—that is, if it were insoluble. But it is not.

Hardin favors private ownership as the solution (either through private property or the selling of pollution rights). But, of course, there are solutions other than private ownership; and private ownership itself is no guarantee of carefully husbanded resources.

One alternative to private ownership of the commons is communal ownership of the sheep—or, in general, of the mechanisms and industries that exploit the resource—combined with communal planning for management. (Note, again, how the metaphor favors one solution: perhaps the "tragedy" lay not in the commons but in the sheep. "The Tragedy of the Privately Owned Sheep" lacks zing, unfortunately.) Public ownership of a commons has been tried in Peru to the benefit of the previously privately owned anchoveta fishery (Gulland 1975). The communally owned agriculture of China does not seem to have suffered any greater overexploitation than that of other Asian nations.

Another alternative is cooperation combined with regulation. For example, Gulland (1975) has shown that Antarctic whale stocks (perhaps the epitome of a commons since they are internationally exploited and no one owns them) are now being properly managed, and stocks are increasing. This has been achieved through cooperation in the International Whaling Commission, which has by agreement set limits to the catch of each nation.

In passing, Hardin's private ownership argument is not generally applicable to nonrenewable resources. Given discount rates, technology substitutes, and no more than an average regard for posterity, privately owned nonrenewable resources, like oil, coal and minerals, are mined at rates that produce maximum profits, rather than at those rates that preserve them for future generations.

Thus, we must reject the temptation to use the commons metaphor as a substitute for analysis. Not all commons are the same: they differ in their origin, their nature, the type and seriousness of the problems they cause, the solutions that are appropriate for them, and the difficulty of implementing those solutions. In particular, we cannot rule out a proposal just because someone calls it a commons; a "solved" or benign commons may be the correct approach to some problems.

ON MALIGN NEGLECT
Hardin implies that nonhelp policies offer a solution to the world population-food problem. But what sort of solution would in fact occur?

Nonhelp policies would have several effects not clearly described in "Lifeboat" (Hardin 1974). First, it is not true that people in poor countries "convert extra food into extra babies" (p. 564). They convert it into longer lives. Denying them food will not lower birth rates; it will increase death rates.

These increases might not take effect immediately after the withdrawal of aid. Increases in local food production and improvements in sanitation and medicine would probably allow populations to continue growing for some time. (Death rates would need to increase almost three-fold to stabilize them.) Thus, in the future we could expect much larger populations in poor countries, living in greater misery than today. The negative relation between well-being and family size could easily lead to even higher birth rates. A "solution" that puts us back to prewar birth and death rates, at even higher population levels, is certainly not a satisfactory permanent solution.

Second, the rich countries cannot remain indifferent to events in poor countries. A poor country or a group of poor countries that controls supplies of a vital raw material, for example, may well want to use this leverage to its advantage; it may be very uncompromising about it, especially if its need is desperate and its attitude resentful, as would be likely. Just how intolerable this situation would be to the rich countries can be guessed at by recent hints of war being an acceptable means for the United States to ensure itself adequate supplies of oil at a "reasonable" price.

War is an option open to poor countries, too. China and India have nuclear weapons; others can be expected to follow. With Hardin's policies, they may feel they have little to lose, and the rich countries have a great deal to lose.

Thus we could look foward to continuing, and probably increasing, interference in and manipulation of the increasingly miserable poor countries by the rich countries. We do not believe this is a stable situation. One or more poor countries will surely want to disrupt it; recent events show that our ability to prevent this is limited. Alternatively, in the future, one or more of the rich countries may decide to help poor countries reduce their birth rates, but will then be faced with an even greater problem than we face today. In sum, malign neglect

of poor nations is not likely to cause the problem to go away.

If Hardin's proposals are so defective, why are they attractive to so many people? We have already discussed Hardin's use of oversimplified metaphors, but there are other temptations.

An obvious one is the presentation of false choices: either we continue what we are doing, or we do nothing. Aid is either effective or ineffective; much of our aid has been ineffective, so all aid is, and it always will be. Such absolute positions are tempting because they save thought, justify inaction, never need reconsideration, and convey an impression of sophisticated cynicism. But they do not conform to the facts. Intelligent and effective aid, though difficult, is possible.

The apparent callousness of Hardin's proposals is itself a temptation. There is an implication that these policies are so brutal that they would not be proposed without good reasons. Conversely, those who argue for increased aid can be dismissed as "highly vocal humanitarian apologists" or "guilt addicts" (Hardin 1974, pp. 563 and 562). The implication is that these views *could* arise from unreasoning emotion, so therefore they *must* arise this way. Proposals for increased aid are then "plaintive cries" produced by guilt, bad conscience, anxiety, and misplaced Christian or Marxist idealism. But such argument by association is plainly misleading. Benign policies can also be the most rational; callous policies can be foolish.

BIRTH RATES: AN ALTERNATIVE VIEW

Is the food-population spiral inevitable? A more optimistic, if less comfortable, hypothesis, presented by Rich (1973) and Brown (1974a), is increasingly tenable: contrary to the "ratchet" projection, population growth rates are affected by many complex conditions beside food supply. In particular, a set of socioeconomic conditions can be identified that motivate parents to have fewer children; under these conditions, birth rates can fall quite rapidly, sometimes even before birth control technology is available. Thus, population growth can be controlled more effectively by intelligent human intervention that sets up the appropriate conditions than by doing nothing and trusting to "natural population cycles."

These conditions are: parental confidence about the future, an improved status of women, and literacy. They require low infant mortality rates, widely available rudimentary health care, increased income and employment, and an adequate diet above subsistence levels.... Expenditure on schools (especially elementary schools), appropriate health services (especially rural paramedical services), and agricultural reform (especially aid to small farmers) will be needed, and foreign aid can help here. It is essential that these improvements be spread across the population; aid can help here, too, by concentrating on the poor nations' poorest people, encouraging necessary institutional and social reforms, and making it easier for poor nations to use their own resources and initiative to help themselves. It is *not* necessary that per capita GNP be very high, certainly not as high as that of the rich countries during their gradual demographic transition. In other words, low birth rates in poor countries are achievable long before the conditions exist that were present in the rich countries in the late 19th and early 20th centuries.

Twenty or thirty years is not long to discover and assess the factors affecting birth rates, but a body of evidence is now accumulating in favor of this hypothesis. Rich (1973) and Brown (1974a) show that at least 10 developing countries have managed to reduce their birth rates by an average of more than one birth per 1,000 population per year for periods of 5 to 16 years. A reduction of one birth per 1,000 per year would bring birth rates in poor countries to a rough replacement level of about 16/1,000 by the turn of the century, though age distribution effects would prevent a smooth population decline. We have listed these countries together with three other nations, including China, that are poor and yet have brought their birth rates down to 30 or less, presumably from rates of over 40 a decade or so ago.

These data show that rapid reduction in birth rates is possible in the developing world. No doubt it can be argued that each of these cases is in some way special. Hong Kong and Singapore are relatively rich; they, Barbados, and Mauritius are also tiny. China is able to exert great social pressure on its citizens; but China is particularly significant. It is enormous; its per capita GNP is almost as low as India's; and

it started out in 1949 with a terrible health system. Also, Egypt, Chile, Taiwan, Cuba, South Korea, and Sri Lanka are quite large, and they are poor or very poor....In fact, these examples represent an enormous range of religion, political systems, and geography and suggest that such rates of decline in the birth rate can be achieved whenever the appropriate conditions are met. "The common factor in these countries is that the *majority* of the population has shared in the economic and social benefits of significant national progress....[M]aking health, education and jobs more broadly available to lower income groups in poor countries contribute[s] significantly toward the motivation for smaller families that is the prerequisite of a major reduction in birth rates" (Rich 1973).

The converse is also true. In Latin America, Cuba (annual per capita income $530), Chile ($720), Uruguay ($820), and Argentina ($1,160) have moderate to truly equitable distribution of goods and services and relatively low birth rates (27, 26, 23 and 22, respectively). In contrast, Brazil ($420), Mexico ($670), and Venezuela ($980) have very unequal distribution of goods and services and high birth rates (38, 42, and 41, respectively). Fertility rates in poor and relatively poor nations seem unlikely to fall as long as the bulk of the population does not share in increased benefits.

We have tried briefly to bring the major evidence before the reader. However, there is a large literature, well summarized by Rich, and the details of the evidence are well worth reading in their entirety.

This evidence is certainly not overwhelming. Its accuracy varies. There are many unmeasured variables. Some measured variables, like income and literacy, are highly interrelated. We have no evidence that we can extrapolate to other countries or to still lower birth rates. By the standards of scientific experiment, these data are not conclusive. But policy decisions such as those discussed here are always based on uncertainty, and this evidence is at least as convincing as simple projections of average birth and death rates now prevailing in poor nations. Certainly the evidence is good enough that we need to treat the reduction of birth rates as a viable alternative to nonhelp.

A useful evaluation of the demographic transition hypothesis is provided by Beaver (1975), whose book became available only after we had completed the final revision of this article. Beaver restates the hypothesis as a set of assumptions, yielding specific predictions that can be tested against recent population data. These assumptions are similar to those given here, with some additional details and emphases. In particular, Beaver stresses the importance of a time lag of about 10 to 15 years before factors which tend to reduce birth rates can take effect. For example, both mortality decline and economic development reduce birth rates in the long run by raising expectations and confidence in the future, but both can increase birth rates in the short run by simply making it possible, physically and economically, for parents to have more children. The demographic transition hypothesis receives "strong empirical support" from a variety of statistical tests using recent Latin American data. Furthermore, the recent declines in natality in Latin America have been much more rapid than the declines in Europe during its demographic transition (see also Teitelbaum 1975).

COSTS, GAINS, AND DIFFICULTIES

We have neither the space nor the expertise to propose detailed food-population policies. Our main concern has been to help set the stage for serious discussion by disposing of simplistic proposals and irrelevant arguments, outlining some of the complexities of the problem, and indicating the existence of a large quantity of available data.

However, some kind of positive statement seems called for, if only to provide a target for others. We approach this task with trepidation. A full discussion of aid possibilities would require detailed consideration of political, social, and cultural complexities in a wide variety of recipient and donor countries. A thorough cost accounting would require detailed, quantitative knowledge about the relation between social conditions and the motivation for smaller families. Here we merely list some forms of aid, crudely estimate their costs, indicate some of their benefits and briefly discuss their feasibility.

Brown (1974a) estimates that $5 billion per year could provide:

- family planning services to the poor nations (excluding China, which already provides

them); the cost includes training personnel and providing transportation facilities and contraceptives;
- literacy for all adults and children (a five-year program); and
- a health care program for mothers and infants (again excluding China).

To this we could add the following:

- 10 million metric tons of grain at annual cost of $2 billion;
- 1.5 million metric tons of fertilizer, which is the estimated amount of the "shortfall" last year in the poor countries (U.N. 1974); the cost, including transportation, is roughly %1 billion; and
- half of the estimated annual cost of providing "adequate" increases in the area of irrigated and cultivated land in the poor countries (U.N. 1974), about $2 billion.

These costs may well be too low, although, according to Abelson (1975), the annual cost of an "effective" global food reserve is only $550 million to $800 million, compared with the $2 billion cited above. The estimates do suggest that aid on this scale, *properly designed and properly used in the recipient nations*, could make a sizeable improvement in social well-being.

The total cost is $10 billion. Still, these estimates are very crude. Let us suppose the real cost is $20 billion. Other wealthy countries could (and should) provide at least half of this. This leaves about $10 billion to be provided by the United States. Can the United States afford it?

In the past, U.S. aid has not normally been free. Indeed, India is now a net exporter of capital to the United States because it pays back more interest and principal on previous aid loans than it receives in aid. However, even giving away $10 billion is likely to have only minor effects on the U.S. economy and standard of living. It is about 1% of the GNP, about 10% of current military expenditure. It would decrease present and future consumption of goods and services in the United States by slightly more than 1% (because the cost of government accounts for about 25% of the GNP). It could result in a slight lowering of the value of the dollar abroad, unless other rich nations were also contributing proportionately. The most noticeable effects within the United States would be on the relative prices of goods and services and, as a consequence, on the poor in this country. Those items most in demand by poor countries would increase in price relative to "luxury" goods, so that the poor in the United States would be hurt more than the rich unless counter-measures were taken.

In short, although we must take care that the burden is equitably borne, the additional aid could be provided with only minor effects on the well-being of the U.S. population. Such a reduction in living standard is hardly "suicidal" or a matter of "human survival" in the United States, to use Hardin's terms. It is not a question of "them or us," as the lifeboat metaphor implies. This simple-minded dichotomy may account for the appeal of Hardin's views, but it bears no relation to reality.

The six measures suggested above should encourage economic growth as well as lower birth rates in poor countries...Adequate diet and health care improve work performance and reduce medical costs and lost work days. There is evidence (Owens and Shaw 1972) that agricultural improvements made available to small farmers can lead not only to improved diets and increased employment but also to greater productivity per hectare than occurs on large, capital-intensive farms, and that the poor can save at very high rates provided they own or rent their economic facilities (e.g., farms) and are integrated into the national economy through a network of financial institutions. Since small farms are labor-intensive, agricultural improvements that concentrate on them are not only well suited to poor countries but make them less vulnerable to fluctuations in energy supplies and costs.

Improved living conditions probably would first decrease the death rate. Does this mean that the decrease in the birth rate must be very great just to compensate? Infant mortality is the major part of the death rate that can still be decreased easily in poor countries. Suppose a poor country has a birth rate of 40/1,000 per population and an infant mortality rate of 150/1,000 live births; India is close to this. These six dead infants (15% of 40) help motivate parents to have many babies. Suppose, in the

next decade, conditions improve so much that infant mortality drops to zero—a ludicrous hope. This decrease would be exactly balanced if the birth rate dropped from 40/1,000 to 34/1,000. All 10 of the countries dropped this many points (and greater percentages) in five years or less. Further, once mortality rates are very low, every reduction in the birth rate reduces population growth. These calculations are oversimplified, but they illustrate that even a great decrease in poverty-related deaths can be balanced by a modest decrease in births.

We can gauge the effect of lowered birth rates upon the food-population ratio. [Consider] currently projected rates of population growth and food production for the major areas of the world (U.N. 1974). These projections assume continued improvement in food production at previous rates; they do not assume increased success in programs against high birth rates. For the next decade, the annual percentage increase of population would be 0.2 to 0.4 greater than that of food supply in Africa, noncommunist Asia, and Latin America (although for the world in general food grows faster than population). A successful program that reduced births by 0.5/1,000 or more per year would quickly remove the projected imbalance between food and population, even allowing for increased survival. This effect would accelerate as gains in survival gradually declined, thus vastly reducing the amount of aid that would be needed.

Will the aid in fact be used in ways that help reduce birth rates? As a disillusioning quarter-century of aid giving has shown, the obstacles to getting aid to those segments of the population most in need of it are enormous. Aid has typically benefitted a small rich segment of society, partly because of the way aid programs have been designed but also because of human and institutional factors in the poor nations themselves (Owens and Shaw 1972). With some notable exceptions, the distribution of income and services in poor nations is extremely skewed—much more uneven than in rich countries. Indeed, much of the population is essentially outside the economic system. Breaking this pattern will be extremely difficult. It will require not only aid that is designed specifically to benefit the rural poor, but also important institutional changes such as decentralization of decision making and the development of greater autonomy and stronger links to regional and national markets for local groups and industries, such as cooperative farms.

Thus, two things are being asked of rich nations and of the United States in particular: to increase nonmilitary foreign aid, including food aid, and to give it in ways, and to governments, that will deliver it to the poorest people and will improve their access to national economic institutions. These are not easy tasks, particularly the second, and there is no guarantee that birth rates will come down quickly in all countries. Still, many poor countries have, in varying degrees, begun the process of reform, and recent evidence suggests that aid and reform together can do much to solve the twin problems of high birth rates and economic underdevelopment. The tasks are far from impossible. Based on the evidence, the policies dictated by a sense of decency are also the most realistic and rational.

REFERENCES

Abelson, P. H. 1975. The world's disparate food supplies. *Science* 187: 218.

Barraclough, G. 1975. The great world crisis I. *The N.Y. Rev. Books* 21: 20–29.

Beaver, S. E. 1975. *Demographic Transition Theory Reinterpreted*. Lexington Books, Lexington, Mass. 177 pp.

Brown, L. R. 1974a. *In the Human Interest*, W. W. Norton & Co., Inc., New York. 190 pp.

———. 1974b. *By Bread Alone*. Praeger, New York. 272 pp.

Davis, K. 1963. Population. *Sci. Amer.* 209(3): 62–71.

Demeny, P. 1974. The populations of the underdeveloped countries. *Sci. Amer.* 231(3): 149–159.

Gulland, J. 1975. The harvest of the sea. Pages 1–67-189 *in* W. W. Murdoch, ed. *Environment: Resources, Pollution and Society*, 2nd ed. Sinauer Assoc., Sunderland, Mass.

Hardin, G. 1968. The tragedy of the commons. *Science* 162: 1243–1248.

———. 1969. Not peace, but ecology. *In* Diversity and Stability in Ecological Systems. *Brookhaven Symp. Biol.* 22: 151–161.

———. 1974. Living on a lifeboat. *BioScience* 24(10): 561–568.

Owens, E., and R. Shaw. 1972. *Development Reconsidered*. D. C. Heath & Co., Lexington, Mass. 190 pp.

Rich, W. 1973. *Smaller Families Through Social and Economic Progress*. Overseas Development Council, Monograph #7, Washington, D.C. 73 pp.

Teitelbaum M. S. 1975. Relevance of demographic transition theory for developing countries. *Science* 188:420–425.

Transnational Institute. 1974. *World Hunger: Causes and Remedies*. Institute for Policy Studies, 1520 New Hampshire Ave., NW, Washington, D.C.

United Nations Economic and Social Council. 1974. Assessment present food situation and dimensions and causes of hunger and malnutrition in the world. E/Conf. 65/Prep/6, 8 May 1974.

University of California Food Task Force. 1974. *A Hungry World: The Challenge to Agriculture*. University of California, Division of Agricultural Sciences. 303 pp.

ARGUMENT 26 ESSAY QUESTIONS

1. Is Hardin's analysis of world hunger and our moral obligations simplistic as some critics say? What do Murdoch and Oaten say about Hardin's view?

2. Will aiding the poor invariably increase their suffering? Are some ways better than others? Explain.

3. Do you have a duty to give aid to the needy in other countries? Why or why not?

27. SINGER'S UTILITARIAN ARGUMENT FOR AIDING THE POOR

In "Famine, Affluence, and Morality," Peter Singer advocates a fundamental shift in the attitudes of people in affluent countries toward the poor and starving of the Third World. His argument is that (1) suffering and death from lack of food and other necessities are bad; (2) "if it is in our power to prevent something bad from happening" without excessive sacrifice, we have a moral duty to do it[8]; therefore, (3) we have a moral duty to help the poor and starving of the world (regardless of their proximity to us or how many other people are in a position to help). If this argument is sound, it shows that giving to famine relief and similar causes is not an act of charity (and therefore optional)—it is a stringent moral obligation.

The second premise comes in two forms, strong and weak. The strong version says that we have a duty to prevent something bad from happening if we can do it without "sacrificing anything of comparable moral importance."[9] This principle requires us to give aid to the level of "marginal utility"—to the point where we could not give any more without causing as much suffering to ourselves or our families as we would ease by our giving. We must reduce our circumstances almost to the same degree of hardship experienced by those we are trying to aid.

Singer thinks the strong principle is the correct one, but he believes the weak version would also transform how we view our obligations to the needy. According to this less stringent principle, we have a duty to prevent something bad from happening if we can do it without "sacrificing anything morally significant."[10] It requires us not to sacrifice to the point of marginal utility, but to stop spending money on comparatively trivial things. It would have us give money to famine relief instead of spending it on a new car or new clothes.

A common criticism of Singer's view is that the strong principle allows the needs of others to outweigh or overrule our own legitimate rights and needs. "An adequate moral theory must make room for self-regarding reasons," says Louis Pojman. "I am required to make *reasonable* sacrifices for others, but not at the cost of what would severely detract from the quality of my own life."[11]

---

[8] Peter Singer, "Famine, Affluence, and Morality."
[9] Peter Singer, "Famine, Affluence, and Morality."
[10] Peter Singer, "Famine, Affluence, and Morality."
[11] Louis Pojman, 178.

Some critics also insist that while we have a duty to help needy people in faraway places, we also have special duties to those close at hand—members of our family, friends, and neighbors. As Pojman puts it,

> I may have a duty to give of my surplus to help save drowning children in a distant land, but I have a stronger duty to help those with whom I have intimate or contractual ties.[12]

Famine, Affluence, and Morality

PETER SINGER

As I write this, in November 1971, people are dying in East Bengal from lack of food, shelter, and medical care. The suffering and death that are occurring there now are not inevitable, not unavoidable in any fatalistic sense of the term. Constant poverty, a cyclone, and a civil war have turned at least nine million people into destitute refugees; nevertheless, it is not beyond the capacity of the richer nations to give enough assistance to reduce any further suffering to very small proportions. The decisions and actions of human beings can prevent this kind of suffering. Unfortunately, human beings have not made the necessary decisions. At the individual level, people have, with very few exceptions, not responded to the situation in any significant way. Generally speaking, people have not given large sums to relief funds; they have not written to their parliamentary representatives demanding increased government assistance; they have not demonstrated in the streets, held symbolic fasts, or done anything else directed toward providing the refugees with the means to satisfy their essential needs. At the government level, no government has given the sort of massive aid that would enable the refugees to survive for more than a few days. Britain, for instance, has given rather more than most countries. It has, to date, given £14,750,000. For comparative purposes, Britain's share of the nonrecoverable development costs of the Anglo-French Concorde project is already in excess of £275,000,000, and on present estimates will reach £440,000,000. The implication is that the British government values a supersonic transport more than thirty times as highly as it values the lives of the nine million refugees. Australia is another country which, on a per capita basis, is well up in the "aid to Bengal" table. Australia's aid, however, amounts to less than one-twelfth of the cost of Sydney's new opera house. The total amount given, from all sources, now stands at about £65,000,000. The estimated cost of keeping the refugees alive for one year is £464,000,000. Most of the refugees have now been in the camps for more than six months. The World Bank has said that India needs a minimum of £300,000,000 in assistance from other countries before the end of the year. It seems obvious that assistance on this scale will not be forthcoming. India will be forced to choose between letting the refugees starve or diverting funds from her own development program, which will mean that more of her own people will starve in the future.[1]

These are the essential facts about the present situation in Bengal. So far as it concerns us here, there is nothing unique about this situation except

"Famine, Affluence, and Morality" by Peter Singer, *Philosophy and Public Affairs*. Copyright © 1972. Reproduced with permission of Blackwell Publishing Ltd.

[12] Louis P. Pojman, *Life and Death* (Belmont, CA: Wadsworth, 2000), 180.

its magnitude. The Bengal emergency is just the latest and most acute of a series of major emergencies in various parts of the world, arising both from natural and from man-made causes. There are also many parts of the world in which people die from malnutrition and lack of food independent of any special emergency. I take Bengal as my example only because it is the present concern, and because the size of the problem has ensured that it has been given adequate publicity. Neither individuals nor governments can claim to be unaware of what is happening there.

What are the moral implications of a situation like this? In what follows, I shall argue that the way people in relatively affluent countries react to a situation like that in Bengal cannot be justified; indeed, the whole way we look at moral issues—our moral conceptual scheme—needs to be altered, and with it, the way of life that has come to be taken for granted in our society.

In arguing for this conclusion I will not, of course, claim to be morally neutral. I shall, however, try to argue for the moral position that I take, so that anyone who accepts certain assumptions, to be made explicit, will, I hope, accept my conclusion.

I begin with the assumption that suffering and death from lack of food, shelter, and medical care are bad. I think most people will agree about this, although one may reach the same view by different routes. I shall not argue for this view. People can hold all sorts of eccentric positions, and perhaps from some of them it would not follow that death by starvation is in itself bad. It is difficult, perhaps impossible, to refute such positions, and so for brevity I will henceforth take this assumption as accepted. Those who disagree need read no further.

My next point is this: if it is in our power to prevent something bad from happening, without thereby sacrificing anything of comparable moral importance, we ought, morally, to do it. By "without sacrificing anything of comparable moral importance" I mean without causing anything else comparably bad to happen, or doing something that is wrong in itself, or failing to promote some moral good, comparable in significance to the bad thing that we can prevent. This principle seems almost as uncontroversial as the last one. It requires us only to prevent what is bad, and not to promote what is

good, and it requires this of us only when we can do it without sacrificing anything that is, from the moral point of view, comparably important. I could even, as far as the application of my argument to the Bengal emergency is concerned, qualify the point so as to make it: if it is in our power to prevent something very bad from happening, without thereby sacrificing anything morally significant, we ought, morally, to do it. An application of this principle would be as follows: if I am walking past a shallow pond and see a child drowning in it, I ought to wade in and pull the child out. This will mean getting my clothes muddy, but this is insignificant, while the death of the child would presumably be a very bad thing.

The uncontroversial appearance of the principle just stated is deceptive. If it were acted upon, even in its qualified form, our lives, our society, and our world would be fundamentally changed. For the principle takes, firstly, no account of proximity or distance. It makes no moral difference whether the person I can help is a neighbor's child ten yards from me or a Bengali whose name I shall never know, ten thousand miles away. Secondly, the principle makes no distinction between cases in which I am the only person who could possibly do anything and cases in which I am just one among millions in the same position.

I do not think I need to say much in defense of the refusal to take proximity and distance into account. The fact that a person is physically near to us, so that we have personal contact with him, may make it more likely that we *shall* assist him, but this does not show that we *ought* to help him rather than another who happens to be further away. If we accept any principle of impartiality, universalizability, equality, or whatever, we cannot discriminate against someone merely because he is far away from us (or we are far away from him). Admittedly, it is possible that we are in a better position to judge what needs to be done to help a person near to us than one far away, and perhaps also to provide the assistance we judge to be necessary. If this were the case, it would be a reason for helping those near to us first. This may once have been a justification for being more concerned with the poor in one's own town than with famine victims in India. Unfortunately for those who like to keep their moral responsibilities limited, instant communication and swift transportation have changed the situation. From the moral point of view, the development of the world into a "global village" has made an important, though still unrecognized, difference to our moral situation. Expert observers and supervisors, sent out by famine relief organizations or permanently stationed in famine-prone areas, can direct our aid to a refugee in Bengal almost as effectively as we could get it to someone in our own block. There would seem, therefore, to be no possible justification for discriminating on geographical grounds.

There may be a greater need to defend the second implication of my principle—that the fact that there are millions of other people in the same position, in respect to the Bengali refugees, as I am, does not make the situation significantly different from a situation in which I am the only person who can prevent something very bad from occurring. Again, of course, I admit that there is a psychological difference between the cases; one feels less guilty about doing nothing if one can point to others, similarly placed, who have also done nothing. Yet this can make no real difference to our moral obligations.[2] Should I consider that I am less obliged to pull the drowning child out of the pond if on looking around I see other people, no further away than I am, who have also noticed the child but are doing nothing? One has only to ask this question to see the absurdity of the view that numbers lessen obligation. It is a view that is an ideal excuse for inactivity; unfortunately most of the major evils—poverty, overpopulation, pollution—are problems in which everyone is almost equally involved.

The view that numbers do make a difference can be made plausible if stated in this way: if everyone in circumstances like mine gave £5 to the Bengal Relief Fund, there would be enough to provide food, shelter, and medical care for the refugees; there is no reason why I should give more than anyone else in the same circumstances as I am; therefore I have no obligation to give more than £5. Each premise in this argument is true, and the argument looks sound. It may convince us, unless we notice that it is based on a hypothetical premise, although the conclusion is not stated hypothetically. The argument would be sound if the conclusion were: if everyone in circumstances like mine were to give £5, I would

have no obligation to give more than £5. If the conclusion were so stated, however, it would be obvious that the argument has no bearing on a situation in which it is not the case that everyone else gives £5. This, of course, is the actual situation. It is more or less certain that not everyone in circumstances like mine will give £5. So there will not be enough to provide the needed food, shelter, and medical care. Therefore by giving more than £5 I will prevent more suffering than I would if I gave just £5.

It might be thought that this argument has an absurd consequence. Since the situation appears to be that very few people are likely to give substantial amounts, it follows that I and everyone else in similar circumstances ought to give as much as possible, that is, at least up to the point at which by giving more one would begin to cause serious suffering for oneself and one's dependents—perhaps even beyond this point to the point of marginal utility, at which by giving more one would cause oneself and one's dependents as much suffering as one would prevent in Bengal. If everyone does this, however, there will be more than can be used for the benefit of the refugees, and some of the sacrifice will have been unnecessary. Thus, if everyone does what he ought to do, the result will not be as good as it would be if everyone did a little less than he ought to do, or if only some do all that they ought to do.

The paradox here arises only if we assume that the actions in question—sending money to the relief funds—are performed more or less simultaneously, and are also unexpected. For if it is to be expected that everyone is going to contribute something, then clearly each is not obliged to give as much as he would have been obliged to had others not been giving too. And if everyone is not acting more or less simultaneously, then those giving later will know how much more is needed, and will have no obligation to give more than is necessary to reach this amount. To say this is not to deny the principle that people in the same circumstances have the same obligations, but to point out that the fact that others have given, or may be expected to give, is a relevant circumstance: those giving after it has become known that many others are giving and those giving before are not in the same circumstances. So the seemingly absurd consequence of the principle I have put forward can occur only if people are in error about the actual circumstances—that is, if they think they are giving when others are not, but in fact they are giving when others are. The result of everyone doing what he really ought to do cannot be worse than the result of everyone doing less than he ought to do, although the result of everyone doing what he reasonably believes he ought to do could be.

If my argument so far has been sound, neither our distance from a preventable evil nor the number of other people who, in respect to that evil, are in the same situation as we are, lessens our obligation to mitigate or prevent that evil. I shall therefore take as established the principle I asserted earlier. As I have already said, I need to assert it only in its qualified form: if it is in our power to prevent something very bad from happening without thereby sacrificing anything else morally significant, we ought, morally, to do it.

The outcome of this argument is that our traditional moral categories are upset. The traditional distinction between duty and charity cannot be drawn, or at least, not in the place we normally draw it. Giving money to the Bengal Relief Fund is regarded as an act of charity in our society. The bodies which collect money are known as "charities." These organizations see themselves in this way—if you send them a check, you will be thanked for your "generosity." Because giving money is regarded as an act of charity, it is not thought that there is anything wrong with not giving. The charitable man may be praised, but the man who is not charitable is not condemned. People do not feel in any way ashamed or guilty about spending money on new clothes or a new car instead of giving it to famine relief. (Indeed, the alternative does not occur to them.) This way of looking at the matter cannot be justified. When we buy new clothes not to keep ourselves warm but to look "well-dressed" we are not providing for any important need. We would not be sacrificing anything significant if we were to continue to wear our old clothes, and give the money to famine relief. By doing so, we would be preventing another person from starving. It follows from what I have said earlier that we ought to give money away, rather than spend it on clothes which we do not need to keep us warm. To do so is not charitable, or generous. Nor is it the kind of

act which philosophers and theologians have called "supererogatory"—an act which it would be good to do, but not wrong not to do. On the contrary, we ought to give the money away, and it is wrong not to do so.

I am not maintaining that there are no acts which are charitable, or that there are no acts which it would be good to do but not wrong not to do. It may be possible to redraw the distinction between duty and charity in some other place. All I am arguing here is that the present way of drawing the distinction, which makes it an act of charity for a man living at the level of affluence which most people in the "developed nations" enjoy to give money to save someone else from starvation, cannot be supported. It is beyond the scope of my argument to consider whether the distinction should be redrawn or abolished altogether. There would be many other possible ways of drawing the distinction—for instance, one might decide that it is good to make other people as happy as possible, but not wrong not to do so.

Despite the limited nature of the revision in our moral conceptual scheme which I am proposing, the revision would, given the extent of both affluence and famine in the world today, have radical implications. These implications may lead to further objections, distinct from those I have already considered. I shall discuss two of these.

One objection to the position I have taken might be simply that it is too drastic a revision of our moral scheme. People do not ordinarily judge in the way I have suggested they should. Most people reserve their moral condemnation for those who violate some moral norm, such as the norm against taking another person's property. They do not condemn those who indulge in luxury instead of giving to famine relief. But given that I did not set out to present a morally neutral description of the way people make moral judgments, the way people do in fact judge has nothing to do with the validity of my conclusion. My conclusion follows from the principle which I advanced earlier, and unless that principle is rejected, or the arguments shown to be unsound, I think the conclusion must stand, however strange it appears.

It might, nevertheless, be interesting to consider why our society, and most other societies, do judge differently from the way I have suggested they should. In a well-known article, J. O. Urmson suggests that the imperatives of duty, which tell us what we must do, as distinct from what it would be good to do but not wrong not to do, function so as to prohibit behavior that is intolerable if men are to live together in society.[3] This may explain the origin and continued existence of the present division between acts of duty and acts of charity. Moral attitudes are shaped by the needs of society, and no doubt society needs people who will observe the rules that make social existence tolerable. From the point of view of a particular society, it is essential to prevent violations of norms against killing, stealing, and so on. It is quite inessential, however, to help people outside one's own society.

If this is an explanation of our common distinction between duty and supererogation, however, it is not a justification of it. The moral point of view requires us to look beyond the interests of our own society. Previously, as I have already mentioned, this may hardly have been feasible, but it is quite feasible now. From the moral point of view, the prevention of the starvation of millions of people outside our society must be considered at least as pressing as the upholding of property norms within our society.

It has been argued by some writers, among them Sidgwick and Urmson, that we need to have a basic moral code which is not too far beyond the capacities of the ordinary man, for otherwise there will be a general breakdown of compliance with the moral code. Crudely stated, this argument suggests that if we tell people that they ought to refrain from murder and give everything they do not really need to famine relief, they will do neither, whereas if we tell them that they ought to refrain from murder and that it is good to give to famine relief but not wrong not to do so, they will at least refrain from murder. The issue here is: Where should we drawn the line between conduct that is required and conduct that is good although not required, so as to get the best possible result? This would seem to be an empirical question, although a very difficult one. One objection to the Sidgwick-Urmson line of argument is that it takes insufficient account of the effect that moral standards can have on the decisions we make. Given a society in which a wealthy man who gives five percent of his income to famine relief is regarded as most generous, it is not surprising that a proposal that we all ought to give away half our incomes will be thought to be absurdly unrealistic. In a society which held that no man should have more than enough while others have less than they need, such a proposal might seem narrow-minded. What it is possible for a man to do and what he is likely to do are both, I think, very greatly influenced by what people around him are doing and expecting him to do. In any case, the possibility that by spreading the idea that we ought to be doing very much more than we are to relieve famine we shall bring about a general breakdown of moral behavior seems remote. If the stakes are an end to widespread starvation, it is worth the risk. Finally, it should be emphasized that these considerations are relevant only to the issue of what we should require from others, and not to what we ourselves ought to do.

The second objection to my attack on the present distinction between duty and charity is one which has from time to time been made against utilitarianism. It follows from some forms of utilitarian theory that we all ought, morally, to be working full time to increase the balance of happiness over misery. The position I have taken here would not lead to this conclusion in all circumstances, for if there were no bad occurrences that we could prevent without sacrificing something of comparable moral importance, my argument would have no application. Given the present conditions in many parts of the world, however, it does follow from my argument that we ought, morally, to be working full time to relieve great suffering of the sort that occurs as a result of famine or other disasters. Of course, mitigating circumstances can be adduced— for instance, that if we wear ourselves out through overwork, we shall be less effective than we would otherwise have been. Nevertheless, when all considerations of this sort have been taken into account, the conclusion remains: we ought to be preventing as much suffering as we can without sacrificing something else of comparable moral importance. This conclusion is one which we may be reluctant to face. I cannot see, though, why it should be regarded as a criticism of the position for which I have argued, rather than a criticism of our ordinary standards of behavior. Since most people are self-interested to some degree, very few of us are likely to do everything that we ought to do. It would however, hardly be honest to take this as evidence that it is not the case that we ought to do it.

It may still be thought that my conclusions are so wildly out of line with what everyone else thinks and has always thought that there must be something wrong with the argument somewhere. In order to show that my conclusions, while certainly contrary to contemporary Western moral standards, would not have seemed so extraordinary at other times and in other places, I would like to quote a passage from a writer not normally thought of as a way-out radical, Thomas Aquinas.

> Now, according to the natural order instituted by divine providence, material goods are provided for the satisfaction of human needs. Therefore the division and appropriation of property, which proceeds from human law, must not hinder the satisfaction of man's necessity from such goods. Equally, whatever a man has in superabundance is owed, of natural right, to the poor for their sustenance. So Ambrosius says, and it is also to be found in the *Decretum Gratiani:* "The bread which you withhold belongs to the hungry; the clothing you shut away, to the naked; and the money you bury in the earth is the redemption and freedom of the penniless."[4]

I now want to consider a number of points, more practical than philosophical, which are relevant to the application of the moral conclusion we have reached. These points challenge not the idea that we ought to be doing all we can to prevent starvation, but the idea that giving away a great deal of money is the best means to this end.

It is sometimes said that overseas aid should be a government responsibility, and that therefore one ought not to give to privately run charities. Giving privately, it is said, allows the government and the noncontributing members of society to escape their responsibilities.

This argument seems to assume that the more people there are who give to privately organized famine relief funds, the less likely it is that the government will take over full responsibility for such aid. This assumption is unsupported, and does not strike me as at all plausible. The opposite view—that if no one gives voluntarily, a government will assume that its citizens are uninterested in famine relief and

would not wish to be forced into giving aid—seems more plausible. In any case, unless there were a definite probability that by refusing to give one would be helping to bring about massive government assistance, people who do refuse to make voluntary contributions are refusing to prevent a certain amount of suffering without being able to point to any tangible beneficial consequence of their refusal. So the onus of showing how their refusal will bring about government action is on those who refuse to give.

I do not, of course, want to dispute the contention that governments of affluent nations should be giving many times the amount of genuine, no-strings-attached aid that they are giving now. I agree, too, that giving privately is not enough, and that we ought to be campaigning actively for entirely new standards for both public and private contributions to famine relief. Indeed, I would sympathize with someone who thought that campaigning was more important than giving oneself, although I doubt whether preaching what one does not practice would be very effective. Unfortunately, for many people the idea that "it's the government's responsibility" is a reason for not giving which does not appear to entail any political action either.

Another, more serious reason for not giving to famine relief funds is that until there is effective population control, relieving famine merely postpones starvation. If we save the Bengal refugees now, others, perhaps the children of these refugees, will face starvation in a few years' time. In support of this, one may cite the now well-known facts about the population explosion and the relatively limited scope for expanded production.

This point, like the previous one, is an argument against relieving suffering that is happening now, because of a belief about what might happen in the future; it is unlike the previous point in that very good evidence can be adduced in support of this belief about the future. I will not go into the evidence here. I accept that the earth cannot support indefinitely a population rising at the present rate. This certainly poses a problem for anyone who thinks it important to prevent famine. Again, however, one could accept the argument without drawing the conclusion that it absolves one from any obligation to do anything to prevent famine. The conclusion that should be drawn is that the best means of preventing famine, in the long run, is population control. It would then follow from the position reached earlier that one ought to be doing all one can to promote population control (unless one held that all forms of population control were wrong in themselves, or would have significantly bad consequences). Since there are organizations working specifically for population control, one would then support them rather than more orthodox methods of preventing famine.

A third point raised by the conclusion reached earlier relates to the question of just how much we all ought to be giving away. One possibility, which has already been mentioned, is that we ought to give until we reach the level of marginal utility—that is, the level at which, by giving more, I would cause as much suffering to myself or my dependents as I would relieve by my gift. This would mean, of course, that one would reduce oneself to very near the material circumstances of a Bengali refugee. It will be recalled that earlier I put forward both a strong and a moderate version of the principle of preventing bad occurrences. The strong version, which required us to prevent bad things from happening unless in doing so we would be sacrificing something of comparable moral significance, does seem to require reducing ourselves to the level of marginal utility. I should also say that the strong version seems to me to be the correct one. I proposed the more moderate version—that we should prevent bad occurrences unless, to do so, we had to sacrifice something morally significant—only in order to show that even on this surely undeniable principle a great change in our way of life is required. On the more moderate principle, it may not follow that we ought to reduce ourselves to the level of marginal utility, for one might hold that to reduce oneself and one's family to this level is to cause something significantly bad to happen. Whether this is so I shall not discuss, since, as I have said, I can see no good reason for holding the moderate version of the principle rather than the strong version. Even if we accepted the principle only in its moderate form, however, it should be clear that we would have to give away enough to ensure that the consumer society, dependent as it is on people spending on trivia rather than giving to famine relief, would slow down and perhaps disappear entirely. There

are several reasons why this would be desirable in itself. The value and necessity of economic growth are now being questioned not only by conservationists, but by economists as well.[5] There is no doubt, too, that the consumer society has had a distorting effect on the goals and purposes of its members. Yet looking at the matter purely from the point of view of overseas aid, there must be a limit to the extent to which we should deliberately slow down our economy; for it might be the case that if we gave away, say, forty percent of our Gross National Product, we would slow down the economy so much that in absolute terms we would be giving less than if we gave twenty-five percent of the much larger GNP that we would have if we limited our contribution to this smaller percentage.

I mention this only as an indication of the sort of factor that one would have to take into account in working out an ideal. Since Western societies generally consider one percent of the GNP an acceptable level for overseas aid, the matter is entirely academic. Nor does it affect the question of how much an individual should give in a society in which very few are giving substantial amounts.

It is sometimes said, though less often now than it used to be, that philosophers have no special role to play in public affairs, since most public issues depend primarily on an assessment of facts. On questions of fact, it is said, philosophers as such have no special expertise, and so it has been possible to engage in philosophy without committing oneself to any position on major public issues. No doubt there are some issues of social policy and foreign policy about which it can truly be said that a really expert assessment of the facts is required before taking sides or acting, but the issue of famine is surely not one of these. The facts about the existence of suffering are beyond dispute. Nor, I think, is it disputed that we can do something about it, either through orthodox methods of famine relief or through population control or both. This is therefore an issue on which philosophers are competent to take a position. The issue is one which faces everyone who has more money than he needs to support himself and his dependents, or who is in a position to take some sort of political action. These categories must include practically every teacher and student of philosophy in the universities of the

Western world. If philosophy is to deal with matters that are relevant to both teachers and students, this is an issue that philosophers should discuss.

Discussion, though, is not enough. What is the point of relating philosophy to public (and personal) affairs if we do not take our conclusions seriously? In this instance, taking our conclusion seriously means acting upon it. The philosopher will not find it any easier than anyone else to alter his attitudes and way of life to the extent that, if I am right, is involved in doing everything that we ought to be doing.

At the very least, though, one can make a start. The philosopher who does so will have to sacrifice some of the benefits of the consumer society, but he can find compensation in the satisfaction of a way of life in which theory and practice, if not yet in harmony, are at least coming together.

NOTES

1. There was also a third possibility: that India would go to war to enable the refugees to return to their lands. Since I wrote this paper, India has taken this way out. The situation is no longer that described above, but this does not affect my argument, as the next paragraph indicates.

2. In view of the special sense philosophers often give to the term, I should say that I use "obligation" simply as the abstract noun derived from "ought," so that "I have an obligation to" means no more, and no less, than "I ought to." This usage is in accordance with the definition of "ought" given by the *Shorter Oxford English Dictionary*: "the general verb to express duty or obligation." I do not think any issue of substance hangs on the way the term is used; sentences in which I use "obligation" could all be rewritten, although somewhat clumsily, as sentences in which a clause containing "ought" replaces the term "obligation."

3. J. O. Urmson, "Saints and Heroes," in *Essays in Moral Philosophy*, ed. Abraham I. Melden (Seattle and London, 1958), p. 214. For a related but significantly different view see also Henry Sidgwick, *The Methods of Ethics*, 7th edn. (London, 1907), pp. 220–221, 492–493.

4. *Summa Theologica*, II–II, Question 66, Article 7, in *Aquinas, Selected Political Writings*, ed. A. P. d'Entreves, trans. J. G. Dawson (Oxford, 1948), p. 171.

5. See, for instance, John Kenneth Galbraith, *The New Industrial State* (Boston, 1967); and E. J. Mishan, *The Costs of Economic Growth* (London, 1967).

World Hunger and Population

LOUIS P. POJMAN

[Everyone has] the right to a standard of living adequate for the health and well being of himself and his family, including food.

United Nations Declaration on Human Rights, 1948

Feeding the hungry in some countries only keeps them alive longer to produce more hungry bellies and disease and death.

Joseph Fletcher, "Give If It Helps But Not If It Hurts"

More than one third of the world goes to bed hungry each night. Ten thousand people starve to death each day. Nearly a quarter of the human race lives in absolute poverty, with incomes less than one dollar a day. Eight hundred forty-one million people are chronically undernourished, and the United Nations

From *Life and Death*, 2nd ed., by Louis P. Pojman. © 2000 Wadsworth, a part of Cengage Learning, Inc. Reproduced by permission. Notes deleted.

Food and Agriculture Organization (FAO) estimates that almost half of these are children. In Africa the *number* of hungry people has more than doubled, and the *proportion* of the population that is hungry has increased 13 percent in the past twenty-five years. The FAO predicts that if current trends continue, 265 million Africans (the size of the present population of the United States) will suffer hunger in 2010, an increase from 148 million in 1981 and 215 million in 1992. While famines have ravaged parts of Africa and Asia, another third of the world, the industrialized West, lives in relative affluence, wasting food or over-eating. The rich get richer and the poor get poorer.

World hunger is one of the most intractable problems facing humankind today. It is an environmental issue because it is tied to population growth, deforestation, soil erosion, and the just distribution of resources. Poor farmers in the rainforest cannot afford to worry about saving endangered species or the rainforest itself, because they are compelled to work to feed their families, even at the expense of the environment. World hunger is a global environmental issue. What can be done about it? What obligations, if any, do we in the affluent West have to distant, needy people, those who are hungry or starving? To what extent should population policies be tied to hunger relief? These are the questions discussed in this chapter.

I will discuss three responses to these questions: (1) the neo-Malthusian response set forth by Garrett Hardin; (2) the conservative (or libertarian) response represented by Thomas Hoboes, Robert Nozick, and others; and (3) the liberal response, exemplified by Peter Singer and Richard Watson. After this I will suggest alternative positions, taking into consideration the valid insights of each of these other positions.

FOUR ETHICAL RESPONSES TO WORLD HUNGER

The contrast between neo-Malthusians and liberals can hardly be greater. Liberals assert that we have a duty to feed the hungry in famine-ridden areas either because the hungry have a right to it or because of utilitarian reasons maximizing welfare or happiness. Neo-Malthusians deny such a right and assert that we have an opposite utilitarian duty to refrain from feeding the hungry in famine-ridden areas. Conservatives take the middle road in this debate, asserting that although we do not have a duty to feed the hungry, it is permissible and praiseworthy to do so. It is an act of supererogation, an act going beyond the call of duty. We begin with the neo-Malthusians.

Neo-Malthusianism

The Reverend Thomas Malthus (1766–1834) held that population size tends to outrun food production, leading to misery, until war, disease, famine and other disasters restore a natural balance. Partly due to modern agricultural technology and the spread of birth control devices, Malthus's predictions haven't been universally fulfilled. In the United States and Canada, for example, food production has been substantially above what is needed for their populations. Neo-Malthusians arc ecologists who accept Malthus's basic thesis but modify it in the light of technological innovation. A nation that is not maintaining the proper food-to-population ratio should not be helped from the outside by increments of food. To feed such sick societies is, to quote Alan Gregg, former vice president of the Rockefeller Foundation, like feeding a cancer. "Cancerous growths demand food; but, as far as I know, they have never been cured by getting it."

The most prominent neo-Malthusian today is Garrett Hardin, Emeritus Professor of Human Biology at the University of California at Santa Barbara, who in a series of articles set forth the idea of Lifeboat Ethics. Hardin's position can be succinctly stated through three metaphors that he has made famous: "lifeboat," "tragedy of the commons," and "the ratchet." Let us examine his use of each of these.

I. Lifeboat

The world is compared to a sea in which a few lifeboats (the affluent nations) are surrounded by hordes of drowning people (the populations of the poor nations). Each lifeboat has a limited carrying capacity, which is such that it cannot possibly take on more than a tiny fraction of the drowning without jeopardizing the lives of its passengers. Besides, the need for a safety factor always dictates that we ought to leave a healthy margin between the actual number on board and the possible number. The optimum population is somewhat below the maximum population. According to Hardin, the affluent nations currently are right around that optimum figure, probably beyond it, so it is self-destructive to rescue the world's poor. Not only must we adhere to a population policy of zero-growth, but we must have stringent immigration policies that prevent immigrants from swamping our boat.

2. Tragedy of the Commons

Imagine a public field (a "commons") where shepherds have been grazing their sheep for centuries. Because of the richness of the field and the poverty of the shepherds, the field is never overgrazed. Now there comes a time when the carrying capacity of the field is reaching its limit. At this point it is in the short-term rational self-interest of each farmer to add one more sheep to the commons in spite of its limitations. The farmer reasons that by grazing yet one more sheep, he will be reaping a positive factor of I (the value brought on by the extra sheep) and losing only a fraction of the negative unit I, the loss of the field's resources, since all of the herdsmen share that equally whether they participate in overgrazing or not. So it is in each shepherd's interest to overgraze, but if too many shepherds act in their short-term self-interest in this way it soon will be against their interest, for the pasture will be ruined. Hence the tragedy of the commons! A similar tragedy is occurring in our use of natural resources. We are in danger of depleting the world's resources through wanton overuse. To prevent such a tragedy, we must have mutually agreed upon, mutually coercive laws that govern population increase, overgrazing, overfishing, deforestation, pollution, and the like. Each nation must manage its own commons, and if one fails to do so, it must be left to its own misery. Benevolent intervention on the part of misguided do-gooders is likely only to increase the overall misery. This leads to the next metaphor.

3. The Ratchet

Hardin argues that there is a natural relationship in ecosystems such that once a species has overshot the environment's carrying capacity, nature takes care of the situation by causing a die-back on the population of the species and eventually restores a balance.... For example, when there is a serious decline in the natural predators of deer in an area,

the deer population tends to increase exponentially until it overshoots the carrying capacity of the land for deer. The land cannot provide for this increase, so the deer begin to starve, causing a die-back in their population, until conditions are such that they can again increase at a normal pace. The same relationship applies to human population systems. Once people in a given area have exceeded the carrying capacity of the environment, there will come a period of scarcity, resulting, à la Malthus, in famine, disease, and war over scarce resources, which results in a die-back or lowering of the population below the level of the carrying capacity. Nature will take care of the tragedy of the commons. When people refuse to constrain their procreative instincts, nature intervenes and does it for them.

Now let some well-meaning altruists intervene to thwart nature's iron law. The altruists send food to the starving, fending off the effects of famine for a time. But what happens? The people procreate and the population increases even further beyond the carrying capacity of the land. Soon there are even more people starving, so another even greater altruistic effort is needed to stave off the worsening situation. A herculean effort is accomplished, and the population is saved once again. But where does this process lead? Only to an eventual disaster. The ratchet effect keeps raising the level of the population without coming to terms with the natural relationship of the population to its environment, and that is where Malthus's law is valid.... Sending food to those who are not taking voluntary steps to curb their population size is like feeding a cancer.

For Hardin, it is wrong to give aid to those who are starving in overpopulated countries because of the ratchet effect. It only causes more misery in the long run. "How can we help a foreign country to escape overpopulation? Clearly the worst thing we can do is send food.... Atomic bombs would be kinder. For a few moments the misery would be acute, but it would soon come to an end for most of the people, leaving a very few survivors to suffer thereafter."

Furthermore, we have a natural duty to our children and to posterity to maintain the health of the planet as a whole. By using resources now for this short-term fix, we rob our children and future generations of their rightful inheritance. The claims of future people in this case override those of distant people.

In summary, Hardin has three arguments against giving aid to the poor in distant lands: (1) It will threaten our lifeboat by affecting the safety factor and causing our carrying capacity to become strained; (2) It will only increase the misery due to the ratchet effect; and (3) It will threaten the welfare of our descendants to whom we have prior obligations. For all of these reasons we are morally required not to give aid to the hungry.

What can be said about this kind of reasoning? Is Hardin right about the world's situation? Let us examine the arguments more closely. Consider (1), the lifeboat argument. Is the metaphor itself appropriate? Are we really so nicely separate from the poor of the world? Or are we vitally interdependent, profiting from the same conditions that contribute to the misery of the underdeveloped nations? Haven't colonialization and commercial arrangements worked to increase the disparity between the rich and the poor nations of the earth? We extract cheap raw materials from poor nations and sell those nations expensive manufactured goods (for example, radios, cars, computers, and weapons) instead of appropriate agricultural goods and training. The structure of tariffs and internal subsidies discriminates selectively against underdeveloped nations. Multinational corporations place strong inducements on poor countries to produce cash crops such as coffee and cocoa instead of food crops needed to feed their own people. Besides this, the United States and other Western nations have often used foreign aid to bolster dictatorships such as the Somoza regime in Nicaragua and the military juntas in Chile and El Salvador, which have resisted social change that would have redistributed wealth more equitably. For example, in 1973 when President Allende of Chile requested aid from the United States, not only was he turned down, but our government also aided in bringing his reformist government to ruin. When the military junta that replaced Allende took power and promised to maintain American business interests, eight times the amount of aid Allende had asked for was given to that government.

Hardin's lifeboat metaphor grimly obscures the fact that we have profited and are profiting from the economic conditions in the third world. Perhaps a more apt metaphor than "lifeboat" might be "octopus"—a powerful multinational corporation octopus with tentacles clutching weapons and reaching out into diverse regions of the globe. Our nation protects, encourages, and even intervenes in the affairs of other nations on the basis of its relations to these corporations. But if that is the case, how can we dissociate ourselves from the plight of people in these countries? Keeping the poor out of our lifeboats might be permissible if we hadn't built the boats out of rubber taken from them in the first place. The fact is, even if you can justify the commercial dealings we have with the rest of the world, we are already involved with the hungry of the world in a way that the lifeboat metaphor belies.

The question of distributive justice haunts Hardin's argument. He admits that ofttimes survival policies are unjust, but he argues as a utilitarian that survival overrides justice, that it is better for some to survive unjustly than to be just and let everyone perish. "Complete injustice, complete catastrophe." But this fails to consider a whole middle range of possibilities where justice could be at least a contributing factor to a solution that would take the need for one's own survival into consideration. Justice would demand that some attention be given to redistributing the world's wealth. At present the United States, with less than 4.5 percent of the world's population, consumes some 35 percent of its food (much of it thrown into garbage cans or rotting in storage silos) and 38 percent of its energy and is responsible for creating 33 percent of the world's pollution. If Hardin is so concerned about preserving the world's purity and resources for posterity, justice would require that we sacrifice the overfed, overweight, over-nourished, overconsuming, overpolluting, greedy Americans who throw into garbage cans more food than some nations eat.

Regarding the carrying capacity and ratchet effect considerations, several objections are in order. First of all, how does Hardin know which nations have exceeded their carrying capacity? The very notion of the carrying capacity, given our technological ability to produce new varieties of food, is a flexible one. Perhaps experts can identify some regions of the earth (for example, deserts) where the land can sustain only a few people, but one ought to be cautious in pronouncing that Bangladesh or India or some region of the Sahal in Africa are in that condition. Too many variables abound. New agricultural or fishing methods or cultural practices may offset the validity of technical assessments.

Second, Hardin is too dogmatic in proclaiming the lawlike dictum that to aid the poor is to cause the escalation of misery. Granted, we can make things worse by merely giving food handouts, and a population policy is needed to prevent the ratchet effect against which Hardin rightly warns. However, intelligent ways exist to aid, such as providing agricultural instruction and technological know-how to nations committed to responsible population policies, promoting mutually beneficial international trade agreements, and seeking ways to eradicate conditions that cause famine and malnutrition. We should also set a good example of what a just, disciplined, frugal society should be. But to dismiss these options out of hand and simply advocate pushing people off our lifeboat is as oversimplistic as it is cruel.

Finally, Hardin's food-population theory ignores the evidence that, contrary to ratchet projections, population growth is affected by many complex conditions besides food. Specifically, a number of socioeconomic conditions can be identified that cause parents to have fewer offspring. Birth rates can fall quite rapidly, sometimes before modern birth control devices are available. These conditions include parental security and faith in the future, the improved status of women in society, literacy, and lower infant mortality. Procuring these conditions requires agricultural reform, some redistribution of wealth, increased income and employment opportunities, better health services, and fresh expenditures on education. Evidence suggests that people who perceive the benefits of a smaller family will act prudently. The theory that favorable socioeconomic conditions cause a natural decrease in birth rates is called "the Benign Demographic Transition theory" (BDT). Although it is controversial, it may give us some reason to hope that population growth will level off. How much hope? That issue is discussed below in more detail. We now turn to the second philosophical theory on world hunger, liberalism.

Liberalism

The liberal position on world hunger is that we have a duty to help the poor in distant lands. There is something inherently evil about affluent people's failing to come to the aid of the poor when they could do so without great sacrifice. Liberal theorists on this issue come in several varieties. Some are utilitarians who argue that sharing our abundance and feeding the poor very likely maximizes utility or happiness. Some are deontologists who argue that we have a fundamental duty to use our surplus to aid those less well-off. Some deontologists simply find it self-evident that the needy have a right to our resources. Witness the report of the Presidential Commission on World Hunger: "Whether one speaks of human rights or basic human needs, the right to food is the most basic of all....The correct moral and ethical position on hunger is beyond debate." Others appeal to the principle of justice, arguing that the notion of fairness requires that we aid the least well-off in the world. Still others are radical egalitarians—perhaps the label "liberal" doesn't strictly apply to them—who argue that the principle of equality overrides even the need for survival, so we should redistribute our resources equitably even if it means that all of us will be malnourished and risk perishing. I think that we can capture most of what is vital to the liberal program if we examine Peter Singer's theory, which covers the first two types of liberalism, and Richard Watson's theory, which is a version of radical egalitarianism.

Peter Singer's article "Famine, Affluence, and Morality," written on the eve of the 1971 famine in Bangladesh, sets forth two principles, either of which would drastically alter our lifestyles and require that we provide substantial assistance to distant, poor and hungry people. The *Strong principle* states that "if it is in our power to prevent something bad from happening without thereby sacrificing anything of *comparable* importance, we ought morally to do it." Although this has similarities to utilitarian principles, it differs from them in that it does not require the maximizing of happiness, simply the amelioration of suffering through sacrifice of our goods to the point that we are at almost the same place as the sufferer. The idea behind this principle is utilitarian: diminishing marginal utility, which states that transferring goods from those with surplus to those with needs generally increases total utility. For example, if you have $100 for your daily food allowance and I have no allowance at all, your giving me some of your money will actually increase the good that the money accomplishes, for my gain of, say, $10 will enable me to survive, thus outweighing the loss you suffer. But there will come a point where giving me that extra dollar will not make a difference to the total good. At that point you should stop giving. If we were to follow Singer's strong principle, we would probably be giving a vast proportion of our GNP (gross national product) to nonmilitary foreign aid instead of the present 0.21 percent or the 0.7 percent advocated by the United Nations as a fair share for rich countries.

Singer's *Weak principle* states that we ought to act to prevent bad things from happening if doing so will not result in our sacrificing anything *morally significant*. He asks you to suppose that you are walking past a shallow pond and see a child drowning. You can save the child with no greater inconvenience than wading into the water and muddying your suit or dress. Should you not jump into the pond and rescue the child? Singer thinks it is self-evident that nothing morally significant is at stake in the sacrifice.

Although Singer prefers the Strong principle, he argues that the Weak principle is sufficient to ground our duty to aid needy, distant people, for what difference does it make whether the drowning child is in your home town or in Africa or Asia? "It makes no moral difference whether the person I can help is a neighbor's child 10 yards away or a Bengali whose name I shall never know, 10,000 miles away." He or she is still a human being, and the same minimal sacrifice is required. Furthermore, the principle makes no distinction between cases in which I am the only person who can do anything and cases in which I am just one among many who can help. I have a duty in either case to see that what is needed is accomplished. Call this the "No-Exception proviso."

Singer's two principles have generated considerable debate, and many ethicists have accepted one or both of them, but there are problems with each. John Arthur has noted in his critique of Singer that the Strong principle is too strong and the Weak principle is too weak. With the Strong principle, our rights to our property and lifestyles are too easily overridden by the needs of others. For example, if I meet a stranger who is going blind and I could

prevent her becoming completely blind by giving her one of my eyes, I should take steps to have my eye removed—even, according to the No-Exception proviso, if there are others on whom she has a greater claim to some assistance than she has on me. Likewise, if I meet a man about to lose his kidneys or lung functions, I have a *prima facie* duty to give him one of my kidneys or lungs, a duty that can be overridden only by finding someone on whom he has a stronger claim, who will donate his or her organ. Woe the person who meets someone in need of all three of these organs—an eye, a lung, and a kidney! If no one else is doing his or her duty, you are left with the responsibility of yielding your organs, even if this results, as it surely will, in a severe change in your lifestyle. So long as you have not reduced your lot to the level of the other person's, you must go on sacrificing, even for strangers.

Richard Watson's position is more severe than Singer's. From a deontological perspective, he argues that the principle of equal worth of individuals calls for the equal distribution of the world's food. "All human beings are moral equals with equal rights to the necessities of life. Differential treatment of human beings thus should be based only on their freely chosen actions and not on accidents of their birth and environment." It is our sacred duty to share scarce resources with every needy person, even if this means that we all will be malnourished, even if no one will get sufficient food, and everyone perishes. Equality trumps survival, even the survival of the human race.

Watson's Equality-Absolute has problems. The equal absolute right of each person to life's necessities needs a defense, which Watson fails to afford. I don't see why I am obligated to sacrifice the lives of my children and myself simply because there is not enough food to feed all of us. Suppose you and your family and friends (50 people in all) work hard and grow enough food to feed 100 people for the next six months. If you feed only your 50 people, you will have enough food for a year, after which a new crop can be harvested. But there are 200 people who need food. If you share your food with all 200, you will all die. If you share it with 50 others besides your family (100 in all), you all can survive for the next six months but must hope for outside aid after that. What is the morally correct thing to do? (1) Feed only our community (50 people who did the work)? (2) Feed these 50 and another 50 outsiders? (3) Feed all 200 and perish together? (4) Draw lots to determine who should get the food and live? I think we are morally permitted to opt for (1), because we have a right to try to survive and flourish so long as we are not unjustly harming others. As we argued in this book, we have a *prima facie* right to the fruits of our labor, so we need not divest ourselves of life's necessities to help others.

An adequate moral theory must make room for self-regarding reasons. I am required to make *reasonable* sacrifices for others, but not at the cost of what would severely detract from the quality of my own life. Watson explicitly rejects the notion of reasonableness in morality. Morality is often unreasonable, according to him, but I see no reason to accept that verdict. If morality were truly unreasonable, rational people would be advised to opt out of it and choose a more rational Quasi-Morality in its place. My thesis throughout this book is that moral principles are reasonable requirements. In general they are in our long-term interest.

Of course, you are free to go beyond the call of duty and donate your organs to strangers. It is certainly noble of you to volunteer to do so. But such supererogatory acts are not duties of as such. Extreme utilitarians and absolutist egalitarians confuse morality with extreme altruism or saintliness.

We turn now to Singer's Weaker principle: If we can prevent an evil by sacrificing something not morally significant, we should do so. This seems closer to the truth, but John Arthur has argued that it is too weak, for what is morally significant varies from person to person. For example, my record collection or collection of rare pieces of art might be a significant part of what makes life worth living for me, so to sacrifice them for the poor would be of moral significance. Is owning a television set or possessing a nice car or having a nice wardrobe morally significant? For many people they are. Nevertheless, there are occasions when sacrificing these things for the poor or needy might be morally required. Even when a child is drowning in a pond, you could refuse to jump into the water to save the child, using Singer's Weak principle, for you could argue that having clean, unspoiled clothes is morally significant for you. Of course, it would really

have to be the case that they are morally significant, but for some people they are.

Singer could respond that Arthur's objection fails because he is overly relativizing morally significance to the individual. There is an objective truth to the matter of whether something really is morally significant. Singer would have to qualify his principle of what is morally significant by relational terms: In situation S, object O is morally significant to person P (whether he or she realizes it or not). Compared to saving someone's life, wearing clean, unspoiled clothes is not morally significant, whatever the misguided dandy might think to the contrary. Not every supposed morally significant trait is really so. If I believe that burning witches is the way to save our nation from the devil and I go around burning those who fit my description, I am simply misguided. Likewise, if I think that my baseball card collection is more important than saving my best friend's life, I have a bad set of priorities—friends really are more valuable than baseball cards. If I fail to realize this, I am missing a deep moral truth.

Singer's Weak principle, suitably qualified, can survive the kind of attack that philosophers like Arthur hurl at it, but it may not be good enough to get him the hunger relief that he advocates. Other factors have to be addressed. For example, do needy strangers have rightful claims on my assets even though I have done nothing to cause their sorry state? Do the starving have rights to my property? We turn now to the conservative position.

Conservativism

Conservatives on world hunger argue that we have no duty at all to give aid to distant needy people. Representatives of the view in question are such libertarians as John Hospers, Robert Nozick, and Ayn Rand, and contractualists such as Thomas Hobbes and, more recently, Gilbert Harman, Howard Kahane and William Nelson. Typically, conservatives, in the minimalist sense I am using the term, reject the notion that we have positive rights that entail duties on the part of others to come to our aid or promote our good unless there is a contractual agreement between us. The one right we have is that of freedom: the right not to be interfered with, the right to possess our property in peace. So long as I have a legitimate claim on my property (that is, I have not acquired it through fraud or coercion) no one may take it from me, and I may refuse to share it regardless of how needy others are.

We may not positively harm others, but we need not help them either. No moral duty obligates you to dirty your clothes by trying to save the child drowning in the muddy pond. Of course, it shows bad character not to save the child, and we should endeavor to be charitable with our surplus and support good causes, but these are not strictly moral duties. They are optional ideals. It follows that if hungry Esau is prompted to sell his birthright to that feisty chef, Jacob, so much the worse for Esau; and if a poor African country decides to contract with a Western corporation to shift from growing a high protein crop to a cash crop such as coffee, so long as no external force was used in the agreement, the contract is entirely just. The corporation need feel no guilt when the poor nation undergoes a famine and finds itself unable to supply its people with adequate protein. No rights have been violated. The country simply made a foolish choice.

If you believe that the contractual approach to ethics, examined in an earlier chapter, is the correct approach, the conservative position will appeal to you. It may have considerable merit, but it also has certain weaknesses. Contractualism, unless it is supplemented with a theory of natural duties, limits moral obligations to agreements made. But, as I suggested, morality, in large part, has to do with the promotion of human flourishing and ameliorating suffering, so we have some duties to help others, even when we have not contracted ahead of time to do so. If a poor country agrees to accept hazardous waste from a rich country, morality has nothing more to say about the matter. Following the contractualist model, the thirty-eight people who for thirty-five minutes watched Kitty Genovese being beaten to death, who did not lift a finger to call the police or lift their windows to shout at the assailant, did nothing wrong. However, if we have a duty to promote human flourishing and ameliorate suffering, these onlookers did have a duty to do something on Ms. Genovese's behalf, and they are to be faulted for not coming to her aid.

It would seem, then, that there are positive duties as well as negative ones. Both utilitarian and deontological theories are better than contractual theories at recognizing positive duties to help others and promote human flourishing, even when no contract is in force.

A Moderate Alternative

There is a moderate position between the liberal and the conservative that accepts part of each position but rejects other parts. It goes as follows: morality originates in group living, tribes. People discover that certain rules are necessary for survival and happiness, such as rules against killing each other, promise breaking, violating property rights, lying, and cheating, and rules promoting justice, cooperation, respect for others, and beneficence. Members of a society implicitly agree to live by this Core Morality. They resolve their conflicts of interest through compromise or impartial third bodies—the primitive origins of law. But they notice that some other groups do not respect their lives or property and that there is no way to resolve differences through impartial review. The Other is the enemy to whom the rules do not apply. Indeed, it is only by not respecting the enemy's life and property that one can survive and flourish.

Eventually, the two groups learn to accept an intertribal Core Morality. They begin with a mutual nonaggression pact, respect each other as equals, cooperate instead of fight with each other, and subject their differences to an impartial review. Nevertheless, in many situations, members of a tribe feel a greater responsibility to aid members of their own family and tribe rather than members of a neighboring one. If my child, a neighboring child, and a child of another tribe all need a pair of shoes, and I have only enough resources to procure one pair, I will feel a duty to give them to my child. If I can procure two pairs easily, I will give the first pair to my child but sell the second pair at a low price to my neighbor. If I go into the shoemaking business, I will still be likely to give favored treatment to my neighbor over the person from the neighboring tribe. Greater opportunity for reciprocity arises with my neighbor than with the family of the neighboring tribe, so it makes sense to treat that family as special.

Moderate moral theory recognizes special responsibilities to family, friends, and neighbors.

This is the reason Singer's drowning child example is misleading. I can do only so much good. I can save only so many drowning children. I may have a duty to give of my surplus to help save drowning children in a distant land, but I have a stronger duty to help those with whom I have intimate or contractual ties.

This said, the other side of the coin must be turned over and the liberal program acknowledged, for another aspect of morality is the enlargement of the circle of benevolence and flourishing, the utilitarian aspect of maximizing good. We need to expand the small circle of moral consideration and commitment from family, community, and country to include the whole world. We need to do this for two reasons. First, it is simply good to do so. Helping as many people (and animals) as possible without harming yourself is part of the meaning of promoting the flourishing of sentient beings. Second, it is in our self-interest to do so. Unless we learn to live together on this small planet, we may all perish. Humanity is no longer innocent. Technology, through its inventions of atomic weapons, biological weapons, poisonous chemicals, and so forth, is available to destroy all sentient life. One nation's adverse environmental impact can affect the rest of the world. If one nation pollutes the air through spreading sulphur dioxide or carbon dioxide, the rest of the world suffers the effects. If the Brazilian or Peruvian farmers cut down large segments of the Amazon Rain Forest, we all lose oxygen and ecological diversity. We are all in each other's debt. If we don't hang together, we *hang* alone.

So the same considerations that led to mutual cooperation between the original tribes must inform our global policies. A rational Core Morality must reign internationally. Although we will still have priority commitments to family and friends, we cannot allow selfishness to hinder generous dealings with the rest of the world. Hardin's metaphor of nations as lifeboats has only limited applicability. It may justify careful immigration policies that prevent overcrowding, but it should not prevent assistance to other nations that may be helped and that someday may be able to help us. In a sense the whole earth is one great lifeboat in which we'll sink or float together.

However, something must be said in Hardin's behalf. He points to a crucial problem that deserves our concentrated attention: population policy. Even if we finally opt for the Benign Demographic Transition theory, many situations may not wait for that policy to take effect. The population of the world is multiplying at an exponential rate. Since 1930 the earth's population has increased from 2 billion to 6 billion by 1999. In 1968 Paul and Anne Ehrlich wrote *Population Bomb,* warning that the population of the world (then 3.5 billion) was growing exponentially at a rate of 70 million per year and that if strong measures were not taken, we would likely have Malthusian problems of famine and disease. Critics pejoratively labeled such cautioners "doomsdayers," but they have been proved correct.

Crowded conditions prevail in many parts of the world. Famines have become worse in areas of Africa and Bangladesh. Today the global population is growing not by 70 million per year, but by 90 million. The growth rate is 1.7 percent, which means that the earth's population is likely to double in 41 years. It is projected to rise to about 11.2 billion by 2050 unless significant population control policies are implemented. A slight increase in the growth rate would result in a world population density like that of present-day New York City by the year 2300. Add to this the following: The innovative technological development of food has leveled off, top soil is being depleted, pesticide-resistant strains of pest destroyers are appearing throughout the earth's agricultural areas, and there is evidence of changing weather patterns, probably brought on by the greenhouse effect, causing diminished farm production. And, as though this were not serious enough, the ocean fish harvests are declining.

I noted in the critique of Hardin that the Benign Demographic Transition theory (BDT) holds that we should concentrate on the root causes of population growth and let the process solve this problem. How does this theory work? It idealizes population changes in four stages. In stage 1, the *preindustrial stage,* the severe living conditions give rise to a high average birthrate and a high average deathrate, resulting in very little, if any, population increase. In stage 2, the *mortality transition stage,* the deathrate falls while the birthrate remains high, so the population increases. In stage 3, the *fertility transition* (or *industrial stage*), the average birthrate decreases due to availability of birth control, the improved status of women, lower infant mortality, general education, and the rising cost of raising children. In stage 4, the *postindustrial stage,* the average rates for both birth and death are low, tending toward zero growth. The population has leveled out but is much larger than it was at stage 1. There is some evidence that validates the BDT. Separate studies by Revelle, Brown, Eberstadt, and Rich have shown that several countries that have progressed in these areas have cut their birthrates dramatically. Some demographers point to the fact that in the 1970s, China has brought its birthrate down from 40 per 1,000 people to 30 in about five years and Cuba has brought its birthrate down to 27 per 1,000. The conclusion is that we should go to the causes of overpopulation (the activities mentioned in stage 3) and not punish countries for their "overpopulation."

Others have argued that the Benign Demographic Transition theory has severe problems. Demographer Joel Cohen points out that some countries decreased their birthrates before industrialization or educational development. In other cases, improved public health measures caused an enormous rise in higher life expectancy in developing countries without significantly reducing the birthrate. Furthermore, after China and India made significant progress toward cutting their fertility rates in the 1970s in spite of the growing benefits of industrialization, their fertility rates increased in the 1980s. Referring to the 1980s and 1990s, Cohen notes that population growth rates are rising. Seventy-eight million people live in countries with a total fertility rate above seven children per woman, and 708 million live in countries with six or more children per woman. Why did the trend reverse? For several reasons, one being China's softening of its austere one-child policy and another India's relaxation of its family planning policy. The point is that the BDT is too idealized a model. It may indicate a tendency in industrialization to lead to population stabilization, but there is no lawlike necessity about it. People must understand that it is to their advantage to have fewer children, and effective techniques of fertility reduction must be available. Even with the benefits of industrialization and the availability of birth control, a high average birthrate may continue for a long time, increasing the population at a very high rate, putting a stress on the ecosystem, and exceeding the carrying capacity of the land. Famines in the coming years could have devastating effects.

We have cause for alarm, and if the shouts of neo-Malthusians such as Hardin and Ehrlich are needed to wake us up, let us thank them for waking us up—even as we work for kinder, more just solutions to the problem. The point is that hard choices must be made, and food aid should be tied to responsible population control for the survival and well-being of humanity.

A proposal that improves on Hardin's Lifeboat Ethics is the triage approach first set forth by Paul and William Paddock in *Famine—1975* and advocated by Joseph Fletcher. The term *triage* (French for "sorting") comes from wartime medical policies. With a scarcity of physicians and resources to cope with casualties of battle, the wounded were divided into three groups: those who would probably survive without medical treatment, those who would not survive even with treatment, and those for whom treatment would make the decisive difference. Only this last group would receive medical aid. The Paddocks and Fletcher urge us to apply the same policy to world hunger. Given limited ability and scarce resources to help, we should not aid nations that will survive without our aid or those who will not be able to sustain themselves even with our help. We should direct all of our attention to nations for which our input could make a decisive difference. The aim should be to enable these people to become self-sufficient, responsive to the carrying capacity of their environment As a Chinese proverb says, "Give a man a fish today and he will eat for a day. Teach him how to fish, and he will eat for the rest of his days."

As repulsive as the triage strategy may seem, it should not be dismissed out of hand. Perhaps at present no nation is hopeless and we still have time to forestall the nefarious effects of overpopulation. We should give the Benign Demographic Transition theory a chance to work, supporting social reform at home and abroad with our actions and our pocketbooks, but if we cannot effect global changes, the time for triage may soon be upon us. The doomsdayers are to be taken seriously. They may not be correct, but their warnings should be heeded.

Meanwhile, the broad-based Core Morality, outlined in the first chapters of this book, seems to require that we personally contribute to hunger relief organizations and urge that national policy provide appropriate agricultural know-how and technological assistance to nations in dire need. At the same time, we should support family planning programs both here and abroad, aiming to provide everyone with as high a quality of life as is possible. The option is not food *or* population control, but food *and* population control. The world must see these as two sides of the same coin, a coin that is the entrance fee to a better future for all people.

If the preceding discussion is correct, we do have a duty to give aid to the needy, both in our own country and in other lands. It is a duty to exercise benevolence to ameliorate suffering and promote human flourishing. We do not have a duty to reduce our lot to an equal poverty as Watson and Singer's Strong principle advocates, but we should be giving more than most of us are. No one can tell another person just how much he or she should be donating, but each of us must consult his or her conscience. We should be living as personal examples of ecological responsibility, as good stewards of the earth's resources, and we should call upon our leaders to increase nonmilitary aid to underdeveloped countries where the need is greatest.

ARGUMENT 27 ESSAY QUESTIONS

1. If we adopted Singer's strong principle, how would our lives change?
2. Do we have obligations to ourselves and to our family and friends that we would have to abandon if we adopted Singer's notion of duties to the needy? Are we mistaken about the strength of these duties as Singer implies? Explain.
3. Pojman takes a moderate position on giving to the needy of other lands. Contrast his view with Singer's. Which approach to the needy seems more reasonable?

SUGGESTIONS FOR FURTHER READING

William Aiken and Hugh LaFollette, ed., *World Hunger and Morality* (Englewood Cliffs, NJ: Prentice Hall, 1996).

John Arthur, "Equality, Entitlements, and Distribution of Income," in *Philosophy for the 21st Century* (New York: Oxford University Press, 2003), 675–84.

John Arthur, "Rights and the Duty to Bring Aid," in *World Hunger and Moral Obligation,* ed. William Aiken and Hugh LaFollette (Englewood Cliffs, NJ: Prentice Hall, 1977).

Nigel Dower, "World Poverty," in *A Companion to Ethics,* ed. Peter Singer (Oxford: Blackwell, 1993), 273–83.

Garrett Hardin, "Lifeboat Ethics: The Case Against Helping the Poor," *Psychology Today Magazine* (1974).

Onora O'Neill, "The Moral Perplexities of Famine and World Hunger," in *Matters of Life and Death,* ed. Tom Regan (New York: Random House, 1986), 322–29.

Onora O'Neill, *Faces of Hunger: An Essay on Poverty, Justice, and Development* (London: Unwin Hyman, 1986).

Thomas Pogge, *World Poverty and Human Rights: Cosmopolitan Responsibilities and Reforms* (Cambridge, England: Polity Press, 2002).

Michael J. Sandel, ed., *Justice: A Reader* (New York: Oxford University Press, 2007).

Debra Satz, "International Economic Justice," in *The Oxford Handbook of Practical Ethics* (Oxford: Oxford University Press, 2003), 620–69.

abolitionist One who wishes to do away with capital punishment.

abortion The ending of a pregnancy.

active euthanasia Euthanasia involving an action that directly causes someone to die; mercy killing.

act-utilitarianism A form of utilitarianism in which the rightness of actions depends solely on the relative good produced by individual actions.

animal rights Moral status for nonhuman animals that cannot be easily overridden.

anthropocentrism The doctrine that humans alone have moral status.

antiwar pacifism The view that war is never morally justified.

applied ethics The application of moral principles, virtues, or theories to real-life cases or issues.

argument A pattern of statements in which at least one of them (a premise) provides support for another one (the conclusion).

beneficence, duty of The moral obligation to do good to others and avoid harming them.

biocentrism The view that all living things have some degree of moral status.

capital punishment Officially sanctioned punishment by death for very grievous (capital) crimes.

chromosome A stringlike, gene-containing molecule in the nucleus of a cell.

cloning The asexual production of a genetically identical entity from an existing one.

conclusion In an argument, the statement that the premises are intended to support.

consequentialist theory A moral theory in which the rightness of actions depends solely on their consequences or results.

contractarianism A moral theory based on the idea of a social contract, or agreement, among individuals for mutual advantage.

critical thinking The systematic evaluation or formulation of beliefs, or statements, by rational standards.

cultural relativism The view that right actions are those endorsed by one's culture.

deductive argument An argument intended to give logically conclusive support for its conclusion.

deontological (or nonconsequentialist) theory A moral theory in which the rightness of actions is determined not solely by their consequences but partly or entirely by their intrinsic nature.

descriptive ethics The study of morality using the methodology of science.

distributive justice Justice concerning the fair distribution of society's advantages and disadvantages, such as jobs, income, taxes, rights, and welfare aid.

divine command theory The doctrine that God is the creator of morality.

doctrine of double effect The principle that performing a bad action to bring about a good effect is never morally acceptable but that performing a good action may sometimes be acceptable even if it produces a bad effect.

erotica Sexually explicit material that does not demean women but depicts them as consenting, equal partners in sexual activity.

ethical egoism The view that right actions are those that further one's own best interests.

ethics (moral philosophy) The study of morality using the methods of philosophy.

eugenics The deliberate attempt to improve the genetic makeup of humans by manipulating reproduction.

euthanasia The direct or indirect bringing about of the death of another person for that person's sake.

gene The fundamental unit of biological inheritance.

gene therapy The manipulation of someone's genetic material to prevent or treat disease.

genome An organism's entire complement of DNA.

homosexuality Sexual relations between members of the same sex.

induced abortion The intentional termination of pregnancy through drugs or surgery; commonly known simply as *abortion*.

inductive argument An argument in which the premises are intended to give probable support to its conclusion.

involuntary euthanasia Euthanasia performed against a person's will or without asking for her consent while she is competent to decide.

justice, egalitarian theory of The doctrine that the important benefits and burdens of society should be distributed equally.

justice, libertarian theory of The doctrine that the benefits and burdens of society should be distributed through the fair workings of a free market and the exercise of liberty rights of noninterference.

justice, utilitarian theory of The doctrine that a just distribution of the benefits and burdens of society is one that maximizes the net good for society.

just war theory The theory that war may be justified provided that certain conditions are met.

Kant's theory The theory that right actions are those that accord with the categorical imperative.

legal moralism The view that a community's basic moral standards should be enshrined in law and enforced by the state.

managed care A system for providing care to a particular group of patients (members of the system) using regulatory restraints to control costs and increase efficiency.

metaethics The study of the fundamental assumptions, concepts, and reasoning involved in the field of ethics.

moral objectivism The view that there are moral standards that are true or correct for everyone.

moral relativism The view that moral standards do not have independent status but are relative to what individuals or cultures believe.

moral status (or moral considerability) The property of being eligible for moral concern or respect, regardless of any relationship to others.

moral theory A theory that explains why an action is right or wrong or why a person or a person's character is good or bad.

morality Beliefs about right and wrong actions and good and bad persons or character.

natural law theory The view that right actions are those that conform to moral standards discerned in nature through human reason.

nontraditional view (of sexual morality) The belief that we should not judge the morality of sex acts by whether they fulfill a particular natural purpose.

nonvoluntary euthanasia Euthanasia performed when patients are not competent to choose death for themselves and have not previously (while competent) disclosed their preferences.

normative ethics The philosophical exploration and evaluation of moral norms (principles, virtues, values, and theories).

obscenity A property thought to render sexually explicit words or images morally or legally illicit.

passive euthanasia Allowing someone to die by not doing something that would prolong life.

physician-assisted suicide A patient's taking her or his own life with the aid of a physician.

pornography Sexually explicit words or images intended to provoke sexual arousal.

premise In an argument, a statement, or reason, given in support of the conclusion.

prima facie moral principles Moral principles that apply in relevant circumstances unless exceptions are warranted (as when two principles conflict and one must be given more weight than the other).

psychological egoism The empirical claim that people always act out of self-interest.

quickening A pregnant woman's experience of fetal movement inside her.

realism (regarding war) The view that morality does not apply to warfare, that the categories of right and wrong are irrelevant to actions occurring in war.

reproductive cloning Cloning aimed at the live birth of an individual.

retentionist One who wishes to retain the death penalty as part of a system of legal punishment.

retributivism The doctrine that people should be punished simply because they deserve it and that the punishment should be proportional to the crime.

rights, negative A person's rights not to be interfered with in obtaining something.

rights, positive A person's rights that obligate others to help him or her obtain something.

rule-utilitarianism A form of utilitarianism in which a right action is one conforming to a rule that, if followed consistently, would create for everyone involved the most beneficial balance of good over bad.

speciesism Discrimination against nonhuman animals purely because of their species.

spontaneous abortion Abortion that is due to natural causes—birth defect or injury, for example; miscarriage.

statement An assertion that something is or is not the case.

subjective relativism The view that right actions are those endorsed by an individual.

terrorism The deliberate use or threat of physical violence against noncombatants to advance political, religious, or ideological aims.

therapeutic abortion Abortion performed to preserve the life or health of the mother.

therapeutic (or research) cloning Cloning done for purposes other than producing a live individual.

torture An act of intentionally inflicting severe pain or suffering on a person for purposes of coercion, punishment, intimidation, or extraction of information.

traditional view (of sexual morality) The belief that sex is morally permissible only within the conventional institution of marriage, which presupposes a monogamous union of a man and a woman.

utilitarianism The view that right actions are those that result in the most beneficial balance of good over bad consequences for everyone involved.

viability The development stage at approximately twenty-three to twenty-four weeks of pregnancy when the fetus may survive outside the uterus.

virtue ethics A moral theory that focuses on the development of virtuous character.

voluntary euthanasia Euthanasia in which a competent patient voluntarily requests or agrees to euthanasia, communicating his wishes either while competent or through instructions to be followed if he becomes incompetent.

Oaten, Allan. *See* "A Critique of Lifeboat
    Ethics"
Obama, Barack, 403
obligation. *See also* global obligations,
    economic justice and
    conditional, 165–66
    defined, 690*n*2
    norms of, 3
    numbers not lessening, 685
    rights and, 165–66, 589–90
O'Brien, William, 433, 436–37
obscenity
    defined, 469–70, 490, 514, 702
    laws, 470, 487–88, 514–15, 519–20
Odysseus, 248
offense, harm and, 502
offensive expression, 506–8
O'Heare, Anthony, 435
"On Deterrence and the Death Penalty"
    (van den Haag)
    causes of crime in, 384–85
    deterrence argument in, 380–88
    "doing" justice in, 381–82
    irrevocability in, 382, 385, 387
    utilitarianism in, 380
On Liberty (Mill), 242, 245–46
    free speech and, 473–78, 479*n*1, 499
    infallibility in, 475–78
    liberty argument against censorship and,
    473–79
Only Words (MacKinnon), 523–26
"On the Moral and Legal Status of
    Abortion" (Warren)
    "Abortion: A Defense of the Personhood
    Argument" defending, 140–47
    "The Being in the Womb Is a Person"
    arguing against, 131–32, 136–37
    fetal development and, 128–29
    human defined in, 126
    moral community defined in, 126–28, 131
    overview of, 125
    personhood argument in, 125–30
    right to life and, 128–30
    virtue ethics and, 214*n*12
open future, right to, 325, 340
open-future argument, against cloning
    in "Cloning Human Beings," 335–42
    Feinberg and, 340
    introduction to, 334–35
    in "A Life in the Shadow," 344–46
open mind, in reading arguments, 17–18
oppression, terrorism and, 442–46. *See
    also* "Pornography, Oppression, and
    Freedom"
Oregon
    assisted suicide in, 265, 297–98
    Medicaid in, 555–56
organization, sensationalism and, 534–35
original position, Rawls's, 72

ornithine transcarboxylase deficiency
    (OTCD), 316–17
osteoporosis, 330
OTCD. *See* ornithine transcarboxylase
    deficiency
"Our Duties to Animals" (Kant), 595
overridingness, as characteristic of
    morality, 2

pacifism. *See* antiwar pacifism
"Pacifism" (Lackey)
    pacifist argument in, 404–13
    prohibition against killing in, 407–9
    right to life in, 408–9
    sacredness of life and, 407–8
    varieties of pacifism in, 406–7
"Pacifism: A Philosophical Analysis"
    (Narveson)
    duty in, 414–17
    pacifist argument in, 405, 413–20
pacifist argument, against war
    introduction to, 404–5
    in "Pacifism," 404–13
    in "Pacifism: A Philosophical Analysis,"
    405, 413–20
Paddock, Paul, 666, 699
Paddock, William, 666, 699
pain
    animals feeling, 584–85, 609–10, 622–27
    humans feeling, 608–10
    in "Moral Vegetarianism and the
    Argument from Pain and Suffering,"
    622–27
    torture and, 608
    wanton infliction of, 153–54
Pakistan, terrorist attacks in, 402
Palestinian terrorism, 436, 439*n*36
Pally, Marcia, 535
Palmer, Julie Gage, 329–30
Parfit, Derek, 166
partial autonomy, 612
partial-birth abortion. *See* intact dilation
    and extraction
Partial-Birth Abortion Ban Act, 124
partiality, 75
particular-interests principle, 165–68, 172
passive euthanasia, 264–66, 702. *See also*
    "Active and Passive Euthanasia"
passive nonvoluntary euthanasia, 266
passive voluntary euthanasia, 266
paternalism. *See also* paternalism, argument
    against
    autonomy and, 221
    decriminalization and, 241–42
    defined, 242–44
    impure, 244
    laws and, 243, 251
    principle, 220–22
    pure, 237, 244

utilitarianism and, 241, 246–47
"Paternalism" (Dworkin, G.)
    argument against paternalism in, 242–51
    Mill in, 241–42, 244–47, 251
    utilitarianism and, 246–47
paternalism, argument against
    overview of, 241–42
    in "Paternalism," 242–51
    in "What Libertarianism Is," 252–59
payback retributivism, 365–66
Pearson, Geoffrey, 227
Pearson, Lester, 384
Peek, Anthony Ray, 379
PEG. *See* polyethylene glycol
"People or Penguins" (Baxter), 652–56
personality disorders, 384
personhood argument, for abortion
    in "Abortion: A Defense of the
    Personhood Argument," 140–47
    in "The Being in the Womb Is a Person,"
    130–39
    in "On the Moral and Legal Status of
    Abortion," 125–30
    overview of, 123–25
    potential personhood in, 128–30, 138,
    144–45
    self-defense argument and, 182, 191–92
    standards for, 125, 127, 131–32
    in "Why Abortion Is Immoral," 148–55
personhood-at-conception argument,
    against abortion
    in "An Almost Absolute Value in
    History" (Noonan), 156–61
    "In Defense of Abortion and Infanticide"
    and, 162–73
    overview of, 155–57
    potential personhood in, 156–57,
    169–72
    "The Scope of the Prohibition Against
    Killing" and, 173–81
    self-defense argument and, 182, 191–92
persons
    being and functioning as, 132–39,
    145–47
    concept of, 614
    defined, 122, 125–27, 131–32, 136, 177
    handicapped, 136–37
    moral, 437–38
    norms of value applied to, 3
    potential, 128–30, 138, 144–45
    principle of respect for, 69
    reality of, seen through love, 137
persuasion, argument contrasted with, 9
pets, 615
"The Philosophers' Brief" (Dworkin, R.,
    et al.)
    autonomy argument in, 269–78
    *Cruzan v. Director, Missouri Department
    of Health* in, 271, 273–75

rape (*continued*)
   sperm donor and, 197
   vans, 535
ratchet effect, 666–68, 675, 677, 691–94
rationality
   ethics and, 55–60
   human superiority and, 638
   limits of, 57–60
   moral rules and, 202
   natural law theory and, 70
   respect for trees and, 644–46, 648n13
   virtue ethics and, 202–3
rational soul, 157
rationing
   health care and, 545–48, 555–56, 559–70
   moral complicity and, 564–65
   transplantation, 545–48, 559–70
   utilitarianism and, 545–46
rationing by moral worthiness, argument
     for
   in "Alcoholics and Liver
     Transplantation," 558–60, 566–70
   in "Fault and the Allocation of Spare
     Organs," 560–65
   introduction to, 559–60
R.A.V. v. City of St. Paul, 501
Rawls, John, 113. *See also* "The
     Philosophers' Brief"
   contractarianism of, 72–73, 81
   health care and, 73, 548
   original position of, 72
   A Theory of Justice by, 102–8, 600
   "Utilitarianism" by, 81–84
realism, 395, 702
real-will theory, 248
reason driven, as characteristic of morality, 3
reasoning, 125, 127. *See also* moral
     reasoning
recreational drug use, 236
rectificatory justice, 560–61, 563, 565
reductionism, 203
Regan, Tom, 596–615
rehabilitation, 381, 388n11
Reich, Robert, 330–31
relativism. *See also* moral relativism
   cultural relativism, 6–9, 701
   ethical, 36–38, 41–43
   subjective, 6–8, 141, 703
religion, ethics and, 4–6. *See also*
     Christianity
religious terrorism, 399
Reno, Janet, 378
repression, as response to terrorism, 444
reproduction, in "Living on a Lifeboat,"
     664–65
reproductive cloning, 318–21, 703
reproductive freedom, right to, 336–37
reproductive technologies. *See* assisted
     reproductive technologies

research
   animal, 582–84, 588–94
   cloning, 319–20
resourcefulness, in moral problem solving,
     78–81
respect for nature, 629–36, 640–41, 644–47,
     648n13. *See also* "The Ethics of
     Respect for Nature"
respect for persons, principle of, 69
restaurant bombing, Hamas, 401
restitution, nonpunitive principle of,
     561–63
retaliation
   as response to terrorism, 444
   right of, 356
retaliatory terrorism, 433–34
retentionists, of capital punishment, 348,
     350–52, 703
retreat, duty to, 389
retributivism. *See also* Kant's retributivism
     argument, for death penalty
   defined, 351, 703
   equality, 364
   payback, 365–66
   proportional, 364–65
"Reverence for Life" (Schweitzer), 649–52
Revolutionary War, 398, 412
Richards, David, 238
right
   action, 63, 202–3
   intention, 397, 451
   wrong and, 3–4
"The Right of Punishing" (Kant), 354–56
rights. *See also* animal rights; human rights;
     right to health care, argument for
   autonomy and, 610–12
   censorship undermining, 488–89
   of children, 612–13
   Civil Rights Movement and, 484–85
   to cloning, 321, 336–37
   competing claims and, 640
   conferred, 612
   content of, 597
   to death, 269–70
   defined, 189–90, 543
   derivative, 543
   of drug users, 224, 239–40
   government protecting, 257–59
   to happiness, 609
   to ignorance, 334–35, 340
   infanticide and, 178–81
   interest and, 163–65
   justice and, 213n10
   legal, moral rights vs., 550
   in libertarianism, 252–60
   to liberty, 257, 473–74, 608–10
   to life, 128–30, 163–69, 172, 186–92,
     257, 358, 408–9, 438, 589, 609–10,
     613, 619–20

   natural, 147, 612
   negative, 547–49, 660, 703
   of nonparadigm humans, 610–12
   obligations and, 165–66, 589–90
   to open future, 325, 340
   of political sovereignty, 423
   positive, 549–51, 660, 703
   to privacy, 141–42, 150
   to property, 254–59
   of punishment, 354–54
   to reproductive freedom, 336–37
   of retaliation, 356
   to self-determination, 269–70, 449–50,
     473
   social, 147
   state, 421
   strength of, 597
   of territorial integrity, 423
   terrorism and, 437–38
   transfer of, 284–85
   view, 596, 602–604
   welfare, 551
   women's, 206–7, 210–11
"The Rights of Animals and Unborn
     Generations" (Feinberg), 163
"The Rights of the Nonhuman World"
     (Warren)
   animal rights in, 605–14
   nonparadigm humans in, 611–12
"The Right to a Decent Minimum of Health
     Care" (Buchanan), 557–58
right to health care, argument for, 541–44
   health care as bottomless pit and, 552
   introduction to, 548–49
   in "Is There a Right to Health Care and,
     if so, What Does It Encompass?",
     548–56
   legal *vs.* moral rights in, 550
   positive *vs.* negative rights in, 549–51
   in "The Right to a Decent Minimum of
     Health Care," 557–58
   scope of, 550–51, 553–55
"The Ring of Gyges" (Plato), 26–30
Robbin, Debra, 534
Robertson, Pat, 367
Robins, Lee, 225
Rockefeller Foundation, 668
Roe, Jane, 278
Roe v. Wade, 119, 122
Roman Catholic Church
   abortion and, 118, 140, 143, 161n1, 169,
     193n4, 193n6, 296n1
   ethics, 70–71
   free speech and, 477
   natural law theory and, 70–71
Roper v. Simmons, 350–51
Rothman, Stanley, 375
RU-486. *See* mifepristone
rules, of war, 397–98. *See also* moral rules

rule-utilitarianism
  defined, 64, 703
  euthanasia and, 66
  torture and, 459–60
Russell, Bertrand, 412
Ryder, Richard, 143

sacredness of life, 407–8
sacrifices, reasonable, 682, 684, 696
Saldano, Victor, 379
Sanger, Margaret, 487
Saudi Arabia, truck bomb attacks in, 401
Scanlon, Thomas. *See* "The Philosophers'
  Brief"
Schlafly, Phyllis, 531
Schmidtz, David, 628. *See also* "Are All
  Species Equal?"
Schur, H., 141
Schwarz, Stephen, 140, 145, 198. *See also*
  "The Being in the Womb Is a Person"
Schweitzer, Albert, 406, 649–52
SCID. *See* severe combined
  immunodeficiency
science
  addiction and, 232
  ethics and, 51–55
  of good for man, 94–95
scientific criteria of adequacy, 77
scientific theories, moral theories and, 77
SCNT. *See* somatic cell nuclear transfer
"The Scope of the Prohibition Against
  Killing" (Devine)
  infanticide in, 177–81
  intuitions in, 177–78
  personhood-at-conception argument
    and, 173–81
  potentiality principle in, 173
  present enjoyment principle in, 173,
    176–77
  species principle in, 173–76
  Tooley in, 177–81
Scruton, Roger, 614–15
seajacking, *Achille Lauro*, 437, 439nn39–40
Secession (Buchanan), 449
secular terrorism, 399
self-concepts, 125, 127
self-consciousness, 175, 586–87
self-defense
  aggression and, 389
  analogy, death penalty and, 388–89
  restitution and, 562–63
  terrorism and, 431
  violence and, 389
self-defense argument, for abortion
  "Arguments from Bodily Rights" and,
    193–201
  in "A Defense of Abortion," 182–93
  overview of, 182–83
  personhood arguments and, 182, 191–92

"Virtue Theory and Abortion" and,
  201–14
self-defense argument, for war, 396–97, 409
  introduction to, 420–21
  in "The Legalist Paradigm," 420–24
  in "When War Is Unjust," 424–29
self-determination
  right to, 269–70, 449–50, 473
  right to reproductive freedom and, 337
  in "Voluntary Active Euthanasia," 305–6
  in "When Self-Determination Runs
    Amok," 279–80
self-esteem, cumulative harm to, 504
self-inflicted harm, 562
self-interest, 66
self-regarding conduct, 251
self-respect, 645–47
Sellin, Thorsten, 385–86, 388n9
sensationalism, as organizing tool, 534–35
"Sense and Censorship" (Pally), 535
September 11, 2001, 401, 403, 458, 463
severe combined immunodeficiency
  (SCID), 317
sex discrimination
  laws, 511
  pornography as, 531–32
sexism
  men damaged by, 512
  pornography and, 497
sexual abuse, 511–13, 519–20. *See also* rape
sexual expression, censorship of, 487–88
sexual morality, 490–91, 702–703
Shaw, Anthony, 289
sheep, cloned, 319–20, 335, 339
Sherlock Holmes (fictional character), 669
Shiro, Thomas, 524
Shonagon, Sei, 615
sight, humanity of others and, 158
"Silver Blaze" (Doyle), 669
Singer, Peter, 138–39, 143, 575, 596, 606.
  See also "All Animals Are Equal";
  "all animals are equal" argument;
  "Famine, Affluence, and Morality";
  utilitarian argument, for aiding poor
  Animal Liberation and Practical Ethics
    by, 622–23
  global obligations and, 659
  Practical Ethics by, 577
  "Utilitarianism and vegetarianism" by,
    625–26
slavery, 579, 611, 621–22
sleeping, functioning during, 132–33, 137,
  145
slippery slope, 183
  animal rights and, 587–88
  censorship and, 500, 505
  torture and, 460
slippery-slope argument, against euthanasia
  overview of, 297–98

in "Voluntary Active Euthanasia,"
  303–13
in "Why Doctors Must Not Kill,"
  297–303
slums, crime rate in, 384, 388n7
Smart, Brian. *See* "Fault and the Allocation
  of Spare Organs"
Smith and Jones thought experiment, 288,
  290–91, 294–96
smoking, 250, 563–65
social reformers, 8
social right, 147
social value, of lives, 547
social visibility, 159
society
  character formed by, 233, 238–39
  class-structured, 637
  international, 421–23
Socrates
  divine command theory and, 5, 22
  free speech and, 478–79
soldiers, killing of, 409–10
solidarity, group, 502–503
somatic-cell gene therapy, 316, 318–19, 326
somatic cell nuclear transfer (SCNT), 319
sound deductive arguments, 11–12
Spaceship Earth, 663
specialist version, of discrimination,
  374–75
species chauvinism, 174
species egalitarianism, 641–44, 647, 647n1.
  See also equality of all life, argument
  for
speciesism, 124, 143, 154, 611
  "All Animals Are Equal" on, 578–84
  animals as food and, 581–82
  arbitrariness of, 646
  in "Are All Species Equal?", 643–44
  "The Case for the Use of Animals in
    Biomedical Research" defending,
    591–92
  defined, 575, 703
  experimenting on animals and, 582–84
  in practice, 581–84
  racism and, 578–81
species principle, 173–76
sperm donor, 197
spheres of freedom objective, 653
spontaneous abortion, 120, 703
sports, dangerous, 564
Standard Belief, 173
starvation, death by, 684
state-mandated agenda, of feminism,
  200–201
statement, 9, 703
state rights, 421
Stein, Eric, 485
Sterba, James, 648n12
Stevenson, Bryan, 372, 375–79

Printed in the USA/Agawam, MA
July 8, 2020

757816.021